ANTITRUST LAW DEVELOPMENTS (FIFTH)

Volume II

Defending Liberty
Pursuing Justice

American Bar Association

This volume should be officially cited as:

ABA Section of Antitrust Law,
Antitrust Law Developments (5th ed. 2002)

Library of Congress Catalog Card Number: 2001133216
ISBN: 1-59031-063-2

Discounts are available for books ordered in bulk. Special consideration is given to state bars, CLE programs, and other bar-related organizations. Inquire at ABA Book Publishing, American Bar Association, 750 North Lake Shore Drive, Chicago, Illinois 60611.

07 06 05 04 03   5 4 3 2 1

CONTENTS

VOLUME I

Chapter I—Restraints of Trade

Chapter II—Monopolization and Related Offenses

Chapter III—Mergers and Acquisitions

Chapter IV—Joint Ventures

Chapter V—Robinson-Patman Act

Chapter VI—Relevant Market

Chapter VII—The Federal Trade Commission

Chapter VIII—Department of Justice Administration and Enforcement

Chapter IX—State Enforcement

Chapter X—Private Antitrust Suits

VOLUME II

Chapter XI—Antitrust Issues Involving Intellectual Property

Chapter XII—Antitrust and International Commerce

Chapter XIII—General Exemptions and Immunities

Chapter XIV—Regulated Industries

Appendixes

CHAPTER XI

ANTITRUST ISSUES INVOLVING INTELLECTUAL PROPERTY

A. Introduction

This chapter addresses the antitrust issues that arise from the acquisition, use, and enforcement of rights in intellectual property, i.e., patents, copyrights, trademarks, trade secrets, and other statutorily created rights.[1]

1. The Nature of Patents and Copyrights

Article I, Section 8, Clause 8 of the U.S. Constitution grants Congress the power to create a patent system. It provides: "The Congress shall have Power . . . [t]o promote the Progress of Science and useful Arts, by securing for limited Times to Authors and Inventors the exclusive Right to their respective Writings and Discoveries."

A patent gives the inventor of any "new and useful process, machine, manufacture, or composition of matter," any "distinct and new variety of plant," any "new, original and ornamental design for an article of manufacture," or any patentable improvements to any of them, the right to exclude others from making, using, or selling the invention throughout the United States.[2] Patents have the

---

1. For example, Congress has given creators of certain semiconductor "mask works" used in the fabrication of integrated circuits a right to prohibit, for a limited time, the importation, reproduction, and distribution of such works. 17 U.S.C. §§ 901-914 (2000). In addition, state statutes can create intellectual property rights, although those rights are qualified in that any state law that is inconsistent with the federal patent system is preempted. *See generally* Bonito Boats, Inc. v. Thunder Craft Boats, Inc., 489 U.S. 141 (1989). However, state law can, and does, create intellectual property rights not preempted by the patent laws, such as trademarks and trade secrets.
2. *See* 35 U.S.C. §§ 101, 154, 161, 171 (1994 & Supp. 1999). The exclusive rights provided for in the patent laws are intended to offer an incentive for inventors to take risks in performing research and development (R&D). *See, e.g.,* Kewanee Oil Co. v. Bicron Corp., 416 U.S. 470, 480-81, 484 (1974); Sears, Roebuck & Co. v. Stiffel Co., 376 U.S. 225, 229-30 (1964); Johnson & Johnson, Inc. v. Wallace A. Erickson & Co., 627 F.2d 57, 59 (7th Cir. 1980); S.C. Johnson, Inc. v. Carter-Wallace, Inc., 225 U.S.P.Q. (BNA) 968, 973 (S.D.N.Y. 1985), *aff'd in part and vacated in part,* 228 U.S.P.Q. (BNA) 367 (Fed. Cir. 1986). The patent laws also are intended to encourage the disclosure of new ideas to the public, which in turn may lead to the development of further advances. *See* Troxel Mfg. Co. v. Schwinn Bicycle Co., 465 F.2d 1253, 1258 (6th Cir. 1972), *later appeal,* 489 F.2d 968 (6th Cir. 1973), *cert. denied,* 416 U.S. 939 (1974); Dart Indus. v. Banner, 200 U.S.P.Q. (BNA) 656, 664 (D.D.C. 1978), *rev'd on other grounds,* 636 F.2d 684 (D.C. Cir. 1980). When the patent expires, the invention becomes freely available to the public without restriction. *See, e.g.,* Brulotte v. Thys Co., 379 U.S. 29, 31 (1964); Special Equip. Co. v. Coe, 324

attributes of personal property.[3]   The period of exclusivity of a U.S. patent is normally twenty years from the date on which the application for the patent was filed.[4]

Each patent contains one or more "claims." The claims are analogous to the "metes and bounds" of a deed. The claims alone define the scope of exclusivity granted to the patentee. The remainder of the disclosure in the patent, while required to comply with the statutory formalities for a patent, confers no exclusive rights.[5] To obtain a patent, the patent applicant must persuade a Patent and Trademark Office examiner that his invention meets the statutory standards of novelty, utility, and nonobviousness.[6] Conflicts between patent applications or an application and an existing patent may be resolved through an inter partes administrative proceeding known as an interference, which determines the priority of invention.[7]

Copyrights are federal statutory grants[8] that protect "original works of authorship fixed in any tangible medium of expression."[9] Others may use the ideas expressed in a copyrighted work,[10] but those who copy the original author's expression of those ideas may be liable as copyright infringers. There is no copyright infringement liability if an identical work is independently created, in contrast to patent law, where infringement can occur even if it was the result of independent creation.[11] Copyright

U.S. 370, 378 (1945). A patentee's remedies for infringement are specified in 35 U.S.C. § 271 (1994 & Supp. 1999), and include rights against importers and exporters of goods covered by the patent. In addition, under § 337 of the Tariff Act of 1930, *as amended*, 19 U.S.C. § 1337 (1994 & Supp. 1999), a patentee may seek relief through the U.S. International Trade Commission against the importation of products that infringe a U.S. patent, subject to certain threshold requirements relating to the existence of a domestic industry practicing the patent.

3.   *See* 35 U.S.C. § 261 (1994). The statutory provision was enacted to negate any inference that a patent was a "public trust" or "privilege." *See, e.g.*, Precision Instrument Mfg. Co. v. Automotive Maint. Mach. Co., 324 U.S. 806, 816 (1945).

4.   35 U.S.C. § 154(a)(2) (1994). The term of a patent that was in force on, or that results from an application filed after, June 8, 1995 is the greater of the 20-year period provided in § 154(a)(2) or 17 years from the grant of the patent. *Id.* § 154(c). Under certain circumstances, a patent's term may be extended if the issuance of the patent is delayed by an interference proceeding or by appellate review of the decision to grant the patent, or if the patentee was subject to regulatory review prior to commercial marketing or use of the patented product. *Id.* §§ 154(b), 156.

5.   *See, e.g., id.* § 112 (1994).

6.   *See id.* §§ 101, 103, 120 (1994 & Supp. 1999).

7.   *Id.* § 102(g) (Supp. 1999) (priority may be based upon the dates of conception and reduction to practice of an invention and the diligence of the person who was the first to conceive of the invention).

8.   *See generally* 17 U.S.C. §§ 101-121 (2000). The 1976 revision of the Copyright Act specifically provides for federal preemption of all state laws directed to copyrightable subject matter. *Id.* § 301. Copyrights, as patents, are provided for in Article I, Section 8, Clause 8 of the Constitution.

9.   *Id.* § 102(a) (2000).

10. *Id.* § 102(b) (2000) ("In no case does copyright protection for an original work of authorship extend to any idea, procedure, process, system, method of operation, concept, principle, or discovery."). *See also* Mazer v. Stein, 347 U.S. 201, 217 (1954) ("protection is given only to the expression of the idea—not the idea itself").

11. *Mazer*, 347 U.S. at 218 ("Absent copying there can be no infringement of copyright."); *cf.* Kewanee Oil Co. v. Bicron Corp., 416 U.S. 470, 477-78 (1974) (stating that patent protection goes "not only to copying the subject matter, which is forbidden under the Copyright Act, . . . but also to independent creation"). *Compare* 17 U.S.C. §§ 106-118, 501 (2000) (copyright), *with* 35 U.S.C. § 271(a) (1994 & Supp. 1999) (patent).

protection, moreover, "has never accorded the copyright owner complete control over all possible uses of his work."[12] For example, copyright law contains a doctrine of fair use which, in certain circumstances, allows others to make limited use of the copyright holder's original work.[13] Patent law, by contrast, contains no similar right to use patented material for any commercial purpose without the permission of the patent holder.

In spite of the differences between patents and copyrights, the Supreme Court has relied on its patent antitrust decisions when resolving conflicts between the copyright and antitrust laws. In *United States v. Paramount Pictures*,[14] for example, the Court held that producers and distributors of motion picture films engaged in an unlawful practice by requiring theaters to maintain minimum admission prices. The Court reasoned that "a copyright may no more be used than a patent to deter competition between rivals in the exploitation of their licenses."[15] Similarly, the Department of Justice and the Federal Trade Commission have stated that they will apply the same antitrust principles to patents, copyrights, and trade secrets.[16]

2. Judicial and Agency Approaches to the Intersection between Antitrust and Intellectual Property Laws

Judicial views on the nature of the relationship between antitrust and intellectual property rights have varied significantly over time and from court to court. Thus, one early case allowed owners of competing patent rights to form a pool and fix the price of their otherwise competing products.[17] Later cases, however, tended to view intellectual property, and particularly patents, as conferring a "monopoly," but one

---

12. Sony Corp. v. Universal City Studios, Inc., 464 U.S. 417, 435 (1984).

13. 17 U.S.C. § 107 (2000). *See generally* Campbell v. Acuff-Rose Music, Inc., 510 U.S. 569 (1994) ("The market for potential derivative uses [protectible by copyright] includes only those that creators of original works would in general develop or license others to develop. Yet the unlikelihood that creators of imaginative works will license critical reviews or lampoons of their own productions removes such uses from the very notion of a potential licensing market.").

14. 334 U.S. 131 (1948).

15. *Id.* at 144. Despite many similarities with respect to antitrust, patents and copyrights are not subject to uniform competition analysis in all contexts. For example, the Seventh Circuit considered the differences between patents and copyrights when it declined to adopt analogous patent doctrine in a copyright case. *See* Saturday Evening Post Co. v. Rumbleseat Press, Inc., 816 F.2d 1191, 1200 (7th Cir. 1987) (distinguishing Lear, Inc. v. Adkins, 395 U.S. 653 (1969), to hold that a no-contest clause in a copyright license is enforceable unless it violates the Sherman Act); *see also* Straus & Straus v. American Publishers' Ass'n, 231 U.S. 222, 234 (1913). In another context, the Court, while acknowledging "the historic kinship between patent and copyright law," has cautioned that "[t]he two areas of the law are, naturally, not identical twins, and we exercise the caution which we have expressed in the past in applying doctrine formulated in one area to the other." Sony, 464 U.S. at 439 & n.19 (1983).

16. *See* U.S. DEP'T OF JUSTICE & FEDERAL TRADE COMM'N, ANTITRUST GUIDELINES FOR THE LICENSING OF INTELLECTUAL PROPERTY § 1 (1995) [hereinafter INTELLECTUAL PROPERTY GUIDELINES], *reprinted in* 4 Trade Reg. Rep. (CCH) ¶ 13,132 *and* Appendix E to this treatise.

17. E. Bement & Sons v. National Harrow Co., 186 U.S. 70, 91-92 (1902) ("The fact that the conditions in the contracts keep up the monopoly or fix prices does not render them illegal.").

ANTITRUST LAW DEVELOPMENTS (FIFTH)

that had to be narrowly construed.[18] Under these cases, various practices, such as tying,[19] were condemned as falling outside the protection of the patent law.[20]

More recently, the enforcement agencies and some courts have de-emphasized the apparent conflict between intellectual property and antitrust and instead characterized them as "two bodies of law [that] are actually complementary, as both are aimed at encouraging innovation, industry and competition."[21] As part of this shift in emphasis, courts and the agencies have sometimes expressly repudiated ideas underlying earlier decisions concerning the relationship between antitrust and intellectual property, such as the presumption that intellectual property confers market or monopoly power.[22] Congress also implicitly rejected the equation of a patent with market power by amending the Patent Act to provide that it is not patent misuse to condition a patent license on the purchase of another product unless "the patent owner has market power in the relevant market for the patent or patented product on which the license or sale is conditioned."[23] At the same time, courts[24] and enforcement officials[25] argued that restraints involving intellectual property should be analyzed using the same principles of antitrust applied in other contexts.

Also reflecting this view, the Department of Justice and Federal Trade Commission jointly issued *Antitrust Guidelines for the Licensing of Intellectual*

18. *See, e.g.*, Sears, Roebuck & Co. v. Stiffel Co., 376 U.S. 225, 230 (1964) ("Once the patent issues, it is strictly construed, it cannot be used to secure any monopoly beyond that contained in the patent, the patentee's control over the product when it leaves his hands is sharply limited, and the patent monopoly may not be used in disregard of the antitrust laws.") (internal citations omitted); United States v. Masonite Corp., 316 U.S. 265 (1942) (condemning price restraints imposed by a patent holder on its licensees); United States v. Line Material, 333 U.S. 287 (1948) (same).

19. Morton Salt Co. v. G.S. Suppiger Co., 314 U.S. 488, 491 (1942).

20. Bruce B. Wilson, *Patent and Know-How License Agreements: Field of Use, Territorial, Price and Quantity Restrictions, in* ANTITRUST PRIMER: PATENTS, FRANCHISING, TREBLE DAMAGE SUITS 11, 12-14 (1970) (listing what came to be known as the "Nine No-Nos" of intellectual property licensing); *see also* Ky P. Ewing, Jr., Dep'y Ass't Att'y Gen., Antitrust Div., *Patent-Antitrust Enforcement, reprinted in* [1969-1983 Transfer Binder] Trade Reg. Rep. (CCH) ¶ 50,398, at 55,883, 55,887 & n.34 (May 5, 1979).

21. Atari Games Corp. v. Nintendo, Inc., 879 F.2d 1572, 1576 (Fed. Cir. 1990); INTELLECTUAL PROPERTY GUIDELINES, *supra* note 16, § 1.0 ("The intellectual property laws and the antitrust laws share the common purpose of promoting innovation and enhancing consumer welfare.").

22. *See, e.g.*, Abbott Labs. v. Brennan, 952 F.2d 1346, 1354 (Fed. Cir. 1991) ("[a] patent does not of itself establish a presumption of market power in the antitrust sense"), *cert. denied*, 505 U.S. 1205 (1992).

23. 35 U.S.C. § 271(d)(5) (1994).

24. For example, in *United States v. Studiengesellschaft Kohle, mbH*, 670 F.2d 1122 (D.C. Cir. 1981), the D.C. Circuit criticized as "formalistic" a lower court analysis that "in effect, applied a *per se* rule" to condemn a license agreement that authorized the licensee to grant sublicensees to use a patented process, but not sell the product produced by the patented process. *Id.* at 1133-34. In testing the reasonableness of the restraint, the court observed that "analysis of the arrangement itself demonstrates that it is no more restrictive than a legal exclusive license, and in fact has certain procompetitive effects not created by such a license." *Id.* at 1135.

25. *See, e.g.*, Sheila F. Anthony, *Antitrust and Intellectual Property Law: From Adversaries to Partners*, 28 AIPLA Q.J. 1, 8 (2000) ("intellectual property has important characteristics that distinguish it, such as ease of misappropriation. The antitrust analysis undertaken in cases involving intellectual property takes such differences into account. Nonetheless, the governing antitrust principles are the same."); Abbott Lipsky, *Current Antitrust Division Views on Patent Licensing Practices*, 50 ANTITRUST L.J. 515, 520 (1981) (resale restrictions on patented goods "ought to be judged by the same general standards as those that ought to be in use outside the patent field").

Property (Intellectual Property Guidelines),[26] which articulate three general principles underlying the agencies' antitrust analysis of intellectual property licensing transactions: (1) for the purpose of antitrust analysis, the agencies regard intellectual property as being essentially comparable to any other form of property; (2) the agencies do not presume that intellectual property creates market power; and (3) the agencies recognize that intellectual property licensing allows firms to combine complementary factors of production and is generally procompetitive.[27] The *Guidelines* also announced an intention to use methods of market definition similar to those described by the 1992 *Merger Guidelines*[28] to define "goods markets," "technology markets," and "innovation markets" in order to evaluate the extent to which a particular patent or innovative new technology may confer market power.[29] To the extent that the agencies or the courts have relied on the analysis suggested by the *Intellectual Property Guidelines*, this is noted in the discussion below.

B. Patent and Copyright Antitrust Issues

1. Acquisition of Patents as an Antitrust Violation

a. PATENTS OBTAINED BY GRANT, PURCHASE, OR ASSIGNMENT

Judicial decisions concerning the legality of patent acquisitions under the antitrust laws have turned in part on whether the patents are acquired by grant to the inventor or by purchase or assignment from another private party. In the context of a challenge to acquisition by grant, the Supreme Court has stated that "mere accumulation of patents, no matter how many, is not in and of itself illegal."[30] Whether by purchase, assignment, or grant, the acquisition of a patent is not rendered illegal simply because the patent will convey monopoly power in a relevant economic market.[31]

---

26. INTELLECTUAL PROPERTY GUIDELINES, *supra* note 16, § 2.0. In late 2001, the Federal Trade Commission (FTC) and Department of Justice (DOJ) announced public hearings, titled "Competition and Intellectual Property Law and Policy in the Knowledge-Based Economy," to focus primarily on the implications of antitrust and patent law for innovation and other aspects of consumer welfare. 66 Fed. Reg. 58,146 (FTC Nov. 20, 2001).
27. *Id.*
28. U.S. DEP'T OF JUSTICE & FEDERAL TRADE COMM'N, HORIZONTAL MERGER GUIDELINES § 1 (1992), *reprinted in* 4 Trade Reg. Rep. (CCH) ¶ 13,104 *and* Appendix C to this treatise. Those *Guidelines* are discussed in Chapter III.
29. INTELLECTUAL PROPERTY GUIDELINES, *supra* note 16, § 3.2.1-3.2.3. The agencies' method of defining markets and safe harbors that may apply to certain licensing arrangements are discussed in part B.3.a of this chapter. The agencies' market definition methodology also may have implications for the analysis of other conduct in addition to licensing, including the acquisition of intellectual property.
30. Automatic Radio Mfg. Co. v. Hazeltine Research, Inc., 339 U.S. 827, 834 (1950); *accord* Cole v. Hughes Tool Co., 215 F.2d 924, 934 (10th Cir. 1954), *cert. denied*, 348 U.S. 927 (1955); Procter & Gamble Co. v. Paragon Trade Brands, Inc., 61 F. Supp. 2d 102, 110-11 (D. Del. 1996) (policy of building a "patent thicket" by soliciting and obtaining multiple patents from the Patent and Trademark Office (PTO) immune from antitrust challenge, unless shown to fit within the sham exception to the *Noerr* doctrine). The *Noerr* doctrine is discussed in part C of Chapter XIII.
31. *See, e.g.*, SCM Corp. v. Xerox Corp., 645 F.2d 1195, 1206 (2d Cir. 1981) ("the procurement of a patent . . . will not violate § 2 even where it is likely that the patent monopoly will evolve into an

The assignment of a patent to another by the patentee is specifically authorized by the Patent Act.[32] Nonetheless, an assignment may violate the Sherman Act where the assignment constitutes unlawful monopolization or is part of an agreement by competitors to restrain trade. For example, in *United States v. Singer Manufacturing Co.*,[33] the Supreme Court found that, in the context of a broader monopolistic scheme, the transfer of a patent from a Swiss manufacturer to its U.S. licensee to facilitate bringing infringement actions against Japanese competitors violated Section 1. Similarly, in *Kobe, Inc. v. Dempsey Pump Co.*,[34] the Tenth Circuit found that the acquisition, nonuse, and enforcement of "every important patent" in the field with a purpose to exclude competition, together with other anticompetitive acts, constituted a violation of Section 2 of the Sherman Act.[35]

The courts have recognized that patent acquisitions may allow firms to achieve significant efficiencies such as the introduction of a new product to the market. In *SCM Corp. v. Xerox Corp.*,[36] the Second Circuit recognized that investors who purchase patents may play a beneficial role in "both the inventive process and commercialization of inventions" that should be accommodated by the antitrust laws.[37]

Patents and copyrights are "assets" for the purpose of Section 7 of the Clayton Act.[38] An exclusive license under a patent or a copyright is also an asset for that

---

economic monopoly"), *cert. denied*, 455 U.S. 1016 (1982); Cole v. Hughes Tool Co., 215 F.2d 924, 937 (10th Cir. 1954), *cert. denied*, 348 U.S. 927 (1955); United States v. Aluminum Co. of Am., 148 F.2d 416 (2d Cir. 1945); Chisholm-Ryder Co. v. Mecca Bros., 1983-1 Trade Cas. (CCH) ¶ 65,406 (W.D.N.Y. 1982); United States v. E.I. duPont de Nemours & Co., 118 F. Supp. 41, 214 (D. Del. 1953) (powers "granted under a valid patent are not powers on which plaintiff may rely to establish monopolization"), *aff'd*, 351 U.S. 377 (1956); *see also* Eastman Kodak Co. v. Goodyear Tire & Rubber Co., 114 F.3d 1547, 1558 (Fed. Cir. 1997) ("Acquisition and enforcement of a patent do not in and of themselves constitute patent misuse."), *overruled on other grounds*, Cybor Corp. v. FAS Tech., Inc., 138 F.3d 1448 (Fed. Cir. 1998); Kaspar Wire Works, Inc. v. K-Jack Eng'g Co., Nos. 95-1095, 95-1115, 1995 U.S. App. LEXIS 33145 (Fed. Cir. Nov. 9, 1995) (unpublished opinion) (to prevail on monopolization claim based on the acquisition of patents, alleged infringer must show that patent holder possessed "dominant market power in the relevant market prior to the purchase of the patents"); *cf.* DiscoVision Assocs. v. Disc Mfg., Inc., 42 U.S.P.Q.2d (BNA) 1749, 1757 (D. Del. 1997) (filing series of patent continuation applications with the specific intent to monopolize or maintain a monopoly may form a basis for antitrust liability).

32. 35 U.S.C. § 261 (1994).
33. 374 U.S. 174 (1963).
34. 198 F.2d 416 (10th Cir.), *cert. denied*, 344 U.S. 837 (1952).
35. *Id.* at 423-24. Prior to *Kobe*, numerous cases dealt with patents in the context of broader monopolization schemes. *See, e.g., Singer*, 374 U.S. 174, United States v. United States Gypsum Co., 333 U.S. 364 (1948); Hartford-Empire Co. v. United States, 323 U.S. 386, *clarified*, 324 U.S. 570 (1945); United States v. Besser Mfg. Co., 96 F. Supp. 304 (E.D. Mich. 1951), *aff'd*, 343 U.S. 444 (1952); United States v. General Elec. Co., 82 F. Supp. 753, 816 (D.N.J. 1949); United States v. Vehicular Parking, Ltd., 54 F. Supp. 828, 839-40 (D. Del.), *modified*, 56 F. Supp. 297 (1944), *modified*, 61 F. Supp. 656 (1945); Stewart-Warner Corp. v. Staley, 42 F. Supp. 140, 146 (W.D. Pa. 1941).
36. 645 F.2d 1195 (2d Cir. 1981), *cert. denied*, 455 U.S. 1016 (1982).
37. *Id.* at 1206 n.9.
38. *See, e.g.*, Crucible, Inc. v. Stora Kopparbergs Bergslags AB, 701 F. Supp. 1157, 1162-63 (W.D. Pa. 1988); SCM Corp. v. Xerox Corp., 463 F. Supp. 983 (D. Conn. 1978), *remanded on other grounds*, 599 F.2d 32 (2d Cir. 1979); *In re* Yarn Process Patent Validity & Antitrust Litig., 398 F. Supp. 31, 35 (S.D. Fla. 1974), *aff'd in part and rev'd in part*, 541 F.2d 1127 (5th Cir. 1976),

purpose.[39] In their *Intellectual Property Guidelines*, the agencies state that the principles and standards used to analyze mergers will be used to analyze outright sales of intellectual property and the acquisition of exclusive rights in intellectual property whether by grant, sale, or other transaction.[40] The *Guidelines* state that such transactions will be analyzed under Section 7 of the Clayton Act, Sections 1 and 2 of the Sherman Act, and Section 5 of the Federal Trade Commission Act (FTC Act).

Applying Sixth Circuit law, the Federal Circuit held that an alleged infringer lacks standing to challenge its competitors' acquisition of the exclusive right to enforce a patent covering an aspect of the manufacturing process of the product both firms produced.[41] In reaching this conclusion, the court noted that the plaintiff alleged injuries stemming only from the enforcement of the patent, not injuries caused by an actual lessening of competition.[42]

The acquisition of patent rights in connection with certain research and development (R&D) joint ventures is covered by the National Cooperative Research and Production Act.[43] The act provides that the legality of joint ventures covered by the statute, including the acquisition of patent rights in connection with the venture, is to be judged under the rule of reason.[44] Moreover, if the parties file the prescribed notice and fit within certain statutory criteria, treble damages will not be available in an action challenging the conduct of the venture.[45]

b.   PATENTS OBTAINED BY GRANTBACKS

Patentees frequently require that licensees grant the patent holder exclusive or nonexclusive rights to any improvements or subsequently developed patents. Such a provision in a patent license is called a "grantback."

Grantbacks permit a patentee to license its technology without the risk that it will be foreclosed from the market by subsequent developments by its licensees. The Supreme Court has found that grantbacks may raise antitrust concerns primarily because of the possibility that they will discourage invention by the licensee.[46] In *Transparent-Wrap Machine Corp. v. Stokes & Smith Co.*,[47] the Supreme Court held that a rule of reason analysis should be used to test the grantback provision in an exclusive license agreement on a patented packaging machine. The grantback provision required the licensee to assign to the licensor all patents for improvements applicable to the patented machine, leaving the licensee with only a nonexclusive,

cert. denied, 433 U.S. 910 (1977); Dole Valve Co. v. Perfection Bar Equip., Inc., 311 F. Supp. 459, 463 (N.D. Ill. 1970); United States v. Lever Bros. Co., 216 F. Supp. 887, 889 (S.D.N.Y. 1963).
39.   *See, e.g.*, United States v. Columbia Pictures Corp., 189 F. Supp. 153, 181-82 (S.D.N.Y. 1960).
40.   INTELLECTUAL PROPERTY GUIDELINES, *supra* note 16, § 5.7.
41.   Eastman Kodak Co. v. Goodyear Tire & Rubber Co., 114 F.3d 1547, 1558 (Fed. Cir. 1997).
42.   *Id.* at 1558-59.
43.   15 U.S.C. §§ 4301-4305 (2000). The coverage of the act (first passed as the National Cooperative Research Act of 1984) initially was limited to research joint ventures. Its protections were extended to production joint ventures by the National Cooperative Production Amendments of 1993, Pub. L. No. 103-42, 107 Stat. 117. The act is discussed in part C.2 of Chapter IV.
44.   15 U.S.C. § 4302 (2000). The rule of reason also may apply to joint ventures that do not fit within the definition set forth in the National Cooperative Research and Production Act. The antitrust analysis of joint ventures is discussed in Chapter IV.
45.   15 U.S.C. § 4303 (2000).
46.   Hartford-Empire Co. v. United States, 323 U.S. 386, 400 (1945).
47.   329 U.S. 637 (1947).

royalty-free license on the improvements. The Court recognized "the possibilities of abuse" and emphasized that it was holding only that grantbacks do not constitute per se violations.[48]

In *United States v. National Lead Co.*,[49] the Supreme Court approved a limited grantback provision in a decree against two defendants that together sold over 90 percent of titanium pigments in the United States.[50] The decree required the defendants to grant to any applicant a nonexclusive license under certain applicable patents at a "uniform, reasonable royalty," but it permitted such licenses to "be conditioned upon the reciprocal grant of a license . . . at a reasonable royalty, under any and all patents covering titanium pigments . . . now issued or pending, or issued within five years from the date of this decree, if any, owned or controlled by such applicant."[51]

In applying a rule of reason analysis to grantback provisions, the courts have identified a number of relevant factors: (1) whether the grantback is exclusive or nonexclusive; (2) if exclusive, whether the licensee retains the right to use the improvements; (3) whether the grantback precludes, permits, or requires the licensor to grant sublicenses; (4) whether the grantback is limited to the scope of the licensed patents or covers inventions which would not infringe the licensed patent; (5) the duration of the grantback; (6) whether the grantback is royalty free; (7) the market power of the parties; (8) whether the parties are competitors; and (9) the effect of the grantback on the incentive for developmental research.[52] Similarly, the agencies have expressed concern that "a [patent] pooling arrangement that requires members to grant licenses to each other for current and future technology at minimal cost may reduce the incentives of its members to engage in research and development because members of the pool have to share their successful research and development and each of the members can free ride on the accomplishments of other pool members."[53]

Many cases hold that in the absence of anticompetitive intent or restrictive practices, the grantback of a nonexclusive license does not violate the antitrust laws

48. *Id.* at 646-48. On remand, the court of appeals found no illegality. Stokes & Smith Co. v. Transparent-Wrap Mach. Co., 161 F.2d 565 (2d Cir.), *cert. denied*, 331 U.S. 837 (1947).

49. 332 U.S. 319 (1947).

50. *Id.* at 335-36, 359-60.

51. *Id.* at 336.

52. *See, e.g.*, Santa Fe-Pomeroy, Inc. v. P & Z Co., 569 F.2d 1084, 1101 (9th Cir. 1978) ("the grant-back was limited in time and subject matter . . . and therefore had no restrictive or 'chilling' effect on any improvements"); International Nickel Co. v. Ford Motor Co., 166 F. Supp. 551, 565-66 (S.D.N.Y. 1958); United States v. Associated Patents, Inc., 134 F. Supp. 74, 82 (E.D. Mich. 1955) (outside parties were foreclosed from obtaining improvement licenses but technological developments were discouraged), *aff'd mem. sub nom.* Mac Inv. Co. v. United States, 350 U.S. 960 (1956); United States v. E.I. duPont de Nemours & Co., 118 F. Supp. 41, 224 (D. Del. 1953) (grantback agreements did not enhance duPont's market power; scope of agreements was limited, no proof of refusal to license by duPont), *aff'd*, 351 U.S. 377 (1956); United States v. Besser Mfg. Co., 96 F. Supp. 304, 310-11 (E.D. Mich. 1951) (purpose of unlawful agreements was "to make certain that these two giants of the industry didn't battle each other over patents any more"); United States v. General Elec. Co., 82 F. Supp. 753, 815-16 (D.N.J. 1949) (defendant acquired patents "to perpetuate a control over the incandescent electric lamp long after its basic patents expired"); United States v. National Lead Co., 63 F. Supp. 513, 524 (S.D.N.Y. 1945) (unlawful "agreements applied to patents not yet issued and to inventions not yet imagined"), *aff'd*, 332 U.S. 319 (1947).

53. INTELLECTUAL PROPERTY GUIDELINES, *supra* note 16, § 5.5 (citing cases).

or constitute misuse.[54] Exclusive grantbacks, standing alone, also have been upheld.[55] Where license agreements combine grantbacks with other restrictions, both exclusive and nonexclusive grantbacks have been held to be illegal.[56]

The *Intellectual Property Guidelines* recognize the potential competitive benefits of grantbacks:

> Grantbacks can have procompetitive effects, especially if they are nonexclusive. Such arrangements provide a means for the licensee and the licensor to share risks and reward the licensor for making possible further innovation based on or informed by the licensed technology, and both promote innovation in the first place and promote the subsequent licensing of the results of the innovation.[57]

However, the *Guidelines* also warn that grantbacks may have an anticompetitive effect "if they substantially reduce the licensee's incentives to engage in research and development and thereby limit rivalry in innovation markets."[58]

2. *Enforcement of Intellectual Property Rights as an Antitrust Violation*

a. INTELLECTUAL PROPERTY OBTAINED BY FRAUD OR INEQUITABLE CONDUCT

The mere procurement of a patent from the Patent and Trademark Office does not violate the antitrust laws.[59] The procurement of a patent through fraud on that office, however, will render all of the claims of the patent unenforceable in an infringement

---

54. *See, e.g.*, Binks Mfg. Co. v. Ransburg Electro-Coating Corp., 281 F.2d 252, 259 (7th Cir. 1960), *cert. dismissed*, 366 U.S. 211 (1961); Barr Rubber Prods. Co. v. Sun Rubber Co., 277 F. Supp. 484, 506 (S.D.N.Y. 1967), *aff'd in part and rev'd in part*, 425 F.2d 1114 (2d Cir.), *cert. denied*, 400 U.S. 878 (1970); Well Surveys, Inc. v. McCullough Tool Co., 199 F. Supp. 374, 395 (N.D. Okla. 1961), *aff'd*, 343 F.2d 381 (10th Cir. 1965), *cert. denied*, 383 U.S. 933 (1966); *International Nickel*, 166 F. Supp. at 565.

55. *See, e.g.*, *Santa Fe-Pomeroy*, 569 F.2d at 1101-02 (many competitive alternatives and no evidence that the grantback had deterred improvements); Zajicek v. KoolVent Metal Awning Corp. of Am., 283 F.2d 127, 131-32 (9th Cir. 1960), *cert. denied*, 365 U.S. 859 (1961); Swofford v. B & W, Inc., 251 F. Supp. 811, 820-21 (S.D. Tex. 1966), *aff'd*, 395 F.2d 362 (5th Cir.), *cert. denied*, 393 U.S. 935 (1968); Sperry Prods. v. Aluminum Co. of Am., 171 F. Supp. 901, 936-38 (N.D. Ohio 1959), *aff'd in part and rev'd in part*, 285 F.2d 911 (6th Cir. 1960), *cert. denied*, 368 U.S. 890 (1961). *But see* Duplan Corp. v. Deering Milliken, Inc., 444 F. Supp. 648, 700 (D.S.C. 1977) (requirement that a licensee assign patents broader than those of licensor "substantially enhanced and extended" monopoly of the licensed patent), *aff'd in part and rev'd in part*, 594 F.2d 979 (4th Cir. 1979), *cert. denied*, 444 U.S. 1015 (1980).

56. *See, e.g.*, United States v. Aluminum Co. of Am., 91 F. Supp. 333, 410 (S.D.N.Y. 1950); *General Elec.*, 82 F. Supp. at 815-16 (nonexclusive grantbacks held illegal where court also found a broad scheme to monopolize an industry and to eliminate competition after basic patents expired); United States v. General Elec. Co., 80 F. Supp. 989, 1005-06 (S.D.N.Y. 1948) (grantbacks in conjunction with price-fixing agreements held to violate the antitrust laws).

57. INTELLECTUAL PROPERTY GUIDELINES, *supra* note 16, § 5.6.

58. *Id.*

59. *See, e.g.*, FMC Corp. v. Manitowoc Co., 835 F.2d 1411, 1418 & n.16 (Fed. Cir. 1987); Brunswick Corp. v. Riegel Textile Corp., 752 F.2d 261, 265 (7th Cir. 1984), *cert. denied*, 472 U.S. 1018 (1985); Oetiker v. Jurid Werke, GmbH, 556 F.2d 1 (D.C. Cir. 1977).

action,[60] and it may expose the patentee to liability for the defendant's attorneys' fees under the Patent Act.[61] Such fraud may form the basis for a criminal prosecution under Sections 1 and 2 of the Sherman Act[62] and also may support an action for cancellation of the patent at the request of the United States.[63] Exploitation of a fraudulently procured patent also may constitute a violation of Section 5 of the FTC Act.[64]

In *Walker Process Equipment, Inc. v. Food Machinery & Chemical Corp.*,[65] the Supreme Court ruled that the enforcement of a patent procured by fraud may form the basis for a cause of action under Section 2 of the Sherman Act, exposing the patentee to a treble-damage claim under Section 4 of the Clayton Act. In *Walker Process*, the defendant alleged that the patentee had procured the patent in suit by filing a false oath that failed to disclose to the Patent and Trademark Office that a statutory bar to patentability existed.[66] The Supreme Court held that these allegations were sufficient to state a claim under Section 2 provided the remaining elements of a monopolization claim were proven.[67] The theory of *Walker Process* has been applied to enforcement of fraudulently obtained copyrights as well.[68]

---

60. *See, e.g.*, Kingsdown Med. Consultants v. Hollister Inc., 863 F.2d 867, 877 (Fed. Cir. 1988) (en banc portion of decision), *cert. denied*, 490 U.S. 1067 (1989); Jack Frost Lab. v. Physicians & Nurses Mfg., 901 F. Supp. 718, 728 (S.D.N.Y. 1995), *aff'd without op.*, 124 F.3d 229 (Fed. Cir. 1997). This rule applies to inequitable conduct in obtaining reissue patents. *See* Hewlett-Packard Co. v. Bausch & Lomb, Inc., 882 F.2d 1556, 1563 (Fed. Cir. 1989), *cert. denied*, 493 U.S. 1076 (1990); *see also* 35 U.S.C. § 288 (1994) ("Whenever, *without deceptive intention*, a claim of a patent is invalid, an action may be maintained for the infringement of a claim of the patent which may be valid.") (emphasis added); Conceptual Eng'g Assocs. v. Aelectronic Bonding, Inc., 714 F. Supp. 1262 (D.R.I. 1989).

61. Fraud or inequitable conduct may form the basis for a finding that a patent case is "exceptional," justifying an award of attorneys' fees under 35 U.S.C. § 285 (1994). *See* Kimberly-Clark Corp. v. Johnson & Johnson, 745 F.2d 1437, 1458 (Fed. Cir. 1984). "The trial standard of proving 'exceptional' is 'clear and convincing.'" Loctite Corp. v. Ultraseal Ltd., 781 F.2d 861, 878 n.12 (Fed. Cir. 1985), *overruled on other grounds by* Nobelpharma AB v. Implant Innovations, Inc., 141 F.3d 1059, 1068 (Fed. Cir.) (en banc portion of decision), *cert. denied*, 525 U.S. 876 (1998).

62. *See* United States v. Union Camp Corp., 1969 Trade Cas. (CCH) ¶ 72,689 (E.D. Va. 1969) (consent decree) (indictment charged fraud on the courts in maintaining a patent infringement suit on a patent known to be invalid), *final judgment terminated*, 1990-1 Trade Cas. (CCH) ¶ 69,000 (E.D. Va. 1990); *see also* United States v. Markham, 537 F.2d 187 (5th Cir. 1976) (fraudulent statement and forged documents filed in an interference proceeding in the PTO to determine priority of invention), *cert. denied*, 429 U.S. 1041 (1977).

63. *See* United States v. American Bell Tel. Co., 128 U.S. 315 (1888); United States v. Saf-T-Boom Corp., 164 U.S.P.Q. (BNA) 283 (E.D. Ark.), *aff'd per curiam*, 431 F.2d 737 (8th Cir. 1970).

64. 15 U.S.C. § 45 (2000); *see* Charles Pfizer & Co. v. FTC, 401 F.2d 574, 579 (6th Cir. 1968), *cert. denied*, 394 U.S. 920 (1969); American Cyanamid Co. v. FTC, 363 F.2d 757 (6th Cir. 1966).

65. 382 U.S. 172 (1965).

66. *Id.* at 174. Under 35 U.S.C. § 102(b) (1994), an applicant is not entitled to a patent if his invention has been on sale for more than one year prior to the time the application for patent is made. At the time *Walker Process* was decided, the patent applicant was obligated to file an oath averring that no such on-sale bar existed. The allegation in *Walker Process* was that the patentee signed this oath with knowledge that an on-sale bar existed.

67. 382 U.S. at 178.

68. *See, e.g.*, Michael Anthony Jewelers v. Peacock Jewelry, 795 F. Supp. 639 (S.D.N.Y. 1992); Knickerbocker Toy Co. v. Winterbrook Corp., 554 F. Supp. 1309, 1321 (D.N.H. 1982); Vogue Ring Creations, Inc. v. Hardman, 410 F. Supp. 609, 616 (D.R.I. 1976).

In an attempted monopolization case under a *Walker Process* theory, some type of enforcement conduct must be shown.[69] In addition, a plaintiff must prove that (1) the patent was procured by fraud,[70] (2) the party asserting the patent was aware of the fraud when it initiated the lawsuit,[71] (3) the patent would not have been granted to the defendant absent the fraud,[72] (4) there is a dangerous probability of the patentee obtaining monopoly power in a properly defined relevant market,[73] and (5) that the party asserting the claim has antitrust standing and has suffered damages.[74] The

---

69. *See, e.g.*, Brunswick Corp. v. Riegel Textile Corp., 752 F.2d 261, 265 (7th Cir. 1984), *cert. denied*, 472 U.S. 1018 (1985); Oetiker v. Jurid Werke, GmbH, 671 F.2d 596 (D.C. Cir. 1982) (dictum); Handgards, Inc. v. Ethicon, Inc., 601 F.2d 986, 993 (9th Cir. 1979) (no *Walker Process* claim established where plaintiff did not contend that defendant sought to enforce a fraudulently obtained patent), *cert. denied*, 444 U.S. 1025 (1980); K-Lath, Div. of Tree Island Wire, Inc. v. Davis Wire Corp., 15 F. Supp. 2d 952, 964 (C.D. Cal. 1998) (dismissing *Walker Process* claim for lack of "threat or reasonable apprehension of an infringement suit"); Silva v. Mamula, 1994-1 Trade Cas. (CCH) ¶ 70,555 (E.D. Pa. 1994) (mere acquisition of patent by fraud is insufficient to satisfy requirements of Sherman Act § 2: "it is the use of that patent in illegal antitrust behavior that gives rise to liability"); Northlake Mktg. & Supply v. Glaverbel, S.A., 861 F. Supp. 653, 658 (N.D. Ill. 1994) (dismissing *Walker Process* claim because plaintiff failed to present sufficient evidence that defendant, an exclusive licensee, had threatened to enforce the patent), *amended*, No. 92 C 2732, 1994 U.S. Dist. LEXIS 13990 (N.D. Ill. Sept. 29, 1994); Struthers Scientific & Int'l Corp. v. General Foods Corp., 334 F. Supp. 1329, 1332 (D. Del. 1971) (dictum).
70. *See infra* notes 87-92 and accompanying text.
71. *Nobelpharma AB*, 141 F.3d at 1069 ("the plaintiff in the patent infringement suit must also have been aware of the fraud when bringing suit"); T&T Geotechnical, Inc. v. Union Pac. Res. Co., 944 F. Supp. 1317, 1324 (N.D. Tex. 1996) (granting summary judgment for, inter alia, lack of evidence defendant knew patent was fraudulently procured).
72. *See, e.g.*, *Brunswick*, 752 F.2d at 265; E.I. duPont de Nemours & Co. v. Berkley & Co., 620 F.2d 1247, 1274 (8th Cir. 1980); United States Movidyn Corp. v. Hercules, Inc., 388 F. Supp. 1146, 1155 (D. Minn. 1975); *see also* Norton v. Curtiss, 433 F.2d 779, 794 (C.C.P.A. 1970) (analyzing the concept of the "materiality" of the fraud). In *Brunswick*, the Seventh Circuit reasoned that unless the invention was not patentable at all, whatever exclusionary power the patent confers is not a concern of the antitrust laws.
73. *See, e.g.*, *Walker Process*, 382 U.S. at 178; Technicon Instr. Corp. v. Alpkem Corp., 866 F.2d 417 (Fed. Cir. 1989); Hennessy Indus. v. FMC Corp., 779 F.2d 402, 405 (7th Cir. 1985); American Hoist & Derrick Co. v. Sowa & Sons, 725 F.2d 1350, 1366-67 (Fed. Cir.), *cert. denied*, 469 U.S. 821 (1984); *Brunswick*, 752 F.2d at 265; *see also* Mitsubishi Elec. v. IMS Tech., 44 U.S.P.Q.2d (BNA) 1904 (N.D. Ill. 1997) (*Walker Process* claim failed for lack of sufficient market power allegation); B.V. Optische v. Hologic, Inc., 909 F. Supp. 162 (S.D.N.Y. 1995) (dismissing complaint for failure to plead a relevant market); Publications Int'l v. Western Publ'g Co., 1994-1 Trade Cas. (CCH) ¶ 70,540 (N.D. Ill. 1994) (the existence of a noninfringing substitute does not necessarily preclude a finding of market power); Re-Alco Indus. v. National Ctr. for Health Educ., Inc., 812 F. Supp. 387 (S.D.N.Y. 1993) (dismissing attempted monopolization claim based on enforcement of invalid copyright because plaintiff did not adequately allege a relevant product market).
74. The party asserting the claim must have antitrust standing. *See, e.g.*, Indium Corp. of Am. v. Semi-Alloys, Inc., 781 F.2d 879 (Fed. Cir. 1985) (no standing where plaintiff is not prepared to manufacture product covered by patent), *cert. denied*, 479 U.S. 820 (1986); *Brunswick*, 752 F.2d at 266-68 (no standing where no consumer interest is harmed); *Handgards, Inc.*, 743 F.2d at 1295-97 (finding standing); *Silva*, 1994-1 Trade Cas. (CCH) ¶ 70,555 (no antitrust injury where parties against whom allegedly unlawful infringement suit was brought were not competitors of the patent holder); D.L. Auld Co. v. Park Electrochem. Corp., 1986-2 Trade Cas. (CCH) ¶ 67,309 (E.D.N.Y. 1986) (shareholder lacked standing). Proof of damages also is an essential element. *See, e.g.*, Grip-Pak, Inc. v. Illinois Tool Works, Inc., 651 F. Supp. 1482 (N.D. Ill. 1986); Indium Corp. of Am. v. Semi-Alloys, Inc., 611 F. Supp. 379 (N.D.N.Y.), *aff'd*, 781 F.2d 879 (Fed. Cir. 1985), *cert. denied*, 479 U.S. 820 (1986); *cf.* Hu-Friedy Mfg. Co. v. Peerless Int'l, Inc., 1986-2 Trade Cas.

allegations of fraud must comply with Rule 9(b) of the Federal Rules of Civil Procedure.[75]

Walker Process claims often are raised as counterclaims in patent infringement actions, and, as a result, most cases involving these counterclaims are appealed to the Federal Circuit. In *Nobelpharma AB v. Implant Innovations, Inc.*,[76] the Federal Circuit held that "whether conduct in procuring or enforcing a patent is sufficient to strip a patentee of its immunity from the antitrust laws is to be decided as a question of Federal Circuit law."[77] The court explained that this holding "applies equally to all antitrust claims premised on the bringing of a patent infringement suit."[78]

Nobelpharma also clarified the relationship between *Walker Process* and the *Noerr* doctrine.[79] Implant Innovations alleged that Nobelpharma was attempting to enforce a patent Nobelpharma knew to be invalid as a result of the inventor's intentional failure to disclose certain prior art to the patent examiner in the course of prosecuting the patent before the Patent and Trademark Office.[80] The Federal Circuit reasoned that *Walker Process* and the sham exception to *Noerr* "provide alternative legal grounds on which a patentee may be stripped of its immunity from the antitrust laws; both legal theories may be applied to the same conduct."[81] To reach this holding, the court rejected Nobelpharma's argument that *Professional Real Estate Investors, Inc. v. Columbia Pictures Industries*[82] (which holds that a lawsuit is not a sham if a reasonable litigant could realistically expect a favorable outcome) required Implant Innovations to show, as an element of its *Walker Process* claim, that Nobelpharma's infringement allegations were "objectively baseless."[83] Other courts have adopted various views with respect to the relationship between *Walker Process*

(CCH) ¶ 67,197 (N.D. Ill. 1986) (ordinary requirements of § 2 case apply to attempted monopolization claim based on bad faith assertion of a trademark).

75. A conclusory assertion that the patentee withheld material information "about pertinent prior art affecting the patentability and validity of said Letters Patent, and . . . knowingly and willfully present[ed] false and/or misleading arguments and materials . . . and in so doing perpetrated a fraud on [the PTO]" is insufficient. Papst Motoren GmbH v. Kanematsu-Goshu (U.S.A.) Inc., 629 F. Supp. 864, 871-72 (S.D.N.Y. 1986); *see also* Rolite, Inc. v. Wheelabrator Envtl. Sys., 958 F. Supp. 992, 1005 (E.D. Pa. 1997) (finding plaintiff stated fraudulent omission claim with sufficient particularity to meet Rule 9(b)'s requirements without deciding whether the rule applies to *Walker Process* claims); *Publications Int'l*, 1994-1 Trade Cas. (CCH) ¶ 70,540 (allegation that product covered by patent was sold more than a year prior to patent filing, that those involved in the filing and prosecution knew of the prior sales, and that they knowingly failed to disclose them to the PTO stated a claim under Rule 9(b)); Erie Technological Prods. v. JFD Elec. Components Corp., 198 U.S.P.Q. (BNA) 179, 186 (E.D.N.Y. 1978).

76. 141 F.3d 1059, 1068 (Fed. Cir.), *cert. denied*, 525 U.S. 876 (1998).

77. *Id.* at 1068 (en banc portion of decision). *Nobelpharma* expressly overruled the Federal Circuit's prior decisions in *Cygnus Therapeutics Sys v. ALZA Corp.*, 92 F.3d 1153, 1161 (Fed. Cir. 1996); *Loctite Corp. v. Ultraseal Ltd.*, 781 F.2d 861, 875 (Fed. Cir. 1985); and *Atari, Inc. v. JS & A Group*, 747 F.2d 1422, 1438-40 (Fed. Cir. 1984) (en banc). See part F.2 of this chapter for a discussion of choice of law rules in the Federal Circuit.

78. 141 F.3d at 1068.

79. The *Noerr* doctrine protects the good faith institution of litigation from serving as the basis for finding antitrust liability; absent a finding that the litigation was a sham, such litigation is lawful. The *Noerr* doctrine is discussed in part C of Chapter XIII.

80. 141 F.3d at 1064-65.

81. *Id.* at 1071.

82. 508 U.S. 49, 60-61 n.6 (1993) (*PRE*).

83. 141 F.3d at 1071-72.

and *Noerr*.[84] The Supreme Court has declined an opportunity to address this question.[85]

The Federal Circuit has applied *Nobelpharma* to prelitigation enforcement conduct, holding that a patent owner's efforts to exclude others from a market by threatening patent infringement lawsuits cannot form the basis for antitrust liability absent a showing that the patent was obtained by fraud or that the threatened lawsuits were shams.[86]

To establish the fraud element of a *Walker Process* claim, courts have required the proof to adhere closely to the elements of common-law fraud: clear and convincing evidence of a misrepresentation of a material fact, intentionally made to deceive, that is reasonably relied upon by the party to whom the misrepresentation was made.[87] For example, in *Nobelpharma* the Federal Circuit required "a misrepresentation or omission [that] . . . evidence[s] a clear intent to deceive the [patent] examiner and thereby cause[s] the PTO to grant an invalid patent."[88] The

84. *See, e.g.*, Rohm & Haas Co. v. Dawson Chem. Co., 635 F. Supp. 1211, 1222 (S.D. Tex. 1986) ("The *Walker Process* Doctrine is an exception to the *Noerr-Pennington* Doctrine."); *cf.* Whelan v. Abell, 48 F.3d 1247, 1255 (D.C. Cir. 1995) ("However broad the First Amendment right to petition may be, it cannot be stretched to cover petitions based on known falsehoods."); Liberty Lake Invs., Inc. v. Magnuson, 12 F.3d 155, 159 (9th Cir. 1993) ("In a case involving a fraudulently-obtained patent, that which immunizes the predatory behavior from antitrust liability (the patent) is, in effect, a nullity because of the underlying fraud . . . . *Professional Real Estate Investors* . . . does not obviate application of the Court's two-part test for determining sham litigation in the absence of proof that a party's knowing fraud upon, or its intentional misrepresentations to, the court deprive the litigation of its legitimacy."), *cert. denied*, 513 U.S. 818 (1994).

85. *See PRE*, 508 U.S. at 72 n.6 (refusing to decide whether *Noerr* permits antitrust liability for litigant's fraud or misrepresentations). Prior to *Nobelpharma*, the Federal Circuit had declined several opportunities to address the relationship of *Walker Process* to the *Noerr* doctrine. Filmtec Corp. v. Hydranautics, 67 F.3d 931, 939 n.2 (Fed. Cir. 1995), *cert. denied*, 519 U.S. 814 (1996); Carroll Touch, Inc. v. Electro Mech. Sys., 15 F.3d 1573, 1583 n.3 (Fed. Cir. 1993); *see also* Hydranautics v. FilmTec Corp., 70 F.3d 533 (9th Cir. 1995); United States Gypsum Co. v. National Gypsum Co., No. 89 C 7533, 1994 U.S. Dist. LEXIS 458 (N.D. Ill. Jan. 20, 1994), *aff'd*, 74 F.3d 1209 (Fed. Cir. 1996).

86. *See* Glass Equip. Dev., Inc. v. Besten, Inc., 174 F.3d 1337, 1343 (Fed. Cir. 1999). Prelitigation threats and other conduct incidental to litigation are discussed in part B.2.b of this chapter.

87. *See, e.g.*, *Walker Process*, 382 U.S. at 177; Argus Chem. Corp. v. Fibre Glass-Evercoat Co., 812 F.2d 1381, 1383-86 (Fed. Cir. 1987); Korody-Colyer Corp. v. General Motors Corp., 828 F.2d 1572, 1577-78 (Fed. Cir. 1987); Kearney & Trecker Corp. v. Cincinnati Milacron, Inc., 562 F.2d 365, 373 (6th Cir. 1977); Cataphote Corp. v. DeSoto Chem. Coatings, Inc., 450 F.2d 769, 770-71 (9th Cir. 1971), *cert. denied*, 408 U.S. 929 (1972); Jack Winter, Inc. v. Koratron Co., 375 F. Supp. 1, 67 (N.D. Cal. 1974).

88. 141 F.3d at 1070; *see also* C.R. Bard, Inc. v. M3 Sys., 157 F.3d 1340 (Fed. Cir. 1998), *cert. denied*, 526 U.S. 1130 (1999) (evidence of several alleged misstatements or omissions in the patent prosecution, including incorrectly naming the inventors, not supplying samples of the product, failing to provide to the PTO additional material provided to the Food and Drug Administration, failing to disclose certain related patents and co-pending patents, and not disclosing all evidence with respect to the on-sale issue were not sufficient to support a jury's finding of *Walker-Process* liability); Miller Pipeline v. British Gas PLC, 69 F. Supp. 2d 1129, 1136 (S.D. Ind. 1999) (insufficient evidence of intent to deceive examiner); Baxa Corp. v. McGaw, Inc., 996 F. Supp. 1044, 1050 (D. Colo. 1997) (granting summary judgment on *Walker Process* claim for lack of evidence of fraud), *aff'd without op.*, 185 F.3d 883 (Fed. Cir. 1999); CVD, Inc. v. Raytheon Co., 769 F.2d 842, 849 (1st Cir. 1985), *cert. denied*, 475 U.S. 1016 (1986); Oetiker v. Jurid Werke, GmbH, 671 F.2d 596 (D.C. Cir. 1982); Handgards, Inc. v. Ethicon, Inc., 601 F.2d 986, 996 (9th Cir. 1979), *cert. denied*, 444 U.S. 1025 (1980); Scripto-Tokai Corp. v. Gillette Co., 1994-2 Trade

Federal Circuit compared this standard to the lesser offense of inequitable conduct (which renders the patent unenforceable but does not give rise to an antitrust claim):[89] "[a] finding of *Walker-Process* fraud requires higher threshold showings of both intent and materiality than does a finding of inequitable conduct."[90] The court rejected "an equitable balancing of lesser degrees of materiality and intent," instead requiring "independent and clear evidence of deceptive intent together with a clear showing of reliance, *i.e.*, that the patent would not have issued but for the misrepresentation or omission."[91] Other courts likewise have held that specific intent to commit fraud, and not some lesser standard such as gross negligence, is necessary to establish a *Walker Process* claim.[92]

Inequitable conduct describes a class of less egregious conduct than *Walker-Process* fraud that can render a patent unenforceable. "The concept of inequitable conduct in patent procurement derives from the equitable doctrine of unclean hands: that a person who obtains a patent by intentionally misleading the PTO can not enforce the patent."[93] The availability of this defense in a patent infringement or declaratory judgment action has been clear since at least 1945, when the Supreme

---

Cas. (CCH) ¶ 70,821 (C.D. Cal. 1994); Minnesota Mining & Mfg. Co. v. Research Med., Inc., 691 F. Supp. 1305, 1309 (D. Utah 1988).

89. *See infra* notes 93-106 and accompanying text.

90. 141 F.3d at 1070-71; *see also* Litton Indus. Prods. v. Solid State Sys., 755 F.2d 158, 166 n.19 (Fed. Cir. 1985) ("the offensive use of such conduct before the PTO generally requires a higher level of materiality than that required for defensive purposes"; looking to Ninth Circuit law for guidance in interpreting Washington state law).

91. 141 F.3d at 1071; *Scripto-Tokai*, 1994-2 Trade Cas. (CCH) ¶ 70,821 (granting summary judgment on *Walker Process* claim where alleged misrepresentations regarding prior art and the results of certain performance tests were not sufficiently material); Al-Site Corp. v. Opti-Ray, Inc., 28 U.S.P.Q.2d (BNA) 1058, 1062 (E.D.N.Y. 1993) ("in determining whether a party has stated a cognizable antitrust counterclaim, the undisclosed prior art is only material if 'but for' the omission or misrepresentation, the patent would not have issued"); Rohm & Haas Co. v. Dawson Chem. Co., 635 F. Supp. 1211, 1218 (S.D. Tex. 1986) ("The fraud must be material *in an antitrust sense* in that the alleged infringer/antitrust counterclaimant must show that but for the fraud no patent would have been issued to anyone.").

92. *See Scripto-Tokai Corp.*, 1994-2 Trade Cas. (CCH) ¶ 70,821 (summary judgment granted dismissing *Walker Process* claims where alleged misrepresentations regarding prior art and the results of certain performance tests were not made with the requisite deliberate intent to deceive); *In re* Recombinant DNA Tech. Patent & Contract Litig., 874 F. Supp. 904, 914-15 (S.D. Ind. 1994) (university's representation that a nonexclusive license appeared unattractive and request that federal agency grant an exclusive license for patents resulting from agency-funded research was not actionable as fraud on agency); Papst Motoren GmbH v. Kanematsu-Goshu (U.S.A.) Inc., 629 F. Supp. 864, 870 (S.D.N.Y. 1986) ("*Walker* and its progeny emphasize that to sustain [defendant's] antitrust counterclaim, 'deliberate fraud' is required: 'there must be allegations and proof of knowing, willful and intentional acts of misrepresentation to the Patent Office.'") (quoting Erie Tech. Prods. v. JFD Elec. Components Corp., 198 U.S.P.Q. (BNA) 179, 185 (E.D.N.Y. 1978)). *But cf. Litton Indus. Prods.*, where the court stated:

    Wholly inadvertent errors or honest mistakes, which are caused by neither fraudulent intent *nor by the patentee's gross negligence*, do not constitute the requisite level of intent. . . . This level of intent for *Walker Process* actions, where inequitable conduct . . . is used offensively for recovering damages, apparently corresponds to the level of intent required under Federal Circuit case law for asserting inequitable conduct defensively to render a patent unenforceable.

755 F.2d at 166 & n.18 (emphasis added) (citations omitted) (looking to Ninth Circuit law for guidance in interpreting Washington state law).

93. Demaco Corp. v. F. Von Langsdorff Licensing Ltd., 851 F.2d 1387, 1394 (Fed. Cir.), *cert. denied*, 488 U.S. 956 (1988).

Court said in *Precision Instrument Manufacturing Co. v. Automotive Maintenance Machinery Co.*[94] that patent applicants have "an uncompromising duty to report to [the PTO] all facts concerning possible fraud or inequitableness underlying the applications in issue."[95] Because the defense of inequitable conduct is rooted in equity, the determination is made by the court. If, however, the defense is coupled with a *Walker Process* counterclaim, the Federal Circuit has held that a counterclaiming defendant is entitled to a jury trial for fact finding common to both the antitrust counterclaim and the defense of inequitable conduct.[96]

To establish an inequitable conduct defense, the accused infringer must show, again by "clear and convincing evidence,"[97] a failure by the applicant[98] to disclose to the Patent and Trademark Office material information known to him or submission of false material information with an intent to act inequitably.[99] Several district

---

94. 324 U.S. 806 (1945).
95. *Id.* at 818 (failure to disclose to PTO the existence of perjury in an interference proceeding); *see also* Kingsland v. Dorsey, 338 U.S. 318, 319 (1949) (concealment of participation of applicant's attorney in preparation of article used to support application); Shawkee Mfg. Co. v. Hartford-Empire Co., 322 U.S. 271, 273-74 (1944) (submission of fraudulent article to deceive PTO); Hazel-Atlas Glass Co. v. Hartford-Empire Co., 322 U.S. 238, 240-51 (1944) (article used in support of a pending application was written by applicant under a different name to deceive PTO); Semiconductor Energy Lab. Co. v. Samsung Elec. Co., 204 F.3d 1368, 1377 (Fed. Cir. 2000) (misleadingly incomplete translation of prior art, which was offered in original foreign language, "constructively withheld the reference from the PTO"), *cert. denied*, 531 U.S. 1190 (2001).
96. Cabinet Vision v. Cabnetware, 129 F.3d 595, 600 (Fed. Cir. 1997). Similarly, one court delayed considering an inequitable conduct defense so as not to interfere with the constitutional right to a jury trial for the legal claim that the patent was unenforceable due to prior art, which presented common factual elements to the equitable conduct defense. Herman v. William Brooks Shoe Co., 49 U.S.P.Q.2d (BNA) 1361 (S.D.N.Y. 1998) (granting motion to reconsider prior order separating bench trial on issues on inequitable conduct from jury trial of issues of patent validity and infringement).
97. *See, e.g.,* SmithKline Diagnostics, Inc. v. Helena Lab., 859 F.2d 878, 891 (Fed. Cir. 1988); Specialty Composites v. Cabot Corp., 845 F.2d 981, 991 (Fed. Cir. 1988); FMC Corp. v. Manitowoc Co., 835 F.2d 1411, 1415 (Fed. Cir. 1987); J.P. Stevens & Co. v. Lex Tex Ltd., 747 F.2d 1553, 1559 (Fed. Cir. 1984), *cert. denied*, 474 U.S. 822 (1985); Dometic Sales Corp. v. Intertherm, No. S87-81, 1988 U.S. Dist. LEXIS 19362 (N.D. Ind. Mar. 28, 1988).
98. Knowledge of others having substantive involvement in the application is chargeable to the applicant. *See* 37 C.F.R. § 1.56(a) (2000); Stark v. Advanced Magnetics, Inc., 119 F.3d 1551, 1556 (Fed. Cir. 1997) ("Misdeeds of co-inventors, or even a patent attorney, can affect the property rights of an otherwise innocent individual."); *FMC Corp.*, 835 F.2d at 1415 n.8; Kimberly-Clark Corp. v. Johnson & Johnson, 745 F.2d 1437, 1449-50 (Fed. Cir. 1984).
99. *See, e.g.,* Merck & Co. v. Danbury Pharmacal, Inc., 873 F.2d 1418, 1420 (Fed. Cir. 1989); *FMC Corp.*, 835 F.2d at 1415; Transmatic, Inc. v. Gulton Indus., 849 F. Supp. 526, 541 (E.D. Mich. 1994), *aff'd in part, rev'd in part, and vacated in part*, 53 F.3d 1270 (Fed. Cir. 1995). In cases concerning inequitable omissions, "proof of inequitable conduct may be rebutted by a showing that: (a) the prior art was not material; (b) if the prior art was material, a showing that the applicant did not know of that art; (c) if the applicant did know of that art, a showing that the applicant did not know of its materiality; or (d) a showing that the applicant's failure to disclose the art did not result from an intent to mislead the PTO." Elk Corp. v. GAF Bldg. Materials Corp., 168 F.3d 28, 30 (Fed. Cir.) (citing *FMC Corp.*, 835 F.2d at 1415), *cert. denied*, 528 U.S. 873 (1999); *see also* Jeneric/Pentron, Inc. v. Dillion Co., No. 3:98CV818 (EBB), 2001 U.S. Dist. LEXIS 15308, at *84-85 (D. Conn. Aug. 27, 2001) (where an existing patent was disclosed to the examiner, but certain calculations relating to a component of that patent were not, the "evidence does not support an inference of intent to deceive sufficient to eliminate any triable issue of fact"); *In re* VISX, Inc., No. 9286, 1999 FTC LEXIS 113 (1999) (finding that FTC complaint counsel failed to establish that applicant acted inequitably by not presenting certain pieces of prior art to the patent examiner).

courts have held that allegations of inequitable conduct must comply with Rule 9(b) of the Federal Rules of Civil Procedure.[100] A specific intent to commit fraud is not required.[101] The Federal Circuit defines the degree of materiality required to establish the defense of inequitable conduct with reference to the Patent and Trademark Office regulation establishing a patent applicant's duty to disclose information to the patent examiner.[102]

The Federal Circuit mandates a two-step inquiry for finding inequitable conduct. First, the trial court must determine whether the misstatement or omission meets a threshold level of materiality. Second, the court must determine whether the evidence reveals a threshold level of intent to mislead the Patent and Trademark Office.[103] The Federal Circuit reviews these findings under the clearly erroneous

---

100. Moore U.S.A., Inc. v. Standard Register Co., 139 F. Supp. 2d 348, 359 (W.D.N.Y. 2001); Rhone-Poulenc Argo S.A. v. Monsanto Co., 73 F. Supp. 2d 537, 539 (M.D.N.C. 1999); Videojet Sys. Int'l, Inc. v. Eagle Inks, Inc., 14 F. Supp. 2d 1046, 1049 (N.D. Ill. 1998) ("Allegations of inequitable conduct must be plead [sic] with the particularity required by Federal Rule of Civil Procedure 9(b)."); Sun Microsystems, Inc. v. Dataram Corp., Civ. No. 96-20708 SW, 1997 U.S. Dist. LEXIS 4557, at *9 (N.D. Cal. Feb. 4, 1997); Elkhart Brass Mfg. v. Task Force Tips, Inc., 867 F. Supp. 782, 784 (N.D. Ind. 1994) (finding that the standard of Rule 9(b) was met).

101. See Argus Chem. Corp. v. Fibre Glass-Evercoat Co., 759 F.2d 10, 12 n.3 (Fed. Cir.), cert. denied, 474 U.S. 903 (1985); Burlington Indus. v. Dayco Corp., 849 F.2d 1418, 1421 (Fed. Cir. 1988). In J.P. Stevens, the Federal Circuit said:

> Conduct before the PTO that may render a patent unenforceable is broader than "common law fraud." It includes failure to disclose material information, or submission of false material information, with an intent to mislead. Because the "fraud" label can be confused with other forms of conduct, this opinion avoids that label and uses "inequitable conduct" as a more accurate description of the proscribed activity, it being understood that the term encompasses affirmative acts of commission, e.g., submission of false information as well as omission, e.g., failure to disclose material information.

747 F.2d at 1559 (citation omitted). The Federal Circuit has held that a finding of gross negligence does not compel a finding that a patentee's conduct was inequitable. See Halliburton Co. v. Schlumberger Tech. Corp., 925 F.2d 1435, 1442-43 (Fed. Cir. 1991) ("Gross negligence does not of itself justify an inference of intent to deceive. This court has clarified that negligent conduct can support an inference of intent only when, 'viewed in light of all the evidence, including evidence indicative of good faith,' the conduct is culpable enough 'to require a finding of intent to deceive.'") (citing and quoting Kingsdown Med. Consultants v. Hollister, Inc., 863 F.2d 867, 876 (Fed. Cir. 1988) (en banc portion of decision)).

102. Semiconductor Energy Lab., 204 F.3d at 1374 (quoting and citing Rule 56(b), 37 C.F.R. § 1.56(b)); Critikon, Inc. v. Becton Dickinson Vascular Access, Inc., 120 F.3d 1253, 1257 (Fed. Cir. 1997) (same), cert. denied, 523 U.S. 1071 (1998). Rule 56(b) provides:

(b) Under this section, information is material to patentability when it is not cumulative to information already of record or being made of record in the application, and

  (1) It establishes, by itself or in combination with other information, a prima facie case of unpatentability of a claim; or

  (2) It refutes, or is inconsistent with, a position the applicant takes in:

    (i) Opposing an argument of unpatentability relied on by the Office, or

    (ii) Asserting an argument of patentability.

On January 17, 1992, the PTO amended Rule 56(b) to clarify an applicant's disclosure duty. Duty of Disclosure, 57 Fed. Reg. 2021 (PTO Jan. 17, 1992). For patent applications prosecuted prior to this amendment, the Federal Circuit asks whether the misrepresentation or omission "would merely have been considered important to the patentability of a claim by a reasonable examiner." Nobelpharma AB v. Implant Innovations, Inc., 141 F.3d 1059, 1070 (Fed. Cir.), cert. denied, 525 U.S. 876 (1998).

103. Baxter Int'l, Inc. v. McGaw, Inc., 149 F.3d 1321, 1327 (Fed. Cir. 1998) (citing Halliburton, 925 F.2d at 1439).

standard of Federal Rule of Civil Procedure 52(a).[104] If both thresholds are established, the trial court must then weigh materiality and intent:[105] the more material the misstatement or omission, the less evidence of intent is required to support a finding of inequitable conduct.[106] The Federal Circuit reviews the trial court's ultimate determination as to whether the patent is enforceable under an abuse of discretion standard.[107]

While inequitable conduct defenses and *Walker Process* counterclaims are frequently brought together, conduct sufficient to support an inequitable conduct defense, but not rising to the level of common-law fraud, will not support a claim under Section 2.[108] The *Intellectual Property Guidelines* state, however, that such conduct may violate Section 5 of the FTC Act.[109]

b.   BAD FAITH ENFORCEMENT OF INTELLECTUAL PROPERTY RIGHTS

It is not a violation of the Sherman Act to bring a patent infringement suit in good faith, even if it is determined in the suit that the patent is invalid.[110] However, the commencement of litigation to enforce a patent known to be invalid may give rise to antitrust liability, irrespective of whether the patent was obtained by fraud on the Patent and Trademark Office.[111] In such a case, the specific intent required to

---

104. *Id.* at 1327 (citing *Kingsdown Med. Consultants*, 863 F.2d at 872); *see also Elk Corp.*, 168 F.3d at 32 (affirming finding of intent to mislead under clearly erroneous standard).
105. *Baxter*, 149 F.3d at 1327 (citing Molins PLC v. Textron, Inc., 48 F.3d 1172, 1178 (Fed. Cir. 1995)).
106. *Id.* (citing N.V. Akzo v. E.I. duPont de Nemours, 810 F.2d 1148, 1153 (Fed. Cir. 1987)).
107. *Id.* (citing, inter alia, Kolmes v. World Fibers Corp., 107 F.3d 1534, 1541 (Fed. Cir. 1997)); *see also Elk Corp.*, 168 F.3d at 32 (affirming inequitable conduct determination under abuse of discretion standard).
108. *See, e.g.*, FMC Corp. v. Manitowoc Corp., 835 F.2d 1411, 1417-18 (Fed. Cir. 1987); Korody-Colyer Corp. v. General Motors Corp., 828 F.2d 1572, 1578 (Fed. Cir. 1987); Argus Chem. Corp. v. Fibreglass Evercoat Co., 812 F.2d 1381, 1384-85 (Fed. Cir. 1987); American Hoist & Derrick Co. v. Sowa & Sons, 725 F.2d 1350, 1368 (Fed. Cir.), *cert. denied*, 469 U.S. 821 (1984); Al-Site Corp. v. Opti-Ray Inc., 28 U.S.P.Q.2d (BNA) 1058, 1061-62 (E.D.N.Y. 1993) (noting that although omitted prior art was not material for purposes of defendant's antitrust counterclaim, it was material for purposes of its inequitable conduct defense); INTELLECTUAL PROPERTY GUIDELINES, *supra* note 16, § 6.
109. INTELLECTUAL PROPERTY GUIDELINES, *supra* note 16, § 6; *see also* American Cyanamid Co., 72 F.T.C. 623, 684-85 (1967), *aff'd sub. nom.* Charles Pfizer & Co., 401 F.2d 574 (6th Cir. 1968), *cert. denied*, 394 U.S. 920 (1969); *In re* VISX, Inc., No. 9286, 1999 FTC LEXIS 113 (1999) (rejecting inequitable conduct allegations brought pursuant to § 5 of the FTC Act).
110. *See, e.g.*, Atari Games Corp. v. Nintendo of Am., Inc., 897 F.2d 1572, 1576 (Fed. Cir. 1990) ("Congress has specifically granted patent owners the right to commence a civil suit in order to protect their inventions."); Colortronic Reinhard & Co. v. Plastic Controls, Inc., 668 F.2d 1, 9 (1st Cir. 1981); Handgards, Inc. v. , Inc., 601 F.2d 986, 993 (9th Cir. 1979) ("[p]atentees must be permitted to test the validity of their patents"), *cert. denied*, 444 U.S. 1025 (1980).
111. *See, e.g.*, Handgards, Inc. v. Ethicon, Inc., 743 F.2d 1282, 1288-89 (9th Cir. 1984) ("[a]ll that is required for a finding of bad faith in the context of an infringement suit is that the patent holder . . . knew that its patent was invalid"), *cert. denied*, 469 U.S. 1190 (1985); *Handgards*, 601 F.2d at 992-96 (presumption of good faith in filing infringement action can be overcome by clear and convincing evidence to the contrary); Baxa Corp. v. McGaw, Inc., 996 F. Supp. 1044, 1050 (D. Colo. 1997) (granting summary judgment on sham litigation claim for lack of clear and convincing evidence plaintiff in infringement lawsuit knew patent was invalid), *aff'd*, 185 F.3d 883 (Fed. Cir. 1999); Hart-Carter Co. v. J.P. Burroughs & Son, 605 F. Supp. 1327, 1347-48 (E.D. Mich. 1985) (patentee attempting to establish an illegal monopoly by misuse of patent should not be permitted

support a Section 2 attempt to monopolize claim exists because the patentee instituted or maintained the litigation in bad faith, i.e., with knowledge of the invalidity of the patent.[112] The other elements of the claim are the same as under the *Walker Process* theory.[113] The patentee's bad faith must be proven by clear and convincing evidence.[114] Because the overt act allegedly causing harm to the plaintiff is a lawsuit, the statute of limitations on an antitrust claim based on that lawsuit may begin to run as of the termination of the lawsuit.[115]

The close relation between a *Walker Process* Section 2 claim and one for bad faith enforcement of a patent is demonstrated by *Handgards, Inc. v. Ethicon, Inc.*,[116] where the Ninth Circuit found that a violation of Section 2 occurred when a patentee instituted litigation with knowledge that its patent was invalid due to an on-sale bar.[117] An on-sale bar was the same basis on which invalidity was alleged in *Walker Process*, i.e., that the alleged antitrust violation occurred because the patentee sought to enforce a patent in court knowing it was procured by fraud before the Patent and Trademark Office.[118] In a *Handgards*-type action, the plaintiff need not show that the

---

      to further goal by means of infringement suit); *see also* Kearney & Trecker Corp. v. Cincinnati Milacron, Inc., 562 F.2d 365, 372 (6th Cir. 1977) (deception in reissue proceedings tainted patent "to the same degree as if the original patent had been procured by fraud"); Duplan Corp. v. Deering Milliken, Inc., 444 F. Supp. 648, 701 (D.S.C. 1977) (no antitrust violation where it was not established by clear and convincing proof that the patent infringement suit was fraudulent), *aff'd in part and rev'd in part*, 594 F.2d 979 (4th Cir. 1979), *cert. denied*, 444 U.S. 1015 (1980); *cf.* CVD, Inc. v. Raytheon Co., 769 F.2d 842, 860 (1st Cir. 1985) (bad faith assertion of trade secret claims known to be invalid, with the intention of restraining competition, violated antitrust laws), *cert. denied*, 475 U.S. 1016 (1986); Kellogg Co. v. National Biscuit Co., 71 F.2d 662, 665-66 (2d Cir. 1934) (bad faith enforcement of trademark states a claim under § 2).

112.   *See, e.g., Handgards*, 601 F.2d at 990; Tennant Co. v. Hako Minuteman, Inc., 651 F. Supp. 945, 958-59 (N.D. Ill. 1986); *see also* Rohm & Haas Co. v. Dawson Chem. Co., 635 F. Supp. 1211, 1218 (S.D. Tex. 1986) ("[*Handgards*] held that the offense which is sanctioned by the antitrust laws is *not* the fraudulent procurement of a patent in circumstances that create monopoly power *but* the bringing of groundless suits for patent infringement."); *see also* T&T Geotech., Inc. v. Union Pac. Resources Co., 944 F. Supp. 1317 (N.D. Tex. 1996) (no liability where patent owner did not know patent was invalid).

113.   *See, e.g.,* Neumann v. Reinforced Earth Co., 786 F.2d 424, 427-30 (D.C. Cir.), *cert. denied*, 479 U.S. 851 (1986); Brunswick Corp. v. Riegel Textile Corp., 752 F.2d 261, 264-65 (7th Cir. 1984), *cert. denied*, 472 U.S. 1018 (1985); *Handgards*, 743 F.2d at 1288-89.

114.   *See, e.g.,* Loctite Corp. v. Ultraseal Ltd., 781 F.2d 861, 876 (Fed. Cir. 1985), *overruled on other grounds by* Nobelpharma AB v. Implant Innovations, Inc., 141 F.3d 1059, 1068 (Fed. Cir.) (en banc portion of decision), *cert. denied*, 525 U.S. 876 (1998); *Handgards*, 743 F.2d at 1294; *Handgards*, 601 F.2d at 996; Bendix Corp. v. Balax, Inc., 471 F.2d 149, 153 (7th Cir. 1972), *cert. denied*, 414 U.S. 819 (1973). In *Argus Chem. Corp. v. Fibre Glass-Evercoat Co.*, 645 F. Supp. 15, 17 (C.D. Cal. 1986), *aff'd*, 812 F.2d 1381 (Fed. Cir. 1987), the district court stated the elements of a § 2 attempt to monopolize claim under the *Handgards* theory: "the defendant must prove (1) by clear and convincing evidence that the patent suit was pursued in bad faith; (2) that plaintiff had a specific intent to monopolize the relevant market; and (3) that a dangerous probability of success existed." *Accord T&T Geotech.*, 944 F. Supp. at 1322.

115.   *See, e.g.,* Northern Trust Co. v. Ralston Purina Co., 1995-1 Trade Cas. (CCH) ¶ 70,874 (N.D. Ill. 1994) (holding statute of limitations began to run as of settlement of the complained-of litigation).

116.   601 F.2d 986 (9th Cir. 1979), *cert. denied*, 444 U.S. 1025 (1980). *See also In re* Independent Serv. Org. Antitrust Litig., 203 F.3d 1322 (Fed. Cir. 2000) (recognizing sham patent enforcement litigation as an established grounds for antitrust liability), *cert. denied*, 531 U.S. 1143 (2001).

117.   *Id.* at 992. The patentee's refusal to dismiss the litigation when invalidity became clear, together with certain discovery misconduct, were also factors relied on by the court in finding a violation. *Id.*

118.   *See supra* notes 65-68 and accompanying text.

patent was procured by fraud; rather, it is sufficient that the defendant learned sometime before suit was filed that the patent was not valid. Similarly, it has been held that institution of patent litigation against a defendant known by the patentee not to infringe may violate Section 2.[119]

Because the overt act in this type of case, filing a lawsuit, enjoys protection under the *Noerr* doctrine, parties challenging the enforcement of a patent against them will often assert that the patent infringement action is a sham not exempt from antitrust scrutiny.[120] In *Professional Real Estate Investors, Inc. v. Columbia Pictures Industries (PRE)*,[121] a copyright infringement case that involved an antitrust counterclaim, the Supreme Court set forth a two-pronged test for determining whether litigation is a sham and therefore not entitled to *Noerr* immunity: (1) "the lawsuit must be objectively baseless in the sense that no reasonable litigant could realistically expect success on the merits"; and (2) if the suit was found to be objectively baseless (and only then), the "court should focus on whether the baseless suit conceals an 'attempt to interfere *directly*' with a competitor's business relationships . . . through the 'use [of] the governmental process—as opposed to the *outcome* of that process—as an anticompetitive weapon.'"[122] Applying this test, the

119. *See* Hoffmann-La Roche Inc. v. Genpharm Inc., 50 F. Supp. 2d 367, 380 (D.N.J. 1999) (denying motion to dismiss sham litigation counterclaim where counterclaimant alleged defendant did not undertake a reasonable search to determine whether its patents were infringed before filing suit, and court determined the reasonableness of any search was a question of fact); United States v. Besser Mfg. Co., 96 F. Supp. 304, 312 (E.D. Mich. 1951), *aff'd*, 343 U.S. 444 (1952). *But see* Glaverbel S.A. v. Northlake Mktg. & Supply, 45 F.3d 1550 (Fed. Cir. 1995) (no bad faith where alleged infringer did not dispute prelitigation tests showing infringement and where alleged infringer's witnesses could not unequivocally deny infringement).

120. *See* Skinder-Strauss Assocs. v. Massachusetts Continuing Legal Educ., Inc., 870 F. Supp. 8, 9-10 (D. Mass. 1994) (holding that a single lawsuit could fall within the sham exception to the *Noerr* doctrine).

121. 508 U.S. 49 (1993).

122. *Id.* at 60-61 (citation omitted); *see also* Glass Equip. Dev., Inc. v. Besten, Inc., 174 F.3d 1337, 1343-44 (Fed. Cir. 1999) (affirming grant of summary judgment on sham litigation counterclaim based on threats of enforcement and initiation of two lawsuits); FilmTec Corp. v. Hydranautics, 67 F.3d 431 (Fed. Cir. 1995) (denying motion to amend to add sham litigation counterclaim because the underlying infringement suit was not objectively baseless), *cert. denied*, 519 U.S. 814 (1996); U.S. Philips Corp. v. Sears Roebuck & Co., 55 F.3d 592, 597 (Fed. Cir.) (rejecting bad faith litigation claim because patent holder had prevailed on patent issues in prior litigation), *cert. denied*, 516 U.S. 1010 (1995); *Glaverbel S.A.*, 45 F.3d at 1558-59 (rejecting bad faith litigation claim where plaintiff offered some evidence of infringement and there was no evidence of intent to harass); Jarrow Formulas, Inc. v. International Nutrition Co., Civ. 3:01CV00478, 2001 U.S. Dist. LEXIS 19414, at *31-38 (D. Conn. Nov. 16, 2001) (refusing to dismiss on the pleadings allegation that prior litigation was baseless and concealed an attempt to interfere with competitor's business); Moore U.S.A., Inc. v. Standard Register Co., 139 F. Supp. 2d 348 (W.D.N.Y. 2001) (refusing to dismiss on the pleadings allegations that licensor entered two licenses for purpose of initiating sham litigation against a competitor whose product did not infringe the licensed patent); Knoll Pharm. Co. v. Teva Pharm. Co., Case No. 01 C 146, 2001 U.S. Dist. LEXIS 12999, at *12 (N.D. Ill. Aug. 21, 2001) (refusing to dismiss sham litigation claim based on an allegation that the "lawsuit was filed with the sole intention of prolonging [the] monopoly . . . during the time this lawsuit is pending"); Pennpac Int'l, Inc. v. Rotonics Mfg., Inc., 2001-1 Trade Cas. (CCH) ¶ 73,282 (E.D. Pa. 2001) (granting motion for summary judgment on sham litigation claim where undisputed evidence showed that patent holder investigated whether product in fact infringed before bringing suit); Open LCR.com v. Rates Tech., Inc., 112 F. Supp. 2d 1223 (D. Colo. 2000) (denying motion to dismiss sham litigation claim that adequately pled that lawsuit was brought without a realistic expectation of success); Novell, Inc. v. CPU Distrib., Inc., Civ. A. No. H-97-

Court concluded that the copyright owner's enforcement suit was not a sham where, in the absence of factual disputes, the owner stated a reasonable basis for its claim in an "unsettled" area of law.[123] *PRE* did not explain how the sham litigation test should be applied in the typical *Handgards* situation, where the defendant alleges the plaintiff possessed facts or information that should have persuaded it that its patent was invalid or not infringed. The Court stated in a footnote that it did not decide "whether and, if so, to what extent *Noerr* permits the imposition of antitrust liability for a litigant's fraud or other misrepresentations."[124]

Following *PRE*, the lower courts have disagreed as to whether the Supreme Court's sham litigation test applies to repetitive lawsuits filed by a plaintiff against a series of defendants. The Second and Ninth Circuits have rejected the suggestion that *PRE*'s two-part analysis applies to a pattern of filing suits without regard to their individual merit,[125] but one district court has held that Federal Circuit law requires application of *PRE* to claims of improper repetitive filing.[126]

2326, 2000 U.S. Dist. LEXIS 9952, at *18 (S.D. Tex. May 12, 2000) (a single contrary decision in a district court in another circuit did not render baseless a suit brought on a "complex" issue of copyright law); Syncsort Inc. v. Sequential Software, Inc., 50 F. Supp. 2d 318, 334 (D.N.J. 1999) (dismissing sham litigation counterclaim where "there was a basis to initiate the proceedings"); Victus Ltd. v. Collezione Europa U.S.A., Inc., 26 F. Supp. 2d 772, 777 (M.D.N.C. 1998) (granting sua sponte summary judgment for defendant on sham litigation claim); Mitek Surgical Prods. v. Arthrex, Inc., 21 F. Supp. 2d 1309, 1318 (D. Utah 1998) (granting summary judgment for lack of "clear and convincing evidence to establish that the infringement lawsuit was objectively baseless"), *aff'd without op.*, 230 F.3d 1383 (Fed. Cir. 2000); Boston Scientific Corp. v. Schneider (Europe) AG, 983 F. Supp. 245, 272-73 (D. Mass. 1997) ("I doubt that the sham litigation exception to the *Noerr-Pennington* doctrine applies to independent claims as opposed to an entire suit."); In re Circuit Breaker Litig., 984 F. Supp. 1267, 1274 (C.D. Cal. 1997) (finding as a matter of law that trademark infringement actions were not objectively baseless); Novo Nordisk of N. Am. v. Genentech, Inc., 885 F. Supp. 522, 525-27 (S.D.N.Y. 1995) (applying *PRE* to bad faith litigation claim based on previous proceedings in International Trade Commission); Bio-Technology Gen. Corp. v. Genentech, Inc., 886 F. Supp. 377, 380-82 (S.D.N.Y. 1995) (same); Montgomery County Ass'n of Realtors v. Realty Photo Master Corp., 878 F. Supp. 804, 816 (D. Md. 1995) (copyright infringement suit by itself did not provide basis for antitrust counterclaim), *aff'd*, 1996-2 Trade Cas. (CCH) ¶ 71,509 (4th Cir. 1996) (unpublished opinion); Scripto-Tokai Corp. v. Gillette Co., 1994-2 Trade Cas. (CCH) ¶ 70,821 (C.D. Cal. 1994) (bad faith litigation claim dismissed because there was no evidence that infringement claim was objectively baseless or that patent holder filed the infringement claim with the subjective intent to interfere with alleged infringer's business); TRW Fin. Sys. v. Unisys Corp., 835 F. Supp. 994, 1011-14 (E.D. Mich. 1993) (relying on *PRE* to dismiss bad faith litigation claim based on patent infringement suit); *see also* Darda, Inc. USA v. Majorette Toys (U.S.) Inc., 627 F. Supp. 1121 (S.D. Fla. 1986) (holding, prior to *PRE*, that if the patent in suit is found valid, no antitrust counterclaim can be maintained), *aff'd in part and rev'd in part on other grounds*, 824 F.2d 976 (Fed. Cir. 1987). Recognizing that patentees normally are entitled to rely on the statutory presumption of validity of patents, 35 U.S.C. § 282 (1994), several courts prior to *PRE* had held that proof of the patentee's bad faith in bringing infringement litigation must be made by clear and convincing evidence. *See supra* note 111.

123. 508 U.S. at 64-65.
124. *Id.* at 61 & n.6.
125. PrimeTime 24 Joint Venture v. NBC, 219 F.3d 92, 101 (2d Cir. 2000); USS-POSCO Indus. v. Contra Costa County Bldg. & Constr. Trades Council, AFL-CIO, 31 F.3d 800, 811 (9th Cir. 1994).
126. Travelers Express Co. v. American Express Integrated Payment Sys., 80 F. Supp. 2d 1033, 1042 (D. Minn. 1999) (reading the Federal Circuit's decision in *Glass Equip. Dev., Inc. v. Besten, Inc.*, 174 F.3d 1337 (Fed. Cir. 1999), to instruct that where a sham claim is based upon a series of lawsuits, "the appropriate inquiry is to determine whether each of the prior lawsuits was objectively baseless").

The Federal Circuit has held that the sending of infringement notices is immune from antitrust liability unless it falls within the sham exception articulated by *PRE*.[127] Most courts that have considered antitrust challenges to infringement notices in other contexts have agreed.[128]   One court has suggested that *Noerr* immunity may not protect certain postlitigation conduct.[129]

In *Kobe, Inc. v. Dempsey Pump Co.*,[130] a case decided prior to *PRE*, the Tenth Circuit held that an infringement action commenced for the purpose of monopolizing a market, combined with other anticompetitive conduct, may violate Section 2 of the Sherman Act even where there is a legitimate belief in validity and infringement. The court found that a plan of acquiring all present and future patents relevant to an entire industry, obtaining covenants not to compete from the sellers of the patents, threatening suits against all who dealt with infringers, and widely publicizing infringement suits violated the Sherman Act.[131]   In such a case, however, the market the defendant sought to monopolize must be more than that which he may control by

127. Virginia Panel Corp. v. MAC Panel Co., 133 F.3d 860 (Fed. Cir. 1997) (issuance of infringement notices and threatening of lawsuits could not form basis of antitrust claim because patent owner had a good faith belief that its patents were infringed), *cert. denied*, 525 U.S. 815 (1998); *see also* Zenith Elec. Corp. v. Exzec, Inc., 182 F.3d 1340, 1353 (Fed. Cir. 1999) ("35 U.S.C. § 287 . . . makes . . . specific notice to the accused infringer a prerequisite to the recovery of damages").

128. *PrimeTime 24 Joint Venture*, 219 F.3d at 100 (prelitigation conduct protected); Cardtoons, L.C. v. Major League Baseball Players Ass'n, 208 F.3d 885, 893 (10th Cir.) (en banc) (stating that prelitigation notices are exempt from liability under the Sherman Act, but holding that *Noerr* did not preclude liability under state law), *cert. denied*, 531 U.S. 873 (2000); McGuire Oil Co. v. Mapco, Inc., 958 F.2d 1552, 1560 (11th Cir. 1992) (threats of suit protected); Coastal States Mktg., Inc. v. Hunt, 694 F.2d 1358 (5th Cir. 1983) (prelitigation communications with potential defendants and third parties protected); Gardner v. Clark, 101 F. Supp. 2d 468, 473 (N.D. Miss. 2000) (activities "directly attributable to litigation" protected); eBay Inc. v. Bidder's Edge Inc., 56 U.S.P.Q.2d (BNA) 1856, 1858 (N.D. Cal. 2000) ("cease-and-desist letters and proposed license agreements" may be protected); Miller Pipeline Corp. v. British Gas PLC, 69 F. Supp. 2d 1129, 1138 (S.D. Ind. 1999) ("activities . . . which manifest the patent holder's intent to protect its rights through judicial action" protected); Barq's, Inc. v. Barq's Beverages, Inc., 677 F. Supp. 449, 453 (E.D. La. 1987) ("threatened litigation and attending publicity" are protected); *see also* F.B. Leopold Co. v. Roberts Filter Mfg. Co., 882 F. Supp. 433 (W.D. Pa. 1995) (finding no evidence to support defendant's counterclaim that patent holder had conspired to make false and misleading representations of infringement), *aff'd without op.*, 119 F.3d 15 (Fed. Cir. 1997); Thermos Co. v. Igloo Prods., 1996-1 Trade Cas. (CCH) ¶ 71,323 (N.D. Ill. 1995) (sending cease and desist letters prior to a trademark infringement lawsuit not a violation of the antitrust laws); *cf.* Biovail Corp. v. Hoechst AG, 49 F. Supp. 2d 750, 770-71 (D.N.J. 1999) (refusing to dismiss on the pleadings antitrust allegation based upon public threats to bring patent litigation despite covenant not to sue). *But see* Laitram Mach., Inc. v. Carnitech A/S, 901 F. Supp. 1155 (E.D. La. 1995) (*Noerr* doctrine does not extend to sending letters to a competitor's customers alleging violations of trade secrets and patent infringement).

129. *Compare* Johnson v. Con-Vey/Keystone, Inc., 856 F. Supp. 1443 (D. Or. 1994) (if incidental to the prior lawsuit, the sending of warning letters to an infringer's customers is not a separate and distinct basis for antitrust liability), *with* Unique Coupons, Inc. v. Northfield Corp., No. 99 C 7445, 2000 U.S. Dist. LEXIS 6767, at *7 (N.D. Ill. May 16, 2000) (distinguishing unprotected "misrepresentations as to the content and import of past litigation" from protected actions incidental to anticipated litigation).

130. 198 F.2d 416 (10th Cir.), *cert. denied*, 344 U.S. 837 (1952).

131. *Id.* at 423-24; *cf.* Kellogg Co. v. National Biscuit Co., 71 F.2d 662 (2d Cir. 1934) (involving trademarks); CVD, Inc. v. Raytheon Co., 769 F.2d 842, 860 (1st Cir. 1985) (involving trade secrets), *cert. denied*, 475 U.S. 1016 (1986).

the exercise of his patent rights and the overt acts must be demonstrated independently and must consist of more than the filing of the infringement suit.[132]

The Sixth Circuit held that a trade dress infringement action with respect to a design feature previously covered by an expired utility patent was not baseless merely because the suit sought to protect a feature no longer protected by patent.[133] On the other hand, one court described as "potentially viable" a sham litigation claim based upon a suit to enforce patents protected by an illegal settlement and cross-licensing agreement, which resulted in the maintenance or issuance of overly broad patents.[134] In an enforcement action alleging inequitable conduct in a standard-setting context, the Federal Trade Commission charged Dell Computer Corp. with violating Section 5 of the FTC Act by voting to approve an industry standard computer interface and certifying that the standard did not infringe Dell's intellectual property, and, after the standard became successful, asserting an earlier-issued patent against several computer manufacturers using the standard.[135]

At least one court has held that expenses of defending infringement actions are not recoverable as antitrust damages.[136] Other courts, however, have permitted the recovery of such expenses.[137]

3.   *Licensing Intellectual Property as an Antitrust Violation*

a.   INTELLECTUAL PROPERTY GUIDELINES

The *Intellectual Property Guidelines* set out a general approach to analyzing licensing arrangements, a series of safety zones, and a description of the analysis applicable to specific practices. The *Guidelines* recognize that certain restrictions in intellectual property licenses may raise antitrust concerns, such as restrictions on goods or technologies other than the licensed technology and contractual provisions that penalize licensees for dealing with suppliers of substitute technologies or for developing their own competing technology. In reviewing licensing arrangements,

---

132. *See, e.g.*, Handgards, Inc. v. Ethicon, Inc., 601 F.2d 986, 996 (9th Cir. 1979), *cert. denied*, 444 U.S. 1025 (1980); Bendix Corp. v. Balax, Inc., 471 F.2d 149, 153 (7th Cir. 1972), *cert. denied*, 414 U.S. 819 (1973).

133. Marketing Displays, Inc. v. TrafFix Devices, Inc., 200 F.3d 929, 941-42 (6th Cir. 1999), *rev'd on other grounds*, 532 U.S. 23 (2001).

134. Boston Scientific Corp. v. Schneider (Europe) AG, 983 F. Supp. 245, 273 (D. Mass. 1997). Another court held that a policy of building a "patent thicket" by soliciting and obtaining multiple patents from the PTO was immune from antitrust challenge under *Noerr*, unless shown to fit within the sham exception. *See* Procter & Gamble Co. v. Paragon Trade Brands, Inc., 61 F. Supp. 2d 102, 110-11 (D. Del. 1996).

135. *In re* Dell Computer Corp., 121 F.T.C. 616 (1996), *see also* Rambus, Inc. v. Infineon Tech. Corp., 164 F. Supp. 2d 743 (E.D. Va. 2001) (denying a motion for judgment as a matter of law following jury verdict that Rambus was liable for patent-related, state law fraud in the context of industry standard setting for certain semiconductor products).

136. *See* Ansul Co. v. Uniroyal, Inc., 448 F.2d 872, 882-83 (2d Cir. 1971), *cert. denied*, 404 U.S. 1018 (1972).

137. *See, e.g.*, Handgards, Inc. v. Ethicon, Inc., 743 F.2d 1282, 1297-98 (9th Cir. 1984), *cert. denied*, 469 U.S. 1190 (1985); Kearney & Trecker Corp. v. Cincinnati Milacron, Inc., 562 F.2d 365, 374 (6th Cir. 1977); Kearney & Trecker Corp. v. Giddings & Lewis, Inc., 452 F.2d 579, 597 (7th Cir. 1971), *cert. denied*, 405 U.S. 1066 (1972); American Infra-Red Radiant Co. v. Lambert Indus., 360 F.2d 977 (8th Cir.), *cert. denied*, 385 U.S. 920 (1966); Hart-Carter Co. v. J.P. Burroughs & Son, 605 F. Supp. 1327, 1347 (E.D. Mich. 1985).

the agencies' analysis focuses primarily upon whether the particular licensing arrangement "harms competition among entities that would have been actual or likely potential competitors . . . in the absence" of the arrangement.[138]

The *Guidelines* describe the agencies' approach to the definition of relevant markets within which the competitive impact of license arrangements will be analyzed. The agencies will analyze the competitive effects of the arrangement in the relevant goods market(s) if possible. Certain transactions, however, may require the delineation of "technology markets" or "innovation markets."[139]

Under the *Guidelines*, technology markets consist of the intellectual property licensed and the technology that may be substituted for that intellectual property.[140] The agencies identify substitutes by looking to the smallest group of technologies or goods over which a hypothetical monopolist could exercise market power. If the necessary data are not available for such an analysis because the relevant technology is not licensed in a way that is quantifiable in monetary terms, the agencies will define the relevant market by identifying other technologies and goods that buyers would substitute at a cost comparable to that of using the licensed technology.[141]

The *Guidelines* provide that "[i]f a licensing arrangement may adversely affect competition to develop new or improved goods or processes, the Agencies will analyze such an impact either as a separate competitive effect in relevant goods or technology markets, or as a competitive effect in a separate innovation market."[142] For this purpose, "[a]n innovation market consists of the research and development directed to particular new or improved goods or processes, and the close substitutes for that research and development."[143] The agencies will attempt to define an innovation market only when the capability to engage in relevant R&D can be linked to specialized assets or characteristics of specific firms.

The *Guidelines* also create an antitrust "safety zone" for restraints in licensing arrangements if (1) the restraints are not facially anticompetitive, and (2) the licensor and licensee collectively account for no more than 20 percent of each relevant market significantly affected by the restraint.[144] The *Guidelines* characterize as "facially anticompetitive" those restraints that generally warrant per se treatment, as well as any other restraints that would always or almost always tend to restrict output or increase prices.[145] Examples of such restraints include horizontal price fixing, output restraints and market allocations, resale price maintenance, and certain group boycotts.

The agencies also set forth alternative safety zone criteria for situations in which available goods market data are insufficient or do not accurately represent competitive significance. In such situations, the agencies generally will not

---

138. INTELLECTUAL PROPERTY GUIDELINES, *supra* note 16, § 3.1; *see also id.* § 2.3 & Example 1.
139. *Id.* § 3.2.
140. *Id.* § 3.2.1. At least two district courts have recognized technology markets as possible loci of anticompetitive effects. *See In re* Pabst Licensing Patent Litig., Civ. A. No.: MDL Dkt. No. 1298, Ref. C.A. 99-3118, 2000 U.S. Dist. LEXIS 12076, at *19-20 (E.D. La. Aug. 10, 2000); DiscoVision Assocs. v. Disc Mfg., Inc., Civ. A. No. 95-21-SLR, Consol. Civ. A. No. 95-345-SLR, 1997 U.S. Dist. LEXIS 7507, at *3-4 & n.2 (D. Del. Apr. 3, 1997).
141. *Id.*
142. *Id.* § 3.2.3.
143. *Id.*
144. *Id.* § 4.3.
145. *Id.* § 4.3 n.30.

challenge licensing arrangements that may affect competition in a technology market if (1) the arrangement is not facially anticompetitive, and (2) there are four or more independently controlled technologies that are adequate substitutes for the technologies controlled by the parties to the arrangement. Also, the agencies generally will not challenge a licensing arrangement that may affect competition in an innovation market if (1) the restraint is not facially anticompetitive, and (2) there are four or more independently controlled entities in addition to the parties to the licensing agreement that possess the required assets or characteristics and the incentive to engage in R&D that is a close substitute for the R&D activities of the parties to the licensing agreement.[146]

With respect to restrictions falling outside of these safety zones, the *Guidelines* note that the vast majority of licensing arrangements will be analyzed under the rule of reason.[147] They also explain the antitrust analysis that the agencies will apply to particular practices—horizontal restraints, resale price maintenance, tying arrangements, exclusive dealing, cross-licensing, grantbacks, and the acquisition of intellectual property rights—if the conditions of the safety zones are not satisfied. The *Guidelines* analysis applicable to a particular practice is noted in this chapter in the section concerning that practice.

b. EXCLUSIVITY

The Patent Act expressly provides that a patent is assignable: the patent owner may "grant and convey an exclusive right under his application for patent, or patents, to the whole or any specified part of the United States."[148] Although not expressly authorized in the statute, courts have long held that a patentee also may issue one or more patent licenses by agreeing to forbear from asserting his exclusive rights in an invention, typically in exchange for royalties.[149] Such licenses may be either exclusive or nonexclusive. A nonexclusive license is simply the patent owner's contractual waiver of his right to exclude the licensee from making, using, or selling the invention.[150] Such a license may arise from a course of conduct with no formal agreement.[151] In an exclusive license, the patent owner also agrees not to license

---

146. *Id.* § 4.3.
147. For a discussion of the rule of reason analysis generally, see part B.3.b of Chapter I.
148. 35 U.S.C. § 261 (1994).
149. *See, e.g.*, Zenith Radio Corp. v. Hazeltine Research, Inc., 395 U.S. 100, 135-36 (1969); Genentech, Inc. v. Eli Lilly & Co., 998 F.2d 931, 949 (Fed. Cir. 1993) ("the grant of an exclusive license is a lawful incident of the right to exclude provided by the Patent Act"), *cert. denied*, 510 U.S. 1140 (1994), *abrogated on other grounds*, Wilton v. Seven Falls Co., 515 U.S. 277 (1995); United States v. Studiengesellschaft Kohle, m.b.H., 670 F.2d 1122, 1127 (D.C. Cir. 1981); United States v. Westinghouse Elec. Corp., 648 F.2d 642, 647 (9th Cir. 1981) ("The right to license [a] patent, exclusively or otherwise, or to refuse to license at all, is 'the untrammeled right' of the patentee.") (quoting Cataphote Corp. v. DeSoto Chem. Coatings, Inc., 450 F.2d 769, 774 (9th Cir. 1971)).
150. *See* General Talking Pictures Corp. v. Western Elec. Co., 304 U.S. 175, 181 ("The Transformer Company . . . was a mere licensee under a nonexclusive license, amounting to no more than 'a mere waiver of the right to sue.'") (quoting De Forest Radio Tel. & Tel. Co. v. United States, 273 U.S. 236, 242 (1927)), *aff'd on reh'g*, 305 U.S. 124 (1938).
151. *See De Forest Radio Tel. & Tel.*, 273 U.S. at 241 ("No formal granting of a license is necessary in order to give it effect."); Met-Coil Sys. Corp. v. Korners Unlimited, Inc., 803 F.2d 684, 686-87 (Fed. Cir. 1986); *cf.* Hunt v. Armour & Co., 185 F.2d 722, 729 (7th Cir. 1950) ("A mere sale does not import a license except where the circumstances plainly indicate that the grant of a license should be inferred."); RCA v. Andrea, 90 F.2d 612, 615 (2d Cir. 1937) (same).

others (and, not uncommonly, not to practice the patent himself).[152]   An exclusive license, as such, does not violate the antitrust laws or constitute patent misuse.[153]   The agencies have expressed concern, however, where, but for the exclusive license, the licensor and the licensee, or two or more licensees, would be actual or potential competitors, and the exclusive license serves to create or enhance the exercise of market power.[154]   The agencies analyze the acquisition of exclusive rights in intellectual property whether by grant, sale, or other transaction under the same principles and standards used to analyze mergers.[155]   Also, an exclusive patent license is treated as an asset acquisition for purposes of the reporting requirements of the Hart-Scott-Rodino Antitrust Improvements Act of 1976.[156]

In the *Intellectual Property Guidelines*, the agencies also distinguish exclusive dealing as a second type of exclusivity in patent licenses that can give rise to antitrust concerns. According to the *Guidelines*, exclusive dealing may exist where express terms or incentives created by the license "prevent[] or restrain[] the licensee from licensing, selling, distributing, or using competing technologies."[157]   In evaluating such agreements, the agencies will apply similar antitrust principles to those applied to exclusive dealing outside of the licensing context, but "the fact that intellectual property may in some cases be misappropriated more easily than other forms of property may justify the use of some restrictions that might be anticompetitive in other contexts."[158]   Some older cases held that it is per se patent misuse to require a licensee to refrain from dealing in competitive products;[159] however, at least one

152. *See* E. Bement & Sons v. National Harrow Co., 186 U.S. 70, 94 (1902); Rail-Trailer Co. v. ACF Indus., 358 F.2d 15, 16-17 (7th Cir. 1966); *cf.* Sanofi, S.A. v. Med-Tech Veterinarian Prods., 222 U.S.P.Q. (BNA) 143 (D. Kan. 1983) (patent holder could not grant implied license to defendants to sell pharmaceutical product in United States, in derogation of rights of plaintiff, given its previous grant of exclusive license to plaintiff).

153. *See, e.g.*, Virtue v. Creamery Package Mfg. Co., 227 U.S. 8, 36-37 (1913); *Genentech*, 998 F.2d at 949; Miller Insituform, Inc. v. Insituform of N. Am., Inc., 830 F.2d 606, 607-09 (6th Cir. 1987), *cert. denied*, 484 U.S. 1064 (1988); Sheet Metal Duct Inc. v. Lindab Inc., 55 U.S.P.Q.2d (BNA) 1480, 1484 (E.D. Pa. 2000); SCM Corp. v. Xerox Corp., 463 F. Supp. 983, 1005-06 (D. Conn. 1978), *remanded*, 599 F.2d 32 (2d Cir.); United States v. E.I. duPont de Nemours & Co., 118 F. Supp. 41, 224 (D. Del. 1953), *aff'd*, 351 U.S. 377 (1956); *cf.* Smith Int'l, Inc. v. Kennametal, Inc., 621 F. Supp. 79, 89-90 (N.D. Ohio 1985) (arrangement by which licensor granted licensee right to make, use, and sell the patented goods, and licensee granted licensor exclusive territorial distributorship for goods in return for licensor's agreement to purchase its requirements of product from licensee would be evaluated under the rule of reason; denying motion for summary judgment); *see also* Levi Case Co. v. ATS Prods., 788 F. Supp. 428, 431-32 (N.D. Cal. 1992) (patentee and its exclusive licensee were legally incapable of conspiring where the exclusive nature of the license prevented the patent holder from functioning as the licensee's competitor).

154. *See* INTELLECTUAL PROPERTY GUIDELINES, *supra* note 16, § 4.1.2; *see also* United States v. American Nat'l Can Co., 1996-2 Trade Cas. (CCH) ¶ 71,641 (D.D.C. 1996) (DOJ challenged exclusive license between competitors where licensor relinquished right to sell its technology and equipment in North America in exchange for licensee's agreement to license and purchase all related technology or equipment from licensor alone); United States v. S.C. Johnson & Son, 1995-1 Trade Cas. (CCH) ¶ 70,884 (N.D. Ill. 1994) (DOJ challenged license between competitors where licensor did not license product to others and licensee was given the right of first refusal for exclusive rights on future product developments).

155. INTELLECTUAL PROPERTY GUIDELINES, *supra* note 16, § 5.7.

156. ABA SECTION OF ANTITRUST LAW, PREMERGER NOTIFICATION PRACTICE MANUAL 45 (1991).

157. *See* INTELLECTUAL PROPERTY GUIDELINES, *supra* note 16, §§ 4.1.2, 5.4.

158. *Id.*

159. *See, e.g.*, Berlenbach v. Anderson & Thompson Ski Co., 329 F.2d 782 (9th Cir.), *cert. denied*, 379 U.S. 830 (1964); McCullough v. Kammerer Corp., 166 F.2d 759 (9th Cir.), *cert. denied*, 335 U.S.

court has concluded that these holdings were superseded by the 1988 Patent Misuse Reform Act.[160]

In *United States v. Microsoft Corp.*,[161] the D.C. Circuit affirmed a district court's finding that Microsoft had illegally maintained its monopoly power in the market for Intel-compatible personal computer operating systems by, inter alia, imposing certain exclusive and other exclusionary provisions in licenses for its copyrighted Windows operating system with computer manufacturers and Internet access providers. Among the license restrictions found illegal were certain limitations on altering the appearance of the Windows desktop[162] and exclusive supply agreements with "the leading" Internet access providers.[163] The court found that these provisions were not justified by a valid business purpose and hampered the distribution of competing products that otherwise might have posed a threat to Microsoft's operating system monopoly.[164] However, the D.C. Circuit reversed the lower court's determination that the Windows license prohibition against causing any user interface other than the Windows desktop to launch automatically was a basis for liability because this restraint was justified by Microsoft's legitimate interest in preventing a "substantial alteration" of its copyrighted work.[165]

c.   PRICE AND QUANTITY LIMITATIONS

In 1926, in *United States v. General Electric Co.*,[166] the Supreme Court held that General Electric did not violate the Sherman Act by granting Westinghouse a license to make and sell patented lamps at prices established by General Electric. The Court stated the rationale for permitting the price restrictions as follows:

> Conveying less than title to the patent, or part of it, the patentee may grant a license to make, use, and vend articles under the specifications of his patent for any royalty, or upon any condition the performance of which is reasonably within the reward which the patentee by the grant of the patent is entitled to secure . . . . [M]ay [the patentee] . . . limit the selling by limiting the method of sale and the price? We think he may do so, provided the conditions of sale are normally and reasonably adapted to secure pecuniary reward for the patentee's monopoly.[167]

The Court thus held that it was reasonable for a patent owner who himself manufactures and sells the patented product to establish the price at which a licensee

---

813 (1948); National Lockwasher Co. v. George K. Garrett Co., 137 F.2d 255 (3d Cir. 1943); Krampe v. Ideal Indus., 347 F. Supp. 1384 (N.D. Ill. 1972).

160. Recombinant DNA Tech. Patent & Contract Litig., 850 F. Supp. 769, 777 (S.D. Ind. 1994) (concluding that 35 U.S.C. § 271's requirement of market power applies equally to tie ins and tie outs); *see also* Beal Corp. Liquidating Trust v. Valleylab, Inc., 927 F. Supp. 1350, 1367 (D. Colo. 1996) (genuine issues of fact exist as to whether patent license agreement prohibiting licensee from purchasing products from outside sources is part of a larger horizontal market allocation scheme).

161. 253 F.3d 34, 59-71 (D.C. Cir.), *cert. denied*, 122 S. Ct. 350 (2001).

162. *Id.* at 59-64.

163. *Id.* at 67-71 ("a monopolist's use of exclusive contracts, in certain circumstances, may give rise to a § 2 violation even though the contracts foreclose less than the 40% or 50% share usually required in order to establish a § 1 violation").

164. *Id.* at 60-64, 71.

165. *Id.* at 63.

166. 272 U.S. 476 (1926).

167. *Id.* at 489-90.

sells the product, because that price "will necessarily affect" the price at which the patent owner can sell his own goods.[168]

The *General Electric* decision has been limited by subsequent decisions. In 1948, in *United States v. Line Material Co.*,[169] the Supreme Court held that where patents are cross-licensed a provision in a sublicense establishing the sublicensee's price violated Section 1 of the Sherman Act.[170] The Court distinguished *General Electric* but declined to overrule it.[171] In 1965, in *United States v. Huck Manufacturing Co.*,[172] an equally divided Supreme Court again refused to overrule *General Electric*. In 1956, the Third Circuit in *Newburgh Moire Co. v. Superior Moire Co.*[173] held that the grant of multiple licenses containing price restrictions does not fit within the scope of the *General Electric* rule and, without more, violates Section 1.[174] In *LucasArts Entertainment Co. v. Humongous Entertainment Co.*,[175] however, a district court held that a price restriction imposed on the resale of videogames by a copyright licensor fell within the safe harbor of *General Electric* because the provision was "reasonably adapted to secure pecuniary reward for the [copyright owner's] . . . monopoly."[176]

General Electric notwithstanding, a patent owner's ability to establish a licensee's prices for a patented product clearly does not include the right to do so in concert with other licensees or patentees, and price restraints resulting from such combinations have been found to be per se violations of the Sherman Act.[177] Moreover, it is clear that *General Electric* does not permit the patent owner to fix the

---

168. *Id.* at 490.
169. 333 U.S. 287 (1948).
170. *See id.* at 293-97, 305-15. More specifically, the Court indicated that the overlapping nature of the cross-licensing relationship improperly allowed the patentees to exercise powers beyond those granted to them by virtue of their individual patents. *Id.* at 307-13.
171. *See id.* at 299-304; *accord In re* Yarn Processing Patent Validity Litig., 541 F.2d 1127, 1135-36 (5th Cir. 1976) (*General Elec.* rule does not apply "where two or more patentees fix the prices of products incorporating several independently owned patents"), *cert. denied*, 433 U.S. 910 (1977).
172. 382 U.S. 197 (1965).
173. 237 F.2d 283 (3d Cir. 1956).
174. *Id.* at 291-94; *see* Tinnerman Prods. v. George K. Garrett Co., 185 F. Supp. 151, 157-59 (E.D. Pa. 1960) ("[I]f a patentee grants more than one license containing price-fixing provisions, such licenses constitute a violation of the antitrust laws . . . ."), *modified*, 188 F. Supp. 815 (E.D. Pa. 1960), *aff'd*, 292 F.2d 137 (3d Cir.), *cert. denied*, 368 U.S. 833 (1961); *see also* Royal Indus. v. St. Regis Paper Co., 420 F.2d 449, 453-54 (9th Cir. 1969) (*General Elec.* "limited to a situation where the 'patentee licenses another to make and vend and retains the right to continue to make and vend on his own account'") (citation omitted) (Carter, J., concurring); Ansul Co. v. Uniroyal, Inc., 306 F. Supp. 541, 558-59 (S.D.N.Y. 1969) (contracts imposing territorial field-of-use restrictions and imposition by defendant of vigorously enforced "suggested" retail prices violated Sherman Act), *aff'd in part, rev'd in part, and remanded*, 448 F.2d 872 (2d Cir. 1971), *cert. denied*, 404 U.S. 1018 (1972). *But see* Westinghouse Elec. Corp. v. Bulldog Elec. Prods. Co., 179 F.2d 139, 143 (4th Cir. 1950) (observing, in dicta, that "[t]here is no reason . . . why [a patentee] . . . should be restricted to a price maintenance agreement with a single licensee, . . . and the reasoning which permits licensing by grantees of patents and price maintenance provisions in maintenance contracts is clearly to the contrary").
175. 870 F. Supp. 285 (N.D. Cal. 1993).
176. *Id.* at 288-89 (quoting *General Elec.*, 272 U.S. at 490).
177. *See, e.g.*, United States v. New Wrinkle, Inc., 342 U.S. 371, 378-80 (1952); United States v. United States Gypsum Co., 333 U.S. 364, 399-401 (1948); United States v. Masonite Corp., 316 U.S. 265, 276-82 (1942); *Newburgh Moire*, 237 F.2d at 292-93; United States v. Vehicular Parking, Ltd., 54 F. Supp. 828, 837-38 (D. Del.), *modified*, 56 F. Supp. 297 (1944), *modified*, 61 F. Supp. 656 (1945). The agencies have challenged price and quantity restraints in the context of cross-licenses or pooling of allegedly competing patented technologies.

price of unpatented products of patented machines or processes.[178] Nor does *General Electric* permit a patent owner to establish resale prices by expressly licensing "resale" of the patented product separately from its manufacture, initial sale, and use. In *United States v. Univis Lens Co.*[179] and *Ethyl Gasoline Corp. v. United States*,[180] the Supreme Court declared unlawful practices whereby patent owners granted licenses to resell products which the patent holder had sold to the licensees, and fixed the prices at which the products were to be resold. In *Ethyl*, the patent owner directly (or by one licensee) made and sold the patented product to another licensee for resale. In *Univis*, the patent owner sold the licensee an unpatented product useful only in making a finished, patented product. In such situations, it is commonly said that the first sale of a product made under the teachings of a patent "exhausts" the patentee's exclusive rights, and that restrictions on subsequent sales cannot be supported by reliance on such rights.[181]

In the *Intellectual Property Guidelines*, the agencies cite *General Electric* but point out that it has been distinguished by lower courts in various contexts and note that "[i]t has been held per se illegal for a licensor of an intellectual property right in a product to fix a licensee's *resale* price of that product."[182]

A number of cases indicate that a patent owner may limit the quantities of patented products produced by a licensee[183] and that quantity limitations in a patent license are not illegal per se.[184] Limitations on the quantity of unpatented products produced by a patented process also have been upheld.[185] However, in a 1949 case involving an alleged conspiracy among a patent owner and licensees, it was held that

---

178. *See, e.g.*, Cummer-Graham Co. v. Straight Side Basket Corp., 142 F.2d 646, 647 (5th Cir.), *cert. denied*, 323 U.S. 726 (1944); Barber-Colman Co. v. National Tool Co., 136 F.2d 339, 343-44 (6th Cir. 1943).

179. 316 U.S. 241, 243-45, 249-51 (1942).

180. 309 U.S. 436, 446-48, 452, 457 (1940).

181. *See, e.g.*, *Univis*, 316 U.S. at 249-51; *Ethyl Gasoline*, 309 U.S. at 457; *see also* B. Braun Med., Inc. v. Abbott Labs., 124 F.3d 1419, 1426 (Fed. Cir. 1997) ("As a general matter . . . an unconditional sale of a patented device exhausts the patentee's right to control the purchaser's use of the device thereafter. The theory behind this rule is that in such a transaction, the patentee has bargained for, and received, an amount equal to the full value of the goods.") (citations omitted).

182. INTELLECTUAL PROPERTY GUIDELINES, *supra* note 16, § 5.2 & n.33. During the 1960s, the DOJ sought a case in which to urge the overruling of *General Electric*. *See* Donald F. Turner, *Patents, Antitrust and Innovations*, 28 U. PITT. L. REV. 151 (1966); *Conflicts between Patent and Antitrust Laws—A Panel*, 10 IDEA 33-35 (1966) (remarks of Donald F. Turner). More recently, Robert Pitofsky, then Chairman of the FTC, observed that "[m]inimum resale price maintenance is treated aggressively because it may be a facilitating practice for cartel behavior among sellers or a direct cartel arrangement among dealers." Robert Pitofsky, Chairman, Federal Trade Comm'n, Challenges of the New Economy: Issues at the Intersection of Antitrust and Intellectual Property, Remarks Before the American Antitrust Institute Conf. (June 15, 2000), *available at* www.ftc.gov/speeches/pitofsky/000615speech.htm. However, Chairman Pitofsky also noted that cross-licensing arrangements involving agreements on price have been allowed where competitors control patents that include legitimate conflicting claims.

183. *See, e.g.*, United States v. E.I. duPont de Nemours & Co., 118 F. Supp. 41, 226 (D. Del. 1953), *aff'd*, 351 U.S. 377 (1956); United States v. Parker-Rust-Proof Co., 61 F. Supp. 805, 812 (E.D. Mich. 1945); *cf.* Aspinwall Mfg. Co. v. Gill, 32 F. 697, 698-99 (C.C.D.N.J. 1887).

184. *See* Atari Games Corp. v. Nintendo of Am., Inc., 897 F.2d 1572, 1578 (Fed. Cir. 1990) (dictum).

185. *See, e.g.*, Ethyl Corp. v. Hercules Powder Co., 232 F. Supp. 453, 460 (D. Del. 1963); Q-Tips, Inc. v. Johnson & Johnson, 109 F. Supp. 657, 660-61 (D.N.J. 1951), *modified*, 207 F.2d 509 (3d Cir. 1953), *cert. denied*, 347 U.S. 935 (1954).

a provision causing royalties to increase as quantity increased violated the antitrust laws.[186]

d. ROYALTIES

A patent owner has the right to exploit his invention by requiring royalty payments[187] and, in general, he may charge as high a royalty as he can obtain.[188]

(1) Royalty Base

A patent owner may base the formula for royalty payments on many different criteria. Royalties on patented articles manufactured by a licensee or on patented machines or processes used for manufacture are commonly based on utilization, either a fixed amount per unit on goods manufactured by the licensee under the patents or a fixed percentage of revenues received by the licensee for such goods. The criteria used to establish the royalty rate may raise antitrust or misuse issues where the royalty calculation is unrelated to the licensee's utilization of the patent. In *Zenith Radio Corp. v. Hazeltine Research, Inc.*,[189] the Supreme Court held that "conditioning the grant of a patent license upon payment of royalties on products which do not use the teaching of the patent" was unlawful.[190] The Court stated that "patent misuse inheres in a patentee's insistence on a percentage-of-sales royalty, regardless of use, and his rejection of licensee proposals to pay only for actual use."[191]

The Court in *Zenith*, however, was careful to note that royalties may be measured by sales of other than the patented products alone when the "convenience of the parties rather than patent power dictates the total-sales royalty provision" and that no adverse inference is to be drawn from a total sales formula standing alone.[192] The Court thus clarified its earlier holding in *Automatic Radio Manufacturing Co. v.*

---

186. *See* United States v. General Elec. Co., 82 F. Supp. 753, 814 (D.N.J. 1949). *But see E.I. duPont de Nemours*, 118 F. Supp. at 226 ("As a patentee duPont had right to fix royalties at graduated scales on amount of Sylvania's production.").

187. *See, e.g.*, Hartford-Empire Co. v. United States, 323 U.S. 386, 413-16, *clarified*, 324 U.S. 570 (1945); Standard Oil Co. v. United States, 283 U.S. 163, 172, 179 (1931).

188. *See, e.g.*, Brulotte v. Thys Co., 379 U.S. 29, 33 (1964); W.L. Gore & Assocs. v. Carlisle Corp., 529 F.2d 614, 623 (3d Cir. 1976); Warner-Jenkinson Co. v. Allied Chem. Corp., 477 F. Supp. 371, 397 (S.D.N.Y. 1979), *aff'd without op.*, 633 F.2d 208 (2d Cir. 1980). *But see* American Photocopy Equip. Co. v. Rovico, Inc., 359 F.2d 745 (7th Cir.) (issue of whether royalty was exorbitant remanded for trial), *on remand*, 257 F. Supp. 192, 201 (N.D. Ill. 1966) (royalty not exorbitant), *aff'd*, 384 F.2d 813 (7th Cir. 1967), *cert. denied*, 390 U.S. 945 (1968).

189. 395 U.S. 100 (1969).

190. *Id.* at 135; *accord* United States v. United States Gypsum Co., 333 U.S. 364, 385-86, 397 (1948) (royalty provision that provided for percentage royalties based upon the sales of both patented and unpatented board held unlawful because purpose was to stabilize the price of patented board by eliminating the competition of unpatented board). *But cf.* Miller Insituform, Inc. v. Insituform of N. Am., Inc., 605 F. Supp. 1125, 1133-34 (M.D. Tenn. 1985) (upholding, without regard to reasonableness, royalty based on percentage of total contract price where contract was for patented process but also for preparatory and finishing work and nonpatented materials), *aff'd*, 830 F.2d 606 (6th Cir. 1987), *cert. denied*, 484 U.S. 1064 (1988).

191. 395 U.S. at 139.

192. *Id.* at 138.

Hazeltine Research, Inc.,[193] in which it had upheld a royalty measured by total sales irrespective of whether any patents applied.[194]

In *United States v. Microsoft Corp.*,[195] the government challenged an allegedly dominant operating system provider's practice of requiring computer manufacturers to pay a license fee for each computer shipped regardless of whether the computer contained the provider's copyrighted product. The complaint charged that these "per processor licenses discourage [computer manufacturers] from licensing competing operating systems and/or cause [computer manufacturers] to raise the price of [computers] with a competing operating system to recoup the fee paid to Microsoft."[196] The government also challenged the software manufacturer's practice of entering into long-term license agreements, which also allegedly "foreclosed [computer manufacturers] from licensing operating systems from Microsoft's competitors."[197] In a consent decree, Microsoft agreed, inter alia, to enter per copy licenses (as opposed to per processor licenses), not to enforce certain minimum commitments, and not to enter licenses with a term greater than one year.[198]

(2) Different or Discriminatory Royalties

Generally, a patent owner is permitted to charge different licensees different royalties. Absent any anticompetitive purpose or effect, charging different royalty rates will not constitute misuse or an antitrust violation.[199] The Seventh Circuit has

---

193. 339 U.S. 827 (1950).
194. *Id.* at 834. In *Western Elec. Co. v. Stewart-Warner Corp.*, 631 F.2d 333, 339 (4th Cir. 1980), *cert. denied*, 450 U.S. 971 (1981), the Fourth Circuit held that it was reasonable to base a royalty on the sale price of the finished products where substantially all the market value of the finished product was derived from the patented feature. *See also* Kearney & Trecker Corp. v. Giddings & Lewis, Inc., 306 F. Supp. 189, 200-01 (E.D. Wis. 1969), *rev'd on other grounds*, 452 F.2d 579 (7th Cir. 1971), *cert. denied*, 405 U.S. 1066 (1972).
195. 56 F.3d 1448 (D.C. Cir. 1995).
196. United States v. Microsoft Corp., 159 F.R.D. 318, 323 (D.D.C.) (summarizing the complaint; rejecting proposed consent decree because it did not adequately remedy the alleged harm to competition from the conduct charged in the complaint and from other allegedly anticompetitive conduct), *rev'd*, 56 F.3d 1448 (D.C. Cir. 1995).
197. 159 F.R.D. at 323 (summarizing the complaint).
198. 1995-2 Trade Cas. (CCH) ¶ 71,096 (D.D.C. 1995).
199. *See, e.g.*, Standard Oil Co. v. United States, 283 U.S. 163, 179 (1931); USM Corp. v. SPS Techs., Inc., 694 F.2d 505 (7th Cir. 1982), *cert. denied*, 462 U.S. 1107 (1983); Carter-Wallace, Inc. v. United States, 449 F.2d 1374, 1381-82 (Ct. Cl. 1971); La Salle St. Press, Inc. v. McCormick & Henderson, Inc., 445 F.2d 84, 95 (7th Cir. 1971); Novell, Inc. v. CPU Distrib., Inc., Civ. A. No. H-97-2326, 2000 U.S. Dist. LEXIS 9952, at *20-22 (S.D. Tex. May 12, 2000) (granting summary judgment on claim challenging software licensor's practice of charging a lower royalty to existing customers than to new customers because there was no evidence that the practice harmed competition); Honeywell, Inc. v. Sperry Rand Corp., 180 U.S.P.Q. (BNA) 673, 763 (D. Minn. 1973); Mobil Oil Corp. v. W.R. Grace & Co., 367 F. Supp. 207, 251 (D. Conn. 1973); Congoleum Indus. v. Armstrong Cork Co., 366 F. Supp. 220, 232 (E.D. Pa. 1973), *aff'd*, 510 F.2d 334 (3d Cir.), *cert. denied*, 421 U.S. 988 (1975); Bela Seating Co. v. Poloron Prods., 297 F. Supp. 489, 509 (N.D. Ill. 1968), *aff'd*, 438 F.2d 733, 738-39 (7th Cir.), *cert. denied*, 403 U.S. 922 (1971); Hanks v. Ross, 200 F. Supp. 605, 623 (D. Md. 1961); Pemco Prods. v. General Mills, Inc., 155 F. Supp. 433, 437 (N.D. Ohio 1957), *aff'd*, 261 F.2d 302 (6th Cir. 1958); *cf.* Akzo v. United States Int'l Trade Comm'n, 808 F.2d 1471, 1488-89 (Fed. Cir. 1986) (approving "value in use" pricing), *cert. denied*, 482 U.S. 909 (1987); Hennessy Indus. v. FMC Corp., 779 F.2d 402, 403-05 (7th Cir. 1985) (denying license unless prospective licensee paid a royalty higher than royalties being paid by others was not antitrust violation); *In re* Independent Serv. Orgs. Antitrust Litig., 964 F. Supp.

stated that "there is no antitrust prohibition against a patent owner's using price discrimination to maximize his income from the patent."[200] Other courts have indicated that in order to demonstrate that a differential royalty licensing regime violates Section 2, the challenger must demonstrate an adverse effect on competition.[201] The patent owner normally is permitted to agree that a licensee will be given so-called most favored nation status, i.e., the benefit of more favorable terms granted in subsequent licenses.[202]

In the *Shrimp Peelers* cases, several courts condemned a practice whereby a patentee with monopoly power in the market for shrimp-cleaning machines licensed and leased his patented shrimp-cleaning machines at different rates in different parts of the country.[203] In a related proceeding, the Federal Trade Commission found that the discriminatory rates tended to insulate the patentee's own downstream shrimp-cleaning business from competition from licensees and lessees of its machines, thereby violating Section 5 of the FTC Act.[204] To the extent that the *Shrimp Peelers* cases have been read to suggest that differential royalty rates standing alone violate the antitrust laws, the decisions have been criticized.[205]

Differential treatment of royalties in patent licenses does not implicate the Robinson-Patman Act where no commodities are sold with the license.[206]

1479, 1491 (D. Kan. 1997) (patentee may license its product to some and not to others and may price its patented products at different prices to different customers). *But cf.* Allied Research Prods. v. Heatbath Corp., 300 F. Supp. 656, 657 (N.D. Ill. 1969) (patent owner's refusal to grant a license without a valid business justification constituted unfair discrimination).

200. *USM Corp.*, 694 F.2d at 512; *accord* Bela Seating Co. v. Poloron Prods., 438 F.2d 733, 738 (7th Cir.), *cert. denied*, 403 U.S. 922 (1971).

201. *See, e.g.*, National Foam Sys. v. Urquhart, 202 F.2d 659, 663-64 (3d Cir. 1953); Barber Asphalt Corp. v. La Fera Grecco Contracting Co., 116 F.2d 211, 214-16 (3d Cir. 1940); *Honeywell, Inc.*, 180 U.S.P.Q. (BNA) 673.

202. *See, e.g.*, General Tire & Rubber Co. v. Firestone Tire & Rubber Co., 349 F. Supp. 333, 344-45 (N.D. Ohio 1972); Technograph Printed Circuits, Ltd. v. Bendix Aviation Corp., 218 F. Supp. 1, 51 (D. Md. 1963), *aff'd per curiam*, 327 F.2d 497 (4th Cir.), *cert. denied*, 379 U.S. 826 (1964); *see also* United States v. United States Gypsum Co., 333 U.S. 364, 389 (1948).

203. *See, e.g.*, Peelers Co. v. Wendt, 260 F. Supp. 193 (W.D. Wash. 1966); Laitram Corp. v. King Crab, Inc., 244 F. Supp. 9 (D. Alaska), *modified*, 245 F. Supp. 1019 (1965). *But cf.* Laitram Corp. v. Depoe Bay Fish Co., 549 F. Supp. 29 (D. Or. 1982) (rejecting argument that uniform royalty on unpeeled shrimp, where effect is unequal royalty on a peeled shrimp basis, is misuse).

204. *See* Grand Caillou Packing Co., 65 F.T.C. 799 (1964), *aff'd in part and rev'd in part sub nom.* LaPeyre v. FTC, 366 F.2d 117 (5th Cir. 1966).

205. *See, e.g.*, *USM Corp.*, 694 F.2d at 513; Official Airline Guides, Inc. v. FTC, 630 F.2d 920 (2d Cir. 1980), *cert. denied*, 450 U.S. 917 (1981); Carter-Wallace, Inc. v. United States, 167 U.S.P.Q. (BNA) 667, 673 n.10 (Ct. Cl. 1970) (the *Shrimp Peelers* cases "stand[] the antimonopoly laws on their head").

206. *See, e.g.*, La Salle St. Press, Inc. v. McCormick & Henderson, Inc., 293 F. Supp. 1004 (N.D. Ill. 1968), *aff'd in part and rev'd in part*, 445 F.2d 84 (7th Cir. 1971); KMG Kanal-Muller-Gruppe Int'l, GmbH v. Inliner U.S.A., 1999-2 Trade Cas. (CCH) ¶ 72,628, at 85,641 (S.D. Tex. 1999) ("The license at issue is not a commodity and the Robinson-Patman Act is inapplicable."); *Honeywell, Inc.*, 180 U.S.P.Q. (BNA) 673.

(3) Preissuance and Postexpiration Royalties

In *Brulotte v. Thys Co.*,[207] the Supreme Court held that a patentee's collection of royalties beyond the expiration of the licensed patent constitutes misuse.[208] The Court concluded that to collect such royalties was to "enlarge the monopoly of the patent" in a manner analogous to a patent-tying arrangement.[209] The Sixth, Seventh, and Eleventh Circuits have held such patent licenses are unenforceable beyond the life of the patents.[210] The Sixth Circuit has held that it constitutes misuse to provide for postexpiration royalties whether or not such royalties were collected.[211] The Second Circuit has indicated, however, that a licensee may still collect royalties up to the expiration of the patent, even if the *Brulotte* rule would invalidate the postexpiration portion of the license.[212]

Some courts have held that preissuance royalties for anticipated patents do not constitute misuse.[213] Where the license in question is a hybrid covering both trade secrets and anticipated patents, courts have held that the collection of preissuance royalties is not misuse.[214]

---

207. 379 U.S. 29 (1964).

208. *Id.* at 30-33; *see also* Virginia Panel Corp. v. MAC Panel Co., 133 F.3d 860, 869 (Fed. Cir. 1997) (stating in dicta that "[t]he courts have identified certain specific practices as constituting *per se* patent misuse, including . . . arrangements in which a patentee effectively extends the term of its patent by requiring post-expiration royalties"), *cert. denied*, 525 U.S. 815 (1998); Ar-Tik Sys. v. Dairy Queen, Inc., 302 F.2d 496, 510 (3d Cir. 1962); Shields-Jetco, Inc. v. Torti, 314 F. Supp. 1292 (D.R.I. 1970), *aff'd*, 436 F.2d 1061 (1st Cir. 1971). *But cf.* Sunrise Med. HHG, Inc. v. AirSep Corp., 95 F. Supp. 2d 348, 458 (W.D. Pa. 2000) ("[T]he royalty rate need not diminish as patents included in a package license expire, as long as the licensee is not coerced."); A.C. Aukerman Co. v. R.L. Chaides Constr. Co., 20 U.S.P.Q.2d 1054, 1058 (N.D. Cal. 1993) ("*Brulotte* has been held inapplicable to package licensing agreements containing expired patents if the licensee was not coerced to enter the arrangement.").

209. 379 U.S. at 33.

210. *See, e.g.*, Meehan v. PPG Indus., 802 F.2d 881 (7th Cir. 1986), *cert. denied*, 479 U.S. 1091 (1987); Boggild v. Kenner Prods., 776 F.2d 1315 (6th Cir. 1985), *cert. denied*, 477 U.S. 908 (1986); Pitney Bowes, Inc. v. Mestre, 701 F.2d 1365 (11th Cir.), *cert. denied*, 464 U.S. 893 (1983). *But cf.* Chromalloy Am. Corp. v. Fischmann, 716 F.2d 683 (9th Cir. 1983) ("hybrid" transfer of patent and of ongoing business unenforceable subsequent to repudiation of invalid patent, but compensation allowed for nonpatent assets such as know-how).

211. *See* Rocform Corp. v. Acitelli-Standard Concrete Wall, Inc., 367 F.2d 678 (6th Cir. 1966) (injunctive relief in an infringement action denied because license agreement provided for postexpiration royalties). Some courts have found misuse when royalties remained at a constant rate until the last of several licensed patents expired. *See, e.g., id.*; Duplan Corp. v. Deering Milliken, Inc., 444 F. Supp. 648, 697-99 (D.S.C. 1977), *aff'd in part and rev'd in part*, 594 F.2d 979 (4th Cir. 1979), *cert. denied*, 444 U.S. 1015 (1980); *cf.* Clayton Mfg. Co. v. Cline, 427 F. Supp. 78 (C.D. Cal. 1976) (contract for royalties based on future sale of an entire line of products is not a per se violation of the Sherman Act); *but see* Hull v. Brunswick Corp., 704 F.2d 1195 (10th Cir. 1983).

212. *See* Modrey v. American Gage & Mach. Co., 478 F.2d 470, 474-75 (2d Cir. 1973); *accord* Veltman v. Norton Simon, Inc., 425 F. Supp. 774 (S.D.N.Y. 1977).

213. *See, e.g.*, Painton & Co. v. Bourns, Inc., 442 F.2d 216, 223 (2d Cir. 1971); Congoleum Indus. v. Armstrong Cork Co., 366 F. Supp. 220, 234 (E.D. Pa. 1973), *aff'd*, 510 F.2d 334 (3d Cir.), *cert. denied*, 421 U.S. 988 (1975).

214. *See, e.g.*, Aronson v. Quick Point Pencil Co., 440 U.S. 257 (1979); San Marino Elec. Corp. v. George J. Meyer Mfg. Co., 155 U.S.P.Q. (BNA) 617 (C.D. Cal. 1967), *aff'd*, 422 F.2d 1285 (9th Cir. 1970); *cf.* Reich v. Reed Tool Co., 582 S.W.2d 549 (Tex. Civ. App. 1979), *cert. denied*, 446 U.S. 946 (1980).

(4) Royalties Based upon Use of an Article Purchased from the Patent Owner or His Licensee

Generally, once a patentee sells a patented article, an action for infringement will not lie against subsequent purchasers (and royalties cannot be collected from such purchasers).[215] In *Mallinckrodt, Inc. v. Medipart, Inc.*,[216] however, the Federal Circuit held that a patentee may sell a patented article and place restrictions on its postsale use so long as the restrictions are reasonably within the scope of the patent grant and do not violate some other law or policy.[217] Under the reasoning in *Mallinckrodt*, a patentee may have an action for infringement against a subsequent purchaser that violates the restrictions if that subsequent purchaser had knowledge of the restrictions.

Moreover, a patentee may license use separately from manufacture and sale and on that basis has been allowed to collect royalties for the use of a machine even though the patentee or manufacturer of the machine had sold it.[218] Finally, wholly apart from the patent, a patent holder may be able to place such vertical restraints on purchasers as the antitrust laws permit with respect to the sale of tangible goods and services and to enforce those restraints using traditional contract remedies.[219]

(5) Sharing or Fixing Royalties

In *Standard Oil Co. v. United States*,[220] the Supreme Court applied a rule of reason analysis to license agreements that required licensees to share sublicense royalties with the patent owners.[221] However, in *In re Yarn Processing Patent Validity Litigation*,[222] the Fifth Circuit held that, on the particular facts, a royalty-sharing arrangement involving royalties several times the magnitude of other costs

---

215. *See, e.g.*, Adams v. Burke, 84 U.S. (17 Wall.) 453, 457 (1873) ("when [patented coffins] are once lawfully made and sold, there is no restriction on their *use* to be implied for the benefit of the patentee"); Bloomer v. McQuewan, 55 U.S. (14 How.) 539, 549 (1852) ("when the machine passes to the hands of the purchaser, it is no longer within the limits of the monopoly"). The patentee may, however, have a contract remedy if privity requirements are met.

216. 976 F.2d 700 (Fed. Cir. 1992).

217. *Id.* at 708; *see* B. Braun Med., Inc. v. Abbott Labs., 124 F.3d 1419, 1426-27 (Fed. Cir. 1997) (error to charge jury that any postsale restriction on use of patented goods was misuse).

218. *See, e.g.*, *In re* Yarn Processing Patent Validity Litig., 541 F.2d 1127 (5th Cir. 1976), *cert. denied*, 433 U.S. 910 (1977); Duplan Corp. v. Deering Milliken, Inc., 444 F. Supp. 648, 671-72 (D.S.C. 1977) (separately licensing the right to manufacture and sell and the right to use is permissible, so long as there is no effect of fixing prices among competitors), *aff'd in part and rev'd in part*, 594 F.2d 979 (4th Cir. 1979), *cert. denied*, 444 U.S. 1015 (1980); Cold Metal Process Co. v. McLouth Steel Corp., 41 F. Supp. 487, 489-90 (E.D. Mich. 1941); *see also* General Talking Pictures Corp. v. Western Elec. Co., 304 U.S. 175 (notice of field of use restriction with purchase is enforceable), *aff'd on reh'g*, 305 U.S. 124 (1938); Extractol Process v. Hiram Walker & Sons, 153 F.2d 264, 267-68 (7th Cir. 1946) (Sherman Act not intended to restrict patentee's control over using the patented articles); *cf.* Brulotte v. Thys Co., 379 U.S. 29, 33 (1964) (only that part of the license calling for royalties after all patents had expired was held unenforceable). *But cf.* PSC Inc. v. Symbol Tech., Inc., 26 F. Supp. 2d 505, 510 (W.D.N.Y. 1998) ("[C]ollection of royalties from two parties for the same product improperly broadens the scope of the rights [patentee] has under its patents.").

219. *See generally* part D of Chapter I.

220. 283 U.S. 163 (1931).

221. *Id.* at 170-71.

222. 541 F.2d 1127 (5th Cir. 1976), *cert. denied*, 433 U.S. 910 (1977).

constituted an unlawful price-fixing agreement. In *Congoleum Industries v. Armstrong Cork Co.*,[223] a district court held that a patent owner may agree with its licensee as to the royalty rate to be charged to sublicensees.[224]

e. TERRITORIAL AND CUSTOMER RESTRICTIONS

The Patent Act specifically provides that a patentee may grant exclusive licenses under its patent for use in the entire United States or "any specified part of the United States."[225] In *Ethyl Gasoline Corp. v. United States*,[226] the Supreme Court held that a patentee may grant a license limiting the licensee's ability to make, use, and sell the patented invention to a particular territory within the United States, its territories, and possessions.[227] In *Brownell v. Ketcham Wire & Manufacturing Co.*,[228] the Ninth Circuit held that a license to a U.S. licensee may prohibit exporting the product.[229] In addition, many courts have held that location clauses in licenses of patented processes are not per se unlawful.[230] The agencies have recognized the possible procompetitive ends served by territorial restrictions.[231]

Where territorial restraints in patent licenses have been struck down, it has often been because the license was found to be a pretext or sham shielding a horizontal market division scheme between licensors and licensees that, but for the license,

---

223. 366 F. Supp. 220 (E.D. Pa. 1973), *aff'd*, 510 F.2d 334 (3d Cir.), *cert. denied*, 421 U.S. 988 (1975).

224. *Id.* at 229; *see also* Hennessy Indus. v. FMC Corp., 779 F.2d 402 (7th Cir. 1985) (upholding agreement among patentee, its licensee, and its former licensee to deny license to industry leader unless that firm paid a disproportionately high royalty).

225. 35 U.S.C. § 261 (1994). For the definition of "United States" in the Patent Act, see *id.* § 100(c).

226. 309 U.S. 436 (1940).

227. *Id.* at 456 (a patentee "may grant licenses to make, use or vend, restricted in point of space or time . . . save only that . . . he may not enlarge his monopoly"); *see also* E. Bement & Sons v. National Harrow Co., 186 U.S. 70, 92-93 (1902); Brownell v. Ketcham Wire & Mfg. Co., 211 F.2d 121, 128 (9th Cir. 1954) ("It is a fundamental rule of patent law that the owner of a patent may license another and prescribe territorial limitations."); Miller Insituform, Inc. v. Insituform of N. Am., Inc., 605 F. Supp. 1125, 1130 (M.D. Tenn. 1985) ("as a matter of law, a patent licensor's use of geographic restrictions in a sublicensing scheme to divide territories into ones of primary or exclusive jurisdiction constitutes a lawful application of the rights derived from a patent grant"), *aff'd*, 830 F.2d 606 (6th Cir. 1987), *cert. denied*, 484 U.S. 1064 (1988); *cf.* Smith Int'l, Inc. v. Kennametal, Inc., 621 F. Supp. 79, 89-90 (N.D. Ohio 1985) (quoting *Brownell* with approval but denying defense motion for summary judgment in case involving exclusive license, reciprocal exclusive distributorship, and requirements contract).

228. 211 F.2d 121 (9th Cir. 1954); Atari Games Corp. v. Nintendo of Am., 897 F.2d 1572, 1578-79 (Fed. Cir. 1990) (citing *Brownell*).

229. 211 F.2d at 129 (holding that license prohibiting export of patented product does not violate the antitrust laws); *cf. Atari Games Corp.*, 897 F.2d at 1578 (restriction judged under rule of reason). The amendments to 35 U.S.C. § 271(f) (1994) tend to reinforce the correctness of this result. *But see* Extractol Process, Ltd. v. Hiram Walker & Sons, 153 F.2d 264, 267-68 (7th Cir. 1946) (suggesting that sale in the United States for use outside the United States is not infringement).

230. *See, e.g.*, United States v. Studiengesellschaft Kohle, mbH, 670 F.2d 1122 (D.C. Cir. 1981) (no per se violation of Sherman Act in limiting field of use of unpatented product made by patented process); Robintech, Inc. v. Chemidus Wavin, Ltd., 628 F.2d 142 (D.C. Cir. 1980); *see also In re* Amtorg Trading Corp., 75 F.2d 826 (C.C.P.A.) (a patented process used outside the United States by a nonpatentee to make and export to the United States a nonpatented product is not an unfair method of competition), *cert. denied*, 296 U.S. 576 (1935).

231. INTELLECTUAL PROPERTY GUIDELINES, *supra* note 16, § 2.3 & Example 1 (recognizing procompetitive effects of territorial restrictions).

would have been competitors.[232] Some decisions also have held unlawful a territorial restraint imposed by a licensor in agreement with one or more of its licensees to insulate the licensees from competition amongst themselves.[233] In these situations, the characterization of the conduct as horizontal or vertical, which is central to an evaluation of its lawfulness, turned in large part upon whether the restraint originated with the patentee or its licensees. By comparison, the *Intellectual Property Guidelines* define such a restraint as horizontal if the licensees "would have been actual or likely potential competitors . . . in the absence of the license."[234]

A patentee may require a manufacturing licensee to sell only to prescribed customers,[235] to licensees under other patents,[236] or to licensees under different claims of the same patent.[237]

The right of a patentee to impose territorial and/or customer restraints on its licensees may be limited by the exhaustion doctrine.[238] Following the first authorized sale of a patented product, further restrictions on use and resale of a product implicate the law of vertical restraints addressed by the Supreme Court in *Continental T.V., Inc. v. GTE Sylvania Inc.*[239]

f. FIELD OF USE RESTRICTIONS

Where a patent owner licenses the patent but restricts its use to a particular market or application, the limitation is sometimes termed a "field of use" restriction. In *General Talking Pictures Corp. v. Western Electric Co.*,[240] the owner of patents on amplifiers licensed a subsidiary to make and sell equipment using the amplifiers for theaters and licensed others to make and sell radio receivers using the amplifiers solely for use in private homes. The defendant, with actual notice of the limited license, purchased theater equipment from one of those licensed to sell only to the

232. *See, e.g.*, Timken Roller Bearing Co. v. United States, 341 U.S. 593, 598-99 (1951); United States v. Crown Zellerbach Corp., 141 F. Supp. 118, 126 (N.D. Ill. 1956); United States v. National Lead Co., 63 F. Supp. 513, 527 (S.D.N.Y. 1945), *aff'd*, 332 U.S. 319 (1947); INTELLECTUAL PROPERTY GUIDELINES, *supra* note 16, Example 7.
233. *See, e.g.*, International Wood Processors v. Power Dry, Inc., 792 F.2d 416, 429 (4th Cir. 1986); Mannington Mills, Inc. v. Congoleum Indus., 610 F.2d 1059, 1071-72 (3d Cir. 1979); United States v. CIBA Geigy Corp., 508 F. Supp. 1118 (D.N.J. 1976); *Crown Zellerbach*, 141 F. Supp. at 127-28; *cf.* United States v. Sealy, Inc., 388 U.S. 350 (1967) (considering territorial restraints imposed as part of a trademark license).
234. INTELLECTUAL PROPERTY GUIDELINES, *supra* note 16, §§ 3.1, 3.3.
235. *See, e.g.*, *In re* Yarn Processing Patent Validity Litig., 541 F.2d 1127, 1135 (5th Cir. 1976) (a license under product patents to make machinery and sell only to persons licensed by the patent owner to use the machinery does not violate the Sherman Act), *cert. denied*, 433 U.S. 910 (1977); Westinghouse Elec. & Mfg. Co. v. Cutting & Washington Radio Corp., 294 F. 671 (2d Cir. 1923).
236. *See, e.g.*, Deering, Milliken & Co. v. Temp-Resisto Corp., 160 F. Supp. 463, 478-82 (S.D.N.Y. 1958), *aff'd in part and rev'd in part*, 274 F.2d 626 (2d Cir. 1960). *But see* United States v. Univis Lens Co., 316 U.S. 241 (1942); Ethyl Gasoline Corp. v. United States, 309 U.S. 436 (1940).
237. *See* SCM Corp. v. RCA, 318 F. Supp. 433 (S.D.N.Y. 1970).
238. *See* part B.3.c of this chapter.
239. 433 U.S. 36 (1977), discussed in part D of Chapter I; *see also* Munters Corp. v. Burgess Indus., 450 F. Supp. 1195, 1207-08 (S.D.N.Y. 1977). DOJ and FTC officials have suggested that resale restrictions ought to be subject to the same standards whether or not goods are subject to a patent. *See supra* note 25 and accompanying text.
240. 304 U.S. 175, *aff'd on reh'g*, 305 U.S. 124 (1938).

private home market. The Supreme Court upheld the field of use restriction and held both the offending licensee and the purchaser liable for infringement.[241]

Numerous cases have approved field of use restrictions in patent licenses.[242] Likewise, the agencies have recognized the procompetitive aspects of field of use restrictions.[243] A field of use restriction that goes beyond the scope of the patent grant may, however, raise more significant antitrust concerns.[244] Likewise, as with territorial restraints, field of use restrictions may be illegal if they are a pretext used to conceal a horizontal market allocation scheme.[245]

In *United States v. Studiengesellschaft Kohle, mbH*,[246] the D.C. Circuit held that field of use restrictions on unpatented products made by a patented process or machine are to be tested by a rule of reason analysis.[247] In *Mallinckrodt, Inc. v. Medipart, Inc.*,[248] the Federal Circuit reversed a trial court's holding that a restriction on reuse of a patented medical device was per se unlawful.[249] The Federal Circuit first inquired whether the restraint was considered per se illegal under governing Supreme Court precedent. Distinguishing the restriction on reuse from traditional per se offenses, such as "price fixing or tying," the court remanded to the lower court with the instruction that the "appropriate criterion is whether Mallinckrodt's restriction is reasonably within the patent grant, or whether the patentee has ventured

---

241. 304 U.S. at 181 ("Patent owners may grant licenses extending to all uses or limited to use in a defined field.").

242. *See, e.g.*, B. Braun Med., Inc. v. Abbott Labs., 124 F.3d 1419, 1426 (Fed. Cir. 1997); Automatic Radio Mfg. Co. v. Hazeltine Research, 176 F.2d 799, 802-03 (1st Cir. 1949), *aff'd*, 339 U.S. 827 (1950); Turner Glass Corp. v. Hartford-Empire Co., 173 F.2d 49, 53 (7th Cir.) (restriction limiting licensee's use of patented machinery to make certain types of glassware upheld), *cert. denied*, 338 U.S. 830 (1949); Smith Int'l, Inc. v. Kennametal, Inc., 621 F. Supp. 79 (N.D. Ohio 1985); United States v. CIBA Geigy Corp., 508 F. Supp. 1118, 1149-51 (D.N.J. 1976); Bela Seating Co. v. Poloron Prods., 297 F. Supp. 489, 503-04, 509-10 (N.D. Ill. 1968) (upholding requirement that chairs manufactured using the patent shall "be the same as or similar to the chairs currently manufactured by [the licensee]"), *aff'd*, 438 F.2d 733 (7th Cir.), *cert. denied*, 403 U.S. 922 (1971); Reliance Molded Plastics, Inc. v. Jiffy Prods., 215 F. Supp. 402, 405, 408-09 (D.N.J. 1963), *aff'd per curiam*, 337 F.2d 857 (3d Cir. 1964); Benger Lab. v. R.K. Laros Co., 209 F. Supp. 639 (E.D. Pa. 1962), *aff'd per curiam*, 317 F.2d 455 (3d Cir.), *cert. denied*, 375 U.S. 833 (1963); *In re* Reclosable Plastic Bags, 192 U.S.P.Q. (BNA) 674, 679 (U.S. Int'l Trade Comm'n 1977).

243. *See* INTELLECTUAL PROPERTY GUIDELINES, *supra* note 16, § 2.3 & Example 1.

244. *See, e.g.*, Ethyl Gasoline Corp. v. United States, 309 U.S. 436, 456 (1940) (patentee "may grant licenses to make, use or vend, restricted in point of space or time, or with any other restriction upon the exercise of the granted privilege, save only that by attaching a condition to his license he may not enlarge his monopoly and thus acquire some other which the statute and the patent together did not give"); Amgen, Inc. v. Chugai Pharm. Co., 808 F. Supp. 894, 903 (D. Mass. 1992), *aff'd sub nom.* Ortho Pharm. Corp. v. Genetics Inst., 52 F.3d 1026 (Fed. Cir.), *cert. denied*, 516 U.S. 907 (1995).

245. *See, e.g.*, Hartford-Empire Co. v. United States, 323 U.S. 386, 400 (1945) (condemning a patent pooling arrangement in the glass container industry that entailed patent licenses with field of use restrictions).

246. 670 F.2d 1122 (D.C. Cir. 1981).

247. *Id.* at 1128. *But see* Robintech, Inc. v. Chemidus Wavin, Ltd. 628 F.2d 142, 147-49 (D.C. Cir. 1980) (holding invalid an export restriction imposed on the sale of an unpatented product produced by a patented process).

248. 976 F.2d 700 (Fed. Cir. 1992).

249. *Id.* at 708. *But see* United States v. Glaxo Group, 302 F. Supp. 1, 4-11 (D.D.C. 1969) (agreement that licensee-purchaser of patented drug in bulk form "will not, without first obtaining [the seller's] consent, resell, or re-deliver in bulk" violated Sherman Act), *rev'd on other grounds*, 410 U.S. 52 (1973).

beyond the patent grant and into behavior having an anticompetitive effect not justifiable under the rule of reason."[250]

g.   TYING ARRANGEMENTS

(1)   Tying as an Antitrust Violation

As discussed in Chapter I of this treatise, a tying arrangement occurs when a seller offers a desired item, the tying item, only on the condition that the purchaser also purchase another item, the tied item.   In general, establishing a tying arrangement that is per se unlawful under Section 1 of the Sherman Act and Section 3 of the Clayton Act requires proof that (1) two separate products or services are involved, (2) there is a sale or agreement to sell one product or service "conditioned" on the purchase of another, (3) the seller has sufficient economic power in the market for the tying product to enable it to restrain trade in the market for the tied product, and (4) a not insubstantial amount of interstate commerce in the tied product is affected.[251]   In the cases discussed in this section, the "tying" item is in some way covered by a patent or copyright.   That is, the tying item is either a license under a patent owned by the licensor or a product made under a patent owned or licensed to the tying seller.

For many years, courts presumed that the seller had sufficient power over the tying product where the tying item was patented or copyrighted.[252]   In 1936, in *IBM v. United States*,[253] the Supreme Court held that the lease of a patented tabulating machine on the condition the lessee also purchase paper cards for use in the machine violated Section 3 of the Clayton Act.   Likewise, in 1947 the Court held in *International Salt Co. v. United States*[254] that a similar tying arrangement violated

---

250.   976 F.2d at 708. *See* B. Braun Med., Inc. v. Abbott Labs., 124 F.3d 1419, 1426 (Fed. Cir. 1997) ("[F]ield of use restrictions (such as those at issue in the present case) are generally upheld, . . . and any anticompetitive effects they may cause are reviewed in accordance with the rule of reason.") (citation omitted); Monsanto Co. v. Trantham, 156 F. Supp. 2d 855, 864-65 (W.D. Tenn. 2001) (upholding as not beyond the scope of the patent restrictions on genetically modified seeds that prevent farmers from saving seeds grown from the modified seeds for replanting in a later growing season); Carter v. Variflex, Inc., 101 F. Supp. 2d 1261, 1266-68 (C.D. Cal. 2000) (cross-licensing agreement with a field of use restriction analyzed under the rule of reason to assess anticompetitive effects).

251.   *See* part D.3.a of Chapter I.   Some courts have imposed additional prerequisites for illegality, including some showing of harm to competition in the tied product market. *See id.*   The enforcement agencies have likewise stated in the INTELLECTUAL PROPERTY GUIDELINES, *supra* note 16, § 5.3, that they will "consider both anticompetitive effects and the efficiencies attributable to a tie-in." *See infra* note 273 and accompanying text.

252.   *See* United States v. Loew's, Inc., 371 U.S. 38, 45 (1962) ("The requisite economic power is presumed when the tying product is patented or copyrighted.") (citations omitted); International Salt Co. v. United States, 332 U.S. 392, 395 (1947) (patented machine); Duplan Corp. v. Deering Milliken, Inc., 444 F. Supp. 648, 673 (D.S.C. 1977), *aff'd in part and rev'd in part*, 594 F.2d 979 (4th Cir. 1979), *cert. denied*, 444 U.S. 1015 (1980); *see also* Northern Pac. Ry. v. United States, 356 U.S. 1, 10 n.8, 18 (1958) (although "it is common knowledge that a patent does not always confer a monopoly over a particular commodity," the Court has held proof of competitive substitutes to be irrelevant); Standard Oil Co. v. United States, 337 U.S. 293, 307 (1949) ("although in fact there may be many competing substitutes for the patented article, [a patent] is at least *prima facie* evidence of [market] control").

253.   298 U.S. 131 (1936).

254.   332 U.S. 392 (1947).

Section 1 of the Sherman Act. In *Jefferson Parish Hospital District No. 2 v. Hyde*,[255] a majority of the Court reaffirmed, in dictum, that a presumption of market power arises when the tying product is the subject of a patent.[256]

The presumption that a patent or copyright confers sufficient market power in a tying case has been questioned by lower courts,[257] by four justices of the Supreme Court,[258] and by the agencies.[259] Proponents of this view argue that whether or not a patent truly confers any market power on its holder depends upon the availability of substitutes in the relevant market and is not properly the subject of a blanket presumption.[260] Whether the presence of a patent is dispositive in allowing the plaintiff to meet its burden to establish the market power element of a tying claim, the other elements of the offense must still be established as if the tying product were not patented.[261]

255. 466 U.S. 2 (1984).

256. *Id.* at 16 ("[I]f the Government has granted the seller a patent or similar monopoly over a product, it is fair to presume that the inability to buy the product elsewhere gives the seller market power."); *see also* Virtual Maint., Inc. v. Prime Computer, Inc., 11 F.3d 660, 666 (6th Cir. 1993) (licensee had market power in the derivative aftermarket for software support by virtue of its exclusive software license and a manufacturer's requirement that all suppliers use the licensed software), *cert. dismissed*, 512 U.S. 1216 (1994); Digidyne Corp. v. Data Gen. Corp., 734 F.2d 1336, 1341-45 (9th Cir. 1984) (presuming defendant's computer software enjoyed market power because it was copyrighted).

257. *See, e.g.*, C.R. Bard, Inc. v. M3 Sys., Inc., 157 F.3d 1340, 1367 & n.7 (Fed. Cir. 1998), *cert. denied*, 526 U.S. 1130 (1999) (citing, inter alia, A.I. Root Co. v. Computer/Dynamics, Inc., 806 F.2d 673, 676 (6th Cir. 1986)); Abbott Labs. v. Brennan, 952 F.2d 1346, 1354 (Fed. Cir. 1991) ("[a] patent does not of itself establish a presumption of market power in the antitrust sense"), *cert. denied*, 505 U.S. 1205 (1992); Mozart Co. v. Mercedes-Benz of N. Am., Inc., 833 F.2d 1342, 1346 n.4 (9th Cir. 1987) (noting that presumption of market power in copyright cases has been rejected by several courts and commentators), *cert. denied*, 488 U.S. 870 (1988); *A.I. Root Co.*, 806 F.2d at 676 (holding that a copyright did not confer a presumption of market power for tying purposes; dismissing as "overbroad" the language in *Loew's, Inc.* to the contrary); American Hoist & Derrick Co. v. Sowa & Sons, 725 F.2d 1350, 1367 (Fed. Cir.) ("patent rights are not *legal monopolies* in the antitrust sense of that word"), *cert. denied*, 469 U.S. 821 (1984); Northlake Mktg. & Supply v. Glaverbel S.A., 861 F. Supp. 653, 662 (N.D. Ill. 1994), *amended*, No. 92 C 2732, 1994 WL 542771 (N.D. Ill. Oct. 3, 1994); Rockbit Indus. U.S.A. v. Baker Hughes, Inc., 802 F. Supp. 1544, 1549 n.3 (S.D. Tex. 1991).

258. *See Jefferson Parish*, 466 U.S. at 37 n.7 (O'Connor, J., concurring) ("a patent holder has no market power in any relevant sense if there are close substitutes for the patented product"); *cf.* Data Gen. Corp. v. Digidyne Corp., 473 U.S. 908, 909 (1985) (White and Blackmun, JJ., dissenting from denial of certiorari) ("this case raises several substantial questions of antitrust law and policy, including . . . what effect should be given to the existence of a copyright or other legal monopoly in determining market power").

259. *See* INTELLECTUAL PROPERTY GUIDELINES, *supra* note 16, § 5.3 ("[t]he Agencies will not presume that a patent, copyright, or trade secret necessarily confers market power upon its owner").

260. *See id.* The presumption, moreover, may have been implicitly rejected by Congress in the context of patent misuse. See discussion of 35 U.S.C. § 271(d)(5), *infra* notes 276-86 and accompanying text; *see also* Schlafly v. Caro-Kann Corp., 1998-1 Trade Cas. (CCH) ¶ 72,138 (Fed. Cir. 1998) (applying 35 U.S.C. § 271(d) to hold that where patentee was not shown to have market power within a relevant market, licensing restrictions did not violate § 1 of the Sherman Act). In § 2 cases, the Supreme Court has not presumed market power from the existence of a patent; for example, *Walker Process Equip. Inc. v. Food Mach. & Chem. Corp.*, 382 U.S. 172 (1965), required independent proof of market power despite the existence of a patent.

261. *See, e.g.*, Intergraph Corp. v. Intel Corp., 195 F.3d 1346, 1362 (Fed. Cir. 1999) ("Commercial negotiations to trade patent property rights for other consideration in order to settle a patent dispute is neither tying nor coercive reciprocity in violation of the Sherman Act."); Virginia Panel Corp. v.

To prevail on a tying claim in the intellectual property context, a plaintiff must show an agreement conditioning an intellectual property license on some additional transaction.[262] Courts often describe the harm caused by such tying arrangements as the extension of the intellectual property right beyond its proper, statutory scope.[263]

A patent owner who sells unpatented materials together with a license to practice a patent can avoid a claim of unlawful tying by offering a separate license under the patent for using materials, parts, or components supplied by others. In general, the terms of the separate license must be definite and as favorable as the terms of the license which the patent owner grants to his purchasers.[264] Moreover, several courts

---

MAC Panel Co., 133 F.3d 860, 871 (Fed. Cir. 1997) (mere proposal of licensing agreement conditioned on purchase of unpatented products cannot constitute patent misuse), *cert. denied*, 525 U.S. 815 (1998); Southtrust Corp. v. Plus Sys., 913 F. Supp. 1517 (N.D. Ala. 1995) ("plus systems" trademark was not sufficiently distinct from the allegedly tied product—the ATM services—to be separate products).

262. In several cases involving computer parts or software, courts have rejected claims that a copyright owner's refusal to license to competing computer maintenance firms amounts to an illegal tying agreement. *See, e.g.*, PSI Repair Servs., Inc. v. Honeywell, Inc., 104 F.3d 811, 815-17 (6th Cir.), *cert. denied*, 520 U.S. 1265 (1997); In re Data Gen. Corp. v. Grumman Sys. Support Corp., 36 F.3d 1147, 1180-81 (1st Cir. 1994); Service & Training, Inc. v. Data Gen. Corp., 963 F.2d 680 (4th Cir. 1992); Advanced Computer Servs. v. MAI Sys., 845 F. Supp. 356 (E.D. Va. 1994); Triad Sys. Corp. v. Southeastern Exp. Co., 1994-2 Trade Cas. (CCH) ¶ 70,837 (N.D. Cal. 1994), *aff'd in part and rev'd in part*, 64 F.3d 1330 (9th Cir. 1995), *cert. denied*, 516 U.S. 1145 (1996).

263. *See, e.g.*, Eastman Kodak Co. v. Image Technical Servs., Inc., 504 U.S. 451, 480 & n.29 (1992) ("The Court has held many times that power gained through some natural and legal advantage such as a patent, . . . can give rise to liability if a seller exploits his dominant position in one market to expand his empire to the next.") (internal quotation omitted); In re Independent Serv. Orgs. Antitrust Litig., 203 F.3d 1322, 1327 (Fed. Cir. 2000) ("undisputed premise that the patent holder cannot use his statutory right to refuse to sell patented parts to gain a monopoly in a market beyond the scope of the patent"), *cert. denied*, 531 U.S. 1143 (2001); Atari Games Corp. v. Nintendo of Am., Inc., 897 F.2d 1572, 1576 (Fed. Cir. 1990) ("[A] patent owner may not take the property right granted by a patent and use it to extend his power in the marketplace improperly, *i.e.* beyond the limits of what Congress intended to give in the patent laws.").

264. *Compare* National Foam Sys. v. Urquhart, 202 F.2d 659, 662-64 (3d Cir. 1953) (separate license constituted misuse where royalty was not as favorable as for patentee's license), Dehydrators, Ltd. v. Petrolite Corp., 117 F.2d 183 (9th Cir. 1941) (separate license constituted misuse where terms not equivalent to patentee's license), Barber Asphalt Corp. v. La Fera Grecco Contracting Co., 116 F.2d 211, 214-16 (3d Cir. 1940) (license fee charged when contractors purchase unpatented goods from another source is misuse), Discovision Assocs. v. Disc Mfg., Inc., 42 U.S.P.Q.2d (BNA) 1749, 1759 (D. Del. 1997) (allegation of "economic coercion" sufficient to state conditioning element of a tying claim where defendant threatened prospective licensees and their customers with lawsuits unless they accepted a package license), Ansul Co. v. Uniroyal, Inc., 306 F. Supp. 541, 563-64 (S.D.N.Y. 1969) (misuse where the offer to competitors to sell the unpatented material was unreasonable and discriminatory), *aff'd in part, rev'd in part, and remanded*, 448 F.2d 872 (2d Cir. 1971), *cert. denied*, 404 U.S. 1018 (1972), *and* Urquhart v. United States, 109 F. Supp. 409, 411-12 (Ct. Cl. 1953) (licensing scheme is misuse where license fee depended upon source of unpatented goods), *with* United States Gypsum Co. v. National Gypsum Co., 387 F.2d 799, 802 (7th Cir. 1967) ("there could be no misuse if the terms on which a license is available to those wishing to use [unpatented] tape manufactured by others are reasonably comparable to the terms for one who uses the patentee's tape"), *cert. denied*, 390 U.S. 988 (1968), Rohm & Haas Co. v. Owens-Corning Fiberglass Corp., 196 U.S.P.Q. (BNA) 726, 734, 742-43 (N.D. Ala. 1977) (license upheld where patentee did not attempt to extend scope of patent claim to unpatented staple goods), Watson Packer, Inc. v. Dresser Indus., 193 U.S.P.Q. (BNA) 552, 559-60 (N.D. Tex. 1977), *and* Congoleum Indus. v. Armstrong Cork Co., 366 F. Supp. 220, 236 (E.D. Pa. 1973) (license upheld where patentee did not attempt to collect royalties after expiration of the patent), *aff'd*, 510 F.2d 334 (3d Cir.), *cert. denied*, 421 U.S. 988 (1975).

have found that the bundling or packaging of licenses could not be challenged where the licensee never asked for a separate, unbundled license and hence the patentee had no opportunity to offer one.[265] In such a circumstance, the availability of unbundled licenses would negate the inference that the sale or license of one was conditional on the other.

Similarly, a court may reject a tying claim where there is no evidence that the licensee was coerced into satisfying the alleged tying condition in order to get a license. For example, in *Data General Corp. v. Grumman Systems Support Corp.*,[266] a copyright infringement case, the defendant asserted a counterclaim alleging that Data General's policy of giving licenses only to equipment owners who maintained their own machines improperly tied the software license to an agreement not to use third-party maintenance organizations. The First Circuit rejected this claim, finding no evidence that any equipment owner had unwillingly chosen to maintain its own equipment in order to get a license.[267]

In *United States v. Microsoft Corp.*,[268] the D.C. Circuit vacated the lower court's determination that "Microsoft's contractual and technological bundling" of its Internet browser with its dominant operating system "resulted in a tying arrangement that was per se unlawful."[269] Observing that there is "no close parallel in prior antitrust cases" to the integration of added functionality into computer "software that serves as a platform to third-party applications," the D.C. Circuit instructed that, on remand, the government's tying claim should be considered under the rule of reason.[270] The court explained that while the standard approach for determining the existence of separate products under the per se rule may serve as an adequate proxy for net efficiencies in other contexts, it risked underestimating the real benefits of product integrations "in technologically dynamic markets where product development is especially unlikely to follow an easily foreseen linear pattern."[271] While acknowledging that its reasoning might be thought to apply to other markets with rapidly evolving technologies, the court cautioned that its "judgment regarding the comparative merits of the per se rule and the rule of reason is confined to the tying arrangement before us, where the tying product is software whose major purpose is to serve as a platform for third-party applications and the tied product is complementary software functionality."[272] The additional elements required to

---

265. *See, e.g.*, Rex Chainbelt, Inc. v. Harco Prods., 512 F.2d 993, 1001 n.2 (9th Cir.) ("the fact that no one has yet asked . . . for a direct license (and consequently no one was refused one) is evidence that there is no economic tying effect or misuse present; however, it is not conclusive of the point") (citations omitted), *cert. denied*, 423 U.S. 831 (1975); Federal Sign & Signal Corp. v. Bangor Punta Operations, Inc., 357 F. Supp. 1222, 1240 (S.D.N.Y. 1973); *Ansul Co.*, 306 F. Supp. at 562-63. *But see* B.B. Chem. Co. v. Ellis, 117 F.2d 829, 837-38 (1st Cir. 1941) (available license must not be on unreasonable and discriminatory terms), *aff'd*, 314 U.S. 495 (1942).

266. 36 F.3d 1147 (1st Cir. 1994).

267. *Id.* at 1181; *see also* Engel Indus. v. Lockformer Co., 96 F.3d 1398, 1408 (Fed. Cir. 1996) ("royalties may be based on unpatented components if that provides a convenient means for measuring the value of the license"); Beal Corp. Liquidating Trust v. Valleylab, Inc., 927 F. Supp. 1350, 1368 (D. Colo. 1996) ("When the record contains no evidence of customer coercion, summary judgement is appropriate on a tying arrangement claim.").

268. 253 F.3d 34 (D.C. Cir.), *cert. denied*, 122 S. Ct. 350 (2001).

269. *Id.* at 84-97.

270. *Id.* at 84.

271. *Id.* at 85-88, 94.

272. *Id.* at 95.

establish a violation under the rule of reason are (1) demonstrating that the tying arrangement had an adverse affect on competition in the relevant market for the tied product, and (2) balancing the efficiency justifications for the tie against its anticompetitive effects.[273]

Some courts have found that if the tied product is also covered by a patent, and thus both products are within the seller's control, the requisite restraint of trade in the tied product is missing.[274] In the *IBM* case, however, the Supreme Court suggested that a patent on the tied product—paper cards—would not have made any difference to IBM's liability for tying under Section 3 of the Clayton Act.[275]

(2) Tying as a Misuse

In 1988, Congress amended the Patent Act to provide that tying will not constitute patent misuse or "illegal extension of the patent right" unless the patentee has market power in the tying product.[276] The amendment added Section 271(d)(5), which provides:

> No patent owner otherwise entitled to relief for infringement or contributory infringement of a patent shall be denied relief or deemed guilty of misuse or illegal extension of the patent right by reason of his having done one or more of the following: . . . (5) conditioned the license of any rights to the patent or the sale of the patented product on the acquisition of a license to rights in another patent or purchase of a separate product, unless, in view of the circumstances, the patent owner has

---

273. *Id.* at 95-97. The agencies have stated that, as a matter of prosecutorial discretion, they will consider both of these factors before challenging tying arrangements as an illegal restraint. INTELLECTUAL PROPERTY GUIDELINES, *supra* note 16, § 5.3. Prior to *Microsoft*, at least one other court had evaluated the extent of foreclosure in the tied product market when evaluating a tying arrangement in an intellectual property license. DiscoVision Assocs. v. Disc Mfg., Inc., 42 U.S.P.Q.2d (BNA) 1749, 1758 (D. Del. 1997) (allegation that "tying arrangement forecloses competition in the [market for the tied technology] by reducing the incentive to design around [the licensor's] technology and by reducing the demand for alternative technologies" sufficiently states foreclosure element of tying offense). For a discussion of tying cases that consider competitive effect and justification outside the confines of intellectual property cases, see part D.3.a of Chapter I.

274. *See, e.g.*, Federal Sign & Signal Corp. v. Bangor Punta Operations, Inc., 357 F. Supp. 1222, 1228 (S.D.N.Y. 1973) (no misuse where "plaintiff was proceeding in good faith to rely upon the validity of its Liston patent, which covers the VASCAR [tied] device" and had "never refused to grant any prospective purchaser a license under the [tying] patent"); United States v. Consolidated Car-Heating Co., 87 U.S.P.Q. (BNA) 20, 23-24 (S.D.N.Y. 1950) (no Sherman Act violation where a patent owner agreed to "loan" its licensee a patented electric furnace and required licensee to purchase patented alloy for use in the furnace); *see also* part B.3.h of this chapter (discussing package licensing).

275. IBM v. United States, 298 U.S. 131, 136-38 (1936); *see also* Baldwin-Lima-Hamilton Corp. v. Tatnall Measuring Sys., 169 F. Supp. 1, 31 (E.D. Pa. 1958) ("The monopoly which the patent law grants with respect to an article covered by one patent may not be utilized to aid the patentee to exploit another article even though it is covered by another patent."), *aff'd per curiam*, 268 F.2d 395 (3d Cir.), *cert. denied*, 361 U.S. 894 (1959); *cf.* Ethyl Gasoline Corp. v. United States, 309 U.S. 436, 459 (1940) ("The patent monopoly of one invention may no more be enlarged for the exploitation of a monopoly of another than for the exploitation of an unpatented article or for the exploitation or promotion of a business not embraced within the patent.") (citations omitted).

276. 35 U.S.C. § 271(d)(5) (1994) (as enacted by Pub. L. No. 100-703, 102 Stat. 4676 (1988)).

market power in the relevant market for the patent or patented product on which the license or sale is conditioned.[277]

Thus, to establish the claim of patent misuse, a defendant in a patent infringement action must show that the patentee had market power in the tying item in the same fashion that it must be shown in a nonpatent antitrust case.[278]

Section 271(d)(5) appears to abrogate several Supreme Court decisions holding that the tying of an unpatented article to a patented article or patent license without more constitutes misuse.[279] Previously, misuse had been found where the lessor of a patented machine required the lessee to use only "staple" materials[280] purchased from the patent owner with the machine,[281] where the patent tied unpatented materials for use in a patented process together with a license to use the patented process,[282] and where the patent owner sold an unpatented element of a patented combination together with notice to customers that the purchase carried a license on the patented combination.[283] Section 271(d)(5) could be interpreted as requiring a showing of market power in the patented (tying) product in these situations as well.[284] At least one court has held that Section 271(d)(5)'s market power requirement applies to "tie-

---

277. *Id.*

278. *See* 134 CONG. REC. H10646-02 (daily ed. Oct. 20, 1988) (statement of Rep. Kastenmeier) (expecting that with respect to market power "the courts will be guided—though not bound—by the past and future decisions of the Supreme Court in the context of antitrust analysis of unlawful tie-ins"); *see also* Virginia Panel Corp. v. MAC Panel Co., 133 F.3d 860, 869 (Fed. Cir. 1997) ("in the absence of market power, even a tying arrangement does not constitute patent misuse"), *cert. denied*, 525 U.S. 815 (1998); Sunrise Med. HHG, Inc. v. AirSep Corp., 95 F. Supp. 2d 348, 458 (W.D. Pa. 2000) ("35 U.S.C. § 271(d) . . . removes any per se illegality from tying arrangements absent a showing of market power on the part of the licensor"); Texas Instruments, Inc. v. Hyundai Elec. Indus. Co., 49 F. Supp. 2d 893, 912 (E.D. Tex. 1999) ("Patent Misuse Reform Act of 1988 removed the doctrine of per se patent misuse due to tying"); Sinclair Int'l Ltd. v. FMC Corp., No. C97-01885 CAL, 1997 U.S. Dist. LEXIS 14963 (N.D. Cal. Sept. 10, 1997) (finding that defendant presented insufficient evidence to establish market power in a relevant market to support patent misuse defense).

279. *See, e.g.*, Morton Salt Co. v. G.S. Suppiger Co., 314 U.S. 488, 490, 494 (1942); B.B. Chem. Co. v. Ellis, 314 U.S. 495 (1942).

280. A staple article or commodity is one that is suitable for a "substantial noninfringing use." 35 U.S.C. § 271(c) (Supp. 1999). A nonstaple article or commodity, by contrast, is one that is "especially adapted for use in an infringement of [a] patent." *Id.*; *accord* Dawson Chem. Co. v. Rohm & Haas Co., 448 U.S. 176, 186 n.6 (1980).

281. *See, e.g.*, *Morton Salt*, 314 U.S. at 491; Senza-Gel Corp. v. Seiffhart, 803 F.2d 661, 665 (Fed. Cir. 1986). *But see* Binks Mfg. Co. v. Ransburg Electro-Coating Corp., 281 F.2d 252, 259 (7th Cir. 1960) (no misuse where "the leasing arrangement is not imposed as a condition of licensing and licenses are available without equipment being leased from the defendant"), *cert. dismissed*, 366 U.S. 211 (1961).

282. *See, e.g.*, *B.B. Chem. Co.*, 314 U.S. at 496-97; Leitch Mfg. Co. v. Barber Co., 302 U.S. 458, 460-63 (1938).

283. *See, e.g.*, Mercoid Corp. v. Mid-Continent Inv. Co., 320 U.S. 661, 664-65 (1944); Mercoid Corp. v. Minneapolis-Honeywell Regulator Co., 320 U.S. 680, 682-84 (1944); B.B. Chem. Co. v. Ellis, 117 F.2d 829, 834-35 (1st Cir. 1941), *aff'd*, 314 U.S. 495 (1942); Philad Co. v. Lechler Lab., 107 F.2d 747 (2d Cir. 1939).

284. In *Dawson Chem. Co. v. Rohm & Haas Co.*, 448 U.S. 176, 200-15 (1980), the Supreme Court read other parts of § 271(d) to effectuate Congress's intent even though the precise language of the statute did not cover the acts in question.

outs"—the grant of a license on the condition that the licensee not use competing products—as well as "tie-ins."[285]

An agreement by a patentee not to deal in other unpatented goods in competition with its licensee's goods has been found unenforceable.[286]

h.   PACKAGE LICENSING OF PATENTS AND COPYRIGHTS

Patent and copyright licenses frequently grant the licensee rights to practice under more than one of the licensor's patents or copyrights. The antitrust treatment of such "package" licenses depends in large part on whether the licensee has been forced to accept the package as a condition for receiving one or more desired licenses.

In general, consensual package licenses, which do not involve tying-like coercion to accept undesired licenses, are lawful and do not constitute misuse. For example, in *Automatic Radio Manufacturing Co. v. Hazeltine Research, Inc.*,[287] the Supreme Court found no misuse where there was a single license for a number of patents and a fixed royalty based on a percentage of the licensee's sales that did not vary regardless of how many of the patents were used. Absent proof that the patent owner refused to grant individual licenses, the Court refused to hold that the licensing scheme constituted misuse.[288] Similarly, in *International Manufacturing Co. v. Landon, Inc.*,[289] the Ninth Circuit found no violation of the Sherman Act in package licensing where activities under one patent could not be carried out without infringing all patents in the group.[290]

When package licenses of intellectual property have been challenged, the concern has been that the licensor has leveraged its power over some patents to force the licensee to take less desirable licenses. That is, the licensor has "tied" the purchase of a desired license to the acceptance of an undesired license. In that regard, a line of Supreme Court decisions held that "block booking" of separately copyrighted films constituted a violation of Section 1 of the Sherman Act.[291] In *MCA Television Ltd. v.*

---

285.   See *In re* Recombinant DNA Tech. Patent & Contract Litig., 850 F. Supp. 769, 777 (S.D. Ind. 1994); *see also* Texas Instruments, Inc. v. Hyundai Elec. Indus. Co., 49 F. Supp. 2d 893, 905 (E.D. Tex. 1999) (applying § 271(d)(5) in the analysis of a "unique sales-cap termination clause [which] operates to 'tie out' [licensee's] sales [of product not covered by the license]").

286.   See McCullough v. Kammerer Corp., 166 F.2d 759 (9th Cir.), *cert. denied*, 335 U.S. 813 (1948).

287.   339 U.S. 827 (1950), *overruled on other grounds by* Lear, Inc. v. Adkins, 395 U.S. 653 (1969).

288.   *Id.* at 831.

289.   336 F.2d 723 (9th Cir. 1964), *cert. denied*, 379 U.S. 988 (1965).

290.   *Id.* at 729-30; *see also* North Am. Philips Co. v. Stewart Eng'g Co., 319 F. Supp. 335, 350 (N.D. Cal. 1970); Binks Mfg. Co. v. Ransburg Electro-Coating Corp., 122 U.S.P.Q. (BNA) 74, 88 (S.D. Ind. 1959), *aff'd in part and rev'd in part*, 281 F.2d 252 (7th Cir. 1960), *cert. dismissed*, 366 U.S. 211 (1961); INTELLECTUAL PROPERTY GUIDELINES, *supra* note 16, § 5.3 (package licensing may be efficiency enhancing "[w]hen multiple licenses are needed to use any single item of intellectual property").

291.   *See, e.g.*, United States v. Loew's, Inc., 371 U.S. 38 (1962); United States v. Paramount Pictures, 334 U.S. 131, 156-59 (1948). In *Broadcast Music, Inc. v. CBS*, 441 U.S. 1, 24 (1979), the Supreme Court, without specifically addressing the package license question, held that agreements whereby holders of rights under numerous musical copyrights granted only "blanket" licenses covering multiple copyrights for a single royalty were not per se violations of § 1. The licenses were nonexclusive, i.e., the individual owners retained the right to grant individual licenses. On remand, the defendant prevailed. CBS v. American Soc'y of Composers, Authors & Publishers, 620 F.2d 930 (2d Cir. 1980), *cert. denied*, 450 U.S. 970 (1981); *see also* Buffalo Broad. Co. v.

Public Interest Corp.,[292] the Eleventh Circuit held that a licensor's conditioning of a license for desired television programs upon acceptance of a new program was illegal per se under this settled Supreme Court authority.[293]

Decisions regarding the evidence needed to establish coercion have sometimes turned on whether the licensee requested and was refused an unbundled license. Some courts have found unlawful packaging where the licensor refused to license separately.[294] Other courts have approved multiple licensing arrangements where the licensee failed to prove that it was refused the opportunity of taking licenses under less than all of the patents in the package.[295]

Section 271(d)(5) of the Patent Act specifically applies to package licenses.[296] Thus, when package licenses of patents are challenged as a misuse, the challenger must show that the licensor possesses market power in the market for the tying patent.[297] The statute, by its terms, does not apply to copyrights, nor does it apply to actions under the Sherman Act.

The agencies have said that they will analyze package licensing as a tying arrangement where the licensing of one product is conditioned on the acceptance of a license of another, separate product.[298]

i. AGREEMENT NOT TO CONTEST VALIDITY

A licensee is permitted to challenge the validity of the licensed patent.[299] While a license provision barring a licensee from contesting validity may be unenforceable,

American Soc'y of Composers, Authors & Publishers, 744 F.2d 917 (2d Cir. 1984), *cert. denied*, 469 U.S. 1211 (1985).

292. 171 F.3d 1265, 1277-79 (11th Cir. 1999).
293. *Id.* at 1277-79; *see also* Six W. Retail Acquisition, Inc. v. Sony Theatre Mgmt. Corp., 97-Civ. 5499, 2000 U.S. Dist. LEXIS 2604, at *53 (S.D.N.Y. Mar. 9, 2000) (claim for block booking adequately alleged where pleadings establish that theater may have been forced to accept unwanted films).
294. *See, e.g.*, Hazeltine Research, Inc. v. Zenith Radio Corp., 388 F.2d 25, 33-35 (7th Cir. 1967), *aff'd in part and rev'd in part*, 395 U.S. 100 (1969); American Securit Co. v. Shatterproof Glass Corp., 268 F.2d 769, 775-77 (3d Cir.), *cert. denied*, 361 U.S. 902 (1959); *see also* Beckman Instruments, Inc. v. Technical Dev. Corp., 433 F.2d 55, 60 (7th Cir. 1970) (stating that if plaintiff could prove coercion, it would have established misuse), *cert. denied*, 401 U.S. 976 (1971). *But see Loew's, Inc.*, 371 U.S. at 55 (seller can try to sell a package and refuse to deal individually for a limited period while he exhausts possibility of a package sale).
295. *See, e.g.*, Hensley Equip. Co. v. Esco Corp., 383 F.2d 252, 265 n.24 (5th Cir.), *modified per curiam*, 386 F.2d 442 (1967); McCullough Tool Co. v. Well Surveys, Inc., 343 F.2d 381, 408-10 (10th Cir. 1965), *cert. denied*, 383 U.S. 933 (1966); Apex Elec. Mfg. Co. v. Altorfer Bros., 238 F.2d 867, 871-72 (7th Cir. 1956); Sunrise Med. HHG, Inc. v. AirSep Corp., 95 F. Supp. 2d 348, 458-59 (W.D. Pa. 2000) (no evidence that license was "coercively condition[ed]"); Eversharp, Inc. v. Fisher Pen Co., 204 F. Supp. 649, 675 (N.D. Ill. 1961); Carter Prods. v. Colgate-Palmolive Co., 164 F. Supp. 503, 525-26 (D. Md. 1958), *aff'd*, 269 F.2d 299 (4th Cir. 1959).
296. 35 U.S.C. § 271(d)(5) (1994) is applicable, inter alia, to cases where the patentee has "conditioned the license of any rights to the patent . . . on the acquisition of a license to rights in another patent."
297. *Id.*
298. *See* INTELLECTUAL PROPERTY GUIDELINES, *supra* note 16, § 5.3.
299. *See, e.g.*, Lear, Inc. v. Adkins, 395 U.S. 653, 671 (1969) (overruling the "licensee estoppel" doctrine which precluded licensees from challenging the validity of the licensed patent). The Seventh Circuit has held that no-contest clauses in copyright licensing agreements may be valid where the issue of "copyrightability" is present and that the *Lear* decision did not apply to copyrights. *See* Saturday Evening Post Co. v. Rumbleseat Press, Inc., 816 F.2d 1191 (7th Cir.

courts have been reluctant to hold that such provisions violate the Sherman Act or constitute misuse.[300]

Consent judgments entered in settlement of litigation that acknowledge validity and infringement have been given res judicata effect.[301] Courts have disagreed on whether licensees under agreements entered in settlement of litigation may challenge validity and also retain the license.[302]

4. *Nonuse and Refusal to License Patents or Copyrights*

United States patent law contains no requirement that the patentee use or license its invention and creates no sanction for a patentee's nonuse or mere refusal to license its invention.[303] Rather, the essence of a patentee's right is the ability to

---

1987). *But see* Twin Books Corp. v. Walt Disney Co., 877 F. Supp. 496 (N.D. Cal. 1995) (distinguishing *Rumbleseat,* applying *Lear* in a copyright licensing case), *rev'd on other grounds,* 83 F.3d 1162 (9th Cir. 1996).

300. *See, e.g.,* Bendix Corp. v. Balax, Inc., 471 F.2d 149, 158 (7th Cir. 1972) (possible misuse because of postexpiration no-contest agreement), *cert. denied,* 414 U.S. 819 (1973); Panther Pumps & Equip. Co. v. Hydrocraft, Inc., 468 F.2d 225, 232 (7th Cir. 1972), *cert. denied,* 411 U.S. 965 (1973); Congoleum Indus. v. Armstrong Cork Co., 366 F. Supp. 220, 233 (E.D. Pa. 1973), *aff'd,* 510 F.2d 334 (3d Cir.), *cert. denied,* 421 U.S. 988 (1975); *see also* Windsurfing Int'l, Inc. v. AMF, Inc., 782 F.2d 995 (Fed. Cir.) (agreement not to contest the validity of a trademark license found not a misuse), *cert. denied,* 477 U.S. 905 (1986).

301. *See, e.g.,* Foster v. Hallco Mfg. Co., 947 F.2d 469 (Fed. Cir. 1991); American Equip. Corp. v. Wikomi Mfg. Co., 630 F.2d 544, 548 (7th Cir. 1980); Wallace Clark & Co. v. Acheson Indus., 532 F.2d 846, 849 (2d Cir.), *cert. denied,* 524 U.S. 976 (1976); Schlegel Mfg. Co. v. USM Corp., 525 F.2d 775 (6th Cir. 1975), *cert. denied,* 425 U.S. 912 (1976); Glasstech, Inc. v. AB Kyro Oyo, 11 U.S.P.Q.2d (BNA) 1703 (N.D. Ohio 1989); USM Corp. v. Standard Pressed Steel Co., 453 F. Supp. 743, 747-48 (N.D. Ill. 1978), *aff'd in part and vacated in part,* 694 F.2d 505 (7th Cir. 1982), *cert. denied,* 462 U.S. 1107 (1983). *But see* Kaspar Wire Works, Inc. v. Leco Eng'g & Mach., 575 F.2d 530 (5th Cir. 1978) (consent judgment dismissing action by alleged infringer to declare patent invalid denied preclusive effect on question of validity); Crane Co. v. Aeroquip Corp., 504 F.2d 1086, 1092 (7th Cir. 1974) ("Defendant was within its rights to test validity after entering into the consent judgment of validity."); Kray v. Nat'l Distillers & Chem. Corp., 502 F.2d 1366, 1369 (7th Cir. 1974) (licensee "is not stopped from challenging the validity of the patent, even though a prior consent decree incorporated an understanding not to challenge the validity of the patent").

302. *Compare* Hemstreet v. Spiegel, Inc., 851 F.2d 348, 350 (Fed. Cir. 1988) (settlement agreement providing for payment of royalties even if patent later declared unenforceable bars litigation of validity), *and* Ransburg Elector-Coating Corp. v. Spiller & Spiller, Inc., 489 F.2d 974, 978 (7th Cir. 1973) (*Lear* inapplicable in case involving settlement for past infringement), *with* Massillon-Cleveland-Akron Sign Co. v. Golden State Advert. Co., 444 F.2d 425, 427 (9th Cir.) (deeming void a clause in settlement agreement acknowledging validity and infringement and covenanting to refrain from directly or indirectly contesting the validity of the patent), *cert. denied,* 404 U.S. 873 (1971), *and* Dilemmatic Mfg. Corp. v. Packaging Indus., 381 F. Supp. 1057, 1061 (S.D.N.Y. 1974) (same), *appeal dismissed,* 516 F.2d 975 (2d Cir.), *cert. denied,* 423 U.S. 913 (1975); *see also* C.R. Bard, Inc. v. Schwartz, 716 F.2d 874, 879-82 (Fed. Cir. 1983) (discussing conflicting authority concerning licensee standing to seek a declaratory judgment of invalidity).

303. Many countries impose some obligation on a patentee to use its invention in the country or to license its use in the country. This is often referred to as a "working" requirement. In these countries, failure to "work" the patent within a specified number of years normally makes it available to others in some fashion, either through revocation of the patent, compulsory license, or some other relief. *See, e.g.,* Centrafarm B.V. v. Sterling Drug, Inc., 1974 Eur. Comm. Ct. J. Rep. 1147, [1974 Transfer Binder] Common Mkt. Rep. (CCH) ¶ 8246.

exclude others from making, using, or selling the claimed invention.[304] Congress has specifically provided that it is not patent misuse for a patentee to refuse to use or license its invention.[305] Unilateral refusals to license are generally lawful, with some exceptions.[306] Concerted refusals to license, however, have been condemned on a number of occasions, sometimes as per se lawful.

a.   UNILATERAL REFUSALS TO USE OR LICENSE

It has long been held that a simple unilateral refusal to use or license a patent or copyright cannot form the basis for an antitrust claim.[307] In *Continental Paper Bag Co. v. Eastern Paper Bag Co.*,[308] the Supreme Court held that it was not unreasonable for a patent owner to use old machines rather than build new patented machines and that there was no requirement to license others to build the new ones:

> As to the suggestion that competitors were excluded from the use of the new patent, we answer that such exclusion may be said to have been of the very essence of the right conferred by the patent, as it is the privilege of any owner of property to use or not use it, without question of motive.[309]

In *Hartford-Empire Co. v. United States*,[310] the Supreme Court set aside a decree provision that barred the defendant from applying for patents with an intent not to use the invention or to withhold it from others:

> A patent owner is not in the position of a quasi-trustee for the public or under any obligation to see that the public acquires the free right to use the invention. He has no obligation either to use it or to grant its use to others. If he discloses the invention in his application so that it will come into the public domain at the end of the 17-year

---

304. *See* 35 U.S.C. § 154 (1994 & Supp. 1999).

305. *See id.* § 271(d)(4).

306. *See infra* notes 313-21 and accompanying text.

307. *See, e.g.*, Standard Oil Co. v. United States, 283 U.S. 163, 179 (1931); United States v. United Shoe Mach. Corp., 247 U.S. 32, 57-58 (1918); SCM Corp. v. Xerox Corp., 645 F.2d 1195, 1209 (2d Cir. 1981), *cert. denied*, 455 U.S. 1016 (1982); Extractol Process, Ltd. v. Hiram Walker & Sons, 153 F.2d 264, 268 (7th Cir. 1946); Corsearch, Inc. v. Thomson & Thomson, 792 F. Supp. 305, 322 (S.D.N.Y. 1992); *see also* INTELLECTUAL PROPERTY GUIDELINES, *supra* note 16, § 2.2 (even where intellectual property owner has market power, that market power does not "impose on the intellectual property owner an obligation to license the use of that property to others"). *But cf.* Allied Research Prods. v. Heatbath Corp., 300 F. Supp. 656, 657 (N.D. Ill. 1969) (dictum) (citing "public policy" for the proposition—which has not been followed in other cases—that patentee was required to use its patent, or to license an applicant when it has already granted a license to the applicant's competitor, in order to be able to assert its rights under the patent laws). This dictum from *Allied Research* was rejected expressly in *Minnesota Mining & Mfg. Co. v. Research Med., Inc.*, 679 F. Supp. 1037, 1065 (D. Utah 1987), in which the court noted that *Allied Research* included no citations to precedent, had not been followed in any jurisdiction, and was directly contrary to binding precedent.

308. 210 U.S. 405 (1908).

309. *Id.* at 429. *Continental Paper Bag* was cited in *Dawson Chem. Co. v. Rohm & Haas Co.*, 448 U.S. 176 (1980), where the Supreme Court noted that compulsory licensing is "a rarity in our patent system." *Id.* at 215 (footnote omitted). *Dawson Chem.* refused to find a requirement that a patentee license suppliers of goods used to practice a patented process. *Id.* at 186.

310. 323 U.S. 386, *clarified*, 324 U.S. 570 (1945).

period of exclusive right he has fulfilled the only obligation imposed by the statute. This has been settled doctrine since at least 1896.[311]

Even where the patent owner has monopoly power in a relevant market, its refusal to license a patent to others generally will not provide the basis for holding the patentee has violated Section 2 of the Sherman Act.[312]

In *Data General Corp. v. Grumman Systems Support Corp.*,[313] however, the First Circuit refused to hold that the unilateral refusal to license a copyrighted work is per se lawful. Instead, the court created a rebuttable presumption that such a refusal to license is permissible.[314] In *Image Technical Services, Inc. v. Eastman Kodak Co.*,[315] the Ninth Circuit established a similar presumption, holding that a patentee's exercise of the statutory right to exclude is a presumptively valid business justification under the Sherman Act but that this presumption could be rebutted by evidence of pretext. The court found that the jury would more likely than not have found such pretext in the instant case, where testimony established that Kodak's patents "never crossed [the] mind" of the employee responsible for the policy at issue, and where evidence showed that Kodak's blanket refusal to license covered "thousands of parts, of which only 65 were patented."[316]

In *In re Independent Service Organizations Antitrust Litigation*,[317] the Federal Circuit declined to embrace the Ninth Circuit's holding in *Image Technical Services*.

311. *Id.* at 432-33 (footnote omitted). More recent decisions reaffirm the patentee's right to refuse to license. *See, e.g.*, United States v. Westinghouse Elec. Corp., 648 F.2d 642, 647 (9th Cir. 1981) (refusal to license does not violate the antitrust laws); Cataphote Corp. v. DeSoto Chem. Coatings, Inc., 450 F.2d 769, 774 (9th Cir. 1971) (calling this refusal to license an "untrammeled right" of the patentee), *cert. denied*, 408 U.S. 929 (1972); E.I. duPont de Nemours & Co., 96 F.T.C. 705 (1980). *But cf.* Foster v. American Mach. & Foundry Co., 492 F.2d 1317, 1324 (2d Cir.) (nonuse considered relevant in denying injunction for infringement), *cert. denied*, 419 U.S. 833 (1974).

312. *See, e.g.*, Miller Insituform, Inc. v. Insituform of N. Am., Inc., 830 F.2d 606, 609 (6th Cir. 1987), *cert. denied*, 484 U.S. 1064 (1988); SCM Corp. v. Xerox Corp., 645 F.2d 1195 (2d Cir. 1981), *cert. denied*, 455 U.S. 1016 (1982); Chisholm-Ryder Co. v. Mecca Bros., 1983-1 Trade Cas. (CCH) ¶ 65,406 (W.D.N.Y. 1982); GAF Corp. v. Eastman Kodak Co., 519 F. Supp. 1203, 1233 (S.D.N.Y. 1981); *see also* INTELLECTUAL PROPERTY GUIDELINES, *supra* note 16, § 2.2 (market power imposes no obligation on an intellectual property owner to license its technology to others).

313. 36 F.3d 1147 (1st Cir. 1994); *see also* Eastman Kodak Co. v. Image Tech. Servs., 504 U.S. 451, 479-80 n.29 (1992) ("[P]ower gained through some natural and legal advantage such as a patent . . . can give rise to liability if a seller exploits his dominant position in one market to expand his empire into the next.") (internal quotation omitted).

314. 36 F.3d at 1184-87. *But cf.* Montgomery County Ass'n of Realtors v. Realty Photo Master Corp., 878 F. Supp. 804 (D. Md. 1995) (association of realtors not obligated to grant photographic service access to copyrighted multiple listing database under essential facilities doctrine or group boycott theory), *aff'd*, 1996-2 Trade Cas. (CCH) ¶ 71,509 (4th Cir. 1996) (unpublished opinion); Tricom, Inc. v. Electronic Data Sys. Corp., 902 F. Supp. 741, 743 (E.D. Mich. 1995) ("[u]nder patent and copyright law, [defendant] may not be compelled to license its proprietary software to anyone"); Advanced Computer Servs. v. MAI Sys., 845 F. Supp. 356, 368-69 (E.D. Va. 1994) (within copyright owner's discretion to selectively license copyrighted software); Corsearch, Inc. v. Thomson & Thomson, 792 F. Supp. 305 (S.D.N.Y. 1992) (competitor denied a license failed to prove that copyrighted trademark database was essential facility to which the copyright owner must grant access); *see also* Morris Communs. v. PGA Tour, Inc., 117 F. Supp. 2d 1322, 1330 (M.D. Fla. 2000) (refusing to grant preliminary injunction where PGA's refusal to allow access to current golf scores may have been justified by interest in protecting legitimate property interests).

315. 125 F.3d 1195 (9th Cir. 1997).

316. *Id.* at 1219.

317. 203 F.3d 1322 (Fed. Cir. 2000), *cert. denied*, 531 U.S. 1143 (2001).

Applying its own law, the Federal Circuit refused to inquire into the subjective motivations of the patent holder in refusing to sell or license its patented works, even though such a refusal "may have an anticompetitive effect, so long as that anticompetitive effect is not illegally extended beyond the statutory patent grant."[318] In holding that Xerox was under no obligation to sell or license its patented parts to independent service organizations that wished to service and repair Xerox copiers, the court noted: "In the absence of any indication of illegal tying, fraud on the PTO, or sham litigation, the patent holder may enforce the statutory right to exclude others from making, using, or selling the claimed invention free from liability under the antitrust laws."[319] Its motives in doing so would be irrelevant. The Federal Circuit also relied upon the Supreme Court's opinion in *Eastman Kodak Co. v. Image Technical Services, Inc.*[320] for the proposition that "the power gained through some natural and legal advantage such as a patent . . . can give rise to liability if a seller exploits his dominant position in one market to expand his empire into the next"— though the court commented that this statement should be viewed in the context of the tying case then before the Court.

In *United States v. Microsoft Corp.*,[321] the D.C. Circuit affirmed a finding that Microsoft's licensing restrictions prevented, inter alia, original equipment manufacturers from promoting rival browsers, thus illegally protecting Microsoft's operating system monopoly from a nascent form of competition. The court characterized as "bordering on the frivolous" Microsoft's argument that the license restrictions were justified by Microsoft's copyright, explaining:

---

318. *Id.* at 1325, 1327-28; *see also* Intergraph Corp. v. Intel Corp., 195 F.3d 1346, 1362 (Fed. Cir. 1999) (acknowledging that "intellectual property does not confer . . . a privilege or immunity to violate the antitrust laws," but also stating that "the antitrust laws do not negate the patentee's right to exclude others from patent property") (internal quotation marks omitted); Intergraph Corp. v. Intel Corp., 88 F. Supp. 2d 1288, 1293 (N.D. Ala. 2000) (finding no antitrust liability for refusal to license and quoting Federal Circuit's standard approvingly); *In re* Independent Serv. Orgs. Antitrust Litig., 114 F. Supp. 2d 1070, 1086, 1088-89 (D. Kan.) (holding that "where a patent has been lawfully acquired, subsequent conduct permissible under the patent laws cannot give rise to liability under the antitrust laws," and that "[a] patentee may unilaterally exclude others . . . even if such conduct allows the patentee to obtain monopolies in multiple markets"), *aff'd*, 203 F.3d 1322 (Fed. Cir. 2000), *cert. denied*, 531 U.S. 1143 (2001); *cf.* Townshend v. Rockwell Int'l Corp., 2000-1 Trade Cas. (CCH) ¶ 72,890 (N.D. Cal. 2000) (where patent holder seeks unfair royalty rates, double-charging of customers and manufacturers, mandatory cross-licenses, and reservation of the right to condition licenses on the resolution of litigation before it will grant license to its patent, court reasons that "[b]ecause a patent holder has the legal right to refuse to license his or her patent on any terms, the existence of a predicate condition to a license agreement cannot state an antitrust violation").

319. 203 F.3d at 1327-28. The Federal Circuit's "sweeping language" in *In re Independent Serv. Orgs. Antitrust Litig.* was criticized by Robert Pitofsky, when chairman of the FTC, who decried the decision's "extremely narrow limits on a virtually unfettered right of a patent holder to refuse to deal in order to achieve an anticompetitive objective." *See* Pitofsky, *supra* note 182 (providing hypotheticals wherein Federal Circuit's categorical approach might be problematic). In contrast, the Solicitor General, in an amicus brief joined by the DOJ (but not by the FTC), suggested that the Federal Circuit's decision need not be read as holding that a § 2 claim may never be based on a unilateral refusal to sell or license intellectual property (aside from the three circumstances expressly recognized by the court). Brief for the United States as Amicus Curiae at 8, CSU, L.L.C. v. Xerox Corp., 531 U.S. 922 (2000) ("While it is conceivable that the court of appeals intended to go that far, its opinion does not compel that conclusion.").

320. 504 U.S. 451, 480 n.29 (1992) (internal quotation omitted).

321. 253 F.3d 34 (D.C. Cir.), *cert. denied*, 122 S. Ct. 350 (2001).

The company claims an absolute and unfettered right to use its intellectual property as it wishes: "If intellectual property rights have been lawfully acquired," it says, then "their subsequent exercise cannot give rise to antitrust liability." That is no more correct than the proposition that use of one's personal property, such as a baseball bat, cannot give rise to tort liability. As the Federal Circuit succinctly stated: "Intellectual property rights do not confer a privilege to violate the antitrust laws."[322]

b. CONCERTED REFUSALS TO LICENSE

The antitrust analysis of a concerted refusal to license—which implicates Section 1 of the Sherman Act—is quite different from the analysis of a unilateral refusal to license. Several courts have recognized that agreements among competitors to restrict patent licensing, or to subject a patent owner's licensing decisions to a competing firm's "veto" right, raise substantial antitrust concerns and are unlawful if they unreasonably restrain trade or tend to create or maintain a monopoly position.[323]

In *United States v. Krasnov*,[324] for example, two dominant sellers of furniture slip covers settled a patent infringement suit with an agreement that cross-licensed several patents and provided that no further licenses would be granted under their respective competing patents without the consent of the other party. The district court, which was affirmed per curiam by the Supreme Court, condemned this aspect of the arrangement and granted summary judgment to the government:

> [T]he Court notes here a situation where no one, the patentee, the assignee, or the licensee, can create any rights under the patent in any other person without the consent of the other two. The owner of the patent and the two dominant manufacturers in the trade have so bound themselves. Although these facts are not identical with those in [*United States v. Besser*], I think the evil which the court there struck down exists here, namely, (1) the veto power over licensing rights granted to a licensee and (2) the contractual arrangement which created the power to restrict competition by requiring joint consent before others could be licensed.[325]

---

322. *Id.* at 63 (citation omitted) (quoting *In re Independent Serv. Orgs.*, 203 F.3d at 1325).
323. *See, e.g.*, Mannington Mills, Inc. v. Congoleum Indus., 610 F.2d 1059, 1072-73 (3d Cir. 1979) (dictum); Moraine Prods. v. ICI Am., Inc., 538 F.2d 134, 138-45 (7th Cir.), *cert. denied*, 424 U.S. 968 (1976); Clapper v. Original Tractor Cab Co., 165 F. Supp. 565, 577 (S.D. Ind. 1958), *aff'd in part and rev'd in part on other grounds*, 270 F.2d 616 (7th Cir. 1959), *cert. denied*, 361 U.S. 967 (1960); Mason City Tent & Awning Co. v. Clapper, 144 F. Supp. 754, 767-68 (W.D. Mo. 1956); United States v. Krasnov, 143 F. Supp. 184, 199 (E.D. Pa. 1956), *aff'd per curiam*, 355 U.S. 5 (1957); United States v. Besser Mfg. Co., 96 F. Supp. 304, 311 (E.D. Mich. 1951), *aff'd*, 343 U.S. 444 (1952); United States v. National Lead Co., 63 F. Supp. 513, 524 (S.D.N.Y. 1945), *aff'd*, 332 U.S. 319 (1947); *In re* Summit Tech. Inc., No. 9286 (complaint), 1998 FTC LEXIS 29, at *3 (1998) (challenging patent pool in which participants relinquished right to license their patents unilaterally), 1999 FTC LEXIS 24 (1999) (final order).
324. 143 F. Supp. 184 (E.D. Pa. 1956), *aff'd per curiam*, 355 U.S. 5 (1957).
325. *Id.* at 201-02 (referring to United States v. Besser Mfg. Co., 343 U.S. 444 (1952)); *cf.* Boston Scientific Corp. v. Schneider (Europe) AG, 983 F. Supp. 245, 271-72 (D. Mass. 1997) (granting motion to dismiss complaint that alleged a concerted refusal to license where settlement agreement results in parties possessing overlapping patents—such that each party was effectively precluded from licensing its own patent unless the other party agreed to license its patent as well—since "the complaint might successfully allege a refusal to deal in concert, but not a concerted refusal to deal").

Following *Krasnov*, some courts have indicated that concerted refusals to license are per se illegal.[326] Other courts have decided that, in certain circumstances, concerted restrictions on licensing should be analyzed under the rule of reason.[327] It has also been held that an agreement between two owners of a patent to refuse to license their jointly owned patent without mutual consent may be permissible.[328]

5. Cross-Licensing and Patent Pools

When two or more owners of different patents agree to license one another or mutually license third parties under their respective patents, such an agreement may be termed a "patent pool," "cross-license," or a "patent interchange."[329] Patent pools may be challenged under Sections 1 or 2 of the Sherman Act. Under Section 1, patent pools generally are analyzed under the rule of reason, though, under some circumstances, restraints on price or output may be deemed illegal per se. Claims under Section 2 must state the elements of the appropriate monopolization offense. In either case, the legality of a pooling arrangement will turn on the characteristics of the pool or the specific terms of the agreement among the pool participants.

In *Standard Oil Co. v. United States*,[330] the Supreme Court held lawful a patent pool among competing oil companies. The agreements were accorded rule of reason treatment and were considered reasonable because they were essential to permit each party to practice its own inventions. The patents were so-called blocking patents, that is, one party could not practice under its patents without infringing the other parties' patents.[331] Similarly, in *Carpet Seaming Tape Licensing Corp. v. Best Seam, Inc.*,[332] the Ninth Circuit noted that a "well-recognized legitimate purpose for a pooling agreement is exchange of blocking patents."[333]

---

326. *See, e.g.*, *Clapper*, 165 F. Supp. at 576 ("An agreement by a patentee which gives a non-exclusive licensee a veto power in the selection of other licensees is invalid according to Sherman Act standards, §§ 1 and 2."). *Mason City*, 144 F. Supp. at 767 (same); *see also* PrimeTime 24 Joint Venture v. NBC, 219 F.3d 92, 102-03 (2d Cir. 2000) (reversing dismissal of antitrust claims and noting that "[a]lthough coordinated efforts to enforce copyrights against a common infringer may be permissible, copyright holders may not agree to limit their individual freedom of action in licensing future rights to such an infringer before, during, or after the lawsuit").

327. *See, e.g.*, *Moraine Prods.*, 538 F.2d at 145-48 (reversing directed verdict dismissing an antitrust claim and remanding for rule of reason analysis); Polysius Corp. v. Fuller Co., 709 F. Supp. 560, 577-79 (E.D. Pa.) (rejecting antitrust claim after a nonjury trial established that there was insufficient proof of anticompetitive effect), *aff'd without op.*, 889 F.2d 1100 (Fed. Cir. 1989).

328. *See* Malco Mfg. Co. v. National Connector Corp., 151 U.S.P.Q. (BNA) 255, 263 (D. Minn. 1966), *aff'd in part and rev'd in part*, 392 F.2d 766 (8th Cir.), *cert. denied*, 393 U.S. 923 (1968).

329. Patent interchanges are sometimes carried out by assigning the patents to a specially created entity. *See, e.g.*, Baker-Cammack Hosiery Mills, Inc. v. Davis Co., 181 F.2d 550, 568 (4th Cir.), *cert. denied*, 340 U.S. 824 (1950); United States v. Vehicular Parking, Ltd., 54 F. Supp. 828 (D. Del.), *modified*, 56 F. Supp. 297 (1944), *modified*, 61 F. Supp. 656 (1945).

330. 283 U.S. 163 (1931).

331. *Id.* at 170-77; Boston Scientific Corp. v. Schneider (Europe) AG, 983 F. Supp. 245, 271 (D. Mass. 1997) (dismissing on the pleadings a challenge to a nonexclusive cross-license and settlement involving blocking patents despite allegation that invalid or overly broad patent claims had an anticompetitive effect), *dismissed by consent*, 152 F.3d 947 (Fed. Cir. 1998); *see* Apex Elec. Mfg. Co. v. Aloofer Bros., 238 F.2d 867, 873 (7th Cir. 1956).

332. 616 F.2d 1133 (9th Cir. 1980).

333. *Id.* at 1142; *accord* International Mfg. Co. v. Landon, Inc., 336 F.2d 723, 729 (9th Cir. 1964) ("In a case involving blocking patents such an arrangement is the only reasonable method for making the invention available to the public.") (citations omitted), *cert. denied*, 379 U.S. 988 (1965);

Because they often involve horizontal agreements among competitors, the purpose of patent pools and cross-licenses may be important in a rule of reason analysis.[334] Thus, in *Duplan Corp. v. Deering Milliken, Inc.*,[335] the Fourth Circuit held that settlement of patent litigation by cross-licensing agreement was lawful if entered into to resolve legitimate conflicting patent claims.[336] On remand, however, the district court found that the settlement violated Sections 1 and 2 because the parties had entered into the agreements to fix and preserve their royalty structures and strengthen themselves against unlicensed outsiders.[337]

A second important factor in determining the legality of a patent pool is whether the patents confer market or monopoly power in a relevant market. In *United States v. Krasnov*,[338] for example, companies that together had monopoly power formed a patent pool and agreed to refrain from licensing others without mutual consent, to allocate customers, to maintain prices established by the licensor, and to determine jointly the institution and maintenance of infringement suits. The district court held that this pool violated Sections 1 and 2 of the Sherman Act.[339] In *United States v. National Lead Co.*,[340] the district court held illegal an agreement between the two largest companies in the titanium dioxide industry involving the exchange of nonexclusive licenses under all their patents, present and future, with the knowledge that such an arrangement would strengthen both parties to the exclusion of outsiders.[341]

A third important factor in determining legality is whether the pool is exclusive, i.e., whether the participants give up the right to license their own patents separately. In *Zenith Radio Corp. v. Hazeltine Research, Inc.*,[342] the Supreme Court held that exclusive patent pools may violate Section 1 of the Sherman Act even in the absence of monopoly power.[343] *Zenith* involved a pool of Canadian patents formed to prevent

---

INTELLECTUAL PROPERTY GUIDELINES, *supra* note 16, § 5.5 (describing "clearing blocking positions" as a benefit of cross-licenses).

334. Many courts consider the purpose or intent behind a restraint relevant to a rule of reason analysis only to the extent it helps predict the effects of the restraint. *See* part B.3.b of Chapter I.

335. 540 F.2d 1215 (4th Cir. 1976).

336. Procter & Gamble Co. v. Paragon Trade Brands, Inc., 61 F. Supp. 2d 102, 107-08 (D. Del. 1996) (rejecting claim that settlement of patent disputes between the largest diaper manufacturers amounted to an illegal patent pool designed to raise costs of other manufacturers). *But see* CCPI Inc. v. American Premier, Inc., 967 F. Supp. 813, 820 (D. Del 1997) (private allocation of conflicting patent claims may support viable antitrust claim). In *Carpet Seaming Tape Licensing Corp.*, 694 F.2d 570, the Ninth Circuit held that the intent among pooling owners merely to enforce their patents was not sufficiently anticompetitive to support a claim of misuse.

337. Duplan Corp. v. Deering Milliken, Inc., 444 F. Supp. 648, 683 (D.S.C. 1977), *aff'd in part and rev'd in part*, 594 F.2d 979 (4th Cir. 1979), *cert. denied*, 444 U.S. 1015 (1980).

338. 143 F. Supp. 184 (E.D. Pa. 1956), *aff'd per curiam*, 355 U.S. 5 (1957).

339. *Id.* at 199-200, 202; *see also* Carter v. Variflex, Inc., 101 F. Supp. 2d 1261, 1267-68 (C.D. Cal. 2000) (summary judgment granted where parties to challenged cross-license not shown to possess market power); United States v. Besser Mfg. Co., 96 F. Supp. 304, 311 (E.D. Mich. 1951) (patentees joining hands with two large competitors to make it impossible for others to obtain rights under the patents was illegal), *aff'd*, 343 U.S. 444 (1952).

340. 63 F. Supp. 513 (S.D.N.Y. 1945), *aff'd*, 332 U.S. 319 (1947).

341. *Id.* at 531-32; *see also* United States v. Singer Mfg. Co., 374 U.S. 174 (1963); United States v. United States Gypsum Co., 333 U.S. 364 (1948); Hartford-Empire Co. v. United States, 323 U.S. 386, *clarified*, 324 U.S. 570 (1945).

342. 395 U.S. 100 (1969).

343. *Id.* at 113; *see also* Boston Scientific Corp. v. Schneider (Europe) AG, 983 F. Supp. 245, 271-77 (D. Mass. 1997) (cross-licensing agreement providing that neither party would sublicense the

the shipment of radio and television apparatus into Canada. "Once Zenith demonstrated that its exports from the United States had been restrained by pool activities, the treble-damage liability of the domestic company [Hazeltine] participating in the conspiracy was beyond question."[344] Likewise, pooling agreements that restrict their participants from developing technologies outside of the pool are more likely to raise antitrust concern than agreements that allow pool participants to independently develop alternative technologies.[345]

Fourth, patent pools that combine so-called competing patents are more likely to raise antitrust concern than pools that combine blocking or complementary patents.[346] Complementary patents cover different aspects of the same technology, process, or product. Competing patents give their owners alternative noninfringing means of accomplishing the same ends. Prospective participants to pooling agreements may reduce the risk of antitrust challenge by employing a disinterested expert to review the patents at issue and selecting only those complementary patents reasonably necessary to effectuate the underlying purpose of the patent pool.[347] Such procedural safeguards may help pool participants avoid later second-guessing of their judgment as to whether particular patents were complementary or competing. However, some older cases suggest that the complementary relationship of pooled patents may not always be dispositive. For example, price-fixing clauses in cross-licenses have been held illegal even though the patents covered complementary, noncompeting products or processes.[348] Likewise, agreements mutually to restrict such licenses to particular territories have been ruled illegal.[349]

In the *Intellectual Property Guidelines*, the agencies note that cross-licensing and pooling arrangements may have procompetitive effects:

---

other's patents held legal, despite "overlapping" nature of the patents), *dismissed by consent*, 152 F.3d 947 (Fed. Cir. 1998); Honeywell, Inc. v. Sperry Rand Corp., 1974-1 Trade Cas. (CCH) ¶ 74,874 (D. Minn. 1973) (cross-license found to be "de facto exclusive"); Mason City Tent & Awning Co. v. Clapper, 144 F. Supp. 754 (W.D. Mo. 1956). *But see* Kaiser Indus. v. Jones & Laughlin Steel Corp., 181 U.S.P.Q. (BNA) 193 (W.D. Pa. 1974) (where noninfringing processes could produce the same product as patented process, the industry was not dominated by the pooled patents and exclusive pooling agreement was lawful even if royalties charged were onerous), *rev'd on other grounds*, 515 F.2d 964 (3d Cir.), *cert. denied*, 423 U.S. 876 (1975).

344. 395 U.S. at 114 n.8.

345. INTELLECTUAL PROPERTY GUIDELINES, *supra* note 16, § 5.5 (discussing arrangements that may reduce pool participants' incentives to engage in R&D).

346. *See, e.g.*, Dep't of Justice, Business Review Letter to Hitachi, Ltd., 1999 DOJBRL LEXIS 7, at *13-15 (June 10, 1999) (declining to challenge pool containing complementary patents); Dep't of Justice, Business Review Letter to Koninklijke Philips Elec., N.V., 1998 DOJBRL LEXIS 15, at *21-30 (Dec. 16, 1998) (same); U.S. Dep't of Justice, Business Review Letter to Trustees of Columbia Univ., 1997 DOJBLR LEXIS 14, at *20-23 (June 26, 1997) (same); *In re* Summit Tech., Inc., No. 9286, 63 Fed. Reg. 46,452 (FTC Aug. 21, 1998) (aid to public comment) (describing consent agreement resolving agency's allegations that pool illegally combined competing patents), 1999 FTC LEXIS 24 (1999) (final order).

347. U.S. Dep't of Justice, Business Review Letter to Trustees of Columbia Univ., 1997 DOJBRL LEXIS 14, at *23 (June 26, 1997).

348. *See* United States v. Line Material Co., 333 U.S. 287, 305-15 (1948); United States v. New Wrinkle, Inc., 342 U.S. 371, 380 (1952) (applying *Line Material* where one pool participant was not a manufacturer of the product covered by the patents); *see also* part B.3.c of this chapter.

349. *See, e.g.*, United States v. Holophane Co., 119 F. Supp. 114, 117-19 (S.D. Ohio 1954), *aff'd per curiam*, 352 U.S. 903 (1956); United States v. Imperial Chem. Indus., 100 F. Supp. 504, 519-31 (S.D.N.Y. 1951).

These arrangements may provide procompetitive benefits by integrating complementary technologies, reducing transaction costs, clearing blocking positions, and avoiding costly infringement litigation. By promoting the dissemination of technology, cross-licensing and pooling arrangements are often procompetitive.[350]

However, the *Intellectual Property Guidelines* also warn that such arrangements may be challenged if they are mechanisms to accomplish price fixing or market allocation, if they diminish rivalry or discourage participants from engaging in R&D, or if they significantly disadvantage competitors not admitted into the pool.[351]

In *United States v. Automobile Manufacturers Ass'n*,[352] the government alleged a violation of the Sherman Act by reason of royalty-free cross-licensing of patents pertaining to emission control devices by the principal domestic automobile manufacturers where the purpose of the cross-license was to delay technical advancement.[353] The consent decree prohibited certain exchanges of technical information and royalty-free patent licenses among defendants. The *Intellectual Property Guidelines* cite *Automobile Manufacturers* favorably for the proposition that "possible anticompetitive effect of pooling arrangements may occur if the arrangement deters or discourages participants from engaging in research and development, thus retarding innovation."[354]

In August 1998, the Federal Trade Commission settled through a consent agreement its allegations that a pooling agreement between holders of patents covering photorefractive keratectomy (PRK), a surgical technique involving the use of lasers to reshape the cornea and correct vision disorders, violated Section 5 of the FTC Act. The agency alleged that the patent pool was between competitors and characterized it as a horizontal restraint because it combined competing patents, and, but for the pool, its participants would have challenged each other's patents, avoided or invented around each other's patents, or combined both tactics to develop rival, noninfringing technologies. The pool was allegedly structured to give the two firms "veto" power over any decision to license the pooled patents to any other licensees, and to set a fee for each PRK procedure performed by their sublicensees.[355] According to the Federal Trade Commission, the pool reduced or eliminated competition between its two participants with respect to selling PRK lasers and licensing PRK technology, deterred entry and, as a result of the set "per procedure" fee, raised the cost of using PRK technology.[356]

---

350. INTELLECTUAL PROPERTY GUIDELINES, *supra* note 16, § 5.5.

351. *Id.*

352. 307 F. Supp. 617 (C.D. Cal. 1969), *aff'd in part and appeal dismissed in part sub nom.* City of New York v. United States, 397 U.S. 248 (1970), *modified sub nom.* United States v. Motor Vehicle Mfrs. Ass'n, 1982-83 Trade Cas. (CCH) ¶ 65,008 (C.D. Cal. 1982).

353. A private action, based on the same theory, was dismissed for failure to show an unreasonable restraint of trade. *In re* Multidistrict Vehicle Air Pollution, 367 F. Supp. 1298, 1303 (C.D. Cal. 1973), *aff'd*, 538 F.2d 231 (9th Cir. 1976).

354. INTELLECTUAL PROPERTY GUIDELINES, *supra* note 16, § 5.5.

355. *In re* Summit Tech., Inc., No. 9286, 63 Fed. Reg. 46,452, 46,453 (FTC Aug. 21, 1998) (aid to public comment). In response to the argument that the pool "reduced the uncertainty and expense associated with the patent litigation that would have inevitably ensued without [it]," the FTC said that the pool participants "could have achieved these efficiencies by any number of significantly less restrictive means, including simple licenses or cross-licenses that did not dictate prices to users or restrict entry." *Id.* at 46,453-54.

356. *In re* Summit Tech. Inc, No. 9286 (complaint at ¶¶ 25-28), 1998 FTC LEXIS 29 (1998).

1084   ANTITRUST LAW DEVELOPMENTS (FIFTH)

In contrast to the PRK pool, a patent pool for certain video compression technology, which was reviewed by the Department of Justice, contained only patents useful for that technology in conjunction with the other patents in the pool, was designed to facilitate licensing to a broad spectrum of users on nondiscriminatory terms, and did not restrict the pool participants' unilateral power to license their own intellectual property. Based on the parties' description of these and other safeguards, the Department of Justice indicated its intention not to challenge the formation this pool.[357]

6. Group Boycott by Infringers or Licensees

The Third Circuit has distinguished between a mere "agreement to challenge the validity" of a patent and the formation of a group for the purpose of "refusing to negotiate" with the patent holder for licenses, holding the latter to be illegal.[358] In *Gould v. Control Laser Corp.*,[359] the district court held that competitors can agree to share the costs of litigating to have a patent declared invalid "even if the goal of the litigation is clearly anti-competitive."[360] However, if the agreement goes further than sharing costs and restricts the rights of the parties to settle individually, antitrust liability could exist.[361] The Federal Circuit has held that challenges to boycott-type conduct by possible infringers under state unfair competition laws are not preempted by federal patent law.[362]

7. Settlement of Infringement Actions and Interference Proceedings

In general, courts favor settlement of infringement and interference proceedings involving "legitimately conflicting [patent] claims."[363] When patent and other intellectual property rights are involved, settlements often include exclusive or restricted licenses, cross-licenses, patent pools and other arrangements discussed in other sections of this chapter.[364] In most circumstances, these settlement provisions

---

357. U.S. Dep't of Justice, Business Review Letter to Trustees of Columbia Univ., 1997 DOJBRL LEXIS 14, at *6-18, *34 (June 26, 1997).

358. Jones Knitting Corp. v. Morgan, 361 F.2d 451, 459 (3d Cir. 1966). *See also* Sony Elec., Inc. v. Soundview Techs., 157 F. Supp. 2d 180, 190 (D. Conn. 2001) (denying motion to dismiss claim that potential licensees engaged in price fixing and a concerted refusal to deal by establishing a maximum price for a license to a collection of patents related to television "v-chip" technology mandated by federal law).

359. 462 F. Supp. 685 (M.D. Fla. 1978), *aff'd in part and appeal dismissed in part*, 650 F.2d 617 (5th Cir. 1981).

360. 462 F. Supp. at 693.

361. *See, e.g.*, *Jones Knitting*, 361 F.2d at 459-60; Lemelson v. Bendix Corp., 621 F. Supp. 1122 (D. Del. 1985), *aff'd*, 800 F.2d 1135 (3d Cir. 1986).

362. Rodime PLC v. Seagate Tech., Inc., 174 F.3d 1294, 1299 (Fed. Cir. 1999), *cert. denied*, 528 U.S. 1115 (2000).

363. *See, e.g.*, Standard Oil Co. v. United States, 283 U.S. 163, 170-71 (1931); Duplan Corp. v. Deering Milliken, Inc., 540 F.2d 1215, 1220 (4th Cir. 1976). *But cf.* Duplan Corp. v. Deering Milliken, Inc., 444 F. Supp. 648, 687 (D.S.C. 1977) (finding violation where settlement included terms beyond the scope of the underlying patent dispute), *aff'd in part and rev'd in part*, 594 F.2d 979 (4th Cir. 1979), *cert. denied*, 444 U.S. 1015 (1980).

364. *See* part B.5 of this chapter.

are analyzed under ordinary antitrust principles applicable to the particular restraint at issue.[365] The Patent Act provides that all settlements of interference proceedings must be notified to the Patent and Trademark Office, allowing it to make an independent assessment of whether the agreement reasonably resolves legitimately conflicting patent rights.[366]

Evidence that a settlement agreement was entered into to allow the parties to share in the exclusionary effect of a patent they believed to be unenforceable may support a finding that the settlement agreement was an unlawful conspiracy in restraint of trade.[367] In *United States v. Singer Manufacturing Co.*,[368] the Supreme Court found that the dominant purpose of a settlement was not to settle priority but to exclude a mutual competitor of the parties.[369] At least two courts have rejected the argument that settlement of a patent litigation is conduct protected by the *Noerr-Pennington* doctrine from serving as a basis for antitrust liability.[370]

In the pharmaceutical industry, settlements of patent infringement litigation between pioneer manufacturers of patented drugs and manufacturers of unpatented bioequivalent drugs (called generics) has prompted antitrust challenge by the government and private plaintiffs. The challenged settlements were reached in the context of the unique mechanism of the Drug Price Competition and Patent Term Restoration Act of 1984 (commonly called the Hatch-Waxman Act amendments),[371] which established a method for obtaining expedited Food and Drug Administration

---

365. *See* INTELLECTUAL PROPERTY GUIDELINES, *supra* note 16, § 5.5 (the agencies will consider the competitive effect of settlements among competitors that involve cross-licensing).

366. 35 U.S.C. § 135(c) (Supp. 1999). Failure to file a settlement agreement resolving a patent interference may render the agreement and related patents unenforceable. *Id.; see also* CTS Corp. v. Piher Int'l Corp., 727 F.2d 1550, 1555 (Fed. Cir. 1984) (§ 135(c) is "a means to prevent anti-competitive settlements between parties involved in patent interferences"). In 1997, Acting Assistant Attorney General Joel I. Klein suggested that a similar notification system be established to inform the antitrust agencies of significant patent infringement litigations and settlements of certain infringement claims most likely to raise competition concerns. Joel I. Klein, Acting Ass't Att'y Gen., Antitrust Div., Cross-Licensing and Antitrust Law, Remarks Before the American Intellectual Property Ass'n (May 2, 1997), *available at* www.usdoj.gov/atr/public/speeches/1123.htm.

367. *See Duplan Corp.*, 444 F. Supp. at 686-87.

368. 374 U.S. 174, 199 (1963) (considering evidence that the settlement was intended to conceal prior art that might result in the invalidation of one or more of the parties' patents).

369. *See also* Hartford-Empire Co. v. United States, 323 U.S. 386, *clarified*, 324 U.S. 570 (1945) (interference settlement held unlawful as part of a scheme to monopolize). *But cf.* American Cyanamid Co. v. FTC, 363 F.2d 757 (6th Cir. 1966) (insufficient evidence of collusive settlement), *on remand*, 72 F.T.C. 618 (1967), *later appeal sub nom.* Charles Pfizer & Co. v. FTC, 401 F.2d 574 (6th Cir. 1968), *cert. denied*, 394 U.S. 920 (1969); Hutzler Bros. v. Sales Affiliates, 164 F.2d 260 (4th Cir. 1947).

370. The *Noerr* doctrine is discussed in part C of Chapter XIII. *Compare* Andrx Pharm., Inc. v. Biovail Corp., 256 F.3d 799, 817-19 (D.C. Cir. 2001) (holding that an interim settlement between private parties may be subject to antitrust challenge), *and In re* Cardizem CD Antitrust Litig., 105 F. Supp. 2d 618, 633 (E.D. Mich. 2000) (same), *with* Columbia Pictures Indus., Inc. v. Professional Real Estate Investors, 944 F.2d 1525, 1528 (9th Cir. 1991) ("A decision to accept or reject an offer of settlement is conduct incidental to the prosecution of the suit and not a separate and distinct activity which might form the basis for antitrust liability."), *aff'd*, 508 U.S. 49 (1993), *and* Hise v. Philip Morris, Inc., 2000-1 Trade Cas. (CCH) ¶ 72,797 (10th Cir.) (unpublished opinion) (tobacco company defendants' settlement with over 40 state Attorneys General protected by *Noerr* doctrine), *cert. denied*, 531 U.S. 959 (2000).

371. 21 U.S.C. § 335 (1994). *See generally* Mova Pharm. Corp. v. Shalala, 140 F.3d 1060 (D.C. Cir. 1998) (discussing procedure established by Hatch-Waxman Act).

approval for generic drugs that do not infringe valid patents. If the holder of the patent for the relevant pioneer drug files a timely infringement action against the potential generic entrant, Food and Drug Administration approval is stayed for thirty months, effectively granting the patent holder an automatic preliminary injunction against the sale of the competing generic product. The Hatch-Waxman Act amendments also grant a successful challenger the right to market its generic versions without competition from other generic versions for a limited period. In several cases, infringement actions commenced under this mechanism have settled and the resulting agreements imposed varying restrictions on the generic manufacturer.

The Federal Trade Commission brought enforcement actions against three such settlement agreements. In two cases, the generic challengers had agreed in exchange for substantial payments from the pioneer firms not to market the allegedly infringing products pending the outcome of patent litigation and also to refrain from relinquishing their rights to market their products without competition from other generic products, with the alleged effect of blocking entry by all other generic drug manufacturers.[372] In both cases, the defendants entered consent decrees requiring agreements involving payments to the generic company to be approved by the court with notice to the Federal Trade Commission, and barring agreements between brand name drug companies and potential generic competitors that restrict the generic from relinquishing its right to a period of exclusivity or from entering the market with a noninfringing product.[373] The third enforcement action challenged settlements between a branded manufacturer and two different generic manufacturers that had applied for Food and Drug Administration approval to market competing products.[374] In addition to charging the branded manufacturer with monopolization, the Federal Trade Commission alleged that both of these settlements were unreasonably broad because, inter alia, they prevented the challengers either from marketing any generic version of the product, whether or not it infringed, or from assisting others from inventing noninfringing alternatives. The Federal Trade Commission also challenged payments made by the branded company to the generic manufacturer, alleging that although the payments were ostensibly made for the license of other products from the generic manufacturer to the branded company, the payments were in fact unrelated to the products covered by the license, which were "of little value to" the branded manufacturer.

Two courts have concluded that, in appropriate circumstances, a generic competitor alleging it was excluded from the market may have standing to attack settlement agreements between a branded manufacturer and generic manufacturer.[375] Where they have reached the merits, two courts have found certain aspects of

---

372. *In re* Abbott Labs., Nos. C-3945, C-3946 (complaint), 2000 FTC LEXIS 65 (2000); *In re* Hoechst Marion Roussel, Inc., No. C-9293 (complaint), 2000 FTC LEXIS 16 (2000).

373. *E.g., In re Abbott Labs.*, 2000 FTC LEXIS 65, at *41-44.

374. *In re* Schering-Plough Corp., No. C-9297 (complaint), 2001 FTC LEXIS 39 (2001).

375. *Andrx Pharm. Inc.*, 256 F.3d at 806-16 (affirming trial court's determination that, where there was no allegation of plaintiff's preparedness to enter the market, injury was not adequately pled, but concluding that plaintiff could allege an antitrust injury sufficient to give it standing to attack a settlement between the branded patent holder and a rival generic); Biovail Corp. Int'l v. Hoechst AG, 49 F. Supp. 2d 750, 766-69, 772-73 (D.N.J. 1999) (excluded generic drug manufacturer had standing to challenge an allegedly collusive settlement agreement; complaint challenging various conduct, including the settlement, stated violations of the Sherman Act).

particular settlements illegal per se, while a third court found as a matter of law that another settlement did not constitute patent misuse.[376]

8. *Foreign Patent and Know-How Licensing*

a. INTRODUCTION

Assuming jurisdictional requirements are met,[377] foreign patent and know-how licenses are subject to scrutiny under the U.S. antitrust laws. For example, in *United States v. Pilkington plc*,[378] the Department of Justice filed a complaint against Pilkington, a British firm, challenging various licensing agreements covering the technology used to manufacture flat glass. Pilkington allegedly used the license agreements at issue—which related to expired patents and trade secret claims—to allocate territories, prevent the use of competing technologies, restrict licensees' ability to sublicense, impose grantback obligations on licensees, and restrict exports to and from the United States. The Department of Justice and Pilkington entered into a consent decree that eliminated all territorial and use limitations on U.S. licensees and allowed licensees to use the technology, or sublicense any third party to do so, anywhere in the world, free of charge. The decree also allowed any U.S. firm that was not a licensee to use the technology free of liability to Pilkington, except in certain limited circumstances. Finally, the decree enjoined conduct having the effect of restricting exports to the United States or limiting the use of the technology in North America.[379]

Competitive restrictions in international license agreements also are affected by a number of statutes enacted in recent years that limit the scope or operation of the antitrust laws. These statutes include (1) the National Cooperative Research and Production Act,[380] which ensures rule of reason treatment for certain research and production joint ventures; (2) the Export Trading Company Act of 1982,[381] under which recipients of export trade certificates from the Department of Commerce can obtain limited immunity under the antitrust laws for international licensing activities specified in the certificate; (3) the Foreign Trade Antitrust Improvements Act,[382] which contains jurisdictional limitations on the application of the Sherman Act to

---

376. *Compare In re* Cardizem CD Antitrust Litig., 105 F. Supp. 2d 682, 707 (E.D. Mich. 2000) (granting partial summary judgment to plaintiffs consumers on issue of antitrust liability because certain aspects of the settlement between branded and generic drug manufacturers amounted to a per se illegal horizontal market allocation), *and In Re* Terazosin Hydrochloride Antitrust Litig., No. 99-MDL-1317, 2000 U.S. Dist. LEXIS 20477 (S.D. Fla. Dec. 13, 2000), *with* Zeneca Ltd. v. Pharmachemie B.V., 37 F. Supp. 2d 85, 93 (D. Mass. 1999) (settlement during pendency of appeal, which vacated trial court finding that patent was unenforceable, did not extend the physical or temporal scope of the patent and was not patent misuse).

377. For a discussion of the application of the antitrust laws to trade or commerce with foreign nations, see Chapter XII.

378. 1994-2 Trade Cas. (CCH) ¶ 70,842 (D. Ariz. 1994) (consent decree).

379. *Id.*

380. 15 U.S.C. §§ 4301-4305 (2000), discussed in part B.2 of Chapter IV.

381. 15 U.S.C. §§ 4001-4053 (2000).

382. 15 U.S.C. § 6a (2000) (discussed in part B.1.a of Chapter XII); *see also* Eurim-Pharm GmbH v. Pfizer Inc., 593 F. Supp. 1102 (S.D.N.Y. 1984) (discussing this statute in connection with dismissal of claim involving an exclusive patent license).

nonimport foreign commerce; and (4) the Federal Arbitration Act,[383] together with the Convention on the Recognition and Enforcement of Foreign Arbitral Awards,[384] which, as construed by *Mitsubishi Motors Corp. v. Soler Chrysler-Plymouth, Inc.,*[385] permit arbitration of antitrust aspects of international licensing disputes.

International patent and know-how license agreements also may be affected by antitrust statutes and regulations in other jurisdictions. The most comprehensive of these foreign regulatory systems is that implemented by the European Union under Article 81 of the Treaty Establishing the European Community.[386]

b.   TERRITORIAL RESTRICTIONS

A patentee is generally permitted to license the manufacture and sale of a product under its patents in one country but not another and to provide by agreement that a foreign licensee will not infringe the licensor's U.S. patents. In *United States v. Westinghouse Electric Corp.,*[387] the Ninth Circuit approved reciprocal license agreements between Westinghouse and a Japanese electrical equipment manufacturer, Mitsubishi. Under the agreements, Westinghouse granted Mitsubishi an exclusive license for the manufacture of certain products in Japan under its patents and Mitsubishi granted Westinghouse nonexclusive licenses under Mitsubishi's patents and know-how to manufacture, use, and sell certain products in all countries other than Japan. Concluding that "Westinghouse has done no more than to license some of its patents and refuse to license others,"[388] the Ninth Circuit affirmed the district court's dismissal of the government's case. In *Dunlop Co. v. Kelsey-Hayes Co.,*[389] the Sixth Circuit ruled that agreements between a licensor and its licensees in various foreign countries that forbade exportation of licensed products to the United States did not violate the antitrust laws. The court concluded that these were "merely territorial licenses granted by a patentee such as are permitted by 35 U.S.C. § 261."[390]

Territorial restraints in international patent or know-how licensing arrangements have been held unlawful when they have brought about a division of markets substantially beyond the scope and terms of the patents or involved pervasive

---

383.   9 U.S.C. §§ 1-16 (2000).
384.   9 U.S.C. § 201 (2000).
385.   473 U.S. 614 (1985).
386.   The primary European Community legislation directly dealing with license agreements is the *Technology Transfer Block Exemption Regulation,* which applies to certain categories of patent and/or know-how license agreements. *See* Commission Regulation 240/96 of 31 January 1996 on the Application of Article 85(3) of the Treaty to Certain Categories of Technology Transfer Agreements, 1996 O.J. (L 31/2). The regulation sets out categories of restrictive or potentially restrictive conditions in license agreements that generally do not infringe European Community competition law in light of European Commission practice and European Court of Justice jurisprudence. As of 2001, the European Commission was considering whether to amend the Technology Transfer Block Exemption Regulation. Insofar as the license agreement is part of an R&D agreement, the *R&D Block Exemption* may also apply. *See* Commission Regulation (EC) No. 2659/2000 of 29 November 2000 on the application of Article 81(3) of the Treaty to Categories of Research and Development Agreements, 2000 O.J. (L 304/7).
387.   648 F.2d 642 (9th Cir. 1981).
388.   *Id.* at 647.
389.   484 F.2d 407 (6th Cir. 1973), *cert. denied,* 415 U.S. 917 (1974).
390.   *Id.* at 417.

schemes to restrain U.S. and foreign commerce.[391]   Also, a patent pool among
Canadian manufacturers who agreed not to license importers has been held to violate
the U.S. antitrust laws.[392]

Actions to bar the import of trademarked or copyrighted products generally are
not found to conflict with the antitrust laws. While there have been substantial
disputes as to the scope of exclusionary rights for imports of trademarked goods
under Section 1526 of the Tariff Act of 1930,[393] it has become clear that the antitrust
laws do not impede the exercise of rights under that section.[394] However, the use of
trademarks as part of a broad scheme involving U.S. domestic or import commerce
to limit output and raise prices is unlawful.[395] Some courts have held that bars to
importation of copyrighted products do not raise antitrust concerns.[396]

9.   *Government Licensing and State Sovereign Immunity*

Government entities, including state universities, often engage in or fund
scientific research. When this research results in the issuance of a patent, a
government agency may become involved in deciding whether and how to license
that patent. In cases where the government's role in the licensing decision is a
subject of litigation, issues of sovereign or Eleventh Amendment immunity may
arise.[397]

---

391. *See, e.g.*, United States v. Singer Mfg. Co., 374 U.S. 174 (1963); United States v. Imperial Chem.
      Indus., 100 F. Supp. 504 (S.D.N.Y. 1951); United States v. Pilkington plc, 1994-2 Trade Cas.
      (CCH) ¶ 70,842 (D. Ariz. 1994) (consent decree). Territorial restrictions in foreign know-how and
      trade secret arrangements will be subject to the same scrutiny as other forms of intellectual
      property arrangements. *See* United States v. Timken Roller Bearing Co., 83 F. Supp. 284 (N.D.
      Ohio 1949), *modified*, 341 U.S. 593 (1951); United States v. General Elec. Co., 82 F. Supp. 753
      (D.N.J. 1949); United States v. National Lead Co., 63 F. Supp. 513 (S.D.N.Y. 1945), *aff'd*, 332
      U.S. 319 (1947); *see also* INTELLECTUAL PROPERTY GUIDELINES, *supra* note 16, Example 7. As
      discussed in Chapter XII, the Sherman Act does not apply to restraints of export commerce which
      do not have a direct, substantial, and reasonably foreseeable effect on U.S. domestic or export
      commerce. *See* Foreign Trade Antitrust Improvements Act, 15 U.S.C. § 6a (2000).
392. Zenith Radio Corp. v. Hazeltine Research, Inc., 401 U.S. 321, 326 (1971).
393. 19 U.S.C. § 1526 (1994 & Supp. 1999); *see* K-Mart Corp. v. Cartier, Inc., 486 U.S. 281 (1988).
394. *See* United States v. Eighty-Nine (89) Bottles of "Eau de Joy," 797 F.2d 767, 770 (9th Cir. 1986)
      ("Congress intended to make genuine goods excludable under Sec. 1526 unless the American
      trademark owner consents to their importation."). In *Coalition to Preserve the Integrity of Am.
      Trademarks v. United States*, 790 F.2d 903, 916 (D.C. Cir. 1986), *aff'd in part and rev'd in part
      sub nom.* K-Mart Corp. v. Cartier, Inc., 486 U.S. 281 (1988), the DOJ and the Customs Service
      filed a joint amicus brief maintaining "that Section 1526 raised no antitrust concerns." *See also*
      Osawa & Co. v. B & H Photo, 589 F. Supp. 1163, 1177-78 (S.D.N.Y. 1984).
395. *See* United States v. Topco Assocs., 405 U.S. 596 (1972); *Timken Roller Bearing Co.*, 341 U.S.
      593.
396. *See, e.g.*, Hearst Corp. v. Stark, 639 F. Supp. 970, 981 (N.D. Cal. 1986); CBS v. Scorpio Music
      Distribs., 569 F. Supp. 47, 49-50 (E.D. Pa. 1983) (importer violated Copyright Act, 17 U.S.C.
      § 602), *aff'd without op.*, 738 F.2d 424 (3d Cir. 1984).
397. The Eleventh Amendment provides: "The Judicial Power of the United States shall not be
      construed to extend to any suit in law or equity, commenced or prosecuted against one of the
      United States by Citizens of another State, or by Citizens or Subjects of any Foreign State."

In 1992, Congress in the Patent Remedy Act expressly abolished state immunity from suit in federal court for patent infringement or any other violation of the Patent Act.[398]   In *Florida Prepaid Postsecondary Education Expense Board v. College Savings Bank*,[399] however, the Supreme Court held that Congress did not have the authority to abrogate state sovereign immunity through such legislation.[400]   Although Congress clearly expressed its intention to eliminate the states' immunity, it did not act "pursuant to a valid exercise of power" under Article I, either the Commerce Clause or the Patent Clause.[401]   While Congress retains the authority to abrogate state sovereign immunity pursuant to the Fourteenth Amendment,[402] the Supreme Court found that the "Patent Remedy Act does not respond to a history of 'widespread and persisting deprivation of constitutional rights' of the sort Congress has faced in enacting proper prophylactic § 5 legislation."[403]   Thus, the Patent Remedy Act could not be sustained under Section 5 of the Fourteenth Amendment.[404]

---

398. Pub. L. No. 102-560, 106 Stat. 4230 (1992) (codified as amended at 35 U.S.C. §§ 271(h), 296(a), 296(b) (1994)).

399. 527 U.S. 627 (1999).

400. *Id.* at 648.

401. To determine whether Congress has validly abrogated state sovereign immunity, two questions must be answered: "first, whether Congress has 'unequivocally expressed its intent to abrogate the immunity,' . . . and second, whether Congress has acted 'pursuant to a valid exercise of power.'" *Id.* at 635 (quoting Seminole Tribe of Fla. v. Florida, 517 U.S. 44, 55 (1996)).

402. *Id.* at 636. The Fourteenth Amendment provides in relevant part: "§ 1. . . . No State shall . . . deprive any person of life, liberty, or property, without due process of law . . . § 5. The Congress shall have power to enforce, by appropriate legislation, the provisions of this article." For Congress to invoke § 5, it must identify conduct transgressing the Fourteenth Amendment's substantive provisions and must tailor its legislative scheme to remedying or preventing such conduct. *Id.* at 639. The Supreme Court noted that patents are included within the "property" of which no person may be deprived by a state without due process of law, and that Congress may legislate against their deprivation without due process under § 5. *Id.* at 642.

403. *Id.* at 645 (quoting City of Boerne v. Flores, 521 U.S. 507, 526 (1997)). "The underlying conduct at issue here is state infringement of patents and the use of sovereign immunity to deny patent owners compensation for the invasion of their patent rights. . . . In enacting the Patent Remedy Act, however, Congress identified no pattern of patent infringement by the States, let alone a pattern of constitutional violations." *Id.* at 640.

404. *Id.* at 647. "The statute's apparent and more basic aims were to provide a uniform remedy for patent infringement and to place States on the same footing as private parties under that regime. These are proper Article I concerns, but that Article does not give Congress the power to enact such legislation after *Seminole Tribe*." *Id.* at 647-48. In a companion case to *Florida Prepaid*, the Supreme Court held that Congress did not have the power to abrogate state sovereign immunity under the Trademark Remedy Clarification Act, 106 Stat. 3567 (1992) (codified as amended at 15 U.S.C. §§ 1114, 1122 (2000)). College Sav. Bank v. Florida Prepaid Postsecondary Educ. Expense Bd., 527 U.S. 666, 675 (1999); *cf.* Chavez v. Arte Publico Press, 204 F.3d 601, 607-08 (5th Cir. 2000) (holding that Congress did not have the power to abrogate state sovereign immunity under the Copyright Remedy Clarification Act); Idaho Potato Comm'n v. M&M Produce Farms & Sales, 95 F. Supp. 2d 150, 155-56 (S.D.N.Y. 2000), *aff'd sub nom.* Hapco Farms, Inc. v. Idaho Potato Comm'n, 283 F.3d 468 (2d Cir. 2001) (Eleventh Amendment shielded state agency from counterclaims of antitrust violations and trademark invalidity). *But cf.* New Star Lasers, Inc. v. Regents of Univ. of Cal., 63 F. Supp. 2d 1240, 1244-45 (E.D. Cal. 1999) (Regents waived Eleventh Amendment immunity to declaratory suit of patent invalidity and noninfringement by acquiring patent).

C. Patent and Copyright Misuse

1. *The Patent Misuse Doctrine*

a. OVERVIEW OF THE DOCTRINE—RELATION TO ANTITRUST

The term "patent misuse" normally refers to conduct by the patentee that constitutes a defense to an action to enforce patent rights, either an infringement action[405] or a contract action to collect royalties due under a license.[406] The misuse doctrine grew out of the equitable doctrine of "unclean hands."[407] In *Morton Salt Co. v. G.S. Suppiger Co.*,[408] a patentee that tied the lease of its patented machines to the purchase of unpatented materials for use in the machines was found to have misused its patent. Invoking the unclean hands doctrine, the Supreme Court refused to enforce the patent against an infringer.[409] The limits of the misuse doctrine have never been well defined. The Federal Circuit has stated that "[t]he key inquiry is whether, by imposing conditions that derive their force from the patent, the patentee has impermissibly broadened the scope of the patent grant with anticompetitive effect."[410] As discussed in this section, the decided cases reveal some continuing uncertainty as to the relationship between misuse and similar antitrust doctrine.

Certain limitations on antitrust actions, such as standing and injury requirements, have not been applied in misuse cases, and the defense of misuse has been found to be available to one who is not directly affected by the patentee's conduct.[411] It

---

405. *See, e.g.*, Morton Salt Co. v. G.S. Suppiger Co., 314 U.S. 488, 492-94 (1942); B.B. Chem. Co. v. Ellis, 314 U.S. 495, 498 (1942).

406. *See, e.g.*, United States Gypsum Co. v. National Gypsum Co., 352 U.S. 457, 465 (1957); Park-In Theatres v. Paramount-Richards Theatres, 90 F. Supp. 730, 735 (D. Del.), *aff'd per curiam*, 185 F.2d 407 (3d Cir. 1950), *cert. denied*, 341 U.S. 950 (1951).

407. The Federal Circuit has suggested that an unclean hands defense exists separate and apart from established misuse authority. *See* Consolidated Aluminum Corp. v. Foseco Int'l Ltd., 910 F.2d 804, 809-12 (Fed. Cir. 1990); *see also* Keystone Driller Co. v. General Excavator Co., 290 U.S. 240, 245-46 (1933) ("[courts of equity] are not bound by formula or restrained by any limitation that tends to trammel the free and just exercise of discretion"); *see also* Zeneca Ltd. v. Pharmachemie B.V., 37 F. Supp. 2d 85, 93-94 (D. Mass. 1999) (addressing an unclean hands defense separate from the patent misuse defense).

408. 314 U.S. 488 (1942).

409. *Id.* at 491. The *Morton Salt* Court viewed the patentee's conduct as an extension of the patentee's "monopoly." It stated: "[A] patent affords no immunity for a monopoly not within the grant . . . and the use of it to suppress competition in the sale of an unpatented article may deprive the patentee of the aid of a court of equity to restrain an alleged infringement." *Id.* (citations omitted); *accord* United States Gypsum Co. v. National Gypsum Co., 352 U.S. 457, 465 (1957).

410. C.R. Bard., Inc. v. M3 Sys., Inc., 157 F.3d 1340, 1372 (Fed. Cir. 1998); *see also* Virginia Panel Corp. v. MAC Panel Co., 133 F.3d 860, 868 (Fed. Cir. 1997); *Zeneca Ltd.*, 37 F. Supp. 2d at 92 (following Federal Circuit standard); Raines v. Switch Mfg., 44 U.S.P.Q.2d (BNA) 1195, 1198 (N.D. Cal. 1997) (same).

411. *See Morton Salt*, 314 U.S. at 493-94; *see also* Ansul Co. v. Uniroyal, Inc., 448 F.2d 872, 880 (2d Cir. 1971) (holding patent unenforceable based upon territorial restraints and resale price fixing in marketing the patented product), *cert. denied*, 404 U.S. 1018 (1972); F.C. Russell Co. v. Consumers Insulation Co., 226 F.2d 373, 375-76 (3d Cir. 1955) (patent unenforceable based upon restrictions in distribution agreements); F.C. Russell Co. v. Comfort Equip. Corp., 194 F.2d 592, 596 (7th Cir. 1952) (patent unenforceable based upon restrictions in distribution agreements). The *F.C. Russell* cases were criticized in REPORT OF THE ATTORNEY GENERAL'S NATIONAL COMMITTEE TO STUDY THE ANTITRUST LAWS 251 (1955). The defense apparently can be denied

generally has been held, however, that the challenged misuse must relate to the patent in suit.[412] Patent misuse also has been found in certain circumstances in which conduct did not rise to the level of an antitrust violation.[413] For example, certain exclusive dealing[414] and tying arrangements where the tying product was patented[415] historically were condemned as patent misuse whether or not the conduct was also challengeable under the antitrust laws.[416]

The misuse doctrine has been applied to a variety of practices that also raise potential antitrust concern. For example, misuse has been found where a patentee compelled a licensee of a patented process to purchase unpatented goods to use in the process,[417] compelled a licensee of one patent to take unwanted licenses under others,[418] compelled the payment of royalties regardless of the licensee's use of the

---

to a defendant who himself has acted inequitably and restrained trade. *See* Touchett v. EZ Paintr Corp., 150 F. Supp. 384, 389 (E.D. Wis. 1957).

412. *See, e.g., Morton Salt*, 314 U.S. at 492-93; Kolene Corp. v. Motor City Metal Treating, Inc., 440 F.2d 77, 84 (6th Cir.) ("The misuse must be of the patent in suit.") (citations omitted), *cert. denied*, 404 U.S. 886 (1971); McCullough Tool Co. v. Well Surveys, Inc., 395 F.2d 230, 238-39 (10th Cir.), *cert. denied*, 393 U.S. 925 (1968); Republic Molding Corp. v. B.W. Photo Utils., 319 F.2d 347, 349 (9th Cir. 1963) ("misconduct in the abstract, unrelated to the claim against which it is asserted as a defense, does not constitute unclean hands"); Binks Mfg. Co. v. Ransburg Electro-Coating Corp., 281 F.2d 252, 259 (7th Cir. 1960), *cert. dismissed*, 366 U.S. 211 (1961); Sperry Prods. v. Aluminum Co. of Am., 171 F. Supp. 901, 940 (N.D. Ohio 1959) (misuse renders patents unenforceable), *aff'd in part and rev'd in part*, 285 F.2d 911 (6th Cir. 1960), *cert. denied*, 368 U.S. 890 (1961); Carter-Wallace, Inc. v. United States, 449 F.2d 1374, 1385-86 (Ct. Cl. 1971) (agreements relating to foreign patents do not render U.S. patents unenforceable).

413. *See, e.g.*, Transparent-Wrap Mach. Corp. v. Stokes & Smith Co., 329 U.S. 637, 641 (1947); *Morton Salt*, 314 U.S. 488; *Zenith Radio Corp.*, 39 U.S. at 140-41; *C.R. Bard*, 157 F.3d at 1372 (noting that patent misuse may arise when the conditions of antitrust violation are not met); *Virginia Panel*, 133 F.3d at 872 (noting that violation of the antitrust laws requires more exacting proof than suffices to demonstrate patent misuse); Berlenbach v. Anderson & Thompson Ski Co., 329 F.2d 782, 784 (9th Cir.), *cert. denied*, 379 U.S. 830 (1964); Hunter Douglas, Inc. v. Comfortex Corp., 44 F. Supp. 2d 145, 156 (N.D.N.Y. 1999) (a patentee's action, although not qualifying as an antitrust violation, may still be subject to the patent misuse defense); Jack Winter, Inc. v. Koratron Co., 375 F. Supp. 1, 71 (N.D. Cal. 1974). *Compare* United States v. Studiengesellschaft Kohle, m.b.H., 670 F.2d 1122 (D.C. Cir. 1981) (no antitrust violation where patentee placed restrictions on sale of goods manufactured through use of patented process), *with* Robintech, Inc. v. Chemidus Wavin, Ltd., 628 F.2d 142, 146-49 (D.C. Cir. 1980) (patent misuse found where holder of process patent imposed territorial restrictions on licensee's sales of unpatented goods).

414. *See* National Lockwasher Co. v. George K. Garrett Co., 137 F.2d 255, 255-56 (3d Cir. 1943).

415. *See* Motion Picture Patents Co. v. Universal Film Mfg. Co., 243 U.S. 502 (1917). *But see* discussion of 35 U.S.C. § 271(d) (1994), which imposed a market power requirement for finding patent misuse, *supra* notes 276-84.

416. *See* USM Corp. v. SPS Techs., Inc., 694 F.2d 505, 511 (7th Cir. 1982), *cert. denied*, 462 U.S. 1107 (1983). The impact of patent misuse law in certain Supreme Court tying cases was noted in the concurring opinion in *Jefferson Parish Hosp. Dist. No. 2 v. Hyde*, 466 U.S. 2, 37 n.7 (1984) (O'Connor, J., concurring).

417. *See, e.g.*, B.B. Chem. Co. v. Ellis, 314 U.S. 495 (1942).

418. *See, e.g.*, Hazeltine Research, Inc. v. Zenith Radio Corp., 388 F.2d 25 (7th Cir. 1967), *aff'd in part and rev'd in part*, 395 U.S. 100 (1969); American Securit Co. v. Shatterproof Glass Corp., 268 F.2d 769 (3d Cir.), *cert. denied*, 361 U.S. 902 (1959). *But cf.* Windsurfing Int'l, Inc. v. AMF, Inc., 782 F.2d 995, 1001-02 (Fed. Cir.) (not misuse to include in patent license an acknowledgment of the validity of the registered trademarks later found to be generic, or an agreement to avoid their use), *cert. denied*, 477 U.S. 905 (1986).

patent,[419] extended its rights beyond the normal seventeen-year life of the patent,[420] or collected two royalties—from the licensee and its manufacturer customers—for the same patents used in the same product.[421] Misuse defenses, however, have been rejected where a patentee has only proposed licensing terms or has refused to license a patent,[422] where both parties voluntarily agreed to a license agreement with royalties based on unpatented components where it provided a convenient means for measuring the value of the license,[423] and where both parties in settlement negotiations agreed to a "sales cap" termination provision that counted sale of product not covered by the license toward the sales under the cap.[424]

In the 1980s, two courts of appeals found that antitrust standards govern application of the patent misuse defense unless the Supreme Court's misuse decisions specifically condemn a practice. In *USM Corp. v. SPS Technologies, Inc.*,[425] the Seventh Circuit held that, beyond "the conventional, rather stereotyped boundaries [of the patent misuse doctrine]," misuse is tested by conventional antitrust principles, in particular the rule of reason. The court found no misuse because the party challenging the license failed to prove an "actual or probable anticompetitive effect in a relevant market," which would be required under the rule of reason.[426]

The Federal Circuit, applying Seventh Circuit law in *Windsurfing International, Inc. v. AMF, Inc.*,[427] found that a patent owner did not misuse its patent by requiring the licensee to acknowledge the validity of certain trademarks of the patent owner and to agree not to use them in any way. The court said:

> To sustain a misuse defense involving a licensing arrangement not held to have been per se anticompetitive by the Supreme Court, a factual determination must reveal that the overall effect of the license tends to restrain competition unlawfully in an appropriately defined relevant market.[428]

419. *See, e.g.*, Zenith Radio Corp. v. Hazeltine Research, Inc., 395 U.S. 100, 133-40 (1969).
420. *See, e.g.*, Brulotte v. Thys Co., 379 U.S. 29, 32 (1964) ("[W]e conclude that a patentee's use of a royalty agreement that projects beyond the expiration date of the patent is unlawful per se.").
421. *See, e.g.*, PSC Inc. v. Symbol Techs., Inc., 26 F. Supp. 2d 505, 510-11 (W.D.N.Y. 1998) (finding that "the collection of royalties from two parties for the same product improperly broadens the scope of the rights Symbol has under its patents" and has "strong anticompetitive effect[s] on the market for scan engines" resulting in an unreasonable restraint on competition).
422. *See* Townshend v. Rockwell Int'l Corp., 2000-1 Trade Cas. (CCH) ¶ 72,890, at 87,636 (N.D. Cal. 2000) (there is no anticompetitive conduct where patentee proposes licensing terms, indicating a willingness to license in accordance with those terms.)
423. *See* Engel Indus., Inc. v. Lockformer Co., 96 F.3d 1398, 1408 (Fed. Cir. 1996) (reasoning that the voluntariness of the licensee's agreement to the royalty provisions is a key consideration); *see also* Zenith Radio Corp., 395 U.S. at 138 (stating "[i]f convenience of the parties rather than patent power dictates the total-sales royalty provisions, there are no misuse of the patents and no forbidden conditions attached to the license").
424. *See* Texas Instruments, Inc. v. Hyundai Elec. Indus. Co., 49 F. Supp. 2d 893, 907-13 (E.D. Tex. 1999).
425. 694 F.2d 505 (7th Cir. 1982), *cert. denied*, 462 U.S. 1107 (1983).
426. *Id.* at 511; *see also* C.R. Bard, Inc. v. M3 Sys., Inc., 157 F.3d 1340, 1373 (Fed. Cir. 1998) (stating that the "misuse doctrine is 'too vague a formulation to be useful'") (quoting *USM Corp.*, 694 F.2d at 510). *But see* Lasercomb Am., Inc. v. Reynolds, 911 F.2d 970 (4th Cir. 1990) (in recognizing the defense of copyright misuse, the court stated that such misuse need not rise to the level of a violation of the antitrust laws to constitute a defense to infringement).
427. 782 F.2d 995 (Fed. Cir.), *cert. denied*, 477 U.S. 905 (1986).
428. *Id.* at 1001 (footnote omitted).

The court in *Windsurfing* questioned whether any licensing practices should be considered per se misuse: "Recent economic analysis questions the rationale behind holding any licensing practice per se anticompetitive."[429] In *Senza-Gel Corp. v. Seiffhart*,[430] however, the Federal Circuit made clear that it was "bound . . . to adhere to existing Supreme Court guidance in the area until otherwise directed by Congress or by the Supreme Court."[431]

Consistent with *Windsurfing*, the Federal Circuit has applied antitrust rule of reason principles to analyze practices that have not previously been found per se unlawful by the Supreme Court. In *Mallinckrodt, Inc. v. Medipart, Inc.*,[432] a case involving a single-use-only restriction on a patented medical device, the Federal Circuit held that the threshold inquiry in a non-per se patent misuse case is whether the challenged restriction "is reasonably within the patent grant, or whether the patentee has ventured beyond the patent grant and into behavior having an anticompetitive effect not justifiable under the rule of reason."[433] Under that test, if the restriction or practice is found to be within the scope of the patent grant there is no misuse.[434] However, if the restriction is found to have "anticompetitive effects extending beyond the patentee's statutory right to exclude, these effects do not automatically impeach the restriction."[435] Under *Mallinckrodt*, in a patent misuse case any anticompetitive conduct that is not per se illegal must be reviewed under the antitrust rule of reason.[436]

In *C.R. Bard, Inc. v. M3 Systems, Inc.*,[437] the Federal Circuit held that alleged "wrongful" enforcement of patents by a patent owner is protected under the *Noerr* doctrine and such conduct is not subject to collateral attack as a new grounds for patent misuse.[438] District courts that have considered whether litigation brought by a patent holder can amount to patent misuse have essentially followed the standards set forth for evaluating whether there is bad faith enforcement of a patent.[439] Thus, a party alleging misuse must show that the litigation is objectively baseless in the sense that no litigant could realistically expect success on the merits.[440]

---

429. *Id.* at 1001 n.9.

430. 803 F.2d 661 (Fed. Cir. 1986).

431. *Id.* at 665; *see also* 1988 Patent Misuse Reform Act, 35 U.S.C. § 271(d) (1994); Texas Instruments, Inc. v. Hyundai Elec. Indus. Co., 49 F. Supp. 2d 893, 907-12 (E.D. Tex. 1999) (concluding that per se patent misuse no longer exists after the 1988 Patent Misuse Reform Act).

432. 976 F.2d 700 (Fed. Cir. 1992).

433. *Id.* at 708.

434. *Id.*; *see also* C.R. Bard, Inc. v. M3 Sys., Inc., 157 F.3d 1340, 1373 (Fed. Cir. 1998) (finding no evidence that patent holder's conduct, including the enforcement of patent rights, "were either per se patent misuse or that they were not reasonably within patent grant") (internal quotation and citation omitted).

435. 976 F.2d at 708.

436. *Id*; *C.R. Bard*, 157 F.3d at 1373 (citing *Mallinckrodt*, 976 F.2d at 708); Virginia Panel Corp. v. MAC Panel Co., 133 F.3d 860, 869 (Fed. Cir. 1997). The rule of reason is discussed in part B.3.b of Chapter I.

437. 157 F.3d 1340 (Fed. Cir. 1998).

438. *Id.* at 1373 ("It is not patent misuse to bring suit to enforce patent rights not fraudulently obtained, nor is otherwise legal competition such behavior as to warrant creation of a new class of prohibited commercial conduct when patents are involved."); *accord Virginia Panel*, 133 F.3d at 868-71 (rejecting allegations of misuse based on threats to enforce patent rights).

439. *See* part B.2.b of this chapter.

440. *See* Moore U.S.A., Inc. v. Standard Register Co., 139 F. Supp. 2d 348 (W.D.N.Y. 2001); Hoffmann-La Roche, Inc. v. Genpharm, Inc., 50 F. Supp. 2d 367, 378-380 (D.N.J. 1999) (citing

A 1988 amendment to Section 271(d) of the Patent Act provides that certain types of conduct shall not constitute "misuse or illegal extension of the patent right."[441] Such conduct includes refusals to license a patent and certain acts relating to enforcement of a patent against contributing infringers.[442]

With regard to misuse claims based on tying, Section 271(d)(5) provides that the

> license of any rights to [a] patent or . . . sale of [a] patented product on the [condition that the buyer take another] license to rights in another patent or purchase a separate product [shall not constitute misuse] unless, in view of the circumstances, the patent owner has market power in the relevant market for the patented product [which is the tying product].[443]

Thus, this statute places patented goods on a par with other tying products for misuse purposes, requiring evidence of market power.[444]

b. REMEDIES FOR MISUSE

Patent misuse is an affirmative defense to a claim of infringement, rendering the patent unenforceable.[445] Misuse generally does not give rise to an independent claim for money damages.[446] In *B. Braun Medical Inc. v. Abbott Laboratories*,[447] the Federal Circuit reversed a district court decision that held that a finding of patent

---

Professional Real Estate Investors, Inc. v. Columbia Pictures Indus., Inc., 508 U.S. 49, 60 (1993)); *see also* Raines v. Switch Mfg., 44 U.S.P.Q.2d (BNA) 1195, 1199 (N.D. Cal. 1997) (dismissing patent misuse claim where defendant failed to provide some factual basis for the allegation that plaintiff knew the patent was invalid or unenforceable when plaintiff filed the infringement action); Undersea Breathing Sys. v. Nitrox Techs., Inc., 985 F. Supp. 752, 780 (N.D. Ill. 1997) (finding no patent misuse where patentee was seeking to enforce his patent rights against infringement), *appeal dismissed,* 155 F.3d 574 (Fed. Cir. 1998).

441. 35 U.S.C. § 271(d) (1994) (as amended by Pub. L. No. 100-703, 102 Stat. 4676 (1988)).

442. *Id.* The misuse doctrine as it applies to contributory infringement actions is the subject of part C.1.c of this chapter.

443. 35 U.S.C. § 271(d)(5). At least one court has applied § 271(d)(5) to tie-outs where, for example, a license is given on the condition that the licensee not use competitors' products, as well as tie-ins. *See In re* Recombinant DNA Tech. Patent & Contract Litig., 850 F. Supp. 769, 777 (S.D. Ind. 1994).

444. *See* Schlafly v. Caro-Kann Corp., 1998-1 Trade Cas. (CCH) ¶ 72,138, at 81,903 (Fed. Cir. 1998) (holding that 35 U.S.C. § 271(d)(5) requires evidence of market power to find a patent misuse violation); Sinclair Int'l Ltd. v. FMC Corp., No. C97-01885 CAL, 1997 U.S. Dist. LEXIS 14963 (N.D. Cal. Sept. 10, 1997) (finding that defendant presented insufficient evidence to establish market power in a relevant market to support patent misuse defense). The Supreme Court's decision in *Jefferson Parish Hosp. Dist. No. 2 v. Hyde,* 466 U.S. 2 (1984), requires a showing of market power in the tying product before a tying arrangement will be found per se illegal under the Sherman Act. *See* part D.3.a of Chapter I. One district court has concluded that per se patent misuse no longer exists after the 1988 Patent Misuse Reform Act. *See Texas Instruments,* 49 F. Supp. 2d at 907-12. For a discussion of tying involving patents, see part B.3.g of this chapter.

445. *See, e.g.,* Morton Salt Co. v. G.S. Suppiger Co., 314 U.S. 488, 492 (1942); *C.R. Bard,* 157 F.3d at 1372 (a holding of patent misuse renders the patent unenforceable until the misuse is purged, but does not by itself invalidate the patent); Senza-Gel Corp. v. Sieffhart, 803 F.2d 661, 668 (Fed. Cir. 1986); W.L. Gore & Assocs. v. Carlisle Corp., 529 F.2d 614, 622 (3d Cir. 1976).

446. *See, e.g.,* CMI, Inc. v. Intoximeters, Inc., 918 F. Supp. 1068, 1090-91 (W.D. Ky. 1995), *appeal dismissed,* 95 F.3d 1168 (Fed. Cir. 1996), *cert. denied,* 522 U.S. 817 (1997); Transitron Elec. Corp. v. Hughes Aircraft Co., 487 F. Supp. 885, 893 (D. Mass. 1980).

447. 124 F.3d 1419 (Fed. Cir. 1997).

misuse could support an award of money damages as an element of providing declaratory relief.[448]   While the court recognized that a district court entering a declaratory judgment that a patent is unenforceable due to misuse may hold a hearing to permit the defendant to state a substantive claim for damages under a contract or antitrust theory, it rejected the notion that monetary damages may be awarded under a declaratory judgment counterclaim based on patent misuse.[449]

Misuse renders a patent unenforceable, but the period of unenforceability ends if the patent owner can demonstrate "purge" of the misuse, i.e., that the misuse has been abandoned and the consequences of the misuse fully dissipated.[450]   The courts divide on whether ceasing enforcement of an offending provision in a license or contract is sufficient to constitute abandonment of the offending agreement. Some find it sufficient.[451]   In *Berlenbach v. Anderson & Thompson Ski Co.*,[452] however, the Ninth Circuit held that the patentee's failure to enforce an offending clause did not purge the misuse because the clause remained in effect. Similarly, in *Ansul Co. v. Uniroyal, Inc.*,[453] the Second Circuit held that relaxation of price policing activities, without affirmative steps to convince distributors of their freedom to set prices, did not purge the misuse. A purge may effectively restore enforceability during the pendency of the infringement suit or after adjudication.[454]

c.   PATENT MISUSE AND CONTRIBUTORY INFRINGEMENT

To directly infringe a patent, it is necessary that a defendant make, use, or sell an article that meets each and every element of a claim of the patent in suit.[455]   Where a defendant sells an article that contains less than all of the elements of a claim,

---

448. *Id.* at 1427-28.

449. *Id.* ("[T]he defense of patent misuse may not be converted to an affirmative claim for damages simply by restyling it as a declaratory judgment counterclaim").

450. *See, e.g.*, United States Gypsum Co. v. National Gypsum Co., 352 U.S. 457, 465, 472-73 (1957); *Morton Salt Co.*, 314 U.S. at 492-94; B.B. Chem. Co. v. Ellis, 314 U.S. 495, 498 (1942); Preformed Line Prods. Co. v. Fanner Mfg. Co., 328 F.2d 265, 278-79 (6th Cir.) (affirming findings that a patentee had abandoned misuse of patent and that the consequences had been dissipated by the date of the hearing on the purge question), *cert. denied*, 379 U.S. 846 (1964); White Cap Co. v. Owens-Illinois Glass Co., 203 F.2d 694, 698 (6th Cir.) (affirming a finding that misuse had been purged where the objectionable clause in a contract was canceled and a showing made that there were no adverse effects to be dissipated), *cert. denied*, 346 U.S. 876 (1953); Campbell v. Mueller, 159 F.2d 803, 807 (6th Cir. 1947) (no misuse where a minimum price clause included in a contract was never acted upon and had been canceled upon renegotiation); Koratron Co. v. Lion Unif., Inc., 409 F. Supp. 1019 (N.D. Cal. 1976) (misuse not purged until last of licenses containing tying provision had expired); Printing Plate Supply Co. v. Crescent Engraving Co., 246 F. Supp. 654, 672-73 (W.D. Mich. 1965) (misuse purged by abandonment of offending practice where there had been no showing by defendant that there were effects to be dissipated).

451. *See, e.g.*, Westinghouse Elec. Corp. v. Bulldog Elec. Prods. Co., 179 F.2d 139, 145 (4th Cir. 1950) (misuse purged by abandoning all efforts to enforce unlawful price control provisions); *cf.* Metals Disintegrating Co. v. Reynolds Metals Co., 228 F.2d 885, 889 (3d Cir. 1956) (no misuse where illegal provisions in a license agreement were not enforced).

452. 329 F.2d 782, 784-85 (9th Cir.), *cert. denied*, 379 U.S. 830 (1964).

453. 448 F.2d 872, 881-82 (2d Cir. 1971), *cert. denied*, 404 U.S. 1018 (1972).

454. *See, e.g.*, Hensley Equip. Co. v. Osco Corp., 383 F.2d 252, 261 (5th Cir.), *modified per curiam*, 386 F.2d 442 (5th Cir. 1967); Eastern Venetian Blind Co. v. Acme Steel Co., 188 F.2d 247, 253-54 (4th Cir.), *cert. denied*, 342 U.S. 824 (1951); *see also Printing Plate Supply*, 246 F. Supp. at 672-73 (collecting decisions).

455. 35 U.S.C. § 271(a) (Supp. 1999).

infringement liability may still exist under the doctrine of contributory infringement. The Patent Act provides:

> Whoever . . . sells . . . a component of a patented machine, manufacture, combination or composition, or a material or apparatus for use in practicing a patented process, constituting a material part of the invention, knowing the same to be especially made or especially adapted for use in an infringement of such patent, and not a staple article or commodity of commerce suitable for substantial noninfringing use, shall be liable as a contributory infringer.[456]

The fact that contributory infringement liability may permit a patentee to prevent defendants from selling unpatented components of patented inventions historically caused some courts to conclude that patent misuse could occur by "extension of the patent monopoly" to reach unpatented products.[457]

In the Patent Act, Congress specifically provided that certain conduct relating to the enforcement of a patent shall not constitute patent misuse, including collecting royalties from acts that would constitute contributory infringement without a license and filing suit against contributing infringers.[458] The legislative history of the statute makes it clear that Congress sought to overturn inconsistent prior decisions that had held the assertion of a patent against a contributing infringer to constitute misuse.[459] The Supreme Court considered the effect of Section 271(d) on the misuse defense in *Dawson Chemical Co. v. Rohm & Haas Co.*[460] In *Dawson*, the Court concluded that Section 271(d) confers upon a patentee "a limited power to exclude others from competition in nonstaple goods."[461] It further concluded that it was not patent misuse for the holder of a process patent to sue manufacturers and sellers of an unpatented chemical specially adapted for use in the process and having no other substantial use.[462] The patentee's refusal to grant licenses separately to those who wished to

---

456. *Id.* § 271(c) (Supp. 1999).

457. *See, e.g.*, Mercoid Corp. v. Mid-Continent Inv. Co., 320 U.S. 661 (1944); Mercoid Corp. v. Minneapolis-Honeywell Regulator Co., 320 U.S. 680 (1944); Leitch Mfg. Co. v. Barber Co., 302 U.S. 458 (1938). In *Carbice Corp. of Am. v. American Patents Dev. Corp.*, 283 U.S. 27, 34 (1931), the Supreme Court not only held that a contributory infringement action would not preclude the sale of unpatented dry ice, but also suggested that an attempt to do so would violate the Sherman Act. The earliest Supreme Court case on a similar point is *Henry v. A.B. Dick Co.*, 224 U.S. 1, 25-36 (1912). There, the Court enjoined, as contributory infringement, the sale of unpatented ink for use in a patented mimeograph machine. Thereafter, in *Motion Picture Patents Co. v. Universal Film Mfg. Co.*, 243 U.S. 502, 528 (1917), the Court overruled *A.B. Dick* and refused to enjoin, as contributory infringement, the sale of unpatented films for use with a patented motion picture projector. The Court relied in part on antitrust principles, including the enactment of the Clayton Act which had taken place in the five-year period between the two cases. The development of the doctrine of contributory infringement is traced in *Dawson Chem. Co. v. Rohm & Haas Co.*, 448 U.S. 176, 187-97 (1980).

458. 35 U.S.C. § 271(d) (1994).

459. Cases finding the assertion of a patent against contributing infringers to constitute a misuse include the Supreme Court's *Mercoid* cases, *supra* note 457. The legislative history of § 271(d) is discussed in *Dawson*, 448 U.S. at 202-12.

460. 448 U.S. 176 (1980).

461. *Id.* at 201.

462. *Id.* at 186.

purchase the unpatented chemical from others and its insistence upon supplying all of the chemical for use in the process itself did not change the result.[463]

2. *The Copyright Misuse Doctrine*

The doctrine of misuse is less well established in copyright cases than in patent cases. Although the Supreme Court has made passing reference to the misuse of a copyright,[464] the Court has never squarely ruled that a copyright is rendered unenforceable because it has been "misused." In *Broadcast Music, Inc. v. CBS*,[465] the Court reversed a ruling of the Second Circuit that blanket copyright licenses were per se violations of the Sherman Act and constituted copyright misuse.[466] The Court remanded the case for an analysis under the rule of reason; the misuse question was not before the Court and was not mentioned by the Second Circuit on remand.[467]

Several circuits have acknowledged the existence of a doctrine of copyright misuse as a valid defense to copyright infringement. In *Lasercomb America, Inc. v. Reynolds*,[468] the Fourth Circuit reversed a damage award for copyright infringement on the ground that the plaintiff had engaged in copyright misuse by inserting a clause in its license prohibiting the licensee from developing competing software for ninety-nine years.[469] In expressly adopting a copyright misuse defense, the Fourth Circuit stated that copyright misuse need not rise to the level of an antitrust violation to constitute a defense.[470] It further held that the defense—like the patent misuse defense—was available to one who was not a direct victim of the offending conduct.[471] Likewise, in *Tempo Music, Inc. v. Myers*,[472] the Fourth Circuit reversed a district court holding of infringement, ruling that the copyright owners had unclean hands for failing to notify licensees of beneficial provisions the owners were compelled to offer under a prior antitrust consent decree.[473]

---

463. *Id.*; *see also* Miller Insituform, Inc. v. Insituform of N. Am., Inc., 605 F. Supp. 1125, 1136 (M.D. Tenn. 1985) ("[A] tie-in usually would not exist when a patentee (or its licensee) conditions the right to use his patented process upon the vendee's purchase of nonpatented commodities that are necessary to the process, if such commodities have no effective, noninfringing use other than application in the patented process."), *aff'd*, 830 F.2d 606 (6th Cir. 1987), *cert. denied*, 484 U.S. 1064 (1988); Lifescan, Inc. v. Polymer Tech. Int'l Corp., 35 U.S.P.Q.2d (BNA) 1225 (W.D. Wash. 1995) (patent holder could restrain trade in nonstaple components even if others had an implied license to use the components). On remand in *Dawson*, the district court found that § 271(d) also precluded a finding of an antitrust violation. Rohm & Haas Co. v. Dawson Chem. Co., 557 F. Supp. 739, 835-36 (S.D. Tex.), *rev'd on other grounds*, 722 F.2d 1556 (Fed. Cir. 1983), *cert. denied*, 469 U.S. 851 (1984).

464. Mazer v. Stein, 347 U.S. 201, 206, 218 (1954).

465. 441 U.S. 1 (1979).

466. CBS v. American Soc'y of Composers, Authors & Publishers, 562 F.2d 130, 141 n.29 (2d Cir. 1977), *rev'd and remanded sub nom.* Broadcast Music, Inc. v. CBS, 441 U.S. 1 (1979).

467. CBS v. American Soc'y of Composers, Authors & Publishers, 607 F.2d 543 (2d Cir. 1979).

468. 911 F.2d 970 (4th Cir. 1990).

469. *Id.* at 979.

470. *Id.* at 978.

471. *Id.* at 979.

472. 407 F.2d 503 (4th Cir. 1969).

473. *Id.* at 507; *see also* PRC Realty Sys. v. National Ass'n of Realtors, 1992 Copyright L. Dec. (CCH) ¶ 26,961 (4th Cir. 1992) (clause in copyright license requiring licensee to use best efforts to convince consumers to utilize licensor's services held misuse because it would suppress any independent expression of the idea at issue); *see also* Religious Tech. Ctr. v. Lerma, Civ. No. 95-

In *DSC Communications Corp. v. DGI Technologies, Inc.*,[474] the Fifth Circuit expressly adopted the Fourth Circuit's characterization of the copyright misuse defense as stated in *Lasercomb*, analogizing it to the patent misuse defense.[475] Subsequently, the Fifth Circuit held in *Alcatel USA, Inc. v. DGI Technologies, Inc.*,[476] that the copyright misuse doctrine barred injunctive relief where the plaintiff licensed its software to customers to be used only in conjunction with the plaintiff's hardware. The court reasoned that such a restriction was an attempt by the plaintiff to obtain patent-like protection of its hardware through enforcement of its software copyright.[477] The court reached this conclusion despite a finding by the jury that the defendant acted with "unclean hands in its acquisition and use" of the plaintiff's copyrighted material.[478] The court reasoned that since the plaintiff was seeking equitable relief, it was the plaintiff's "hands alone that must pass the hygenic test," which it failed as a result of its copyright misuse.[479] The defendant's unclean hands did not bar its copyright misuse defense.[480]

The Ninth Circuit also examined the doctrine of copyright misuse in its decision in *Practice Management Information Corp. v. American Medical Ass'n.*[481] The court held that although copyright misuse does not invalidate a copyright, it furnishes a defense to infringement by precluding the enforcement of the copyright during the period of its misuse.[482] The court found that the defendant had established as a matter of law a defense of copyright misuse where the plaintiff conditioned a license of the copyrighted material on the defendant's promise not to use its competitor's products.[483] The court also agreed with the Fourth Circuit that a defendant in a copyright infringement suit need not prove an antitrust violation to prevail on a copyright misuse defense.[484] In *A&M Records, Inc. v. Napster, Inc.*,[485] the Ninth Circuit affirmed the trial court's preliminary rejection of the affirmative defense of misuse where the evidence indicated only that the plaintiff record companies sought "to control reproduction and distribution of their copyrighted works, exclusive rights of copyright holders."[486]

In *United Telephone Co. v. Johnson Publishing Co.*,[487] the Eighth Circuit stated that a claim of copyright misuse rising to the level of an antitrust violation may be used as a defense to a charge of copyright infringement. One district court also

1107-A, 1996 U.S. Dist. LEXIS 15454, at *32-35 (E.D. Va. Oct. 4, 1996) (describing copyright misuse as "somewhat analogous to the prohibition against 'tying' in the patent law").

474. 81 F.3d 597 (5th Cir. 1996); *see also* Elec. Data Sys. Corp. v. Computer Assoc. Int'l, Inc., 802 F. Supp. 1463, 1466 (N.D. Tex. 1992) (permitting assertion of a copyright misuse defense).

475. 81 F.3d at 601.

476. 166 F.3d 772 (5th Cir. 1999).

477. *Id.* at 793.

478. *Id.* at 794.

479. *Id.*

480. *Id.* at 795. *But see* Data Gen. Corp. v. Grumman Sys. Support Corp., 36 F.3d 1147, 1170 n.43 (1st Cir. 1994) ("[i]f copyright misuse is an equitable defense, a defendant that has itself acted inequitably may not be entitled to raise such a defense").

481. 121 F.3d 516 (9th Cir.), *cert. denied*, 522 U.S. 933 (1997).

482. *Id.* at 520 n.9.

483. *Id.* at 521.

484. *Id.*

485. 239 F.3d 1004 (9th Cir. 2001).

486. *Id.* at 1026-27.

487. 855 F.2d 604, 611 (8th Cir. 1988).

required that a copyright misuse defense assert misuse that constitutes an antitrust violation.[488]

The First Circuit, in *Data General Corp. v. Grumman Systems Support Corp.*,[489] declined to decide whether copyright misuse was a valid defense. It noted, however, that although "it is often more difficult to prove an antitrust violation when the claim rests on the questionable market power associated with a copyright, . . . that would not be a reason to prohibit a defendant from attempting to meet its burden of proof, and would be a poor reason to refrain entirely from recognizing a copyright misuse defense."[490]

The status of the copyright misuse defense in the Seventh Circuit is somewhat uncertain. In *F.E.L. Publications v. Catholic Bishop*,[491] the court reversed a district court ruling that a copyright holder had engaged in illegal licensing and tying arrangements and thus could not enforce a claim of infringement. Although the copyright misuse defense was recognized by the court of appeals, it held that misuse gives rise to a valid defense against infringement only after a "balancing of equities."[492] In *Reed-Union Corp. v. Turtle Wax, Inc.*,[493] however, the Seventh Circuit stated that the validity of the copyright misuse defense is an "open issue in this court," noting that "copyrights do not exclude independent expression and therefore create less market power than patents."[494]

Prior to *Lasercomb*, many district courts had rejected the argument that a federal antitrust law violation provides the basis for an unclean hands defense to a copyright infringement suit.[495] Some district courts in circuits where the court of appeals has

---

488. Nihon Keizai Shimbun, Inc. v. Camline Bus. Data, Inc., No. 98 Civ. 641, 1998 U.S. Dist. Lexis 6806, at *50 (S.D.N.Y. Apr. 14, 1998) (copyright misuse available as an affirmative defense only where the copyright conferred "market dominance" and the copyright owner engaged in an unreasonable restraint of trade, such as by tying).

489. 36 F.3d 1147 (1st Cir. 1994).

490. *Id.* at 1170 (dictum); *see also* Broadcast Music, Inc. v. Hampton Beach Casino Ballroom, 1995 Copyright L. Dec. (CCH) ¶ 27,459 (D.N.H. 1995) (granting summary judgment dismissing copyright misuse defense because alleged infringer could provide no evidence of an antitrust violation or a violation of the public policies underlying the copyright laws). In *BellSouth Advert. & Publ'g Corp. v. Donnelley Info. Publ'g*, 933 F.2d 952, 960-61 (11th Cir. 1991), the Eleventh Circuit suggested that it might apply the copyright misuse doctrine in an appropriate case. The panel decision was vacated when rehearing was granted, 977 F.2d 1435 (11th Cir. 1992), and the decision on rehearing did not address the issue, 999 F.2d 1436 (1993) (en banc), *cert. denied*, 510 U.S. 1101 (1994). *See also* Eastern Publ'g & Advert., Inc. v. Chesapeake Publ'g & Advert., Inc., 831 F.2d 488, 493 (4th Cir. 1987), *vacated on other grounds*, 492 U.S. 913 (1989); Mitchell Bros. Film Group v. Cinema Adult Theater, 604 F.2d 852, 865 (5th Cir. 1979) ("In an appropriate case a misuse of the copyright statute that in some way subverts the purpose of the statute—the promotion of originality—might constitute a bar to judicial relief."), *cert. denied*, 445 U.S. 917 (1980); Edward B. Marks Music Corp. v. Colorado Magnetics, Inc., 497 F.2d 285, 290-91 (10th Cir. 1974), *cert. denied*, 419 U.S. 1120 (1975); K-91, Inc. v. Gershwin Publ'g Corp., 372 F.2d 1, 4 (9th Cir. 1967), *cert. denied*, 389 U.S. 1045 (1968).

491. 1982-1 Trade Cas. (CCH) ¶ 64,632 (7th Cir.), *cert. denied*, 459 U.S. 859 (1982).

492. *Id.* at 73,464 n.9; *see also* qad. inc. v. ALN Assocs., 974 F.2d 834, 836 (7th Cir. 1992) (dictum) (copyright misuse "has its historical roots in the unclean hands defense and is a complete bar to enforcement of one's copyright").

493. 77 F.3d 909 (7th Cir. 1996).

494. *Id.* at 913.

495. *See, e.g.*, Buck v. Cecere, 45 F. Supp. 441 (W.D.N.Y. 1942); Buck v. Newsreel, Inc., 25 F. Supp. 787, 789 (D. Mass. 1938); Vitagraph, Inc. v. Grobaski, 46 F.2d 813, 814 (W.D. Mich. 1931); M. Witmark & Sons v. Pastime Amusement Co., 298 F. 470, 480 (E.D.S.C.), *aff'd*, 2 F.2d 1020 (4th

yet to resolve the issue may still be reluctant to recognize the copyright misuse defense.[496] Other courts have recognized the copyright misuse defense generally but rejected it in the case at hand.[497] The defense has been successful, however, in a

---

Cir. 1924); Harms v. Cohen, 279 F. 276, 280-81 (E.D. Pa. 1922). Those decisions predate *Morton Salt Co. v. G.S. Suppiger Co.*, 314 U.S. 488, 493-94 (1942), where the Court refused to enforce a patent that had been misused. A number of district courts reached the same result, however, subsequent to *Morton Salt*. *See, e.g.*, Orth-O-Vision, Inc. v. Home Box Office, 474 F. Supp. 672, 686 (S.D.N.Y. 1979) ("As a general rule, it is no defense to a copyright infringement claim that the copyright owner is violating the antitrust laws."); Foreign Car Parts, Inc. v. Auto World, Inc., 366 F. Supp. 977, 979 (M.D. Pa. 1973) (doubtful that an antitrust violation creates a defense to an action for copyright infringement); Harms, Inc. v. Sansom House Enters., 162 F. Supp. 129, 135 (E.D. Pa. 1958), *aff'd sub nom.* Leo Feist, Inc. v. Lew Tendler Tavern, Inc., 267 F.2d 494 (3d Cir. 1959). In certain of these cases, the decision may be based on the absence of any relationship between the intellectual property and the antitrust violation in question. In *Morton Salt*, there was such a relationship between the intellectual property and the violation. However, in *United Artists Associated v. NWL Corp.*, 198 F. Supp. 953, 958 (S.D.N.Y. 1961), the court, after carefully reviewing *Morton Salt* and noting the connection between the patent and the antitrust violation, concluded that "it is a substantial question whether a like rule . . . is applicable to an action for infringement of *copyright*."

496. *See, e.g.*, Microsoft Corp. v. Compusource Distrib., 115 F. Supp. 2d 800, 809 (E.D. Mich. 2000) (rejecting the argument that the findings of fact in *United States v. Microsoft Corp.*, 84 F. Supp. 2d 9 (D.D.C. 1999), supported defense of copyright or trademark misuse because defendant in infringement action had not demonstrated "any causal nexus" between any antitrust violation and defendant's competitive position); Telecomm Tech. Servs., Inc. v. Siemens Rolm Communs., 66 F. Supp. 2d 1306, 1324 (N.D. Ga. 1998) (noting that the Eleventh Circuit has not recognized the copyright misuse defense and that even if the court were to recognize the defense, such a defense would be inappropriate where the court cannot conclude that plaintiff's claims are "objectively meritless"); Syncsort Inc. v. Sequential Software, Inc., 50 F. Supp. 2d 318, 336 (D.N.J. 1999) (reasoning that "[w]hether this Circuit recognizes copyright misuse as an independent antitrust violation is irrelevant to the disposition of the Motion . . . because [defendant] did not allege facts evidencing copyright misuse, much more an antitrust violation").

497. *See, e.g.*, Triad Sys. Corp. v. Southeastern Express Co., 64 F.3d 1330, 1337 (9th Cir. 1995) (rejecting copyright misuse defense based on manufacturer's refusal to license diagnostic software to independent service providers), *cert. denied*, 516 U.S. 1145 (1996); Data Gen. Corp. v. Grumman Sys. Support Corp., 36 F.3d 1147 (1st Cir. 1994); Atari Games Corp. v. Nintendo of Am., Inc., 975 F.2d 832 (Fed. Cir. 1992); Service & Training, Inc. v. Data Gen. Corp., 963 F.2d 680, 690 (4th Cir. 1992) (defendants offered no evidence that the copyright holder "did anything beyond limiting the use of the software to repair and maintenance of specific computer hardware, activity that is protected as an exclusive right of a copyright owner"); *In re* Independent Serv. Orgs. Antitrust Litig., 85 F. Supp. 2d 1130, 1176 (D. Kan. 2000) (finding that copyright holder's unilateral refusal to license its copyrights does not constitute misuse); Sony Computer Entm't Am., Inc. v. Gamemasters, 87 F. Supp. 2d 976, 988-89 (N.D. Cal. 1999) (rejecting copyright misuse claim where plaintiff's copyright claim is sound); Dream Dealers Music v. Parker, 924 F. Supp. 1146, 1152 (S.D. Ala. 1996); Advanced Computer Servs. of Mich., Inc. v. MAI Sys. Corp., 845 F. Supp. 356, 368-69 (E.D. Va. 1994) (rejecting copyright misuse defense because "[i]t is within MAI's discretion to protect its copyrighted works, and this discretion includes the right to license its software to whomever it chooses"); Mastercraft Fabrics Corp. v. Dickson Elberton Mills Inc., 821 F. Supp. 1503 (M.D. Ga. 1993); Sega Enters. v. Accolade, Inc., 785 F. Supp. 1392 (N.D. Cal.), *aff'd in part and rev'd in part on other grounds*, 977 F.2d 1510 (9th Cir. 1992); Budish v. Gordon, 784 F. Supp. 1320 (N.D. Ohio 1992); National Cable Television Ass'n v. Broadcast Music, Inc., 772 F. Supp. 614 (D.D.C. 1991); qad. inc. v. ALN Assocs., 770 F. Supp. 1261 (N.D. Ill. 1991), *appeal dismissed in relevant part*, 974 F.2d 834 (7th Cir. 1992); Coleman v. ESPN, Inc., 764 F. Supp. 290 (S.D.N.Y. 1991); Basic Books, Inc. v. Kinko's Graphics Corp., 758 F. Supp. 1522 (S.D.N.Y. 1991); Allen-Myland, Inc. v. IBM, 746 F. Supp. 520 (E.D. Pa. 1990), *recons. denied*, 770 F. Supp. 1004 (1991), *vacated on other grounds*, 33 F.3d 194 (3d Cir.), *cert. denied*, 513 U.S. 1066 (1994); Georgia Television Co. v. TV News Clips of Atlanta, Inc., 1991-2 Trade Cas. (CCH)

growing number of cases.[498] To establish a copyright misuse defense, most courts that recognize the defense have required that the defendant show either (1) that the copyright holder violated the antitrust laws, or (2) that the copyright holder extended its right to exclusivity beyond the scope of the copyright or violated the public policies underlying the copyright laws.[499]

Additionally, two courts specifically have rejected copyright misuse as an affirmative claim for relief.[500]

D. Trademarks and Antitrust

A trademark consists of "any word, name, symbol, or device or any combination thereof" used by a manufacturer or seller to distinguish his products from those of others.[501] Rights in a trademark are established by using the mark commercially on goods or with respect to services. In general, the first user of a mark is entitled to exclude others from using the same or a similar trademark where confusion of the purchasing public is likely.[502] A trademark differs significantly from a patent in that a trademark gives the owner no exclusive right to make, use, or sell any good or

¶ 69,516 (N.D. Ga. 1991); Broadcast Music, Inc. v. Hearst/ABC Viacom Entm't Servs., 746 F. Supp. 320 (S.D.N.Y. 1990).

498. *See* Alcatel USA, Inc. v. DGI Techs., Inc., 166 F.3d 772, 793 (5th Cir. 1999) (upholding jury finding of copyright misuse where copyrighted software was licensed to customers to be used only in conjunction with plaintiff's manufactured hardware); Practice Mgmt. Info. Corp. v. American Med. Ass'n, 121 F.3d 516, 520 (9th Cir.) (concluding that plaintiff misused its copyright by licensing a copyrighted coding system to defendant in exchange for defendant's agreement not to use competing coding systems), *cert. denied*, 522 U.S. 933 (1997); PRC Realty Sys. v. National Ass'n of Realtors, 1992 Copyright L. Dec. (CCH) ¶ 26,961 (4th Cir. 1992) (best efforts clause held to be misuse); *qad. inc.*, 770 F. Supp. at 1267-71 (finding that copyright owner misused its copyright by attempting to enforce rights in litigation as to material over which it had no copyright, and by engaging in inequitable conduct during litigation); *cf.* DSC Communs. Corp. v. DGI Techs., Inc., 81 F.3d 597 (5th Cir. 1996) (district court did not abuse discretion in narrowing injunction because of possibility of successful copyright misuse defense).

499. *See, e.g.*, Lasercomb Am., Inc. v. Reynolds, 911 F.2d 970, 978 (4th Cir. 1990); *In re Independent Serv. Orgs. Antitrust Litig.*, 85 F. Supp. 2d at 1175; *see also Alcatel*, 166 F.3d at 792 (noting that the copyright misuse doctrine "'forbids the use of the [copyright] to secure an exclusive right or limited monopoly not granted by the [Copyright] Office'") (quoting *Lasercomb*, 911 F.2d at 976).

500. Novell, Inc. v. CPU Distrib. Inc., Civ. A. No. H-97-2326, 2000 U.S. Dist. LEXIS 9952, at *16 (S.D. Tex. May 12, 2000) (refusing to recognize copyright misuse as a claim for affirmative relief "except on clear authority from the appellate court"); Warner/Chappel Disc, Inc. v. Pilz Compact Disc, Inc., 52 U.S.P.Q.2d (BNA) 1942, 1947 n.5 (E.D. Pa. 1999) (stating that there is "no authority" in the Third Circuit and "virtually no authority" in any circuit permitting an affirmative claim of copyright misuse).

501. 15 U.S.C. § 1127 (2000). A trademark refers to a mark used in connection with goods. A mark used in connection with services is called a service mark. For convenience, the term "trademark" will be used in this section to refer to both trademarks and service marks.

502. *See* 15 U.S.C. § 1114 (2000); United Drug Co. v. Theodore Rectanus Co., 248 U.S. 90, 97-98 (1918); Hanover Star Milling Co. v. Metcalf, 240 U.S. 403, 412-15 (1916); *In re* Trade-Mark Cases, 100 U.S. 82, 92, 94 (1879).

service.[503] In fact, the functional aspects of a product cannot be protected as a trademark.[504]

Because trademarks, unlike patents, do not confer exclusionary power over products or services, excluding others from the use of a trademark will not support an attempt to monopolize claim.[505] Similarly, the fact that a brand is protected by a trademark does not imply that the brand or trademark constitutes an antitrust product market for the purposes of the rule of reason analysis in a Section 1 claim.[506] Additionally, the filing of a trademark infringement action may enjoy antitrust immunity under the *Noerr* doctrine.[507]

The owner of a trademark may license others to use the mark, but as with patents and copyrights, restraints in the license agreement are subject to challenge under the antitrust laws. Thus, in *United States v. Sealy, Inc.*,[508] the Court struck down a territorial trademark licensing scheme in which the individual licensees jointly owned the licensor organization on the ground that it constituted a horizontal market division.[509] Similarly, resale price maintenance cannot be justified on the ground that

---

503. *See, e.g.*, Clorox Co v. Sterling Winthrop, Inc., 117 F.3d 50, 56 (2d Cir. 1997); Car-Freshner Corp. v. Auto Aid Mfg. Corp., 438 F. Supp. 82, 86 (N.D.N.Y. 1977); Seven-Up Co. v. No-Cal Corp., 183 U.S.P.Q. (BNA) 165, 166 (E.D.N.Y. 1974); Carl Zeiss Stiftung v. V.E.B. Carl Zeiss, Jena, 298 F. Supp. 1309, 1314 (S.D.N.Y. 1969), *modified on other grounds*, 433 F.2d 686 (2d Cir. 1970), *cert. denied*, 403 U.S. 905 (1971). The DOJ and the FTC chose not to include treatment of trademark issues in the *Intellectual Property Guidelines* because the *Guidelines* were designed to "deal with technology transfer and innovation-related issues that typically arise with respect to patents, copyrights, trade secrets and know-how agreements, rather than with product-differentiation issues that typically arise with respect to trademarks." INTELLECTUAL PROPERTY GUIDELINES, *supra* note 16, § 1 n.2.
504. *See* Mechanical Plastics Corp. v. Titan Techs., Inc., 823 F. Supp. 1137, 1147 (S.D.N.Y. 1993), *aff'd without op.*, 33 F.3d 50 (2d Cir. 1994).
505. *See, e.g.*, Seven-Up Co. v. No-Cal Corp., 183 U.S.P.Q. (BNA) 165, 166 (E.D.N.Y. 1974); Alberto-Culver Co. v. Andrea Dumon, Inc., 295 F. Supp. 1155, 1158 (N.D. Ill. 1969), *aff'd in part and rev'd in part*, 466 F.2d 705 (7th Cir. 1972); Borden, Inc., 92 F.T.C. 669 (1978) (respondent not required to license ReaLemon trademark in spite of monopoly), *aff'd*, 674 F.2d 498 (6th Cir. 1982), *vacated and remanded for entry of consent judgment*, 461 U.S. 940 (1983); *see also* Marketing Displays, Inc. v. TrafFix Devices, Inc., 967 F. Supp. 953, 965 (E.D. Mich. 1997) (mere assertion of trade dress rights after the expiration of a patent does not give rise to a claim for attempted monopolization), *aff'd*, 200 F.3d 929 (6th Cir. 1999), *rev'd on other grounds*, 532 U.S. 23 (2001); VMG Enter. v. F. Quesada & Franco, 788 F. Supp. 648, 658 (D.P.R. 1992) (recognizing that the exclusivity that inheres in a trademark could not preclude competition in any meaningful way). *But see* Kellogg Co. v. National Biscuit Co., 71 F.2d 662, 665-66 (2d Cir. 1934); Clorox Co. v. Sterling Winthrop, 836 F. Supp. 983 (E.D.N.Y. 1993).
506. *See, e.g.*, Generac Corp. v. Caterpillar, Inc., 172 F.3d 971 (7th Cir. 1999); Weber v. NFL, 112 F. Supp. 2d 667, 673-74 (N.D. Ohio 2000); *see also* Queen's City Pizza v. Domino's Pizza, Inc., 124 F.3d 430, 437-40 (3d Cir. 1997) (discussing Eastman Kodak Co. v. Image Tech. Servs., Inc., 504 U.S. 451, 482 (1992)), *cert. denied*, 523 U.S. 1059 (1998); Adidas America, Inc. v. NCAA, 64 F. Supp. 2d 1097 (D. Kan. 1999).
507. *See* Hartford Life Ins. Co. v. Variable Annuity Life Ins. Co., 964 F. Supp. 624 (D. Conn. 1997) (granting motion to dismiss for failure to allege facts establishing the lack of any objective basis for pursing a trademark infringement action and holding that presence of equitable defenses does not make an infringement suit baseless); Credit Counseling Ctrs. of Am. v. National Found. of Consumer Credit, No. 3:94-CV-1855-D, 1997 U.S. Dist. LEXIS 4957 (N.D. Tex. Apr. 2, 1997) (dismissing antitrust claim on summary judgment but granting plaintiff the opportunity to gather discovery from intervenors).
508. 388 U.S. 350 (1967).
509. *Id.* at 356; *see also* United States v. Topco Assocs., 405 U.S. 596 (1972); Timken Roller Bearing Co. v. United States, 341 U.S. 593 (1951); Instructional Sys. Dev. Corp. v. Aetna Cas. & Sur. Co.,

a product is trademarked.[510]   However, in accordance with recent jurisprudence relating to vertical nonprice restraints,[511] vertical licensing agreements that grant trademark exclusivity in particular territories are analyzed under the rule of reason and have been found lawful. For example, in *Generac Corp. v. Caterpillar, Inc.*,[512] the Seventh Circuit found, under a rule of reason analysis, that a vertical arrangement did not violate Section 1 of the Sherman Act even though it granted one party an exclusive license to sell products bearing a particular trademark in certain territories and restricted that licensee's ability to compete with the licensor in other territories.[513]

Although a number of cases have questioned whether trademark misuse may be used as a defense to an infringement action[514] (with an early case holding that it could not[515]), certain courts have recognized the defense as valid.[516] Because of the significant differences between the exclusionary effects of patents and trademarks, the availability of any trademark misuse defense generally will be limited to situations in which the trademark "itself has been the basic and fundamental vehicle required and used to accomplish the [antitrust] violation."[517]

---

787 F.2d 1395 (10th Cir. 1986) (in reversing a grant of summary judgment for defendant, the court held that restrictions in a joint venture agreement beyond what was necessary to effectuate a trademark license (*e.g.*, market division) could violate § 1 under the rule of reason), *modified on other grounds*, 817 F.2d 639 (1987). A district court decision finding a probable violation of the *Sealy* consent decree and granting a preliminary injunction was reversed in *Sealy Mattress Co. v. Sealy, Inc.*, 789 F.2d 582 (7th Cir. 1986).

510. *See* United States v. Bausch & Lomb Optical Co., 321 U.S. 707, 721 (1944). Maximum resale price restraints are now subject to the rule of reason. *See* State Oil Co. v. Khan, 522 U.S. 3 (1997) (overruling in part *Albrecht v. Herald Co.*, 390 U.S. 145 (1968)). *See* part D.1.a(2) of Chapter I.

511. *See, e.g.,* Continental T.V., Inc. v. GTE Sylvania Inc., 433 U.S. 36 (1977).

512. 172 F.3d 971 (7th Cir. 1999).

513. *Id.* at 977. The Seventh Circuit noted that competition would not be harmed extensively because the agreement left the other party free to sell differently branded products in the exclusive territories and "product markets are not defined in terms of one trademark or another." *Id.* The court also pointed out that the contract was entered into to establish "more efficient promotion of the covered products and better sales." *Id. See also* Clorox Co v. Sterling Winthrop, Inc., 117 F.3d 50 (2d Cir. 1997) (upholding a settlement agreement under the rule of reason, even though it regulated the parties' use of trademarks, because it did not restrict Clorox "from producing and selling products that compete directly with the Lysol brand, so long as they are marketed under a brand name other than Pine-Sol").

514. *See* Microsoft Corp. v. Compusource Distributors, Inc., 115 F. Supp. 2d 800 (E.D. Mich. 2000) (noting that the Sixth Circuit has not addressed the issue of trademark misuse defense and that "courts in other circuits have questioned" its existence; awarding summary judgment to the plaintiff due to the absence of any evidence of trademark misuse); Northwestern Corp. v. Gabriel Mfg. Co., 48 U.S.P.Q.2d (BNA) 1902, 1909 (N.D. Ill. 1998) (if a trademark misuse defense exists at all, it is likely meant only to cover instances where the trademark is not an effective identifier of source, but rather is misleading to potential purchasers); Juno Online Servs. v. Juno Lighting, Inc., 979 F. Supp. 684 (N.D. Ill. 1997) (a trademark misuse defense is less justifiable than a patent misuse defense because "in trademark law, the mark holder usually does not have the ability to destroy competition").

515. Folmer Graflex Corp. v. Graphic Photo Serv., 41 F. Supp. 319, 320 (D. Mass. 1941). The court did remark that such misuse may be a factor in determining equitable relief for the plaintiff.

516. *See, e.g.,* Black & Decker, Inc. v. Hoover Serv. Ctr., 765 F. Supp. 1129, 1133 (D. Conn. 1991); Phi Delta Theta Fraternity v. J.A. Buchroeder & Co., 251 F. Supp. 968 (W.D. Mo. 1966); *see also* Coca-Cola Co. v. Howard Johnson Co., 386 F. Supp. 330, 336 n.4 (N.D. Ga. 1974) (citing cases).

517. Carl Zeiss Stiftung v. V.E.B. Carl Zeiss, Jena, 298 F. Supp. 1309, 1315 (S.D.N.Y. 1969), *modified on other grounds*, 433 F.2d 686 (2d Cir. 1970), *cert. denied*, 403 U.S. 905 (1971); *see also* Estee Lauder, Inc. v. Fragrance Counter, Inc., 189 F.R.D. 269, 272 (S.D.N.Y. 1999); G. Heileman

Section 33(b) of the Lanham Act provides that a mark that has become incontestable is conclusive evidence of the registrant's ownership, except when "the mark has been or is being used to violate the antitrust laws of the United States."[518] Some courts have suggested that Section 33(b) provides authority for finding trademark misuse.[519] These cases, however, have not discussed or recognized the difference between a possible defense to incontestability, which does not necessarily defeat the trademark owner's right to prevail, and a defense of misuse, which can defeat an infringement action.[520]

A variety of cases have discussed whether a trademark can be considered a separate product for the purpose of a tying analysis and the related question whether a trademark can be presumed to confer economic power. The Ninth Circuit held in *Siegel v. Chicken Delight, Inc.*[521] that a franchisor could not license franchisees to use its trademark and business methods on condition that the franchisees purchase supplies and equipment from the franchisor. The court rejected the argument that the tying arrangement was justified by the franchisor's need to maintain quality control in connection with the use of its trademark, and held the trademark to constitute a distinct tying product.[522] The court also held that the presumption of economic power in patent cases applies equally to trademarks.[523]

Subsequent decisions, however, have limited the holding of *Chicken Delight*. In *Krehl v. Baskin-Robbins Ice Cream Co.,*[524] the Ninth Circuit distinguished a "business format" franchise of the type in *Chicken Delight* from a "distribution type system," holding that the trademark in the latter was inseparable from the product.[525]

Brewing Co. v. Anheuser-Busch Inc., 676 F. Supp. 1436, 1473 (E.D. Wis. 1987) (the test to be applied in determining whether a particular trademark use constitutes a § 2 violation is the same as in any other case where an unlawful monopoly or attempt to monopolize is alleged; § 2 is violated only when the trademark owner's "actions have led to or resulted in a dangerous probability that it will gain a monopoly over the relevant market"), *aff'd*, 873 F.2d 985 (7th Cir. 1989); Coca-Cola Co. v. Howard Johnson Co., 386 F. Supp. 330, 335-37 (N.D. Ga. 1974).

518. 15 U.S.C. § 1115(b)(7) (2000).

519. *See, e.g.*, G.D. Searle & Co. v. Institutional Drug Distribs., 151 F. Supp. 715, 720 (S.D. Cal. 1957); *Carl Zeiss Stiftung*, 298 F. Supp. at 1314.

520. *See* Coca-Cola Co. v. Howard Johnson Co., 386 F. Supp. 330, 335 (N.D. Ga. 1974).

521. 448 F.2d 43 (9th Cir. 1971), *cert. denied*, 405 U.S. 955 (1972); *see also* Subsolutions, Inc. v. Doctor's Assoc., Inc., 62 F. Supp. 2d 616, 623-24 (D. Conn. 1999) (Subway trademark could constitute tying product for tie covering computerized sales system used in Subway sandwich shops); Little Caesar Enter. v. Smith, 34 F. Supp. 2d 459, 467 (E.D. Mich. 1998) (franchise could serve as tying product where it is efficient for a firm to provide the tied items separately from the franchise); Maryland Staffing Servs., Inc. v. Manpower, Inc., 936 F. Supp. 1494, 1504 (E.D. Wis. 1996) (alleged tie of franchise and insurance purchased by franchisor for the franchisees stated a claim for illegal tying).

522. 448 F.2d at 51; *see also* Northern v. McGraw-Edison Co., 542 F.2d 1336, 1345 (8th Cir. 1976), *cert. denied*, 429 U.S. 1097 (1977); Warriner Hermetics, Inc. v. Copeland Refrigeration Corp., 463 F.2d 1002, 1012-15 (5th Cir.), *cert. denied*, 409 U.S. 1086 (1972). *But see* Susser v. Carvel Corp., 332 F.2d 505, 519-20 (2d Cir. 1964) (the franchisor's trademark did not confer economic power and that tying arrangements were justified by the franchisor's need for quality control), *cert. dismissed*, 381 U.S. 125 (1965). The Lanham Act imposes an affirmative duty upon the trademark licensor to control the quality of goods and services. 15 U.S.C. §§ 1055, 1127 (2000).

523. 448 F.2d. at 47, 49-50.

524. 664 F.2d 1348 (9th Cir. 1982).

525. *Id.* at 1353; *see also* Power Test Petroleum Distribs. v. Calcu Gas, Inc., 754 F.2d 91, 98 (2d Cir. 1985); Jack Walters & Sons Corp. v. Morton Bldg., Inc., 737 F.2d 698, 704 (7th Cir.), *cert. denied*, 469 U.S. 1018 (1984); Hamro v. Shell Oil Co., 674 F.2d 784, 788 (9th Cir. 1982) ("the nexus

Similarly, in *Redd v. Shell Oil Co.*,[526] the Tenth Circuit refused to find the defendant's trademark to be separate from petroleum products sold under the mark, stating that "permissive trademark use did not . . . transform the mark into a separate product to be sold to plaintiff."[527] In *Principe v. McDonald's Corp.*,[528] the Fourth Circuit held that a McDonald's franchise and the store location were not separate products. The court explicitly disagreed with *Chicken Delight*'s conclusion that trademarks were the essence of a franchise, stating that "[w]here the challenged aggregation is an essential ingredient of the franchised system's formula for success, there is but a single product and no tie-in exists as a matter of law."[529]

Other cases have strongly questioned any presumption of economic power that is based solely on the possession of a trademark. In *Capital Temporaries, Inc. v. Olsten Corp.*,[530] the Second Circuit refused to uphold a tying claim that required the presumption of the existence of economic power based on a trademark (the allegedly tying product).[531] Similarly, in *Valley Products Co. v. Landmark*,[532] the Sixth Circuit rejected the conclusion that a trademark license could be a tying product used to coerce franchisees into purchasing tied supplies from specific sources. The court stated that the contrary holding in *Chicken Delight* "ignores the obvious differences between patents and trademarks—a patented product is necessarily unique . . . while a trademarked product is not."[533]

E. Trade Secrets and Antitrust

State law, not federal law, protects trade secrets and know-how.[534] In *Kewanee Oil Co. v. Bicron Corp.*,[535] the Supreme Court held that trade secret protection is not preempted by federal patent law.[536] Unlike patent license restrictions, however,

---

between the trademark and [gasoline] is sufficiently close to warrant treating them as one product"); Smith v. Mobil Oil Corp., 667 F. Supp. 1314 (W.D. Mo. 1987).

526. 524 F.2d 1054 (10th Cir. 1975), *cert. denied*, 425 U.S. 912 (1976).

527. *Id.* at 1057. *But see* Bogosian v. Gulf Oil Corp., 561 F.2d 434 (3d Cir. 1977), *cert. denied*, 434 U.S. 1086 (1978).

528. 631 F.2d 303 (4th Cir. 1980), *cert. denied*, 451 U.S. 970 (1981).

529. *Id.* at 309. *But see* Roberts v. Elaine Powers Figure Salons, 708 F.2d 1476 (9th Cir. 1983) (franchise and bookkeeping service are separate products).

530. 506 F.2d 658 (2d Cir. 1974).

531. *Id.* at 663; *see also* Queen's City Pizza v. Domino's Pizza, Inc., 124 F.3d 430, 440 (3d Cir. 1997) (dismissing on the pleadings a tying claim that defined the tying product market solely with reference to defendant's trademark), *cert. denied*, 523 U.S. 1059 (1998); Chawla v. Shell Oil Co., 75 F. Supp. 2d 626, 642 (S.D. Tex. 1999).

532. 128 F.3d 398 (6th Cir. 1997).

533. *Id.* at 405.

534. The terms "trade secrets" and "know-how" are used interchangeably in this section. A trade secret can consist of any confidential information used by one firm in the conduct of business that gives that firm a competitive advantage over firms that do not have the information. *See, e.g.*, Kewanee Oil Co. v. Bicron Corp., 416 U.S. 470, 474-75 (1974); Telex Corp. v. IBM, 510 F.2d 894, 928 (10th Cir.), *cert. dismissed*, 423 U.S. 802 (1975). The essence of trade secret protection stems from a motive to protect express or implied agreements to keep business information confidential. Unlike patents, trade secret law provides no rights against a person who independently develops or properly obtains the confidential information. *See, e.g.*, Kewanee Oil, 416 U.S. at 490; Dr. Miles Med. Co. v. John D. Park & Sons & Co., 220 U.S. 373, 400-02 (1911).

535. 416 U.S. 470 (1974).

536. *Id.* at 491-92. In *Aronson v. Quick Point Pencil Co.*, 440 U.S. 257, 265-66 (1979), the Supreme Court held that the patent laws do not preempt state enforcement of a contract for payment for

restrictions in trade secret licenses cannot be justified on the ground that they serve the purposes of the patent statute or policy. In *CVD, Inc. v. Raytheon Co.*,[537] the First Circuit held that the bad faith assertion of trade secret claims, i.e., with the knowledge that no trade secrets exist, may violate both Sections 1 and 2 of the Sherman Act.[538]

The agencies have indicated that they will apply the same antitrust principles to trade secrets as they do to patents and copyrights.[539]

Licenses to use trade secrets are lawful, as are restrictions that are reasonable and ancillary to such licenses. As the Ninth Circuit stated, "[t]he critical question in an antitrust context is whether the restriction may fairly be said to be ancillary to a commercially supportable licensing arrangement, or whether the licensing scheme is a sham set up for the purpose of controlling competition while avoiding the consequences of the antitrust laws."[540] Field of use restrictions in a know-how license have been upheld,[541] as have territorial restrictions in know-how licenses where the restrictions were not an integral part of a general scheme to suppress competition.[542] In other cases, territorial restraints, when used as a part of a larger conspiracy to divide markets, have been held unlawful.[543] Package licenses involving trade secrets may raise antitrust concerns where the licensing of trade secrets has been conditioned upon the licensing of patents and other trade secrets.[544]

---

know-how. In *Bonito Boats, Inc. v. Thunder Craft Boats, Inc.*, 489 U.S. 141, 157 (1989), the Supreme Court held that a state law (a Florida law that prohibited the use of a direct molding process to duplicate unpatented boat hulls) was preempted under the Supremacy Clause of the Constitution and thus reaffirmed the holdings in *Sears, Roebuck & Co. v. Stiffel Co.*, 376 U.S. 225 (1964), and *Compco Corp. v. Day-Brite Lighting, Inc.*, 376 U.S. 234 (1964).

537. 769 F.2d 842 (1st Cir. 1985), *cert. denied*, 475 U.S. 1016 (1986).

538. *Id.* at 851 (plaintiff required to "prove, in addition to the other elements of an antitrust violation, by clear and convincing evidence, that the defendant asserted trade secrets with the knowledge that no trade secrets existed" where litigation "would have proved ruinous" to a new corporation and would have "effectively foreclosed competition"; the court held that "the threat of unfounded trade secrets litigation in bad faith is sufficient to constitute a cause of action under the antitrust laws"). *But cf.* Boeing Co. v. Sierracin Corp., 108 Wash. 2d 38, 738 P.2d 665 (1987) (good faith and confidentiality clauses are lawful).

539. *See* INTELLECTUAL PROPERTY GUIDELINES, *supra* note 16, § 1.

540. A. & E. Plastik Pak Co. v. Monsanto Co., 396 F.2d 710, 715 (9th Cir. 1968).

541. *See id.* at 715; *see also* Syncsort Inc. v. Sequential Software, Inc., 50 F. Supp. 2d 318, 336 (D.N.J. 1999) (holding copyright license restriction not to be a basis for an attempted monopolization claim because restriction was meant to protect the licensor's trade secrets, not to "control competition"; there was no restriction on licensee's ability to develop competing products that did not make use of the licensor's trade secrets). *Cf.* Lasercomb Am. v. Reynolds, 911 F.2d 970, 978-79 (4th Cir. 1990) (finding copyright license restriction to be excessively broad).

542. *See, e.g.*, Thoms v. Sutherland, 52 F.2d 592, 594-96 (3d Cir. 1931); Foundry Servs. v. Beneflux Corp., 110 F. Supp. 857, 860-62 (S.D.N.Y.), *rev'd on other grounds*, 206 F.2d 214 (2d Cir. 1953); *see also* United States v. E.I. duPont de Nemours & Co., 118 F. Supp. 41, 219 (D. Del. 1953), *aff'd*, 351 U.S. 377 (1956); Shin Nippon Koki Co. v. Irvin Indus., 186 U.S.P.Q. (BNA) 296, 298 (N.Y. Sup. Ct. 1975).

543. *See, e.g.*, United States v. Imperial Chem. Indus., 100 F. Supp. 504, 519-31 (S.D.N.Y. 1951); United States v. Timken Roller Bearing Co., 83 F. Supp. 284, 315-16 (N.D. Ohio 1949), *modified and aff'd*, 341 U.S. 593 (1951) (the Supreme Court did not discuss the know-how issue); *see also* United States v. Pilkington plc, 1994-2 Trade Cas. (CCH) ¶ 70,842 (D. Ariz. 1994) (consent decree).

544. *See, e.g.*, Technograph Printed Circuits, Ltd. v. Bendix Aviation Corp., 218 F. Supp. 1, 50 (D. Md. 1963), *aff'd per curiam*, 327 F.2d 497 (4th Cir.), *cert. denied*, 379 U.S. 826 (1964).

Additionally, unlike a patentee, the owner of a trade secret may collect royalties even after the trade secret has "expired" through public disclosure.[545]

Apart from licensing, trade secrets have also been at issue in litigation and enforcement actions involving tying and refusals to deal. In *In re Data General Corp. Antitrust Litigation*,[546] a district court held that a trade secret does not necessarily convey the economic power required to establish unlawful tying. In 1998, the Federal Trade Commission brought an enforcement action against Intel Corporation, charging that the company withheld competitively critical trade secret information concerning its microprocessors from three customers as a means of coercing them into licensing their patented innovations to Intel.[547]

F. Procedural Aspects of the Antitrust-Intellectual Property Interface

1. Jurisdiction

The U.S. Court of Appeals for the Federal Circuit has exclusive appellate jurisdiction over any complaint involving an antitrust claim and a claim arising under the patent laws.[548] Federal Circuit choice of law rules with respect to cases raising both antitrust and intellectual property issues are discussed in the next section.[549]

In *Christianson v. Colt Industries Operating Corp.*,[550] the Supreme Court ruled that 28 U.S.C. § 1295(a)(1) jurisdiction is evaluated by determining whether a claim arises under the patent law under 28 U.S.C. § 1338(a) in accordance with the well-pleaded complaint rule, which is based upon "'what necessarily appears in the plaintiff's statement of his own claim in the bill or declaration, unaided by anything alleged in anticipation or avoidance of defenses which it is thought that the defendant

---

545. *See, e.g.*, Warner-Lambert Pharm. Co. v. John J. Reynolds, Inc., 178 F. Supp. 655, 663-67 (S.D.N.Y. 1959) (plaintiff's obligation to pay royalties under trade secret agreement was not relieved by the fact that the "secret" formula had been disclosed to the public), *aff'd*, 280 F.2d 197 (2d Cir. 1960); *see also* Aronson v. Quick Point Pencil Co., 440 U.S. 257, 266 (1979) (where a contract provided for a 5% royalty if a patent was granted and a 2.5% royalty otherwise, plaintiff was not precluded from collecting the 2.5% royalty despite the fact that the patent was denied and the product "ceased to have any secrecy as soon as it was first marketed"). *But see Pilkington PLC*, 1994-2 Trade Cas. (CCH) ¶ 70,842 (patent and know-how licensing agreements with likely competitors for the manufacture of flat glass by proprietary process were unreasonably restrictive).

546. 529 F. Supp. 801 (N.D. Cal. 1981), *aff'd in part and rev'd in part sub nom.* Digidyne Corp. v. Data Gen. Corp., 734 F.2d 1336 (9th Cir. 1984), *cert. denied*, 473 U.S. 908 (1985).

547. *In re* Intel Corp., No. C-9288, 1998 FTC LEXIS 65 (FTC June 8, 1998) (complaint). Intel entered into a consent agreement with the FTC requiring, inter alia, that, unless a customer seeks an injunction against Intel selling its microprocessors, Intel will not withhold technical information from customers who enforce their own intellectual property rights against Intel. *In re* Intel Corp., No. C-9288, 64 Fed. Reg. 20134 (FTC Apr. 23, 1999).

548. *See* 28 U.S.C. § 1295(a) (1994 & Supp. 1999); Atari, Inc. v. JS & A Group, 747 F.2d 1422, 1428-40 (Fed. Cir. 1984) (citing cases), *overruled on other grounds by* Nobelpharma AB v. Implant Innovations, Inc., 141 F.3d 1059, 1069 (Fed. Cir.), *cert. denied*, 525 U.S. 876 (1998); *see also* Handgards, Inc. v. , Inc., 743 F.2d 1282, 1285-88 (9th Cir. 1984) (exploring but not resolving reach of this "perplexing statute"), *cert. denied*, 469 U.S. 1190 (1985).

549. *See* part F.2 of this chapter.

550. 486 U.S. 800 (1988).

may interpose.'"[551] A suggestion that expired patents owned by Colt were invalid did not make the case one "arising under" the patent law.[552] The Seventh Circuit insisted that the Federal Circuit had appellate jurisdiction and the Federal Circuit insisted that the Seventh Circuit had jurisdiction. The Supreme Court agreed with the Federal Circuit.[553]

The Federal Circuit and the First Circuit have held that where a nonfrivolous compulsory counterclaim for patent infringement is filed in an antitrust action, exclusive appellate jurisdiction rests in the Federal Circuit notwithstanding the traditional rule that the plaintiff's complaint establishes the basis for district court jurisdiction.[554] The Federal Circuit later held that "any counterclaim [including permissive counterclaims] raising a nonfrivolous claim of patent infringement is sufficient to support this court's appellate jurisdiction."[555] Likewise, the court's jurisdiction extends to state law claims containing a falsity element that requires the plaintiff to prove patent infringement, invalidity, or unenforceability.[556]

Where the antitrust and patent claims are severed in the district court under Rule 42 of the Federal Rules of Civil Procedure, appellate jurisdiction over the antitrust claims normally will remain in the Federal Circuit.[557] Where, however, all patent claims and counterclaims are voluntarily dismissed without prejudice in the district court, thus effectively amending the complaint to exclude patent claims, the Federal Circuit does not have exclusive jurisdiction over the appeal of the remaining nonpatent issues.[558] On the other hand, dismissals reflecting a judgment on the merits of the patent claims, which will have a res judicata effect, do not effectively amend the complaint, so jurisdiction remains with the Federal Circuit.[559]

---

551. *Id.* at 809 (quoting Franchise Tax Bd. v. Construction Laborers Vacation Trust, 463 U.S. 1, 10 (1983)).

552. *Id.* at 806, 812-13.

553. *Id.* at 818-19.

554. Aerojet-General Corp. v. Machine Tool Works, 895 F.2d 736, 740-45 (Fed. Cir. 1990) (en banc) (distinguishing *Christianson*); Xeta, Inc. v. Atex, Inc., 825 F.2d 604 (1st Cir. 1987).

555. DCS Communs. v. Pulse Communs., 170 F.3d 1354, 1359 (Fed. Cir.), *cert. denied*, 528 U.S. 923 (1999). *But see* Leatherman Tool Group v. Cooper Indus., 131 F.3d 1011, 1015 (Fed. Cir. 1997) (transferring appeal) (on appeal of preliminary injunction issued in trade dress infringement action, held affirmative defense and counterclaim that design was in public domain as a result of failed design patent application did not create an action arising under the patent laws).

556. *See* Hunter Douglas, Inc. v. Harmonic Design, 153 F.3d 1318 (Fed. Cir. 1998) (state claims raising issues of invalidity or unenforceability), *cert. denied*, 525 U.S. 1143 (1999), *overruled on other grounds by* Midwest Indus. v. Karavan Trailers, Inc., 175 F.3d 1356, 1360-61 (Fed. Cir.), *cert. denied*, 528 U.S. 1019 (1999) (applying Federal Circuit law to determine whether patent law preempts state causes of action); Additive Controls & Measurement Sys. v. Flowdata, Inc., 986 F.2d 476 (Fed. Cir. 1993) (state business disparagement claim involving accuracy of claims of infringement); *see also* Scherbatskoy v. Halliburton Co., 52 U.S.P.Q.2d (BNA) 1461 (Fed. Cir. 1999) (unpublished opinion) (following transfer of case from the Fifth Circuit, accepting as not "clearly erroneous" that court's determination that the Federal Circuit had jurisdiction over state contract claim involving issue of patent infringement); U.S. Valves, Inc. v. Dray, 190 F.3d 811, 815 (7th Cir. 1999) (transferring state contract claim involving patent infringement claim to the Federal Circuit).

557. *See* Korody-Colyer Corp. v. General Motors Corp., 828 F.2d 1572 (Fed. Cir. 1987).

558. *See* Gronholz v. Sears, Roebuck & Co., 836 F.2d 515, 518 (Fed. Cir. 1987); *see also* Nilssen v. Motorola, Inc., 203 F.3d 782, 785 (Fed. Cir. 2000) ("fact that the dismissal of . . . patent claims was without prejudice is ultimately what matters" to jurisdiction).

559. Zenith Elec. Corp. v. Exzec, Inc., 182 F.3d 1340, 1346 (Fed. Cir. 1999). The Ninth Circuit held that where all patent claims had been dismissed by the district court, an appeal of a partial final

2. *Choice of Law*

The Federal Circuit applies its own law with respect to issues of patent law, which fall within its exclusive jurisdiction.[560] Prior to 1998, the Federal Circuit applied the law of the circuit from which the case originated with respect to other questions of law, including all antitrust issues.[561] In a series of decisions beginning with *Pro-Mold & Tool Co. v. Great Lakes Plastics, Inc.*,[562] however, the simple distinction between patent and nonpatent law was replaced with more subtle choice of law rules, which have extended the breadth of Federal Circuit law into areas of antitrust. *Pro-Mold & Tool* held as a matter of Federal Circuit law that inequitable conduct in the prosecution of a patent application did not constitute a claim under the Lanham Act.[563] The court decided to apply its own law even though "unfair competition is not unique to [its] jurisdiction" because the issue "clearly does impact our exclusive jurisdiction."[564]

In *Nobelpharma AB v. Implant Innovations, Inc.*,[565] the Federal Circuit held that "whether conduct in procuring or enforcing a patent is sufficient to strip a patentee of its immunity from the antitrust laws is to be decided as a question of Federal Circuit law."[566] This choice of law holding is limited, however, to just those listed elements of antitrust claims; regional circuit law still applies to other elements of antitrust

judgment granted under Rule 54(b) on certain nonpatent issues was not within the exclusive jurisdiction of the Federal Circuit. Denbicare U.S.A., Inc. v. Toys "R" Us, Inc., 84 F.3d 1143, 1147-48 (9th Cir.), *cert. denied*, 519 U.S. 873 (1996).

560. *See, e.g.*, Midwest Indus. v. Karavan Trailers, Inc., 175 F.3d 1356, 1359 (Fed. Cir.) (en banc portion of decision), *cert. denied*, 528 U.S. 1019 (1999).

561. Cygnus Therapeutics Sys. v. ALZA Corp., 92 F.3d 1153, 1161 (Fed. Cir. 1996); Loctite Corp. v. Ultraseal Ltd., 781 F.2d 861, 875 (Fed. Cir. 1985); Atari, Inc. v. JS & A Group, 747 F.2d 1422, 1438-40 (Fed. Cir. 1984) (en banc). These decisions were all overruled by the choice of law rule announced in *Nobelpharma AB v. Implant Innovations, Inc.*, 141 F.3d 1059, 1068 (Fed. Cir.) (en banc portion of decision), *cert. denied*, 525 U.S. 876 (1998); *see also* Cable Elec. Prods. v. Genmark, Inc., 770 F.2d 1015, 1029, 1033 (Fed. Cir. 1985) (regional circuit law applies to question of whether patent law preempts particular state law causes of action or conflicts with rights created by other federal statutes), *overruled by Midwest Indus.*, 175 F.3d at 1358-62 (en banc portion of decision).

562. 75 F.3d 1568, 1574-75 (Fed. Cir. 1996).

563. *Id.* (noting that "[t]he established remedy for inequitable conduct is unenforceability of the patent" or, when the other elements of a monopolization offense are present, relief is available pursuant to § 2 of the Sherman Act). *But see* Spotless Enter. v. Carlisle Plastics, Inc., 56 F. Supp. 2d 274, 281-82, 285 n.11 (E.D.N.Y. 1999) (distinguishing *Pro-Mold & Tool* to permit Lanham Act claim for false assertions of patent infringement and questioning the Federal Circuit's intrusion upon issues of law not within its exclusive jurisdiction).

564. 75 F.3d at 1574. *But see In re* Filmtec Corp., 155 F.3d 573 (table), 1998 U.S. App. LEXIS 17322 (Fed. Cir. July 7, 1998) (unpublished opinion) (*Nobelpharma*'s choice of law holding did not give Federal Circuit power to issue mandamus relief in antitrust action not within the court's appellate jurisdiction).

565. 141 F.3d 1059, 1068 (Fed. Cir.), *cert. denied*, 525 U.S. 876 (1998).

566. *Id.*; *see also* Travelers Express Co. v. American Express Integrated Payment Sys., 80 F. Supp. 2d 1033, 1041-42 (D. Minn. 1999) (applying Federal Circuit law to determine whether conduct challenged in attempted monopolization claim fell within the sham exception to the *Noerr* doctrine); *cf.* Dow Chem. Co. v. Exxon Corp., 30 F. Supp. 2d 673, 692 n.31 (D. Del. 1998) ("[i]n the absence of Third Circuit precedent addressing this issue," applying Federal Circuit law as instructed by *Nobelpharma* to decide whether RICO claims based solely upon allegedly fraudulent petitioning conduct before the PTO were precluded by the *Noerr* doctrine).

claims in patent cases, such as market definition or proof of market power.[567] Noting
that these suits will most frequently be appealed to it, the Federal Circuit adopted this
rule because "[it is] in the best position to create a uniform body of federal law on
this subject and thereby avoid the 'danger of confusion [that] might be enhanced if
this court were to embark on an effort to interpret the laws' of the regional
circuits."[568] The Federal Circuit also has applied its own law to the review of
antitrust claims arising from a refusal to sell patented parts.[569]

3. Procedure

When a suit involves both antitrust and patent claims, the case is frequently
bifurcated for separate discovery or trial. A court is normally more willing to grant a
motion for bifurcation if potentially dispositive issues are present. Antitrust issues
are often postponed until patent rights are determined.[570] In some cases alleging
unenforceability due to inequitable conduct in the procurement of the patent, thus
challenging the enforceability of the patent, this matter is addressed early in the
proceedings.[571] In *Baxter International, Inc. v. Cobe Laboratories*,[572] the court stayed

---

567. 141 F.3d at 1068 (mentioning relevant market, market power, and damages as issues decided with
reference to regional circuit law). *But see In re* Spalding Sports Worldwide, Inc., 203 F.3d 800,
804-08 (Fed. Cir. 2000) (applying Federal Circuit law to decide whether attorney-client privilege
applies to invention record submitted for patent evaluation and concluding that a showing of
inequitable conduct did not establish the crime/fraud exception to the attorney-client privilege).

568. 141 F.3d at 1068 (quoting and citing Forman v. United States, 767 F.2d 875, 880 n.6 (Fed. Cir.
1985)).

569. *In re* Independent Serv. Orgs. Antitrust Litig., 203 F.3d 1322, 1325 (Fed. Cir. 2000), *cert. denied*,
531 U.S. 1143 (2001). The Federal Circuit applies its own law to decide whether federal patent
law conflicts with rights created under other federal statutes, such as the Lanham Act, or preempts
state causes of action for unfair competition and other business torts. Midwest Indus. v. Karavan
Trailers, Inc., 175 F.3d 1356, 1357 (Fed. Cir.), *cert. denied*, 528 U.S. 1019 (1999). The court's
decisions with respect to unfair competition law do not address issues of antitrust law, and, hence,
are beyond the scope of this chapter.

570. *See, e.g., In re* Innotron Diagnostics, 800 F.2d 1077 (Fed. Cir. 1986) (bifurcating patent
infringement claims from antitrust counterclaims in the interests of economy and avoidance of
prejudice); Ecrix Corp. v. Exabyte Corp., 191 F.R.D. 611, 614 (D. Colo. 2000) ("bifurcation is
appropriate in the interest of economy and to expedite the trial"); Hunter Douglas, Inc. v.
Comfortex Corp., 44 F. Supp. 2d 145, 157 (N.D.N.Y. 1999) (ordering trifurcated trial in which
issues of patent infringement liability and damages would be decided before patent misuse defense
and antitrust and state tort counterclaims); Hewlett-Packard v. Genrad, Inc., 882 F. Supp. 1141 (D.
Mass. 1995) (bifurcating patent infringement claim from antitrust and unfair competition
counterclaims because failure to prove inequitable conduct in procuring the patent would eliminate
the basis for the counterclaim); Virginia Panel Corp. v. MAC Panel Co., 887 F. Supp. 880 (W.D.
Va. 1995) (postponing trial on both patent misuse and antitrust issues until after a trial on
infringement), *aff'd*, 133 F.3d 860 (Fed. Cir. 1997), *cert. denied*, 525 U.S. 815 (1998).

571. *See, e.g.,* Gardco Mfg. v. Herst Lighting Co., 820 F.2d 1209 (Fed. Cir. 1987) (inequitable conduct
hearing by court in advance of scheduled jury trial); Hemstreet v. Burroughs Corp., 666 F. Supp.
1096 (N.D. Ill. 1987) (summary judgment on inequitable conduct), *rev'd in part on other grounds
and appeal dismissed in part mem.*, 861 F.2d 728 (Fed. Cir. 1988).

572. No. 89 C 9460, 1992 U.S. Dist. LEXIS 5660 (N.D. Ill. Apr. 7, 1992); *see also* Knoll Pharm. Co. v.
Teva Pharm. USA, Inc., Case No. 01 C 1646, 2001 U.S. Dist. LEXIS 12998, at *4-6 (N.D. Ill.
Aug. 21, 2001) (ordering bifurcated trials of infringement claims and antitrust counterclaims but
refusing to separate issues of willfulness and damages from issues of validity and infringement);
Implant Innovations Inc. v. Nobelpharma AB, No. 93-C-7489, 1996 U.S. Dist. LEXIS 14495, at *3
(N.D. Ill. Oct. 2, 1996) (ordering separate trials for patent claims and antitrust and unfair

consideration of an antitrust counterclaim based on bad faith enforcement because otherwise the plaintiff would have been forced to abandon a good faith argument or rely upon the testimony of patent counsel to show good faith and thereby disqualify counsel and waive the attorney-client privilege.

Some license agreements provide for arbitration of disputes arising in connection with the agreement. The Ninth and Tenth Circuits have held that any antitrust claims directly related to such a license are subject to mandatory arbitration.[573]

4. Remedies

In antitrust actions brought by the Department of Justice alleging unlawful provisions in patent and copyright licenses, courts often have enjoined the defendant from further enforcement of the offending provisions or from entering into similar agreements.[574] Compulsory licensing is an important additional remedy in such cases.   In *United States v. Glaxo Group*,[575] the Supreme Court stated that "[m]andatory selling on specified terms and compulsory patent licensing at reasonable charges are recognized antitrust remedies."[576] While noting that "'[t]he framing of decrees should take place in the District rather than in Appellate Courts,'" the Court recognized "'an obligation to intervene in this most significant phase of the case' when necessary to assure that the relief will be effective."[577]

A number of early consent decrees call for royalty-free licensing.[578] A few courts have ordered royalty-free licensing or the dedication of existing patents to the public.[579] Other lower courts have chosen not to order such remedies.[580]

competition claims and staying discovery of the antitrust and unfair competition claims until after resolution of the patent issues); *cf.* eBay Inc. v. Bidder's Edge Inc., 56 U.S.P.Q.2d (BNA) 1856, 1859 (N.D. Cal. 2000) (refusing to bifurcate trial and stay discovery on sham litigation counterclaim "where complete discovery will educate the parties on the strengths and weaknesses of their positions and facilitate settlement").

573. *See* Simula, Inc. v. Autoliv, Inc., 175 F.3d 716, 721-22 (9th Cir. 1999); Coors Brewing Co. v. Molson Breweries, 51 F.3d 1511, 1515 (10th Cir. 1995).

574. *See, e.g.*, United States v. Glaxo Group, 410 U.S. 52, 64 (1973); United States v. United States Gypsum Co., 340 U.S. 76 (1950); United States v. Paramount Pictures, 334 U.S. 131 (1948); Hartford-Empire Co. v. United States, 323 U.S. 386, *clarified*, 324 U.S. 570 (1945); Ethyl Gasoline Corp. v. United States, 309 U.S. 436 (1940).

575. 410 U.S. 52 (1973).

576. *Id.* at 64; *cf.* Image Technical Servs., Inc. v. Eastman Kodak Co., 125 F.3d 1195, 1224-25 (9th Cir. 1997) (affirming injunction requiring sale of parts, including parts covered by patents, to certain customers at a reasonable price), *cert. denied*, 523 U.S. 1094 (1998); United States v. Imperial Chem. Indus., 105 F. Supp. 215 (S.D.N.Y. 1952) (requiring grant of reasonable royalty licenses with immunity under foreign patents). For a construction of the immunity provision, see United States v. Imperial Chem. Indus., 1956 Trade Cas. (CCH) ¶ 68,435 (S.D.N.Y. 1956). The Seventh Circuit upheld a lower court's refusal to prohibit a defendant from further use of a trademark used to violate the antitrust laws. Switzer Bros. v. Locklin, 297 F.2d 39, 48 (7th Cir. 1961), *cert. denied*, 369 U.S. 851 (1962).

577. 410 U.S. at 64 (quoting International Salt Co. v. United States, 332 U.S. 392, 400-01 (1947), and *United States Gypsum Co.*, 340 U.S. at 89.

578. *See, e.g.*, United States v. General Motors, 1965 Trade Cas. (CCH) ¶ 71,624 (E.D. Mich. 1965) (royalty-free licenses on existing patents; reasonable royalties on patents obtained within five years); United States v. Pitney-Bowes, Inc., 1959 Trade Cas. (CCH) ¶ 69,235 (D. Conn. 1959); United States v. RCA, 1958 Trade Cas. (CCH) ¶ 69,164 (S.D.N.Y. 1958) (royalty-free licenses on existing patents, reasonable royalties on future patents); United States v. IBM, 1956 Trade Cas. (CCH) ¶ 68,245 (S.D.N.Y. 1956) (partly royalty-free, partly at reasonable royalties, depending on

The Supreme Court has never ruled on whether dedication or compulsory royalty-free licensing is a proper remedy. In *Hartford-Empire Co. v. United States*,[581] the Court expressly declined to order dedication on the ground that "a patent is property, protected against appropriation both by individuals and by government."[582] Later, however, in *United States v. National Lead Co.*,[583] the Court declared the issue concerning dedication and royalty-free licensing to be undecided.[584]

When certain joint R&D ventures and joint production ventures are reported in advance to the agencies, the plaintiffs challenging conduct (such as licensing) within the scope of such notification may recover only actual damages, plus costs (including reasonable attorneys' fees) and interest from the date of injury.[585]

Compulsory disclosure of know-how also has been ordered.[586] In doing so, however, courts have recognized the importance of secrecy to the property right.[587]

5. Counterclaims

Antitrust counterclaims are frequently filed in response to patent infringement actions. An antitrust counterclaim may or may not be compulsory.[588] In *Xerox Corp. v. SCM Corp.*,[589] the Third Circuit held that a patent infringement action was not a

---

product); United States v. Western Elec. Co., 1956 Trade Cas. (CCH) ¶ 68,246 (D.N.J. 1956) (partly royalty-free, partly at reasonable royalties, depending on identity of patentee); United States v. American Steel Foundries, 1955 Trade Cas. (CCH) ¶ 68,156 (N.D. Ohio 1955) (royalty-free licenses on existing patents).

579. *See, e.g.*, United States v. Greyhound Corp., 1957 Trade Cas. (CCH) ¶ 68,756, at 73,089 (N.D. Ill. 1957) (dedication of existing patents); United States v. General Elec. Co., 115 F. Supp. 835, 843-44 (D.N.J. 1953) (same); United States v. American Can Co., 1950-51 Trade Cas. (CCH) ¶ 62,679, at 63,972-73 (N.D. Cal. 1950) (royalty-free license).

580. *See, e.g.*, United States v. General Instrument Corp., 1953 Trade Cas. (CCH) ¶ 67,574 (D.N.J. 1953) (the government sought the dedication of defendants' patents; the court concluded that such drastic relief was unnecessary); *Imperial Chem. Indus.*, 105 F. Supp. at 225 ("We hold that in the circumstances before us, compulsory royalty free licensing may not be decreed in the absence of legislative authority and the sanction of explicit interpretation of existing statutes by higher courts affirmatively permitting such action."); United States v. Vehicular Parking, Ltd., 61 F. Supp. 656, 657 (D. Del. 1945) ("I am unable to agree with the government's reading of Hartford-Empire . . . , that the court has power to mandate a royalty-free license where the patent has been used as an instrument in violation of the anti-trust laws.").

581. 323 U.S. 386, *clarified*, 324 U.S. 570 (1945).

582. *Id.* at 415.

583. 332 U.S. 319 (1947).

584. *Id.* at 338; *see also* Data Gen. Corp. v. Grumman Sys. Support Corp., 761 F. Supp. 185, 194 (D. Mass. 1991) (noting that the remedy for a successful essential facilities claim based on refusal to grant an intellectual property license is compulsory licensing), *aff'd*, 36 F.3d 1147 (1st Cir. 1994).

585. *See* National Cooperative Research and Production Act, 15 U.S.C. §§ 4301-4305 (2000). *See also* part C.2 of Chapter IV.

586. *See, e.g.*, United States v. United Shoe Mach. Corp., 110 F. Supp. 295 (D. Mass. 1953), *aff'd per curiam*, 347 U.S. 521 (1954); United States v. General Elec. Co., 115 F. Supp. 835, 853-55 (D.N.J. 1953); United States v. Minnesota Mining & Mfg. Co., 1950-51 Trade Cas. (CCH) ¶ 62,724, at 64,115-16 (D. Mass. 1950); United States v. American Can Co., 1950-51 Trade Cas. (CCH) ¶ 62,679, at 63,974 (N.D. Cal. 1950).

587. *See, e.g.*, United States v. National Lead Co., 332 U.S. 319, 357-58 (1947); Imperial Chem. Indus. v. National Distillers & Chem. Corp., 342 F.2d 737 (2d Cir. 1965); United States v. Imperial Chem. Indus., 254 F. Supp. 685 (S.D.N.Y. 1966).

588. *See* FED. R. CIV. P. 13(a).

589. 576 F.2d 1057 (3d Cir. 1978).

compulsory counterclaim to a "massive antitrust suit" challenging "virtually every aspect of its business conduct."[590] Similarly, in *Hydranautics v. FilmTec Corp.*,[591] the Ninth Circuit held that it was permissible for a defendant in a patent infringement case to delay suing the plaintiff for predatory patent litigation until after the defendant had prevailed in the patent case.[592] Some courts have held, however, that antitrust claims are compulsory counterclaims in related patent infringement actions.[593]

Antitrust counterclaims also have been held to be compulsory where the complaint alleged copyright infringement and unfair trade practices, and the defendants claimed that the plaintiff's suit was "one of a series of harassing maneuvers designed to interfere with defendants' proper exploitation of rights."[594]

Under Federal Rule of Civil Procedure 42(b), infringement issues may be tried separately from antitrust counterclaims and misuse issues.[595]

---

590. *Id.* at 1061; *see also* Mercoid Corp. v. Mid-Continent Inv. Co., 320 U.S. 661, 670-71 (1944) (antitrust counterclaim not compulsory in patent infringement action); Tank Insulation Int'l v. Insultherm, Inc., 104 F.3d 83, 86-88 (5th Cir.) (antitrust counterclaim based on initiation of infringement action not compulsory), *cert. denied*, 522 U.S. 907 (1997). *But see* Longwood Mfg. v. Wheelabrator Clean Water Sys., 954 F. Supp. 17, 18 (D. Me. 1997) (following *Mercoid* while questioning the continuing validity of its holding); Boston Scientific Corp. v. Schneider (Europe) AG, 983 F. Supp. 245, 267 (D. Mass. 1997) (questioning the continuing validity of *Mercoid*).

591. 70 F.3d 533 (9th Cir. 1995).

592. *Id.* at 536-37.

593. *See, e.g.,* Critical-Vac Filtration Corp. v. Minuteman Int'l, Inc., 233 F.3d 697, 703 (2d Cir. 2000) (distinguishing *Mercoid* and finding antitrust claim is compulsory counterclaim when based on patentee's attempt to enforce an invalid patent), *cert. denied*, 121 S. Ct. 1958 (2001); Genentech, Inc. v. Regents of the Univ. of Cal., 143 F.3d 1446, 1456 (Fed. Cir. 1998) (affirming determination that federal antitrust claims were compulsory counterclaims in patent infringement suit), *judgment vacated on other grounds*, 527 U.S. 1031 (1999); American Packaging Corp. v. Golden Valley Microwave Foods, Inc., 1995-1 Trade Cas. (CCH) ¶ 71,009 (E.D. Pa. 1995) (antitrust counterclaim was compulsory in prior patent infringement action), *aff'd without op.*, No. 95-1386, 1996 U.S. App. LEXIS 12061 (3d Cir. Apr. 8, 1996).

594. United Artists Corp. v. Masterpiece Prods., 221 F.2d 213, 216 (2d Cir. 1955); *accord* Harley-Davidson Motor Co. v. Chrome Specialties, Inc., 173 F.R.D. 250, 252-53 (E.D. Wis. 1997) (antitrust claim based upon initiation of "frivolous" trademark litigation was compulsory).

595. *See, e.g.,* Triad Sys. Corp. v. Southeastern Express Co., 64 F.3d 1330, 1338 (9th Cir. 1995), *cert. denied*, 516 U.S. 1145 (1996); *In re* Innotron Diagnostics, 800 F.2d 1077, 1084-85 (Fed. Cir. 1986); Helene Curtis Indus. v. Church & Dwight Co., 560 F.2d 1325, 1334-37 (7th Cir. 1977), *cert. denied*, 434 U.S. 1070 (1978); Hewlett-Packard Co. v. Genrad, Inc., 882 F. Supp. 1141, 1158 (D. Mass. 1995); Components, Inc. v. Western Elec. Co., 318 F. Supp. 959, 965-68 (D. Me. 1970); Western Geophysical Co. of Am. v. Bolt Assocs., 50 F.R.D. 193 (D. Conn. 1970), *appeal dismissed*, 440 F.2d 765 (2d Cir. 1971); Henan Oil Tools, Inc. v. Engineering Enters., 262 F. Supp. 629 (S.D. Tex. 1966); Fischer & Porter Co. v. Sheffield Corp., 31 F.R.D. 534, 539-40 (D. Del. 1962); Zenith Radio Corp. v. Radio Corp. of Am., 106 F. Supp. 561, 576-77 (D. Del. 1952); Container Co. v. Carpenter Container Corp., 9 F.R.D. 89 (D. Del. 1949); *see also supra* note 570. *But cf.* ACS Communications v. Plantronics, Inc., No. CIV. 95-20294 SW, 1995 U.S. Dist. LEXIS 22188 (N.D. Cal. Dec. 1, 1995) (denying motion for separate trials).

CHAPTER XII

ANTITRUST AND INTERNATIONAL COMMERCE

A. Introduction

The application of U.S. antitrust laws to international trade or commerce raises a variety of special issues. First, this application often raises fundamental questions concerning national jurisdiction to prescribe rules of law governing persons and conduct beyond national borders. Second, the international dimension of economic activity sometimes calls for the application of special substantive rules not appropriate in the purely domestic context. Third, antitrust is but one of a number of national policies affecting international trade and these other national policies may at times be in tension with antitrust policies.[1] Fourth, the competition policies of other countries are not always in accord with U.S. antitrust policies and, even where they are, multinational coordination of enforcement poses challenging issues. This chapter discusses these and related issues.

B. Subject Matter Jurisdiction and Related Issues

1. Sherman Act

a.   JURISDICTION

The Sherman Act applies to "every contract, combination . . . or conspiracy, in restraint of trade" and to every person who shall "monopolize, or attempt to

---

1.   Apart from the Sherman, Clayton, Robinson-Patman, and Federal Trade Commission Acts, other U.S. competition or trade policy statutes applicable to foreign commerce include: the Omnibus Trade and Competitiveness Act of 1988, 19 U.S.C. §§ 2901-2906 (1994); the Export Trading Company Act of 1982, 15 U.S.C. §§ 4001-4021 (2000); the Webb-Pomerene Act, 15 U.S.C. §§ 61-66 (2000); the Wilson Tariff Act, 15 U.S.C. §§ 8-11 (2000); the Panama Canal Act, 15 U.S.C. § 31 (2000); § 801 of the Revenue Act, 15 U.S.C. §§ 71-77 (2000); § 337 of the Tariff Act of 1930, 19 U.S.C. § 1337 (1994); the countervailing duties law, 19 U.S.C. §§ 1671-1671h (1994); the antidumping provisions of the Trade Agreements Act of 1979, 19 U.S.C. §§ 1673-1677g (1994); §§ 301-306 of the Trade Act, 19 U.S.C. §§ 2411-2416 (1994); the antitrust provisions of the Shipping Act, 46 U.S.C. App. §§ 801-842 (1994); and the Merchant Marine Act of 1920, 46 U.S.C. App. § 885 (1994). The international policies of the Department of Justice (DOJ) and the Federal Trade Commission (FTC) are described in their joint guidelines. U.S. DEP'T OF JUSTICE & FEDERAL TRADE COMM'N, ANTITRUST ENFORCEMENT GUIDELINES FOR INTERNATIONAL OPERATIONS (1995) [hereinafter INTERNATIONAL ANTITRUST GUIDELINES], *reprinted in* 4 Trade Reg. Rep. (CCH) ¶ 13,107 *and* Appendix D to this treatise.

monopolize, or combine or conspire . . . to monopolize" trade or commerce "among the several States, or with foreign nations." Congress limited the scope of this language by enacting the Foreign Trade Antitrust Improvements Act of 1982 (FTAIA),[2] which amended the Sherman Act to preclude its application to conduct involving trade or commerce (other than import trade or commerce) with foreign nations unless two jurisdictional prerequisites are met. First, the conduct must have a "direct, substantial, and reasonably foreseeable" effect on domestic U.S. commerce or U.S. import trade, or on the export commerce of a person engaged in such commerce in the United States.[3] Second, the "direct, substantial, and reasonably foreseeable" effect on U.S. domestic or foreign commerce must "give rise to" a Sherman Act claim.[4]

Historically, Sherman Act jurisdiction over foreign trade or commerce has been interpreted in various ways by a number of courts. The issue first came before the Supreme Court in *American Banana Co. v. United Fruit Co.*,[5] where the Sherman Act was construed to be inapplicable to the defendant's inducement of a military seizure of property outside the United States. In rejecting the claim, Justice Holmes wrote:

> [T]he acts causing the damage were done, so far as appears, outside the jurisdiction of the United States . . . . It is surprising to hear it argued that they were governed by the act of Congress . . . . [T]he general and almost universal rule is that the character of an act as lawful or unlawful must be determined wholly by the law of the country where the act is done.[6]

This strict territorial interpretation of Sherman Act jurisdiction was eroded in subsequent cases[7] and then largely rejected in 1945 in *United States v. Aluminum Co. of America (Alcoa)*.[8] In *Alcoa*, the Second Circuit[9] held that the Sherman Act reached agreements entered into and consummated outside the United States by foreign companies "if they were intended to affect [U.S.] imports and did affect them."[10] Judge Learned Hand wrote that "it is settled law—as [the defendant] itself agrees—that any state may impose liabilities, even upon persons not within its allegiance, for conduct outside its borders that has consequences within its borders

---

2.　Pub. L. No. 97-290, title IV, § 402, 96 Stat. 1246 (1982), codified at 15 U.S.C. § 6a (2000).

3.　15 U.S.C. § 6a(1).

4.　15 U.S.C. § 6a(2).

5.　213 U.S. 347 (1909).

6.　*Id*. at 355-56 (citations omitted).

7.　*See, e.g.*, United States v. Sisal Sales Corp., 274 U.S. 268 (1927) (fact that control of production was aided by discriminatory legislation of foreign country did not prevent exercise of jurisdiction and punishment of forbidden results of the conspiracy within United States); Thomsen v. Cayser, 243 U.S. 66 (1917) (exercising jurisdiction with respect to combination formed abroad that was put into operation in United States and affected U.S. foreign commerce); United States v. Pacific & Arctic Ry. & Navigation Co., 228 U.S. 87 (1913) (exercising jurisdiction with respect to agreement between U.S. and Canadian firms to monopolize transportation routes partly in Canada); United States v. American Tobacco Co., 221 U.S. 106 (1911) (exercising jurisdiction with respect to contracts dividing world markets executed in the United Kingdom by U.S. and British companies doing business in United States).

8.　148 F.2d 416 (2d Cir. 1945).

9.　The case was certified by the Supreme Court to the Second Circuit for want of a quorum. *Id*. at 421.

10.　*Id*. at 444.

which the state reprehends; and these liabilities other states will ordinarily recognize."[11]

Notwithstanding the Second Circuit's view of the "settled law," *Alcoa*'s assertion of antitrust jurisdiction over wholly foreign conduct on the basis of the economic effects of that conduct within the United States proved controversial among foreign governments.[12] It was nevertheless adopted by most U.S. courts and validated by the Supreme Court in *Hartford Fire Insurance Co. v. California*: "[I]t is well established by now that the Sherman Act applies to foreign conduct that was meant to produce and did in fact produce some substantial effect in the United States."[13] This holding also has been extended to criminal proceedings. In *United States v. Nippon Paper Industries Co.*,[14] the First Circuit held that the Supreme Court's ruling in *Hartford Fire* that Congress intended the Sherman Act to apply to wholly extraterritorial conduct in some circumstances was controlling in the criminal context as well because the same statutory language creates both civil and criminal liability.[15]

After *Alcoa*, however, varying standards were developed for determining the magnitude and type of domestic effect necessary for jurisdiction under U.S. antitrust laws.[16] For example, in 1977, the Department of Justice adopted the enforcement

---

11. *Id.* at 443 (citations omitted).
12. The United Kingdom, for example, has described the extraterritorial application of U.S. law as "exorbitant." RESTATEMENT (THIRD) OF THE FOREIGN RELATIONS LAW OF THE UNITED STATES § 403 reporters' note 1 (1987) [hereinafter RESTATEMENT (THIRD)]; *see also* ABA SECTION OF ANTITRUST LAW, REPORT OF THE SPECIAL COMMITTEE ON INTERNATIONAL ANTITRUST 150 (1991) (noting that nations whose nationals have been sued in U.S. courts have complained of extraterritorial jurisdiction).
13. 509 U.S. 764, 796 (1993) (finding subject matter jurisdiction where alleged activity of foreign reinsurers outside United States produced a substantial effect in United States). Other formulations for finding subject matter jurisdiction have been devised. *See, e.g.,* Fleischmann Distilling Corp. v. Distillers Co., 395 F. Supp. 221, 226 (S.D.N.Y. 1975) ("direct and material adverse effect on interstate or foreign commerce"); Todhunter-Mitchell & Co. v. Anheuser-Busch, Inc., 383 F. Supp. 586, 587 (E.D. Pa. 1974) ("flow of commerce . . . was directly restrained"); Sabre Shipping Corp. v. American President Lines, 285 F. Supp. 949, 953 (S.D.N.Y. 1968) ("'directly and materially affect . . . foreign commerce'") (citation omitted), *cert. denied*, 407 F.2d 173 (2d Cir.), *cert. denied*, 395 U.S. 922 (1969); United States v. Watchmakers of Switzerland Info. Ctr., Inc., 1963 Trade Cas. (CCH) ¶ 70,600, at 77,456 (S.D.N.Y. 1962) ("direct and substantial restraint on interstate and foreign commerce of the United States"), *order modified*, 1965 Trade Cas. (CCH) ¶ 71,352 (S.D.N.Y. 1965); United States v. General Elec. Co., 82 F. Supp. 753, 891 (D.N.J. 1949) ("direct and substantial effect upon trade").
14. 109 F.3d 1 (1st Cir. 1997), *cert. denied*, 522 U.S. 1144 (1998).
15. *See id.* at 6. The court noted that application of the Sherman Act to foreign conduct in a criminal context was "uncharted terrain" and was "aware of no authority directly on point." *Id.* at 4. The court therefore relied on *Hartford Fire* and canons of statutory interpretation, concluding that "reading the language in a manner consonant with a prior Supreme Court decision is irresistible." *Id.* at 5. On remand, however, the district court granted an acquittal based on lack of jurisdiction, holding that in price-fixing cases based entirely on foreign conduct, the government is subject to a higher standard when proving substantial impact on the U.S. market. 62 F. Supp. 2d 173 (D. Mass. 1999). The court adopted a "'per se plus' test, adding to the traditional analysis the requirement that the government show . . . a substantial connection to the U.S. market." *Id.* at 195.
16. *See, e.g.,* Timberlane Lumber Co. v. Bank of Am. Nat'l Trust & Sav. Ass'n, 749 F.2d 1378 (9th Cir. 1984) (in addition to finding effect on U.S. commerce of the type and magnitude to be cognizable as a violation of antitrust laws, before exercising jurisdiction courts weigh comity and fairness factors, including the relative significance of the effects on the United States as compared to those elsewhere), *cert. denied*, 472 U.S. 1032 (1985); National Bank of Canada v. Interbank Card Ass'n, 666 F.2d 6 (2d Cir. 1981) (jurisdiction existed only where effect upon U.S. commerce was foreseeable and appreciable). In enacting the FTAIA, Congress adopted an approach that

position that the Sherman Act applied only to transactions that had a "substantial and foreseeable effect on U.S. commerce."[17]

Motivated in part by the goal of articulating a uniform test for determining whether U.S. antitrust jurisdiction exists over particular international conduct, in 1982 Congress passed the FTAIA, which established an objective standard for determining the existence of "intended effects" under *Alcoa*.[18] As noted above, the FTAIA eliminates U.S. antitrust jurisdiction over conduct involving trade or commerce (other than import trade or import commerce)[19] with foreign nations unless "(1) such conduct has a direct, substantial and reasonably foreseeable effect (A) on [domestic or import commerce]; or (B) on export trade or export commerce . . . of a person engaged in such trade or commerce in the United States; and (2) such effect gives rise to a [Sherman Act claim]."[20]

---

closely followed that of the Second Circuit in *National Bank of Canada*. Various tests of antitrust subject matter jurisdiction that developed among the circuits are described in *Zenith Radio Corp. v. Matsushita Elec. Indus. Co.*, 494 F. Supp. 1161, 1177-89 (E.D. Pa. 1980), *aff'd in part and rev'd in part sub nom. In re* Japanese Elec. Prods. Antitrust Litig., 723 F.2d 238 (3d Cir. 1983), *rev'd sub nom.* Matsushita Elec. Indus. Co. v. Zenith Radio Corp., 475 U.S. 574 (1986).

17. *See* U.S. DEP'T OF JUSTICE, ANTITRUST GUIDE FOR INTERNATIONAL OPERATIONS (1977) [hereinafter 1977 INTERNATIONAL ANTITRUST GUIDE], *reprinted in* 4 Trade Reg. Rep. (CCH) ¶ 13,110, at 20,645.

18. H.R. REP. NO. 97-686, at 2-3 (1982), *reprinted in* 1982 U.S.C.C.A.N. 2487, 2487-88. A second impetus to the passage of the FTAIA was a desire to ensure that U.S. antitrust laws did not act as a "barrier to joint export activities that promote efficiencies in the export of American goods and services." *Id.* at 2, 1982 U.S.C.C.A.N. at 2487.

19. Because conduct involving "import trade or import commerce" is excepted from the FTAIA, the judicially created "effects" test continues to determine whether jurisdiction exists over such conduct. *See* Eskofot A/S v. E.I. duPont de Nemours & Co., 872 F. Supp. 81, 85 (S.D.N.Y. 1995) (because the "Sherman Act continue[s] to apply to import trade and import commerce" and "plaintiff's pleading alleges an impact on import trade and import commerce . . . [r]ather than the FTAIA's 'direct, substantial and reasonably foreseeable' standard, the Court must determine whether the challenged conduct has, or is intended to have, any anticompetitive effect upon United States commerce"). As explained by one district court, the "import trade or import commerce" exception has consistently been applied "only to domestic importers," thus exempting from the FTAIA "those claims that involve the business of United States firms that import goods into the United States and not all claims involving the export of goods to the United States from abroad." United Phosphorus Ltd. v. Angus Chem. Co., 131 F. Supp. 2d 1003, 1023 (N.D. Ill. 2001). *See also* Kruman v. Christie's Int'l PLC, 129 F. Supp. 2d 620, 627 (S.D.N.Y. 2001) (the import trade and commerce exception applies to cases where the challenged conduct involves "the trade in and subsequent movement of the goods that were purchased and sold").

20. 15 U.S.C. § 6a (2000). Notwithstanding the FTAIA's explicit language permitting the exercise of jurisdiction over conduct impacting U.S. export commerce, the DOJ initially took the position that, as an enforcement matter, it "is concerned only with adverse effects on competition that would harm U.S. consumers by reducing output or raising prices." U.S. DEP'T OF JUSTICE, ANTITRUST ENFORCEMENT GUIDELINES FOR INTERNATIONAL OPERATIONS § 4.1 n.159 (1988) [hereinafter 1988 INTERNATIONAL ANTITRUST GUIDELINES], *reprinted in* 4 Trade Reg. Rep. (CCH) ¶ 13,109. In 1992, the DOJ officially rescinded that enforcement policy and announced it would take action against conduct overseas that restrains U.S. exports where the jurisdiction requirements under the FTAIA and any other prerequisites to enforcement action are met. DOJ Press Release (Apr. 3, 1992). This policy is incorporated by reference in the DOJ's current enforcement guidelines. *See* INTERNATIONAL ANTITRUST GUIDELINES, *supra* note 1, § 3.122 n.62. In a subsequent investigation, the DOJ issued civil investigative demands (CIDs) seeking information regarding the control of performance rights societies abroad that were allegedly engaging in price fixing and other unfair practices that impeded U.S. music video programming broadcasters from exporting their services. *See* United States v. Time Warner, Inc., 1997-1 Trade Cas. (CCH) ¶ 71,702 (D.D.C. 1997). The district court enforced the CIDs, holding that the FTAIA does not exempt conduct that

Where jurisdiction is based only on subparagraph (B) of the statute, the antitrust laws apply to that conduct "only for injury to export business in the United States."[21] Even where the allegedly unlawful conduct takes place in the United States, the courts interpret the language of the FTAIA literally,[22] holding that conduct lacking the requisite domestic effect is not within the subject matter jurisdiction of the U.S. antitrust laws.[23] Where the conduct at issue takes place wholly in foreign markets, the requisite domestic effects can be in the form of injuries to U.S. exporters resulting from such conduct, provided that the injuries to U.S. exporters meet the FTAIA's direct, substantial, and reasonably foreseeable standard.[24]

Courts have provided some contours to the direct, substantial, and reasonably foreseeable standard. A domestic effect is direct if it "'follows as an immediate consequence of the defendant's activity.'"[25] A domestic effect may be substantial if

---

has the effect of injuring U.S. exporters, even if that conduct has no spillover effect on domestic markets. *Id.* at 78,991.

21. 15 U.S.C. § 6a. *See* The 'In' Porters, S.A. v. Hanes Printables, Inc., 663 F. Supp. 494, 500 (M.D.N.C. 1987) (holding French distributor of U.S. goods could not recover for injury suffered in France and could not piggyback onto the alleged injury of U.S. exporters; plaintiff itself had to be within the class of injured U.S. exporters).

22. *See, e.g.*, United Phosphorus, Ltd. v. Angus Chem. Co., No. 94-C-2078, 1994 U.S. Dist. LEXIS 14786, at *22 (N.D. Ill. Oct. 18, 1994) ("conduct on American soil is not always sufficient to prove effect on domestic commerce because it is the situs of the effect, not the conduct, which is crucial"; nevertheless, "broad, conclusory allegations . . . of antitrust injury in the United States" sufficient to withstand motion to dismiss for lack of jurisdiction under the FTAIA). *But see* Filetech S.A. v. France Telecom S.A., 157 F.3d 922 (2d Cir. 1998) ("sparse and largely conclusory allegations" of impact on competition in the United States were insufficient to establish jurisdiction; case remanded to the trial court to look beyond the pleadings to resolve the disputed factual questions of the nature and amount of commercial activity in the United States), *on remand*, 2001-1 Trade Cas. (CCH) ¶ 73,228, at 90,018 (S.D.N.Y. 2001) (dismissing claim under the Foreign Sovereign Immunities Act and stating in dicta that the FTAIA could not be satisfied where defendant made minimal U.S. sales, did not solicit U.S. customers, and did not obtain U.S. sales by placing its directory over the Internet).

23. *See, e.g.*, McGlinchy v. Shell Chem. Co., 845 F.2d 802, 814, 815 (9th Cir. 1988) (antitrust claim dismissed for lack of subject matter jurisdiction where plaintiff failed to allege requisite effect under the FTAIA); *Kruman*, 129 F. Supp. 2d at 627 (observing that the FTAIA applies to conspiracies that operate both domestically and abroad and dismissing claim lacking the requisite domestic effect); Optimum, S.A. v. Legent Corp., 926 F. Supp. 530 (W.D. Pa. 1996) (antitrust claims dismissed for lack of subject matter jurisdiction where actions of U.S. corporation's wholly owned subsidiary in Argentina did not have "the requisite effect on commerce in the United States"); Caribbean Broad. Sys. v. Cable & Wireless PLC, 1996-1 Trade Cas. (CCH) ¶ 71,263, at 76,150 (D.D.C. 1995) ("'the concern of the antitrust laws is protection of American consumers and American exporters, not foreign consumers or producers'") (quoting PHILLIP E. AREEDA & HERBERT HOVENKAMP, ANTITRUST LAW 305 (1993 Supp.)), *rev'd in part*, 148 F.3d 1080 (D.C. Cir. 1998); Coors Brewing Co. v. Miller Brewing Co., 889 F. Supp. 1394, 1398 (D. Colo. 1995) ("with the exception of claims brought by domestic importers, the Sherman Act will not apply to conduct affecting foreign markets, consumers or producers unless there is also a direct, substantial, and reasonably foreseeable effect on the domestic market"); McElderry v. Cathay Pac. Airways, 678 F. Supp. 1071, 1077 (S.D.N.Y. 1988) (antitrust claims dismissed for failure to meet requirements of the FTAIA and for reasons of comity); Eurim-Pharm GmbH v. Pfizer Inc., 593 F. Supp. 1102, 1107 (S.D.N.Y. 1984) (district court lacked jurisdiction when plaintiff failed to establish anticompetitive effect under the FTAIA).

24. *See* Access Telecom Inc. v. MCI Telecommuns. Corp., 197 F.3d 694 (5th Cir.) (finding subject matter jurisdiction over actions in Mexico by Mexican long-distance telephone company that prevented U.S. company from exporting long-distance service to Mexican consumers), *cert. denied*, 531 U.S. 917 (2000).

25. Lantec, Inc. v. Novell, Inc., No. 2:95-CV-97, 2000 U.S. Dist. LEXIS 19905, at *16 (D. Utah Sept. 15, 2000) (quoting *Filetech S.A*, 157 F.3d at 931). *Cf. Optimum*, 926 F. Supp. at 533 ("an

it involves a sufficient volume of U.S. commerce and is not a mere "spillover effect."[26] And although the standard articulated by Judge Hand in *Alcoa* refers to "intended effects," the FTAIA employs the phrase "reasonably foreseeable." The legislative history also reflects that the standard adopted by Congress is "an objective one . . . [designed] to avoid—at least at the jurisdictional stage—inquiries into the actual, subjective motives of defendants."[27] The legislative history formulates the test, therefore, as "whether the effects [of the alleged unlawful conduct] would have been evident to a reasonable person making practical business judgments, [and] not whether actual knowledge or intent can be shown."[28]

In 1995, the Department of Justice and the Federal Trade Commission released joint *Antitrust Enforcement Guidelines for International Operations* (*International Antitrust Guidelines*).[29] The *International Antitrust Guidelines* replaced the 1988 international antitrust guidelines (1988 *International Antitrust Guidelines*)[30] and set forth the enforcement agencies' current policies and priorities in this area. The *International Antitrust Guidelines* outline the positions of the enforcement agencies with respect to jurisdiction over several types of conduct and provide illustrative examples.

With respect to subject matter jurisdiction, the *International Antitrust Guidelines* state that "anticompetitive conduct that affects U.S. domestic or foreign commerce may violate the U.S. antitrust laws regardless of where such conduct occurs or the nationality of the parties involved."[31] For example, as to conduct involving import commerce, the *International Antitrust Guidelines* refer to the Supreme Court's 1993 decision in *Hartford Fire Insurance Co. v. California*[32] and state that "imports into the United States by definition affect the U.S. domestic market directly, and will, therefore, almost invariably satisfy the intent part of the *Hartford Fire* test. Whether they in fact produce the requisite substantial effects will depend on the facts of each case."[33] In an accompanying illustrative example involving a cartel formed by foreign producers with no U.S. subsidiaries or production to raise the prices of products imported into the United States, the *International Antitrust Guidelines*

allegation that income flows between corporations [impacted by the challenged conduct] is insufficient to establish the requisite domestic effect").

26. *See, e.g.*, United Phosphorus, Ltd. v. Angus Chem. Co., 131 F. Supp. 2d 1003, 1011-12 (N.D. Ill. 2001) (finding volume of impacted U.S. sales inadequate and relying on Eurim-Pharm GmbH v. Pfizer, Inc., 593 F. Supp. 1102, 1106-07 (S.D.N.Y. 1984), for the proposition that a spillover U.S. effect is inadequate).

27. H.R. REP. NO. 97-686, *supra* note 18, at 9; *see also McElderry*, 678 F. Supp. at 1077; *Eurim-Pharm GmbH*, 593 F. Supp. at 1106 n.4.

28. H.R. REP. NO. 97-686, *supra* note 18, at 9.

29. INTERNATIONAL ANTITRUST GUIDELINES, *supra* note 1.

30. 1988 INTERNATIONAL ANTITRUST GUIDELINES, *supra* note 20.

31. INTERNATIONAL ANTITRUST GUIDELINES, *supra* note 1, § 3.11.

32. 509 U.S. 764 (1993).

33. INTERNATIONAL ANTITRUST GUIDELINES, *supra* note 1, § 3.11. *See also* Caribbean Broad. Sys. v. Cable & Wireless PLC, 148 F.3d 1080 (D.C. Cir. 1998) (holding that FTAIA conferred jurisdiction over a foreign radio station's complaint alleging anticompetitive conduct by another foreign radio station based on injuries to U.S. advertisers); Betterware PLC v. Tupperware Corp., 1998-1 Trade Cas. (CCH) ¶ 72,158 (S.D.N.Y. 1998) (allegations that defendant filed sham trademark actions abroad to keep foreign plaintiff out of the U.S. market were sufficient to support jurisdiction in civil suit because this conduct had a foreseeable effect on U.S. commerce); *but see* S. Megga Telecommuns. v. Lucent Tech., C.A. No. 96-357-SUR, 1997 U.S. Dist. LEXIS 2312 (D. Del. Feb. 14, 1997) (dismissing foreign manufacturers' complaint alleging attempt to monopolize U.S. market for cordless telephones, holding that FTAIA requires injury to a U.S. plaintiff).

indicate that Sherman Act jurisdiction is clear because there was an intended and foreseeable effect on U.S. commerce.[34]

The *International Antitrust Guidelines* refer to the FTAIA in considering conduct involving foreign commerce other than (direct) imports.[35] In Illustrative Example B, a foreign cartel sells its products into the United States only through unrelated foreign intermediaries, knowing that the goods will be imported into the United States. The *International Antitrust Guidelines* state that the FTAIA standard of direct, substantial, and reasonably foreseeable effects on U.S. domestic or import commerce will be applied in these circumstances. Also relevant, according to the agencies, is the Supreme Court's test for jurisdiction in cases involving interstate commerce articulated in *Summit Health, Ltd. v. Pinhas*,[36] which looks to the "potential harm that would ensue if the conspiracy were successful, not . . . whether the actual conduct in furtherance of the conspiracy had in fact the prohibited effect upon interstate or foreign commerce."[37]

As noted above, to establish subject matter jurisdiction under the FTAIA, a plaintiff must also show that "such effect"—i.e., the direct, substantial, and reasonably foreseeable anticompetitive domestic effect—"gives rise to" a Sherman Act claim.[38] Courts have long read paragraph (2) of the FTAIA to provide "that the effect required for jurisdictional nexus must be an anticompetitive effect in the domestic market."[39] Recently, several courts squarely addressed whether paragraph (2) requires that the plaintiff's injury be tied to the anticompetitive domestic effect.[40] Those courts that have addressed the issue, including one appellate court, have held that the FTAIA does not confer jurisdiction over all injuries arising out of a course of conduct that has a direct, substantial, and reasonably foreseeable U.S. effect. Rather, jurisdiction exists only when the injury for which the plaintiff seeks redress arises from the direct, substantial, and reasonably foreseeable U.S. effect.[41]

34. INTERNATIONAL ANTITRUST GUIDELINES, *supra* note 1, Illustrative Example A.
35. *Id.* § 3.12.
36. 500 U.S. 322, 330-31 (1991).
37. INTERNATIONAL ANTITRUST GUIDELINES, *supra* note 1, § 3.121; *id.* Illustrative Example B.
38. 15 U.S.C. § 6a(2) (2000).
39. *See* Liamuiga Tours v. Travel Impressions, Ltd., 617 F. Supp. 920, 924 (E.D.N.Y. 1985) (citing H.R. REP. NO. 97-686, *supra* note 18, at 11-12, *reprinted in* 1982 U.S.C.C.A.N. 2487, 2496-97). *See also* McElderry v. Cathay Pac. Airways, Ltd., 678 F. Supp. 1071, 1077-78 (S.D.N.Y. 1988) (dismissing an American consumer's antitrust claim, in part, because the alleged domestic injury was a monetary injury to herself and other similarly situated plaintiffs, and not to the U.S. market or U.S. competition).
40. *See* Den Norske Stats Oljeselskap As v. HeereMac Vof, 241 F.3d 420, 429 & n.13 (5th Cir. 2001) (noting that prior to its decision, no circuit court and only three district courts had interpreted paragraph (2) of the FTAIA); *cf. In re* Copper Antitrust Litig., 117 F. Supp. 2d 875, 863 (W.D. Wis. 2000) (observing that prior to the passage of the FTAIA, "courts had no occasion to address" whether plaintiff's injury must be tied to the anticompetitive domestic effect "because in each [pre-FTAIA] case, the plaintiffs' injuries arose out of the same effects experienced by the markets").
41. *See Den Norske*, 241 F.3d at 429; Kruman v. Christie's Int'l PLC, 129 F. Supp. 2d 620, 625 (S.D.N.Y. 2001) ("[T]he FTAIA permits suit . . . only where the conduct complained of had 'direct, substantial and reasonably foreseeable effects' in the United States and the effects giving rise to jurisdiction also are the basis for the alleged injury."); *In re* Microsoft Corp. Antitrust Litig., 127 F. Supp. 2d 702, 715 (D. Md. 2001) ("foreign consumers who have not participated in any way in the U.S. market have no right to institute a Sherman Act claim" arising out of defendant's alleged worldwide monopolistic conduct); *In re Copper Antitrust Litig.*, 117 F. Supp. 2d at 888 ("Unless [plaintiff's] injury arises out of an effect on an American market, there is no jurisdictional nexus that allows the United States to apply its laws to extraterritorial conduct."); *cf.* Turicento,

In *Den Norske Stats Oljeselskap As v. HeereMac Vof*,[42] the Fifth Circuit considered an alleged conspiracy to fix bids and allocate customers, territories, and projects for heavy-lift barge services in the Gulf of Mexico, the North Sea, and the Far East. The foreign plaintiff, however, operated and allegedly sustained injury only in the North Sea. In determining whether the district court properly found no subject matter jurisdiction, the Fifth Circuit held that the first prong of the FTAIA's jurisdictional test was satisfied by the plaintiff's allegation that the conspiracy caused U.S. purchasers to pay artificially inflated prices for heavy-lift services in the Gulf of Mexico and artificially inflated oil prices.[43] Relying on the plain language and legislative history of the FTAIA, as well as the limited body of case law, the Fifth Circuit nonetheless affirmed the district court's dismissal of the plaintiff's Sherman Act claim because the plaintiff's injury did not "arise from" or "stem from" the alleged anticompetitive domestic effect.[44]

The Fifth Circuit expressly rejected the plaintiff's contention that paragraph (2) of the FTAIA simply required "that there be some anticompetitive, harmful effect in [the United States]—not just a positive or neutral domestic effect."[45] That interpretation, the Fifth Circuit reasoned, would run contrary to Congress's explicit intent to "'require that the "effect" providing the jurisdictional nexus must also be the basis for the injury alleged under the antitrust laws.'"[46] The court concluded that simply requiring that the defendants' domestic conduct give rise to an antitrust claim was an overly expansive reading of the FTAIA, which would encourage foreign plaintiffs "to flock to United States federal courts" to recover treble damages.[47] Thus, "regardless of the situs of the plaintiff's injury" and whether some of the

---

S.A. v. American Airlines, Inc., 152 F. Supp. 2d 829, 833 (E.D. Pa. 2001) ("plain language of the FTAIA precludes subject matter jurisdiction over claims by foreign plaintiffs against defendants where the situs of the injury is overseas and that injury arises from effects in a non-domestic market"); United Phosphorus, Ltd. v. Angus Chem. Co., 131 F. Supp. 2d 1003, 1009 (N.D. Ill. 2001) (the "alleged conduct underlying plaintiffs' claims can have had no effect on any United States commerce").

42.   241 F.3d 420 (5th Cir. 2001).

43.   *Id.* at 422, 426-27. Although the plaintiff exported a substantial volume of oil into the United States, it did not allege any injury to itself derived from those exports. *Id.* at 422 n.4.

44.   *Id.* at 421, 427. Although acknowledging that a "close relationship" may exist between the domestic injury and the plaintiff's claim, i.e., high service prices in the Gulf of Mexico and high service prices in the North Sea, the court stated that the FTAIA sets a higher standard. *Id.* at 427. *See also In re Copper Antitrust Litig.*, 117 F. Supp. 2d at 879, 886-87 (it is not enough that plaintiff traded in a foreign market closely tied to U.S. markets and that "[b]y artificially driving up copper prices on the [London Metal Exchange], where 95% of the world's copper futures are traded, defendants directly and predictably increased prices . . . in the United States").

45.   *Den Norske*, 241 F.3d at 425. In dissent, Judge Higginbotham accepted the plaintiff's contention, emphasizing that the FTAIA uses the indefinite article, "a claim," and reasoning that requiring the domestic effect to "give rise" to a plaintiff's particular injury would render the FTAIA's final proviso redundant. *See id.* at 432-33. The majority, however, found no redundancy because it interpreted the final proviso to add an additional requirement that recovery for an injury suffered in export commerce under paragraph 1(b) be limited "to injuries occurring in the United States." *Id.* at 426.

46.   *Den Norske*, 241 F.3d at 426 (quoting H.R. REP. NO. 97-686, *supra* note 18, at 12, *reprinted in* 1982 U.S.C.C.A.N. at 2497). *See also* Kruman v. Christie's Int'l PLC, 129 F. Supp. 2d 620, 623 (S.D.N.Y. 2001) (Congress never intended "to establish an antitrust regime to cover the world").

47.   *Den Norske*, 241 F.3d at 427-28. *Cf. Kruman*, 129 F. Supp. 2d at 625 (dismissing claim even though "'conduct' [allegedly] took place in substantial part in the United States," because it is not the overall course of conduct but "[t]he precise acts that caused injury" that are the focus of the jurisdictional inquiry under paragraph (2) of the FTAIA).

anticompetitive conduct took place in the United States, the necessary step is to determine whether the plaintiff's injury arose "from the anticompetitive effects on United States commerce."[48]

Most district courts that have interpreted paragraph (2) of the FTAIA have done so in the context of an alleged global conspiracy, and have concluded, as the Fifth Circuit did in *Den Norske*, that "[t]he assumed existence of a single, unified, global conspiracy does not relieve [a plaintiff] of its burden of alleging that its injury arose from the conspiracy's proscribed effects on United States commerce."[49] Where "at least some aspect of the [plaintiff's individual] sales transaction took place in the United States," however, some courts have held that the jurisdictional nexus is sufficiently alleged to withstand a motion to dismiss.[50]

---

48. *Den Norske*, 241 F.3d at 427-28. (reasoning that the inquiry, framed as such, "produces the precise result intended by Congress—that 'foreign purchasers should enjoy the protection of [U.S.] antitrust laws in the domestic marketplace, just as [U.S.] citizens do'") (quoting H.R. REP. NO. 97-686, *supra* note 18, at 10-11). *See also In re* Microsoft Corp. Antitrust Litig., 127 F. Supp. 2d 702, 715 (D. Md. 2001) (analyzing the same provision of the legislative history and finding intent was to protect foreign purchasers in the U.S. domestic marketplace and not in foreign marketplaces).

49. *Den Norske*, 241 F.3d at 427 n.24. In *Kruman*, the court dismissed the claims of foreign and domestic plaintiffs who purchased goods in Christie's and Sotheby's auctions in London because, although plaintiffs' damages were "influenced by a conspiracy with important U.S. elements," those damages arose out of "entirely foreign transactions" in a foreign market. 129 F. Supp. 2d at 627. The plaintiffs had claimed that some of the products were displayed and most of the anticompetitive conduct occurred in the United States, that most of the auction houses' revenue was derived from U.S. sales, that many class members were U.S. citizens, and that the auction services market is international. *Id.* at 622-23. In *In re Copper Antitrust Litig.*, the defendants allegedly had conspired to corner the market in copper for immediate delivery on the London Metal Exchange (LME), thereby artificially increasing LME copper prices. 117 F. Supp. 2d at 878-79. Although the same price inflation that caused the plaintiffs' injury on the LME also caused price inflation in the U.S. markets, the plaintiffs' claim was dismissed because "it was not those [latter] effects that injured plaintiffs." *Id.* at 887. In *In re Microsoft Corp. Antitrust Litig.*, the court dismissed the claims of foreign plaintiffs who had purchased Microsoft software product licenses abroad at allegedly inflated prices. 127 F. Supp. 2d at 715-16. Although the plaintiffs alleged that Microsoft's monopolistic conduct was intentionally and necessarily international so that Microsoft could maintain its domestic U.S. monopoly, the key fact leading to dismissal was that the plaintiffs did not participate in any way in a U.S. market. *Id. See also* Sniado v. Bank Austria AG, No. 00 Civ. 9123 (AGS), 2001 U.S. Dist. LEXIS 19800 (S.D.N.Y. Nov. 30, 2001) (dismissing claims under FTAIA of conspiracy to fix foreign exchange rates); Ferromin Int'l Trade Corp. v. UCAR Int'l, Inc., 153 F. Supp. 2d 700, 702, 705 (E.D. Pa. 2001) (FTAIA permits jurisdiction only when the "anticompetitive effect on the domestic marketplace gave rise to [plaintiffs'] injuries" and dismissing claims seeking recovery for purchases of graphite electrodes that "had no connection whatsoever to the United States"); Empagran S.A. v. F. Hoffman-La Roche, Ltd., Civ. No. 00-1686 (TFH), 2001 U.S. Dist. LEXIS 20910, at *5 (D.D.C. June 7, 2001) (dismissing claim of foreign plaintiffs arising out of global vitamins price-fixing conspiracy because plaintiffs' "precise injuries" did not stem from artificially inflated U.S. vitamin prices, but from vitamins purchased "for delivery outside the United States" and that were not otherwise connected with U.S. commerce); *In re* Vitamins Antitrust Litig., 2001-2 Trade Cas. (CCH) ¶ 73,325, at 90,852 (D.D.C. 2001) ("plaintiffs must also allege that the injuries which they seek to remedy 'arise' from an anticompetitive effect of defendants' conduct on U.S. commerce").

50. *See In re Microsoft Corp. Antitrust Litig.*, 127 F. Supp. 2d at 715 (but finding those facts not alleged in that case). *Cf. Ferromin Int'l Trade Corp.*, 153 F. Supp. 2d at 706 (plaintiffs' allegation that their purchases of graphite electrodes were manufactured and more importantly invoiced in the United States "satisfies the causal requirement that these . . . plaintiffs were injured as the result of higher prices for graphite electrodes in the United States market"); *In re Vitamins Antitrust Litig.*, 2001-2 Trade Cas. (CCH) ¶ 73,325, at 90,852 & n.3 (allegations sufficient under the FTAIA where U.S. companies and their foreign subsidiaries claimed their substantial purchases of "vitamins for delivery both in the United States and abroad [were] part of a global procurement strategy

b.   STANDING

Under Section 4 of the Clayton Act, only persons or corporations injured while trading in U.S. foreign or domestic commerce have standing to bring claims for antitrust violations involving foreign commerce.[51]   In *de Atucha v. Commodity Exchange*,[52] the district court held that plaintiffs who traded exclusively on a foreign market did not have standing under U.S. antitrust law.   Similarly, the district court in *Galavan Supplements, Ltd. v. Archer Daniels Midland Co.*[53] dismissed a class action suit filed by persons and entities outside the United States who purchased citric acid from the defendants' overseas facilities, holding that the plaintiffs were neither consumers nor competitors in the U.S. market and therefore had no standing under the U.S. antitrust laws.[54]   In *United Phosphorus, Ltd. v. Angus Chemical Co.*,[55] the district court held that the foreign plaintiffs had standing to sue because their alleged injury was partially suffered in the United States where they had intended to enter the market but were thwarted by the defendants' actions.

In actions involving U.S. export trade, the FTAIA permits recovery only for "injury to export business in the United States."   Therefore, to have standing to sue under U.S. antitrust law, a plaintiff must demonstrate not only the requisite effect on U.S. export trade but also that it is within the class of injured U.S. exporters.[56]

---

formulated and directed by United States parent corporations" and caused direct and ultimate "financial injury in the United States").

51.   *See, e.g., Empagran S.A.*, 2001 U.S. Dist. LEXIS 20910 (reserving ruling on standing pending amended complaint where domestic plaintiffs had provided insufficient detail regarding the transactions at issue for the court to determine whether plaintiffs "were competitors or consumers in the U.S. domestic market"); Information Resources, Inc. v. Dun & Bradstreet Corp., 127 F. Supp. 2d 411, 417 (S.D.N.Y. 2001) (despite U.S. company's allegation that it performed a "unitary function" with its foreign subsidiaries and suffered diminished demand for its U.S. services, U.S. company had no standing to recover for those diminished services as they resulted from injuries sustained by foreign affiliates in foreign markets); Lantec, Inc. v. Novell, Inc., No. 2:95-CV-97, 2000 U.S. Dist. LEXIS 19905, at *18-19 (D. Utah Sept. 15, 2000) (plaintiff that is not a participant in the relevant U.S. market cannot establish standing by showing that its injury is "inextricably intertwined" with a U.S. domestic injury); Transnor (Berm.) Ltd. v. BP N. Am. Petroleum, 738 F. Supp. 1472, 1476 (S.D.N.Y. 1990); de Atucha v. Commodity Exch., 608 F. Supp. 510, 517-18 (S.D.N.Y. 1985). For a detailed discussion of standing requirements under § 4 of the Clayton Act, 15 U.S.C. § 15 (2000), see part C of Chapter X.

52.   608 F. Supp. 510, 518 (S.D.N.Y. 1985) ("Congress did not contemplate recovery under the antitrust laws by an individual who traded, and was injured entirely outside of United States commerce.").

53.   No. C97-3259 FMS, 1997 U.S. Dist. LEXIS 18585 (N.D. Cal. Nov. 18, 1997).

54.   *Id.* at *4. The defendants had already settled a class action brought on behalf of those who directly purchased citric acid from the defendants' U.S. facilities. *Id.* at *1. Plaintiffs have acquired U.S. antitrust standing where the international transactions in which they were involved had even very slight ties to U.S. commerce, particularly when those transactions have been able to avoid the "exclusively foreign" label because the market traded upon was deemed to be located in the United States. In *Transnor (Berm.) Ltd.*, 738 F. Supp. at 1476, the location of the trading market was the relevant consideration; the location of the production, delivery, and contract points were considered much less relevant where the trading market itself was considered a U.S. market. *Cf. In re Copper Antitrust Litig.*, 117 F. Supp. 2d at 886-87 (despite alleged substantial nexus between the LME and U.S. copper futures market, plaintiff trading on LME traded only on foreign market because that market "is located in London and all but one of its brokers have offices in England").

55.   No. 94-C-2078, 1994 U.S. Dist. LEXIS 14786 (N.D. Ill. Oct. 13, 1994).

56.   *See* United Phosphorous, Ltd. v. Angus Chem. Ltd., 131 F. Supp. 2d 1003, 1019 (N.D. Ill. 2001) (foreign plaintiffs could not establish FTAIA jurisdiction over "export-related injuries" suffered by a U.S. plaintiff); The 'In' Porters, S.A. v. Hanes Printables, Inc., 663 F. Supp. 494, 500 (M.D.N.C.

c. COMITY CONSIDERATIONS

Prior to the enactment of the FTAIA, some courts had supplemented the *Alcoa* "effects" test by requiring an analysis of international comity and other factors.[57] A leading decision was *Timberlane Lumber Co. v. Bank of America National Trust & Savings Ass'n*,[58] in which the Ninth Circuit stated that the "effects test by itself is incomplete because it fails to consider other nations' interests" and because it fails to take into account the relationship between the actors involved and the United States.[59] The court therefore set forth three requirements for Sherman Act subject matter jurisdiction, explicitly including principles of international comity: (1) "that there be *some* effect—actual or intended—on American foreign commerce before the federal courts may legitimately exercise subject matter jurisdiction"; (2) that the restraint be "of such a type and magnitude so as to be cognizable as a violation of the Sherman Act"; and (3) that "[a]s a matter of international comity and fairness, . . . extraterritorial jurisdiction of the United States [should] be asserted to cover [the restraint]."[60]

While some courts adopted the *Timberlane* approach,[61] others weighed *Timberlane*-type comity factors as discretionary factors to be applied once subject matter jurisdiction has been established.[62] In *Mannington Mills, Inc. v. Congoleum*

1987) ("a foreign company can not demonstrate the domestic injury requirement by 'piggy-backing' onto the injury of a United States exporter").

57. Comity has been defined as "neither a matter of absolute obligation, on the one hand, nor of mere courtesy and good will, upon the other. But it is the recognition which one nation allows within its territory to the legislative, executive or judicial acts of another nation, having due regard both to international duty and convenience, and to the rights of its own citizens or of other persons who are under the protection of its laws." Hilton v. Guyot, 159 U.S. 113, 163-64 (1895). Comity considerations that arise from general considerations involving international relations should therefore be distinguished from the narrower act of state doctrine (discussed in part D.2 of this chapter).

58. 549 F.2d 597 (9th Cir. 1976).

59. *Id.* at 611-12.

60. *Id.* at 613-15. The factors to be weighed in making this third determination, according to *Timberlane*, include (1) the degree of conflict with foreign law or policy, (2) the nationality or allegiance of the parties and the locations or principal places of business of corporations, (3) the extent to which enforcement by either state can be expected to achieve compliance, (4) the relative significance of effects on the United States as compared with those elsewhere, (5) the extent to which there is explicit purpose to harm or affect U.S. commerce, (6) the foreseeability of such effect, and (7) the relative importance to the violations charged of conduct within the United States as compared with conduct abroad.

61. *See, e.g.*, Montreal Trading Ltd. v. Amax, Inc., 661 F.2d 864 (10th Cir. 1981), *cert. denied*, 455 U.S. 1001 (1982); Dominicus Americana Bohio v. Gulf & W. Indus., 473 F. Supp. 680 (S.D.N.Y. 1979).

62. The distinction between conduct that does not confer subject matter jurisdiction under the Sherman Act and conduct that does not give rise to a cognizable claim is important because there are significant procedural differences between a dismissal for lack of subject matter jurisdiction and a dismissal for failure to state a claim. Most importantly, a dismissal for lack of subject matter jurisdiction is not a judgment on the merits and thus has no res judicata effect, whereas a dismissal for failure to state a claim, if leave to amend pleadings is not granted, results in a judgment on the merits. *See, e.g.*, Industrial Inv. Dev. Corp. v. Mitsui & Co., 671 F.2d 876, 884-85 n.7 (5th Cir. 1982) (defendants failed to show that *Timberlane* factors required summary judgment), *vacated on other grounds and remanded*, 460 U.S. 1007, *reaff'd*, 704 F.2d 785 (5th Cir.), *cert. denied*, 464 U.S. 961 (1983); *Timberlane*, 549 F.2d at 601-02 (discussing procedural differences between dismissal for lack of subject matter jurisdiction and dismissal for failure to state a claim); Zenith Radio Corp. v. Matsushita Elec. Indus. Co., 494 F. Supp. 1161, 1171-77 (E.D. Pa. 1980)

Corp.,[63] the Third Circuit applied the *Alcoa* intended effects test but ordered the district court on remand to engage in what it termed the *Timberlane* "balancing process" to determine "whether jurisdiction should be exercised."[64] In addition to the *Timberlane* factors, the Third Circuit held that the jurisdictional analysis should consider any treaties governing the conduct at issue, the degree of harm to U.S. foreign policy that might result from asserting jurisdiction, the problems that might be created by any relief granted, and the availability of remedies abroad.[65] Similarly, the Seventh Circuit in *In re Uranium Antitrust Litigation*[66] ruled that subject matter jurisdiction should be determined under the *Alcoa* intended effects test and, if that test is satisfied, a court "should consider additional factors to determine whether the exercise of that jurisdiction is appropriate," with the *Mannington Mills* factors providing an "adequate framework for such a determination."[67]

In *Industrial Investment Development Corp. v. Mitsui & Co.*,[68] however, the Fifth Circuit took issue with the Seventh Circuit's suggestion in *In re Uranium Antitrust Litigation* that exercising jurisdiction is discretionary, holding that, as a matter of law (but not as an issue of subject matter jurisdiction), a court "should not apply the antitrust laws to foreign conduct or foreign actors if such application would violate principles of comity, conflicts of law, or international law."[69] Other courts had taken a variety of approaches to jurisdiction prior to enactment of the FTAIA.[70]

(summarizing the "confused and anomalous" state of the law governing the relationship between dismissal for failure to state a claim and dismissal for lack of subject matter jurisdiction), *aff'd in part and rev'd in part sub nom. In re* Japanese Elec. Prods. Antitrust Litig., 723 F.2d 238 (3d Cir. 1983), *rev'd sub nom.* Matsushita Elec. Indus. Co. v. Zenith Radio Corp., 475 U.S. 574 (1986).

63.   595 F.2d 1287 (3d Cir. 1979).

64.   *Id.* at 1292, 1297 (citations omitted); *cf. id.* at 1301-02 n.9 (Adams, J., concurring) (such discretionary abstention is narrowly limited).

65.   *Id.* at 1297-98; *see also* Rivendell Forest Prods. v. Canadian Forest Prods., 810 F. Supp. 1116, 1119-20 (D. Colo. 1993) (comity analysis considered whether activity at issue was also a matter of ongoing dispute between nations).

66.   617 F.2d 1248 (7th Cir. 1980).

67.   *Id.* at 1255. The court affirmed a district court's exercise of jurisdiction over defaulting foreign defendants based on the complexity of the litigation, the seriousness of the antitrust charges, and, especially, the recalcitrance of the nonappearing parties. *See also* Pillar Corp. v. Enercon Indus. Corp., 694 F. Supp. 1353, 1361 (E.D. Wis. 1988) (denying defendant's motion to dismiss for lack of subject matter jurisdiction for failure to present evidence pertinent to the factors adopted in *In re Uranium Antitrust Litig.*).

68.   671 F.2d 876 (5th Cir. 1982), *vacated on other grounds and remanded*, 460 U.S. 1007, *reaff'd*, 704 F.2d 785 (5th Cir.), *cert. denied*, 464 U.S. 961 (1983).

69.   *Id.* at 884. One district court summarily rejected the plaintiffs' comity argument that customary international law condemned what they called "certain basic anticompetitive activities," including price fixing. Kruman v. Christie's Int'l PLC, 129 F. Supp. 2d 620, 627 (S.D.N.Y. 2001) (noting the absence of international agreement on the issue).

70.   The Second Circuit expressly rejected the *Timberlane* jurisdictional test in *National Bank of Canada v. Interbank Card Ass'n*, 666 F.2d 6, 8-9 (2d Cir. 1981), finding that more than "some" effect upon U.S. commerce should be necessary to warrant jurisdiction under the U.S. antitrust laws. The court found that it did not have subject matter jurisdiction because the plaintiffs had failed to demonstrate that the allegedly unlawful conduct could be foreseen as having any "appreciable" anticompetitive effect upon U.S. foreign or interstate commerce. While the Second Circuit had applied comity factors apart from its jurisdictional analysis in deciding whether to dismiss an antitrust action against a foreign corporation in *Joseph Muller Corp. Zurich v. Société Anonyme de Gerance et D'Armement*, 451 F.2d 727 (2d Cir. 1971), *cert. denied*, 406 U.S. 906 (1972), it did not expressly sanction the comity factors set forth in *Timberlane* when it decided *National Bank of Canada*. *See also* Bulk Oil (ZUG) A.G. v. Sun Co., 583 F. Supp. 1134 (S.D.N.Y. 1983) (following *National Bank of Canada* jurisdictional test and finding no subject

In enacting the FTAIA, Congress indicated neutrality on the role of comity. The House Report accompanying the bill that became the FTAIA stated that "the bill is intended neither to prevent nor to encourage additional judicial recognition of the special international characteristics of transactions."[71] Citing *Timberlane*, the House Report noted that if "a court determines that the requirements for subject matter jurisdiction are met, this bill would have no effect on the courts' ability to employ notions of comity . . . or otherwise to take account of the international character of the transactions."[72] Thus, the FTAIA does not prevent courts from employing notions of comity to decline jurisdiction even where the requirements of the FTAIA have been satisfied.[73]

The *Restatement (Third) of the Foreign Relations Law of the United States*,[74] which followed the enactment of the FTAIA, would preclude "unreasonable"

---

matter jurisdiction), *aff'd without op.*, 742 F.2d 1431 (2d Cir.), *cert. denied*, 469 U.S. 835 (1984); Power E. Ltd. v. Transamerica Delaval Inc., 558 F. Supp. 47 (S.D.N.Y.) (dismissing antitrust claim where activities alleged took place and had their effect outside United States), *aff'd without op.*, 742 F.2d 1439 (2d Cir. 1983). In dicta in *Laker Airways v. Sabena, Belgian World Airlines*, 731 F.2d 909, 938 & nn.106-09, 948 n.145 (D.C. Cir. 1984), the D.C. Circuit indicated that facts relating to comity are appropriately considered both with respect to whether Congress intended to regulate the conduct in question and with respect to whether prescriptive jurisdiction, the jurisdiction to prescribe the law governing a particular controversy, exists. It held, however, that judicial interest balancing was inappropriate to resolve cases in which two nations properly have jurisdiction but their assertions of jurisdiction are contradictory and mutually inconsistent. *Id.* at 948-51.

71. H.R. REP. NO. 97-686, *supra* note 18, at 13.
72. *Id.* (citation omitted).
73. *See In re* Insurance Antitrust Litig., 938 F.2d 919, 932 (9th Cir. 1991) (where the conduct meets the requirements of the FTAIA, comity will require abstention only in unusual cases; because the FTAIA did not completely eliminate comity considerations, *Timberlane* analysis was applied to determine whether jurisdiction should be exercised), *aff'd in part, rev'd in part, and remanded sub nom.* Hartford Fire Ins. Co. v. California, 509 U.S. 764 (1993); Transnor (Berm.) Ltd. v. BP N. Am. Petroleum, 738 F. Supp. 1472, 1477-78 (S.D.N.Y. 1990) (defendant's motion for summary judgment failed when *Timberlane* analysis favored exercise of jurisdiction); McElderry v. Cathay Pac. Airways, 678 F. Supp. 1071, 1078-80 (S.D.N.Y. 1988) (jurisdiction declined on basis of international comity in spite of finding of sufficient anticompetitive effect on U.S. commerce).
74. The *Restatement (Third)* provides as follows:
Limitations on Jurisdiction to Prescribe
(1) Even when one of the bases for jurisdiction under § 402 is present, a state may not exercise jurisdiction to prescribe law with respect to a person or activity having connections with another state when the exercise of such jurisdiction is unreasonable.
(2) Whether exercise of jurisdiction over a person or activity is unreasonable is determined by evaluating all relevant factors, including, where appropriate:
(a) the link of the activity to the territory of the regulating state, i.e., the extent to which the activity takes place within the territory, or has substantial, direct, and foreseeable effect upon or in the territory;
(b) the connections, such as nationality, residence or economic activity, between the regulating state and the person principally responsible for the activity to be regulated, or between that state and those whom the regulation is designed to protect;
(c) the character of the activity to be regulated, the importance of regulation to the regulating state, the extent to which other states regulate such activities, and the degree to which the desirability of such regulation is generally accepted;
(d) the existence of justified expectations that might be protected or hurt by the regulation;
(e) the importance of the regulation to the international political, legal, or economic system;
(f) the extent to which the regulation is consistent with the traditions of the international system;

ANTITRUST LAW DEVELOPMENTS (FIFTH)

1128

exercises of jurisdiction. Although the *Restatement* does not directly invoke comity,
the factors enumerated as relevant to an evaluation of unreasonableness are similar to
those identified in *Timberlane*.

In 1993, the Supreme Court, in *Hartford Fire Insurance Co. v. California*,[75] cast
doubt upon the propriety of discretionary abstention from the exercise of U.S.
antitrust jurisdiction and arguably expanded the federal courts' extraterritorial power.
The Court affirmed, by a five-to-four decision, the Ninth Circuit's holding in *In re
Insurance Antitrust Litigation*[76] that jurisdiction existed over alleged activity by
foreign reinsurers outside the United States and ruled that comity considerations did
not require abstention.

The defendants had argued that comity dictated abstention because U.K. law
permitted (but did not compel) the conduct in question. The Court reasoned that the
"only substantial question" was whether "there is in fact a true conflict between
domestic and foreign law"[77] and found no "true" conflict because the defendants did
not face conflicting demands under the regulatory schemes of the United States and
the United Kingdom.[78] Therefore, the Court stated, it had "no need in this case to
address other considerations that might inform a decision to refrain from the exercise
of jurisdiction on grounds of international comity."[79] It did not consider any of the
Timberlane or *Restatement (Third)* factors. The majority opinion suggests that
comity is not an issue in a federal court's determination whether to exercise
jurisdiction in the absence of a conflict between foreign and domestic law that places
conflicting demands on the defendant.[80]

(g)   the extent to which another state may have an interest in regulating the activity;
and
(h)   the likelihood of conflict with regulation by another state.
(3)   When it would not be unreasonable for each of two states to exercise jurisdiction over a
person or activity, but the prescriptions by the two states are in conflict, each state has an
obligation to evaluate its own as well as the other state's interest in exercising jurisdiction, in
light of all the relevant factors, Subsection (2); a state should defer to the other state if that
state's interest is clearly greater.
RESTATEMENT (THIRD), *supra* note 12, § 403.
75.   509 U.S. 764 (1993).
76.   938 F.2d 919 (9th Cir. 1991).
77.   509 U.S. at 798 (quoting Société Nationale Industrielle Aérospatiale v. United States Dist. Court,
482 U.S. 522, 555 (1987) (Blackmun, J., concurring in part and dissenting in part)).
78.   *Id.* at 798-99; *see also* Filetech S.A. v. France Telecom S.A., 157 F.3d 922 (2d Cir. 1998) (to
establish a "true conflict" for purposes of dismissal on the grounds of comity it must be shown that
"compliance with the regulatory laws of both countries would be impossible"; a "substantial
claim" of true conflict is insufficient as the conflict must be clearly demonstrated); Metro Indus. v.
Sammi Corp., 82 F.3d 839, 847 (9th Cir.) (citing *Hartford Fire*, finding comity concerns
inapplicable because "there is no conflict with foreign law or policy because the [conduct at issue]
was not compelled by the Korean government, even though three Korean government
representatives [were involved in it]"), *cert. denied*, 519 U.S. 868 (1996); Trugman-Nash, Inc. v.
New Zealand Dairy Board, 954 F. Supp. 733 (S.D.N.Y. 1997) (dismissing claim on international
comity considerations, the act of state doctrine, and foreign sovereign compulsion because of
actual conflict of laws in which it would be impossible for New Zealand dairy producers to comply
with both regulatory schemes).
79.   509 U.S. at 799.
80.   In dissent, Justice Scalia balanced the reasonableness factors set forth in *Restatement (Third)*
§ 403(2) and determined that extraterritorial jurisdiction would be unreasonable in light of the
predominant contacts with the United Kingdom. The dissent argued that, in those circumstances, it
was not necessary to consider whether a conflict existed between U.S. and U.K. law, and that, even
if it were necessary to do so, a conflict of laws would exist "[w]here applicable foreign and

Comity considerations continue to play a role in government enforcement decisions.[81] A list of factors similar to that in *Timberlane* is considered by the Department of Justice and the Federal Trade Commission in determining whether to assert jurisdiction in a case involving international commerce.[82] The enforcement agencies state that, "in determining whether to assert jurisdiction to investigate or bring an action, or to seek particular remedies in a given case, each agency takes into account whether significant interests of any foreign sovereign would be affected."[83] The *International Antitrust Guidelines* emphasize, however, that "no conflict exists for purposes of an international comity analysis in the courts if the person subject to regulation by two states can comply with the laws of both," as the Supreme Court reasoned in *Hartford Fire*.[84]

In the 1988 *International Antitrust Guidelines*, the Department of Justice asserted that, in suits to which the United States is a party, courts are precluded from ordering dismissal on the basis of comity because

[a] decision by the Department to prosecute an antitrust action amounts to a determination by the Executive Branch that the interests of the United States supersede the interests of any foreign sovereign and that the challenged conduct is more harmful to the United States than any injury to foreign relations that might result from the antitrust action.[85]

---

domestic laws provide different substantive rules of decision to govern the parties' dispute." *Id.* at 821.

81. *See* part G.2 of this chapter.

82. In such an analysis, the *International Antitrust Guidelines* indicate that the enforcement agencies will consider "all relevant factors," including (1) the relative significance to the alleged violation of conduct within the United States, as compared to conduct abroad; (2) the nationality of the persons involved in or affected by the conduct; (3) the presence or absence of a purpose to affect U.S. consumers, markets, or exporters; (4) the relative significance and foreseeability of the effects of the conduct on the United States as compared to the effects abroad; (5) the existence of reasonable expectations that would be furthered or defeated by the action; (6) the degree of conflict with foreign law or articulated foreign economic policies; (7) the extent to which the enforcement activities of another country with respect to the same persons, including remedies resulting from those activities, may be affected; and (8) the effectiveness of foreign enforcement as compared to U.S. enforcement action. INTERNATIONAL ANTITRUST GUIDELINES, *supra* note 1, § 3.2. The last two factors were not mentioned in the 1988 *International Antitrust Guidelines* but are derived from the antitrust cooperation agreement between the United States and the European Community. *See* Agreement between the European Communities and the Government of the United States of America Regarding the Application of their Competition Laws [hereinafter 1991 EC Agreement], 30 I.L.M. 1491 (Nov. 1991), *reprinted in* 4 Trade Reg. Rep. (CCH) ¶ 13,504. A similar list of factors is included in the cooperation agreement with Canada, which is patterned after the 1991 EC Agreement. Agreement between the Government of Canada and the Government of the United States of America Regarding the Application of Their Competition and Deceptive Marketing Practices Laws (Aug. 3, 1995) [hereinafter Canadian Agreement], *reprinted in* 4 Trade Reg. Rep. (CCH) ¶ 13,503.

83. INTERNATIONAL ANTITRUST GUIDELINES, *supra* note 1, § 3.2.

84. *Id.*

85. 1988 INTERNATIONAL ANTITRUST GUIDELINES, *supra* note 20, § 5 n.167; *see also In re* Grand Jury Proceedings Bank of Nova Scotia, 740 F.2d 817, 832 n.23 (11th Cir. 1984) (act of state doctrine does not apply where executive branch announces that it does not oppose judicial inquiry), *cert. denied*, 469 U.S. 1106 (1985); Brief for the United States as Amicus Curiae at 23-24, Matsushita Elec. Indus. Co. v. Zenith Radio Corp., 475 U.S. 574 (1986) (No. 83-2004) (sovereign compulsion doctrine should not apply in suits brought by the United States).

This position is retained in the 1995 *International Antitrust Guidelines*, which note that, while the agencies may consult with foreign governments through diplomatic channels rather than bring an enforcement action, the decision by the Department of Justice to bring an action "represents a determination by the Executive Branch that the importance of antitrust enforcement outweighs any relevant foreign policy concerns" and that it is not "the role of the courts to 'second-guess the executive branch's judgment as to the proper role of comity concerns under these circumstances.'"[86]   In at least one case, a district court deferred to the State Department's consideration of a foreign government's objections,[87] and a number of other cases contain language that supports such deference.[88]

Even if a U.S. court has jurisdiction, a foreign court also may lawfully exercise jurisdiction.[89] A court may not exercise its jurisdiction by ordering acts in another country where compliance with such an order would subject a person to liability in the other country.[90] When a court exercises jurisdiction over a matter that is also pending before a foreign court, however, it may, in its discretion, stay its proceedings pending the outcome of the foreign litigation.[91] Comity issues also arise when a court considers antisuit injunctions sought against parties proceeding simultaneously in domestic and foreign courts.[92]

---

86.   INTERNATIONAL ANTITRUST GUIDELINES, *supra* note 1, § 3.2 (footnotes omitted). The *Guidelines* recognize that this reasoning does not apply to actions brought by the FTC because it is not part of the executive branch, but they note that the FTC also "considers comity issues and consults with foreign antitrust authorities." *Id.* n.78.

87.   United States v. Baker Hughes Inc., 731 F. Supp. 3, 6 n.5 (D.D.C.) ("It is not the Court's role to second-guess the executive branch's judgment as to the proper role of comity concerns."), *aff'd*, 908 F.2d 981 (D.C. Cir. 1990).

88.   In the 1976 *Timberlane* decision, for example, the Ninth Circuit specifically distinguished government cases, noting that in private suits "there is no opportunity for the executive branch to weigh the foreign relations impact, nor any statement implicit in the filing of the suit that that consideration has been outweighed." Timberlane Lumber Co. v. Bank of Am. Nat'l Trust & Sav. Ass'n, 549 F.2d 597, 613 (9th Cir. 1976); *cf.* Laker Airways v. Sabena, Belgian World Airlines, 731 F.2d 909, 944 (D.C. Cir. 1984) (absence of executive branch's intervention or expression of affirmative U.S. interest does not bar or impede private plaintiff's antitrust suit against foreign corporation); United States v. Vetco Inc., 691 F.2d 1281, 1289 n.9 (9th Cir.) (enforcement of Internal Revenue Service summons), *cert. denied*, 454 U.S. 1098 (1981); Arthur Andersen & Co. v. Finesilver, 546 F.2d 338, 342 (10th Cir. 1976) (defendant cannot speak for United States in asserting international comity as a basis for its failure to comply with discovery order where such order could cause the defendant to violate foreign law), *cert. denied*, 429 U.S. 1096 (1977).

89.   *See* RESTATEMENT (THIRD), *supra* note 12, § 403 comments d-e (stating that one state's exercise of jurisdiction to prescribe is not conclusive that it is unreasonable for another state to exercise its own jurisdiction, but where the states' regulations conflict, each state in exercising jurisdiction is required to evaluate both its interests and those of the other state and to defer if the other state's interests are clearly greater); Laker Airways v. Pan Am. World Airways, 559 F. Supp. 1124 (D.D.C. 1983), *aff'd sub nom.* Laker Airways v. Sabena, Belgian World Airlines, 731 F.2d 909, 921-26 (D.C. Cir. 1984).

90.   Reebok Int'l Ltd. v. McLaughlin, 49 F.3d 1387 (9th Cir.), *cert. denied*, 516 U.S. 908 (1995); RESTATEMENT (THIRD), *supra* note 12, § 441(1). Nevertheless, the *Restatement (Third)* position maintains that a court may exercise its jurisdiction by ordering acts within that country where compliance with such an order would subject a person to liability in another country. *Id.* § 441(2).

91.   *See, e.g.*, Mul-T-Lock Corp. v. Mul-T-Lock Ltd., 1984-1 Trade Cas. (CCH) ¶ 65,855 (E.D.N.Y. 1984).

92.   *See, e.g.*, Shell Offshore, Inc. v. Heeremac, 33 F. Supp. 2d 1111 (S.D. Tex. 1999) (denying injunction to bar foreign defendants from prosecuting litigation in England designed to compel plaintiffs in U.S. action to have their claims heard in England because (1) no comity concerns were present, and (2) there was no threat of imminent and irreparable injury justifying issuance of an

2. The Federal Trade Commission, Robinson-Patman, and Clayton Acts

Section 5 of the Federal Trade Commission Act (FTC Act) prohibits unfair methods of competition and unfair or deceptive acts or practices "in or affecting commerce."[93] Commerce is defined to include "commerce . . . with foreign nations."[94] In 1982, as part of the FTAIA, however, the FTC Act was amended to prohibit only unfair methods of competition involving domestic commerce and import commerce, and other foreign commerce where the "methods of competition have a direct, substantial, and reasonably foreseeable effect" on U.S. domestic or import commerce, or on the export commerce of a person so engaged in the United States.[95]

In *Branch v. FTC*,[96] the FTC Act was held to apply to false advertising overseas.[97] The Seventh Circuit reasoned that although the FTC Act did not protect overseas consumers from Branch's false statements, it did protect his U.S. competitors from the effects of his unfair practices.[98]

Section 1 of the Clayton Act defines commerce to include "commerce . . . with foreign nations."[99] Because Section 7 of the act was amended in 1980 to apply to acquisitions or mergers between persons engaged "in commerce" or in activities "affecting commerce,"[100] it now covers many acquisitions and mergers involving foreign companies.[101]

---

injunction); Umbro Int'l, Inc. v. Japan Prof'l Football League, 1998-2 Trade Cas. (CCH) ¶ 72,245 (D.S.C. 1997) (enjoining foreign defendant in U.S. antitrust action from prosecuting parallel litigation in a Japanese court).

93. 15 U.S.C. § 45(a)(1) (2000).
94. *Id.* § 44 (2000).
95. *Id.* § 45(a)(3)(A) (2000).
96. 141 F.2d 31 (7th Cir. 1944).
97. *See also* FTC v. Compagnie de Saint-Gobain-Pont-A-Mousson, 636 F.2d 1300, 1322 (D.C. Cir. 1980) (dictum) (FTC has jurisdiction under § 5 to investigate and regulate any activities of a foreign corporation that affect U.S. commerce); *but see* Nieman v. Dryclean U.S.A. Franchise Co., 178 F.3d 1126 (11th Cir. 1999) (without considering FTAIA, holding that the FTC Act does not authorize extraterritorial application of the Franchise Rule and dismissing complaint of Argentine citizen against U.S. company based on conduct solely in Argentina), *cert. denied*, 528 U.S. 1118 (2000).
98. Foreshadowing later repercussions abroad over the extension of U.S. jurisdiction to matters involving foreign commerce, the *Branch* court was careful to claim that its exercise of jurisdiction was "no invasion of the sovereignty of any other country or any attempt to act beyond the territorial jurisdiction of the United States." 141 F.2d at 35.
99. 15 U.S.C. § 12 (2000).
100. *Id.* § 18 (2000); *see* Antitrust Procedural Improvements Act of 1980, Pub. L. No. 96-349, 94 Stat. 1154.
101. Even before its amendment, when § 7 applied only to mergers involving corporations "engaged in commerce," the Clayton Act was applied both to acquisitions by U.S. companies of foreign companies with U.S. subsidiaries, *see, e.g., United States v. Jos. Schlitz Brewing Co.*, 253 F. Supp. 129 (N.D. Cal.), *aff'd per curiam*, 385 U.S. 37 (1966), and to acquisitions by foreign companies of U.S. companies, *see, e.g., British Oxygen Co.*, 86 F.T.C. 1241 (1975), *set aside on other grounds and remanded sub nom. BOC Int'l Ltd. v. FTC*, 557 F.2d 24 (2d Cir. 1977). For example, in a challenge to an acquisition of a Japanese corporation by a U.S. corporation pursuant to a joint venture agreement, the FTC held that the Japanese corporation, which existed solely for the purpose of manufacturing motors for sale to its parent corporations (which were clearly engaged in U.S. commerce and which imported most of those motors into the United States for resale), was engaged in commerce under the Clayton Act. Brunswick Corp., 94 F.T.C. 1174, 1264-65 (1979),

Section 3 of the Clayton Act and Section 2(a) of the Robinson-Patman Act, on the other hand, reach only transactions in which the commodities or goods involved are sold "for use, consumption or resale in the United States."[102] In *In re Japanese Electronic Products Antitrust Litigation*,[103] the Third Circuit ruled that both sales that form the basis of a price discrimination claim under Section 2(a) must meet this test.[104] In *Paceco, Inc. v. Ishikawajima-Harima Heavy Industries Co.*,[105] the district court suggested that the "use" requirement could be satisfied where the goods that were the subject of the challenged discrimination were imported into the United States after sale and then incorporated into a product sold in the United States. One district court has held that the "resale" requirement is met when the goods are sold in the United States and then resold domestically before being sold abroad, i.e., where two or more sales precede the export transaction.[106] Unlike Section 2(a), Robinson-Patman Act Sections 2(c), (d), (e), and (f) contain no requirement that the goods involved be used or resold in the United States. Thus, some courts have found that the limitation to domestic sales and imports in Section 2(a) is not applicable to Section 2(c).[107] In *Baysoy v. Jessop Steel Co.*,[108] for example, the district court specifically held that Section 2(c) applies to the sale of goods or commodities for export.

C. Special Substantive/Analytical Rules Applicable in the International Context

The substantive antitrust rules governing transactions in U.S. foreign commerce are generally identical to those applicable to domestic commerce. Thus, price fixing,[109] output restriction,[110] and market division[111] generally have been condemned

---

aff'd as modified sub nom. Yamaha Motor Co. v. FTC, 657 F.2d 971 (8th Cir. 1981), *cert. denied*, 456 U.S. 915 (1982).

102. 15 U.S.C. §§ 13(a), 14 (2000); *see also* Shulton, Inc. v. Optel Corp., 1987-1 Trade Cas. (CCH) ¶ 67,436, at 59,816 & n.9 (D.N.J. 1986); C.E.D. Mobilephone Communs. v. Harris Corp., 1985-1 Trade Cas. (CCH) ¶ 66,386, at 64,894-95 (S.D.N.Y. 1985).

103. 723 F.2d 238 (3d Cir. 1983), *rev'd on other grounds sub nom.* Matsushita Elec. Indus. Co. v. Zenith Radio Corp., 475 U.S. 574 (1986).

104. *Id.* at 316-17. *See also* General Chems., Inc. v. Exxon Chem. Co., USA, 625 F.2d 1231, 1234 (5th Cir. 1980); O. Hommel Co. v. Ferro Corp., 472 F. Supp. 793, 794-95 (W.D. Pa. 1979), *rev'd on other grounds*, 659 F.2d 340 (3d Cir. 1981), *cert. denied*, 455 U.S. 1017 (1982); Fimex Corp. v. Barmatic Prods. Co., 429 F. Supp. 978, 980 (E.D.N.Y.) (U.S. firm purchasing for export has no cause of action), *aff'd*, 573 F.2d 1289 (2d Cir. 1977).

105. 468 F. Supp. 256, 260 (N.D. Cal. 1979). Although *Paceco* was brought under § 2(f) of the Robinson-Patman Act, which prohibits a buyer from inducing unlawful price discrimination, the court read into this section the jurisdictional requirements contained in § 2(a). It did so to conform with the Supreme Court's ruling that buyer liability under § 2(f) is dependent on seller liability under § 2(a). *See* Great Atl. & Pac. Tea Co. v. FTC, 440 U.S. 69, 75-77 (1979).

106. *See* Raul Int'l Corp. v. Sealed Power Corp., 586 F. Supp. 349, 352-55 (D.N.J. 1984).

107. *See, e.g.*, Canadian Ingersoll-Rand Co. v. D. Loveman & Sons, 227 F. Supp. 829, 833-34 (N.D. Ohio 1964).

108. 90 F. Supp. 303, 305-06 (W.D. Pa. 1950). *But cf. Paceco*, 468 F. Supp. at 259-60 n.7 (§ 2(f) incorporates the jurisdictional requirements of § 2(a)).

109. *See, e.g.*, United States v. Timken Roller Bearing Co., 83 F. Supp. 284 (N.D. Ohio 1949), *modified*, 341 U.S. 593 (1951); United States v. General Elec. Co., 80 F. Supp. 989 (S.D.N.Y. 1948); *see also* part C.1 and D.1 of Chapter I.

110. *See, e.g.*, United States v. General Elec. Co., 82 F. Supp. 753 (D.N.J. 1949), *supplemental op.*, 115 F. Supp. 835 (1953).

as illegal per se, whereas vertical nonprice restraints,[112] joint ventures,[113] and mergers[114] generally have been examined under a rule of reason standard. There is a split in the circuit courts, however, as to whether a per se rule or rule of reason analysis is appropriate for price fixing that occurs in a foreign country. In *Metro Industries v. Sammi Corp.*,[115] the Ninth Circuit rejected a claim that a Korean registration system constituted a per se illegal market division, in part because "application of the per se rule is not appropriate where conduct in question occurred in another country."[116] In *United States v. Nippon Paper Industries*,[117] however, the First Circuit held that the per se rule applied to an alleged conspiracy between Japanese firms to fix prices of thermal fax paper sold in the United States. On remand, the district court explicitly rejected the reasoning of *Metro Industries* and held that the per se rule may be applied to price fixing in a foreign country where that conduct had "substantial effects" in the United States.[118]

Substantive rules aside, there are a variety of distinct jurisdictional, analytical, and procedural considerations that arise in foreign commerce settings. First, as noted in part B of this chapter, considerations of jurisdiction, comity, or prosecutorial discretion may limit the application of U.S. antitrust laws even where blatant cartel activity is involved if the activity is directed solely to overseas markets and has only incidental effects on U.S. commerce.[119]

Second, in evaluating market power, it may be necessary to consider circumstances peculiar to the international setting that may affect the competitive significance of foreign firms.[120] The 1992 *Merger Guidelines* issued by the Federal Trade Commission and Department of Justice start from the proposition that "market shares will be assigned to foreign competitors in the same way in which they are

---

111. *See, e.g., Timken*, 83 F. Supp. at 307; United States v. National Lead Co., 63 F. Supp. 513, 523 (S.D.N.Y. 1945), *aff'd*, 332 U.S. 319 (1947); United States v. Aluminum Co. of Am., 148 F.2d 416 (2d Cir. 1945); United States v. Holophane Co., 119 F. Supp. 114 (S.D. Ohio 1954), *aff'd per curiam*, 352 U.S. 903 (1956); *see also* part C.2 of Chapter I.

112. *See, e.g.*, Continental T.V., Inc. v. GTE Sylvania Inc., 433 U.S. 36, 54-57 (1977); *see also* parts D.2 and D.3 of Chapter I.

113. *See, e.g., In re* Brunswick Corp., 94 F.T.C. 1174 (1979), *aff'd as modified sub nom.* Yamaha Motor Co. v. FTC, 657 F.2d 971 (8th Cir. 1981), *cert. denied*, 456 U.S. 915 (1982); *see also* Chapter IV.

114. United States v. General Dynamics Corp., 415 U.S. 486 (1974); *see also* Chapter III.

115. 82 F.3d 839 (9th Cir.), *cert. denied*, 519 U.S. 868 (1996).

116. *Id.* at 844-45.

117. 109 F.3d 1, 7 (1st Cir. 1997), *cert. denied*, 522 U.S. 1044 (1998).

118. United States v. Nippon Paper Indus., 62 F. Supp. 2d 173, 194-95 (D. Mass. 1999).

119. *See Metro Indus.*, 82 F.3d at 845-47; Montreal Trading Ltd. v. Amax Inc., 661 F.2d 864, 869-70 (10th Cir. 1981), *cert. denied*, 455 U.S. 1001 (1982); Alfred Bell & Co. v. Catalda Fine Arts, Inc., 74 F. Supp. 973 (S.D.N.Y. 1947), *interlocutory decree aff'd*, 86 F. Supp. 399 (S.D.N.Y. 1949), *modified*, 191 F.2d 99 (2d Cir. 1951). An anticompetitive agreement need not expressly include the United States to risk antitrust exposure if it is clear from the participants' actions that they intend to include the United States in their arrangement. *See, e.g.*, United States v. United States Alkali Export Ass'n, 86 F. Supp. 59 (S.D.N.Y. 1949); United States v. Timken Roller Bearing Co., 83 F. Supp. 284, 304-07 (N.D. Ohio 1949), *modified*, 341 U.S. 593 (1951). The legislative history of the FTAIA noted that a U.S. export cartel may have a "spillover" effect that in time would have a direct, substantial, and reasonably foreseeable effect on domestic commerce. H.R. REP. NO. 97-686, *supra* note 18, at 13.

120. *See generally* part B.1 of Chapter III.

assigned to domestic competitors."[121]   Nevertheless, the 1992 *Merger Guidelines*
recognize that foreign competition may be subject to certain variables not normally
encountered in a purely domestic context and that these variables may affect the
quantitative weight to be accorded to potential foreign supply response in any given
case. The 1992 *Merger Guidelines* identify three "special factors" that may affect
the treatment of foreign competition: (1) where exchange rates fluctuate
significantly, "the Agency may measure market shares over a period of longer than
one year";[122] (2) an import quota will be treated as a ceiling for imports in market
share calculation,[123] and where percentage quotas exist, "actual import sales and data
will be reduced for the purpose of calculating market shares";[124] and (3) "[a] single
market share may be assigned to a country or a group of countries if firms in that
country or group of countries act in coordination."[125]

In addition to the factors listed in the 1992 *Merger Guidelines*, other factors also
may be found to affect the competitive significance of a foreign firm's activities as
an actual or potential U.S. market participant. The current absence of imports is not
considered determinative because it "may simply indicate that local prices are
currently competitive, whereas, if prices rose, foreign (or non-local) shipments of the
relevant product would enter the market."[126] On the other hand, regulatory approvals
and testing, inexperience with marketing in the United States, and other "political
factors"[127] and "economic factors"[128] may disproportionately burden some foreign
firms.[129] Certain of these factors may be unique to foreign firms, while others may
simply represent unrecoverable costs that impact foreign firms more than domestic
firms.[130]

Under the 1992 *Merger Guidelines*, market shares for each market participant are
assigned "based on the total sales or capacity currently devoted to the relevant

---

121. U.S. DEP'T OF JUSTICE & FEDERAL TRADE COMM'N, HORIZONTAL MERGER GUIDELINES § 1.41
     (1992) [hereinafter 1992 MERGER GUIDELINES], *reprinted in* 4 Trade Reg. Rep. (CCH) ¶ 13,104
     and Appendix C to this treatise.
122. 1992 MERGER GUIDELINES, *supra* note 121, § 1.43. *See also* Olin Corp., 113 F.T.C. 400 (1990),
     aff'd, 986 F.2d 1295 (9th Cir. 1993), *cert. denied*, 510 U.S. 1110 (1994).
123. 1992 MERGER GUIDELINES, *supra* note 121, § 1.43. Voluntary export quotas are evaluated in the
     same manner as formal import quotas for purposes of calculating market shares. *See*
     ANTICIPATING THE 21ST CENTURY: COMPETITION IN THE NEW HIGH-TECH GLOBAL
     MARKETPLACE 15 (May 1996) [hereinafter FTC STAFF REPORT], *reprinted in* 70 Antitrust &
     Trade Reg. Rep. (BNA) No. 1765 (1996).
124. 1992 MERGER GUIDELINES. *supra* note 121, § 1.43.
125. *Id.*
126. FTC STAFF REPORT, *supra* note 123, at 10.
127. Political factors include national security concerns, domestic ownership restrictions, and "buy
     American" preferences *See* FTC STAFF REPORT, *supra* note 123, at 14-16; *see also* United States
     v. General Elec. Co., 1986-2 Trade Cas. (CCH) ¶ 67,382 (D.D.C. 1986) (consent order settling
     challenge to acquisition of RCA Corp. by General Electric in "buy American" defined market for
     silicon target vidicon tubes for military application).
128. Other economic factors include customer convenience and preference, including localized product
     differentiation and language/translation factors. *See* FTC STAFF REPORT, *supra* note 123, at 16-
     19; *see also* FTC v. Owens-Illinois, Inc., 681 F. Supp. 27, 51 (D.D.C.), *vacated as moot*, 850 F.2d
     694 (D.C. Cir. 1988) (foreign suppliers not viable alternative for reasons including quality
     concerns, breakage, and unreliability of supply).
129. FTC STAFF REPORT, *supra* note 123, at 11.
130. Under the 1992 *Merger Guidelines*, significant unrecoverable costs include "market-specific
     investments in production facilities, technologies, marketing, research and development, regulatory
     approvals and testing." 1992 MERGER GUIDELINES, *supra* note 121, § 1.32.

market together with that which likely would be devoted" in response to a price increase.[131] As applied to foreign firms, the following factors have been identified as potentially relevant considerations in making this determination: (1) a foreign firm might be deterred by the threat that diverting a substantially increased portion of its production to a single export destination would result in the imposition of trade restrictive measures such as tariffs, quotas, import bans, or other punitive actions by the importing country;[132] (2) if the foreign firm's products were subsidized, the foreign government might be unwilling to continue or extend those subsidies if that future support were to flow to foreign consumers;[133] and (3) a foreign producer's marginal cost of supplying additional units in the relevant geographic area may be greater than nonlocal domestic producers if the foreign firm must rely on third-party distributors.[134]

The implementing regulations under the Hart-Scott-Rodino Antitrust Improvements Act of 1976 (H-S-R Act)[135] exempt certain otherwise reportable "foreign" transactions from the act's reporting requirements, depending upon (1) where the acquiring person is organized and has its principal offices; (2) where the issuer of securities being acquired is organized and has its principal offices; (3) whether that issuer holds assets located in the United States, has a U.S. subsidiary, and/or made sales in or into the United States; (4) whether assets that are being acquired are located outside the United States; and (5) whether such assets generated sales in or into the United States.[136]

In addition, an acquisition by a foreign state, foreign government, or agency thereof (other than a corporation engaged in commerce) is not reportable,[137] nor is an acquisition, made by or from an entity "controlled" by a foreign state, foreign government, or agency thereof, of either assets located in that foreign state, or voting securities of an issuer organized under the law of that foreign state.[138] However, according to the International Competition Policy Advisory Committee to the Attorney General and Assistant Attorney General for Antitrust (ICPAC), established in 1997 to recommend measures "that would contribute to achieving the integration of markets,"[139] even the H-S-R Act's exemptions of certain foreign transactions allow "many more transactions than may be necessary [to] come within the U.S. merger review net."[140]

Finally, cases involving intellectual property are affected by the fact that the protection of intellectual property is governed by separate national regimes. Thus, "corresponding" or "parallel" patents—that is, patents in different countries covering

---

131. *Id.* § 1.41.
132. FTC STAFF REPORT, *supra* note 123, at 12-13. *See also* Olin Corp., 113 F.T.C. 400, 615-16 (1990), *aff'd*, 986 F.2d 1295 (9th Cir. 1993), *cert. denied*, 510 U.S. 1110 (1994).
133. FTC STAFF REPORT, *supra* note 123, at 13.
134. *Id.*
135. 15 U.S.C. § 18a (2000). See also part D.1 of Chapter III for a description of the premerger notification requirements under the H-S-R Act.
136. 16 C.F.R. §§ 802.50, 802.51 (2001). The FTC issued a notice of proposed rulemaking to both narrow and expand these rules in 2001. 66 Fed. Reg. 8723, 8725-26 (FTC Feb. 1, 2001).
137. *Id.* § 801.1(a)(2) (2001).
138. *Id.* § 802.52 (2001). "Control" is defined at 16 C.F.R. § 801.1(b) (2001).
139. *See* INTERNATIONAL COMPETITION POLICY ADVISORY COMMITTEE TO THE ATTORNEY GENERAL AND ASSISTANT ATTORNEY GENERAL FOR ANTITRUST, FINAL REPORT, at 2 (Feb. 2000) [hereinafter ICPAC REPORT], *available at* www.usdoj.gov/atr/icpac/finalreport.htm.
140. *Id.* at 126.

the same invention—can be used in an international licensing arrangement to effect a territorial division of markets.   The Department of Justice's 1977 *International Antitrust Guide* stated that an international territorial division created by selectively licensing patents in different countries would not itself be illegal under the antitrust laws.[141]   In the 1988 *International Antitrust Guidelines*, the Department of Justice suggested that such arrangements should initially be analyzed as an acquisition of technology and that possible impact on other markets should be addressed under its merger analysis standards.[142]   The 1995 *International Antitrust Guidelines* do not address these substantive issues, but the *Intellectual Property Guidelines* provide that:

> The principles of antitrust analysis described in these Guidelines apply equally to domestic and international licensing arrangements.   However, as described in the [*International Antitrust Guidelines*], considerations particular to international operations, such as jurisdiction and comity, may affect enforcement decisions when the arrangement is in an international context.[143]

The issues raised by international patent licensing and patent pools are more fully discussed in Chapter XI.

D. Defenses and Exemptions to Application of Antitrust Laws in Foreign Commerce

1. Sovereign Immunity

A foreign sovereign's immunity from suit in U.S. courts has long been recognized in the United States.[144]   Until 1976, questions of sovereign immunity were often addressed by both the executive and judicial branches of the government, with the views of the executive commonly regarded as binding on the courts.[145]   Since 1976,

---

141. 1977 INTERNATIONAL ANTITRUST GUIDE, *supra* note 17, Cases H-I; *see also* DEP'T OF JUSTICE, GUIDELINES FOR THE ISSUANCE OF EXPORT TRADE CERTIFICATES OF REVIEW, Part V.C, 50 Fed. Reg. 1786, 1798-99 (Jan. 11, 1995) [hereinafter EXPORT TRADE CERTIFICATES GUIDELINES], *reprinted in* 4 Trade Reg. Rep. (CCH) ¶ 13,300, at 21,116-17.

142. 1988 INTERNATIONAL ANTITRUST GUIDELINES, *supra* note 20, Case 11.

143. DEP'T OF JUSTICE & FEDERAL TRADE COMM'N, ANTITRUST GUIDELINES FOR THE LICENSING OF INTELLECTUAL PROPERTY (1995), *reprinted in* 4 Trade Reg. Rep. (CCH) ¶ 13,132 *and* Appendix E to this treatise.

144. Foreign sovereign immunity was first recognized in *The Schooner Exch. v. M'Faddon*, 11 U.S. (7 Cranch) 116 (1812) (Marshall, C.J.)   *See also* L'Invincible, 14 U.S. (1 Wheat.) 238 (1816).

145. *See, e.g.*, Republic of Mexico v. Hoffman, 324 U.S. 30, 38 (1945); *Ex parte* Republic of Peru, 318 U.S. 578, 588-89 (1943); *cf.* United States v. Deutsches Kalisyndikat Gesellschaft, 31 F.2d 199, 201-02 (S.D.N.Y. 1929) (defense of sovereign immunity rejected where there were private shareholders in a mining company controlled by the French government, French law permitted suits against the company in France, and the State Department had been silent). *But cf. In re* Grand Jury Investigation of the Shipping Indus., 186 F. Supp. 298, 318-20 (D.D.C. 1960) (court reserved decision where State Department refused to recommend extension of sovereign immunity to shipping line nationalized by the Philippine government); *In re* Investigation of World Arrangements with Relation to the Prod., Transp., Ref., and Distrib. of Petroleum, 13 F.R.D. 280, 288-91 (D.D.C. 1952) (sovereign immunity compelled quashing subpoena where oil company was found to be "indistinguishable" from the British government, which owned 35% of the capital investment, controlled one-half of the voting stock, and had formed the company to assure an

however, questions of sovereign immunity have been addressed through the application of the Foreign Sovereign Immunities Act (FSIA).[146] The FSIA is "the exclusive source of subject matter jurisdiction over suits involving foreign states or their instrumentalities."[147] It applies to all actions, of any nature, against foreign sovereigns. Moreover, since sovereign immunity is a matter of jurisdiction, a party may raise it at any time during litigation.[148]

Under the FSIA, foreign sovereigns are "presumptively immune" from the jurisdiction of the courts of the United States unless a specified exception to immunity applies.[149] A defendant pleading sovereign immunity must produce evidence of its status as a foreign state. The burden of proof then shifts to the plaintiff to present evidence that one of the FSIA's exceptions to immunity applies.[150] Once the plaintiff has met this burden, the burden shifts back to the foreign state to prove "by a preponderance of the evidence that the exception does not apply."[151] If the plaintiff cannot produce evidence that an exception applies, the foreign state cannot be sued in the United States.[152]

---

adequate supply of petroleum to the British fleet). *See generally* H.R. REP. NO. 94-1487 (1976), *reprinted in* 1976 U.S.C.C.A.N. 6604 (report accompanying bill that became the FSIA).

146. 28 U.S.C. §§ 1330, 1602-1611 (1994 & Supp. 1999), *amended by* Pub. L. No. 106-386, Div. C., § 2002, 114 Stat. 1543 (2000). With the statute, Congress intended to codify the restrictive theory of sovereign immunity, under which a state is immune from the jurisdiction of foreign courts as to its sovereign or public acts, but not as to those that are private or commercial in character. *See* Verlinden B.V. v. Central Bank of Nigeria, 461 U.S. 480 (1983). In *Djordjevich v. Bundesminister Der Finanzen, F.R.G.*, 827 F. Supp. 814 (D.D.C. 1993), the court confirmed that the FSIA has retroactive effect only to 1952. That case involved a claim against the German government for failure to return gold coins taken during World War II in occupied Yugoslavia. The court cited alternative grounds for dismissal based on the lack of a direct effect in the United States. *Id.* at 817.

147. *See* Republic of Argentina v. Weltover, Inc., 504 U.S. 607, 611 (1992) (the FSIA "provides the sole basis for obtaining jurisdiction over a foreign sovereign in the United States"); Argentine Republic v. Amerada Hess Shipping Corp., 488 U.S. 428, 434 (1989); Adler v. Federal Republic of Nigeria, 219 F.3d 869, 874 (9th Cir. 2000) ("The FSIA 'provides the sole basis for obtaining jurisdiction over a foreign state in the courts of this country.'") (citing *Argentine Republic*, 488 U.S. at 443); Dewhurst v. Telenor Invest A.S., 83 F. Supp. 2d 577, 586 (D. Md. 2000) ("The FSIA provides the sole basis for federal courts to assert subject matter jurisdiction over claims against a foreign sovereign."). *See also* H.R. REP. NO 94-1487, at 12 (1976), *reprinted in* 1976 U.S.C.C.A.N. 6604, 6610 (noting that the FSIA "sets forth the sole and exclusive standards to be used in resolving questions of sovereign immunity raised by foreign states").

148. *See* FED. R. CIV. P. 12(h)(3) ("whenever it appears by suggestion of the parties or otherwise that the court lacks jurisdiction over the subject matter, the court shall dismiss the action"). *Cf.* Ferdman v. Consulate Gen. of Israel, No. 98C 1555, 1999 U.S. Dist. LEXIS 1775, at *1 n.1 (N.D. Ill. Feb. 16, 1999).

149. *See* Saudi Arabia v. Nelson, 507 U.S. 349, 355 (1993); *Weltover*, 504 U.S. at 610-11; *Adler*, 219 F.3d at 874.

150. Kelly v. Syra Shell Petroleum Dev. B.V., 213 F.3d 841, 847 (5th Cir. 2000).

151. *Adler*, 219 F.3d at 874. *See also* Cabiri v. Republic of Ghana, 165 F.3d 193, 196 (2d Cir. 1999) ("Once the defendant presents a prima facie case that it is a foreign sovereign, the plaintiff has the burden of going forward with evidence showing that, under exceptions to the FSIA, immunity should not be granted, although the ultimate burden of persuasion remains with the alleged foreign sovereign.") (internal citations omitted).

152. A threshold issue is whether the determination of the party's sovereign status should be based on the time of the alleged wrongdoing or the time the suit is brought. Three of the four courts of appeals that expressly considered the issue concluded that the status at the time of the alleged wrongdoing should control. *See* Pare v. Nuovo Pignone, Inc., 150 F.3d 477 (5th Cir. 1998); General Elec. Capital Corp. v. Grossman, 991 F.2d 1376, 1380-82 (8th Cir. 1993); Gould, Inc. v. Pechiney Ugine Kuhlmann, 853 F.2d 445, 450 (6th Cir. 1988). The Ninth Circuit, on the other

The exceptions to foreign sovereign immunity are primarily set forth in Section 1605(a) of the FSIA. This section provides that a foreign sovereign is not entitled to immunity if (1) it has waived its immunity either explicitly or by implication; (2) it is engaged in commercial activity having a certain nexus to the United States; (3) it has expropriated property in violation of international law and such property is present in the United States in connection with a commercial activity carried on in the United States; (4) it has acquired rights to property situated in the United States; (5) it has committed certain noncommercial tortious acts in the United States; (6) it has agreed to arbitrate a dispute concerning subject matter capable of settlement by arbitration under the laws of the United States; or (7) in certain cases, it has caused personal injury or death through an act of torture, extrajudicial killing, aircraft sabotage, or hostage taking.[153]

Section 1605(a)(2) of the FSIA provides that foreign sovereign immunity does not extend to suits arising out of commercial activity in the United States by a foreign sovereign.[154] It also provides that immunity does not extend to acts

---

hand, concluded that the time of the complaint should control, *see Straub v. AP Green, Inc.*, 38 F.3d 448 (9th Cir. 1994), as did one district court, *see Gardiner Stone Hunter Int'l v. Iberia Lineas Aereas de Espana, S.A.*, 896 F. Supp. 125 (S.D.N.Y. 1995). These decisions were addressed in *Belgrade v. Sidex Int'l Furniture Corp.*, 2 F. Supp. 2d 407, 412-14 (S.D.N.Y. 1998), where the district court concluded that "[a]lthough these cases at first appear inconsistent, they can be woven into a unified approach consistent with the objectives of the FSIA." After reviewing the apparent conflict, the court determined that "the focus on the potential liability or the propriety of the conduct of a foreign sovereign is the key to understanding why some cases appear to hold that the relevant time of inquiry is the time of the underlying conduct while other cases focus on the time the lawsuit was filed." *Id.* According to the district court, "the correct approach under the FSIA is to ask whether the underlying conduct took place on the foreign state's watch, even if that state is no longer in control of the party by the time of the lawsuit, or, alternatively, whether the defendant [is] currently a foreign state, regardless of its status at the time of the underlying conduct." *Id.*

153. 28 U.S.C. § 1605(a) (1994 & Supp. 1999). In addition, § 1605(b) provides that a foreign state is not entitled to immunity "in any case in which a suit in admiralty is brought to enforce a maritime lien against a vessel or cargo of the foreign state, which maritime lien is based upon a commercial activity of the foreign state." *Id.* § 1605(b) (1994). Section 1605(d) provides an exception in situations in which an action is brought to foreclose a preferred mortgage, *see id.* § 1605(c), as defined in the Ship Mortgage Act. *See* 46 U.S.C. § 31322 (1994). Finally, Section 1607 provides an exception in connection with certain counterclaims. 28 U.S.C. § 1607 (1994). If a court determines that one or more of these exceptions apply, the foreign state is, subject to restrictions with respect to punitive damages, otherwise "liable in the same manner and to the same extent as a private individual under like circumstances." *Id.* § 1606.

154. 28 U.S.C. § 1605(a)(2) (1994); Ministry of Supply, Cairo v. Universe Tankships, Inc., 708 F.2d 80, 83-84 (2d Cir. 1983); *see also* Alfred Dunhill of London, Inc. v. Republic of Cuba, 425 U.S. 682, 701-02 (1976) (White, J., plurality opinion) (noting U.S. policy is to decline to extend sovereign immunity to the "commercial dealings of foreign governments"); Hanil Bank v. PT. Bank Negara Indonesia, 148 F.3d 127, 131 (2d Cir. 1998) (acts of the state are in connection with a commercial activity when there is a substantive connection or causal link between the acts and the commercial activity); Barkanic v. General Admin. of Civil Aviation of People's Republic of China, 822 F.2d 11, 13 (2d Cir.) ("a nexus is required between the commercial activity in the United States and the cause of action"), *cert. denied*, 484 U.S. 964 (1987); Tonoga, Ltd. v. Ministry of Pub. Works and Housing of the Kingdom of Saudi Arabia, 135 F. Supp. 2d 350, 355-57 (N.D.N.Y. 2001) (holding that a foreign state's assumption of liability under a collection of performance guarantee bonds constituted commercial activity); Mann v. Hanil Bank, 900 F. Supp. 1077, 1089 (E.D. Wis. 1995) (claim is "based upon" commercial activities in the United States if those activities establish a legal element of claim); RESTATEMENT (THIRD), *supra* note 12, § 451 ("Under international law, a state or state instrumentality is immune from the jurisdiction of the courts of another state, except with respect to claims arising out of activities of the kind that may be carried on by private persons.").

performed in the United States in connection with a commercial activity elsewhere, or to acts performed outside the United States in connection with a commercial activity elsewhere where "that act causes a direct effect in the United States."[155]

With respect to commercial activity carried on in the United States, the district court, in its decision in *United States Fid. & Guar. Co. v. Braspetro Oil Servs. Co.*, 97 Civ. 6124 (JGK), 1999 U.S. Dist. LEXIS 7236 (S.D.N.Y. May 17, 1999), *aff'd*, 199 F.3d 94 (2d Cir. 1999), stated that "[t]he focus is 'not on whether the foreign state generally engages in commercial activity in the United States, but on whether the particular conduct giving rise to the claim is a part of a commercial activity having substantial contact with the United States.'" *Id.* at *39.

155. 28 U.S.C. § 1605(a)(2) (1994); *see, e.g.*, Republic of Argentina v. Weltover, Inc., 504 U.S. 607, 617-19 (1992) ("An effect is 'direct' if it follows from an immediate consequence of the defendant's activity, the effect need not be substantial or foreseeable.") (issuance of dollar bonds to stabilize Argentinean currency and repudiation of obligation to deliver proceeds to New York bank was commercial activity that caused direct effect in the United States); Verlinden B.V. v. Central Bank of Nigeria, 461 U.S. 480, 498 n.23 (1983) (overseas repudiation of letter of credit did not cause direct effect in United States); Reiss v. Societe Centrale du Groupe des Assurances Nationales, 235 F.3d 738, 747 (2d Cir. 2000) (remanding case for determination through discovery of facts determining whether sufficient nexus between commercial activity by French government instrumentality and employment of plaintiff); *Adler*, 219 F.3d at 876 (bribery of the Nigerian government and certain officials had a direct effect in United States because plaintiff used U.S. mail and telephones to violate Foreign Corrupt Practices Act); Filetech S.A. v. France Telecom S.A., 157 F.3d 922, 930-31 (2d Cir. 1998) (for commercial activity in the United States to satisfy the requirements of the exception, a significant nexus must exist between the commercial activity and plaintiff's cause of action; such nexus exists when the activity causes a nontrivial direct effect in the United States); *Hanil Bank*, 148 F.3d at 133 (to establish a direct effect in the United States, the United States "need not be the location where the most direct effect is felt, simply *a* direct effect"); Commercial Bank of Kuwait v. Rafidain Bank, 15 F.3d 238, 241 (2d Cir. 1994) ("The failure of [defendants] to remit funds in New York, as they were contractually bound to do, had a direct effect in the United States."); United World Trade, Inc. v. Mangyshlakneft Oil Prod. Ass'n, 33 F.3d 1232, 1236-39 (10th Cir. 1994) (actions of state agencies in a contract dispute in an overseas oil transaction with the government of Kazakhstan did not have a direct effect in the United States, even though payment under the contract required conversion of funds through a U.S. bank into U.S. dollars and lost profits and other injury were suffered in the United States), *cert. denied*, 513 U.S. 1112 (1995); Antares Aircraft, LP. v. Federal Republic of Nigeria, 999 F.2d 33 (2d Cir. 1993) ("the fact that an American . . . firm suffers some financial loss . . . cannot, standing alone, suffice to trigger the [direct effect] exception" since that "would in large part eviscerate the FSIA's provision of immunity for foreign states"); NYSA-ILA Pension Trust Fund v. Garuda Indonesia, 7 F.3d 35, 38 (2d Cir. 1993) (must be "significant nexus" between plaintiff's cause of action and "the commercial activity in this country upon which the exception is based"); Texas Trading & Milling Corp. v. Federal Republic of Nigeria, 647 F.2d 300, 313 (2d Cir. 1981) ("The question is, was the effect sufficiently 'direct' and sufficiently 'in the United States' that Congress would have wanted an American court to hear the case?"), *cert. denied*, 454 U.S. 1148 (1982); Carey v. National Oil Corp., 592 F.2d 673, 676 (2d Cir. 1979) (per curiam) (dismissing action against Libyan government-owned oil company because the challenged conduct, consisting of alleged overcharges and breach of contract, concerned a contract between a foreign state (the oil company) and a Bahamian corporation and because no "direct effect in the United States" had been shown, even though the Bahamian corporation was a subsidiary of a U.S. corporation; direct effect language "embodies the standard set out in *International Shoe*," and an indirect effect on a U.S. parent corporation did not meet this standard) (citing International Shoe Co. v. Washington, 326 U.S. 310, 316 (1945)); Rodriguez v. Republic of Costa Rica, 99 F. Supp. 2d 157, 166 (D.P.R. 2000) (in order for the commercial activity exception to apply, there must be a nexus between the plaintiff's action and the commercial activity); *see also* Dominican Energy Ltd. v. Dominican Republic, 903 F. Supp. 1507, 1514 (M.D. Fla. 1995) (no direct effect where contractual negotiations involving U.S. plaintiff did not result in an agreement and where the proposed contract called for payment in United States); Wyle v. Bank Melli, 577 F. Supp. 1148, 1158-60 (N.D. Cal. 1983) (demand on shipping company's U.S. bank by Iranian guarantor bank for payment of a letter of credit was held to cause a direct effect in the United States because assets

ANTITRUST LAW DEVELOPMENTS (FIFTH)

The determination of whether an activity is commercial is central to cases involving the FSIA. The FSIA defines commercial activity as "either a regular course of commercial conduct or a particular commercial transaction or act," with its character to be determined "by reference to the nature of the course of conduct or particular transaction or act, rather than by reference to its purpose."[156] Therefore, the fact that a foreign state has engaged in an act for a public purpose does not, by itself, render the act noncommercial.

In *Republic of Argentina v. Weltover, Inc.*,[157] the Supreme Court unanimously held that

> when a foreign government acts, not as regulator of a market, but in the manner of a private player within it, the foreign sovereign's actions are "commercial" within the meaning of the FSIA. Moreover, because the FSIA provides that the commercial character of an act is to be determined by reference to its "nature" rather than its "purpose," the question is not whether the foreign government is acting with a profit motive or instead with the aim of fulfilling uniquely sovereign objectives. Rather, the issue is whether the particular actions that the foreign state performs (whatever the motive behind them) are the *type* of actions by which a private party engages in "trade and traffic or commerce."[158]

Similarly, in *Saudi Arabia v. Nelson*,[159] the Court held Saudi Arabia immune under the FSIA with respect to tort claims by a U.S. plaintiff who had been recruited in the United States for a position at a state-owned hospital in Saudi Arabia and then allegedly was unlawfully detained and tortured by government agents for reporting safety violations at the hospital. The majority held that the commercial activity exception did not apply because the legal claims were not "based upon" commercial activity but on the allegedly tortious conduct.[160]

---

would be removed from the United States and because a U.S. bankruptcy estate would experience the loss).

156. 28 U.S.C. § 1603(d) (1994). In *Texas Trading & Milling Corp.*, 647 F.2d at 308-10, the Second Circuit relied on the act's legislative history, the case law in existence when it was passed, and international law in finding that commercial activity included a government purchase of cement on the open market, regardless of the purpose to which the cement was put. *See also* Gibbons v. Udaras na Gaeltachta, 549 F. Supp. 1094, 1110-11 (S.D.N.Y. 1982) ("Where . . . the commercial activity in question centers on the formation of a contract, the United States will be found to have had a substantial contact with that activity if substantial contractual negotiations occurred here . . . or if substantial aspects of the contract were to be performed here.").

157. 504 U.S. 607 (1992).

158. *Id.* at 614 (citations omitted).

159. 507 U.S. 349 (1993).

160. *Id.* at 355-58. Three dissenting justices disagreed, arguing that the plaintiff's "failure to warn" claim should not have been dismissed because it was based upon the hospital's recruiting activity within the United States. *Id.* at 371-76; *see also* General Elec. Capital Corp. v. Grossman, 991 F.2d 1376, 1382-86 (8th Cir. 1993) (foreign sovereign operation of an airline did not destroy immunity where the suit alleged that the airline conspired to inflate the price of an unrelated business sold to plaintiff because most of the allegedly improper acts occurred in Canada; activities conducted in the United States in connection with the sale were too minimal to result in jurisdiction). In *United States Fid. & Guar. Co. v. Braspetro Oil Servs. Co.*, 199 F.3d 94, 98 (2d Cir. 1999), the Second Circuit held that a "state engages in 'commercial activity' for the purposes of the FSIA when it acts not in its governmental or public role, but rather as a private player in the marketplace."

Classification of activity as sovereign or commercial is necessarily fact-specific.[161] In *Outboard Marine Corp. v. Pezetel*,[162] suit was brought against a

161. *See, e.g.,* Janini v. Kuwait Univ., 43 F.3d 1534 (D.C. Cir. 1995) (termination by decree of a government employment contract was not a sovereign act immune under the FSIA but a commercial act among "the *type* of actions by which a private party engages in 'trade and traffic or commerce'") (citation omitted); Princz v. Federal Republic of Germany, 26 F.3d 1166, 1172 (D.C. Cir. 1994) (whether forced labor for private industry under Nazi regime constituted commercial activity was a "close question"), *cert. denied*, 513 U.S. 1121 (1995); *In re* Estate of Marcos, Human Rights Litig., 25 F.3d 1467, 1470-72 (9th Cir. 1994) (acts of torture instigated by the former president of the Philippines were done in an individual, not a governmental, capacity, so the estate was not eligible for immunity), *cert. denied*, 513 U.S. 1126 (1995); Walter Fuller Aircraft Sales, Inc. v. Republic of the Philippines, 965 F.2d 1375, 1380-86 (5th Cir. 1992) (seizure and sale of a leased airplane by the Philippine commission charged with locating and retrieving property of a former president was a commercial act supporting jurisdiction over title claims by a U.S. firm on the airplane pursuant to the *Weltover* holding that the purpose of the act is irrelevant, but remanded for fact-finding on the issue of whether the commission was an alter ego of the Philippine government); Siderman de Blake v. Republic of Argentina, 965 F.2d 699, 708-09 (9th Cir. 1992) (marketing to tourists in the United States of an expropriated hotel and the receipt and use of revenues from U.S. tourists constituted commercial activity within and directly affecting the United States under the FSIA), *cert. denied*, 507 U.S. 1017 (1993); Rush-Presbyterian-St. Luke's Med. Ctr. v. Hellenic Republic, 877 F.2d 574, 581 (7th Cir.) (Greek government's execution of contract to reimburse physicians and organ bank for requested kidney transplants performed on Greek nationals in U.S. facilities was commercial activity under FSIA), *cert. denied*, 493 U.S. 937 (1989); Millen Indus. v. Coordination Council for N. Am. Affairs, 855 F.2d 879, 883-86 (D.C. Cir. 1988) (remanded to determine whether defendant, an instrumentality of the Taiwanese government, was engaged in commercial activity or immune sovereign activity when soliciting U.S. citizens to establish commercial ventures in Taiwan); West v. Multibanco Comermex, S.A., 807 F.2d 820, 824-25 (9th Cir.) (Mexican bank's issuance of certificates of deposit was held to be commercial activity despite the Mexican government's institution of currency exchange controls), *cert. denied*, 482 U.S. 906 (1987); Practical Concepts, Inc. v. Republic of Bolivia, 811 F.2d 1543, 1549-50 (D.C. Cir. 1987) (a consulting contract between a U.S. firm and a foreign government was held to be commercial activity; the commercial activity exception was determined by the essential character of the activity in issue); Millicom Int'l Cellular, S.A. v. Republic of Costa Rica, 995 F. Supp. 14 (D.D.C. 1998) (exclusion of plaintiffs from the Costa Rican cellular telephone market did not qualify for commercial activity exception to FSIA); Bryks v. Canadian Broad. Corp., 906 F. Supp. 204, 207-08 (S.D.N.Y. 1995) (television broadcasting is a commercial activity); Dominican Energy Ltd. v. Dominican Republic, 903 F. Supp. 1507, 1513 (M.D. Fla. 1995) (soliciting bids for financing, construction, and operation of electrical power generation facility is a commercial activity); Bybee v. Oper der Standt Bonn, 899 F. Supp. 1217, 1220 (S.D.N.Y. 1995) (engaging an opera singer to perform constitutes a commercial activity); EAL Corp. v. European Org. for the Safety of Air Navigation, No. 93-578-SLR, 1994 U.S. Dist. LEXIS 20528, at *20-33 (D. Del. Aug. 3, 1994) (the imposition and collection of navigation charges levied pursuant to an international agreement on users of air navigation services were sovereign, not commercial, activities); Eckert Int'l, Inc. v. Sovereign Democratic Republic of Fiji, 834 F. Supp. 167 (E.D. Va. 1993) (Fiji's entering into a contract is a private act and thus commercial activity), *aff'd*, 32 F.3d 77 (4th Cir. 1994); Caribbean Trading & Fidelity Corp. v. Nigerian Nat'l Petroleum Co., No. 90 Civ. 4169 (JFK), 1993 U.S. Dist. LEXIS 18242 (S.D.N.Y. Dec. 28, 1993) (the settlement of a contract dispute on the sale and disposition of crude oil constituted a commercial activity for the purposes of jurisdiction where the alleged direct effect in the United States was the discharge of attorneys' liens and the deprivation of U.S. law firms of fees); Zveiter v. Brazilian Nat'l Superintendency of Merchant Marine, 833 F. Supp. 1089, 1093 (S.D.N.Y.), *supplemental op.*, 841 F. Supp. 111, 112 (1993) (an allegation of sexual harassment in the New York office of a Brazilian state-owned company based upon an act, the employment of a secretary, which was commercial in nature and not "peculiarly sovereign in nature," but on rehearing the case, the court noted that the outcome may have been different if plaintiff had been hired in Brazil, given her dual citizenship); Optopics Lab. Corp. v. Savannah Bank of Nigeria, 816 F. Supp. 898, 907 n.5 (S.D.N.Y. 1993) (no immunity for Nigerian state-owned bank's failure to pay on a dollar-denominated letter of credit ostensibly due to foreign currency exchange restrictions imposed by Nigeria, because the letter was a

Polish government trade organization engaged in the manufacture and sale of golf carts that were imported into the United States. The district court held that this activity was inherently commercial.[163]

By contrast, in *International Ass'n of Machinists v. OPEC*,[164] the commercial activity exception was found inapplicable. The plaintiff argued that the defendants' price-fixing activities were commercial and thus susceptible to antitrust suits in U.S. courts. The district court disagreed, ruling that establishing terms and conditions for the removal of natural resources was a governmental prerogative entitled to sovereign immunity. Because the Organization of Petroleum Exporting Countries (OPEC) was composed of a collection of countries "coming together to agree upon how they will carry on that activity," the district court found the cartel to be involved in noncommercial activities,[165] and the suit was accordingly dismissed. The Ninth Circuit affirmed, but did so on act of state grounds, expressly avoiding deciding whether OPEC's activities were commercial.[166]

Whether criminal activity falls within the commercial activity exception to the FSIA was addressed by the Ninth Circuit in *Adler v. Federal Republic of Nigeria*.[167] In *Adler*, the majority held that "an illegal contract constitutes commercial activity under the FSIA."[168] The majority, however, was careful to note that not all illegal

---

commercial activity "entered into entirely independently of any [political] actions taken by the government of Nigeria to restrict foreign currency exchange"); Ampac Group v. Republic of Honduras, 797 F. Supp. 973, 976-77 (S.D. Fla. 1992) (commercial activity consisted of those acts customarily engaged in for profit by private persons, without regard to purpose), *aff'd without op.*, 40 F.3d 389 (11th Cir. 1994); Morgan Guar. Trust Co. v. Republic of Palau, 702 F. Supp. 60, 62-63 (S.D.N.Y. 1988) (a loan by a U.S. company to a foreign government was held to be a commercial activity), *vacated on other grounds*, 924 F.2d 1237 (2d Cir. 1991); American Bonded Warehouse Corp. v. Compagnie Nationale Air France, 653 F. Supp. 861, 864 (N.D. Ill. 1987) (an alleged scheme by defendant to eliminate competition in the freight forwarding industry was held to constitute commercial activity).

162. 461 F. Supp. 384 (D. Del. 1978).

163. *Id.* at 395-96. The court also held that the defendant, a state agency, was not protected from treble-damage liability by 28 U.S.C. § 1606 (1994 & Supp. 1999), which provides that "a foreign state except for an agency or instrumentality thereof shall not be liable for punitive damages" in most circumstances. *Id.* at 394-95.

164. 477 F. Supp. 553 (C.D. Cal. 1979), *aff'd on other grounds*, 649 F.2d 1354 (9th Cir. 1981), *cert. denied*, 454 U.S. 1163 (1982).

165. *Id.* at 569.

166. 649 F.2d at 1358. In *Prewitt Enters., Inc. v. OPEC*, 2001-1 Trade Cas. (CCH) ¶ 73,246 (D. Ala. 2001), however, the district court held that certain "agreements to restrict output and thereby affect prices of [a] commodity vital to United States trade and commerce . . . are plainly commercial in nature because they are acts that, while illegal, can be performed by private persons as well as sovereign states . . . . Accordingly, there can be no sovereign immunity with respect to such acts." *Id.* at 90,131. In addition, the district court found that OPEC, unlike its individual members, "is not itself a foreign state or an agency or instrumentality of a foreign state; rather, by its own description, OPEC is a 'voluntary intergovernmental organization' based in Vienna, Austria." *Id.* As a result, neither the FSIA nor the act of state doctrine had any application to the action. *See also Prepared Statement of the Federal Trade Commission on Solutions to Competitive Problems in the Oil Industry Before the House Comm. on the Judiciary*, 106th Cong. (statement of Richard G. Parker, Dir., Bureau of Competition, Federal Trade Comm'n), *available at* www.ftc.gov/os/2000/03/opectestimony.htm.

167. 219 F.3d 869 (9th Cir. 2000).

168. *Id.* at 871. *See also* Gould, Inc. v. Mitsui Mining & Smelting Co., 750 F. Supp. 838, 843-44 (N.D. Ohio 1990) (no criminal jurisdiction over agency of French government). *But see* United States v. Hendron, 813 F. Supp. 973, 975 (E.D.N.Y. 1993) (immunity applies only to civil proceedings).

activity falls within the commercial activity exception. Illegal activity "devoid of any commercial component," for example, does not fall within the exception.[169]

The courts have divided on the issue of whether intermediate subsidiaries of a foreign state are entitled to immunity under the FSIA.[170] An intermediate subsidiary will be entitled to immunity under the FSIA if it can demonstrate that it is "an organ of a foreign state or political subdivision thereof."[171] In determining whether these criteria are satisfied, courts look to whether the entity's purpose and functions are integral to and controlled by the foreign state.[172]

An individual also may qualify for immunity under the FSIA if he is employed by a foreign state and was acting in his official capacity and within the scope of his authority when he engaged in the acts in question.[173]

---

169. 219 F.3d at 874.
170. The Ninth Circuit has held that "tiering" should not be allowed; that is, a subsidiary should not qualify as a foreign state simply because its parent qualifies as an agency or instrumentality of a foreign state by virtue of being owned by the foreign state. *See* Gates v. Victor Fine Foods, 54 F.3d 1457, 1461-62 (9th Cir.), *cert. denied*, 516 U.S. 869 (1995). The Seventh Circuit has held that tiering is allowed, and it has granted the presumption of immunity for this type of indirectly owned entity. *See, e.g., In re* Air Crash Disaster near Roselawn, Ind., 909 F. Supp. 1083, 1094 (N.D. Ill. 1995) ("so long as the corporate intermediaries standing between a foreign state and a defendant seeking to invoke foreign-state status are themselves majority-owned by a statutorily-defined 'foreign state' (which, to be explicit, includes an agency or instrumentality of a foreign state), such tiering of ownership interests will not deprive the defendant of foreign state status"), *aff'd*, 96 F.3d 932 (7th Cir. 1996).

   Several district courts have agreed with the reasoning of the Ninth Circuit. *See, e.g.*, Southern Ocean Seafood Co. v. Holt Cargo Sys., Inc., No. 96-5217, 1997 U.S. Dist. LEXIS 12159 (E.D. Pa. Aug. 11, 1997); Lucas v. Dow Chem. Co., No. 95-3212, 1996 U.S. Dist. LEXIS 13180 (E.D. La. Sept. 4, 1996); Gardiner Stone Hunter Int'l v. Iberia Lineas Aereas de Espana, S.A., 896 F. Supp. 125 (S.D.N.Y. 1995). Others have agreed with the reasoning of the Seventh Circuit. *See, e.g.*, Filetech S.A. v. France Telecom S.A, 2001-1 Trade Cas. (CCH) ¶ 73,228, at 90,012 (S.D.N.Y. 2001) ("The FSIA applies to the instant case because the principal defendant, France Telecom, S.A., is an instrumentality of a foreign sovereign, the Republic of France. Accordingly that defendant's wholly-owned subsidiary, defendant France Telecom, Inc., has the same status. The defendants remain instrumentalities of France, notwithstanding France Telecom's recent transformation from an entity wholly owned and operated by the French government to a publicly traded company in which the government is the majority shareholder."). *See also* Dewhurst v. Telenor Invest A.S., 83 F. Supp. 2d 577 (D. Md. 2000); Millicom Int'l Cellular, S.A. v. Republic of Costa Rica, 995 F. Supp. 14, 18 n.5 (D.D.C. 1998); Delgado v. Shell Oil Co., 890 F. Supp. 1315, 1318 n.5 (S.D. Tex. 1995), *aff'd*, 231 F.3d 165 (5th Cir. 2000), *cert. denied*, 121 S. Ct. 1603 (2001); Credit Lyonnais v. Getty Square Assocs., 876 F. Supp. 517 (S.D.N.Y. 1995); Talbot v. Saipem A.G., 835 F. Supp. 352, 353 n.2 (S.D. Tex. 1993); Trump Taj Mahal v. Costuzioni Aeronautiche Geovanni, 761 F. Supp. 1143, 1150 (D.N.J. 1991), *aff'd*, 958 F.2d 365 (3d Cir.), *cert. denied*, 506 U.S. 826 (1992); Richmark Corp. v. Timber Falling Consultant, Inc., 747 F. Supp. 1409, 1411-12 (D. Or. 1990), *aff'd*, 937 F.2d 1444 (9th Cir. 1991), *cert. denied*, 506 U.S. 903 (1992).

   Numerous courts, including the Seventh Circuit, also have held that "pooling" is allowed. *See Roselawn*, 96 F.3d at 937-39 (an entity may qualify as a foreign state even if not majority owned by a single foreign government); LeDonne v. Gulf Air, Inc., 700 F. Supp. 1440 (E.D. Va. 1988).

171. 28 U.S.C. § 1603(b)(2) (1994). The factors considered by the courts in making this determination include the following: (1) whether the foreign state created the entity for a national purpose, (2) whether the foreign state actively supervises the entity, (3) whether the foreign state requires the hiring of public employees and compensates them, (4) whether the entity holds exclusive rights to some right in the country, and (5) whether the entity is treated as a part of the government under the laws of the foreign state. *Southern Ocean Seafood*, 1997 U.S. Dist. LEXIS 12159, at *12.

172. *See* Hyatt Corp. v. Stanton, 945 F. Supp. 675, 679 (S.D.N.Y. 1996).

173. *Id. See also* Chuidian v. Philippine Nat'l Bank, 912 F.2d 1095 (9th Cir. 1990).

The *International Antitrust Guidelines* emphasize the limits of sovereign immunity for antitrust violations. They state: "As a practical matter, most activities of foreign government-owned corporations operating in the commercial marketplace will be subject to U.S. antitrust laws to the same extent as the activities of foreign privately-owned firms."[174]

2. *Act of State*

The "act of state" doctrine, like the principle of sovereign immunity, has long been recognized in the United States.[175] However, unlike sovereign immunity, which exempts the sovereign itself from suit by virtue of its sovereign status, the act of state doctrine does not exempt any party from the process of the courts.[176] Rather, "[t]he act of state doctrine . . . merely requires that . . . the acts of foreign sovereigns taken within their own jurisdictions shall be deemed valid."[177] Where a plaintiff's theory turns on the invalidity of such acts, this doctrine may permit a private or governmental party to avoid liability. Unlike foreign sovereign immunity, parties cannot contractually preclude the application of the act of state doctrine.[178]

---

174. INTERNATIONAL ANTITRUST GUIDELINES, *supra* note 1, § 3.31.

175. *See* Underhill v. Hernandez, 168 U.S. 250, 252 (1897) ("Every sovereign State is bound to respect the independence of every other sovereign State, and the courts of one country will not sit in judgment on the acts of the government of another done within its own territory."). *See also* Banco Nacional de Cuba v. Sabbatino, 376 U.S. 398, 401 (1964) ("The act of state doctrine in its traditional formulation precludes the courts of this country from inquiring into the validity of the public acts a recognized sovereign power committed within its own territory."); International Ass'n of Machinists v. OPEC, 649 F.2d 1354, 1358 (9th Cir. 1981) ("The act of state doctrine declares that a United States court will not adjudicate a politically sensitive dispute which would require the court to judge the legality of the sovereign act of a foreign state.").

176. *See* Ricaud v. American Metal Co., 246 U.S. 304, 309 (1918) ("[The act of state doctrine] does not deprive the courts of jurisdiction once acquired over a case. It requires only that, when it is made to appear that the foreign government has acted in a given way on the subject-matter of the litigation, the details of such action or the merit of the result cannot be questioned but must be accepted by our courts as a rule for their decision. To accept a ruling authority and to decide accordingly is not a surrender or abandonment of jurisdiction but is an exercise of it.")

177. W.S. Kirkpatrick & Co. v. Environmental Tectonics Corp., Int'l, 493 U.S. 400, 409 (1990). In *Kirkpatrick*, the Court recognized "that the policies underlying the act of state doctrine should be considered in deciding whether, despite the doctrine's technical availability, it should nonetheless not be invoked." *Id.* Thus, the presumption of validity of the conduct in issue may be rebuttable or inapplicable. *See infra* notes 194-97 and accompanying text. *See also* Banco Nacional de Cuba v. Sabbatino, 376 U.S. 398, 428 (1964) (the Court "will not examine the validity of a taking of property within its own territory by a foreign sovereign government"); RESTATEMENT (THIRD), *supra* note 12, § 443(1) ("In the absence of a treaty or other unambiguous agreement regarding controlling legal principles, courts in the United States will generally refrain from examining the validity of a taking by a foreign state of property within its own territory, or from sitting in judgment on other acts of a governmental character done by a foreign state within its own territory and applicable therein.").

178. Unlike the defense of sovereign immunity, the act of state doctrine is not waivable by parties to a litigation. A court may apply the doctrine sua sponte, *cf. Frolova v. Union of Soviet Socialist Republics*, 761 F.2d 370, 371 (7th Cir. 1985), and U.S. case law reveals many instances in which the courts have refused to decide a matter on the basis of the act of state doctrine. In *Occidental Petroleum Corp. v. Buttes Gas & Oil Co.*, 461 F.2d 1261 (9th Cir. 1972), the Ninth Circuit invoked the act of state doctrine to avoid adjudicating which of two competing sheikdoms had superior authority to grant a concession. Since the plaintiffs' asserted claim arose through rights granted by a foreign government, the act of state doctrine was applied. Similarly, in *Compania de Gas de Nuevo Laredo v. Entex*, 686 F.2d 322 (5th Cir. 1982), the act of state doctrine precluded

Whatever its original premises may have been,[179] the act of state doctrine is now seen primarily as an aspect of the separation of powers.[180] According to this view, a judicial declaration that an act of a foreign state is invalid, even for the limited purpose of adjudicating a dispute under U.S. law, may adversely affect the conduct of foreign relations[181]—a subject that the Constitution commits to the executive branch.[182] Thus, the act of state doctrine is concerned with the potential embarrassment not of foreign states[183] but of the U.S. government in its relations with foreign states.[184] The doctrine also is concerned with ensuring that the courts do not make decisions that are at odds with the policies of the executive branch.[185]

---

consideration of a tort claim. These decisions were unaffected by the fact that the sovereign rulers were not named as parties. Thus, even in situations where both parties to a suit wish to see the action adjudicated, the act of state doctrine may prevent them from doing so.

179. For other suggested rationales of the doctrine and its history, *see* First Nat'l City Bank v. Banco Nacional de Cuba, 406 U.S. 759, 765-68 (1972); *Sabbatino*, 376 U.S. at 421-25; Oetjen v. Central Leather Co., 246 U.S. 297 (1918); Ricaud v. American Metal Co., 246 U.S. 304 (1918); American Banana Co. v. United Fruit Co., 213 U.S. 347 (1909); Underhill v. Hernandez, 168 U.S. 250 (1897).

180. *See, e.g.*, Environmental Tectonics Corp., Int'l v. W.S. Kirkpatrick, Inc., 847 F.2d 1052, 1058 (3d Cir. 1988) ("The core concern of modern act of state jurisprudence is preserving the separation of powers between the federal judiciary and the political branches of our government—especially, the executive branch, where primary responsibility for the conduct of foreign affairs is lodged."), *aff'd*, 493 U.S. 400 (1990); Industrial Inv. Dev. Corp. v. Mitsui & Co., 594 F.2d 48, 51 (5th Cir. 1979) (act of state doctrine "has emerged as independently based on concerns of separation of powers"), *cert. denied*, 445 U.S. 903 (1980); *see also Sabbatino*, 376 U.S. at 421, 423 ("We do not believe that this doctrine is compelled either by the inherent nature of sovereign authority, as some of the earlier decisions seem to imply, or by some principle of international law." Rather, the doctrine "arises out of the basic relationships between branches of government in a system of separation of powers.") (citations omitted); Associated Container Transp. (Australia) Ltd. v. United States, 705 F.2d 53, 61 (2d Cir. 1983) ("In essence, courts have recognized that the conduct of foreign relations is within the province of the executive branch and have refused under certain circumstances to become embroiled in international political controversies."); International Ass'n of Machinists v. OPEC, 649 F.2d 1354, 1358-59 (9th Cir. 1981) (doctrine "addresses concerns central to our system of government"), *cert. denied*, 454 U.S. 1163 (1982); Linseman v. World Hockey Ass'n, 439 F. Supp. 1315, 1324 (D. Conn. 1977) (doctrine based on "realization that the judiciary may hinder the executive in its conduct of foreign affairs" if it were to interfere); Occidental Petroleum Corp. v. Buttes Gas & Oil Co., 331 F. Supp. 92, 108-09 (C.D. Cal. 1971) (doctrine reflects "executive's primary competency in foreign affairs" and possibility that judiciary might "hinder or embarrass" foreign relations if it interfered), *aff'd per curiam*, 461 F.2d 1261 (9th Cir.), *cert. denied*, 409 U.S. 950 (1972).

181. *Kirkpatrick*, 493 U.S. at 404.

182. *See, e.g.*, *International Ass'n of Machinists*, 649 F.2d at 1358-59. The act of state doctrine is akin to the "political question" doctrine, which also occasionally may be implicated in antitrust suits involving foreign policy considerations. Unlike the act of state doctrine, however, the political question doctrine, if applicable, renders the entire dispute nonjusticiable. *See, e.g.*, Occidental of Umm al Qaywayn, Inc. v. A Certain Cargo of Petroleum, 577 F.2d 1196, 1203 (5th Cir. 1978) (a suit in conversion for crude oil extracted from the disputed territory was nonjusticiable; "The ownership of lands disputed by foreign sovereigns is a political question of foreign relations, the resolution or neutrality of which is committed to the executive branch by the Constitution."), *cert. denied*, 442 U.S. 928 (1979). *See generally* Goldwater v. Carter, 444 U.S. 996 (1979); Baker v. Carr, 369 U.S. 186 (1962).

183. *See Kirkpatrick*, 493 U.S. at 409.

184. *See* Banco Nacional de Cuba v. Sabbatino, 376 U.S. 398, 423 (1964) (the judiciary's "engagement in the task of passing on the validity of foreign acts of state may hinder rather than further this country's pursuit of goals, both for itself and for the community of nations"). *See also International Ass'n of Machinists*, 649 F.2d at 1358 ("The political branches of our government are able to consider the competing economic and political considerations and respond to the public

The precise scope of the act of state doctrine remained uncertain for many years.[186] Lower courts generally had engaged in a "case by case analysis of the extent to which the separation of powers concerns on which the doctrine is based [were] implicated."[187] Courts were more likely to apply the doctrine where a foreign state nationalized private property,[188] where the government conduct that was being questioned was public rather than commercial in nature,[189] or where a judicial pronouncement might have potentially serious foreign policy ramifications,[190] such as

---

will in order to carry on foreign relations in accordance with the best interests of the country as a whole. The courts, in contrast, focus on single disputes and make decisions on the basis of legal principles. . . . When the courts engage in piecemeal adjudication of the legality of sovereign acts of states, they risk disruption of our country's international diplomacy."). As the Second Circuit stated in *Bigio v. Coca-Cola Co.*:

> We begin with the proposition that the function of the court in applying the act of state doctrine is to 'weigh in balance the foreign policy interests that favor or disfavour [its] application.' *Republic of the Philippines v. Marcos*, 806 F.2d 344, 359 (2d Cir. 1986). We have noted that the policy concerns underlying the doctrine require that the political branches be preeminent in the realm of foreign relations . . . . The applicability of the doctrine depends on the likely impact on international relations that would result from judicial consideration of the foreign sovereign's act. If adjudication would embarrass or hinder the executive in the realm of foreign relations, the court should refrain from inquiring into the validity of the foreign state's act.

239 F.3d 440, 452 (2d Cir. 2000).

185. *See International Ass'n of Machinists*, 649 F.2d at 1358 (concluding that the act of state doctrine arises from recognition that "to participate adeptly in a global community, the United States must speak with one voice and pursue careful and deliberate foreign policy").

186. The Supreme Court first addressed the act of state doctrine in an antitrust context in *American Banana Co. v. United Fruit Co.*, 213 U.S. 347 (1909), in which the plaintiff alleged that its competitor had induced the Costa Rican military to seize the plaintiff's banana plantations. The Court held that the antitrust laws had no extraterritorial application. While this rendered unnecessary any consideration of the act of state doctrine, Justice Holmes nevertheless admonished that "a seizure by a state is not a thing that can be complained of elsewhere in the courts." *Id.* at 357-58. Persuading a foreign government to make such a seizure could not be illegal, according to Justice Holmes, because "it is a contradiction in terms to say that within its jurisdiction it is unlawful to persuade a sovereign power to bring about a result that it declares by its conduct to be desirable and proper." *Id.* at 358.

The Supreme Court reversed the jurisdictional holding of *American Banana* in *Continental Ore Co. v. Union Carbide & Carbon Corp.*, 370 U.S. 690, 704 (1962). In *Kirkpatrick*, the Court described the act of state discussion in *American Banana* as dictum that did not survive *United States v. Sisal Sales Corp.*, 274 U.S. 268 (1927). *See infra* notes 201-04 and accompanying text.

187. Texas Trading & Milling Corp. v. Federal Republic of Nigeria, 647 F.2d 300, 316 n.38 (2d Cir. 1981), *cert. denied*, 454 U.S. 1148 (1982); *see also* Republic of the Philippines v. Marcos, 862 F.2d 1355, 1361 (9th Cir. 1988), *cert. denied*, 490 U.S. 1035 (1989); Allied Bank Int'l v. Banco Credito Agricola de Cartago, 757 F.2d 516, 521 (2d Cir.), *cert. dismissed*, 473 U.S. 934 (1985); Williams v. Curtiss-Wright Corp., 694 F.2d 300, 303-05 (3d Cir. 1982); Rasoulzadeh v. Associated Press, 574 F. Supp. 854, 856 (S.D.N.Y. 1983), *aff'd without op.*, 767 F.2d 908 (2d Cir. 1985); Sage Int'l, Ltd. v. Cadillac Gage Co., 534 F. Supp. 896, 898-903 (E.D. Mich. 1981).

188. *See* RESTATEMENT (THIRD), *supra* note 12, § 443 comment c (the doctrine "has been applied predominantly" to acts involving the taking of private property by foreign states); *cf. Williams*, 694 F.2d at 304. *But see infra* note 218.

189. *See infra* notes 221-26 and accompanying text.

190. *See International Ass'n of Machinists*, 649 F.2d at 1360-61 (noting that "'the crucial element' is the potential for interference with our foreign relations") (citation omitted); Clayco Petroleum Corp. v. Occidental Petroleum Corp., 712 F.2d 404, 407-08 (9th Cir. 1983) (per curiam), *cert. denied*, 464 U.S. 1040 (1984); Hunt v. Mobil Oil Corp., 550 F.2d 68, 78 (2d Cir.), *cert. denied*, 434 U.S. 984 (1977); *cf. Texas Trading & Milling*, 647 F.2d at 316 n.38 (the act of state doctrine was not applied because defendants' challenged conduct did not threaten to embarrass the executive branch in its conduct of foreign relations).

where a court was asked to inquire into the validity of a foreign government's actions.[191]

In *Alfred Dunhill of London, Inc. v. Republic of Cuba*,[192] the Supreme Court indicated that the act of state doctrine protects only the "public act of those with authority to exercise sovereign power."[193] Therefore, the act of a sovereign agent, standing alone, may not be sufficient to establish an act of state defense if the act is either private or unauthorized.

In *W.S. Kirkpatrick & Co. v. Environmental Tectonics Corp., International*,[194] a unanimous Supreme Court clarified several aspects of the act of state doctrine. The plaintiff alleged that a competitor had conspired, in violation of the Robinson-Patman, RICO, and New Jersey RICO Acts, to bribe Nigerian officials in order to obtain a government construction contract.[195] Although the Court assumed that the award of the contract was a sovereign act, Nigeria was not a party to the litigation and no one argued that the award of the contract was invalid. Instead, the plaintiff sought judgment based on the defendant's conduct in obtaining the contract. The Court held that because the validity of the contract award was not in issue, the act of state doctrine did not apply.[196] The Court suggested that to place validity in issue, a party must seek relief or invoke a defense that "declare[s] invalid the official act of a foreign sovereign."[197] The Court also indicated that it is not enough for a sovereign act to merely be related to the litigation; instead, the sovereign act must be the subject matter of the judgment.

Kirkpatrick thus resolved a conflict among the circuits over whether the doctrine permits judicial inquiry into the motivations of the relevant state actors[198] or whether

---

In some cases, courts have declined to apply the act of state doctrine where the executive branch has stated that its application would not advance foreign policy interests. *See infra* notes 227-30 and accompanying text.

191. *See, e.g.*, Alfred Dunhill of London, Inc. v. Republic of Cuba, 425 U.S. 682, 697, 706 (1976) (plurality op.) (White, J.) (the act of state doctrine "'precludes the courts of this country from inquiring into the validity'" of public acts of a foreign sovereign committed within its own territory) (citation omitted); Banco Nacional de Cuba v. Sabbatino, 376 U.S. 398, 428 (1964); *cf.* Associated Container Transp. (Australia) Ltd. v. United States, 705 F.2d 53, 61 (2d Cir. 1983) (the doctrine is not applicable where the court is not required to inquire into validity of foreign statutes).

192. 425 U.S. 682 (1976).

193. *Id.* at 694.

194. 493 U.S. 400 (1990).

195. *Id.* at 401-02.

196. *Id.* at 405 ("Nothing in the present suit requires the Court to declare invalid, and thus ineffective as 'a rule of decision for the courts of this country,' . . . the official act of a foreign sovereign.") (citation omitted).

197. *Id.*

198. *See, e.g.*, Clayco Petroleum Corp. v. Occidental Petroleum Corp., 712 F.2d 404, 407-08 (9th Cir. 1983); Hunt v. Mobil Oil Corp., 550 F.2d 68, 73-79 (2d Cir. 1977); Occidental Petroleum Corp. v. Buttes Gas & Oil Co., 331 F. Supp. 92, 110 (C.D. Cal. 1971), *aff'd per curiam*, 461 F.2d 1261 (9th Cir. 1972).

In *Hunt*, for example, an independent oil producer alleged that the major oil companies, acting in concert, had manipulated their dealings with Libya so as to prompt the nationalization of the plaintiff's Libyan oil interests. The plaintiff did not allege any wrongful conduct by the Libyan government. The Second Circuit nevertheless ruled that Libya's action was a necessary element in one of the antitrust counts, and Hunt's claim was "admittedly not viable unless the judicial branch examine[d] the motivation of the Libyan action and that inevitably involve[d] its validity"—which, under the act of state doctrine, a court should not do. 550 F.2d at 76-77. The court relied on a State Department analysis of the nationalization, in part to support its conclusion that the issues of

the doctrine is limited to questions of validity of the foreign state's act.[199] Relying
upon the judicial duty to decide cases and controversies, the Court adopted the latter
view:

> Act of state issues only arise when a court *must decide*—that is, when the outcome of
> the case turns upon—the effect of the official action by a foreign sovereign . . . .
>
> The short of the matter is this: Courts in the United States have the power, and
> ordinarily the obligation, to decide cases and controversies properly presented to them.
> The act of state doctrine does not establish an exception for cases and controversies
> that may embarrass foreign governments, but merely requires that, in the process of
> deciding, the acts of foreign sovereigns taken within their own jurisdictions shall be
> deemed valid.[200]

---

motivation and validity were inextricably intertwined, and in part to show that the State
Department had already decided those issues and thus a judicial inquiry "could only be fissiparous,
hindering or embarrassing the conduct of foreign relations"—relations that the oil crises had
moved to a delicate stage. *Id.* at 77-78.

   Similar concerns about judging the validity and motivation of acts of foreign governments led
several other courts, often relying on *Hunt*, to invoke the doctrine. *See* O.N.E. Shipping Ltd. v.
Flota Mercante Grancolombiana, S.A., 830 F.2d 449, 452-53 (2d Cir. 1987) (antitrust claims
arising from foreign cargo preference laws dismissed on the basis of the act of state doctrine), *cert.
denied*, 488 U.S. 923 (1988); International Ass'n of Machinists v. OPEC, 649 F.2d 1354, 1358-59
(9th Cir. 1981); General Aircraft Corp. v. Air Am., Inc., 482 F. Supp. 3, 6 (D.D.C. 1979)
(following Occidental Petroleum Corp. v. Buttes Gas & Oil Co., 331 F. Supp. 92, 110 (C.D. Cal.
1971)); *Occidental Petroleum*, 331 F. Supp. at 110 (challenge of conduct "catalyzing" foreign
sovereign's disruption of Mideast oil operations would require inquiry "into the authenticity and
motivation of the acts of foreign sovereigns"); Bokkelen v. Grumman Aerospace Corp., 432 F.
Supp. 329 (E.D.N.Y. 1977) (challenge to allegedly improper influencing of Brazil export license
denial); *see also* RESTATEMENT (THIRD), *supra* note 12, § 443 & reporters' note 7.

199. *See, e.g.*, Associated Container Transp. (Australia) Ltd. v. United States, 705 F.2d 53, 61-62 (2d
Cir. 1983); Williams v. Curtiss-Wright Corp., 694 F.2d 300, 304 & n.5 (3d Cir. 1982); Industrial
Inv. Dev. Corp. v. Mitsui & Co., 594 F.2d 48, 54 (5th Cir. 1979), *cert. denied*, 445 U.S. 903
(1980); Sage Int'l, Ltd. v. Cadillac Gage Co., 534 F. Supp. 896, 901-03, 909 (E.D. Mich. 1981);
INTERNATIONAL ANTITRUST GUIDELINES, *supra* note 1, § 3.33. The DOJ and the FTC have taken
the position that the act of state doctrine should apply only in cases where the conduct "complained
of is a public act of the foreign sovereign within its territorial jurisdiction on matters pertaining to
its governmental sovereignty." *Id.*

200. *Kirkpatrick*, 493 U.S. at 406, 409; *see also* Walter Fuller Aircraft Sales, Inc. v. Republic of the
Philippines, 965 F.2d 1375, 1387-88 (5th Cir. 1992) (holding act of state doctrine inapplicable
because there was no challenge to validity of any acts of the Philippine government); Richmark
Corp. v. Timber Falling Consultants, 959 F.2d 1468 (9th Cir.) (act of state doctrine inapplicable to
a dispute over the effect of blocking statutes because validity of the statutes was not in dispute),
cert. dismissed, 506 U.S. 948 (1992); Lamb v. Phillip Morris, Inc., 915 F.2d 1024, 1025-27 (6th
Cir. 1990) (donations by U.S. firms to a Venezuelan charitable organization in exchange for tax
deductions, the elimination of price controls on cigarettes, and a pledge not to raise excise taxes in
Venezuela did not involve the doctrine because the adjudication "merely call[ed] into question
the . . . parties' motivations and the resulting anticompetitive effects of their agreement, not the
validity of any foreign sovereign act"), *cert. denied*, 498 U.S. 1086 (1991); Alpha Lyracom Space
Communs. v. Communications Satellite Corp., 1993-1 Trade Cas. (CCH) ¶ 70,184, at 69,863
(S.D.N.Y. 1993) (act of state doctrine not applicable where the only issue was whether a U.S.
company had reached agreements with foreign state-owned companies in violation of the antitrust
law); Norwest Corp. v. Commissioner, 63 T.C.M. (CCH) ¶ 3023 (U.S. Tax Ct. 1992) (act of state
doctrine inapplicable to decision interpreting the effect, but not validity, of Brazilian tax
provision), *aff'd*, 69 F.3d 1404 (8th Cir. 1995), *cert. denied*, 517 U.S. 1203 (1996); *see also*
Pittsburgh-Corning Corp. v. Askewe, 823 S.W.2d 759, 761 (Tex. Ct. App. 1992) (act of state

The Court characterized as dictum[201] its previous discussion of the act of state doctrine in *American Banana Co. v. United Fruit Co.*[202] and made clear that, in any event, that dictum had not survived *United States v. Sisal Sales Corp.*[203] *Sisal* involved an alleged conspiracy that culminated in the enactment of discriminatory tax legislation in Mexico. The Supreme Court ruled that the antitrust laws applied notwithstanding the act of state doctrine where a conspiracy was formed in the United States, the conspirators took actions in the United States to further the conspiracy, and the restraint of trade resulted not from foreign sovereign acts alone but from the "deliberate acts, here and elsewhere," of private parties.[204]

Further, indicating a restricted view of the act of state doctrine, the Court in *Kirkpatrick* suggested that, in cases where a judicial inquiry into the validity of the act of a foreign state would not compromise the principles of comity, sovereignty, and the separation of powers that underlie the doctrine, a court may decline to invoke the doctrine.[205] While this ad hoc "balancing approach" may be deployed to operate "against application of the doctrine, for example, if the government that committed the 'challenged act of state' is no longer in existence,"[206] the Court emphasized that "it is something quite different to suggest that those underlying policies are a doctrine unto themselves, justifying expansion of the act of state doctrine . . . into new and uncharted fields."[207] In other words, courts have some discretion to contract but not to expand the scope of the doctrine.

Despite the Supreme Court's clarification of the act of state doctrine in *Kirkpatrick*, various threshold questions remain uncertain. These include determining whether the challenge is to an act of state. For example, in *Timberlane Lumber Co. v. Bank of America National Trust & Savings Ass'n*,[208] the defendants were alleged to have conspired to block the plaintiff's efforts to set up a plant in Honduras. The complaint alleged that the defendants had instituted proceedings in Honduran courts for the sole purpose of interfering with the operations of the plant. The district court

---

doctrine inapplicable in dispute over antisuit injunction because validity of foreign governmental action was not at issue).

201. 493 U.S. at 407-08.
202. 213 U.S. 347 (1909).
203. 274 U.S. 268 (1927). Although the Court did not discuss the act of state doctrine by name, its reasoning in *Sisal* appears to have been based on the doctrine.
204. *Id.* at 276; *see also* United Nuclear Corp. v. General Atomic Co., 629 P.2d 231, 258 (N.M. 1980) (mere fact that foreign government played role in anticompetitive scheme is not dispositive; courts must examine "the nature of the role played by the foreign government"), *appeal dismissed*, 451 U.S. 901 (1981).
205. 493 U.S. at 408-09; *see also* Grupo Protexa, S.A. v. All Am. Marine Slip, 20 F.3d 1224, 1236-39 (3d Cir.) (the validity of a foreign governmental act may be examined where none of the underlying policies of the act of state doctrine was present in a challenge to a Mexican decision to remove a sunken wreck from the bay off the coast of Mexico), *cert. denied*, 513 U.S. 986 (1994).
206. *See, e.g.*, Republic of the Philippines v. Marcos, 806 F.2d 344, 359 (2d Cir. 1986) (rationale for considering a change in government is that "the danger of interference with the Executive's conduct of foreign policy is surely much less than the typical case where the act of state is that of the current foreign government"). *See also* Bigio v. Coca-Cola Co., 239 F.3d 440, 453 (2d Cir. 2000) (decision not to invoke act of state doctrine would not offend government of Egypt or interfere with the relationship between Egypt and the United States because "there is little doubt that the Egyptian government that is now in power is far removed in time and circumstance from that which seized the Bigios' property. The expropriation took place thirty-four or more years ago; President Nasser has been dead for thirty years.").
207. 493 U.S. at 409.
208. 549 F.2d 597 (9th Cir. 1976).

ANTITRUST LAW DEVELOPMENTS (FIFTH)

dismissed the suit on the ground that the judicial decree that caused the plaintiff's injury was an act of state. The Ninth Circuit reversed. Noting that the suit did not challenge any policy of the Honduran government, that a judicial determination of the legality of the offensive conduct would not threaten relations between Honduras and the United States, and that the judicial proceedings were not instituted by the sovereign, the court concluded that a foreign court judgment in a private civil suit was not an act of state.[209]

Similarly, in *Mannington Mills, Inc. v. Congoleum Corp.*,[210] the Third Circuit held that the act of state doctrine did not preclude judicial consideration of allegedly fraudulent methods used to obtain foreign patents. The court reasoned that the "ministerial" act of granting a patent was "not the kind of governmental action contemplated by the act of state doctrine."[211] Rather, the court observed that judicial abstention generally has been required only when the conduct being challenged is "a result of a considered policy determination by a government to give effect to its political and public interests—matters that would have a significant impact on American foreign relations."[212]

In *Biovail Corp. International v. Hoechst Aktiengesellschaft*,[213] a Canadian drug manufacturer sued several pharmaceutical companies under the Sherman Act for, among other things, allegedly interfering with the Canadian drug regulatory process in order to delay approval of a new drug by Canada's Health Protection Board (HPB). In moving for dismissal, the defendants argued that "the chain of causation between their acts and [the plaintiff's] alleged injury is 'irrevocably destroyed' because evaluating the chain would necessarily entail questioning the correctness of

---

209. *Id.* at 608; *see also* Dominicus Americana Bohio v. Gulf & W. Indus., 473 F. Supp. 680 (S.D.N.Y. 1979).

210. 595 F.2d 1287 (3d Cir. 1979).

211. *Id.* at 1294. In *Williams v. Curtiss-Wright Corp.*, 694 F.2d 300, 303 (3d Cir. 1982), the Third Circuit clarified that it did not create a "ministerial exception" in *Mannington Mills.*

212. 595 F.2d at 1294 (citation omitted); *see also* Remington Rand Corp.-Del. v. Business Sys., 830 F.2d 1260, 1265 (3d Cir. 1987) (act of state doctrine did not apply to foreign debtor's bankruptcy trustees because they were not government officials); American Indus. Contracting v. Johns-Manville Corp., 326 F. Supp. 879 (W.D. Pa. 1971) (statute of Province of Quebec was not covered by the doctrine because Quebec is not a nation state). *Compare* Bernstein v. Van Heyghen Frères S.A., 163 F.2d 246, 249-52 (2d Cir.) (Hand, J.) (the subsequent war against, and destruction of, the Nazi regime did not retroactively deprive prewar actions by Nazi officials of act of state status), *cert. denied*, 332 U.S. 772 (1947), *with* Underhill v. Hernandez, 168 U.S. 250 (1897) (seizures by a then-unrecognized revolutionary party, which by the time of suit had become the recognized government of Venezuela, accorded act of state status).

 Acts deemed to have been committed by foreign officials in their private capacity are not acts of state and thus receive no protection under the doctrine. *See, e.g.*, Republic of the Philippines v. Marcos, 806 F.2d 344, 358-59 (2d Cir. 1986) (drawing a distinction between "acts of Marcos as head of state, which may be protected from judicial scrutiny even if illegal under Philippine law, and his purely private acts," but noting the difficulty of distinguishing between the two); Jimenez v. Aristeguieta, 311 F.2d 547, 557-58 (5th Cir. 1962) (a former Venezuela dictator, seeking to block extradition for embezzlement, could not invoke the doctrine because his acts "were not acts of Venezuelan sovereignty" but for "private . . . benefit" only and "constituted common crimes committed by the Chief of State . . . . They are as far from being an act of state as rape . . . ."), *cert. denied*, 373 U.S. 914 (1963); United States v. Noriega, 746 F. Supp. 1506, 1521-22 (S.D. Fla. 1990) (a former Panamanian dictator's participation in a conspiracy to import cocaine into the United States and protect money launderers was but "a series of private acts committed by the defendant for his own personal financial enrichment" and thus not immunized from prosecution by the act of state doctrine).

213. 49 F. Supp. 2d 750 (D.N.J. 1999).

the regulatory approval decision of a foreign sovereign, namely the Canadian HPB."[214] The district court disagreed. The court first stated that it would "not, under the 'act of state' doctrine, inquir[e] into the validity of the public acts of a recognized sovereign power committed within its own territory."[215] It then noted that it did not appear that the plaintiff was challenging the activities of the HPB but merely contending that the defendants were liable for the actions that they took in trying to impermissibly influence the HPB. The defendants were not insulated from liability simply because their allegedly anticompetitive conduct was directed at a foreign government's regulatory process.[216]

Other threshold questions include whether the sovereign in question is one to whom the U.S. judiciary owes deference,[217] and whether the conduct has occurred within the foreign sovereign's jurisdiction.[218]

There are also several possible exceptions to the doctrine. Congress created one such exception with the Second Hickenlooper Amendment,[219] which reversed the Supreme Court's holding in *Banco Nacional de Cuba v. Sabbatino*[220] and required courts to determine the validity of expropriations under international law.

The precise status of other exceptions is less clear. In *Alfred Dunhill of London, Inc. v. Republic of Cuba*,[221] a four-justice plurality of the Supreme Court declared the act of state doctrine inapplicable to sovereign action involving a commercial, rather

214. *Id.* at 770.
215. *Id.*
216. *Id.*
217. *See* Banco Nacional de Cuba v. Sabbatino, 376 U.S. 398, 408-12, 437-38 (1964). The Supreme Court rejected the argument that the severance of diplomatic relations, imposition of an embargo, and freezing of assets manifested such hostility toward Cuba as to deprive that country of the privilege of suing in U.S. courts or raising the act of state doctrine as a defense: "This Court would hardly be competent to undertake assessments of varying degrees of friendliness . . . we are constrained to consider any relationship, short of war, with a recognized sovereign power" as sufficient. *Id.* at 410; *see also Bernstein*, 163 F.2d at 249-51 (doctrine applied to prewar acts of Nazi officials); *cf.* Republic of the Philippines v. Marcos, 862 F.2d 1355, 1360-61 (9th Cir. 1988) (a deposed head of state cannot invoke the doctrine to immunize his past activities from inquiry in U.S. courts where the reigning sovereign authority is suing to reclaim assets allegedly misappropriated in violation of its municipal law), *cert. denied*, 490 U.S. 1035 (1989).
218. The act of state doctrine does not apply to extraterritorial assertions of jurisdiction by the foreign sovereign. Thus, when a foreign state attempts to seize the property of its nationals located in the United States, "our courts will give effect to acts of state 'only if they are consistent with the policy and law of the United States.'" Republic of Iraq v. First Nat'l City Bank, 353 F.2d 47, 51 (2d Cir.) (citation omitted) (Iraqi seizure of assets abroad), *aff'g* 241 F. Supp. 567, 574 (S.D.N.Y. 1965), *cert. denied*, 382 U.S. 1027 (1966); *see also Sabbatino*, 376 U.S. at 447 n.7 (White, J., dissenting) (collecting cases); Bandes v. Harlow & Jones, Inc., 852 F.2d 661, 666 (2d Cir. 1988) ("When another state attempts to seize property held here, our jurisdiction is paramount."); Tchacosh Co. v. Rockwell Int'l Corp., 766 F.2d 1333, 1336 (9th Cir. 1985) ("Notions of territoriality run deep through the doctrine. . . . When property is located within United States territory . . . 'the policies mandating a hands-off attitude no longer apply with the same force.'") (citation omitted); United Bank v. Cosmic Int'l, Inc., 542 F.2d 868 (2d Cir. 1976) (holding act of state doctrine inapplicable to Bangladesh's extraterritorial seizures); Eckert Int'l v. Sovereign Democratic Republic of Fiji, 834 F. Supp. 167, 172 (E.D. Va. 1993) (contract could not have been completed within Fiji); Optopics Lab. Corp. v. Savannah Bank of Nigeria, 816 F. Supp. 898, 906 (S.D.N.Y. 1993) (right to receive payment was in United States); Drexel Burnham Lambert Group v. Committee of Receivers for A.W. Galadari, 810 F. Supp. 1375, 1391 (S.D.N.Y. 1993) (U.S. situs of debt), *rev'd on other grounds*, 12 F.3d 317 (2d Cir. 1993), *cert. denied*, 511 U.S. 1069 (1994).
219. 22 U.S.C. § 2370(e)(2) (1994).
220. 376 U.S. 398 (1964).
221. 425 U.S. 682, 695-706 (1976) (White, J., with Burger, C.J., Powell, J. & Rehnquist, J.).

than a governmental, function.[222]   The Second Circuit and some other courts have adopted this commercial activity exception.[223]   Other courts, however, have discounted the authority of the *Dunhill* plurality.[224]   The Ninth Circuit took the strongest position against the exception in *International Ass'n of Machinists v. OPEC*,[225] stating that

> the act of state doctrine is not diluted by the commercial activity exception which limits the doctrine of sovereign immunity. While purely commercial activity may not rise to the level of an act of state, certain seemingly commercial activity will trigger act of state considerations . . . [W]hen the state qua state acts in the public interest, its sovereignty is asserted. The courts must proceed cautiously to avoid an affront to that sovereignty . . . [W]e find that the act of state doctrine remains available when such caution is appropriate, regardless of any commercial component of the activity involved.[226]

---

222. *Id.* at 695 (the act of state doctrine does not protect "the repudiation of a purely commercial obligation owed by a foreign sovereign or by one of its commercial instrumentalities"). The FSIA contains a commercial activity exception. 28 U.S.C. § 1605(a)(2) (1994); *see also* part D.1 of this chapter.

223. *See, e.g.*, Hunt v. Mobil Oil Corp., 550 F.2d 68, 73 (2d Cir.), *cert. denied*, 434 U.S. 984 (1977); *see also* Walter Fuller Aircraft Sales, Inc. v. Republic of the Philippines, 965 F.2d 1375, 1388 (5th Cir. 1992) (commercial activities exception to the act of state doctrine allowed U.S. courts to adjudicate the dispute); Northrop Corp. v. McDonnell Douglas Corp., 705 F.2d 1030, 1048 n.25 (9th Cir.) (stating that purely commercial activity ordinarily does not require judicial forbearance), *cert. denied*, 464 U.S. 849 (1983); Texas Trading & Milling Corp. v. Federal Republic of Nigeria, 647 F.2d 300, 316 n.38 (2d Cir. 1981) (declining to apply the doctrine in part because the governmental conduct was commercial), *cert. denied*, 454 U.S. 1148 (1982); *Eckert Int'l*, 834 F. Supp. at 171 (act of state doctrine does not apply to private commercial activity outside a sovereign's territory); *Drexel Burnham*, 810 F. Supp. at 1391 (the repudiation of debts located in the United States was held to be commercial activity and thus the act of state doctrine was inapplicable); Ampac Group v. Republic of Honduras, 797 F. Supp. 973, 978 (S.D. Fla. 1992) (the doctrine does not apply where governmental action is commercial in nature), *aff'd without op.*, 40 F.3d 389 (11th Cir. 1994); Sage Int'l, Ltd. v. Cadillac Gage Co., 534 F. Supp. 896, 905 (E.D. Mich. 1981) ("the better reasoned conclusion is that consideration of the commercial nature of a given act is compelled if the doctrine is to be applied correctly").

224. *See, e.g.*, Bokkelen v. Grumman Aerospace Corp., 432 F. Supp. 329, 333 (E.D.N.Y. 1977).

225. 649 F.2d 1354 (9th Cir. 1981).

226. *Id.* at 1360. The Ninth Circuit's decision was distinguished in *Prewitt Enters., Inc. v. OPEC*, 2001-1 Trade Cas. (CCH) ¶ 73,246 (N.D. Ala. 2001). In *Prewitt*, the district court entered default judgment against OPEC, holding that the actions of OPEC "consisting of crafting, developing, coordinating, monitoring, entering into, implementing and/or enforcing agreements regarding the production and export of crude oil are . . . unlawful contracts, combinations or conspiracies in restraint of United States or foreign commerce in violation of § 1 of the Sherman Act." *Id.* at 90,133. With respect to the application of the act of state doctrine, the district court wrote that "because the acts are commercial in nature, they are not protected from judicial scrutiny by virtue of the act of state doctrine, which is a judge-made rule based largely on separation of powers concerns suggesting a reluctance to determine the legality of acts of foreign states taken within their own territories." *Id.* The court noted its awareness of *International Ass'n of Machinists*, where "the Ninth Circuit concluded that it was barred under the act of state doctrine from determining whether OPEC's members had violated the Sherman Act with respect to a series of earlier acts in restraint of trade," but found that decision distinguishable because, inter alia, "the defendants were the OPEC members not OPEC" and because "the Ninth Circuit did not give meaningful weight to the decision of the plurality of the Supreme Court in *Alfred Dunhill*. . . ." *Id.* at 90,134.

In *First National City Bank v. Banco Nacional de Cuba*,[227] a three-justice plurality adopted an exception that the Second Circuit had recognized in *Bernstein v. N.V. Nederlandsche-Amerikaansche Stoomvaart-Maatschappij*,[228] holding that courts need not invoke the doctrine where the executive branch has formally represented (in a so-called *Bernstein* letter) that its application "would not advance the interests of American foreign policy."[229] Because the act of state doctrine did not apply to the facts of *Kirkpatrick*, the Court declined to address either the commercial activity or *Bernstein* letter exceptions.[230]

An act of state issue is a matter of federal law whether it arises in a federal or state court.[231] The doctrine is not jurisdictional, however, but is a substantive rule of decision.[232] Thus, as a matter of procedure, a motion to dismiss on act of state grounds lies under Rule 12(b)(6) of the Federal Rules of Civil Procedure, not under Rule 12(b)(1).[233] The stage of the proceeding at which the doctrine is raised may affect its applicability. In *Associated Container Transportation (Australia) Ltd. v. United States*,[234] the Second Circuit reversed the district court's decision to quash civil investigative demands (CIDs) of the Department of Justice on *Noerr*[235] and act

---

227. 406 U.S. 759 (1972) (Rehnquist, J., with Burger, C.J. & White, J.).
228. 210 F.2d 375 (2d Cir. 1954).
229. *First Nat'l City Bank*, 406 U.S. at 768; *see also Sabbatino*, 376 U.S. at 462 (White, J., dissenting); *cf.* Environmental Tectonics Corp., Int'l v. W.S. Kirkpatrick Inc., 847 F.2d 1052, 1061-62 (3d Cir. 1988) (the State Department's views are "entitled to substantial respect"), *aff'd on other grounds*, 493 U.S. 400 (1990). As with the commercial activity exception, courts have split on whether to adopt the *Bernstein* letter exception. *Compare* United Nuclear Corp. v. General Atomic Co., 629 P.2d 231, 263-64 (N.M. 1980) (state antitrust action) (executive branch representations, while relevant, are not dispositive with respect to the applicability of the act of state doctrine), *appeal dismissed*, 451 U.S. 901 (1981), *and* Republic of the Phillipines v. Marcos, 806 F.2d 344, 358 (2d Cir. 1986) ("'Whether to invoke the act of state doctrine is ultimately and always a judicial question.'") (citation omitted), *with In re* Grand Jury Proceedings the Bank of Nova Scotia, 740 F.2d 817, 832 n.23 (11th Cir. 1984) (act of state doctrine does not apply where the executive announces that it has no objection to a judicial examination), *cert. denied*, 469 U.S. 1106 (1985).

The acquiescence or tacit consent of the State Department also may lessen a court's sensitivity to asserted foreign policy concerns. *See, e.g.*, Associated Container Transp. (Australia) Ltd. v. United States, 705 F.2d 53, 61 n.11 (2d Cir. 1983) ("State Department's failure to intervene on either side, however, makes us less wary of permitting the Justice Department" to proceed with its request for records of communications between the defendants and the governments of Australia and New Zealand), *rev'g* 502 F. Supp. 505 (S.D.N.Y. 1980).

230. *Kirkpatrick*, 493 U.S. at 404-05. Courts also have declined to apply the act of state doctrine to infamous conduct. *See, e.g.*, Liu v. Republic of China, 892 F.2d 1419, 1432-34 (9th Cir. 1989) (a foreign intelligence officer who allegedly ordered an assassination in the United States could not raise the doctrine as a defense in a wrongful death action brought by a widow), *cert. dismissed*, 497 U.S. 1058 (1990); Filartiga v. Pena-Irala, 630 F.2d 876, 889-90 (2d Cir. 1980) (dictum) (torture committed by a Paraguayan official was not protected by the act of state doctrine, even though it was committed within the territory of a foreign state, because torture is a violation of universally recognized human rights); Letelier v. Republic of Chile, 488 F. Supp. 665, 671-74 (D.D.C. 1980) (assassination in Washington, D.C., allegedly ordered by foreign government).

231. *See, e.g.*, *Sabbatino*, 376 U.S. at 425-27.
232. *See, e.g.*, *Kirkpatrick*, 493 U.S. at 405-07 (noting that the act of state doctrine is a rule of decision that prevents courts in the United States from invalidating a foreign sovereign's completed domestic acts).
233. *See, e.g.*, Ricaud v. American Metal Co., 246 U.S. 304, 309 (1918); Lamb v. Phillip Morris, Inc., 915 F.2d 1024, 1026 n.3 (6th Cir. 1990), *cert. denied*, 498 U.S. 1086 (1991); Timberlane Lumber Co. v. Bank of Am. Nat'l Trust & Sav. Ass'n, 549 F.2d 597, 602 (9th Cir. 1976).
234. 705 F.2d 53 (2d Cir. 1983).
235. The *Noerr* doctrine is discussed in part D.5 of this chapter and part C of Chapter XIII.

of state grounds, holding that CIDs could be enforced to compel production of
communications to the Federal Maritime Commission and New Zealand and
Australian government agencies. The court emphasized that it was premature to
foreclose inquiry and specifically noted that its decision "in no way indicates that
these doctrines may not properly be invoked at a later state of these proceedings
should the Justice Department decide to bring formal charges."[236] The burden of
proof is on the party asserting the act of state doctrine.[237]

The *International Antitrust Guidelines* take a narrow view of the act of state
doctrine. They state that the government may refrain from taking action when a
restraint on competition arises directly from the act of a foreign government, and that
foreign acts of state will not be challenged where (1) the specific conduct is a public
act of the sovereign, (2) the act took place within the territorial jurisdiction of the
sovereign, and (3) the matter is governmental rather than commercial.[238] The federal
enforcement agencies will apply the doctrine "when the validity of the acts of a
foreign government is an unavoidable issue in a case."[239]

3. Foreign Sovereign Compulsion

Courts generally will not impose antitrust liability on a private party if the
offending conduct is compelled by a foreign sovereign.[240] In cases of compelled
conduct, the acts of the private party "become effectively acts of the sovereign."[241]

The defense of foreign sovereign compulsion reflects a judicial recognition that it
would be unfair to impose liability upon a private party compelled to act by the
command of a foreign sovereign, at least where a refusal to comply with the
sovereign's command would result in the imposition of significant penalties or in the
denial of significant benefits.[242]

The sovereign compulsion defense has generally not been applied to private
conduct that was simply sanctioned or assisted by a foreign government but not

236. 705 F.2d at 62; *see also* Cofinco, Inc. v. Angola Coffee Co., 1975-2 Trade Cas. (CCH) ¶ 60,456
(S.D.N.Y. 1975) (denying summary judgment motion because genuine issues of material fact
existed concerning the act of state defense). *But see In re* Investigation of World Arrangements
with Relation to Prod., Transp., Ref. & Distrib. of Petroleum, 13 F.R.D. 280 (D.D.C. 1952)
(quashing grand jury subpoena in DOJ oil cartel investigation).

237. *See, e.g.*, Alfred Dunhill of London, Inc. v. Republic of Cuba, 425 U.S. 682, 691 (1976); Republic
of the Philippines v. Marcos, 806 F.2d 344, 359 (2d Cir. 1986); Linseman v. World Hockey Ass'n,
439 F. Supp. 1315, 1323 (D. Conn. 1977).

238. INTERNATIONAL ANTITRUST GUIDELINES, *supra* note 1, § 3.33.

239. *Id.*

240. *See, e.g.*, Mannington Mills, Inc. v. Congoleum Corp., 595 F.2d 1287, 1293 (3d Cir. 1979);
Timberlane Lumber Co. v. Bank of Am. Nat'l Trust & Sav. Ass'n, 549 F.2d 597, 606 (9th Cir.
1976), Interamerican Ref. Corp. v. Texaco Maracaibo, Inc., 307 F. Supp. 1291, 1296-98 (D. Del.
1970); United States v. Watchmakers of Switzerland Info. Ctr., Inc., 1963 Trade Cas. (CCH)
¶ 70,600, at 77,456 (S.D.N.Y. 1962), *order modified*, 1965 Trade Cas. (CCH) ¶ 71,352 (S.D.N.Y.
1965); *see also* Letter from Attorney Gen. W.F. Smith to Ambassador Y. Okawara of Japan (May
7, 1981), *in* 1981-1 Trade Cas. (CCH) ¶ 63,998 (compliance with Japanese automobile export
limitations would not violate the U.S. antitrust laws).
     The Supreme Court indicated in *Hartford Fire Ins. Co. v. California*, 509 U.S. 764, 798-99
(1993), that foreign sovereign compulsion was one of two bases for determining that a "true"
conflict of laws existed between U.S. laws and foreign laws.

241. *Interamerican Ref.*, 307 F. Supp. at 1298.

242. *Id.* at 1297-98; *see also* INTERNATIONAL ANTITRUST GUIDELINES, *supra* note 1, § 3.32;
RESTATEMENT (THIRD), *supra* note 12, § 441 comment a.

compelled.[243] For example, in *United States v. Watchmakers of Switzerland Information Center, Inc.*,[244] Swiss watch manufacturers and sellers entered into private agreements in an attempt to protect the Swiss watch industry. One agreement, the Collective Convention, was devised in part to impede the growing watch industry in the United States. Although the companies were not compelled to enter into the convention, the consortium was clearly sanctioned by the Swiss government. One company involved in the formulation of the convention was owned by a corporation in which the Swiss government had a 37 percent interest. The government also adopted legislation to facilitate the implementation of the convention. The district court conceded that the agreements were approved by the government and were recognized in Switzerland as "facts of economic and industrial life."[245] However, absent a showing that the companies were forced to organize by the Swiss government, the foreign sovereign compulsion defense was held inapplicable.[246] Similar results have been reached in other cases.[247]

The sovereign compulsion defense was pleaded successfully in *Interamerican Refining Corp. v. Texaco Maracaibo, Inc.*[248] In that case, the defendants were ordered by the Venezuelan government not to sell oil to the plaintiff. In granting summary judgment to the defendants, the district court stated:

> When a nation compels a trade practice, firms there have no choice but to obey. Acts of business become effectively acts of the sovereign . . . . Anticompetitive practices compelled by foreign nations are not restraints of commerce, as commerce is

---

243. *See, e.g., Mannington Mills*, 595 F.2d at 1293; *Watchmakers of Switzerland*, 1963 Trade Cas. (CCH) ¶ 70,600, at 77,456-57; *cf.* Continental Ore Co. v. Union Carbide & Carbon Corp., 370 U.S. 690, 704-07 (1962) (conduct was not immunized merely because the alleged conspiracy involved some legal acts of the Canadian government where there was no indication that the Canadian government would have approved of the alleged conspiracy).

244. 1963 Trade Cas. (CCH) ¶ 70,600.

245. *Id.* at 77,456.

246. *Id.*

247. *See, e.g.*, Richmark Corp. v. Timber Falling Consultants, 959 F.2d 1468 (9th Cir.) (sanctions for failure to provide discovery were appropriate and not barred by the sovereign compulsion doctrine because there was no evidence that the defendant sought, in good faith, a waiver of China's secrecy laws; and the defendant could have avoided hardship by simply posting an appeal bond to eliminate the need for discovery), *cert. dismissed*, 506 U.S. 948 (1992).

In *Continental Ore*, 370 U.S. 690, the Supreme Court held that a corporation was not immunized from antitrust liability by virtue of its position as an agent for the Canadian government. Although the alleged antitrust violation occurred while the corporation was acting as an agent, the Court found that the Canadian government had neither directed nor approved of the anticompetitive conduct and that the conduct was not compelled by Canadian law. Absent compulsion, the corporation's actions were held susceptible to judicial scrutiny. *Id.* at 706-07.

A number of cases arising out of an alleged uranium cartel considered, but refused to apply, the sovereign compulsion defense on motions to dismiss. *See, e.g., In re* Uranium Antitrust Litig., 480 F. Supp. 1138 (N.D. Ill. 1979); United Nuclear Corp. v. General Atomic Co., 629 P.2d 231, 260-63 (N.M. 1980), *cert. denied*, 451 U.S. 901 (1981). Although the evidence showed extensive governmental involvement in the cartel, the courts were unable to find the requisite compulsion. This inquiry, however, was made more difficult by the refusal of the host governments of some of the defendants to permit those defendants to participate fully in the discovery process. *See, e.g., In re Uranium Antitrust Litig.*, 480 F. Supp. at 1154; *United Nuclear Corp.*, 629 P.2d at 259-61.

248. 307 F. Supp. 1291 (D. Del. 1970).

understood in the Sherman Act, because refusal to comply would put an end to commerce.[249]

The court also noted that compulsion by a foreign sovereign is a complete defense to an antitrust action.

The district court's decision in *Interamerican Refining Corp.* has been criticized by other courts because it allows for the application of the sovereign compulsion defense even though the compelled action takes place outside the foreign sovereign's territory.[250]

The *International Antitrust Guidelines* recognize the defense where there is actual compulsion and the refusal to comply with the foreign command would result in the imposition of penal or other severe sanctions.[251] This latter condition is important because the federal enforcement agencies will not recognize a defense of foreign compulsion if there are no penalties for not complying with the request of the foreign government.[252] Also, as with the act of state defense, the *International Antitrust Guidelines* state that, for the foreign sovereign compulsion defense to apply, the compulsion normally must take place within the territory of the foreign sovereign, must compel action entirely within the foreign sovereign's territory, and must constitute governmental, rather than commercial, action.[253] If the compelled conduct takes place in the United States, the U.S. antitrust enforcement agencies will not recognize this defense.

4. *Restraints Approved by the U.S. Executive Branch*

A defendant in an antitrust suit may seek to raise the defense that the challenged acts are requested or authorized by directives of the U.S. government. In contrast to the directives of foreign governments, domestic government directives immunize conduct only if they originate from statutory exceptions or from executive authority to permit activities that otherwise contravene U.S. antitrust laws.[254]

In *Consumers Union of U.S., Inc. v. Rogers*,[255] the extent of executive authority to immunize conduct was raised in an action charging violations of the Sherman Act in the steel import quota program, under which various foreign steel producers voluntarily limited sales into the United States.[256] The State Department and the president actively participated in the negotiation of the voluntary steel import quotas. The Department of Justice argued that the challenged restraints were valid,

---

249. *Id.* at 1298 (citation omitted).
250. *See* Sabre Shipping Corp. v. American President Lines, 285 F. Supp. 949, 954 (S.D.N.Y. 1968) (even if sovereign compulsion were established, it "would not necessarily immunize [the defendants] from prosecution or civil responsibility for acts done in United States commerce"), *cert. denied*, 407 F.2d 173 (2d Cir.), *cert. denied*, 395 U.S. 922 (1969).
251. INTERNATIONAL ANTITRUST GUIDELINES, *supra* note 1, § 3.32.
252. *Id.* Illustrative Example K.
253. *Id.* § 3.32. The enforcement agencies do indicate, however, that they will consider comity as a factor in such situations. *Id.* § 3.32 n.96.
254. *See, e.g.*, United States v. Socony-Vacuum Oil Co., 310 U.S. 150, 225-28 (1940).
255. 352 F. Supp. 1319 (D.D.C. 1973), *modified sub nom.* Consumers Union v. Kissinger, 506 F.2d 136 (D.C. Cir. 1974), *cert. denied*, 421 U.S. 1004 (1975).
256. Section 607 of the Trade Act of 1974, 19 U.S.C. § 2485 (1994), precludes state or federal antitrust liability arising from the voluntary limitation of steel exports to the United States at the request of the Secretary of State if the arrangement terminated prior to 1975.

representing the lawful exercise of the president's constitutional powers, and thus could not violate the Sherman Act. By stipulation among the parties, the antitrust claim was dismissed. Nonetheless, the district court, ruling on motions for summary judgment, stated unequivocally that:

> The President clearly has no authority to give binding assurances that a particular course of conduct, even if encouraged by its representatives, does not violate the Sherman Act or other related congressional enactments any more than he can grant immunity under such laws.[257]

Acknowledging that the question was not directly before the court because of the stipulation, the court concluded that "very serious questions can and should be raised as to the legality of the arrangements" under the Sherman Act.[258]

On appeal, the holding of the district court concerning the president's authority to negotiate the agreements was upheld.[259] However, the D.C. Circuit repudiated the lower court's discussion of the antitrust issues and vacated that portion of the decision. Noting that "complex questions of fact and law" were raised by the antitrust claim, the appellate court determined that the potential antitrust ramifications from the agreement restricting imports were not ripe in view of the plaintiff's decision to abandon that claim.[260]

The Department of Justice has taken the position that U.S. government officials negotiating import restraints by foreign governments should not incur antitrust liability.[261] The most recent letter expressing this view went so far as to suggest that even private participants in such negotiations should not incur antitrust liability.[262]

The *International Antitrust Guidelines* reiterate the prevailing view that the settlement of trade disputes that follow the procedures set out in the U.S. import relief laws enjoy an implied immunity under the antitrust laws. The *Guidelines* add that agreements between competitors that do not comply with the import relief laws, or that go beyond the measures authorized by law, enjoy no immunity and that the encouragement or involvement of U.S. or foreign government officials in such arrangements will not provide immunity.[263]

---

257. 352 F. Supp. at 1323.
258. *Id.* at 1324.
259. 506 F.2d at 143-44.
260. *Id.* at 141, 144.
261. *See* Letter from Assistant Att'y Gen. Anne K. Bingaman to Ambassador Ira Shapiro (May 17, 1996); Letter from Associate Att'y Gen. J. Shenefield to Senator C. Levin (Dec. 29, 1980), *in* [Current Comment—1969-1983 Transfer Binder] Trade Reg. Rep. (CCH) ¶ 50,422.
262. *See* Letter from Assistant Att'y Gen. Anne K. Bingaman to Ambassador Ira Shapiro (May 17, 1996) ("[W]e believe the [softwood lumber export limitations] agreement (including the representations by U.S. trade associations, producers and unions . . .) and its implementation . . . would be consistent with the U.S. antitrust law."); *see also* Letter from Attorney Gen. W.F. Smith to Ambassador Y. Okawara of Japan (May 7, 1981), *in* 1981-1 Trade Cas. (CCH) ¶ 63,998 (foreign firms would not incur antitrust liability by complying with government directives).
263. INTERNATIONAL ANTITRUST GUIDELINES, *supra* note 1, § 3.4. The *International Antitrust Guidelines* provide two illustrations of how the DOJ and the FTC would analyze these issues. *Id.* Illustrative Examples M and N; *cf.* Hammons v. Alcan Aluminum Corp., 1997-1 Trade Cas. (CCH) ¶ 71,714 (C.D. Cal. 1996) (complaint alleging that a memorandum of understanding regarding Russian aluminum production negotiated among government officials from Russia, the European Community, and the United States—including the participation of three attorneys from the DOJ— was part of a conspiracy by U.S. aluminum producers to restrict production and increase prices of aluminum in violation of a state antitrust statute was dismissed under political question, act of

5. Noerr *Doctrine*

A related question involves the extent to which the *Noerr* doctrine[264] immunizes activities of private parties that are designed to influence a foreign government to engage in conduct that would be in conflict with U.S. antitrust laws. The courts are in disagreement as to the applicability of this doctrine in the international context.[265]

In *Coastal States Marketing, Inc. v. Hunt*,[266] the Fifth Circuit found that the act of filing or joining in numerous foreign lawsuits was protected petitioning activity because at least one of the purposes of filing such suits was to establish ownership of the product involved.[267] The *Noerr* doctrine protects the petitioning of foreign governments, the court reasoned, because the doctrine "reflects not only first amendment concerns but also a limitation on the scope of the Sherman Act."[268]

Other courts also have evidenced some willingness to employ the doctrine in an international context. In *United States v. AMAX Inc.*,[269] the district court suggested that the doctrine could be applied to an attempt by U.S. corporations to influence the Canadian government. It chose not to do so, however, because the defendants' conduct, involving alleged private acts in the United States, was deemed beyond "the scope of the protection afforded by *Noerr-Pennington*."[270] In *Continental Ore Co. v. Union Carbide & Carbon Corp.*,[271] the Ninth Circuit applied *Noerr* to find that efforts to influence a private corporation that was acting as an agent of the Canadian government were protected from the Sherman Act.[272] The Supreme Court reversed. It distinguished *Noerr*, but without mentioning the nationality of the government; instead, the Court pointed to the commercial nature of the activity being challenged.[273]

One court has declined to apply the doctrine to the petitioning of a foreign government. In *Occidental Petroleum Corp. v. Buttes Gas & Oil Co.*,[274] the district court declined to apply the *Noerr* doctrine to allegations that the defendant, through various activities designed to influence the foreign governments involved, had provoked a border dispute in order to effect the displacement of the plaintiff from an oil concession. The district court ruled that the attempted persuasion of Middle Eastern states was "a far cry from the political process with which *Noerr* is concerned," and thus the "wholesale application" of the *Noerr* doctrine appeared

---

state, and *Noerr* doctrines), *aff'd without op.*, 132 F.3d 39 (9th Cir. 1997), *cert. denied*, 525 U.S. 948 (1998).

264. *See* Eastern R.R. Presidents Conf. v. Noerr Motor Freight, Inc., 365 U.S. 127 (1961). For a more extensive discussion of this doctrine, see part C of Chapter XIII.

265. *See, e.g.*, Associated Container Transp. (Australia) Ltd. v. United States, 705 F.2d 53, 60 n.10 (2d Cir. 1983) (declining to resolve the question but ruling that the doctrine should not block the discovery in issue).

266. 694 F.2d 1358 (5th Cir. 1983).

267. *Id.* at 1372.

268. *Id.* at 1364.

269. 1977-1 Trade Cas. (CCH) ¶ 61,467 (N.D. Ill. 1977).

270. *Id.* at 71,799.

271. 289 F.2d 86 (9th Cir. 1961), *vacated and remanded*, 370 U.S. 690 (1962).

272. *Id.* at 94.

273. 370 U.S. at 707 ("Respondents were engaged in a private commercial activity, no element of which involved seeking to procure the passage or enforcement of laws.").

274. 331 F. Supp. 92 (C.D. Cal. 1971), *aff'd per curiam*, 461 F.2d 1261 (9th Cir.), *cert. denied*, 409 U.S. 950 (1972).

"inappropriate."[275] Another district court stated that it is "questionable" whether the *Noerr* doctrine protects attempts to influence foreign governments.[276] Yet another district court expressed doubt about the applicability of *Noerr* directly but declined on comity grounds to examine under the antitrust laws the petitioning of a foreign government.[277] A question also has arisen over the applicability of *Noerr* where the petitioning entity is itself owned by the foreign government.[278] Further, *Noerr* has been found not to prevent Department of Justice CIDs that seek discovery against foreign firms regarding conduct that involves, at least in part, the petitioning of a foreign government.[279]

The *International Antitrust Guidelines* reiterate the government's long-standing position that it regards the doctrine as applying in the same manner to the petitioning of foreign governments as it does to the petitioning of the U.S. government.[280]

6. Statutory Exemptions Relating to Foreign Commerce

a.   WEBB-POMERENE ACT

The Webb-Pomerene Act[281] provides a limited exemption to the provisions of the Sherman Act for associations formed solely for the purpose of engaging in export trade, defined as "trade or commerce in goods, wares, or merchandise exported, or in the course of being exported" from the United States.[282] The statutory exemption,

---

275. *Id.* at 108.

276. Bulkferts Inc. v. Salatin Inc., 574 F. Supp. 6, 9 (S.D.N.Y. 1983) (disputed issues of fact prevented summary judgment); *see also* Dominicus Americana Bohio v. Gulf & W. Indus., 473 F. Supp. 680, 690 n.3 (S.D.N.Y. 1979) (*Noerr*'s applicability to lobbying foreign governments is an "open question," but attempts to influence the Dominican government were corrupt and coercive and thus would have fallen within the *Noerr* sham exception).

277. Laker Airways v. Pan Am. World Airways, 604 F. Supp. 280, 287 n.20 (D.D.C. 1984).

278. In an earlier decision in *Laker Airways*, the district court questioned whether an entity owned by a foreign government would have the same right to petition as would a private party, or whether the government's pecuniary interest might vitiate the arm's-length relationship normally assumed in petitioning. Laker Airways v. Pan Am. World Airways, 596 F. Supp. 202, 204 n.9 (D.D.C. 1984).

279. *See* Associated Container Transp. (Australia) Ltd. v. United States, 705 F.2d 53, 59-60 (2d Cir. 1983) (enforcing CIDs because *Noerr* does not bar enforcement of such demands at discovery stage of proceeding because the exercise of expertise is necessary to determine whether antitrust laws have been violated or whether *Noerr* immunizes the impugned conduct); *see also* Australia/Eastern U.S.A. Shipping Conf. v. United States, 537 F. Supp. 807, 812 (D.D.C. 1982) (enforcing CIDs because "[t]he Justice Department now explains that although the *Noerr* doctrine is applied in foreign contexts in some cases for non-constitutional reasons . . . it is not applied across the board to all dealings with foreign governments"), *modifying* 1982-1 Trade Cas. (CCH) ¶ 64,721, at 74,071 n.6 (D.D.C. 1981).

280. INTERNATIONAL ANTITRUST GUIDELINES, *supra* note 1, § 3.34.

281. 15 U.S.C. §§ 61-66 (2000).

282. *Id.* §§ 61-62. The product exported must be U.S.-produced and members must be U.S. citizens. *See In re* Phosphate Export Ass'n, 42 F.T.C. 555, 849-50 (1946). Membership in an association by a U.S. company owned or controlled by foreign interests does not, in and of itself, vitiate the exemption. *See* International Raw Materials, Ltd. v. Stauffer Chem. Co., 716 F. Supp. 188, 193 (E.D. Pa. 1989), *vacated on other grounds*, 898 F.2d 946, 950 (3d Cir. 1990); FTC Advisory Opinion, 83 F.T.C. 1840 (1973). Also, § 4 of the Webb-Pomerene Act, 15 U.S.C. § 64, subjects these associations to scrutiny under § 5 of the FTC Act, 15 U.S.C. § 45 (2000). In *International Raw Materials, Ltd. v. Stauffer Chemical Co.*, 978 F.2d 1318, 1325 (3d Cir. 1992), the Third Circuit held that U.S. subsidiaries owned by or affiliated with foreign firms are also entitled to protection under the Webb-Pomerene Act.

which was originally recommended by the Federal Trade Commission to permit U.S. companies to compete more effectively against foreign cartels,[283] is conditioned upon the export association not being in restraint of trade within the United States, not restraining the export trade of any of its domestic competitors, and not acting so as to artificially or intentionally affect prices within the United States or substantially lessen competition therein.[284]

Few decisions have interpreted the Webb-Pomerene Act.[285] The decisions have generally involved joint conduct that did not qualify for the Webb-Pomerene exemption because it involved restraints on the export activity of other domestic firms or impermissible anticompetitive restraints within the United States. It also has been held that the act does not immunize cartel agreements entered into between a U.S. export association and foreign competitors.[286]

The most widely cited discussion of the Webb-Pomerene exemption is contained in *United States v. Minnesota Mining & Manufacturing Co.*[287] In that case, the district court found that the Webb-Pomerene Act did not grant Sherman Act immunity to an association that established and jointly operated manufacturing facilities abroad and thereafter restricted its exports in favor of making more profitable sales of products manufactured overseas.[288] The court then went on, however, to describe a wide variety of export practices that would be immunized by

---

283. *See* FEDERAL TRADE COMM'N, REPORT ON COOPERATION IN AMERICAN EXPORT TRADE (1916). *See generally* Federal Trade Comm'n, *Webb-Pomerene Associations: Ten Years Later* (Staff Analysis Nov. 1978); Federal Trade Comm'n, *Webb-Pomerene Associations: A 50-Year Review* (Staff Report 1967).

284. 15 U.S.C. § 62. *But cf.* United States v. Minnesota Mining & Mfg. Co., 92 F. Supp. 947, 965 (D. Mass. 1950) ("Now it may very well be that every successful export company does inevitably affect adversely the foreign commerce of those not in the joint enterprise and does bring the members of the enterprise so closely together as to affect adversely the members' competition in domestic commerce. Thus every export company may be a restraint. But if there are only these inevitable consequences an export association is not an unlawful restraint.").

285. *See, e.g.*, United States v. Concentrated Phosphate Export Ass'n, 393 U.S. 199, 208-10 (1968) (association cannot make foreign aid sales); *International Raw Materials*, 716 F. Supp. at 190, 194 (an association can consolidate members' goods, arranging joint shipment and distribution thereof for export); United States v. Anthracite Export Ass'n, 1970 Trade Cas. (CCH) ¶ 73,348 (M.D. Pa. 1970); *Minnesota Mining & Mfg. Co.*, 92 F. Supp. 947; United States v. Elec. Apparatus Export Ass'n, 1946-47 Trade Cas. (CCH) ¶ 57,546 (S.D.N.Y. 1947); United States v. United States Alkali Export Ass'n, 58 F. Supp. 785 (S.D.N.Y. 1944), *aff'd*, 325 U.S. 196, 211-12 (1945) (DOJ as well as FTC can sue), *later proceeding*, 86 F. Supp. 59, 70, 74 (S.D.N.Y. 1949) (an association cannot join an overseas cartel, nor can an association attempt to control any terms or conditions of sale by members within the United States); Phosphate Rock Export Ass'n, [FTC Complaints & Orders— 1983-1987 Transfer Binder] Trade Reg. Rep. (CCH) ¶ 22,059 (FTC 1983) (advisory opinion approving commodity barter arrangement); In re Carbon Black Export, Inc., 46 F.T.C. 1245, 1417 (1949) (office operations conducted jointly with domestic trade association are not permitted); In re Pipe Fittings & Valve Export Ass'n, 45 F.T.C. 917 (1948); In re General Milk Co., 44 F.T.C. 1355, 1420 (1947) (agreements not allowed which precluded use of trademarks or labels within the United States); In re Sulfur Export Corp., 43 F.T.C. 820, 978-79 (1947) (nonmember exports cannot be deducted from an association's export quota); In re Export Screw Ass'n of the United States, 43 F.T.C. 980 (1947); In re Phosphate Export Ass'n, 42 F.T.C. 555, 845-7 (1946) (essential loading terminal use restricted to association members not covered).

286. *See United States Alkali Export Ass'n*, 325 U.S. at 198, 212.

287. 92 F. Supp. 947 (D. Mass. 1950).

288. *Id.* at 960, 963. While an association may not itself own overseas production operations, individual members may, provided they keep those operations fully independent so as to avoid any artificial or intentional impact on domestic prices traceable to their foreign operations. *See id.* at 962-63; FTC Advisory Opinion, *summarized at* 70 F.T.C. 1874-75 (1966).

the act, including the creation of an export association by four-fifths of the firms in an industry, the use of an association as the exclusive foreign outlet of its members, the establishment of association export prices for its members' products, the allocation of export orders among association members, and the establishment of resale price and exclusive dealing restrictions on foreign distributors of the association's products. The district court found all of these to be normal and essential features of any joint export enterprise and permissible under the act, absent unfairness or oppressive character in a particular setting.[289]

In *International Raw Materials, Ltd. v. Stauffer Chemical Co.*,[290] the district court upheld an association's efforts to reduce distribution costs by consolidating goods and jointly negotiating for terminaling services. It held that such activities were within the Webb-Pomerene Act's goals to promote economies of scale and that the act's concerns about domestic trade restraints were aimed at protecting the interests of consumers, not domestic export service industries. In dismissing claims of horizontal price fixing and boycott brought by a terminal operator (who alleged he was forced to charge the association lower prices), the district court further held that even if the association were found to be acting outside the scope of its exemption in other areas, that would not destroy the exemption for conduct in the course of export trade.[291]

In order to obtain the antitrust immunity provided by the Webb-Pomerene Act, associations must register with the Federal Trade Commission and file annual reports.[292] Association activities outside the scope of the immunity may be challenged at any time by the antitrust enforcement agencies or by private parties.[293]

b. CERTIFICATES OF REVIEW

Title III of the Export Trading Company Act of 1982[294] creates a procedure by which any person engaged in export trade may request a certificate of review from the Secretary of Commerce that confers partial antitrust immunity.[295] Under Sections 4013(a) and 4013(b) of the act, the Secretary of Commerce, with the concurrence of the Attorney General, must issue a certificate of review to any applicant (including a foreign applicant) that establishes that its export trade, export trade activities, and methods of operation will (1) result in neither a substantial lessening of competition or restraint of trade within the United States nor a substantial restraint of the export trade of any competitor of the applicant; (2) not unreasonably enhance, stabilize, or depress prices within the United States of the class of goods, wares, merchandise, or services exported by the applicant; (3) not constitute unfair methods of competition against competitors who are engaged in the export of goods, wares, merchandise, or

---

289. 92 F. Supp. at 965.

290. 716 F. Supp. 188 (E.D. Pa. 1989), *vacated on other grounds*, 898 F.2d 946 (3d Cir. 1990).

291. *Id.* at 191-92.

292. 15 U.S.C. § 65 (2000); 16 C.F.R. § 1.42 (2001). As of December 2001, 12 associations were registered with the FTC. There has been a steady decrease in the number of associations registered: in August 1996, 16 were registered; in January 1992, 21 were registered; at the end of 1985, 25 were registered.

293. *See, e.g.*, United States v. United States Alkali Exports Ass'n, 58 F. Supp. 785, 786 (S.D.N.Y. 1944).

294. 15 U.S.C. §§ 4011-4021 (2000).

295. Rules for applications for certificates of review are published at 15 C.F.R. pt. 325 (2001).

services of the class exported by the applicant; and (4) not include any act that may reasonably be expected to result in the sale for consumption or resale within the United States of the goods, wares, merchandise, or services exported by the applicant.[296] Export trade is defined in the act as the "trade or commerce in goods, wares, merchandise, or services exported, or in the course of being exported, from the United States or any territory thereof to a foreign nation."[297]

To a large extent, standards for certification are a codification of the Webb-Pomerene Act exemption discussed above.[298] Unlike the Webb-Pomerene Act, however, a certificate of review can cover export of services, including the licensing of technology.[299] Export trade certification also affords some significant additional procedural safeguards and limitations of liability (discussed below). The Secretary of Commerce has issued guidelines that discuss the eligibility requirements, certification standards, and analytical approach that the Departments of Commerce and Justice will utilize in determining whether to issue an export trade certificate of review.[300]

If the certificate of review is granted,[301] the holder is protected against criminal and treble damage liability under the antitrust laws for all conduct specified in the certificate that occurred while it was in effect.[302] Of course, only conduct that is specified in and complies with the terms of the certificate of review is protected from criminal sanctions and civil enforcement suits under the antitrust laws, and a certificate procured by fraud is void ab initio.[303] The grant, denial, revocation, or modification of a certificate of review is subject to judicial review, based on and limited to the administrative record developed during the application process at the Department of Commerce.[304] Denial of any application, in whole or in part, is not admissible in evidence in any proceeding in support of any claim under the antitrust laws.[305]

Private parties injured by conduct engaged in under a certificate of review may seek "injunctive relief, actual [single] damages, the loss of interest on actual damages, and the cost of suit (including a reasonable attorney's fee) for the failure to

296. 15 U.S.C. § 4013(a), (b).
297. Id. § 4021(1).
298. See H.R. REP. NO. 637, pt. I, 97th Cong., 2d Sess. 18-19 (1982), reprinted in 1982 U.S.C.C.A.N. 2431, 2440-41; see also S. REP. NO. 27, 97th Cong., 1st. Sess. 10 (1981).
299. 15 U.S.C. §§ 4002(a)(2), (a)(3) (2000).
300. EXPORT TRADE CERTIFICATES GUIDELINES, supra note 141. These guidelines contain several examples illustrating application of the certification standards to specific export trade conduct, including the use of vertical and horizontal restraints and technology licensing agreements. As of the end of 2001, the Department of Commerce had issued certificates to approximately 184 holders.
301. The Secretary of Commerce must publish notice of the application and must act within 90 days of receiving the application. 15 U.S.C. §§ 4012(b1), 4013(b) (2000). Expedited action is permitted where a special need for prompt disposition is indicated. Id. § 4013(c). The Secretary of Commerce must state his reasons for denying an application and an applicant may request reconsideration. Id. § 4013(d).
302. 15 U.S.C. § 4016(a) (2000). Antitrust laws are defined to include "any State antitrust or unfair competition law." Id. § 4002(a)(7) (2000).
303. Id. §§ 4016(a), 4013(f) (2000).
304. Id. § 4015(a) (2000); see Horizons Int'l, Inc. v. Baldrige, 811 F.2d 154 (3d Cir. 1987). The Third Circuit in Horizons observed, however, that a challenge to a certified export trading company's conduct is not limited to the administrative record or standards. Id. at 167.
305. 15 U.S.C. § 4015(c) (2000).

comply with the standards" of Section 4013(a).[306] There is a presumption, however, that conduct specified in a certificate of review complies with those standards, and if a court finds that challenged conduct does so comply, it "shall award [the defendant] the cost of suit . . . (including a reasonable attorney's fee)."[307]

A certificate holder who violates the relevant conditions of a certificate does not thereby become liable under the antitrust laws. Rather, he becomes liable to the prescriptions of the Export Trading Company Act, which provides that

> any action commenced . . . shall proceed as if it were an action commenced under section 15 or section 26 of this title, except that the standards of section 4013(a) of this title [which gives the four conditions of the Export Trading Company Act as set out above] and the remedies provided in this paragraph shall be the exclusive standards and remedies applicable.[308]

In addition, the act provides that the Attorney General also may bring suit pursuant to Section 15 of the Clayton Act "to enjoin conduct threatening clear and irreparable harm to the national interest."[309]

c. NATIONAL DEFENSE

Section 708 of the Defense Production Act of 1950, as amended,[310] provides antitrust immunity for participation, at the request of the president, in national defense programs relating to preparedness, production, capacity, and supply. Since its enactment, the act has been used, on a number of occasions, to grant antitrust immunity to joint action by U.S. oil companies in their dealings with foreign petroleum suppliers and tanker capacity, as well as for various national emergencies.[311] Acting in response to the 1973 oil embargo, Congress expanded the "national defense" exemption by providing immunity for voluntary agreements and plans of action for international allocation of petroleum products.[312] Suppliers participating in such allocation programs were required to comply with an elaborate system of recordkeeping, and their agreements were subject to close monitoring by the antitrust enforcement agencies.[313] The expansion of the national defense exemption, however, was repealed by Congress in 1991.[314]

---

306. *Id.* § 4016(b)(1) (2000). By allowing suits that allege unfair methods of competition, the Export Trading Company Act permits, for the first time, a private cause of action under a federal "unfairness" standard that may be similar to that of § 5 of the FTC Act. The FTC standard of unfairness is discussed in Chapter VII. The Department of Commerce has stated that the Export Trading Company Act standard of unfairness is "narrower" than the FTC standard, and any decisions expanding § 5 of the FTC Act beyond the Sherman and Clayton Acts and applying to conduct only because of its effect on competitors, "while illustrative, have no precedential significance." EXPORT TRADE CERTIFICATES GUIDELINES, *supra* note 141, at 21,108.
307. 15 U.S.C. §§ 4016(b)(3), (b)(4) (2000).
308. *Id.* § 4016(b)(1).
309. *Id.* § 4016(b)(5) (2000).
310. 50 U.S.C. App. § 2158 (1994).
311. *See* U.S. DEP'T OF JUSTICE, REPORT OF THE TASK GROUP ON ANTITRUST IMMUNITIES 18 (1977).
312. 50 U.S.C. App. 2158a (repealed 1991).
313. *Id.*
314. Defense Production Act Extension and Amendments of 1991, Pub. L. No. 102-99, § 4, 105 Stat. 187.

E. Procedural Issues in Foreign Commerce

The authority of U.S. courts to compel foreign individuals or corporations to appear and answer antitrust allegations involves three distinct but interrelated concepts: venue, personal jurisdiction, and service of process. Generally, these concepts have the same meanings in the antitrust context as they do in other areas of the law. The antitrust laws, however, contain several special venue provisions which provide the starting point for analysis in this area. Courts have interpreted these provisions so expansively that in antitrust cases the issues of venue, service of process, and personal jurisdiction, in the constitutional sense, have become "virtually congruent."[315]

The application of other procedural doctrines such as forum non conveniens and the enforceability of arbitration clauses are relative newcomers in the foreign commerce antitrust field and are discussed at the end of this section.

1. Venue

The special antitrust venue provisions are contained in Sections 4 and 12 of the Clayton Act.[316] Section 4, which applies to individuals as well as corporations, authorizes private damage actions in any district "in which the defendant resides or is found or has an agent."[317] Section 12 provides that a suit against a corporation "may be brought not only in the judicial district whereof it is an inhabitant, but also in any district wherein it may be found or transacts business."[318] In cases involving foreign individuals or corporations, the critical terms of these provisions are "found," "agent," and "transacts business."

To be found within a district, a corporation must be doing business in such a manner and to such an extent that actual presence is established.[319] This has been

---

315. Pacific Tobacco Corp. v. American Tobacco Co., 338 F. Supp. 842, 844 (D. Or. 1972); *accord* Cascade Steel Rolling Mills, Inc. v. C. Itoh & Co. (Am.), 499 F. Supp. 829, 835 (D. Or. 1980); *see also* Icon Indus. Controls Corp. v. Cimetrix, Inc., 921 F. Supp. 375, 377-78 (W.D. La. 1996) (the issues of personal jurisdiction and venue in antitrust cases are not easily separated because the Clayton Act is the basis for both); Square D Co. v. Niagara Frontier Tariff Bureau, 1984-1 Trade Cas. (CCH) ¶ 65,825, at 67,455 (D.D.C. 1984) (determination of personal jurisdiction also determinative of venue); Smokey's of Tulsa, Inc. v. American Honda Motor Co., 453 F. Supp. 1265, 1267 (E.D. Okla. 1978) ("the jurisdictional issue hinges upon the determination regarding venue, to wit: if venue is proper so is in personam jurisdiction"); Humid-Aire Corp. v. J. Levitt, Inc., 1978-1 Trade Cas. (CCH) ¶ 61,846, at 73,534 (N.D. Ill. 1977) (three-part test for evaluating minimum contacts for jurisdiction purposes also determines whether venue is proper); Industria Siciliana Asfalti, Bitumi, SpA v. Exxon Research & Eng'g Co., 1977-1 Trade Cas. (CCH) ¶ 61,256, at 70,786 & n.10 (S.D.N.Y. 1977); Zenith Radio Corp. v. Matsushita Elec. Indus. Co., 402 F. Supp. 262, 328 (E.D. Pa. 1975); Flank Oil Co. v. Continental Oil Co., 277 F. Supp. 357, 359 (D. Colo. 1967). *But see* Dunham's, Inc. v. National Buying Syndicate, 614 F. Supp. 616, 624 (E.D. Mich. 1985) (concept of transacting business more lenient than minimum contacts standard); 28 U.S.C. § 1391(c) (1994) ("For purposes of venue under this chapter, a defendant that is a corporation shall be deemed to reside in any judicial district in which it is subject to personal jurisdiction at the time the action is commenced.").

316. 15 U.S.C. §§ 15, 22 (2000). The general federal venue statute that allows an alien to be sued in any judicial district, 28 U.S.C. § 1391 (1994), is discussed later in this section.

317. 15 U.S.C. § 15(a).

318. *Id.* § 22.

319. *See, e.g.*, Eastman Kodak Co. v. Southern Photo Materials Co., 273 U.S. 359, 371 (1927). An individual defendant is found in a district, within the meaning of § 4, if he is physically present

held to require "proof of continuous local activities" in the district and consideration of whether the forum is "unfairly inconvenient."[320]

A corporation (or individual) has an agent in a district under Section 4 if an employee or other representative conducts business there on its behalf.[321]

The most expansive and, consequently, the most important basis for venue over corporations is provided by the transacts business language of Section 12. The leading case applying this language to a foreign corporation is *United States v. Scophony Corp. of America.*[322] In *Scophony*, a British corporation asserted, and the district court agreed, that it did not transact business in the Southern District of New York within the meaning of Section 12 because its business was "manufacturing, selling and licensing of television apparatus," and, although a 50 percent-owned U.S. subsidiary was engaged in this activity, Scophony was engaged only in protecting its interest as an investor.[323]

The Supreme Court reversed. Referring to its landmark decision applying the transacts business test to domestic corporations,[324] the Supreme Court observed that it had "sloughed off the highly technical distinctions" that had previously governed venue determinations and instead "substituted the practical and broader business conception of engaging in any substantial business operations . . . . The practical, everyday business or commercial concept of doing or carrying on business, of any substantial character, became the test of venue."[325] The Court thus applied the transacts business test to foreign as well as domestic corporations. The Court said that the determination of whether a corporation transacts business should not "be made for such an enterprise by atomizing it into minute parts or events, in disregard of the actual unity and continuity of the whole course of conduct."[326] In *Scophony*,

there when served with process. *See, e.g.*, Freeman v. Bee Mach. Co., 319 U.S. 448, 453-54 (1943).

320. United States v. Watchmakers of Switzerland Info. Ctr., Inc., 133 F. Supp. 40, 43-46 (S.D.N.Y. 1955) (two Swiss corporations were found in the Southern District of New York, within the meaning of § 12, in view of the continuous activities in the district of their jointly-owned subsidiary which was found to have no independent business of its own and to have acted exclusively as the agent of its Swiss parents); *see also In re* Chicken Antitrust Litig., 407 F. Supp. 1285, 1299 (N.D. Ga. 1975) (out-of-state partnership was not found in the Northern District of Georgia within the meaning of § 4 because sporadic sales and purchases within the district did not constitute "continuous local activities").

321. *See, e.g.*, Fooshee v. Interstate Vending Co., 234 F. Supp. 44, 48-52 (D. Kan. 1964); Goldlawr, Inc. v. Shubert, 169 F. Supp. 677 (E.D. Pa. 1958), *aff'd*, 276 F.2d 614 (3d Cir. 1960). In cases involving corporate defendants, the presence of an agent in the district is most often discussed as evidence that the corporation is "transacting business" there within the meaning of § 12, rather than as a separate basis for venue under § 4. *See, e.g.*, Sunrise Toyota, Ltd. v. Toyota Motor Co., 55 F.R.D. 519, 524 (S.D.N.Y. 1972).

At one time, some courts employed the "agent" language of § 4 to conclude that a resident coconspirator was the agent of nonresident coconspirators for purposes of establishing venue. *See, e.g.*, Giusti v. Pyrotechnic Indus., 156 F.2d 351, 354 (9th Cir.), *cert. denied*, 329 U.S. 787 (1946); Ross-Bart Port Theatre v. Eagle Lion Films, 140 F. Supp. 401, 402-03 (E.D. Va. 1954). This line of reasoning has since been repudiated. *See* Piedmont Label Co. v. Sun Garden Packing Co., 598 F.2d 491, 492-95 (9th Cir. 1979) (citing cases).

322. 333 U.S. 795 (1948).

323. United States v. Scophony Corp. of Am., 69 F. Supp. 666, 669 (S.D.N.Y. 1946), *rev'd*, 333 U.S. 795 (1948).

324. Eastman Kodak Co. v. Southern Photo Materials Co., 273 U.S. 359 (1927).

325. 333 U.S. at 807.

326. *Id.* at 817.

the test was satisfied because a series of investment and licensing agreements "called for continuing exercise of supervision over and intervention in" the subsidiary's affairs[327] and individuals acting at least in part as Scophony's agents actively pursued its interests, beyond mere investment interests, in New York.

Determining whether a corporation transacts business is a qualitative process requiring an analysis of the corporation's activities in the district in which venue is sought.[328] Among the factors courts consider in making this determination are (1) whether the activities of a defendant in the district are continuous and substantial;[329] (2) whether any contracts have been negotiated or consummated by the defendant in the district;[330] (3) whether the relationship between the defendant and a domestic subsidiary (or some related entity located in the district) is such that the related entity is merely carrying on the defendant's business in the district as its alter ego;[331] (4)

---

327. *Id.* at 814 (declining to decide whether Scophony could be found in New York by virtue of these agreements alone).

328. *See, e.g.*, Buckeye Assocs. v. Fila Sports, Inc., 616 F. Supp. 1484, 1489-91 (D. Mass. 1985) (venue improper under § 12 where Italian parent firm had no contacts with Massachusetts and subsidiary domestic firm did not have systematic, continuous, or substantial contact with the state, although some products made their way into state); Chrysler Corp. v. General Motors Corp., 589 F. Supp. 1182, 1195-99 (D.D.C. 1984) (venue proper in Washington, D.C. even though government contact discounted); Zenith Radio Corp. v. Matsushita Elec. Indus. Co., 402 F. Supp. 262, 317-28 (E.D. Pa. 1975) (venue proper over corporations with relationships of sufficient intimacy with corporations transacting business in the relevant districts that the former may be said to be transacting business there as well); Lippa & Co. v. Lenox Inc., 305 F. Supp. 175 (D. Vt. 1969).

329. *See, e.g., Scophony*, 333 U.S. 795; *Eastman Kodak*, 273 U.S. at 370; Black v. Acme Mkts., Inc., 564 F.2d 681, 686-87 (5th Cir. 1977); Hunt v. Mobil Oil Corp., 410 F. Supp. 4, 8 (S.D.N.Y. 1975), *aff'd*, 550 F.2d 68 (2d Cir.), *cert. denied*, 434 U.S. 984 (1977).

330. *See, e.g., Hunt*, 410 F. Supp. at 8.

331. *See, e.g., Scophony*, 333 U.S. at 814 (defendant transacting business in district where controls over partially-owned subsidiary amounted to "continuing exercise of supervision over and intervention in [subsidiary's] affairs"); Campos v. Ticketmaster Corp., 140 F.3d 1166, 1173 (8th Cir. 1998) ("Sufficient control over the operations of a subsidiary renders the subsidiary the instrument, rather than merely the investment, of the parent, and supports the conclusion that the parent is transacting business in a district."), *cert. denied*, 525 U.S. 1102 (1999); Tiger Trash v. Browning-Ferris Indus., 560 F.2d 818, 822-24 (7th Cir. 1977) ("[O]nce a sufficient level of control is established, the fact that the subsidiary is not controlled to an ultimate degree is irrelevant to the decision to pierce the corporate veil for venue purposes."), *cert. denied*, 434 U.S. 1034 (1978); San Antonio Tel. Co. v. AT&T, 499 F.2d 349, 352 (5th Cir. 1974) (venue not proper with respect to 22 telephone operating companies despite fact that company within district dictates general policies, where daily business affairs are responsibility of the operating companies); Frank Sexton Enters., Inc. v. Societe de Diffusion Internationale Agro-Alimentaire (SODIAAL), 1999-2 Trade Cas. (CCH) ¶ 72,638 (E.D. Pa. 1999) ("Where, however, the subsidiary is merely the 'alter ego' of the parent corporation, its forum contacts may be attributed to the parent"); Gallagher v. Mazda Motor of Am., Inc., 781 F. Supp. 1079, 1085 (E.D. Pa. 1992) ("[J]urisdictional contacts of a subsidiary corporation should be imputed to the corporate parent when the subsidiary corporation is engaged in functions that, but for the existence of the subsidiary, the parent would have to undertake."); Omega Homes, Inc. v. Citicorp Acceptance Co., 656 F. Supp. 393, 398 (W.D. Va. 1987) (continual supervision of and intervention in subsidiary's affairs allows court to find that parent "transacts business" in subsidiary's district); Codex Corp. v. Racal-Milgo, Inc., 1984-1 Trade Cas. (CCH) ¶ 65,853, at 67,562 (D. Mass. 1984) (venue proper where defendant had three wholly-owned subsidiaries qualified to do business in district, at least one of which conducted substantial business in district); *Chrysler Corp.*, 589 F. Supp. at 1200-03 (venue properly asserted over parent corporation where subsidiary in district was merely alter ego of parent); MCI Communs. Corp. v. AT&T, 1983-2 Trade Cas. (CCH) ¶ 65,652, at 69,330-41 (D.D.C. 1983) (parent amenable to suit in district based on "unified hierarchy" of subsidiaries that transacted business in district); Sportmart, Inc. v. Frisch, 537 F. Supp. 1254, 1258-59 (N.D. Ill. 1982) (venue not appropriate over foreign defendant where

whether the relationship between the defendant and any seemingly unrelated company—an exclusive distributor, for example—is such that the company, in fact, is acting as the defendant's agent;[332] (5) the volume of sales the defendant is making, directly, in the district;[333] (6) whether the defendant carries on patent licensing activities in the district;[334] (7) whether the defendant has solicited business in the district,[335] maintains offices or employees in the district,[336] makes purchases in the district,[337] or advertises in the district;[338] and (8) whether its officers and executives have made business trips into the district.[339] Courts also will evaluate the defendant's activities in the district as they relate to the specific allegations upon which the cause of action is based.[340]

In addition to the special antitrust venue provisions, the general federal venue statute[341] may provide a basis for venue in an antitrust action.[342] With respect to

company within district, in which it held a minority ownership interest, could not be considered its alter ego); Star Lines v. Puerto Rico Maritime Shipping Auth., 442 F. Supp. 1201, 1206-07 (S.D.N.Y. 1978) (corporation transacting business for purposes of establishing venue where its day-to-day operations are controlled by corporation within district that acts as its agent); Williams v. Canon, Inc., 432 F. Supp. 376, 379-80 (C.D. Cal. 1977) (finding that foreign defendant transacts business in district for venue purposes requires not only that defendant controls local company, but that it actively manages its day-to-day operations); Zenith Radio, 402 F. Supp. at 327-38 (detailing factors considered in determining whether subsidiary's presence in district means that defendant is transacting business there, including whether, absent subsidiary, defendant would perform subsidiary's activities itself); Fisher Baking Co. v. Continental Baking Corp., 238 F. Supp. 322 (D. Utah 1965) (corporation not transacting business in district of subsidiary where subsidiary operated separately on a day-to-day basis, corporate forms meticulously observed, and interorganizational contacts did not merge activities); see also Dunham's, Inc. v. National Buying Syndicate, 614 F. Supp. 616, 624-25 (E.D. Mich. 1985) (venue proper where members of defendant buying syndicate are located in the district).

332. See, e.g., Hoffman Motors Corp. v. Alfa Romeo S.p.A., 244 F. Supp. 70, 75-77 (S.D.N.Y. 1965); but see Athletes Foot of Del., Inc. v. Ralph Libonati Co., 445 F. Supp. 35, 44 (D. Del. 1977).

333. See, e.g., Sunbury Wire Rope Mfg. Co. v. United States Steel Corp., 129 F. Supp. 425, 427 (E.D. Pa. 1955).

334. See, e.g., Scophony, 333 U.S. 795.

335. See, e.g., School Dist. v. Kurtz Bros., 240 F. Supp. 361, 363 (E.D. Pa. 1965); cf. AG Bliss Co. v. United Carr Fastener Co. of Can., 116 F. Supp. 291, 293-94 (D. Mass. 1953) (foreign subsidiary of Massachusetts firm not doing business in Massachusetts where it has no place of business or employees in the state and does not solicit business there), aff'd, 213 F.2d 541 (1st Cir. 1954).

336. See, e.g., Chrysler Corp., 589 F. Supp. at 1199-1203; see also AG Bliss Co., 116 F. Supp. at 294 (where Canadian corporation was subsidiary of Massachusetts corporation, the fact that it had Massachusetts residents as officers did not make it subject to service of process in Massachusetts).

337. See, e.g., McCrory Corp. v. Cloth World, Inc., 378 F. Supp. 322, 324-25 (S.D.N.Y. 1974).

338. See, e.g., Runnels v. TMSI Contractors, Inc., 764 F.2d 417, 421 (5th Cir. 1985) (advertising in two Louisiana newspapers over a five-year period constituted a contact). But cf. GTE New Media Servs. Inc. v. Bellsouth Corp., 199 F.3d 1343, 1350 (D.C. Cir. 2000) (defendant did not "transact business" in the district—and that, therefore, there was no personal jurisdiction over it—merely by advertising through an Internet Web site accessible from the district); San Antonio Tel. Co., 499 F.2d at 351 n.5 (national advertising that reaches a district is insufficient).

339. See, e.g., C.C.P. Corp. v. Wynn Oil Co., 354 F. Supp. 1275, 1279 (N.D. Ill. 1973).

340. See, e.g., Chrysler Corp., 589 F. Supp. at 1203-06 (Toyota had sufficient joint venture-related contacts with forum); In re Uranium Antitrust Litig., 1980-81 Trade Cas. (CCH) ¶ 63,678, at 77,637 (N.D. Ill. 1980) (alleged conspiratorial meetings took place in the district); In re Chicken Antitrust Litig., 407 F. Supp. 1285, 1291-92 & n.2 (N.D. Ga. 1975). But cf. Sportmart, Inc. v. Frisch, 537 F. Supp. 1254, 1259 (N.D. Ill. 1982) ("[t]he fact that Sportmart may have suffered injury here, without more, will not support the exercise of personal jurisdiction or create venue").

341. 28 U.S.C. § 1391 (1994 & Supp. 1999).

342. See, e.g., Sportmart, Inc., 537 F. Supp. at 1257 (dictum); H & S Distribs. v. Cott Corp., 1980-2 Trade Cas. (CCH) ¶ 63,358, at 75,831 (D. Conn. 1980) (dictum); Ohio-Sealy Mattress Mfg. Co. v.

foreign defendants, whether individuals or corporations, the most pertinent provision of that statute is Section 1391(d), which provides that "[a]n alien may be sued in any district."[343] In *Brunette Machine Works, Ltd. v. Kockum Industries*,[344] a patent infringement action, the Supreme Court observed that Section 1391(d) "is properly regarded, not as a venue restriction at all, but rather as a declaration of the long-established rule that suits against aliens are wholly outside the operation of all the federal venue laws, general and special."[345] Consistent with this rule, courts in antitrust cases have applied Section 1391(d) in rejecting claims of improper venue asserted by alien defendants, both individual[346] and corporate.[347]

The general venue statute, Section 1391(b), also permits venue in an antitrust suit to be laid in (1) a judicial district where any defendant resides, if all defendants reside in the same state; (2) a judicial district in which a substantial part of the events or omissions giving rise to the claim occurred, or a substantial part of property that is the subject of the action is situated; or (3) a judicial district in which any defendant

---

Kaplan, 429 F. Supp. 139, 141 (N.D. Ill. 1977); ABC Great States, Inc. v. Globe Ticket Co., 310 F. Supp. 739 (N.D. Ill. 1970); Edward J. Moriarty & Co. v. General Tire & Rubber Co., 289 F. Supp. 381, 386-87 (S.D. Ohio 1967); Hoffman Motors Corp. v. Alfa Romeo S.p.A., 244 F. Supp. 70, 84 (S.D.N.Y. 1965). *But see GTE New Media Servs. Inc.*, 199 F.3d at 1350-51 (plaintiff may not use other venue statutes if § 12 of the Clayton Act was used for service of process).

343. 28 U.S.C. § 1391(d) (1994).
344. 406 U.S. 706 (1972).
345. *Id.* at 714. The constitutionality of § 1391(d) was challenged by the defendants but not decided by the district court in *Zenith Radio Corp. v. Matsushita Elec. Indus. Co.*, 402 F. Supp. 262, 330 & n.39 (E.D. Pa. 1975).
346. *See, e.g.*, Scriptomatic, Inc. v. Agfa-Gevaert, Inc., 1973-1 Trade Cas. (CCH) ¶ 74,594, at 94,632 (S.D.N.Y. 1973); *Edward J. Moriarty*, 289 F. Supp. at 389.
347. *See, e.g.*, Miller Pipeline Corp. v. British Gas plc, 901 F. Supp. 1416, 1420 (S.D. Ind. 1995); Square D Co. v. Niagara Frontier Tariff Bureau, 1984-1 Trade Cas. (CCH) ¶ 65,825, at 67,454-55 (D.D.C. 1984) (venue in any district proper as to Canadian corporations); General Elec. Co. v. Bucyrus-Erie Co., 550 F. Supp. 1037, 1040-41 (S.D.N.Y. 1982); Centronics Data Computer Corp. v. Mannesmann, A.G., 432 F. Supp. 659, 661-64 (D.N.H. 1977); *Hoffman Motors*, 244 F. Supp. at 84.

The D.C. Circuit has approached the issue in a different fashion, holding that if a plaintiff uses the worldwide service of process provisions of § 12 of the Clayton Act it must also satisfy the venue provisions of § 12 and may not rely on supplemental venue statutes such as § 1391(d). *See GTE New Media Servs. Inc.*, 199 F.3d at 1351; *In re* Vitamins Antitrust Litig., 94 F. Supp. 2d 26, 30 (D.D.C. 2000).

A conclusion that venue with respect to an alien defendant is properly laid under § 1391(d) does not necessarily mean that the defendant is amenable to suit. The jurisdictional question would still remain. *See, e.g.*, Chrysler Corp. v. Fedders Corp., 643 F.2d 1229, 1237-38 (6th Cir.), *cert. denied*, 454 U.S. 893 (1981); SCM Corp. v. Brother Int'l Corp., 316 F. Supp. 1328, 1334 (S.D.N.Y. 1970) (in patent infringement suit, Japanese parent corporation, with respect to which venue was properly laid under § 1391(d), also was found amenable to suit in the forum district because it had "sufficient contacts and activities in this jurisdiction to require [it] to defend an action commenced in this forum"); *see also* O.S.C. Corp. v. Toshiba Am., Inc., 491 F.2d 1064, 1068 (9th Cir. 1974) (after concluding that defendant Japanese corporation was not transacting business in the district, the court rejected venue based on § 1391(d) because plaintiff had not shown that the alien corporation was amenable to suit in any U.S. district from a jurisdictional standpoint); Williams v. Canon, Inc., 432 F. Supp. 376 (C.D. Cal. 1977) (following *O.S.C.*). As discussed in part E.2 of this chapter, answering the jurisdictional question entails analysis of the alien defendant's contacts with the forum district and, perhaps, the United States as a whole, an analysis that does not significantly differ from that required by § 12 of the Clayton Act.

may be found, if there is no district in which the action may otherwise be brought.[348] Prior to a 1990 amendment, Section 1391(b) permitted venue to lie where "the claim arose."[349] The previous language implied that there was only one district where the claim arose and thus encouraged litigation over which forum was proper in a multiforum transaction. Under the amended clause, venue may be proper in more than one district in a multiforum transaction.[350]

Under Section 1391(c), a corporate defendant may be sued in any district in which it is subject to personal jurisdiction at the time the action is commenced.[351] If a corporation is amenable to jurisdiction in a state with several districts, venue is proper in the district with which the defendant has the most significant contacts.[352]

Finally, Section 1391(f) establishes special venue rules for civil actions against foreign states.[353] Under these rules, venue in such actions may be laid in, among other places, any U.S. judicial district in which a substantial part of the events or omissions giving rise to the claim occurred, the district in which a substantial part of the property subject to the action is located, or in the District of Columbia.[354]

---

348. 28 U.S.C. § 1391(b) (1994). Subsection (a) of the statute applies only in cases in which jurisdiction is founded solely on diversity and thus is not applicable to federal antitrust claims, which always present a federal question. *Id.* § 1391(a).

349. 28 U.S.C. § 1391(b) (1988). Under the pre-1990 statute, two tests existed for determining whether or not a claim arose in a particular district: (1) the "target area" test under which the claim arose in the district in which the target of the alleged violation suffered injury to its business, *see, e.g.,* *Centronics Data Computer,* 432 F. Supp. at 661; and (2) the "weight of the contact" test under which courts would look not only to the place in which the injury allegedly occurred, but also to other contacts between the defendants and the forum districts, *see, e.g.,* Caribe Trailer Sys. v. Puerto Rico Maritime Shipping Auth., 475 F. Supp. 711, 718-19 (D.D.C. 1979), *aff'd mem.,* 1980 WL 130478 (D.C. Cir. Jul. 3, 1980), *cert. denied,* 450 U.S. 914 (1981).

350. *See* H.R. REP. No. 734, 101st Cong., 2d Sess. 23 (1990), *reprinted in* 1990 U.S.C.C.A.N. 6860, 6869.

351. Rule 4(k)(2) of the Federal Rules of Civil Procedure increases the choices of venue in which plaintiffs, including foreign plaintiffs, can sue corporate defendants pursuant to 28 U.S.C. § 1391(c) (1994). FED. R. CIV. P. 4(k)(2).

352. 28 U.S.C. § 1391(c) (1994) provides that:
    For purposes of venue under this chapter, a defendant that is a corporation shall be deemed to reside in any judicial district in which it is subject to personal jurisdiction at the time the action is commenced. In a State which has more than one judicial district and in which a defendant that is a corporation is subject to personal jurisdiction at the time an action is commenced, such corporation shall be deemed to reside in any district in that State within which its contacts would be sufficient to subject it to personal jurisdiction if that district were a separate State, and, if there is no such district, the corporation shall be deemed to reside in the district within which it has the most significant contacts.

353. 28 U.S.C. § 1391(f) (1994). This provision codifies part of the Foreign Sovereign Immunities Act of 1976, Pub. L. No. 94-583, 90 Stat. 2891.

354. *See, e.g.,* Kalamazoo Spice Extraction Co. v. Provisional Military Gov't of Socialist Ethiopia, 616 F. Supp. 660, 666 (W.D. Mich. 1985) (venue proper where accounts receivable totaling $2 million were located in the district and constituted a substantial portion of the assets of expropriated company that were subject matter of action); Schmidt v. Polish People's Republic, 579 F. Supp. 23, 28 (S.D.N.Y) (negotiation of original loan, negotiations after default, execution of agreement, and payment of notes together make up a substantial part of events that give rise to claim to recover on defaulted notes, and all took place in the district), *aff'd,* 742 F.2d 67 (2d Cir. 1984).

2. *Personal Jurisdiction*

No special rules of personal jurisdiction govern antitrust actions. As in other areas of law, *International Shoe Co. v. Washington*[355] provides the guiding principle: due process "requires only that in order to subject a defendant to a judgment *in personam*, if he be not present within the territory of the forum, he have certain minimum contacts with it such that the maintenance of the suit does not offend 'traditional notions of fair play and substantial justice.'"[356] In decisions subsequent to *International Shoe*, this principle evolved into a two-pronged test. The first requirement is that there must be some "minimum contact" with the forum state (or district) resulting from an affirmative act of the defendant by which he "purposefully avails" himself of the privilege of conducting activities there and invokes the benefits and protections of the forum's laws.[357] The second requirement is that it be fair and

---

355. 326 U.S. 310 (1945).

356. *Id.* at 316 (citations omitted). *International Shoe* involved consideration of the adjudicatory power of state courts under the Due Process Clause of the Fourteenth Amendment. Technically, in federal question cases, the Due Process Clause of the Fifth Amendment controls. Even in such cases, courts frequently consult the Supreme Court's pronouncements on the jurisdiction of state courts for the "clearest guidance" on when the exercise of personal jurisdiction is permissible. *See, e.g.*, Max Daetwyler Corp. v. Meyer, 762 F.2d 290, 293 (3d Cir.), *cert. denied*, 474 U.S. 980 (1985); Buckeye Assocs. v. Fila Sports, Inc., 616 F. Supp. 1484, 1488 n.5 (D. Mass. 1985); Japan Gas Lighter Ass'n v. Ronson Corp., 257 F. Supp. 219, 232 (D.N.J. 1966). *But see* Dunham's, Inc. v. National Buying Syndicate, 614 F. Supp. 616, 619-23 (E.D. Mich. 1985) (stating that in a federal antitrust action, personal jurisdiction is guided by standards of due process under the Fifth Amendment rather than an *International Shoe* standard of minimum contacts with the forum; the proper inquiry is therefore whether service of process was adequate to give notice of the proceeding); *cf.* First Flight Co. v. National Carloading Corp., 209 F. Supp. 730, 736-37 (E.D. Tenn. 1962) (stating that it is anomalous to limit federal court action by a constitutional provision applicable only to state action).

  International Shoe considerations are applicable even for actions against foreign states. Under the FSIA, discussed in part D.1 of this chapter, personal jurisdiction is established whenever a court has subject matter jurisdiction and process has been served pursuant to the act but the courts have imposed a due process review. *See, e.g.*, Texas Trading & Milling Corp. v. Federal Republic of Nigeria, 647 F.2d 300, 308-10 (2d Cir. 1981), *cert. denied*, 454 U.S. 1148 (1982); *Kalamazoo Spice*, 616 F. Supp. at 665-66; Transamerican S.S. Corp. v. Somali Democratic Republic, 590 F. Supp. 968, 976 (D.D.C. 1984), *aff'd in part and rev'd in part*, 767 F.2d 998 (D.C. Cir. 1985); *Schmidt*, 579 F. Supp. at 28; Ruiz v. Transportes Aereos Militares Ecuadorianos, 103 F.R.D. 458, 459 (D.D.C. 1984) (applying national contacts test for service made under § 1608 of the FSIA).

357. *See, e.g.*, Burger King Corp. v. Rudzewicz, 471 U.S. 462, 474 (1985) ("the constitutional touchstone remains whether the defendant purposefully established 'minimum contacts' in the forum State"). In *Burger King*, the Supreme Court determined that personal jurisdiction in Florida over a Michigan franchisee for breach of the franchise agreement was proper where the defendant entered into a 20-year relationship with wide-ranging contacts with Burger King's Miami headquarters and agreed that disputes would be governed by Florida law. These actions indicated a deliberate affiliation with the forum state and the reasonable foreseeability of possible litigation there. *See also* Chandler v. Barclays Bank PLC, 898 F.2d 1148, 1151 (6th Cir. 1990) (issuance of a letter of credit naming a state resident as beneficiary is generally insufficient to confer jurisdiction). *Compare* World-Wide Volkswagen Corp. v. Woodson, 444 U.S. 286, 298 (1980) (dictum) (act of delivering one's products "into the stream of commerce with the expectation that they will be purchased by consumers in the forum State" subjects one to the assertions of jurisdiction by courts in that state), Ruston Gas Turbines, Inc. v. Donaldson Co., 9 F.3d 415, 420 (5th Cir. 1993) ("*Asahi* does not provide clear guidance on the 'minimum contacts' prong, and therefore we will continue to follow the stream of commerce analysis in *World-Wide Volkswagen*"), FMC Corp. v. Varonos, 892 F.2d 1308 (7th Cir. 1990) (faxed transmissions into a forum, coupled with an attempt to avail oneself of that forum's benefits, provides sufficient basis

reasonable to require the defendant to come into the forum state (or district) and defend the action.[358] A determination of whether the exercise of jurisdiction is reasonable will turn upon "the burden on the defendant, the interests of the forum state, and the plaintiff's interest in obtaining relief."[359]

The jurisdictional analysis required to evaluate due process is similar to the analysis required by the transacting business test for determining whether venue is proper under Section 12 of the Clayton Act. The factors that courts consider are virtually identical, including (1) the continuity of the defendant's activities in the district;[360] (2) the volume of the defendant's business in the district;[361] (3) the relationship between the defendant's activities in the district and the nature of the cause of action;[362] (4) activities in the district by a subsidiary controlled by the

---

for jurisdiction), *and* Carter v. Trafalgar Tours Ltd., 704 F. Supp. 673, 675-77 (W.D. Va. 1989) (sending travel brochures into forum sufficient to exercise jurisdiction), *with* Asahi Metal Indus. Co. v. Superior Court, 480 U.S. 102, 112 (1987) (O'Connor, J., plurality) (mere placement of goods into the "stream of commerce," with awareness that they would eventually reach the forum state, is not sufficient to satisfy minimum contact requirement), Hanson v. Denckla, 357 U.S. 235, 252-55 (1958) (defendant trustee did not "purposefully avail itself of the privilege of conducting activities within the forum state" simply by sending checks to the settlor of the trust, who moved to the forum state after having established the trust in defendant's home state), *and* Coblentz GMC/Freightliner, Inc. v. General Motors Corp., 724 F. Supp. 1364, 1368-70 (M.D. Ala. 1989) (foreseeability of effect within a forum, absent intent, does not entitle the forum to exercise jurisdiction), *aff'd without op.*, 932 F.2d 977 (11th Cir. 1991).

358. *See, e.g.*, Congoleum Corp. v. DLW A.G., 729 F.2d 1240, 1243 (9th Cir. 1984) (would not "comport with fair play and substantial justice to assert jurisdiction over a West German corporation in the distant forum of California on a claim that arises out of activities in Europe, where the corporation had no contact with California" other than sales and sales promotion by independent nonexclusive sales representatives unrelated to the cause of action); Metrix Warehouse, Inc. v. Daimler-Benz A.G., 1984-2 Trade Cas. (CCH) ¶ 66,129 (D. Md. 1984), *aff'd*, 828 F.2d 1033 (4th Cir. 1987), *cert. denied*, 486 U.S. 1017 (1988); *see also* McGee v. International Life Ins. Co., 355 U.S. 220, 223 (1957) (noting that "modern transportation and communications have made it much less burdensome for a party sued to defend itself in a State where he engages in economic activity").

359. *Asahi*, 480 U.S. at 113.

360. *See, e.g.*, Keeton v. Hustler Magazine, Inc., 465 U.S. 770, 779-81 (1984) (out-of-state publisher's continuous and deliberate exploitation of the forum state market—i.e., regular monthly sales of thousands of magazines—was sufficient to support an assertion of jurisdiction in a libel action that arose out of the very activity being conducted in the forum state, regardless of plaintiff's limited contacts with the state); Helicopteros Nacionales de Colombia, S.A. v. Hall, 466 U.S. 408, 416-18 (1984) (in wrongful death action concerning helicopter crash in Peru, a contract negotiation session, helicopter purchases, and related training trips were insufficient contacts for the state of Texas to exercise general personal jurisdiction over Colombian corporation unrelated to forum contacts); Perkins v. Benguet Consol. Mining Co., 342 U.S. 437, 447-49 (1952); International Shoe Co. v. Washington, 326 U.S. 310, 320 (1945); GTE New Media Servs. Inc. v. Bellsouth Corp., 199 F.3d 1343 (D.C. Cir. 2000) (no personal jurisdiction based on access to foreign Web site); Harran Transp. Co. v. National Trailways Bus Sys., 1985-2 Trade Cas. (CCH) ¶ 66,723, at 63,458-60 (D.D.C. 1985) ($37,800 in parts sales, four service calls, and sales of 36 buses not sufficient to meet more substantial contacts required for exercise of general jurisdiction); United States v. Imperial Chem. Indus., 100 F. Supp. 504 (S.D.N.Y. 1951); *In re* Shipowners Litig., 361 N.W.2d 112 (Minn. Ct. App. 1985) (personal jurisdiction lacking over state antitrust counterclaim against foreign counterdefendant where only contact with forum was a single meeting, instituted by counterclaimant, to discuss possible settlement of contract dispute).

361. *See, e.g.*, *International Shoe*, 326 U.S. at 320.

362. *See, e.g.*, *Perkins*, 342 U.S. at 447-48; *International Shoe*, 326 U.S. at 320; Pillar Corp. v. Enercon Indus. Corp., 1989-1 Trade Cas. (CCH) ¶ 68,597, at 61,178-79 (E.D. Wis. 1989) (court could exercise personal jurisdiction over West German firm because firm's contacts with the forum, though minimal, gave rise to the cause of action). *Compare Burger King*, 471 U.S. at 472-73,

defendant;[363] (5) local telephone or other listings by the defendant in the district;[364] (6) the convenience of the forum chosen by the plaintiff and the availability of other forums;[365] (7) the existence of directors' meetings, business correspondence, banking,

---

Keeton, 465 U.S. at 775-77; Calder v. Jones, 465 U.S. 783, 788-90 (1984) (personal jurisdiction was proper in California over Florida reporter and editor of National Enquirer where California was the deliberate focal point of the story and of the harm suffered by plaintiff), *and* Widger Chem. Corp. v. Chemfil Corp., 601 F. Supp. 845, 848-49 (E.D. Mich. 1985) (personal jurisdiction proper in Michigan where entering into licensing agreement and meeting to map out strategy, the activities that were the basis of antitrust and other claims, occurred in Michigan), *with Congoleum Corp.*, 729 F.2d 1240 (cause of action not related to defendant's activities in district), Mizlou Television Network v. NBC, 603 F. Supp. 677, 681-83 (D.D.C. 1984) (fact that party received legal advice regarding the transaction from attorney who operated from the district was not sufficient to confer personal jurisdiction), *and* McGlinchy v. Shell Chem. Co., 1985-2 Trade Cas. (CCH) ¶ 66,672 (N.D. Cal. 1984) (no contacts related to the cause of action on which personal jurisdiction could be based), *aff'd*, 845 F.2d 802 (9th Cir. 1988).

363. *See, e.g.,* In re Cardizem CD Antitrust Litig., 105 F. Supp. 2d 618, 675 (E.D. Mich. 2000) (personal jurisdiction over German parent corporation properly alleged based in part on control of activities of U.S. indirect subsidiary); Frank Sexton Enter. v. Societe de Diffusion Internationale, 1999-2 Trade Cas. (CCH) ¶ 72,638 (E.D. Pa. 1999) (denying personal jurisdiction over foreign parent of U.S. defendant where no evidence after jurisdictional discovery that foreign parent controlled affairs of U.S. subsidiary); Kalamazoo Spice Extraction Co. v. Provisional Military Gov't of Socialist Ethiopia, 616 F. Supp. 660, 666 (W.D. Mich. 1985) (activities of expropriated company attributed to foreign state which exercised direct control over operations by appointing majority of board of directors, requiring a government-approved director to sign checks, and approving invoices); Dunlop Tire & Rubber Corp. v. PepsiCo, Inc., 591 F. Supp. 88, 90 (N.D. Ill. 1984) (jurisdiction exists where foreign firm owned 100% of U.S. subsidiaries, appointed common directors and holders of various high positions, and exercised control over capital expenditure and financial operations); Call Carl, Inc. v. BP Oil Corp., 391 F. Supp. 367, 371 (D. Md. 1975), *aff'd in part and rev'd in part*, 554 F.2d 623 (4th Cir.), *cert. denied*, 434 U.S. 923 (1977); United States v. Watchmakers of Switzerland Info. Ctr., Inc., 133 F. Supp. 40, 43-46 (S.D.N.Y. 1955); United States v. Imperial Chem. Indus., 100 F. Supp. 504, 511 (S.D.N.Y. 1951); *cf.* Behagen v. Amateur Basketball Ass'n, 744 F.2d 731, 733-34 (10th Cir. 1984) (international association regulating amateur basketball maintained continuous and substantial activity in forum state through the actions of its members), *cert. denied*, 471 U.S. 1010 (1985). *But cf.* Cannon Mfg. Co. v. Cudahy Packing Co., 267 U.S. 333 (1925) (no personal jurisdiction over parent company though it dominates and exerts commercial and financial control over local subsidiary immediately and completely); Miller v. Honda Motor Co., 779 F.2d 769, 772 (1st Cir. 1985) (no personal jurisdiction over foreign parent in personal injury suit even though domestic subsidiary was wholly owned, sold the parent's products, and had two common board members with parent); Kramer Motors, Inc. v. British Leyland, Ltd., 628 F.2d 1175, 1177 (9th Cir.) (per curiam) (no jurisdiction despite common directors between British parent and U.S. subsidiary where parent did not exercise day-to-day control), *cert. denied*, 449 U.S. 1062 (1980); Perfumer's Workshop, Ltd. v. Roure Bertrand du Pont, Inc., 737 F. Supp. 785, 788 (S.D.N.Y. 1990) (no personal jurisdiction over parent corporation of U.S. subsidiary where parent neither supplied product to, asserted control over, nor derived financial benefit from subsidiary); Savin Corp. v. Heritage Copy Prods., 661 F. Supp. 463, 471 (M.D. Pa. 1987) (no personal jurisdiction over parent that was not alter ego of subsidiary); Camellia City Telecasters, Inc. v. Tribune Broad. Co., 1984-2 Trade Cas. (CCH) ¶ 66,114, at 66,224-25 (D. Colo. 1984) (being part of national network of corporation insufficient to establish personal jurisdiction unless facts justify piercing the corporate veil); Sportmart, Inc. v. Frisch, 537 F. Supp. 1254, 1258 (N.D. Ill. 1982) (jurisdiction denied where U.S. subsidiary was not "alter ego" of parent); Jamesbury Corp. v. Kitamura Valve Mfg. Co., 484 F. Supp. 533, 535 (S.D. Tex. 1980) (dictum) (unless subsidiary acts as an agent or parent lacks distinct legal existence, "mere transaction of business through a wholly owned subsidiary" is insufficient).

364. *See, e.g.,* Glick v. Empire Box Corp., 119 F. Supp. 224 (S.D.N.Y. 1954).

365. *See, e.g.,* Travelers Health Ass'n v. Virginia, 339 U.S. 643, 648-49 (1950); Latimer v. S/A Industrias Reunidas F. Matarazzo, 175 F.2d 184, 186 (2d Cir.), *cert. denied*, 338 U.S. 867 (1949).

stock transfers, payment of salaries, and purchasing of machinery in the district;[366] and (8) the attendance by the defendant at alleged conspiratorial meetings in the district.[367]

If a defendant challenges jurisdiction but fails to comply with discovery orders aimed at establishing jurisdictional facts, a court may sanction the noncompliance by finding that jurisdiction is established.[368]

Supreme Court decisions have expanded the exercise of personal jurisdiction over nonresident individuals who purposefully direct activity toward the forum jurisdiction.[369] In *Keeton v. Hustler Magazine, Inc.*[370] and *Calder v. Jones*,[371] the Court held that an individual who publishes an allegedly libelous article may be subject to the personal jurisdiction of a state in which the defamed individual lives,[372] does business, or otherwise may have suffered harm from the libelous act.[373]

This "purposeful activity" doctrine has been applied in antitrust actions involving foreign defendants. For example, in *Consolidated Gold Fields, PLC v. Anglo American Corp. of South Africa*,[374] the purposeful activity doctrine was held to establish personal jurisdiction over a foreign defendant in the absence of general jurisdiction, where the defendant allegedly attempted to monopolize the international and U.S. gold market through a hostile tender offer that violated U.S. antitrust and securities laws. The district court held that

> where [the defendant's] "intentional and allegedly . . . [unlawful], actions were expressly aimed at" the United States . . . and the company knew and intended that its actions would have a direct impact on [the acquired entity] with whatever consequences that impact might have for competition in the United States, [the defendant] "must 'reasonably anticipate being haled into court there' to answer for" its actions.[375]

---

366. *See, e.g., Perkins*, 342 U.S. at 447-48; Lanier v. American Bd. of Endodontics, 843 F.2d 901, 907 (6th Cir.), *cert. denied*, 488 U.S. 926 (1988). *But see* Helicopteros Nacionales de Colombia, S.A. v. Hall, 466 U.S. 408, 411, 418 (1984) (mere purchases, even if they included training sessions and were made at regular intervals, did not establish general in personam jurisdiction; nor was it proper to consider the acceptance of checks drawn on a bank in the forum state in determining the existence of significant contacts, where the bank was unilaterally selected by another party).

367. *See, e.g.,* Ohio-Sealy Mattress Mfg. Co. v. Kaplan, 429 F. Supp. 139, 141 (N.D. Ill. 1977); *cf.* McDonald v. St. Joseph's Hosp., 574 F. Supp. 123, 127-28 (N.D. Ga. 1983) (allegedly defamatory statements made in telephone conversations with the forum state, which were not initiated by the nonresident defendant, not sufficient contact).

368. *See, e.g.,* Insurance Corp. of Ireland v. Compagnie des Bauxites de Guinee, 456 U.S. 694, 704-07 (1982); English v. 21st Phoenix Corp., 590 F.2d 723, 728 (8th Cir.), *cert. denied*, 444 U.S. 832 (1979).

369. *See, e.g.,* Burger King Corp. v. Rudzewicz, 471 U.S. 462 (1985); Keeton v. Hustler Magazine, Inc., 465 U.S. 770 (1984); Calder v. Jones, 465 U.S. 783 (1984). *But cf.* Karsten Mfg. Corp. v. United States Golf Ass'n, 728 F. Supp. 1429, 1433-34 (D. Ariz. 1990) (foreseeability that activity might cause injury to the forum state is not sufficient to impose personal jurisdiction against one who did not purposefully direct its activities at the forum state).

370. 465 U.S. 770 (1984).

371. 465 U.S. 783 (1984).

372. *Id.* at 788-89.

373. *Keeton*, 465 U.S. at 777.

374. 698 F. Supp. 487 (S.D.N.Y. 1988), *aff'd in part and rev'd in part sub nom.* Consolidated Gold Fields PLC v. Minorco, S.A., 871 F.2d 252 (2d Cir.), *cert. dismissed*, 492 U.S. 939 (1989).

375. *Id.* at 496 (quoting *Calder*, 465 U.S. at 789, and World-Wide Volkswagen Corp. v. Woodson, 444 U.S. 286, 297 (1980)).

In federal question cases, courts traditionally have held that the appropriate jurisdictional question is whether the nonresident defendant has had sufficient contacts with the forum district.[376] In such cases, when there is no federal statute authorizing nationwide service of process, courts are required to obtain personal jurisdiction under the long-arm statutes of the state in which they are sitting.[377]

When a federal statute authorizes nationwide service of process, however, many courts have adopted a jurisdictional theory using an "aggregate" or "national" contacts test to determine whether jurisdiction may be asserted over foreign defendants.[378] This approach is based on the theory that if the defendant has sufficient cumulative contacts with the sovereign of which the court is an arm, the absence of contacts with the particular portion of that sovereign's physical territory in which the court sits raises a question of venue rather than jurisdiction.[379]

---

376. *See generally World-Wide Volkswagen Corp.*, 444 U.S. at 297 ("critical to due process analysis . . . is that the defendant's conduct and connection with the forum state are such that he should reasonably anticipate being haled into court there"); International Shoe Co. v. Washington, 326 U.S. 310, 316 (1945) (assertion of personal jurisdiction requires that "certain minimum contacts" exist between the nonresident defendant and the forum "such that maintenance of the suit does not offend traditional notions of fair play and substantial justice").

377. *See, e.g.*, Omni Capital Int'l v. Rudolf Wolff & Co., 484 U.S. 97 (1987) (jurisdiction of federal court, even in federal question cases, in the absence of a statutory provision for nationwide service of process, is determined according to the jurisdiction provisions of the forum state); Max Daetwyler Corp. v. Meyer, 762 F.2d 290, 297 (3d Cir. 1985) (same); United States v. M/V Santa Clara I, 859 F. Supp. 980, 987-88 (D.S.C. 1994) (same).

378. *See, e.g.*, Securities Investors Protection Corp. v. Vigman, 764 F.2d 1309 (9th Cir. 1985) (when a federal statute authorizes nationwide service of process, "the question becomes whether the party has sufficient contacts with the United States, not any particular state"); Trans-Asiatic Oil Ltd. v. Apex Oil Co., 743 F.2d 956 (1st Cir. 1984) (service under federal admiralty provision and federal jurisdiction being national in scope, due process requires only sufficient contacts within the United States as a whole); Fitzsimmons v. Barton, 589 F.2d 330 (7th Cir. 1979) (same; service under § 27 of the Securities Exchange Act of 1934); Kalamazoo Spice Extraction Co. v. Provisional Military Gov't of Socialist Ethiopia, 616 F. Supp. 660, 665 (W.D. Mich. 1985) (application of national contacts standard to foreign state); Transamerican S.S. Corp. v. Somali Democratic Republic, 590 F. Supp. 968, 976-77 (D.D.C. 1984) (same with respect to foreign state shipping agency), *aff'd in part and rev'd in part*, 767 F.2d 998 (D.C. Cir. 1985); Ruiz v. Transportes Aereos Militares Ecuadorianos, 103 F.R.D. 458, 459-60 (D.D.C. 1984) (applying national contacts test for service made under § 1608 of the FSIA); *cf. In re* Marc Rich & Co., 707 F.2d 663, 667 (2d Cir.) (personal jurisdiction over enforcement of grand jury subpoena should have been based on national contacts), *cert. denied*, 463 U.S. 1215 (1983); Texas Trading & Milling Corp. v. Federal Republic of Nigeria, 647 F.2d 300, 314 (2d Cir. 1981) (when service is made under § 1608 of the FSIA, "the relevant area in delineating contacts is the entire United States, not merely New York"), *cert. denied*, 454 U.S. 1148 (1982).

379. *See, e.g.*, First Flight Co. v. National Carloading Corp., 209 F. Supp. 730, 738 (E.D. Tenn. 1962); *see also* Courtesy Chevrolet, Inc. v. Tennessee. Walking Horse Breeders' & Exhibitors' Ass'n of Am., 344 F.2d 860, 865 (9th Cir. 1965) (considering defendant's contacts with California in determining proper venue). The Supreme Court has declined to rule on whether the aggregation of national contacts comports with the due process requirements of the Fifth Amendment. *See* Asahi Metals Indus. Co. v. Superior Court, 480 U.S. 102, 113 (1987) ("We have no occasion here to determine whether Congress could, consistent with the Due Process Clause of the Fifth Amendment, authorize federal court personal jurisdiction over alien defendants based on the aggregate of national contacts, rather than on the contacts between the defendant and the State in which the federal court sits.") However, on an earlier occasion the Court appeared to undermine the sovereignty approach to jurisdiction upon which the aggregate of contacts theory is premised. *See* Insurance Corp. of Ireland v. Compagnie des Bauxites de Guinee, 456 U.S. 694, 702 (1982) ("The personal jurisdiction requirement recognizes and protects an individual liberty interest. It represents a restriction on judicial power not as a matter of sovereignty, but as a matter of individual liberty."); *accord* Bamford v. Hobbs, 569 F. Supp. 160, 165 (S.D. Tex. 1983).

Accordingly, because the Clayton Act authorizes worldwide service of process,[380] several courts have adopted the aggregate contacts theory in antitrust cases.[381] Other courts, however, have rejected the aggregate contacts theory in the antitrust context,[382] and still others consider the aggregate of a defendant's national contacts in the context of a range of general principles of fair play and substantial justice.[383]

---

380. 15 U.S.C. § 22 (2000).

381. See, e.g., Access Telecom, Inc. v. MCI Telecommuns. Corp., 197 F.3d 694, 718 (5th Cir. 1999) (applying national contacts test but holding no personal jurisdiction), cert. denied, 531 U.S. 917 (2000); Go-Video, Inc. v. Akai Elec. Co., 885 F.2d 1406, 1413-17 (9th Cir. 1989); United Phosphorus, Ltd. v. Argus Chem. Co., 43 F. Supp. 2d 904, 911 (N.D. Ill. 1999); Miller Pipeline Corp. v. British Gas plc, 901 F. Supp. 1416, 1421-22 (S.D. Ind. 1995); In re Plastic Bag Prod. Patent & Antitrust Litig., 1987-1 Trade Cas. (CCH) ¶ 67,561, at 60,370 (D. Mass. 1987); Newport Components, Inc. v. NEC Home Elecs. (U.S.A.), Inc., 671 F. Supp. 1525, 1537-38 (C.D. Cal. 1987); Amtrol, Inc. v. Vent-Rite Valve Corp., 646 F. Supp. 1168, 1172 (D. Mass. 1986) ("Where a defendant is served pursuant to a congressional authorization of worldwide service of process, due process requires only that the defendant's aggregate contacts with the United States as a whole are such that "maintenance of the suit does not offend traditional notions of fair play and substantial justice.") (quoting International Shoe Co. v. Washington, 326 U.S. 310, 316 (1945) (internal quotations omitted)); Dunham's, Inc. v. National Buying Syndicate, 614 F. Supp. 616, 622-23 (E.D. Mich. 1985); General Elec. Co. v. Bucyrus-Erie Co., 550 F. Supp. 1037, 1043 (S.D.N.Y. 1982); Scriptomatic, Inc. v. Agfa-Gevaert, Inc., 1973-1 Trade Cas. (CCH) ¶ 74,594, at 94,633 (S.D.N.Y. 1973) (contacts with forum district also shown).

382. See, e.g., GTE New Media Servs. Inc. v. Bellsouth Corp., 199 F.3d 1343 (D.C. Cir. 2000) (§ 12 of Clayton Act authorizes worldwide service of process only where defendants inhabit or transact business in forum where case is brought); Columbia Metal Culvert v. Kaiser Indus. Corp., 526 F.2d 724, 730 (3d Cir. 1975) (applying state long arm statute); O.S.C. Corp. v. Toshiba Am., Inc., 491 F.2d 1064, 1068 (9th Cir. 1974) (considering state contacts); In re Vitamins Antitrust Litig., 94 F. Supp. 2d 26 (D.D.C. 2000) (questioning local contacts theory but regarding itself bound by D.C. Circuit precedent in GTE New Media Servs. Inc. and thus overruling prior opinion to the contrary); Sportmart, Inc. v. Frisch, 537 F. Supp. 1254, 1260 (N.D. Ill. 1982); Neumann v. Vidal, 1982-2 Trade Cas. (CCH) ¶ 64,933, at 72,772 (D.D.C. 1981); Superior Coal Co. v. Ruhrkohle, A.G., 83 F.R.D. 414, 418-19 (E.D. Pa. 1979) (holding that absent a federal statute or amendment of the Federal Rules of Civil Procedure evidencing a congressional intent to allow an aggregation of national contacts, courts are without authority to extend personal jurisdiction); Humid-Aire Corp. v. J. Levitt, Inc., 1978-1 Trade Cas. (CCH) ¶ 61,846 (N.D. Ill. 1977) (relying on Illinois jurisdictional laws); cf. Chrysler Corp. v. General Motors Corp., 589 F. Supp. 1182, 1202 n.11 (D.D.C. 1984) (explicitly noting that its finding of jurisdiction was not based on the "aggregation of national contacts theory accepted by some courts").

383. See, e.g., Entek Corp. v. Southwest Pipe & Supply Co., 683 F. Supp. 1092, 1099-1103 (N.D. Tex. 1988); Bamford, 569 F. Supp. at 166 (exercise of personal jurisdiction should not be decided solely on the basis of minimum contacts with the United States but on general principles of fair play and substantial justice, including the burden on defendant of litigation in a distant forum, the character of defendant's business as national or regional, plaintiff's interest in obtaining convenient and effective relief, and forum's interest in effective resolution of controversies); see also Chrysler Corp. v. Fedders Corp., 643 F.2d 1229, 1238 (6th Cir.) (dictum) (stating that under certain circumstances it "may well be neither unfair nor unreasonable as a matter of due process to aggregate the nonforum contacts of an alien corporate defendant in order to establish personal jurisdiction"), cert. denied, 454 U.S. 893 (1981); Harley-Davidson, Inc. v. Columbia Tristar Home Video, Inc., 851 F. Supp. 1265, 1269 (E.D. Wis. 1994) (considering both defendants' forum state activities and their national contacts); Centronics Data Computer Corp. v. Mannesmann, A.G., 432 F. Supp. 659, 664 (D.N.H. 1977) ("Where an alien defendant is sued by an American plaintiff, and where there is no particular inconvenience due to the specific forum state, the fact that the defendant is an alien and that there is no other forum in which to litigate the claim should be taken into consideration for purposes of determining whether a finding of jurisdiction meets the requisite constitutional standards of fair play."); Edward J. Moriarty & Co. v. General Tire & Rubber Co., 289 F. Supp. 381, 390 (S.D. Ohio 1967) (adopting aggregate contacts theory but holding that, in absence of federal statute providing for service upon an alien corporation, state long-arm statute

Rule 4(k)(2) of the Federal Rules of Civil Procedure, adopted in 1993, introduces a federal long-arm provision that allows personal jurisdiction over a foreign defendant "who is not subject to the jurisdiction of the courts of general jurisdiction of any state" where that jurisdiction is consistent with federal laws and the U.S. Constitution. Thus, a federal court may exercise personal jurisdiction over foreign antitrust defendants if such jurisdiction complies with the due process requirements of the Fifth Amendment and the foreign defendants are not subject to a state long-arm statute or amenable to service of process in any state.[384]

3. Service of Process

A federal court's power to exercise authority over a defendant is limited not only by constitutional considerations but also by the means granted by statute for securing the defendant's attendance. In the case of a typical corporate defendant, Section 12 of the Clayton Act authorizes service of process "in the district of which it is an inhabitant, or wherever it may be found."[385] Section 12 authorizes extraterritorial service of process.[386] In *Hoffman Motors Corp. v. Alfa Romeo SpA*,[387] this authorization was held to permit service of process upon an alien corporation at its headquarters abroad.[388]

Under Rule 4(f), service may be made on a defendant located abroad unless prohibited by federal law, and without the invocation of a state long-arm statute.

---

will control, thereby requiring an analysis of contacts with the forum state); *cf.* Busch v. Buchman, Buchman & O'Brien, Law Firm, 11 F.3d 1255 (5th Cir. 1994) (securities case; when statute authorizes nationwide service of process, look to national contacts and fulfillment of traditional notions of fair play and substantial justice).

384. *See In re* Vitamins Antitrust Litig., 94 F. Supp. 2d 26, 34-35 (D.D.C. 2000) (Rule 4(k)(2) not applicable where defendants are subject to personal jurisdiction in various states even if personal jurisdiction not available in forum state); Eskofot A/S v. E.I. duPont de Nemours & Co., 872 F. Supp. 81, 86-87 (S.D.N.Y. 1995) ("no undue surprise or prejudice" from applying Rule 4(k)(2) to action filed three months before effective date of rule with motion to dismiss filed two months after the effective date; due process satisfied by minimum contacts with the United States at large).

385. 15 U.S.C. § 22 (2000). Some cases hold that § 12 authorizes service of process only in cases where venue is established under that section or another venue statute. *See, e.g., GTE New Media Servs. Inc.*, 199 F.3d 1343 (plaintiff who uses worldwide service of process provisions of § 12 also must satisfy the venue provisions of that section); *Go-Video, Inc.*, 885 F.2d at 1417 (service of process may be effectuated under § 12 although venue is proper under § 1391(d)); *Miller Pipeline Corp.*, 901 F. Supp. at 1420-21; *General Elec. Co.*, 550 F. Supp. at 1042; *Scriptomatic, Inc.*, 1973-1 Trade Cas. (CCH) ¶ 74,594, at 94,632; *cf.* Goldlawr, Inc. v. Heiman, 288 F.2d 579, 581 (2d Cir. 1961) (extraterritorial service of process under § 12 permitted only where requirements of § 12 are met), *rev'd on other grounds*, 369 U.S. 463 (1962).

386. *See, e.g.,* Black v. Acme Mkts., Inc., 564 F.2d 681, 685 (5th Cir. 1977); C.C.P. Corp. v. Wynn Oil Co., 354 F. Supp. 1275, 1278 (N.D. Ill. 1973); Luria Steel & Trading Corp. v. Ogden Corp., 327 F. Supp. 1345, 1348-49 (E.D. Pa. 1971); Goldlawr, Inc. v. Shubert, 169 F. Supp. 677, 688 (E.D. Pa. 1958), *aff'd*, 276 F.2d 614 (3d Cir. 1960).

387. 244 F. Supp. 70 (S.D.N.Y. 1965).

388. *Id.* at 79-80; *see also* Intermountain Ford Tractor Sales Co. v. Massey-Ferguson Ltd., 210 F. Supp. 930, 939 (D. Utah 1962) (denying motions to quash return of service of process on officers of U.S. subsidiary deemed agents of Canadian corporation and finding that plaintiffs also may serve Canadian parent at home office in Canada), *aff'd per curiam*, 325 F.2d 713 (10th Cir. 1963), *cert. denied*, 377 U.S. 931 (1964); *cf.* Omni Capital Int'l, Ltd. v. Rudolf Wolff & Co., 484 U.S. 97, 104-08 (1987) (in case arising under the Commodity Exchange Act, statutory limits on service of process held applicable; extraterritorial service of process improper where not specifically authorized by statute). *But see GTE New Media Servs. Inc.*, 199 F.3d at 1343.

Furthermore, such service may be made according to "any internationally agreed means reasonably calculated to give notice, such as those means authorized by the Hague Convention on the Service Abroad of Judicial and Extrajudicial Documents."[389] If such means of service do not exist, or an international agreement allows for other means of service, other service provisions still may apply so long as they are reasonably calculated to give notice.[390] Finally, service also may be made "by other means not prohibited by international agreement as may be directed by the court."[391] Thus, authorization by state or federal law, as required by former Rules 4(e) and 4(i), is no longer necessary for extraterritorial service of a summons and complaint.[392]

Rule 4 also now contains a waiver-of-service provision that imposes a duty to save costs of service on a party receiving, by "first-class mail or other reliable means," notice of an action and a request for waiver of service of process.[393] A timely return of the waiver may affect favorably the time period in which the defendant is allowed to respond to the complaint.[394]

Finally, the activities of a foreign parent's subsidiary in a district may support the conclusion that the parent is found in that district, within the meaning of Section 12 of the Clayton Act, or that the subsidiary is acting as the parent's general agent, within the meaning of Rule 4(d)(3).[395] In either case, service of process upon the

---

389. FED. R. CIV. P. 4(f)(1) (referring to the treaty entered into force by the United States on Feb. 10, 1969, 20 UST 361, TIAS 6638, *reprinted in* MARTINDALE HUBBELL INTERNATIONAL LAW DIGESTS at IC-1 (2001).

390. *See* FED. R. CIV. P. 4(f)(2).

391. FED. R. CIV. P. 4(f)(3).

392. Service of process on foreign states is authorized by 28 U.S.C. § 1608 (1994) and may be made, among other ways, by having the court clerk mail a translated copy of a complaint, signed receipt required.

393. FED. R. CIV. P. 4(d)(2). Rule 4(d) replaced former Rule 4(c)(2)(C)(ii), (D), and (E) regarding service by mail. While not expressly excluding a defendant foreign state or political subdivision, agency, or instrumentality thereof from the waiver-of-service provision, Rule 4(j) states that the special provisions of the FSIA apply to service upon foreign government entities. FED. R. CIV. P. 4(j).

394. Although the costs of service may shift to a defendant that fails to comply with a waiver request without good cause, this rule does not apply to a defendant located outside the United States. *See* FED. R. CIV. P. 4(d)(2).

395. *See, e.g.,* Volkswagenwerk A.G. v. Schlunk, 486 U.S. 694, 707-08 (1988) (Hague Convention on the Service Abroad of Judicial and Extrajudicial Documents (*Hague Service Convention*) need not be used to serve process on a foreign corporation when service can be made on a U.S. subsidiary with a sufficiently close relationship to overseas parent); United States v. Scophony Corp. of Am., 333 U.S. 795 (1948); Frank Sexton Enter. v. Societe de Diffusion Internationale, 1998-2 Trade Cas. (CCH) ¶ 72,264, at 82,696-98 (E.D. Pa. 1998) (service on U.S. subsidiary sufficient where subsidiary is agent or alter ego of foreign defendant); Lamb v. Volkswagenwerk A.G., 104 F.R.D. 95, 97-101 (S.D. Fla. 1985) (control exercised by German parent corporation over wholly-owned U.S. subsidiary sufficient basis for finding that parent transacted business in Florida or that subsidiary acted as parent's agent; objection of Federal Republic of Germany to direct mail service pursuant to *Hague Service Convention* inapplicable when service accomplished upon alter ego within United States); Zisman v. Sieger, 106 F.R.D. 194, 199-200 (N.D. Ill. 1985) (service accomplished within United States on local agent of foreign defendant renders *Hague Service Convention* inapplicable); *In re* Siemens & Halske A.G., 155 F. Supp. 897 (S.D.N.Y. 1957) (service upon U.S. subsidiary found to be agent and alter ego of German parents upheld). *But cf.* Southmark Corp. v. Life Investors, Inc., 851 F.2d 763, 773-74 (5th Cir. 1988) (where "wholly-owned subsidiary is operated as a distinct corporation, its contacts with the forum cannot be imputed to the parent"); FDIC v. British-American Corp., 726 F. Supp. 622, 629-30 (E.D.N.C. 1989) (presence of wholly owned subsidiary does not definitively establish that foreign parent

parent at the subsidiary's offices would be effective. In other courts, the multinational character of corporate defendants has been considered relevant under the "convenience" prong of the *International Shoe* due process test.[396]

4. *Forum Non Conveniens*

In the international context, where the doctrine of forum non conveniens, rather than change of venue under 28 U.S.C. § 1404 would normally be applied, courts traditionally have ruled that the doctrine is not applicable to suits under the U.S. antitrust laws due to the special nature of those laws.[397]

The general requirements for the application of the doctrine of forum non conveniens are set forth in the Supreme Court's decisions in *Piper Aircraft Co. v. Reyno*[398] and *Gulf Oil Corp. v. Gilbert.*[399] In general, courts dismiss cases pursuant to forum non conveniens where there is another available forum that has superior contacts to the litigation and is more conducive to adjudicating the case. The Supreme Court has cautioned that dismissal normally is not appropriate if the alternative forum does not permit litigation of the subject matter of the dispute or the remedy in the alternative forum "is so clearly inadequate or unsatisfactory that it is no remedy at all."[400] The mere fact, however, that the alternative forum provides a less favorable remedy normally is not relevant.[401]

The first, and so far only, case dismissing a U.S. antitrust case pursuant to forum non conveniens is *Capital Currency Exchange, N.V. v. National Westminster Bank PLC.*[402] In that case, a Dutch financial services firm brought antitrust claims against two British banks for allegedly conspiring to destroy the plaintiff's British banking affiliate. The court applied traditional forum non conveniens factors and held that the private interests involved favored dismissal since most of the evidence and witnesses were located in England and the real parties in interest were both British corporations.[403] The court further held that the plaintiff's claims could be brought in English courts under the competition provisions of the European Community, thus

---

corporation is subject to forum's jurisdiction); Williams v. Canon, Inc., 432 F. Supp. 376, 379-80 (C.D. Cal. 1977) (venue not established as to parent merely by allegation that it participated in conspiracy with its subsidiaries).

396. *See, e.g.*, Centronics Data Computer Corp. v. Mannesmann, A.G., 432 F. Supp. 659, 664 (D.N.H. 1977) (that "an alien defendant is sued by an American plaintiff . . . and that there is no other forum in which to litigate the claim should be taken into consideration for purposes of determining whether a finding of jurisdiction meets the requisite constitutional standards of fair play").

397. *See, e.g.*, Industrial Dev. Corp. v. Mitsui & Co., 671 F.2d 876, 890 (5th Cir. 1982), *vacated on other grounds and remanded*, 460 U.S. 1007, *reaff'd*, 704 F.2d 785 (5th Cir.), *cert. denied*, 464 U.S. 961 (1983); The 'In' Porters, S.A. v. Hanes Printables, Inc., 663 F. Supp. 494, 504-06 (M.D.N.C. 1987); Laker Airways v. Pan Am. World Airways, 568 F. Supp. 811, 813-16 (D.D.C. 1983); El Cid, Ltd. v. New Jersey Zinc Co., 444 F. Supp. 845, 846 n. 1 (S.D.N.Y. 1977) (motion denied "as frivolous since the plaintiffs could not institute a Sherman Act or a comparable suit in Bolivia"); *Centronics Data Computer Corp.*, 432 F. Supp. 659. *Cf.* American Rice, Inc. v. Growers Co-op. Ass'n, 701 F.2d 408, 416-17 (5th Cir. 1983) (denying forum non conveniens motion on the merits).

398. 454 U.S. 235 (1981).

399. 330 U.S. 501 (1947).

400. *Reyno*, 454 U.S. at 254 & n.22.

401. *Id.* at 247.

402. 155 F.3d 603 (2d Cir. 1998), *cert. denied*, 526 U.S. 1067 (1999).

403. *Id.* at 611-12.

assuring both an adequate alternative forum and an adequate potential remedy for the plaintiff.[404]

5. Arbitration

Although lower courts had long held that claims arising under the antitrust laws are not arbitrable, the Supreme Court in *Mitsubishi Motors Corp. v. Soler Chrysler-Plymouth, Inc.*[405] ruled that an agreement to resolve antitrust claims by arbitration is enforceable when that agreement arises from an international transaction. The Court declared that

> concerns of international comity, respect for the capacities of foreign and transnational tribunals, and sensitivity to the need of the international commercial system for predictability in the resolution of disputes require that we enforce the parties' agreement, even assuming that a contrary result would be forthcoming in a domestic context.[406]

Some lower courts have since extended that ruling to the domestic context, allowing arbitration of rights under the antitrust laws regardless of whether the agreement to arbitrate arises from an international transaction.[407]

In *Simula, Inc. v. Autoliv, Inc.*,[408] the Ninth Circuit addressed the application to alleged antitrust claims of arbitration clauses requiring arbitration by the International Chamber of Commerce (ICC) in Switzerland. The case arose out of a contract between the parties relating to the development and marketing of new side-impact air bag technology. Following suit by the plaintiffs which included antitrust claims, the defendants sought to compel arbitration pursuant to a clause in the contract requiring "all disputes arising in connection with this agreement" to be submitted to ICC arbitration. The Ninth Circuit concluded that the plaintiffs' antitrust allegations required arbitration because resolution of the antitrust claims would necessitate interpreting the contract.[409]

The Ninth Circuit rejected the plaintiffs' argument that the choice-of-law and arbitration clauses violated public policy because the ICC might not apply American antitrust law. The court rejected as dictum cautionary language from *Mitsubishi* that suggested the Supreme Court might reject arbitration clauses that effectively barred a party from pursuing statutory antitrust remedies.[410] The Ninth Circuit stated: "The

---

404. *Id.* at 610. The court acknowledged that treble damages and some of the plaintiff's common-law claims would not be available in an English tort action applying European Community competition rules, but said the unavailability of treble damages or identical causes of action does not render a forum inadequate. *Id.* at 610-11.

405. 473 U.S. 614 (1985).

406. *Id.* at 629. *See also In re* Hops Antitrust Litig., 832 F.2d 470 (8th Cir. 1987); High Strength Steel, Inc. v. Svenskt Stal Aktiebolag, 1985-2 Trade Cas. (CCH) ¶ 66,884 (N.D. Ill. 1985).

407. *See, e.g.*, Seacoast Motors of Salisbury, Inc. v. DaimlerChrysler Motors Corp., 271 F.3d 6 (1st Cir. 2001); Kotam Elecs. v. JBL Consumer Products, Inc., 93 F.3d 724 (11th Cir. 1996) (en banc), *cert. denied*, 519 U.S. 1110 (1997); Nghiem v. NEC Elec., Inc., 25 F.3d 1437, 1441-42 (9th Cir.), *cert. denied*, 513 U.S. 1044 (1994); Sanjuan v. American Bd. of Psychiatry and Neurology, Inc., 40 F.3d 247 (7th Cir. 1994); Syscomm Int'l Corp. v. SynOptics Communs. Inc., 856 F. Supp. 135 (E.D.N.Y. 1994).

408. 175 F.3d 716 (9th Cir. 1999).

409. *Id.* at 712-22.

410. *Id.* at 723 (interpreting 473 U.S. at 637 n.19).

applicable standard should be whether the law of the transferee court is so deficient that the plaintiffs would be deprived of any reasonable recourse."[411] It held that the ICC would afford sufficient remedies and that the plaintiff would receive sufficient protection if Swiss law applied, even if those protections were not identical to the remedies under U.S. law.

F. Discovery and the Conduct of Litigation in Foreign Commerce Cases

1. *Discovery outside the United States*

Courts in the United States ordering discovery abroad or otherwise ordering or prohibiting conduct abroad affecting litigation in the United States often encounter conflicts with laws of foreign nations.[412] Extraterritorial application of U.S. discovery laws has given rise to considerable friction among nations.[413]

a. PROCEDURES UNDER U.S. LAW FOR OBTAINING DOCUMENTS LOCATED ABROAD

Rule 34 of the Federal Rules of Civil Procedure provides that when documents sought are in the "possession, custody, or control" of a party to the action, and the court has jurisdiction over the party, the location of the documents is not determinative of whether they must be produced.[414] The position of the United States

---

411. *Id.*
412. RESTATEMENT (THIRD), *supra* note 12, § 442 reporters' note 1. Several countries have enacted legislation to restrict or prohibit altogether persons or corporations under their control from complying with foreign discovery orders. *Id. See also* part F.1.b of this chapter.
413. A British court enjoined a British corporation from pursuing a U.S. antitrust action against two British defendants in *British Airways Bd. v. Laker Airways*, [1983] 3 W.L.R. 544, 588-91 (C.A. July 26, 1983). The decision was based in part on, and upheld, the Protection of Trading Interests Act, which prohibited the British defendants from producing certain documents and information in the U.S. proceeding. *See* Protection of Trading Interests Act, 1980, ch. 11 (Eng.), *as amended by* Civil Jurisdiction and Judgments Act, 1982, ch. 27, *and* Statute Law (Repeals) Act, 1993, ch. 50, Sch. 1 pt. XIV. The U.S. court responded to the British court's injunction by enjoining the other defendants "from taking any action in a foreign forum that would impair or interfere with the jurisdiction of this Court." Laker Airways v. Pan Am. World Airways, 559 F. Supp. 1124, 1139 (D.D.C. 1983), *aff'd sub nom.* Laker Airways v. Sabena, Belgian World Airlines, 731 F.2d 909, 922 (D.C. Cir. 1984) (stating that where two or more states have legitimate interests in a controversy, jurisdiction is not mutually exclusive; under principles of international law, territoriality and nationality often give rise to concurrent jurisdiction). The House of Lords discharged the British court's injunction on appeal. British Airways Bd. v. Laker Airways, [1984] 3 W.L.R. 413, 414, *reprinted in* 23 I.L.M. 727 (C.A. July 19, 1984); *see also* American Home Assurance Co. v. Insurance Corp. of Ireland, 603 F. Supp. 636, 642-43 (S.D.N.Y 1984) (enjoining litigants from pursuing suits simultaneously in U.S. and foreign forums where resolution of one suit is dispositive of the other); Smith Kline & French Lab. v. Bloch, [1983] 1 W.L.R. 730 (C.A. May 13, 1982) (English Court of Appeals upheld injunction against U.S. antitrust complaint by English person against English subsidiary of U.S. company arising out of contract in England; amended complaint naming only U.S. parent allowed to proceed).
414. *See, e.g., In re* Grand Jury Proceedings Bank of Nova Scotia, 740 F.2d 817, 828 & n.17 (11th Cir. 1984) (law of situs of documents does not necessarily control in cases of conflict), *cert. denied*, 469 U.S. 1106 (1985); *In re* Marc Rich & Co., 707 F.2d 663, 667 (2d Cir.) ("test for the production of documents is control, not location"), *cert. denied*, 463 U.S. 1215 (1983); Cooper Indus. v.

is that persons who do business in the United States or otherwise bring themselves within the jurisdiction of U.S. courts are subject to the burdens as well as the benefits of U.S. law, including the laws on discovery.[415] The national interests of the state in which the documents are kept, however, may affect a court's decision whether to

---

British Aerospace, Inc., 102 F.R.D. 918, 920 (S.D.N.Y. 1984) (custody or control, not possession or location, is determinative); *In re* Uranium Antitrust Litig., 480 F. Supp. 1138, 1144 (N.D. Ill. 1979) (ordering production of documents located abroad that are under the control of defendants); *In re* Grand Jury Subpoenas Duces Tecum Addressed to Canadian Int'l Paper Co., 72 F. Supp. 1013, 1020 (S.D.N.Y. 1947) (corporate resolution maintaining custody of corporation's documents in Canada and prohibiting disclosure elsewhere provides no defense to properly served subpoena).

Section 442 of the *Restatement (Third)* would require discovery requests for documents or information located abroad to be issued by a court or agency authorized by statute or rule of court, not just a private party, and would impose a stricter relevancy test than is applicable to domestic discovery. RESTATEMENT (THIRD), *supra* note 12, § 442. The Attorney General and the Assistant Attorney General in charge of the Antitrust Division are authorized by statute to issue CIDs or subpoenas to persons outside the United States. Antitrust Civil Process Act, 15 U.S.C. § 1312(d)(2) (2000).

In foreign commerce cases, the most common dispute is whether a court may order a U.S. corporation to produce documents in the hands of a foreign affiliate. No general test of "possession, custody, or control" emerges from the case law. Whether or not a party has access to the documents in the ordinary course of business is one indication of whether that party controls the documents. United States v. King, No. 94-CR 455, 1997 U.S. Dist. LEXIS 14356 (S.D.N.Y. Sept. 19, 1997). Other indicia of control include common ownership, exchange or intermingling of directors, officers or employees, and any benefit or involvement by the nonparty corporation in the transaction or litigation. *See, e.g.*, United States v. Ericsson, Inc., 181 F.R.D. 302 (M.D.N.C. 1998). Courts have ordered production from foreign subsidiaries controlled by U.S. corporations. *See, e.g.*, *In re Uranium Antitrust Litig.*, 480 F. Supp. at 1144-45 (ordering production from subsidiaries located in Australia, South Africa, Switzerland, and Canada); *In re* Investigation of World Arrangements with Relation to the Prod., Transp., Ref. & Distrib. of Petroleum, 13 F.R.D. 280, 285 (D.D.C. 1952) (stating that parent corporations, having the power to control the directors of their subsidiaries, have the control necessary to secure documents). Where the U.S. corporation is a subsidiary of a foreign corporation, however, the courts have split on whether the U.S. company controls the foreign parent for Rule 34 purposes. *Compare In re Uranium Antitrust Litig.*, 480 F. Supp. at 1145 (stating that the test of control is less clear when an order is directed to a U.S. subsidiary of a foreign corporation, and rests finally on questions of fact), *with* United States v. Ciba Corp., 1972 Trade Cas. (CCH) ¶ 74,026, at 92,253-54 (D.N.J. 1971) (requiring corporation to make good faith attempt to secure pertinent material in hands of foreign parent). *See also In re* Messerschmitt Bolkow Blohm GmbH, 757 F.2d 729, 733-34 (5th Cir. 1985) (no evidence that subsidiary was sham or alter ego or that it had custody or control of documents), *cert. granted and decision vacated and remanded sub nom.* Messerschmitt Bolkow Blohm, GmbH v. Walker, 483 U.S. 1002 (1987); Laker Airways v. Pan Am. World Airways, 607 F. Supp. 324 (S.D.N.Y. 1985) (with respect to nonparties, documents regularly maintained in the United Kingdom could not be obtained by serving U.S. branch office that had no connection with matters in issue); Compagnie Française d'Assurance Pour le Commerce Exterieur v. Phillips Petroleum Co., 105 F.R.D. 16, 33-35 (S.D.N.Y. 1984) (where agency of French government is plaintiff and is affirmatively seeking benefit of U.S. law, it is not inappropriate to require discovery of documents in possession of other agencies of French government).

415. RESTATEMENT (THIRD), *supra* note 12, § 442 reporters' note 1; *see also* United States v. Germann, 370 F.2d 1019, 1023 (2d Cir.) ("[A]nyone within the jurisdiction of the court may be subpoenaed .... It makes no difference where he is resident or of what country he is a citizen."), *vacated and remanded on other grounds*, 389 U.S. 329 (1967); McKesson Corp. v. Islamic Republic of Iran, 185 F.R.D. 70, 80 (D.D.C. 1999) (finding that Iran must accept reasonable burdens imposed on it in defending a lawsuit, including discovery, so that plaintiffs are not denied fair process); *cf.* CFTC v. Nahas, 738 F.2d 487, 493-95 (D.C. Cir. 1984) (in the absence of clear congressional direction to the contrary, statute authorizing court to enforce investigational subpoenas by Commodities Future Trading Commission did not authorize enforcement of subpoena served on foreign citizen in foreign country in contravention of principles of international law).

exercise its power to order production or penalize nonproduction. Thus, before a court compels discovery, it may evaluate the importance of the requested discovery, the specificity of the request, the country of origin of the requested information, the availability of an alternative means of obtaining the requested information, and the extent to which important interests of the United States or a foreign country would be undermined by compliance or noncompliance.[416]

U.S. courts also may order production of documents in the possession of nonparties in the United States.[417] Moreover, Section 1783 of the Judicial Code authorizes service of subpoenas upon nonparties located abroad if they are U.S. citizens or residents.[418]

In addition, courts may obtain documents located abroad by letters rogatory.[419] When documents are in the possession of a party, or a nonparty that can be served with a subpoena under Rule 45, a letter rogatory offers an additional method for obtaining the documents.[420] A letter rogatory is the only method available for obtaining documents from nonparties who cannot be served with subpoenas. Federal Rule of Civil Procedure 28(b) authorizes the district court to issue a letter rogatory on the request of a party to the action.[421] The letter may be transmitted directly to the foreign tribunal or it may be sent via the Department of State.[422]

The Hague Convention on the Taking of Evidence Abroad in Civil or Commercial Matters (*Hague Evidence Convention*) expressly provides for the use of

---

416. *See* Société Nationale Industrielle Aérospatiale v. United States Dist. Court, 482 U.S. 522, 546 (1987) (cautioning courts to exercise "special vigilance" to protect foreign litigants against undue burden and intrusiveness); *see also* RESTATEMENT (THIRD), *supra* note 12, § 442(1)(c); *cf.* United States v. First Nat'l City Bank, 396 F.2d 897, 901-03 (2d Cir. 1968) (affirming validity of subpoena requiring New York bank to produce documents located at its branch in Frankfurt pursuant to the conclusion that U.S. interest in antitrust enforcement outweighed German bank secrecy doctrine).

417. Discovery from nonparties is governed by Federal Rule of Civil Procedure 45, which sets out the rules for the issuance and service of a subpoena.

418. 28 U.S.C. § 1783(a) (1994) provides:

A court of the United States may order the issuance of a subpoena requiring the appearance as a witness before it, or before a person or body designated by it, of a national or resident of the United States who is in a foreign country, or requiring the production of a specified document or other thing by him, if the court finds that particular testimony or the production of the document or other thing by him is necessary in the interest of justice, and, in other than a criminal action or proceeding, if the court finds, in addition, that it is not possible to obtain his testimony in admissible form without his personal appearance or to obtain the production of the document or other thing in any other manner.

419. A letter rogatory has been described as

the medium, in effect, whereby one country, speaking through one of its courts, requests another country, acting through its own courts and by methods of court procedure peculiar thereto and entirely within the latter's control, to assist the administration of justice in the former country; such request being made, and being usually granted, by reason of the comity existing between nations in ordinary peaceful times.

Tiedemann v. The Signe, 37 F. Supp. 819, 820 (E.D. La. 1941).

420. Thus, for example, where a party sought enforcement of a subpoena for bank records located in Canada and the parties differed on whether Canadian bank secrecy laws barred disclosure of the documents, the Second Circuit directed the party seeking the documents to proceed by letter rogatory in order to allow a Canadian court to decide the matter. *See* Ings v. Ferguson, 282 F.2d 149, 152 (2d Cir. 1960).

421. Rule 28 permits an applicable treaty or convention to govern the taking of depositions. FED. R. CIV. P. 28.

422. 28 U.S.C. § 1781 (1994). Department of State regulations governing letters rogatory and related matters are set forth in 22 C.F.R. pt. 92 (2001).

letters rogatory, which it terms "letters of request."[423]   Twenty-five countries, including the United States, are parties to the *Hague Evidence Convention.*[424] Chapter 1 of the *Convention* sets out the procedures for issuing and executing letters of request.[425] Although the *Convention* provides procedures for obtaining evidence abroad, the current state of practice under the convention varies from country to country.

The *Hague Evidence Convention*'s facilitation of discovery through letters of request is tempered by several provisions that limit its usefulness in providing access to material for use in litigation in the United States. Most significant is Article 23, which permits a contracting state to declare that it will not execute letters of request that seek to obtain "pretrial discovery of documents as known in Common Law countries."[426] Of the twenty-five signatories, only Barbados, the Czech and Slovak Republics, Israel, Latvia, and the United States have not issued such a declaration.[427] Estonia has not issued such a declaration, but will only fulfill a request for documents under certain conditions.[428] The tendency to make Article 23 declarations apparently arose from a widespread misunderstanding that U.S. lawyers might seek, prior to the filing of a case, to determine whether evidence exists that could support the filing of an action.[429]   Notwithstanding their Article 23 declarations, many

---

423. Hague Convention on the Taking of Evidence Abroad in Civil or Commercial Matters, Mar. 18, 1970, art. 2 [hereinafter HAGUE EVIDENCE CONVENTION], 23 U.S.T. 2555, T.I.A.S. No. 7444, *reprinted in* MARTINDALE HUBBELL INTERNATIONAL LAW DIGESTS at IC-20 (2001) (entered into force for the United States Oct. 7, 1972). With respect to countries that are signatories to the *Hague Evidence Convention*, letters of request are sent not to the foreign tribunal but to a Central Authority designated by each signatory. The Central Authority will transmit the request to the judicial authority competent to execute it.

424. TREATY AFFAIRS STAFF, U.S. DEP'T OF STATE, TREATIES IN FORCE, A LIST OF TREATIES AND OTHER INTERNATIONAL AGREEMENTS OF THE UNITED STATES IN FORCE ON JANUARY 1, 1999, at 399 (1999). The signatories are Argentina, Australia, Barbados, China (applicable only to Hong Kong), Cyprus, the Czech Republic, Denmark, Estonia, Finland, France, Federal Republic of Germany, Israel, Italy, Latvia, Luxembourg, Mexico, Monaco, the Netherlands, Norway, Poland, Portugal, Singapore, the Slovak Republic, South Africa, Spain, Sweden, Switzerland, the United Kingdom, the United States, and Venezuela. The *Hague Evidence Convention* is the latest in a series of multilateral treaties governing the collection of evidence abroad. The earlier two treaties, to which the United States is not a party, essentially codified existing international practice at the time. Because so few countries have acceded to the latest treaty, the earlier two are still important in international practice. They are the Convention Relating to Civil Procedure, *ratified* Apr. 24, 1909, 99 British and Foreign State Papers 990 (1910), and the Convention Relating to Civil Procedure, Mar. 1, 1954, 286 U.N.T.S. 266 (1958).

425. HAGUE EVIDENCE CONVENTION, *supra* note 423, arts. 1-14. The issuing country must indicate in the letter the nature of the action for which the evidence is sought, the parties to the action, and whether any documents are sought. *Id.* art. 3(b), (c), (g). The country receiving the letter "shall apply the appropriate measures of compulsion in the instances and to the same extent as are provided by its internal law" for enforcing the letter. *Id.* art. 10.

426. HAGUE EVIDENCE CONVENTION, *supra* note 423, art. 23.

427. *Id.*

428. The conditions are (1) the process has been launched; (2) the documents have been reasonably identified according to the dates, contents, or other information; and (3) the circumstances have been indicated giving grounds to presume that the documents are in the property or possession of the person or are known to him. HAGUE EVIDENCE CONVENTION, *supra* note 423.

429. Report on the Work of the Special Commission on the Operation of the Convention of 18 March 1970 on the Taking of Evidence Abroad in Civil or Commercial Matters, 17 I.L.M. 1425, 1428 (1978); Report of the United States Delegation to the Special Commission on the Operation of the Convention of 18 March 1970 on the Taking of Evidence Abroad in Civil or Commercial Matters, 17 I.L.M. 1417, 1421 (1978).

contracting states will execute carefully drafted, specific document requests, particularly when the letter of request specifies that the requested documents are relevant to matters that will be in issue at trial. Indeed, after the civil law countries became aware that U.S. discovery typically occurs only in a pending action, several clarified their Article 23 declarations, making it clear that they will execute requests for specific and identified documents.[430] In addition, Article 23 applies only to letters of request seeking documents. Thus, requests for deposition discovery by letters of request are not restricted by Article 23. Moreover, pretrial discovery of documents may be sought through consular or commissioner channels from voluntary witnesses where the compulsory power of the foreign state is not needed.[431]

The *Hague Evidence Convention* also provides that the person from whom the testimony or material is sought may refuse to give evidence insofar as he may claim a privilege under the law of the state sending the letter or the law of the state where execution is sought. In addition, a country may declare that it will respect privileges and duties existing under the laws of other countries.[432] Finally, Article 12 states that a nation may refuse to execute a letter if it "considers that its sovereignty or security may be prejudiced thereby."[433]

Some foreign courts have relied on the *Hague Evidence Convention*'s limitations on letters of request to deny discovery requests from U.S. courts. For example, in *Rio Tinto Zinc Corp. v. Westinghouse*,[434] the British House of Lords cited the *Convention* in denying enforcement of a letter of request presented by Westinghouse in the *Uranium Antitrust Litigation*. Canadian courts also relied on the *Hague Evidence Convention* in refusing to enforce letters of request seeking evidence concerning an alleged uranium cartel.[435]

---

430. For example, the U.K. declaration under Article 23 states that:
    In accordance with Article 23 Her Majesty's Government declare that the United Kingdom will not execute Letters of Request issued for the purpose of obtaining pre-trial discovery of documents. Her Majesty's Government further declare that Her Majesty's Government understand "Letters of Request issued for the purpose of obtaining pre-trial discovery of documents" for the purposes of the foregoing Declaration as including any Letter of Request which requires a person:
        a. to state what documents relevant to the proceedings to which the Letter of Request relates are, or have been, in his possession, custody or power; or
        b. to produce any documents other than particular documents specified in the Letter of Request as being documents appearing to the requested court to be, or to be likely to be, in his possession, custody or powers.
    United Kingdom instruction of ratification, cl. 3, deposited July 16, 1976, *reprinted in* MARTINDALE HUBBELL INTERNATIONAL LAW DIGESTS at IC-31 (2001). Singapore, the Netherlands, Sweden, Finland, Norway, and Denmark have made similar modifications to their Article 23 declarations. France subsequently modified its declaration to state that it will honor document requests that are "enumerated limitatively in the Letter of Request and have a direct and precise link with the object of the procedure." The Federal Republic of Germany and Italy have ratified the convention while making broad reservations under Article 23. The various countries' declarations are reprinted in MARTINDALE HUBBELL INTERNATIONAL LAW DIGESTS, at IC-22-33 (2001).
431. HAGUE EVIDENCE CONVENTION, *supra* note 423, art. 2.
432. *Id.* art. 11.
433. *Id.* art. 12(b).
434. [1978] 2 W.L.R. 81 (H.L. 1977).
435. Gulf Oil Corp. v. Gulf Can. Ltd., [1980] 2 S.C.R. 39, 1980-1 Trade Cas. (CCH) ¶ 63,285 (Can. 1980); *cf. In re* Westinghouse Elec. Corp., 16 O.R.2d 273 (Ont. H. Ct. J. 1977).

In *Société Nationale Industrielle Aérospatiale v. United States District Court*,[436] the Supreme Court held, by a vote of five-to-four, that the *Hague Evidence Convention* does not displace the Federal Rules of Civil Procedure in matters of foreign discovery but provides an alternative or supplementary means of obtaining information located abroad.[437] The decision directed the lower courts to engage in a detailed comity analysis in order to determine whether to order use of *Convention* procedures or to conduct discovery under the Federal Rules of Civil Procedure. Factors considered in the analysis include (1) the competing interests of the governments involved (e.g., the U.S. interest in full discovery versus foreign principles of judicial sovereignty and the interest of all signatories in maintaining a smoothly functioning international legal system); (2) the likelihood that *Convention* procedures would be effective; (3) the intrusiveness of the discovery requests (e.g., whether the requests seek trade secrets or matters affecting the national defense of a foreign sovereign); (4) the origin of the information being sought; (5) the costs of transporting the witnesses, documents, or other evidence to the United States; (6) the skill with which the requests are drafted (i.e., whether they are clear, specific, and limited to obtaining relevant information); (7) the importance to the litigation of the documents or information sought; and (8) the availability of alternative means of securing the information.[438]

The Court also stated that "[t]he exact line between reasonableness and unreasonableness in each case must be drawn by the trial court, based on its knowledge of the case and of the claims and interests of the parties and the governments whose statutes and policies they invoke."[439] The Court emphasized the importance of careful supervision of discovery requests propounded to foreign litigants, cautioning courts to exercise "special vigilance to protect [them] from the danger that unnecessary, or unduly burdensome, discovery may place them in a disadvantageous position."[440]

Lower courts interpreting *Aérospatiale* have reached inconsistent conclusions in allocating the burden of persuasion on whether to apply *Hague Evidence Convention* procedures or U.S. procedural rules.[441] Opinions also diverge as to whether foreign

---

436. 482 U.S. 522 (1987).
437. *Id.* at 538. Before *Aérospatiale*, courts were divided over the proper relationship between the *Hague Evidence Convention* and the federal rules. *Compare* Compagnie Française d'Assurance Pour le Commerce Exterieur v. Phillips Petroleum Co., 105 F.R.D. 16, 26-36 (S.D.N.Y. 1984) (*Hague Evidence Convention* was the preferred means of conducting foreign discovery), *and* TH. Goldschmidt A.G. v. Smith, 676 S.W.2d 443 (Tex. Ct. App. 1984) (requiring litigants to pursue *Hague Evidence Convention* procedures as a matter of first resort), *with In re* Anschuetz & Co., 754 F.2d 602, 615 (5th Cir. 1985), *cert. granted and vacated sub nom.* Anschuetz & Co. v. Mississippi River Bridge Auth., 483 U.S. 1002 (1987) (discovery should ordinarily be conducted under the Federal Rules of Civil Procedure if the party is subject to the court's personal jurisdiction).
438. 482 U.S. at 555-68.
439. *Id.* at 546.
440. *Id. See also* Belmont Textile Mach. Co. v. Superba, S.A., 48 F. Supp. 2d 521 (W.D.N.C. 1999).
441. *Compare In re* Vitamins Antitrust Litig., 120 F. Supp. 2d 45, 52 (D.D.C. 2000) (burden of persuasion lies with the party requesting that discovery proceed under the *Hague Evidence Convention* rather than the Federal Rules of Civil Procedure), Valois of Am., Inc. v. Risdon Corp., 183 F.R.D. 344, 346 (D. Conn. 1997) (same), Rich v. KIS Cal., Inc., 121 F.R.D. 254, 257 (M.D.N.C. 1988) (same), *and* Benton Graphics v. Uddelholm Corp., 118 F.R.D. 386, 389 (D.N.J. 1987) (same), *with* Hudson v. Hermann Pfauter GmbH & Co., 117 F.R.D. 33, 38 (N.D.N.Y. 1987) ("the burden should be placed on the party opposing the use of Convention procedures to

defendants objecting to U.S. court jurisdiction are subject to discovery under the federal rules on that issue.[442]

b. FOREIGN LAWS REGULATING DISCOVERY ABROAD

Efforts by U.S. litigants to obtain discovery abroad may conflict with the laws or interests of the country where the material sought is located. Several countries have enacted statutes that limit the extent to which a corporation or person subject to its jurisdiction may comply with requests for information abroad. In some instances, the legislative history of these laws makes it clear that the primary reason for passage was to block U.S. discovery requests.[443]

Among the countries that have passed blocking statutes are Australia, Canada, the United Kingdom, and France. Ontario and Quebec have passed their own statutes. The statutes vary greatly in scope and application. Some may be waived by government consent, while others may not. Some block discovery of material relating to certain industries; others apply to all commercial information. The Business Records Protection Act of Ontario[444] and the Business Concerns Record Act of Quebec[445] appear to bar absolutely the removal of any documents from businesses in these two provinces in response to any judicial order. Statutes like the United Kingdom's Protection of Trading Interests Act,[446] Australia's Foreign Proceedings (Excess of Jurisdiction) Act,[447] and Canada's Foreign Extraterritorial Measures Act[448] permit removal unless a government official prohibits it. In addition, French law prohibits a French citizen, a resident of France, a French company, or a company with an establishment in France from providing documents or information of an

---

demonstrate that those procedures would frustrate" the interests of domestic litigants in pursuing evidence), *and* Knight v. Ford Motor Co., 260 N.J. Super. 110, 118-21 (N.J. Super. Ct. Law Div. 1992) (placing burden of persuasion on party opposing use of the *Hague Evidence Convention*).

442. *Compare In re Vitamins Antitrust Litig.*, 120 F. Supp. 2d at 55 (allowing discovery on jurisdictional issue to proceed under the federal rules based on the *Aérospatiale* factors), *In re* Aircrash Disaster Near Roselawn, Ind., 172 F.R.D. 295, 309-10 (N.D. Ill. 1997) (same), Fishel v. BASF Group, 175 F.R.D. 525, 529 (S.D. Iowa 1997) (allowing limited discovery to proceed under the federal rules despite German company's claim that the court lacked personal jurisdiction), *and Rich*, 121 F.R.D. 254 (allowing limited discovery to proceed under the federal rules where a French company challenged court's jurisdiction), *with* Jenco v. Martech Int'l, Inc., Civ. No. 86-4229, 1988 U.S. Dist. LEXIS 4727 (E.D. La. May 19, 1988) (holding that evidence on the jurisdictional question regarding a Norwegian defendant should be taken under the *Hague Evidence Convention*), *and Knight*, 260 N.J. Super. at 119 ("If jurisdiction does not exist over a foreign party . . . the Convention may provide the only recourse for obtaining evidence.").

443. This is reflected most clearly in the legislative history of the United Kingdom's Protection of Trading Interests Act, 1980, ch. 11 (Eng.), *as amended* by Civil Jurisdiction and Judgments Act, 1982, ch. 27, and Statute of Law (Repeals) Act, 1993, ch. 50, Sch. 1, pt. XIV. *See* 404 PARL. DEB. H.L. (5th ser.) 554-60 (1980) (remarks of Lord Mackay); 2.973 PARL. DEB., H.C. (5th ser.) 1533-38, 1546 (1979) (remarks of John Nott).

444. R.S.O. ch. B.19 (1990) (Ont.). *But see In re* Inter-City Truck Lines (Can.), 133 D.L.R.3d 134, 138 (Ont. H. Ct. J. 1982) (Ontario attorney general did not object to removal of photocopies).

445. R.S.Q. ch. D-12 (1977) (Que.), *as amended* by S.Q. ch. 4, pt. 388 (1990), *and* S.Q. ch. 61, pt. 267 (1992).

446. Protection of Trading Interests Act, 1980, ch. 11, § 2, *as amended*.

447. Foreign Proceedings (Excess of Jurisdiction) Act, No. 3, §§ 7-8 (1984) (Austl.), *as amended by* Foreign Judgments Act, No. 112 (1991).

448. Foreign Extraterritorial Measures Act, R.S.C., ch. F-29, § 3 (1984) (Can.), *as amended by* Department of External Affairs Act, 1995, ch. 5, 1994-1995 S.C. *and by* Foreign Extraterritorial Measures Act, 1996, ch. 28, 1995-1996 S.C.

economic, commercial, industrial, financial, or technical nature that might threaten France's sovereignty, security, or basic economic interests.[449]

c. THE EFFECT OF FOREIGN LAWS AND COMITY CONSIDERATIONS ON U.S. DISCOVERY

Under U.S. law, the effect of a foreign nondisclosure law, or of other foreign interests in conflict with discovery, is decided on a case-by-case basis.[450] The starting point is *Société Internationale Pour Participations Industrielles et Commerciales, S.A. v. Rogers.*[451] In that case, Swiss bank secrecy laws had prevented the plaintiff from fully complying with the defendant's document request under Rule 34 of the Federal Rules of Civil Procedure. The plaintiff had sought a waiver of the Swiss law and had been partially successful; nonetheless, the plaintiff was unable to produce all the documents sought. As a result, the district court granted the defendant's motion under Rule 37 to dismiss the action with prejudice.

The Supreme Court reversed, stressing that the plaintiff's inability to produce the documents was "fostered neither by its own conduct nor by circumstances within its control."[452] Rule 37 should not be construed as authorizing dismissal, the Court said, where "noncompliance . . . has been due to inability, and not to willfulness, bad faith, or any fault of petitioner."[453] The Court stated, however, that the plaintiff should not be allowed to benefit from nonproduction and that on remand the district court possessed wide discretion, including the power to draw inferences adverse to the plaintiff, to fashion an appropriate remedy.

In *Société Internationale*, the Court drew a distinction between the power to order production in the face of a foreign nondisclosure law—which had been properly exercised—and the appropriate sanctions to apply for noncompliance. The Court found that the existence of the foreign law barring disclosure, and the plaintiff's attempt to have it waived, "can hardly affect the fact of noncompliance and are relevant only to the path which the District Court might follow in dealing with petitioner's failure to comply."[454] This language led some courts to conclude that considerations of international comity are not relevant until the sanctions phase of the discovery proceeding.[455] That interpretation, however, does not appear to survive *Société Nationale Industrielle Aérospatiale v. United States District Court,*[456] which

---

449. Law concerning the Communication of Economic, Commercial, Industrial, Financial or Technical Documents or Information, Law No. 80-538, 1980 Journal Officiel de la République Française [J.O.] 1799 (July 16, 1980). Switzerland also has a nondisclosure law. *See* STGB, CP, Cod. Pen. art. 273 (disclosure of business or manufacturing secret prohibited except where all those with interest consent).

450. SEC v. Banner Fund Int'l, 211 F.3d 602, 612 (D.C. Cir. 2000).

451. 357 U.S. 197 (1958).

452. *Id.* at 211.

453. *Id.* at 212 (footnote omitted).

454. *Id.* at 208.

455. *See, e.g.*, Arthur Andersen & Co. v. Finesilver, 546 F.2d 338, 342 (10th Cir. 1976) ("[*Société Internationale*] only indicates that the foreign law question goes to the imposition of a sanction for noncompliance with local law."), *cert. denied*, 429 U.S. 1096 (1977); Lasky v. Continental Prods. Corp., 569 F. Supp. 1227, 1228-29 (E.D. Pa. 1983) (stating in dictum that "while a court may have the power to order actions which are in violation of the laws of a foreign sovereign, the court must weigh considerations of international comity in determining . . . sanctions").

456. 482 U.S. 522 (1987).

stated that U.S. courts should supervise pretrial proceedings with "special vigilance" in accordance with the demands of comity.[457] Other courts have held that the obligation of comity must yield to strong domestic policy interests.[458]

---

457. *Id.* at 545-46. Although the Supreme Court did not articulate specific rules in *Aérospatiale* to guide this analysis, numerous courts, before and after *Aérospatiale*, engaged in a comity analysis in deciding whether to order production in the first instance. *See, e.g., In re* Grand Jury Proceedings Bank of Nova Scotia, 740 F.2d 817, 826-29 (11th Cir. 1984) (in affirming contempt fine, court approved district court's balancing of factors under § 40 of *Restatement (Second) of the Foreign Relations Law of the United States* (1965) to determine whether subpoena enforcement was proper), *cert. denied*, 469 U.S. 1106 (1985); Alfadda v. Fenn, 149 F.R.D. 28, 35 (S.D.N.Y. 1993) (mem.) (deposition testimony ordered where strength of the Swiss national interest in the outcome uncertain because official letter clarifying the requirements of Swiss bank secrecy laws was "not the expression of a view regarding th[e] motion" for a protective order, and Swiss law did not prevent disclosure of the information sought); Minpeco, S.A. v. Conticommodity Servs., 116 F.R.D. 517, 521-22 (S.D.N.Y.) (comity analysis performed before deciding whether to order discovery barred by Swiss secrecy laws), *aff'd sub nom.* Korwek v. Hunt, 827 F.2d 874 (2d Cir. 1987); Garpeg, Ltd. v. United States, 588 F. Supp. 1237 (S.D.N.Y. 1984) (refusing to quash Internal Revenue Service (IRS) summons after balancing respective interests of each state); United States v. Chase Manhattan Bank, 584 F. Supp. 1080, 1085-87 (S.D.N.Y. 1984) (enforcing IRS summons after examining *Restatement (Second)* § 40 factors); Garpeg, Ltd. v. United States, 583 F. Supp. 789, 795-96 (S.D.N.Y. 1984) (noting that factors other than those in § 40 suggested by the *Restatement (Second)*, while relevant, have not yet been adopted by the Second Circuit); Soletanche & Rodio, Inc. v. Brown & Lambrecht Earth Movers, Inc., 99 F.R.D. 269 (N.D. Ill. 1983) (declining to vacate order compelling answers to interrogatories after balancing § 40 factors); *In re* Uranium Antitrust Litig., 480 F. Supp. 1138, 1148 (N.D. Ill. 1979) (issuance of production order held to be a "discretionary" act which, under *Société Internationale*, should be determined primarily by consideration of three factors: the importance of the U.S. statutes underlying plaintiff's claims, the importance of the information sought to the prosecution of such claims, and the degree of flexibility in the foreign nation's nondisclosure laws; all other considerations of comity deferred for sanctions hearing); *see also* Richmark Corp. v. Timber Falling Consultants, 959 F.2d 1468, 1474, 1479 (9th Cir.) (comity considered in decision to impose sanctions on company owned by government of People's Republic of China for failure to comply with discovery, despite state secrecy law prohibiting production of financial information about worldwide operations, where failure to assert state secrecy law in timely fashion waived issue of the validity of the discovery request), *cert. dismissed*, 506 U.S. 948 (1992); Trade Dev. Bank v. Continental Ins. Co., 469 F.2d 35, 41-42 (2d Cir. 1972) (affirming decision not to order Swiss bank to seek customers' waivers of bank secrecy laws); United States v. First Nat'l City Bank, 396 F.2d 897, 904-05 (2d Cir. 1968) (potential civil liability in Germany for production of documents did not justify disobeying subpoena when German government did not oppose compliance); *In re* Chase Manhattan Bank, 297 F.2d 611 (2d Cir. 1962); Ings v. Ferguson, 282 F.2d 149, 152-53 (2d Cir. 1960) (declining to call for production of bank records located in Canada when bank was merely a witness); Graco, Inc. v. Kremlin, Inc., 101 F.R.D. 503, 515 (N.D. Ill. 1984) (foreign state's flexibility should be considered at the sanctions stage).

458. Johnson v. United States, 971 F. Supp. 862, 873-74 (D.N.J. 1997) (U.S. interest in investigating violations of its criminal laws outweighed Cayman Islands' interest in maintaining confidentiality of records under bank secrecy law); American Indus. Contracting v. Johns-Manville Corp., 326 F. Supp. 879, 880 (W.D. Pa. 1971) (notwithstanding Canadian blocking statute, U.S. public policy demanded answers to interrogatories concerning Canadian subsidiaries of U.S. corporation when the subsidiaries sold their products in the United States); *see also* Laker Airways v. Sabena, Belgian World Airlines, 731 F.2d 909, 937 (D.C. Cir. 1984). A strong public interest often exists in actions brought pursuant to statutes that have the intended effect of enforcing the law by means of private attorneys general, for example, actions asserting rights under the antitrust, commodities, and racketeering statutes. *See* United States v. Dentsply Int'l Inc., 2000-1 Trade Cas. (CCH) ¶ 72,919, at 87,827 (D. Del. 2000) (citing "a general policy of allowing liberal discovery in antitrust cases" in granting discovery regarding defendant's competitive position and strategy in foreign markets) (citation omitted); First Am. Corp. v. Price Waterhouse LLP, 988 F. Supp. 353, 364 (S.D.N.Y. 1997) (U.S. interest in resolving bank fraud action outweighed any interest held by

A party relying on foreign law bears the burden of demonstrating that such law actually bars production.[459] Once that showing is made, a range of comity factors similar to those set forth in Section 442 of the *Restatement (Third) of the Foreign Relations Law of the United States*[460] generally will be considered by most courts at some stage of the proceedings prior to ordering sanctions for noncompliance with the discovery order.[461] When only the absence of permission by foreign authorities

England or the Cayman Islands in absolute preservation of their confidentiality laws), *aff'd*, 154 F.3d 16 (2d Cir. 1998).

459. SEC v. Banner Fund Int'l, 211 F.3d 602 (D.C. Cir. 2000) (citations omitted) (one who relies on foreign law assumes the burden of showing that such law prevents compliance with the court's order); *In re* Vitamins Antitrust Litig., 2001-2 Trade Cas. (CCH) ¶ 73,338, at 90,932 (D.D.C. 2001); SEC v. Euro Sec. Fund, No. 98 CIV 7347, 1999 U.S. Dist. LEXIS 4046 (S.D.N.Y. Apr. 2, 1999) (same); Al Fadda v. Fenn, 149 F.R.D. 28, 34 (S.D.N.Y. 1993) (same). *See also* Coca-Cola Foods v. Empresa Comercial Int'l de Frutas S.A., No. 96-358-CIV-T-17C, 1997 U.S. Dist. LEXIS 9295, at *9 (M.D. Fla. June 12, 1997) (defendants did not adequately show that production on the issue of personal jurisdiction was prohibited by Swiss law).

460. Section 442 would require a court to evaluate several factors before issuing an order compelling discovery, such as the importance of the information to the litigation, the degree of specificity of the request, the availability of alternative means of securing the information, and the interests of the countries involved. RESTATEMENT (THIRD), *supra* note 12, § 442. Where foreign law prohibits compliance with the discovery request, the party to whom the discovery is directed would be expected to make a good faith effort to secure permission for the discovery. When the party makes a good faith effort, the only sanction the *Restatement (Third)* would allow a court to consider for noncompliance is the entry of adverse fact findings. *Id.* § 442(b).

461. *See, e.g.*, United States v. Vetco Inc., 691 F.2d 1281, 1288 (9th Cir.) ("Courts must balance competing interests in determining whether foreign illegality ought to preclude enforcement of an IRS summons.") (summons enforced), *cert. denied*, 454 U.S. 1098 (1981); *In re* Westinghouse Elec. Corp. Uranium Contracts Litig., 563 F.2d 992, 997-98 (10th Cir. 1977) (contempt citation vacated); *In re* Grand Jury Proceedings, 532 F.2d 404, 407 (5th Cir.) (contempt order affirmed), *cert. denied*, 429 U.S. 940 (1976); SEC v. Banca Della Svizzera Italiana, 92 F.R.D. 111 (S.D.N.Y. 1981) (discovery ordered). The case for sanctions is particularly strong where the nonproducing party has acted in bad faith, deliberately seeking a nondisclosure order or otherwise attempting to impede the discovery process. *See, e.g.*, General Atomic Co. v. Exxon Nuclear Co., 90 F.R.D. 290, 296 (S.D. Cal. 1981) (sanctions ordered where crucial documents were located only in Canada through the fault of defendant and to the prejudice of plaintiff); United Nuclear Corp. v. General Atomic Co., 629 P.2d 231 (N.M. 1980), *appeal dismissed*, 451 U.S. 901 (1981); *cf.* Cochran Consulting v. Uwatec USA, Inc., 102 F.3d 1224 (Fed. Cir. 1996) (vacating sanction order where party prohibited by Swiss court from producing documents); *In re* Sealed Case, 825 F.2d 494, 497-99 (D.C. Cir.) (reversing civil contempt order to grand jury witness where production of documents located in a foreign country would violate that country's laws), *cert. denied*, 484 U.S. 963 (1987); Sharon v. Time, Inc., 599 F. Supp. 538, 558-60 (S.D.N.Y. 1984) (plaintiff would not be precluded from testifying at trial about certain subjects in light of the extent and significance of the testimony given in discovery, the lesser importance of the testimony withheld, and the absence of prejudice to defendant). *But cf. In re* Grand Jury Proceedings Bank of Nova Scotia, 740 F.2d 817, 828-29 (11th Cir. 1984) (comity factors considered, but court noted that it is not unfair for bank—which was not a target of the grand jury investigation—to have to choose between the conflicting commands of two sovereigns because it accepted that risk by electing to do business in numerous foreign host countries), *cert. denied*, 469 U.S. 1106 (1985); *In re* Marc Rich & Co., 736 F.2d 864, 866-67 (2d Cir. 1984) (consideration of foreign secrecy law barred by prior agreement of parties; however, contemnor would still be permitted to show that it was physically impossible to comply with grand jury subpoena because Swiss government had seized documents); United States v. Chase Manhattan Bank, 590 F. Supp. 1160, 1162 (S.D.N.Y. 1984) (good faith and comity had been considered at enforcement stage and were not relevant to contempt sanctions); Garpeg, Ltd. v. United States, 588 F. Supp. 1240 (S.D.N.Y. 1984) (party held in contempt despite making good faith effort to dissolve injunction by Hong Kong barring discovery where injunction by Hong Kong premised on finding that it would place party in no "real jeopardy" of contempt proceedings).

interferes with discovery, courts often will expect persons from whom discovery is sought to make a good faith effort to secure permission.[462] A party's lack of good faith in requesting permission to comply with discovery may result in sanctions.[463] When foreign secrecy laws require the consent by a subject of a grand jury investigation before permitting a third party to respond to a subpoena, some courts have compelled the subject to give consent.[464] In cases where the target of an investigation has sought to prevent disclosure through litigation in a foreign jurisdiction, some courts have compelled the target to terminate the foreign litigation.[465]

In one case, the Federal Trade Commission found a compromise between U.S. and German interests. As an alternative to quashing or enforcing a subpoena for German documents, the Federal Trade Commission allowed the documents to be transmitted to the German Foreign Office, ordering the parties to negotiate a depository arrangement permitting Federal Trade Commission complaint counsel to view but not take possession of the documents, so that the degree of confidentiality

---

462. *See, e.g.*, Reinsurance Co. of Am. v. Administratia Asigurarilor de Stat, 902 F.2d 1275, 1282 (7th Cir. 1990) (district court may require a good faith effort from the parties to seek a waiver of any blocking provisions); *see also* United States v. First Nat'l Bank, 699 F.2d 341 (7th Cir. 1983) (order enforcing IRS summons reversed, but trial court directed to consider order requiring good faith effort); *In re* Grand Jury Proceedings, 691 F.2d 1384, 1388-89 (11th Cir. 1982) (contempt order affirmed where no good faith effort to comply), *cert. denied*, 462 U.S. 1119 (1983); *Graco*, 101 F.R.D. at 503, 516 (ordering compliance with certain discovery requests and noting that potential sanctions may depend on whether party made reasonable attempt to secure permission); *Soletanche & Rodio, Inc.*, 99 F.R.D. at 271 (compulsion order required party to seek waiver); Compagnie Française d'Assurance Pour le Commerce Exterieur v. Phillips Petroleum Co., No. 81 Civ. 4463-CLB, slip op. at 13-14 (S.D.N.Y. Jan. 23, 1983), *summarized in* Compagnie Française d'Assurance Pour le Commerce Exterieur v. Phillips Petroleum Co., 105 F.R.D. 16, 23-24 (S.D.N.Y. 1984) (motion to compel held in abeyance while party directed to make good faith effort to obtain waivers); United States v. Standard Oil Co. (N.J.), 23 F.R.D. 1, 4 (S.D.N.Y. 1958) (defendants ordered to make good faith attempt to obtain information; failure will result in hearing to determine how to proceed); RESTATEMENT (THIRD), *supra* note 12, § 442(2)(a) (providing that if a foreign law blocks discovery, a court may require the person to whom the order is directed to make a good faith effort to secure permission to make the information available).

463. Remington Prods., Inc. v. North Am. Philips Corp., 107 F.R.D. 642, 653 (D. Conn. 1985) (sanctions ordered where application for exemption from Dutch blocking statute suggested requesting party did not support the exemption). Note that a party may be required to seek a waiver of secrecy law to allow production even if the waiver requires a financial commitment. *See* Shamis v. Ambassador Factors Corp., 34 F. Supp. 2d 879 (S.D.N.Y. 1999) (party required to seek waiver of secrecy law despite fact that grant of waiver predicated on agreement to indemnify).

464. *See, e.g.*, *In re* United States Grand Jury Proceedings, 767 F.2d 1131 (5th Cir. 1985); United States v. Davis, 767 F.2d 1025, 1033-36 (2d Cir. 1985); United States v. Ghidoni, 732 F.2d 814 (11th Cir.), *cert. denied*, 469 U.S. 932 (1984). *But cf.* Senate Select Comm. v. Secord, 664 F. Supp. 562, 564-66 (D.D.C.) (witness cannot be compelled to consent to ordering foreign banks to produce information), *vacated*, Misc. No. 87-0090, 1987 U.S. Dist. LEXIS 10705 (D.D.C. Nov. 16, 1987); *In re* Grand Jury Investigation, 599 F. Supp. 746, 748 (S.D. Tex. 1984) (compelled waiver would acknowledge existence of and signatory authority over account and would violate Fifth Amendment), *aff'd*, 812 F.2d 1404 (5th Cir. 1987), *aff'd sub nom.* Doe v. United States, 487 U.S. 201 (1988); Garpeg, Ltd. v. United States, 583 F. Supp. 789, 799 (S.D.N.Y. 1984) (foreign corporation that was not a defendant or a target of an investigation would not be compelled to waive its rights under foreign bank secrecy law; bank would be compelled to respond to summons without benefit of waiver).

465. *Davis*, 767 F.2d at 1036-39 (citing cases). *But see Garpeg*, 583 F. Supp. at 797-99 (injunction denied where the issues in the two actions were not the same and the right of secrecy sought to be enforced in the foreign court was one arising under foreign law; bank would be compelled to respond to subpoena without being relieved of foreign suit by its customer).

insisted upon by the German government could be maintained at least through most of the discovery period.[466]

2. Discovery within the United States in Actions outside the United States

Under Section 1782 of the Judicial Code, a U.S. district court may assist a foreign or international tribunal, or litigant before such a tribunal, by ordering a nonparty within its district to give testimony or provide documents in response to a letter rogatory or request from the foreign entity.[467] The term foreign tribunal includes foreign bodies other than conventional courts, provided that they are "adjudicative" in nature.[468] Additionally, the proceeding for which the discovery will be used need not be pending at the time of the request so long as it is very likely that the proceeding will soon commence.[469]

U.S. courts are split as to whether the information sought pursuant to Section 1782 must be discoverable under the laws of the foreign jurisdiction.[470] However, if the applicant is the foreign tribunal itself, some courts will presume discoverability from the foreign tribunal's request.[471]

G. International Antitrust Enforcement

1. Bilateral and Multilateral Cooperation

a. COOPERATION AGREEMENTS

The United States has entered into bilateral agreements on antitrust cooperation with Germany (1976),[472] Australia (1982 and 1999),[473] the European Communities

---

466. Volkswagen of Am., Inc., 103 F.T.C. 536 (1984).
467. 28 U.S.C. § 1782(a) (1994 & Supp. 1999).
468. *See, e.g.*, NBC v. Bear Stearns & Co., 165 F.3d 184, 191 (2d Cir. 1999); Euromepa v. R. Esmerian, Inc., 154 F.3d 24, 27 (2d Cir. 1998); Republic of Kazakhstan v. Biederman Int'l, 168 F.3d 880, 883 (5th Cir. 1999); *In re* Letters Rogatory Issued by Dir. of Inspection of Gov't of India, 385 F.2d 1017 (2d Cir. 1967).
469. *Compare In re* Request for International Judicial Assistance for the Federative Republic of Brazil, 936 F.2d 702, 706 (2d Cir. 1991) (proceeding must be "imminent"), *with In re* Letter of Request from Crown Prosecution Serv. of the United Kingdom, 870 F.2d 686, 691 (D.C. Cir. 1989) (proceeding must be "within reasonable contemplation").
470. *Compare Euromepa*, 154 F.3d at 28 (no discoverability requirement in Second Circuit), *and In re* Application of Bayer, 146 F.3d 188, 195 (3d Cir. 1998), *with In re* Application of Asta Medica, S.A., 981 F.2d 1, 7 (1st Cir. 1992) (discoverability requirement), *and In re* Request for Assistance from Ministry of Legal Affairs of Trinidad & Tobago, 848 F.2d 1151, 1156 (11th Cir. 1988) (same).
471. *See, e.g.*, United States v. Morris, 82 F.3d 590, 592 (4th Cir. 1996); *In re* Letter Rogatory from the First Court of First Instance in Civil Matters, Caracas, Venezuela, 42 F.3d 308, 310-11 (5th Cir. 1995).
472. Agreement Relating to Mutual Cooperation Regarding Restrictive Business Practices, June 23, 1976, U.S.-Federal Republic of Germany, 27 U.S.T. 1956, T.I.S. No. 8291, *reprinted in* 4 Trade Reg. Rep. (CCH) ¶ 13,501.
473. Agreement between the Government of the United States of America and the Government of Australia Relating to Cooperation on Antitrust Matters, June 29, 1982, U.S.-Australia, T.I.A.S. No. 10365, *reprinted in* 4 Trade Reg. Rep. (CCH) ¶ 13,502; Agreement between the Government of the

(EC) (1991 and 1998),[474] Canada (1984 and 1995),[475] Israel (1999),[476] Japan (1999),[477] Brazil (1999),[478] and Mexico (2000).[479] These agreements have been motivated by a mutual desire to cooperate and coordinate more closely in antitrust enforcement and to avoid or manage possible conflict arising from the application of antitrust laws to international business conduct.

Under U.S. law, these bilateral agreements are executive agreements. Although they represent formal and binding international agreements for the U.S. authorities, they do not have the legal status of treaties in the U.S. system. As a result, the agreements do not supplant domestic laws that, for example, prohibit sharing confidential information without the submitter's consent.[480] However, the Department of Justice and the Federal Trade Commission have found that the agreements often provide a catalyst for broader and deeper cooperation with the foreign antitrust agencies.[481]

While there are some variations among these agreements, they generally provide for the following types of communication and cooperation: (1) notification to the other party of an enforcement investigation or proceeding that may affect its important interests; (2) sharing information relevant to each other's investigations or proceedings to the extent permitted by domestic law; (3) coordination of parallel investigations, for example, when each party is investigating the same firm, conduct, or transaction; and (4) consultation to resolve issues arising from enforcement

United States of America and the Government of Australia on Mutual Antitrust Enforcement Assistance, April 27, 1999, *reprinted in* 4 Trade Reg. Rep. (CCH) ¶ 13,502A.

474. 1991 EC Agreement, *supra* note 82; Agreement between the Government of the United States of America and the European Communities on the Application of Positive Comity Principles in the Enforcement of Their Competition Laws, June 4, 1998 [hereinafter 1998 EC Agreement], *reprinted in* 4 Trade Reg. Rep. (CCH) ¶ 13,504A.

475. Memorandum of Understanding as to Notification, Consultation, and Cooperation with Respect to the Application of National Antitrust Laws, March 9, 1984, U.S.-Canada, *reprinted in* 4 Trade Reg. Rep. (CCH) ¶ 13,503A; Canadian Agreement, *supra* note 82.

476. Agreement between the Government of the United States of America and the Government of the State of Israel Regarding the Application of Their Competition Laws, March 15, 1999, *reprinted in* 4 Trade Reg. Rep. (CCH) ¶ 13,506.

477. Agreement between the Government of the United States of America and the Government of Japan Concerning Cooperation on Anticompetitive Activities, October 7, 1999, *reprinted in* 4 Trade Reg. Rep. (CCH) ¶ 13,507.

478. Agreement between the Government of the United States of America and the Government of the Federative Republic of Brazil Regarding Cooperation between Their Competition Authorities in the Enforcement of their Competition Laws, October 26, 1999, *reprinted in* 4 Trade Reg. Rep. (CCH) ¶ 13,508.

479. Agreement between the Government of the United States of America and the Government of the United Mexican States Regarding the Application of Their Competition Laws, July 11, 2000, *reprinted in* 4 Trade Reg. Rep. (CCH) ¶ 13,509.

480. *See* Anne K. Bingaman, Ass't Att'y Gen., Antitrust Div., The Clinton Administration: Trends in Criminal Antitrust Enforcement, Address Before the Corporate Counsel Inst. 21 (Nov. 30, 1995), *available at* www.usdoj.gov/atr/public/speeches/speech.n30.htm.

481. *Id.* at 21-22 (stating that bilateral antitrust cooperation agreements have aided DOJ in prosecuting foreign firms and individuals); Gary R. Spratling, Dep'y Ass't Att'y Gen., Antitrust Div., Criminal Antitrust Enforcement Against International Cartels, Remarks at the Advanced Criminal Antitrust Workshop 6 (Feb. 21, 1997), *available at* www.usdoj.gov/atr/public/speeches/grs97221.htm (stating that bilateral antitrust agreements maximize the evidence available to cooperating countries and increase resources for prosecuting international conspiracies); *see also* ABA SECTION OF ANTITRUST LAW, COMPETITION LAWS OUTSIDE THE UNITED STATES Overview-116 (2001) (stating that cooperation between U.S. and foreign enforcement agencies has increased through bilateral agreements).

activities or any other matter arising from the agreement. These agreements also provide for periodic meetings to exchange information on the parties' current enforcement activities and priorities, economic sectors of common interest, policy changes under consideration, and other matters of mutual interest relating to the application of antitrust laws.

The 1991 U.S.-EC agreement was the first bilateral agreement to include a "positive comity" provision.[482] Under such a provision, one party can request that the other party investigate conduct within its territory which is having anticompetitive effects in the requesting party's territory and which also violates the requested party's laws.[483] Agreements entered into subsequent to the EC agreement with Canada, Israel, Japan, Brazil, and Mexico also include a positive comity provision.

In June 1998, the United States and the European Commission entered into a new agreement elaborating on the positive comity provisions of the 1991 agreement.[484] The new agreement clarifies the circumstances under which the parties will refer cases of anticompetitive activities to each other and sets forth the circumstances under which one party normally will defer to the other to investigate alleged anticompetitive practices in the other's territory. It spells out the obligations that the antitrust authorities undertake in handling these cases, while preserving the right of each authority to act independently. The agreement excludes notified mergers because of the short time frames in which they must be reviewed and because statutory obligations to review certain mergers preclude deferring to the other jurisdiction's authority. In addition, the agreement contemplates that the parties may pursue separate enforcement activities where—as in the case of international cartels—anticompetitive conduct affecting both countries justifies the imposition of penalties in both.

There has been limited practical experience to date with these positive comity provisions. One case was formally referred by the Department of Justice to the European Commission under the 1991 agreement, involving allegations that anticompetitive conduct by European airline owners of a European-based computer reservation system impeded competition from U.S.-based airline computer reservation systems; the EC authorities closed their investigation in July 2000 after agreements were reached between the complaining U.S. computer reservation system and a number of the European airlines.[485] There have been no announced cases to date under the 1998 agreement.[486]

482. 1991 EC Agreement, *supra* note 82.
483. *See* ABA SECTION OF ANTITRUST LAW, COMPETITION LAWS OUTSIDE THE UNITED STATES, *supra* note 481, Overview–114-15 (defining positive comity)
484. 1998 EC Agreement, *supra* note 474.
485. *See* Commission Press Release IP (00)835 (25 July 2000); *see also* ABA SECTION OF ANTITRUST LAW, COMPETITION LAWS OUTSIDE THE UNITED STATES, *supra* note 481, Overview–115-16 (stating that EC authorities closed investigations based on undertakings by Air France to abide by the "Code of Good Behaviour").
486. Some cases also have been handled informally following positive comity principles. The FTC decided not to take any action against a group of Italian Parma ham producers who had agreed on a production quota limiting exports because the Italian antitrust authority was investigating the matter and eventually imposed an effective remedy. Robert Pitofsky, Chairman, Federal Trade Comm'n, Statement Before the Senate Judiciary Committee, Subcommittee on Antitrust, Business Rights and Competition, 105th Cong. (Oct. 2, 1998) (stating that FTC encouraged Italian competition authorities to investigate Parma ham producers), *reprinted in* FEDERAL NEWS SERVICE (Oct. 2, 1998). The DOJ, in late 1996, closed its investigation into the way AC Nielsen

b.   INTERNATIONAL ANTITRUST ENFORCEMENT ASSISTANCE ACT

To encourage international cooperation in civil and criminal antitrust matters, Congress enacted the International Antitrust Enforcement Assistance Act of 1994 (IAEAA).[487] This legislation authorizes the Department of Justice and Federal Trade Commission to enter into bilateral antitrust mutual assistance agreements with foreign governments that authorize the agencies to share confidential information obtained in the agencies' investigations and to use their respective investigatory powers to gather evidence on behalf of foreign antitrust authorities.[488]

The law is conditioned on mutuality—both parties must have comparable authority to provide assistance.[489] Congress also required that both parties have laws adequate to protect materials provided in confidence from unauthorized public disclosure.[490] Thus, included as part of the agreement must be a listing of the relevant laws respecting confidentiality of both parties.[491] Confidentiality also is addressed in provisions requiring the return to the United States of all evidence—and all copies of evidence—at the conclusion of the proceeding, assuming that it is still "under the control" of the foreign antitrust authority.[492] If a breach of confidentiality occurs and adequate action is not taken by the foreign government to minimize the harm that resulted and to ensure that no breach will occur again, the agreement must be terminated.[493] Furthermore, if a breach occurs, the foreign agency must notify the Department of Justice or Federal Trade Commission promptly, and the U.S. authority in question must notify the party who provided the evidence.[494]

Information shared pursuant to bilateral agreements made pursuant to the statute can be used only for law enforcement purposes.[495] The IAEAA does not cover information provided to the U.S. agencies under their premerger notification provisions.[496] Also excluded is information protected under grand jury secrecy rules absent a showing of particularized need with respect to the foreign enforcer,[497] classified national security information, and information classified under the Atomic Energy Act.[498]

The IAEAA grants the Department of Justice and the Federal Trade Commission the authority to assist foreign antitrust authorities in investigating and obtaining evidence regarding possible violations of foreign antitrust laws.[499] A request for

---

Co. contracted its services for tracking retail sales because the company had reached an agreement with the European Commission that alleviated any anticompetitive concerns. *See* DOJ Press Release, Justice Department Closes Investigation into the Way AC Nielsen Co. Contracts its Services for Tracking Retail Sales (Dec. 3, 1996).

487. 15 U.S.C. §§ 6201-6212 (2000).
488. ABA SECTION OF ANTITRUST LAW, COMPETITION LAWS OUTSIDE THE UNITED STATES, *supra* note 481, Overview-114. IAEAA agreements must be placed on the public record for a 45-day public comment period. 15 U.S.C. § 6206.
489. 15 U.S.C. § 6211(2)(A).
490. *Id.* § 6211(2)(B).
491. *Id.* § 6211(2)(C).
492. *Id.* § 6211(2)(F).
493. *Id.* § 6211(2)(G).
494. *Id.* § 6211(2)(H).
495. *Id.* § 6211(2)(E).
496. *Id.* § 6204(1).
497. *Id.* § 6204(2).
498. *Id.* § 6204(3), (4).
499. *Id.* § 6202(b).

investigative assistance by a foreign antitrust authority must be made to the Attorney General, who may deny all or part of it.[500] If a request is granted, the Department of Justice and the Federal Trade Commission may obtain and forward information sought by the foreign authorities relating to possible violations of foreign antitrust laws without regard to whether the conduct investigated would violate any U.S. antitrust laws.[501] Before assistance is provided to another country under an IAEAA agreement, the Department of Justice or the Federal Trade Commission, as the case may be, must make a determination that to do so would not be contrary to the public interest of the United States.[502]

The United States currently has one IAEAA agreement in effect—with Australia.[503]

c. MUTUAL LEGAL ASSISTANCE TREATIES

Since the 1970s, the Department of Justice and the State Department have made it a high priority to negotiate mutual legal assistance treaties (MLATs), which provide for comprehensive reciprocal assistance between the United States and foreign governments in criminal matters. Among other things, MLATs provide for obtaining documents, physical evidence, and testimony located in foreign countries for use in U.S. criminal prosecutions.[504] As of 2001, the United States had MLATs in force with thirty countries, with twenty-one others awaiting Senate approval.[505]

The Department of Justice has acknowledged using the U.S.-Canada MLAT to receive and/or provide judicial assistance in several prosecutions.[506] Department of Justice officials have indicated that its prosecutors have invoked MLATs in other antitrust investigations.[507] The specifics of such additional uses, however, have not been made public.

d. INFORMAL COOPERATION

Informal communication and cooperation occurs among competition enforcement agencies on a wide range of issues. Officials of both the Department of Justice and

---

500. *Id.* § 6202(a).
501. *Id.* § 6202(c).
502. *Id.* § 6207(a)(3).
503. Agreement between the Government of the United States of America and the Government of Australia on Mutual Antitrust Enforcement Assistance, April 27, 1999, *reprinted in* 4 Trade Reg. Rep. (CCH) ¶ 13,502A. This agreement entered into force in November 1999.
504. *See* ABA SECTION OF ANTITRUST LAW, COMPETITION LAWS OUTSIDE THE UNITED STATES, *supra* note 481, at Overview-117. Judicial assistance can, in some instances, be obtained from countries with which the United States does not have an MLAT through the letter rogatory process. *See* part F.1.a of this chapter.
505. ICPAC REPORT, *supra* note 139, at 181 n.57.
506. Charles A. James, Ass't Att'y Gen., Antitrust Div., International Antitrust in the Bush Administration, Address Before the Canadian Bar Ass'n (Sept. 21, 2001), *available at* www.usdoj. gov/atr/public/speeches/9100.htm (discussing antitrust prosecution cooperation with Canada made possible by MLAT); *see also* ABA SECTION OF ANTITRUST LAW, COMPETITION LAWS OUTSIDE THE UNITED STATES, *supra* note 481, Overview-117 (stating that the U.S.-Canada MLAT played a significant role in the investigations of suspected cartels in the disposable plastic dinnerware and ductile pipe industries).
507. Spratling, *supra* note 481, at 5 (stating that the DOJ is beginning to invoke MLATs with countries other than Canada).

the Federal Trade Commission have described the frequent communication that takes place between their professional staffs and those of foreign competition authorities, particularly those of the European Commission and individual European countries, in the context of merger investigations.[508]

Communication also takes place between U.S. agency officials and officials of foreign competition authorities about other substantive and operational matters. This may involve explaining how the Department of Justice investigates and prosecutes cartel cases, how the agencies approach a merger investigation, or rules of practice and procedure that could assist those authorities in setting up an administrative enforcement agency.[509]

In late 2001, numerous countries agreed to participate in an "International Competition Network," which is intended to serve as a venue for senior antitrust officials from participating countries to work to reach consensus on proposals for procedural and substantive convergence in antitrust enforcement.[510]

2. *Comity Considerations*

The comity considerations the Department of Justice and the Federal Trade Commission apply to their enforcement decisions are set out in the agencies' *International Antitrust Guidelines*.[511] The *Guidelines* state that the agencies do take comity considerations into account in their enforcement decisions and enumerate a list of relevant factors.[512]

The *Guidelines* also articulate the Department of Justice's position that a decision by the United States to prosecute an antitrust case represents a determination by the executive branch that the importance of antitrust enforcement outweighs any relevant foreign policy concerns, and that it is therefore not the proper role of the courts to second-guess such a determination.[513]

3. *International Criminal Enforcement*

The Department of Justice (through its Antitrust Division) has undertaken the prosecution of international[514] cases since the early 1900s.[515] One example of an

---

508. *See* part G.4 of this chapter.
509. *See* Spratling, *supra* note 481, at 4-5 (discussing technical assistance provided by the DOJ to nascent foreign antitrust authorities seeking to draft and enforce antitrust laws).
510. FTC Press Release, U.S. and Foreign Antitrust Officials Launch International Competition Network (Oct. 25, 2001). Officials already agreeing to participate include those from Australia, Canada, the European Commission, France, Germany, Israel, Italy, Japan, Korea, Mexico, South Africa, the United Kingdom, the United States, and Zambia.
511. *See* INTERNATIONAL ANTITRUST GUIDELINES, *supra* note 1.
512. *Id.* § 3.2.
513. *Id.* This position was articulated by the DOJ and accepted by the court in *United States v. Baker Hughes, Inc.*, 731 F. Supp. 3, 6 n.5 (D.D.C. 1990), *aff'd*, 908 F.2d 981 (D.C. Cir. 1990). *See also* part B.1.c of this chapter.
514. The definition for "international matters" developed in fiscal year 1997 by the DOJ for data collection associated with its performance measurement efforts is as follows:
    An international matter—that is, investigation or case—is so defined if it involves possible anticompetitive impact on U.S. domestic or foreign commerce, and if any one of the following criteria is met, leading to increased complexity and greater resource requirements than would otherwise be the case: one or more involved parties* is not a U.S. citizen or a U.S. business;

early (1907) antitrust case raising international issues, although in a civil context, was *United States v. American Tobacco*,[516] which involved, inter alia, a territorial allocation agreement among British and U.S. firms. The Supreme Court ultimately held that the conduct of both the U.S. and British defendants was illegal.[517] The Department of Justice continued to file both civil and criminal international antitrust cases against international cartels, and those cases were particularly numerous in the 1940s and early 1950s.[518] However, between 1950 and the early 1990s, the Department of Justice reduced its enforcement efforts against international cartels in favor of domestic prosecutions.[519]

In the early 1990s, the Department of Justice made international antitrust enforcement a priority and began aggressively prosecuting international cartels.[520] The intensity of this focus on international prosecutions increased yearly, so that as of 2001 the Department of Justice stated that since 1997 it had obtained over $1.7 billion in criminal fines, well over 90 percent of which was imposed in connection with the prosecution of international cartel activity.[521] Department of Justice officials have stated that they sought to increase corporate deterrence through these very substantial fines.[522] In fiscal year 2000 alone, approximately thirty ongoing grand

---

one or more involved parties* is not located in the U.S.; potentially relevant information is located outside the U.S.; conduct potentially illegal under U.S. law occurred outside the U.S.; or substantive foreign government consultation or coordination is undertaken in connection with the matter. [* . . . where "involved party" may be an individual or corporation that is the subject or target, or potential subject or potential target, of a criminal or civil non-merger investigation or case; a party to a merger or an acquisition; or otherwise a participant or potential participant in an investigation or case].

U.S. Dep't of Justice, Antitrust Div., Executive Office (Dec. 1999) (emphasis omitted).

515. *See* ICPAC REPORT, *supra* note 139, ch. 4.
516. 221 U.S. 106 (1911).
517. *Id.* at 184.
518. ICPAC REPORT, *supra* note 139, at 166.
519. *Id.*
520. *See* Anne K. Bingaman, Ass't Att'y Gen., Antitrust Div., Change and Continuity in Antitrust Enforcement, Address Before the Fordham Corporate Law Inst. 1-5 (Oct. 21, 1993), *available at* www.usdoj.gov/atr/public/speeches/93-10-21.htm (stating that her first priority is to respond to an increasingly global economy by enhancing international antitrust enforcement, in particular by seeking additional mechanisms to reach foreign-located information and witnesses and to emphasize international issues in the DOJ's organization and operations); Bingaman, *supra* note 480; *see also* Joel I. Klein, Ass't Att'y Gen., Antitrust Div., Statement Before the Subcomm. on Antitrust, Business Rights, and Competition, Comm. on the Judiciary, U.S. Senate, 105th Cong., at 3 (May 4, 1999), *available at* www.usdoj.gov/atr/public/testimony/2413.htm (vigorous enforcement against international cartels continues to be a top priority because international cartels typically pose a greater threat to U.S. businesses and consumers than do domestic cartels since they tend to be highly sophisticated and extremely broad in their geographic reach and economic impact).
521. James M. Griffin, Dep'y Ass't Att'y Gen., Antitrust Div., Status Report, Presented to ABA Antitrust Section Criminal Practice and Procedure Comm. (Mar. 28, 2001), *available at* www.usdoj.gov/ atr/public/speeches/8063.htm.
522. *See, e.g.*, Gary R. Spratling, Dep'y Ass't Att'y Gen., Antitrust Div., The Trend Towards Higher Corporate Fines: It's A Whole New Ball Game (Mar. 7, 1997), *available at* www.usdoj.gov/ atr/public/speeches/4011.htm. The DOJ was able to obtain these record fines in part because of legislation which raised Sherman Act fines. In 1990, Congress increased the fine for Sherman Act offenses from $1 million to $10 million for corporations, and from $100,000 to $350,000 for individual defendants. 15 U.S.C. § 1 (2000). Furthermore, the DOJ began using the Criminal Fine Improvements Act, which establishes a new maximum criminal fine equal to twice the gain derived from a crime or twice the loss suffered by the victims of the crime, if either of those

jury investigations involved international cartels extending to twenty countries and five continents.[523] Prosecutions of foreign cartels increased from a negligible percentage of Department of Justice actions in the early 1990s to almost two-thirds in 1998.[524] As of February 2000, it was estimated that the Department of Justice had prosecuted nearly twenty international cartels, charging more than eighty corporate and sixty individual defendants in the process.[525] Moreover, approximately 25 percent of the more than 625 criminal antitrust cases filed by the Department of Justice since fiscal year 1990 were international in scope.[526] Many worldwide industries spawned the cartels targeted in these cases, including food and feed additives, chemicals, vitamins, graphite electrodes, and marine construction and transportation services.[527]

As part of its focus on international activity, the Department of Justice modified certain of its enforcement procedures in order to promote detection of international cartels, encourage cooperation of foreign national witnesses, and facilitate obtaining documents located overseas. One such change, which impacted the Department of Justice's ability to negotiate plea agreements with foreign citizens, was a memorandum of understanding between the Department of Justice and the Immigration and Naturalization Service in which the immigration authorities agreed to adjudicate the immigration status of cooperating foreign national defendants in antitrust cases before those individuals enter into plea agreements.[528] Several foreign citizens have taken part in this process and received written assurances that they may travel to the United States freely after conviction.[529]

Another change in the Department of Justice's enforcement procedures which positively impacted its ability to undertake international enforcement involved the Corporate Leniency Policy.[530] First announced by the Department of Justice in 1978, the Corporate Leniency Policy was expanded in 1993 to increase the opportunities and incentives for companies to report criminal activity and cooperate with the

---

amounts is greater than the fine specified in the statute establishing the offense, to obtain corporate fine levels above the $10 million fine provided for in the Sherman Act. 18 U.S.C. § 3571(d) (2000).

523. See id; see also ICPAC REPORT, supra note 139, at 167-68.

524. ICPAC Meeting Addresses Comity, Cooperation, and Antitrust Enforcement, 75 Antitrust & Trade Reg. Rep. (BNA) 326 (1998).

525. ICPAC REPORT, supra note 139, at 167 & Annex 4-A.

526. Id. at 167.

527. See id. at 171-73; see also Griffin, supra note 521.

528. U.S. Dep't of Justice, Memorandum of Understanding Between the Antitrust Division and the Immigration and Naturalization Service (Mar. 15, 1996); see also Spratling, supra note 481. In the past, foreign citizens convicted of antitrust offenses could be banned from traveling to the United States by the immigration service. This potential travel ban negatively impacted the individual defendant's incentive to cooperate with an investigation.

529. See, e.g., United States v. Yamamoto, No. 96-CR 520, 6 Trade Reg. Rep. (CCH) ¶ 45,090, at 45,113 (N.D. Ill. Jan. 14, 1997) (plea agreement); United States v. Hartmann, Crim. No. 97-0019, 6 Trade Reg. Rep. (CCH) ¶ 45,097, at 45,303 (N.D. Cal. Jan. 29, 1997) (plea agreement); United States v. Haas, Crim. No. 97-00083, 6 Trade Reg. Rep. (CCH) ¶ 45,097, at 45,310 (N.D. Cal. Mar. 26, 1997) (plea agreement); United States v. Bichlbauer, Crim. No. 97-0084, 6 Trade Reg. Rep. (CCH) ¶ 45,097, at 45,310 (N.D. Cal. Mar. 26, 1997) (plea agreement).

530. Antitrust Div., U.S. Dep't of Justice, Corporate Leniency Policy, reprinted in 4 Trade Reg. Rep. (CCH) ¶ 13,113. See part C.4.f of Chapter VIII for a more extended discussion of the DOJ's leniency program.

Department of Justice. The 1993 revisions applied to three major areas.[531] First, the policy was changed to ensure that leniency is automatic (if the applicant meets the program's requirements) as long as there is no preexisting investigation; second, in some cases leniency is available even if cooperation begins after an investigation is commenced; third, if a corporation qualifies for automatic leniency, all directors, officers, and employees who come forward with the corporation and agree to cooperate will also receive automatic leniency. In addition, executives of a corporation seeking leniency after an investigation has begun will be given serious consideration for lenient treatment in exchange for full cooperation.[532]

Department of Justice policy is that it will not disclose to any other party, including foreign antitrust agencies, information obtained from an leniency application unless the applicant first agrees to the disclosure or unless the Department of Justice is legally required to do so.[533] In late 1999, the Department of Justice reported it had received approximately two leniency applications per month over the course of that year—more than twenty times the application rate under the old leniency program.[534]

When international firms and their representatives do not qualify for leniency, the Department of Justice may nevertheless, pursuant to a plea agreement, recommend reduced sentences for defendants who cooperate early in an investigation or who secure the cooperation of other coconspirators.[535] In 1999, the Department of Justice articulated policies concerning recurring issues arising during international cartel plea negotiations:[536] (1) the Department of Justice requires cooperating defendants to

---

531. *See* Antitrust Div., U.S. Dep't of Justice, Status Report: Corporate Leniency Program (May 2001) [hereinafter DOJ May 2001 Status Report], *available at* www.usdoj.gov/atr/public/criminal/8278.htm; Gary R. Spratling, Dep'y Ass't Att'y Gen., Antitrust Div., The Corporate Leniency Policy: Answers to Recurring Questions, Remarks at the ABA Antitrust Section 1998 Spring Meeting (Apr. 1, 1998), *available at* www.usdoj.gov/atr/public/speeches/1626.htm.

532. DOJ May 2001 Status Report, *supra* note 531; *see also* Gary R. Spratling, Dep'y Ass't Att'y Gen., Antitrust Div., Are the Recent Titanic Fines in Antitrust Cases Just the Tip of the Iceberg?, Address Before the 12th Annual Institute on White Collar Crime, ABA Criminal Justice Section (Mar. 6, 1998), *available at* www.usdoj.gov/atr/public/speeches/1583.htm [hereinafter Spratling, Titanic Fines].

533. DOJ May 2001 Status Report, *supra* note 531; Gary R. Spratling, Dep'y Ass't Att'y Gen., Antitrust Div., Making Companies an Offer They Shouldn't Refuse: The Antitrust Division's Corp. Leniency Policy—An Update, Remarks at the Bar Ass'n of the Dist. of Columbia's 35th Annual Symposium on Associations and Antitrust, at 5-7 (Feb. 16, 1999), *available at* www.usdoj.gov/atr/public/speeches/2247.pdf.

534. Spratling, *supra* note 533, at 1-2. Leniency applicants can receive significant financial advantages by virtue of their cooperation, in many situations paying no fines when coconspirators were subject to very substantial ones. *See* DOJ May 2001 Status Report, *supra* note 531; Antitrust Div., U.S. Dep't of Justice, Status Report: Criminal Fines (May 2001), *available at* www.usdoj.atr/public/criminal/8270.htm.

535. *See, e.g.,* United States v. Haarmann & Reimer Corp., No. CR 97-00019 (THE), 6 Trade Reg. Rep. (CCH) ¶ 45,097, at 45,303 (N.D. Cal. 1997) (firm's cooperation in securing the cooperation of other citric acid cartel participants and in the investigation resulted in Antitrust Division requesting a downward departure for the firm's fine, calculated under the U.S. Sentencing Guidelines); *see also* Spratling, *supra* note 481, at 12 (describing the Antitrust Division's new policy in this regard and cautioning that "there is a maximum of only one such 'extra credit' per investigation, and it goes to the firm that takes the lead in securing multi-firm cooperation").

536. *See* Gary R. Spratling, Dep'y Ass't Att'y Gen., Antitrust Div., Negotiating the Waters of International Cartel Prosecutions: Antitrust Division Policies Relating to Plea Agreements in International Cases, Remarks at the ABA Criminal Justice Section's 13th Annual National Institute on White Collar Crime (Mar. 4, 1999), *available at* www.usdoj.gov/atr/public/speeches/2275.htm.

provide all documents it requests in connection with its investigation, wherever located, and requires corporate defendants to make available key employees for interviews and testimony;[537] (2) the Department of Justice does not agree to restrictions in plea agreements that limit its ability to provide U.S. or foreign governments with information obtained from cooperating defendants;[538] (3) the Department of Justice generally does not enter into plea agreements that provide for a no jail sentence for an individual defendant, although it may make exceptions for foreign nationals over whom it has no reasonable means of obtaining personal jurisdiction;[539] (4) the Department of Justice may petition the Immigration and Naturalization Service to preadjudicate the immigration status of a cooperating alien before the individual enters into a plea agreement, thus allowing the Department of Justice to guarantee that a conviction pursuant to a plea agreement will not be used by the immigration service as a basis for deportation or permanent exclusion from the United States;[540] (5) the Department of Justice no longer includes provisions in plea agreements that require it to wait five days after giving a defendant notice of its intention to void a plea agreement before taking action against any individuals subject to the plea agreement;[541] (6) the Department of Justice normally uses the volume of U.S. commerce affected by the defendant's participation in a conspiracy when calculating that defendant's Sentencing Guidelines fine range, unless that amount understates the seriousness of the defendant's role in the offense and its impact on U.S. businesses and consumers;[542] and (7) in choosing whether to prosecute a U.S. subsidiary or its overseas parent, the Department of Justice prefers to prosecute the most culpable party involved in the conspiracy.[543] However, the Department of Justice may accept a plea from either the U.S. or foreign-based entity so long as it has a solid factual basis for the plea and the entity that pleads had a substantial level of involvement in the conspiracy.[544] The Department of Justice regards foreign-located documents produced by a cooperating party pursuant to a plea agreement as subject to the secrecy and disclosure provisions of Rule 6(e) of the Federal Rules of Criminal Procedure, as long as the documents are also responsive to an outstanding subpoena.[545]

The intensity of the Department of Justice's enforcement activity directed at international cartels is reflected in the record criminal fines which have been imposed.[546] The 1990s also saw the first instances of jail time for foreign nationals

---

537. *See id.* § II.
538. *See id.* § III.A.
539. *See id.* § IV.A.
540. *See id.* § IV.B.
541. *See id.*
542. *See id.* § V.A.
543. *See id.* § VI.B.
544. *Id.*
545. *See id.* § II.C.
546. For example, in 1996 Archer Daniels Midland, a U.S. firm, agreed to pay $100 million—$30 million for its participation in a worldwide cartel to fix the price and divide the market of the food additive citric acid, and $70 million for its participation in a worldwide cartel to fix the price and divide the market of the feed additive lysine. *See* Press Release, U.S. Dep't of Justice, Antitrust Div., Archer Daniels Midland Co. to Plead Guilty and Pay $100 Million for Role in Two International Price-Fixing Conspiracies (Oct. 15, 1996). In April 1998, the DOJ obtained a $110 million fine from UCAR, International, a U.S. company that participated in an international cartel to fix the price and allocate the volume of graphite electrodes. *See U.S. Company Will Pay $110 Million Fine in International Price Fixing Conspiracy*, 74 Antitrust & Trade Reg. Rep. (BNA) 353

for violating the Sherman Act. In 1995, two Canadian defendants who participated in a cartel in the disposable plastic dinnerware industry agreed to serve time in U.S. prisons for violations of the Sherman Act.[547] Furthermore, of the individual defendants charged in the investigation into the vitamins cartel, several German and Swiss citizens agreed to serve prison terms and pay substantial fines.[548]

The Department of Justice has taken the position that valid service of a criminal summons alone may be sufficient to convey personal jurisdiction and that subject matter jurisdiction attaches to any price-fixing conspiracy, wherever formed, that intends to and does affect U.S. commerce.[549]

4. *Multijurisdictional Merger Review*

The marked increase in the number of jurisdictions that have adopted merger review regimes means that international mergers and acquisitions are often subject to review by multiple competition authorities. During fiscal year 1999, roughly one-fifth of the notifications that the U.S. antitrust authorities received under the H-S-R Act[550] involved a foreign party.[551] Furthermore, cases involving international aspects account for a significant percentage of U.S. antitrust authorities' enforcement actions against proposed mergers.[552]

In multijurisdictional mergers, the types of issues that parties must consider include the following: (1) what jurisdictions may review the merger; (2) which of those jurisdictions require premerger notification; (3) which of those jurisdictions require payment of a filing fee; (4) what documentation must be submitted to the reviewing authorities; (5) when the premerger notification must be filed; (6) how long the review process may take in each jurisdiction; (7) what restrictions apply during the review period; (8) what cooperation may occur, and what information may be shared, among the reviewing authorities; and (9) how parties can avoid conflicting decisions by the reviewing authorities. A complete depiction of the variety of merger review rules is beyond the scope of this treatise.[553]

(1998). This case also resulted in the largest antitrust fine ever imposed against an individual, a $10 million fine paid by an executive of SGL. *See* DOJ Press Release, German Company and Chief Executive Officer Each Agree to Pay Record Fines for International Conspiracy (May 4, 1999). Also in 1999, F. Hoffman-La Roche, a Swiss company, pleaded guilty to participating in a worldwide conspiracy to fix prices and allocate market share for certain vitamins and paid a fine of $500 million, the largest criminal fine in U.S. history. *See* DOJ Press Release, F. Hoffman-LaRoche and BASF Agree to Pay Record Criminal Fines for Participating in International Vitamin Cartel (May 20, 1999). A German company, BASF Aktiengesellschaft, pleaded guilty to the same conspiracy and paid a $225 million fine. *Id. See generally* Spratling, Titanic Fines, *supra* note 532.

547. *See* ICPAC REPORT, *supra* note 139, at 170.
548. *See* DOJ Press Release, Four Foreign Executives of Leading European Vitamin Firms Agree to Plead Guilty to Participating in International Vitamin Cartel (Apr. 6, 2000).
549. *See* INTERNATIONAL ANTITRUST GUIDELINES, *supra* note 1.
550. 15 U.S.C. § 18a (2000).
551. *See* INTERNATIONAL ANTITRUST GUIDELINES, *supra* note 1.
552. *Id.* at 47.
553. *See generally* ABA SECTION OF ANTITRUST LAW, COMPETITION LAWS OUTSIDE THE UNITED STATES, *supra* note 481.

H. Extraterritorial Remedies and Relief

U.S. courts have broad authority to order remedies, either monetary damages or equitable relief, designed to cure or deter foreign-based anticompetitive conduct affecting U.S. commerce.[554] Applying U.S. remedies to conduct undertaken abroad, however, often reaches into the domain of foreign law and policy. Increasingly, expansive unilateral enforcement has continued to provoke conflict, spurring defensive reactions by some foreign nations[555] and raising questions of comity by U.S. courts and antitrust enforcement agencies.

1. Enforcement of Foreign Judgments

a. JUDGMENTS

Private antitrust plaintiffs that are able to establish jurisdiction over foreign defendants, obtain evidence sufficient to meet the elements of an antitrust violation, and win a judgment on the merits must overcome yet another hurdle: successful enforcement of the judgment. In a similar vein, a plaintiff that wins an antitrust judgment abroad may need to enforce that judgment in U.S. federal or state courts. Although U.S. federal courts are authorized to order relief addressing anticompetitive conduct in foreign countries, they often lack authority to enforce their own remedies abroad.

The United States is not a party to any generally applicable treaties or conventions regarding the recognition of foreign judgments. Nonetheless, foreign court judgments have long been recognized in the United States on the basis of comity, as defined by the Supreme Court's 1895 decision in *Hilton v. Guyot*.[556] In *Hilton*, the Court set forth various criteria of fairness that must be met for a foreign judgment to be enforced, including the opportunity for a full and fair trial abroad before a court of competent jurisdiction, a system of jurisprudence likely to yield an impartial result between its citizens and noncitizens, no evidence of prejudice in the court or in the legal system in which the court was sitting, and reciprocity by the foreign court in giving effect to U.S. judgments.[557]

Although comity serves as the basis for enforcing foreign judgments in federal courts, thirty-one states have adopted the Uniform Foreign Money Judgments Recognition Act,[558] which outlines several criteria upon which a state court will evaluate the enforcement of a foreign money judgment.[559] These criteria generally track the principles set forth in *Hilton*, although some states have dropped the requirement of reciprocity by the foreign court in enforcing U.S. judgments.[560]

---

554. *See* United States v. Imperial Chem. Indus., 100 F. Supp. 504 (S.D.N.Y. 1951), *supplemental op. on remedies*, 105 F. Supp. 215, 238 (S.D.N.Y. 1952).

555. *See, e.g.*, The United Kingdom's Protection of Trading Interest Act, 1980, ch. 11, (Eng.), *as amended* (limiting recognition of foreign multiple damage judgments).

556. 159 U.S. 113 (1895).

557. *See* Kohn v. American Metal Climax, Inc., 458 F.2d 255, 302 (3d Cir. 1972) (summarizing *Hilton* criteria).

558. 13 U.L.A. 94 (Supp. 2001).

559. *Id.* § 4.

560. *See* Tahan v. Hodgson, 662 F.2d 862, 867 (D.C. Cir. 1981).

Because the United States is not party to any treaties for the recognition of foreign judgments, enforceability of U.S. antitrust judgments in foreign countries is governed by the laws of the country where enforcement is sought. Most civil-law and common-law foreign courts are willing to enforce U.S. judgments when it is established that the U.S. court had jurisdiction that would have satisfied the enforcing court's standards and that the foreign defendant appeared in the U.S. court and defended on the merits.[561]

b. ARBITRAL AWARDS

The United States is one of over ninety countries to sign the New York Convention on the Recognition and Enforcement of Foreign Arbitral Awards (*New York Convention*),[562] which provides the general rule in favor of enforceability and a number of clearly delineated exceptions.

One such exception to enforceability is set forth in Article V(2)(a) of the *Convention*, which authorizes a court to refuse to recognize and enforce an award when the subject matter of the dispute is not capable of settlement by arbitration under the law of the country where enforcement is sought. Since the Supreme Court ruled in *Mitsubishi Motors Corp. v. Soler Chrysler-Plymouth, Inc.*[563] that an agreement to resolve antitrust claims by arbitration is enforceable when that agreement arises from an international transaction, Article V(2)(a) appears to have been reduced as an obstruction to enforcement of arbitral awards in international antitrust disputes.

2. *Injunctions and Equitable Relief*

The object of injunctive remedies in antitrust cases generally is to terminate unlawful anticompetitive activity, prevent its revival, and destroy its effects by reestablishing competitive conditions insofar as they pertain to U.S. market conditions. Comity concerns may influence the structuring and enforcement of injunctive and other equitable relief in the international context.

a. JUDICIAL TREATMENT

Although U.S. antitrust courts tend to give deference to foreign laws and interests under comity principles, they often will order foreign defendants, as well as U.S. defendants with business activities abroad, to take remedial action when necessary to redress U.S. antitrust violations.

---

561. *See* LAWRENCE W. NEWMAN & DAVID ZASLOWSKI, LITIGATING INTERNATIONAL COMMERCE DISPUTES § 13.4, at 186-87 (1996) (indicating that "[g]reater scrutiny is given to judgments obtained by default than to those obtained in proceedings in which there has been an appearance by the defendant," although this should not matter where due process has occurred). There are some countries, however, that are apt to deny effect to U.S. judgments because, without the United States having signed any bilateral or multilateral recognition treaties, there is no guarantee that U.S. courts will recognize and enforce foreign judgments.
562. 9 U.S.C. § 201 (2000) (referring to *New York Convention*, *reprinted in* MARTINDALE HUBBELL INTERNATIONAL LAW DIGESTS at IC-15 (2001)).
563. 473 U.S. 614 (1985).

The Supreme Court in *United States v. Holophane Co.*[564] affirmed the authority of U.S. courts to order injunctive relief abroad. In *Holophane*, a U.S. defendant was party to an international cartel that had allocated the world market for prismatic glassware. The district court found that the allocation agreements violated Section 1 of the Sherman Act and ordered the defendant to breach the unlawful agreements by using "reasonable efforts" to sell its products in countries from which the agreements had excluded it. A unanimous Supreme Court, realizing that compliance with the district court's decree would subject the U.S. company to suits in foreign countries for breach of the underlying contracts, nonetheless affirmed the judgment.[565]

Following the Supreme Court's lead, lower courts have required foreign entities to license U.S. patents,[566] to refrain from enforcing foreign patents,[567] and to divest joint ownership interests in companies based in third countries.[568] Courts also have ordered U.S. companies to divest themselves of stockholdings in foreign corporations,[569] to encourage their foreign subsidiaries to export to the United States,[570] to undertake reasonable efforts to sell abroad,[571] to restrict the flow of

564. 119 F. Supp. 114 (S.D. Ohio) (findings and conclusions), 1954 Trade Cas. (CCH) ¶ 67,679 (S.D. Ohio 1954) (judgment), *aff'd per curiam*, 352 U.S. 903 (1956).

565. 352 U.S. 903 (1956) (per curiam); *see also* United States v. National Lead Co., 332 U.S. 319, 335 (1947) (upholding a decree enjoining performance and renewal of anticompetitive agreements among U.S. companies, ordering compulsory licensing of patents, and requiring divestiture of stockholdings and other financial interests in foreign companies).

566. *See, e.g.*, United States v. S.C. Johnson & Son, 1995-1 Trade Cas. (CCH) ¶ 70,884 (N.D. Ill. 1994) (consent decree requiring Bayer to offer licenses to produce and sell cyfluthrin in the United States on reasonable and nondiscriminatory terms); United States v. Imperial Chem. Indus., 105 F. Supp. 215, 227 (S.D.N.Y. 1952), *supplementing* 100 F. Supp. 504 (S.D.N.Y. 1951) (requiring British company to license its U.S. patents to redress antitrust violations arising from denial of licensing because of intervention and objection of U.S. company).

567. *See, e.g.*, United States v. Pilkington plc, 1994-2 Trade Cas. (CCH) ¶ 70,842 (D. Ariz. 1994) (consent decree prohibiting assertion of rights in public domain technology, enforcement of license restrictions and fees); United States v. Inco Ltd., 1978-1 Trade Cas. (CCH) ¶ 61,869, at 73,640 (E.D. Pa. 1978) (consent decree requiring defendants to license their patents and granting immunity to licensees of defendants' patent rights from suit under any other patent belonging to defendants); *Imperial Chem.*, 105 F. Supp. at 228 (requiring British company to grant immunity under its British patents to licensees of its corresponding U.S. patents).

568. *See Imperial Chem.*, 105 F. Supp. at 237 (noting that "'the harsh remedy of divestiture'" was necessary not only to remove the means to further restrain the market but also to eliminate the incentive not to compete) (citation omitted).

569. *See, e.g.*, United States v. National Lead Co., 332 U.S. 319, 363 (1947) (upholding decree requiring U.S. company to present a divestment plan because the foreign stock acquisitions had been part of territorial allocation agreements regarding the market for titanium products); *cf.* Pilkington Bros. plc, 103 F.T.C. 707 (1984) (consent order under which British company agreed to sell certain interests in and forego certain control over float glass producers in Canada and Mexico, not to acquire any float glass producers in North America for 10 years, and to keep detailed records regarding certain business dealings abroad).

570. *See, e.g.*, United States v. Everest & Jennings Int'l, 1979-1 Trade Cas. (CCH) ¶ 62,508, §§ VIII-X (C.D. Cal. 1979) (consent decree requiring manufacturer to take affirmative action to encourage its subsidiaries to export to the United States and to help them develop a distribution system).

571. *See, e.g.*, United States v. Diebold, Inc., 1977-2 Trade Cas. (CCH) ¶ 61,736, § VI (N.D. Ohio 1977) (consent decree requiring defendant to "promote in good faith" the firm's products in the United Kingdom and requiring a written explanation for every foreign sale refused); *see also* United States v. Norman M. Morris Corp., 1976-1 Trade Cas. (CCH) ¶ 60,894, § VII(C) (S.D.N.Y. 1976) (obliging firm to notify distributors of their right to export), *decree terminated by consent*, 1983-1 Trade Cas. (CCH) ¶ 65,442 (S.D.N.Y. 1981); United States v. R. Hoe & Co., 1955 Trade Cas. (CCH) ¶ 68,215, § IX(A)-(B) (S.D.N.Y. 1955) (requiring defendant to advertise the availability of its product abroad).

competitively sensitive information between a U.S. and non-U.S. corporation that were partners in a joint venture,[572] and to license foreign patents royalty-free.[573]

Despite their power to apply U.S. antitrust law to conduct in foreign countries, U.S. courts have often shown deference to foreign interests, particularly when a foreign government expresses concern. For example, in *United States v. Watchmakers of Switzerland Information Center, Inc.*,[574] the district court modified its initial decree to accommodate concerns that the Swiss government articulated as amicus curiae after the court had entered the decree.[575] Similarly, in *United States v. General Electric Co.*,[576] the district court permitted Canada to consult on the terms of the proposed consent decree, although it did not yield to all of Canada's concerns.

b.   ENFORCEMENT AGENCY TREATMENT

It is the formal policy of the Federal Trade Commission and the Department of Justice to consider comity when crafting remedial enforcement decrees. The *International Antitrust Guidelines* expressly provide that "in determining whether to . . . seek particular remedies in a given case, each Agency takes into account whether significant interests of any foreign sovereign would be affected."[577]

Further, the U.S.-EC bilateral agreement[578] commits the parties to take six *Timberlane*-like factors[579] into account when considering enforcement actions that affect the other: (1) the relative significance to the anticompetitive activities involved of conduct within the enforcing party's territory as compared to conduct within the other party's territory; (2) the presence or absence of a purpose on the part of those engaged in the anticompetitive activities to affect consumers, suppliers, or competitors within the enforcing party's territory; (3) the relative significance of the effects of the anticompetitive activities on the enforcing party's interests as compared to the effects on the other party's interests; (4) the existence or absence of reasonable expectations that would be furthered or defeated by the enforcement activities; (5) the degree of conflict or inconsistency between the enforcement activities and the other party's laws or articulated economic policies; and (6) the extent to which enforcement activities of the other party with respect to the same persons, including judgments or undertakings resulting from such activities, may be affected.

---

572. *See, e.g.*, United States v. MCI Communs. Corp., 1994-2 Trade Cas. (CCH) ¶ 70,730 (D.D.C. 1994) (consent decree prohibiting U.S. telecommunications firm and its joint venture with foreign telecommunications firm from receiving proprietary information from foreign firm regarding competing telecommunications providers to avoid possibility that U.S. firm would gain access to proprietary information regarding its competitors serving the United Kingdom); *see also* United States v. Sprint Corp., 1996-1 Trade Cas. (CCH) ¶ 71,300 (D.D.C. 1996) (consent decree providing same relief as in *MCI* with respect to telecommunications services in France and Germany).

573. *See, e.g.*, United States v. Inco Ltd., 1978-1 Trade Cas. (CCH) ¶ 61,869, at 73,640 (E.D. Pa. 1978) (consent decree requiring U.S. and foreign battery manufacturers to license their patents without charge to anyone making a written request).

574. 1963 Trade Cas. (CCH) ¶ 70,600 (S.D.N.Y. 1962), *order modified*, 1965 Trade Cas. (CCH) ¶ 71,352 (S.D.N.Y. 1965).

575. 1965 Trade Cas. (CCH) ¶ 71,352, at 80,492-93 (S.D.N.Y. 1965).

576. 1962 Trade Cas. (CCH) ¶¶ 70,342, 70,428, 70,546 (S.D.N.Y. 1962) (enjoining home entertainment firms from undertaking activity restricting exports from the United States to Canada).

577. INTERNATIONAL ANTITRUST GUIDELINES, *supra* note 1, § 3.2 (footnote omitted).

578. *See* 1991 EC Agreement, *supra* note 82.

579. Timberlane Lumber Co. v. Bank of Am. Nat'l Trust & Sav. Ass'n, 749 F.2d 1378 (9th Cir. 1984).

Although the Federal Trade Commission and the Department of Justice are committed to taking comity into account in the exercise of their prosecutorial discretion, neither agency has hesitated to impose extraterritorial relief when deemed necessary.

(1) International Cartel Prosecution Remedies

Since the early 1990s, the Department of Justice has made international cartel prosecutions a top priority. Alongside increasing corporate fines, prison terms and fines for individuals show the extent of antitrust enforcement against foreign defendants in recent years.[580]

(2) International Merger Investigation Remedies

In the merger context, the U.S. antitrust enforcement agencies have, with increasing regularity, required foreign defendants to undertake remedial actions to address likely anticompetitive effects in the United States.[581] With increased globalization of commerce, more and more firm assets and production facilities may be located outside U.S. borders. Approximately half of the Federal Trade Commission's second-stage merger investigations in 1999 had an important international component such as a foreign-based party, essential information located abroad, or a foreign asset critical to an effective remedy.[582]

At one time, merger enforcement had the potential to create conflict with other countries when remedies were imposed in a foreign country that deemed such relief

---

580. *See* part G.3 of this chapter.
581. *See, e.g.,* Mannesman, A.G., 115 F.T.C. 412 (1992) (consent order requiring divestiture of U.S. subsidiary), *terminated* 120 F.T.C. 814 (1995); Hanson plc, 115 F.T.C. 342 (1992) (consent order requiring divestiture of interest in U.S. company); Hoechst Celanese Corp., 114 F.T.C. 720 (1991) (consent order requiring removal of constraints on the operation of a joint venture in Japan in order to facilitate the expansion of the venture's acetal business into the United States); Institut Merieux S.A., 113 F.T.C. 742 (1990) (consent order requiring divestiture of Canadian rabies vaccine business), *modified by* 117 F.T.C. 473 (1999). *See also* United States v. MCI Communs. Corp., 62 Fed. Reg. 37,594 (DOJ July 14, 1997) (modification of final judgment) (requiring remedial action similar to that in *Sprint*); United States v. Cargill, Inc., 62 Fed. Reg. 26,559 (DOJ May 14, 1997) (final judgment ordering divestiture of U.S. salt mine and a U.S. evaporated salt plant prior to acquisition of Dutch firm's Western Hemisphere salt operations by U.S. company); American Home Prods. Corp., 123 F.T.C. 1279 (1997) (consent agreement ordering American firm to divest assets relating to acquired Belgian firm's canine lyme, canine corona virus combination, and feline leukemia combination vaccines); Baxter Int'l Inc., Dkt. No. C-3726, 1997 FTC LEXIS 84 (1997) (consent agreement requiring American firm to divest its Factor VIII inhibitor treatment, and license acquired firm's fibrin sealant product in development); Insilco Corp., 62 Fed. Reg. 47,209 (FTC Sept. 8, 1997) (aid to public comment) (consent agreement requiring U.S. acquiror of the assets of U.S. subsidiary of German corporation to divest two welded seam aluminum tube mills, and prohibiting certain premerger information exchanges), 125 F.T.C. 293 (1998) (decision and order); United States v. Sprint Corp., 61 Fed. Reg. 3970 (DOJ Feb. 2, 1996) (requiring disclosure of information and transparency, and prohibiting parties from inappropriately using any confidential information Deutsche Telekom and France Telecom obtained from Sprint's competitors).
582. *See* William J. Baer, Dir., Bureau of Competition, Federal Trade Comm'n, Report from the Bureau of Competition, Address Before the ABA Antitrust Section (Apr. 15, 1999), *available at* www.ftc.gov/speeches/other/baerspaba99.htm.

unnecessary.[583]   For example, in a 1990 investigation of a proposed merger of a
Canadian firm and a French firm, the Federal Trade Commission did not inform
Canadian merger authorities before obtaining a consent agreement from a Canadian
company that required divestiture of Canadian assets.[584]   More recently,
extraterritorial merger enforcement by the U.S. agencies has become increasingly
characterized by cooperation and coordination with foreign merger review
authorities, particularly the European Commission, and particularly in the area of
remedies.[585]   The staffs of the U.S. and EC agencies typically share their individual
assessments of a transaction's anticompetitive effects—with the parties' consent—in
order to determine if they have overlapping concerns.   Examples of transactions in
which U.S. and EC (or certain of its member state) officials cooperated extensively
to fashion complementary remedies include Ciba-Giegy–Sandoz,[586] Zeneca-Astra,[587]
ABB-Elsag,[588] Federal Mogul-TNN,[589] Dresser-Halliburton,[590] WorldCom-Sprint,[591]
and Oerlikon-Bührle–Leybold.[592]   The few instances of conflict, such as the 1997
merger of Boeing and McDonnell Douglas,[593] and the blocked 2001 merger of
General Electric and Honeywell,[594] have been the exception rather than the rule.[595]

---

583.   See ICPAC REPORT, *supra* note 139, at 54-55.

584.   Institut Merieux, 113 F.T.C. 742 (1990) (requiring divestiture despite neither firm having relevant
       production assets in the United States).

585.   See Robert Pitofsky, Chairman, Federal Trade Comm'n, EU and U.S. Approaches to International
       Mergers—Views from the Federal Trade Commission, Remarks Before the International Bar
       Ass'n (Sept. 15, 2000), *available at* www.ftc.gov/speeches/pitofsky/pitintermergers.htm; Debra A.
       Valentine, General Counsel, Federal Trade Comm'n, Merger Enforcement: Multijurisdictional
       Review and Restructuring Remedies, Remarks Before the International Bar Ass'n (Mar. 24, 2000),
       available at www.ftc.gov/speeches/other/dvmergerenforcement.htm. *See also* ICPAC REPORT,
       supra note 139, at 76 ("The coordination of remedies is particularly important when remedies
       could affect conduct in more than one jurisdiction or the feasibility of remedies being considered
       by other jurisdictions. The goal at the remedies phase should lie in avoiding conflicting remedies
       as well as avoiding a mix of remedies that may overly burden an otherwise competitively benign or
       efficiency-enhancing transaction.").

586.   Ciba-Geigy Ltd., Dkt. No. C-3725 (Mar. 24, 1997), [FTC Complaints & Orders 1997-2001
       Transfer Binder] Trade Reg. Rep. (CCH) ¶ 24,182; Ciba-Giegy/Sandoz, EC Case No. IV/M.737
       (July 17, 1997).   There, complementary remedies alleviated EC concern regarding Sandoz's
       monopoly of methoprene and assured FTC and Canadian officials that the buyer of Sandoz's flea
       control business would have stable methoprene supply.

587.   Zeneca Group plc, Dkt. No. C-3880 (June 7, 1999), [FTC Complaints & Orders 1997-2001
       Transfer Binder], Trade Reg. Rep. (CCH) ¶ 24,521 (worldwide market for long-acting local
       anaesthetics); *see also* Astra/Zeneca, EC Case No. IV/M.1403 (Feb. 26, 1999).

588.   ABB/Elsag Baily, Dkt No. C-3867 (Apr. 22, 1999), [FTC Complaints & Orders 1997-2001 Trade
       Reg. Rep. (CCH) ¶ 24,521 (worldwide market for gas chromatographs and gas spectrometers); *see
       also* ABB/Elsag Bailey, EC Case No. IV/M.1339 (Dec. 16, 1998).

589.   Federal-Mogul Corp., Dkt. No. C- 3836 (Apr. 22, 1999), [FTC Complaints & Orders 1997-2001
       Transfer Binder] Trade Reg. Rep. (CCH) ¶ 24,400 (worldwide market for thinwall bearings used in
       cars, trucks, and heavy equipment engines).

590.   United States v. Halliburton Co., 64 Fed. Reg. 7248 (Feb. 12, 1999).

591.   United States v. WorldCom, Inc., No. 1:00CV01526, *reported in* 6 Trade Reg. Rep. (CCH)
       ¶ 45,100 at 45,588 (June 27, 2000).

592.   Oerlikon-Bührle Holding AG, Dkt. No. C-3555 (Feb. 1, 1995), [FTC Complaints & Orders 1993-
       1997 Transfer Binder] Trade Reg. Rep. (CCH) ¶ 23,697 (U.S. market for turbomolecular pumps
       used in semiconductors; worldwide market for compact disc metallizer machines).

593.   Boeing/McDonnell Douglas, EC Case No. IV/M.877 (July 30, 1997).   The FTC cleared the
       transaction without condition after determining that the merger was unlikely to pose substantial
       adverse effects to commercial airlines that purchased planes from the merging parties. *See* The
       Boeing Co., Joint Statement closing investigation of the proposed merger and separate statement of
       Commissioner Mary L. Azcuenaga, File No. 971-0051 (July 1, 1997), [FTC Complaints & Orders

3.   *Reactions by Foreign Countries*

The willingness of U.S. courts to enforce antitrust laws extraterritorially often has engendered concern on the part of foreign countries. An early case, *United States v. Imperial Chemical Industries*,[596] illustrates the negative reaction of some foreign countries to perceived intrusion by U.S. courts. *Imperial Chemical* was an action brought by the Department of Justice against several international chemical companies for dividing world markets for chemicals and explosives. The court ruled in favor of the Department of Justice and, as part of the remedy for the antitrust violations, enjoined Imperial Chemical Industries (ICI), a British company, from enforcing its English patents against licensees of its corresponding U.S. patents. ICI, however, had assigned its English patent rights to another British company. The assignee sued in an English court, which upheld the contract rights of the assignee, in effect partially overturning the U.S. decree.[597]

Some countries have passed blocking statutes limiting the extraterritorial application of U.S. antitrust judgments. Foreign blocking statutes may be motivated by the potential for the award of treble damages to private plaintiffs resulting from conduct outside the United States that may even have been condoned or encouraged by a foreign government.[598] Blocking statutes may limit discovery, the enforcement of U.S. judgments, or both.

Among the countries that have acted to bar enforcement of U.S. judgments are the Philippines, the United Kingdom, Canada, Australia, and South Africa.[599]   The

1997-2001 Transfer Binder] Trade Reg. Rep. (CCH) ¶ 24,295. The European Commission ultimately cleared the deal, subject to conditions agreed to by Boeing. *See* ICPAC REPORT, *supra* note 139, at 55-56.

594. General Electric/Honeywell, EC Case No. COMP/M.2220 (July 3, 2001). The DOJ cleared the transaction as modified by agreed remedies. *See* DOJ Press Release, Statement by Assistant Attorney General Charles A. James on the EU's Decision Regarding the GE/Honeywell Acquisition (July 3, 2001), *available at* www.usdoj.gov/atr/public/press_releases/2001/8510.htm. The European Commission decided to prohibit the proposed acquisition following an investigation into the markets for aero-engines, avionics, and other aircraft components and systems. In adopting its decision, the European Commission opined that the merger would create or strengthen dominant positions on several markets and that the remedies proposed by GE were insufficient to resolve the competition concerns resulting from the proposed acquisition. *See* Commission Press Release IP/01/939 (July 3, 2001).

595. *See* Debra A. Valentine, General Counsel, Federal Trade Comm'n, Merger Enforcement: Multijurisdictional Review and Restructuring Remedies, Remarks Before the International Bar Ass'n (Mar. 24, 2000), *available at* www.ftc.gov/speeches/other/dvmergerenforcement.htm (observing that recent cross-border merger enforcement has, in most cases, cooperated sufficiently to avoid placing "inconsistent burdens" on transacting parties).

596. 100 F. Supp. 504 (S.D.N.Y. 1951), *supplemental op. on remedies*, 105 F. Supp. 215 (S.D.N.Y. 1952).

597. *See* British Nylon Spinners Ltd. v. Imperial Chem. Indus., [1953] 1 Ch. 19, 26 (C.A. 1952) (Eng.) ("[patents are] a species of property . . . which is English in character and is subject to the jurisdiction of the English courts; and . . . plaintiffs have at least established a prima facie case for saying that it is not competent for the courts of the United States or of any other country to interfere with those rights").

598. *See, e.g.*, Brief for Amicus Curiae Government of Australia, *In re* Uranium Antitrust Litig., 617 F.2d 1248 (7th Cir. 1980) (No. 79-1427) (complaining that the treble damage litigation will have "a very serious and detrimental effect on the [Australian] national interest").

599. Litigation against foreign uranium producers for participation in an alleged government-organized international uranium cartel was the major impetus for much of this legislation. Several governments stated in amicus briefs filed in a U.S. antitrust action stemming from the cartel's

Philippines's statute prohibits enforcement of foreign judgments for multiple damages without clearance from the Philippine President's representative.[600] In the United Kingdom, the Secretary of Trade may bar enforcement of foreign judgments for multiple damages, and British companies that have paid a "multiple damage" award may sue the successful plaintiff in an English court to recover the "excess" damages.[601] Canadian law permits its Attorney General to declare a foreign antitrust judgment nonrecognizable, or recognizable only up to a certain amount, and permits Canadian citizens, residents, and corporations to sue the successful plaintiff for the damages collected under the nonrecognizable portion of a judgment.[602] Australia's blocking statute allows its Attorney General to declare a judgment rendered in a foreign antitrust proceeding not recognizable in Australia,[603] and it authorizes Australians to recover the full amount—not just the noncompensatory portion—of multiple damages imposed in foreign countries.[604] South Africa's Protection of Business Act provides that no foreign decree or judgment may be enforced at all in South Africa without the consent of the Minister of Economic Affairs.[605] Multiple and punitive damage awards are never enforceable in South Africa, and, as in Britain and Canada, those who have paid damage awards imposed by foreign judgments may recover the noncompensatory portion.[606]

I. Relationship of U.S. International Trade Laws to Antitrust Laws

1. Antidumping Act of 1916

Section 801 of the Revenue Act of 1916, more commonly known as the Antidumping Act of 1916, creates a private cause of action for treble damages against importers and others that import or sell comparable articles in the United States at substantially less than their wholesale price or actual market value in their market of production (or other export market), where such pricing is "common" or "systematic" and is done with anticompetitive intent.[607] It also includes a

---

alleged activities that it was their policy that private uranium producers cooperate in those activities. *See, e.g.*, Brief for Amicus Curiae Government of Australia at 3-4, *In re* Uranium Antitrust Litig., 617 F.2d 1248 (7th Cir. 1980) (No. 79-1427); Brief for Amicus Curiae Government of Canada at 3-4, *In re* Uranium Antitrust Litig., 473 F. Supp. 382 (N.D. Ill. 1979) (No. 76-C-3830).

600. Presidential Decree No. 1718 (1980) (Phil.).

601. Protection of Trading Interests Act, 1980, ch. 11, §§ 5-6 (Eng.), *as amended.*

602. Foreign Extraterritorial Measures Act, R.S.C., F-29, §§ 8-9 (1984) (Can.), *as amended.* A U.S. district court, in dictum, has indicated that U.S. courts should not normally interfere with such "clawback" recoveries. Laker Airways v. Pan Am. World Airways, 559 F. Supp. 1124, 1136-37 (D.D.C. 1983), *aff'd sub nom.* Laker Airways v. Sabena, Belgian World Airlines, 731 F.2d 909 (D.C. Cir. 1984).

603. Foreign Proceedings (Excess of Jurisdiction) Act, No. 3, cl. 9(1), (2) (1984) (Austl.), *as amended.*

604. *Id.* cl. 10.

605. Protection of Business Act, No. 99, § 1 (1978) (S. Afr.), *as amended.*

606. *Id.* §§ 1A, 1B.

607. 15 U.S.C. § 72 (2000). The statute describes the requisite intent as "the intent of destroying or injuring an industry in the United States, or of preventing the establishment of an industry in the United States, or of restraining or monopolizing any part of trade and commerce in such articles in the United States." *Id.*

misdemeanor criminal offense, punishable by up to one year in prison and a $5,000 fine, for violations or conspiracies to violate its prohibition.[608]

Although its legislative sponsors intended the 1916 Act to protect domestic industries from an onslaught of cheap goods from Europe after World War I,[609] few civil or criminal cases have been pursued under the statute.[610] Courts have consistently viewed its intent requirement as very difficult to meet.[611] As a result, although the 1916 Act remains on the books, new mechanisms for prosecuting antidumping claims through administrative duties largely supplanted the act when Congress passed other antidumping statutes beginning in 1921.[612]

The few courts that have considered the 1916 Act's private right of action disagree on the act's relationship to domestic antitrust laws. After completing the most thorough reported review of the act's history and purpose, the district court in *Zenith Radio Corp. v. Matsushita Electric Industrial Corp.*[613] granted partial summary judgment for Japanese consumer electronic manufacturers in an action brought by U.S. television manufacturers. The court considered the 1916 Act "functionally similar" to the Clayton Act, as amended by the Robinson-Patman Act, and held that "the statute should be interpreted whenever possible to parallel the 'unfair competition' law applicable to domestic commerce."[614] Reversing the district court on other grounds, the Third Circuit also described the statute as the

---

608. *Id.*
609. The legislation's sponsor noted that "the same unfair competition law which now applies to the domestic trader should apply to the foreign import trader." 53 Cong. Rec. App. 1938 (July 6, 1916) (statement of Rep. Kitchin). *See also* H.R. REP. NO. 922, 64th Cong., 1st Sess. at 9 (1916) (explaining purpose of act was to place foreign sellers "in the same position as our manufacturers with reference to unfair competition").
610. No criminal enforcement attempts have been successful, and none has resulted in a reported judicial decision. The reported civil decisions under the 1916 Act focus largely on jurisdictional and procedural issues, although they make some references to interpretive principles for the Act. *See, e.g.,* Western Concrete Structures Co. v. Mitsui & Co. (U.S.A.), 760 F.2d 1013, 1019 (9th Cir. 1985) (standing); Helmac Prods. Corp. v. Roth (Plastics) Corp., 814 F. Supp. 560, 567 (E.D. Mich. 1992) (limitations period); Isra Fruit Ltd. v. Agrexco Agric. Export Co., 631 F. Supp. 984, 988-89 (S.D.N.Y. 1986) (standing); Jewel Foliage Co. v. Uniflora Overseas Fla., Inc., 497 F. Supp. 513, 517 (M.D. Fla. 1980) (standing); Schwimmer v. Sony Corp. of Am., 471 F. Supp. 793, 796-97 (E.D.N.Y. 1979), *aff'd*, 637 F.2d 41 (2d Cir. 1980) (standing); Outboard Marine Corp. v. Pezetel, 461 F. Supp. 384, 408-09 (D. Del. 1978) (requirement of foreign sale); Bywater v. Matsushita Elec. Indus. Co., 1971 Trade Cas. (CCH) ¶ 73,759 (S.D.N.Y. 1971) (standing). Even when parties have litigated the more substantive elements of the 1916 Act, no plaintiff has won an award of treble damages and costs, as permitted under the act. United States Anti-Dumping Act of 1916, Report No. 00-2118 (May 29, 2000 World Trade Organization).
611. *See* Zenith Radio Corp. v. Matsushita Elec. Indus. Co., 494 F. Supp. 1190, 1224-25 (E.D. Pa. 1980); Geneva Steel Co. v. Ranger Steel Supply Corp, 980 F. Supp. 1209, 1220 (D. Utah 1997). *See also* UNITED STATES TARIFF COMMISSION ANN. REP. at 10-12 (1919); UNITED STATES TARIFF COMMISSION, DUMPING AND UNFAIR FOREIGN COMPETITION IN THE UNITED STATES AND CANADA'S ANTIDUMPING LAW at 18-21 (1919) (reporting that proof of intent is "extremely difficult to establish" because such intent is "not necessarily present" in profit-driven international commercial dealings where other incentives exist).
612. *Zenith*, 494 F. Supp. at 1224-25; *Geneva Steel*, 980 F. Supp. at 1220. The Tariff Act of 1930 provides the modern procedure for seeking administrative duties against foreign firms that dump products into the United States, a process that involves the U.S. International Trade Commission and the Department of Commerce. 19 U.S.C. §§ 1673-1673i (1994 & Supp. 1999) (including portions of the 1921 Act as amended by the Trade Agreements Act of 1979, Pub. L. No. 96-39).
613. 494 F. Supp. 1190 (E.D. Pa. 1980).
614. *Id.* at 1213, 1223.

ANTITRUST AND INTERNATIONAL COMMERCE 1211

international analogue to the Robinson-Patman Act, prohibiting anticompetitive discriminatory pricing in international commerce.[615]

In *Geneva Steel Co. v. Ranger Steel Supply Corp.*,[616] however, another district court saw the 1916 Act as advancing both antitrust and trade protection principles. The defendants, two steel importers, asserted that the plaintiff, a U.S. steel producer, had not properly alleged predatory pricing under *Brooke Group Ltd. v. Brown & Williamson Tobacco Corp.*[617] Distinguishing *Zenith* and also citing the act's legislative history, the court noted that *Brooke Group*'s requirement of recoupment did not always apply to the 1916 Act since the act's intent element could be either trade-oriented (intent to destroy, injure, or prevent the establishment of a U.S. industry) or antitrust-oriented (intent to restrain or monopolize trade or commerce). Since the plaintiff had asserted a trade-oriented intent, the intent to injure the U.S. steel industry, the court denied the defendants' motion to dismiss. Another court reached a similar conclusion and declined automatically to apply competition law principles to the act, but has acknowledged "the applicability of [antitrust] jurisprudence."[618]

In *Wheeling-Pittsburgh Steel Corp. v. Mitsui & Co.*,[619] the court agreed with *Geneva Steel* that *Brooke Group*'s predatory pricing standards were not applicable to an action alleging a trade-related intent on the part of the alleged dumping party. The court recognized that the Sherman, Clayton, and Robinson-Patman Acts "share a similarity" with the 1916 Act, but distinguished them based on the 1916 Act's explicit intent element.[620] The court did not foreclose, however, the applicability of antitrust principles under other circumstances.[621]

The district court also held that a remedy of injunctive relief did not exist under the act.[622] This holding was subsequently affirmed by the Sixth Circuit, which limited plaintiffs to "the remedies expressly provided for in the statute—treble damages, attorneys' fees and costs" because of Congress's implication that no additional relief would be appropriate under the act, plaintiff's request for such relief not being based on traditional principles of equitable relief, and the existence of other federal antidumping remedies.[623]

A third district court decision agreed with the reasoning of *Geneva Steel* and *Wheeling-Pittsburgh* that antitrust principles do not necessarily apply to a claim under the act.[624] The court reached this conclusion despite evidence that the U.S.

---

615. Zenith Radio Corp. v. Matsushita Elec. Indus. Co. (*In re* Japanese Electronic Products Antitrust Litigation), 723 F.2d 319, 324 (3d Cir. 1983). The Supreme Court's ultimate consideration of the case did not involve any 1916 Act issues. Matsushita Elec. Indus. Co. v. Zenith Radio Corp., 475 U.S. 574 (1986).

616. 980 F. Supp. 1209 (D. Utah 1997).

617. 509 U.S. 209 (1993).

618. Helmac Prods. Corp. v. Roth (Plastics) Corp., 814 F. Supp. 560, 574 (E.D. Mich. 1992) (recognizing validity of price suppression damages as in antitrust law). *See also* Helmac Prods. Corp. v. Roth (Plastics) Corp., 814 F. Supp. 581, 591 (E.D. Mich. 1993) (applying antitrust damages principles).

619. 35 F. Supp. 2d 597, 602-06 (S.D. Ohio 1999).

620. *Id.*

621. *Id.* at 603.

622. Wheeling-Pittsburgh Steel Corp. v. Mitsui & Co., Case No. C2-98-1122 (S.D. Ohio May 27, 1999) (unpublished opinion).

623. Wheeling-Pittsburgh Steel Corp. v. Mitsui & Co., 221 F.3d 924, 926-28 (6th Cir. 2000).

624. Goss Graphic Sys., Inc. v. Man Roland Druckmaschinen Aktiengesellschaft, 139 F. Supp. 2d 1040, 1048 (N.D. Iowa 2001).

Trade Representative believed the act "should be interpreted in the same manner as the predatory intent requirement of domestic price discrimination claims under the Robinson-Patman Act and predatory pricing claims under the Sherman Act."[625]

Despite the act's infrequent use, two arbitration panels of the World Trade Organization (WTO) in 2000 concluded that the 1916 Act violates the General Agreement on Tariffs and Trade (GATT).[626] Responding to complaints by the European Commission and Japan, the panels held that the 1916 Act impermissibly allows U.S. courts—instead of the U.S. government—to punish foreign companies for alleged dumping of manufactured products. The U.S. government filed an appeal of the decisions, but the WTO's Dispute Settlement Body adopted the WTO Appellate Body's acceptance of the panel decisions.[627]

2. *Use and Abuse of U.S. Trade Law*

A variety of trade laws, including those imposing customs duties to neutralize the effects of dumping[628] and subsidization[629] of imports, and imposing duties or quotas on imports that seriously injure a domestic industry,[630] may be invoked by U.S. companies. Where a trade law claim is baseless or a sham and is used primarily to erect barriers to competition from foreign-origin products, such a claim could be the basis of antitrust liability.[631]

One court of appeals also has held that the sale of imported products at prices below a level that could give rise to liability under the antidumping law could be an antitrust violation. In *Western Concrete Structures Co. v. Mitsui & Co. (U.S.A.)*,[632] the Ninth Circuit held that causes of action under Sections 1 and 2 of the Sherman Act as well as the Wilson Tariff Act were stated by a complaint alleging that a company had conspired with a supplier to import an input at a price below the lawfully established antidumping trigger price, thus allowing the defendant to underbid the plaintiff and other competitors.

---

625. *Id.* at 1048-50.
626. United States Anti-Dumping Act of 1916, Report No. 00-1257 (WTO Mar. 31, 2000); United States Anti-Dumping Act of 1916, Report No. 00-2118 (WTO May 29, 2000).
627. United States Anti-Dumping of 1916, Report No. 00-3369 (WTO Aug. 28, 2000) (Appellate Body report); United States Anti-Dumping Act of 1916, Report No. 00-3996 (WTO Oct. 2, 2000) (Dispute Settlement Body decision). Although the United States opposed the WTO's determinations, it subsequently participated in WTO-sponsored arbitration to determine a timetable for implementing legislative measures to address the WTO's concerns. United States Anti-Dumping Act of 1916, Report No. 01-0980 (WTO Feb. 28, 2001) (defining "reasonable period of time" for implementation as expiring July 26, 2001). A variety of proposals to amend the 1916 Act have been introduced in recent sessions of Congress. *See, e.g.*, S. 528 & H.R. 1201, 106th Cong. (1999); S. 1148, 104th Cong. (1995); S. 99 & 332, 103d Cong. (1993).
628. 19 U.S.C. §§ 1673-1673i (1994 & Supp. 1999).
629. *Id.* §§ 1671-1671h (1994 & Supp. 1999).
630. *Id.* §§ 2251-2254 (1994 & Supp. 1999).
631. *See* part C.2.a of Chapter XIII. The *International Antitrust Guidelines* set forth the DOJ's and FTC's concerns and caution that the settlement of such an action may pose even greater peril to competition. INTERNATIONAL ANTITRUST GUIDELINES, *supra* note 1, § 3.4 & Illustrative Example M; *see also Task Force Report on the Interface Between International Trade Law and Policy and Competition Law and Policy*, 56 ANTITRUST L.J. 461 (1987) (discussing the issues raised by the interplay of competition and trade law).
632. 760 F.2d 1013, 1016-18 (9th Cir. 1985).

CHAPTER XIII

GENERAL EXEMPTIONS AND IMMUNITIES

A. Introduction

In areas where federal, state, and local governments have adopted economic or social policies that conflict with free and open competition, Congress sometimes has resolved these conflicts by creating explicit statutory exemptions—often industry specific—from the antitrust laws.[1] In other instances, the federal courts have defined categories of exempt or immune conduct, or developed related doctrines of deference to government decision making, based upon the need to harmonize the mandates of the federal antitrust laws with local, state, or federal regulation. This chapter discusses judicially created exemptions and immunities as well as doctrines of deference applicable to conduct involving government action.

B. The State Action Doctrine

Under the "state action" doctrine, the Supreme Court has permitted state governments and certain private economic actors to show that the operation of a state regulatory scheme precludes the imposition of antitrust liability. Today, the state action doctrine primarily comes into play when conduct by state or private actors undertaken pursuant to a state regulatory program is challenged under the federal antitrust laws.

The foundation for state action jurisprudence is *Parker v. Brown,*[2] where the Supreme Court upheld, as an "act of government which the Sherman Act did not undertake to prohibit,"[3] a California program that regulated the marketing of raisins. Principles of federalism immunized such state action from antitrust attack. "In a dual system of government," the Court explained, "in which, under the Constitution, the states are sovereign, save only as Congress may constitutionally subtract from their authority, an unexpressed purpose to nullify a state's control over its officers and agents is not lightly to be attributed to Congress."[4] The Court found no such purpose underlying the antitrust laws.

---

1. These statutory exemptions are addressed in Chapter XIV.
2. 317 U.S. 341 (1943).
3. *Id.* at 352.
4. *Id.* at 351; *see also* City of Columbia v. Omni Outdoor Advert., Inc., 499 U.S. 365, 370 (1991) (stating that *Parker* relied on "principles of federalism and state sovereignty" to hold that "the Sherman Act did not apply to anticompetitive restraints imposed by the States 'as an act of government'").

1. State Action Analysis of Private Conduct— A Two-Part Framework

The Supreme Court in *California Retail Liquor Dealers Ass'n v. Midcal Aluminum, Inc.*[5] explained that there are "two standards for antitrust immunity" under the *Parker* doctrine: (1) the challenged restraint must be "one clearly articulated and affirmatively expressed as state policy," and (2) "the policy must be 'actively supervised' by the state itself."[6]

Midcal's two-pronged test has supplied the analytical framework within which subsequent decisions have determined the availability of immunity to private parties. Disputes concerning the application of the state action doctrine have focused upon satisfaction of the "clear articulation" and "active supervision" requirements, and the treatment of policies that emanate from public entities other than a state legislature.

a. THE CLEAR ARTICULATION REQUIREMENT

The requirement that the challenged conduct be undertaken "pursuant to a 'clearly articulated and affirmatively expressed state policy' to replace competition with regulation"[7] serves to ensure that the state has authorized departures from free market competition. In *Southern Motor Carriers Rate Conference, Inc. v. United States*,[8] the Supreme Court explained that "a state policy that expressly *permits*, but does not compel, anticompetitive conduct may be 'clearly articulated' within the meaning of *Midcal*."[9] In other words, the state need not explicitly authorize specific conduct for that conduct to satisfy the first prong of the *Midcal* test: "[I]f the State's intent to establish an anticompetitive regulatory program is clear, . . . the State's failure to describe the implementation of its policy in detail will not subject the program to the restraints of the federal antitrust laws."[10]

---

5.   445 U.S. 97 (1980).

6.   *Id.* at 105 (citation and footnote omitted).

7.   Hoover v. Ronwin, 466 U.S. 558, 569 (1984) (four-to-three decision) (citation omitted).

8.   471 U.S. 48 (1985).

9.   *Id.* at 61 (footnote omitted); *see also* Snake River Valley Elec. Ass'n v. PacificCorp., 238 F.3d 1189, 1192 (9th Cir. 2001) (rejecting plaintiff's argument that state action doctrine protects anticompetitive conduct only if compelled by state regulation).

10.   471 U.S. at 64-65 (citation omitted). *See also* Trigen-Oklahoma City Energy v. Oklahoma Gas & Elec. Co., 244 F.3d 1220, 1226 (10th Cir.) (sales by regulated electric utility entitled to state action immunity even though there was no specific, detailed legislative authorization), *cert. denied*, 122 S. Ct. 459 (2001); Omega Homes, Inc. v. City of Buffalo, 171 F.3d 755 (2d Cir. 1999) (general delegation of authority for urban renewal to municipality sufficient authorization for exclusive contracts); FTC v. Hospital Bd. of Dirs., 38 F.3d 1184, 1191-92 (11th Cir. 1994) (board's acquisition of another hospital was state action where Florida legislature had knowledge of market at time relevant statute enacted, and thus could foresee board's action); Yeager's Fuel, Inc. v. Pennsylvania Power & Light Co., 22 F.3d 1260, 1270 (3d Cir. 1994) (electric utility's program promoting builder's installation of electric heat pumps was expressly authorized through legislation and regulation by the Pennsylvania Utilities Commission); Sandy River Nursing Care v. Aetna Cas., 985 F.2d 1138, 1146-47 (1st Cir.) (private insurance companies immune from liability for alleged conspiracy to charge maximum rates authorized but not compelled by state), *cert. denied*, 510 U.S. 818 (1993); Nugget Hydroelectric, L.P. v. Pacific Gas & Elec. Co., 981 F.2d 429, 434-35 (9th Cir. 1992) (defendant utility's actions received immunity as a foreseeable result of state's policy), *cert. denied*, 508 U.S. 908 (1993). *Cf.* Surgical Care Ctr. v. Hospital Serv. Dist. No. 1, 171 F.3d 231 (5th Cir. 1999) (no clear articulation for exclusive contracts even though legislation authorized contracts and was to be construed broadly to rectify competitive

The requisite state authority need not always antedate the challenged activity. For example, the Ninth Circuit has concluded that the state's authorizing legislation can shield conduct that occurred well before the measure was enacted,[11] and the Eleventh Circuit has upheld immunity for conduct that, while not expressly sanctioned under preexisting state law, had been undertaken for years with the knowledge and approval of state regulators.[12] Private parties also may qualify for immunity by demonstrating reasonable reliance upon a state statute that the state's courts subsequently declare to be unconstitutional.[13] However, when a state deregulates an industry, it is not yet clear whether this change in state policy precludes granting immunity under the state action doctrine.[14]

b.   THE ACTIVE SUPERVISION REQUIREMENT

Midcal's active supervision requirement is intended to ensure that state action immunity "will shelter only the particular anticompetitive acts of private parties that, in the judgment of the State, actually further state regulatory policies."[15]   The

---

disadvantages between defendant and private hospitals); Hardy v. City Optical Inc., 39 F.3d 765, 768-70 (7th Cir. 1994) (state law requiring that optometrists be personally involved in the follow-up care of their patients was not a clearly articulated policy that would immunize optometrists who refused to furnish lens specifications to their patients); *Nugget Hydroelectric, L.P.*, 981 F.2d at 435 (no clear articulation of state policy for public utility's interconnection plan).

11.   *See, e.g.*, California Aviation, Inc. v. City of Santa Monica, 806 F.2d 905, 909 n.5 (9th Cir. 1986) ("[s]tatutes enacted after allegedly anticompetitive conduct [may] express[] pre-existing state policies to displace competition"); Mercy-Peninsula Ambulance, Inc. v. County of San Mateo, 791 F.2d 755, 757-58 (9th Cir. 1986) (giving effect to statutory intent to immunize conduct occurring before statute's enactment). *But see* Columbia Steel Casting Co. v. Portland Gen. Elec. Co., 103 F.3d 1446, 1461 (9th Cir. 1996) (retroactive amendment by Public Utilities Commission of a 1972 order cannot satisfy *Midcal* clear articulation test by declaring that it had intended to displace competition 20 years earlier).

12.   *See* TEC Cogeneration Inc. v. Florida Power & Light Co., 76 F.3d 1560, 1568 (11th Cir.) (requisite state authorization for particular private anticompetitive conduct could be inferred from the state's action after the original state authorization was given), *modified on other grounds*, 86 F.3d 1028 (11th Cir. 1996); Praxair, Inc. v. Florida Power & Light, 64 F.3d 609, 611 (11th Cir. 1995) (electric utilities' division of state was immune where division had existed with state's permission for 25 years after state's original order), *cert. denied*, 510 U.S. 1012 (1996). *But see Columbia Steel Casting Co.*, 103 F.3d at 1456 (rejecting state action immunity for electric utility that had been operating pursuant to a belief that a 1972 public utilities commission order authorized exclusive service territories; court held that the order was not sufficiently clear on the exclusivity issue to satisfy the first prong of the *Midcal* test); Tambone v. Memorial Hosp., 635 F. Supp. 508, 513-15 (N.D. Ill. 1986) (subsequent enactment of supervisory mechanism for peer review system could not be said to endorse policies implicit in statutes in effect at time of challenged conduct), *aff'd*, 825 F.2d 1132 (7th Cir. 1987).

13.   *See, e.g.*, Lease Lights, Inc. v. Public Serv. Co., 849 F.2d 1330, 1334 (10th Cir. 1988) ("The constitutional invalidity of the attempted state regulation is not an appropriate basis for disregarding state action immunity.... Rather, there should be a defense for those reasonably relying on the appearance of legality when a state agency's exercise of power is unauthorized.") (citations omitted), *cert. denied*, 488 U.S. 1019 (1989); Davis v. Southern Bell Tel. & Tel. Co., 755 F. Supp. 1532, 1542 (S.D. Fla. 1991) (immunity available if defendant reasonably relies upon what ultimately proves to be erroneous regulatory decision).

14.   *See* New York *ex rel.* Spitzer v. Saint Francis Hosp., 94 F. Supp. 2d 399, 409 (S.D.N.Y. 2000) (dictum) ("Were we to rule today that a change in state policy [i.e., hospital deregulation] has no impact on defendants' immunity, we would blunt the impact of the State's legislation.").

15.   Patrick v. Burget, 486 U.S. 94, 100-01 (1988). Most circuits have concluded that municipal supervision is sufficient to satisfy the active supervision requirement. *See, e.g.*, Tri-State Rubbish, Inc. v. Waste Mgmt., Inc., 998 F.2d 1073, 1079 (1st Cir. 1993); Tom Hudson & Assocs. v. City of

Supreme Court has emphasized that the active supervision prong of the *Midcal* test is closely related to the clear articulation prong in that "[b]oth are directed at ensuring that particular anticompetitive mechanisms operate because of a deliberate and intended state policy."[16]   Specifically, the purpose of the active supervision requirement "is to determine whether the State has exercised sufficient independent judgment and control so that the details of the rates or prices have been established as a product of deliberate state intervention, not simply by agreement among private parties."[17] The test is similar to causation inquiries in tort cases in that the analysis asks whether the state regulators have played a "substantial role in determining the specifics of the economic policy."[18]

Numerous state programs have failed to afford immunity due to a lack of supervision. For example, in *324 Liquor Corp. v. Duffy*,[19] the Supreme Court considered the implementation of a New York statute that promoted industry-wide resale price maintenance. The Court held that state action did not immunize the liquor wholesalers. A clearly articulated and affirmatively expressed state policy satisfied the *Midcal* test's first requirement, but there was no active state supervision of the prices set by the wholesalers. The state simply authorized the actions of the wholesalers.[20] Similarly, in *Patrick v. Burget*,[21] the Supreme Court ruled that state action immunity did not apply to Oregon physicians who served on hospital peer review committees. The Oregon peer review process failed to provide the requisite active supervision because the state's role was limited essentially to regulating peer review procedures. To meet the active supervision test, state officials must "have and exercise power to review particular anticompetitive acts of private parties and disapprove those that fail to accord with state policy."[22]

2. *Actions Taken by Subordinate Government Entities*

The predicate for state action immunity is a policy decision by the state to authorize the adoption of competition-suppressing practices. The decisions of only some instrumentalities can provide the requisite authority to restrict competition. It is well established that the state legislature and the state's highest court (when it performs nonjudicial functions) have independent authority to permit departures

---

Chula Vista, 746 F.2d 1370, 1374 (9th Cir. 1984), *cert. denied*, 472 U.S. 1028 (1985); Gold Cross Ambulance & Transfer v. City of Kansas City, 705 F.2d 1005, 1014-15 (8th Cir. 1983), *cert. denied*, 471 U.S. 1003 (1985). *But see* Riverview Invs., Inc. v. Ottawa Cmty. Improvement Corp., 774 F.2d 162, 163 (6th Cir. 1985).

16.   FTC v. Ticor Title Ins. Co., 504 U.S. 621, 636 (1992).

17.   *Id.* at 634.

18.   *Id.* at 635.

19.   479 U.S. 335 (1987).

20.   *Id.* at 344-45. A state's comprehensive regulation of liquor distribution within its boundaries would be entitled to immunity, but even a simple "minimum markup" statute might be enough. *Id.* at 344 n.6. *See also* TFWS, Inc. v. Schaefer, 242 F.3d 198, 210-11 (4th Cir. 2001) (following *324 Liquor Corp.* to invalidate Maryland's liquor pricing statute).

21.   486 U.S. 94 (1988).

22.   *Id.* at 101. *See also* Snake River Valley Elec. Ass'n v. PacificCorp., 238 F.3d 1189, 1194-95 (9th Cir. 2001) (state utility statute was not sufficiently self-policing that active supervision unnecessary); A.D. Bedell Wholesale Co. v. Philip Morris, Inc., 263 F.3d 239, 254-66 (3d Cir. 2001) (rejecting state action defense to multistate tobacco settlement agreement because monitoring by states did not cover pricing and other claimed anticompetitive actions).

from competition.[23]   State action immunity for other instrumentalities of the state varies depending upon the particular type of instrumentality under scrutiny.

a.   STATE EXECUTIVE DEPARTMENTS, AGENCIES, OR SPECIAL AUTHORITIES

The status of decisions by state executive departments, agencies, or special authorities was addressed in *Southern Motor Carriers Rate Conference, Inc. v. United States*.[24]   There, the Supreme Court rejected the argument that a state public service commission's mere approval of collective ratemaking could constitute state authorization of departures from competition.   "*Parker* immunity is available only when the challenged activity is undertaken pursuant to a clearly articulated policy of the State itself, such as a policy approved by a state legislature . . . or a State Supreme Court."[25]   The Court found that the requisite authorization existed in this instance by virtue of a state statute that permitted the state public service commission to set just and reasonable rates.[26]

---

23.   Southern Motor Carriers Rate Conf., Inc. v. United States, 471 U.S. 48, 62-63 (1985); Hoover v. Ronwin, 466 U.S. 558, 568 n.17 (1984) (suggesting that decisions by the governor of a state will be deemed actions of the state); *cf.* Midwest Constr. Co. v. Illinois Dep't of Labor, 684 F. Supp. 991, 994 (N.D. Ill.) (acts of state legislature and state's highest court "are deemed acts of state in its sovereign capacity; and therefore, are exempt from federal antitrust scrutiny"; however, "state agency, municipality, or other subdivision must show that it was acting pursuant to 'a clearly articulated state policy'"), *vacated in part on other grounds*, No. 88 C 957, 1988 WL 148605 (N.D. Ill. Dec. 30, 1988) (citing *Hoover*).

24.   471 U.S. 48 (1985).

25.   *Id.* at 62-63.

26.   *Id.* at 63, 65.   Lower court decisions have reached varied results in considering whether state executive departments or agencies should be accorded a status similar to a state legislature or the highest state court.   Some courts have concluded that state agencies are equivalent to the sovereign and require no additional authorization for their decisions to constitute state action. *See* Neo Gen Screening, Inc. v. New England Newborn Screen Program, 187 F.3d 24, 28-29 (1st Cir.) (the term "state" includes officials of the executive branch), *cert. denied*, 528 U.S. 1061 (1999); Charley's Taxi Radio Dispatch Corp. v. SIDA of Hawaii, Inc., 810 F.2d 869, 876 (9th Cir. 1987) (decisions of the Hawaii Department of Transportation and its director were "entitled to *Parker* immunity for actions taken pursuant to their constitutional or statutory authority, regardless of whether these particular actions or their anticompetitive effects were contemplated by the legislature"); Green v. State Bar, 27 F.3d 1083, 1087 (5th Cir. 1994) (counsel for state committee on unauthorized practice of law, created by Texas statute, is a state agency entitled to *Parker* immunity); Berger v. Cuyahoga County Bar Ass'n, 983 F.2d 718, 722 (6th Cir.) (enforcement of attorney disciplinary rules by state bar pursuant to a state constitutional grant of power was entitled to state action immunity), *cert. denied*, 508 U.S. 940 (1993); Ralph Rosenberg Court Reporters, Inc. v. Fazio, 811 F. Supp. 1432, 1440 (D. Haw. 1993) (state supreme court's rule on court reporters' pricing practices was state action for purposes of antitrust immunity); Board of Governors v. Helpingstine, 714 F. Supp. 167, 176 (M.D.N.C. 1989) (treating state university as sovereign for state action purposes; noting that university was created in the North Carolina constitution to carry out "state purposes").   A number of decisions have declined to equate certain state agencies and other public entities with the state, chiefly on the ground that the public instrumentality is not controlled by, or acts independently from, the state. *See, e.g.*, Washington State Elec. Contractors Ass'n v. Forrest, 930 F.2d 736, 737 (9th Cir.) (apprenticeship council that set minimum wage rates is not a "state agency" because "[t]he council has both public and private members, and the private members have their own agenda which may or may not be responsive to state labor policy"), *cert. denied*, 502 U.S. 968 (1991); Benton, Benton & Benton v. Louisiana Pub. Facilities Auth., 897 F.2d 198, 203 (5th Cir. 1990) (special purpose public authority is a public corporation eligible for state action immunity, but the public authority is not the state itself), *cert. denied*, 499 U.S. 975 (1991); Bolt v. Halifax Hosp. Med. Ctr., 891 F.2d 810, 824 (11th Cir.) (concluding that hospital district is not the state for *Parker* purposes), *cert. denied*, 495 U.S. 924 (1990); Hass v. Oregon State Bar, 883 F.2d

b.   CITIES, COUNTIES, AND MUNICIPALITIES

Political subdivisions such as cities, counties, municipalities, and townships are not entitled to the same immunity from the antitrust laws as a state itself. In *City of Lafayette v. Louisiana Power & Light Co.*,[27] a four-justice plurality concluded that "[c]ities are not themselves sovereign."[28] *Lafayette* held that "the *Parker* doctrine exempts only anticompetitive conduct engaged in as an act of government by the State as sovereign, or, by its subdivisions, pursuant to state policy to displace competition with regulation or monopoly public service."[29] The Court explained that a state's political subdivisions are entitled to immunity only when "the State authorized or directed a given municipality to act as it did."[30] When the state itself has not authorized an anticompetitive practice, "the State's subdivisions in exercising their delegated power must obey the antitrust laws."[31]

The Supreme Court further narrowed the exemption available to a state's political subdivisions in *Community Communications Co. v. City of Boulder*.[32] Although Colorado's home rule statute granted extensive powers to municipalities and may have authorized the city of Boulder to regulate cable television, the statute did not sufficiently articulate a state policy to confer immunity from the antitrust laws. The Court characterized the statute as an expression of "mere *neutrality*" and held that when a state "allows its municipalities to do as they please [it] can hardly be said to have 'contemplated' the specific anticompetitive actions for which municipal liability is sought."[33] The Court held that the general authority provided under Colorado's home rule statute did not immunize the city of Boulder from antitrust attack.[34]

1453, 1456 (9th Cir. 1989) (state bar was not the state but "merely an instrumentality of the state judiciary"), *cert. denied*, 494 U.S. 1081 (1990); FTC v. Monahan, 832 F.2d 688, 689 (1st Cir. 1987) (Board of Registration in Pharmacy deemed not to be the sovereign but a "subordinate governmental unit"), *cert. denied*, 485 U.S. 987 (1988); Cine 42nd St. Theater Corp. v. Nederlander Org., 790 F.2d 1032, 1044 (2d Cir. 1986) (urban development corporation is not the state for *Parker* purposes).

27.   435 U.S. 389 (1978).
28.   *Id.* at 412.
29.   *Id.* at 413.
30.   *Id.* at 414.
31.   *Id.* at 416; *see also* Commuter Transp. Sys. v. Hillsborough County Aviation Auth., 801 F.2d 1286, 1291 (11th Cir. 1986) (to defeat *Parker* defense, plaintiff "must show a conspiracy not authorized by state law and thus beyond protection of state action immunity"); Central Telecommuns. v. City of Jefferson City, 589 F. Supp. 85, 88-89 (W.D. Mo. 1984) (where actions exceed grant of authority, no immunity exists).
32.   455 U.S. 40 (1982).
33.   *Id.* at 55; *see also* Heitz Corp. v. City of New York, 1 F.3d 121, 128 (2d Cir. 1993) (city ordinance prohibiting rental car companies from imposing higher fees based on a person's residence is not immune under the state action doctrine because the state of New York had not granted New York City authority over car rental companies and the city could not rely on its general home rule powers), *cert. denied*, 510 U.S. 1111 (1994).
34.   Several courts have addressed the issue of whether a special purpose agency, such as one governing a particular business or profession, constitutes a political subdivision for state action purposes. *See* Earles v. State Bd. of Certified Pub. Accountants, 139 F.3d 1033, 1041 (5th Cir.) (Board of Certified Public Accountants was functionally equivalent to a municipality), *cert. denied*, 525 U.S. 982 (1998); Bankers Ins. Co. v. Florida Residential Prop. & Cas. Joint Underwriting Ass'n, 137 F.3d 1293, 1296-97 (11th Cir. 1998) (per curiam) (association of insurers entitled to be treated as a public subdivision); Ehlinger & Assocs. v. Louisiana Architects Ass'n,

Following *Boulder*, Congress passed the Local Government Antitrust Act of 1984 (LGAA)[35] that expressly bars antitrust damage actions against local governments. Protection is afforded to any "city, county, parish, town, township, village, or any other general function governmental unit established by State law"[36] as well as to "a school district, sanitary district, or any other special function governmental unit established by State law in one or more States."[37] The LGAA also precludes the recovery of antitrust damages from any local government official or employee "acting in an official capacity."[38] Private persons also enjoy immunity from damages under the act in specified circumstances. No claim against a private party can be "based on any official action directed by a local government, or official or employee thereof acting in an official capacity."[39] The LGAA, however, does not affect injunction actions against local governments,[40] nor does it preclude the recovery of attorneys' fees by plaintiffs who "substantially prevail."[41]

(1) Clear Articulation

In *Town of Hallie v. City of Eau Claire*,[42] the Supreme Court considered "how clearly a state policy must be articulated for a municipality to be able to establish that its anticompetitive activity constitutes state action."[43] Unincorporated townships

---

989 F. Supp. 775, 780-83 (E.D. La. 1998) (Louisiana Architects Selection Board entitled to state action immunity), *aff'd without op.*, 167 F.3d 537 (5th Cir. 1998).

35. 15 U.S.C. §§ 34-36 (2000).
36. *Id.* § 34(1)(A).
37. *Id.* § 34(1)(B). *See* Shapiro v. Middlesex County Mun. Joint Ins. Fund, 704 A.2d 1316 (N.J. Super. Ct. App. Div. 1998) (County Joint Insurance Fund was entitled to LGAA protection as a special function government unit established by state law).
38. 15 U.S.C. § 35(a). *See also* Thatcher Enters. v. Cache County Corp., 902 F.2d 1472, 1477-78 (10th Cir. 1990) (LGAA immunized public officials from damage liability for acts in their public capacity); Martin v. Stites, 31 F. Supp. 2d 926, 930 (D. Kan. 1998) (finding that officials had acted in their official capacity despite allegations that they had received gratuities and free services from those awarded contracts for county work); Lamminen v. City of Cloquet, 987 F. Supp. 723, 733-34 (D. Minn. 1997) (LGAA applied to city council members acting in their official capacity despite allegations that they ignored competitive bidding statutes), *aff'd without op.*, 162 F.3d 1164 (8th Cir. 1998); Command Force Sec., Inc. v. City of Portsmouth, 968 F. Supp. 1069, 1073 (E.D. Va. 1997) (affirmative grant of authority not required for public official to be immune); Forest Ambulance Serv. v. Mercy Ambulance, Inc., 952 F. Supp. 296, 301 (E.D. Va. 1997) (city council entitled to LGAA immunity).
39. 15 U.S.C. § 36(a). *Compare* Sandcrest Outpatient Servs. v. Cumberland County Hosp. Sys., 853 F.2d 1139, 1143-46 (4th Cir. 1988) (LGAA immunity held applicable to private hospital management company whose contract with county hospital's board of trustees permitted company to choose the hospital's suppliers, subject to review of individual decisions by the board of trustees), *and* Montauk-Caribbean Airways v. Hope, 784 F.2d 91, 94-95 (2d Cir.) (LGAA precludes damage suit against town board), *cert. denied*, 479 U.S. 872 (1986), *with* City Communs. v. City of Detroit, 660 F. Supp. 932, 935-36 (E.D. Mich. 1987) (LGAA immunity deemed inapplicable to private cable television firm).
40. *See, e.g.*, Wicker v. Union County Gen. Hosp., 673 F. Supp. 177, 186 (N.D. Miss. 1987) (equitable claims against a county hospital were allowed to proceed; damages claims were barred); Montauk-Caribbean Airways, Inc. v. Hope, 1985-2 Trade Cas. (CCH) ¶ 66,660, at 63,104 (E.D.N.Y. 1985) (equitable claim against public officials could proceed), *aff'd on other grounds*, 784 F.2d 91 (2d Cir.), *cert. denied*, 479 U.S. 872 (1986).
41. *See, e.g.*, Lancaster Cmty. Hosp. v. Antelope Valley Hosp. Dist., 940 F.2d 397, 404 n.14 (9th Cir. 1991), *cert. denied*, 502 U.S. 1094 (1992).
42. 471 U.S. 34 (1985).
43. *Id.* at 40.

located next to the City of Eau Claire alleged that the city had violated the Sherman Act by using "its monopoly over sewage treatment to gain an unlawful monopoly over the provision of sewage collection and transportation services."[44]   After examining the Wisconsin statutes that authorized cities to operate sewage systems, to determine the districts to be served, and to refuse service to unincorporated areas, the Supreme Court rejected the contention that without express mention of anticompetitive conduct there was no evidence of a state policy to displace competition. Instead, the challenged conduct was deemed "a foreseeable result of empowering the City to refuse to serve unannexed areas."[45]   The Court said "it is clear that anticompetitive effects logically would result from this broad authority to regulate."[46]

The "foreseeable result" test was reaffirmed in *City of Columbia v. Omni Outdoor Advertising, Inc.*[47] in a dispute over a city restriction on billboard advertising. The Supreme Court explained that the impact of the challenged zoning regulation was foreseeable because "[t]he very purpose of zoning regulation is to displace unfettered business freedom in a manner that regularly has the effect of preventing normal acts of competition, particularly on the part of new entrants."[48]   In recent years, courts increasingly have found that the clear articulation test as applied to political subdivisions is satisfied by general statutory authorizations to regulate.[49]

---

44.   *Id.* at 37.

45.   *Id.* at 42.

46.   *Id.*; *see also* Trigen-Oklahoma City Energy v. Oklahoma Gas & Elec. Co., 244 F.3d 1220, 1226 (10th Cir.) (electric utility subject to state regulation entitled to state action immunity), *cert. denied*, 122 S. Ct. 459 (2001); Crosby v. Hospital Auth., 93 F.3d 1515, 1525-32 (11th Cir. 1996) (hospital authority and members of peer review panel are instrumentalities of the state entitled to immunity under *Hallie* single-prong test), *cert. denied*, 510 U.S. 1116 (1997); Martin v. Memorial Hosp., 86 F.3d 1391, 1399 (5th Cir. 1996) (hospital subdivision of municipal corporation established under state law is immune from antitrust claims flowing from exclusive contract arrangement; suppression of competition was the foreseeable result of state regulatory program); A-1 Ambulance Serv. v. County of Monterey, 90 F.3d 333, 335 (9th Cir. 1996) (county's creating exclusive operating areas for emergency medical service providers contemplated by legislation); McCallum v. City of Athens, 976 F.2d 649, 652-55 (11th Cir. 1992) (city dividing up waterworks market territory was foreseeable considering state's enabling legislation); Fisichelli v. Town of Methuen, 956 F.2d 12, 15 (1st Cir. 1992) (municipal board's denial of an issuance of bonds for the construction of a shopping mall was "a logical and necessary outcome of authority to grant industrial revenue bonds") (citation omitted); Paragould Cablevision, Inc. v. City of Paragould, 930 F.2d 1310, 1313-14 (8th Cir.) (city's decision to enter cable television business in competition with existing private franchisee deemed "necessary and reasonable" consequence of state authorization for city to enter cable television business), *cert. denied*, 502 U.S. 963 (1991); Jacobs, Visconsi & Jacobs, Co. v. City of Lawrence, 927 F.2d 1111, 1121 (10th Cir. 1991) (statutory power to rezone has foreseeable anticompetitive effects); Todorov v. DCH Healthcare Auth., 921 F.2d 1438, 1461-62 (11th Cir. 1991) ("it is fair to say that Alabama's legislature could foresee that DCH, or hospitals like DCH, would rely upon the recommendations of its medical staff in processing applications for privileges to practice in DCH's medical departments").

47.   499 U.S. 365 (1991).

48.   *Id.* at 373.

49.   *See, e.g.*, Redwood Empire Life Support v. County of Sonoma, 190 F.3d 949 (9th Cir. 1999) (the clear articulation requirement was satisfied by a general statutory authorization conferring authority on counties to award exclusive contracts for emergency ambulance services), *cert. denied*, 528 U.S. 1116 (2000); Omega Homes, Inc. v. City of Buffalo, 171 F.3d 755, 757 (2d Cir.) (state legislature, in delegating general authority over urban renewal to municipalities, contemplated the displacement of market forces through exclusive contracts), *cert. denied*, 528 U.S. 874 (1999); North Star Steel Co. v. MidAmerican Energy Holdings Co., 184 F.3d 732 (8th Cir.) (legislation authorizing a state board to establish exclusive service territories in which

(2) Active Supervision

The Supreme Court's *Hallie* decision held that state supervision of local government activities was unnecessary. The Court explained that after "it is clear that the state authorization exists, there is no need to require the State to supervise actively the municipality's execution of what is a properly delegated function."[50] Thus, the conduct of local government entities is immune even though the state does not supervise the exercise of authority it has delegated.[51] Several lower courts have concluded that *Hallie*'s logic dictates the same result for state agencies and departments.[52] Courts continue to apply *Midcal*'s active supervision requirement, however, to private actors seeking immunity under the state action doctrine.[53]

3. Conspiracy, Bribery, or Commercial Activity

In *City of Columbia v. Omni Outdoor Advertising, Inc.*,[54] the Supreme Court considered whether *Parker* withheld immunity for anticompetitive conspiracies

---

specific electric utilities would provide the sole means of service to customers reflected a policy to displace competition in the market for generating electricity as well as service to retail customers), *cert. denied*, 528 U.S. 1046 (1999); Zimomra v. Alamo Rent-A-Car, 111 F.3d 1495, 1502-03 (10th Cir.) (reasonably foreseeable that county would require car rental companies to pay airport usage fees to ensure payment of bonds), *cert. denied*, 522 U.S. 948 (1997); Four T's Inc. v. Little Rock Airport Comm'n, 108 F.3d 909 (8th Cir. 1997) (legislation granting commission unlimited authority to operate airport reflected a state policy to displace competition). *But see* Surgical Care Ctr. v. Hospital Serv. Dist. No. 1, 171 F.3d 231 (5th Cir.) (en banc) (a general statutory authorization, which did not reflect an intent to displace competition, did not satisfy the clear articulation requirement), *cert. denied*, 528 U.S. 964 (1999).

50. *Hallie*, 471 U.S. at 47.
51. *See also* Tri-State Rubbish, Inc. v. Waste Mgmt., Inc., 998 F.2d 1073, 1079 (1st Cir. 1993) (nonprofit corporation created by municipalities to construct and operate a municipal waste facility was not subject to active supervision prong); Askew v. DCH Reg'l Health Care Auth., 995 F.2d 1033, 1037-38 (11th Cir.) (public health care authority held not subject to active supervision requirement), *cert. denied*, 510 U.S. 1012 (1993); Porter Testing Lab. v. Board of Regents, 993 F.2d 768, 772 (10th Cir.) (active supervision requirement did not apply to state colleges), *cert. denied*, 510 U.S. 932 (1993).
52. *See, e.g.*, *Zimomra*, 111 F.3d 1445 (active supervision prong was inapplicable because city and county were the effective decision makers); Benton, Benton & Benton v. Louisiana Pub. Facilities Auth., 897 F.2d 198, 203-04 (5th Cir. 1990) (conduct of special purpose public corporation need not be actively supervised by state), *cert. denied*, 499 U.S. 875 (1991); Hass v. Oregon State Bar, 883 F.2d 1453, 1460-61 (9th Cir. 1989) (state bar association deemed to be state agency and need not be supervised separately), *cert. denied*, 494 U.S. 1081 (1990); Ambulance Serv. of Reno, Inc. v. Nevada Ambulance Servs., Inc., 819 F.2d 910, 913 (9th Cir. 1987) (regional emergency medical services corporation created by the state for a county board of health deemed similar to a municipality; supervision not required); Interface Group v. Massachusetts Port Auth., 816 F.2d 9, 13 (1st Cir. 1987) (state port authority treated as similar to municipality; supervision not required); Cine 42nd St. Theater Corp. v. Nederlander Org., 790 F.2d 1032, 1047 (2d Cir. 1986) (because urban development corporation was political subdivision of state, active state supervision not required).
53. *See* New York *ex rel.* Spitzer v. Saint Francis Hosp., 94 F. Supp. 2d 399, 411 (S.D.N.Y. 2000) ("The rationale behind requiring the second prong of the *Midcal* test for private actors while municipalities and other subsections of the State do not have to meet this test is that 'where a private party is engaging in the anticompetitive activity, there is a real danger that he is acting to further his own interests, rather that the governmental interests of the State.'") (quoting *Hallie*, 471 U.S. at 47).
54. 499 U.S. 365 (1991).

between private actors and public officials. The Court ruled that "[t]here is no such conspiracy exception" to the state action doctrine.[55] The Court expressed concern that adopting a "public interest" standard would engage judges in "the sort of deconstruction of the governmental process and probing of the official 'intent' that we have consistently sought to avoid."[56]

The Court also rejected, in dicta, the argument that state action immunity should be denied to government action procured by means of bribery or other unlawful behavior. The Court gave two reasons for this position. First, the existence of unlawful, corrupt conduct does not establish that governmental action ultimately taken is not in the public interest.[57] Second, the Sherman Act was not designed to ensure that public officials abide by "principles of good government."[58]

Although it repudiated a conspiracy exception to the state action doctrine, *Omni* suggested that immunity might not extend to public intervention when the state acts not as a regulator but instead behaves as a commercial entity. The Court observed: "We reiterate that, with the possible market participant exception, *any* action that qualifies as state action is '*ipso facto* . . . exempt from the operation of the antitrust laws.'"[59] With little elaboration, the Court interpreted *Parker* to mean that "immunity does not necessarily obtain where the State acts not in a regulatory capacity but as a commercial participant in a given market."[60] The significance of this brief mention of a possible "commercial" or "market participant" exception is uncertain.[61] Courts addressing the issue subsequent to *Omni* have rejected a market participant exception to the state action doctrine.[62]

---

55.   *Id.* at 374.

56.   *Id.* (footnote omitted).

57.   *Id.* at 378.

58.   *Id.*; *see also* Trigen-Oklahoma City Energy v. Oklahoma Gas & Elec. Co., 244 F.3d 1220, 1227 (10th Cir.) (defendant's "lavish entertainment" of customers did not waive state action immunity), *cert. denied*, 122 S. Ct. 459 (2001); Hedgecock v. Blackwell, 1995-1 Trade Cas. (CCH) ¶ 70,960, at 74,374-75 (9th Cir. 1995) (unpublished opinion) (motive of actors was irrelevant where water district's anticompetitive actions were foreseeable result of legislative delegation of authority); Sandy River Nursing Care v. Aetna Cas., 985 F.2d 1138, 1144 (1st Cir.) (rejecting argument that state action immunity does not apply because legislation was allegedly motivated by economic boycott of workers' compensation insurance market), *cert. denied*, 510 U.S. 818 (1993); Nugget Hydroelectric, L.P. v. Pacific Gas & Elec. Co., 981 F.2d 429, 434 (9th Cir. 1992) (defendant utility's force majeure policy conformed from an objective standpoint with a clearly articulated state standard, making motivation irrelevant), *cert. denied*, 508 U.S. 908 (1993); Buckley Constr., Inc. v. Shawnee Civic & Cultural Dev. Auth., 933 F.2d 853, 856 (10th Cir. 1991) ("Once a municipality establishes that it is entitled to state action immunity, the subjective motivation of the actors involved in the decisionmaking process should not come into play."); Consolidated Television Cable Serv. v. City of Frankfort, 857 F.2d 354, 362 (6th Cir. 1988) ("the sovereignty of state action must be respected without reference to the subjective motivations of persons implementing the state's policy"), *cert. denied*, 489 U.S. 1082 (1989).

59.   499 U.S. at 379 (citation omitted).

60.   *Id.* at 374-75.

61.   *Compare* Paragould Cablevision, Inc. v. City of Paragould, 930 F.2d 1310, 1312-13 (8th Cir.) (*Omni*'s "market participant exception is merely a suggestion and is not a rule of law"), *cert. denied*, 502 U.S. 963 (1991), *with* Genentech, Inc. v. Eli Lilly & Co., 998 F.2d 931, 948 (Fed. Cir. 1993) (stating, in dicta, that "the policies underlying *Parker* do not extend to circumstances where the state acts not in a legislative/regulatory capacity but as a 'commercial participant in a given market'") (quoting *Omni*, 499 U.S. at 374-75), *cert. denied*, 510 U.S. 1140 (1994).

62.   *See, e.g.*, *Paragould Cablevision*, 930 F.2d at 1312-13; Helen Brett Enters. v. New Orleans Metro. Convention & Visitors Bureau, 1996-2 Trade Cas. (CCH) ¶ 71,529, at 77,800 (E.D. La. 1996).

C. Solicitation of Government Action

Competitors sometimes petition government entities to restrict the ability of their rivals to compete in the marketplace. When successful, these entreaties can have significant anticompetitive effects, particularly when firms persuade government authorities to exclude competitors from commercial opportunities. Even though such petitioning can have anticompetitive results, courts have conferred "petitioning immunity" upon a wide range of activities designed to induce government bodies to restrain competition.

1. Basic Framework and Evolution of Noerr Immunity

The foundation for antitrust immunity for efforts to solicit competition-restricting government action is the Supreme Court's decision in *Eastern Railroad Presidents Conference v. Noerr Motor Freight, Inc.*[63] *Noerr* established the groundwork for judicial efforts to define the circumstances in which private efforts to elicit rivalry-suppressing government action are immune from antitrust challenge.

a.   EFFORTS TO INFLUENCE LEGISLATIVE PROCESSES

In *Noerr*, the Court considered the application of the Sherman Act to a publicity and lobbying effort conducted by a group of railroads to obtain legislation to restrict competition from the trucking industry. The railroads carried out their campaign against the truckers through deceptive and unethical means,[64] and their sole aim in pursuing legislation was to destroy the competitive capability of the truckers.[65] Because "the railroads were making a genuine effort to influence legislation and law enforcement practices," the Court held that their conduct enjoyed absolute antitrust immunity,[66] regardless of any anticompetitive motive that prompted the petitioning activities.[67]

The Court in *Noerr* did not specify how much its refusal to impose liability stemmed from its assessment of the aims of the Sherman Act or its solicitude for

---

63.   365 U.S. 127 (1961).

64.   *Id.* at 145.

65.   *Id.* at 129.

66.   *Id.* at 144.

67.   *Id.* at 129. Subsequent decisions have reiterated *Noerr*'s observation that the defendant's anticompetitive motive does not invalidate efforts to elicit government intervention. In *United Mine Workers v. Pennington*, 381 U.S. 657, 670 (1965), the Court stated that "*Noerr* shields from the Sherman Act a concerted effort to influence public officials regardless of intent or purpose." *See also* City of Columbia v. Omni Outdoor Advert., Inc., 499 U.S. 365, 380 (1991) ("[t]hat a private party's political motives are selfish is irrelevant"); Davric Maine Corp. v. Rancourt, 216 F.3d 143, 147-48 (1st Cir. 2000) (efforts to "bury" rival through lobbying state legislature for action adverse to rival's business protected by *Noerr*); *In re* Burlington N., Inc., 822 F.2d 518, 526 (5th Cir. 1987) (regardless of defendant's motives, filing of lawsuit was protected activity), *cert. denied*, 484 U.S. 1007 (1988); Razorback Ready Mix Concrete Co. v. Weaver, 761 F.2d 484, 487-88 (8th Cir. 1985) (petitioner's "invocation of adjudicative process to press legitimate claims is protected even though its purpose in doing so is to eliminate competition"; concluding that it is "immaterial" that petitioner's motives "may have been selfish or altruistic or mixed"); Greenwood Utils. Comm'n v. Mississippi Power Co., 751 F.2d 1484, 1499 (5th Cir. 1985) ("Nor does the possibility that the companies had selfish or anticompetitive ends in mind when seeking to influence the government deprive them of *Noerr-Pennington* protection.").

First Amendment rights.[68]   The Court reasoned that to condemn the lobbying campaign "would impute to the Sherman Act a purpose to regulate, not business activity, but political activity, a purpose which would have no basis whatever in the legislative history of that Act."[69]   At the same time, the Court stated that to hold otherwise would hinder the process by which constituents convey opinions to government officials and "would raise important constitutional questions."[70]   This ambiguity has proven significant where differing conceptions about *Noerr*'s constitutional and nonconstitutional bases have affected judicial opinions about the applicability of *Noerr* immunity.[71]

As it shielded genuine efforts to shape government policy, the Court in *Noerr* cautioned that immunity would not extend to all activities seemingly designed to influence government behavior. The Court said "[t]here may be situations in which a publicity campaign, ostensibly directed toward influencing governmental action, is a mere sham to cover what is actually nothing more than an attempt to interfere directly with the business relationships of a competitor and the application of the Sherman Act would be justified."[72]   Subsequent cases have demonstrated that the bounds of *Noerr* immunity depend heavily upon how courts interpret this "sham" exception.[73]

---

68. Since *Noerr* immunity is based in part on an interpretation of the Sherman Act, the Tenth Circuit has concluded that applying it outside the antitrust context requires an independent application of the First Amendment. Cardtoons, L.C. v. Major League Baseball Players Ass'n, 208 F.3d 885, 888-91 (10th Cir. 2000). Other courts, however, have applied *Noerr* to state law and other nonantitrust claims. *See, e.g.*, Hydranautics v. FilmTec, 204 F.3d 880, 887 (9th Cir. 2000) (applying *Noerr* to patent and state law claims); Bristol Myers Squibb Co. v. IVAX Corp., 77 F. Supp. 2d 606, 616 (D.N.J. 2000) ("the [Third] Circuit recently . . . held, with the D.C. and Ninth Circuits, that state law claims . . . are barred by *Noerr-Pennington* immunity) (citing Cheminor Drugs, Ltd. v. Ethyl Corp., 168 F.3d 119, 128-29 (3d Cir. 1999)), *aff'd in part and vacated in part*, 246 F.3d 1368 (Fed. Cir. 2001).

69. 365 U.S. at 137.

70. *Id.* at 137-38.

71. *See, e.g.*, Whelan v. Abell, 48 F.3d 1247, 1253-54 (D.C. Cir. 1995) (describing Supreme Court's varying explanations of the basis for *Noerr* immunity). This lack of clarity has created a conflict among the lower courts when determining whether *Noerr* immunity applies to the petitioning of foreign governments. *Compare* Coastal States Mktg., Inc. v. Hunt, 694 F.2d 1358, 1364 (5th Cir. 1983) (*Noerr* deemed applicable to filing of foreign lawsuits because *Noerr* "reflects not only First Amendment concerns but also a limit on the scope of the Sherman Act"), *with* United States v. AMAX Inc., 1977-1 Trade Cas. (CCH) ¶ 61,467, at 71,799 (N.D. Ill. 1977) (*Noerr* immunity no protection for attempts to influence Government of Canada), Occidental Petroleum Corp. v. Buttes Gas & Oil Co., 331 F. Supp. 92, 107-08 (C.D. Cal. 1971) (declining to extend *Noerr* to petitioning of foreign governments because concern that Sherman Act would "trespass upon the First Amendment right to petition" was limited with foreign governments), *aff'd per curiam on other grounds*, 461 F.2d 1261 (9th Cir.), *cert. denied*, 409 U.S. 950 (1972), *and* Bulkferts Inc. v. Salatin Inc., 574 F. Supp. 6, 9 (S.D.N.Y. 1983) (same). *Cf.* Laker Airways v. Pan Am. World Airways, 604 F. Supp. 280, 287-94 & n.20 (D.D.C. 1984) (First Amendment does not prevent enjoining a party from petitioning a foreign government, but declining to issue such an injunction on comity grounds). In the *Antitrust Enforcement Guidelines for International Operations*, the Department of Justice and the Federal Trade Commission stated that their policy is to "apply [the doctrine] in the same manner to the petitioning of foreign governments and the U.S. Government." U.S. DEP'T OF JUSTICE & FEDERAL TRADE COMM'N, ANTITRUST ENFORCEMENT GUIDELINES FOR INTERNATIONAL OPERATIONS (1995), *reprinted in* 4 Trade Reg. Rep. (CCH) ¶ 13,107 *and* Appendix D of this treatise.

72. 365 U.S. at 144.

73. *See* part C.2.a of this chapter.

b. EFFORTS TO INFLUENCE ADMINISTRATIVE PROCESSES

In *United Mine Workers v. Pennington*,[74] the Supreme Court extended *Noerr* to attempts to influence government administrative processes. In *Pennington*, large coal mine operators and the union collaborated to persuade the Secretary of Labor to establish higher minimum wages for workers supplying coal to the Tennessee Valley Authority.[75] The Court held this concerted activity to be exempt from the Sherman Act, stating: "Joint efforts to influence public officials do not violate the antitrust laws even though intended to eliminate competition. Such conduct is not illegal, either standing alone or as part of a broader scheme itself violative of the Sherman Act."[76] The Court reached this conclusion even though there was considerable evidence that, in addition to seeking government intervention, the union and large coal operators had engaged in a number of anticompetitive acts that did not involve petitioning activity.[77]

c. EFFORTS TO INFLUENCE ADJUDICATORY PROCESSES

In *California Motor Transport Co. v. Trucking Unlimited*,[78] the Supreme Court held that the *Noerr* doctrine applies to attempts to influence judicial and other adjudicatory actions.[79] However, because the plaintiffs contended that the defendants, without regard to the merits of their claims, initiated court and administrative actions to defeat the plaintiffs' applications to obtain and transfer motor operating rights,[80] the Court went on to find that the conduct alleged would fall outside *Noerr*'s protection as a sham.[81] The Court said that "a pattern of baseless, repetitive claims . . . effectively barring respondents from access to the agencies and

---

74. 381 U.S. 657 (1965). *See also* Kottle v. Northwest Kidney Ctrs., 146 F.3d 1056 (9th Cir. 1998) (applying *Noerr* to certificate of need administrative proceedings), *cert. denied*, 525 U.S. 1140 (1999); Bristol-Myers Squibb Co. v. IVAX Corp., 77 F. Supp. 2d 606, 611 (D.N.J. 2000) (noting that petitioning activity can take many forms), *aff'd in part and vacated in part*, 246 F.3d 1368 (Fed. Cir. 2001).
75. 381 U.S. at 660-61.
76. *Id.* at 670.
77. *Id.* at 660.
78. 404 U.S. 508 (1972).
79. Subsequent lower court decisions have extended *Noerr* to petitioning designed to elicit intervention by law enforcement bodies. *See, e.g.*, King v. Idaho Funeral Serv. Ass'n, 862 F.2d 744, 745 (9th Cir. 1988) (*Noerr* immunizes trade association's efforts to alert state licensing agency that firm was retailing caskets illegally); Ottensmeyer v. Chesapeake & Potomac Tel. Co., 756 F.2d 986, 993 (4th Cir. 1985) (*Noerr* immunizes defendant's cooperation with police where such action yields anticompetitive result so long as actions were not taken purely for purpose of harassment); Forro Precision, Inc. v. IBM, 673 F.2d 1045, 1059-60 (9th Cir. 1982) (*Noerr* immunizes reports to police about alleged theft).

   There is a split among the courts as to whether *Noerr* protection extends to nonparties who fund a litigation from behind the scenes. *Compare In re* Burlington N., Inc., 822 F.2d 518, 531 & n.11 (5th Cir. 1987) (defendant that lacked standing to bring lawsuit which was the basis for antitrust claim could not claim *Noerr* protection for help to party to that lawsuit), *with* Baltimore Scrap Corp. v. David J. Joseph Co., 237 F.3d 394, 400-01 (4th Cir.) (upholding *Noerr* protection because "[f]unding of litigation by a non-party can be petitioning to the same extent that filing a lawsuit itself is petitioning"), *cert. denied*, 121 S. Ct. 2521 (2001).
80. 404 U.S. at 509.
81. *See* discussion of sham litigation in part C.2.a of this chapter.

courts" would not qualify for immunity under the "umbrella of 'political expression.'"[82]

Whether *Noerr* immunity extends to prelitigation threats was the subject of the Tenth Circuit decision in *Cardtoons, L.C. v. Major League Baseball Players Ass'n.*[83] In *Cardtoons*, the defendant had sent letters to the plaintiff threatening litigation if the plaintiff continued to produce trading cards that featured caricatures of active major league baseball players. The plaintiff filed a declaratory relief action, and the district court entered judgment in its favor on the grounds that the cards were protected by the First Amendment. The plaintiff then pursued remaining state law damage claims against the defendant alleging, among other things, that the prelitigation letters were defamatory. The defendant asserted that the letters were protected by *Noerr*. Although the district court had granted *Noerr* immunity and a Tenth Circuit panel previously had affirmed that decision,[84] the Tenth Circuit reversed on rehearing en banc. The en banc court reasoned that "[a] letter from one private party to another private party simply does not implicate the right to petition, regardless of what the letter threatens."[85] The court thus refused to extend *Noerr* immunity to a letter threatening litigation "because there was no petition of the government."[86]

---

82. 404 U.S. at 513; *see also* Otter Tail Power Co. v. United States, 410 U.S. 366, 380 (1973) (*California Motor Transport* "held that the principle of *Noerr* may also apply to the use of administrative or judicial processes where the purpose to suppress competition is evidenced by repetitive lawsuits carrying the hallmark of insubstantial claims and thus is within the 'mere sham' exception"); Primetime 24 Joint Venture v. NBC, 219 F.3d 92, 100-01 (2d Cir. 2000) (allegation that television networks and affiliates brought numerous baseless challenges against signal re-transmitter stated an antitrust claim).

83. 208 F.3d 885 (10th Cir.) (en banc), *cert. denied*, 531 U.S. 873 (2000).

84. 182 F.3d 1132 (10th Cir. 1999). The Tenth Circuit cited four other circuit courts as holding that *Noerr* protected prelitigation threats. Glass Equip. Dev., Inc. v. Besten, Inc., 174 F.3d 1337 (Fed. Cir. 1999); McGuire Oil Co. v. Mapco, Inc., 958 F.2d 1552 (11th Cir. 1992); CVD, Inc. v. Raytheon Co., 769 F.2d 842 (1st Cir. 1985); Coastal States Mktg., Inc. v. Hunt, 694 F.2d 1358 (5th Cir. 1983). It noted, however, that three decisions predated *Professional Real Estate Investors, Inc. v. Columbia Pictures Indus.*, 508 U.S. 49 (1993), and had failed to provide a uniform standard as to when a threat to litigate is worthy of *Noerr* protection. *See also* Gardner v. Clark, 101 F. Supp. 2d 468, 473 (N.D. Miss. 2000) (*Noerr* protects activities "directly attributable to litigation"); Miller Pipeline Corp. v. British Gas PLC, 69 F. Supp. 2d 1129 (S.D. Ind. 1999) (extending *Noerr* immunity to prelitigation activities such as notice of infringement letters); Barq's, Inc. v. Barq's Beverages, Inc., 677 F. Supp. 449, 453 (E.D. La. 1987).

85. 208 F.3d at 891.

86. *Id. See also* Unique Coupons, Inc. v. Northfield Corp., No. 99 C 7445, 2000 U.S. Dist. LEXIS 6767, at *7-8 (N.D. Ill. May 16, 2000) (recognizing ambiguity of applicable case law in light of *Cardtoons;* refusing to grant *Noerr* immunity because plaintiff "does not seek to impose liability for any action incident to or attendant future litigation, but for misrepresentations as to the content and import of past litigation"); Alexander Binzel Corp. v. Nu-Tecsys Corp., 2000-1 Trade Cas. (CCH) ¶ 72,906, at 87,701 (N.D. Ill. 2000) (refusing to apply *Noerr* doctrine to provide immunity to a letter that contained statements the jury found literally false and that went beyond the legal and factual bases of the lawsuit); Republic Tobacco, L.P. v. North Atl. Trading Co., 2000-1 Trade Cas. (CCH) ¶ 72,782, at 86,744 n.2 (N.D. Ill. 1999) ("[I]t is not clear that [defendant's] communications [regarding false threats of litigation] were so connected with intended litigation at the time they were made that any litigation privilege applies. Not all of the statements were included in defendant's later judicial pleadings, and the third parties to whom they were addressed have not been sued.").

Courts have applied *Noerr*'s protections to settlement efforts. *See* Hise v. Philip Morris, Inc., 208 F.3d 226 (10th Cir.) (unpublished opinion) (litigation settlements are within the ambit of *Noerr* immunity so that defendants' actions in negotiating and entering the multistate tobacco

d.   EFFORTS TO INFLUENCE PRIVATE ORGANIZATIONS

Noerr's protection does not extend to efforts to influence private organizations, at least by economically interested parties.   In *Allied Tube & Conduit Corp. v. Indian Head, Inc.*,[87] the Supreme Court considered the standard-setting activities of the National Fire Protection Association (NFPA), a private trade association that sets performance standards for electrical products.   The NFPA standards are often incorporated into municipal fire codes.   The Court ruled that *Noerr* did not protect attempts to influence the association's standard-setting activities.[88]   The Court explained that the antitrust significance of efforts to suppress competition by influencing government bodies "depends . . . on the source, context, and nature of the anticompetitive restraint at issue."[89]   The "source" element of the Court's test focused upon whether the trade restraint flowed from governmental or private action.   The injury in *Allied Tube* resulted from the plaintiff's exclusion from the NFPA's model code and not from any government body's adoption of the code.   The Court concluded that the "relevant context is thus the standard-setting process of a private association," an entity whose conduct ordinarily is subject to antitrust review.[90]

The Court also considered and rejected the argument that the NFPA should be treated as a "quasi-legislature" for purposes of *Noerr* analysis.[91]   Although it found that the challenged restriction resulted from "private action,"[92] the Court said that *Noerr* immunity nonetheless might be available if the trade association's refusal to

---

settlement agreement are immunized from suit under the *Noerr* doctrine), *cert. denied*, 531 U.S. 959 (2000); *see also* A.D. Bedell Wholesale Co. v. Philip Morris, Inc., 263 F.3d 239, 250-54 (3d Cir. 2001) (same); Forces Action Project L.L.C. v. California, No. C 99-0607 MJJ, 2000 U.S. Dist. LEXIS 163, at *25-27 (N.D. Cal. Jan. 5, 2000) (same), *aff'd in part and rev'd in part*, 2001 U.S. App. LEXIS 18676 (9th Cir. Aug. 15, 2001) (unpublished opinion).

87.   486 U.S. 492 (1988).

88.   *Id.* at 509-10.

89.   *Id.* at 499.

90.   *Id.* at 500; *see also* Massachusetts Sch. of Law v. American Bar Ass'n, 107 F.3d 1026 (3d Cir.) (court distinguished *Allied Tube* and held that efforts of the American Bar Association (ABA) to persuade states to prohibit graduates of unaccredited law schools from taking bar examination were entitled to *Noerr* immunity and any stigma on unaccredited schools was incidental to that petitioning activity), *cert. denied*, 522 U.S. 907 (1997); Schachar v. American Acad. of Ophthalmology, Inc., 870 F.2d 397, 399-400 (7th Cir. 1989) (rejecting antitrust liability where professional association provided information but did not constrain others to adopt its views); Clamp-All Corp. v. Cast Iron Soil Pipe Inst., 851 F.2d 478, 488-89 (1st Cir. 1988) (declining to find antitrust liability for efforts to petition private standard-setting entity; plaintiff failed to prove that defendant's conduct constituted "a significant abuse of [the entity's] procedural standards or practices"), *cert. denied*, 488 U.S. 1007 (1989).

In *Sessions Tank Liners, Inc. v. Joor Mfg.*, 17 F.3d 295, 299 (9th Cir.), *cert denied*, 513 U.S. 813 (1994), the Ninth Circuit held that the defendant's lobbying activities were immune under *Noerr* despite allegations that it had procured change in a standard-setting organization's model fire code through deliberate misrepresentations because, unlike in *Allied Tube*, there was no proof of stigma against the plaintiff's tank lining procedure in jurisdictions that did not enforce the model code's tank lining ban. The Ninth Circuit concluded that the only harm to plaintiff was that which flowed directly from governmental action in adopting the organization's model code, a harm for which private actors could not be liable under *Noerr*.

91.   486 U.S. at 501-02; *see also* Preferred Physicians Mut. Risk Retention Group v. Cuomo, 865 F. Supp. 1057, 1072 (S.D.N.Y. 1994) (National Association of Insurance Commissioners is not a governmental body, and thus efforts to influence it do not come within *Noerr*'s protections), *vacated in part*, 85 F.3d 913 (2d Cir. 1996).

92.   486 U.S. at 501-02.

endorse the use of the plaintiff's conduit was "incidental to a valid effort to influence governmental action."[93] Even though the restriction stemmed from private action, *Noerr* immunity would apply if the nature of the conduct was chiefly political rather than commercial.[94]

The Supreme Court, moreover, has drawn a distinction between collaborative arrangements undertaken to achieve noneconomic ends and boycotts to serve the economic interests of the participants. *NAACP v. Claiborne Hardware Co.*[95] involved a state tort law challenge to an agreement by black citizens to deny their patronage to white merchants to induce government officials and business leaders to meet a list of demands for equality and racial justice.[96] The Court ruled that the First Amendment shielded the boycott against the tort claim, even though the participants anticipated and intended that the boycott would impose economic harm upon the merchants. The Court suggested that it might have reached a different result if the boycott's participants had been economic competitors.[97] The Court emphasized the political distinction in *FTC v. Superior Court Trial Lawyers Ass'n*,[98] where it evaluated the defendant lawyers' concerted efforts to induce the District of Columbia to raise the hourly fees paid for representing indigent criminal defendants. The Court distinguished the trial lawyers from the *Claiborne Hardware* defendants:

> *Claiborne Hardware* is not applicable to a boycott conducted by business competitors who "stand to profit financially from a lessening of competition in the boycotted market." No matter how altruistic the motives of respondents may have been, it is undisputed that their immediate objective was to increase the price that they would be paid for their services. Such an economic boycott is well within the category that was expressly distinguished in the *Claiborne Hardware* opinion itself.[99]

2. *Qualifications to* Noerr *Immunity*

Courts have devoted substantial effort to defining the limits of *Noerr*'s protection. As a general matter, decisions have tended to confer immunity more expansively when the government body is performing nonadjudicatory functions and less expansively when the government body is executing adjudicatory responsibilities.[100]

---

93. *Id.* at 502.
94. The Court acknowledged problems that might arise in attempting to distinguish conduct that is primarily political from conduct that is primarily commercial. 486 U.S. at 507-08 n.10. The Court noted that the activities in question in *Noerr* had taken place in the "open political arena, where partisanship is the hallmark of decisionmaking." *Id.* at 506.
95. 458 U.S. 886 (1982).
96. The Mississippi Supreme Court previously had dismissed an antitrust cause of action. Thus, only the state tort claim was before the U.S. Supreme Court. *Id.* at 894.
97. 458 U.S. at 915 (boycott had been motivated neither by "parochial economic interests" nor "organized for economic ends").
98. 493 U.S. 411 (1990).
99. *Id.* at 427 (quoting *Allied Tube*, 486 U.S. at 508); *see also* Sandy River Nursing Care v. Aetna Cas., 985 F.2d 1138, 1142-43 (1st Cir.) (*Noerr* immunity denied to alleged boycott of Maine's workers' compensation insurance market by insurance companies seeking to force legislation increasing workers' compensation premiums), *cert. denied*, 510 U.S. 818 (1993).
100. In *California Motor Transport Co. v. Trucking Unlimited*, 404 U.S. 508 (1972), the Court observed that misrepresentations "condoned in the political arena, are not immunized when used in the adjudicatory process." *Id.* at 513; *accord* Clipper Express v. Rocky Mountain Motor Tariff Bureau, 690 F.2d 1240, 1261 (9th Cir. 1982) (misrepresentations to adjudicatory bodies treated

Specific, recurring issues relating to the scope and applicability of *Noerr* protection are identified and treated in this section.

a. SHAM EXCEPTION

Decisions invoking the sham exception announced in *Noerr* and *California Motor Transport* to withhold immunity for petitioning activity ordinarily have concluded that the defendants' conduct was not designed to secure the benefits of government intervention but rather to impose burdens upon rivals, regardless of the outcome, by forcing them to defend themselves or to incur substantial costs to gain access to the processes of government. A finding of sham conduct by itself ordinarily does not suffice to establish antitrust liability, as courts usually require the plaintiff to satisfy all elements of the asserted theory of antitrust liability.[101]

Courts have applied the sham exception in a variety of circumstances. Sham exception arguments have succeeded most frequently where the challenged conduct involves the alleged misuse of adjudicatory processes.[102] Sham behavior has been found where the defendant filed baseless requests that a government body deny a rival's petition for regulatory approval,[103] commenced administrative proceedings to impede a rival's access to government processes,[104] or instituted administrative proceedings to inflict substantial costs of defense upon a rival.[105]

---

more severely because adjudicatory tribunals, unlike legislatures, depend more heavily on parties to verify the accuracy of information provided), *cert. denied*, 459 U.S. 1227 (1983).

101. *See, e.g.*, Neumann v. Reinforced Earth Co., 786 F.2d 424, 428 (D.C. Cir.) ("even if the litigation was a sham . . . [plaintiff] must still prove the other elements of an illegal attempt to monopolize"), *cert. denied*, 479 U.S. 851 (1986).

102. *See, e.g.*, Hufsmith v. Weaver, 817 F.2d 455, 459 (8th Cir. 1987) (filing baseless state law claim for tortious interference with contractual relations); CVD, Inc. v. Raytheon Co., 769 F.2d 842, 851 (1st Cir. 1985) (despite knowing it lacked a valid claim, defendant filed trade secret infringement suit to impede new entrant), *cert. denied*, 475 U.S. 1016 (1986); Handgards, Inc. v. Ethicon, Inc., 743 F.2d 1282, 1294 (9th Cir. 1984) (filing suit "without probable cause and in complete disregard of the law to interfere with the business relationships of a competitor"), *cert. denied*, 469 U.S. 1190 (1985); Winterland Concessions Co. v. Trela, 735 F.2d 257, 263 (7th Cir. 1984) (strategically filing and withdrawing "John Doe" injunction actions); Energy Conservation, Inc. v. Heliodyne, Inc., 698 F.2d 386, 389 (9th Cir. 1983) (filing lawsuit to focus adverse media attention upon rival); Alexander v. National Farmers Org., 687 F.2d 1173, 1200 (8th Cir. 1982) (mailing copies of complaint to rival's customers), *cert. denied*, 461 U.S. 937 (1983).

103. *See, e.g.*, Litton Sys. v. AT&T, 700 F.2d 785, 811-12 (2d Cir. 1983) (despite having no realistic prospect for success, defendant sought to have regulatory agency deny plaintiff permission to interconnect equipment with defendant's telephone network), *cert. denied*, 464 U.S. 1073 (1984); *Clipper Exxpress*, 690 F.2d at 1253-54 (without regard to the merits of its actions, defendant consistently and automatically opposed rival's rate filings with administrative body); Knology, Inc. v. Insight Communs. Co., 2001-2 Trade Cas. (CCH) ¶ 73,375 (W.D. Ky. 2001) (refusing to dismiss antitrust claim when allegedly baseless court action automatically stayed the grant of a cable franchise to a competitor).

104. *See, e.g.*, Hospital Bldg. Co. v. Trustees of Rex Hosp., 691 F.2d 678, 687 (4th Cir. 1982) (defendants participated in federal and state regulatory processes to prevent rivals from gaining access to government bodies), *cert. denied*, 464 U.S. 904 (1983); City of Kirkwood v. Union Elec. Co., 671 F.2d 1173, 1181 (8th Cir. 1982) (same), *cert. denied*, 459 U.S. 1170 (1983).

105. *See, e.g.*, Greenwood Utils. Comm'n v. Mississippi Power Co., 751 F.2d 1484, 1498 n.9 (5th Cir. 1985) (commencement of regulatory proceedings intended to impose burdens upon competitor rather than elicit favorable government action); MCI Communs. Corp. v. AT&T, 708 F.2d 1081, 1156 (7th Cir.) (forcing plaintiff to participate in proceedings before a multiplicity of forums in order to establish its rights), *cert. denied*, 464 U.S. 891 (1983); Landmarks Holding Corp. v.

In *City of Columbia v. Omni Outdoor Advertising, Inc.*,[106] the Supreme Court was invited to apply the sham exception in a legislative context to a situation in which the plaintiff alleged that a competitor and the city of Columbia, South Carolina, had restricted the plaintiff's ability to compete in the market for outdoor advertising by enacting a zoning ordinance that impeded the plaintiff's efforts to construct new billboards.[107] The Court concluded that the defendants' behavior did not fall within *Noerr*'s sham exception. The Court explained that the sham exception "encompasses situations in which persons use the governmental *process*—as opposed to the *outcome* of that process—as an anticompetitive weapon"[108] and reiterated *Allied Tube*'s holding that sham conduct "involves a defendant whose activities are 'not genuinely aimed at procuring favorable government action'" at all.[109] The *Omni* defendants clearly had desired to exclude the plaintiff, but they "sought to do so not through the very process of lobbying, or of causing the city council to consider zoning measures, but rather through the ultimate *product* of that lobbying and consideration, viz., the zoning ordinances."[110] The sham exception applied only to "a context in which the conspirators' participation in the governmental process was itself claimed to be a 'sham,' employed as a means of imposing cost and delay."[111]

In *Professional Real Estate Investors, Inc. v. Columbia Pictures Industries* (*PRE*),[112] the Supreme Court clarified the proper criteria to evaluate sham conduct in the context of adjudicatory activity. There, the Court was confronted with a choice between subjective and objective standards for evaluating allegedly sham litigation. The Court set out a two-part definition of sham litigation: First, the lawsuit must be "objectively baseless."[113] In other words, if an objective, reasonable litigant could realistically expect a favorable outcome of the suit on the merits, then the suit is entitled to *Noerr* immunity and any antitrust claim based on the sham exception must fail.[114] If, on the other hand, the challenged suit is objectively baseless, the court must then examine the subjective motivation of the party bringing the questioned suit to determine whether the baseless lawsuit constitutes an attempt to interfere directly with a competitor's business by using the governmental process, rather than the outcome of that process, as an anticompetitive weapon.[115]

Bermant, 664 F.2d 891, 896 (2d Cir. 1981) (defendant repeatedly commenced proceedings despite knowledge that it lacked standing).

106.   *Id.* 499 U.S. 365 (1991).

107.   *Id.* at 368.

108.   *Id.* at 380.

109.   *Id.* (quoting Allied Tube & Conduit Corp. v. Indian Head, Inc., 486 U.S. 492, 500 n.4 (1988)).

110.   *Id.* at 381.

111.   *Id.* at 381-82. The Court explained that to extend the sham exception "to a context in which the regulatory process is being invoked genuinely, and not in a 'sham' fashion, would produce precisely the conversion of antitrust law into regulation of the political process that we have sought to avoid." *Id.* at 382.

112.   508 U.S. 49 (1993).

113.   *Id.* at 60-61.

114.   *Id.* at 63. The Court implied that the standard for determining whether a violation of Federal Rule of Civil Procedure 11 has occurred might assist in the determination of whether there is an objective basis for asserting an allegedly sham claim. *Id.* at 65. However, Justice Souter, in his concurring opinion, explained that the Court's reference to Rule 11 was not intended "to signal the importation [into the objective test of sham petitioning] of every jot and tittle of the law of attorney sanctions." *Id.* at 67.

115.   *Id.* In rejecting a purely subjective test, *PRE* requires a finding of objective baselessness before the subjective motivation of the plaintiff is relevant. Consequently, the *PRE* Court denied discovery

Elaborating upon the objective prong of its definition, the Court explained that the analysis under the objective part of its test was akin to determining probable cause in the common law tort of malicious prosecution, which requires "a 'reasonabl[e] belie[f] that there is a chance that [a] claim may be held valid upon adjudication.'"[116] Thus, under the Court's test, a sham lawsuit cannot exist where the plaintiff has probable cause to sue. Although *PRE* resolved the evaluative criteria for determining "sham" in the context of a single allegedly sham lawsuit, lower courts continue to try to determine whether and to what extent *PRE*'s definition will be applied in other allegedly "sham" contexts.[117]

The Second and Ninth Circuits have rejected the application of *PRE* to the repetitive filings of lawsuits, limiting it to a single or small number of such suits. In *USS-POSCO Industries v. Contra Costa County Building & Construction Trades Council*,[118] the Ninth Circuit resolved what it perceived as a conflict between *California Motor Transport* and *PRE* by reading them as applying to different situations. According to the Ninth Circuit, *PRE*'s two-step test is used "to assess whether a single action constitutes sham petitioning."[119] *California Motor Transport*, the Ninth Circuit noted, "deals with the case where the defendant is accused of bringing a whole series of legal proceedings."[120] Similarly, in *Prime Time 24 Joint Venture v. NBC*,[121] the Second Circuit held that *PRE* applies to determine whether a single lawsuit is a sham, and not to repetitive filings. If there are repetitive filings, the test is prospective, not retroactive, and is whether the filings are part of a pattern or practice.[122]

---

into subjective intent and affirmed summary judgment for the defendants because the threshold objective portion of the sham test had not been satisfied. *Id.* at 65-66. *See also* Bayou Fleet, Inc. v. Alexander, 26 F. Supp. 2d 894, 897 (E.D. La. 1998) (sham exception inapplicable because defendant "was not interested in the [governmental] process itself as a weapon, but in actually obtaining the agency decisions that would effectively close Bayou Fleet's sand pit operation").

116. 508 U.S. at 62-63 (quoting Hubbard v. Beatty & Hyde, Inc., 178 N.E.2d 485, 488 (Mass. 1961)).

117. In *Associated Bodywork & Massage Prof'ls v. American Massage Therapy Ass'n*, 897 F. Supp. 1116 (N.D. Ill. 1995), the court rejected a claim of sham petitioning relating to efforts by a not-for-profit massage therapy association to petition state legislatures for the enactment of certification standards for the industry. The court held that the "narrow" sham exception applies, in the legislative context, "only if Defendant had no reasonable expectation of obtaining the favorable legislation." *Id.* at 1120. The court further rejected the argument that the sham exception applies where the defendant used "improper means" (in this case, libel) when recommending the challenged legislation. *Id.* This case did not cite or discuss the *PRE* decision. *See also* Cheminor Drugs, Ltd. v. Ethyl Corp. 168 F.3d 119 (3d Cir. 1999) (applying *PRE* to proceedings before International Trade Commission); Greater Rockford Energy & Tech. Corp. v. Shell Oil Co., 998 F.2d 391, 397 (7th Cir. 1993) (successful lobbying efforts are not a sham and are protected), *cert. denied*, 510 U.S. 1111 (1994).

118. 31 F.3d 800 (9th Cir. 1994). *Accord* Kottle v. Northwest Kidney Ctrs., 146 F.3d 1056, 1059-60 (9th Cir. 1998), *cert. denied*, 525 U.S. 1140 (1999).

119. 31 F.3d at 810-11. *But see* Glass Equip. Dev., Inc. v. Besten, Inc., 174 F.3d 1337 (Fed. Cir. 1999) (applying *PRE* test to two lawsuits); Music Ctr. S.N.C. DiLuciano Pisoni & C. v. Prestini Musical Instrument Corp., 874 F. Supp. 543, 549 (E.D.N.Y. 1995) (applying *PRE*'s two-part test to allegations that antitrust defendant had filed multiple sham antidumping petitions with the Department of Commerce).

120. 31 F.3d at 811.

121. 219 F.3d 92 (2d Cir. 2000).

122. *Id.* at 101. *But see* Travelers Express Co. v. American Express Integrated Payment Sys., 80 F. Supp. 2d 1033, 1042-43 (D. Minn. 1999) (refusing to follow Ninth Circuit because the potential immunity of a patentee under the antitrust laws is a question of Federal Circuit law; defendant had

The scope of the sham exception in patent cases was addressed by the Federal Circuit in *Nobelpharma AB v. Implant Innovations, Inc.*[123] There, the Federal Circuit held that a patentee who brings an infringement action can be stripped of antitrust immunity for the anticompetitive effects of that suit in two ways: (1) by proof that the patent was obtained through knowing and willful fraud within the meaning of *Walker Process Equipment, Inc. v. Food Machinery & Chemical Corp.*,[124] or (2) by proof that the patent infringement action is a sham under *Noerr* and its progeny.[125] In *Nobelpharma*, the jury found in favor of a Section 2 counterclaimant based upon the plaintiff's attempt to enforce a patent obtained through fraud on the patent office.[126] Affirming the jury verdict, the Federal Circuit rejected the plaintiff's argument that the counterclaimant alleging fraud was required to satisfy the two-part test of *PRE* before the plaintiff patent holder lost its right to enforce the patent under *Noerr*.[127] Instead, the Federal Circuit found that "*PRE* and *Walker Process* provide alternative grounds on which a patentee may be stripped of its immunity from the antitrust laws; both theories may be applied to the same conduct."[128]

In *Independent Service Organizations Antitrust Litigation*,[129] independent servicers of Xerox copiers sued Xerox under the antitrust laws for its policies intended to restrict their access to Xerox parts. Xerox counterclaimed for patent and copyright infringement. The district court granted summary judgment for Xerox on the grounds that its refusal to sell or license its patented invention could not violate the antitrust laws regardless of Xerox's intent or the competitive effects of its decision.[130] The Federal Circuit again held that *PRE* and *Walker Process* were separate and independent doctrines with respect to patent enforcement.[131] Since there was no claim of fraud on the patent office, or that Xerox's enforcement of its patents was a sham, neither *Walker Process* nor *PRE* justified denying Xerox *Noerr* protection. The Federal Circuit concluded that unless it can be shown that the infringement suit is objectively baseless, an antitrust defendant's subjective motivation is immaterial.[132]

b.   SUPPLYING FALSE INFORMATION

Noerr litigation sometimes involves claims that private parties have distorted government decision making by providing public officials with false or misleading information. *Noerr* held that a deceptive publicity campaign designed to persuade

---

failed under the *PRE* test to present evidence that created a genuine issue of material fact that any of a series of lawsuits involving the patented technology at issue were objectively baseless).
123. 141 F.3d 1059 (Fed. Cir. 1998).
124. 382 U.S. 172 (1965). *Walker Process* holds that a plaintiff who knowingly enforces a patent obtained by fraud on the patent office is subject to liability under the Sherman Act if the other requirements for antitrust liability are met. *Id.* at 178.
125. 141 F.3d at 1068.
126. *Id.* at 1063.
127. *Id.* at 1071.
128. *Id.*
129. 203 F.3d 1322 (Fed. Cir. 2000), *cert. denied*, 531 U.S. 1143 (2001).
130. CSU, L.L.C. v. Xerox Corp., 23 F. Supp. 2d 1242 (D. Kan. 1999), *aff'd*, 203 F.3d 1322 (Fed. Cir. 2000), *cert. denied*, 531 U.S. 1143 (2001).
131. 203 F.3d at 1326.
132. *Id. See also* Hartford Life Ins. Co. v. Variable Annuity Life Ins. Co., 964 F. Supp. 624, 628 (D. Conn. 1997) (dismissing counterclaim asserting sham trademark enforcement activity).

legislators and executive branch officials was immune from antitrust challenge.[133] *California Motor Transport* later observed that "[m]isrepresentations, condoned in the political arena, are not immunized when used in the adjudicatory process."[134] In *Allied Tube & Conduit Corp. v. Indian Head, Inc.*,[135] the Supreme Court also observed in dicta that "unethical and deceptive practices can constitute abuses of administrative or judicial processes that may result in antitrust violations."[136]

In *PRE*, the Supreme Court noted that the question presented by the case did not require the Court to decide "whether and, if so, to what extent *Noerr* permits the imposition of antitrust liability for a litigant's fraud or other misrepresentations."[137] At least one court of appeals, however, has concluded that *PRE*'s test applies even in the face of allegations of abuse of the litigation process, at least in the absence of a fraud or misrepresentation that "deprive the litigation of its legitimacy."[138]

Lower court decisions have emphasized the forum in which petitioning occurs in determining the antitrust significance of false statements. Misrepresentations designed to influence government bodies in performing what can be characterized as

---

133. 365 U.S. at 140-41 ("Insofar as [the Sherman] Act sets up a code of ethics at all, it is a code that condemns trade restraints, not political activity, and, . . . a publicity campaign to influence governmental activity falls clearly into the category of political activity.").

134. 404 U.S. at 513. In *Walker Process Equip., Inc. v. Food Mach. & Chem. Corp.*, 382 U.S. 172, 174 (1965), the Supreme Court held that the enforcement of a patent obtained through fraud on the Patent Office may violate § 2 of the Sherman Act. *Walker Process* contained no mention of the Court's earlier decisions in *Noerr* and *Pennington*, but it has provided a basis upon which some courts have concluded that providing spurious information to adjudicatory bodies can be actionable as monopolization or attempted monopolization. *See, e.g.*, Clipper Exxpress v. Rocky Mountain Motor Tariff Bureau, 690 F.2d 1240, 1261 (9th Cir. 1982) ("We hold that the fraudulent furnishing of false information to an agency in connection with an adjudicatory proceeding can be the basis for antitrust liability, if the requisite predatory intent is present and the other elements of an antitrust claim are proven."), *cert. denied*, 459 U.S. 1227 (1983); Woods Exploration & Producing Co. v. Aluminum Co. of Am., 438 F.2d 1286, 1298 (5th Cir. 1971) (providing false information to state regulatory body performing adjudicatory tasks was "abuse of the administrative process" and did not warrant antitrust immunity), *cert. denied*, 404 U.S. 1047 (1972).

135. 486 U.S. 492 (1988).

136. *Id.* at 499-500 (citations omitted); *cf.* City of Columbia v. Omni Outdoor Advert., Inc., 499 U.S. 365, 383-84 (1991) (noting that in *Noerr*, "where the private party 'deliberately deceived the public and public officials' in its successful lobbying campaign, we said that 'deception, reprehensible as it is, can be of no consequence so far as the Sherman Act is concerned'") (quoting *Noerr*, 365 U.S. at 145).

137. 508 U.S. at 61-62 n.6 (citing *Walker Process Equip.*, 382 U.S. at 176-77). The Federal Circuit, however, has concluded that *PRE* established a separate and independent basis for antitrust liability apart from *Walker Process* claims. Nobelpharma v. Implant Innovations, Inc., 141 F.3d 1059, 1068 (Fed Cir. 1998). Also, in *Hydranautics v. Filmtec Corp.*, 70 F.3d 533, 538 (9th Cir. 1995), the Ninth Circuit held that a patent infringement action will be considered to lack probable cause and be deemed sham where the patent holder obtained the patent by "intentional fraud" as opposed to "technical fraud." *But see* Hydranautics v. Filmtec Corp., 67 F.3d 931, 938-39 (Fed. Cir. 1995) (holding in parallel suit that patent infringement lawsuit was not objectively baseless), *cert. denied*, 519 U.S. 814 (1996).

138. Liberty Lake Invs., Inc. v. Magnuson, 12 F.3d 155, 159 (9th Cir. 1993), *cert. denied*, 513 U.S. 818 (1994). The Ninth Circuit distinguished *Walker Process*, to which the Court in *PRE* referred in its footnote 6, as applying to situations where the fraud—such as fraudulently obtaining a patent—went to the core of the litigation's legitimacy. *Id.* at 159; *see also Hydranautics*, 70 F.3d at 537 (same); Baltimore Scrap Corp. v. The David J. Joseph Co., 81 F. Supp. 2d 602, 617 (D. Md. 2000) (adopting *Liberty Lake*'s "core of a lawsuit's legitimacy" standard), *aff'd*, 237 F.3d 394, 401-04 (4th Cir.), *cert. denied*, 121 S. Ct. 2521 (2001).

"legislative functions" tend to qualify for *Noerr* immunity.[139] By contrast, efforts to mislead officials performing adjudicatory functions in many instances have been denied *Noerr*'s protection[140] and may remain subject to antitrust scrutiny.[141] Where *Noerr* immunity is denied, plaintiffs nonetheless may be required to show that the false information materially affected the government body's decision making and caused the injury at issue.[142]

The Third Circuit has applied *Noerr* immunity to willful misrepresentations to a state certifying agency, reasoning that the antitrust laws simply do not reach such conduct. In *Armstrong Surgical Center, Inc. v. Armstrong County*,[143] the defendants had successfully persuaded the state Department of Health to deny the plaintiff's application for a certificate of need to build a new medical facility. The plaintiff contended, however, that the sham exception to *Noerr* immunity applied because the defendants had made willful misrepresentations to the Department of Health. The Third Circuit emphasized that because the plaintiff did not claim that the petitioning conduct was for any purpose but to obtain favorable government action, the

---

139. *See, e.g.*, Sessions Tank Liners, Inc. v. Joor Mfg., 17 F.3d 295, 301 (9th Cir.) (private parties are not liable for injury brought about by government adoption of model fire code that banned plaintiff's tank lining procedure even though government action occurred as a result of misrepresentations), *cert. denied*, 513 U.S. 813 (1994); Lawline v. American Bar Ass'n, 956 F.2d 1378, 1383 (7th Cir. 1992) (ABA is immune under *Noerr* for adopting model rule prohibiting lawyers from assisting nonlawyers in the unauthorized practice of law and urging adoption of model rule by state's supreme court), *cert. denied*, 510 U.S. 992 (1993); Aurora Cable Communs. v. Jones Intercable, Inc., 720 F. Supp. 600, 602 (W.D. Mich. 1989) ("misrepresentation in the *political* arena, as distinct from the judicial arena, is outside the scope of the Sherman Act") (citations omitted).

140. *See* Clipper Exxpress v. Rocky Mountain Motor Tariff Bureau, 690 F.2d 1240, 1261 (9th Cir. 1982) ("In the adjudicatory sphere, . . . information supplied by the parties is relied on as accurate for decision making and dispute resolving. The supplying of fraudulent information thus threatens the fair and impartial functioning of these agencies and does not deserve immunity from the antitrust laws."), *cert. denied*, 459 U.S. 1227 (1983). *See also* Kottle v. Northwest Kidney Ctrs., 146 F.3d 1056, 1060–62 (9th Cir. 1998) (different standards for applicability of sham exception depending on whether legislative or judicial proceeding; sham exception broader for behavior in adjudicatory proceedings, including certificate of need determinations), *cert. denied*, 525 U.S. 1140 (1999); St. Joseph's Hosp. v. Hospital Corp. of Am., 795 F.2d 948, 955 (11th Cir. 1986) ("When a governmental agency such as [the State Health Planning Agency] is passing on specific certificate applications it is acting judicially. Misrepresentations under these circumstances do not enjoy *Noerr* immunity."); DeLoach v. Philip Morris Cos., 2001-2 Trade Cas. (CCH) ¶ 73,409 (M.D.N.C. 2001) (*Noerr* protects defendants' efforts to change tobacco policy but not submission of false information to agency setting tobacco quotas).

141. To the extent *Noerr* rests on the First Amendment, such denial of *Noerr* protection appears to be in keeping with Supreme Court decisions denying First Amendment protection to deliberate misrepresentations of fact. *See, e.g.*, Hustler Magazine, Inc. v. Falwell, 485 U.S. 46, 52 (1988) ("[f]alse statements of fact are particularly valueless; they interfere with the truth-seeking function of the marketplace of ideas").

142. *Compare* Cheminor Drugs Ltd. v. Ethyl Corp., 168 F.3d 119, 124-27 (3d Cir. 1999) (defendant's alleged false representations were not material and court determined that Ethyl's petition was not objectively baseless without regard to allegedly misrepresented facts), *and* Interstate Properties v. Pyramid Co., 586 F. Supp. 1160, 1162-63 (S.D.N.Y. 1984) (misrepresentation to environmental agency that is not considered material to agency's decision making and eventual conclusion deemed insufficient to constitute sham conduct), *with* Clipper Exxpress, 690 F.2d at 1261 (even if false information did not mislead government agency, "the fraudulent furnishing of false information to an agency in connection with an adjudicatory proceeding can be the basis for antitrust liability").

143. 185 F.3d 154 (3d Cir. 1999).

subjective prong of *PRE* could not be satisfied.[144] Since all of the plaintiff's injuries resulted from the department action denying the certificate of need, the court concluded that no liability could be imposed on a private party who induced this state action by means of concerted anticompetitive activity. As to the alleged misrepresentations, the Third Circuit concluded that the antitrust laws, as opposed to other laws, do not and should not reach conduct such as bribery, corruption, or misrepresentations.[145] The court reasoned that while such conduct may be reprehensible and unlawful, it is for reasons having nothing to do with antitrust policies; therefore, the sham exception did not apply.

c. CONSPIRACIES WITH PUBLIC OFFICIALS

In *City of Columbia v. Omni Outdoor Advertising, Inc.*,[146] the Supreme Court refused to recognize an exception to *Noerr* immunity "when government officials conspire with a private party to employ government action as a means of stifling competition."[147] For the same reasons that it rejected a conspiracy exception to state action immunity, the Court held that no such exception was available under *Noerr*.[148] The Court explained that "[i]t would be unlikely that any effort to influence a legislative action could succeed unless one or more members of the legislative body became . . . 'co-conspirators' in *some* sense with the private party urging such action."[149]

Omni thus disavowed a conspiracy exception to *Noerr*.[150] Moreover, the *Omni* Court suggested in dicta that *Noerr* immunity would extend to government intervention obtained by means of bribery or other illicit agreements between private actors and public officials.[151] *Omni* intimated that other regulatory mechanisms (such as antibribery statutes or conflict of interest prohibitions) are superior to the antitrust laws as tools for policing behavior in the political marketplace.[152] *Omni* thus

---

144. *Id.* at 158 & n.2 (citing *PRE*, 508 U.S. at 61). *See also* Bayou Fleet, Inc. v. Alexander, 68 F. Supp. 2d 734 (E.D. La. 1999) (where defendants used administrative and legislative channels to try to put competitor out of business, actions were not a sham because defendants genuinely sought to achieve the outcome of the processes they used), *aff'd*, 234 F.3d 852 (5th Cir. 2000).

145. 185 F.3d at 161-62. *See also* Bristol Myers Squibb Co. v. IVAX Corp., 77 F. Supp. 2d 606, 612-13 (D.N.J. 2000) (concluding that a variety of tortious conduct did not defeat immunity), *aff'd in part and vacated in part*, 246 F.3d 1368 (Fed. Cir. 2001).

146. 499 U.S. 365 (1991).

147. *Id.* at 382. Some lower court decisions previously had recognized a conspiracy exception to *Noerr*. *See, e.g.*, Affiliated Capital Corp. v. City of Houston, 735 F.2d 1555, 1566-68 (5th Cir. 1984) (en banc), *cert. denied*, 474 U.S. 1053 (1986); Duke & Co. v. Foerster, 521 F.2d 1277, 1282 (3d Cir. 1975).

148. 499 U.S. at 383.

149. *Id.* (quoting Metro Cable Co. v. CATV of Rockford, Inc., 516 F.2d 220, 230 (7th Cir. 1975)).

150. *Id.*; *see also* Municipal Utils. Bd. v. Alabama Power Co., 934 F.2d 1493, 1505 (11th Cir. 1991) ("[T]he Supreme Court has recently held that there is no 'public co-conspirator' exception to the *Noerr-Pennington* doctrine. *Omni, supra.* Accordingly, the Cities' claim under this theory is now foreclosed."); Omega Homes, Inc. v. City of Buffalo, 4 F. Supp. 2d 187, 193-94 (W.D.N.Y. 1998) *aff'd*, 171 F.3d 755 (2d Cir.) (rejecting the conspiracy exception), *cert. denied*, 528 U.S. 874 (1999).

151. 499 U.S. at 378.

152. *Id.* at 378-79, 383.

contradicts, albeit in dicta, the Court's earlier suggestion in *Allied Tube* that bribery might not be entitled to *Noerr* protection.[153]

d.   GOVERNMENT ACTING IN COMMERCIAL CAPACITY

Some courts have recognized a commercial exception to *Noerr* immunity where the government body acts in a purely commercial or proprietary capacity. Although it rejected a conspiracy exception to the *Noerr* and state action immunity doctrines, *Omni* mentioned in dicta that state action immunity might be denied if the government acts "as a commercial participant in a given market."[154] Because the Court used essentially the same reasoning in evaluating a proposed conspiracy exception under the *Noerr* and state action doctrines, *Omni* may suggest a commercial participant exception to *Noerr* immunity.[155]

Lower courts have taken divergent paths in considering a commercial exception to *Noerr*. A seminal decision recognizing a commercial exception is *George R. Whitten, Jr., Inc. v. Paddock Pool Builders, Inc.*[156] In *Whitten*, the First Circuit addressed the defendant's efforts to persuade government purchasing agencies to specify its products for procurement under competitive bidding statutes. The court concluded that "the immunity for efforts to influence public officials in the enforcement of laws does not extend to efforts to sell products to public officials acting under competitive bidding statutes."[157]

Other courts have found *Noerr* immunity even when the governmental activity is commercial.[158] Representative of this view is *Greenwood Utilities Commission v.*

---

153. In *Allied Tube*, the Court said "one could imagine situations where the most effective means of influencing government officials is bribery, and we have never suggested that that kind of attempt to influence the government merits protection." 486 U.S. at 504; *see also* California Motor Transport Co. v. Trucking Unlimited, 404 U.S. 508, 513 (1972) (noting existence of "forms of illegal and reprehensible practice which may corrupt the administrative or judicial processes and which may result in antitrust violations").

154. 499 U.S. at 374-75; *see also id.* at 379 (describing "the possible market participant exception" to state action immunity).

155. In *Allied Tube*, the Court did not directly address the possibility of treating commercial activities differently. However, its "source, context, and nature" formula might be interpreted to withhold immunity when the government acts essentially as a commercial entrepreneur. 486 U.S. at 507.

156. 424 F.2d 25, 33 (1st Cir.), *cert. denied*, 400 U.S. 850 (1970).

157. *Id.*; *accord* Ticor Title Ins. Co. v. FTC, 998 F.2d 1129, 1138 (3d Cir. 1993) (*Noerr* immunity unavailable where "collective rate setting efforts can 'more aptly be characterized as commercial activity with a political impact' . . . than as political activity with a commercial impact") (citation omitted), *cert. denied*, 510 U.S. 1190 (1994); Todorov v. DCH Healthcare Auth., 921 F.2d 1438, 1447 (11th Cir. 1991) (declining to apply *Noerr* where the lobbying activity "is more economic than political in nature"); Federal Prescription Serv. v. American Pharm. Ass'n, 663 F.2d 253, 263 (D.C. Cir. 1981), *cert. denied*, 455 U.S. 928 (1982), Israel v. Baxter Lab., 466 F.2d 272, 275-77 (D.C. Cir. 1972) (using *Whitten* framework to evaluate drug producers' efforts to persuade Food and Drug Administration to bar plaintiff's products from market). *But see* United States v. Johns Manville Corp., 259 F. Supp. 440, 452-53 (E.D. Pa. 1966) (immunity recognized for efforts to influence public officials to draft procurement specifications so narrowly that rivals are excluded).

158. *See, e.g.*, TEC Cogeneration Inc. v. Florida Power & Light Co., 76 F.3d 1560, 1572-73 (11th Cir.) (rejecting a commercial exception to *Noerr* immunity), *modified on other grounds*, 86 F.3d 1028 (11th Cir. 1996); Independent Taxicab Drivers' Employees v. Greater Houston Transp. Co., 760 F.2d 607, 612-13 (5th Cir.) (actions of taxicab company in obtaining exclusive control over airport's transportation service through contract with city upheld under *Noerr* despite commercial nature of firm's relationship with city), *cert. denied*, 474 U.S. 903 (1985); *In re* Airport Car Rental Antitrust Litig., 693 F.2d 84, 88 (9th Cir. 1982) ("There is no commercial exception to *Noerr-*

Mississippi Power Co.,[159] in which the Fifth Circuit evaluated an electric utility's efforts to contract with a federal agency to purchase all the agency's output of electric power. Despite the defendant's anticompetitive aims in gaining exclusive access to the agency's generation capacity, the court held that *Noerr* immunized the conduct. The Fifth Circuit found "no reason why the result should be different when the government's decision is embodied in a contract with a private entity rather than in a regulation or statute."[160] Administering a commercial exception to *Noerr* immunity would be "difficult, if not impossible, . . . in a case . . . where the government engages in a policy decision and at the same time acts as a participant in the marketplace."[161]

Related to the question of a commercial exception is the problem of whether *Noerr* applies when regulated firms submit tariffs to regulatory authorities. In such cases, regulated firms may assert that *Noerr* immunizes the preparation and filing of tariffs with government regulators. Some courts have declined to recognize *Noerr* immunity in this context. In *Litton Systems v. AT&T*,[162] for example, an AT&T tariff compelled use of an AT&T interface device to connect non-AT&T telephone equipment into the Bell System network. AT&T had filed the challenged tariff with the Federal Communications Commission, which had not evaluated the propriety of the interconnection requirement. The Second Circuit concluded that *Noerr* was inapplicable because the "fact that the FCC might ultimately set aside a tariff filing does not transform AT&T's independent decisions as to how it will conduct its business into a request for governmental action or an expression of political opinion."[163] Nonetheless, some decisions have identified circumstances in which *Noerr* immunity extends to tariff filings and related activities.[164]

Pennington."), *cert. denied*, 462 U.S. 1133 (1983); Bristol-Myers Squibb Co. v. IVAX Corp., 77 F. Supp. 2d 606, 614-15 (D.N.J. 2000) (no commercial exception where the injury flows from government action), *aff'd in part and vacated in part*, 246 F.3d 1368 (Fed. Cir. 2001); Forest City Ambulance Serv. v. Mercy Ambulance of Richmond, Inc., 952 F. Supp. 296 (E.D. Va. 1997) (no commercial exception).

159. 751 F.2d 1484 (5th Cir. 1985).
160. *Id.* at 1505.
161. *Id.*
162. 700 F.2d 785 (2d Cir. 1983), *cert. denied*, 464 U.S. 1073 (1984).
163. *Id.* at 807-08 (citation and footnotes omitted); *accord* Columbia Steel Casting Co. v. Portland Gen. Elec. Co., 103 F.3d 1446, 1465 (9th Cir. 1996) ("Applying to an administrative agency for approval of an anticompetitive contract is not lobbying activity within the meaning of the *Noerr-Pennington* doctrine."); Jack Faucett Assocs. v. AT&T, 744 F.2d 118, 122-24 (D.C. Cir. 1984), *cert. denied*, 469 U.S. 1196 (1985); City of Kirkwood v. Union Elec. Co., 671 F.2d 1173, 1181 (8th Cir. 1982) (tariff filing "may not be used as pretext to achieve otherwise unlawful results"), *cert. denied*, 459 U.S. 1170 (1983); *In re* Wheat Rail Freight Rate Antitrust Litig., 579 F. Supp. 517, 537-38 (N.D. Ill. 1984) (ordinary tariff filing with Interstate Commerce Commission does not constitute request for government action and is not immune under *Noerr*), *aff'd*, 759 F.2d 1305 (7th Cir. 1985), *cert. denied*, 476 U.S. 1158 (1986).
164. *See, e.g.*, MCI Communs. Corp. v. AT&T, 708 F.2d 1081, 1155 (7th Cir.) (*Noerr* immunity applies to tariff filings unless the filing is "a pro forma publication perhaps required by law"), *cert. denied*, 464 U.S. 891 (1983); Clipper Exxpress v. Rocky Mountain Motor Tariff Bureau, 690 F.2d 1240, 1253-54 (9th Cir. 1982), *cert. denied*, 459 U.S. 1227 (1983); *cf.* United States v. Southern Motor Carriers Rate Conf., Inc., 672 F.2d 469, 477 (5th Cir. 1982) (*Noerr* immunity extends to rate filings and joint activities before public regulatory authorities, but not to prefiling collective efforts to devise proposed rates), *modified en banc on other grounds*, 702 F.2d 532 (1983), *rev'd on other grounds*, 471 U.S. 48 (1985). In *TEC Cogeneration Inc. v. Florida Power & Light Co.*, 76 F.3d 1560 (11th Cir.), *modified on other grounds*, 86 F.3d 1028 (11th Cir. 1996), the court refused to reject state action immunity for the activities of the regulated entity leading up to, and in

D. Relationship between Antitrust and Government Regulation

The role of the antitrust laws in industries regulated under federal statutory schemes reflects the extent to which Congress intended to replace the antitrust regime with the regulatory regime. Where Congress has explicitly stated that the antitrust laws do not apply at all, or that they do not apply under the circumstances set forth in the regulatory statute, an express exemption is said to exist.[165] There also are limited circumstances in which, despite the absence of an express statutory direction, exemption from the antitrust laws must be implied to preserve the integrity of a congressionally mandated regulatory scheme. In still other circumstances, the possible application of the antitrust laws will be deferred under the doctrine of primary jurisdiction while the administrative agency with regulatory responsibility for the industry or area of commerce in question makes an initial determination of the dispute or an essential element thereof. These concepts are discussed in this section.

In addition, courts have ruled that federal agencies and officials acting in their official capacities are exempt from antitrust claims;[166] some courts have applied the same exemption to private parties when they engage in conduct required by a government contract.[167] However, the mere fact that federal officials knew of or induced challenged private conduct is not sufficient to create immunity.[168]

---

preparation for, the state regulatory hearing. 76 F.3d at 1569-70. In the *Noerr* portion of its opinion, the court did not consider the parallel question whether *Noerr* protection shields meetings leading up to, and in preparation for, otherwise protected lobbying activities.

165. Express exemptions are discussed in Chapter XIV.

166. *See, e.g.*, Name.Space, Inc. v. Network Solutions, Inc., 202 F.3d 573, 581 (2d Cir. 2000) (National Science Foundation has "absolute immunity from the antitrust laws"); Lawline v. American Bar Ass'n, 956 F.2d 1378, 1384 (7th Cir. 1992) (executive committee of U.S. district court and the U.S. Trustee were immune from antitrust liability for role in adopting ABA model rule prohibiting lawyers from assisting nonlawyers in the unauthorized practice of law), *cert. denied*, 510 U.S. 992 (1993); Rex Sys. v. Holiday, 814 F.2d 994, 997 (4th Cir. 1987) (Department of Navy and two Navy officials acting in their official capacities are not "persons" capable of being sued under the Sherman Act); Sea-Land Serv. v. Alaska R.R., 659 F.2d 243, 246-47 (D.C. Cir. 1981) (entity owned and operated by United States is immune from antitrust liability), *cert. denied*, 455 U.S. 919 (1982).

167. The Second Circuit has held that private parties may sometimes be immune from the antitrust laws with respect to conduct required by a government contract. *Name.Space*, 202 F.3d at 581 (defendant awarded a contract by federal government agency to act as exclusive registrar of domain names over the Internet; Second Circuit formulated a "conduct based" federal instrumentality immunity where conduct is compelled by the explicit terms of the government contract and by government policies). *Cf.* Thomas v. Network Solutions, Inc., 176 F.3d 500 (D.C. Cir. 1999) (declining to apply federal instrumentality doctrine to private party), *cert. denied*, 528 U.S. 1115 (2000).

168. In *United States v. Socony-Vacuum Oil Co.*, 310 U.S. 150 (1940), the Supreme Court rejected the argument that antitrust immunity was conferred by federal officials' knowledge of and acquiescence in the defendants' collaborative efforts to stabilize the price of refined petroleum products. Subsequent decisions have reiterated that federal officials have no independent authority to exempt conduct from the antitrust laws. *See* Otter Tail Power Co. v. United States, 410 U.S. 366, 378-79 (1973) (rejecting electric utility's argument that federal officials had immunized its conduct by approving contractual restrictions that municipally owned distribution companies claimed violated the antitrust laws).

1. Implied Exemptions

A finding that an activity is exempt from the antitrust laws is not limited to matters in which agencies have express authority to approve and thereby immunize the activity. Where it appears to a court that antitrust enforcement would "disrupt" or be "repugnant" to a pervasive regulatory scheme, the court may hold that the activity is impliedly immune. *Gordon v. New York Stock Exchange*[169] illustrates this principle, where the plaintiffs challenged agreements by which New York Stock Exchange brokers fixed commission charges. Although these agreements were allowed under exchange rules, the Securities and Exchange Commission had statutory authority to alter the rules. The Supreme Court held that this authority to alter exchange rules, supplemented by the Securities and Exchange Commission's actual review of commission charges, was sufficient to imply antitrust immunity for the commission-fixing agreements. The Court found that immunity was necessary to avoid the possibility of collision between the Securities and Exchange Commission's instructions to the exchange and limits that might be imposed on the exchange by an antitrust court. The mere existence of complex regulation, however, is not sufficient to give rise to implied immunity.[170]

The courts have repeatedly relied on the Supreme Court's instruction that "[r]epeals of the antitrust laws by implication from a regulatory statute are strongly disfavored, and have only been found in cases of plain repugnancy between the antitrust and regulatory provisions."[171] The implication of repeal will be limited to the activity challenged and will not extend to other conduct regulated by the same agency. As the Supreme Court emphasized in *Silver v. New York Stock Exchange*,[172]

169. 422 U.S. 659 (1975). *See also In re* Stock Exchanges Options Trading Antitrust Litig., 2001-1 Trade Cas. (CCH) ¶ 73,186 (S.D.N.Y. 2001) (implied repeal of antitrust laws with respect to the trading and listing of equity options since Securities and Exchange Commission has broad, plenary jurisdiction in this area and its active exercise of that jurisdiction conflicted with operation of antitrust laws)

170. *See, e.g.*, United States v. Rockford Mem'l Corp., 898 F.2d 1278, 1281 (7th Cir.) (hospitals not immune from antitrust merger restrictions), *cert. denied*, 498 U.S. 920 (1990); *In re* Wheat Rail Freight Rate Antitrust Litig., 759 F.2d 1305, 1313 (7th Cir. 1985) ("[i]t was not true that rail carriers' activities were so pervasively regulated that the 'paradigm of competition' had been foresworn by Congress for the rail industry"), *cert. denied*, 476 U.S. 1158 (1986); Southern Pac. Communs. Co. v. AT&T, 740 F.2d 980, 999-1000 (D.C. Cir. 1984) (no pervasive regulatory control over rates and interconnection decisions so as to conflict with antitrust laws), *cert. denied*, 470 U.S. 1005 (1985).

171. United States v. Philadelphia Nat'l Bank, 374 U.S. 321, 350-51 (1963) (footnotes omitted); *see also* North Carolina *ex rel.* Edmisten v. P.I.A. Asheville, Inc., 740 F.2d 274, 281 (4th Cir. 1984) (antitrust immunity not implied in regulatory structure established by National Health Planning and Resources Department Act), *cert. denied*, 471 U.S. 1003 (1985); City of Kirkwood v. Union Elec. Co., 671 F.2d 1173, 1178 (8th Cir. 1982) (no implied immunity because electric utility regulatory scheme and antitrust laws not "plainly repugnant" to each other), *cert. denied*, 459 U.S. 1170 (1983); Phonetele, Inc. v. AT&T, 664 F.2d 716, 731-35 (9th Cir. 1982) (perceived repugnancy between antitrust laws and regulatory laws insufficient to establish finding of implied immunity; actual repugnancy must exist), *cert. denied*, 459 U.S. 1145 (1983). *But see* Strobl v. New York Mercantile Exch., 768 F.2d 22, 27-29 (2d Cir.) (antitrust laws may not apply when they would prohibit an action the regulatory scheme might allow), *cert. denied*, 474 U.S. 1006 (1985); Waldo v. North Am. Van Lines, 669 F. Supp. 722, 732-33 (W.D. Pa. 1987) (exclusivity provisions in portions of trucking company's operating agreement with driver mandated by regulatory scheme of Interstate Commerce Commission, thereby providing antitrust immunity).

172. 373 U.S. 341 (1963). Decisions applying these principles to various industries are discussed in Chapter XIV.

"[r]epeal is to be regarded as implied only if necessary to make the [regulatory statute] work, and even then only to the minimum extent necessary. This is the guiding principle to reconciliation of the two statutory schemes."[173]

In *National Gerimedical Hospital & Gerontology Center v. Blue Cross*,[174] the Supreme Court applied this standard to refuse to exempt from antitrust scrutiny Blue Cross's exclusion of the plaintiff from an insurance plan, even though the decision was made in furtherance of a local health care planning scheme created in response to national health planning legislation. The plaintiff had not sought approval of its plans to construct a hospital from the local advisory group created under the statute, and on this ground Blue Cross had rejected the plaintiff's application to participate in the plan.[175] The Supreme Court denied Blue Cross immunity for its decision because, among other reasons, the local advisory group, although created and funded under federal law, was a private planning body, not a government agency charged with implementing a regulatory statute, and because no "clear repugnancy" between application of the antitrust laws to Blue Cross's decision and any provision of the statute or regulatory order was demonstrated.[176] The Court also expressly declined to create a blanket exemption for all conduct taken in response to the health planning process under the statute, finding this result consistent with its decisions in other industrial contexts.[177]

2.   *The Filed Rate Doctrine*

In *Keogh v. Chicago & Northwestern Railway*,[178] the Supreme Court held that a private shipper could not recover treble damages against railway companies that had set uniform rates duly filed with, and approved by, the Interstate Commerce Commission.[179] The Court did not give the railway companies complete immunity from the antitrust laws—the Court expressly noted that Interstate Commerce Commission approval would not bar government antitrust proceedings[180]—but it held that a shipper could not recover antitrust damages from a carrier based on allegedly unreasonable filed rates.

---

173. 373 U.S. at 357. *See also* Hecht v. Pro-Football, Inc., 444 F.2d 931, 944 (D.C. Cir. 1971) (although Congress authorized the District of Columbia armory board to provide a stadium suitable for holding athletic events "without regard to any other provision of law," this did not place the activities of the board in doing so beyond the reach of the antitrust laws).

174. 452 U.S. 378, 393 (1981).

175. *Id.* at 381.

176. *Id.* at 390-91.

177. *Id.* at 392 (citing Carnation Co. v. Pacific Westbound Conf., 383 U.S. 213, 217-19 (1966) (maritime industry) and Otter Tail Power Co. v. United States, 410 U.S. 366, 373-74 (1973) (electric power industry)); *see also* City of Long Beach v. Standard Oil Co., 872 F.2d 1401, 1409 (9th Cir.) (federal price control regulations do not supplant antitrust laws), *amended*, 886 F.2d 246 (1989), *cert. denied*, 493 U.S. 1076 (1990). For a decision giving wide latitude to private regulatory bodies in amateur sports, *see* Behagen v. Amateur Basketball Ass'n, 884 F.2d 524, 529 (10th Cir. 1989) (Amateur Sports Act directs "monolithic" control of amateur sports, therefore the actions of this association cannot be challenged on antitrust grounds), *cert. denied*, 495 U.S. 918 (1990).

178. 260 U.S. 156 (1922).

179. *Id.* at 161.

180. *Id.* at 162.

The vitality of the filed rate doctrine developed in *Keogh* was reconfirmed by the Supreme Court in *Square D Co. v. Niagara Frontier Tariff Bureau.*[181] *Square D* involved a suit by shippers against the collective rate-making activities of an association of motor carriers. The Supreme Court determined that the carriers' rates had been duly filed with the Interstate Commerce Commission and hence were lawful rates "in the same sense that the rates filed in *Keogh* were lawful."[182] The Court reiterated, however, the limits of the filed rate doctrine, noting that *Keogh* does not create broad antitrust immunity, but merely precludes treble damage recovery in an action by a private shipper arising from rates approved by the agency.[183]

The Supreme Court has continued to voice skepticism about the wisdom of the filed rate doctrine, but it has been unwilling to substitute its policy preferences for the dictates of the governing statutes.[184] Consequently, the doctrine continues to shield regulated industry defendants against antitrust damage claims based on conduct undertaken pursuant to a filed tariff.[185]

Recent filed rate doctrine decisions have consistently held that the doctrine applies as much to regulation by state agencies as to federal regulation.[186] As the Second Circuit stated in *Wegoland Ltd. v. NYNEX Corp.*,[187] "courts have uniformly held, and we agree, that the rationales underlying the filed rate doctrine apply equally strongly to regulation by state agencies."[188] Similarly, the lower courts have

---

181. 476 U.S. 409 (1986).

182. *Id.* at 417; *see also* County of Stanislaus v. Pacific Gas & Elec. Co., 1996-1 Trade Cas. (CCH) ¶ 71,305, at 76,436 (E.D. Cal. 1995) (lawfully filed rates preclude antitrust damage actions regardless of the absence of a regulatory challenge to the rates or of an explicit determination by the regulator that the rates were proper), *aff'd*, 114 F.3d 848 (9th Cir. 1997).

183. 476 U.S. at 422. The Supreme Court most recently reaffirmed the filed rate doctrine (outside the antitrust context) in *AT&T Corp. v. Central Office Tel., Inc.*, 524 U.S. 214 (1998). *See also* Daleure v. Kentucky, 119 F. Supp. 2d 683, 689 (W.D. Ky. 2000) ("The Supreme Court has at least arguably extended the scope of the filed rate doctrine as recently as 1998.").

184. *See, e.g.*, MCI Telecommuns. Corp. v. AT&T, 512 U.S. 218, 234 (1994) (noting—outside of the antitrust context—the "considerable 'debate in other forums about the wisdom of the filed rate doctrine,'" but acknowledging that "[f]or better or worse, the [Federal Communications] Act establishes a rate-regulation, filed-tariff system"); Security Servs. v. Kmart Corp., 511 U.S. 431, 435 (1994); *see also* County of Stanislaus v. Pacific Gas & Elec Co., 114 F.3d 858, 862 (9th Cir. 1997) (Supreme Court "acknowledged criticism of the doctrine, but affirmed its vitality").

185. *See, e.g.*, Miranda v. Michigan, 141 F. Supp. 2d 747 (E.D. Mich. 2001) (barring claims based on rates charged for collect telephone calls from prisoners); Florida Mun. Power Agency v. Florida Power & Light Co., 839 F. Supp. 1563, 1571 (M.D. Fla. 1993) (plaintiff cannot recover damages based upon a regulated utility's refusal to sell transmission services because "any award of damages would require an assumption regarding what type of rate/service terms would have been approved by FERC"), *vacated in part and remanded in part*, 64 F.3d 614 (11th Cir. 1995). Some courts have applied the filed rate doctrine outside the antitrust context. *See, e.g.*, Evanns v. AT&T Corp., 229 F.3d 837 (9th Cir. 2000) (breach of contract and tort claims); Sun City Taxpayers' Ass'n v. Citizens Utils. Co., 45 F.3d 58, 61-62 (2d Cir.) (applying doctrine to RICO claims), *cert. denied*, 514 U.S. 1064 (1995); Wegoland Ltd. v. NYNEX Corp., 27 F.3d 17, 21 (2d Cir. 1994) (RICO); MCI Telecommuns. Corp. v. Graphnet, Inc., 881 F. Supp. 126, 133 (D.N.J. 1995) (breach of contract claims).

186. *See, e.g.*, *Daleure*, 119 F. Supp. 2d at 688 n.15; Uniforce Temp. Personnel, Inc. v. National Council on Compensation Ins., Inc., 892 F. Supp. 1503, 1512 n.10 (S.D. Fla. 1995), *aff'd*, 87 F.3d 1296 (11th Cir. 1996); Calico Trailer Mfg. Co. v. Insurance Co. of N. Am., 1995-1 Trade Cas. (CCH) ¶ 71,022, at 74,794 (E.D. Ark. 1994).

187. 27 F.3d 17 (2d Cir. 1994).

188. *Id.* at 20 (citing Taffett v. Southern Co., 967 F.2d 1483, 1494 (11th Cir.) (en banc), *cert. denied*, 506 U.S. 1021 (1992)); *accord* H.J., Inc. v. Northwestern Bell Tel. Co., 954 F.2d 485, 494 (8th Cir.), *cert. denied*, 504 U.S. 957 (1992). In fact, one court has held that "[a]fter agency approval of

consistently rejected arguments that the doctrine does not apply where the regulated party is alleged to have defrauded the regulator in connection with the promulgation of the filed rate.[189]

The courts of appeals are divided, however, on the applicability of the filed rate doctrine to actions brought by competitors rather than customers. Those declining to apply the doctrine to competitor lawsuits have held the view that the regulatory goal of achieving rate uniformity for customers is not undercut by affording the treble damage remedy in competitor suits.[190] The Sixth Circuit, however, extended the filed rate doctrine to a competitor lawsuit in *Pinney Dock & Transport Co. v. Penn Central Corp.*[191] Acknowledging that "the anti-discrimination arguments behind the *Keogh* doctrine lose their force" in lawsuits brought by competitors, the Sixth Circuit interpreted the Interstate Commerce Act as reflecting an assumption that the Interstate Commerce Commission takes competition policy into account in approving rates.[192] The court also noted that the plaintiffs in the matter before it had the right to complain to the Interstate Commerce Commission about the challenged rates.[193] Analyzing the plaintiffs' claims, the court held that those claims unrelated to the reasonableness of filed rates should be allowed to proceed, and that the plaintiffs should be afforded opportunity to amend their complaint to clarify their allegations where the court could not determine whether *Keogh* applied.[194]

3. *Primary Jurisdiction*

Even when the antitrust laws are not entirely displaced by a regulatory scheme and a court declines to find that agency jurisdiction is expressly or impliedly exclusive, a court may defer consideration of antitrust issues until one or more

---

filed rates, even unregulated conduct which results in fixing the amount of the rate cannot be the subject of an antitrust complaint." County of Stanislaus v. Pacific Gas & Elec. Co., 1996-1 Trade Cas. (CCH) ¶ 71,305, at 76,436 (E.D. Cal. 1995), aff'd, 114 F.3d 858 (9th Cir. 1997).

189. *See, e.g.*, *Wegoland*, 27 F.3d at 20 ("every court that has considered the plaintiffs' argument has rejected the notion that there is a fraud exception to the filed rate doctrine"); *Taffett*, 967 F.2d at 1494-95; *H.J., Inc.*, 954 F.2d at 489; Lifschultz Fast Freight, Inc. v. Consolidated Freightways Corp., 805 F. Supp. 1277, 1295 (D.S.C. 1992), aff'd, 998 F.2d 1009 (4th Cir.), *cert. denied*, 510 U.S. 993 (1993); Cullum v. Arkla, Inc., 797 F. Supp. 725, 728-29 (E.D. Ark. 1992), aff'd, 994 F.2d 842 (8th Cir. 1993).

190. *See, e.g.*, Cost Mgmt. Servs. v. Washington Natural Gas Co., 99 F.3d 937, 948 (9th Cir. 1996); City of Kirkwood v. Union Elec. Co, 671 F.2d 1173, 1179 (8th Cir. 1982), *cert. denied*, 459 U.S. 1170 (1983); City of Groton v. Connecticut Power & Light Co., 662 F.2d 921, 929 (2d Cir. 1981); Essential Communs. Sys. v. AT&T, 610 F.2d 1114, 1121 (3d Cir. 1979). The First Circuit also has declined to extend a "competitor" exception to the filed rate doctrine on the basis that the factual situation before the court did not support such exception. *See* Town of Norwood, Mass. v. New England Power Co., 202 F.3d 408, 420 (1st Cir. 2000). The court found that "[a]lthough Norwood may be in limited competition with New England Power affiliates, it is primarily a consumer challenging a filed rate that it does not want to pay." *Id.*

191. 838 F.2d 1445 (6th Cir.), *cert. denied*, 488 U.S. 880 (1988).

192. *Id.* at 1457.

193. *Id.*

194. *Id.* at 1457-58; *see also* County of Stanislaus v. Pacific Gas & Elec. Co., 114 F.3d 858 (9th Cir. 1997) (applying filed rate doctrine to dismiss claims against entities engaged in importation of Canadian natural gas on grounds that the prices and alleged exclusionary conduct had been subject to multiple layers of federal and state regulatory review); Paladin Assocs., Inc. v. Montana Power Co., 97 F. Supp. 2d 1013 (D. Mont. 2000) (filed rate doctrine did not bar monopolization claims which did not challenge the filed rate as unreasonable).

regulatory agencies with "primary jurisdiction" has had an opportunity to consider a dispute. In *Ricci v. Chicago Mercantile Exchange*,[195] the Supreme Court set forth the circumstances under which a court should await initial agency review of an issue before deciding antitrust questions. Ricci claimed that the Chicago Mercantile Exchange had conspired with an exchange member to prevent his trading on the exchange. The action alleged a restraint of trade and a violation of the Commodity Exchange Act. The Supreme Court held that the antitrust action should be stayed until the Commodity Exchange Commission had acted. It concluded that the antitrust court ultimately would have to determine whether any provisions of the Commodity Exchange Act were incompatible with antitrust enforcement and that because "some facets" of the dispute were within the statutory jurisdiction of the Commodity Exchange Commission, that agency's adjudication of the dispute "promise[d] to be of material aid [to the court] in resolving the immunity question."[196] Thus, the Court established that deferral of an antitrust action pending administrative proceedings is proper when agency consideration of matters within the agency's jurisdiction will materially aid the court in resolving the antitrust issue.[197]

Consistent with the *Ricci* standard, courts will not employ the doctrine of primary jurisdiction if the agency determination will not affect the status of the antitrust claim.[198] Thus, in *International Travel Arrangers v. Western Airlines*,[199] the Eighth Circuit declined to apply the primary jurisdiction doctrine because a determination by the Civil Aeronautics Board on unfair competition, an issue that fell within the regulatory authority, would not have clarified the antitrust questions presented.[200] Similarly, in *American Ass'n of Cruise Passengers v. Cunard Line*,[201] the D.C. Circuit held that there were no common regulatory issues between those claims that came under the exclusive jurisdiction of the Federal Maritime Commission and those claims that did not. Accordingly, the court concluded that "there is no chance that a cruise line will be subject to different regulations and different sanctions for the same act" if parts of its conduct were scrutinized by the regulatory agency while others were scrutinized by the district court.[202] The court therefore ruled that "the district

---

195. 409 U.S. 289 (1973).
196. *Id.* at 302. The Court noted that "the question of immunity, as such, will not be before the agency; but if Ricci's complaint is sustained, the immunity issue will dissolve, whereas if it is rejected and the conduct of the Exchange warranted by a valid membership rule, the court will be in a much better position to determine whether the antitrust action should go forward." *Id.* at 306.
197. In *Arsberry v. Illinois*, 244 F.3d 558, 563-64 (7th Cir. 2001), *cert. denied*, 2001 U.S. LEXIS 10940 (U.S. Dec. 3, 2001), Judge Posner described the primary jurisdiction doctrine as encompassing two concepts: (1) exclusive agency jurisdiction over lawsuits involving regulated firms brought under the regulatory statute; and (2) deference by a court to an agency that knows more about an issue, even if the agency's jurisdiction is not exclusive.
198. *See, e.g.*, Telecom Plus v. Local No. 3, 719 F.2d 613, 615 (2d Cir. 1983) (deferral not appropriate where controlling issue in antitrust claim against union was wholly unrelated to the issue before the labor board); International Travel Arrangers v. Western Airlines, 623 F.2d 1255, 1259 (8th Cir.), *cert. denied*, 449 U.S. 1063 (1980). *See also* Cost Mgmt. Servs., Inc. v. Washington Natural Gas Co., 99 F.3d 937, 949 (9th Cir. 1996) (primary jurisdiction doctrine is "inapplicable" at pleading stage where allegations of complaint must be accepted as true).
199. 623 F.2d 1255 (8th Cir.), *cert. denied*, 449 U.S. 1063 (1980).
200. *Id.* at 1259.
201. 31 F.3d 1184 (D.C. Cir. 1994).
202. *Id.* at 1187.

court ought to have retained jurisdiction over that part of the suit within its exclusive jurisdiction."[203]

Courts also may refuse to defer to an agency if the questions involved are essentially legal and not factual, and thus are not peculiarly within the agency's special expertise.[204] In these circumstances, courts have no need to "avail themselves of the aid implicit in the agency's superiority in gathering the relevant facts and in marshaling them into a meaningful pattern."[205]

---

203. *Id.*
204. *See, e.g.,* I.C.C. v. Big Sky Farmers & Ranchers Mktg. Coop., 451 F.2d 511, 515 (9th Cir. 1971); *see also* TransKentucky Transp. R.R. v. Louisville & N. R.R., 581 F. Supp. 759, 772 (E.D. Ky. 1983) (court refused to refer case to Interstate Commerce Commission under doctrine of primary jurisdiction where resolution of issues did not require special competence of agency).
205. Ricci v. Chicago Mercantile Exch., 409 U.S. 289, 305-06 (1973) (quoting Federal Maritime Bd. v. Isbrandtsen Co., 356 U.S. 481, 498 (1958)).

CHAPTER XIV

REGULATED INDUSTRIES

A. Agriculture

1. Introduction

Concern about the economic well-being of U.S. farmers and ranchers has been a factor in passage of most of the nation's major antitrust legislation. Historically, farmers and ranchers have been particularly vulnerable to the effects of concentration of market power by suppliers, processors, and transporters and have sought help in the form of legislation. In addition to the general antitrust laws, there are two areas of legislation specifically directed to the agricultural sector of the economy. First, agricultural cooperatives are not considered illegal combinations for purposes of the antitrust laws, and members of cooperatives are permitted to act in concert with one another in preparing and marketing their products.[1] Second, the livestock, meat, and poultry industries are subject to the provisions of the Packers and Stockyards Act of 1921 (PSA) prohibiting anticompetitive behavior by meat packers and poultry dealers and by stockyards, marketing agents, and dealers.[2]

Notwithstanding this existing legislation, the high level of concentration in several parts of the agricultural sector (including meat packing, grain trading, and transportation), the accelerating pace of agribusiness mergers, and the generally poor economic condition of smaller farmers and ranchers have spurred calls for more comprehensive regulation of merger activity in this sector. A number of bills were introduced in 1999 and 2000 to try to address these concerns, but as of the date of publication, no significant legislation had been passed.[3] However, in an effort to respond to the demand for more action, in 1999, the Department of Justice, the Federal Trade Commission, and the Department of Agriculture entered into a memorandum of understanding providing that the agencies would coordinate and confer on issues relating to competitive conditions in the agricultural marketplace.[4]

---

1. *See* part A.2 of this chapter.
2. *See* part A.3 of this chapter.
3. Proposed legislation included an 18-month moratorium on agribusiness mergers (*e.g.*, S. 1739, The Agribusiness Merger Moratorium and Antitrust Review Act of 1999, introduced Oct. 15, 1999) and creation of a position within the Department of Agriculture with responsibility for reviewing all mergers in the agriculture sector (*e.g.*, S. 2252, Agriculture Competition Enhancement Act, introduced Mar. 20, 2000).
4. Memorandum of Understanding between the Antitrust Division, Department of Justice, and the Federal Trade Commission and the Department of Agriculture Relative to Cooperation With Respect To Monitoring Competitive Conditions in the Agriculture Marketplace (Aug. 31, 1999), *available at* www.usdoj.gov/atr/public/guidelines/3675.htm. The memorandum provides that the three agencies will confer regularly and share information consistent with applicable

In addition, in January 2000, a new position of Special Counsel for Agriculture was created within the Antitrust Division of the Department of Justice to "help look out for the interests of farm families, rural communities, and consumers."[5] In light of the pressure from Congress and these actions by the agencies, it is likely that mergers and allegations of anticompetitive activity within the agricultural sector will face substantial scrutiny for the next several years.[6]

2.   *Antitrust Immunity for Agricultural Cooperatives*

Congress has enacted a series of statutes granting agricultural producers the right to combine into associations and to engage in cooperative functions without violating the antitrust laws. From its inception in 1914, the Clayton Act has provided:

> Nothing contained in the antitrust laws shall be construed to forbid the existence and operation of . . . agricultural or horticultural organizations, instituted for the purposes of mutual help, and not having capital stock or conducted for profit, or to forbid or restrain individual members of such organizations from lawfully carrying out the legitimate objects thereof; nor shall such organizations, or the members thereof, be held or construed to be illegal combinations or conspiracies in restraint of trade, under the antitrust laws.[7]

In 1922, Congress expanded the cooperative exemption in the Capper-Volstead Act,[8] Section 1 of which provides:

---

confidentiality restrictions. *Id.* ¶¶ 3, 4. The memorandum also provides that each of the three agencies shall designate a primary contact person to facilitate communications. *Id.* ¶ 3.

5.   78 Antitrust & Trade Reg. Rep. (BNA) 45 (Jan. 21, 2000).

6.   For example, in 2000, the proposed acquisition by Cargill, Inc. (the second largest grain trader in North America) of the worldwide grain trading business of Continental Grain Company (formerly the third largest grain trader in North America) faced intense opposition by farming interests. Although the merger eventually was permitted, the Department of Justice (DOJ) required substantial divestitures, including divestiture of grain elevators held by either Continental or Cargill in each of nine geographic markets where the DOJ believed the consolidation would give grain companies the power to artificially depress prices. The parties also were required to divest elevators on the Illinois River to ensure that concentrations among firms controlling the Chicago Board of Trade (CBOT) authorized delivery points did not provide opportunities for manipulation of CBOT corn and soybean futures prices. *See* United States v. Cargill, Inc., Civ. No. 99-1875 (GK) (D.D.C. June 30, 2000) (final judgment).

7.   15 U.S.C. § 17 (2000). The legislative histories of the Clayton Act § 6 and the Capper-Volstead Act, 7 U.S.C. §§ 291-292 (2000), are discussed in *Maryland & Va. Milk Producers Ass'n v. United States*, 362 U.S. 458, 464-67 (1960), and *Fairdale Farms v. Yankee Milk, Inc.*, 635 F.2d 1037, 1040-44 (2d Cir. 1980), *cert. denied*, 454 U.S. 818 (1981). See generally *Tigner v. Texas*, 310 U.S. 141 (1940), where the Court summarized the agricultural exemption legislation as follows:
> [A]n impressive legislative movement bears witness to general acceptance of the view that the differences between agriculture and industry call for differentiation in the formulation of public policy . . . .
> At the core of all these enactments lies a conception of price and production policy for agriculture very different from that which underlies the demands made upon industry and commerce by antitrust laws.
Id. at 145-46 (footnote omitted).

8.   7 U.S.C. §§ 291-292 (2000). In 1934, fishermen were also granted the right to form cooperatives by the Fisherman's Collective Marketing Act, 15 U.S.C. §§ 521-522 (2000), which was patterned after the Capper-Volstead Act.

Persons engaged in the production of agricultural products as farmers, planters, ranchmen, dairymen, nut and fruit growers may act together in associations, corporate or otherwise, with or without capital stock, in collectively processing, preparing for market, handling, and marketing in interstate and foreign commerce, such products of persons so engaged. Such associations may have marketing agencies in common; and such associations and their members may make the necessary contracts and agreements to effect such purposes [subject to specified limitations on the organizational structure of the cooperative].[9]

Section 2 of the act, however, authorizes the Secretary of Agriculture to proceed against cooperative associations that have monopolized or restrained trade "to such an extent that the price of any agricultural product is unduly enhanced."[10]

Additional statutory exemptions have followed. The Cooperative Marketing Act of 1926 authorizes agricultural producers and associations to acquire and exchange "past, present and prospective" pricing, production, and marketing data.[11] Internal payments by cooperatives to their members are exempt from the Robinson-Patman Act.[12] The Agricultural Marketing Agreement Act of 1937 grant an exemption from the antitrust laws for marketing agreements between the Secretary of Agriculture and processors, producers, associations of producers, and others engaged in the handling of any agricultural commodity or product.[13] In another aid to agricultural cooperatives, the Agricultural Fair Practices Act of 1967 makes it unlawful for "handlers"—defined to include both processors and producer associations—to coerce any producer in the decision whether to join a cooperative.[14]

The Supreme Court addressed the Capper-Volstead exemption as well as Section 6 of the Clayton Act in *Maryland & Virginia Milk Producers Ass'n v. United States*,[15] in which it concluded that a cooperative is not protected by the Capper-Volstead exemption when it monopolizes or attempts to monopolize by engaging in predatory or otherwise anticompetitive practices.[16] In such cases, a cooperative is subject to the same antitrust liability as nonexempt entities.[17]

---

9.   7 U.S.C. § 291.

10.   *Id.* § 292.

11.   *Id.* § 455 (2000).

12.   15 U.S.C. § 13b (2000); 7 U.S.C. § 207(f) (2000).

13.   7 U.S.C. § 608(b) (2000); *see, e.g.*, United States v. Rock Royal Coop., 307 U.S. 533 (1939); *In re* Midwest Milk Monopolization Litig., 380 F. Supp. 880, 885 (W.D. Mo. 1974) (limiting exemption to marketing agreements and not marketing orders). *But see* Chiglades Farm v. Butz, 485 F.2d 1125, 1131 (5th Cir. 1973) (exemption also applies to marketing orders), *cert. denied*, 417 U.S. 968 (1974). *See generally* Berning v. Gooding, 820 F.2d 1550, 1552 (9th Cir. 1987) (administrative committee not liable under Clayton Act for its recommendations to Secretary of Agriculture pursuant to Agricultural Adjustment Act, 7 U.S.C. §§ 601-626 (2000)); United States v. Maryland & Va. Milk Producers Ass'n, 90 F. Supp. 681, 687-88 (D.D.C. 1950), *rev'd on other grounds*, 193 F.2d 907 (D.C. Cir. 1951).

14.   7 U.S.C. §§ 2301-2306 (2000). *See* Michigan Canners & Freezers Ass'n v. Agricultural Mktg. & Bargaining Bd., 467 U.S. 461, 478 (1984) (act preempts Michigan statute that accredited cooperative association as exclusive bargaining agent for all producers of a commodity); Newark Gardens, Inc. v. Michigan Potato Indus. Comm'n, 847 F.2d 1201, 1210 (6th Cir. 1988) (act does not preempt Michigan statute requiring payment of mandatory assessment to state commission for generic promotion of commodity).

15.   362 U.S. 458 (1960).

16.   *Id.* at 463-67.

17.   *Id.*

Following the lead of the Supreme Court, lower courts have found the Clayton Act Section 6 and Capper-Volstead exemptions inapplicable to charges of boycott,[18] predatory refusal to deal,[19] unfair rebates to favored customers,[20] discriminatory pricing,[21] coercion through picketing,[22] coerced membership,[23] acts of violence,[24] or other "predatory practices."[25] The courts have held that, absent predatory activity, the Capper-Volstead Act and Section 6 of the Clayton Act permit producers to seek, maintain, and exercise monopoly power through the formation, growth, and combination of cooperatives.[26] At least one court has held that the Capper-Volstead exemption is inapplicable—even absent evidence of predatory acts—when an otherwise exempt association "used its legitimately acquired monopoly power to stifle competition in violation of Section 2."[27]

---

18. *See* Boise Cascade Int'l, Inc. v. Northern Minn. Pulpwood Producers Ass'n, 294 F. Supp. 1015, 1023-24 (D. Minn. 1968).

19. *See* Agritronics Corp. v. National Dairy Herd Ass'n, 914 F. Supp. 814, 826 (N.D.N.Y. 1996) (denying Capper-Volstead protection where defendants were charged with entering into exclusive relationships and imposing discriminatory restrictions with respect to the sale of bull semen); North Tex. Producers Ass'n v. Metzger Dairies, 348 F.2d 189, 194, 196 (5th Cir. 1965), *cert. denied*, 382 U.S. 977 (1966).

20. *See* Knuth v. Erie-Crawford Dairy Coop. Ass'n, 463 F.2d 470 (3d Cir. 1972).

21. *See* Bergjans Farm Dairy Co. v. Sanitary Milk Producers, 241 F. Supp. 476, 484 (E.D. Mo. 1965), *aff'd*, 368 F.2d 679 (8th Cir. 1966); *see also* Holly Sugar Corp. v. Goshen County Coop. Beet Growers Ass'n, 725 F.2d 564, 569 (10th Cir. 1984) (dictum).

22. *See* Otto Milk Co. v. United Dairy Farmers Coop. Ass'n, 388 F.2d 789, 797 (3d Cir. 1967).

23. *See* Gulf Coast Shrimpers & Oystermans Ass'n v. United States, 236 F.2d 658, 665 (5th Cir.), *cert. denied*, 352 U.S. 927 (1956).

24. *See* Cincinnati Milk Sales Ass'n v. National Farmers' Org., 1967 Trade Cas. (CCH) ¶ 72,092 (S.D. Ohio 1967).

25. *See* Maryland & Va. Milk Producers Ass'n v. United States, 362 U.S. 458, 463 (1960); *Holly Sugar Corp.*, 725 F.2d at 569; Treasure Valley Potato Bargaining Ass'n v. Ore-Ida Foods, Inc., 497 F.2d 203, 216 (9th Cir.), *cert. denied*, 419 U.S. 999 (1974).

26. *See* Fairdale Farms v. Yankee Milk, Inc., 715 F.2d 30 (2d Cir. 1983), *cert. denied*, 464 U.S. 1043 (1984); L. & L. Howell, Inc. v. Cincinnati Coop. Milk Sales Ass'n, 1983-2 Trade Cas. (CCH) ¶ 65,595 (6th Cir. 1983), *cert. denied*, 466 U.S. 904 (1984); Fairdale Farms v. Yankee Milk, Inc., 635 F.2d 1037, 1045 (2d Cir. 1980), *cert. denied*, 454 U.S. 818 (1981); Amarel v. Connel, 1994-1 Trade Cas. (CCH) ¶ 70,632, at 74,429 (N.D. Cal. 1993) (defendants are exempt under the Capper-Volstead Act from Sherman Act § 2 liability unless predatory acts can be demonstrated); GVF Cannery, Inc. v. California Tomato Growers Ass'n, 511 F. Supp. 711 (N.D. Cal. 1981) (no claims against cooperative under Sherman Act § 2 without pleading and proof of predatory acts); Kinnett Dairies v. Dairymen, Inc., 512 F. Supp. 608, 642-43 (M.D. Ga. 1981) (judgment for defendant cooperative absent showing of predatory practices), *aff'd per curiam*, 715 F.2d 520 (11th Cir. 1983), *cert. denied*, 465 U.S. 1051 (1984); *see also* Marketing Assistance Plan v. Associated Milk Producers, 338 F. Supp. 1019, 1023 (S.D. Tex. 1972) (plaintiff's allegations of predatory commercial activities could not be dismissed for failure to state a claim under antitrust laws); Cape Cod Food Prods. v. National Cranberry Ass'n, 119 F. Supp. 900, 907 (D. Mass. 1954) (jury instructed that it "is not unlawful under the anti-trust acts for a Capper-Volstead cooperative . . . to try to acquire even 100 percent of the market if it does it exclusively through marketing agreements approved under the Capper-Volstead Act") (citation omitted). *But see* Alexander v. National Farmers Org., 687 F.2d 1173, 1183 (8th Cir. 1982) ("Whether a co-op's given business practice is unlawful . . . is not merely a question of whether it is 'predatory' in a strict sense, *e.g.*, lacking a legitimate business justification."), *cert. denied*, 461 U.S. 937 (1983); United States v. Dairymen, Inc., 660 F.2d 192, 195 (6th Cir. 1981) ("An anticompetitive practice may have economic justification, but its use may be undertaken with unlawful intent and in the desire to achieve an unlawful goal. . . . However, the most important inquiry is whether these contracts were intended to stifle competition or were intended to meet legitimate business purposes.").

27. Agritronics Corp. v. National Dairy Herd Ass'n, 1994-2 Trade Cas. (CCH) ¶ 70,758, at 73,199 (N.D.N.Y. 1994); *see also* Agritronics Corp. v. National Dairy Herd Ass'n, 914 F. Supp. 814, 825

In actions concerning an alleged price-fixing conspiracy among California lettuce producers, the Federal Trade Commission and the Ninth Circuit have ruled that the activity of a cooperative that was formed and operated solely for the purpose of setting prices for its members' products was protected from attack under Section 1 of the Sherman Act.[28] The separate opinions rely heavily on an earlier Ninth Circuit case which held that associations of producers whose activities are confined to bargaining for prices are exempt from antitrust liability under Section 1 of the Sherman Act because setting a price for the sale of members' produce, without more, is "marketing" as that term is used in the Capper-Volstead Act.[29]

Capper-Volstead immunity may impact the analysis of mergers in the agricultural sector. The Department of Justice filed suit in 2000 to block the proposed acquisition of Société de Diffusion Internationale Agro-Alimentaire (SODIAAL) by Dairy Farmers of America, Inc. In its complaint, the Department of Justice alleged that the merger would have a negative impact on the butter market in New York City and Philadelphia because it would leave only Dairy Farmers and Land O'Lakes, both cooperatives under the Capper-Volstead Act, as competitors in those markets.[30] The complaint further alleged that the general concern for coordinated pricing in a duopoly market was greater in the case of this merger because, as cooperatives, Dairy Farmers and Land O'Lakes could legally collude and fix prices.[31] The complaint was settled when Dairy Farmers agreed to spin off a noncooperative subsidiary to compete in those markets.[32]

Although the Capper-Volstead Act permits members of cooperatives to act in concert, it does not permit cooperatives to collude with others who do not enjoy immunity. In *United States v. Borden Co.*,[33] the Supreme Court upheld an indictment under Section 1 of the Sherman Act charging a dairy cooperative with having conspired with milk processors and distributors, a union, and local health officials to fix milk prices. The Court held that the Capper-Volstead Act did not authorize a

---

(N.D.N.Y. 1996) (farmers are not immune when they use "legitimately acquired monopoly power in such a manner as to smother competition under Section 2 of the Sherman Act").

28. *See* Northern Cal. Supermarkets v. Central Cal. Lettuce Producers Coop., 580 F.2d 369 (9th Cir. 1978), *cert. denied*, 439 U.S. 1090 (1979); Central Cal. Lettuce Producers Coop., 90 F.T.C. 18 (1977); *accord* Fairdale Farms v. Yankee Milk, Inc., 635 F.2d 1037, 1039-40 (2d Cir. 1980), *cert. denied*, 454 U.S. 878 (1981).

29. *See* Treasure Valley Potato Bargaining Ass'n v. Ore-Ida Foods, Inc., 497 F.2d 203 (9th Cir.), *cert. denied*, 419 U.S. 999 (1974); *see also Agritronics Corp.*, 914 F. Supp. at 825 (entities in the business of testing milk and providing "official" milk production records for dairy farmers are engaged in "marketing" under the Capper-Volstead Act); Holly Sugar Corp. v. Goshen County Coop. Beet Growers Ass'n, 725 F.2d 564, 568-69 (10th Cir. 1984) (no antitrust violation stated where bargaining cooperative sought to take legal action to enforce marketing agreement with members); Washington Crab Ass'n, 66 F.T.C. 45, 105-14 (1964) (Capper-Volstead immunity applicable to cooperative that did not process, handle, or sell members' products in competition with each other); *cf. L. & L. Howell, Inc.*, 1983-2 Trade Cas. (CCH) ¶ 65,595 (upholding joint proposing of handling fees to be paid).

30. United States v. Dairy Farmers of America, Inc., C.A. No. 00-CV-1633, ¶¶ 25-30 (E.D. Pa. Mar. 3, 2000) (complaint).

31. *Id.* ¶ 31.

32. *See* United States v. Dairy Farmers of America, Inc., 65 Fed. Reg. 44,820 (DOJ July 19, 2000) (proposed final judgment and competitive impact statement), 2001-1 Trade Cas. (CCH) ¶ 73,136 (E.D. Pa. 2000) (final judgment).

33. 308 U.S. 188 (1939).

cooperative to combine or conspire with persons outside the cooperative to fix prices or restrain trade.[34]

In three separate cases, the Supreme Court has sought to refine the *Borden* rule regarding concerted action with "outsiders." In *Sunkist Growers v. Winckler & Smith Citrus Products Co.*,[35] the Supreme Court held that Capper-Volstead immunity barred conspiracy charges against three agricultural cooperatives that were legally separate entities but that had substantially the same members. The Court reasoned that the three cooperatives were, in substance, a single economic unit and that the organizational distinctions between the groups were not of legal significance because at any time the individual members and their cooperatives could have formed a single organization incapable of conspiring with itself.[36] Subsequently, upon a more complete record, the Court in *Case-Siwayne Co. v. Sunkist Growers*[37] held that the same "economic unit" was ineligible for exemption under the Capper-Volstead Act because 15 percent of its members were nonfarm corporations or partnerships rather than producers. Similarly, in its most recent consideration of the agricultural cooperative exemption, *National Broiler Marketing Ass'n v. United States*,[38] the Supreme Court refused to grant the protection of the exemption to associations whose members could not all be classified as "farmers." The lower courts have attempted to construe this limitation on the application of the exemption under a variety of distinct circumstances.[39]

---

34. *Id.* at 204-05; *see also* Tillamook Cheese & Dairy Ass'n v. Tillamook County Creamery Ass'n, 358 F.2d 115, 117-18 n. 4 (9th Cir. 1966); Farmland Dairies v. New York Farm Bureau, 1996-1 Trade Cas. (CCH) ¶ 71,423, at 77,147-48 (N.D.N.Y. 1996); *cf.* Allen Gradley Co. v. Local 3, IBEW, 325 U.S. 797 (1945) (discussing parallel exemption for labor organization). In *Borden*, 308 U.S. at 203-04, the Supreme Court also rejected the contention that under § 2 of the Capper-Volstead Act the Secretary of Agriculture has exclusive or primary jurisdiction over antitrust violations involving agricultural cooperatives, a position that was followed in *Maryland & Va. Milk Producers Ass'n v. United States*, 362 U.S. 458, 462-63 (1960). *See also* Sunkist Growers v. FTC, 464 F. Supp. 302, 304, 312 (C.D. Cal. 1979) (dismissing action to restrain Federal Trade Commission (FTC) administrative proceedings).

35. 370 U.S. 19 (1962).

36. *Id.* at 29; *see also* Ripplemeyer v. National Grape Coop. Ass'n, 807 F. Supp. 1439, 1458 (W.D. Ark. 1992) (incorporated agricultural cooperative is incapable of conspiring with its wholly owned subsidiary); Hudson's Bay Co. Fur Sales v. American Legend Coop., 651 F. Supp. 819, 839 (D.N.J. 1986) (cooperative association of mink ranchers is incapable of conspiring with its subsidiary auction house).

37. 389 U.S. 384 (1967).

38. 436 U.S. 816 (1978). The Court ruled that in order for an association to enjoy the limited exemption of the Capper-Volstead Act, all of its members must be qualified as "farmers, planters, ranchmen, dairymen, nut or fruit growers." *Id.* at 823. Producers who own neither a breeder flock nor a hatchery and who maintain no grow-out facility do not qualify and, therefore, the cooperative association of which they are members is not protected by the exemption. *Id.* at 827; *see also* Holly Sugar Corp. v. Goshen County Coop. Beet Growers Ass'n., 725 F.2d 564, 569 (10th Cir. 1984). *But see* Alexander v. National Farmers Org., 687 F.2d 1173, 1186-87 (8th Cir. 1982) (de minimis nonproducer membership of cooperative does not invalidate exemption when cooperative's activities were "conducted exclusively for true dairy farmers"), *cert. denied*, 461 U.S. 937 (1983).

39. *See, e.g.*, Ewald Bros v. Mid-America Dairymen, Inc., 877 F.2d 1384, 1390 (8th Cir. 1989) (dairy cooperative did not forfeit exemption by contracting with nonmember proprietary dairies to obtain milk for standby pool, because nonmembers played no role in managing the cooperative or the standby pool, and because the volume of noncooperative milk was always less than the volume of milk supplied by the member cooperatives); Green v. Associated Milk Producers, Inc., 692 F.2d 1153, 1157 (8th Cir. 1982) (exemption does not apply where cooperative conspires with noncooperative); Agritronics Corp. v. National Dairy Herd Ass'n, 914 F. Supp. 814, 824

3. *The Packers and Stockyards Act of 1921*

The PSA was enacted in the face of a Federal Trade Commission investigation into the substantial amount of control a handful of firms exercised over the meat-packing industry. The PSA is intended "to assure fair competition and fair trade practices in livestock marketing and in the meatpacking industry[,] . . . to safeguard farmers and ranchers[,] . . . to protect consumers[,] . . . [and to protect] members of the livestock, meat, and poultry industries from unfair, deceptive, unjustly discriminatory, and monopolistic practices."[40] The PSA is remedial legislation and courts consistently have held that it should be liberally construed.[41] However, one court has cautioned that the general outlines of basic antitrust law must be kept in mind when enforcing the PSA.[42]

Section 202 of the PSA makes it unlawful for "any packer[43] with respect to livestock, meats, meat food products, or livestock products in unmanufactured form, or any live poultry dealer with respect to live poultry," to engage in or use any "unfair, unjustly discriminatory, or deceptive practice or device."[44] In addition to this general prohibition, the statute specifically bars undue or unreasonable preferences, market allocation, price manipulation, and restraint of commerce by regulated entities.[45] The PSA also bars conspiracies between a regulated entity and "any other person" to (1) apportion territory for carrying on business, (2) to apportion purchases

---

(N.D.N.Y. 1994) (same); United States v. Hinote, 823 F. Supp. 1350, 1359 (S.D. Mills. 1993) (companies involved in leasing fish ponds and acting as middlemen in the purchase and sale of catfish held not to be "producers of agricultural products" subject to Capper-Volstead Act protection); *Ripplemeyer*, 807 F. Supp. at 1457 (presence of a nonfarmer grape processor in a grape marketing cooperative abrogates Capper-Volstead immunity because the middleman role of the grape processor "exceeds the conduct Congress intended to permit through the Capper-Volstead exemption").

40. H.R. REP. NO. 85-1048 (1957), *reprinted in* 1958 U.S.C.C.A.N. 5213.

41. *See, e.g.*, Stafford v. Wallace, 258 U.S. 495, 521 (1922); Safeway Stores, Inc. v. Freeman, 369 F.2d 952, 956 (1966); Swift & Co. v. United States, 393 F.2d 247, 253 (7th Cir. 1968); Bruhn's Freezer Meats of Chicago, Inc. v. USDA, 438 F.2d 1332, 1337 (8th Cir. 1971).

42. Armour & Co. v. United States, 402 F.2d 712 (7th Cir. 1968). In finding that promotional coupons distributed by Armour to consumers did not violate the PSA, the court noted:
    While Section 202(a) of the Packers and Stockyards Act may be broader than antecedent antitrust legislation found in the Sherman, Clayton, Federal Trade Commission and Interstate Commerce Acts, there is no showing that there was any intent to give the Secretary of Agriculture complete and unbridled discretion to regulate the operations of packers. . . . Congress gave the secretary no mandate to ignore the general outline of long-time antitrust policy by condemning practices which are neither destructive nor injurious to competition nor intended to be so by the party charged.
    Id. at 722.

43. "Packer" is defined as "any person engaged in the business (a) of buying livestock in commerce for purposes of slaughter, or (b) of manufacturing or preparing meats or meat food products for sale of shipment in commerce, or (c) of marketing meats, meat food products, or livestock products in an unmanufactured form acting as a wholesale broker, dealer or distributor in commerce." 7 U.S.C. § 191 (2000).

44. *Id.* § 192(a) (2000).

45. *Id.* §§ 192(b), (c), (d) and (e) (2000). The Department of Agriculture regulations barr particular practices. *See, e.g.*, 9 C.F.R. § 201.69 (2001) (barring packers, dealers, and marketing agents from providing buying information to competitors for purposes of restricting or limiting competition, manipulating prices, or controlling the movement of livestock), § 201.70 (2001) (requiring each packer or dealer engaged in purchasing livestock to act independently of other packers and dealers). It also has issued several policy statements concerning implementation and enforcement of the PSA. 9 C.F.R. pt. 203 (2001).

or sales of any article, (3) to manipulate or control prices, or (4) to do, or aid and abet any act made unlawful under any provision of the section.[46]

Section 312 of the PSA contains a prohibition against any "unfair, unjustly discriminatory, or deceptive practice or device" by "any stockyard owner, market agency, or dealer" that is "in connection with determining whether persons should be authorized to operate at the stockyards, or with the receiving, marketing, buying, or selling on a commission basis or otherwise, feeding, watering, holding, delivery, shipment, weighing, or handling of livestock."[47] Unlike Section 202, Section 312 does not enumerate any specific types of activities that are unlawful, nor does it contain a conspiracy clause.

Both Section 202 and Section 312 are enforced by the Department of Agriculture's Grain Inspection, Packers and Stockyards Administration. The agency may enforce the statute through administrative proceedings[48] or through the Department of Justice in federal district court.[49] The PSA also grants the Secretary of Agriculture investigative powers, including subpoena power, so that the agency may effectively execute the provisions of the PSA and provide information to Congress.[50] Upon an administrative finding of a violation, the Secretary of Agriculture may issue a cease and desist order and assess civil penalties of up to $11,000 per violation.[51] Such orders are appealable to the court of appeals.[52] If a cease and desist order issued pursuant to Section 202 is affirmed by a court of appeals, a person who violates the order is subject to criminal prosecution and faces a fine of between $550 and $11,000 and imprisonment of between six months and five years.[53] A violation of an order issued pursuant to Section 312 subjects the violator to a forfeiture of $550 per day.[54]

Section 308 of the PSA provides a private right of action for any person who has been injured by conduct that is unlawful under the PSA or that violates any order of the Secretary of Agriculture under the act.[55] Under the statute, an injured party may enforce this liability either through filing a complaint with the Secretary of

---

46. 7 U.S.C. §§ 192(f), (g) (2000).
47. Id. § 213(a) (2000). Under the PSA, stockyards are regulated like public utilities. See id.§ 203 (2000); Stafford v. Wallace, 258 U.S. 495, 516 (1922) ("The act, therefore, treats the various stockyards of the country as great national public utilities to promote the flow of commerce from the ranges and farms of the West to the consumers in the East.").
48. 7 U.S.C. § 193 (2000); id. § 213(b) (2000).
49. Id. § 224 (2000). Because of what appears to be a statutory anomaly, violations of the PSA by live poultry dealers may be enforced only through district court action. See, e.g., Jackson v. Swift Eckrich, Inc., 53 F.3d 1452, 1457-58 (8th Cir. 1995).
50. 7 U.S.C. § 222 (2000); 15 U.S.C. §§ 46, 48-50 (2000).
51. 7 U.S.C. §§ 193(b), 213(b) (2000); 7 C.F.R. § 3.91 (2001) (adjusting civil monetary penalties to take account of inflation every four years).
52. 7 U.S.C. §§ 194, 213(b) (2000); 7 C.F.R. § 3.91 (2001) (adjusting civil monetary penalties to take account of inflation every four years).
53. 7 U.S.C. § 195 (2000); 7 C.F.R. § 3.91 (2001) (adjusting civil monetary penalties to take account of inflation every four years).
54. 7 U.S.C. § 215 (2000); 7 C.F.R. § 3.91 (2001) (adjusting civil monetary penalties to take account of inflation every four years).
55. 7 U.S.C. § 209 (2000). See Gerace v. Utica Veal Co., 580 F. Supp. 1465 (N.D.N.Y. 1984) (state commissioner of agriculture could seek private damage remedy in federal district court for alleged violations of PSA).

Agriculture or by suit in U.S. district court. However, courts have from time to time invoked the doctrine of primary jurisdiction in actions filed in court.[56]

Types of conduct that have been held to violate the PSA include price refunds resulting in the customer obtaining a price advantage over his competitors,[57] price discounts,[58] purchasing agreements among competitors,[59] conspiracies to affect terms of contracts between packers and producers,[60] and refusals to deal.[61] The Department of Agriculture has held that Section 202 should be read liberally enough to reach types of anticompetitive practices deemed unfair under Section 45 of the Federal Trade Commission Act, and also to reach any special mischief and injuries inherent in livestock and poultry traffic.[62]

No showing of actual injury is necessary to find liability under the PSA.[63] However, the agency and the courts tend to look at the actual or possible results of the conduct, or the accused party's apparent intent, and not the type of conduct itself in order to determine whether the PSA has been violated. Thus, a price refund has been held not to violate the act when it did not result in an anticompetitive advantage

56. *See, e.g.*, Kelly v. Union Stockyards & Transit Co. of Chicago, 190 F.2d 860, 863 (7th Cir. 1951); Shannon v. Chambers, 212 F. Supp. 620, 622 (S.D. Ind. 1962) (finding that, notwithstanding the provisions of 7 U.S.C. § 209(b)(2), the case presented matters for the Secretary of Agriculture's expertise that should be addressed by him in the first instance); *but see* McCleneghan v. Union Stock Yards Co. of Omaha, 298 F.2d 659, 667 (8th Cir. 1962) (primary jurisdiction "is not an inevitable barrier to court jurisdiction" in all cases arising under PSA). Under the PSA, the agency has the authority to issue an order awarding money damages to a person injured by a violation of the PSA, *see* 7 U.S.C. § 210(e) (2000), and those orders are enforceable in federal district courts and state courts or general jurisdiction. *Id.* § 210(f) (2000).

57. *See, e.g.*, Trunz Pork Store, Inc. v. Wallace, 70 F.2d 688 (2d Cir. 1934) (upholding cease and desist order prohibiting "set-up" broker from refunding part of commission to customer, thereby giving customer price advantage).

58. *See, e.g.*, Wilson & Co., Inc. v. Benson, 286 F.2d 891 (7th Cir. 1961) (upholding cease and desist order concerning price discounts given to hotels where discounts were found to have no relationship to costs or to prices of competitors).

59. *See, e.g.*, Swift & Co. v. United States, 308 F.2d 849 (7th Cir. 1962).

60. *See, e.g.*, De Jong Packing Co. v. USDA, 618 F.2d 1329, 1336 (9th Cir.) (conspiracy by packers to force auction stockyards to change terms of sale so that risk of loss from failure to pass government inspection fell on packers and not sellers constituted unfair practice under § 202(a), even though it did not violate the conspiracy provision of § 202(g)), *cert. denied*, 449 U.S. 1061 (1980).

61. *See, e.g.*, Swift & Co. v. United States, 393 F.2d 247, 253 (1968) (finding that prohibitions of PSA "are broader and more far-reaching than the Sherman Act or even Section 5 of the Federal Trade Commission Act," and that petitioners' refusals to buy from certain lamb producers under the circumstances did violate § 202) (citations omitted); Baldree v. Cargill, Inc., 758 F. Supp. 704 (M.D. Fla. 1990) (court preliminarily enjoined unilateral termination of contract with poultry producer where plaintiff alleged termination was part of effort to discourage plaintiff from supporting producers' association), *aff'd without opinion*, 925 F.2d 1474 (11th Cir. 1991).

62. *In re* Walti, Schilling Co., 39 Ag. Dec. 119 (1978).

63. *See, e.g.*, IBP, Inc. v. Glickman, 187 F.3d 974, 977 (8th Cir. 1999) (potential for injury is sufficient to support a cease and desist order, but right of first refusal packer obtained from producer in that case did not potentially suppress or reduce competition sufficiently to be proscribed by the act); Wilson & Co. v. Benson, 286 F.2d 891, 895 (7th Cir. 1961); Bowman v. USDA, 363 F.2d 81, 85 (5th Cir. 1966); *cf.* Central Coast Meats, Inc. v. USDA, 541 F.2d 1325, 1327 (9th Cir. 1976) (even assuming no proof of injury is required, the Secretary of Agriculture must show that the conduct in question is likely to produce the sort of injury § 202 is designed to prevent).

for a customer.[64]   Similarly, a price discount that appeared to result from the competitive nature of business has been held not to violate the PSA.[65]

The PSA is intended to provide remedies in addition to those provided under other antitrust statutes, and does not supplant those other statutes.[66] The PSA also explicitly defines the roles of the Department of Agriculture and the Federal Trade Commission in investigating anticompetitive conduct in the industries regulated by the PSA. In particular, the PSA provides that the Federal Trade Commission shall have jurisdiction over a matter "involving meat, meat food products, livestock products in unmanufactured form, or poultry products" (1) when the Secretary of Agriculture requests the Federal Trade Commission to investigate; (2) when the Federal Trade Commission determines that the effective exercise of its jurisdiction with respect to retail sales of meat, meat food products, or livestock products will otherwise be impaired; or (3) when the matter involves transactions in margarine or poultry products or retail sales of meat, meat food products, and livestock products.[67]

B.   Communications

1.   *Broadcasting*

Since the early 1980s, the Federal Communications Commission has moved away from extensive regulation of broadcasters and broadcast services and eliminated a variety of regulations.[68]

---

64.   Wilmington Provision Co. v. Wallace, 72 F.2d 989 (3d Cir. 1934) (cease and desist order set aside where broker's practice of remitting part of brokerage fee to customer did not result in price advantage to the customer).

65.   Swift & Co. v. Wallace, 105 F.2d 848 (7th Cir. 1939) (whether a discount amounts to an "unreasonable preference" in violation of § 202(b) must be determined by evaluation of the circumstances; discounts and other trade practices that can be justified by the standards of business are not prohibited by § 202).

66.   *See* 7 U.S.C. § 209(b) (2000) (private right of action under PSA "shall not in anyway abridge or alter remedies now existing at common law or by statute, but the provisions of this chapter are in addition to such remedies"); *id.* § 225 (2000) (providing that nothing in PSA is intended to prevent or interfere with the enforcement of, among other things, the Sherman Act or Clayton Act).

67.   *Id.* § 227(b) (2000). If the FTC determines it needs to investigate such matters under subsection (2), the FTC is required to notify the Secretary of Agriculture and may not proceed if within 10 days of such notice the Secretary of Agriculture notifies the FTC that he is already investigating the matter. *Id.* Conversely, the Secretary of Agriculture may investigate matters falling under subsection (3) (except those concerning poultry products) if he determines it is necessary for the effective exercise of his jurisdiction under the PSA and the FTC, upon notice of his determination, does not notify him that the FTC already is investigating the matter. *Id.* § 227(d) (2000). The Secretary of Agriculture's jurisdiction to investigate matters involving poultry products is very limited. *Id.* § 227(e) (2000).

68.   *See, e.g.*, Review of the Prime Time Access Rule, § 73.658(k) of the Federal Communications Commission's (FCC) Rules, Report and Order, 11 F.C.C.R. 546 (1996) (eliminating prime time access rule); Review of the Syndication and Financial Interest Rules, § 73.659-73.663 of the FCC's Rules, Report and Order, 10 F.C.C.R. 12,165 (1995) (eliminating syndication and financial interest rules); Review of the FCC's Regulations Governing Television Broadcasting, Report and Order, 10 F.C.C.R. 4538 (1995) (eliminating network station relationship rule and secondary affiliation rule); Amendment of Part 26, Subpart J, § 76.501 of the FCC's Rules Relative to Elimination of the Prohibition on Common Ownership of Cable Television Systems and National Television Networks, 7 F.C.C.R. 6156 (1992), *recons.*, 8 F.C.C.R. 1184 (1993); Deregulation of Radio, 84 F.C.C.2d 968 (1981) (eliminating guidelines regarding nonentertainment programming, commercial levels, and certain record-keeping requirements), *aff'd in part and remanded in part*

Section 313(a) of the Communications Act of 1934 (1934 Act)[69] makes "all laws of the United States relating to unlawful restraints and monopolies and to combinations, contracts, or agreements in restraint of trade" applicable to interstate and foreign radio and television communications.[70] Section 313(a) also provides that if a Federal Communications Commission licensee is found guilty in a civil or criminal suit of violating the antitrust laws, the court may revoke its license.[71] Section 313(b) directs the Federal Communications Commission to refuse a license to any person whose license has been revoked by a court under this section.[72] The section does not prevent the Federal Communications Commission from granting a license transfer during the pendency of an antitrust suit, but the new licensee may be joined as a party defendant in the antitrust suit.[73]

The Federal Communications Commission does not have the statutory power to decide antitrust issues. In *United States v. Radio Corp. of America (RCA)*,[74] the Supreme Court held that in broadcasting, where "there [was] no pervasive regulatory scheme, and no rate structures to throw out of balance," there was no need to defer to the agency's expertise.[75] The Court thus concluded that the Federal Communications Commission's approval of an agreement to exchange radio stations did not warrant dismissal on primary jurisdiction grounds of an antitrust action challenging the exchange. Nevertheless, subsequent to *RCA*, courts have on occasion deferred to pending agency action in cases involving antitrust claims.[76] The Federal Communications Commission, in turn, has sometimes deferred to antitrust enforcement agencies and the courts on issues of antitrust policy. For example, the agency dismissed a complaint alleging that a licensee unlawfully monopolized the broadcasting of sporting events because, in the agency's view, the Department of Justice, the Federal Trade Commission, or the courts were better equipped to deal with the antitrust analysis required.[77] Similarly, the Federal Communications Commission dismissed a petition by an association of theater owners to direct a

---

sub nom. Office of Communication of United Church of Christ v. FCC, 707 F.2d 1413 (D.C. Cir. 1983), *modified on remand*, 96 F.C.C.2d 930 (1984), *vacated and remanded*, 779 F.2d 702 (D.C. Cir. 1985), *modified on remand*, 104 F.C.C.2d 505 (1986); Revision of Programming and Commercialization Policies, Ascertainment Requirements, and Program Log Requirements for Commercial Television Stations, 98 F.C.C.2d 1076 (1984), *recons. denied*, 104 F.C.C.2d 357 (1986), *aff'd in part and remanded in part sub nom.* Action for Children's Television v. FCC, 821 F.2d 741 (D.C. Cir. 1987); Revision of Applications for Renewal of License of Commercial and Noncommercial AM, FM and Television Licensees, 87 F.C.C.2d 1127 (1981) (streamlining renewal application process), *aff'd sub nom.* Black Citizens for a Fair Media v. FCC, 719 F.2d 407 (D.C. Cir. 1983), *cert. denied*, 467 U.S. 1255 (1984); Elimination of Unnecessary Broadcast Regulation, 50 Fed. Reg. 5583 (1985).

69.   47 U.S.C. § 313(a) (1994).

70.   *Id.* § 313(b) (1994).

71.   *Id.* § 313(a) (1994). Section 313(a) is the only provision of the Communications Act under which a body other than the FCC may revoke an FCC license.

72.   *Id.* § 313(b).

73.   A.H. Belo Corp., 43 F.C.C.2d 336, 338 (1973).

74.   358 U.S. 334, 346 (1959).

75.   *Id.* at 350; *see also* United States v. ABC, 1977-2 Trade Cas. (CCH) ¶ 61,580, at 72,371 (C.D. Cal. 1977); United States v. CBS, 1977-1 Trade Cas. (CCH) ¶ 61,327, at 71,139 (C.D. Cal. 1977); United States v. NBC, 1974-1 Trade Cas. (CCH) ¶ 74,885, at 95,922 (C.D. Cal. 1973).

76.   *See, e.g.*, Writers' Guild of Am. v. ABC, 609 F.2d 355 (9th Cir. 1979), *cert. denied*, 449 U.S. 824 (1980); Levitch v. CBS, 495 F. Supp. 649, 658 (S.D.N.Y. 1980), *aff'd*, 697 F.2d 495 (2d Cir. 1983).

77.   Cahill v. Kaswell, 37 Rad. Reg. 2d (P&F) 197, 200-01 (1976).

program producer to cease exhibiting motion pictures on pay cable television.[78] The agency held that the petition was tantamount to a request for interpretation and enforcement of an antitrust consent decree and thus was brought in the wrong forum.[79]

The Federal Communications Commission historically has recognized that "competitive considerations are an important element of the 'public interest' standard" that governs its decision making.[80] In affirming the Federal Communications Commission's duty to consider competitive factors in its regulation of broadcasting, the Supreme Court has suggested that "in a given case the FCC might find that antitrust considerations alone would keep the statutory standard from being met."[81]

The Federal Communications Commission has discretion to determine the appropriate weight that should be accorded competitive considerations in particular circumstances. The agency has demonstrated an increased willingness to rely on case-by-case enforcement by private parties and the antitrust enforcement agencies, as opposed to broad, prophylactic rules and policies that may inhibit otherwise efficient conduct.[82] The Federal Communications Commission has noted that its "overriding responsibility is not to foster the maximum level of competition in the industry but rather to promote the public interest."[83]

The Federal Communications Commission has considered competitive factors primarily in its regulation of licensing and certain aspects of broadcast industry behavior and structure.

a. LICENSING

Prior to 1986, in considering whether the grant of a particular application for a broadcast license was in the public interest, the Federal Communications Commission weighed, among other factors, whether the applicant had been prosecuted or convicted under the antitrust laws.[84] In 1986, however, the agency

---

78. Warner Communs., 51 F.C.C.2d 1079, 1081-82 (1975).
79. *Id.* at 1081.
80. United States v. FCC, 652 F.2d 72, 81-82 (D.C. Cir. 1980) (en banc) (quoting Northern Natural Gas Co. v. FPC, 399 F.2d 953, 961 (D.C. Cir. 1968)); *accord* NBC v. United States, 319 U.S. 190, 223-24 (1943); *CBS*, 1977-1 Trade Cas. (CCH) ¶ 61,327, at 71,135.
81. United States v. RCA, 358 U.S. 334, 351 (1959).
82. *See* Elimination of Unnecessary Broadcast Regulation, 50 Fed. Reg. 5583, 5588 n.19 (FCC 1985). Regulation of certain types of competitive practices by the FCC was found to be "unnecessary and possibly counterproductive. To the extent the policies cover areas regulated by the antitrust laws, other agencies such as the Department of Justice or the Federal Trade Commission have primary enforcement responsibility." *Id.* at 5588 (footnote omitted).
83. United States Cellular Operating Co., 3 F.C.C.R. 5345, 5346 n.3 (1988).
84. Report on Uniform Policy as to Violation by Applicants of Laws of United States, 42 F.C.C.2d 399 (1951) [hereinafter 1951 REPORT]; *see also NBC*, 319 U.S. 190 (stating FCC might infer past acts of monopoly or unfair competition make applicant unfit licensee); RKO Gen., Inc. (WNAC-TV), 78 F.C.C.2d 1, 116-18 (1980) (antitrust considerations were important to FCC's denial of RKO's license renewal application), *aff'd in part and rev'd in part*, 670 F.2d 215 (D.C. Cir. 1981), *cert. denied*, 456 U.S. 927 (1982). The fate of RKO's licenses took several lengthy and tangled turns before the FCC approved settlement agreements whereby RKO would sell its facilities and the stations were placed in the hands of "an unquestionably qualified licensee." *See* RKO Gen., Inc. (KHJ-TV), 3 F.C.C.R. 5057, 5060 (1988), *appeal dismissed sub nom.* Los Angeles Television v. FCC, No. 88-1673 (D.C. Cir. Aug. 4, 1989) (settlement of KHJ-TV, Los Angeles proceeding); *see also* RKO Gen., Inc. (WHBQ), 3 F.C.C.R. 5055 (1988) (settlement of WHBQ, Memphis

radically altered its treatment of competitive factors as part of the regulation of licensing.[85] Instead of considering whether the applicant has been prosecuted or convicted for any antitrust violation,[86] the agency generally will restrict its inquiry to antitrust convictions for broadcast-related activities.[87] The agency will use these criteria primarily in comparative licensing proceedings.

b. LICENSEE SALES PRACTICES

In passing on the qualifications of broadcast license applicants, the Federal Communications Commission in the past has taken into consideration behavior that, although not necessarily violative of the antitrust laws, may nevertheless tend to restrain competition.[88] A variety of sales practices of broadcast licensees were the subject of scrutiny under this aspect of the agency's public interest standard. However, many of these rules and practices of the Federal Communication Commission have been eliminated or abandoned.[89]

c. OWNERSHIP OF BROADCAST LICENSES

The Federal Communications Commission has pursued a structural approach to broadcast regulation. Its rules limit ownership of broadcast facilities by limiting the number of broadcast licenses a single entity can hold[90] and by limiting the extent to

proceeding); RKO Gen., Inc. (WGMS), 3 F.C.C.R. 5262 (1988) (settlement of WGMS and WGMS-FM, Bethesda proceeding); RKO Gen., Inc. (WRKO), 3 F.C.C.R. 6603 (1988) (settlement of WRKO and WROR-FM, Boston proceeding).

85. Policy Regarding Character Qualifications in Broadcast Licensing, 102 F.C.C.2d 1179 (1986) [hereinafter 1986 POLICY STATEMENT], recons. denied, 1 F.C.C.R. 421 (1986), appeal dismissed sub nom. National Ass'n for Better Broad. v. FCC, No. 86-1179 (D.C. Cir. June 11, 1987).

86. Factors that previously were relevant to the weight and significance of a given antitrust violation included whether the violation was willful or not, recurring or isolated, and recent or remote in time, and whether the antitrust judgment was final or on appeal. 1951 REPORT, supra note 84, at 402-03.

87. If the licensee or applicant allegedly engaged in nonbroadcast-related anticompetitive activity, the inquiry will be limited to adjudicated violations of the law involving fraudulent misconduct before a government agency or criminal felony convictions involving false statements or dishonesty. 1986 POLICY STATEMENT, supra note 85, at 1200-01.

88. See, e.g., Metropolitan Television Co. v. FCC, 289 F.2d 874, 876 (D.C. Cir. 1961) ("it is settled that practices which present realistic dangers of competitive restraint are a proper consideration for the Commission in determining the 'public interest, convenience, and necessity'") (citations and footnote omitted); cf. supra note 80 and accompanying text.

89. See, e.g., Elimination of Unnecessary Broadcast Regulation, 51 Fed. Reg. 11,914 (FCC 1986) (eliminating rules concerning combination advertising rates and joint sales practices among separately owned stations serving same geographic areas); Representation of Stations by Representatives Owned by Competing Stations in the Same Area, 87 F.C.C.2d 668, 682-83 (1981) (eliminating prior prohibition against sales representative with common ownership with one broadcast station from representing another similar broadcast station in same area); Elimination of Unnecessary Broadcast Regulation, 50 Fed. Reg. 5583, 5587 (FCC 1985) (abandoning practice of scrutinizing licensee use of broadcast facilities to further nonbroadcast activities, finding antitrust laws a more proper recourse for any such improper activity); United States v. National Ass'n of Broadcasters, 1982-83 Trade Cas. (CCH) ¶¶ 65,049-50 (D.D.C. 1982) (consent decree) (National Association of Broadcasters agreed to abolish certain advertising standards provisions in its self-regulatory code that DOJ alleged violated the Sherman Act because they constituted agreement among broadcasters to limit availability of commercial advertising time).

90. Under the FCC's multiple ownership rules, a single person or entity can own any number of UHF and VHF television stations as long as the television stations, in the aggregate, do not reach more

which a broadcast licensee can have an interest in other media or media-related entities.[91] These multiple and cross-ownership rules are designed to further two basic policies: (1) diversification of programming sources and viewpoints, and (2) prevention of economic concentration in the broadcast industry.[92] The Supreme Court has upheld both the Federal Communications Commission's power to restrict multiple ownership and the validity of those policy goals.[93]

These ownership rules, however, have been relaxed in light of the general deregulatory environment under the Telecommunications Act of 1996 (1996 Act).[94] This has led to a number of mergers and acquisitions, which have been subjected to Department of Justice scrutiny. One example is the merger between Clear Channel Communications, Inc. and AMFM Inc.[95] In 2000, these two companies agreed to sell ninety-nine radio stations in twenty-seven markets nationwide to satisfy Department of Justice antitrust concerns.[96]

---

than 35% of the national audience according to Nielsen Designated Market Area (DMA) market ratings. 47 C.F.R. § 73.3555(e)(1) (2000). The rule "discounts" the reach of UHF stations, so that owners of UHF stations are attributed only 50% of the television households in their DMA market. *Id.* § 73.3555(e)(2)(i) (2000). Limitation on the number of radio stations nationwide that could be owned were eliminated by the Telecommunications Act of 1996, Pub. L. No. 104-104, § 202, 110 Stat. 87.

91. The FCC's cross-ownership rules prohibit the ownership of both a broadcast facility and a daily newspaper in the same community. 47 C.F.R. § 73.3555 (2000); *see also* FCC v. National Citizens Comm. for Broad., 436 U.S. 755, 802 (1978) (upholding these rules). The FCC, however, has granted temporary waivers of these rules upon a showing that the owner will have to sell at a distressed price, when separate ownership and operation of the newspaper and station cannot be supported in the locality, or when "for whatever reason" the purposes of the rule will be best served by continued joint ownership. Multiple Ownership, 50 F.C.C.2d 1046, 1085 (1975); *see also* Owosso Broad. Co., 60 Rad. Reg. 2d (P&F) 99 (1986) (granting temporary waiver of 11 months); Metromedia Radio & Television, Inc., 102 F.C.C.2d 1334 (1985) (granting 24-month waiver), *aff'd sub nom.* Health & Med. Policy Research Group v. FCC, 807 F.2d 1038 (D.C. Cir. 1986). The cross-ownership rules also prohibit the ownership of a broadcast facility and a cable television system in the same community. 47 C.F.R. § 76.501 (2000).

   In addition to its rules restricting multiple ownership of broadcast licenses, the FCC has granted a preference in comparative licensing proceedings to applicants who have no other media interests. *See* Policy Statement, Reexamination of the Commission's Cross-Interest Policy, 4 F.C.C.R. 2208 (1989). For firms with other media interests, however, a substantial broadcast record in the public interest can outweigh the absence of diversification. *See* Policy Statement on Comparative Broadcast Hearings, 1 F.C.C.2d 393, 394-99 (1965).

92. *See* Multiple Ownership Rules, 22 F.C.C.2d 306, 307 (1970).

93. *See* United States v. Storer Broad. Co., 351 U.S. 192, 203-05 (1956).

94. Modifications in these rules are continuing. The FCC in late 2001 announced plans to review existing limitations on the number of radio stations that can be owned in local markets. *See* 66 Fed. Reg. 56,107 (FCC Nov. 6, 2001).

95. United States v. Clear Channel Communs., Inc., 66 Fed. Reg. 12,544 (DOJ Feb. 27, 2001) (proposed final judgment and competitive impact statement), Civ. 1:00CV02063 (TPF) (D.D.C. 2001).

96. After the merger, the combined entity would own or operate 898 stations. *Id.* The DOJ also required the combined company to sell AMFM's 29% interest in Lamar Advertising Co. *Id.* Other mergers that have been modified to overcome DOJ objections include the 2001 acquisition of Chris-Craft, Indus., Inc. by The News Corp. Ltd., which required Chris-Craft to divest one television station in Salt Lake City, United States v. The News Corp., 66 Fed. Reg. 29,997 (DOJ June 4, 2001) (notice of filing of proposed final judgment); 1999 acquisition of Triathlon Broadcasting Co. by Capstar Broadcasting Corp., which required Capstar's divestiture of five radio stations in Wichita, Kansas; United States v. Capstar Broad. Corp., 64 Fed. Reg. 31,612 (DOJ June 11, 1999) (proposed final judgment and competitive impact statement); acquisition of SFX Broadcasting, Inc. by Capstar Broadcasting Partners in 1998, which required Capstar to divest radio stations in South Carolina, Texas, Mississippi, and New York, United States v. Hicks, Muse,

d. NETWORKS

In the past, the Federal Communications Commission was concerned with the economic power of the three major commercial television networks and sought to limit the influence of the networks (ABC, CBS, and NBC) over their affiliated stations in order to make the stations more independent.[97] However, because of the multitude of nonnetwork sources for television programming today, many of the agency's rules governing the networks have been eliminated.[98] The courts, on the other hand, have stepped in to prevent improper activity by the networks.[99]

e. CABLE CARRIAGE OF BROADCAST STATIONS

In 1993, the Federal Communications Commission adopted rules to implement the mandatory television broadcast signal carriage and retransmission consent provisions of the Cable Television Consumer Protection and Competition Act of 1992.[100] These provisions require broadcasters either to demand carriage of their signals ("must-carry")[101] or to state their intention to enter compensation agreements for carriage ("retransmission consent")[102] once very three years.[103]

2. *Common Carriers*

a. OVERVIEW

Competition among telecommunications common carriers has been dramatically affected by the landmark 1996 Act.[104] Congress intended the 1996 Act to establish a "procompetitive, deregulatory national policy framework" for the

---

Tate & Furst, Inc., 63 Fed. Reg. 18,214 (DOJ Apr. 14, 1998) (proposed final judgment and competitive impact statement).

97. *See generally* FCC Network Inquiry Special Staff, FCC Rules Governing Commercial Television Network Practices (1979).

98. *See, e.g.*, Review of the Prime Time Access Rule, Section 73.658(k) of the Commission's Rules, Report and Order, 11 F.C.C.R. 546 (1996) (eliminating the "prime time access" rule); Review of the Syndication and Financial Interest Rules, Section 73.658-73.663 of the Commission's Rules, Report and Order, 10 F.C.C.R. 12, 165 (1995) (eliminating the "financial interest and syndication" rules); Review of Rules and Policies Concerning Network Broadcasting by Television Stations: Elimination or Modification of Section 73.658(c), 4 F.C.C.R. 2755 (1989) (eliminating rules relating to the duration of affiliation agreements between television station licensees and television networks); *see also* 66 Fed. Reg. 32,242 (FCC June 14, 2001) (amending 47 C.F.R. § 73,658(g) to permit one of the four major television networks (ABC, CBS, NBC and Fox) to own, operate, maintain, or control the WB or UPN television networks).

99. *See, e.g.*, PrimeTime 24 Joint Venture v. NBC, 219 F.3d 92, 98, 103 (2d Cir. 2000) (remanding a satellite broadcaster's antitrust claims that the networks and their affiliates engaged in concerted baseless challenges under the Satellite Home Viewers Act of 1988 to stifle competition and refuse to negotiate copyright licenses with the satellite broadcaster).

100. Pub. L. No. 102-385, 106 Stat. 1460.

101. 47 U.S.C. § 534 (1994 & Supp. 1999).

102. *Id.* § 325(b) (Supp. 1999).

103. *See* Implementation of the Cable Television Consumer Protection and Competition Act of 1992, Report and Order, 8 F.C.C.R. 2965 (1993), *recons.*, 9 F.C.C.R. 6723 (1994), *aff'd sub nom.* Turner Broad. Sys. v. FCC, 910 F. Supp. 734 (D.D.C. 1995) (three-judge court), *aff'd*, 520 U.S. 180 (1997). While retransmission consent provisions apply to both television and radio stations, must-carry requirements are applicable only to television stations.

104. Pub. L. No. 104-104, 110 Stat. 56 (1996).

telecommunications industry.[105] But while there has been a general decrease in regulation and a concomitant increase in reliance on market forces to shape this industry, telecommunications common carriers remain extensively regulated both by the Federal Communications Commission and by state regulatory agencies.

The 1996 Act, though informed by the industry's extensive regulatory history, substantially rewrote many of the rules. Among other things, the 1996 Act expressly repealed the 1982 decree in *United States v. AT&T*[106] and established a framework promoting competition in local telecommunications markets as well as a mechanism to allow the regional Bell operating companies (RBOCs) to provide interexchange long-distance service in the states in which they are local exchange carriers (LECs). In general, that framework has begun to blur the traditional lines between providers of local telecommunications services and interstate telecommunications services. While the 1996 Act contains an express antitrust savings clause,[107] recent decisions have raised questions about the extent, if any, to which the 1996 Act limits telecommunications common carriers' antitrust liability for failure to adhere to the requirements of the 1996 Act.[108]

b.   THE TELECOMMUNICATIONS ACT OF 1996

(1)   Overview

The 1996 Act substantially amended the 1934 Act with the overriding goal of promoting competition in all telecommunications markets. Title I of the 1996 Act is devoted to telecommunications services and contains two subtitles. The first subtitle is primarily aimed at promoting competition in the provision of local telephone service by seeking to eliminate technological, economic, and regulatory barriers to competitive entry. The 1996 Act envisions that competitive local telephone service in a given geographic area could be provided by, among others, local telephone companies that currently serve other geographic areas, long-distance telephone companies, cable television companies, and electric utilities. The 1996 Act also eliminates state and local barriers to competitive entry.[109]

105. H.R. CONF. REP. NO. 104-458, at 1 (1996), *reprinted in* 1996 U.S.C.C.A.N. 124 [hereinafter CONF. REP.].
106. *See* 47 U.S.C. § 152, note (a)(1) (Supp. 1999). The decision adopting the consent decree is reported at 552 F. Supp. 131 (D.D.C. 1982), *aff'd sub nom.* Maryland v. United States, 460 U.S. 1001 (1983). This decree, sometimes referred to as the AT&T Decree or the Modification of Final Judgment (MFJ), was entered as a modification of a 1956 consent decree that had been entered in an earlier monopolization case brought by the government. United States v. Western Elec. Co., 1956 Trade Cas. (CCH) ¶ 68,246 (D.N.J. 1956). In addition, the 1996 Act provides that conduct previously subject to a consent decree in connection with United States v. GTE Corp., Civ. No. 83-1298 (D.D.C. Dec. 21, 1984), and a proposed consent decree regarding United States v. AT&T Corp. and McCaw Cellular Communications, Inc., Civ. No. 94-01555 (D.D.C. July 15, 1994), would no longer be subject to those decrees but would be governed by the 1996 Act. Congress intended that the courts retain jurisdiction over these decrees for the limited purpose of examining conduct that predates the enactment of the 1996 Act. CONF. REP., *supra* note 105, at 198-99. The AT&T Decree was terminated nunc pro tunc as of February 8, 1996. United States v. Western Elec. Co., 1996-1 Trade Cas. (CCH) ¶ 71,364 (D.D.C. 1996).
107. 47 U.S.C. § 152, note (b)(1) (Supp. 1999).
108. *See, e.g.,* Goldwasser v. Ameritech Corp., 222 F.3d 390 (7th Cir. 2000); part B.2.b(2)(a) of this chapter.
109. 47 U.S.C. § 253(a) (Supp. 1999).

Section 251(a) of the 1996 Act generally imposes a duty on telecommunications carriers to interconnect their facilities with the facilities of other telecommunications carriers.[110] Section 251(b) places additional obligations on LECs, which are required, among other things, to permit resale of their telecommunications services and to provide "number portability" and "dialing parity."[111]

Section 251(c) imposes further obligations on incumbent LECs (ILECs).[112] ILECs are required to interconnect their facilities with the facilities of competing LECs (CLECs) at any technically feasible point within the incumbent's network.[113] Interconnection is required to be at least equal in quality to that provided by the ILEC to itself, an affiliate, or any other party and is to be provided on just, reasonable, and nondiscriminatory rates and terms.[114] The ILEC also must provide competing telephone companies with access to requested network elements at any technically feasible point, on an "unbundled basis," and at reasonable and nondiscriminatory rates.[115] The 1996 Act specifies that rates for interconnection and access to network elements are to be based on the cost of providing the interconnection or network element and may include a reasonable profit.[116]

An ILEC also must offer its retail services at wholesale rates for purposes of resale.[117] The 1996 Act specifies that wholesale rates are to be based on retail rates minus any costs (such as marketing or billing) that are avoided by the ILEC as a result of not providing the service to its customers at retail.[118] In addition, an ILEC is required to provide for physical collocation of a competitor's equipment necessary for interconnection or access on the ILEC's premises.[119]

The 1996 Act requires ILECs and CLECs requesting interconnection/access to negotiate in good faith the terms of agreements that satisfy the requirements of

110. *Id.* § 251(a) (Supp. 1999).
111. *Id.* § 251(b) (Supp. 1999). Number portability generally refers to the ability of a customer who remains at the same location to retain the same telephone number when switching to a different telephone company. *Id.* § 153(30) (Supp. 1999). Under the 1996 Act, dialing parity means that customers will be able to have their calls routed automatically to the telecommunications service provider of their choice, without the need to dial an access code. *Id.* § 153(15) (Supp. 1999).
112. The 1996 Act defines the "incumbent" LEC as the LEC that, on the date of the act's enactment, was providing local telephone service in a given geographic area and was deemed to be a member of the exchange carrier association. *Id.* § 251(h)(1) (Supp. 1999).
113. *Id.* § 251(c)(2)(B) (Supp. 1999). The FCC's order implementing this and other provisions of §§ 251 and 252 is discussed in part B.2.b(3) of this chapter.
114. 47 U.S.C. § 251(c)(2)(C), (D) (Supp. 1999).
115. *Id.* § 251(c)(3) (Supp. 1999). An "unbundled basis" means that a particular element can be obtained individually, without having to be taken as part of a package of elements. For a telephone company seeking to compete with an ILEC, the choice between interconnection and access is generally determined by the extent to which the competitor is using its own facilities. That is, a competing local telephone company is likely to request interconnection for its own facilities and request access for those network components it does not seek to duplicate.
116. *Id.* § 252(d)(1)(A), (B) (Supp. 1999). The act, however, does not define "cost" other than to state that cost shall be "determined without reference to a rate-of-return or other rate-based proceeding." *Id.* § 252(d)(1)(A)(i).
117. *Id.* § 251(c)(4) (Supp. 1999).
118. *Id.* § 252(d)(3) (Supp. 1999).
119. *Id.* § 251(c)(6) (Supp. 1999); *see infra* notes 175-79. *See also* US West Communs., Inc. v. Hamilton, 224 F.3d 1049, 1056 (9th Cir. 2000) (1996 Act permits a state commission to require collocation of remote switching on the ILEC's premises); MCI Telecommuns. Corp. v. US West Communs., Inc., 204 F.3d 1262, 1272 (9th Cir. 2000) (affirming validity of provision requiring collocation of remote switching units on ILEC's premises).

Sections 251(b) and (c).[120] Under Section 252 of the act, however, an agreement arrived at voluntarily is not required to meet the standards of Sections 251(b) and (c).[121] At any time during the negotiating process, any party may ask a state commission to mediate any disputes.[122] In addition, after the negotiation process has been given a substantial amount of time to succeed, the 1996 Act provides a window of time when any party may petition a state commission to arbitrate any disputes.[123]

All interconnection agreements, whether negotiated or arbitrated, must be submitted to the appropriate state commission for approval.[124] The 1996 Act establishes time frames within which a state must act and specifies the grounds under which a state commission may reject an agreement.[125] The act preempts state court review of a state commission's approval or rejection of an agreement and provides for federal court review of such determinations.[126] In cases where the state refuses to act on a submitted agreement, the Federal Communications Commission is authorized to act.[127]

Aside from the provisions involving negotiated or arbitrated agreements, the 1996 Act also permits a Bell operating company (BOC) to submit for approval to a state commission a statement of the terms and conditions it generally offers to parties requesting interconnection within the state.[128] In order to be approved, the BOC's statement must comply with the requirements of Sections 251 and 252(d).[129]

The second subtitle of Title I of the 1996 Act contains provisions specifically applicable to the BOCs. Chief among these provisions are those that govern the offering of interLATA service by the BOCs.[130] The act divides interLATA service

---

120. 47 U.S.C. § 251(c)(1) (Supp. 1999).
121. *Id.* § 252(a)(1) (Supp. 1999).
122. *Id.* § 252(a)(2) (Supp. 1999).
123. *Id.* § 252(b)(1) (Supp. 1999). The window for petitioning a state commission to arbitrate runs from the 135th to the 160th day after the ILEC receives a request to negotiate an interconnection agreement. *Id.*
124. *Id.* § 252(e)(1) (Supp. 1999). Courts have held that the grant to states of this authority to approve, as well as that to mediate or arbitrate disputes regarding interconnection agreements necessarily implies the authority to interpret and enforce them. *See* Southwestern Bell Tel. Co. v. Brooks Fibercommuns. of Okla., Inc., 235 F.3d 493, 497 (10th Cir. 2000); Southwestern Bell Tel. Co. v. Public Util. Comm'n of Tex., 208 F.3d 475, 479-80 (5th Cir. 2000); Iowa Util. Bd. v. FCC, 120 F.3d 753, 804 (8th Cir. 1997), *aff'd in part and rev'd in part on other grounds sub nom.* AT&T v. Iowa Util Bd., 525 U.S. 366 (1999).
125. 47 U.S.C. § 252(e)(2), (4) (Supp. 1999).
126. *Id.* § 252(e)(6) (Supp. 1999). Courts have interpreted § 252(e)(6) broadly to hold that federal jurisdiction extends to review of state commission rulings on complaints pertaining to interconnection agreements, and that such jurisdiction is not restricted to mere approval or rejection of the agreements. *See Southwestern Bell Tel. Co.*, 208 F.3d at 480-81; *see also* Illinois Bell Tel. Co. v. Worldcom Techs., Inc., 179 F.3d 566, 571 (7th Cir. 1999) (recognizing exclusive federal jurisdiction to review "actions" by state commissions); *but see* GTE South, Inc. v. Breathitt, 963 F. Supp. 610 (E.D. Ky. 1997) (§ 252(e)(6) does not extend the scope of federal court review to determinations prior to the stage of approval or rejection of the agreement or statement).
127. 47 U.S.C. § 252(e)(4)-(6) (Supp. 1999).
128. *Id.* § 252(f) (Supp. 1999).
129. *Id.* § 252(f)(2) (Supp. 1999).
130. *See id.* § 271 (Supp. 1999). InterLATA is defined in 47 U.S.C. § 153(21) (Supp. 1999). Section 271 applies to the provision of interLATA services by the BOCs and their affiliates. *See* part B.2.b(4) of this chapter. Under the 1996 Act, an affiliate involves an equity interest of greater than 10%. 47 U.S.C. § 153(1) (Supp. 1999).

into three categories—in-region, out-of-region, and incidental.[131]   Section 271 permits a BOC to provide out-of-region and incidental interLATA services immediately.[132] With respect to in-region interLATA services, however, a BOC must apply to the Federal Communications Commission for approval to provide such services, on a state-by-state basis.[133] In order to obtain approval to provide in-region interLATA service in a given state, a BOC either must be providing interconnection and access to at least one "facilities-based" CLEC in the state under an agreement approved under Section 252 or must be generally offering interconnection and access to prospective CLECs in the state under a statement of terms and conditions approved under Section 252(f).[134] In addition, the interconnection and access being provided or generally offered by the BOC must satisfy a fourteen-point "competitive checklist."[135]   The competitive checklist contained in Section 271 generally incorporates the obligations imposed on ILECs under Sections 251(b) and (c) and 252(d), with some additional requirements such as offering white pages directory listings for the CLEC's customers.[136]

After receiving an application from a BOC for authority to provide in-region interLATA service, the Federal Communications Commission must approve or reject the application within ninety days.[137] To approve the application, the agency must find that the petitioning BOC is either providing or generally offering access and interconnection to competitors under terms that satisfy all fourteen elements of the competitive checklist.[138] In addition, the agency must find that the application is in the public interest.[139]

In reviewing applications submitted by a BOC, the Federal Communications Commission is required to consult with the Department of Justice. The Department of Justice is to evaluate the application using any standard it deems appropriate.[140] The Federal Communications Commission is required to give "substantial weight" to the Department of Justice's evaluation, although this evaluation does not have preclusive effect on the Federal Communications Commission.[141]   The Federal

---

131. 47 U.S.C. § 271(b). "In-region" interLATA services are those interLATA services that originate in states within which the BOC provides wireline local telephone service. *Id.* § 271(b)(1), (i). "Out-of-region" interLATA services are those that originate outside the BOC's region. *Id.* § 271(b)(2). "Incidental" interLATA services are defined as the interLATA provision of, among other things, cellular and other commercial mobile services, video programming services, and alarm monitoring services. *Id.* § 271(g). Incidental interLATA services may originate in any state. *Id.* § 271(b)(3).

132. *Id.* § 271(b)(2), (3).

133. *Id.* § 271(b)(1).

134. *Id.* § 271(c)(1) (Supp. 1999). A facilities-based competitor is one that provides local exchange service exclusively or predominantly over its own facilities. *Id.* § 271(c)(1)(A). The "generally offering" alternative is applicable only if the BOC has not received an interconnection/access request from a facilities-based CLEC within the time frame specified in the statute. *Id.* § 271(c)(1)(B).

135. *Id.* § 271(c)(2)(A), (B) (Supp. 1999).

136. *Id.* § 271(c)(2)(B).

137. *Id.* § 271(d)(3) (Supp. 1999).

138. *Id.* § 271(d)(3)(A).

139. *Id.* § 271(d)(3)(C). A BOC that receives approval to provide in-region interLATA service must do so through a separate subsidiary. *Id.* § 272(a) (Supp. 1999). If a BOC is authorized to provide in-region interLATA service pursuant to § 271, it is also then permitted to manufacture and provide telecommunications equipment, including premises equipment. *Id.* § 273(a) (Supp. 1999).

140. *Id.* § 271(d)(2)(A).

141. *Id.*

Communications Commission also is required to consult with the appropriate state commission to verify BOC compliance with the checklist.[142]

With respect to federal review of mergers between telephone companies, the 1996 Act repeals the section of the Communications Act that gave the Federal Communications Commission the ability to confer antitrust immunity on telephone company mergers that were submitted to the agency for review.[143] As a result, telephone company mergers will be subject to the regular Hart-Scott-Rodino Act (H-S-R Act) premerger review process.[144]

The 1996 Act requires the Federal Communications Commission to undertake biennial reviews of all regulations issued under the Communications Act that apply to the activities of any telecommunications service provider[145] and requires the agency to "repeal or modify any regulation it determines to be no longer necessary in the public interest."[146] The 1996 Act also directs the agency to forbear from applying any regulation or any provision of the Communications Act if the Federal Communications Commission determines that (1) enforcement is not necessary to ensure just, reasonable, and nondiscriminatory rates; (2) enforcement is not necessary to protect consumers; and (3) forbearance is consistent with the public interest.[147] In making the public interest determination, the agency is to consider whether forbearance will promote competitive market conditions.[148]

(2) Judicial Interpretation of the 1996 Act

(a) The Interplay between the Antitrust Laws and the 1996 Act

Much debate has centered on the impact of the 1996 Act on the reach of the antitrust laws. The Seventh Circuit, in *Goldwasser v. Ameritech Corp.*,[149] concluded that a class of end-users of local telephone services could not state a Section 2 claim that was based entirely on alleged violations of the 1996 Act. The Seventh Circuit reasoned that Congress had chosen to impose "a host of special duties" on ILECs in order to "jump-start the development of competitive local markets."[150] Because it found the duties Congress imposed in the 1996 Act "go well beyond anything the antitrust laws would mandate on their own," it concluded that it would be "both illogical and undesirable to equate a failure to comply with the 1996 Act with a failure to comply with the antitrust laws."[151]

The Seventh Circuit made clear, however, that it was not finding that the 1996 Act immunized any ILEC conduct, noting that such an approach "would be

---

142. *Id.* § 271(d)(2)(B).
143. *Id.* § 152, note (b)(2) (Supp. 1999) (repealing 47 U.S.C. § 221(a)). The 1996 Act also amends the last paragraph of § 7 of the Clayton Act by removing the FCC from the list of agencies whose approval of a transaction exempts the transaction from § 7. 47 U.S.C. § 152, note (b)(3) (amending 15 U.S.C. § 18).
144. 15 U.S.C. § 18a (2000). *See* CONF. REP., *supra* note 105, at 200-01.
145. 47 U.S.C. § 161(a)(1) (Supp. 1999).
146. *Id.* § 161(b) (Supp. 1999).
147. *Id.* § 160(a) (Supp. 1999).
148. *Id.* § 160(b) (Supp. 1999).
149. 222 F.3d 390, 402 (7th Cir. 2000).
150. *Id.* at 399.
151. *Id.* at 400.

troublesome at best given the antitrust savings clause in the statute."[152] Because the plaintiffs had not alleged any wrongful conduct that was separable from Ameritech's duties under the 1996 Act, the court dismissed the antitrust claims in their entirety. A number of lower courts have considered similar motions to dismiss based on *Goldwasser*. The majority have followed *Goldwasser* and dismissed antitrust claims that are based on violations of duties imposed by the 1996 Act.[153] A minority of courts have denied *Goldwasser* motions, sustaining antitrust claims based, in part, on conduct that also violates the 1996 Act.[154]

(b) *Iowa Utilities Board* and the Limits of the Federal Communications
     Commission's Local Competition Authority

The courts also have struggled with the extent of the Federal Communications Commission's jurisdiction to regulate local telephone competition under the 1996 Act. In *AT&T Corp. v. Iowa Utilities Board*,[155] the Supreme Court reversed much of two Eighth Circuit opinions upholding challenges by a number of ILECs and state utility commissions to the federal agency's initial order and implementing regulations meant to bring competition to local telecommunications markets.[156] The main thrust of the challenges was that the states, not the Federal Communications Commission, were responsible for implementing the local competition provisions of the 1996 Act.[157] The Eighth Circuit had held that the rulemaking authority conferred upon the agency by the 1934 Act extended only to interstate matters and not intrastate matters, which were under the province of the state commissions.[158]

The Supreme Court reversed the Eighth Circuit's holding on jurisdiction, finding that Congress had expressly directed the Federal Communications Commission to "prescribe such rules and regulations as may be necessary" in the 1934 Act, and had expressly extended this rulemaking authority to provisions in the 1996 Act.[159] The Court rejected the ILECs' and state commissions' argument that the rulemaking authority is limited to provisions dealing with purely interstate and foreign matters, and did not include local competition provisions.[160] In particular, the Court held that the Federal Communications Commission has jurisdiction over pricing and pre-

---

152. *Id.* at 401.
153. *See, e.g.*, MGC Communs., Inc. v. BellSouth Telecommuns., Inc., 146 F. Supp. 2d 1344 (S.D. Fla. 2001); Supra Telecommuns. & Info. Sys., Inc. v. BellSouth Telecommuns., Inc., No. 99-1706-CIV (S.D. Fla. June 8, 2001); Covad Communs. Co. v. BellSouth Corp., No. 1:00-CV-3414 BBM (N.D. Ga. July 6, 2001); Law Offices at Curtis V. Trinko LLP v. Bell Atlantic Corp., 123 F. Supp. 2d 738 (S.D.N.Y. 2000); Intermedia Communs., Inc. v. BellSouth Telecommuns., Inc., No. 8:00-CIV-1410-T-24 (N.D. Fla. Dec. 15, 2000).
154. *See, e.g.*, Stein v. Pacific Bell, No. C00-2915 SI (N.D. Cal. Feb. 14, 2001); MGC Communs. Corp. v. Sprint Corp., No. CV-S-00-0948-PMP (D. Nev. Dec. 12, 2000); Bell Atlantic Network Servs., Inc. v. Ntegrity Telecontent Servs., Inc., No. 99-5366 (AET) (D.N.J. Nov. 1, 2000); CalTech Int'l Telecom Corp. v. Pacific Bell, No. C97-2105-CAL (N.D. Cal. Oct. 25, 2000); Electronet Intermedia Consulting, Inc. v. Sprint-Fla., Inc., No. 4:00-CV-0176-RH (N.D Fla. Sept. 20, 2000).
155. 525 U.S. 366 (1999).
156. Iowa Util. Bd. v. FCC, 120 F.3d 753 (8th Cir. 1997), *and* California v. FCC, 124 F.3d 934 (8th Cir. 1997).
157. 525 U.S. at 374.
158. *See id.* at 374-75.
159. *See id.* at 377-78.
160. *See id.* at 378-83.

existing interconnection agreements between ILECs and other carriers.[161] The Court further held that the Eighth Circuit erroneously considered respondents' claim that the federal agency does not have authority to review agreements already approved by state commissions because the claim was not ripe.[162]

The Court also considered the extent to which ILECs must share their networks with potential competitors.[163] The ILECs objected to the Federal Communications Commission's broad definition of "network elements" that must be provided to competitors.[164] The Court upheld the agency's network element list—which includes operator services, directory assistance, operational support systems, and vertical switching functions such as caller ID, call forwarding, and call waiting—finding it consistent with the broad definition in the 1934 Act.[165]

The Court found, however, that the agency did not adequately consider the "necessary and impair" requirements of the 1996 Act when it gave new carriers blanket access to these same network elements.[166] Section 251(d)(2) of the 1996 Act requires the Federal Communications Commission to consider whether "(a) access to such network elements as are proprietary in nature is necessary; and (b) the failure to provide access to such network elements would impair the ability of the telecommunications carrier seeking access to provide the services that it seeks to offer."[167] The Court found that Section 251 "requires the FCC to apply *some* limiting standard, rationally related to the goals of the Act, which it has simply failed to do."[168] Under the standard the Federal Communications Commission set, entrants to the market, rather than the federal agency, could determine whether network elements met the necessary and impair requirements, without even considering the availability of elements outside ILECs' networks, which is inconsistent with the 1996 Act.[169] The Court found the 1996 Act requires the agency to make a rational determination of what network elements must be made available, considering the availability of elements outside the network, and the increased cost or decreased service quality if the element were not made available.[170]

A number of lower courts have applied *Iowa Utilities Board* to further delineate the Federal Communications Commission's local competition jurisdiction.[171] On remand, the Eighth Circuit again reviewed the merits of several of the agency's rules interpreting and implementing the local competition provisions of the 1996 Act, particularly as they relate to costing principles.[172] In *Southwestern Bel Tel. Co. v. FCC*,[173] the Eighth Circuit re-interpreted the definition of a network element as well as the scope of the unbundled access requirement in light of the Supreme Court's

---

161. *Id.* at 383-84.
162. *See id.* at 385-86.
163. *See id.* at 386 87.
164. *Id.*
165. *Id.*
166. *See id.* at 387-92.
167. *Id.* at 388 (citing 47 U.S.C. § 251(d)(2)).
168. *Id.*
169. *See id.* at 389.
170. *Id.*
171. *See, e.g.*, AT&T Communs. of Va., Inc. v. Bell Atlantic-Virginia, Inc., 35 F. Supp. 2d 493 (E.D. Va. 1999).
172. *See* Iowa Util. Bd. v. FCC, 219 F.3d 744 (8th Cir. 2000) (vacating FCC's forward-looking economic cost rule).
173. 199 F.3d 996, 997-98 (8th Cir. 1999).

decision. The Eighth Circuit refused to hold that mere status as a network element requires that ILECs must offer it to competitors on an unbundled basis.[174]

The D.C. Circuit also analyzed ILECs' duty to share space in central offices (known as collocation) under Section 251(c)(6) of the 1996 Act,[175] holding that the Federal Communications Commission's collocation rules[176] improperly favored competitors of ILECs. The court remanded the case to the agency on the grounds that its rules embraced "unduly broad definitions of 'necessary' and 'physical collocation.'"[177] The court noted that the agency's interpretations of necessary and physical collocation seem "to diverge from any realistic meaning of the statute, favoring the competitors of LECs in ways that exceed what is necessary to achieve reasonable physical collocation and in ways that may result in unnecessary taking of LEC property."[178] The D.C. Circuit concluded that ILECs were only required to "provide collocation of . . . equipment that is directly related to and thus, necessary, required, or indispensable to interconnection or access to unbundled network elements."[179]

(3) Federal Communications Commission Implementation of the 1996 Act

The Federal Communications Commission issued a report and order adopting regulations that implement Sections 251 and 252 of the 1996 Act (local competition order)[180] in which it attempted to create a new jurisdictional paradigm regarding local competition. Under the new paradigm, the agency's primary responsibility is to establish national rules. The primary role of the states is to administer these rules, although the states may adopt additional rules that are critical to promoting local competition, so long as they do not conflict with national rules.

The local competition order established national rules for interconnection, resale of services, and access to unbundled network elements. The Federal Communications Commission determined that interconnection under the 1996 Act referred to the physical linking of two networks for the mutual exchange of traffic and mandated that interconnection be provided at any point that is "technically feasible."[181] The agency identified a minimum set of five points in the local network where interconnection is deemed to be technically feasible.[182] Similarly, the agency

---

174. *Id.*; *see also* MCI Telecommuns. Corp. v. US West Communs., 204 F.3d 1262 (9th Cir. 2000) (requiring ILECs to offer combinations of otherwise separate network elements); GTE South, Inc. v. Morrison, 199 F.3d 733 (4th Cir. 1999) (rejecting argument that ILECs have a "vested right" to recover their "historic costs" in pricing to competitors).

175. *See* GTE Serv. Corp. v. FCC, 205 F.3d 416, 427 (D.C. Cir. 2000).

176. Deployment of Wireline Services Offering Advanced Telecommunications Capability, 14 F.C.C.R. 4761 (1999) (First Report and Order and Further Notice of Proposed Rulemaking).

177. *See* GTE Serv., 205 F.3d at 427.

178. *See id.*

179. *Id.* at 424.

180. Implementation of the Local Competition Provisions in the Telecommunications Act of 1996; Interconnection between Local Exchange Carriers and Commercial Mobile Radio Service Providers, 11 F.C.C.R. 15,499 (1996).

181. Local Competition Order ¶¶ 174-176, 11 F.C.C.R. 15,588-90; *see id.* at 15,599-15,607 for the definition of technical feasibility.

182. The FCC identified these points where interconnection was technically feasible: (1) the line side of a local switch, (2) the trunk side of a local switch, (3) the trunk interconnection points on a tandem switch, (4) central office cross-connect points, and (5) out-of-band signaling facilities. *Id.* ¶¶ 207-212, 11 F.C.C.R. at 15,607-09.

determined a minimum number of unbundled network elements that ILECs are required to provide.[183] The Federal Communications Commission proscribed ILECs from imposing restrictions on the use of unbundled network elements and required them to provide access to such elements in a manner that allows requesting carriers to combine them as they choose.[184]

As part of their obligations under the agency's rules, ILECs must provide any technically feasible method of interconnection or access to an unbundled element. The Federal Communications Commission determined that technically feasible methods included physical collocation, virtual collocation, and interconnection at "meet" points.[185]

In addition to establishing national rules concerning the implementation of Section 251, the Federal Communications Commission established pricing rules to be applied by the states during arbitration proceedings conducted under Section 252 of the 1996 Act. The agency concluded that the price telecommunications carriers should pay for interconnection and unbundled elements should be based on the ILEC's total element long-run incremental cost plus a share of forward-looking joint and common costs.[186] For states that would be unable to complete a cost study within the arbitration period set forth in the 1996 Act, the agency established, by state, default price ceilings that the states could apply on an interim basis.[187]

The Federal Communications Commission has refined and implemented the new jurisdictional paradigm through a number of other orders enacted in the wake of the Local Competition Order. Following remand by the Supreme Court in *AT&T Corp. v. Iowa Utilities Board*,[188] the agency issued an order revisiting the issue of which local telephone network elements may be characterized properly as unbundled network elements consistent with Section 251(d)(2).[189] The Federal Communications Commission declined to apply a strict essential facilities test to the determination of unbundled network elements. Indeed, it found that the necessary and impair requirements under Section 251(d)(2) are distinct, and that "'necessary' modifies elements that are 'proprietary in nature' while . . . 'impair' modifies all other network elements."[190] A network element is "necessary" if, taking into account other available alternatives, "lack of access to that element would, as a practical, economic, and operational matter, *preclude* a requesting carrier from providing the services it seeks to offer."[191] A network element meets the "impair" standard if, again taking

---

183. The FCC identified these unbundled network elements as local loops, local and tandem switches, interoffice transmission facilities, network interface devices, signaling and call-related database facilities, operations support systems functions, and operator and directory assistance facilities. *Id.* ¶¶ 366-541, 11 F.C.C.R. at 15,683-775.
184. *Id.* ¶¶ 342-365, 11 F.C.C.R. at 15,671-83.
185. *Id.* ¶¶ 542-617, 11 F.C.C.R. at 15,776-811.
186. *Id.* ¶¶ 630-673, 11 F.C.C.R. at 15,817-44. Total element long-run incremental cost is commonly referred to as TELRIC.
187. *Id.* ¶¶ 766-771, 11 F.C.C.R. at 15,883-84.
188. 525 U.S. 366 (1999); *see generally supra* notes 155-70 and accompanying text.
189. Implementation of the Local Competition Provisions of the Telecommunications Act of 1996, 15 F.C.C.R. 3696 (1999) (Third Report and Order).
190. *Id.* ¶ 31, 15 F.C.C.R. at 3715.
191. *Id.* ¶ 44, 15 F.C.C.R. at 3721.

into account available alternatives, "lack of access to that element materially diminishes a requesting carrier's ability to provide the services it seeks to offer."[192]

The 1996 Act requires LECs "to establish reciprocal compensation arrangements for the transport and termination of telecommunications."[193] The issue of whether LECs are entitled to reciprocal compensation for traffic delivered to information service providers, particularly Internet service providers (ISPs), developed into a highly controversial issue before the Federal Communications Commission. Some have argued that, in the context of Internet-related traffic, reciprocal compensation is not mutual, but instead a one-way form of compensation that leads to significant windfalls for carriers with ISP customers.[194] In 1999, the agency ruled that dial-up calls to ISPs were largely long-distance, and therefore the act did not require the payment of reciprocal compensation.[195] However, the Federal Communications Commission also ruled that parties are bound by their interconnection agreements, including any reciprocal compensation provisions in those agreements.[196]

In March 2000, the D.C. Circuit vacated and remanded the agency's reciprocal compensation ruling.[197] It held that the Federal Communications Commission had not adequately justified the application of its end-to-end analysis, which focuses on the end-points of the communication.[198] The agency in April 2001 again issued an order that ISP-bound traffic is interstate in nature and not subject to traditional reciprocal compensation obligations, and implemented a program to migrate to a new compensation regime within thirty-six months.[199]

The Federal Communications Commission also has issued a number of other orders designed to regulate the interactions among ILECs and CLECs, including orders requiring ILECs to provide unbundled access to the high frequency portion of the local loop (a practice known as "time-sharing"),[200] adjusting the federal charges for access to local networks historically used to support universal service,[201] defining ILECs' obligations to provide cageless collocation (that is, collocation without a physical barrier, or cage, separating the CLECs' equipment from the ILECs'

192. *Id.* ¶ 51, 15 F.C.C.R. at 3725. In formulating this standard, the FCC specifically rejected suggestions that the ability of a single competitor to survive without the requested element per se means that the element does not meet the impair standard (*id.* ¶ 53, 15 F.C.C.R. at 3725) and that the impair standard should be equivalent to the essential facilities standard of antitrust law. *Id.* ¶¶ 57-61, 15 F.C.C.R. at 3728-30.
193. 47 U.S.C. § 251(b)(5) (Supp. 1999); *see also* Implementation of the Local Competition Provisions in the Telecommunications Act of 1996, 15 F.C.C.R. 3696 (1999); Intercarrier Compensation for ISP-Bound Traffic, 14 F.C.C.R. 3689 (1999) [hereinafter Reciprocal Compensation Order].
194. Reciprocal Compensation Order, *supra* note 193, 14 F.C.C.R. at 3693-95.
195. *Id.* at 3701-03. The 1996 Act requires reciprocal compensation only for calls classified as local. 47 C.F.R. § 51.701 (2000).
196. Reciprocal Compensation Order, *supra* note 193, at 14 F.C.C. R. 3703-06.
197. Bell Atlantic Tel. Cos. v. FCC, 206 F.3d 1, 3-6 (D.C. Cir. 2000).
198. *Id.* at 22.
199. Intercarrier Compensation for ISP-Bound Traffic, 16 F.C.C.R. 9151 (2001).
200. Deployment of Wireline Services Offering Advanced Telecommunications Capability (Third Report and Order); Implementation of the Local Competition Provisions of the Telecommunications Act of 1996 (Fourth Report and Order), 14 F.C.C.R. 20,912, 20,941 (1999).
201. Access Charge Reform; Price Cap Performance Review for Local Exchange Carriers; Low-Volume Long-Distance Users; Federal-State Joint Board On Universal Service, 15 F.C.C.R. 12,962 (2000).

equipment),[202] and requiring ILECs to use "best efforts" to obtain necessary third-party intellectual property rights for CLECs to utilize ILEC network elements.[203]

(4) Provision of In-Region Long-Distance

A prominent feature of the 1996 Act is that it allows RBOCs to offer in-region long-distance service, so long as they meet a competitive checklist.[204] A number of RBOCs have applied for permission to offer in-region long-distance under Section 271.[205]　In *AT&T Corp. v. FCC*,[206] the D.C. Circuit affirmed a Federal Communications Commission order[207] approving Bell Atlantic's application to provide in-region long-distance service in New York.[208] AT&T had challenged the agency's approval of Bell Atlantic's application on four grounds: (1) Bell Atlantic's prices did not conform to the appropriate pricing methodology, (2) Bell Atlantic failed to provide competitors nondiscriminatory access to certain loops, (3) Bell Atlantic imposed use restrictions that violated the act, and (4) Bell Atlantic's proposal for handling calls regarding service conflicted with Section 272's nondiscrimination safeguards.[209]　The court, however, found the Federal Communications Commission had "demanded real evidence that Bell Atlantic had complied with all checklist requirements, but at the same time, it did not allow 'the infeasible perfect to oust the feasible good.'"[210]

In June 2000, the Federal Communications Commission approved SBC Communications's application under Section 271 of the 1996 Act to provide in-region long-distance service in Texas,[211] finding that its affiliate Southwestern Bell satisfied the competitive checklist in Section 271(d)(3) for opening its network to competition.[212] For the first time, both the Department of Justice and the relevant

---

202. *See* Deployment of Wireline Services Offering Advanced Telecommunications Capability; Implementation of the Local Competition Provisions of the Telecommunications Act of 1996, 15 F.C.C.R. 17,806 (2000).

203. Petition of MCI for Declaratory Ruling that New Entrants Need Not Obtain Separate License or Right-to-Use Agreements Before Purchasing Unbundled Elements; Implementation of the Local Competition Provisions in the Telecommunications Act of 1996, 15 F.C.C.R. 13,896 (2000).

204. 47 U.S.C. § 271 (Supp. 1999).

205. The FCC in 2001 updated the general procedural requirements that apply to its processing of applications under § 271. *See* Updated Filing Requirements for Bell Operating Company Applications under Section 271 of the Communications Act, 16 F.C.C.R. 6923 (2001).

206. 220 F.3d 607 (D.C. Cir. 2000).

207. Application of Bell Atlantic New York for Authorization Under Section 271 of the Communications Act to Provide In-Region, InterLATA Service in the State of New York, 15 F.C.C.R. 3953 (1999) (memorandum opinion and order).

208. 220 F.3d at 610.

209. *Id.* at 615.

210. *See id.* at 633 (citations omitted).

211. Application by SBC Communs., Inc., Southwestern Bell Tel. Co., and Southwestern Bell Communs. Services, Inc. d/b/a Southwestern Bell Long Distance Pursuant to Section 271 of the Telecommunications Act of 1996 To Provide In-Region, InterLATA Services in Texas, 15 F.C.C.R. 18,354 (2000) (memoranda opinion and order). For FCC approval of another application under § 271, *see* Application of Verizon New York, Inc., Verizon Long Distance, Verizon Enterprise Solutions, Verizon Global Networks, Inc. and Verizon Select Servs., Inc. for Authorization to Provide In-Region, InterLATA Services in Connecticut, 16 C.F.F.R. 14,147 (2001) (memorandum opinion and order).

212. *Application by SBC Communs.*, memorandum and order at ¶¶ 2-3, 15, 18, 15 F.C.C.R. at 18,357, 18,363-64. The FCC strongly encourages states to establish a collaborative process, in conjunction with incumbent and competing carriers, for measuring and reporting performance in certain areas:

state commission, in this case the Texas Public Utility Commission, supported the Section 271 application.[213] The Texas commission spent over two years overseeing Southwestern Bell's implementation of Section 271's requirements.[214] Specifically, the Texas commission defined performance measurements and standards, adopted a performance remedy plan, and implemented a six-month review process to monitor performance measurements.[215] The Federal Communications Commission particularly relied on the state agency's efforts and expertise in Section 271 compliance and on the degree of entry by competitors into the local exchange market.[216]

c. MERGER REVIEW

The 1996 Act has been followed by a period of intense industry consolidation, including combinations that would not have been practicable or approved before passage of the 1996 Act. Since 1997, the Federal Communications Commission has approved SBC Communications's mergers with both Pacific Telesis[217] and Ameritech Corporation,[218] Bell Atlantic's merger with both NYNEX[219] and GTE Corporation,[220] MCI Communications's merger with WorldCom, Inc.,[221] and AT&T Corporation's mergers with Teleport Communications Group[222] and Media One.[223]

On January 22, 2001, the Federal Communications Commission also granted approval, with conditions, to the proposed merger between America Online (AOL) and Time Warner.[224] The Federal Communications Commission approved the

"An extensive and rigorous evaluation of the BOC's performance by the states provides greater certainty that barriers to competition have been eliminated and the local markets in a state are open to competition." *Id.* at ¶ 54, 15 F.C.C.R. at 18,377.

213. *Id.* at ¶¶ 2, 19-20, 15 F.C.C.R. at 18,357, 18,364-65.
214. *Id.* at ¶ 3, 15 F.C.C.R. at 18,357.
215. *Id.* at ¶¶ 3, 11, 13-14, 15 F.C.C.R. at 18,357, 18,360-62.
216. *Id.* at ¶¶ 4-5, 15 F.C.C.R. at 18,358. According to the DOJ, competitors captured about 8% of access lines in Southwestern Bell's territory in Texas. *Id.* at ¶ 5, 15 F.C.C.R. at 18,358.
217. Application of Pacific Telesis Group and SBC Communs., 12 F.C.C.R. 2624 (1997) (memorandum opinion and order).
218. Application of Ameritech Corp. and SBC Communs., 14 F.C.C.R. 14,712 (1999) (memorandum opinion and order). A private plaintiff's challenge to the transaction under § 7 of the Clayton Act subsequently was rejected on the ground that since the two RBOCs did not actually compete to provide local service, that statute did not apply. South Austin Coalition Cmty. Council v. SBC Communs. Inc., No. 00-1864, 2001 U.S. App. LEXIS 26885 (7th Cir. Dec. 19, 2001) (Easterbrook, J.).
219. Application of Nynex Corp. and Bell Atlantic Corp., 12 F.C.C.R. 19,985 (1997) (memorandum opinion and order).
220. Application of GTE Corp. and Bell Atlantic Corp. For Consent to Transfer Control of Domestic and International Sections 214 and 310 Authorizations and Application to Transfer Control of a Submarine Cable Landing License, 15 F.C.C.R. 14,032 (2000) (memorandum opinion and order).
221. Application of WorldCom, Inc. and MCI Communs. Corp., 13 F.C.C.R. 18,025 (1998) (memorandum opinion and order).
222. Application of Teleport Communs. Group and AT&T Corp., 13 F.C.C.R. 15,236 (1998) (memorandum opinion and order).
223. Applications for Consent to the Transfer of Control of Licenses and Section 214 Authorizations from MediaOne Group, Inc. to AT&T Corp, 15 F.C.C.R. 9816 (2000) (memorandum opinion and order).
224. Applications for Consent to the Transfer of Control of Licenses and Section 214 Licenses of Time Warner, Inc. and America Online, Inc., Transferors, to AOL Time Warner, Inc., Transferee, CS Dkt. No. 00-30, 2001 FCC LEXIS 432 (Jan. 22, 2001) (memorandum opinion and order). The

merger subject to four main categories of conditions designed to protect competition: (1) AOL must ensure that nonaffiliated ISPs are able to gain nondiscriminatory access to AOL's network; (2) because AOL would enjoy a potentially dominant position in the provision of advanced, instant message-based high-speed services (AIHS),[225] AOL was prohibited from offering any new streaming video AIHS services "until it interoperates";[226] (3) as a result of concern that AOL's indirect ownership interest in DirecTV, through its $1.5 billion investment in General Motors Corporation, would give AOL "excessive purchasing power" in the video programming market,[227] AOL was required to provide written notice of any transactions that would have the effect of increasing AOL's ownership in General Motors or Hughes Electronics (the parent corporation of DirecTV);[228] and (4) AOL may not seek, and AT&T may not contract or agree to provide, any AOL ISP affiliate exclusive access or any other preferential access, or "otherwise disadvantage AOL's competitors with respect to access to AT&T's cable systems."[229]

In March 2000, the Federal Communications Commission also approved a merger between Qwest Communications and US West.[230] Although the Qwest-US West combination resulted in a smaller merged entity than in some other recent mergers, the agency had concerns because Qwest provided interLATA services within US West's service area. Because US West is one of the original RBOCs, it cannot provide interLATA services within its service area.[231] To avoid this obstacle to their merger, Qwest and US West submitted a divestiture plan that provided for Qwest-US West to "cease providing all interLATA services originating in the US West region."[232]

The GTE-Bell Atlantic merger was also scrutinized closely, due to three potential public interest harms. First, the merger would remove GTE "as one of the most significant potential" local telephone competitors within Bell Atlantic's region.[233] Second, the merger would reduce the Federal Communications Commission's ability to benchmark as a way of determining competitiveness in the industry.[234] And finally, the merger would increase "the incentive and ability of the merged entity to discriminate against its rivals, particularly with respect to the provision of advanced

---

FTC also approved the transaction subject to conditions. *See* America Online, Inc., 2001 FTC LEXIS 44 (2001).

225. *Id.* at ¶ 130.
226. *Id.* at ¶¶ 190, 325.
227. *Id.* at ¶ 210.
228. *Id.* at ¶¶ 251, 330.
229. *Id.* at ¶¶ 273, 331-32.
230. Qwest Communs. Int'l Inc. and US WEST, Inc. Applications for Transfer of Control of Domestic and International Sections 214 and 310 Authorizations and Application to Transfer Control of a Submarine Cable Landing License, 15 F.C.C.R. 5376 (2000) (memorandum opinion and order).
231. *Id.* at ¶¶ 6, 11, 15 F.C.C.R. at 5380, 5382.
232. *Id.* at ¶ 14, 15 F.C.C.R. at 5383. The FCC found that the proposed divestiture of Qwest's interLATA in-region services, customers, and assets in the 14-state US West service region was consistent with the requirements of § 271. Qwest Communs. Int'l Inc. and US WEST, Inc. Applications for Transfer of Control of Domestic and International Sections 214 and 310 Authorizations and Application to Transfer Control of a Submarine Cable Landing License, 15 F.C.C.R. 5376 (2000).
233. Application of GTE Corp. and Bell Atlantic Corp. For Consent to Transfer Control of Domestic and International Sections 214 and 310 Authorizations and Application to Transfer Control of a Submarine Cable Landing Business, 15 F.C.C.R. 14,032, 14,037 (2000) (memorandum opinion and order).
234. *Id.* at 14,037-38.

telecommunications services."[235] The agency approval of the merger, therefore, was based on additional conditions designed to advance one of the agency's public interest goals, i.e., to promote advanced services, to open local markets to competition, to foster out-of-region competition, and to improve residential service.[236] These conditions were "patterned closely" after the conditions imposed as part of the 1999 merger of SBC and Ameritech.[237]

Only weeks before the Federal Communications Commission approved the GTE-Bell Atlantic merger, it approved AT&T's merger with MediaOne.[238] The merger combined the nation's largest phone company and largest cable operator, AT&T, with the nation's fourth largest cable operator, MediaOne.[239] In addition, MediaOne held a significant interest in the nation's second largest cable operator, Time Warner Entertainment.[240] Despite the concentration of cable ownership (or perhaps because of it), the agency approved the merger. The Federal Communications Commission ruled that "the merger is likely to accelerate competition among providers of local telephony, video, and broadband services in the service areas of MediaOne, AT&T, and other cable operators with whom the merged entity may enter telephony joint ventures or other contractual arrangements."[241]

d. WIRELESS AUCTIONS

In 1993, Congress amended the Communications Act to change the statutory system of licensing and regulating wireless telecommunications services.[242] Congress defined all mobile telecommunications services that are provided for profit and make interconnected service available to the public as "commercial mobile radio service," or CMRS.[243] CMRS encompasses cellular telephone service and paging as well as most specialized mobile radio service.[244] It also includes the growing narrowband and broadband "personal communications services," or PCS.[245] One of the effects of Congress's action was the promotion of consistent regulation of CMRS by, among other things, preempting state regulation of rates and entry into CMRS.[246]

235. *Id.* at 14,038.
236. *Id.* at App. D, Market Opening Conditions.
237. *Id.* at 14,144. The SBC/Ameritech merger conditions are reported at 14 F.C.C.R. 14,712, 14,854-925 (1999), ¶¶ 348-518 (section of the order discussing the conditions); App. C, Conditions, *id.* at 14,964-15,172.
238. Applications for Consent to the Transfer of Control of Licenses and Section 214 Authorizations from MediaOne Group, Inc. to AT&T Corp, 15 F.C.C.R. 9816 (2000) (memorandum opinion and order).
239. *Id.* at 9832.
240. *Id.*
241. *Id.* at 9886.
242. Omnibus Budget Reconciliation Act of 1993, Pub. L. No. 103-66, Title VI, § 6002, 107 Stat. 312 (codified in principal part at 47 U.S.C. § 332 (1994)).
243. *See* 47 U.S.C. §§ 153(27), 332(c)(1) (Supp. 1999).
244. *See* Implementation of Sections 3(n) and 332 of the Communications Act—Regulatory Treatment of Mobile Services, 9 F.C.C.R. 1411, 1468 (1994) (Second Report and Order).
245. PCS is a category of wireless services that the FCC has defined as a "wide array of mobile, portable and ancillary communications services to individuals and businesses." *See, e.g.,* Implementation of Section 309(j) of the Communications Act—Competitive Bidding, 8 F.C.C.R. 7635, 7654 (1993) (notice of proposed rulemaking).
246. 47 U.S.C. § 332(c)(3) (Supp. 1999). In May 1995, the FCC considered and denied the petitions of the seven states that had sought to continue their regulation of CMRS rates, finding that the states had not shown that continued regulation was necessary to protect consumers. The orders, all of

One of the most widely used commercial mobile radio services is cellular telephone service. In each major geographic area, the Federal Communications Commission has licensed two carriers to provide cellular service[247] and has required those carriers to permit "resellers" to compete with them in providing service at the retail level to the public.[248] Broadband PCS service, using frequencies roughly twice as high as cellular frequencies, has emerged as an alternative to traditional cellular service.[249] The Federal Communications Commission awarded licenses for the provision of broadband PCS through an auction process, allowing as many as six service providers in each geographic area.[250] The PCS auction process proved controversial, with serious questions arising as to the integrity of various license auctions. Suspect bidding practices, including alleged "bid signaling" in which bidders used complex numerical codes to allocate territories, led to consent decrees with a number of bidders.[251]

e.   STATE REGULATION

Like the Federal Communications Commission, state regulators have had to adapt quickly to the massive changes wrought by the 1996 Act. The 1996 Act created a complex jurisdictional landscape in which the division of authority among the states and the Federal Communications Commission has not always been clear. In the wake of the Supreme Court's clarification of the federal agency's power to set local competition rules in *AT&T v. Iowa Utilities Board*,[252] the states have featured most prominently in two areas: arbitration of disputes over the terms of interconnection

---

which were released May 19, 1995, are reported at 10 F.C.C.R. 7824 (Arizona); 10 F.C.C.R. 7486 (California); 10 F.C.C.R. 7025 (Connecticut), *aff'd*, Connecticut Dep't of Pub. Util. Control v. FCC, 78 F.3d 842 (2d Cir. 1996); 10 F.C.C.R. 7872 (Hawaii); 10 F.C.C.R. 7898 (Louisiana); 10 F.C.C.R. 7842 (Ohio); *and* 10 F.C.C.R. 8187 (New York).

247. One of the two licenses in each area was initially granted to the "wireline" carrier, i.e., the LEC. Implementation of Section 6002(b) of the Omnibus Budget Reconciliation Act of 1993; Annual Report and Analysis of Competitive Market Conditions with Respect to Commercial Mobile Services, 12 F.C.C.R. 11,266, 11,279 (1997).

248. Cellular Communs. Sys., 86 F.C.C.2d 469 (1981), *recons. granted in part*, 89 F.C.C.2d 58 (1982), *further recons. granted in part*, 90 F.C.C.2d 571 (1982), *aff'd sub nom.* MCI Cellular Tel. Co. v. FCC, 738 F.2d 1322 (D.C. Cir. 1984).

249. Cellular service uses frequencies slightly below 900 MHz. Broadband PCS uses the 1850-1990 MHz spectrum.

250. The development of the FCC's concept of and implementation of broadband PCS is set forth in Amendment of the Commission's Rules to Establish New Personal Communications Services, 7 F.C.C.R. 5676, Erratum, 7 F.C.C.R. 5779 (1992) (notice of proposed rule making and tentative decision); 8 F.C.C.R. 7700 (1993) (Second Report and Order); 9 F.C.C.R. 4957 (1994), Erratum, Mimeo No. 44006 released July 22, 1994 (memorandum opinion and order); 9 F.C.C.R. 6908 (1994) (Third Memorandum Opinion and Order); Implementation of Section 309(j) of the Communications Act—Competitive Bidding, 10 F.C.C.R. 11,872 (1995), Erratum released June 26, 1995 (further notice of proposed rule making); 11 F.C.C.R. 136 (1995), Erratum, DA-1614, released July 19, 1995 (Sixth Report and Order).

251. *See, e.g.*, United States v. Mercury PCS II, LLC, 63 Fed. Reg. 65,228 (DOJ Nov. 25, 1998) (proposed consent decree and competitive impact statement), 1999-2 Trade Cas. (CCH) ¶ 72,707 (D.D.C. 1999) (final judgment); US West Communs. for Facilities in the Broadband Personal Communs. Sys. in the D, E and F Blocks, 13 F.C.C.R. 8286 (1998) (notice of apparent liability for forfeiture).

252. 525 U.S. at 378-79 n.6 (noting Congress had "unquestionably" "taken the regulation of local telecommunications competition away from the States"); *see* part B.2.b(2) of this chapter.

agreements pursuant to Section 252 of the 1996 Act,[253] and review of BOCs' requests to provide in-region long-distance service pursuant to Section 271.[254] BOCs have pushed for a broader interpretation of the states' regulatory powers and, as a result, a small number of lower court decisions have held that state regulators have exclusive original jurisdiction over all disputes over implementation and breach of interconnection agreements.[255]

Unlike Federal Communications Commission regulation, state regulation of common carriers may provide immunity from federal antitrust laws under the state action doctrine first enunciated in *Parker v. Brown*.[256] However, as state statutes change to promote new telecommunications competition, and as states change the nature of regulation, the extent to which the state action doctrine immunizes common carrier conduct may change as well.[257]

3. Cable Television

a. STATUTORY REGULATION UNIQUE TO CABLE TELEVISION

The pervasive statutory regulation of the cable television industry imports unique factors into cable television antitrust analysis. The cable television industry is regulated concurrently at the federal and local levels according to the statutory framework established in the 1934 Act,[258] principally with respect to cable communications by the Cable Communications Policy Act of 1984 (1984 Cable Act),[259] the Cable Television Consumer Protection and Competition Act of 1992 (1992 Cable Act)[260] and the 1996 Act.

The federal statutory framework addresses matters such as the types of programming cable systems must carry, compulsory leased access to cable systems, rates charged by cable systems, limits on vertically integrated cable operators, and limits on vertically integrated cable programmers. In contrast, local authorities regulate cable operators through the issuance of cable franchises, renewal of cable franchises, and through oversight of requested transfers of cable franchises. In some

253. 47 U.S.C. § 252(e)(6) (Supp. 1999). The 1996 Act provides for federal district court review of state regulators' decisions concerning arbitration agreements. *Id. See also supra* note 126.
254. 47 U.S.C. § 271(d)(2)(A) (Supp. 1999).
255. *See, e.g.*, Covad Communs. Co. v. BellSouth Corp., No. 1:00-CV-3414 BBM (N.D. Ga. July 6, 2001); Intermedia Communs., Inc. v. BellSouth Telecommuns., Inc., No. 8:00-CIV-1410-T-24 (M.D. Fla. Dec. 15, 2000). No court of appeal has yet addressed this issue.
256. 317 U.S. 341 (1943); *see also* DFW Metro Line Servs. v. Southwestern Bell Tel. Corp., 988 F.2d 601 (5th Cir. 1993); Capital Tel. Co. v. New York Tel. Co., 750 F.2d 1154 (2d Cir. 1984) (affirming judgment on pleadings on ground of state action immunity), *cert. denied*, 471 U.S. 1101 (1985).
257. See part B of Chapter XIII for a discussion of the state action doctrine.
258. Title VI of the Communications Act of 1934, as amended, addresses cable communications and is codified at 47 U.S.C. §§ 521-573 (Supp. 1999).
259. Pub. L. No. 98-549, 98 Stat. 2785 (codified in various sections of 47 U.S.C. §§ 521-559 (Supp. 1999)). The 1984 Cable Act represented Congress's first attempt to comprehensively regulate the cable television industry.
260. Pub. L. No. 102-385, 106 Stat. 1460 (codified in various sections of 47 U.S.C. §§ 521-559). The 1992 Cable Act was designed to curb the market power of cable operators, protect broadcast television, and promote competition to cable television by new technologies for the distribution of video programming. *Id.* § 2(a), (b).

instances, both federal and local regulators share oversight responsibility for cable television.[261]

Importantly for mergers and acquisitions, the Federal Communications Commission must approve any transfers of cable television ownership interests. First, the agency has statutory authority over transfers of cable television relay service (CARS) licenses.[262] In determining whether a proposed transfer serves "the public interest, convenience, and necessity," the Federal Communications Commission "must weigh the potential public interest harms and benefits."[263] The agency's public interest analysis evaluates possible competitive effects of the transfer, but it is not limited by traditional antitrust principles.[264] This is one reason given by the Federal Communications Commission for its determination not to defer to the Department of Justice when considering the competitive impact of license transfers.[265] Second, the transfer of cable television ownership interests that implicate the Federal Communications Commission's ban on cross-ownership of broadcast stations and cable systems in the same market also requires agency approval.[266]

Although federal legislation extensively regulates the cable industry, in these enactments Congress has made clear that the industry remains subject to federal and state antitrust laws.[267] The same holds true for consumer protection statutes "if not inconsistent" with federal regulations.[268] In fact, the 1996 Act eliminated the exemption from the antitrust laws previously afforded by the Clayton Act for transactions "duly consummated" pursuant to the authority of the Federal Communications Commission.[269]

---

261. *See, e.g.,* 47 U.S.C. § 552(d) (Supp. 1999) (allowing local authorities to promulgate consumer protections in addition to, but not inconsistent with, consumer protections established by FCC).

262. 47 U.S.C. § 308 (1994 & Supp. 1999), § 310(d) (1994). CARS licenses allow cable operators to use specially designated radio frequencies to transport video programming from antennae locations to headends. Most cable systems rely on a CARS license for their operations.

263. Applications for Consent to the Transfer of Control of Licenses and Section 214 Authorizations from Tele-Communications, Inc., Transferor, to AT&T Corp., Transferee, 14 F.C.C.R. 3160, 3168 (1999).

264. *Id.*

265. *See, e.g.,* Tele-Communs., Inc. & Liberty Media Corp., 9 F.C.C.R. 4783 (1994) (declining to truncate FCC review of CARS license transfer in deference to DOJ's prior review).

266. 47 C.F.R. § 75.501(a) (2000).

267. The 1992 Cable Act provided that nothing therein "shall be construed to alter or restrict in any manner the applicability of Federal or State antitrust law." 47 U.S.C. § 521 note (1994). The 1996 Act contains a similar provision. 47 U.S.C. § 152 note (Supp. 1999). *See also* Total TV v. Palmer Communs., 69 F.3d 298 (9th Cir.) (California law prohibiting predatory pricing is a state "antitrust law" not preempted by 1992 Cable Act), *cert. dismissed,* 517 U.S. 1152 (1996).

268. 47 U.S.C. § 552(d) (Supp. 1999); *see also* Shaw v. TCI/TKR of N. Ky., Inc., 67 F. Supp. 2d 712 (W.D. Ky. 1999) (state consumer protection claim not preempted); *cf.* Time Warner Cable v. Doyle, 66 F.3d 867 (7th Cir. 1994), *cert. denied,* 516 U.S. 1141 (1996) (Wisconsin consumer protection action enjoined on preemption grounds where it interferes with execution of FCC's cable rate regulations).

269. 47 U.S.C. § 152 note (Supp. 1999). *See also* Cableamerica Corp. v. FTC, 795 F. Supp. 1082, 1092 (N.D. Ala. 1992) (FCC regulatory power to approve cable system mergers does not immunize merger from challenge under the antitrust laws).

b. MARKET DEFINITION ISSUES

Product markets in the context of the cable television industry have been defined most often by referring to the delivery of video programming to cable television subscribers and to the sale or license of video programming to cable operators. Recent technological advances have created new products that have been recognized as constituting new product markets, such as the provision of Internet access service and interactive television services.

Geographic market definition for cable television services, on the other hand, has to date occasioned neither extended comment nor controversy in judicial decisions or elsewhere. Where delivery of programming to subscribers is at issue, the geographic market is usually defined with respect to the service area of the cable operator and, accordingly, is most often characterized as local.[270] With respect to the sale or license of programming to cable operators, the market is defined as local, national, or international.[271]

Congress has expressed as one of its objectives the promotion of competition in "cable communications."[272] "Cable system" is defined to mean "cable service which includes video programming and which is provided to multiple subscribers within a community."[273] Addressing competition in the distribution and acquisition of programming in the 1992 Cable Act, Congress directed the Federal Communications Commission to promote "the development of competition in local and national multichannel video programming distribution markets."[274]

The 1992 Cable Act assigned to the Federal Communications Commission responsibility for resolving many of the issues that had accounted for the largest number of court opinions discussing product market definition in the context of cable television. Product market definition is also discussed in less numerous but also recurring decisions in actions by cable operators alleging restraints on their initial entry into, or expansion into, geographic markets. The product market adopted most frequently in all of these cases has been defined as the market for "retail cable

---

270. *See, e.g.*, Cable Holdings of Georgia, Inc. v. Home Video, Inc., 825 F.2d 1559 (11th Cir. 1987) ("passive visual entertainment" in Cobb County, Georgia); Central Telecommuns. v. TCI Cablevision, Inc., 800 F.2d 711 (8th Cir. 1986) (cable television in Jefferson City, Missouri), *cert. denied*, 480 U.S. 910 (1987); Aventura Cable Corp. v. Rifkin/Narragansett South Florida CATV Ltd. P'ship, 941 F. Supp. 1189 (S.D. Fla. 1996) (satellite services providers alleging defendant restrained entry to "Miami Beach highrise market").

271. *See, e.g.*, Viacom Int'l, Inc. v. Time Inc., 785 F. Supp. 371 (S.D.N.Y. 1992) (claim of monopoly leveraging from local markets for cable television into national market for sale of pay television programming).

272. 47 U.S.C. § 521(6) (1994).

273. *Id.* § 522(7) (Supp. 1999).

274. *Id.* § 548(c)(4)(A) (Supp. 1999). Where a cable operator has an attributable interest in the programming vendor, exclusive agreements limiting distribution of such programming to areas not served by cable are prohibited, and they are valid elsewhere only if the FCC finds that they are in the public interest. *Id.* § 548(c)(2) (1994). The FCC is directed in making such determinations to assess, among other factors, the impact of those agreements on "the development of competition in local and national multichannel video programming distribution markets." *Id.* at § 548(c)(4) (1994). In compliance with the 1992 Cable Act, the FCC adopted rules prohibiting unfair and discriminatory programming distribution practices by vertically integrated cable operators. 47 C.F.R. §§ 76.1000-76.1003 (2000).

television sales," or defined in very similar terms, with the geographic market defined as the area in which the plaintiff either does or intends to offer service.[275]

Litigations challenging exclusivity or other restrictions on programming supply also have produced opinions which approve both broader product market definitions, such as "leisure and entertainment,"[276] and narrower definitions, such as the broadcast of "cream" or "major" events.[277] Intermediate positions have also been approved in these cases, i.e., by defining the market as pay television offering both movie and sports programming.[278]

Competition for advertising revenues by cable operators has been acknowledged by the courts.[279] As yet that competition has not, however, produced any significant volume of antitrust litigation.[280]

Some older decisions defined product markets consisting of both distribution facilities and receiving equipment associated with cable television. Litigation brought by cable operators alleging the wrongful refusal of utilities to permit the use of the utility's poles or rights of way produced decisions recognizing a market for cable television distribution facilities and the distribution of cable television signals.[281] Federal legislation now addresses many of these issues.[282] A market

---

275. *See, e.g., Central Telecommuns.*, 800 F.2d 711; *Aventura Cable Corp.*, 941 F. Supp. 1189 (satellite services providers alleging defendant restrained entry to "Miami Beach highrise market"); Futurevision Cable Sys. v. Multivision Cable TV Corp., 789 F. Supp. 760, 767 n.4 (S.D. Miss. 1992); *Viacom Int'l, Inc.*, 785 F. Supp. 371 (claim of monopoly leveraging from local markets for cable television into national market for sale of pay television programming).

276. Satellite Television & Associated Resources, Inc. v. Continental Cablevision, 714 F.2d 351 (4th Cir. 1983) (affirming a lower court finding of fact); *see also* Cable Holdings v. Home Video, Inc., 825 F.2d 1559 (11th Cir. 1987) (affirming jury verdict based on defendant's definition of market consisting of "passive visual entertainment" including cable television, satellite television, video cassette recordings, and over-the-air television.

277. *See* Storer Cable Communs. v. City of Montgomery, 826 F. Supp. 1338, 1355 (M.D. Ala.), *order vacated pursuant to stipulation and settlement*, 866 F. Supp. 1376 (M.D. Ala. 1993). In so ruling, the district court followed *Eastman Kodak Co. v. Image Technical Servs., Inc.*, 504 U.S. 451, 482 (1992), where the Supreme Court held that "one brand of a product can constitute a relevant market." *But see* TV Communs. Network v. Turner Network Television, 964 F.2d 1022, 1023-24 (10th Cir.) (market definition limited to the defendant's single channel, the TNT channel, held "defective as a matter of law"), *cert. denied*, 506 U.S. 999 (1992).

278. *See, e.g., Z* Channel Ltd. v. Home Box Office, 931 F.2d 1338 (9th Cir. 1991) ("market for pay television offering both movies and sports programming"); Fort Wayne Telsat v. ESPN, 753 F. Supp. 109 (S.D.N.Y. 1990) (market for "subscription television programming services for quality sports programming"); New York Citizens Comm. v. Manhattan Cable TV, Inc., 651 F. Supp. 802, 807-08 (S.D.N.Y. 1986) ("television movie and non-sports entertainment services"); Crimpers Promotions, Inc. v. Home Box Office, 724 F.2d 290 (2d Cir. 1983) ("market for programming to cable pay-television industry"). Subscriptions to "premium" tiers of cable service were implicitly accepted as separate markets in an opinion granting summary judgment for the cable operator on a subscriber's tying complaint in *Friedman v. Adams Russell Cable Servs.*, 624 F. Supp. 1568, 1573 (D. Kan. 1985), where the court found no impact on competition in the market for the tied product.

279. Turner Broad. v. FCC, 910 F. Supp. 734 (D.D.C. 1995) (upholding the must-carry rules against constitutional challenge), *aff'd*, 520 U.S. 180 (1997).

280. In *Thompson Everett, Inc. v. National Cable Advert.*, 850 F. Supp. 470, 477-78 (E.D. Va. 1994), where an advertising sales representative challenged exclusive representation agreements between the plaintiff's competitors and cable television operators, the court accepted the plaintiff's market definition of "spot" advertising on cable television but entered summary judgment for defendants.

281. *See, e.g.,* Continental Cablevision v. American Elec. Power Co., 715 F.2d 1115, 1120 (6th Cir. 1983); TV Signal Co. of Aberdeen v. AT&T, 617 F.2d 1302, 1310 (8th Cir. 1980).

282. The 1996 Act established a right of access by cable operators to any pole, duct, conduit, or right of way of any utility on terms that are nondiscriminatory, just, and reasonable. 47 U.S.C. § 224(f) (Supp. 1999).

defined in a monopolization counterclaim as equipment for viewing satellite signals survived a motion to dismiss by cable operators accused by the equipment manufacturer of bringing copyright infringement claims in bad faith.[283]

The Federal Communications Commission also has provided its views on defining product markets associated with the cable industry. In its 2000 *Competition Report* to Congress addressing competition in the cable industry, the agency analyzed competition in "markets for the delivery of video programming." The *Competition Report* also recognized a market for the purchase of video programming.[284]

Merger review by the antitrust enforcement agencies has required definition of cable television product markets. In 1996, the Federal Trade Commission accepted a consent decree resolving antitrust concerns arising from the acquisition of Turner Broadcasting System by Time Warner.[285] The Federal Trade Commission alleged that by acquiring Turner, Time Warner might (1) acquire market power in the product market described as "the sale of cable television programming services," meaning "satellite-delivered video programming that is offered, alone or with other services, to Multichannel Video Programming Distributors (MVPDs) in the United States"; and (2) harm competition among MVPDs by denying rival MVPDs access, or access on nondiscriminatory terms, to cable television programming services.[286]

In 2000, the Department of Justice reviewed the acquisition of MediaOne Group, Inc. by AT&T.[287] The Department of Justice expressed concern that the proposed acquisition would lessen "competition in the nationwide market for the aggregation, promotion, and distribution of residential broadband content."[288] Also in 2000, the Federal Trade Commission accepted a consent decree resolving its objections to the merger between AOL and Time Warner.[289] According to the Federal Trade Commission's complaint, the merger would (1) lessen competition in the residential broadband Internet access market, (2) lessen competition in the Internet transport service market, and (3) restrain competition in the market for interactive television.[290]

c.   PREVENTION OF ACQUISITION OR EXERCISE OF MONOPOLY POWER

Congress and the courts have recognized in a variety of contexts that cable operators can exercise monopoly power in the market for the delivery of video signals. Congress declared in the 1992 Cable Act, for example, that regulation was required to control the "undue market power" available to cable operators in their dealings with subscribers.[291] Among the explanations for this power cited by

---

283. Air Capital Cablevision v. Starlink Communs. Group, Inc., 601 F. Supp. 1568, 1573 (D. Kan. 1985) ("providing facilities for home use viewing of satellite-transmitted television signals").
284. Seventh Annual Report, In the Matter of Annual Assessment of the Status of Competition in the Market for the Delivery of Video Programming, 16 F.C.C.R. 6005, 6007, 6070-78 (2000) [hereinafter 2000 COMPETITION REPORT].
285. Time Warner, Inc., 61 Fed. Reg. 50,301 (FTC Sept. 25, 1996) (proposed consent order), 123 F.T.C 171 (1997) (decision and order).
286. 123 F.T.C. at 172, 180.
287. United States v. AT&T Corp., 65 Fed. Reg. 38,584 (DOJ June 21, 2000) (proposed final judgment and competitive impact statement), Civ. No. 00CV01176 (RCL) (D.D.C. 2000).
288. 65 Fed. Reg. at 38,584; *see infra* notes 359-60 and accompanying text.
289. America Online, Inc., 65 Fed. Reg. 79,861 (FTC Dec. 20, 2000) (aid to public comment), 2001 FTC LEXIS 44 (2001) (decision and order).
290. 2001 FTC LEXIS 44, at *9-11.
291. 47 U.S.C. § 521 note (1994).

Congress is the cost of entry—the "extraordinary expense of constructing more than one cable television system to serve a particular geographic area."[292]

Section 532(a) of the Communications Act contains provisions intended "to promote competition in the delivery of diverse sources of video programming and to assure that the widest possible diversity of information sources are made available to the public."[293] The statute prohibits local jurisdictions from awarding exclusive franchises for cable systems.[294] It also prohibits cable operators from owning multichannel multipoint distribution services (wireless cable) licenses or offering satellite master antenna television service within their franchise areas.[295] To mitigate further what Congress perceived to be the monopoly power of cable operators over the delivery of video signals, it also enacted the must-carry provisions of the 1992 Cable Act. These require cable operators to retransmit at no charge signals of certain local broadcast stations.[296]

The progressively expanding presence of alternatives to cable delivery of video signals, principally delivery by direct broadcast satellite (DBS) services,[297] has been noted annually by the Federal Communications Commission in its report on the status of competition for the delivery of video programming. For 1998 the agency reported, for example, that 85 percent of subscribers receiving services from a MVPD did so from a franchised cable operator as compared with 87 percent a year earlier.[298] As reported by the agency for 2000, this had dropped to 80 percent.[299] DBS subscribers, meanwhile, represented 9.4 percent of the total as of 1998,[300] and 15.4 percent as of 2000.[301] Nevertheless, the Federal Communications Commission concluded that the market for the delivery of video programming to households "continues to be highly concentrated and characterized by substantial barriers to entry."[302]

---

292. The monopoly power of cable operators was cited by the D.C. Circuit as a justification for upholding the rate regulation provisions of the 1992 Cable Act. In identically captioned but separate cases, the court cited "bottleneck, or gatekeeper control" that cable operators possess over programming delivered to homes, and "the absence of effective competition" for cable operators. Time Warner Entm't Co. v. FCC, 56 F.3d 151, 182-83 (D.C. Cir. 1995), cert. denied, 516 U.S. 1112 (1996); Time Warner Entm't Co. v. FCC, 93 F.3d 957, 967 (D.C. Cir. 1996).

293. 47 U.S.C § 532(a) (1994).

294. Id. § 541(a)(1) (1994).

295. Id. § 533(a) (Supp. 1999).

296. Id. § 535 (1994). When the Supreme Court upheld the must-carry provisions against a First Amendment challenge in Turner Broad. Sys. v. FCC, 512 U.S. 622 (1994), the Court agreed that cable operators possessed monopoly power over the transmission of video programming stating, e.g., that the rules were "justified by . . . the bottleneck monopoly power exercised by cable operators." Id. at 661. This was reconfirmed by the Court in Turner Broad. Sys., Inc. v. FCC, 520 U.S. 180, 197 (1997).

297. "The growth of non-cable MVPD subscribers continues to be primarily attributable to the growth of DBS." 2000 COMPETITION REPORT, supra note 284, at 6008. Other alternatives are wireless cable systems using frequencies in the multichannel multipoint distribution service (MMDS), satellite master antenna television (SMATV), and, to an extent, broadcast television. See, e.g., Fifth Annual Report, Annual Assessment of the Status of Competition in the Market for the Delivery of Video Programming, 13 F.C.C.R. 24,284, 24,286 (1998) [hereinafter 1998 COMPETITION REPORT].

298. 1998 COMPETITION REPORT, supra note 297, at 24,287.

299. 2000 COMPETITION REPORT, supra note 284, at 6008.

300. 1998 COMPETITION REPORT, supra note 297, at 24,287.

301. 2000 COMPETITION REPORT, supra note 284, at 6008. The FCC reported that DBS "appears to attract former cable subscribers and consumers not previously subscribing to an MVPD." See id.

302. Id. at 6066.

These findings notwithstanding, in *Time Warner Entertainment Co. v. FCC*,[303] the D.C. Circuit found the risks of undue concentration in the cable industry insufficient to justify a "subscriber cap" imposed by the Federal Communications Commission as directed by Congress.[304] The cap limited to 30 percent the number of MVPD subscribers that a single "multi-system operator" may serve.[305] The court struck down the cap on First Amendment grounds, noting that, according to the agency's own data, DBS operators are adding subscribers at almost three times the rate of cable operators.[306] The court thus reasoned that any Federal Communications Commission regulations limiting cable television ownership will have to take into account the impact of DBS on cable operators' market power.[307]

The inability of DBS operators to retransmit copyrighted broadcasts without a license from the network or broadcaster that holds the copyright could constrain the ability of DBS to compete with wire line cable operators.[308] Under the Satellite Home Viewer Improvement Act,[309] however, enacted in November 1999, satellite providers may retransmit network and network affiliate signals into local markets subject to retransmission consent rules similar to those established for cable operators.[310]

The 1996 Act included provisions removing barriers to entry by LECs into the market for delivery of video programming by creating the "open video system" framework.[311] The Federal Communications Commission reports, however, that the "expected technological convergence" that would permit the use of telephone facilities for video service had not occurred as of 2000.[312]

Conversely, cable operators have begun to offer telephone service using traditional telephone switching equipment, according to the Federal Communications Commission, and some testing of Internet Protocol telephony has begun.[313] The agency characterizes the pairing of Internet service with other services as "the most significant convergence of service offerings."[314] This is accompanied by increasing

---

303. 240 F.3d 1126 (D.C. Cir. 2001).

304. 47 U.S.C. § 533(f)(1)(A) (1994).

305. Implementation of Section 11(c) of the Cable Television Consumer Protection and Competition Act of 1992, 14 F.C.C.R. 19,098 (1999) (Third Report and Order).

306. 240 F.3d at 1133. The statute authorizing the FCC's ownership cap had previously been upheld against a facial challenge under the First Amendment in *Time Warner Entm't Co. v. United States*, 211 F.3d 1313 (D.C. Cir. 2000), *cert. denied*, 531 U.S. 1183 (2001).

307. 240 F.3d at 1134.

308. This limitation appeared in the Satellite Home Viewers Act, Pub. L. No. 100-667, § 202, 102 Stat. 3935 (1988).

309. Pub. L. No. 106-113, 115 Stat. 1501 (1999). This statute was upheld against constitutional and other challenges in *Satellite Broad. & Communs. Ass'n v. FCC*, No. 01-1151, 01-1271, 01-1272, 01-1818, 2001 U.S. App. LEXIS 26120 (4th Cir. Dec. 7, 2001).

310. For six months following enactment of the legislation, retransmission was permitted without consent. 47 U.S.C. § 325(b)(2)(E) (Supp. 1999). The FCC is required to establish election time periods for satellite carrier retransmission consent consistent with those established pursuant to the 1992 Cable Act. *Id.* § 325(b)(3)(C)(i) (Supp. 1999).

311. *Id.* § 573 (Supp. 1999).

312. 2000 COMPETITION REPORT, *supra* note 284, at 6009. LEC entry into this market is increasing, but through ownership of traditional franchised cable assets. *Id.*

313. *Id.*

314. *Id.*

litigation associated with demands for access to the broadband networks of cable operators.[315]

(1)   The Market for Delivery of Programming to Subscribers

The rates for basic cable service offered by cable operators not subject to "effective competition"[316] are regulated either by the local franchising authority or by the Federal Communications Commission.[317] The agency presumes that effective competition is absent, and places on the cable operator the burden to demonstrate otherwise by petition to the Federal Communications Commission.[318] The rates for video services other than basic cable service are no longer subject to regulation.[319]

Operators not subject to "effective competition" also are prohibited from charging discriminatory subscriber rates.[320] While state law also may provide a remedy against discriminatory rates,[321] the Robinson-Patman Act does not because courts have held that the delivery of cable is a service rather than a "commodity."[322]

State antitrust laws also have been used to attack other instances in which cable operators allegedly exercised monopoly power or something approaching it. Overcoming the defense that the claims were preempted, the plaintiff was able to invoke state law to challenge subscriber rates on the grounds that they were below cost and therefore predatory,[323] and, although the claim was unsuccessful, to allege that subscriptions to premium programming were tied to subscriptions to other programming "tiers."[324]

---

315. *See* part B.3.d of this chapter.

316. Federal law provides that "effective competition" exists where (1) less than 30% of the households in the operator's franchise area subscribe to cable service, (2) where other providers of multichannel video programming have penetrated the market to prescribed levels, (3) a municipal cable system competes at prescribed levels with the operator, or (4) the LEC offers comparable services. 47 U.S.C. § 543(l)(1) (1994 & Supp. 1999).

317. *Id* § 543(a)(2)(A) (1994). Local franchising authorities may become certified to regulate rates. *Id.* §§ 543(a)(3), (4) (1994). Otherwise, cable operators are subject to rate requirements of the Communications Act and the FCC's rules, including regulation of unreasonable basic cable service rates, 47 C.F.R. § 76.922 (2000), and a uniform rate structure requirement. 47 U.S.C. § 543(d) (Supp. 1999); 47 C.F.R. § 76.984 (2000).

318. 47 C.F.R. §§ 76.906, 76.911(b)(1) (2000).

319. 47 U.S.C. § 543(c)(4) (Supp. 1999).

320. *Id.* § 543(d) (Supp. 1999); *see* Time Warner Entm't Co. v. FCC, 56 F.3d 151, 191-92 (D.C. Cir.) (no "meeting competition" defense to a claim alleging rate discrimination in violation of the 1992 Cable Act), *cert. denied*, 516 U.S. 1112 (1996).

321. Dunlap v. Colorado Springs Cablevision, 829 P.2d 1286 (Colo. 1992) (permitting discriminatory pricing claim under Colorado Unfair Practices Act).

322. *See, e.g.*, Gall v. Home Box Office, 1992-2 Trade Cas. (CCH) ¶ 69,949 (S.D.N.Y. 1992); TV Communs. Network v. ESPN, 767 F. Supp. 1062, 1075-76 (D. Colo. 1991), *aff'd*, 964 F.2d 1022 (10th Cir. 1992); Rankin County Cablevision v. Pearl River Valley Water Dist., 692 F. Supp. 691 (S.D. Miss. 1988); Satellite T Assoc. v. Continental Cablevision of Va., Inc., 586 F. Supp. 973 (E.D. Va. 1982), *aff'd sub nom.* Satellite Television & Associated Resources v. Continental Cablevision, 714 F.2d 351 (4th Cir.), *cert. denied*, 465 U.S. 1027 (1984).

323. Total TV v. Palmer Communs., Inc., 69 F.3d 298 (9th Cir. 1995) (1992 Cable Act does not preempt prohibition against below-cost pricing in California Unfair Practices Act), *cert. dismissed*, 517 U.S. 1152 (1996).

324. In *Morrison v. Viacom, Inc.*, 78 Cal. Rptr. 2d 133 (Cal. App. 1998), the plaintiffs alleged that, but for the tying arrangement, they would have purchased from the defendant only satellite and "premium" channel services, but not broadcast channels. The plaintiffs alleged a violation of California's Cartwright Act, CAL. BUS. & PROF. CODE § 16700 *et seq.* Affirming dismissal on the pleadings, the appellate court held that the plaintiffs failed to show any foreclosure in the market

(2) The Programming Supply Market

Assuring nondiscriminatory access by cable operators to programming is a
critical issue in an industry in which ownership interests frequently overlap among
cable operators and programming producers, distributors, and vendors.[325]
Accordingly, with respect to programming distributed by satellite,[326] vertically
integrated programming vendors and cable operators are, absent a finding by the
Federal Communications Commission that the agreement is in the public interest,
prohibited from entering into exclusive contracts[327] and from engaging in either
price[328] or nonprice[329] discrimination. The agency may award damages for these
"program access" violations.[330]

Copyright is another source of power in the market for programming. In the
Satellite Home Viewer Act (SHVA),[331] Congress elaborated on the protection
afforded to copyrighted broadcast programming. Until the SHVA was amended in
1999,[332] with limited exceptions copyrighted programming could not be retransmitted
by satellite delivery, i.e., by DBS services, without a license from the broadcaster.[333]
A series of suits against a particular satellite provider brought by television broadcast
networks to enforce this restriction[334] led to allegations by the satellite provider in
Primetime 24 Joint Venture v. NBC[335] that the broadcast networks had engaged in a
concerted refusal to deal. Notwithstanding the fact that the networks were successful
in many of those prior actions, the Second Circuit reversed the lower court's
judgment dismissing Primetime 24's complaint. The court held that allegations of
"simultaneous and voluminous challenges" brought under the SHVA "without regard
to whether the challenges had merit" brought the case within the sham exception to
the *Noerr* doctrine.[336] While allowing that coordinated efforts to enforce copyrights

---

for the tied product—broadcast television—nor could they do so since those signals are available
at no cost. *See also* Friedman v. Adams Russell Cable Servs., 624 F. Supp. 1568 (D. Kan. 1985)
(summary judgment for defendant on claim that premium tiers unlawfully tied).

325. In enacting the 1992 Cable Act, Congress found that as a result of increased vertical integration
between cable operators and cable programmers, vertically integrated program suppliers have "the
incentive and ability to favor their affiliated cable operators over nonaffiliated cable operators and
programming distributors using other technologies." 47 U.S.C. § 521 note (1994).
326. 47 U.S.C. § 548(i) (1994).
327. *Id.* § 548(c)(2)(D) (1994).
328. *Id.* § 548(b) (1994).
329. Implementation of Sections 12 and 19 of the Cable Television Consumer Protection and
Competition Act of 1992: Development of Competition and Diversity in Video Programming
Distribution and Carriage, 8 F.C.C.R. 3359 (1993). The 1996 Act also prohibits "unfair methods
of competition or unfair or deceptive acts or practices" that significantly hinder or prevent access
by operators to programming distributed by satellite. 47 U.S.C. § 548(b) (Supp. 1999).
330. Implementation of the Cable Television Consumer Protection and Competition Act of 1992, 13
F.C.C.R. 15,822 (1998).
331. Pub. L. No. 100-667, § 202, 102 Stat. 3935 (1988).
332. Pub. L. No. 106-113, 115 Stat. 1501 (1999). *See supra* notes 309-10 and accompanying text.
333. The Satellite Home Viewer Act provides for a statutory license in favor of satellite carriers for
retransmission to "unserved households." 17 U.S.C. § 119(a)(2)(B) (2000). This is a household
that cannot receive the over-the-air signal of a primary network station affiliate of Grade B
intensity as defined by the FCC, in addition to other conditions. *Id.* at § 119(d)(10) (2000).
334. ABC v. Primetime 24, 184 F.3d 348 (4th Cir. 1999) (affirming judgment for plaintiff except as to
moot claims); CBS v. Primetime 24, 9 F. Supp. 2d 1333 (S.D. Fla. 1998).
335. 219 F.3d 92 (2d Cir. 2000).
336. *Id.* at 101. The *Noerr* doctrine and the sham exception to it are discussed in part C of Chapter XIII.

against a common infringer may be permissible, the court held that an agreement by the copyright holders "to limit their individual freedom of action in licensing future rights to such an infringer" is not. Citing *Klor's, Inc. v. Broadway-Hale Stores, Inc.*,[337] the court concluded that "[a] concerted refusal to license copyright programming . . . in order to prevent competition" violates the Sherman Act.[338]

d. OPEN ACCESS

Beginning in 1999, several actions were brought against cable television operators to require them to allow the use of their cable facilities by unaffiliated entities for the provision of Internet access service (a remedy termed by its proponents "open access"). AT&T's acquisition of TCI cable franchises in the Portland, Oregon, metropolitan area resulted in the first court decision on the issue.[339] To implement the acquisition of TCI by AT&T the parties applied, where contractually required, for the consent of the local franchising authorities to the "change in control" of TCI's franchises. The city of Portland, Oregon, and Multnomah County conditioned their approval of the change of control on the agreement of the parties to carry on their network ISPs and other third-party online services that compete with the parties' own services. The parties refused and the local authorities disapproved the franchise transfer. AT&T and TCI filed suit alleging that the transfer conditions were inconsistent with various provisions of the Federal Communications Act[340] and that the conditions were therefore preempted and invalid.[341] The district court held that AT&T and TCI could be required to permit "access" to their broadband network because the local authorities had the power to declare such access is an "essential facility."[342] The court further found that federal law did not preempt the authority of the local authorities to require third-party access to that network as a condition to permitting the franchise transfer.[343]

---

337. 359 U.S. 207, 212 (1959).
338. 219 F.3d at 102-04.
339. The FCC has yet to take any action to create "rights of access" to broadband systems of cable television operators. Inquiry Concerning the Deployment of Advanced Telecommunications Capability to All Americans in a Reasonable and Timely Fashion, and Possible Steps to Accelerate Such Deployment Pursuant to Section 706 of the Telecommunications Act of 1996, 14 F.C.C.R. 2398 (1999).
340. For example, the complaint alleged that 47 U.S.C. § 544(b)(1) (Supp. 1999) prohibits local franchising authorities from establishing requirements for programming or other information services, and that 47 U.S.C. § 541(b)(3)(D) (Supp. 1999), prohibits a franchising authority from requiring an operator, as a condition to the transfer of a franchise, to provide "any telecommunications service or facilities." The complaint also alleged, and prayed for a judicial declaration, that neither AT&T nor TCI is subject to the unbundling provisions of 47 U.S.C. § 251(c)(3) (Supp. 1999) applicable to ILECs.
341. *See* 47 U.S.C. § 556(c) (1994).
342. AT&T Corp. v. City of Portland, 43 F. Supp. 2d 1146 (D. Or. 1999), *rev'd*, 216 F.3d 871 (9th Cir. 2000).
343. *Id.* at 1151-55. First, citing 47 U.S.C. § 556 (1994 & Supp. 1999), and particularly subparagraph (b), the court found that "Congress intended to interfere as little as possible" with local regulation of cable services. 43 F. Supp. 1151-52. Second, the court found that Congress "specifically recognizes" the power of local government to preserve competition for cable services. *Id.* at 1152, citing 47 U.S.C. § 533(d) (1994) (state and local governments may prohibit ownership where "the acquisition of such a cable system may eliminate or reduce competition").

On appeal, the Ninth Circuit reversed and voided the open access conditions sought by the local authorities.[344] The court held that Internet access services provided by AT&T over its cable television facilities did not satisfy the definition of "cable services" under the 1934 Act.[345] On that basis, local jurisdictions lacked statutory authority to directly regulate Internet services through their franchising authority.[346] The court also held that local jurisdictions are prohibited under the 1934 Act from imposing conditions on the provision of Internet service through the franchise transfer approval authority that local jurisdictions possess.[347]

The second court to address the issue reached the same conclusion.[348] The Fourth Circuit held that local requirements to provide open access are preempted by Communications Act provisions that prohibit local franchise authorities from requiring cable operators to provide telecommunications services.[349]

A district court has invalidated open access requirements imposed locally on First Amendment grounds.[350] Applying both strict scrutiny and intermediate scrutiny analysis, the district court held that Broward County's ordinance imposing open access requirements on cable operators "invidiously impacts a cable operator's ability to participate in the information market"[351] and does not further a substantial governmental interest.[352]

e. MERGER ACTIVITY

To prevent undue concentration nationally in the cable industry, Congress directed the Federal Communications Commission, in a statute adopted in 1992, to "prescribe rules and regulations establishing reasonable limits on the number of cable subscribers a person is authorized to reach through cable systems owned by such person, or in which such person has an attributable interest."[353] This statutory direction to the Federal Communications Commission survived a facial challenge when the D.C. Circuit held that the subscriber cap authority assigned to the agency did not violate the First Amendment.[354]

As implemented,[355] the subscriber cap prohibits cable operators from serving more than 30 percent of all multichannel video programming subscribers nationwide.[356] The rules also require any cable operator serving 20 percent or more of multichannel video programming subscribers to certify to the agency, prior to acquiring additional systems, that the acquisition will not violate the national

344. AT&T Corp. v. City of Portland, 216 F.3d 871 (9th Cir. 2000).
345. *Id.* at 877.
346. *Id.*
347. *Id.* at 878.
348. MediaOne Group v. County of Henrico, Va., 257 F.3d 356 (4th Cir. 2001). The court also considered whether the local open access requirement was barred by Virginia law and found that it was not. *Id.* at 362.
349. *See* 47 U.S.C. § 541(b)(3)(D) (Supp. 1999).
350. Comcast Cablevision v. Broward County, 124 F. Supp. 2d 685 (S.D. Fla. 2000).
351. *Id.* at 693.
352. *Id.* at 698.
353. 47 U.S.C. § 533(f)(1)(A) (1994).
354. Time Warner Entm't Co. v. United States, 211 F.3d 1313, 1320 (D.C. Cir. 2000), *cert. denied*, 531 U.S. 1183 (2001).
355. Implementation of Section 11(c) of the Cable Television Consumer Protection and Competition Act of 1992, 14 F.C.C.R. 19,098 (1999) (Third Report and Order).
356. 47 C.F.R. § 76.503(a) (2000).

subscriber limits.[357] The D.C. Circuit subsequently vacated these rules on several grounds, including that, under an intermediate scrutiny First Amendment analysis, the agency had failed to show that the limits it chose did not burden substantially more speech than necessary to further the governmental interest in ownership limits.[358]

Both the Department of Justice and the Federal Trade Commission have reviewed and conditioned cable industry mergers based upon concerns of increased horizontal concentration. The Department of Justice recently approved the merger between AT&T and MediaOne Group subject to AT&T divesting its interest in the operating entity providing broadband Internet access under the trade name "Road Runner" acquired through the MediaOne merger.[359] Based on AT&T's existing control of the nation's largest provider of residential broadband Internet access, Excite@Home, and AT&T's potential ownership of 34 percent of the Road Runner operation, the Department of Justice alleged that the merger would result in a lessening of "competition in the nationwide market for the aggregation, promotion, and distribution of residential broadband content."[360]

In 2000, the Federal Trade Commission announced a consent agreement imposing conditions on the merger between AOL and Time Warner.[361] According to the complaint drafted by the Federal Trade Commission, an unconditioned merger between AOL and Time Warner would have anticompetitive effects in three product markets: (1) the market for broadband Internet access; (2) the market for residential broadband Internet transport services, or "last mile" access; and (3) the market for interactive television services.[362] The settlement required the combined entity to make available in those systems the services of alternative, nonaffiliated broadband ISPs.[363] The consent agreement also prohibited Time Warner from interfering with content passed along the bandwidth used by nonaffiliated ISPs.[364]

C. Energy

1. Natural Gas

The natural gas industry—although still regulated at the pipeline transportation level—in many other respects is now unregulated in key competitive elements. The federal and state regulatory framework for the natural gas industry can be understood

---

357. *Id.* at § 76.503(g) (2000).
358. Time Warner Entm't Co. v. FCC, 240 F.3d 1126, 1139 (D.C. Cir. 2001), *cert. denied sub nom.* Consumer Fed'n of Am. v. FCC, 70 U.S.L.W. 3372 (Dec. 3, 2001).
359. United States v. AT&T Corp., 65 Fed. Reg. 38,584 (DOJ June 21, 2000) (proposed final judgment and competitive impact statement), 2000-2 Trade Cas. (CCH) ¶ 73,096 (D.D.C. 2000).
360. 65 Fed. Reg. at 38,590.
361. America Online, Inc. 65 Fed. Reg. 79,861 (FTC Dec. 20, 2000) (aid to public comment), 2001 FTC LEXIS 44 (Apr. 17, 2001) (decision and order).
362. 2001 FTC LEXIS 44, at *9-11.
363. *Id.* at *24-25. Time Warner must first make available in those systems broadband Internet service offered by Earthlink, Inc.; within 90 days of offering AOL's broadband Internet service in certain identified cable systems, Time Warner must enter into agreements for access to those systems with two other nonaffiliated broadband ISPs; and in cable systems not identified in the consent agreement, Time Warner must enter into agreements with three nonaffiliated ISPs for access to cable facilities.
364. *Id.* at *35-36.

with reference to the three distinct sectors of the industry: (1) the production and gathering of natural gas in the field, where the "wellhead price" is generally set; (2) the interstate and intrastate transportation of gas by pipeline from the producing field to local distribution companies or large end-users; and (3) the local distribution of the gas to consumers.

At the federal level, the natural gas industry is regulated by the Federal Energy Regulatory Commission pursuant to the Natural Gas Act (NGA).[365] Under the NGA, the Federal Energy Regulatory Commission has the power to implement price controls on wellhead sales,[366] establish rates and review practices in interstate transportation, and regulate asset acquisitions and changes in facilities and services by natural gas companies.[367] While carrying out Congress's public interest directive, the agency must consider federal antitrust policies.[368]

Traditionally, the Federal Energy Regulatory Commission required producers and gatherers to sell wellhead gas at "just and reasonable" rates, but the gas shortages of the early 1970s fostered a push to deregulate gas prices. In 1989, Congress took the final step toward deregulating the wellhead price of natural gas with the passage of the Natural Gas Wellhead Decontrol Act.[369] The deregulation of the wholesale sales market, along with the related development of financial instruments, revolutionized trading in natural gas. As the Federal Energy Regulatory Commission decontrolled competition at the wellhead, the demand for pipeline supply increased and the transportation of gas became the focus for regulators.

Prior to deregulation, interstate gas pipelines bought gas from producers, and the customers of interstate pipelines—local distribution companies (LDCs) and certain large gas users such as industrial customers—purchased a package of regulated gas and regulated transportation. As gas supplies became more plentiful and market prices began to drop, LDCs and large end-users sought to purchase natural gas directly from producers as opposed to their traditional pipeline suppliers. These purchasers sought to have their gas supplies transported by pipelines on a nondiscriminatory, open access basis. The Federal Energy Regulatory Commission mandated open access in a series of orders beginning with Order No. 636, which required that all pipelines provide open access transportation and that all contracts for sales of gas and transportation be "unbundled."[370] Today, the agency primarily

---

365. 15 U.S.C. §§ 717-717z (2000).

366. The NGA does not explicitly cover production, gathering, and local distribution, but the Supreme Court held in *Philips Petroleum Co. v. Wisconsin*, 347 U.S. 672 (1954), that the Federal Power Commission (FPC), the predecessor to the Federal Energy Regulatory Commission (FERC), had jurisdiction to regulate the wellhead price of natural gas.

367. *See, e.g.*, 15 U.S.C. § 717c (rates and charges); § 717f (issuance of certificates authorizing operations).

368. Maryland People's Counsel v. FERC, 760 F.2d 318 (D.C. Cir. 1985); Alabama Power Co. v. FPC, 511 F.2d 383 (D.C. Cir. 1974); Northern Natural Gas Co. v. FPC, 399 F.2d 953 (D.C. Cir. 1968).

369. Pub. L. No. 101-60, 103 Stat. 157 (1989). This act called for a relatively quick transition to a completely deregulated market at the wellhead. Any gas supplies still regulated as of January 1, 1993, were completely decontrolled on that date. FERC implemented the provisions of the Wellhead Decontrol Act by regulations promulgated in Order No. 523, issued on April 18, 1990. [Regs. Preamble] (1986-1990) F.E.R.C. Stats. & Regs. (CCH) ¶ 30,887 (1990).

370. Order 636, Pipeline Service Obligations and Revisions to Regulations Governing Self-Implementing Transportation; and Regulation of Natural Gas Pipelines After Partial Wellhead Decontrol, 57 Fed. Reg. 15,267 (Apr. 16, 1992), III F.E.R.C. (CCH) Stats. & Regs. [Regs. Preambles] ¶ 30,950 (Aug. 3, 1992); *order on reh'g*, Order No. 636-B, 57 Fed. Reg. 57,911 (Dec. 8, 1992), 61 F.E.R.C. (CCH) ¶ 61,007 (1993).

regulates transportation prices of interstate pipeline companies and imposes operational and conduct rules to ensure open and nondiscriminatory access to, and use of, pipeline facilities by all shippers.[371]

a.   REFUSING ACCESS TO TRANSPORTATION

The nature of the gas transportation industry has made it a target for federal regulation.   Pipeline transportation is capital intensive, embodies large-scale economies, and requires special rights of way.   As a result, the Federal Energy Regulatory Commission believes that gas transportation systems are susceptible to monopoly control and will continue to require some form of economic regulation for the foreseeable future.[372]

Recent agency regulatory initiatives focus on promoting and ensuring open access to pipeline facilities.   The pre-Order 636 litigation over pipeline access issues is no longer directly applicable to many current disputes.   Nonetheless, the older cases established principles that remain relevant in an increasingly deregulated environment.   For example, pipelines may not indirectly deny access by imposing burdensome operational or credit requirements or offering services only at the maximum rate.[373]

Monopolization claims under Section 2 of the Sherman Act for denial of access to transportation facilities have met with mixed success.   In an early case, *Woods Exploration & Producing Co. v. Aluminum Co. of America*,[374] defendants Alcoa and a subsidiary owned a pipeline that was used to transport gas from the producing field to an Alcoa plant.   The defendants also marketed gas that had been produced in the producing field and sold to a third party.   The plaintiffs, leaseholders in the field, requested that Alcoa transport their gas and "unitize" the field.   Alcoa refused both

---

371. Order No. 637, Regulation of Short-Term Natural Gas Transportation Services, and Regulation of Interstate Natural Gas Transportation Services, 65 Fed. Reg. 10,156 (Feb. 25, 2000), III F.E.R.C. (CCH) Stats. & Regs. [Regs. Preambles] ¶ 31,091 (Feb. 9, 2000); Order No. 637-A, 65 Fed. Reg. 35,706 (June 5, 2000), III F.E.R.C. (CCH) Stats. & Regs. [Regs. Preambles] ¶ 31,099 (May 19, 2000), *order denying reh'g*, Order No. 637-B, 92 F.E.R.C. (CCH) ¶ 61,062 (2000). Order 637 was FERC's response to the increase in competitiveness following the deregulation of wellhead price controls and the implementation of open access to pipeline transportation. The order revised the agency's pricing policy by waiving price ceilings for short-term released capacity for a two-year period and permitting pipelines to file for peak/off-peak and term differentiated rate structures. The order changed regulations regarding scheduling procedures, capacity segmentation, and pipeline penalties and narrowed the right of first refusal for long-term capacity customers.

372. Even this sector of the industry has been exhibiting indicia of competitive markets, including trading of firm capacity rights by pipeline shippers in competition with the pipeline's sales of firm and interruptible capacity; lifting of rate caps on such "secondary" capacity releases under certain circumstances; introducing innovative transportation and storage services; and charging negotiated and market-based rates upon a showing that a company can mitigate or lacks market power.

373. *Cf.* Southern California Co. v. FERC, 172 F.3d 74 (D.C. Cir. 1999) (allegations of withholding of capacity from the secondary capacity market, thereby artificially increasing its value, by a shipper that offered to release capacity at an above-market—albeit below the maximum tariff rate—price to unaffiliated parties). *See also* Process Gas Consumers Group v. FERC, 177 F.3d 995 (D.C. Cir. 1999) (FERC gave too much weight to a pipeline's ability to increase its revenues while ignoring potentially serious anticompetitive effects of the transaction at issue); Public Util. Comm'n of the State of Cal. v. El Paso Natural Gas Co., Dkt. No. RP00-342-000, 97 F.E.R.C. (CCH) ¶ 63,004 (2001) (allegation of withholding capacity, thereby creating anticompetitive effect on the delivered price of gas and the wholesale electric market).

374. 438 F.2d 1286 (5th Cir. 1971), *cert. denied*, 404 U.S. 1047 (1972).

requests, and the plaintiffs began construction of a pipeline. The defendants then attempted to thwart the construction of the pipeline by forcing the plaintiffs to file condemnation proceedings to gain right of way. The Fifth Circuit reinstated a jury verdict finding that the defendants had violated Section 2.

Two cases addressed the issue of whether a pipeline had "legitimate business justifications" for its refusal to transport gas purchased by its customers from third parties. In *Illinois ex rel. Hartigan v. Panhandle Eastern Pipe Line Co.*,[375] the state, suing on behalf of itself and a class of residential and industrial natural gas consumers, alleged that Panhandle monopolized the sale of natural gas within central Illinois by refusing to transport gas purchased directly from independent producers by LDCs.[376] The LDCs were full requirements sales customers of Panhandle pursuant to Panhandle's federally approved "zero-tariff" rate schedule, and as such they were contractually committed to purchase all of their gas from the pipelines, which also transported the supplies. Panhandle justified its refusal to transport nonsystem gas for these zero-tariff customers on the ground that enabling them to obtain gas from other sources would dramatically reduce demand for the expensive gas Panhandle was contractually obligated to purchase, and thus would expose it to enormous take-or-pay liability.

The district court, after a bench trial, found that Panhandle had monopoly power over natural gas sales to LDCs for use by residential and commercial customers within central Illinois and that federal regulation did not effectively constrain Panhandle's ability to exercise monopoly power with respect to the practices at issue.[377] The court held, however, that Panhandle's insistence on enforcing its federally approved tariff during a period of regulatory turmoil and uncertainty did not constitute willful maintenance of monopoly power, but merely a "lawful refusal to cut its own throat."[378]

In affirming, the Seventh Circuit emphasized that because Panhandle acted with a legitimate business purpose in refusing to permit its customers to avoid their contractual obligations when to do so would be to expose it to enormous take-or-pay obligations, its conduct could not be characterized as anticompetitive.[379] The Seventh Circuit also affirmed the district court's dismissal of the state's essential facilities claim. The court found that access to Panhandle's pipeline was not essential for other gas sellers to compete because it was economically feasible for competitors to duplicate much of Panhandle's system by means of interconnections with competing pipelines and the construction of new ones.[380] Moreover, the court held that denying access to an essential facility is actionable only if providing access is feasible, and

---

375. 730 F. Supp. 826 (C.D. Ill. 1990), *aff'd sub nom.* Illinois *ex rel.* Bunt v. Panhandle E. Pipe Line Co., 935 F.2d 1469 (7th Cir. 1991), *cert. denied*, 502 U.S. 1094 (1992).

376. The complaint, brought under both federal and Illinois antitrust laws, alleged unlawful monopolization, attempted monopolization, monopoly leveraging, an unlawful denial of access to an essential facility, and an unlawful tie of gas transportation to gas purchases. 730 F. Supp. at 834.

377. *Id.* at 871, 876. The court found, however, that Panhandle did not possess monopoly power with respect to industrial end-users capable of using alternate fuels. *Id.* at 874.

378. *Id.* at 882-83, 918.

379. 935 F.2d at 1483-85 & n.13. The Seventh Circuit thus rejected the district court's view that Panhandle's concern about take-or-pay liability was "not a legitimate business justification for antitrust purposes." *Id.* at 1483 n.13.

380. *Id.* at 1482-83.

the economic exposure created by the take-or-pay contracts rendered it unfeasible in this case.[381]

In *City of Chanute v. Williams Natural Gas Co.*,[382] the district court held that a natural gas pipeline had a legitimate business reason for reversing its policy of interim open access "given the uncertainty and chaotic conditions in the natural gas industry at the time and the potential take-or-pay liability it was facing," and the court granted summary judgment against monopolization and attempted monopolization claims brought by various cities seeking access.[383] Many of Williams's sales customers took advantage of its interim open access policy to buy cheaper natural gas from producers. The customers' conversion from sales service[384] to transportation service resulted in a dramatic increase in Williams's exposure under its take-or-pay contracts with producers. When Williams's efforts to negotiate take-or-pay relief with its producers failed, Williams "closed" its pipeline to transportation of third-party gas. The court found that Williams's decision was reasonable, holding: "It is the potential seriousness of the take-or-pay exposure which provides Williams with a legitimate business rationale for reversing its policy of interim open access."[385] It noted that failure to take measures to check such significant exposure "could certainly affect a pipeline's ability to provide reliable services to its customers."[386]

The court also granted summary judgment against the cities' essential facilities claim. It held that the cities could not show that they had no feasible alternative to use of Williams's facilities for open access transportation of third-party gas. It found that both the purchase of gas from producers pursuant to regulation and the purchase of Williams's own sales gas, which was reasonably priced, were feasible alternatives for the cities.[387] On appeal, the Tenth Circuit affirmed that, as a matter of law, the defendant's supply of gas at federally regulated prices provided the cities with "reasonable access to the pipelines."[388] The court found that although Williams had monopoly power, it had a legitimate business justification for its refusal to provide access because it wanted to prevent take-or-pay liability and prevent conversion of sales service in a period of regulatory turmoil.[389]

In *Consul, Ltd. v. Transco Energy Co.*,[390] the court also addressed an essential facilities claim against a natural gas pipeline. Consul, a natural gas broker, alleged that Transco had violated Section 2 by refusing to transport gas brokered by Consul.

381. *Id.* at 1483.
382. 743 F. Supp. 1437 (D. Kan. 1990), *aff'd*, 955 F.2d 641 (10th Cir.), *cert. denied*, 506 U.S. 831 (1992).
383. *Id.* at 1459. Earlier, the district court had granted a preliminary injunction requiring Williams to keep its pipeline open for transportation of gas purchased by the cities from third parties. City of Chanute v. Williams Natural Gas Co., 678 F. Supp. 1517 (D. Kan. 1988).
384. Such sales service included a bundled product—gas supplies plus their transportation.
385. 743 F. Supp. at 1454.
386. *Id.* at 1460.
387. *Id.* at 1461; *cf.* Reynolds Metals Co. v. Columbia Gas Sys., No. 87-0446-K (E.D. Va. Aug. 17, 1988) (dismissing essential facility claim by natural gas end-user against pipeline on ground that the essential facilities doctrine is available only to competitors and not to consumers). *Chanute* also rejected the cities' monopoly leveraging claim. It reasoned that the Tenth Circuit would not recognize monopoly leveraging as a separate offense under § 2 of the Sherman Act. Thus, because the cities could not establish the "willful maintenance" element of their general monopolization claim, their monopoly leveraging claim also failed. 743 F. Supp. at 1461-62.
388. 955 F.2d at 649.
389. *Id.* at 655-56.
390. 805 F.2d 490 (4th Cir. 1986), *cert. denied*, 481 U.S. 1050 (1987).

The Fourth Circuit rejected Consul's contention that a plaintiff claiming denial of access to an essential facility need not define a relevant market and establish the defendant's market power in that market.[391] It held that Consul's Section 2 claim was defeated by its inability to show that Transco possessed market power in the market for natural gas at the wellhead or in the nationwide market in which Consul and Transco competed as brokers.[392]

b. TYING

Several pipeline cases also have addressed the issue of tying. For example, in *Continental Trend Resources, Inc. v. OXY USA, Inc.*,[393] the Tenth Circuit affirmed a grant of summary judgment for a defendant accused of tying gas processing and compression services to another company's gathering and transportation services. The court found that the defendant lacked market power in the tying service of gathering and processing. The court also rejected a conspiracy claim because the agreement between the two companies did not limit the plaintiffs to using only the defendant's processing and compression services.[394]

In *United States v. El Paso Natural Gas Co.*,[395] the Department of Justice brought a Section 1 tying complaint alleging that El Paso forced operators seeking to connect natural gas wells to El Paso's gas-gathering system to also purchase meter installation service, although the operators might otherwise have preferred to purchase that service elsewhere or on different terms. The well operator generally had to agree to pay El Paso a flat fee for the construction and installation of the meter equipment necessary to connect the well to El Paso's system. In many instances, El Paso had taken a longer time to complete meter installation than it would have taken if the well operator had been able to use an alternative service provider.[396]

The Department of Justice and El Paso settled the case with entry of a consent decree that ordered the company to refrain from these tying practices. Additionally, it prohibited El Paso from setting and implementing standards and procedures related to meter installation for wells connected to the company's gathering system that would enable it to discriminate against other providers of meter installation in favor of its own meter installation services. El Paso was permitted to continue to provide meter installation, but it was required affirmatively to inform its gathering customers that they had the option of using third-party service providers. The consent decree also contained provisions to ensure that El Paso did not disadvantage well operators who chose competing meter installation providers. In recognition of El Paso's safety and liability concerns, El Paso could impose upon such third parties reasonable specifications for the construction and installation of metering facilities.[397]

---

391. *Id.* at 494.
392. *Id.* at 495-96.
393. 44 F.3d 1465 (10th Cir. 1995), *vacated and remanded*, 517 U.S. 1216 (1996). The case was remanded by the Supreme Court to allow the lower court to reconsider the amount of punitive damages awarded to the plaintiff on its tort and contract claims in light of *BMW of North Am., Inc. v. Gore*, 517 U.S. 559 (1996) (reversing an award of punitive damages as grossly excessive).
394. 44 F.3d at 1482-83.
395. 60 Fed. Reg. 5217, 5218 (DOJ Jan. 26, 1995) (proposed final judgment and competitive impact statement), CIV. 1:95 CV00067 (D.D.C. 1995) (final judgment).
396. *Id.* at 5218-19.
397. *Id.* at 5219, 5223-24.

c.   MERGERS AND ACQUISITIONS

The Federal Energy Regulatory Commission has no regulatory authority over acquisitions of voting securities of natural gas companies. Its power attaches only to the extent of Section 7(c) of the NGA,[398] which prohibits the operation of acquired assets without a certificate of public convenience and necessity. In *California v. FPC*,[399] the Supreme Court concluded that the authority granted in Section 7(c) does not deprive the federal courts of jurisdiction to enforce the antitrust laws with respect to the natural gas industry. Hence, the Department of Justice, the Federal Trade Commission, and private parties remain free to challenge acquisitions under the antitrust laws, even after approval by the Federal Energy Regulatory Commission.

Many of these challenges have arisen in the context of combinations of pipeline operations.[400] For example, in *United States v. El Paso Natural Gas Co.*,[401] the government challenged El Paso's acquisition of Pacific Northwest Pipeline, which at the time was one of the two major interstate pipelines serving the Rocky Mountain states. At the time of the acquisition, El Paso was the "only actual supplier of out-of-state gas" to the California market.[402] Pacific Northwest had never sold gas in the California market, but it was nevertheless found to "have been a substantial factor in the California market."[403] Accordingly, the Supreme Court held that the effect of the merger may be substantially to lessen competition within the meaning of Section 7 of the Clayton Act, and it ordered the lower court to require El Paso to divest itself of the acquired pipeline.[404]

The Federal Trade Commission has challenged several mergers involving gas pipelines and has obtained consent decrees modifying the transactions.[405] In two

---

398. 15 U.S.C. § 717f (2000).
399. 369 U.S. 482 (1962).
400. In addition, the FTC and DOJ have challenged convergence mergers concerning the combination of natural gas distributors and electric utility companies. *See* part C.2.e of this chapter.
401. 376 U.S. 651 (1964).
402. *Id.* at 658.
403. *Id.*
404. *Id.* at 662.
405. *See, e.g.*, Chevron Corp., No. 001-0011, 66 Fed. Reg. 48,136 (FTC Sept. 18, 2001) (alleging that merger of Chevron and Texaco would cause market for transportation in Central Gulf of Mexico region to become significantly more concentrated) (consent order requiring divestiture of Texaco's interest in pipeline system in that region and Texaco's resignation as operator of that system); El Paso Energy Corp., No. 001-0086, 66 Fed. Reg. 9399 (FTC Feb. 7, 2001) (alleging that merger of El Paso and Coastal would eliminate competition in 20 sections of the country, increase concentration in already highly concentrated markets for gas transportation) (consent decree requiring divestiture of interest in 10 pipelines and one pipeline yet to be constructed); El Paso Energy Corp., No. 00-0121, 65 Fed. Reg. 83,035 (FTC Dec. 19, 2000) (alleging that acquisition of two Pacific Gas & Electric subsidiaries by El Paso would lessen competition for transportation of natural gas in three markets) (consent order requiring divestitures of interest in several gas pipelines); Arkla Inc., [FTC Complaints & Orders 1987-1993 Transfer Binder] Trade Reg. Rep. (CCH) ¶ 22,686 (FTC Oct. 10, 1989) (alleging that Arkla's acquisition of pipeline from TransArk might lessen actual and potential competition in pipeline transportation of gas out of Arkansas portion of Arkoma Basin and transportation of gas into the Conway-Morrilton-Russellville corridor) (consent decree requiring divestiture), *modified*, Arkla, Inc., 119 F.T.C. 413 (1995) (changes in the industry that expanded capacity and entry decreased potential for competitive harm; previously ordered divestiture requirement dropped); Panhandle E. Corp., [FTC Complaints & Orders 1987-1993 Transfer Binder] Trade Reg. Rep. (CCH) ¶ 22,680 (FTC July 17, 1989) (alleging that acquisition of Texas Eastern might substantially lessen competition in the pipeline transportation of natural gas out of portions of the Gulf of Mexico; consent decree required

recent cases, the Federal Trade Commission obtained consent decrees requiring divestitures to address concerns created by the mergers. The agency challenged a merger between Duke Energy Corporation and Phillips Petroleum Company pursuant to which all of Duke's and Phillips's natural gas-gathering and -processing businesses would be combined.[406] Duke also would have acquired certain gas-gathering and -processing assets in central Oklahoma. The Federal Trade Commission identified seven markets in counties in Kansas, Oklahoma, and Texas where gas producers could only turn to the combined Duke-Phillips or, at most, to one other gas gatherer, for gas-gathering services. It alleged that the proposed merger and acquisition would reduce competition in the provision of gas-gathering services in these markets and likely lead to anticompetitive increases in gathering rates and an overall reduction in gas drilling and production.[407] To resolve these concerns, Duke agreed to divest approximately 2,780 miles of gas-gathering pipeline in these markets, eliminating any overlap between its holdings and what it would have acquired from Phillips and another joint venture.[408]

In the case of a proposed merger between El Paso Natural Gas Company and Sonat, the Federal Trade Commission focused on the transportation of natural gas out of producing fields (gathering) and the transportation of natural gas into gas consuming areas (intrastate and/or interstate transmission).[409] The complaint alleged that the effect of the acquisition could be to substantially lessen competition or tend to create a monopoly in the transportation or gathering in the relevant market by eliminating actual and potential competition between El Paso and Sonat, eliminating actual and potential competition among competitors generally, and increasing concentration in the transportation or gathering, thereby increasing the likelihood of collusion.[410] To address these concerns, substantial divestitures were required, including divestiture of two companies that owned natural gas pipelines.[411]

The Federal Trade Commission also has required nondivestiture relief in several recent cases involving gas pipeline mergers. In the case of a merger between the Williams Companies and MAPCO Inc, the agency challenged the transaction on the ground that the merger would have anticompetitive effects in the market for

Panhandle to divest its interest in a pipeline gathering system that competed with a pipeline owned by Texas Eastern); Occidental Petroleum Corp., 109 F.T.C. 167 (1986) (challenging vertical merger between natural gas producer and sole pipeline supplier of gas in St. Louis area on the ground that pipeline could pass on to consumers cost of gas purchased at inflated prices from affiliated producer; consent decree required Occidental to divest pipeline serving St. Louis area); MidCon Corp., 107 F.T.C. 48 (1986) (alleging that acquisition of United Energy Resources would substantially reduce competition in transportation of gas from certain fields and carriage to Baton Rouge/New Orleans area; consent order required divestiture of interest in pipeline); InterNorth, Inc., 106 F.T.C. 312 (1985) (alleging that merger of two gas pipeline companies would lessen competition in purchase and transportation of natural gas from producing areas in the Permian Basin and the Panhandle region, and in transportation and sale of gas in the Texas Gulf Coast consuming area; consent decree required divestiture of certain pipelines and interests in certain pipelines).

406. Duke Energy Corp., File No. 001-0080, 65 Fed. Reg. 18,997 (FTC Apr. 10, 2000) (aid to public comment), 2000 FTC LEXIS 62, 63 (FTC 2000) (decision and order).
407. 65 Fed. Reg. at 18,997.
408. Id.
409. El Paso Energy Corp., File No. 991-0178, 64 Fed. Reg. 59,179 (FTC Nov. 2, 1999) (aid to public comment), 2000 FTC LEXIS 7 (FTC 2000) (decision and order).
410. 64 Fed. Reg. at 59,180-81.
411. El Paso Energy Corp., No. 991-0178, 64 Fed. Reg. 59,179 (FTC Nov. 2, 1999).

transportation by pipeline and terminaling of propane gas, and the market for pipeline transportation of raw mix from Southern Wyoming.[412] Williams owned and operated pipelines that, pursuant to certain agreements with Kinder Morgan Operating L.P., transported propane to terminals owned and operated by Kinder Morgan. The terminals serviced the same markets as MAPCO's terminals.[413] The Federal Trade Commission alleged that the merged company would have the ability and the incentive to hinder Kinder Morgan's access to pipeline capacity and eliminate the company as a competitor in the transportation and terminaling of propane. Accordingly, the Federal Trade Commission primarily required the merged company to comply with the relevant Kinder Morgan agreements to ensure the provision of pipeline capacity to Kinder Morgan so that it could service its terminals. The merged company was not allowed to cancel the agreements except for a few specified reasons and had to enter into, and comply with, similar agreements with any subsequent owner of Kinder Morgan's terminals.[414]

Another challenged transaction included CMS Energy Corporation's acquisition of Duke Energy Company's interests in Panhandle Eastern Pipeline Company.[415] Consumers Energy Company, CMS's principal subsidiary, was a combination electric and gas utility company serving customers in broad sections of Michigan. Panhandle and Truckline, interstate gas transmission pipeline companies, interconnected with Consumers Energy.[416] The Federal Trade Commission claimed that the acquisition would lessen competition in the pipeline transportation of natural gas into Consumers Energy's gas service area comprising all or portions of fifty-four counties in the lower peninsula of Michigan. Consumers Energy received natural gas through interconnections with Panhandle and Trunkline as well as other pipelines in which Consumers Energy would have no financial interest after the proposed acquisition. The agency alleged that Consumers Energy had the ability to unilaterally decide to reduce the Panhandle and Trunkline interconnection capacity or close the interconnection altogether. Post-acquisition, CMS also would have the incentive to close or reduce the interconnection capacity with the non-CMS pipelines. This, in turn, would likely increase demand for transportation service on Panhandle and Trunkline and enable these pipelines to increase their rates. To remedy these potential anticompetitive effects, the Federal Trade Commission required the merged company to allow a customer to use an alternative interconnection on the Consumers Energy system if a requested interconnection point had less than actual design capacity, provided the shipper did not incur increased costs. Alternatively, CMS had to supply gas from its own system to any shipper to which CMS refused transportation because of reduced interconnect capacity.[417]

The Federal Trade Commission also challenged Shell Oil Company's proposed acquisition of ANR Field Services Company's gas-gathering pipeline assets and

412. Williams Cos., Dkt. No. C-38171, 63 Fed. Reg. 16,553 (FTC Apr. 3, 1998) (aid to public comment), 125 F.T.C. 1300 (1998) (decision and order).
413. 125 F.T.C. at 1302.
414. Id. at 1308.
415. CMS Energy Corp., File No. 991-0046, 64 Fed. Reg. 14,725 (FTC Mar. 26, 1999) (aid to public comment), 1999 FTC LEXIS 118 (FTC 1999) (decision and order).
416. 64 Fed. Reg. at 14,726.
417. Id. at 14,726-27.

certain gas-processing and related facilities in Oklahoma, Texas, and Kansas.[418] The Federal Trade Commission alleged that the acquisition would raise competitive concerns in certain overlap counties within which Shell was the largest gatherer and ANR was its substantial competitor. In six areas, Shell and ANR were the only two competitors. The Federal Trade Commission asserted that the acquisition would eliminate competition for gathering of gas from existing and new wells in the relevant market, likely lead to collusion and/or coordinated interaction, give Shell the ability to exact anticompetitive price increases from producers, and producers would be less likely to do exploratory and developmental drilling.[419] As a primary remedy, the Federal Trade Commission required Shell to construct a gathering pipeline connected to an existing ANR gathering pipeline; promptly sell the pipeline and certain related assets; offer the purchaser of the assets the opportunity to have its gas processed by Shell for up to two years; and, until the divestiture, to purchase, gather, and process gas on the same conditions as traditionally offered by ANR.[420]

The Federal Trade Commission challenged a transaction involving Questar Corporation's proposed acquisition of a 50 percent stake in Kern River Gas Transmission Co. Questar was the exclusive transporter of natural gas to Salt Lake City, and Kern River was the only possible competitive alternative for Salt Lake City customers. The Federal Trade Commission sought a preliminary injunction to halt the acquisition based on evidence that potential competition from Questar was already having a pricing impact in the Salt Lake market and that, over time, erosion of Questar's monopoly position would drive prices even lower. The Federal Trade Commission claimed that elimination of competition from Kern River was a prime reason for the deal. The parties ultimately chose to abandon the transaction rather than defend it.[421]

2. Electric Power

The electric power industry traditionally has been regulated by both federal and state authorities. Retail sales of electricity generally are regulated by state public utility commissions, while other aspects of the industry, including wholesale sales, wholesale and interstate transmission service, and mergers, are subject to the jurisdiction of the Federal Energy Regulatory Commission pursuant to the Federal Power Act (FPA).[422] In recent years deregulation and restructuring initiatives at the federal and state levels have broadened the scope of competition significantly. While the transmission and distribution of electricity, the so-called wires functions, remain highly regulated, the Federal Energy Regulatory Commission permits much

---

418. Shell Oil Co., Dkt. No. C-3843, 1998 FTC LEXIS 136 (FTC 1998) (complaint, decision, and order).

419. *Id.* at *1-2.

420. *Cf.* Phillips Petroleum Co., Dkt. No. C-3728, 62 Fed. Reg. 1459 (FTC Jan. 10, 1997) (aid to public comment), 123 F.T.C. 952 (1997) (decision and order) (requiring divestiture of portions of a gathering pipeline system in similar circumstances and based on similar alleged competitive harm); Phillips Petroleum Co., File No. 951-0037, 60 Fed. Reg. 47,376 (Sept. 12, 1995) (consent agreement with analysis to aid public comment), 120 F.T.C. 1129 (1995) (decision and order) (where Phillips and Enron were the only two competitors in gas gathering within the affected counties and would have the largest market share in the relevant market, Phillips prohibited from buying some of the contemplated assets).

421. United States v. Questar Corp., Civ. No. 2:95CV1127S (D. Utah filed Dec. 27, 1995).

422. 16 U.S.C. §§ 791a-828c (2000).

wholesale electricity to be sold at market-based prices, and numerous states have implemented programs for competition in sales of retail electricity.[423]

The public interest standard of the FPA requires the Federal Energy Regulatory Commission to consider antitrust policies.[424] Agency regulation does not, however, confer a blanket immunity from the antitrust laws. In *Otter Tail Power Co. v. United States*,[425] the Supreme Court rejected a utility's implied immunity claim. The Court found a congressional intent to reject

> a pervasive regulatory scheme for controlling the interstate distribution of power in favor of voluntary commercial relationships. When these relationships are governed in the first instance by business judgment and not regulatory coercion, courts must be hesitant to conclude that Congress had intended to override the fundamental national policy embodied in the antitrust laws.[426]

Historically many of the leading antitrust cases involving electric utilities have addressed territorial restrictions, access to transmission lines, and price squeezes. Restructuring and the introduction of open transmission access have changed the regulatory landscape since a number of these cases discussed below were litigated. Nonetheless, the principles they establish retain relevance today as new cases raise questions regarding the use of regulated assets and the role of regulated activities in competitive markets.

a.   ANTICOMPETITIVE AGREEMENTS

Courts have long applied Section 1 of the Sherman Act to address allegedly anticompetitive agreements involving electric utilities. For example, the courts have consistently condemned horizontal territorial agreements entered into by utilities,[427]

---

423. *See, e.g.*, 1998 Ariz. Sess. Laws 209; 1999 Ark. Acts 1556; 1996 Cal. Stat. 854; 1998 Colo. Sess. Laws 234; 1998 Conn. Acts 98-28 (Reg. Sess.); 72 Del. Laws 10 (1999); 1999 D.C. Stat. 107; 1997 Ill. Laws 561; 1997 Me. Laws 316; 1999 Md. Laws 4; 1997 Mass. Acts 164; 2000 Mich. Pub. Acts 141; 1997 Mont. Laws 505; 1999 Nev. Stat. 600; 1996 N.H. Laws 129; 1999 N.J. Laws 23; 1999 N.M. Laws 294; 1999 Ohio Laws 47; 1997 Okla. Sess. Laws 162; 1999 Or. Laws 865; 1996 Pa. Laws 1996-138; 1996 R.I. Pub. Laws 96-316; 1999 Tex. Gen. Laws 405; 1999 Va. Acts ch. 411.

424. *See* Gulf States Utils. Co. v. FPC, 411 U.S. 747, 759-60 (1973); Central Power & Light Co. v. FERC, 575 F.2d 937, 938-39 (D.C. Cir. 1978) (per curiam) (remanding to FERC to conduct a hearing considering antitrust issues under its public interest mandate), *cert. denied*, 439 U.S. 981 (1978). *But see* Northern Cal. Power Agency v. FPC, 514 F.2d 184, 189 (D.C. Cir. 1975) (denying request for a hearing on antitrust issues contained in contracts between a utility and a public power agency), *cert. denied*, 423 U.S. 863 (1975). The Supreme Court held that the power granted FERC's predecessor, the FPC, to regulate the industry "clearly carries with it the responsibility to consider, in appropriate circumstances, the anticompetitive effects of regulated aspects of interstate utility operations," and that the FPC was to serve "the important function of establishing a first line of defense against those competitive practices that might later be the subject of antitrust proceedings." *Gulf States Utils.*, 411 U.S. at 758-59, 760. *See also* XY State Elec. & Gas Corp. v. FERC, 638 F.2d 388, 393-98 (2d Cir. 1980) (holding that FERC had jurisdiction to require modification of contracts containing restrictive resale provisions that FERC found to be anticompetitive), *cert. denied*, 454 U.S. 821 (1981).

425. 410 U.S. 366 (1973).

426. *Id.* at 374.

427. *See* Gainesville Utils. Dep't v. Florida Power & Light Co., 573 F.2d 292, 300 (5th Cir. 1978) (an agreement between utilities to fix prices or divide territories was per se unlawful; relying on *Otter Tail*, the court "saw no reason to assume an antitrust exemption, nor to defer its decision pending

unless protected by the state action doctrine.[428] Section 1 challenges have also been leveled against various other forms of agreements alleged to restrict the proper scope of competition in power sales markets.

In *United States v. Rochester Gas & Electric Corp.*,[429] the Department of Justice charged that Rochester Gas & Electric had offered to supply the University of Rochester with electricity at discounted rates in exchange for an agreement that the university would not compete in the sale of electricity to consumers. According to the government, the reduced rates and reciprocal agreement were designed to stop the university from building its own power plant and selling excess power in competition with the utility.[430] The parties resolved the case through a consent agreement that prohibited Rochester Gas & Electric from enforcing a provision in its power sales agreement with the university, or including similar language in any other flexible rate contract, that prevented the university or another entity from coordinating with other customers to develop alternative sources of electric power or thermal energy. Rochester Gas & Electric also agreed to refrain from enforcing any "covenant or agreement not to compete in the retail sale of electricity with any competitor or potential competitor in the retail sale of electricity" unless such an agreement was "reasonably ancillary" to retail marketing agreements, joint ventures, and the like.[431]

In *United States v. City of Stilwell*,[432] the Department of Justice challenged the city's policy of requiring customers to purchase electric service from the city if they wished to receive water and sewer service. As explained in the agency's competitive impact statement,[433] the city had a "virtual monopoly" on sewer and water service in Stilwell, but faced competition in providing electric service in certain areas of the city. The effect of the policy was to restrict competition for electric service in the areas where the city faced competition. The consent agreement required the city to

---

FPC guidance"), *cert. denied*, 439 U.S. 966 (1978); Pennsylvania Water & Power Co. v. Consolidated Gas, Elec. Light & Power Co., 184 F.2d 552 (4th Cir. 1950) (an agreement between two utilities that allowed one utility to control the prices at which the second could sell electricity to other customers and the territories in which it could operate violated § 1 of the Sherman Act), *cert. denied*, 340 U.S. 906 (1950); United States v. Florida Power Corp., 1971 Trade Cas. (CCH) ¶ 73,637 (M.D. Fla. 1971) (consent decree prohibiting two utilities from agreeing to allocate territories and customers).

428. *See* North Star Steel Co. v. MidAmerican Energy Holdings Co., 184 F.3d 732, 734 (8th Cir.), *cert. denied*, 528 U.S. 1046 (1999) (state action immunity barred antitrust claims against a state regulated electric utility for its refusal to wheel electricity from third-party suppliers to a steel mill over the utility's transmission system because an Iowa statute designated the utility as the only supplier of electricity within the "exclusive service territory" in which the steel mill was located); North Star Steel Texas, Inc. v. Entergy Gulf States, Inc., 33 F. Supp. 2d 557, 567 (S.D. Tex. 1998) (motion to dismiss granted where "Texas has clearly articulated and affirmatively expressed a policy to displace competition with regulation in the electrical power industry. . . . Pursuant to the state action doctrine, the court therefore concludes that Entergy is immune from suit under the federal antitrust laws."). The state action doctrine is discussed in part B of Chapter XIII.

429. 4 F. Supp. 2d 172 (W.D.N.Y. 1998).

430. *Id.* at 173.

431. United States v. Rochester Gas & Elec. Corp., 1998-1 Trade Cas. (CCH) ¶ 72,200 (W.D.N.Y. 1998) (consent judgment).

432. 1999-1 Trade Cas. (CCH) ¶ 72,398 (E.D. Okla. 1998) (final judgment).

433. 63 Fed. Reg. 41,292 (DOJ Aug. 3, 1998) (proposed final judgment and competitive impact statement).

abandon its policy and prohibited it from discriminating against potential customers who did not buy its electricity.[434]

In *City of Pittsburgh v. West Penn Power Co.*,[435] the Third Circuit affirmed the dismissal of the city's antitrust claims against Allegheny Power System. The city claimed Allegheny had violated Section 1 when it entered into a merger agreement with Duquesne Light Company that called for Allegheny's withdrawal of an application to provide power to certain redevelopment zones within the city. Duquesne was the sole authorized provider of electric services for the city, including the redevelopment zones, at all times relevant to the suit. The court found that the city had no standing to pursue an antitrust action because there was no causal connection between Allegheny's conduct and the alleged harm to the city. Allegheny and Duquesne were not competitors at the time of their merger agreement and were subject to the continued regulation of the Pennsylvania Public Utilities Commission. Thus, the city's inability to choose its electric supplier was not caused by Allegheny's agreement with Duquesne but was "an injury visited upon it by the regulated nature of utility service."[436] The court stressed that its analysis turned on the presence of continued regulation of the electric industry. With the advent of competition, the court expected that "future utility arrangements in the free-market atmosphere may well pass muster for purposes of standing under the antitrust laws."[437]

b.   ACCESS TO TRANSMISSION

In *Otter Tail*,[438] the government challenged the refusal of Otter Tail Power to sell wholesale power or wheel bulk power from another source to municipalities formerly served by Otter Tail at retail that wanted to establish municipally owned distribution systems. The Supreme Court affirmed the district court's finding that Otter Tail had monopoly power in retail sales of electric power in its service area and held that by refusing to sell at wholesale or wheel power to the municipalities, Otter Tail violated Section 2 of the Sherman Act by using its strategic dominance in transmission to foreclose potential competition for sales at retail.[439]

Since *Otter Tail*, a number of decisions have addressed Section 2 claims based on refusals to wheel, with plaintiffs frequently invoking the essential facilities doctrine. These cases generally have applied basic Section 2 principles but have turned upon the specific industry facts, including the regulatory requirements facing the utilities in question.[440] For example, the Ninth Circuit issued companion decisions in which it

---

434. *Id.* at 41,293-94.
435. 147 F.3d 256 (3d Cir. 1998).
436. *Id.* at 266.
437. *Id.* at 269.
438. Otter Tail Power Co. v. United States, 410 U.S. 366 (1973).
439. *Id.* at 380-81. The Supreme Court rejected Otter Tail's implied immunity antitrust claim, holding that there was "no basis for concluding that the limited authority of the Federal Power Commission to order interconnections was intended to be a substitute for, or to immunize Otter Tail from, antitrust regulation." *Id.* at 374-75. *See also* City of Chanute v. Kansas Gas & Elec. Co., 754 F.2d 310, 312-13 (10th Cir. 1985) (FERC's limited authority under the Public Utility Regulatory Policies Act of 1978 to order wheeling of power in certain instances did not deprive plaintiffs of a remedy at law for alleged anticompetitive behavior).
440. *See* City of Malden v. Union Elec. Co., 887 F.2d 157, 161 (8th Cir. 1989) (upholding a jury verdict for defendant where there was only one existing electric transmission line accessible to the city,

found legitimate business justifications for Southern California Edison's denial or limitation of access to the Pacific Intertie, a network of high-voltage transmission lines carrying low-cost hydroelectric energy to California.

In *City of Anaheim v. Southern California Edison Co.*,[441] five municipal wholesale electricity customers brought suit against Edison alleging a price squeeze and denial of access to an essential transmission facility. Edison responded that it fully utilized its transmission capacity in the Pacific Intertie to import economical energy; that this energy had become part of its overall system power used to serve all its customers, including the plaintiffs; and that providing access to the plaintiffs would cause Edison to forego its own use of the facility, thus raising its costs of providing electric service. The Ninth Circuit found that Edison had established a legitimate business justification for not allowing access.[442] The court also affirmed the district court's findings that the Pacific Intertie was not an essential facility because power was available from other sources and that the facility did not become essential merely because obtaining access to it would lower the plaintiffs' costs.[443]

In *City of Vernon v. Southern California Edison Co.*,[444] the plaintiff, a customer of Edison for the bulk of its power supplies, alleged that Edison was liable under the antitrust laws for failing to give Vernon "relative size share access" to those facilities.[445] The Ninth Circuit rejected the plaintiff's essential facilities claim, noting that Edison was fully utilizing its share of the Pacific Intertie's capacity and that "the demand that Edison turn over its facility to a city simply because the city could save money by obtaining cheaper power stands the essential facility doctrine on its head."[446] Vernon also had charged Edison with violating Section 2 by refusing to enter into an operating agreement that would have integrated Vernon's power purchases from other suppliers within a reasonable time frame. In prior litigation, the Federal Energy Regulatory Commission had rejected Edison's position that it should be able to determine the timing for integrating resources at its discretion and found three years to be a reasonable integration period.[447] The Ninth Circuit held that Vernon was entitled to injunctive relief on this claim, stressing that integration of Vernon's resources with reasonable notice would benefit both parties.[448]

---

but the city could have "economically provided for an alternative transmission system to convey electrical power"); Greenwood Utils. Comm'n v. Mississippi Power Co., 751 F.2d 1484 (5th Cir. 1985) (plaintiff's inability to obtain power generated by Southeastern Power Administration and transmitted over defendant's lines was a result of activities and relationships between a government agency and defendant that were immunized by the *Noerr* doctrine); Borough of Lansdale v. Philadelphia Elec. Co., 692 F.2d 307 (3d Cir. 1982) (utility's refusal to wheel power did not violate § 2 because utility did not have monopoly power in the relevant market, which included the service areas of other nearby wholesale suppliers); City of Groton v. Connecticut Light & Power Co., 662 F.2d 921 (2d Cir. 1981) (utility's policy of evaluating wheeling requests on a case-by-case basis represented reasonable behavior); Town of Massena v. Niagara Mohawk Power Corp., 1980-2 Trade Cas. (CCH) ¶ 63,526, at 76,823-24 (N.D.N.Y. 1980) (refusal to wheel based on legitimate business reasons did not violate § 2).

441. 955 F.2d 1373 (9th Cir.), *cert. denied*, 506 U.S. 908 (1992).
442. *Id.* at 1379.
443. *Id.* at 1381.
444. 955 F.2d 1361 (9th Cir. 1992), *cert. denied*, 506 U.S. 908 (1992).
445. *Id.* at 1364 & n.3.
446. *Id.* at 1367.
447. *Id.*
448. *Id.* at 1367-68. In a district court case, the Florida Municipal Power Agency (FMPA) sued Florida Power & Light Company (FP&L), accusing the utility of refusing to sell "network" transmission service. (Network transmission service allows for the delivery and receipt of service at multiple

Access issues will remain a potential source of antitrust controversy as long as electric utilities continue to be vertically integrated, regulated firms that control competitively important assets.[449] However, major changes in the law and federal regulatory policy have greatly reduced the scope for future antitrust litigation concerning access to transmission facilities subject to Federal Energy Regulatory Commission jurisdiction. In 2000, that agency issued Orders 2000 and 2000-A,[450] which "require that each public utility that owns, operates, or controls facilities for the transmission of electric energy in interstate commerce make certain filings with respect to following and participating in an RTO [regional transmission organization]."[451] Once fully implemented, these orders will strip public utilities of control over access to their transmission facilities, placing them in the hands of the independent RTOs.

---

points, thereby permitting a utility to integrate its loads and resources and more efficiently supply power.) FP&L provided the FMPA with transmission service, but only on a point-to-point basis under a FERC-approved rate schedule. Florida Mun. Power Agency v. Florida Power & Light Co., 839 F. Supp. 1563 (M.D. Fla. 1993), *vacated and remanded*, 64 F.3d 614 (11th Cir. 1995). The court granted FP&L's motion for summary judgment on the ground that the filed rate or *Keogh* doctrine barred the claim. *Id.* at 1569. (The filed rate and *Keogh* doctrines are discussed in part D.2 of Chapter XIII.) The Eleventh Circuit reversed and remanded the case, however, on the grounds that it was unclear whether network and point-to-point transmission were distinct services. 64 F.3d 614.

    In another case involving FP&L and wheeling, the Eleventh Circuit addressed a refusal by FP&L to provide self-service wheeling. TEC Cogeneration Inc. v. Florida Power & Light Co., 76 F.3d 1560 (11th Cir.), *modified on other grounds*, 86 F.3d 1028 (11th Cir. 1996). The Eleventh Circuit, in reversing a district court decision, found that FP&L was protected by the state action doctrine for its refusal to wheel power (under the state's self-service wheeling provisions) and by the *Noerr* doctrine for its efforts to influence legislators.

449. In *Modesto Irrigation Dist. v. Pacific Gas & Elec. Co.*, the district court declined to find an antitrust violation where Pacific Gas and Electric Co. (PG&E) refused to wheel electric power from Dynergy Power Services to the Modesto Irrigation District that Modesto planned to resell to retail and industrial customers. 61 F. Supp. 2d 1058 (N.D. Cal. 1999). PG&E argued that a transmission services agreement between it and Dynergy barred Dynergy from reselling at retail power transmitted by PG&E. Dynergy and PG&E subsequently reached an agreement that prohibited Dynergy from selling electric power to Modesto for resale at retail. *Id.* at 1061-62. The court dismissed Modesto's § 1 claims because they alleged only a unilateral refusal to deal and failed to identify "the specific agreement that constitutes the basis of the conspiracy claim." *Id.* at 1069. The court likewise denied Modesto's § 2 monopolization claim under the *Noerr* doctrine because PG&E's refusal to wheel electric power to Modesto was incident to a petition filed by PG&E with FERC seeking a declaration that the deal between Dynergy and Modesto was a sham wholesale transaction. *Id.*

450. Regional Transmission Organizations: Final Rule, Order No. 2000, 65 Fed. Reg. 810 (FERC Jan. 6, 2000), *order on reh'g*, Order No. 2000-A, 65 Fed. Reg. 12,088 (FERC Mar. 8, 2000), *appeal pending*, PUD No. 1 of Snohomish County, Wash. v. FERC, No. 01-1395 (D.C. Cir. Sept. 10, 2001), appealing Avista Corp. (RTO West; Transconnect), 96 F.E.R.C. (CCH) ¶ 61,058 (2001). FERC had previously required all public utilities to provide transmission service on a nondiscriminatory basis. *See* Promoting Wholesale Competition Through Open Access Non-Discriminatory Transmission Service by Public Utilities; Recovery of Stranded Costs by Public Utilities and Transmitting Utilities, Order No. 888, 61 Fed. Reg. 21,540 (FERC May 10, 1996), *order on reh'g*, Order No. 888-A, 62 Fed. Reg. 12,274 (FERC Mar. 14, 1997), *order on reh'g*, Order No. 888-B, 62 Fed. Reg. 64,688 (FERC Dec. 7, 1997), *order on reh'g*, Order No. 888-C, 79 F.E.R.C. (CCH) ¶ 61,046 (1998), *aff'd in part sub nom.* Transmission Access Policy Study Group v. FERC, 225 F.3d 667 (D.C. Cir. 2000), *cert. granted sub nom.* New York v. FERC, 531 U.S. 1191 (2001).

451. Order No. 2000, 65 Fed. Reg. 810.

c. LEVERAGING

Claims have been raised on occasion against electrical utilities challenging a utility's use of its market power in the regulated market to monopolize or attempt to monopolize a second, unregulated market. In *Grason Electric Co. v. Sacramento Municipal Utility Dist.*,[452] thirteen electrical contractors brought a Sherman Act case alleging that a municipal electric utility unlawfully used its monopoly power in the retail electrical energy market to "smother competition" in the market for the installation and maintenance of street and outdoor lighting systems.[453] The district court denied the contractors' motion for summary judgment, finding that the utility's use of customer contacts for advertising purposes did not constitute an unlawful use of monopoly power under Section 2 of the Sherman Act.[454] The court observed that a monopolist may lawfully use "legitimate competitive advantages" such as size, integration, foresight, and business acumen if these advantages are available to all businesses of "similar size and sophistication."[455]

In *Yeager's Fuel, Inc. v. Pennsylvania Power & Light Co.*,[456] the plaintiff oil dealers accused a utility of using its market power in electricity to increase its share of the home heating market by offering reduced electric rates to purchasers of all-electric homes and by providing cash incentives to builders to install electric heat pumps. The Third Circuit affirmed summary judgment for the defendant utility on state action grounds with respect to some of the promotional activities but reversed with respect to others. In particular, the Third Circuit declined to permit state action immunity for promotional offers conditioned on agreements by developers that subdivisions would be all electric. The court found that the incentives not linked to such agreements were provided pursuant to a state policy that encouraged energy conservation and load management and that the state supervised the programs.[457] Following remand and an amended complaint, the district court refused to grant the utility's motion for summary judgment on plaintiffs' monopoly leveraging and attempted monopolization claims.[458]

In *Aquatherm Indus., Inc. v. Florida Power & Light Co.*,[459] the Eleventh Circuit affirmed the district court's dismissal of a Sherman Act complaint brought by a manufacturer of solar power heating systems for swimming pools against Florida Power & Light Co., an electric utility and regulated monopoly in Florida that did not sell swimming pool equipment but that promoted the use of electric pool heating

452. 571 F. Supp. 1504 (E.D. Cal. 1983); *see also* Lease Lights, Inc. v. Public Serv. Co., 849 F.2d 1330 (10th Cir. 1988), *cert. denied*, 488 U.S. 1019 (1989).
453. 571 F. Supp. at 1506. The contractors pointed to four allegedly unlawful uses of monopoly power, including the utility's practice of informing its electric customers that it would construct and maintain street lighting systems at no initial cost. *Id.* at 1528.
454. *Id.* at 1528-29.
455. *Id.* The court concluded that physical access to customers constitutes a competitive advantage when "a monopolist can force its customers to accept a product that they would not otherwise purchase at the price tendered, but any firm can use the regular contact it has with its customers to promote a new product." *Id.*
456. 22 F.3d 1260 (3d Cir. 1994).
457. *Id.* at 1267-72.
458. Yeager's Fuel, Inc. v. Pennsylvania Power & Light Co., 953 F. Supp. 617 (E.D. Pa. 1997). *See also* Florida Mun. Power Agency v. Florida Power & Light Co., 81 F. Supp. 2d 1313 (M.D. Fla. 1999) (denying plaintiff's motion for summary judgment on the claim that utility had leveraged transmission monopoly into the market for sale of bulk electricity).
459. 145 F.3d 1258 (11th Cir. 1998), *cert. denied*, 526 U.S. 1050 (1999).

pumps to increase the use of electrical power. Aquatherm asserted that the utility either wrongly attempted to prevent erosion of its electric power monopoly or wrongly interfered with the pool heater market to increase its profits. The claims were dismissed because Aquatherm failed to allege that the utility's actions increased its market share in the electric power market or had erected any barriers to entry into this market, or that Florida Power & Light attempted to monopolize the pool heater market. The court concluded that because the utility did not participate in the pool heater market and did not have the intent to monopolize this market, Aquatherm could not support its claims.[460]

d. PRICE SQUEEZES

Private antitrust actions have involved allegations that vertically integrated utilities that sell electricity at wholesale and also compete with their wholesale customers to supply retail service have engaged in unlawful price squeezes. The wholesale customer, typically a municipal electric distribution system, usually alleges that the differential between its supplier's wholesale price for requirements service and retail rates impairs the customer's ability to compete with the supplier at retail.[461] The Federal Energy Regulatory Commission's imposition of open access transmission principles and the development of competitive bulk power markets has made it more difficult for purchasers of electricity to demonstrate that their supplier possesses the requisite economic power over wholesale supply to effectuate an effective price squeeze.[462]

Courts have rejected claims that the Federal Energy Regulatory Commission's regulation of wholesale rates gives that agency primary or exclusive jurisdiction over price-squeeze allegations in antitrust cases.[463] Courts also have rejected claims of

---

460. Aquatherm's restraint on competition and illegal tying claims likewise failed because Aquatherm did not claim that FP&L's actions harmed competition in the pool heater market and FP&L did not attempt to coerce pool owners into purchasing electric heating pumps.

461. One court has defined a price squeeze for regulatory purposes as "a price differential between [a supplier's] retail and wholesale rates that is not justified by differing costs and which places the wholesale customer at a disadvantage in competing with its own supplier for retail customers." Public Serv. Co. v. FERC, 832 F.2d 1201, 1207 n.6 (10th Cir. 1987).

462. See Town of Norwood v. New England Power Co., 202 F.3d 408, 420-21 (1st Cir.) (expressing skepticism about "what monopoly power Norwood attributes to New England Power, which has now sold its main generating assets and, so far as it may retain a dominant position in transmission, is constrained to wheel power for others under Order No. 888"), cert. denied, 531 U.S. 818 (2000).

463. See City of Kirkwood v. Union Elec. Co., 671 F.2d 1173, 1179 (8th Cir. 1982) (neither FERC nor state regulatory commission had exclusive jurisdiction over a price-squeeze claim; antitrust courts may consider price-squeeze claims without infringing on the regulatory jurisdiction of federal or state regulatory agencies because "the question is not whether the rates themselves are anticompetitive, but whether the defendant utility acted illegally in proposing a certain anticompetitive combination of rates"), cert. denied, 459 U.S. 1170 (1983); City of Mishawaka v. Indiana & Mich. Elec. Co., 560 F.2d 1314 (7th Cir. 1977) (holding that FPC did not have exclusive or primary jurisdiction over a price squeeze claim against a regulated utility), cert. denied, 436 U.S. 922 (1978); Ellwood City v. Pennsylvania Power Co., 570 F. Supp. 553 (W.D. Pa. 1983) (rejecting a claim that FERC had exclusive jurisdiction over price squeeze allegations); City of Newark v. Delmarva Power & Light Co., 467 F. Supp. 763, 769, 771-72 (D. Del. 1979) (rejecting an exclusive jurisdiction claim, and declining to stay court proceedings pending FERC decision on price squeeze issues).

immunity under the state action doctrine based on state regulation of the utility's retail rates.[464] Courts have held that the filed rate doctrine, under which a customer is precluded from recovering damages based on a claim that rates filed with and approved by a regulatory commission are unlawful under the antitrust laws, does not apply to traditional price-squeeze claims involving wholesale and retail rates not regulated by a single agency.[465] In *Town of Concord v. Boston Edison Co.*,[466] however, the First Circuit adopted a qualified rule against antitrust liability for price squeezes where a utility is fully regulated.[467] In *City of Anaheim v. Southern California Edison Co.*,[468] the Ninth Circuit did not follow *Town of Concord*'s conclusion that a utility regulated at both levels was unlikely to effect an anticompetitive price squeeze.[469] However, citing *City of Mishawaka v. American Electric Power Co.*,[470] the court held that proof of a specific intent to monopolize must be established in order to hold a regulated electric utility liable under Section 2.[471]

e.   MERGERS AND ACQUISITIONS

Under Section 203 of the FPA, Federal Energy Regulatory Commission authorization is required for mergers and acquisitions involving public utilities subject to its jurisdiction.[472] The agency is to approve a merger if it finds that the

---

464.   *See City of Kirkwood*, 671 F.2d at 1179-80; *City of Mishawaka*, 560 F.2d at 1319-20.
465.   *See City of Kirkwood*, 671 F.2d at 1179 (doctrine found inapplicable because the allegations are not a direct attack on filed rates, but on the relationship between wholesale and retail rates, and the plaintiff alleged injury as a competitor, not as a customer); City of Groton v. Connecticut Light & Power Co., 662 F.2d 921 (2d Cir. 1981) (doctrine found inapplicable because plaintiff sued as a competitor, not as a customer). In *Town of Norwood*, the First Circuit held that the filed rate doctrine did bar a suit where the alleged price squeeze was accomplished through a contract termination charge and a wholesale standard offer rate, both regulated by FERC. 202 F.3d 418-19.
466.   915 F.2d 17 (1st Cir. 1990), *cert. denied*, 499 U.S. 931 (1991).
467.   *Id.* at 28. The court limited its holding by stating that "normally" a price squeeze will not constitute an exclusionary practice in the context of a fully regulated monopoly, thus leaving open the possibility that liability might be found in cases involving "exceptional circumstances." *Id.* at 29. The court also noted that its holding did not apply to the case where a monopolist is regulated only at one level. *Id.*
468.   955 F.2d 1373 (9th Cir.), *cert. denied*, 506 U.S. 908 (1992).
469.   Antitrust cases based on price squeezes involving wholesale and retail electricity rates are discussed in more detail in part D.3 of Chapter II.
470.   616 F.2d 976 (7th Cir. 1980), *cert. denied*, 449 U.S. 1096 (1981).
471.   955 F.2d at 1378.
472.   16 U.S.C. § 824b (2000); *see* El Paso Elec. Co. and Central & S. W. Servs., 71 F.E.R.C. (CCH) ¶ 63,001 (1995); Cincinnati Gas & Elec. Co. and PSI Energy, Inc., 69 F.E.R.C. (CCH) ¶ 61,005 (1994); Northeast Utils. Serv. Co., 50 F.E.R.C. (CCH) ¶ 61,266 (1990), *aff'd*, 993 F.2d 937 (1st Cir. 1993); Southern Cal. Edison Co., 47 F.E.R.C. (CCH) ¶ 61,196 (1989); Tucson Elec. Power Co., 44 F.E.R.C. (CCH) ¶ 61,441 (1988); Utah Power & Light Co., 41 F.E.R.C. (CCH) ¶ 61,283 (1987). Section 203 of the FPA provides that a public utility must obtain FERC approval in order to "sell, lease, or otherwise dispose of the whole of its facilities subject to the jurisdiction of the Commission, . . . or by any means whatsoever, directly or indirectly, merge or consolidate such facilities or any part thereof with those of any other person." 16 U.S.C. § 824b.

merger "will be consistent with the public interest,"[473] although a positive benefit is not necessary.[474]

The Federal Energy Regulatory Commission examines three factors in evaluating mergers: the effect of the merger on competition, rates, and regulation. In its 1996 *Merger Policy Statement*,[475] the agency endorsed the analytical framework used in the 1992 *Merger Guidelines*[476] to assess the competitive effects of horizontal mergers and in Appendix A to that statement developed a prescribed methodology for calculating changes in market concentration caused by the merger in the relevant destination markets for sales of electricity.[477] In November 2000, the agency affirmed its approach to assessing horizontal competitive effects and articulated a competitive analysis for mergers raising vertical market power concerns.[478]

Under Section 203(b) of the FPA, the Federal Energy Regulatory Commission may condition its approval on "such terms and conditions as it finds necessary or appropriate to secure the maintenance of adequate service and the coordination in the public interest of facilities subject to the jurisdiction of the Commission."[479] For example, the agency has conditioned approval of mergers upon the applicants'

---

473. *Utah Power & Light*, 41 F.E.R.C. (CCH) ¶ 61,283, at 61,752 (quoting 16 U.S.C. § 824b(a)); *see also Northeast Utils.*, 50 F.E.R.C. (CCH) ¶ 61,226, at 61,833; *Southern Cal. Edison*, 47 F.E.R.C. (CCH) ¶ 61,196, at 61,671; *Tucson Elec.*, 44 F.E.R.C. (CCH) ¶ 61,441, at 62,394. FERC is required to find that the transaction taken as a whole is consistent with the public interest. *See, e.g.*, Northeast Utils. Serv. Co. v. FERC, 993 F.2d 937, 951 (1st Cir. 1993); Environmental Action, Inc. v. FERC, 939 F.2d 1057, 1061 (D.C. Cir. 1991). Thus, FERC need not find that no harm to any individual entity can possibly occur. *See* Cincinnati Gas & Elec. Co. and PSI Energy, Inc., 64 F.E.R.C. (CCH) ¶ 61,237 (1993).
474. *Utah Power & Light*, 41 F.E.R.C. (CCH) ¶ 61,283, at 61,752 (citing Pacific Power & Light Co. v. FPC, 111 F.2d 1014, 1017 (9th Cir. 1940)). FERC has found that the standards set forth in the Public Utility Holding Company Act are relevant but not binding on it. *See, e.g.*, *Utah Power & Light*, 41 F.E.R.C. (CCH) ¶ 61,283, at 61,753 ("the policies proscribed by the SEC for dealing with holding companies are not necessarily applicable to the same degree in dealing with operating companies").
475. Inquiry Concerning the Commission's Merger Policy under the Federal Power Act: Policy Statement, Order No. 592, 61 Fed. Reg. 68,595, at 68,596 (1996), *recons. denied*, Order No. 592-A, 62 Fed. Reg. 33,341 (1997).
476. U.S. DEP'T OF JUSTICE & FEDERAL TRADE COMM'N, HORIZONTAL MERGER GUIDELINES (1992) [hereinafter 1992 MERGER GUIDELINES], *reprinted in* 4 Trade Reg. Rep. (CCH) ¶ 13,104 *and* Appendix C to this treatise.
477. *See* Order No. 592, 61 Fed. Reg. at 68,596.
478. *See* Revised Filing Requirements Under Part 33 of the Commission's Regulations: Final Rule, Order No. 642, 65 Fed. Reg. 70,984 (FERC Nov. 28, 2000). FERC adopted an interim method for assessing whether an applicant has generation power, building on the prevously used hub-and-spoke analysis. *See* Order on Triennial Market Power Updates and Announcing New Interim Generation Market Power Screen and Mitigation Policy, 97 F.E.R.C. (CCH) ¶ 61,219 (Nov. 20, 2000). FERC also adopted a four-step analysis to evaluate vertical mergers: (1) define the relevant products traded by the downstream and upstream merging firms, (2) define the relevant downstream and upstream geographic markets, (3) evaluate competitive conditions using market share and concentration statistics in the respective geographic markets, and (4) evaluate the potential adverse effects of the proposed merger in those markets and other factors that can counteract such effects. 65 Fed. Reg. at 71,003.
479. 16 U.S.C. § 824b(b) (2000).

commitment to divest certain generating facilities,[480] waive transmission priorities,[481] join an RTO,[482] or accept standards of conduct requirements governing the sharing of certain kinds of information with affiliates and competitors.[483]

Electric utility mergers and asset acquisitions have been subjected to review by the Federal Trade Commission or the Department of Justice under the H-S-R Act[484] and have resulted in several consent decrees. In February 1998, the Federal Trade Commission required a consent order in the proposed merger between PacifiCorp, both a retail electric provider and a wholesale electric marketer throughout the western United States, and the Energy Group PLC, parent of Peabody Coal Company, a producer of roughly 15 percent of the coal mined in the United States.[485] The Federal Trade Commission expressed concern that Peabody was the exclusive supplier of coal to two large generating stations that competed with PacifiCorp's power plants within the Western Systems Coordinating Council. The agency alleged that after the merger PacifiCorp would have the incentive and ability to increase fuel costs at those generating stations and that doing so would drive up the price of electricity in the western United States.[486] The agency maintained that because the coal-fired plants were the last facilities to be dispatched during periods of low electricity demand, PacifiCorp would be in a position to set the market price at off-peak times. Furthermore, by increasing the price of coal, PacifiCorp could shift coal-fired plants upward along the supply curve and thus affect electricity prices during peak times as well.[487] The consent decree required PacifiCorp to divest the mines in question, although the PacificCorp transaction was later abandoned.[488]

In November 1999, the Federal Trade Commission approved a proposed consent decree in the merger of Virginia Power, owner of 70 percent of electric generating capacity in the commonwealth of Virginia, and Virginia Natural Gas, the primary gas provider in southeastern Virginia.[489] The Federal Trade Commission asserted that the

480. *See* American Elec. Power Co., 90 F.E.R.C. (CCH) ¶ 61,242, at 61,777 (2000), *reh'g dismissed in part, denied in part, and granted in part*, 91 F.E.R.C. (CCH) ¶ 61,129 (2000); Consolidated Edison Co. of N.Y., Inc. and Orange & Rockland Utils., Inc., 86 F.E.R.C. (CCH) ¶ 61,064, at 61,247 (1999).

481. *See American Elec. Power*, 90 F.E.R.C. (CCH) ¶ 61,242, at 61,777; Ohio Edison, 81 F.E.R.C. (CCH) ¶ 61,110, at 61,406 (1997), *reh'g denied*, 85 F.E.R.C. (CCH) ¶ 61,203 (1998).

482. *See* CP&L Holdings, Inc. and Florida Progress Corp., 92 F.E.R.C. (CCH) ¶ 61,023, at 61,055 (2000); *American Elec. Power*, 90 F.E.R.C. (CCH) ¶ 61,242, at 61,777; *Ohio Edison*, 81 F.E.R.C. (CCH) ¶ 61,110, at 61,408.

483. *See* Dominion Res., Inc. and Consolidated Natural Gas Co., 89 F.E.R.C. ¶ 61,162, at 61,478 (1999); San Diego Gas & Elec. Co. and Enova Energy, Inc., 79 F.E.R.C. (CCH) ¶ 61,372, at 62,565 (1997), *reh'g denied*, 85 F.E.R.C. (CCH) ¶ 61,199 (1998).

484. 15 U.S.C. § 18a (2000).

485. 63 Fed. Reg. 9551, 9552 (FTC Feb. 25, 1998) (proposed consent and aid to public comment).

486. *Id.* at 9553.

487. *Id.* at 9554; *cf.* Public Util. Comm'n of Cal. v. El Paso Natural Gas Co., No. RP00-342-000, 97 F.E.R.C. (CCH) ¶ 63,004 (2001) (allegations of withholding capacity, thereby creating anticompetitive effect on the delivered price of gas and the wholesale electric market).

488. 63 Fed. Reg. at 9554-55. The FTC also argued that PacifiCorp through Peabody could gain access to sensitive information regarding coal contracts and supply relationships in the western United States. The FTC contended that PacifiCorp could use that information to predict supply shifts and consequent price movements in the market, giving it a competitive advantage in power marketing. Even the perception of such advantages, the FTC alleged, would discourage new entry and investment in the market.

489. 64 Fed. Reg. 61,645 (FTC Nov. 12, 1999) (aid to public comment), 1999 FTC LEXIS 195 (FTC 1999) (decision and order).

combination could deter new entry into the electric power generation market and allow the resulting entity to exercise unilateral market power in southeastern Virginia. This market power assertedly would lead to higher electricity prices, particularly given the high barriers to entry for electricity generation and gas pipeline services in the area.[490] The consent decree ordered the divestiture of Virginia Natural Gas.[491]

In February 2001, the Federal Trade Commission issued a consent order concerning the formation of Entergy-Koch LP by Entergy Corporation, a registered public utility holding company, and Koch Industries, Inc., a privately held natural gas marketer and transporter.[492] Entergy-Koch acquired Entergy's subsidiary that markets electricity and natural gas in the United States, Koch's natural gas marketer, and Koch's more than 10,000 miles of natural gas pipelines serving parts of Texas, Louisiana, Mississippi, Alabama, and Florida.[493] The Federal Trade Commission asserted that the transaction would reduce competition in areas of Louisiana and western Mississippi where Entergy subsidiaries sold electricity to consumers and in New Orleans and Baton Rouge, Louisiana, where Entergy subsidiaries provided retail natural gas services. The complaint alleged that electricity and natural gas prices were "likely to rise as a result of Entergy passing on inflated costs for natural gas transportation to consumers" and noted the difficulties that regulators will have in reviewing and challenging Entergy's purchase of natural gas transportation.[494] To alleviate the claimed anticompetitive effects of the transaction, the agency ordered Entergy to adopt an open solicitation process for its purchase of natural gas and gas transportation. These measures, the Federal Trade Commission stated, would preclude affiliate bias by Entergy in its purchase of gas supplies and, hence, prevent higher prices.[495]

In March 1998, the Department of Justice filed a complaint and related consent decree regarding the merger of Enova Corporation, parent of San Diego Gas & Electric Company (SDG&E), an electric utility in southern California, and Pacific Enterprises, parent of Southern California Gas Company (SoCalGas), the possessor of a monopoly over natural gas transportation and storage services in that area.[496] The Department of Justice charged that the merger violated the Clayton Act because the merged firm would have the ability and incentive to drive up the price of gas to competing gas-fired generators and thereby increase electric prices.[497] The consent decree addressed the merged entity's incentive to increase prices. First, the decree required Enova to divest its two low-cost, gas-fired power plants. Second, it required the merged firm to seek prior approval from the agency before acquiring ownership or control over existing California generating facilities with more than 500 MW in aggregate capacity and before entering any tolling agreement for electric generation.[498]

---

490. 64 Fed. Reg. at 61,646.
491. *Id.*
492. 66 Fed. Reg. 9342 (FTC Feb. 7, 2001) (aid to public comment).
493. *Id.* at 9343.
494. *Id.*
495. *Id.* at 9342.
496. United States v. Enova Corp., 107 F. Supp. 2d 10 (D.D.C. 2000) (final judgment).
497. *Id.* at 12.
498. *Id.* at 14-15 n.10.

Southern California Edison, a direct competitor of the merged company, challenged the adequacy of the decree in district court, arguing that the decree would be insufficient unless it incorporated one or more of the following alternatives: (1) rejection of the merger, (2) divestiture of the gas pipelines, (3) control of the pipelines by an independent system operator, or (4) a bar against trading electricity derivatives for the Southern California market.[499]   The Department of Justice responded that the incentive to exploit SoCalGas's pipeline monopoly existed whether or not Pacific merged with Enova, and that the decree was designed to address the effects of the merger, not SoCalGas's gas monopoly generally.[500]   The city of Vernon, owner of a municipal gas utility, also contended that the decree was inadequate because the merger would result in reduced competition for gas transportation.   The Department of Justice took the position that its complaint concerned electricity markets, not gas transportation markets.[501]   The district court entered a final judgment approving the consent decree in June 2000.[502]

In March 2001, the Federal Trade Commission challenged a merger between MCN Energy Group, Inc. and DTE Energy Company.[503]   DTE is the parent holding company of the Detroit Edison Company, a public utility serving southeastern Michigan, including the city of Detroit. MCN is the parent company of MichCon, a distributor of natural gas in areas of Michigan. The agency alleged that in areas of overlap, where MichCon was the only distributor of natural gas and Edison the only distributor of electricity, the merger would substantially lessen competition and tend to create a monopoly for the distribution of gas and electricity.[504]   MCN and DTE were viewed by the agency as competitors in the overlap area because natural gas was used to displace electricity in various commercial and industrial applications.[505] In addition, the agency found significant barriers to entry into the distribution of electricity and natural gas.[506] To remedy potential anticompetitive effects, the agency required MichCon to divest certain assets to Exelon Energy Company, one of the largest unregulated suppliers of electricity and natural gas in the country.[507] MichCon was required to convey to Exelon an easement over MichCon's local natural gas distribution system, which would allow Exelon to use five billion cubic feet of annual transportation capacity to distribute and store natural gas in the overlap area.[508]   The consent agreement also contained additional provisions designed to increase Exelon's ability to be a viable competitor in the overlap area.[509]

3. *Competition and Federal Lands*

Much of the nation's unexploited and unexplored energy reserves lie under lands owned or effectively controlled by the federal government. In the mid-1970s,

---

499. *Id.* at 15.
500. *Id.* at 16.
501. *Id.*
502. *Id.* at 19.
503. DTC Energy Co., File No. 001 0067, 66 Fed. Reg. 17,179 (FTC Mar. 19, 2001) (aid to public comment).
504. *Id.* at 17,179.
505. *Id.* at 17,180.
506. *Id.* at 17,179.
507. *Id.* at 17,181.
508. *Id.* at 17,180.
509. *Id.* at 17,181.

Congress established three programs under which the Department of Justice conducts an antitrust review of proposed sales of leases or production from federal lands. These three programs are described individually below. The antitrust review standard employed in each of these programs—whether the proposed lease or sale "would create or maintain a situation inconsistent with the antitrust laws"—is discussed at the end of this section.

a. REGULATORY PROGRAMS SUBJECT TO ANTITRUST REVIEW

(1) Federal Coal Leasing

The federal coal leasing program is managed by the Department of the Interior. Coal reserves are leased either through a competitive sealed-bid lease sale[510] or by "application."[511] Under Section 15 of the Federal Coal Leasing Amendments Act of 1976, the Secretary of the Interior must notify the Attorney General thirty days prior to the proposed issuance, renewal, or readjustment of a federal coal lease and provide the Attorney General with such information as the Attorney General requires to determine whether the proposed lease "would create or maintain a situation inconsistent with the antitrust laws."[512] If the Attorney General advises the Secretary of the Interior that issuance of the proposed lease would create or maintain such a situation, the Secretary of the Interior may not issue the lease unless, after conducting a public hearing on the record, he finds that issuance of the lease "is necessary to effectuate the purposes of the [federal coal leasing laws], that it is consistent with the public interest, and that there are no reasonable alternatives consistent with [the act], the antitrust laws, and the public interest."[513]

Before federal coal leases are actually issued, successful bidders must provide information in a form or a format approved by the Department of Justice.[514] The Department of the Interior may not issue a lease until thirty days after the Attorney General has received the information required to be submitted by the successful bidder.[515]

From 1978 to 1995, the Department of Justice set forth its policies regarding review of federal coal leases in annual reports pursuant to the Federal Coal Leasing

---

510. 43 C.F.R. subpt. 3422 (2000).

511. *Id.* subpt. 3425 (2000). Leasing by application can occur if a tract is outside a designated regional coal production region or if the tract is necessary to maintain production at existing mines, to meet contractual obligations, or to prevent the bypass of federal coal. *Id.*

512. 30 U.S.C. § 1841(l)(2) (1994). Regulations promulgated by the Department of the Interior (DOI) require that lease exchanges and transfers also be reviewed by the DOJ. 43 C.F.R. §§ 3435.3-7; 3453.2-2(e) (2000).

513. 30 U.S.C. § 184(l)(2); 43 C.F.R. § 3422.3-4(e)(2) (2000).

514. 43 C.F.R. § 3422.3-4(a) (2000). Information that must be reported includes total in-place coal reserves, uncommitted in-place coal reserves held by the successful bidder, the characteristics of the coal to be leased, and the identity of any affiliates, subsidiaries, and joint ventures, including affiliations or joint ventures with railroads, electric utilities, and nuclear fuel fabricators or converters. Antitrust Div., U.S. Dep't of Justice (OMB N. 1105-0025). The DOJ has created two reporting forms, one covering federal coal leases in certain western states (Arizona, Colorado, Montana, New Mexico, North Dakota, South Dakota, and Wyoming) and a second form covering leases in certain eastern states (Texas, Nebraska, Iowa, Kansas, Missouri, Oklahoma, Arkansas, Illinois, Indiana, and western Kentucky). These forms are available from the DOI.

515. 43 C.F.R. § 3422.3-4(c) (2000). If the information submitted is incomplete, however, the 30-day period is tolled pending the submission of correct or complete data. *Id.*

Amendments Act of 1976.[516] The Department of Justice's initial report set forth the analytical framework for reviewing federal coal leases and defined the relevant geographic and product markets. The Department of Justice found separate markets for metallurgical coal, utility steam coal, spot coal, and long-term contract coal, although the market for long-term contracts for uncommitted utility steam coal predominated.[517] The agency described four geographic markets in which it would evaluate coal leases: the Appalachian market,[518] the Midwest market, the Northern Plains market,[519] and the Southwest market.[520] In a subsequent report, the Department of Justice somewhat narrowed its geographic market definition, finding a smaller Powder River Region market within the Northern Plains market.[521]

Although the Department of Justice found in its initial report that the nation's coal markets were competitive, it nonetheless announced that it would regard the fact that a winning bidder's share of the relevant market, including the leases under review, exceeds 15 percent of uncommitted nonfederal reserves as prima facie evidence that award of the lease would create or maintain a situation inconsistent with the antitrust laws. The Department of Justice also stated that it would consider relevant mitigating evidence that would demonstrate that the lease sale subject to a prima facie rule would not, in fact, be anticompetitive, although the burden of coming forward with such evidence will rest upon the prospective lease holder.[522] In later reports, the agency announced that it would give special attention to proposed leases to affiliates of the Burlington Northern Railroad, which it found had market power over coal transportation from the Powder River Region,[523] and to leases to electric utilities because of the potential for the evasion of rate regulation.[524]

(2) Outer Continental Shelf Oil and Gas Leasing

Under Section 205 of the Outer Continental Shelf Lands Act Amendments of 1978,[525] the Department of Justice reviews proposed new federal offshore oil and gas leases on the Outer Continental Shelf.[526] Lease sales are conducted by the Secretary of the Interior by competitive bidding under regulations promulgated by that agency.[527] Before the Secretary of the Interior may accept any bids at a proposed sale, he must allow the Attorney General, in consultation with the Federal Trade

516. 30 U.S.C. § 208-2 (1994). The requirement for submission of these reports was repealed in Pub. L. No. 104-66, § 1091(e), 109 Stat. 722 (1995).
517. U.S. DEP'T OF JUSTICE, COMPETITION IN THE COAL INDUSTRY 39-42 (1978).
518. Maryland, Ohio, Pennsylvania, West Virginia, Alabama, Georgia, eastern Kentucky, North Carolina, eastern Tennessee, Virginia, and Michigan. Id. at 48-51.
519. Idaho, Montana, North Dakota, South Dakota, Wyoming, Alaska, Oregon, and Minnesota. Id. at 47-48.
520. Arizona, Colorado, New Mexico, and Utah. Id. at 52-53.
521. U.S. DEP'T OF JUSTICE, COMPETITION IN THE COAL INDUSTRY 47 (1982).
522. U.S. DEP'T OF JUSTICE, COMPETITION IN THE COAL INDUSTRY 130-31 (1978).
523. U.S. DEP'T OF JUSTICE, COMPETITION IN THE COAL INDUSTRY 79-81, 104-06 (1980). Leasing directly to railroad companies is prohibited by § 2(c) of the Mineral Lands Leasing Act of 1920, 30 U.S.C. § 202 (1994). See National Coal Ass'n v. Hodel, 825 F.2d 523, 526 (D.C. Cir. 1987).
524. U.S. DEP'T OF JUSTICE, COMPETITION IN THE COAL INDUSTRY 68-69 (1982).
525. 43 U.S.C. § 1337(c) (1994).
526. The term "Outer Continental Shelf" is defined as submerged lands subject to the control of the United States lying outside a line three miles from the coastline. Id. §§ 1301(a), 1331(a) (1994).
527. Id. § 1337 (1994 & Supp. 1999).

Commission, thirty days to review the results of the sale.[528] The statute grants the Attorney General the discretion to conduct such antitrust review as the Attorney General believes is appropriate, in consultation with the Federal Trade Commission, and the Secretary of the Interior is required to provide such information as they require in order to conduct their antitrust review.[529]

Under Section 205, the Attorney General, in consultation with the Federal Trade Commission, may make such recommendations to the Secretary of the Interior as may be appropriate, including the nonacceptance of any bid. If either the Attorney General (in consultation with the Federal Trade Commission) or the Secretary of the Interior determines that the issuance of the lease "may create or maintain a situation inconsistent with the antitrust laws," the Secretary of the Interior may refuse to issue the lease, notifying the Attorney General and the lessee of the reason for his decision.[530] The statute specifically provides that this antitrust review process leaves unaltered the rights and authority of the Department of Justice, the Federal Trade Commission, or private parties under the antitrust laws.[531]

The Department of Justice has announced that it generally will analyze Outer Continental Shelf lease sales in one of two relevant markets. Leases off the Eastern and Gulf Coasts are considered part of the world crude oil market.[532] The Department of Justice, however, defined a separate geographic market consisting of Alaska, California, Washington, Oregon, Nevada, and Arizona, an area known as "PAD District V," for which lower quality crudes, i.e., crude oil of high sulfur content and viscosity, form a separate product.[533]

The Department of Justice also has announced that it would recommend that the Secretary of the Interior reject any joint bid for a federal offshore lease submitted by two or more of the four largest reserve holders in PAD District V.[534] The Department

---

528. *Id.* § 1337(c)(1). The statute permits the Attorney General and the FTC to agree to a shorter period. *Id.* Under DOI regulations, the Secretary of the Interior also "shall consult with and give due consideration to the views of the Attorney General" prior to approving a transfer or assignment of a lease. 30 C.F.R. § 256.65 (2001). The Attorney General has 30 days to provide those views. *Id.*

529. 43 U.S.C. § 1337(c)(2).

530. *Id.* § 1337(c)(3).

531. *Id.* §§ 1337(c)(4)(A), (B).

532. U.S. DEP'T OF JUSTICE, ADVICE AND RECOMENDATIONS OF THE U.S. DEP'T OF JUSTICE TO THE SECRETARY OF INTERIOR PURSUANT TO SECTION 205 OF THE OUTER CONTINENTAL SHELF LANDS ACT AMENDMENTS OF 1978 at 30-31 (1980) [hereinafter 1980 DOJ REPORT]. The DOJ concluded that in the world oil market all crudes are generally substitutes for one another even though they produce different quantities of the various refined petroleum products. *Id.* at 31 n.37.

533. *Id.* at 21-29. The DOJ's market definition was based in part on the then-existing excess supply of such quality crudes in PAD District V, environmental restrictions, and restrictions on the export of crude oil produced in Alaska. *See* 50 U.S.C. app. § 2403(l) (1994); 30 U.S.C § 185(u) (1994). The FTC defined a more narrow market consisting only of crude oil similar to that produced in Alaska, excluding similar crude oil produced in California. 1980 DOJ REPORT, *supra* note 532, at 30-31. Consistent with this view of the market for Alaskan oil, and in light of other considerations specific to the market positions of BP Amoco L.L.C. and Atlantic Richfield Co. (ARCO), a major feature of the consent decree permitting the recent merger between BP Amoco and ARCO was a requirement that ARCO divest all of its Alaska assets, including all of its federal leases. In the complaint issued by the FTC in connection with that merger, the FTC identified a product market for the "purchase of exploration rights" in the geographic market of "the Alaska North Slope." BP Amoco P.L.C., 65 Fed. Reg. 21,434 (FTC Apr. 21, 2000) (aid to public comment), 2000 FTC LEXIS 56 (FTC 2000) (complaint ¶¶ 44-45).

534. At the time this policy was announced, these four companies were ARCO, BP, Exxon Corporation, and Shell Oil Company. 1980 DOJ REPORT, *supra* note 532, at 67. Presumably, the policy would

of Justice found that the concentration in the relevant market was very high, there were substantial barriers to entry, and the existence of joint ventures made independent action more difficult.[535]

(3) Naval and National Petroleum Reserves

Section 201(11) of the Naval Petroleum Reserves Product Act of 1976[536] makes the sale of petroleum or petroleum leases from the naval petroleum reserves, or the formulation of any leasing or sale plans affecting those reserves, subject to review by the Attorney General "with respect to matters which may affect competition."[537] The Secretary of Energy must notify the Attorney General at least fifteen days prior to the issuance or execution of any contract or operating agreement with respect to any of the naval petroleum reserves. The Secretary of Energy also must provide such information as the Attorney General requires to formulate his advice. If, within the fifteen-day period, the Attorney General advises the Secretary of Energy that "a contract or operating agreement may create or maintain a situation inconsistent with the antitrust laws," the Secretary of Energy may not enter into the proposed contract.[538] The National Petroleum Reserve in Alaska, administered by the Secretary of the Interior, is subject to the same statutory provisions.[539]

In addition, any plans for the exploration, development, and production of the naval and national petroleum reserves must be submitted to Congress and must contain a report by the Attorney General with respect to the anticipated effect of the plans on competition.[540] The Secretary of the Interior has published regulations covering competitive leasing of the National Petroleum Reserve in Alaska, extending the time for the Attorney General to review a proposed lease to thirty days,[541] and requiring prospective bidders to submit such information as required by the Attorney General to conduct an antitrust review.[542]

Although the Department of Justice has not announced any policy with respect to reviews of leases or sales of production from the national and naval petroleum reserves, the geographic and product market definitions and general policies set out with respect to its role in providing advice pursuant to Section 205 of the Outer Continental Shelf Lands Act Amendments of 1978[543] would appear to be applicable to such leasing and sales.

---

now apply to Phillips Petroleum Co. in light of the transfer to Phillips of ARCO's Alaska assets as part of ARCO's merger with BP Amoco. At the time the DOJ announced its policy, BP, Exxon, and Shell all had levels of production that would prevent them from making joint bids with one another under § 105 of the Energy Policy and Conservation Act, 42 U.S.C. § 6213 (1994). It was clear from the DOJ's report, however, that even if Exxon, BP, or Shell were no longer subject to § 105, the DOJ would nonetheless continue to recommend against the acceptance of any joint bid submitted by them. The DOI regulations implementing § 105 are found at 30 C.F.R. §§ 256.38-46, 260.303 (2001).

535. 1980 DOJ REPORT, *supra* note 532, at 36-47.
536. 10 U.S.C. § 7430(g) (2000).
537. *Id.* § 7430(g)(1).
538. *Id.* § 7430(g)(2).
539. 42 U.S.C. § 6506 (1994).
540. *Id.*; 10 U.S.C. § 7431(b)(2) (2000).
541. 43 C.F.R. § 3130.1(c) (2000).
542. *Id.* § 3130.1(b) (2000). Any information submitted must be treated as confidential by the Secretary of the Interior and the Attorney General. *Id.* § 3130.1(f) (2000).
543. 43 U.S.C. § 1337(c) (1994).

b.   THE STATUTORY STANDARD

The standard of antitrust review applicable to each of the three federal energy leasing or sale programs is identical: whether a particular lease or sale "would create or maintain a situation inconsistent with the antitrust laws."[544] The Department of Justice has stated that a recommendation against issuing a lease does not require a finding of a prosecutable antitrust violation. Rather, the agency views its role as advising whether there is a "reasonable probability that issuance of a lease will contravene the policies underlying the antitrust laws or will lead to an antitrust violation."[545]

Although the legislative histories of the relevant statutes are bereft of any expressed purpose underlying the antitrust review standard, provisions incorporating nearly identical language have appeared in various federal statutes since 1944.[546] The legislative history, as well as judicial and administrative interpretations of the antitrust review standard under one of those statutes, Section 105 of the Atomic Energy Act of 1954,[547] supports the Department of Justice's views. In amending Section 105, Congress stated:

> The concept of certainty of contravention of the antitrust laws or the policies clearly underlying these laws is not intended to be implicit in this standard; nor is mere possibility of inconsistency. It is intended that the finding is based on reasonable probability of contravention of the antitrust laws or the policies clearly underlying these laws.[548]

In *Alabama Power Co. v. NRC*[549] the Eleventh Circuit held that this language was intended to reach "situations which would not, if left to fruition, in fact violate any antitrust law."[550] The court added that the reference to "the policies clearly underlying these laws" means that "a traditional antitrust enforcement scheme is not envisioned, and a wider one is put in place."[551]

---

544. 30 U.S.C. § 184(l)(2) (1994); 43 U.S.C. § 1337(c); 10 U.S.C. § 7430(g)(2) (2000).
545. U.S. DEP'T OF JUSTICE, COMPETITION IN THE COAL INDUSTRY 5-7 (1978); 1980 DOJ REPORT, *supra* note 532, at 8.
546. This standard first appeared in the Surplus Property Act of 1944, *amended by* § 207 of the Federal Property and Administrative Services Act of 1949, 40 U.S.C. § 488(a) (1994). *See also* 1970 Amendments to the Atomic Energy Act of 1954, § 105(c)(5), 42 U.S.C. § 2135(c)(5) (1994); Deep Seabed Hard Mineral Resources Act of 1980, §§ 103(d), 104, 30 U.S.C. §§ 1413(d), 1414 (1994); Amendments to the Patent and Trademark Laws, 35 U.S.C. § 209(a)(4), *amended by* Pub. L. No. 106-404, § 4(a), 114 Stat. 1743 (2000); Ocean Thermal Energy Conversion Act of 1980, 42 U.S.C. § 9114 (1994).
547. 42 U.S.C. § 2135 (1994). Under § 105(c)(5) of the Atomic Energy Act of 1954, the DOJ reviews each license for a nuclear electric generating facility to determine "whether the activities under the license would create or maintain a situation inconsistent with the antitrust laws." *Id.* § 2135(c)(5).
548. Report by the Joint Comm. on Atomic Energy, H.R. REP. 91-1470, *reprinted in* 1970 U.S.C.C.A.N. 4981, 4994.
549. 692 F.2d 1362 (11th Cir. 1982), *cert. denied*, 464 U.S. 816 (1983).
550. *Id.* at 1368.
551. *Id.*; *see* Consumers Power Co., [1975-1978 Transfer Binder] Nuclear Reg. Rep. (CCH) ¶ 30,263 (1977); *see also* Louisiana Power & Light Co., 6 A.E.C. 48, 49 (1973). In practice, the DOJ has used the "wider" enforcement scheme envisioned by the statutes only to extend to lease sales by the federal government the incipiency standard of § 7 of the Clayton Act, 15 U.S.C. § 18 (2000), which otherwise would not apply to acquisitions of resources from the government. U.S. DEP'T OF JUSTICE, COMPETITION IN THE COAL INDUSTRY 7 (1978); *see also* 1980 DOJ REPORT, *supra* note 532, at 10.

The Department of Justice and the Federal Trade Commission view Section 7 of the Clayton Act[552] as the appropriate framework within which to analyze lease sales.[553] The Department of Justice analogizes the sale of a federal coal or oil lease to a holder of existing, uncommitted reserves to an acquisition of a potential de novo entrant, rather than a conventional horizontal merger.[554] It reasons that, unlike a horizontal merger, where previously independent productive assets are combined under one seller, a lease sale necessarily expands the potential productive assets in the market.[555] The Department of Justice has stated, however, that even where award of a lease would not alter the existing market structure, it would regard such an award as sufficiently anticompetitive to justify rejection if the proposed buyer is a leading firm in a concentrated market with high entry barriers and the award could "eliminate significant possibilities for eventual deconcentration."[556] In applying this standard, however, the Department of Justice has considered the effect on concentration of the entire lease sale, not only of those leases won by the leading firm.[557] It also has taken into account long lead times needed to develop leases and the uncertainty that oil would be found in sufficient quantities to be produced economically.[558] Finally, the Department of Justice has noted that a variety of factors, other than concentration, may enhance or diminish the likelihood of noncompetitive behavior in a relevant market. These factors include ease of entry, the cost or difficulty of monitoring competitors' actions, the presence of joint ventures, offsetting buyer concentration, the diversity and complexity of products and terms of sale, and the degree to which a firm's market share accurately reflects its competitive significance.[559]

D. Financial Institutions and Markets

1. Financial Institutions

Sections 1 and 2 of the Sherman Act[560] and Section 7 of the Clayton Act[561] apply to banking activities. Congress has not granted financial institutions immunity from

---

552. 15 U.S.C. § 18 (2000).
553. U.S. DEP'T OF JUSTICE, COMPETITION IN THE COAL INDUSTRY 7 (1978); 1980 DOJ REPORT, *supra* note 532, at 10.
554. U.S. DEP'T OF JUSTICE, COMPETITION IN THE COAL INDUSTRY 8 (1978).
555. *Id.*
556. 1980 DOJ REPORT, *supra* note 532, at 13-14. The DOJ nonetheless concluded that the award of a lease to a leading firm, where there was no other bidder, was preferable to withholding those tracts from the market or delaying their development by requiring that they be reoffered at a later sale. *Id.* at 68-69.
557. *Id.* at 69-71 (concluding that leases could be awarded to a leading firm where the award of other leases offered at the same sale would reduce overall concentration by 3-6%).
558. *Id.* at 12, 71.
559. U.S. DEP'T OF JUSTICE, COMPETITION IN THE COAL INDUSTRY 11-14 (1978).
560. *See, e.g.,* United States v. First Nat'l Bank & Trust Co., 376 U.S. 665, 669-70 (1964); Michaels Bldg. Co. v. Ameritrust Co., 848 F.2d 674 (6th Cir. 1988) (complaint provided adequate notice of claim of alleged conspiracy to fix interest rate); Sharon Steel Corp. v. Chase Manhattan Bank, 691 F.2d 1039 (2d Cir. 1982) (concerted activity by indenture trustee banks who were faced with a common breach of indenture agreements by liquidating debtor corporation, and their arrival at a common position, did not violate antitrust laws because there was no anticompetitive purpose or effect), *cert. denied,* 460 U.S. 1012 (1983); Tose v. First Pa. Bank, 648 F.2d 879, 893 (3d Cir.) (affirming district court's rejection of conspiracy by banks to fix interest rates and engage in group

the antitrust laws. Congress has, however, enacted several statutes that apply special antitrust rules to financial institutions and that affect the forums in which such issues are decided. For example, the Bank Merger Acts of 1960[562] and 1966[563] and the Bank Holding Company Act Amendments of 1970[564] incorporate the language and criteria of Section 7 of the Clayton Act, but they also set unique procedures for bank mergers and acquisitions and provide a special defense to antitrust challenges. In addition, Section 106 of the 1970 Bank Holding Company Act Amendments[565] and Section 331 of the Garn-St. Germain Depository Institutions Act of 1982[566] prohibit certain tying arrangements by financial institutions. Of course, many antitrust issues relating to financial institutions have arisen under Sections 1 and 2 of the Sherman Act and have not directly involved the banking regulatory agencies.

a. JOINT VENTURES

Antitrust issues raised by joint ventures among financial institutions, such as bank credit card ventures and automated teller machine networks, have involved fee-setting arrangements and exclusivity requirements.

(1) Bank Credit Card Ventures

Fee-setting arrangements have been the subject of controversy. One type of fee set by bank credit card joint ventures is an interchange fee, paid by the merchant's bank to the cardholder's bank. In *National Bancard Corp. (NaBanco) v. VISA U.S.A., Inc.,*[567] a district court upheld an interchange fee under the rule of reason because it found that prearranged interchange rules are an inescapable consequence of the integration necessary to achieving the efficiencies of a bank card joint venture.[568] The court concluded that the interchange fee was procompetitive because a national bank credit card system could not exist without it.[569]

---

boycott among banks), *cert. denied*, 454 U.S. 893 (1981); Weit v. Continental Ill. Nat'l Bank & Trust Co., 641 F.2d 457 (7th Cir. 1981) (affirming summary judgment for defendants on claim that banks conspired to fix credit card interest rates), *cert. denied*, 455 U.S. 988 (1982); Wilcox Dev. Co. v. First Interstate Bank, 605 F. Supp. 592 (D. Or. 1985) (claim for alleged conspiracy to fix prime rate), *aff'd in part, rev'd in part, and remanded*, 815 F.2d 522 (9th Cir. 1987); United States v. Warren Five Cents Sav. Bank, 1980-81 Trade Cas. (CCH) ¶ 63,772 (D. Mass. 1981) (consent decree in suit based on § 1 violation forbade use of restrictive lease between bank and shopping center); United States v. Northwestern Nat'l Bank, 1964 Trade Cas. (CCH) ¶ 71,022 (D. Minn. 1964) (consent decree prohibited banks from fixing interest rates and exchanging information relating to interest rates); United States v. Hunterdon County Trust Co., 1962 Trade Cas. (CCH) ¶ 70,623 (D.N.J. 1962) (consent decree prohibited banks from fixing uniform service charges and from exchanging information relating to such charges).
561. *See, e.g.*, United States v. Philadelphia Nat'l Bank, 374 U.S. 321, 371-72 (1963).
562. Pub. L. No. 86-463, 74 Stat. 129 (codified as amended at 12 U.S.C. § 1828(c) (2000)).
563. Pub. L. No. 89-356, 80 Stat. 7 (codified as amended as 12 U.S.C. § 1828(c) (2000)).
564. 12 U.S.C. § 1841 *et seq.* (2000).
565. Pub. L. No. 91-607, 84 Stat. 1766 (codified as amended at 12 U.S.C. §§ 1971-1978 (2000)).
566. Pub. L. No. 97-320, § 331, 96 Stat. 1503 (codified at 12 U.S.C. § 1464(q) (2000)).
567. 596 F. Supp. 1231, 1236-38 (S.D. Fla. 1984), *aff'd*, 779 F.2d 592 (11th Cir.), *cert. denied*, 479 U.S. 923 (1986).
568. *Id.* at 1252-56. The Eleventh Circuit considered the interchange fee to be "a potentially efficiency creating agreement among members of a joint enterprise." 779 F.2d at 602.
569. 596 F. Supp. at 1259-60. The court's decision was explicitly influenced by its finding that VISA lacked market power in a market the court labeled as a "nationwide market for payment systems."

Exclusive membership rules, which prohibit a member of one joint venture from belonging to another venture, also are the source of frequent litigation. In the 1970s, National BankAmericard, the predecessor to VISA, sought to exclude members of competing credit card ventures. The rule was challenged by a bank member, and the district court found a per se violation. The Eighth Circuit reversed, holding that a bank card joint venture exclusivity requirement should be analyzed under the rule of reason because of the novelty and complexity of the antitrust issues.[570] When VISA sought to have a subsequent exclusive membership rule approved by the Department of Justice, it refused because of insufficient information and a concern that potential entrants could be deterred.[571]

In the early 1990s, the exclusive membership controversy was revisited. When VISA refused to admit Dean Witter (the issuer of the Discover Card) as a member, Dean Witter sued, claiming that the membership was an illegal group boycott in violation of Section 1. The jury found for Dean Witter, and the district court affirmed. The Tenth Circuit reversed because VISA lacked market power and the exclusion was justified because it promoted intersystem competition.[572] As to market power, the appellate court observed that the district court erred by permitting the definition of the relevant market to be "transformed, equating exclusion from VISA USA to exclusion from the market."[573] The correct market was that of credit card issuance, a market that was "remarkably unconcentrated."[574] The court also held that VISA's rule was "reasonably necessary" to the success of the venture because it prevented competitors from free-riding.[575]

In 1998, the Department of Justice filed suit against VISA and MasterCard to "prevent and enjoin VISA and MasterCard from violating anti-trust laws by restraining competition in the market for general purpose card network products & services."[576] The Department of Justice alleged that certain policies of each association disadvantaged or excluded rival general purpose card networks, such as American Express and Discover, by prohibiting all member banks from doing business with other general purpose card networks. In addition, the agency asserted that VISA and Mastercard were controlled by the same large banks, which allegedly derived substantial profits from issuing the card of the other. The Department of Justice alleged that this dual governance structure was anticompetitive, impeding brand development, advertisement against the other, and innovations such as smart

---

Id. at 1258. As a result, the court concluded that "VISA lacks the ability to impose any restraint detrimental to competition." *Id.*

570. Worthen Bank & Trust Co. v. National BankAmericard, Inc., 485 F.2d 119, 126 (8th Cir. 1973), *cert. denied*, 415 U.S. 918 (1974).

571. Letter from Thomas E. Kauper, Ass't Att'y Gen., Antitrust Div., to Francis R. Kirkham and Allan N. Littman (Oct. 7, 1975). Much earlier, the DOJ obtained a consent decree against the Bank of Virginia ending the bank's practice of allowing merchants to accept its bank card only if the merchants refused to accept all other regional credit cards. United States v. Bank of Va., 1966 Trade Cas. (CCH) ¶ 71,947 (E.D. Va. 1966).

572. SCFC ILC, Inc. v. Visa U.S.A., Inc., 36 F.3d 958 (10th Cir. 1994), *cert. denied sub nom.* MountainWest Fin. Corp. v. Visa U.S.A., Inc., 515 U.S. 1152 (1995).

573. *Id.* at 968.

574. *Id.*

575. *Id.* at 970.

576. United States v. VISA U.S.A., Inc., 163 F. Supp. 2d 322 (S.D.N.Y. 2001).

cards, commercial cards, and systems to provide secure general purpose card transactions over the Internet.[577]

In October 2001, the district court held that the VISA and MasterCard policies prohibiting members from issuing cards from any other general purpose credit card network adversely affected competition among credit card networks and harmed consumers by denying them choice.[578] The court determined that VISA and MasterCard have market power in the general purpose card network market and that their policies inhibited the growth of competing networks such as American Express and Discover.[579] As a result, these other general purpose card networks were denied the scale necessary to provide effective network competition.[580] However, the court also held that the Department of Justice failed to prove that the dual governance structure adversely affected competition or inhibited innovation. Rather, the court found ample evidence that VISA and MasterCard have competed against each other, notwithstanding the duality, and have both introduced numerous innovations benefiting consumers.[581]

(2) Automated Teller Machine Networks

Automated teller machines (ATMs) offer customers access to one or more networks of ATMs. Thus, a customer can draw funds from an account at one bank through an ATM of another bank. These networks face fee-setting and exclusivity disputes similar to credit card networks.

In ATM networks, the customer's bank pays an interchange fee to the bank that operates the ATM used by the customer.[582] An arbitrator examining a fee-setting arrangement under the rule of reason held that when (1) a single interchange fee for an ATM network is set by the joint venture, and (2) the joint venture has market power, the network must provide its members the ability to impose surcharges or grant rebates.[583] One district court reached the opposite conclusion in permitting a national ATM network to prohibit surcharges.[584]

ATM networks also have faced litigation about exclusivity and membership rules. One district court has held that a regional ATM network may forbid its members

---

577. A copy of the complaint is available on the DOJ's Web site at www.usdoj.gov/atr/cases/f1900/1973.htm

578. 163 F. Supp. 2d at 379.

579. Id.

580. Id. at 387-89.

581. Id. at 345-79.

582. For descriptions of ATM networks and interchange and processing fees, see Treasurer, Inc. v. Philadelphia Nat'l Bank, 682 F. Supp. 269 (D.N.J.), aff'd without op., 853 F.2d 921 (3d Cir. 1988); In re Arbitration Between First Tex. Sav. Ass'n & Financial Interchange, Inc., 55 Antitrust & Trade Reg. Rep. (BNA) 340, 341-42 (1988) (Kauper, Arb.).

583. See In re Arbitration Between First Tex. Sav., 55 Antitrust & Trade Reg. Rep. (BNA) at 349-51, 370-72. The arbitrator's finding of market power rested on findings that, at the time of his decision, no other national, regional or combination of local ATM networks offered coverage comparable to that of the respondent ATM network. Id. at 352-56; see also Valley Bank v. PLUS Sys., 749 F. Supp. 223 (D. Nev. 1989) (upholding state statute that required network to offer ability to assess surcharges), aff'd, 914 F.2d 1186 (9th Cir. 1990).

584. See SouthTrust Corp. v. Plus Sys., 913 F. Supp. 1517 (N.D. Ala. 1995).

from joining other competing regional networks.[585] The Department of Justice has declined to challenge the admission into an ATM network of an institution that was already a member of a competing ATM network.[586]

A joint venture that poses no competitive concerns at the time of formation may result in competitive concerns over time, depending on changes in circumstances such as internal reorganization, adoption of new agreements among the parties, changes in the parties, new market conditions, or changes in market share.[587] For example, the *Antitrust Guidelines for Competitor Collaborations* (*Competitor Collaborations Guidelines*) issued by the Department of Justice and Federal Trade Commission in 2000 provide as an example of this rule a joint venture to establish an ATM network.[588] The hypothetical joint venture agreement specified that the participating banks would not participate in any other ATM networks. Over time, the joint venture expanded by adding more bank participants, and the number of competitors fell. In this example, the agencies would focus upon whether the exclusivity rule harmed competition given the change in events.[589] The agencies would consider various factors in making this determination, including whether there was significant sunk investment made in reliance upon the exclusivity rule.[590]

b.   MERGERS AND ACQUISITIONS[591]

Bank mergers are governed by the same legal principles that apply to mergers in other industries. The procedures and forums, however, differ. The applicable statutes—the Bank Merger Acts of 1960 and 1966, the Bank Holding Company Act, and the Gramm-Leach-Bliley Financial Services Modernization Act of 1999—each incorporate the language and standards of Section 7 of the Clayton Act, with the addition of a special defense available only to banks. After the Supreme Court in 1963 applied the Clayton Act to bank mergers in *United States v. Philadelphia National Bank*,[592] Congress amended the Bank Merger Act of 1960[593] to establish substantive standards and procedures for bank mergers and acquisitions. The Bank Merger Act of 1966 incorporated Sherman Act and Clayton Act standards, barring

---

585. *See Treasurer, Inc.*, 682 F. Supp. at 279-80. The district court also held that one regional network lacked standing to challenge a transaction that was, in effect, a merger of two competing regional networks because it failed to make a showing of antitrust injury.

586. *See* Letter from William F. Baxter, Ass't Att'y Gen., Antitrust Div., to Donald I. Baker (Aug. 3, 1983).

587. U.S. DEPT OF JUSTICE & FEDERAL TRADE COMM'N, ANTITRUST GUIDELINES FOR COLLABORATIONS AMONG COMPETITORS (2000) [hereinafter COMPETITOR COLLABORATIONS GUIDELINES], *reprinted in* 4 Trade Reg. Rep. (CCH) ¶ 13,161 *and* Appendix G to this treatise.

588. *Id.* § 2.4, Example 3.

589. *Id.*

590. *Id.*

591. This subsection deals largely with the regulatory structure governing bank mergers and acquisitions. For a discussion of substantive issues that have arisen in bank merger cases, such as geographic and product market definition, see Chapters III and VI (treating such cases together with other merger and market definition cases).

592. 374 U.S. 321 (1963).

593. Pub. L. No. 89-356, 80 Stat. 7 (codified as amended at 12 U.S.C. § 1828(c) (2000)). The Bank Merger Act of 1960, Pub. L. No. 86-463, 74 Stat. 129 (previously codified at 12 U.S.C. § 1828(c)), had directed the Comptroller of the Currency, the Federal Reserve System, and the Federal Deposit Insurance Corporation to take competitive effects into account when evaluating bank mergers and to consider reports on a proposed transaction from the other two bank regulatory agencies and the Attorney General.

the responsible agency from allowing any transaction "whose effect in any section of the country may be substantially to lessen competition, or to tend to create a monopoly, or which in any other manner would be in restraint of trade."[594]   In addition, the responsible agency may not approve any transactions "which would result in a monopoly, or which would be in furtherance of any combination or conspiracy to monopolize or to attempt to monopolize the business of banking in any part of the United States."[595]

The Bank Merger Act of 1966 provides a special defense that permits the responsible agency to "approve transactions, even if they are anticompetitive, if they find that the anticompetitive effects of the proposed transaction are clearly outweighed in the public interest by the probable effect of the transaction in meeting the convenience and needs of the community to be served."[596]   Banks have the burden of proving the convenience and needs defense.[597]   That defense also was applied by a district court to a bank merger challenged by the Department of Justice under the Sherman Act.[598]

Except for certain emergency cases, a bank merger may not be consummated before the thirtieth calendar day after the approval of the relevant banking agency.[599] However, if the banking agency has not received any adverse comment from the Attorney General, the banking agency and Attorney General can agree to a shorter time frame, provided that a bank merger may not be consummated any earlier than the fifteenth calendar day after agency approval.[600]

---

594. 12 U.S.C. § 1828(c)(5)(B).
595. *Id.* § 1828(c)(5)(A). The Community Reinvestment Act (CRA), 12 U.S.C. §§ 2901-2907 (2000), also requires the relevant banking agency to consider whether the bank or bank holding company is serving adequately the credit needs of all segments of the community or communities in which it has deposit-accepting offices. 12 U.S.C. § 2901(a)(3). Since enactment of the CRA, community groups have argued before the banking agencies that banks have not been doing enough to service the low- and moderate-income segments of their communities. In recent years, those challenges have become more sophisticated, with protestants arguing not only the deficiency of the organization on CRA grounds, but the legality of the transaction on antitrust or other grounds under the Bank Merger Act or the Bank Holding Company Act.

      Challenges to banking agency approval by private parties have been largely unsuccessful. In *Lee v. Board of Governors of the Federal Reserve Sys.*, 118 F.3d 905 (2d Cir. 1997), the Second Circuit dismissed an appeal by residents of a community in which the merging organization was located on the ground that these petitioners lacked standing to challenge the approval of the merger. Similarly, in *Inner City Press v. Board of Governors of the Federal Reserve Sys.*, 130 F.3d 1088 (D.C. Cir. 1997) (per curiam), *cert. denied*, 524 U.S. 937 (1998), the D.C. Circuit dismissed an appeal by community groups of the Federal Reserve Board's (FRB) decision to permit a bank merger. The D.C. Circuit held that participating in an administrative proceeding before the FRB was insufficient to establish standing to challenge its actions. The petitioners' appearance before the FRB only established prudential standing and, without more, fell short of the injury-in-fact requirement of Article III of the Constitution. *Id.*
596. 12 U.S.C. § 1828(c)(5)(A). For transactions in which the defense was considered by the Federal Reserve System, see First Nat'l Bankshares, 70 Fed. Res. Bull. 832 (1984) (defense satisfied); First Am. Bank Corp., 70 Fed. Res. Bull. 516 (1984) (same, in part). For judicial consideration of the defense, see United States v. Phillipsburg Nat'l Bank & Trust Co., 399 U.S. 350 (1970); United States v. Third Nat'l Bank, 390 U.S. 171 (1968); United States v. First Nat'l Bank, 310 F. Supp. 157 (D. Md. 1970); United States v. Provident Nat'l Bank, 280 F. Supp. 1 (E.D. Pa. 1968).
597. *See* United States v. First City Nat'l Bank, 386 U.S. 361 (1967).
598. *See* United States v. Central State Bank, 564 F. Supp. 1478 (W.D. Mich. 1983).
599. 12 U.S.C. § 1828(c)(6) (2000).
600. *Id.*

Under the Bank Merger Act of 1966, a court must automatically enter a preliminary injunction against any bank merger challenged by the Attorney General within thirty days of banking agency approval.[601] If the merger is not challenged within thirty days of such approval, it is immune from attack under any antitrust law other than Section 2 of the Sherman Act.[602]

Commercial bank mergers are reviewed by three federal banking agencies. Generally, the Office of the Comptroller of the Currency reviews transactions where the "acquiring, assuming or resulting bank" is a national bank; the Federal Deposit Insurance Corporation reviews transactions where the acquiring or resulting bank will be a federally insured, state-chartered bank that is not a member of the Federal Reserve System; and the Board of Governors of the Federal Reserve System (Federal Reserve Board) reviews transactions where the acquiring or resulting bank will be a state-chartered bank that is a member of the Federal Reserve System.[603] Each regulatory agency is required to conduct its own examination of the transaction and to obtain a report from the Department of Justice before approving the transaction.[604] Transactions governed by the Bank Merger Act are exempt from the premerger notification requirements of the H-S-R Act.[605]

Under the Bank Holding Company Act,[606] the Federal Reserve Board must apply the same standards to mergers and acquisitions involving bank holding companies as those set in the Bank Merger Act of 1966.[607] The Bank Holding Company Act does not require the Federal Reserve Board to obtain a report from the Department of Justice before approving a transaction, although the Department of Justice submits a report as a matter of practice. Nonetheless, such transactions are exempt from the premerger notification procedures of the H-S-R Act.[608] The Bank Holding Company Act does require the Federal Reserve Board to notify the Department of Justice (and in the case of a nonbank acquisition, the Federal Trade Commission as well) of its approval of any merger transaction.[609]

The Bank Holding Company Act requires bank holding companies, that are not also financial holding companies, to obtain Federal Reserve Board approval for any acquisition of a nonbank.[610] To evaluate these transactions, the Federal Reserve

601. *Id.* § 1828(c)(7)(A) (2000). The automatic stay is to be given full effect unless the government's complaint is "frivolous." *See First City Nat'l Bank*, 386 U.S. at 366. The automatic stay provision of 12 U.S.C. § 1828(c)(7)(A) does not apply to antitrust actions brought by private parties. *See* Vial v. First Commerce Corp., 564 F. Supp. 650, 666-67 (E.D. La. 1983).

602. 12 U.S.C. § 1828(c)(7)(C) (2000).

603. *Id.* § 1828(c)(2) (2000).

604. *Id.* § 1828(c)(4) (2000).

605. 15 U.S.C. § 18a(c)(7) (2000).

606. 12 U.S.C. §§ 1841-1850 (2000). The Bank Holding Company Act was amended in 1966 to conform with the Bank Merger Act of 1966. Pub. L. No. 89-485, §§ 1-11, 80 Stat. 236-40 (codified as amended at 12 U.S.C. §§ 1841-1859 (2000)). The Bank Holding Company Act applies to all companies that own 25% or more of the voting stock of a bank, control the election of a majority of a bank's directors, or that the FRB finds exercise a "controlling influence" over a bank. *Id.* § 1841(a).

607. 12 U.S.C. § 1842(c) (2000); *see, e.g.*, County Nat'l Bancorp. v. Board of Governors, 654 F.2d 1253, 1260 (8th Cir. 1981) (FRB may not "deny a merger on competitive grounds absent a finding of an antitrust violation"); Mercantile Tex. Corp. v. Board of Governors, 638 F.2d 1255, 1260-63 (5th Cir. 1981) (FRB may not employ "convenience and needs" consideration to create a more stringent standard than the Clayton Act).

608. 15 U.S.C. § 18a(c)(7).

609. 12 U.S.C. § 1849(b) (2000).

610. *Id.* § 1843(a) (2000).

Board determines whether the activity in which the bank holding company would be engaged as a result of the acquisition "is a proper incident to banking or managing or controlling banks."[611] To make that determination, it considers whether the "benefits to the public, such as greater convenience, increased competition, or gains in efficiency, outweigh possible adverse effects, such as undue concentration of resources, decreased or unfair competition, conflicts of interest, or unsound bank practices."[612] Copies of a bank holding company application to purchase nonbanks must be filed with the Department of Justice and the Federal Trade Commission at least thirty days before consummation of the transaction for it to be exempt from regular H-S-R Act reporting requirements.[613]

The Gramm-Leach-Bliley Financial Services Modernization Act was enacted in 1999.[614] It allows for the affiliation of banking, securities and insurance activities in new financial holding companies.[615] It amends the H-S-R Act to provide the Federal Trade Commission and the Department of Justice with jurisdiction over the antitrust review of nonbank acquisitions by financial holding companies which would not otherwise require approval under Sections 3 and 4 of the Bank Holding Company Act.[616]

The Office of Thrift Supervision regulates the formation of and acquisitions by savings and loan holding companies.[617] A savings and loan holding company is any company that directly or indirectly controls a federally insured savings and loan association.[618] The Director of the Office of Thrift Supervision is required to request and to consider a report from the Attorney General "on the competitive factors involved."[619] Finally, the Director of the Office of Thrift Supervision may not approve an acquisition that would violate codified standards similar to those of Section 7 of the Clayton Act unless he finds the anticompetitive effects of the transaction to be in the public interest by "meeting the convenience and needs of the community."[620] No H-S-R Act filing is required for these transactions.[621]

"Bridge banks" are institutions formed by the Federal Deposit Insurance Corporation that hold assets of one or more banks that are in default or are anticipated to become in default.[622] Bridge bank charters are granted by the Office of the Comptroller of the Currency and expire after two years.[623] The standards and procedures of the Bank Merger Act, including notification of the Department of

---

611. *Id.* § 1843(c)(8).
612. *Id.*
613. 15 U.S.C. § 18a(c)(8) (2000).
614. Pub. L. No. 106-102, 113 Stat. 1341, 1342, 1351, 1359-1361 (1999).
615. 12 U.S.C. § 1843(k) (2000).
616. 15 U.S.C. § 18a(c)(7), (8) (2000).
617. 12 U.S.C. § 1467a(e) (2000). That authority previously resided with the Federal Home Loan Bank Board. The Federal Institutions Reform Recovery Enforcement Act of 1989 abolished the Federal Home Loan Bank Board and transferred the authority to regulate the formation and acquisition of savings and loan holding companies to the newly created Director of the Office of Thrift Supervision. Pub. L. No. 101-73, § 401, 103 Stat. 183, 354.
618. 12 U.S.C. § 1467a(a)(1)(D) (2000).
619. *Id.* § 1467a(e)(2).
620. *Id.*
621. 15 U.S.C. § 18a(c)(7) (2000).
622. 12 U.S.C. § 1821(n) (2000).
623. *Id.* § 1821(n)(2).

Justice, apply to mergers and acquisitions involving bridge banks.[624] The responsible agency may allow the transaction to be consummated immediately to prevent failure.[625]

Congress has not addressed the issue of mergers of federally chartered credit unions or of federally chartered credit unions with state-chartered credit unions. Pursuant to the general regulatory authority granted to the National Credit Union Administration Board,[626] however, this board has promulgated regulations establishing procedures and standards governing consideration of these mergers.[627] Under the regulations, a federal credit union must submit a plan describing a proposed merger to the board. The credit union is not required to include in the merger plan any information regarding the impact on competition of the proposed merger. The plan is limited to information concerning the financial condition of the credit unions.[628] The regulations do not suggest that the board will consider any competitive issues.

While Congress has directed the banking agencies and the Department of Justice to evaluate transactions under the identical standard, in practice each has developed its own approach to examining mergers. The Federal Reserve Board, the Office of the Comptroller of the Currency, and the Department of Justice have jointly promulgated screening guidelines to determine those cases in which competitive consequences may require closer analysis.[629] The screens assume that an institution's locally derived deposits are a proxy for its competitive strength. From that point on, however, the banking agencies, on the one hand, and the Department of Justice, on the other, use different screening techniques that reflect the differing methods of analysis that each employs. In addition, the Federal Trade Commission can use its own guidelines in evaluating transactions with financial holding companies that are not subject to Federal Reserve approval under Sections 3 and 4 of the Bank Holding Company Act.

Both the banking agencies and the Department of Justice begin their analysis by determining the level of concentration in the relevant geographic markets using the Herfindahl-Hirschman Index (HHI).[630] Within each of those relevant geographic markets, the banking agencies include commercial bank deposits at 100 percent, and thrift deposits at 50 percent—the lesser percentage for thrift deposits representing that thrifts, on average, do not provide as many services as commercial banks.[631] The transaction passes the banking agencies' screening test if there is no geographic market in which the transaction increases the HHI by more than 200 points and results in an HHI greater than 1,800 points.[632] The screening tests are broader than

---

624. *Id.* § 1821(n)(8)(A). The DOJ has challenged an acquisition of a bridge bank. *See* United States v. Fleet/Norstar Fin. Group, Civ. No. 91-0021-P (D. Me. filed July 5, 1991).
625. 12 U.S.C. § 1821(n)(8)(A) (2000).
626. *Id.* § 1766.
627. 12 C.F.R. pt. 708b (2001).
628. *Id.*
629. Bank Merger Competitive Review—Introduction and Overview (1995) [hereinafter Screening Guidelines], *available at* www.usdoj.gov.atr.public.guidelines.6472.htm. The Office of the Comptroller of the Currency version of the screening guidelines, dated July 18, 1995, is OCC Advisory Letter 95-4.
630. *Id.* at 6-7. See part B.1.c(2) of Chapter III for a description of the HHI calculation.
631. Screening Guidelines, *supra* note 629, at 6-7.
632. *Id.*

the thresholds in the 1992 *Merger Guidelines*[633] because of the existence of competition from organizations that do not have locally derived deposits.[634]

The Department of Justice initially uses this screen, but it sometimes uses a tighter screen if the agency suspects that the banking agency screen fails to uncover the anticompetitiveness of the proposal.[635] The Department of Justice's tighter screen weights thrift deposits at zero and it uses a more narrow geographic market than the Federal Reserve Board, if justified.[636] As with the first screen, the transaction will not be challenged if the HHI is not raised by more than 200 and results in no market with the HHI exceeding 1800.[637] The Department of Justice on occasion will study more carefully transactions that pass even the tighter screen.[638]

The difference between the two screens is based on the differences between the banking agencies' and the Department of Justice's views of the relevant product and geographic markets. The banking agencies still rely on the *Philadelphia National Bank*[639] definition of the product market as the cluster of services known as commercial banking. The Department of Justice, on the other hand, has disaggregated the cluster into its constituent parts.

Among the markets on which the Department of Justice generally focuses is the market for unsecured loans to small businesses. Because thrifts do not generally offer this service, they are initially excluded from the tighter screen. Since the Department of Justice believes that the geographic market for such loans is very local, the agency will screen based on smaller geographic areas than does the Federal Reserve Board, if data about smaller areas is easily available and justifiable. The Department of Justice's disaggregation of the cluster also affects the sufficiency of the divestitures that it will accept as the solution to a transaction it believes is anticompetitive. Because it focuses on a particular product in concluding that a transaction is anticompetitive, the Department of Justice requires that the divested offices be significant suppliers of that product or service.[640] The banking agencies, on the other hand, require only that the deposits divested reduce the HHI level to that which is appropriate for the transaction.

E. Government Contracts

U.S. government policy is to promote "full and open competition" in the award of government contracts.[641] Though this policy has been codified in the government contracts setting in the Federal Acquisition Regulation (FAR), antitrust law in this area does not differ significantly from antitrust law in the nongovernment contracts

---

633. The 1992 *Merger Guidelines, supra* note 476, are discussed in Chapter III, and that chapter should be consulted for definitions and explanations of the terms and concepts discussed in the accompanying text.

634. Illinois Fin. Servs., 81 Fed. Res. Bull. 480 (May 1995).

635. Screening Guidelines, *supra* note 629, at 1-4.

636. *Id.* at 8-10.

637. *Id.* at 2.

638. *Id.*

639. 374 U.S. 321 (1963).

640. *See* J. Robert Kramer, Chief, Litigation II Section, Antitrust Div., "Mega-Mergers" in the Banking Industry, Remarks Before the ABA Antitrust Section (Apr. 14, 1999), *available at* www. usdoj.gov/atr/public/speeches/2650.htm.

641. Competition in Contracting Act, 10 U.S.C. § 2304 (2000), 41 U.S.C. § 253 (1994 & Supp. 1999). *See generally* 48 C.F.R. subpt. 3.301 (2000) (Federal Acquisition Regulation).

setting. The anticompetitive concerns are the same in regards to such actions as bid rigging,[642] market allocation,[643] and predatory pricing.[644] These types of activities are generally held per se illegal.[645] Additional provisions of FAR are intended to prevent anticompetitive behavior.[646] Although the government generally discourages anticompetitive behavior, when negotiating contracts the government may choose to permit what appears to be an anticompetitive agreement, such as a teaming agreement between the only two competitors, for the purpose of keeping its own costs down.

One concern specific to government contracting is a government contractor's immunity from antitrust laws as a federal instrumentality. This issue was addressed in *Name.Space, Inc. v. Network Solutions, Inc.*[647] In *Name.Space*, the Second Circuit found that Network Solutions, Inc. (NSI), the "master root zone server" for the Internet,[648] was immune under the antitrust law for its assignment of domain names because it is a federal instrumentality. Name.Space argued that NSI "abused its monopoly power over the domain name registration system to maintain its control of an essential facility, namely the root zone file."[649] Name.Space also argued that NSI was not entitled to immunity because none was expressly granted to it by Congress, "because there is no pervasive regulatory scheme over the [domain name system] mandating such immunity," and that a government contracting agent lacks the power to grant such immunity.[650]

The court rejected these arguments. The court refused to apply a status-based theory of sovereign immunity, stating that this type of application is too broad and that it may "improperly insulate NSI and other private entities that are or will be involved in administering the [domain name system] from liability for future anticompetitive conduct."[651] Rather, the court applied a conduct-based test. The court held that in this case the challenged conduct was "compelled by the explicit terms of the NSI's agreement with a government agency and by the government's

---

642. *See* 48 C.F.R. § 3.303(c) (2000) (identifying behavior patterns that are often associated with antitrust violations that are not necessarily improper but are sufficiently questionable to warrant notifying the appropriate authorities); *id.* § 3.301 (2000) (stating that collusive bidding is an anticompetitive practice that "may warrant criminal, civil, or administrative action against the participants").

643. *See* United States v. Koppers Co., Inc., 652 F.2d 290 (2d Cir.), *cert. denied*, 454 U.S. 1083 (1981) (holding that a classic market allocation scheme for government contracts was a per se violation of the Sherman Act).

644. FAR defines this practice as "buying-in." 48 C.F.R. § 3.501-1 (2000). FAR does not expressly make buying-in illegal, but 48 C.F.R. § 3.01-2 (2000) states that "[t]he contracting officer must take appropriate action to ensure buying-in losses are not recovered by the contractor through the pricing of (1) change orders or (2) follow-on contracts subject to cost analysis."

645. *See Koppers*, 652 F.2d 290.

646. For example, 48 C.F.R. § 3.103-1 (2000) provides that contracting officers must insert a Certificate of Independent Price Determination into their solicitations. The requirements for the certificate are outlined at 48 C.F.R. § 52.203-2 (2000). In addition, there are many requirements in FAR regarding "teaming arrangements," discussed *infra* at notes 658-61 and accompanying text.

647. 202 F.3d 573 (2d Cir. 2000).

648. *Id.* at 577.

649. *Id.* at 581.

650. *Id. See also* Otter Tail Power Co. v. United States, 410 U.S. 366, 378-79 (1973) (rejecting defense that anticompetitive actions were pursuant to government contract); Thomas v. Network Solutions, Inc., 176 F.3d 500 (D.C. Cir. 1999) (expressing doubt that a private contractor automatically shares the federal agency's immunity).

651. 202 F.3d at 581.

policies regarding the proper administration of the [domain name system],"[652] and thus NSI is entitled to antitrust immunity as a governmental instrumentality for the specific conduct at issue in this case.

Another concern that arises in connection with government contracts is the impact of the consolidation of the defense industry. In 1994, the Defense Science Board Task Force on Antitrust Aspects of Defense Industry Consolidation recommended that the Department of Defense apply the Department of Justice and Federal Trade Commission 1992 *Merger Guidelines*[653] and that the Department of Defense take an active role in advising the Department of Justice and Federal Trade Commission on defense industry mergers.[654] In May 1997, the Department of Defense's Defense Science Board Task Force on Vertical Integration and Supplier Decisions issued a report addressing vertical mergers within the defense industry. The report stated that while there could be potential problems involved with vertical mergers, there was no evidence that these problems currently existed.[655] The report recommended that the Department of Defense expand its current monitoring of this issue.[656] One year later, the Department of Justice and Department of Defense challenged the proposed merger of Lockheed Martin and Northrop Grumman partially based on vertical concerns.[657]

As a result of the consolidation of the defense industry, the Department of Defense also has refocused on the practice of "teaming." FAR allows for teaming, and even encourages the practice.[658] Nevertheless, the Department of Defense issued a memorandum in 1999 noting the increased use of both horizontal and vertical exclusive teaming arrangements and warning that inadequate competition was a potential result.[659] The memorandum suggested that contractors be advised at government information meetings with potential competitors that preestablished teaming arrangements would be scrutinized for any potential to inhibit competition.[660] Pursuant to this memorandum, the Defense Contract Audit Agency

---

652. *Id.* at 582. *See also* Medical Ass'n of Alabama v. Schweiker, 554 F. Supp. 955, 966 (M.D. Ala.) (dismissing complaint where private parties' actions were "wholly at the direction and with the consent of the federal defendants"), *aff'd*, 714 F.2d 107 (11th Cir. 1983).
653. *See* DEFENSE SCIENCE BOARD, ANTITRUST ASPECTS OF DEFENSE INDUSTRY CONSOLIDATION (1994).
654. *See id.*
655. *See* DEFENSE SCIENCE BOARD, VERTICAL INTEGRATION AND SUPPLIER DECISIONS (1997).
656. *See id.* at viii.
657. United States v. Lockheed Martin Corp. and Northrop Grumman Corp., No. 98-CV-00731 (D.D.C. Mar. 23, 1998) (complaint). Since that time, the DOJ has challenged several additional defense industry mergers and acquisitions where vertical concerns were raised. *See, e.g.*, United States v. Raytheon Co., 1998-1 Trade Cas. (CCH) ¶ 72,054 (D.D.C. 1998) (consent order); United States v. Raytheon Co., 1997-2 Trade Cas. (CCH) ¶ 72,029 (D.D.C. 1997) (consent order).
658. 48 C.F.R. § 9.602 (2000) provides that:
    (a) Contractor team arrangements may be desirable from both a Government and industry standpoint in order to enable the companies involved to (1) complement each other's unique capabilities and (2) offer the Government the best combination of performance, cost, and delivery for the system or product being acquired.
    (b) Contractor team arrangements may be particularly appropriate in complex research and development acquisitions, but may be used in other appropriate acquisitions, including production.
659. *See* Under Secretary of Defense (Acquisition and Technology), Memorandum for Secretaries of the Military Departments, Directors of Defense Agencies, and Director, Defense Procurement, re: Anticompetitive Teaming (Jan. 5, 1999).
660. *Id.*

issued revised audit guidelines regarding anticompetitive exclusive teaming arrangements in 1999.[661]

F. Health Care

1. *Introduction*

Ever since its ruling in *Goldfarb v. Virginia State Bar*[662] that the "learned professions" were not exempt from the antitrust laws, the Supreme Court has affirmed that the antitrust laws apply to the health care industry.[663] The Court has held that the activities of health care providers—both individual providers such as physicians[664] and institutional providers such as hospitals[665]—sufficiently affect interstate commerce to come within the reach of the antitrust laws. Despite arguments that the market for health care goods and services operates differently from other commercial markets, the Court has refused to create special exceptions under the antitrust laws for the health care professions.[666]

To adapt to a rapidly changing marketplace, many individual and institutional providers have undertaken new alliances in the form of joint ventures, mergers, and other collaborative activities. While these alliances may be procompetitive by increasing the providers' efficiency, such collaboration among formerly competing providers also can pose risks of price fixing, group boycotts, market division, monopolization, and other traditional concerns of the antitrust laws.

In 1996, the Department of Justice and the Federal Trade Commission issued nine statements of enforcement policy and analytical principles relating to health care and antitrust (1996 *Health Care Statements*).[667] Superseding earlier statements issued in 1993 and 1994,[668] these statements were designed to provide guidance to the health

---

661. *See* DCAA Memorandum for Regional Directors, Audit Guidance/Management Memorandum No. 00-PFC-084(R), July 26, 1999 (superceding MRD-99-PFC-038(R)).

662. 421 U.S. 773, 786-88 (1975). The Supreme Court applied the antitrust laws to the activities of the American Medical Association in 1943, *see* American Med. Ass'n v. United States, 317 U.S. 519, 528 (1943), but it did not expressly decide whether a physician's medical practice constituted "trade" under the Sherman Act, leaving unsettled the extent to which the antitrust laws could be applied to the activities of the health care professions generally.

663. Issues relating to concerted action under § 1 of the Sherman Act and unilateral conduct under § 2 of the Sherman Act are discussed in Chapters I and II, respectively, of this treatise.

664. *See, e.g.*, Summit Health, Ltd. v. Pinhas, 500 U.S. 322, 332-33 (1991).

665. *See, e.g.*, Hospital Bldg. Co. v. Trustees of Rex Hosp., 425 U.S. 738, 739-40 (1976).

666. *See, e.g.*, Jefferson Parish Hosp. Dist. No. 2 v. Hyde, 466 U.S. 2, 26-29 (1984) (rejecting argument that "market imperfections" and other factors specific to the health care market justified the revocation of the per se rule against tying); Arizona v. Maricopa County Med. Soc'y, 457 U.S. 332, 348-49 (1982) (affirming that Sherman Act establishes rule for price-fixing agreements applicable to all industries). In recent years, attempts have been made at both the federal and the state level to enact legislation providing an antitrust exemption for physicians to negotiate collectively with health plans regarding fees and other terms. While the legislation proposed in Congress has not passed, both Texas and Washington have enacted such exemptions. S.B. 1468, 76th Leg. (Tex. 1999); WASH. REV. CODE § 43.72.310 (1993 & Supp. 1997).

667. U.S. DEP'T OF JUSTICE & FEDERAL TRADE COMM'N, STATEMENTS OF ANTITRUST ENFORCEMENT POLICY IN HEALTH CARE (1996) [hereinafter 1996 HEALTH CARE STATEMENTS], *reprinted in* 4 Trade Reg. Rep. (CCH) ¶ 13,153 *and* Appendix F to this treatise.

668. U.S. DEP'T OF JUSTICE & FEDERAL TRADE COMM'N, STATEMENTS OF ANTITRUST ENFORCEMENT POLICY IN HEALTH CARE (1993), *reprinted in* 4 Trade Reg. Rep. (CCH) ¶ 13,151; U.S. DEP'T OF JUSTICE & FEDERAL TRADE COMM'N, STATEMENTS OF ENFORCEMENT POLICY AND ANALYTICAL

care industry concerning the agencies' enforcement policies and to reduce uncertainty in the application of the antitrust laws to health care mergers, joint ventures, and other potentially procompetitive activities. As part of the 1996 changes, the enforcement agencies updated and expanded the *Statements* dealing with physician and multiprovider network joint ventures.

The *Statements* provide a number of antitrust "safety zones," which describe circumstances under which the enforcement agencies will not challenge certain conduct among health care providers under the antitrust laws absent extraordinary circumstances. The statements also outline the framework that the agencies will use to analyze conduct falling outside of the antitrust safety zones.

The 1996 *Health Care Statements* address the following activities in the health care industry: (1) hospital mergers, (2) hospital joint ventures involving expensive (e.g., high-technology) health care equipment, (3) hospital joint ventures involving expensive (e.g., specialized clinical) health care services, (4) providers' collective provision of non-fee-related information to purchasers of health care services, (5) providers' collective provision of fee-related information to purchasers of health care services, (6) provider participation in exchanges of cost and price information, (7) joint purchasing arrangements among health care providers, (8) physician network joint ventures, and (9) multiprovider networks. The individual statements are discussed below.

More recently, the Federal Trade Commission has pursued enforcement activities against the pharmaceutical industry. Antitrust enforcement in this context has focused primarily on agreements between brand name drug manufacturers and their rival generic companies to delay the introduction of generic alternatives into the marketplace. However, the agency also has demonstrated a willingness to challenge the exclusive licensing practices of generic drug manufacturers that deprive competitors of ingredients necessary for those competitors to effectively compete.

2. Staff Privileges

a. DENIAL, TERMINATION, OR LIMITATION OF STAFF PRIVILEGES

Peer review of physicians holding or applying for hospital or medical staff privileges has given rise to numerous antitrust claims. The courts have recognized that peer review has the potential to be procompetitive by ensuring that only competent, professional, and otherwise qualified practitioners are permitted to practice at health care institutions.[669] On the other hand, staff privileges decisions

---

PRINCIPLES RELATING TO HEALTH CARE AND ANTITRUST (1994) [hereinafter 1994 HEALTH CARE STATEMENTS], *reprinted in* 4 Trade Reg. Rep. (CCH) ¶ 13,152.

669. *See, e.g.,* Willman v. Heartland Hosp. E., 34 F.3d 605, 610 (8th Cir. 1994) (monitoring physician competence through peer review is in public interest, and revocation of privileges because of legitimate concerns about quality care is lawful objective), *cert. denied*, 415 U.S. 1018 (1995); Oksanen v. Page Mem'l Hosp., 945 F.2d 696, 706 (4th Cir. 1991) (en banc) (finding peer review a "legitimate activity designed to enhance the quality of care and to provide a harmonious working environment for all the hospital's staff"), *cert. denied*, 502 U.S. 1074 (1992); Mathews v. Lancaster Gen. Hosp., 883 F. Supp. 1016, 1044 (E.D. Pa. 1995) (terminating staff privileges furthers legitimate interest by avoiding negligence liability), *aff'd*, 87 F.3d 624 (3d Cir. 1996); Vakharia v. Swedish Covenant Hosp., 824 F. Supp. 769, 780 (N.D. Ill. 1993) ("Terminating privileges is not necessarily anticompetitive. Hospitals compete with each other, and the quality of medical care and lower prices resulting from lower malpractice premiums are means of

can raise a risk of anticompetitive abuse insofar as they are typically made upon the recommendations of members of the medical staff who may be direct or indirect competitors of the physician under review. The courts have recognized that a denial or termination of staff privileges arguably can insulate the other medical staff members from competition by the physician under review and therefore can raise conspiracy, group boycott, or other antitrust concerns under Section 1 of the Sherman Act.[670] Exclusions of health care practitioners in certain markets also have resulted in claims of monopolization, attempt or conspiracy to monopolize, or tying in violation of Section 2 of the Sherman Act.[671]

Although a number of courts dismissed earlier cases involving staff privileges decisions on the ground that the plaintiff failed to demonstrate sufficient impact on

---

competition."); Marin v. Citizens Mem'l Hosp., 700 F. Supp. 354, 361 (S.D. Tex. 1988) ("restricting staff privileges to doctors who maintain a basic level of medical competency is ultimately pro-competitive not anti-competitive"); Friedman v. Delaware County Mem'l Hosp., 672 F. Supp. 171, 190 (E.D. Pa. 1987) (finding exclusion of physician procompetitive), aff'd, 849 F.2d 600 (3d Cir. 1988); Quinn v. Kent Gen. Hosp., 617 F. Supp. 1226, 1239 (D. Del. 1985) ("peer review process is arguably procompetitive, for by monitoring the qualifications and performance of physicians it may compensate for the relative lack of information about these matters by consumers").

670. See, e.g., Patrick v. Burget, 800 F.2d 1498, 1506 (9th Cir. 1986) ("The peer review process allows doctors to agree to eliminate a competitor from the market because they believe his or her product is substandard. An analogous scheme would allow General Motors, Chrysler and Ford to review the safety of Toyotas to determine if the public should be allowed to drive them. Clearly such an arrangement would raise antitrust concerns."), rev'd on other grounds, 486 U.S. 94 (1988); Weiss v. York Hosp., 745 F.2d 786, 819-20 (3d Cir. 1984) (holding that a hospital's denial of staff privileges to osteopaths was similar to traditional boycott), cert. denied, 470 U.S. 1060 (1985); Johnson v. Nyack Hosp., 891 F. Supp. 155, 157 (S.D.N.Y. 1995) (recognizing how the power wielded by those that make hospital staff privileges decisions "may be abused for any of a panoply of reasons . . . not the least of them racial, religious and ethnic bias, anticompetitive motives, and personal animus"), aff'd, 86 F.3d 8 (2d Cir. 1996); Pao v. Holy Redeemer Hosp., 547 F. Supp. 484, 490 (E.D. Pa. 1982).

671. See, e.g., Country of Toulomne v. Sonora Cmty. Hosp., 236 F.3d 1148, 1160 (9th Cir. 2001) (affirming summary judgment for defendants on tying and conspiracy to restrain trade claims); Willman, 34 F.3d 605 (affirming summary judgment for defendants on essential facilities and monopoly leveraging claims); Tarabishi v. McAlester Reg'l Hosp., 951 F.2d 1558 (10th Cir. 1991) (affirming judgment for defendants on § 2 claims where plaintiff failed to prove that hospital had monopoly power), cert. denied, 505 U.S. 1206 (1992); Oksanen, 945 F.2d at 710 (affirming summary judgment for defendants on § 2 claims); Beard v. Parkview Hosp., 912 F.2d 138, 144-45 (6th Cir. 1990) (same); McKenzie v. Mercy Hosp., 854 F.2d 365, 368-71 (10th Cir. 1988) (same); Collins v. Associated Pathologists, Ltd., 844 F.2d 473, 480 (7th Cir.) (same), cert. denied, 488 U.S. 852 (1988); Potters Med. Ctr. v. City Hosp. Ass'n, 800 F.2d 568 (6th Cir. 1986) (reversing summary judgment for defendants to determine whether hospital had monopoly power); Weiss, 745 F.2d at 831 (reversing finding of liability on § 2 grounds); Kerth v. Hamot Health Found., 989 F. Supp. 691 (W.D. Pa. 1997) (granting summary judgment on monopoly claims due to lack of evidence of concerted action), aff'd without op., 159 F.3d 1351 (3d Cir.), cert. denied, 525 U.S. 1055 (1998); Farr v. Healtheast, Inc., 1993-1 Trade Cas. (CCH) ¶ 70,294 (E.D. Pa. 1993) (granting summary judgment for defendants on § 2 claims); Robles v. Humana Hosp. Cartersville, 785 F. Supp. 989 (N.D. Ga. 1992) (same); Brown v. Our Lady of Lourdes Med. Ctr., 767 F. Supp. 618, 631 (D.N.J. 1991) (same), aff'd, 961 F.2d 207 (3d Cir. 1992); Bhan v. NME Hosps., 669 F. Supp. 998 (E.D. Cal. 1987) (same), aff'd, 929 F.2d 1404 (9th Cir.), cert. denied, 502 U.S. 994 (1991). The FTC also has brought enforcement actions challenging the exclusion of classes of providers. See Diran M. Seropian, M.D., 115 F.T.C. 891 (1992); Medical Staff of Holy Cross Hosp., 114 F.T.C. 555 (1991); Medical Staff of Broward Gen. Med. Ctr., 114 F.T.C. 542 (1991); Medical Staff of Mem'l Med. Ctr., 110 F.T.C. 541 (1988); Forbes Health Sys. Med. Staff, 94 F.T.C. 1042 (1979).

interstate commerce to establish jurisdiction under the Sherman Act,[672] the Supreme Court in *Summit Health, Ltd. v. Pinhas*[673] found that a single hospital's revocation of an ophthalmologist's staff privileges had a sufficient nexus with interstate commerce to support antitrust jurisdiction. *Summit Health* has made it more difficult for peer review defendants successfully to argue for dismissal of staff privileges cases on the ground that their actions had a de minimis effect on interstate commerce. Subsequent courts have found the plaintiffs in such cases to have met the interstate commerce requirement.[674]

Nevertheless, plaintiffs rarely have successfully invoked the antitrust laws to overturn hospital staffing decisions.[675] Many courts have dismissed the complaint or granted summary judgment on behalf of the defendants in such cases on the ground that the plaintiff did not suffer antitrust injury and hence did not have standing to bring an action under the antitrust laws.[676] For example, where the plaintiff's alleged

---

672. *See, e.g.*, Sarin v. Samaritan Health Ctr., 813 F.2d 755 (6th Cir. 1987); Seglin v. Esau, 769 F.2d 1274 (7th Cir. 1985); Loiterman v. Antani, No. 90-C-983, 1990 WL 91062 (N.D. Ill. June 28, 1990); Thompson v. Wise Gen. Hosp., 707 F. Supp. 849 (W.D. Va. 1989), *aff'd without op.*, 896 F.2d 547 (4th Cir.), *cert. denied*, 498 U.S. 846 (1990); Jaffee v. Horton Mem'l Hosp., 680 F. Supp. 125 (S.D.N.Y. 1988); Rosenberg v. Healthcorp Affiliates, 663 F. Supp. 222 (N.D. Ill. 1987). The requirement of establishing a restraint on interstate commerce is discussed in part B.2 of Chapter I.

673. 500 U.S. 322, 332 (1991).

674. *See, e.g.*, BCB Anesthesia Care, Ltd. v. Passavant Mem'l Area Hosp. Ass'n, 36 F.3d 664, 666 (7th Cir. 1994); Funtes v. South Hills Cardiology, 946 F.2d 196, 201 (3d Cir. 1991); *Oksanen*, 945 F.2d at 702 n.1; Mid-Michigan Radiology Assocs. v. Central Mich. Cmty. Hosp., 1995-1 Trade Cas. (CCH) ¶ 70,943 (E.D. Mich. 1995); Pudlo v. Adamski, 789 F. Supp. 247, 250 n.2 (N.D. Ill. 1992), *aff'd without op.*, 2 F.3d 1153 (7th Cir. 1993), *cert. denied*, 510 U.S. 1072 (1994); *Our Lady of Lourdes Med. Ctr.*, 767 F. Supp. at 627.

675. Peer review plaintiffs have occasionally succeeded at trial on the merits of their antitrust claims. *See, e.g., Patrick*, 486 U.S. 94 (upholding jury award of $650,000 to plaintiff where defendants were found to have violated §§ 1 and 2 by initiating and participating in peer review proceedings to eliminate competition provided by plaintiff); Boczar v. Manatee Hosps. & Health Sys., 993 F.2d 1514 (11th Cir. 1993) (upholding jury award of $150,000 to plaintiff obstetrician/gynecologist whose hospital staff privileges had been suspended); Oltz v. St. Peter's Cmty. Hosp., 861 F.2d 1440 (9th Cir. 1988) (upholding jury verdict on the question of liability for plaintiff nurse anesthetist whose staff privileges were terminated as a result of hospital's submission to pressure from group of competing M.D. anesthesiologists seeking to exclude plaintiff as a competitor); *Weiss*, 745 F.2d 786 (holding plaintiff osteopath entitled to relief on claim that medical staff violated § 1).

   More frequently, plaintiffs' success in staff privileges disputes have been measured by surviving preliminary motions, particularly in cases where (1) the plaintiff was not a physician, *see, e.g.*, Sweeney v. Athens Reg'l Med. Ctr., 709 F. Supp. 1563 (M.D. Ga. 1989) (nurse midwife); Nurse Midwifery Assocs. v. Hibbett, 689 F. Supp. 799 (M.D. Tenn. 1988) (nurse midwives), *aff'd in part and rev'd in part*, 918 F.2d 605 (6th Cir. 1990), *modified*, 927 F.2d 904 (6th Cir. 1990), *cert. denied*, 502 U.S. 952 (1991); (2) the peer review action allegedly lacked fair notice and hearing procedures, *see, e.g.*, Miller v. Indiana Hosp., 843 F.2d 139 (3d Cir.), *cert. denied*, 488 U.S. 870 (1988); or (3) the plaintiff offered evidence that the peer review action was motivated by considerations other than his competence or professional conduct, *see, e.g.*, Bolt v. Halifax Hosp. Med. Ctr., 891 F.2d 810 (11th Cir.) (en banc) (finding a possible inference that defendants acted to achieve ends not dictated by legitimate business concerns), *cert. denied*, 495 U.S. 924 (1990); *Miller*, 843 F.2d 139 (finding a fact issue existed over whether defendants revoked plaintiff's privileges because of concern over his competence or out of anticompetitive motivation); Shah v. Mem'l Hosp., 1988-2 Trade Cas. (CCH) ¶ 68,199 (W.D. Va. 1988) (finding the evidence tended to exclude possibility that defendants acted for procompetitive reasons).

676. *See, e.g.*, Mathews v. Lancaster Gen. Hosp., 87 F.3d 624 (3d Cir. 1996) (affirming summary judgment for defendants where plaintiff showed injury only to a competitor, not to competition); Kumar v. National Med. Enters., 1995-2 Trade Cas. (CCH) ¶ 70,868 (9th Cir. 1994) (per curiam) (affirming summary judgment for defendant because plaintiff failed to show injury to competition

injury reflects "really only harm to the individual doctor, and not to competition within the market place," the plaintiff has not suffered antitrust injury and therefore lacks standing to bring an antitrust claim.[677] Such cases generally have been resolved

in the market for neonatal care); Todorov v. DCH Healthcare Auth., 921 F.2d 1438, 1446, 1454 (11th Cir. 1991); Piccone v. Board of Dirs. of Doctor's Hosp. of Staten Island, Inc., 2000-2 Trade Cas. (CCH) ¶ 73,032 (S.D.N.Y. 2000) (dismissing action where plaintiff alleged only injury to himself as a competitor and made no specific allegations concerning injury to competition); Evac LLC v. Pataki, 89 F. Supp. 2d 250 (N.D.N.Y. 2000) (dismissing complaint for failure to allege market-wide injury resulting from plaintiff's exclusion from the market); Feldman v. Palmetto Gen'l Hosp., 980 F. Supp. 467 (S.D. Fla. 1997) (dismissing complaint because plaintiff failed to allege antitrust injury; plaintiff alleged injury to himself but not to competition within the relevant market); Doctor's Hosp. v. Southeast Med. Alliance, Inc., 889 F. Supp. 879 (E.D. La. 1995) (granting summary judgment for defendant where expert testimony that prices would increase and consumer choice would be reduced was speculative and lacking in factual basis); Leak v. Grant Med. Ctr., 893 F. Supp. 757 (S.D. Ohio 1995) (granting summary judgment for defendant because there was no antitrust injury where plaintiff anesthesiologist still held privileges at other hospitals); Mid-Michigan Radiology Assocs., 1995-1 Trade Cas. (CCH) ¶ 70,943 (complaint dismissed on antitrust standing grounds because plaintiff was replaced by another provider and there was only a reshuffling of competitors); Levine v. Central Fla. Med. Affiliates, 864 F. Supp. 1175 (M.D. Fla. 1994) (affirming summary judgment for defendants because plaintiff internist did not show antitrust injury where plaintiff had privileges at other area hospitals), aff'd on other grounds, 72 F.3d 1538 (11th Cir.), cert. denied, 519 U.S. 820 (1996); Huhta v. Children's Hosp., 1994-1 Trade Cas. (CCH) ¶ 70,619 (E.D. Pa. 1994) (granting summary judgment where plaintiff failed to raise genuine issue as to either antitrust injury or propriety of his status as antitrust enforcer), aff'd, 52 F.3d 315 (3d Cir. 1995); Purgess v. Sharrock, 806 F. Supp. 1102, 1106-08 (S.D.N.Y. 1992) (same), supplemented, 1993-2 Trade Cas. (CCH) ¶ 70,349 (1992); Robles v. Humana Hosp. Centerville, 785 F. Supp. 989, 999 (N.D. Ga. 1992) (same); Colorado Chiropractic Council v. Porter Mem'l Hosp., 650 F. Supp. 231 (D. Colo. 1986); Ivey v. Galen Hosps. of Tex., Inc., 2000-1 Trade Cas. (CCH) ¶ 72,888 (Tex. App. 2000) (granting summary judgment where there was no reduction in the number of medical procedures performed despite plaintiff's exclusion from the market) (unpublished opinion); Zipper v. Health Midwest, 978 S.W.2d 398 (Mo. Ct. App. 1998) (plaintiff failed to show any anticompetitive effect in the market or harm to consumers such as an increase in the cost or decrease in the quality of orthopedic services); see also BCB Anesthesia Care, 36 F.3d at 669 ("A staffing decision does not itself constitute an antitrust injury."). But see Angelico v. Lehigh Valley Hosp., 184 F.3d 268 (3d Cir. 1999) (physician has standing to assert antitrust claims against rival physicians and hospitals based on allegations that they conspired to exclude him from a relevant market); Bhan v. NME Hosps., 669 F. Supp. 998, 1012-15 (E.D. Cal. 1987) (loss of business is an injury antitrust laws were designed to forestall), aff'd, 929 F.2d 1404 (9th Cir.), cert. denied, 502 U.S. 994 (1991); Odom v. Fairbanks Mem'l Hosp., 999 P.2d 123 (Alaska 2000) (plaintiff has standing to sue for antitrust violations where a prima facie case is sufficiently alleged); Odom v. Lee, 999 P.2d 755 (Alaska 2000) (same).

677. Wagner v. Magellan Health Servs., Inc., 121 F. Supp. 2d 673, 681-83 (N.D. Ill. 2000) (neither injury to plaintiff's business and professional interest nor alleged reduction in the number of suppliers sufficient to show harm to competition); Alpern v. Cavorocchi, 1999-1 Trade Cas. (CCH) ¶ 72,514 (E.D. Pa. 1999) (finding the challenged conduct to be procompetitive where it resulted in a net increase in the number of competing physician practice groups); Parks v. Hillsdale Cmty. Health Ctr., 1999-1 Trade Cas. (CCH) ¶ 72,555 (W.D. Mich. 1999) (granting summary judgment where plaintiff showed only injury from normal competition); Huhta, 1994-1 Trade Cas. (CCH) ¶ 70,619 (loss of patient referrals and loss of income); see also Patel v. Scotland Mem'l Hosp., 1996-2 Trade Cas. (CCH) ¶ 71,469 (4th Cir. 1996) (affirming dismissal of a complaint where plaintiff alleged only injury to herself, not to competition in relevant markets); Mathews v. Lancaster Gen. Hosp., 883 F. Supp. 1016, 1044-46 (E.D. Pa. 1995) (granting summary judgment for lack of antitrust standing where plaintiff alleged "essentially harm to himself only. From the standpoint of the consumer, there has been no meaningful change in the market."), aff'd, 87 F.3d 624 (3d Cir. 1996); Levine, 864 F. Supp. 1175 (granting summary judgment on ground that plaintiff had not suffered any antitrust injury because, during the time his privileges were suspended by defendant hospitals, he was able to compete successfully by admitting patients to

on preliminary motions in the defendants' favor on a variety of grounds, including lack of evidence of anticompetitive effects;[678] the defendants' lack of capacity to conspire[679] or absence of evidence of conspiracy-in-fact;[680] the defendants' immunity under the Health Care Quality Improvement Act of 1986 (HCQIA);[681] the state action doctrine;[682] the Local Government Antitrust Act of 1984;[683] the lack of personal jurisdiction over the defendants;[684] the failure to exhaust administrative remedies;[685] and the bar of the statute of limitations.[686]

In order to establish the element of concerted action in a claim under Section 1, the plaintiff must show evidence of an agreement between two or more separate entities. The general rule, sometimes known as the "intraenterprise conspiracy doctrine," is that a corporation and its directors, officers, employees, or other agents constitute a single enterprise and hence are legally incapable of conspiring with each other.[687] Because a hospital board's adverse decision on a physician's staff privileges usually is taken after the board has reviewed the recommendations of the hospital's medical staff committees (whose members may be direct or indirect competitors of the physician), the peer review plaintiff typically seeks to show concerted action by alleging the existence of an unlawful agreement between the hospital and its medical staff, the hospital and individual members of its medical staff, and/or among the individual members of the medical staff. There is a split among the courts as to whether a hospital has the legal capacity to conspire with the members of its medical staff.[688]

---

other hospitals in market); *Robles*, 785 F. Supp. at 997-99 (granting summary judgment where plaintiff alleged only harm to individual doctor, not to competition).

678. *See infra* note 696 and accompanying text.

679. *See, e.g.*, Alba v. Marietta Mem'l Hosp., 2000-1 Trade Cas. (CCH) ¶ 72,774 (6th Cir. 2000) (a hospital and its medical staff cannot conspire as a matter of law); *Patel*, 1996-2 Trade Cas. (CCH) ¶ 71,469 (intracorporate conspiracy doctrine barred cardiologists' peer review claim); Muzquiz v. W.A. Foote Mem'l Hosp., 70 F.3d 422 (6th Cir. 1995) (same); Urdinaran v. Aarons, 115 F. Supp. 2d 484 (D.N.J. 2000) (a hospital and its medical staff cannot conspire as a matter of law); *see also infra* notes 687-88 and accompanying text.

680. *See infra* notes 689-94 and accompanying text.

681. 42 U.S.C. §§ 11101-11152 (1994); *see infra* notes 697-706 and accompanying text.

682. *See infra* notes 892-99 and accompanying text.

683. 15 U.S.C. §§ 34-36 (2000); *see, e.g.*, Cohn v. Bond, 953 F.2d 154, 157-58 (4th Cir. 1991), *cert. denied*, 505 U.S. 1230 (1992); Sandcrest Outpatient Servs. v. Cumberland County Hosp. Sys., 853 F.2d 1139 (4th Cir. 1988); Martin v. Mem'l Hosp., 881 F. Supp. 1087, 1095 (S.D. Miss. 1995), *rev'd on other grounds*, 86 F.3d 1391 (5th Cir. 1996); Crosby v. Hospital Auth., 873 F. Supp. 1568, 1581 (M.D. Ga. 1995), *aff'd*, 93 F.3d 1515 (11th Cir. 1996), *cert. denied*, 520 U.S. 1116 (1997); Scara v. Bradley Mem'l Hospital, 1993-2 Trade Cas. (CCH) ¶ 70,353 (E.D. Tenn. 1993); Sweeney v. Athens Reg'l Med. Ctr., 705 F. Supp. 1556, 1562 (N.D. Ga. 1989).

684. *See, e.g.*, Canady v. National Hosp. for Orthopedics & Rehab., 1995-1 Trade Cas. (CCH) ¶ 71,021 (D.D.C. 1995).

685. *See, e.g.*, Rogers v. Columbia/HCA of Cent. La., 961 F. Supp. 960 (W.D. La. 1997).

686. *See, e.g.*, Johnson v. Nyack Hosp., 86 F.3d 8 (2d Cir. 1996); Mir v. Little Co. of Mary Hosp., 844 F.2d 646 (9th Cir. 1988); Baker v. Chagrin Valley Med. Corp., 1985-1 Trade Cas. (CCH) ¶ 66,622 (N.D. Ohio 1985).

687. *See* Copperweld Corp. v. Independence Tube Corp., 467 U.S. 752, 777 (1984) (parent corporation and wholly owned subsidiary are legally incapable of conspiring). The *Copperweld* doctrine is discussed in part B.1.b of Chapter I.

688. *See* part B.1.b of Chapter I; *see also* Alba v. Marietta Mem'l Hosp., 202 F.3d 267 (6th Cir. 2000) (dismissing § 1 challenge because officers and staff of a single hospital are not separate economic actors); Urdinaran v. Aarons, 115 F. Supp. 2d 484 (D.N.J. 2000) (a hospital and its medical staff cannot conspire as a matter of law); Kerth v. Hamot Health Found., 989 F. Supp. 691 (W.D. Pa. 1997) (granting summary judgment for defendants due to lack of evidence of concerted action

Assuming that a court finds the peer review defendants to have the legal capacity to conspire, the plaintiff also must prove that they did, in fact, conspire.[689] Because a hospital is legally entitled to make unilateral decisions regarding membership on its medical staff,[690] the peer review plaintiff must offer evidence "that tends to exclude the possibility of independent action"[691] by the hospital concerning his staff privileges in order to survive a motion for summary judgment.[692] Evidence concerning the defendants' objectives has been found relevant in determining the plausibility of an inference of conspiracy among them. Lower courts have attempted to distinguish peer review actions undertaken for the procompetitive reasons of

---

among hospital, cardiologists, and competing surgery group to eliminate plaintiff as a competitor), *aff'd without op.*, 159 F.3d 1351 (3d Cir.), *cert. denied*, 525 U.S. 1055 (1998).

689. *See* Le Baud v. Frische, 1998-2 Trade Cas. (CCH) ¶ 72,242 (10th Cir. 1998) (dismissing antitrust claims where there was no evidence of conspiracy and the hospital was found to have acted independently and unilaterally in revoking plaintiff's privileges); Ostrzenski v. Columbia Hosp. for Women Found., 158 F.3d 1289 (D.C. Cir. 1998) (affirming summary judgment for defendants where "no reasonable jury" could find the termination of plaintiffs' hospital privileges was the result of an alleged group boycott); Beyer v. Lakeview Cmty. Hosp., 1998-1 Trade Cas. (CCH) ¶ 72,196 (W.D. Mich. 1998) (finding sufficient evidence that the revocation of plaintiff's privileges resulted from independent action), *aff'd without op.*, 187 F.3d 634 (6th Cir. 1999); *Kerth*, 989 F. Supp. 691 (granting summary judgment for defendants due to lack of evidence of concerted action among hospital, cardiologists, and competing surgery group to eliminate plaintiff as a competitor).

690. BCB Anesthesia Care, Ltd. v. Passavant Mem'l Area Hosp. Ass'n, 36 F.3d 664, 667 (7th Cir. 1994) (hospital has "unquestioned right to exercise some control over the identity and number to whom it accords staff privileges"). Hospitals are not only entitled to make such decisions, they are legally required to exercise reasonable care in the selection, retention, and monitoring of the members of their medical staffs under state law. *See, e.g.*, Insinga v. LaBella, 543 So. 2d 209, 213-14 (Fla. 1989) (at least 17 other states have applied corporate negligence doctrine to hospital's selection and retention of its medical staff); Thomson v. Nason Hosp., 591 A.2d 703, 706-07 (Pa. 1991) (under doctrine of corporate negligence, hospital owes nondelegable duty to patient to, among other things, select and retain only competent physicians). In addition, all 50 states have statutes governing aspects of peer review by hospitals. *See* AMERICAN MED. ASS'N, A COMPENDIUM OF STATE PEER REVIEW IMMUNITY LAWS vi (1988).

691. Monsanto Co. v. Spray-Rite Serv. Corp., 465 U.S. 752, 768 (1984); *see also* County of Tuolumne v. Sonora Cmty. Hosp., 236 F.3d 1148, 1156-57 (9th Cir. 2001) (affirming summary judgment based on lack of evidence that hospital's elaborate reviews of plaintiff's application for privileges was inconsistent with independent, nonconspiratorial conduct); Vakharia v. Swedish Covenant Hosp., 190 F.3d 799 (7th Cir. 1999) (affirming summary judgment against plaintiff who failed to provide any evidence of a conspiracy between defendant hospital and the association that prepared a report upon which hospital relied in terminating plaintiff's staff privileges), *cert. denied*, 530 U.S. 1297.(2000); Oksanen v. Page Mem'l Hosp., 945 F.2d 696, 706 (4th Cir. 1991) (en banc) ("Simply making a peer review recommendation does not prove the existence of a conspiracy; there must be something more such as a conscious commitment by the medical staff to coerce the hospital into accepting its recommendation."); Egan v. Athol Mem'l Hosp., 971 F. Supp. 37 (D. Mass. 1997) (granting summary judgment where court found no evidence that tended to exclude the possibility that the hospital board acted unilaterally in terminating plaintiff's privileges), *aff'd without op.*, 134 F.3d 361 (1st Cir. 1998).

692. *See* Matsushita Elec. Indus. Co. v. Zenith Radio Corp., 475 U.S. 574, 588 (1986) (inference of conspiracy cannot be supported solely by evidence of "conduct [which is] as consistent with permissible competition as with illegal conspiracy"); Payne v. Harris Methodist H-E-B, 2001-1 Trade Cas. (CCH) ¶ 73,169 (N.D. Tex. 2001) (summary judgment granted where plaintiff failed to provide evidence of a conspiracy involving peer review participants).

improving the quality of care or increasing efficiency of hospital operations[693] from those undertaken with an anticompetitive purpose of restraining competition.[694]

Courts generally apply a rule of reason analysis for staff privileges litigation under Section 1.[695] A number of cases have been dismissed under the rule of reason

---

693. *See, e.g.*, Willman v. Heartland Hosp. E., 34 F.3d 605, 610-12 (8th Cir. 1994) (affirming summary judgment where evidence relating to termination of plaintiff's hospital privileges was as consistent with lawful motive of promoting quality care as with anticompetitive motive), *cert. denied*, 515 U.S. 1131 (1995); Todorov v. DCH Healthcare Auth., 921 F.2d 1438, 1456-59 (11th Cir. 1991) (affirming summary judgment where evidence supported board's procompetitive reasons for denial of privileges); Cooper v. Forsyth County Hosp. Auth., 789 F.2d 278, 280-82 (4th Cir.) (affirming summary judgment where plaintiff did not rebut defendants' affidavits that they acted on quality-of-care grounds), *cert. denied*, 479 U.S. 972 (1986); Mathews v. Lancaster Gen. Hosp., 883 F. Supp. 1016, 1037-41 (E.D. Pa. 1995) (granting summary judgment where plaintiff offered no evidence that tended to exclude possibility that hospital acted unilaterally), *aff'd*, 87 F.3d 624 (3d Cir. 1996); Williamson v. Sacred Heart Hosp., No. 89-30084-RV, 1993 WL 543002, at *35-38 (N.D. Fla. May 28, 1993) (granting summary judgment where denial of privileges was "at least as consistent with rational, independent business conduct as with an antitrust conspiracy"), *aff'd*, 1995-1 Trade Cas. (CCH) ¶ 70,905 (11th Cir. 1994) (unpublished opinion), *cert. denied*, 515 U.S. 1131 (1995); Brown v. Our Lady of Lourdes Med. Ctr., 767 F. Supp. 618, 629 (D.N.J. 1991) (granting summary judgment where there was not "a single fact" from which anticompetitive conspiracy could be inferred), *aff'd*, 961 F.2d 207 (3d Cir. 1992); Anesthesia Advantage, Inc. v. Metz Group, 759 F. Supp. 638, 650 (D. Colo. 1991) (granting summary judgment where hospital's exclusion of nurse anesthetists was "consistent with the pursuit of permissible independent business purposes"); Castelli v. Meadville Med. Ctr., 702 F. Supp. 1201, 1205-06 (W.D. Pa. 1988) (granting summary judgment where plaintiff's evidence did not support inference of conspiracy), *aff'd without op.*, 872 F.2d 411 (3d Cir. 1989); Friedman v. Delaware County Mem'l Hosp., 672 F. Supp. 171, 193 (E.D. Pa. 1987) (granting summary judgment where plaintiff failed to exclude possibility that hospital acted for legitimate purpose), *aff'd*, 849 F.2d 600 (3d Cir. 1988); Drs. Steuer & Latham, P.A. v. Nat'l Med. Enters., 672 F. Supp. 1489, 1518 (D.S.C. 1987) (same), *aff'd*, 846 F.2d 70 (4th Cir. 1988); Wright v. Southern Mono Hosp. Dist., 631 F. Supp. 1294, 1321 (E.D. Cal. 1986) (granting summary judgment where plaintiff failed to rebut defendants' evidence of legitimate business reasons for their conduct), *aff'd without op. sub nom.* Stehlik v. Southern Mono Hosp. Dist., 924 F.2d 1063 (9th Cir. 1991).

694. *See, e.g.*, Boczar v. Manatee Hosps. & Health Sys., 993 F.2d 1514, 1518 (11th Cir. 1993) (finding error in granting j.n.o.v. where evidence tended to exclude possibility of independent action because jury could infer defendants fabricated damaging incidents about plaintiff); Bolt v. Halifax Hosp. Med. Ctr., 891 F.2d 810, 819-22 (11th Cir. 1990) (en banc) (directed verdict improperly granted given evidence that peer review proceedings were a sham, which supported inference that hospital and peer review committees "intended to enter into an agreement designed to achieve an end not dictated by legitimate business concerns"), *cert. denied*, 495 U.S. 924 (1990); Miller v. Indiana Hosp., 843 F.2d 139, 144-45 (3d Cir.) (reversing summary judgment for defendants given fact issue as to whether defendants acted out of concern over plaintiff's competence or out of anticompetitive motivation), *cert. denied*, 488 U.S. 870 (1988); Sweeney v. Athens Reg'l Med. Ctr., 709 F. Supp. 1563, 1572-73 (M.D. Ga. 1989) (summary judgment denied where evidence tended to exclude possibility of independent action); Shah v. Memorial Hosp., 1988-2 Trade Cas. (CCH) ¶ 68,199 (W.D. Va. 1988) (summary judgment denied where evidence tended to exclude possibility that defendants acted for procompetitive reasons).

In cases where plaintiffs prevailed after a jury trial, the juries found evidence of anticompetitive purpose or intent. *See, e.g.*, Patrick v. Burget, 486 U.S. 94, 98 (1988) (jury found specific intent to injure or destroy competition); *Boczar*, 993 F.2d at 1518 (evidence supported finding that hospital had economic motive to conspire to restrain plaintiff's practice); Oltz v. St. Peter's Cmty. Hosp., 861 F.2d 1440, 1449 (9th Cir. 1988) (evidence sufficient for jury to infer conspiracy with intent to eliminate plaintiff as a competitor); Weiss v. York Hosp., 745 F.2d 786, 818-20 (3d Cir. 1984) (jury found defendants engaged in policy of discrimination against plaintiff and other osteopaths, and exclusions from staff were not based on qualifications), *cert. denied*, 470 U.S. 1060 (1985).

695. *See, e.g.*, Flegel v. Christian Hosp. Northeast-Northwest, 4 F.3d 682, 686-87 (8th Cir. 1993); Miller v. Indiana Hosp., 843 F.2d 139, 144 (3d Cir. 1988), *cert. denied*, 488 U.S. 870 (1988); *Mathews*, 883 F. Supp. at 1036; Loiterman v. Antani, No. 90-C983, 1990 WL 91062 at *7 (N.D.

on the ground that the plaintiff offered insufficient evidence either that the defendants had market power or that the denial, termination, or limitation of the plaintiff's staff privileges had actual detrimental effects in a properly defined market.[696]

b. THE HEALTH CARE QUALITY IMPROVEMENT ACT

The HCQIA[697] was enacted to address the national problem of increasing medical malpractice by establishing a two-pronged program to identify incompetent physicians throughout the country. One part of the program grants limited legal immunity to those who engage in "professional review actions" that meet certain requirements of the HCQIA.[698] This limited immunity from liability for damages was designed to encourage the medical profession to engage in active, good faith, professional review of its members by curtailing the threat of litigation, especially

---

Ill. June 28, 1990). *But see Weiss*, 745 F.2d at 820 (per se rule applied to discrimination against osteopaths in staff privileges decisions).

696. *See, e.g.*, Benjamin v. Aroostook Med. Ctr., 113 F.3d 1 (1st Cir.) (affirming summary judgment where there was no evidence of harm to competition and plaintiff failed to show that hospital and members of its staff had market power under § 2 or were capable of conspiring under § 1) (per curiam), *cert. denied*, 522 U.S. 1016 (1997); Levine v. Central Fla. Med. Affiliates, 72 F.3d 1538 (11th Cir.) (affirming summary judgment for defendant hospitals, finding that plaintiff failed to prove market power or an actual adverse effect on competition as a result of the suspension of privileges because he exercised privileges at other hospitals), *cert. denied*, 519 U.S. 820 (1996); *Flegel*, 4 F.3d at 688-91 (affirming summary judgment where plaintiff failed to produce sufficient evidence of actual detrimental effects or possession of market power or sufficient market share from which market power could be inferred); Lie v. St. Joseph Hosp., 964 F.2d 567, 570 (6th Cir. 1992) (affirming summary judgment given insufficient evidence of actual detrimental effects or market power); Coffey v. Healthtrust, Inc., 955 F.2d 1388, 1393 (10th Cir. 1992) (affirming summary judgment for defendants where hospital's entering into exclusive radiology contract resulted only in "reshuffling of competitors," not actual detrimental effect on competition); *Oksanen*, 945 F.2d at 709 (en banc) (affirming grant of summary judgment due to insufficient evidence of anticompetitive effects); Bhan v. NME Hosps., 929 F.2d 1404, 1413-14 (9th Cir.) (affirming grant of summary judgment where plaintiff failed to demonstrate actual detrimental effects on competition), *cert. denied*, 502 U.S. 994 (1991); Goss v. Memorial Hosp. Sys., 789 F.2d 353, 355 (5th Cir. 1986) (affirming grant of summary judgment where defendants lacked market power); Villalobos v. Llorens, 137 F. Supp. 2d 44, 47-48 (D.P.R. 2001) (dismissing anesthesiologist's hospital privileges claim for failure to allege a proper geographic market); Urdinaran v. Aarons, 115 F. Supp. 2d 484 (D.N.J. 2000) (finding no evidence of market power and questioning the narrowness of the alleged relevant geographic market); Alpern v. Cavorocchi, 1999-1 Trade Cas. (CCH) ¶ 72,514 (E.D. Pa. 1999) (finding facts alleged insufficient to show the possession or dangerous probability of possessing market power, and also finding the challenged conduct to be procompetitive where it resulted in a net increase in the number of competitors); Farr v. Healtheast, Inc., 1993-1 Trade Cas. (CCH) ¶ 70,294 (E.D. Pa. 1993) (granting summary judgment on grounds that defendant hospital lacked market power and that revocation of plaintiff obstetrician/gynecologist's hospital privileges had little anticompetitive effect where hospital accounted for only 6 out of 208 specialty beds, and 115 out of 3,146 total hospital beds within the relevant market); Jackson v. Radcliffe, 795 F. Supp. 197, 205-06 (S.D. Tex. 1992) (granting summary judgment on antitrust challenge to termination of plaintiff's privileges where there was no evidence that defendants had market power or that termination affected market for radiology services); Bellam v. Clayton County Hosp. Auth., 758 F. Supp. 1488, 1493-94 (N.D. Ga. 1990) (granting summary judgment where plaintiff failed to show an anticompetitive effect on the relevant market).

697. 42 U.S.C. §§ 11101-11152 (1994).

698. *See id.* § 11151(9) (to qualify for immunity, a "professional review action" must be "based on the competence or professional conduct of an individual physician").

treble damage antitrust litigation, against those who review the conduct and qualifications of their peers.[699] The second part of the program established a national computer system for reporting cases of physician malpractice, incompetence, or adverse staff privileges decisions.[700]

Under the HCQIA, peer review participants cannot be held liable in a suit for damages if they undertook a professional review action against a physician:

1. in the reasonable belief that the action was in the furtherance of quality health care,

2. after a reasonable effort to obtain the facts of the matter,

3. after adequate notice and hearing procedures are afforded to the physician involved or after such other procedures as are fair to the physician under the circumstances, and

4. in the reasonable belief that the action was warranted by the facts known after such reasonable effort to obtain facts and after meeting the requirement of paragraph (3).[701]

The HCQIA creates a rebuttable presumption that the peer reviewers' actions meet these four standards of reasonableness and due process.[702]

A number of courts considering staff privileges disputes have found that the defendant hospital and peer review participants qualified for immunity under the HCQIA, and dismissed such cases on preliminary motions.[703] In one case, the court of appeals reversed a $4.2 million judgment in favor of the plaintiff physician on the ground that the case should not have been submitted to the jury in the first place

699. *Id.* § 11101(4) (finding by Congress that threat of treble damage liability under federal antitrust law unreasonably discourages physicians from participating in effective peer review); *id.* § 11101(5) (finding by Congress that there was national need "to provide incentive and protection for physicians engaging in effective professional peer review").

700. *Id.* §§ 11131-11137 (called the National Practitioner Data Bank).

701. *Id.* § 11112(a).

702. The presumption may be rebutted by a preponderance of the evidence. *Id.* The HCQIA does not create an insurmountable bar to discovery of peer materials. *See* Poliner v. Texas Health Sys., 201 F.R.D. 437, 438 (N.D. Tex. 2001).

703. *See, e.g.,* Sugarbaker v. SSM Health Care, 190 F.3d 905 (8th Cir. 1999), *cert. denied,* 528 U.S. 1137 (2000); Brader v. Allegheny Gen. Hosp., 167 F.3d 832 (3d Cir. 1999); Wayne v. Genesis Med. Ctr., 140 F.3d 1145 (8th Cir. 1998); Parsons v. Sanchez, 1995-1 Trade Cas. (CCH) ¶ 70,877 (9th Cir. 1995) (per curiam); Smith v. Ricks, 31 F.3d 1478 (9th Cir. 1994), *cert. denied,* 514 U.S. 1035 (1995); Imperial v. Suburban Hosp. Ass'n, 37 F.3d 1026 (4th Cir. 1994); Austin v. McNamara, 979 F.2d 728 (9th Cir. 1992); Chalal v. Northwest Med. Ctr., 147 F. Supp. 2d 1160 (N.D. Ala. 2001); Payne v. Harris Methodist H-E-B, 2001-1 Trade Cas. (CCH) ¶ 73,169 (N.D. Tex. 2001); Perez v. Pottstown Mem'l Med. Ctr., No. CIV 97-334, 1998 U.S. Dist. LEXIS 12150 (E.D. Pa. Aug. 3, 1998), *aff'd without op.,* 210 F.3d 358 (3d Cir. 2000); Egan v. Athol Mem'l Hosp., 971 F. Supp. 37 (D. Mass. 1997); Johnson v. Greater Southeast Cmty. Hosp., 1996-2 Trade Cas. (CCH) ¶ 71,511 (D.D.C. 1996); Mathews v. Lancaster Gen. Hosp., 883 F. Supp. 1016, 1024-35 (E.D. Pa. 1995), *aff'd,* 87 F.3d 624 (3d Cir. 1996); Crosby v. Hospital Auth., 873 F. Supp. 1568 (M.D. Ga. 1995); Monroe v. AMI Hosps., 877 F. Supp. 1022 (S.D. Tex. 1994); Farr v. Healtheast, Inc., 1993-1 Trade Cas. (CCH) ¶ 70,294 (E.D. Pa. 1993); Fobbs v. Holy Cross Health Sys. Corp., 789 F. Supp. 1054 (E.D. Cal. 1992), *aff'd,* 29 F.3d 1439 (9th Cir. 1994), *cert. denied,* 513 U.S. 1127 (1995).

because, as a matter of law, the defendant hospital was immune under the HCQIA from damages liability in connection with peer review activities.[704]

By contrast, some defendants have been unable to convince the courts that they qualified for immunity under the HCQIA.[705] The courts generally have been reluctant to allow an immediate appeal of a denial of immunity under the HCQIA on the ground that the act provides only immunity from damages liability, not immunity from suit.[706]

Some physicians aggrieved by peer review proceedings have attempted to use the HCQIA offensively to create a private cause of action. Thus far, the courts have consistently held that the act does not provide a private cause of action for plaintiffs whose staff privileges have been adversely affected by a professional review action.[707]

As a deterrent to unfounded litigation over adverse actions by hospitals against physicians' staff privileges, the HCQIA provides for the award of costs and attorneys' fees to substantially prevailing defendants when the plaintiff's claims or conduct during the litigation are "frivolous, unreasonable, without foundation, or in bad faith."[708] In *Smith v. Ricks*,[709] the Ninth Circuit affirmed an award of over $300,000 in costs and attorneys' fees under the HCQIA, finding no abuse of discretion in the district court's determination that the plaintiff's "antitrust claims were at best without foundation, and at worst frivolous."[710]

---

704. *See* Brown v. James E. Holmes Reg'l Med. Ctr., 33 F.3d 1318 (11th Cir. 1994), *cert. denied*, 514 U.S. 1019 (1995); *see also* Nicholas v. North Colo. Med. Ctr., Inc., 27 P.3d 828 (Colo. 2001) (reversing district court decision and finding that the peer review committee acted in accordance with the HCQIA and was therefore immune from suit and liability for damages).

705. *See, e.g.*, Brown v. Presbyterian Healthcare Servs., 101 F.3d 1324 (10th Cir. 1996) (upholding jury verdict denying antitrust immunity under the HCQIA where defendants were found not to have made reasonable efforts to ascertain facts before removing plaintiffs' obstetrical privileges), *cert. denied*, 520 U.S. 1181 (1997); Harris v. Bellin Mem'l Hosp., 13 F.3d 1082 (7th Cir. 1994) (affirming denial of summary judgment on state law claims because professional review actions commenced prior to effective date for the HCQIA immunity); Williamson v. Sacred Heart Hosp., No. 89-30084-RV, 1993 WL 543002 (N.D. Fla. May 28, 1993) (denying summary judgment on HCQIA grounds where genuine issue of fact over whether defendants acted reasonably in furtherance of quality of care), *aff'd mem.*, 41 F.3d 667 (11th Cir. 1994), *cert. denied*, 515 U.S. 1331 (1995); Islami v. Covenant Med. Ctr., 822 F. Supp. 1361 (N.D. Iowa 1992) (denying summary judgment where plaintiff's evidence created factual question over whether hospital provided fair procedures); Manion v. Evans, No. 3:89CV7436, 1991 WL 575715 (N.D. Ohio July 8, 1991) (denying summary judgment where evidence raised genuine issue as to defendants' motives and where defendants failed to meet the act's reporting requirements), *appeal dismissed*, 986 F.2d 1036 (6th Cir.), *cert. denied*, 510 U.S. 818 (1993).

706. *See, e.g.*, Manion v. Evans, 986 F.2d 1036 (6th Cir.), *cert. denied*, 510 U.S. 818 (1993); Decker v. IHC Hosps., 982 F.2d 433 (10th Cir. 1992), *cert. denied*, 509 U.S. 924 (1993).

707. *See, e.g.*, Hancock v. Blue Cross-Blue Shield, 21 F.3d 373 (10th Cir. 1994); Zamanian v. Christian Health Ministry, Civ. A. No. 94-1781, 1994 WL 396179 (E.D. La. July 22, 1994); Goldsmith v. Harding Hosp., 762 F. Supp. 187 (S.D. Ohio 1991); Regualos v. Community Hosp. Ass'n, No. 5:89-CV-113, 1991 WL 239953 (W.D. Mich. Aug. 7, 1991).

708. 42 U.S.C. § 11113 (1994).

709. 31 F.3d 1478 (9th Cir. 1994), *cert. denied*, 514 U.S. 1035 (1995).

710. *Id.* at 1487-88; *see also* Thompson v. Sisters of Providence, No. 97-36025 & 98-35144, 1999 U.S. App. LEXIS 2075, at *5-7 (9th Cir. Feb. 9, 1999) (affirming district court award of attorneys' fees under the HCQIA where district court did not abuse its discretion); Imperial v. Suburban Hosp. Ass'n, No. 96-1978, 1998 U.S. App. LEXIS 893, at *5-6 (4th Cir. Jan. 22, 1998) (per curiam) (awarding attorneys' fees); Rooney v. Medical Ctr. Hosp. of Chillicothe, No. C2-91-1100, 1995 U.S. Dist. LEXIS 18646 (S.D. Ohio Mar. 8, 1995) (granting defendants' motion for costs and attorneys' fees under the HCQIA).

c.   EXCLUSIVE CONTRACTS

A physician may be denied staff privileges at a hospital that has entered into an exclusive contract with another physician or group of physicians providing competing services. These contracts often stipulate that staff privileges to provide the type of service covered by the contract may not be granted to anyone outside the contracting group. Antitrust challenges to such exclusive contracts generally have been unsuccessful.[711]

The Supreme Court established a framework for analyzing exclusive hospital contracts in *Jefferson Parish Hospital District No. 2 v. Hyde*.[712] In declining to apply the per se rule against tying to a contract for anesthesiology services between a hospital and a group of four anesthesiologists,[713] the Court found that the hospital had not exercised market power over the provision of acute care in-patient services to force its patients to buy anesthesiological services that they would otherwise not have purchased.[714] In considering whether the defendants nonetheless unreasonably restrained trade under Section 1, the Court observed that the contract, like any exclusive dealing arrangement, could be unlawful if it foreclosed the group's competitors from so much of the market as to unreasonably restrain competition for anesthesiology services.[715] The plaintiff, however, had failed to make such a

---

711. *See, e.g.*, Minnesota Ass'n of Nurse Anesthetists v. Unity Hosp., 208 F.3d 655 (8th Cir. 2000) (rejecting plaintiffs' claim that their termination by defendant hospitals and the hospitals' subsequent entry into sole source contracts with anesthesiologists were part of a conspiracy to eliminate lower cost, equally competent competitors); Korshin v. Benedictine Hosp., 34 F. Supp. 2d 133 (N.D.N.Y. 1999) (plaintiff physician lacks standing to challenge exclusive contracting arrangement involving competitors where plaintiff alleges only injury due to his exclusion from the rival group). A notable exception to the typical judicial treatment upholding exclusive hospital contracts is *Oltz v. St. Peter's Cmty. Hosp.*, 861 F.2d 1440 (9th Cir. 1988). The *Oltz* court upheld a jury finding that a hospital and a group of anesthesiologists had illegally conspired to enter into an exclusive contract and to terminate a nurse anesthetist's billing contract with the hospital, but remanded the case for a new trial on damages. *See also* Ertag v. Naples Cmty. Hosp., 1997-2 Trade Cas. (CCH) ¶ 71,966 (11th Cir. 1997) (per curiam) (reversing grant of summary judgment for defendants where plaintiffs sought only lost "competitive" profits at a price no higher than Medicare fee levels, and plaintiffs' claimed injury was sufficiently direct and discernible to confer standing); Allen v. Washington Hosp., 34 F. Supp. 2d 958 (W.D. Pa. 1999) (denying summary judgment where defendants conceded that plaintiff incurred antitrust injury and plaintiff is "an" efficient enforcer of the antitrust laws); Higgins v. Medical Coll., 849 F. Supp. 1113, 1119-20 (E.D. Va. 1994) (plaintiffs adequately alleged antitrust injury and therefore had standing to challenge exclusive contract between hospital and two medical schools for provision of radiology oncology services).

712. 466 U.S. 2 (1984). This case is discussed extensively in part D.3.a of Chapter I.

713. The Court treated the relationship between the hospital and the group of anesthesiologists as if governed by an exclusive contract in light of the hospital's continuing treatment of the group as the exclusive provider of anesthesiology services at the hospital, although the group's contract no longer expressly required that no other anesthesiologists be permitted to practice at the hospital. *Jefferson Parish*, 466 U.S. at 6-7. Distinguishing between the legality of the group's contract with the hospital and the legality of the hospital's contract with its patients, the Court found that the group's contract raised only an exclusive dealing question, whereas the "issue here is whether the hospital's insistence that its patients purchase anesthesiological services from [the group] creates a tying arrangement." *Id.* at 18 n.28.

714. *Id.* at 28 ("It is safe to assume that every patient undergoing a surgical operation needs the services of an anesthesiologist; at least this record contains no evidence that the hospital 'forced' any such services on unwilling patients."). The Court refused to infer that the hospital had market power where 70% of patients in the area used other hospitals. *Id.* at 26-27.

715. *Id.* at 30 n.51.

showing or to demonstrate the actual effects of this arrangement on the price or quality of anesthesiology services in the market.

Since *Jefferson Parish*, exclusive hospital contracts have been challenged not only as illegal exclusive dealing arrangements, but also as allegedly unlawful tying arrangements,[716] group boycotts,[717] and monopolistic conduct.[718] Because exclusive dealing arrangements are analyzed under the rule of reason,[719] courts considering the legality of exclusive hospital contracts attempt to balance the purported procompetitive benefits of the contracts against their alleged anticompetitive harms. Exclusive contracts are frequently justified on the ground that they improve the hospital's efficiency and enhance the quality of care its patients receive.[720] In *Jefferson Parish*, for example, benefits from exclusivity were said to include ensuring twenty-four hour coverage of anesthesiology services at the hospital, improving the efficient use of hospital equipment and the standardization of procedures, facilitating flexible scheduling of operations, and increasing the hospital's ability to monitor the quality of anesthesiology services provided to its patients.[721]

Challenges by physicians to exclusive hospital contracts are often unsuccessful because the plaintiff fails to demonstrate either the hospital's market power or actual anticompetitive effects in the market.[722] Although an exclusive contract for health

---

716. *See, e.g.*, Bhan v. NME Hosps., 929 F.2d 1404 (9th Cir.) (tying claim failed in absence of proof of hospital's market power), *cert. denied*, 502 U.S. 994 (1991); Beard v. Parkview Hosp., 912 F.2d 138, 144 (6th Cir. 1990) (tying claim failed where hospital received no direct economic benefit from exclusive radiology contract); Collins v. Associated Pathologists, Ltd., 844 F.2d 473, 478 (7th Cir.) (tying claim failed where pathology services held not to be separate product from hospital services), *cert. denied*, 488 U.S. 852 (1988); White v. Rockingham Radiologists, Ltd., 820 F.2d 98, 103-04 (4th Cir. 1987) (tying claim failed where hospital lacked economic interest in tied product); Scara v. Bradley Mem'l Hosp., 1993-2 Trade Cas. (CCH) ¶ 70,353 (E.D. Tenn. 1993) (same); Castelli v. Meadville Med. Ctr., 702 F. Supp. 1201, 1208-09 (W.D. Pa. 1988) (tying claim failed where hospital did not benefit economically from exclusive radiology contract), *aff'd without op.*, 872 F.2d 411 (3d Cir. 1989); Drs. Steuer & Latham, P.A. v. National Med. Enters., 672 F. Supp. 1489 (D.S.C. 1987) (tying claim failed where hospital lacked market power), *aff'd*, 846 F.2d 70 (4th Cir. 1988).

717. *See, e.g.*, Minnesota Ass'n of Nurse Anesthetists v. Unity Hosp., 208 F.3d 655 (8th Cir. 2000) (rejecting arguments that sole source contracts are per se unlawful group boycotts); Balaklaw v. Lovell, 14 F.3d 793 (2d Cir. 1994) (upholding exclusive anesthesiology contract); Coffey v. Healthtrust, Inc., 955 F.2d 1388 (10th Cir. 1992) (upholding exclusive radiology contract); *Bhan*, 929 F.2d at 1411-12 (upholding hospital policy of excluding nonphysicians); *Collins*, 844 F.2d at 479-80 (upholding contract for pathology services).

718. *See, e.g.*, Ford v. Stroup, 1997-1 Trade Cas. (CCH) ¶ 71,838 (6th Cir. 1997) (per curiam) (unpublished opinion); *Beard*, 912 F.2d at 144-45; *White*, 820 F.2d 98; Allen v. Washington Hosp., 34 F. Supp. 2d 958 (W.D. Pa. 1999); *Castelli*, 702 F. Supp. at 1206-08.

719. Jefferson Parish Hosp. Dist. No. 2 v. Hyde, 466 U.S. 2, 44-45 (1984) (O'Connor, J., concurring); *see also* Diaz v. Farley, 215 F.3d 1175 (10th Cir. 2000) (affirming summary judgment and holding the alleged group boycott was not subject to per se treatment when plaintiffs conceded they did not have sufficient evidence under rule of reason).

720. *See, e.g.*, *Beard*, 912 F.2d at 145; Williamson v. Sacred Heart Hosp., No. 89-30084-RV, 1993 WL 543002 (N.D. Fla. May 28, 1993) (exclusive contract allows hospital "to offer continuous, high quality care with a minimum of administrative effort"), *aff'd mem.*, 41 F.3d 667 (11th Cir. 1994), *cert. denied*, 515 U.S. 1113 (1995).

721. *Jefferson Parish*, 466 U.S. at 43-44 (O'Connor, J., concurring).

722. *See, e.g.*, *Diaz*, 215 F.3d 1175 (finding that plaintiffs did not define a relevant market and thus failed to show that defendants possessed market power and that defendants advanced plausible arguments concerning the procompetitive effects of the agreements); Read v. Medical X-Ray Ctr., 110 F.3d 543 (8th Cir.) (upholding § 1 judgment for defendant and reversing § 2 judgment for

care services might restrain trade unreasonably if a significant portion of providers of those services are "frozen out" of the market,[723] in most cases the plaintiffs, like the plaintiff in *Jefferson Parish*, are unable to demonstrate such a substantial foreclosure.[724] Challenges to exclusive hospital contracts also have failed because the plaintiff failed to demonstrate antitrust injury and therefore lacked standing under the antitrust laws[725] or offered insufficient evidence of a horizontal conspiracy to support a group boycott claim.[726]

plaintiff because failure of plaintiff's radiology practice was not caused by defendant or any harm to legitimate competition), *cert. denied*, 522 U.S. 914 (1997); Baglio v. Baska, 116 F.3d 467 (3d Cir. 1997) (per curiam) (affirming summary judgment in favor of defendant due to lack of injury to competition and resulting antitrust injury to plaintiff); *Ford*, 1997-1 Trade Cas. (CCH) ¶ 71,838 (affirming summary judgment for defendants on attempted monopolization claim of radiation oncologist challenging hospital's termination of exclusive contract with plaintiff in favor of open staff policy for use of hospital's linear accelerator, due to lack of evidence of a dangerous probability that rival practice group would achieve monopoly power due to hospital's actions); *Balaklaw*, 14 F.3d at 797-99; *Coffey*, 955 F.2d at 1393 (upholding exclusive radiology contract that had resulted only in a "reshuffling of competitors," but no actual detrimental effect on competition); Morgan, Strand, Wheeler & Biggs v. Radiology, Ltd., 924 F.2d 1484, 1488-90 (9th Cir. 1991) (upholding exclusive radiology contract where lack of proof of relevant market); *Collins*, 844 F.2d 473 (upholding exclusive pathology service contract that affected only the local market for pathology services where the relevant market was the national market for pathologists); Korshin v. Benedictine Hosp., 34 F. Supp. 2d 133 (N.D.N.Y. 1999) (plaintiff failed to demonstrate antitrust injury where there was no allegation that the contract resulted in higher prices, reduced quality, or decreased consumer choice); Vakharia v. Little Co. of Mary Hosp., 917 F. Supp. 1282 (N.D. Ill. 1996) (upholding exclusive anesthesia contract where no allegation of market power or showing of anticompetitive effects); Bellam v. Clayton County Hosp. Auth., 758 F. Supp. 1488 (N.D. Ga. 1990) (upholding exclusive anesthesiology contract where lack of evidence of anticompetitive impact on market); Kuck v. Bensen, 647 F. Supp. 743, 746 (D. Me. 1986) (upholding exclusive contract for emergency room services where substantial portion of market was unaffected by it); Gonzales v. Insignares, 1985-2 Trade Cas. (CCH) ¶ 66,701 (N.D. Ga. 1985) (upholding exclusive anesthesiology contract where 60% of market was unaffected).

723. *See Jefferson Parish*, 466 U.S. at 45 (O'Connor, J., concurring) ("When the sellers of services are numerous and mobile, and the number of buyers is large, exclusive-dealing arrangements of narrow scope pose no threat of adverse economic consequences.").
724. *See, e.g., Balaklaw*, 14 F.3d at 797-99 (quoting *Coffey*, 955 F.2d at 1393) (finding no foreclosure of competition by hospital's award of exclusive contract for anesthesiology services to provider group that competed with plaintiff, which resulted in "only a reshuffling of competitors" from the consumer's viewpoint and no diminution of competition among anesthesiologists for jobs from the provider's viewpoint); Drs. Steuer & Latham, P.A. v. National Med. Enters., 672 F. Supp. 1489 (D.S.C. 1987) (upholding exclusive pathology contract); *see also* Giampolo v. Somerset Hosp. Ctr. for Health, Inc., No. CIV.A. 95-133J, 1998 U.S. Dist. LEXIS 14388 (W.D. Pa. May 29, 1998), *aff'd without op.*, 189 F.3d 464 (3d Cir. 1999) (finding that the hospital's termination of an exclusive contract and nonrenewal of an employment contract did not cause antitrust injury but was procompetitive because it created an opportunity for new entry, intensified local competition, and led to increased consumer choice).
725. *See, e.g.*, Williamson v. Sacred Heart Hosp., 1995-1 Trade Cas. (CCH) ¶ 70,905 (11th Cir. 1994) (upholding exclusive contract for radiology services) (unpublished opinion), *cert. denied*, 515 U.S. 1131 (1995); *Balaklaw*, 14 F.3d 793 (upholding exclusive anesthesiology contract); Howerton v. Grace Hosp., 1995-2 Trade Cas. (CCH) ¶ 71,208 (W.D.N.C. 1995), *aff'd without op.*, 96 F.3d 1438 (4th Cir. 1996); Leak v. Grant Med. Ctr., 893 F. Supp. 757 (S.D. Ohio 1995), *aff'd per curiam*, 1997-1 Trade Cas. (CCH) ¶ 71,724 (6th Cir. 1996) (unpublished opinion); Mid-Michigan Radiology Assocs. v. Central Mich. Cmty. Hosp., 1995-1 Trade Cas. (CCH) ¶ 70,943 (E.D. Mich. 1995); Scara v. Bradley Mem'l Hosp., 1993-2 Trade Cas. (CCH) ¶ 70,353 (E.D. Tenn. 1993). *But see* Higgins v. Medical Coll., 849 F. Supp. 1113, 1119-20 (E.D. Va. 1994) (plaintiffs had adequately alleged antitrust injury and so had standing to challenge exclusive contract between hospital and two medical schools for provision of radiology oncology services).
726. *See, e.g., Coffey*, 955 F.2d at 1392 (upholding exclusive contract for radiology services).

3. *Health Care Provider Networks and Joint Ventures*

The health care marketplace has witnessed the rapid evolution of hospital, physician, multiprovider, and other health care provider networks and joint ventures. The most prominent antitrust issues raised by provider networks and joint ventures include size and formation, pricing, and exclusionary conduct.[727]

a. SIZE AND FORMATION

The enforcement agencies have attempted to provide guidance about the permissible size of health care joint ventures. The 1996 *Health Care Statements* provide certain safety zones for integrated joint ventures under a certain size, depending upon whether the network is exclusive or nonexclusive.

Pursuant to Statement 8, an exclusive physician network joint venture falls within a safety zone if its physician participants share substantial financial risk and constitute 20 percent or less of the physicians in each physician specialty with active hospital staff privileges who practice in the relevant geographic market.[728] A nonexclusive physician network falls within a safety zone if it includes 30 percent or less of the physicians in each physician specialty with active hospital staff privileges who practice in the relevant geographic market.[729] The agencies caution that participants in a nonexclusive physician network must be sure that the network is nonexclusive in fact, not just in name. In determining the exclusive or nonexclusive nature of the venture, the agencies will focus on the following practical indicia: (1) whether viable competing networks or health plans with adequate provider participation currently exist in the market; (2) whether providers in the network actually participate in or contract with other networks or health plans, or there is other evidence of their willingness and incentive to do so; (3) whether providers in the network earn substantial revenue outside the network; (4) whether there are indications of significant de-participation from other networks in the market; and (5) whether there are indications of coordination among providers in the network regarding price or other competitively significant terms of participation.[730]

Ventures falling outside the safety zone do not necessarily raise substantial antitrust concerns and indeed can be procompetitive under a rule of reason analysis.[731]

Staff advisory opinions and business review letters of the enforcement agencies have approved physician and multiprovider networks involving higher percentages of providers in the posited geographic market than those specified in the safety zones where the circumstances indicated that the network formation or operation would not

727. For a general discussion of the application of antitrust law to joint ventures, see Chapter IV.
728. In markets with fewer than five physicians in a particular specialty, an exclusive network otherwise qualifying for the safety zone may include one physician from that specialty on a nonexclusive basis, even though the inclusion of that physician results in more than 20% of the physicians in the specialty. 1996 HEALTH CARE STATEMENTS, *supra* note 667, Statement 8.A.1.
729. In those markets with fewer than four physicians in a particular specialty, the nonexclusive network otherwise qualifying for the safety zone may include one physician from that specialty. *Id.*, Statement 8.A.2.
730. *Id.*, Statement 8.A.3.
731. *Id.*, Statement 8.B.

appear likely to substantially lessen competition.[732] For example, the agencies have approved physician or multiprovider networks consisting of almost all physicians in the area,[733] 78 percent of all colon and rectal specialists in the county,[734] more than 50 to 70 percent of allergists, endocrinologists, and other specialty physicians in a ten-county area,[735] more than 50 percent of physicians who practice in eight specialties,[736] 54 percent of the podiatrists in the state of New York,[737] up to 50 percent of the chiropractors in the state,[738] 40 to 45 percent of the independent community pharmacies in the county,[739] 44 percent of all board-certified dermatologists in the market,[740] 40 percent of all family practitioners in the market,[741] and 40 percent of area physicians.[742]

Statement 9 on multiprovider networks does not provide safety zones because such networks—including physician-hospital organizations, hospital networks operating at several levels, and management services organizations—involve "a large variety of structures and relationships among many different types of health care providers, and new arrangements are continually developing."[743] Nevertheless, the antitrust principles found in Statement 8 generally also are applicable to multiprovider networks discussed in Statement 9.[744]

As described in Statement 9, multiprovider networks are analyzed in terms of their competitive impact in each market in which they operate. For example, the competitive impact of a physician-hospital organization would be analyzed in each relevant market for hospital services, physician services (or each medical specialty services market), and physician-hospital network services.[745] In addition, vertical arrangements within multiprovider networks, i.e., exclusive and selective

---

732. The DOJ's business review procedure is set forth in 28 C.F.R. § 50.6 (2001). The FTC's advisory opinion procedure is set forth at 16 C.F.R. §§ 1.1-1.4 (2001).

733. U.S. Dep't of Justice, Business Review Letter to Sierra CommCare, Inc., 1996 DOJBRL LEXIS 20 (Aug. 15, 1996).

734. U.S. Dep't of Justice, Business Review Letter to Allied Colon and Rectal Specialists, 1996 DOJBRL LEXIS 6 (July 1, 1996).

735. Federal Trade Comm'n, Staff Advisory Opinion Letter to William T. Harvey (May 19, 1998).

736. U.S. Dep't of Justice, Business Review Letter to Heritage Alliance, 1998 DOJBRL LEXIS 14 (Sept. 15, 1998).

737. U.S. Dep't of Justice, Business Review Letter to Preferred Podiatric Network, Inc., 1994 DOJBRL LEXIS 19 (Sept. 14, 1994).

738. U.S. Dep't of Justice, Business Review Letter to California Chiropractic Ass'n, 1993 DOJBRL LEXIS 27 (Dec. 8, 1993).

739. Federal Trade Comm'n, Staff Advisory Opinion Letter to John A. Cronin, Pham D., J.D. (May 19, 1999) (nonexclusive risk-based network).

740. U.S. Dep't of Justice, Business Review Letter to Dermnet, Inc., 1995 DOJBRL LEXIS 27 (Dec. 5, 1995).

741. U.S. Dep't of Justice, Business Review Letter to Itasca Clinic & Grand Rapids Med. Assocs., 1996 DOJBRL LEXIS 13 (Mar. 19, 1996).

742. Federal Trade Comm'n, Staff Advisory Opinion Letter to Yellowstone Physicians (May 14, 1997).

743. 1996 HEALTH CARE STATEMENTS, supra note 667, Statement 9.

744. Id. at n.44.

745. Id., Statement 9.B.1. See also U.S. Dep't of Justice, Business Review Letter to Midwest Behavioral Healthcare LLC, 2000 DOJBRL LEXIS 7 (Feb. 4, 2000) (identifying separate relevant markets for general psychiatrists, psychologists, nurses, social workers, counselors, foster parents, therapists, technicians, and case managers); U.S. Dep't of Justice, Business Review Letter to Preferred Physicians Med. Group, 1999 DOJBRL LEXIS 5 (July 23, 1999) (identifying separate relevant markets for primary care and specialty physicians).

contracting, are analyzed under the rule of reason to assess both the potential procompetitive justifications and any potential foreclosure effects.[746]

b. PRICING ISSUES FOR PROVIDER NETWORKS

As a general proposition, price-fixing agreements among horizontal competitors are per se illegal.[747] This proposition is at the center of the antitrust concerns raised by the formation of joint ventures, networks, and other collaborative delivery systems among health care providers. To the extent that these health care delivery systems facilitate joint pricing practices among formerly or currently competing providers, they raise the specter of the prohibition against price-fixing agreements.

In *Arizona v. Maricopa County Medical Society*,[748] the Supreme Court held that agreements among the physician members of two not-for-profit medical foundations on the maximum fees that physicians would be allowed to charge patients insured under health plans approved by the foundations were per se illegal. The Court observed that such agreements among "independent competing entrepreneurs . . . fit squarely into the horizontal price-fixing mold."[749] The Court in *Maricopa* distinguished the medical foundations from joint ventures that allow their members to sell a new product or service in the market.[750] It also distinguished the foundations from other "joint arrangements in which persons who would otherwise be competitors pool their capital and share the risks of loss as well as the opportunities for profit," thus creating "a single firm competing with other sellers in the market."[751] Since *Maricopa*, a critical question facing physicians, hospitals, or other competing health care providers who have formed multiprovider networks is how much clinical and/or financial integration is enough to avoid fitting "squarely into the horizontal price-fixing mold." Subsequent case law has not offered much additional guidance on how integrated delivery systems may be structured to avoid such condemnation.[752]

(1) Background: Price Fixing by Unintegrated Providers

The enforcement agencies have made clear their intention to challenge collaborative ventures that engage in collective dealings with third-party payors over fees or other terms of reimbursement but do not create substantial integration among the participating providers. The agencies have challenged unintegrated groups of

---

746. 1996 HEALTH CARE STATEMENTS, *supra* note 667, Statement 9.B.2.b.
747. *See* part C.1.a of Chapter I.
748. 457 U.S. 332 (1982).
749. *Id.* at 357.
750. *Id.* at 356 ("Their combination has merely permitted them to sell their services to certain customers at fixed prices and arguably to affect the prevailing market price of medical care.").
751. *Id.* at 356-57 ("The agreement under attack is an agreement among hundreds of competing doctors concerning the price at which each will offer his own services to a substantial number of consumers. . . . If a clinic offered complete medical coverage for a flat fee, the cooperating doctors would have the type of partnership arrangement in which a price-fixing agreement among the doctors would be perfectly proper.").
752. *But see* Hassan v. Independent Practice Assocs., 698 F. Supp. 679, 688-90 (E.D. Mich. 1988) (distinguishing *Maricopa* where independent practice association (IPA) member physicians shared risks of loss and opportunities for profit and IPA created a "new product: guaranteed comprehensive physician services for a prepaid premium different from fee-for-service physician services").

hospitals,[753] physicians,[754] dentists,[755] and pharmacies[756] that allegedly restrained trade by agreeing on the fees they would charge payors, negotiating collectively with third-

---

753. *See, e.g.*, United States v. Morton Plant Health Sys., Inc., 2000-2 Trade Cas. (CCH) ¶ 73,034 (M.D. Fla. 2000) (settling charges that Morton Plant Health Systems and Mease Hospital violated terms of a September 29, 1994 Final Consent Order which prohibited a merger but permitted the formation of a partnership; finding that the partners coordinated payor contracting and pricing without having created sufficient integration); New York *ex rel.* Spitzer v. St. Francis Hosp., 94 F. Supp. 2d 399 (S.D.N.Y. 2000) (granting summary judgment based on evidence of per se price fixing and market allocation by two hospitals and their joint venture); United States v. Classic Care Network, 59 Fed. Reg. 67,719 (DOJ Dec. 30, 1994) (consent decree and competitive impact statement) (charging that eight Long Island hospitals conspired to form a joint sales agency to coordinate the terms of contracts with health maintenance organizations (HMOs) and other managed care payors, the purpose and effect of which was to prevent discounting off the hospitals' inpatient rates and to limit discounting off their outpatient rates), 1995-1 Trade Cas. (CCH) ¶ 70,997 (E.D.N.Y. 1995) (final judgment).

754. *See, e.g.*, Alaska Healthcare Network, Inc., 65 Fed. Reg. 59,425 (FTC Oct. 5, 2000) (proposed consent and aid to public comment) (settling charges that organization representing 60% of physicians at only private acute care hospital in Fairbanks served as vehicle to negotiate with health plans), 2001 FTC LEXIS 55 (2001) (decision and order); Texas Surgeons, P.A., 65 Fed. Reg. 21,441 (FTC May 18, 2000) (proposed consent and aid to public comment) (settling charges that six practice groups of surgeons attempted to coerce health plans into raising surgical rates by sending identically worded letters terminating agreements based on insurers' "unacceptable" rate reductions and prominently announcing their resignation from Blue Cross in a newspaper advertisement), 2000 FTC LEXIS 68 (2000) (decision and order); Colegio de Cirujanos Dentistas de P.R., 65 Fed. Reg. 17,506 (FTC Apr. 3, 2000) (proposed consent and aid to public comment) (settling charges that the Colegio determined the payors with which the unintegrated physicians would deal, set the prices and terms under which its members would provide services to payors, limited discounts, and generally blocked payors from implementing new health care delivery systems), 2000 FTC LEXIS 14 (2000) (order); Wisconsin Chiropractic Ass'n, 65 Fed. Reg. 13,387 (FTC Mar. 13, 2000) (proposed consent and aid to public comment) (the Wisconsin Chiropractic Association allegedly conspired with its members to fix prices for chiropractic services and to boycott payors to obtain higher prices), 2000 FTC LEXIS 72 (2000) (decision and order); Michael T. Berkley, D.C., 65 Fed. Reg. 13,385 (FTC Mar. 13, 2000) (proposed consent and aid to public comment) (settling charges that two chiropractors conspired to fix prices and to boycott a payor to obtain higher reimbursement rates), 2000 FTC LEXIS 47 (2000) (decision and order); North Lake Tahoe Med. Group, 64 Fed. Reg. 14,730 (FTC Mar. 26, 1999) (proposed consent and aid to public comment) (settling charges that members of the group, who accounted for at least 70% of all physicians in the area, engaged in a group boycott to impede the entry of managed care into the market), 1999 FTC LEXIS 134 (1999) (decision and order); United States v. Federation of Certified Surgeons and Specialists, 64 Fed. Reg. 5,831 (DOJ Feb. 5, 1999) (consent agreement) (settling charges that the federation and the accounting firm it used as messenger engaged in joint negotiations), 1999-1 Trade Cas. (CCH) ¶ 72,549 (M.D. Fla. 1999) (final judgment); FTC v. M.D. Physicians of Southwest Louisiana, Inc., 63 Fed. Reg. 34,423 (FTC June 24, 1998) (proposed consent and aid to public comment) (resolving charges that the group of unintegrated physicians conspired to fix prices and other terms of dealing with payors, and to obstruct the entry of managed care), 1998 FTC LEXIS 89 (1998) (decision and order); Urological Stone Surgeons, Inc., 63 Fed. Reg. 1,867 (FTC Jan. 12, 1998) (proposed consent and aid to public comment) (settling charges that the physicians' practices were not sufficiently integrated to justify the setting of uniform fees for their professional services), 125 F.T.C. 513 (1998) (decision and order); FTC v. Mesa County Physicians Indep. Practice Ass'n, 1998-1 Trade Cas. (CCH) ¶ 24,385 (FTC 1998) (consent order) (alleging that group consisting of at least 85% of private practice physicians and at least 90% of primary care physicians negotiated collectively with payors and encouraged members not to deal with health plans on nonapproved terms without integrating their services to create efficiencies); Physicians Group, 60 Fed. Reg. 25,223, 25,225 (FTC May 11, 1995) (proposed consent and aid to public comment) (settling charges that Virginia corporation and physician members of its board of directors conspired to fix the terms upon which they would deal with third-party payors, including terms of reimbursement and terms by which third-party payors attempt to contain health care costs), 120 F.T.C. 567 (1995) (decision and order); Trauma Assocs., 59 Fed. Reg. 42,051 (FTC

party payors over fees or other reimbursement terms, or threatening to boycott payors unless they dealt with the groups' members on collectively determined terms. These concerted activities often have been aimed at impeding the cost containment efforts of managed care plans or other third-party payors and sometimes have been dissolved under agency consent orders.[757]

Aug. 16, 1994) (proposed consent and aid to public comment) (settling charges that medical group and 10 surgeons conspired to fix fees for trauma services and engaged in a concerted refusal to deal with a local hospital authority operating two trauma centers in Florida), 118 F.T.C. 1130 (1994) (decision and order); United States v. Greater Bridgeport Individual Practice Ass'n, 57 Fed. Reg. 46,874 (FTC Oct. 13, 1992) (proposed consent and aid to public comment) (settling charges that IPA engaged in illegal boycott of HMO by urging its physician members not to contract individually with HMO and to support only joint negotiations through IPA, with result that contract ultimately negotiated between IPA and HMO provided for fees at significantly higher levels than HMO had offered in individual contracts), 57 Fed. Reg. 2913 (FTC Jan. 24, 1992) (consent order); Southbank IPA, Inc., 56 Fed. Reg. 50,912 (FTC Oct. 9, 1991) (proposed consent and aid to public comment) (settling charges that group of Florida obstetrician/gynecologists formed IPA as a vehicle to facilitate their engaging in collective decisions on fees and other terms desired from third-party payors and to jointly coerce the payors to accept those terms, where the physician participants allegedly did not place themselves jointly at financial risk for losses and neither the IPA nor its members offered new or more efficient services as a result of its formation), 114 F.T.C. 783 (1991) (decision and order); Preferred Physicians, Inc., 110 F.T.C. 157, 160 (1988) (consent order) (settling charges that incorporated group of Oklahoma physicians conspired to fix or increase prices charged by physicians in area by engaging in negotiations with third-party payors on behalf of its members with inherent threats that members would refuse to contract with payors if payors did not agree on prices and other terms acceptable to the association, as well as by urging its physician members to enter into agreements with third-party payors only on terms acceptable to the group); cf. United States v. Lake Country Optometric Soc'y, No. W-95-CR-114 (W.D. Tex. Dec. 15, 1995) (optometrists pled guilty to price-fixing charges brought by DOJ); final sentencing, Crim No. W95-CR-114 (July 9, 1996).

755. See, e.g., United States v. Alston, 974 F.2d 1206, 1211 (9th Cir. 1992) (government presented sufficient evidence to enable trier of fact to find dentists guilty beyond reasonable doubt of conspiring to fix prices for dental services provided to members of prepaid dental plans when they organized a letter-writing campaign among area dentists urging the plans to adopt higher copayment fees, after which the plans raised the copayment fees to match the schedules in the letters); Colegio de Cirujanos Dentistas de P.R., 65 Fed. Reg. 17,506 (FTC Apr. 3, 2000) (proposed consent and aid to public comment) (alleging that the unintegrated Colegio, consisting of almost all dentists practicing in Puerto Rico, acted as collective bargaining agent for its members, determined which payors its members would deal with, set prices and terms under which members would provide services, limited fee discounts by payors, and generally blocked payors from implementing new health care delivery systems), 2000 FTC LEXIS 14 (2000) (decision and order); FTC v. Dentists of San Juana Diaz, Coamo & Santa Isabel, P.R., 63 Fed. Reg. 50,573 (FTC Sept. 22, 1998) (consent order) (settling charges that the dentists boycotted a government program for indigent patients in order to obtain increased reimbursement).

756. Asociacion de Farmacias Region de Arecibo, Inc., 63 Fed. Reg. 70,407 (FTC Dec. 21, 1998) (proposed consent and aid to public comment) (settling charges that organization of 125 pharmacies in northern Puerto Rico agreed on prices for contracts with third-party payors), 1999 FTC LEXIS 28 (1999) (decision and order); FTC v. Institutional Pharmacy Network, 63 Fed. Reg. 29,736 (FTC June 1, 1998) (proposed consent and aid to public comment) (settling charges that five institutional pharmacies in Oregon unlawfully fixed prices), 1998 FTC LEXIS 86 (1998) (decision and order).

757. See, e.g., Physicians Group, 60 Fed. Reg. 25,223 (FTC May 11, 1995) (proposed consent and aid to public comment), 120 F.T.C. 567 (1995) (decision and order); Trauma Assocs., 59 Fed. Reg. 42,051 (FTC Aug. 16, 1994) (proposed consent and aid to public comment), 118 F.T.C. 1130 (1994) (decision and order); see also Southbank IPA, Inc., 56 Fed. Reg. 50,912 (FTC Oct. 9, 1991) (proposed consent and aid to public comment), 57 Fed. Reg. 2913 (Jan. 24, 1992) (consent order).

Where a provider group jointly sets fees on behalf of its providers, it must be able to demonstrate that the price setting is an integral part of the group's operations and necessary to make a new product or service available in the market.[758]

Providers who participate in an integrated joint venture[759] may collectively determine fees or other terms upon which the venture will deal with payors. Insofar as medical associations are combinations of unintegrated providers, their collective activities raise antitrust concerns similar to those raised by other groups of unintegrated providers, and also are discussed below.[760]

Groups of unintegrated providers may lessen the risk that their joint activities will be challenged by avoiding any joint setting of fees and protecting against the sharing of fee information.[761]

(2)   The 1996 Health Care Statements

The 1996 *Health Care Statements* specify that provider networks can avoid per se antitrust condemnation where the venture is not, on balance, anticompetitive either by assuring that the participants "share substantial financial risk" or that their economic integration creates "substantial efficiencies."[762] Statement 8 describes the types of risk sharing that qualify for the safety zone and expands (as compared to the 1994 *Health Care Statements*) the types of integration outside the safety zone that enable joint provider pricing within a network to escape per se condemnation. In addition to capitation and risk withholds (which were the focus of the 1994 *Health Care Statements*), examples of physician risk sharing that qualify under the safety zone include (1) the provision of designated services to a health plan "for a predetermined percentage of premium or revenue from the plan"; (2) establishing cost or utilization targets for the network as a whole, with physicians subject to substantial financial rewards or penalties based upon group performance in meeting the target; and (3) "global fee" or "all-inclusive case rate" arrangements.[763]

---

758. *See* part F.3.b of this chapter.
759. The FTC has expressly permitted such collective activity in its consent orders defining an "integrated joint venture" as "a joint arrangement to provide health care services in which all physicians participating in the venture who would otherwise be competitors (1) pool their capital to finance the venture . . . and (2) share a substantial risk of loss from their participation in the venture." Physicians Group, 60 Fed. Reg. 25,223, 25,224, 25,226 (FTC May 11, 1995) (proposed consent and aid to public comment), 120 F.T.C. 567 (1995) (decision and order); Trauma Assocs., 59 Fed. Reg. 42,051 (FTC Aug. 16, 1994) (proposed consent and aid to public comment), 118 F.T.C. 1130 (1994) (decision and order); Southbank IPA, Inc., 56 Fed. Reg. 50,912, 50,916 (FTC Oct. 9, 1991) (proposed consent and aid to public comment), 114 F.T.C. 783 (1991) (decision and order); *see also* United States v. Classic Care Network, 1995-1 Trade Cas. (CCH) ¶ 70,997 (E.D.N.Y. 1995) (prohibitions of final judgment do not extend to membership in integrated joint venture). As noted below, the 1996 *Health Care Statements* expand the agencies' views of the types of integration that may justify rule of reason treatment of joint provider pricing.
760. *See* part F.4.c of this chapter.
761. *See* U.S. Dep't of Justice, Business Review Letter to North Mississippi Health Services, 1987 DOJBRL LEXIS 16 (Apr. 19, 1987); U.S. Dep't of Justice, Business Review Letter to Health Care Management Assocs. (Sept. 21, 1983).
762. 1996 HEALTH CARE STATEMENTS, *supra* note 667, Statement 8.B.1 ("Where competitors economically integrate in a joint venture, however, such agreements [to fix prices or allocate markets], if reasonably necessary to accomplish the procompetitive benefits of the integration, are analyzed under the rule of reason").
763. *Id.*, Statement 8.A.4; *see also* U.S. Dep't of Justice, Business Review Letter to Patrick R. Gordon, 2001 DOJBRL LEXIS 6 (Aug. 29, 2001) (20% fee withhold and preestablished cost containment

Outside the safety zone, joint provider pricing (and other horizontal agreements ancillary to the network) may be justified under rule of reason analysis where the integration provided by the network "is likely to produce significant efficiencies that benefit consumers, and any price agreements . . . are reasonably necessary to realize those efficiencies."[764] Statement 8 points to some examples of such integration, including

> (1) establishing mechanisms to monitor and control utilization of health care services that are designed to control costs and assure quality of care; (2) selectively choosing network physicians who are likely to further these efficiency objectives; and (3) the significant investment of capital, both monetary and human, in the necessary infrastructure and capability to realize the claimed efficiencies.[765]

The 1996 *Health Care Statements* indicate that clinical integration is one way of generating the efficiencies that can justify price agreement within the network. An example provided in both Statements 8 and 9 describes types of clinical integration that may justify such agreements, including the establishment of quality and utilization goals, evaluation of provider performance, modification of provider practices, case management, preauthorization of some services, concurrent and retrospective review of inpatient stays, practice protocols and standards, investment in information systems, and hiring of a medical director and support staff to monitor the foregoing.[766]

Statement 8 also indicates in Example 2 that if a network has both risk-sharing (e.g., capitated) and fee-for-service arrangements with payors, joint provider pricing of the latter arrangements may be analyzed under the rule of reason where the risk-sharing arrangements generate significant network efficiencies, in terms of effectively managing the provision of care, that carry over to the fee-for-service business.[767] Statement 9 does not provide for safety zones for multiprovider network pricing activities due to the multiplicity of structures, arrangements, and relationships such networks involve, but it applies similar analytical principles and identifies similar forms of risk sharing in treating pricing (and other horizontal) issues for such networks.

---

and quality goals); U.S. Dep't of Justice, Business Review Letter to First Priority Health Systems, 1997 DOJBRL LEXIS 19 (Nov. 3, 1997) (capitated payments); Federal Trade Comm'n, Staff Advisory Opinion Letter to New Jersey Pharmacists Ass'n (Aug. 12, 1997) (capitation and "shared risk reward" contracts); U.S. Dep't of Justice, Business Review Letter to Vermont Physicians Clinic, 1997 DOJBRL LEXIS 16 (July 30, 1997) (capitation and fee withholds); U.S. Dep't of Justice, Business Review Letter to Southwest Orthopedic Specialists, 1997 DOJBRL LEXIS 12 (June 10, 1997) (capitated fees and efficiency withholds); Federal Trade Comm'n, Staff Advisory Opinion Letter to Yellowstone Physicians (May 14, 1997) (capitation and substantial fee withholds); U.S. Dep't of Justice, Business Review Letter to Santa Fe Managed Care Org., 1997 DOJBRL LEXIS 3 (Feb. 12, 1997) (capitation and global fee arrangements).

764. 1996 HEALTH CARE STATEMENTS, *supra* note 667, Statement 8.B.1.
765. *Id.*
766. *Id.*, Statement 8.C.1, Statement 9.D.1; *see also* Federal Trade Comm'n, Staff Advisory Opinion Letter to Mobile Health Resources (Jan. 30, 1997) (proposed capitated fees and risk withhold may not be sufficient to entail "financial substantial risk sharing," but network provides substantial economic and functional integration and agreements on price are reasonably necessary to achieve anticipated efficiencies).
767. 1996 HEALTH CARE STATEMENTS, *supra* note 667, Statement 8.C.2.

Where the network is not sufficiently integrated to justify collective price setting, it may use the "messenger model" to create joint contracting efficiencies while avoiding unlawful price agreements among competitors. Under the traditional messenger model, an independent third-party messenger serves as a conduit for exchanging information between payors and network providers about the pricing terms and conditions each is willing to accept, with each provider unilaterally and individually making all pricing decisions. The messenger must avoid becoming a negotiating agent or a vehicle for price agreement among the network providers.[768]

c.   EXCLUSIONARY CONDUCT BY PROVIDER NETWORKS
     AND JOINT VENTURES

(1)   Refusals to Deal

Provider networks often limit their membership for a variety of reasons such as limiting the venture's size; assuring a certain level of proficiency or certification; and seeking to achieve quality control standards, utilization control, and cost containment. The courts typically apply the rule of reason in cases involving exclusion from provider networks. When the rule of reason applies, an antitrust violation will not be found unless the challenged activities have a substantial anticompetitive effect that is not outweighed by procompetitive benefits.[769] The market power of the defendant will weigh heavily in the balance.[770]

For example, in *Capital Imaging Associates v. Mohawk Valley Medical Associates*,[771] a private radiology group brought an antitrust claim against an independent practice association (IPA) and the health maintenance organization (HMO) that contracted for the IPA members' services.[772] The IPA had denied membership to the radiology group. Because the HMO's subscribers were required to go to the IPA's physicians for all of their medical needs, the plaintiff was effectively precluded from serving the segment of the market served by the HMO/IPA.[773] The Second Circuit held that although the plaintiff was injured, it failed to prove an injury to competition within the relevant market. The court noted

---

768. *Id.*, Statement 9.C, Statement 9.D.4; *see also* Levine v. Central Fla. Med. Affiliates, 72 F.3d 1538, 1548-49 (11th Cir.) (approving messenger model featuring provider "opt out" provision, contrary to 1996 *Health Care Statements*), *cert. denied*, 519 U.S. 820 (1996); United States v. HealthCare Partners, 1996-1 Trade Cas. (CCH) ¶ 71,337 (D. Conn 1996) (setting forth relatively restrictive terms for role of messenger); Federal Trade Comm'n, Staff Advisory Opinion Letter to Ohio Ambulance Network (Jan. 30, 1997) (messenger program for pricing determined to be consistent with Statement 9, but cautioning that use of messenger to develop coordinated programs for quality assurance and utilization management would not eliminate the potential for a collective agreement among members on such matters).

769. The rule of reason is discussed in part B.3.b of Chapter I.

770. *See, e.g.*, Hahn v. Oregon Physicians' Serv., 868 F.2d 1022 (9th Cir. 1988), *cert. denied*, 493 U.S. 846 (1989); Randall v. Buena Vista County Hosp., 75 F. Supp. 2d 946 (N.D. Iowa 1999) (denying summary judgment and holding that discovery was necessary to determine whether defendant hospital possessed market power in a relevant market); *see also* Continental Orthopedic Appliances, Inc. v. Health Ins. Plan, 40 F. Supp. 2d 109 (E.D.N.Y. 1999) (declining to grant summary judgment and holding that discovery was necessary to assess the commercial realities of the market).

771. 996 F.2d 537 (2d Cir.), *cert. denied*, 510 U.S. 947 (1993).

772. *Id.*

773. *Id.*

that the defendant HMO included only 2.3 percent of the region's HMO subscribers and 6.75 percent of its physicians. Further, the plaintiff had conceded that, whether or not it was admitted to the IPA, the fees radiologists charged for their services probably would remain constant.

Similarly, in *Levine v. Central Florida Medical Affiliates*,[774] the court rejected an internist's antitrust claims against a preferred provider organization (PPO), a hospital, the hospital's parent corporation, and Central Florida Medical Affiliates, a physicians' advocacy group organized to supply physicians to the PPO. Levine alleged that the defendants unlawfully restricted the size of the provider panel and discouraged providers from referring PPO enrollees to non-PPO physicians. The court, analyzing the alleged restraint under the rule of reason, upheld summary judgment in favor of the defendants, concluding that the plaintiff could not prove that the defendants' behavior had a detrimental effect on competition—particularly because Levine's practice had grown at an extraordinary rate notwithstanding his exclusion.[775]

By contrast, in *Hahn v. Oregon Physicians' Service*,[776] the defendant was a statewide PPO that claimed approximately 90 percent of all eligible physicians as members and 16 percent of Portland's residents as subscribers.[777] Podiatrists were not permitted to become members.[778] The PPO used a two-tiered reimbursement system whereby the rate at which member physicians were reimbursed for services was higher than the rate at which nonmembers were reimbursed.[779] A group of podiatrists claimed that this system constituted a group boycott.[780] They asserted that, due to the two-tiered system, they were unable to compete effectively with member physicians who provided similar services.[781] The court permitted the plaintiffs to go to trial on their group boycott claim, concluding that, under the rule of reason, the PPO would have to show that there was a "justification" for excluding podiatrists.[782] Although the court suggested that valid cost concerns might suffice, it also noted that the evidence indicated that podiatrists actually charged less per patient than the PPO members did.[783]

774. 72 F.3d 1538 (11th Cir.), *cert. denied*, 519 U.S. 820 (1996).
775. *Id.* at 1544, 1551; *see also* Park Ave. Radiology Assoc. v. Methodist Health Sys., Inc., 1999-2 Trade Cas. (CCH) ¶ 72,712 (6th Cir. 1999) (applying the five-factor test for standing as articulated in *Associated Gen. Contractors of Cal. v. California State Council of Carpenters*, 459 U.S. 519 (1983), and finding that plaintiffs failed to sufficiently allege antitrust standing) (unpublished opinion); Doctor's Hosp. v. Southeast Med. Alliance, 123 F.3d 301 (5th Cir. 1997) (affirming summary judgment for defendants where there was no evidence that affiliation with defendant PPO was necessary for plaintiff to compete and there was insufficient evidence of an injury to competition); Finkelstein v. Aetna Health Plans of N.Y., 1997-2 Trade Cas. (CCH) ¶ 71,971 (S.D.N.Y. 1997) (dismissing claims challenging termination without cause provision in HMO contract because plaintiff did not claim contract terms resulted in reduced quality of care or other harm to competition), *aff'd without op.*, 152 F.3d 917 (2d Cir. 1998).
776. 868 F.2d 1022 (9th Cir.), *cert. denied*, 493 U.S. 846 (1989).
777. *Id.* at 1024.
778. *Id.*
779. *Id.* at 1024-25.
780. *Id.* at 1030.
781. *Id.*
782. *Id.* at 1031.
783. *Id.* at 1032. For other cases holding boycotts unlawful in the health care context, see, e.g., Reazin v. Blue Cross & Blue Shield, 899 F.2d 951 (10th Cir.) (Blue Shield-initiated conspiracy to exclude hospital dealing with insurer's competitor), *cert. denied*, 497 U.S. 1005 (1990); Virginia Acad. of Clinical Psychologists v. Blue Shield, 624 F.2d 476 (4th Cir. 1980) (provider-controlled Blue

In general, however, with regard to claims arising out of a network's exclusion of particular providers, courts have recognized that networks must have the freedom to be selective about membership in order to achieve a level of efficiency and quality that makes their product desirable. For the most part, claims asserted by health care providers excluded from physician networks, hospitals, and health plans have failed because courts do not view selectivity as necessarily anticompetitive.[784] In *Hassan v. Independent Practice Associates*,[785] for example, the court held that the defendants' "acts of expulsion and the refusal to readmit plaintiffs are justified by enhancing efficiency and making the market more competitive."[786] *Hassan* involved the claims of two affiliated allergists against an IPA that had been formed in order to contract on a capitated basis with a managed care organization.[787] The allergists were terminated from IPA membership on the ground that they performed excessive, unnecessary tests.[788] Addressing whether to apply a per se analysis, the court examined the procompetitive justifications for the expulsion and stated that "'[i]f an HMO utilizes physicians who disagree with its philosophy of cost containment, that philosophy cannot be realized.'"[789] The court stated that the issue is not whether the IPA's testing guidelines were "correct" but whether they were plausibly intended to enhance efficiency.[790]

The Federal Trade Commission staff also has acknowledged that the exclusion of providers is not necessarily anticompetitive, noting that the foreclosure effect of an overinclusive network "raises far more substantial competitive concerns and antitrust risk" than does the concern that exclusion of providers from the network may constitute a boycott.[791]

Cross refusal to pay for clinical psychologists' services unless billed through physicians), *cert. denied*, 450 U.S. 916 (1981); Griffiths v. Blue Cross & Blue Shield of Alabama, 147 F. Supp. 2d 1203, 1211 (N.D. Ala. 2001) (concerted action giving rise to insurer's policies that favored one class of health care provider over another); Blue Cross v. Kitsap Physicians Serv., 1982-1 Trade Cas. (CCH) ¶ 64,588 (W.D. Wash. 1981) (dominant health insurer's bylaw precluding participating physicians from rendering services to competing HMOs).

784. The excluded provider must establish all of the elements of a claim under the Sherman Act. Thus, these types of claims do not succeed when the physician fails to establish standing, to define the relevant market adequately, or to show the anticompetitive effect of the challenged activities in that market. *See, e.g.*, Morgan, Strand, Wheeler & Biggs v. Radiology, Ltd., 924 F.2d 1484, 1491 (9th Cir. 1991); Ezekwo v. American Bd. of Internal Med., 18 F. Supp. 2d 271 (S.D.N.Y. 1998) (plaintiff failed to establish antitrust injury; the court found no evidence that defendants' refusal to associate with plaintiff eliminate patients' choice of internists); J. Allen Ramey, M.D., Inc. v. Pacific Found. for Med. Care, 999 F. Supp. 1355 (S.D. Cal. 1998) (plaintiff, excluded from defendant PPO, suffered no antitrust injury; plaintiff remained free to set his own prices and to compete on price terms with PPO); Brown v. Our Lady of Lourdes Med. Ctr., 767 F. Supp. 618 (D.N.J. 1991), *aff'd*, 961 F.2d 207 (3d Cir. 1992).

785. 698 F. Supp. 679 (E.D. Mich. 1988).

786. *Id.* at 694.

787. *Id.* at 681-82.

788. *Id.* at 682-83.

789. *Id.* at 694 (quoting defendants' counsel).

790. *Id.*; *see also* Northwest Med. Lab. v. Blue Cross & Blue Shield, 794 P.2d 428 (Or. 1990) (rejecting claims that providers confining referrals to other HMO providers constituted unlawful group boycott, given absence of market power and benefits of exclusivity to effective utilization and quality of care).

791. Federal Trade Comm'n, Staff Advisory Opinion Letter to California Managed Imaging Med. Group, Inc. (Nov. 17, 1993). The 1996 *Health Care Statements* recognize the potential procompetitive effects of membership rules that may exclude certain providers. *See* 1996 HEALTH CARE STATEMENTS, *supra* note 667, Statement 9.B.2.c.

(2) Exclusive and Selective Contracting

A leading case analyzing exclusive dealing arrangements in the context of a health care network is *U.S. Healthcare, Inc. v. Healthsource, Inc.*[792] In that case, the First Circuit upheld an exclusive dealing clause in a contract between an HMO and the doctors who provided primary care for it. Noting that in cases challenging exclusive dealing arrangements "judgments for plaintiffs are not easily obtained," the court focused on one critical question, namely, whether the deal

> "foreclose[s]" so much of the available supply or outlet capacity that existing competitors or new entrants may be limited or excluded and, under certain circumstances, this may reinforce market power and raise prices for consumers.[793]

The plaintiff failed to show that the challenged arrangement resulted in significant foreclosure. The HMO's contracts with physicians were terminable on thirty days' notice and the evidence did not otherwise show that doctors were significantly foreclosed from the market. The court stated that "[n]ormally an exclusivity clause terminable on 30 days' notice would be close to a *de minimus* [sic] constraint."[794] In addition, although the HMO had contracts with 25 percent of the primary care physicians in the state, new doctors were continuously entering the market.[795] The monopolization claim also failed because the plaintiff failed to show that the HMO had market power.[796] Significantly, the court also cited the legitimate purposes often served by exclusive arrangements, including assurance of supply or outlets, enhanced ability to plan, reduced transaction costs, and creation of loyalty.[797]

---

792. 986 F.2d 589, 598 (1st Cir. 1993).

793. *Id.* at 595; *see also* U.S. Dep't of Justice, Business Review Letter to First Priority Health Sys., 1997 DOJBRL 19 (Nov. 3, 1997) (clearing exclusive affiliation by physician organization which includes 30% of area primary care "gatekeepers" with HMO that serves 60% of area enrollees in gatekeeper plans, because plans compete with other health plans and because many other primary care physicians are available to staff these gatekeeper plans).

794. 986 F.2d at 596.

795. *Id.*

796. *Id.* at 599; *see also* Minnesota Ass'n of Nurse Anesthetists v. Unity Hosp., 208 F.3d 655 (8th Cir. 2000) (affirming summary judgment against association attacking exclusive dealing arrangements between three hospitals and two groups of anesthesiologists because defendants did not possess market power and their actions did not harm competition); All Care Nursing Serv. v. High Tech Staffing Servs., 135 F.3d 740 (11th Cir. 1998) (the use of preferred nurse registries did not exclude any competing registries—which continued to receive more than a "trifling portion" of defendants' business—nor create a risk of stabilizing prices), *cert. denied*, 526 U.S. 1016 (1999); Retina Assocs. v. Southern Baptist Hosp., 105 F.3d 1376 (11th Cir. 1997) (per curiam) (affirming summary judgment for defendants on challenge to exclusive referral arrangement due to defendants' lack of market power).

797. *U.S. Healthcare, Inc.*, 986 F.2d at 595. Quality of care and efficiency justifications have supported judicial approval of exclusive arrangements between hospitals and exclusive provider groups in a number of cases. *See, e.g.*, Smith v. Northern Mich. Hosps., 703 F.2d 942 (6th Cir. 1983); Pfenninger v. Exempla, Inc., 116 F. Supp. 2d 1184 (D. Colo. 2000) (finding plausible procompetitive arguments that an agreement between a hospital and several IPAs to require hospital staff privileges as a condition to membership in the IPAs would help payors to obtain lower costs by ensuring that the IPAs would refer patients to a designated hospital); Drug Emporium Inc. v. Blue Cross of Western N.Y., Inc., 104 F. Supp. 2d 184 (W.D.N.Y. 2000) (granting in part defendants' motion to dismiss group boycott claims and denying plaintiff's request for per se condemnation of exclusive pharmacy network as "futile" due to the procompetitive virtue of exclusive networks); Bellam v. Clayton County Hosp. Auth., 758 F. Supp.

The 1996 *Health Care Statements* recognize the potential procompetitive benefits of selective and exclusive contracts involving provider networks.[798]

4. *Other Pricing Issues in Health Care*

a. EXCHANGES OF PRICE AND OTHER INFORMATION

The courts and the enforcement agencies have long recognized both the potential procompetitive benefits and the potential anticompetitive impact of sharing price information.[799] As a general proposition, making price and other information available to purchasers of health care services allows them to make better informed purchasing decisions to react promptly to changes in the market, which encourages competition among providers.[800] On the other hand, exchanges of price data or other competitively significant information among competitors can facilitate collusion on prices or other anticompetitive behavior.[801]

(1) *The 1996* Health Care Statements: *Antitrust Safety Zones*

The 1996 *Health Care Statements* provide three antitrust safety zones for exchanges of information in health care markets. The first safety zone relates to providers' collective provision of non-fee-related information to purchasers of health care services. Absent extraordinary circumstances, the agencies will not challenge (1) a medical society's collection and dissemination of outcome data about a procedure that its members believe should be covered by a health care purchaser, or (2) health care providers' development and dissemination of suggested clinical practice guidelines or "practice parameters."[802] While the agencies recognize that the collective provision of underlying medical data by health care providers may be procompetitive by helping health care purchasers assess the quality or efficacy of particular treatments, the agencies also caution that a collective attempt by providers

---

1488 (N.D. Ga. 1990); *see also* part F.2.c of this chapter regarding exclusive arrangements in the context of medical staff privileges cases.

798. 1996 HEALTH CARE STATEMENTS, *supra* note 667, Statement 9.B.2.b.

799. *See* part C.1.c of Chapter I.

800. *See* U.S. Dep't of Justice, Business Review Letter to AdviNet, Inc., 1995 DOJBRL LEXIS 13 (May 12, 1995) (declining to challenge proposal to establish nationwide database of nursing home services which offered "potential to benefit competition by promoting more informed consumer choice"); U.S. Dep't of Justice, Business Review Letter to Birmingham Cooperative Clinical Benchmarking Demonstration Project, 1994 DOJBRL LEXIS 14 (June 20, 1994) (declining to challenge proposal to exchange cost and patient outcome data among Birmingham-area businesses and hospitals which "has the potential of allowing businesses to make better informed purchasing decisions and should also promote hospital effectiveness and efficiency"); U.S. Dep't of Justice, Business Review Letter to St. Louis Area Business Health Coalition, 1988 DOJBRL LEXIS 9 (Mar. 24, 1988).

801. *See, e.g.,* U.S. Dep't of Justice, Business Review Letter to Hyatt, Imler, Ott & Blount, P.C., 1992 DOJBRL LEXIS 13 (June 15, 1992) (information exchange that facilitated collective action to increase prices would raise antitrust concern); Federal Trade Comm'n, Staff Advisory Opinion Letter to Utah Society of Oral & Maxillofacial Surgeons (June 8, 1985) (while dissemination of truthful, historic range of providers' fee information would generally not raise antitrust concerns, dissemination of average prices for particular procedure may be part of providers' reaching common understanding about prices they will charge).

802. 1996 HEALTH CARE STATEMENTS, *supra* note 667, Statement 4.A.

to coerce a purchaser to adopt their suggestions or recommendations could create antitrust exposure.[803]

The second safety zone for the provision of health care information relates to providers' collective provision of fee-related information to purchasers of health care services, including such information as providers' current or historical fees, discounts, or alternative reimbursement methods that they accept (such as capitation or all-inclusive fees).[804] Absent extraordinary circumstances, the agencies will not challenge the provision of such fee-related information to purchasers if (1) a third party (e.g., consultant, purchaser, or government agency) manages the collection of the information, (2) any information exchanged among the competing providers themselves is historical (i.e., more than three months old), and (3) for any information that is available to the providers, certain precautions are taken to ensure that specific fee information cannot be identified with specific providers.[805] Information about providers' future prices or fees is expressly excluded from the safety zone.[806]

The third safety zone for the provision of health care information relates to provider participation in exchanges of price and cost information.[807] The agencies acknowledge that surveys of providers about the prices they charge for their services or about the salaries, wages, or other benefits they pay their employees can have procompetitive benefits, including increasing an individual provider's ability to price competitively or to attract highly qualified personnel, and helping purchasers to make better informed purchasing decisions.[808] Absent extraordinary circumstances, the agencies will not challenge provider participation in written surveys of either (1) prices for health care services, or (2) wages, salaries, or other benefits of health care personnel if the three conditions delineated in the second safety zone, discussed above, are met.[809] These last two safety zones reflect the agencies' attempt to balance, on the one hand, an individual provider's procompetitive interest in having fee-related, price, and cost information to be able to adjust its own prices or wages in light of market conditions against, on the other hand, the potential that the information could be used by the providers collectively to set or affect prices or employee compensation.

The 1996 *Health Care Statements* also outline the analysis that the agencies will use to review exchanges of information falling outside of the antitrust safety zones.[810]

---

803. *Id.* (citing as an example of such illegal coercion the collective refusal by providers to provide X rays to a purchaser who uses them to make its coverage determination).

804. *Id.*, Statement 5.A.

805. *Id.* Specifically, these precautions are that "there are at least five providers reporting data upon which each disseminated statistic is based, no individual provider's data may represent more than 25 percent on a weighted basis of that statistic, and any information disseminated must be sufficiently aggregated such that it would not allow recipients to identify the prices charged by any individual provider." *Id.*

806. *Id.*, Statement 5.B.

807. *Id.*, Statement 6.A. *See also id.* n. 15 (noting that the term "prices" in connection with health care provider services includes "billed charges for individual services, discounts off billed charges, or per diem, capitated, or diagnosis related group rates").

808. *Id.*, Statement 6.

809. *Id.*, Statement 6.A; *see also infra* note 841.

810. For price, cost, and fee-related exchanges that fall outside the safety zones, the agencies will consider (1) the nature of the information exchanged, (2) the rationale for the exchange, (3) the nature and extent of the communications between the parties, (4) the involvement of a third party

In several business review letters, the Department of Justice has analyzed and declined to challenge information exchanges that did not fully meet the safety zone requirements.[811]

(2) Sellers' Exchanges

Specific factors that have been important in the agencies' review of health care providers' exchanges of price information include whether (1) there was a legitimate, procompetitive purpose for the participants to share the information; (2) the information related to historical prices rather than current or future prices, and it was provided in aggregate form to avoid identification of the specific prices charged by individual providers; (3) an independent third party collected and distributed the data; (4) the information was widely available to interested parties, such as consumers, third-party payors, government agencies, and the public, and not only to competing providers; (5) participation in the exchange was voluntary, and no collective action was taken or suggested in light of the information; and (6) the market in which the exchange occurred was relatively unconcentrated.[812]   The

---

or a public entity, and (5) whether the exchange results in an agreement on prices or on wages paid to employees. *Id.*, Statement 5.B, Statement 6.B.

811. *See, e.g.*, U.S. Dep't of Justice, Business Review Letter to Seeskin, Paas, Blackburn & Co., 1994 DOJBRL LEXIS 15 (June 29, 1994) (although proposal did not meet 1993 safety zone for hospital exchanges of price and cost information, DOJ declined to challenge proposal by accounting firm to publish survey of prices charged by its dentist clients for about 400 dental procedures, undertaken for purpose of allowing participating dentists to compare their list prices with high, low, and average prices of other dentists); U.S. Dep't of Justice, Business Review Letter to New Jersey Hosp. Ass'n and New Jersey Soc'y for Health Care Human Resources Admin., 1994 DOJBRL LEXIS 11 (Feb. 18, 1994) (where proposal "substantially meets" 1993 safety zone for hospital exchanges of price and cost information, DOJ declined to challenge proposal to compile survey and produce report on the wages and salaries of hospital employees).

812. *See, e.g.*, U.S. Dep't of Justice, Business Review Letter to AdviNet, Inc., 1995 DOJBRL LEXIS 13 (May 12, 1995) (declining to challenge proposal of AdviNet, a subsidiary of country's largest provider of long-term care services, to provide consumers access to nationwide database concerning services and other information on nursing home and long-term care providers, some of whom may opt to become "participating providers," undertaken for purpose of meeting consumer need for information about long-term care alternatives nationwide); U.S. Dep't of Justice, Business Review Letter to Seeskin, Paas, Blackburn & Co., 1994 DOJBRL LEXIS 15 (June 29, 1994) (declining to challenge proposal of accounting firm to publish survey of prices charged by its dentist clients for about 400 dental procedures, undertaken for purpose of allowing participating dentists to compare their list prices with those of other dentists); U.S. Dep't of Justice, Business Review Letter to Hotel Employees & Restaurant Employees Int'l Union Welfare Fund, 1994 DOJBRL LEXIS 21 (May 20, 1994) (declining to challenge proposal of union welfare fund to provide a one-time exchange of physician fee information to PPO with which it contracts for physician services, undertaken for purpose of enabling individual physicians to make informed decision whether to accept fund's fee schedule); U.S. Dep't of Justice, Business Review Letter to Transplant Assocs., 1992 DOJBL LEXIS 19 (Oct. 26, 1992) (declining to challenge proposal of Transplant Associates, a provider-based PPO whose member physicians perform kidney and liver transplants, to compile data on members' charges for such transplants and to use such data in PPO's negotiations with third-party payors over capitated contracts); U.S. Dep't of Justice, Business Review Letter to Hyatt, Imler, Ott & Blant, P.C., 1992 DOJBRL LEXIS 13 (June 15, 1992) (declining to challenge proposal of a public accounting firm in Atlanta, Georgia, to compile, analyze, and publish data on the prices charged by Georgia hospitals for specified hospital services undertaken for purpose of assisting hospital administrators in assessing market conditions for provision of hospital services); Federal Trade Comm'n, Staff Advisory Opinion Letter to American Dental Ass'n (Feb. 15, 1990) (declining to challenge proposal of American Dental Association to survey the usual, customary, and reasonable rates of dental insurers for purpose of compiling set of

agencies have not hesitated to oppose exchanges of fee information that appeared to result in coordinated pricing among health care providers.[813]

(3) Buyers' Exchanges

Exchanges of price information also may occur among health care buyers, such as employers or insurance companies. Making price and quality information available to buyers enhances the buyers' ability to make more informed health care purchases and encourages competition among the providers, and hence is generally viewed as procompetitive.[814]

The Department of Justice has acknowledged that in the health care industry, provider-specific and insurer-specific exchanges of information among buyers generally do not raise antitrust concerns so long as they would not facilitate collective or collusive use in bargaining or bidding contexts.[815] The Department of Justice thus encourages efforts to disseminate information to consumers and third-party payors that allows them to make better informed selections of insurance coverages and health care providers.[816] Accordingly, the agency frequently has declined to challenge proposals by groups of health care buyers, such as employers or insurance companies, to exchange information among the groups' members concerning prices charged by providers of health care products or services.[817]

guidelines for insurers to use in establishing fee levels); Federal Trade Comm'n, Staff Advisory Opinion Letter to North Texas Chapter, American College of Surgeons (Dec. 12, 1985) (concluding that serious antitrust concerns were not raised by proposed survey of fees charged by members of surgeons' association for surgical procedures, if undertaken for purpose of enhancing individual negotiations between surgeons and third-party payors); Federal Trade Comm'n, Staff Advisory Opinion Letter to American Dental Ass'n (Aug. 26, 1985) (concluding that serious antitrust concerns were not raised by proposed surveys of dentists' fees in local market areas undertaken for purpose of aiding dental patients or dentists in evaluating dentists' fees or level of dental benefits offered by third-party payors).

    For a decision not to challenge a proposed exchange of non-fee-related information among providers, see U.S. Dep't of Justice, Business Review Letter to American Ass'n of Ophthalmology (July 3, 1979) (involving proposed survey of public's utilization of ophthalmological services for dissemination to association members).

813. *See, e.g.*, United States v. Burgstiner, 56 Fed. Reg. 6681 (DOJ Feb. 19, 1991) (competitive impact statement summarizing complaint) (settling allegations that 22 obstetrician/gynecologists conspired to exchange current and prospective fee information, resulting in higher fees for normal and cesarean section deliveries), 1991-1 Trade Cas. (CCH) ¶ 69,422 (S.D. Ga. 1991) (final judgment); *see also* Federal Trade Comm'n, Staff Advisory Opinion Letter to Northwestern Nevada Orthopaedic Surgery Alliance (July 11, 1995) (cautioning that the use of a messenger as a participant in fee negotiations with payors raises serious antitrust concerns); United States v. Utah Soc'y for Healthcare Human Resources Admin., 59 Fed. Reg. 14,204 (DOJ Mar. 25, 1994) (proposed consent decree), 1994-2 Trade Cas. (CCH) ¶ 70,795 (D. Utah 1994) (consent decree nunc pro tunc).

814. U.S. Dep't of Justice, Business Review Letter to Lexecon Health Serv., 1986 DOJBRL LEXIS 10 (June 20, 1986).

815. U.S. Dep't of Justice, Business Review Letter to Stark County Health Care Coalition, 1985 DOJBRL LEXIS 7 (Aug. 30, 1985).

816. U.S. Dep't of Justice, Business Review Letter to Maryland Health Care Coalition (Feb. 19, 1982).

817. *See, e.g.*, U.S. Dep't of Justice, Business Review Letter to Northwestern Nat'l Life Ins. Co., 1995 DOJBRL LEXIS 3 (Mar. 9, 1995) (declining to challenge insurance company's program to detect medical fraud by exchanging price information with other insurers); U.S. Dep't of Justice, Business Review Letter to St. Louis Area Bus. Health Coalition, 1988 DOJBRL LEXIS 9 (Mar. 24, 1988) (declining to challenge proposal by nonprofit coalition of 34 St. Louis area employers which purchased health care services for their employees to collect and publish information on the

Similarly, it has declined to challenge exchanges of wage or other cost information among health care providers where adequate safeguards against collusion were present.[818]

Although antitrust concerns may not seem as serious when information is exchanged among buyers rather than sellers, similar factors are considered relevant in assessing the antitrust risks of buyer and seller exchanges.[819] The sharing of price information among buyers could facilitate collusion on the prices they will pay or the sellers with whom they will deal, raising the risk of illegal group boycotts or concerted refusals to deal except on collectively agreed-upon terms. These risks are

---

prices of the most frequently used hospital services in 39 area hospitals, undertaken for the purpose of promoting competition among health care providers by giving consumers information to compare prices and identify efficient providers); U.S. Dep't of Justice, Business Review Letter to Lexecon Health Serv., 1986 DOJBRL LEXIS 10 (June 24, 1986) (declining to challenge proposal to compile and publish historical and publicly available provider-specific price and quality health care information, undertaken for the purpose of enhancing consumers' ability to make better informed health care judgments); U.S. Dep't of Justice, Business Review Letter to Stark County Health Care Coalition, 1985 DOJBRL LEXIS 7 (Aug. 30, 1985) (declining to challenge proposal by coalition of 25 employers to collect variety of health care data from members, local hospitals, and members' health care insurance carriers, undertaken for purpose of encouraging members to make informed decisions in the purchase and design of health benefit plans); U.S. Dep't of Justice, Business Review Letter to Southwest Mich. Health Sys. Agency (Mar. 3, 1982) (declining to challenge proposal to gather and publish rates charged for the 25 most frequently used hospital services at 22 area hospitals, undertaken for the purpose of enabling and encouraging consumers to shop for lower priced hospital services); U.S. Dep't of Justice, Business Review Letter to Maryland Health Care Coalition (Feb. 19, 1982) (declining to challenge aspect of proposal of an informal group primarily of employers to collect and analyze a variety of publicly available information on health care utilization, price, and other data undertaken for the purpose of allowing employers to compare their employees' health care costs and utilization and to assess impact of health benefits packages on utilization).

For a favorable consideration of an exchange of price and nonprice information among both sellers and buyers that the DOJ said had the potential to be procompetitive by encouraging hospitals to improve their quality and efficiency and by allowing businesses to make better informed purchasing decisions, see U.S. Dep't of Justice, Business Review Letter to Birmingham Coop. Clinical Benchmarking Demonstration Project, 1994 DOJBRL LEXIS 14 (June 20, 1994) (declining to challenge proposal of a group of Birmingham businesses and hospitals to publish information about the local hospitals' historical costs and clinical effectiveness in providing three particular medical services, undertaken for the purpose of allowing each participating hospital's costs and patient outcomes to be compared with national averages, local averages, and national "benchmark" averages for costs and patient outcomes).

818. *See, e.g.,* U.S. Dep't of Justice, Business Review Letter to Southwest Oncology Group, 1995 DOJBRL LEXIS 25 (Nov. 2, 1995) (declining to challenge proposal by a group of cancer institutes to collect cost information about clinical trials); U.S. Dep't of Justice, Business Review Letter to New Jersey Ass'n & New Jersey Soc'y for Health Care Human Resources Admin., 1994 DOJBRL LEXIS 11 (Feb. 18, 1994); U.S. Dep't of Justice, Business Review Letter to Health & Personal Care Distrib. Conf., Inc., 1993 DOJBRL LEXIS 19 (Oct. 13, 1993) (declining to challenge proposal by a national health care trade association for distributors of health and personal care products to exchange information concerning its members' experience with transportation services). *But see* United States v. Utah Soc'y for Healthcare Human Resources Admin., 59 Fed. Reg. 14,204 (DOJ Mar. 25, 1994) (proposed consent decree and competitive impact statement) (settling charges that eight Utah hospitals and related entities unlawfully conspired to exchange nonpublic information about current and prospective entry wages for registered nurses, allegedly resulting in stabilization of such wages and lower annual wage increases than would have been paid in a competitive market), 1994-2 Trade Cas. (CCH) ¶ 70,795 (D. Utah 1994) (consent decree nunc pro tunc).

819. *See* part F.4.a(2) of this chapter; *see also* Mandeville Island Farms v. American Crystal Sugar Co., 334 U.S. 219, 235-36 (1948) (Sherman Act reaches conspiracies among buyers as well as sellers).

minimized where (1) the buyers are encouraged to make informed, unilateral decisions in their health care purchases by comparing the prices, quality, and other attributes of the services offered by competing providers; and (2) the buyers avoid joint activity on the basis of the shared information, such as attempting to negotiate collectively with providers or to exert collective economic pressure on them to lower prices.[820] As with sellers' exchanges, exchanges of information among health care buyers that appear to have resulted in the stabilization of prices in the market have been condemned.[821]

b. PEER REVIEW OF FEES

Local medical societies or other professional associations may offer informal procedures for the voluntary resolution of fee disputes among patients, providers, and third-party payors. These peer review programs may promote competition in a number of ways, such as by providing useful information to consumers and payors to allow them to make informed health care purchasing decisions,[822] by aiding the payors in their cost containment efforts,[823] and by giving providers an incentive to practice in a cost conscious manner. Both the Federal Trade Commission[824] and the Department of Justice[825] have expressly permitted the peer review of individual physicians' fees in cases where a medical society and individual physicians do not otherwise engage in joint activity over fees.

The professional review of fees may be anticompetitive if the review threatens independent pricing by the providers[826] or if the program effectively coerces providers into adopting, or third-party payors into accepting, particular fee levels or reimbursement systems as determined by the association.[827] The HCQIA expressly excludes from its immunity provisions any peer review actions based on physicians' fees.[828]

---

820. *See generally* cases cited *supra* in notes 800, 813.
821. *See, e.g., Utah Soc'y*, 59 Fed. Reg. at 14,204.
822. *See* Federal Trade Comm'n, Advisory Opinion Letter to American Med. Ass'n & Chicago Med. Soc'y (Feb. 14, 1994) ("Advisory peer review can give patients, and payers, information about the basis for a fee and an informed opinion about its reasonableness, and help them decide whether to pay a disputed bill or to continue to patronize a particular doctor.").
823. *See* Iowa Dental Ass'n, 99 F.T.C. 648 (1982).
824. *See, e.g.,* Southbank IPA, Inc., 56 Fed. Reg. 50,912, 50,914 (FTC Oct. 9, 1991) (proposed consent and aid to public comment), 114 F.T.C. 783 (1991) (decision and order); Michigan State Med. Soc'y, 101 F.T.C. 191, 314 (1983).
825. *See, e.g.,* United States v. Massachusetts Allergy Soc'y, 1992-1 Trade Cas. (CCH) ¶ 69,846 (D. Mass. 1992) (peer review of individual physicians' fees permitted when requested by third party or patient).
826. *See, e.g., Iowa Dental Ass'n*, 99 F.T.C. at 649 ("joint action related to fees can readily threaten independent pricing"); Federal Trade Comm'n, Staff Advisory Opinion Letter to American Podiatry Ass'n (Aug. 18, 1983).
827. *See, e.g.,* Federal Trade Comm'n, Advisory Opinion Letter to American Med. Ass'n and Chicago Med. Soc'y (Feb. 14, 1994) (concluding that aspect of proposal that authorizes a group of physicians to discipline a competing physician on the basis of fee levels alone ("fee gouging") created substantial danger of violating antitrust laws); *see also* Ratino v. Medical Serv. of D.C., 718 F.2d 1260, 1270 (4th Cir. 1983) (peer review of fees may create risk of abuse through intimidating physicians into conformity with fee schedule).
828. 42 U.S.C. § 11151(9)(B) (1994).

Factors that the Federal Trade Commission has identified as mitigating the risk of antitrust challenge to a fee review program include (1) the peer review process is voluntary and advisory, rather than mandatory and binding, for all participants, including patients, providers, and third-party payors;[829] (2) the fee decisions by peer review panels are confidential or given limited disclosure, such as only to the parties to the specific dispute;[830] and (3) the purpose of the program is avowedly procompetitive, such as to assist consumers in resolving fee-related disputes with their providers or assist third-party payors in containing costs.[831]

c.   ASSOCIATION ACTIVITY

Courts have held that a trade or professional association is a combination of its members who, through the association, can conspire to restrain trade illegally.[832] Activities of such professional associations are therefore subject to the same antitrust scrutiny as are other collective activities among competitors.

---

829.   *See, e.g.*, Federal Trade Comm'n, Advisory Opinion Letter to American Med. Ass'n and Chicago Med. Soc'y (Feb. 14, 1994) (favorably reviewing aspects of proposed peer review program which was advisory in nature, voluntary for patients and insurers, and mandatory for physicians); Federal Trade Comm'n, Staff Advisory Opinion Letter to National Capital Soc'y of Plastic & Reconstructive Surgeons (Apr. 23, 1991) (favorably reviewing proposed fee review program which was voluntary and advisory); Federal Trade Comm'n, Advisory Opinion Letter to Tarrant County Med. Soc'y (July 11, 1984) (advisory fee review program less likely to facilitate boycotts or other conspiracies); Federal Trade Comm'n, Staff Advisory Opinion Letter to American Podiatry Ass'n (Aug. 18, 1983) (advisory nature of peer review program mitigates possibilities of coercion or anticompetitive conspiracies); *see also* Iowa Dental Ass'n, 99 F.T.C. 648, 649 (1982) (advising vigilant safeguarding of voluntary and advisory nature of peer review program of dental fees); Federal Trade Comm'n, Staff Advisory Opinion Letter to Passaic County Med. Soc'y (Jan. 3, 1986) (concluding that mandatory and binding aspects of proposed fee review program created anticompetitive risk of coercion of physicians to comply with fee schedule approved by society or of facilitating boycott).

830.   For examples of favorable agency review of fee review programs providing for limited dissemination of fee decisions, see Federal Trade Comm'n, Advisory Opinion Letter to American Med. Ass'n and Chicago Med. Soc'y (Feb. 14, 1994) (concluding that making disciplinary decisions public without disclosing fee in question would be unlikely to violate antitrust laws); Federal Trade Comm'n, Staff Advisory Opinion Letter to National Capital Soc'y of Plastic & Reconstructive Surgeons (Apr. 23, 1991); Federal Trade Comm'n, Staff Advisory Opinion to Tarrant County Med. Soc'y (July 11, 1984); Federal Trade Comm'n, Staff Advisory Opinion Letter to American Podiatry Ass'n (Aug. 18, 1983); *see also Iowa Dental Ass'n*, 99 F.T.C. at 649 (limited dissemination of fee decisions is crucial).

831.   *See, e.g., Iowa Dental Ass'n*, 99 F.T.C. at 649-50 (risk of antitrust challenge arises where purpose or effect of fee review program is to establish "reasonable" fee levels for general use by providers, to discipline providers who advertise or engage in other forms of competition or innovative practices, to determine whether a third-party payor's reimbursement levels were "reasonable," or to pressure third-party payors into accepting certain fee levels as "usual" or "customary").

832.   The Supreme Court frequently has considered antitrust challenges to the activities of professional associations. *See, e.g.*, FTC v. Superior Ct. Trial Lawyers Ass'n, 493 U.S. 411 (1990); Arizona v. Maricopa County Med. Soc'y, 457 U.S. 332 (1982); Goldfarb v. Virginia State Bar, 421 U.S. 773 (1975); *see also* Marrese v. American Acad. of Orthopaedic Surgeons, 1991-1 Trade Cas. (CCH) ¶ 69,398 (N.D. Ill. 1991) (trade association may be found to have engaged in concerted activity), *aff'd*, 977 F.2d 585 (7th Cir. 1992); Michigan State Med. Soc'y, 101 F.T.C. 191, 256-57 (1983) (medical societies with their "many physician members, inherently consist of two or more persons, and are, therefore, combinations").

(1) Discussions with Third-Party Payors

As a general proposition, purely informational discussions between a medical association and third-party payors are lawful.[833] Absent legislative immunity,[834] antitrust risks can arise when such discussions go further and become collective negotiations over fees or other concerted efforts to establish reimbursement levels or criteria. In *Michigan State Medical Society*,[835] the Federal Trade Commission provided guidance regarding the point at which communications between a medical association and a third-party payor can become a restraint of trade. When negotiations between the Michigan State Medical Society (MSMS) and Blue Cross and Blue Shield of Michigan (Blue Cross) over Blue Cross's reimbursement policies failed to produce results desired by the MSMS, the society's leaders encouraged its members to withdraw from Blue Cross in order to pressure the company to accede to the MSMS position. The MSMS argued that its de-participation campaign merely expressed its policy position, and because those views were not binding on its members, it had not engaged in collective action to withhold or withdraw service from Blue Cross.[836]

The Federal Trade Commission disagreed, finding that the MSMS had gone beyond merely informational discussions with third-party payors and had become its members' negotiating agent on reimbursement issues, in effect establishing horizontal agreements among competitors to set the terms on which they would sell their services and to force third-party payors to accept those terms.[837] The final order did not prohibit the MSMS from providing information or views to third-party payors on any issue, including reimbursement issues, but it prohibited the MSMS from reaching or attempting to reach agreement with third-party payors on those issues, whether by negotiation, coercion, or otherwise.[838] The Federal Trade Commission observed:

---

833. *See, e.g.*, Southbank IPA, Inc., 56 Fed. Reg. 50,912, 50,914 (FTC Oct. 9, 1991) (proposed consent and aid to public comment) (prohibitions of consent order do not include provision of information or views by providers, individually or collectively, to third-party payors on any issue including reimbursement), 114 F.T.C. 783 (1991) (decision and order); Federal Trade Comm'n, Staff Advisory Opinion Letter to Medical Soc'y of the County of Erie (Mar. 12, 1984) (medical association may lawfully provide information or present views to third-party payors concerning reimbursement matters, and may receive information from payors about their criteria and methods for determining reimbursement levels).

834. *See supra* note 666 and *infra* note 895.

835. 101 F.T.C. 191 (1983).

836. *Id.* at 280. Counsel for the MSMS characterized its de-participation campaign as "not . . . authorizing the Negotiating Committee to fix prices, but only to argue persuasively with third-party payers." *Id.* at 273.

837. *Id.* at 285-86. The FTC also found that the MSMS's attempts to tamper with the means by which third-party payors set prices was tantamount to tampering with reimbursement levels, even if specific prices were not established. *Id.* at 291.

838. *Id.* at 313-14 (specifically prohibiting MSMS from organizing a collective refusal of its members to enter into participation agreements with third-party payors, from urging its members collectively to withdraw from such agreements, and from threatening third-party payors with mass de-participation from their insurance plans in order to coerce the payors to accept MSMS's views on reimbursement issues or other terms of their participation agreements). Observing that the final order did not outright prohibit the MSMS from expressing its views to third-party payors, the FTC "[s]tated as plainly as possible, [the order] would not preclude communications that fall short of agreements or attempts to reach agreements on reimbursement." *Id.* at 307-08.

In allowing [the MSMS] to engage in non-binding, non-coercive discussions with health insurers, we have attempted to strike a proper balance between the need for insurers to have efficient access to the views of large groups of providers and the need to prevent competitors from banding together in ways that involve the unreasonable exercise of collective market power.[839]

Since *Michigan State Medical Society*, other medical or professional associations have been found to have stepped over the line separating lawful communications with third-party payors from illegal conspiracies to set the terms on which their members would sell their services.[840] Communications over fees or other reimbursement issues are lawful if undertaken for informational purposes and so long as no action is required to be taken on the basis of such information.[841] Medical associations risk antitrust challenge if they attempt to set the fees charged by their

---

839. *Id.* at 295-96.
840. *See, e.g.*, American Council of Certified Podiatric Physicians and Surgeons v. American Bd. of Podiatric Surgery, 185 F.3d 606 (6th Cir. 1999) (reversing the entry of summary judgment in favor of defendants and finding sufficient evidence to support plaintiffs' monopolization and attempted monopolization charges); FTC v. Asociacion de Farmacias Region de Arecibo, Inc., 63 Fed. Reg. 70,407 (FTC Dec. 21, 1998) (proposed consent and aid to public comment) (resolving charges that the group engaged in collective negotiation and obtained increased reimbursement after threatening to boycott a government health care program for the indigent), 1999 FTC LEXIS 28 (Mar. 15, 1999) (decision and order); FTC v. College of Physician-Surgeons of P.R., [FTC Complaints & Orders 1997-2001 Transfer Binder] Trade Reg. Rep. (CCH) ¶ 24,335 (D.P.R. 1997) (proposed consent order) (settling charges that College demanded that a government agency recognize the College as the exclusive bargaining agent of physicians and allow it to collectively negotiate contracts for physicians, and organized eight-day strike when these demands were not met); United States v. Massachusetts Allergy Soc'y, 57 Fed. Reg. 6741 (Feb. 27, 1992) (notice of amended competitive impact statement) (alleging that professional society of allergists and individual members conspired to fix and raise the fees paid for allergy services by certain HMOs by agreeing, among other things, to have society act as joint negotiating agent to obtain higher fees from HMOs, to resist competitive pressures to discount fees, and to adopt a fee schedule for use by society in negotiating higher fees), 1992-1 Trade Cas. (CCH) ¶ 69,846 (D. Mass. 1992) (consent decree) (prohibiting society from entering or attempting to enter into agreements concerning fees with third-party payors, from urging physicians to withdraw or not participate in agreements with third-party payors, and from threatening any third-party payors with de-participation by any physician if any agreement term is not acceptable to society); United States v. North Dakota Hosp. Ass'n, 640 F. Supp. 1028 (D.N.D. 1986) (conspiracy to fix prices for services provided to Native Americans through Indian Health Service).
841. Agency consent decrees and orders with health care providers expressly have excluded from their prohibitions the simple provision of information (including fee information) by health care providers to third-party payors. *See, e.g.*, United States v. Massachusetts Allergy Soc'y, 1992-1 Trade Cas. (CCH) ¶ 69,846 (D. Mass. 1992) (consent decree); Southbank IPA, Inc., 56 Fed. Reg. 50,912 (FTC Oct. 9, 1991) (proposed consent and aid to public comment), 114 F.T.C. 783 (1991) (decision and order). In addition, exchanges of information have been found to promote legitimate shared interests, such as the promotion of research and promulgation of health guidelines. *See, e.g.*, U.S. Dep't of Justice, Business Review Letter to American Heart Ass'n Pharm. Roundtable, 1998 DOJBRL LEXIS 7 (Mar. 20, 1998) (clearing proposed changes to the funding of targeted research programs); DM Research, Inc. v. College of Am. Pathologists, 2 F. Supp. 2d 226 (D.R.I. 1998) (finding insufficient evidence of an anticompetitive scheme and dismissing antitrust claims based on the adoption of guidelines discouraging the use of bottled reagent water), *aff'd*, 170 F.3d 53 (1st Cir. 1999).

members,[842] act as their members' negotiating agent with third-party payors,[843] or encourage their members to refuse to participate in agreements with a third-party payor, or to threaten such mass de-participation, if the payor's policies are not acceptable to the association or its members.[844]

---

842. *See, e.g.*, Arizona v. Maricopa County Med. Soc'y, 457 U.S. 332 (1982) (setting by medical societies of maximum fee schedules for their members held per se illegal); United States v. Lake County Optometric Soc'y, No. W-95-CR-114 (W.D. Tex. Dec. 15, 1995) (DOJ filed criminal charges against professional association of optometrists for price fixing), final sentencing, Crim. No. W95-CR114 (W.D. Tex. July 9, 1996); Wisconsin Chiropractic Ass'n, 65 Fed. Reg. 13,387 (FTC Mar. 13, 2000) (proposed consent and aid to public comment) (alleging that association conspired with some of its members and others to fix prices and boycott third-party payors to obtain higher reimbursement rates), 2000 FTC LEXIS 72 (2000) (decision and order); *cf.* U.S. Dep't of Justice, Business Review Letter to Pharmaceutical Mfrs. Ass'n, 1993 DOJBRL LEXIS 20 (Oct. 1, 1993) (concluding that association's proposal to control rising costs of prescription drugs would, if implemented, be per se illegal where under proposal each association member would agree to limit annual increase in its overall changes in prices for its prescription drug products to a level not higher than the annual increase in the consumer price index).

843. *See, e.g.*, *In re* Colegio de Cirujanos Dentistas de P.R., 65 Fed. Reg. 17,506 (FTC Apr. 3, 2000) (proposed consent and aid to public comment) (alleging that unintegrated Colegio consisting of almost all dentists practicing in Puerto Rico acted as collective bargaining agent for its members, determined which payors its members would deal with, set prices and terms under which members would provide services, limited fee discounts to payors, and generally blocked payors from implementing new health care delivery systems), 2000 FTC LEXIS 14 (2000) (order); United States v. Federation of Physicians and Dentists, Inc., No. 98-475 (D. Del. Aug. 12, 1998) (complaint) (alleging that Federation sought to negotiate on behalf of independent practitioners); McLean County Chiropractic Ass'n, 59 Fed. Reg. 3114, 3116 (FTC Jan. 20, 1994) (proposed consent and aid to public comment) (settling charges that association of Illinois chiropractors unlawfully conspired to fix the maximum fees charged by its members and to negotiate the terms of agreements between its members and third-party payors), 117 F.T.C. 396 (1994) (decision and order). *But cf.* U.S. Dep't of Justice, Business Review Letter to Case W. Reserve Univ. Sch. of Med., 1993 DOJBRL LEXIS 15 (Jan. 7, 1993) (declining to challenge use of single agent to negotiate contract terms with third-party payors on behalf of 19 separate physician practice groups, where groups did not compete with each other and other safeguards against collusion existed). For a view that some collective negotiation may be permissible, see United States v. Alston, 974 F.2d 1206, 1214 (9th Cir. 1992):

> In light of these departures [in health care markets] from a normal competitive market, individual health care providers are entitled to take some joint action (short of price fixing or a group boycott) to level the bargaining imbalance created by [health insurance] plans and provide meaningful input into the setting of the fee schedules. Thus health care providers might pool cost data in justifying a request for an increased fee schedule. . . . Providers might also band together to negotiate various other aspects of their relationship with the plans such as payment procedures, the type of documentation they must provide, the method of referring patients and the mechanism for adjusting disputes. Such concerted actions, which would not implicate the per se rule, must be carefully distinguished from efforts to dictate terms by explicit or implicit threats of mass withdrawals from the plans.

844. *See, e.g.*, FTC v. Asociacion de Farmacias Region de Arecibo, Inc., 63 Fed. Reg. 70,407 (FTC Dec. 21, 1998) (proposed consent and aid to public comment) (resolving charges that the group engaged in collective negotiation and obtained increased reimbursement after threatening to boycott a government health care program for the indigent), 1999 FTC LEXIS 28 (1999) (decision and order); La Asociacion Medica, 60 Fed. Reg. 35,907 (FTC July 12, 1995) (proposed consent and aid to public comment) (resolving claims that medical association, its physiatry section, and individual physicians conspired to organize concerted boycott by physiatrists of a government insurance program in an attempt to obtain higher reimbursement rates and adoption of "exclusive referral" rules under which patients would be reimbursed for physical therapy services only if referred by a physiatrist), 119 F.T.C. 772 (1995) (decision and order); United States v. Montana Nursing Home Ass'n, 47 Fed. Reg. 17,886 (DOJ Apr. 26, 1982) (proposed consent decree and competitive impact statement) (settling charges that nursing home association conspired with others to raise prices of nursing home services paid under Medicaid program by, among other

(2) Peer Review and Relative Value Scales

The antitrust concerns raised by programs of medical associations for the peer review of fees and other aspects of their members' practice can also arise when medical associations promote the use of a relative value scale or guide (RVS) among their members.[845] Although an RVS is not a fee schedule, it could be turned into one by simply multiplying the relative values by a dollar conversion factor.[846]

Historically, the Federal Trade Commission challenged the use of an RVS by a medical association based on concerns that the association and its members would agree to adhere to the RVS in determining their fees, thus potentially restraining trade unreasonably by tampering with market pricing structures.[847] Changes in the federal Medicare program, however, particularly those requiring that resource-based relative value scales (RBRVSs) be used for physician reimbursement under Medicare and contemplating professional participation in the development of RBRVSs, have prompted the Federal Trade Commission to reconsider its views on the dissemination of RVSs among medical association members and, in one case, to set aside a prior order prohibiting such dissemination.[848] The Department of Justice has expressly

---

things, jointly refusing to enter into Medicaid contracts except on collectively determined terms), 1982-1 Trade Cas. (CCH) ¶ 64,852 (D. Mont. 1982) (consent decree); see also Pennsylvania Dental Ass'n v. Medical Serv. Ass'n, 815 F.2d 270, 274-75 (3d Cir.) (denying summary judgment where there was evidence that purpose of dental associations' de-participation movement was to coerce health insurance company to abandon its cost containment efforts), cert. denied, 484 U.S. 851 (1987).

The FTC has settled charges with various pharmaceutical associations that they engaged in concerted refusals to deal with government programs or other third-party payors in order to coerce higher reimbursement. See, e.g., Baltimore Metro. Pharm. Ass'n, 58 Fed. Reg. 65,718, 65,720 (FTC Dec. 16, 1993) (proposed consent and aid to public comment) (alleging that when insurer of employees' prescription drug benefit plan announced that it would lower its reimbursement rate, defendant pharmaceutical associations urged their members not to participate in plan), 117 F.T.C. 95 (1994) (decision and order); Southeast Colo. Pharmacal Ass'n, 57 Fed. Reg. 52,631 (FTC Nov. 4, 1992) (proposed consent and aid to public comment), 116 F.T.C. 51 (1993) (decision and order); Chain Pharmacy Ass'n, 56 Fed. Reg. 12,534 (FTC Mar. 26, 1991) (proposed consent order and analysis to aid public comment), 56 Fed. Reg. 32,575 (FTC July 17, 1991) (consent order); Empire State Pharm. Soc'y, 56 Fed. Reg. 9223 (FTC Mar. 5, 1991) (consent order).

845. An RVS has been defined as "any list or compilation of surgical or medical procedures that states comparative numerical values for those procedures or services." American Acad. of Orthopaedic Surgeons, 60 Fed. Reg. 30,542, 30,543 n.1 (FTC June 9, 1995) (order setting aside order).

846. Federal Trade Comm'n, Advisory Opinion Letter to American Soc'y of Internal Med., 105 F.T.C. 505 (1985).

847. See id. at 512 (declining to approve association's proposal to develop RVSs); see also California Med. Ass'n, 93 F.T.C. 519 (1979) (consent order), modified, 105 F.T.C. 277 (1985); American Coll. of Radiology, 89 F.T.C. 144 (1977) (consent order), modified, 55 Fed. Reg. 23,981 (June 13, 1990); American Acad. of Orthopaedic Surgeons, 88 F.T.C. 968 (1976) (consent order), modified, 105 F.T.C. 248 (1985), set aside, 60 Fed. Reg. 30,542 (June 9, 1995); American Coll. of Obstetricians & Gynecologists, 88 F.T.C. 955 (1976) (consent order), modified, 104 F.T.C. 524 (1984).

848. American Acad. of Orthopaedic Surgeons, 60 Fed. Reg. 30,542, 30,544-45 (June 9, 1995) (order setting aside order) (observing that academy's inability due to prior order to disseminate its research on physician work scales and Medicare RBRVSs to its members and other professional groups was likely to hinder participation in the process sponsored by the Health Care Financing Administration (HCFA) for identifying information relevant to revising Medicare RBRVSs, could increase HCFA's costs in obtaining such information, inhibit the academy's members in contributing to the development of RBRVSs and increase the costs of disseminating information, and was inconsistent with federal Medicare policy). The FTC recognized that setting aside the order did not, however, eliminate the danger that the academy's members would use RVSs as a

permitted the dissemination of an RVS or fee schedule by a medical society to a third-party payor where (1) the dissemination is solely for informational purposes, (2) the third-party payor specifically requests it, and (3) the medical society expressly states that the payor is not required to accept or adopt the RVS or fee schedule.[849] The Federal Trade Commission also has approved the public dissemination of information and analysis developed by a national professional association in preparing recommendations concerning Medicare RBRVSs, noting that such information has value to providers and is not likely to facilitate an agreement on prices.[850]

d. MOST FAVORED NATION CLAUSES

Most favored nation clauses in the health care field have come under increasing antitrust scrutiny. In most cases, provider organizations have entered into consent orders rather than defend the merits of such provisions.[851]

5. *Hospital Mergers*

Until the mid-1990s, the hospital industry was an active source of merger enforcement activities, with the antitrust agencies prevailing in a number of important federal court and administrative proceedings.[852] In more recent years,

---

basis for an unlawful price-fixing agreement and noted that the academy and its members remained subject to the laws against price fixing. *Id.* at 30,545; *see also* California Med. Ass'n, 120 F.T.C. 858 (1995) (order granting petition to modify or set aside consent order) (consent order prohibiting the publication of RVSs modified so that association can publish schedule of fees for network members).

849. United States v. Massachusetts Allergy Soc'y, 1992-1 Trade Cas. (CCH) ¶ 69,846 (D. Mass. 1992) (consent decree).

850. Federal Trade Comm'n, Staff Advisory Opinion Letter to American Med. Ass'n (Mar. 26, 1996).

851. *See, e.g.*, United States v. Delta Dental, 943 F. Supp. 172 (D.R.I. 1996); United States v. Delta Dental of Ariz., 1995-1 Trade Cas. (CCH) ¶ 71,337 (D. Ariz. 1995); RXCare of Tenn., Inc., 121 F.T.C. 762 (1996); United States v. Medical Mutual, 63 Fed. Reg. 52,764 (Oct. 1, 1988) (consent order resolving charges that the use of "most favorable rates" clauses unreasonably restrained competition, stifled the development of health plans, increased prices for hospital and insurance services, and deprived consumers of innovative and less costly alternative health care services); Health Sys. Int'l, No. M95-06-024 (Pa. Ins. Dep't, May 5, 1998) (proposed settlement resolving charges that prudent buyer clauses in Blue Cross contracts created an artificial rate floor). For detailed discussions of this topic, see part D.1.c(4) of Chapter I and part D.1 of Chapter II.

852. *See, e.g.*, FTC v. University Health, Inc., 938 F.2d 1206 (11th Cir. 1991); United States v. Rockford Mem'l Corp., 898 F.2d 1278 (7th Cir. 1990); Hospital Corp. of Am. v. FTC, 807 F.2d 1381 (7th Cir. 1986), *cert. denied*, 481 U.S. 1038 (1987); FTC v. Columbia Hosp. Corp., 1993 WL 183557 (M.D. Fla. 1993); American Med. Int'l, Inc., 104 FTC 1, 239 (1984). *But see* United States v. Carilion Health Sys., 707 F. Supp. 840, 849 (W.D. Va.) (government failed to prove that the proposed merger would constitute unreasonable restraint of trade), *aff'd*, 892 F.2d 1042 (4th Cir. 1989); Adventist Health Sys./West, 117 F.T.C. 224 (1994) (evidence did not support the relevant geographic markets alleged in the FTC's complaint). The agencies also have reviewed, and in some cases challenged, mergers involving physician practice groups and other health care providers. *See, e.g.*, HTI Health Servs. v. Quorum Health Group, Inc., 960 F. Supp. 1104 (S.D. Miss. 1997); United States v. Health Choice of Northwest Missouri, 1996-2 Trade Cas. (CCH) ¶ 71,606 (W.D. Mo. 1996); U.S. Dep't of Justice, Business Review Letter to CVT Surgical Center/Vascular Surgery Assocs. of Baton Rouge, 1997 DOJBRL LEXIS 8 (Apr. 16, 1997); U.S. Dep't of Justice, Business Review Letter to Orthopaedic Associates/Bone & Joint Center of Mobile, 1997 DOJBRL LEXIS 7 (Apr. 16, 1997); U.S. Dep't of Justice, Business Review Letter to Anne Arundel Med. Ctr., 1996 DOJBRL LEXIS 23 (Oct. 17, 1996); U.S. Dep't of Justice,

however, the government has been unable to obtain a preliminary injunction in a hospital merger challenge.[853]

The 1992 *Merger Guidelines* articulate the framework the agencies apply in analyzing mergers and have been endorsed by several courts.[854] In most hospital merger cases, market definition has been the critical issue. The plaintiff's failure to prove a relevant market is fatal to a merger challenge because absent a properly defined market, a merger's effect on competition cannot be evaluated.[855] The relevant product market typically has been defined as the cluster of services provided by general acute care hospitals as a unique package of services.[856] For example, the relevant product market has been defined as general acute care hospital services,[857] primary and secondary care inpatient services,[858] psychiatric hospital services,[859] and outpatient surgery services.[860] In *United States v. Long Island Jewish Medical Center*, the Department of Justice unsuccessfully sought to define a market for "anchor hospitals."[861]

The geographic market definition has been hotly disputed in most hospital merger cases because the size of the geographic market determines the number of competitors in the market, the size of their market shares, and the likelihood of competitive effects.[862] Patient discharge data typically is used as a preliminary measure of the relevant geographic market.[863] Starting with the location of the

---

Business Review Letter to Itasca Clinic and Grand Rapids Med. Assocs., 1996 DOJBRL LEXIS 13 (Mar. 19, 1996).

853. *See* FTC v. Tenet Health Care Corp., 186 F.3d 1045 (8th Cir. 1999); United States v. Long Island Jewish Med. Ctr., 983 F. Supp. 121 (E.D.N.Y. 1997); FTC v. Butterworth Health Corp., 946 F. Supp. 1285 (W.D. Mich. 1996), *aff'd*, 121 F.3d 708 (6th Cir. 1997); FTC v. Freeman Hosp., 911 F. Supp. 1213 (W.D. Mo.), *aff'd*, 69 F.3d 260 (8th Cir. 1995); United States v. Mercy Health Servs., 902 F. Supp. 968 (N.D. Iowa 1995), *vacated as moot*, 107 F.3d 632 (8th Cir. 1997).
854. See Chapter III for a discussion of merger analysis and the 1992 *Merger Guidelines*.
855. *See, e.g., Long Island Jewish Med. Ctr.*, 983 F. Supp. at 140; *Freeman Hosp.*, 911 F. Supp. at 1227; *Mercy Health Servs.*, 902 F. Supp. at 987; *Adventist Health Sys./West*, 117 F.T.C. at 287-97.
856. *Hospital Corp. of Am.*, 807 F.2d 1381; *American Med. Int'l*, 104 F.T.C. at 177. The cluster of services concept also has been applied in physician practices mergers. *See, e.g., Quorum Health Group*, 960 F. Supp. 1104; U.S. Dep't of Justice, Business Review Letter to Itasca Clinic and Grand Rapid Med. Assocs., 1996 DOJBRL LEXIS 13 (Mar. 19, 1996). The Supreme Court first introduced the cluster of services concept with reference to commercial banking in *United States v. Philadelphia Nat'l Bank, Inc.*, 374 U.S. 321, 356 (1963).
857. *Hospital Corp. of Am.*, 807 F.2d at 1384-85; *Butterworth*, 946 F. Supp. at 1291 (specifically including normal childbirth, gynecology, pediatrics, general medicine, and general surgical services); *Mercy Health Servs.*, 902 F. Supp. at 976 (specifically excluding inpatient psychiatric care, substance abuse treatment, rehabilitation services, and open-heart surgery); *Carilion Health Sys.*, 707 F. Supp. at 847-48 (specifically including outpatient services); *Rockford Mem'l Corp.*, 717 F. Supp. 1251 (specifically excluding outpatient services); *American Med. Int'l*, 104 F.T.C. at 194.
858. *Tenet Health Care Corp.*, 17 F. Supp. 2d at 942 (defendants did not dispute FTC's definition of a primary and secondary inpatient services market); *Butterworth*, 946 F. Supp. at 1290 (defining a market consisting of primary care inpatient hospital services).
859. *See, e.g.*, FTC v. Columbia/HCA Healthcare Corp., 61 Fed. Reg. 30,614 (FTC June 17, 1996) (consent order); FTC v. Charter Med. Corp., 60 Fed. Reg. 10,861 (FTC Feb. 28, 1995) (consent order).
860. *See, e.g.*, FTC v. Columbia/HCA Healthcare Corp., 60 Fed. Reg. 464 (FTC Jan. 4, 1995).
861. United States v. Long Island Jewish Med. Ctr., 983 F. Supp. 121, 140 (E.D.N.Y. 1997).
862. *Tenet Health Care Corp.*, 186 F.3d at 1052; FTC v. Freeman Hosp., 69 F.3d 260, 270 n.14 (8th Cir. 1995); *Butterworth*, 946 F. Supp. at 1291; *Mercy Health Servs.*, 902 F. Supp. at 975-76.
863. *Freeman Hosp.*, 69 F.3d at 270 n.14 (8th Cir. 1995); *Tenet Health Care Corp.*, 62 F.3d at 345; *Butterworth*, 946 F. Supp. at 1291-92; *Mercy Health Servs.*, 902 F. Supp. at 977.

merging hospitals, patient origin studies determine (1) the percentage of patients residing within the hospitals' primary and secondary service area who remain in the area for hospital services, and (2) the percentage of patients served by area hospitals who are residents of the area. The preliminary market definition encompasses an area where the percentages of these patient inflow and outflows reach a minimum threshold percentage—somewhere between 75 and 90 percent.[864] However, patient flow data alone provides only a static view of the market, and does not speak to the critical question of where consumers could practicably obtain alternative hospital services in the event of a postmerger price increase.[865] For this reason, it is necessary to assess other factors such as the geographic area that the hospital administrators have identified as the relevant one, the office location and admitting patterns of physicians who practice at the hospital, and the views of managed care payors.[866] Several courts have concluded that the market for hospital services is a local one, except for highly specialized medical services,[867] although others have found that geographic markets may extend to an area as far as fifty-four miles[868] to seventy-five miles away.[869]

In addition to assessing the relevant market, most courts routinely consider efficiencies as either an affirmative defense or as part of their overall assessment of competitive effects. Efficiencies have been rejected where they could be achieved by means other than merger, were not adequately proved, or were not significant net efficiencies once the costs of attaining those efficiencies were offset against the claimed savings.[870] However, several cases have accepted efficiencies claims.[871]

864. *See* Kenneth G. Elzinga & Thomas F. Hogarty, *The Problem of Geographical Market Delineation in Antimerger Suits*, 18 ANTITRUST BULL. 45 (1973).

865. *See Freeman Hosp.*, 69 F.3d at 269 (criticizing FTC's failure to provide a dynamic analysis of the market); *Long Island Jewish Med. Ctr.*, 983 F. Supp. at 138; *Butterworth*, 946 F. Supp. at 1292-94 (concluding that FTC did not rely solely on a static analysis but adequately presented a dynamic analysis); *Mercy Health Servs.*, 902 F. Supp. at 978 (faulting DOJ for failing to provide a fluid analysis of where patients could practicably go to obtain alternate hospital services); Adventist Health Sys./West, 117 F.T.C. 224, 287-97 (1994) (dismissing case because complaint counsel failed to establish geographic market with patient flow data).

866. *See, e.g.*, *Long Island Jewish Med. Ctr.*, 983 F. Supp. at 144-45 (citing testimony of health insurers who believed the merger would not lead to higher prices); *Mercy Health Servs.*, 902 F. Supp. at 983 (citing managed care payor testimony regarding their ability to use financial incentives to induce patients to travel to more distant hospitals); American Med. Int'l, 104 F.T.C. 1, 197 (1984) (hospitals compete for physicians in order to increase admissions). *But see Tenet Health Care Corp.*, 186 F.3d at 1054 (questioning the district court's reliance on the testimony of managed care payors); *Butterworth*, 946 F. Supp. at 1302 (discounting the testimony of managed care payors and noting that their interests "pale" in comparison with those of consumers); *Freeman Hosp.*, 911 F. Supp. at 1220 (rejecting informal, off-the-cuff remarks and anecdotal evidence as no substitute for solid economic analysis), *id.*, 69 F.3d at 269 (views of market participants not always sufficient to establish a relevant market "especially where their testimony fails to specifically address the practicable choices available to consumers").

867. *See, e.g.*, *Butterworth*, 946 F. Supp. at 1291-93 (relevant geographic market for general acute care inpatient hospital services consisted of greater Kent County and relevant market for primary care inpatient services encompassed the "immediate Grand Rapids area"); American Medicorp. v. Humana, Inc., 445 F. Supp. 573, 605 (E.D. Pa. 1977) (relevant geographic market was "in and around Bluefield, West Virginia"); *American Med. Int'l*, 104 F.T.C at 187 (city of San Luis Obispo as well as San Luis Obispo County were relevant geographic markets).

868. *Freeman Hosp.*, 911 F. Supp. at 1219-21.

869. *Mercy Health Servs.*, 902 F. Supp. at 984.

870. *See, e.g.*, FTC v. University Health, 938 F.2d 1206, 1223 (11th Cir. 1991); *Mercy Health Servs.*, 902 F. Supp. at 987-89.

Similarly, courts have been increasingly willing to consider the nonprofit status of the merging hospitals. The nonprofit defense was explicitly rejected in earlier cases.[872] However, in *Butterworth*, the district court concluded that the merging nonprofit hospitals would not be likely to exercise market power to the detriment of consumers because nonprofit hospitals operate differently from profit-maximizing firms.[873] The district court also noted that the boards of the two hospitals were comprised of prominent community leaders, the hospitals had made a commitment to the community to freeze prices and to pass cost savings to consumers, and the merger was likely to produce substantial cost savings and efficiencies.[874] Similarly, in *Long Island Jewish Medical Center*, the court noted that nonprofit status may be considered if "supported by other evidence that such status would inhibit anticompetitive effects."[875] In concluding that the merger would not be likely to harm consumers, the court noted that the two hospitals were nonprofit, had agreed not to raise prices for at least two years after the merger, and had provided millions of dollars of services to their communities for indigent care.[876]

6. Pharmaceuticals and Agreements to Impede Market Entry

The Federal Trade Commission recently has applied antitrust scrutiny to the pharmaceutical industry.[877] The agency's enforcement efforts have focused primarily on private agreements between brand name and generic drug manufacturers to delay competition from generic versions of patent-protected drugs by manipulating certain provisions of Hatch-Waxman Act.[878]

---

871. *See, e.g., Tenet Health Care Corp.*, 186 F.3d at 1054 (noting that district court should have considered evidence of enhanced efficiency in the context of the competitive effects of the merger); *Butterworth*, 946 F. Supp. at 1301; United States v. Carilion, 707 F. Supp. 840, 849 (W.D. Va. 1989).
872. *See University Health*, 938 F.2d at 1224-25; United States v. Rockford Mem'l Corp., 898 F.2d 1278, 1286 (11th Cir. 1990); *Mercy Health Servs.*, 902 F. Supp. at 989. Two district courts noted the nonprofit status of merging hospitals, but both approved the mergers on other grounds. *See Freeman Hosp.*, 911 F. Supp. at 1226-28; *Carilion*, 707 F. Supp. at 847-49.
873. *Butterworth*, 946 F. Supp. at 1302.
874. *Id.; see also Freeman Hosp.*, 911 F. Supp. at 1222 (noting that merging hospitals are nonprofits; boards controlled by persons representing the interests of hospital consumers or other groups that desire competitively priced hospital services).
875. *See* United States v. Long Island Jewish Med. Ctr., 983 F. Supp. 121, 146 (E.D.N.Y. 1997).
876. *Id.*
877. Mergers in the pharmaceutical industry have given rise to antitrust scrutiny and enforcement activities. *See, e.g.,* FTC v. The Hearst Trust, Civ. No. 1:01CV00734 (D.D.C. filed Apr. 5, 2001); Glaxo Wellcome PLC and Smith Kline Beecham PLC, 2001 FTC LEXIS 13 (Jan. 26, 2001) (decision and order); Pfizer Inc. and Warner-Lambert Co., 2000 FTC LEXIS 88 (July 27, 2000) (decision and order); Hoechst AG and Rhone-Poulenc, 2000 FTC LEXIS 3 (Jan. 18, 2000) (decision and order); Zeneca Group PLC, 1999 FTC LEXIS 115 (June 7, 1999) (decision and order); Merck/Medco, 1999 FTC LEXIS 18 (Feb. 18, 1999) (decision and order); FTC v. Cardinal Health, Inc., 12 F. Supp. 2d 34 (D.D.C. 1998); Roche Holding Ltd., 125 F.T.C. 919 (1998) (consent order); Baxter Int'l, Inc., 23 F.T.C. 904 (1997); Ciba-Geigy, Ltd., 123 F.T.C. 842 (1997) (consent order); The Upjohn Co., 121 F.T.C. 44 (1996) (consent order); Hoechst AG, 120 F.T.C. 1010 (1995) (consent order); Glaxo PLC, 119 F.T.C. 815 (1995); Eli Lilly/PCF, 120 F.T.C. 243 (1985) (consent order).
878. In addition, a number of private plaintiffs have filed suits containing similar allegations. *See, e.g.,* Andrx Pharms., Inc. v. Biovail Corp. Int'l, 256 F.3d 799 (D.C. Cir. 2001); Eon Labs Mfg., Inc. v. Watson Pharm., Inc., 164 F. Supp. 2d 350 (S.D.N.Y. 2001); Bristol-Myers Squibb Co. v. Copley Pharm., Inc., 144 F. Supp. 2d 21 (D. Mass. 2000).

The Hatch-Waxman Act allows companies to seek approval from the Food and Drug Administration to market a generic drug before the patent on the brand name version of the drug expires.[879] The generic drug manufacturer certifies in an abbreviated new drug application (ANDA) that the patent for the brand name drug is either invalid or will not be infringed by the generic drug for which the ANDA seeks approval. To encourage competition, the first company to file an ANDA with the Food and Drug Administration is given the exclusive right to market the generic drug for 180 days. In several recent cases, the Federal Trade Commision has challenged agreements between brand name manufacturers and generic manufacturers alleged to have manipulated this provision of the statute to forestall competition.[880]

In one case, the Federal Trade Commission entered into consent orders with Abbott Laboratories and Geneva Pharmaceuticals, Inc., following allegations that Abbott paid Geneva $4.5 million per month to delay bringing to market a generic alternative to Abbott's brand name hypertension and prostate drug, Hytrin. As alleged in the complaint, Geneva was the first company to file an ANDA for the generic version of Hytrin. Abbott sued Geneva for patent infringement of the tablet form of Hytrin, but neglected to make a similar claim regarding the capsule form of Hytrin, thereby paving the way for Food and Drug Administration approval of Geneva's capsule product. Since Geneva was the first to file an ANDA, it retained the 180-day period of market exclusivity.

During the pendency of the patent litigation over the tablet form of the generic version of Hytrin, Abbott agreed to pay Geneva $4.5 million per month not to enter the market with its capsule product. In exchange for the payments, Geneva also agreed not to transfer, assign, or relinquish its 180-day exclusivity right. By agreeing not to sell its generic version, Geneva prevented the start of the 180-day exclusivity period with the result that neither Geneva nor any other company could introduce a generic version of Hytrin into the market. According to the Federal Trade Commission, this $4.5 million per month well exceeded the financial cost to Geneva of foregoing entering the market.

The consent orders prohibited Abbott and Geneva from entering into agreements pursuant to which a first-filing generic company would agree with the brand drug manufacturer to (1) give up or transfer its 180-day exclusivity rights, and (2) not bring a noninfringing drug to market. In addition, the orders required that agreements involving payments to a generic company to stay off the market during the pendency of patent litigation be approved by the court with notice to the Federal Trade Commission. Geneva also was required to waive its right to a 180-day exclusivity period for its generic tablet version of Hytrin so that other generic tablets could immediately enter the market. The Federal Trade Commission, in a statement accompanying the orders, warned that it would consider its entire range of enforcement actions against similar arrangements, including seeking disgorgement of illegally obtained profits.

---

879. 21 U.S.C. § 355(j) (1994 & Supp. 1999).

880. Hoechst Marion Roussel, Inc., 66 Fed. Reg. 18,636 (FTC Apr. 10, 2000) (proposed consent and aid to public comment), 2001 FTC LEXIS 56 (consent order issued May 8, 2001); Abbott Labs., 2000 FTC LEXIS 66 (May 22, 2000) (proposed consent and aid to public comment); Geneva Pharmaceuticals, Inc., 2000 FTC LEXIS 65 (May 22, 2000) (proposed consent and aid to public comment); see also FTC v. Schering Plough Corp., 2001 FTC LEXIS 39 (complaint issued Mar. 30, 2001).

In addition to challenging horizontal agreements between brand name and generic manufacturers, the Federal Trade Commission also has challenged certain exclusive licensing practices of generic drug manufacturers. In *FTC v. Mylan Labs., Inc.*,[881] the agency challenged the licensing practices of Mylan, alleging that Mylan and its suppliers conspired to deny Mylan's competitors ingredients necessary to manufacture two widely prescribed antianxiety drugs, lorazepam and clorazepate. One supplier of the ingredients agreed to supply them exclusively to Mylan, and Mylan agreed to share its profits from the sale of lorazepam and clorazepate. Subsequently, Mylan was able to raise its prices on lorazepam and clorazepate by approximately 2,000-3,000 percent. The Federal Trade Commission and Mylan later entered into the largest monetary settlement in agency history, with Mylan agreeing to pay $100 million in disgorged profits.[882] In announcing the settlement, the Federal Trade Commission stated that it would continue to seek disgorgement sparingly in antitrust cases, but nevertheless upheld the remedy in the *Mylan* case due to the "particularly egregious conduct" of Mylan and its coconspirators.[883]

7. The Noerr-Pennington *and State Action Doctrines*

Under the *Noerr* doctrine, medical associations and other groups of health care providers may lawfully provide government bodies with information, data, and opinions in an effort to influence legislation or otherwise obtain a favorable governmental response in matters of concern to them.[884] Consent decrees and orders with the enforcement agencies routinely provide that the prohibitions against certain communications among health care providers do not prevent providers or their associations from exercising their rights under the First Amendment to petition federal or state government concerning legislation and to participate in any federal or state administrative or judicial proceedings.[885] In addition, the *Noerr* doctrine protects health care providers who appear singly or jointly before administrative and judicial bodies to oppose a competing provider's application for favorable governmental action—for example, the approval of a certificate of need (CON) for hospital building or capital expenditures.[886]

---

881. 62 F. Supp. 2d 25 (D.D.C.), *modified*, 99 F. Supp. 2d 1 (D.D.C. 1999).

882. FTC v. Mylan Labs., Inc., 1:98cv03114 (TFH) (D.D.C. Feb. 9, 2001) (final judgment).

883. Statement of Chairman Pitofsky and Commissioners Sheila F. Anthony and Mozelle W. Thompson (Nov. 29, 2000), *available at* www.ftc.gov/os/2000/11/mylanpitofskystatement.htm.

884. *See, e.g.*, National Bd. for Certification in Occupational Therapy v. American Occupational Therapy Ass'n, 24 F. Supp. 2d 494 (D. Md. 1998) (lobbying legislature to require certification as a prerequisite for state licensure qualifies as "petitioning activity" under *Noerr-Pennington*); Action Ambulance Serv. v. Atlanticare Health Servs., 815 F. Supp. 33, 40 (D. Mass. 1993) (*Noerr* protected bona fide petitioning of city to enter into exclusive agreement with defendants). The *Noerr* doctrine is discussed in part C of Chapter XIII.

885. *See, e.g.*, United States v. Classic Care Network, 1995-1 Trade Cas. (CCH) ¶ 70,997 (E.D.N.Y. 1995) (consent decree); Physicians Group, 60 Fed. Reg. 25,223, 25,224 (FTC May 11, 1995) (proposed consent and aid to public comment), 120 F.T.C. 567 (1995) (decision and order); United States v. Massachusetts Allergy Soc'y, 1992-1 Trade Cas. (CCH) ¶ 69,846 (D. Mass. 1992) (consent decree); Southbank IPA, Inc., 56 Fed. Reg. 50,912, 50,914 (FTC Oct. 9, 1991) (proposed consent and aid to public comment), 114 F.T.C. 783 (1991) (decision and order); *cf.* Michigan State Med. Soc'y, 101 F.T.C. 191, 314 (1983) (litigated order).

886. *See, e.g.*, Armstrong Surgical Ctr. v. Armstrong County Mem'l Hosp., 185 F.3d 154 (3d Cir. 1999) (upholding dismissal of claims challenging defendant's successful opposition to a CON required by plaintiff, regardless of the accuracy of the information or assertions provided by defendants

Some health care providers have been found to exceed the realm of legitimate political lobbying activities or "mere solicitation" of governmental action. The *Noerr* immunity does not cover a provider's sham activities that are not genuinely aimed at securing favorable government action but are designed to interfere with a competitor's use of governmental processes so that governmental action on the merits is delayed or prevented.[887] Further, several circuit courts have held that *Noerr* immunity does not extend to a health care provider's knowing submission of false information to a government body.[888]

Moreover, the *Noerr* doctrine protects only concerted action to petition government officials and to influence government action; it does not extend to attempts to influence nongovernmental bodies whose members may include government officials[889] or to purely private conduct that is not genuinely aimed at prompting governmental action.[890] *Noerr* immunity also does not protect a medical association's activities where they are not limited to advocating change in payor policies but amount to collective decisions over whether to accept or reject those policies or involve threats to de-participate from the payor program if the association's views are not adopted.[891]

during the process); Boulware v. State of Nev., Dep't of Human Resources, 960 F.2d 793 (9th Cir. 1992) (*Noerr* immunized defendants' institution of state court action for plaintiff's alleged failure to comply with CON regulations); Bristol-Myers Squibb Co. v. IVAX Corp., 77 F. Supp. 2d 606 (D.N.J. 2000) (dismissing on *Noerr* grounds allegations that plaintiff unlawfully frustrated defendants' attempts to gain federal approval for new drugs); Forest Ambulance Serv. v. Mercy Ambulance, 952 F. Supp. 296 (E.D. Va. 1997) (dismissing on *Noerr* grounds ambulance service's claim against private rivals for opposing effort to obtain operating permit from city).

887. See City of Columbia v. Omni Outdoor Advert., Inc., 499 U.S. 365, 380 (1991) ("The 'sham' exception to *Noerr* encompasses situations in which persons use the governmental process—as opposed to the outcome of that process—as an anticompetitive weapon."); see also Hospital Bldg. Co. v. Trustees of Rex Hosp., 791 F.2d 288, 292 (4th Cir. 1986) (*Noerr* immunity does not apply if defendants' activity was intended to injure plaintiff directly rather than through governmental decision); Huron Valley Hosp. v. City of Pontiac, 612 F. Supp. 654, 663 (E.D. Mich. 1985) (abuse of process in barring access to agencies or courts falls within sham exception), aff'd on other grounds, 792 F.2d 563 (6th Cir.), cert. denied, 479 U.S. 885 (1986).

888. See, e.g., Kottle v. Northwest Kidney Ctrs., 146 F.3d 1056, 1060-62 (9th Cir. 1998), cert. denied, 525 U.S. 1140 (1999) (intentional misrepresentations fall within sham exception); Potters Med. Ctr. v. City Hosp. Ass'n, 800 F.2d 568, 580 (6th Cir. 1986) (knowing and willful submission of false information to government agency falls within sham exception); St. Joseph's Hosp. v. Hospital Corp. of Am., 795 F.2d 948, 955 (11th Cir. 1986) (furnishing of misinformation to government agency is not entitled to *Noerr* immunity). But see Armstrong Surgical Ctr., Inc., 185 F.3d 154 (party's conduct, even if deceitful, does not fall within the sham exception if the conduct was sincerely intended to procure legislative action); Bristol-Myers Squibb Co., 77 F. Supp. 2d 606 (sham exception does apply due to petitioner's tortious conduct where the injuries arose from government's decision rather than the "lobbying process" itself).

889. See, e.g., Preferred Physicians Mut. Risk Retention Group v. Cuomo, 865 F. Supp. 1057, 1072 (S.D.N.Y. 1994) (finding that National Association of Insurance Commissioners was a private trade association consisting of government regulators from different states to which *Noerr* immunity did not extend), vacated in part on other grounds, 85 F.3d 913 (2d Cir. 1996); see also Allied Tube & Conduit Corp. v. Indian Head, Inc., 486 U.S. 492, 504, 506-07 (1988) (immunity does not extend to anticompetitive efforts to influence private standard-setting body).

890. See, e.g., Wilk v. American Med. Ass'n, 895 F.2d 352, 357-58 (7th Cir.) (*Noerr* did not protect conduct that was aimed at achieving medical association's goal of boycott of chiropractors, rather than obtaining legislative action), cert. denied, 498 U.S. 982 (1990).

891. Michigan State Med. Soc'y, 101 F.T.C. 191, 298-99 (1983); see also United States v. North Dakota Hosp. Ass'n, 640 F. Supp. 1028, 1043 (D.N.D. 1986) (concluding that *Noerr* did not protect collective refusal by hospitals to accept proposal of Indian Health Service for reimbursement rates at Medicaid levels); Chain Pharmacy Ass'n, 56 Fed. Reg. 12,534, 12,541

In litigation over staff privileges, some courts have applied the state action doctrine to hold that peer review participants at a government-operated hospital are immune under state legislation authorizing the construction, operation, or staffing of public hospitals,[892] although courts in other jurisdictions have found otherwise.[893] Most courts have declined to extend state action immunity to peer review participants at private hospitals, however, finding that the state did not engage in active supervision of the peer review process.[894]

Several states have enacted legislation that permits physicians to jointly negotiate with health insurance companies.[895] Whether such statutes actually succeed in conferring such immunity is open to question, particularly on the issue of whether the state exercises active supervision over private activities.[896]

State action immunity has been held applicable, however, to some mergers or acquisitions and joint ventures involving public hospitals.[897] It has also been found to apply to actions undertaken by municipalities that grant licenses (e.g., a CON) to

(FTC Mar. 26, 1991) (proposed consent and aid to public comment) ("For example, [a pharmacy trade association or one of its members] could suggest arguments to present to legislators in criticizing a government-sponsored third-party prescription plan in order to encourage pharmacy firms to lobby for changes in the terms of the plan, so long as it did not do so as a sham to encourage pharmacy firms to boycott a third-party prescription plan."), 56 Fed. Reg. 32,575 (July 17, 1991) (consent order).

892. See, e.g., Bolt v. Halifax Hosp. Med. Ctr., 980 F.2d 1381, 1386-88 (11th Cir. 1993) (Florida); Cohn v. Bond, 953 F.2d 154, 158 (4th Cir. 1991) (North Carolina), cert. denied, 505 U.S. 1230 (1992); Todorov v. DCH Healthcare Auth., 921 F.2d 1438, 1460-62 (11th Cir. 1991) (Alabama); Wee v. Rome Hosp., 1996-1 Trade Cas. (CCH) ¶ 71,429 (N.D.N.Y. 1996) (New York); Crosby v. Hospital Auth., 873 F. Supp. 1568, 1573-80 (M.D. Ga. 1995) (Georgia), aff'd, 93 F.3d 1515 (11th Cir. 1996), cert. denied, 520 U.S. 1116 (1997); Shaw v. Phelps County Reg'l Med. Ctr., 858 F. Supp. 954, 960 (E.D. Mo. 1994) (Missouri); Scara v. Bradley Mem'l Hosp., 1993-2 Trade Cas. (CCH) ¶ 70,353 (E.D. Tenn. 1993) (Tennessee); Bloom v. Hennepin County, 783 F. Supp. 418, 423-26 (D. Minn. 1992) (Minnesota). The state action doctrine is discussed in part B of Chapter XIII.

893. See, e.g., Tambone v. Memorial Hosp., 825 F.2d 1132, 1135 (7th Cir. 1987) (Illinois).

894. See, e.g., Patrick v. Burget, 486 U.S. 94, 105 (1988) (Oregon); Miller v. Indiana Hosp., 930 F.2d 334, 336-39 (3d Cir. 1991) (Pennsylvania); Pinhas v. Summit Health, Ltd., 894 F.2d 1024, 1027-30 (9th Cir. 1989) (California), aff'd, 500 U.S. 322 (1991); Shahawy v. Harrison, 875 F.2d 1529, 1534-36 (11th Cir. 1989) (Florida); Jiricko v. Coffeyville Mem'l Hosp. Med. Ctr., 700 F. Supp. 1559, 1561-63 (D. Kan. 1988) (Kansas); Quinn v. Kent Gen. Hosp., 617 F. Supp. 1226, 1236-40 (D. Del. 1985) (Delaware). But see Ezpeleta v. Sisters of Mercy Health Corp., 800 F.2d 119, 121-22 (7th Cir. 1986) (per curiam) (holding peer review participants at private hospital immune under state action doctrine).

895. For example, a 1999 Texas law permits the joint negotiation of fees. S.B. 1468, 76th Leg. (Tex. 1999). A Washington statute permits physicians to organize and negotiate with payors on matters of patient concern. WASH. REV. CODE § 43.72.310 (1993 & Supp. 1997).

896. See, e.g., New York ex rel. Spitzer v. St. Francis Hosp., 94 F. Supp. 2d 399 (S.D.N.Y. 2000) (finding that the parties' collaborative activities, including allocations of services and joint payor negotiations, were not "actively supervised" by the state); see generally FTC v. Ticor Title Ins. Co., 504 U.S. 621 (1992); North Carolina ex rel. Edmisten v. P.I.A. Asheville, 740 F.2d 274 (4th Cir. 1984) (state approval of merger pursuant to CON legislation inadequate because state did not monitor hospital's action after acquisition).

897. See, e.g., Surgical Care Ctr. of Hammond v. Hospital Serv. Dist. No. 1, 171 F.3d 231 (5th Cir.), cert. denied, 528 U.S. 964 (1999); Martin v. Memorial Hosp., 86 F.3d 1391 (5th Cir. 1996); FTC v. Hospital Bd. of Dirs., 38 F.3d 1184 (11th Cir. 1994); Todorov, 921 F.2d 1438.

operate health care businesses[898] and by public hospitals and state-granted hospital service districts.[899]

G. Insurance

The McCarran-Ferguson Act[900] affords insurers an exemption from the federal antitrust laws under two conditions: (1) the challenged practice must be part of the "business of insurance," and (2) the practice must be "regulated by State law."[901] However, there is an exception to the exemption for acts or agreements of "boycott, coercion, or intimidation."[902]

1. The Business of Insurance

The "business of insurance" standard is a conduct-oriented rather than an entity-oriented test.[903] Thus, not all activities of insurance companies are protected by the exemption, only those that constitute the business of insurance.[904]

In *Union Life Insurance Co. v. Pireno*,[905] the Supreme Court fashioned a tripartite test to determine whether a particular activity qualifies as the business of insurance:

---

898. *See, e.g.*, Redwood Empire Life Support v. County of Sonoma, 190 F.3d 949 (9th Cir. 1999), *cert. denied*, 528 U.S. 1116 (2000) (state action shielded from antitrust liability the county and the private ambulance company with which it proposed to contract on an exclusive basis); Forest Ambulance Serv. v. Mercy Ambulance, 952 F. Supp. 296 (E.D. Va. 1997) (dismissing on state action grounds ambulance service's antitrust challenge to city's refusal to grant operating permit). *But see St. Francis Hosp.*, 94 F. Supp. 2d 399 (state action immunity did not apply to hospitals' joint pricing negotiations and market allocation agreements even though state had issued CON for the joint venture because state did not actively supervise joint activity).

899. *See, e.g.*, Neo Gen. Screening, Inc. v. New England Newborn Screening Program, 187 F.3d 24 (1st Cir.), *cert. denied*, 528 U.S. 1061 (1999) (affirming dismissal on state action grounds of antitrust challenge to the University of Massachusetts' exclusive contract to perform certain blood screening for newborns on behalf of the state); *Surgical Care Ctr.*, 171 F.3d 231 (state action did not apply to antitrust claims against hospital service district); Fremaux v. Board of Comm'rs of Hosp. Serv. Dist. No. 3, 1997-1 Trade Cas. (CCH) ¶ 71,852 (E.D. La. 1997) (dismissing on state action grounds challenge to hospital district's exclusive contract).

900. 15 U.S.C. §§ 1011-15 (2000).

901. *Id.* § 1012(b). The primary purpose of the McCarran Act was to preclude preemption of state insurance regulation by the dormant Commerce Clause or by federal statutes. Thus, under the nonantitrust provisions of the McCarran Act, federal statutes (other than the antitrust laws) that do not "specifically relate[]" to the "business of insurance" do not apply where they would "invalidate, impair, or supersede" a state insurance law. *Id.*

902. *Id.* § 1013(b). Other federal antitrust exemptions of general applicability, such as the state action doctrine and filed rate doctrine, also may apply to insurers. *See, e.g., Ticor Title Ins. Co.*, 504 U.S. 621 (state action doctrine); Sandy River Nursing Care Ctr. v. Aetna Cas. & Sur. Co., 985 F.2d 1138 (1st Cir.), *cert. denied*, 510 U.S. 818 (1993) (state action doctrine); Uniforce Temporary Personnel, Inc. v. National Council on Compensation Ins., Inc., 892 F. Supp. 1503 (S.D. Fla. 1995), *aff'd on other grounds*, 87 F.3d 1296 (11th Cir. 1996) (filed rate doctrine). Some states have statutory exemptions from state antitrust laws specifically applicable to insurers; others have statutory or implied exemptions of general applicability that may apply to insurers. For an overview of state antitrust exemptions, see ABA SECTION OF ANTITRUST LAW, INSURANCE ANTITRUST HANDBOOK 35-38 (1995).

903. Hartford Fire Ins. Co. v. California, 509 U.S. 764, 781 (1993).

904. SEC v. National Secs., Inc., 393 U.S. 453, 459 (1969).

905. 458 U.S. 119 (1982).

[F]irst, whether the practice has the effect of transferring or spreading a policyholder's risk; *second,* whether the practice is an integral part of the policy relationship between the insurer and the insured; and *third,* whether the practice is limited to entities within the insurance industry.[906]

The Court cautioned that "[n]one of these criteria is necessarily determinative in itself."[907] The Supreme Court and lower courts have applied the *Pireno* test to a variety of insurance practices, the most important of which are described below.

One insurance industry practice that raises competition questions is ratemaking. In many lines of insurance, particularly the property and casualty lines, insurers cooperate on rate-related matters, typically as members or subscribers of state-licensed "rating" or "advisory" organizations. Joint activities include the collection of historic loss data according to "risk classifications," calculation of "historic loss costs" for each such classification, development of "prospective loss costs" through "loss development" (projection of future claims under past policies) and "trending" (trends affecting future losses), determination of the "expense component" of rates (designed for recovery of costs not related to losses), and development of "end rates" consisting of the loss cost and expense elements.

A "primary concern" of the McCarran Act antitrust exemption was to protect these "cooperative ratemaking efforts."[908] Accordingly, the courts have determined that a wide variety of ratemaking practices are part of the business of insurance.[909] Allegations that rate cooperation was illegal price fixing or was undertaken beyond the scope of state authorization do not vitiate the exemption because its very purpose is to immunize rate agreements that otherwise would be unlawful under the federal antitrust statutes.[910]

Courts also have addressed whether the standardization of insurance policy forms is covered by the McCarran Act. Insurance rating and advisory organizations usually develop standard policy forms and endorsements for filing with state regulators. Form standardization is closely related to ratemaking because standardized definitions of risk facilitate aggregation and analysis of loss data. As a result, form standardization has been deemed part of the business of insurance.[911]

---

906. *Id.* at 129; *see also* Group Life & Health Ins. Co. v. Royal Drug Co., 440 U.S. 205 (1979).

907. *Pireno,* 458 U.S. at 129.

908. *Royal Drug,* 440 U.S. at 221. *See also National Secs.,* 393 U.S. at 460 ("[c]ertainly the fixing of rates is part of this business"). The McCarran Act exemption was enacted in response to *United States v. South-Eastern Underwriters Ass'n,* 322 U.S. 533 (1944), in which the Supreme Court sustained a criminal antitrust indictment of a rating organization against the argument that insurance was not interstate commerce.

909. *See, e.g., In re Workers' Compensation Ins. Antitrust Litig.,* 867 F.2d 1552 (8th Cir.), *cert. denied,* 493 U.S. 818 (1989); Ohio AFL-CIO v. Insurance Rating Bd., 451 F.2d 1178 (6th Cir. 1971), *cert. denied,* 409 U.S. 917 (1972); Allstate Ins. Co. v. Lanier, 361 F.2d 870 (4th Cir.), *cert. denied,* 385 U.S. 930 (1966); Owens v. Aetna Life & Cas. Co., 654 F.2d 218 (3d Cir.), *cert. denied,* 454 U.S. 1092 (1981); Meicler v. Aetna Cas. & Sur. Co., 506 F.2d 732 (5th Cir. 1975); Bristol Hotel Mgmt. Corp. v. Aetna Cas. & Sur. Co., 20 F. Supp. 2d 1345, 1349 (S.D. Fla. 1998); Grant v. Erie Ins. Exch., 542 F. Supp. 457, 462 (M.D. Pa. 1982), *aff'd without op.,* 716 F.2d 890 (3d Cir.), *cert. denied,* 464 U.S. 938 (1983).

910. *In re Workers' Compensation Ins. Antitrust Litig.,* 867 F.2d at 1556.

911. *National Secs.,* 393 U.S. at 460 (business of insurance includes "the type of policy which could be issued"); UNR Indus. v. Continental Ins. Co., 607 F. Supp. 855, 862 (N.D. Ill. 1984) ("The type of coverage offered directly affects the spreading of risk, is at the very heart of the policy relationship, and the agreement is limited to insurance companies."); Pierucci v. Continental Cas.

Insurers frequently underwrite risks jointly, either through permanent "pools" or through ad hoc arrangements of lesser scope and duration. In addition, most states by statute or regulation create "involuntary" or "residual" markets requiring insurers to cooperate in providing insurance for risks otherwise unable to obtain coverage. Although there are few decisions applying the McCarran Act to joint underwriting arrangements, they typically would qualify as the business of insurance because they involve the assumption of risk from the policyholder and spreading of it to the joint underwriters.[912] More generally, insurer decisions whether to accept or deny applications for insurance are the business of insurance because such decisions "are the essence of 'the underwriting of . . . risk.'"[913]

Insurer marketing and distribution of policies to insureds also can satisfy the *Pireno* standards.[914] However, the courts are divided on the question whether the relationship between an insurer and an independent agent used for the marketing and distribution of policies is the business of insurance.[915]

Another insurance industry practice addressed by the courts is claims handling. Insurers regularly investigate claims reported under their policies in order to determine whether the claim is a covered one and, if so, how much to pay. In *United States Department of Treasury v. Fabe*,[916] the Court held that claims payments were the business of insurance because the performance of the contract was the means by which risk actually was transferred. *Fabe* thus indicates that an insurer's dealings with insureds relating to claims are protected by the McCarran Act exemption.

However, an insurer's dealings with third parties during the claims-handling process generally does not constitute part of the business of insurance even if there is

---

Co., 418 F. Supp. 704, 708 (W.D. Pa. 1976) ("We hold that the issuance of policies and forms which are used by the various companies constitute part of the business of insurance.").

912. *Cf.* Slagle v. ITT Hartford Ins. Group, 102 F.3d 494, 498 (11th Cir. 1996) (joint setting of rates by Florida pool for windstorm risks was the business of insurance). However, ancillary practices of an underwriting pool that do not involve policyholders or the spreading of risk may not qualify as part of the business of insurance.

913. Equifax, Inc., 96 F.T.C. 844, 1100 (1980) (citation omitted), *modified*, 678 F.2d 1047 (11th Cir. 1982); *see also* Feinstein v. Nettleship Co., 714 F.2d 928, 931-33 (9th Cir. 1983); Weatherby v. RCA Corp., 1988-1 Trade Cas. (CCH) ¶ 68,077, at 58,534-35 (N.D.N.Y. 1986).

914. FTC v. National Cas. Co., 357 U.S. 560 (1958) (McCarran Act exempts the advertising of insurance); *National Secs.*, 393 U.S. at 460 (the "selling and advertising of policies" is "within the scope of the [act]").

915. Owens v. Aetna Life & Cas. Co., 654 F.2d 218 (3d Cir. 1981) (business of insurance includes agent's solicitation of customers and decisions on applications), *cert. denied*, 454 U.S. 1092 (1981); Malley-Duff & Assocs. v. Crown Life Ins. Co., 734 F.2d 133 (2d Cir.) (agent termination was not the business of insurance), *cert. denied*, 469 U.S. 1072 (1984); Bogan v. Northwestern Mut. Life Ins. Co., 953 F. Supp. 532, 538 (S.D.N.Y. 1997) (restrictions on agent's ability to transfer to other agencies was not the business of insurance), *aff'd*, 166 F.3d 509 (2d Cir.), *cert. denied*, 528 U.S. 1019 (1999); Gribbin v. Southern Farm Bureau Life Ins. Co., 1984-1 Trade Cas. (CCH) ¶ 65,798, at 67,341-42 (W.D. La. 1984) (contractual limitations on insurer's agents were part of the insurance business), *aff'd without op.*, 751 F.2d 1257 (5th Cir. 1985); American Standard Life & Accident Ins. Co. v. U.R.L., Inc., 701 F. Supp. 527, 532-33 (M.D. Pa. 1988) (insurance agents' attempt to induce customers to switch policies was not the business of insurance). While not uniform, the cases suggest a distinction between those aspects of the insurer/agent relationship that directly involve the insured and those aspects that do not.

916. 508 U.S. 491 (1993). *Fabe* involved the McCarran Act's nonantitrust provisions but it interpreted the same "business of insurance" language used in the antitrust exemption provisions.

a significant indirect effect on the insured. In *Group Life & Health Insurance Co. v. Royal Drug*,[917] the Court held that a health insurer's agreement with pharmacies for the supply of drugs to insureds was not the business of insurance because the agreement did not entail the spreading of risk and involved entities outside the insurance industry. In *Union Labor Life Insurance Co. v. Pireno*,[918] the Court held for similar reasons that an insurer's use of physicians for peer review of medical bills was not the business of insurance.[919]

Reinsurance is the business of insurance because it is insurance for insurers.[920] A financial contract styled as an "insurance policy" will not be regarded as the business of insurance where the writer of the policy assumes no real insurance risk.[921] Similarly, insurer services that are not rendered in performance of an insurance contract, such as third-party claims administration services provided to self-insured employers, are not the business of insurance.[922] Further, certain types of life insurance or annuities may not be deemed part of the insurance business if they are primarily investment products.[923]

---

917. 440 U.S. 205 (1979).

918. 458 U.S. 119 (1982).

919. Following *Royal Drug* and *Pireno*, numerous lower courts have held that vertical arrangements between insurers and third-party providers of claims-related goods and services are not the business of insurance. *See, e.g.*, Proctor v. State Farm Mut. Auto. Ins. Co., 675 F.2d 308, 336-37 (D.C. Cir.) (arrangements with automobile repair shops), *cert. denied*, 459 U.S. 839 (1982); Portland Retail Druggists Ass'n v. Kaiser Found. Health Plan, 662 F.2d 641, 646-47 (9th Cir. 1981) (contractual arrangements with drug manufacturers, wholesalers, and distributors), *cert. denied*, 469 U.S. 1229 (1985); St. Bernard Hosp. v. Hospital Serv., Inc., 618 F.2d 1140, 1145 (5th Cir. 1980) (contract with hospital); Hahn v. Oregon Physician Serv., 689 F.2d 840, 844 (9th Cir. 1982) (contract with provider), *cert. denied*, 462 U.S. 1133 (1983); Rozema v. Marshfield Clinic, 1997-1 Trade Cas. (CCH) ¶ 71,796 (W.D. Wis. 1997) (health plan's refusal to include chiropractor in network of approved providers). A common concern in these cases is that the McCarran exemption not be interpreted to affect competition in health care or other noninsurance markets.

Vertical agreements between an insurer and a third-party provider are distinguishable from the insurer's decision whether to provide coverage to the insured for medical treatment given by certain types of providers. The latter would appear to be part of the contractual relationship with the insured and to involve the scope and type of risk transferred to the insurer. Nevertheless, some courts have held that insurer decisions whether to provide reimbursement for certain types of providers are not the business of insurance. *See, e.g.*, Trident Neuro-Imaging Lab. v. Blue Cross & Blue Shield, 568 F. Supp. 1474 (D.S.C. 1983) (refusal to reimburse for services performed on physician-owned rather than hospital-owned equipment).

920. *In re* Insurance Antitrust Litig., 938 F.2d 919, 927 (9th Cir. 1991), *aff'd in part and rev'd in part on other grounds sub nom.* Hartford Fire Ins. Co. v. California, 509 U.S. 764 (1993).

921. *See, e.g.*, Ticor Title Ins. Co. v. FTC, 998 F.2d 1129 (3d Cir. 1993) (title insurers did not assume any risk of loss but instead performed only title search and examination activities), *cert. denied*, 510 U.S. 1190 (1994).

922. Reazin v. Blue Cross & Blue Shield, Inc., 663 F. Supp. 1360 (D. Kan. 1987), *aff'd in part and remanded in part*, 899 F.2d 951 (10th Cir.), *cert. denied*, 497 U.S. 1005 (1990); *see also* United States v. Title Ins. Rating Bureau, 700 F.2d 1247 (9th Cir. 1983) (real estate escrow services sold by title insurers not the business of insurance), *cert. denied*, 467 U.S. 1240 (1984); Perry v. Fidelity Union Life Ins. Co., 606 F.2d 468 (5th Cir. 1979) (financing of premiums not part of the insurance business), *cert. denied*, 446 U.S. 987 (1980).

923. *See, e.g.*, SEC v. Variable Annuity Life Ins. Co., 359 U.S. 65 (1959); *but see* Blackfeet Nat'l Bank v. Nelson, 171 F.3d 1237 (11th Cir. 1999) ("retirement CD" with an annuity feature was insurance because it shifted "mortality risk" to the issuer).

Courts have treated HMOs' contractual relationships with subscribers as within the business of insurance.[924] Finally, the "tying" of insurance with noninsurance products does not qualify as the business of insurance.[925]

2. Regulated by State Law

The intensity and specificity of state regulation needed to qualify for McCarran Act immunity is less than required for the state action doctrine.[926] The objective of the McCarran Act was to preserve existing forms of state regulation, which typically involved insurance codes delegating administrative power to insurance departments. Thus, the courts have held that the state regulation requirement is satisfied by the existence of a general administrative scheme of regulation affording regulators jurisdiction over the challenged practice, whether or not exercised.[927] It is not necessary for the state law to expressly authorize anticompetitive insurer agreements or the challenged practice.[928] In the case of proposed rates and policy forms, the state need not give affirmative advance approval to insurer filings after a substantive review, as is required for the state action doctrine to apply.[929] The McCarran Act requirement also is satisfied if the insurance department has the power to prohibit the challenged practice under an "unfair insurance practices act" modeled on the Federal Trade Commission Act.[930]

---

924. *See* Washington Physicians Serv. Ass'n v. Gregoire, 147 F.3d 1039, 1047 (9th Cir. 1998) (state law requiring managed care plans to cover specified treatments regulated the business of insurance), *cert. denied*, 525 U.S. 1141 (1999); Anglin v. Blue Shield of Virginia, 693 F.2d 315, 318 (4th Cir. 1982) (refusal to offer HMO coverage is the business of insurance); Ocean State Physicians Health Plan, Inc. v. Blue Cross & Blue Shield of Rhode Island, 883 F.2d 1101, 1107-09 (1st Cir. 1989) (Blue Cross managed care plan qualified as business of insurance), *cert. denied*, 494 U.S. 1027 (1990) (HMO's contracts with subscribers and pricing of services to subscribers were the business of insurance).

925. FTC v. Dixie Fin. Co., 695 F.2d 926, 929-30 (5th Cir.) (tying of credit and credit insurance), *cert. denied*, 461 U.S. 928 (1983); FTC v. Manufacturers Hanover Consumer Servs., Inc., 567 F. Supp. 992, 995-96 (E.D. Pa. 1983) (same).

926. See discussion of state action doctrine in part B of Chapter XIII.

927. *See, e.g.*, Mackey v. Nationwide Ins. Cos., 724 F.2d 491, 420-21 (4th Cir. 1984); Feinstein v. Nettleship Co., 714 F.2d 928, 933 (9th Cir. 1983), *cert. denied*, 466 U.S. 972 (1984); *In re* Insurance Antitrust Litig., 723 F. Supp. 464, 474 (N.D. Cal. 1989), *rev'd on other grounds*, 938 F.2d 919 (9th Cir. 1991), *aff'd in part and rev'd in part on other grounds sub nom.* Hartford Fire Ins. Co. v. California, 509 U.S. 764 (1993).

928. *See, e.g.*, *In re* Workers' Compensation Ins. Antitrust Litig., 867 F.2d 1552, 1557-58 (8th Cir.) (repeal of statute authorizing collective ratemaking did not make the exemption unavailable because the insurance commissioner still had general authority over rating practices), *cert. denied*, 493 U.S. 818 (1989); Maryland v. Blue Cross & Blue Shield Ass'n, 620 F. Supp. 907, 920-21 (D. Md. 1985) (state need not expressly approve territorial market division by health insurers).

929. The majority of decisions have held that "file-and-use" and "use-and-file" laws, or similar "deemed approved" laws, are sufficient state regulation even though rates automatically go into effect if the regulator fails to disapprove. *See, e.g.*, Ohio AFL-CIO v. Insurance Rating Bd., 451 F.2d 1178 (6th Cir. 1971), *cert. denied*, 409 U.S. 917 (1972); Commander Leasing Co. v. Transamerica Title Ins. Co., 477 F.2d 77 (10th Cir. 1973); Lawyer's Title Co. v. St. Paul Title Ins. Corp., 526 F.2d 795 (8th Cir. 1975); *but see* Brown v. Ticor Title Ins. Co., 982 F.2d 386 (9th Cir. 1992) (state regulation requirement not satisfied where rates went into effect without actual review), *cert. dismissed*, 511 U.S. 117 (1994). The state regulation requirement also is satisfied in states that do not require rate or form filing so long as the insurance commissioner has the power to investigate and suspend. *Feinstein*, 714 F.2d 928.

930. Mackey v. Nationwide Ins. Cos., 724 F.2d 419 (4th Cir. 1984); Anglin v. Blue Shield of Virginia, 693 F.2d 315 (4th Cir. 1982); Dexter v. Equitable Life Assurance Soc'y, 527 F.2d 233 (2d Cir.

Challenges to the effectiveness of state regulation have not been permitted.[931] Further, the exemption applies to the conduct of an insurer subject to state regulation even though other alleged participants in that conduct were beyond the regulatory reach of state insurance departments.[932] Nevertheless, the Supreme Court has left open the possibility that a regulatory scheme will not satisfy the McCarran Act where it is a "mere pretense."[933] In addition, because a state cannot regulate extraterritorially, there must be regulation by the state in which the challenged practices occur or have their impact.[934] However, the courts have split on the question whether a noninsurance statute of general applicability, such as a state antitrust law, is sufficient to trigger the exemption.[935]

3. Agreements or Acts of Boycott, Coercion, or Intimidation

In *St. Paul Fire & Marine Insurance Co. v. Barry*,[936] the Supreme Court held that the McCarran Act's boycott exception was not limited to boycotts of competing agents or insurers but included boycotts of policyholders and others as well. Subsequently, in *Hartford Fire Insurance Co. v. California*,[937] the Court defined boycott to mean a concerted refusal to deal in one transaction in order to coerce changes in the terms of a separate and unrelated transaction. "It is this expansion of the refusal to deal beyond the targeted transaction that gives great coercive force to a commercial boycott: unrelated transactions are used as leverage to achieve the terms desired."[938]

Under the *Hartford Fire* test, it is not a boycott for insurers to refuse to engage in a particular transaction until the coverage or other terms of that transaction are agreeable. Thus, an alleged group refusal by reinsurers to provide reinsurance for primary insurance policies containing coverage terms to which the defendants objected was not a boycott because "the terms of the primary coverages are central elements of the reinsurance contract—they are *what is* reinsured."[939]

1975); Klamath-Lake Pharmaceutical Ass'n v. Klamath Med. Serv. Bureau, 701 F.2d 1276 (9th Cir.), *cert. denied*, 464 U.S. 822 (1983).

931. FTC v. National Cas. Co., 357 U.S. 560 (1958) (rejecting FTC's argument that unfair insurance practices laws were insufficient for the exemption where states did not elaborate the statutes through regulations or rulings); *Ohio AFL-CIO*, 451 F.2d at 1184 ("[T]here is nothing in the language of the McCarran Act or in its legislative history to support the thesis that the act does not apply when the state's scheme of regulation has not been effectively enforced.").
932. *Hartford Fire*, 509 U.S. at 784 (U.S. insurers were exempt notwithstanding alleged agreement with foreign reinsurers not subject to state regulation).
933. *National Cas.*, 357 U.S. at 564-65.
934. FTC v. Travelers Health Ass'n, 362 U.S. 293 (1960).
935. *Compare* Fry v. John Hancock Mut. Life Ins. Co., 355 F. Supp. 1151, 1153-54 (N.D. Tex. 1973) (Texas antitrust statute does not satisfy state regulation requirement), *with Klamath-Lake Pharmaceutical Ass'n*, 701 F.2d at 1287 (dicta to effect that Oregon antitrust law satisfies state regulation requirement), Maryland v. Blue Cross & Blue Shield Ass'n, 620 F. Supp. 907, 920-21 (D. Md. 1985) (Maryland antitrust act sufficient state regulation), *and* California League of Independent Ins. Producers v. Aetna Cas. & Sur. Co., 175 F. Supp. 857, 860 (N.D. Cal.) (California antitrust law satisfied state action requirement), *modified on other grounds*, 179 F. Supp. 65 (1959).
936. 438 U.S. 531 (1978).
937. 509 U.S. 764 (1993).
938. *Id.* at 802-03.
939. *Id.* at 806.

Therefore, in determining whether the boycott exception applies, the critical questions are (1) whether the transactions in which the refusal to deal occurs are "related" to or "separate" from the transactions the defendants seek to influence, and (2) whether the purpose of the refusal is "collateral" to the transactions involving the refusal to deal. Thus, in *Hartford Fire*, an alleged refusal to provide reinsurance for one type of coverage sufficiently plead a boycott where the reinsurers' asserted purpose was to influence the terms of separate primary insurance transactions. After *Hartford Fire*, lower courts have dismissed boycott allegations on the pleadings for failure to allege separate transactions.[940]

H. Organized Labor

Certain agreements and activities involving labor are immune from the antitrust laws, based on statutory and nonstatutory exemptions. The statutory labor exemption enables workers to organize to eliminate competition among themselves, and to pursue their legitimate labor interests, so long as they do not combine with a nonlabor group. The nonstatutory labor exemption applies to agreements or concerted action between employees or their labor organizations and employers or other nonlabor entities where the agreement or action is appropriate to achieve the objectives of national labor policy and does not have an unwarranted anticompetitive impact on the business market.

1. The Statutory Exemption

Prior to passage of the Clayton Act in 1914, courts generally held concerted activities by employees aimed at obtaining union recognition to be illegal. In 1908, in *Loewe v. Lawlor* (the Danbury Hatters case),[941] the Supreme Court held that a union violated the Sherman Act when it organized a nationwide secondary boycott of nonunion-made hats as part of an organizational strike against a hat manufacturer. Congress responded in 1914 by granting, as part of the Clayton Act,[942] specific exemptions from the antitrust laws for certain conduct arising out of a "labor dispute." Section 6 of the Clayton Act states:

> The labor of a human being is not a commodity or article of commerce. Nothing contained in the antitrust laws shall be construed to forbid the existence and operation of labor ... organizations, ... or to forbid or restrain individual members of such organizations from lawfully carrying out the legitimate objects thereof; nor shall such organizations, or the members thereof, be held or construed to be illegal combinations or conspiracies in restraint of trade, under the antitrust laws.[943]

---

940. *See, e.g.*, Slagle v. ITT Hartford Ins. Group, 102 F.3d 494, 499 (11th Cir. 1996) (defendant insurers' alleged refusal to sell windstorm insurance except through a joint underwriting pool was not a boycott but merely a demand for higher rates); Uniforce Temporary Personnel, Inc. v. National Council on Compensation Ins., 892 F. Supp. 1503, 1510 (S.D. Fla. 1995) (no boycott where plaintiffs complained only of the premiums they were forced to pay), *aff'd*, 87 F.3d 1296 (11th Cir. 1996).
941. 208 U.S. 274 (1908).
942. Act of Oct. 15, 1914, ch. 323, § 6, 38 Stat. 731 (codified at 15 U.S.C. § 17 (2000)).
943. 15 U.S.C. § 17.

Section 20 of the Clayton Act prohibits the issuance of federal injunctions against strikes, boycotts, or picketing "in any case between an employer and employees, or between employers and employees, or between employees, or between persons employed and persons seeking employment, involving, or growing out of, a dispute concerning terms or conditions of employment," and concludes with the broad prohibition that none "of the acts specified in this paragraph be considered or held to be violations of any law of the United States."[944] Notwithstanding these provisions, the Supreme Court in *Duplex Printing Press Co. v. Deering*[945] upheld an injunction against a secondary boycott conducted by union members against the goods of an employer. The Court held that the immunity granted by the Clayton Act was limited solely to the collective action by employees of the employer with whom the labor dispute existed.[946]

Congress responded to *Duplex Printing* and other antitrust decisions narrowly construing the Clayton Act exemption by enacting the Norris-LaGuardia Act,[947] which was intended "to restore the broad purpose which Congress thought it had formulated in the Clayton Act but which was frustrated, so Congress believed, by unduly restrictive judicial construction."[948] The Norris-LaGuardia Act deprives the federal courts of jurisdiction to issue injunctions "in a case involving or growing out of a labor dispute," except where unlawful acts are threatened or committed.[949] The protection of the Norris-LaGuardia Act extends to all persons "participating or interested" in a labor dispute, including any member of the union whose members are involved in the dispute.[950]

After Congress passed Section 20 of the Clayton Act and the Norris-LaGuardia Act, the Supreme Court, in *United States v. Hutcheson*,[951] articulated the scope of the statutory exemption in the following terms:

> The Norris-LaGuardia Act reasserted the original purpose of the Clayton Act by infusing into it the immunized trade union activities as redefined by the later Act. In this light § 20 removes all such allowable conduct from the taint of being a "violation of any law of the United States," including the Sherman Law.[952]

Although the statutory exemption is broad, it has not been interpreted to immunize labor or union activity in all circumstances.[953] In *Hutcheson*, the Court

---

944. Act of Oct. 15, 1914, ch. 323, § 20, 38 Stat. 738 (codified at 29 U.S.C. § 52 (1994)).
945. 254 U.S. 443 (1921).
946. *Id. See also* Bedford Cut Stone Co. v. Journeymen Stone Cutters' Ass'n, 274 U.S. 37 (1927).
947. Act of Mar. 23, 1932, ch. 90, §§ 1-15, 47 Stat. 70-73 (codified at 29 U.S.C. §§ 101-110, 113-115 (1994)).
948. United States v. Hutcheson, 312 U.S. 219, 236 (1941).
949. 29 U.S.C. §§ 101, 107. *See also* Milk Wagon Drivers v. Lake Valley Farm Products, Inc., 311 U.S. 91 (1940).
950. 29 U.S.C. §§ 104, 105, 113(b). The Norris-LaGuardia Act has been held to insulate unions from Sherman Act injunctive relief in cases involving labor disputes. *See, e.g.,* Burlington N. Santa Fe Ry. Co. v. International Bro. of Teamsters Local 174, 203 F.3d 703 (9th Cir. 2000); Utilities Servs. Eng'g, Inc. v. Colorado Bldg. & Constr. Trades Council, 549 F.2d 173 (10th Cir. 1977).
951. 312 U.S. 219 (1941).
952. *Id.* at 236.
953. It has been argued, based upon *Apex Hosiery Co. v. Leader*, 310 U.S. 469 (1940), that the antitrust laws simply do not apply to labor market restraints. In *Apex Hosiery*, the Court stated in dicta that the Sherman Act was not directed at "an elimination of price competition based on differences in labor standards." *Id.* at 503. *See also* H.A. Artists & Assoc., Inc. v. Actors' Equity Ass'n, 451

found that the exemption applied "[s]o long as a union acts in its self-interest and does not combine with non-labor groups."[954]

Thus, to invoke the statutory exemption, an organization must first be a bona fide "labor group" and must not include commercial competitors.[955] A bona fide labor group seeking protection under the statutory labor exemption also must act in its "self-interest" by limiting its activities to labor market objectives.[956] Lastly, the statutory exemption is unavailable under *Hutcheson* if the bona fide labor group combines with a nonlabor group. In *American Federation of Musicians v. Carroll*,[957] the Supreme Court held that, in resolving this issue, a court must determine whether there was "job or wage competition or some other economic interrelationship affecting legitimate union interests between the union members" and the alleged nonlabor group.[958] The *Carroll* case involved agreements between orchestra leaders and musicians that imposed broad restrictions on orchestra leaders, including restrictions on the hiring and paying of musicians and the use of booking agents. The orchestra leaders sought to invalidate the agreements by arguing that the leaders constituted a nonlabor group and, therefore, were subject to the antitrust laws. The Supreme Court approved the district court's use of an "economic interrelationship" test and sustained its findings that the "orchestra leaders performed work and functions which actually or potentially affected the hours, wages, job security, and

---

U.S. 704, 715 n.16 (1981). However, the Supreme Court has taken a different tack beginning in *Hutcheson* and continuing through its most recent consideration of labor exemption issues in *Brown v. Pro Football*, 518 U.S. 231 (1996), discussed *infra* at notes 978-83 and accompanying text.

954. *Hutcheson*, 312 U.S. at 232.

955. *See H.A. Artists*, 451 U.S. at 717 n.20 ("Of course a party seeking refuge in the statutory exemption must be a bona fide labor organization, and not an independent contractor or entrepreneur."); Columbia River Packers Ass'n v. Hinton, 315 U.S. 143 (1942) (actions of a "union" of fishermen and their employees not protected by Norris-LaGuardia Act because fishermen were independent businessmen); Los Angeles Meat and Provision Drivers Union, Local 626 v. United States, 371 U.S. 94 (1962) (businessmen who combine in an association that would otherwise be properly subject to dissolution under the antitrust laws cannot immunize themselves from that sanction by the simple expedient of calling themselves a labor union).

956. In *H.A. Artists*, the Supreme Court held that unilateral union activity imposing "franchise fees" on theatrical agents was not exempt because the fees were not related to the legitimate union interest in "elimination of wage competition, upholding of the union wage scale, and promotion of fair access to jobs." 451 U.S. at 722. *See also* USS-POSCO Indus. v. Contra Costa County Bldg. and Constr. Trades Council, 31 F.3d 800, 809 (9th Cir. 1994) (work stoppage motivated by well-founded safety concerns at the project site, and picketing and hand billing on the contractor's premises protected by statutory exemption; lawsuits, permit protests, and lobbying activities designed to make an example of the contractor may not be protected); Allied Int'l, Inc. v. International Longshoremen's Ass'n, 640 F.2d 1368, 1380 (1st Cir. 1981), *aff'd*, 456 U.S. 212 (1982) (refusal to unload Russian ships to protest the invasion of Afghanistan did not relate to a legitimate union interest); Collins v. National Basketball Players Ass'n, No. 92-1022, 1992 U.S. App. LEXIS 24069 (10th Cir. Sept. 21, 1992) (National Basketball Players Association was acting in its self-interest when it denied certification to a prospective player agent); Mid-America Reg'l Bargaining Ass'n v. Will County Carpenters Dist. Council, 675 F.2d 881 (7th Cir.), *cert. denied*, 459 U.S. 860 (1992); U.S. Steel Corp. v. Fraternal Ass'n of Steelhaulers, 431 F.2d 1046, 1050 (3d Cir. 1971) ("[t]his unmistakable concern with a return on capital investment, although economically understandable, lends a distinct non-labor character to FASH's operations"); U.S. Steel Corp. v. Fraternal Ass'n of Steel Haulers, 601 F.2d 1269 (3d Cir. 1979); Pan Alaska Trucking v. International Bro. of Teamsters, 621 F. Supp. 800 (D. Alaska 1985).

957. 391 U.S. 99 (1968).

958. *Id.* at 106.

working conditions of [the labor union's] members."[959]   These were held to be matters of traditional, legitimate union concern. Because the orchestra leaders and musicians competed with each other in the same labor market, orchestra leaders were found to constitute a labor group subject to union pressures to maintain labor standards among its own membership. The Court also held that the prohibition against dealing with unlicensed booking agents was justified, despite the lack of competition between musicians and booking agents, because of the effect that the higher fees charged by unlicensed agents would have on musicians' wages.[960]

2. *The Nonstatutory Exemption*

While the statutory exemption has been limited to legitimate organizing and other unilateral activities of employees and their labor unions, the courts have developed a nonstatutory exemption that applies to concerted activities of and agreements between labor and nonlabor parties. The nonstatutory labor exemption is designed to accommodate national labor policy and the antitrust laws. The nonstatutory exemption has been applied to concerted activities and agreements that were intimately related to a mandatory subject of bargaining, i.e., core labor market issues of wages, hours, and working conditions, and did not have "a potential for restraining competition in the business market in ways that would not follow naturally from elimination of competition over wages and working conditions,"[961] and, in most cases, which have arisen in the collective bargaining setting.

The Supreme Court discussed the nonstatutory exemption extensively in *Connell Construction Co. v. Plumbers & Steamfitters* and held that the exemption did not apply to agreements that went beyond legitimate labor market concerns and into a business market.[962]   In *Connell*, a union representing plumbing and mechanical workers picketed Connell, a general contractor, to secure an agreement whereby Connell would subcontract plumbing and mechanical work only to firms that had a current contract with the union. The union did not represent or seek to represent any of Connell's employees. Connell signed the agreement under protest and then

---

959. *Id.* The Supreme Court reaffirmed the economic interrelationship test in *H.A. Artists*, 451 U.S. 704. *Cf.* Local 24 of International Bro. of Teamsters v. Oliver, 358 U.S. 283 (1959).

960. 391 U.S. at 113. Several courts have found a failure to demonstrate that the labor group in question combined with a nonlabor entity. *See* Phoenix Elec. Co. v. National Elec. Contractors Ass'n, 861 F. Supp. 1498 (D. Or. 1994); Imperial Constr. Mgmt. Corp. v. Laborers' Int'l Local 96, 818 F. Supp. 1179 (N.D. Ill. 1993); Paramount Brands, Inc. v. Peerless Importers, Inc., 1992-2 Trade Cas. (CCH) ¶ 70,052 (E.D.N.Y. 1992); Petrochem Insulation, Inc. v. Northern Cal. and N. Nev. Pipe Trades Council, 1992-1 Trade Cas. (CCH) ¶ 69,814 (N.D. Cal. 1992), *aff'd sub nom.* Petrochem Insulation, Inc. v. United Ass'n of Journeymen & Apprentices Local No. 38, 8 F.3d 29 (9th Cir. 1993), *cert. denied*, 510 U.S. 1191 (1994). *But see* Ehredt Underground, Inc. v. Commonwealth Edison Co., No. 91 C 2361, 1992 U.S. Dist. LEXIS 7360 (N.D. Ill. May 27, 1992). In *USS-POSCO*, the Ninth Circuit held that to be a nonlabor group, an entity "must operate in the same market as the [antitrust claimant] to a sufficient degree that it would be capable of committing an antitrust violation against the [claimant], quite independent of the union's involvement." 31 F.3d at 806. This would include a competitor of a claimant, a supplier or purchaser of the claimant's goods or services, or even more remote entities that are deemed to be operating in the same market. *Id.* *But see* Colfax Corp. v. Illinois State Toll Highway Auth., 1994-2 Trade Cas. (CCH) ¶ 70,771, at 73,247 (N.D. Ill. 1994) (affording the protection of the statutory exemption to an agreement between a union and a plaintiff's customer), *aff'd*, 79 F.3d 631 (7th Cir. 1996).

961. Connell Constr. Co. v. Plumbers & Steamfitters, 421 U.S. 616, 635 (1975).

962. *Id.*

brought suit alleging violations of Sections 1 and 2 of the Sherman Act and of state antitrust laws.

After tracing the history of the labor exemptions through three landmark cases, *Allen Bradley Co. v. Local 3, International Brotherhood of Electrical Workers*,[963] *United Mine Workers v. Pennington*,[964] and *Local 189, Amalgamated Meat Cutters v. Jewel Tea Co.*,[965] the Court explained the rationale for the nonstatutory exemption:

> The nonstatutory exemption has its source in the strong labor policy favoring the association of employees to eliminate competition over wages and working conditions. Union success in organizing workers and standardizing wages ultimately will affect price competition among employers, but the goals of federal labor law never could be achieved if this effect on business competition were held a violation of the antitrust laws. The Court therefore has acknowledged that labor policy requires tolerance for the lessening of business competition based on differences in wages and working conditions.[966]

As the Court also observed, however, the scope of the exemption is not unlimited:

> Labor policy clearly does not require, however, that a union have freedom to impose direct restraints on competition among those who employ its members. Thus, while the statutory exemption allows unions to accomplish some restraints by acting unilaterally, the nonstatutory exemption offers no similar protection when a union and a nonlabor party agree to restrain competition in a business market.[967]

In balancing competing antitrust and labor law concerns, the Supreme Court considered and rejected the argument accepted by both the district court and the court of appeals that the agreement at issue was lawful as a matter of federal labor law under the construction industry proviso to Section 8(e) of the National Labor Relations Act (NLRA),[968] and was therefore exempt from antitrust scrutiny.[969] The

---

963. 325 U.S. 797 (1945) (holding that agreements of unions and employer groups that effectively insulated New York area business entities from outside competition in business markets was not protected by the nonstatutory labor exemption).

964. 381 U.S. 657 (1965) (holding that agreement by union to extend wage scale to companies outside the labor market, although facially directed to equalizing labor standards, a labor market objective, was not protected by nonstatutory exemption where objective was to eliminate competition in business markets).

965. *Id.* at 676 (decided the same day as *Pennington*, and holding that agreement to restrict hours of operation, although facially directed to a business rather than a labor market, was protected by nonstatutory exemption because its objective was to limit hours of work, a labor market objective). *Cf. In re* Detroit Auto Dealers Ass'n, 955 F.2d 457 (6th Cir.) (holding that such agreement not protected where entered into among car dealers to forestall unionization), *cert. denied*, 506 U.S. 973 (1992).

966. 421 U.S. at 622.

967. *Id.* at 622-23 (citations omitted).

968. 29 U.S.C. § 158(e) (1994).

969. 421 U.S. at 633-35. Under both *Connell* and *Brown v. Pro Football, Inc.*, 518 U.S. 231 (1996), the relationship between federal labor and antitrust laws is critical to application of the nonstatutory labor exemption. *Connell*, in particular, addresses the relationship between whether an agreement violates § 8(e) of the NLRA, which proscribes "hot cargo" clauses by which an employer refuses to handle nonunion goods (subject to provisos for the construction and garment industries), and the availability of the nonstatutory exemption. In *Kaiser Steel Corp. v. Mullins*, 455 U.S. 72, 85 (1982), the Court commented that in *Connell* it was necessary to decide the § 8(e) issue first in order "to determine whether the agreement was immune from the antitrust laws." *See also* Sheet

1380 ANTITRUST LAW DEVELOPMENTS (FIFTH)

Court emphasized the broad anticompetitive effect of the subcontracting agreement, noting that the union had been able to secure such agreements with other general contractors in the area in addition to Connell.[970] The Court also noted that the effect of these agreements went beyond the elimination of competition in wages, hours, and working conditions by excluding from the bidding process subcontractors whose lower bids might result from cost efficiencies unrelated to the wages they paid to their nonunion employees.[971] Thus, while the sole purpose of the subcontracting agreement appeared to be to organize as many subcontractor employees as possible,[972] the effect was to insulate union subcontracting firms from all types of competition, not merely wage competition.[973] The Court found this to be a substantial anticompetitive effect on the subcontracting business market that did not follow naturally from the collective bargaining process.[974] The Court concluded, therefore, that "[t]he federal policy favoring collective bargaining" could "offer no shelter" to the union's activities.[975]

Lower courts have interpreted the nonstatutory exemption to protect from antitrust scrutiny a wide variety of labor-nonlabor agreements and activities directed at labor market concerns.[976] Such protected activity has included joint employer

---

Metal Div. of Capitol Dist. Sheet Metal, Roofing and Air Conditioning Contractors Ass'n v. Local Union 38 of Sheet Metal Worker's Int'l Ass'n, 208 F.3d 18, 20-22 (2d Cir. 2000); Associated Builders and Contractors, Inc. v. City of Seward, 966 F.2d 492 (9th Cir. 1992), cert. denied, 507 U.S. 984 (1993); Sun-Land Nurseries v. Southern Cal. Dist. Council of Laborers, 793 F.2d 1110 (9th Cir. 1986) (en banc), cert. denied, 479 U.S. 1090 (1987); but see Local 210, Laborers' Int'l Union v. Labor Relations Div. Associated Gen. Contractors, Inc., 844 F.2d 69 (2d Cir. 1988) (although clause was legal under the proviso to § 8(e), this did not necessarily mean that it was beyond the reach of the antitrust laws). Moreover, it has been held that a violation of labor law does not of itself automatically remove the exemption. Richards v. Neilsen Freight Lines, 810 F.2d 898, 906 (9th Cir. 1987) ("The Supreme Court's consideration [in Connell], however, of the actual and potential anticompetitive effects of the agreement independently of the violation of section [8(e)] suggests that the presence of a section [8(e)] violation may not itself decide the exemption issue. . . . Connell does not suggest that every violation of section [8(e)] gives rise to an antitrust suit.").

970. 421 U.S. at 623.
971. Id. at 624.
972. Id. at 625.
973. Id. at 624.
974. See Imperial Constr. Mgmt. Corp. v. Laborers' Int'l Local 96, 818 F. Supp. 1179 (N.D. Ill. 1993).
975. 421 U.S. at 626.
976. See, e.g., Local Union 257 v. Sebastian Elec., 121 F.3d 1890 (8th Cir. 1999) (union "target fund" providing partial reimbursement to employers for wages paid to local union members protected by nonstatutory exemption); Sheet Metal Workers Local Union No. 54 v. E.F. Etie Sheet Metal Co., 1 F.3d 1464 (5th Cir. 1993) (negotiation of arbitration clause by local union and chapter of multiemployer bargaining unit), cert. denied, 510 U.S. 1117 (1994); Continental Maritime of San Francisco, Inc. v. Pacific Coast Metal Trades Dist. Council, 817 F.2d 1391 (9th Cir. 1987) (summary judgment for union defendants upheld on Sherman Act charge of conspiracy to make wage concessions for defendant shipyards); Cannon v. Teamsters & Chauffeurs Union, Local 627, 657 F.2d 173 (7th Cir. 1981) (agreement between union and beer and liquor distributors to restrict hours of delivery of beer and liquor to certain liquor retailers); Amalgamated Meat Cutters, Local 576 v. Wetterau Foods, Inc., 597 F.2d 133 (8th Cir. 1979) (applying the exemption to joint employer activity opposing striking employees of one employer); Detroit Newspaper Publishers Ass'n v. Detroit Typographical Union No. 18, 471 F.2d 872 (6th Cir. 1972), cert. denied, 411 U.S. 967 (1973); Phoenix Elec. Co. v. National Elec. Contractors Ass'n, 861 F. Supp. 1498 (D. Or. 1994) (agreement between electrical contractors' trade association and local union representing electrical workers whereby union workers would contribute percentage of their wages to fund that would then be used to reduce amount that union contractors would pay union workers on specific projects); Petrochem Insulation, Inc. v. Northern Cal. and N. Nev. Pipe Trades Council, 1992-1

activity addressed to collective bargaining issues, even after expiration of the collective bargaining agreement. The scope of this protection was addressed repeatedly in the context of disputes between owners and players in professional sports leagues,[977] and was finally resolved by the Supreme Court in *Brown v. Pro Football, Inc.*[978] In *Brown*, the Court held that the nonstatutory labor exemption protects agreements among members of a multiemployer bargaining association that directly relate to, and arise out of, lawful multiemployer collective bargaining. In *Brown*, the National Football League (NFL) owners adopted a rule, proposed by the owners in negotiations but never agreed to by the NFL players union, that every "developmental squad player" would be paid $1,000 per week.[979] The Supreme Court affirmed the D.C. Circuit's reversal of a $30 million judgment in favor of the players and held that the owners could implement this rule without risk of antitrust liability. The Court's decision broadly exempted multiemployer conduct engaged in pursuant and limited to a lawful, voluntary multiemployer collective bargaining process:

> [W]e hold that the implicit ("nonstatutory") antitrust exemption applies to the employer conduct at issue here. That conduct took place during and immediately after a collective-bargaining negotiation. It grew out of, and was directly related to, the lawful operation of the bargaining process. It involved a matter that the parties were required to negotiate collectively. And it concerned only the parties to the collective-bargaining relationship.[980]

In so holding, the Court found that the nonstatutory labor exemption "reflects both history and logic," and, in particular, rests upon the national labor policy favoring free and private collective bargaining.[981]

The Court emphasized that multiemployer bargaining, including the joint imposition of proposed terms after impasse, is a "well-established, pervasive method of collective bargaining" and that subjecting joint employer conduct during

---

  Trade Cas. (CCH) ¶ 69,814 (N.D. Cal. 1992) (complaint alleging antitrust violation based on agreement between a union and a developer to exclude nonunion subcontractors from certain projects dismissed for failure to plead a sufficient injury to competition to avoid nonstatutory exemption), *aff'd sub nom.* Petrochem Insulation, Inc. v. United Ass'n of Journeymen & Apprentices Local No. 38, 8 F.3d 29 (9th Cir. 1993), *cert. denied*, 510 U.S. 1191 (1994); Home Box Office, Inc. v. Directors Guild of Am., Inc., 531 F. Supp. 578 (S.D.N.Y. 1982) (notice and bargaining provisions in standard television directors' union agreements with pay television production companies held exempt because effect on product market "minimal and probably avoidable where necessary"), *aff'd per curiam*, 708 F.2d 95 (2d Cir. 1983).

977. *See, e.g.*, NBA v. Williams, 45 F.3d 684 (2d Cir. 1995), *cert. denied*, 518 U.S. 1016 (1996); Caldwell v. American Basketball Ass'n, Inc., 66 F.3d 523 (2d Cir. 1995), *cert. denied*, 518 U.S. 1033 (1996); Powell v. NFL, 930 F.2d 1293 (8th Cir. 1989), *cert. denied*, 498 U.S. 1040 (1991); Independent Entm't Group Inc. v. NBA, 853 F. Supp. 333, 335-36 (C.D. Cal. 1994); White v. NFL, 822 F. Supp. 1389 (D. Minn. 1993), *aff'd*, 41 F.3d 402 (8th Cir. 1994), *cert. denied sub nom.* Jones v. NFL, 515 U.S. 1137 (1995); McNeil v. NFL, 790 F. Supp. 871 (D. Minn. 1992); NHL v. National Hockey League Players Ass'n, 789 F. Supp. 288 (D. Minn. 1992); *see also* McCourt v. California Sports, Inc., 600 F.2d 1193 (6th Cir. 1979); Mackey v. NFL, 543 F.2d 606, 614 (8th Cir. 1976), *cert. dismissed*, 434 U.S. 801 (1977); Powell v. NFL, 678 F. Supp. 777 (D. Minn. 1988); Wood v. NBA, 809 F.2d 954 (2d Cir. 1987); Bridgeman v. NBA, 675 F. Supp. 960 (D.N.J. 1987); Zimmerman v. NFL, 632 F. Supp. 398 (D.D.C. 1986).

978. 518 U.S. 231 (1996).

979. *Id.* at 234.

980. *Id.* at 250.

981. *Id.* at 235-36.

bargaining to scrutiny by "antitrust courts" would improperly inhibit the bargaining process.[982] The Court therefore rejected the various boundary lines proposed on behalf of the players and essentially exempted the entire bargaining process. The Court did, however, indicate that there may be an outer limit to the exemption:

> Our holding is not intended to insulate from antitrust review every joint imposition of terms by employers, for an agreement among employers could be sufficiently distant in time and in circumstances from the collective-bargaining process that a rule permitting antitrust intervention would not significantly interfere with that process. We need not decide in this case whether, or where, within these extreme outer boundaries to draw that line. Nor would it be appropriate for us to do so without the detailed views of the [National Labor Relations] Board, to whose "specialized judgement" Congress "intended to leave" many of the "inevitable questions concerning multiemployer bargaining bound to arise in the future."[983]

I. Sports

The business of sports is subject to little regulation, and the sports industry is generally subject to the antitrust principles that govern other industries. The fact that competitive sports cannot exist without some degree of cooperation between competing teams, however, has influenced the development of general antitrust principles.[984] Moreover, the sports industry is subject to two narrow antitrust exemptions discussed below: (1) a statutory exemption relating to sports broadcasting, and (2) a nonstatutory baseball exemption, which recently was modified by statute.

1. Sports Broadcasting Act

The Sports Broadcasting Act (SBA)[985] essentially consists of two separate provisions, the first enacted in 1961 and the second in 1966. The first provision, which exempts certain agreements among professional football, baseball, basketball, or hockey teams to pool their sponsored television broadcast rights for sale as a package, was passed in response to a judicial decision involving the NFL.[986] The second provision was passed to permit the merger of the American Football League (AFL) and the NFL into a single league, which operates under the latter name.

---

982. *Id.* at 240-42.
983. *Id.* at 250 (citations omitted). In *Sage Realty Corp. v. ISS Cleaning Servs. Group, Inc.*, 936 F. Supp. 130 (S.D.N.Y. 1996), citing *Brown*, the court held that the nonstatutory exemption protected an alleged agreement between a multiemployer bargaining association and certain cleaning contractors in a separate bargaining association to not enter into "you too" agreements with a union negotiating with each employer association.
984. Many cases involving standard setting and refusals to deal have focused on the unique characteristics of the sports industry, *see* part C.3.b of Chapter I, as have cases dealing with the question of whether a sports league should be viewed as a single entity or a multiplicity of teams capable of conspiring, *see* part B.1.b of Chapter I.
985. 15 U.S.C. §§ 1291-1295 (2000).
986. *See generally* S. REP. NO. 87-1087 (1961), *reprinted in* 1961 U.S.C.C.A.N. 3042-44; *see also* WTWV, Inc. v. NFL, 678 F.2d 142, 144-45 (11th Cir. 1982) (discussing background and history of the legislation).

a. EXEMPTION FOR POOLING OF TELEVISION BROADCAST RIGHTS

In 1951, the Department of Justice filed a civil antitrust action against the NFL and its member clubs, challenging NFL bylaws that restricted television and radio broadcasting of NFL games. After trial, the district court held that certain of the restrictions were lawful and others violated the Sherman Act,[987] and entered a judgment containing permanent injunctive provisions.[988] The NFL and its member clubs later filed a petition seeking a declaration that an exclusive contract between the NFL and a television network did not violate the previous judgment.[989] The district court held that this "pooling" of broadcast rights by the member clubs eliminated competition between and among those clubs, and thereby violated the prior judgment.[990] At the request of the NFL, Congress responded in 1961 by passing the SBA in order to "overrule the effect of" the court's decision.[991]

The SBA exempts from the antitrust laws agreements by the members of professional baseball, basketball, football, or hockey leagues to pool their sponsored television broadcast rights for sale in a package to purchasers, such as television networks, for broadcast as sponsored television.[992] The exemption comes with several specific limitations. First, the exemption does not apply to agreements with territorial limits on the purchaser's broadcast area, except restrictions that protect a home team from competing games broadcast into its home territory on a day when it is playing a game at home.[993] Second, the exemption does not apply to a pooled agreement that permits telecasting of football games in the vicinity of and on days and at times when college and high school football teams traditionally play their games.[994] Third, the exemption is limited to its express terms and is specifically not intended "to change, determine, or otherwise affect the applicability or nonapplicability of the antitrust laws" to any other aspect of the professional sports identified in the statute.[995]

987. United States v. NFL, 116 F. Supp. 319 (E.D. Pa. 1953).
988. Id. at 330.
989. United States v. NFL, 196 F. Supp. 445 (E.D. Pa. 1961).
990. Id. at 447.
991. Pub. L. No. 87-331, 75 Stat. 732 (1961). See S. REP. NO. 87-1087 (1961), reprinted in 1961 U.S.C.C.A.N. 3042. At that time, teams in the AFL and teams in other professional sport leagues, including the National Basketball Association and the National Hockey League, had been pooling their broadcast rights for sale to television networks, and this created the perception of unequal treatment. Id. at 3042-43. See also NCAA v. Board of Regents, 468 U.S. 85, 104-05 n.28 (1984).
992. 15 U.S.C. § 1291 (2000).
993. Id. § 1292 (2000). Restrictions that protect a home team from competing games in its home territory on days when it plays at home and that allow the home team to "bar" television coverage of nonselling games in its home market are known as "blackout rules." The courts that have heard challenges to the NFL's blackout rules have held that the SBA shields them from antitrust scrutiny. See WTWV, Inc. v. NFL, 678 F.2d 142, 145-46 (11th Cir. 1982); Blaich v. NFL, 212 F. Supp. 319, 321-22 (S.D.N.Y. 1962).
994. 15 U.S.C. § 1293 (2000); see Association of Indep. Television Stations v. College Football Ass'n, 637 F. Supp. 1289, 1300 n.11 (W.D. Okla. 1986). This provision was "designed to provide greater protection for in person attendance at college football contests and carrie[d] out the recommendations of the NCAA." S. REP. NO. 87-1087 (1961), reprinted in 1961 U.S.C.C.A.N. 3042, 3043-44. The 1966 SBA changes extended the prohibition from college games to both high school and college games. See CONF. REP. NO. 89-2308 (1966), reprinted in 1966 U.S.C.C.A.N. 4378.
995. 15 U.S.C. § 1294 (2000).

The scope of the antitrust exemption created by the SBA has been explored in court challenges. Litigated issues include whether the exemption is limited to a single contract with one network,[996] whether the statute should be construed narrowly or broadly,[997] and whether the act exempts league efforts to force an unwilling member club to pool its broadcast rights or whether the act exempts agreements forbidding certain sales of broadcast rights.[998] Another issue involves the scope of the exemption's specification of "sponsored telecasting" and whether it encompasses closed circuit, cable, subscription, or pay-per-view television.[999]

b.   EXEMPTION FOR FOOTBALL LEAGUE MERGERS

The second provision of the SBA was passed in 1966 and is more narrow in scope. It was passed to allow the NFL and AFL to merge without fear of antitrust challenge. The exemption is limited to professional football and exempts agreements by "the member clubs of two or more professional football leagues . . . [to] combine their operations in [an] expanded single league . . . if such agreement increases rather than decreases the number of professional football clubs so operating."[1000] This second provision of the SBA was an amendment to a bill to amend the tax laws and specifies that the antitrust exemption applies to football leagues that are exempt from federal income tax as Section 501(c)(6) not-for-profit organizations.[1001] The legislative history of the provision made it clear that its "sole effect . . . is to permit the combination of the two leagues to go forward without fear of antitrust challenge based upon joint agreement . . . to combine in a single league and conduct their affairs as members of a single league."[1002]

---

996. *See, e.g.*, United States Football League v. NFL, 842 F.2d 1335, 1353-55, 1358-61 (2d Cir. 1988) (exemption not limited to contract with a single network, but if intent and effect of agreements are to exclude a competing league or its members from selling their television rights, they may be unlawful).

997. *Compare id.* at 1354 ("the legislation does contain express limitations on the exemption designed to protect college football from televised competition with the NFL, which suggests by implication that no other limitations exist"), *with* Chicago Professional Sports Ltd. P'ship v. NBA, 95 F.3d 593, 595 (7th Cir. 1996) ("[t]he Sports Broadcasting Act, as a special-interest exception to the antitrust laws, receives a beady-eyed reading. A league has to jump through every hoop; partial compliance doesn't do the trick . . . ."), *and* Chicago Professional Sports Ltd. P'ship v. NBA, 961 F.2d 667, 671-72 (7th Cir.), *cert. denied*, 506 U.S. 954 (1992), *and WTWV, Inc.*, 678 F.2d at 144-45 (exemption should be narrowly construed).

998. *See, e.g., Chicago Professional Sports*, 961 F.2d at 670-74.

999. *See* 15 U.S.C. § 1291 (2000). In *Shaw v. Dallas Cowboys Football Club*, 172 F.3d 299 (3d Cir. 1999), the Third Circuit held that the exemption applies only to "broadcasts which are financed by business enterprises (the 'sponsors') in return for advertising time and are therefore provided free to the general public," and not to satellite rebroadcasts. *See also Chicago Professional Sports*, 808 F. Supp. at 649-50, *and* 874 F. Supp. 856 & n.12 (N.D. Ill. 1995), *vacated and remanded*, 95 F.3d 593 (7th Cir. 1996).

1000. 15 U.S.C. § 1291.

1001. *Id.; see also* 26 U.S.C. § 501(c)(6) (1994). The same 1966 bill also amended the tax laws to specify that "professional football leagues (whether or not administering a pension fund for football players)" are exempt from federal income tax if they are "not organized for profit and no part of the net earnings of which inures to the benefit of any private shareholder or individual." *See* Pub. L. No. 89-800, 80 Stat. 1508; CONF. REP. NO. 89-2308 (1966), *reprinted in* 1966 U.S.C.C.A.N. 4327, 4372, 4377-78. The concern had been that a sports league administering a pension fund for players might not be "not for profit" because the fund's earnings inure to the benefit of football players.

1002. CONF. REP. NO. 89-2308 (1966), *reprinted in* 1966 U.S.C.C.A.N. 4327, 4378.

When the second provision was passed in 1966, Congress also extended the provision of the 1961 act that protected college football from telecasts of professional football games, to make that protection also apply to high school football.[1003]

Plaintiffs suing the NFL under Section 2 of the Sherman Act have sought at various times to introduce evidence concerning the 1966 provision permitting the AFL-NFL merger to support allegations of monopolistic intent or acquisition of monopoly power by unlawful means.[1004] While courts have permitted plaintiffs to offer evidence about the legislation, and have expressly held that abuse of monopoly power acquired as a result of the legislation is not exempt, they generally have held that evidence about the reasons or motives that led the NFL to seek the legislation is not admissible, and the NFL's lobbying efforts related to the passage of that legislation are immune from antitrust challenge under the *Noerr* doctrine.[1005]

As this provision of the SBA is limited to professional football leagues, it did not protect the National Basketball Association and the American Basketball Association from antitrust challenge when they discussed a possible merger.[1006]

2. *The Baseball Exemption*

The Supreme Court has considered the application of the antitrust laws to baseball in a series of cases. In *Federal Baseball Club v. National League of Professional Baseball Clubs*,[1007] the Supreme Court held that the "business [of] giving exhibitions of base ball" did not constitute interstate commerce, even though the competitions were "arranged between clubs from different cities and States" and the league had to induce and pay for players and other personnel to cross state lines.[1008] Accordingly, the Court did not reach the merits, but affirmed the lower court's dismissal of the case.[1009] The Court expressed the view that "personal effort, not related to production, is not a subject of commerce," and that the exhibitions were not interstate, so that neither commerce generally nor interstate commerce in particular was at issue.[1010]

1003. *See* 15 U.S.C. § 1293 (2000) ("interscholastic football contests . . . between secondary schools . . . which . . . offer courses continuing through the twelfth grade"); Conf. Rep. No. 89-2308 (1966), *reprinted in* 1966 U.S.C.C.A.N. 4327, 4378.

1004. *See, e.g.*, United States Football League v. NFL, 842 F.2d 1335, 1358-59 (2d Cir. 1988); Mid-South Grizzlies v. NFL, 720 F.2d 772, 784 (3d Cir. 1983), *cert. denied*, 467 U.S. 1215 (1984).

1005. *See, e.g.*, United States Football League v. NFL, 634 F. Supp. 1155, 1170-71 (S.D.N.Y. 1986); *Mid-South Grizzlies*, 720 F.2d at 784-85 & n.7. The *Noerr* doctrine is discussed in part C of Chapter XIII.

1006. *See* Robertson v. NBA, 1970 Trade Cas. (CCH) ¶ 73,282 (S.N.D.Y. 1970); *see also A Bill to Allow the Merger of Two or More Professional Basketball Leagues: Hearings on S. 2373 Before the Subcommittee on Antitrust and Monopoly of the Senate Committee on the Judiciary*, 92nd Cong., 1st Sess. (1971).

1007. 259 U.S. 200 (1922).

1008. *Id.* at 208-09.

1009. The plaintiff, the only remaining team in baseball's Federal League, had secured a $240,000 verdict after trebling against the National and American Leagues for buying up Federal League teams and inducing teams to leave the Federal League in other ways. On appeal, the D.C. Circuit held the antitrust laws inapplicable and entered judgment for the defendants. National League of Professional Baseball Clubs v. Federal Baseball Club, 269 F. 681, 688 (D.C. Cir. 1920), *aff'd*, 259 U.S. 200 (1922).

1010. 259 U.S. at 208-09.

The Supreme Court next considered the application of the antitrust laws to baseball in *Toolson v. New York Yankees, Inc.*[1011] There the Court dismissed several challenges by players against baseball's reserve system, holding that "Congress had no intention of including the business of baseball within the scope of the Federal antitrust laws."[1012] The *Toolson* majority stated that (1) Congress had been aware that the *Federal Baseball* decision had left professional baseball to develop "on the understanding that it was not subject to existing antitrust legislation," (2) Congress had considered possible responses to that decision, and (3) as a result, "if there are evils in this field which now warrant application to it of the antitrust laws it should be by legislation."[1013]

After *Toolson*, the Supreme Court issued a series of rulings that the antitrust laws apply to the production of theatrical attractions,[1014] championship boxing exhibitions,[1015] professional football,[1016] and professional basketball.[1017] The lower federal courts also have held that other professional sports are not exempt.[1018] Questions were raised about the continued validity of baseball's exemption and the *Federal Baseball* and *Toolson* decisions in light of decisions consistently holding that other sports and exhibition businesses were not exempt from antitrust scrutiny.[1019]

However, when the Supreme Court considered the baseball exemption for the third time in *Flood v. Kuhn*,[1020] the Court again held that the baseball exemption precluded judicial application of the antitrust laws, both state and federal, to another challenge to baseball's reserve system. The *Flood* decision recognized that "[p]rofessional baseball is a business and it is engaged in interstate commerce," and further acknowledged that the affording of an antitrust exemption only to baseball and not to other professional sports is "an anomaly."[1021] Nevertheless, the Court held that the exemption remains and is confined to baseball.[1022]

The *Flood* majority held that even though baseball's exemption from the antitrust laws might be regarded by some as an aberration, "it is an aberration that has been with us now for half a century, one heretofore deemed fully entitled to the benefit of *stare decisis*, and one that has survived the Court's expanding concept of interstate

---

1011. 346 U.S. 356 (1953) (per curiam).
1012. *Id.* at 357.
1013. *Id.*
1014. United States v. Shubert, 348 U.S. 222 (1955).
1015. United States v. International Boxing Club, 348 U.S. 236 (1955).
1016. Radovich v. NFL, 352 U.S. 445 (1957).
1017. Haywood v. NBA, 401 U.S. 1204 (1971).
1018. *See, e.g.*, Deesen v. Professional Golfers' Ass'n, 358 F.2d 165 (9th Cir.), *cert. denied*, 385 U.S. 846 (1966); Petro v. Madison Square Garden Corp., 1958 Trade Cas. (CCH) ¶ 69,106 (S.D.N.Y. 1958) (hockey).
1019. *See, e.g.*, Salerno v. American League of Prof'l Baseball Clubs, 429 F.2d 1003, 1005 (2d Cir. 1970), *cert. denied*, 400 U.S. (1971):
    We freely acknowledge our belief that *Federal Baseball* was not one of Justice Holmes' happiest days, that the rationale of *Toolson* is extremely dubious and that, to use the Supreme Court's own adjectives, the distinction between baseball and other professional sports is "unrealistic," "inconsistent" and "illogical." . . . While we should not fall out of our chairs with surprise at the news that *Federal Baseball* and *Toolson* had been overruled, we are not at all certain the Court is ready to give them a happy d[i]spatch.
1020. 407 U.S. 258 (1972).
1021. *Id.* at 282.
1022. *Id.*

commerce. It rests on a recognition and an acceptance of baseball's unique characteristics and needs."[1023]

The Court held that the baseball exemption remains viable for several reasons. First, for fifty years Congress had allowed professional baseball to develop and expand, and although "[r]emedial legislation has been introduced repeatedly in Congress, . . . none has ever been enacted," thereby evidencing, by "positive inaction," a congressional intent that the exemption should continue.[1024] Second, the majority expressed concern that a "judicial overturning of *Federal Baseball*" could cause confusion and retroactivity problems.[1025] The Court stated that if the exemption is to be changed, it should be by legislative action that "by its nature, is only prospective in operation."[1026]

Since *Flood*, the reported decisions focusing on the baseball exemption have focused on defining its scope. In *Charles O. Finley & Co. v. Kuhn*, the court interpreted the Supreme Court trilogy (*Federal Baseball*, *Toolson*, and *Flood*) as holding "that 'the business of baseball' is exempt from federal antitrust laws."[1027] The dispute at issue in that case concerned the baseball commissioner's disapproval of the assignment of three player contracts, and the *Finley* court held that this conduct was part of the business of baseball and thus exempt from antitrust challenge.[1028] Other courts similarly have held that the scope of the exemption was "the business of baseball"[1029] or have applied a similarly broad formulation in dismissing antitrust challenges.[1030]

Some lower courts have nonetheless found that the scope of the exemption is not without limits. In *Henderson Broadcasting Corp. v. Houston Sports Ass'n*,[1031] the court stated that the baseball exemption has a "narrow scope," does not apply to radio broadcasting of baseball, and does not apply to agreements between baseball teams and nonbaseball business enterprises. It explained that the exemption is limited to conduct or agreements that are "central enough to the 'unique

1023. *Id.*
1024. *Id.* at 283. The Court distinguished its decision issued one year earlier in *Boys Markets, Inc. v. Retail Clerks Union*, 398 U.S. 235, 241-42 (1970), which held that when Congress was urged to modify a Supreme Court decision and responded with congressional silence and inactivity, that was an insufficient reason for the Supreme Court to refuse subsequently to reconsider the decision.
1025. 407 U.S. at 283.
1026. *Id.* at 284 ("If there is any inconsistency or illogic in all this, it is an inconsistency and illogic of long standing that is to be remedied by the Congress and not by this Court.").
1027. 569 F.2d 527, 541 (7th Cir.), *cert. denied*, 439 U.S. 876 (1978).
1028. The court in *Finley* cautioned, however, that the "exemption does not apply wholesale to all cases which may have some attenuated relation to the business of baseball." *Id.* at 541 & n.51.
1029. *See, e.g.*, Professional Baseball Sch. & Clubs v. Kuhn, 693 F.2d 1085, 1086 (11th Cir. 1982) (per curiam) (rejecting an antitrust challenge to the minor league player assignment and franchise location systems and other minor league rules); Salerno v. American League of Prof'l Baseball Clubs, 429 F.2d 1003, 1005 (2d Cir. 1970) (affirming the dismissal of antitrust claims filed by two discharged major league umpires), *cert. denied*, 400 U.S. 1001 (1971).
1030. *See, e.g.*, Portland Baseball Club v. Kuhn, 368 F. Supp. 1004, 1007 (D. Or. 1971), *aff'd per curiam*, 491 F.2d 1101, 1103 (9th Cir. 1974) (major league baseball's agreement with the minor leagues and the rules about territorial allocation and compensation for territorial infringement are protected from federal antitrust challenge). *See also* Minnesota Twins P'ship v. State *ex rel.* Hatch, 592 N.W.2d 847 (Minn.), *cert. denied*, 528 U.S. 1013 (1999) (Minnesota Attorney General lacked authority to investigate possible violations of state antitrust laws in baseball transactions).
1031. 541 F. Supp. 263, 265-72 (S.D. Tex. 1982).

characteristics and needs' of baseball," or are a "part of the sport in the way in which players, umpires, the league structure and the reserve system are."[1032]

The scope of the exemption also was at issue in *Postema v. National League of Professional Baseball Clubs*,[1033] in which the court held that the baseball exemption did not apply to antitrust claims about baseball's employment relations with its umpires. The court followed the *Henderson* court's analysis, seeking to assess whether the challenged conduct was "central enough to baseball to be encompassed in the baseball exemption."[1034] The *Postema* opinion treated *Flood* as an opinion limiting the scope of the exemption to baseball's "unique characteristics and needs" and applied that narrow scope to Postema's claims.

> Unlike the league structure or the reserve system, baseball's relations with non-players are not a unique characteristic or need of the game. Anti-competitive conduct toward umpires is not an essential part of baseball and in no way enhances its vitality or viability.[1035]

More recently, the baseball exemption battleground has concerned whether the scope of the exemption is limited to antitrust claims concerning baseball's reserve clause and other issues concerning players' compensation and freedom to negotiate with a number of professional baseball teams. In *Piazza v. Major League Baseball*,[1036] the court concluded that the Supreme Court's opinion in *Flood* stripped all prior cases of any precedential value except with respect to the reserve clause—the conduct at issue in *Flood*.[1037] The court nevertheless also assessed the scope of the exemption, assuming that the exemption was not limited to the reserve clause. The court concluded that determining which aspects of league structure are "central . . . to the unique characteristics of baseball exhibitions" or which types of league and team decisions or agreements are part of baseball's league structure are factual questions that could be decided only on the basis of a factual record.[1038]

These issues were addressed in the Curt Flood Act of 1998,[1039] which by adding a new provision to the Clayton Act, revoked baseball's antitrust exemption insofar as it relates to the employment of major league players. The statute leaves unchanged the application of the antitrust laws to the minor leagues (including the amateur draft) and to matters not involving player-management relations. Questions regarding the application of the antitrust laws to issues such as franchise relocation, for example, are unaffected by the new legislation.

1032. *Id.* at 268-69.

1033. 799 F. Supp. 1475, 1489 (S.D.N.Y. 1992), *vacated on other grounds*, 998 F.2d 60 (2d Cir. 1993).

1034. *Id.* (quoting *Henderson*, 541 F. Supp. at 265).

1035. *Id.*; *see also* Amateur Softball Ass'n of Am. v. United States, 467 F.2d 312, 314 (10th Cir. 1972) ("amateur softball is not presently entitled to rely on the same unique exemption that organized professional baseball has claimed and achieved for so many years").

1036. 831 F. Supp. 420 (E.D. Pa. 1993).

1037. *Id.* at 435-36.

1038. *Id.* at 441. *But see* McCoy v. Major League Baseball, 911 F. Supp. 454, 456-57 (W.D. Wash. 1995) ("This Court rejects the reasoning and results of *Piazza*."); New Orleans Pelicans Baseball, Inc. v. National Ass'n of Baseball Leagues, Civ. No. 93-253, 1994 U.S. Dist. LEXIS 21468 (E.D. La. Mar. 1, 1994) (expressly rejecting the "cramped view" of *Piazza*).

1039. Pub. L. No. 105-297, 112 Stat. 2824 (1998) (codified at 15 U.S.C. § 27a (2000)).

J.   Transportation

1.   Motor Transportation

Little remains of the once pervasive economic regulation of the motor carrier industry[1040] by the federal and state governments.[1041] Federal licensing of interstate motor carriers is now virtually automatic, with most applicants required to show only that they meet minimum safety and financial responsibility standards.[1042] Household goods carriers must make additional, traditional entry showings.[1043]

Rate regulation also is largely a thing of the past. Generally, the rates, rules, and classifications of a motor carrier, whether set independently or collectively, need not be filed with the government, although they must be made available to a shipper in writing or electronically on request.[1044] Still required to be "reasonable" are rates, classifications, rules, or practices related to movements of household goods; rates by or with a water carrier in noncontiguous domestic trade (i.e., originating in or destined for Alaska, Hawaii, or a U.S. territory); and rates, rules, and classifications

---

1040. The motor carrier industry consists of private and for-hire carriers. Private carriers, companies that carry their own goods, have never been subject to economic regulation, except to the extent they engage in for-hire transportation—for example, on back hauls after delivering the companies' own goods. 49 U.S.C. § 13505 (Supp. 1999). Also exempt from economic regulation is for-hire motor carrier transportation of agricultural products and certain other commodities, or of any commodities when entirely within terminal areas, commercial zones in and around municipalities, or the state of Hawaii. *Id.* §§ 13502, 13503, 13506 (Supp. 1999).

1041. The dismantling of the Motor Carrier Act of 1935's all-encompassing system of federal rate-and-entry regulation began with a series of deregulatory decisions by the Interstate Commerce Commission (ICC) in the late 1970s. *See, e.g.*, Liberty Trucking Co., Ext.-Gen'l Commodities, 131 M.C.C. 573 (1979) (citing May Trucking Co. v. United States, 593 F.2d 1349 (D.C. Cir. 1979)). The Motor Carrier Act of 1980, Pub. L. No. 96-296, 94 Stat. 793, liberalized the formal entry requirements for motor carriers and provided a framework for further ICC deregulation of rates and entry over the next 14 years. In 1994, Congress eliminated many of the ICC's remaining functions applicable to motor carriers. Trucking Industry Regulatory Reform Act of 1994, Pub. L. No. 103-311, § 201, 108 Stat. 1683. A year later, Congress enacted the Interstate Commerce Commission Termination Act of 1995 (ICCTA), Pub. L. No. 104-88, 109 Stat. 803 (codified at 49 U.S.C. § 13101 *et seq.* (Supp. 1999)), abolishing the ICC and dividing all remaining regulatory functions between a new Surface Transportation Board (STB) and the U.S. Department of Transportation (DOT). Most DOT functions are performed by the Federal Motor Carrier Safety Administration.

1042. 49 U.S.C. § 13902(a) (Supp. 1999); 49 C.F.R. § 365.107 (2000). Freight carriers controlled by Mexican citizens are barred altogether from grants of new U.S. domestic operating authority. Section 6(g) of the Bus Regulatory Reform Act of 1982 imposed a moratorium, extended since by successive presidents, on issuance of authority to operate a motor carrier transporting domestic cargo between points within the United States to any carrier "domiciled in . . . or owned or controlled by persons of" Mexico. Pub. L. No. 97-261, 96 Stat. 1102, 1107-08 (codified at 49 U.S.C. § 13902(c) (Supp. 1999)). *Cf.* President's Memorandum of June 5, 2001—Determination Under the ICCTA, 66 Fed. Reg. 30,799 (June 5, 2001) (lifting moratorium to the extent of allowing hauling of international cargo between points in the United States).

1043. Household goods carriers must make additional showings of "public purpose, responsive to a public demand or need" (common carriers) or "public interest" (contract carriers). 49 C.F.R. § 365.107(d), (e) (2000). A general freight carrier that merely hauls a customer packed and loaded shipment of household goods does not constitute a "household goods carrier" subject to rate-and-entry regulation. Letter from Acting Deputy Administrator Julie Anna Cirillo, Federal Motor Carrier Safety Admin., to American Moving & Storage Ass'n, denying petition for declaratory order (June 13, 2001), cited in Household Goods Carriers' Bureau Comm.—Petition for Declaratory Order, STB Dkt. No. 42055, 2001 STB LEXIS 615, at *2-3 (served July 13, 2001).

1044. 49 U.S.C. § 13710(a)(1) (Supp. 1999).

made collectively under agreements approved by the Surface Transportation Board.[1045] Also subject to continuing federal regulation are motor carrier extensions of credit, billing practices, leasing and owner-operator arrangements, loading and unloading practices, financial reporting, security interests in certain motor vehicles, and cargo loss and damage claims.[1046]

Antitrust immunity continues for Surface Transportation Board-approved agreements among motor carriers for collective action on commodity classifications (including uniform bills of lading and packaging rules),[1047] mileage guides, through routes and joint rates, general rate adjustments, rates for the transportation of household goods, and rules and divisions.[1048] The Surface Transportation Board is required to review previously approved agreements every five years.[1049] Congress has forbidden the agency to take any action permitting the establishment of nationwide collective ratemaking.[1050]

Mergers and acquisitions of most motor carriers no longer require prior government approval.[1051] Instead, they are subject to the same H-S-R Act[1052] and other antitrust requirements as similar transactions in other industries, with one possible exception: in the case of motor carriers, the Federal Trade Commission, state attorneys general, and private parties may lack their usual authority to bring suit to enjoin actual and threatened antitrust violations.[1053] The Department of Justice,

---

1045. *Id.* § 13701(a). Only rates applicable to noncontiguous domestic trade must be filed with the STB. *Id.* § 13702 (Supp. 1999). Rates and rules applicable to the movement of household goods must be maintained by carriers in tariffs that are available for inspection by the STB and individual shippers, but need not be filed with the STB. *Id.* Routes, rates, classifications, mileage guides, and rules established collectively through STB-approved agreements must be "published and made available for public inspection upon request." *Id.* § 13703(g)(1)(A) (Supp. 1999).

1046. *Id.* §§ 13706, 13707, 13708, 13710(a)(3), 14102, 14103, 14123, 14701, 14706 (Supp. 1999). In addition, a carrier is permitted to retain possession of property transported until payment for the transportation has been made, and a shipper is barred from contesting billed charges if it does not do so within 180 days of receiving the carrier's freight bill. *Id.* §§ 13707, 13710(a)(3)(B).

1047. *See* Jays Foods, Inc. v. National Classification Comm., 646 F. Supp. 604 (E.D. Va. 1985), *aff'd without op.*, 801 F.2d 394 (4th Cir. 1986) (the mere publication by a motor carrier group of a freight classification for an unregulated commodity, without referring to rates, not a per se violation of § 1 of the Sherman Act).

1048. 49 U.S.C. §§ 13703(a) (Supp. 1999). Any carrier whose "routes, rates, classifications, mileage guides, rules, or packaging are determined or governed by publications established under agreements" approved by the STB must participate in the governing publication for such provisions to apply. *Id.* § 13703(g) (Supp. 1999).

1049. *Id.* § 13703(c) (Supp. 1999). The statute provides that "[a]ny such agreement shall be continued unless the Board determines otherwise." *Id.*

1050. *Id.* § 13703(d) (Supp. 1999).

1051. The ICCTA requires mergers and acquisitions of motor carriers of passengers, but not motor carriers of property, to be submitted to the STB for advance approval and accompanying antitrust immunity. *Id.* § 14303 (Supp. 1999); 49 C.F.R. § 1182 (2000).

1052. 15 U.S.C. § 18a (2000).

1053. Motor "common carriers" are exempt from FTC jurisdiction under both the FTC Act, 15 U.S.C. §§ 45(a)(2), 46(a), (b) (2000), and the Clayton Act, with the latter vesting enforcement power in the STB, 15 U.S.C § 21(a) (2000). These carriers also are exempt from Clayton Act suits for injunctive relief brought by persons other than the United States. 15 U.S.C. § 26 (2000). Although common carriers historically have constituted only one of two categories of regulated motor carriers (the other being "contract carriers"), the ICCTA mandated the eventual elimination of the distinction, 49 U.S.C. §§ 13902(d), 13710(b) (Supp. 1999), and, in the meantime, imposed common carrier-like obligations on all motor carriers, *id.* §14101(a). Thus, although not yet determined by any court, Congress's intent appears to have been to make these enforcement exemptions for common carriers available to all regulated motor carriers.

however, clearly retains such authority.[1054]   Certain motor carrier joint ventures known as pooling agreements must be submitted to the Surface Transportation Board in advance for review.[1055]   If a pooling agreement is approved, any participating carrier is "exempt from the antitrust laws and from all other law, including State and municipal law, as necessary to let that person carry out the arrangement."[1056]

Most state and local economic regulation of motor carriage (except of household goods and all motor carriage in Hawaii) is preempted under a federal statute that became effective on January 1, 1995. The statute reaches any "law, regulation, or other provision having the force or effect of law related to a price, route, or service of any motor carrier, . . . broker, or freight forwarder."[1057]   In enacting this statute, Congress indicated its preference for a broad interpretation of preemption.[1058]   The challenged law must be shown to "frustrate the purpose of deregulation by *acutely* interfering with the forces of competition."[1059]   Exempted from preemption is state and local regulation of nonconsensual towing rates.[1060]   The law also authorizes states to continue regulating the safety of commercial vehicles, routes used for the transportation of hazardous materials or based on the size and weight of a vehicle,

---

1054. 15 U.S.C. §§ 4, 25 (2000). The DOJ also is empowered to participate in STB merger review proceedings. *Id.* § 21(b) (2000).
1055. 49 U.S.C. § 14302 (Supp. 1999); 49 C.F.R. § 1184 (2000).
1056. 49 U.S.C. § 14302(f). In *Rothery Storage & Van Co. v. Atlas Van Lines*, 792 F.2d 210 (D.C. Cir. 1986), *cert. denied*, 479 U.S. 1033 (1987), the D.C. Circuit held that a van line carrier's agreement with its agents did not violate § 1 of the Sherman Act in barring them from using the van line's name, facilities, equipment, and services to haul freight under their own ICC operating authorities in competition with the van line.
1057. Section 601 of the Federal Aviation Administration Authorization Act of 1994, Pub. L. No. 103-305, 108 Stat. 1569 (codified at 49 U.S.C. § 14501(c)(1) (Supp. 1999)).
1058. The legislative history of the motor carrier preemption statute endorsed the "broad preemption interpretation" given to the corresponding airline statute, 49 U.S.C. § 41713(b)(1) (Supp. 1999), in *Morales v. Trans World Airlines, Inc.*, 504 U.S. 374 (1992). *See* H.R. CONF. REP. 103-677, at 83 (1994), *reprinted in* 1994 U.S.C.C.A.N. at 1755.
1059. Californians for Safe and Competitive Dump Truck Transportation v. Mendonca, 152 F.3d 1184, 1189 (9th Cir. 1998), *cert. denied*, 526 U.S. 1060 (1999). In interpreting the preemption statute, courts have upheld state prevailing wage laws, *id.*; antidiscrimination laws, LaRosa v. United Parcel Service, 23 F. Supp. 2d 136 (D. Mass. 1998); a state law authorizing forfeiture of a truck used to transport contraband cigarettes, Robertson v. Washington Liquor Control Bd., 10 P.3d 1079, 1084 (Wash. App. 2000), *petition for review denied*, 21 P.3d 290 (Wash. 2001); and, under the "market participant" ("municipal-proprietor") doctrine, localities' restrictions on nonconsensual towing operations, Petrey v. City of Toledo, 246 F.3d 548, 555-59 (6th Cir. 2001). Courts have struck down state and local laws regulating consensual towing services, Tocher v. City of Santa Ana, 219 F.3d 1040, 1047-48, 1050-52 (9th Cir. 2000), *cert. denied*, 531 U.S. 1146 (2001), even when defended under the market participant doctrine, Stucky v. City of San Antonio, 260 F.3d 424, 432-39 (5th Cir. 2001); municipal criminal code provisions governing the width, length, and weight of commercial motor vehicles, City of Columbus v. Garrett, No. 00AP-610, 2001 Ohio App. LEXIS 1422 (Ohio Ct. App. Mar. 27, 2001); and state common-law claims for fraud, negligence, unjust enrichment, conversion for lost, potentially dangerous, or improperly priced trucking services, Rockwell v. United Parcel Service, Inc., No. 2:99 CV 57, 1999 U.S. Dist. LEXIS 22036 (D. Vt. July 7, 1999), Deerskin Trading Post, Inc. v. United Parcel Service of America, Inc., 972 F. Supp. 665, 672 (N.D. Ga. 1997), Vieira v. United Parcel Service, Inc., No. C-95-04697, 1996 U.S. Dist. LEXIS 11223 (N.D. Cal. Aug. 5, 1996).
1060. 49 U.S.C. § 14501(c)(2)(C) (Supp. 1999). In addition, the federal statute allows states to continue to enact and enforce laws governing intrastate transportation of property with respect to uniform cargo liability, bills of lading, credit rules, antitrust immunity for joint line rates or routes, classifications, mileage guides, pooling, or agent-van line operations—provided that such laws are no more burdensome than their federal counterparts and that a motor carrier has requested they be applicable to its operations. *Id.* § 14501(c)(3) (Supp. 1999).

and matters related to insurance.[1061] Courts are split on whether municipalities, in addition to states, may avail themselves of this safety exemption.[1062]

2.　*Rail Transportation*

From 1887 to 1995, the Interstate Commerce Commission regulated the railroad industry pursuant to the Interstate Commerce Act.[1063] In 1995, the Interstate Commerce Commission Termination Act (ICCTA)[1064] replaced the Interstate Commerce Commission with the Surface Transportation Board.

In three steps since 1976, Congress largely deregulated the railroads. In 1976, it passed the Railroad Revitalization and Regulatory Reform Act (4R Act),[1065] which reduced regulation of rail rates. In 1980, Congress further deregulated rates and other aspects of rail service in the Staggers Rail Act.[1066] The ICCTA effected further modest deregulation. Together, these three acts substantially altered the role of antitrust as it applies to rail carriers.

a.　RAIL TRANSPORTATION POLICY

The Staggers Rail Act added to the Interstate Commerce Act a national rail transportation policy that emphasizes the desirability of competition in the rail transportation system. The Interstate Commerce Act now provides:

> In regulating the railroad industry, it is the policy of the United States Government—
> (1) to allow, to the maximum extent possible, competition and the demand for services to establish reasonable rates for transportation by rail;
> (2) to minimize the need for Federal regulatory control over the rail transportation system and to require fair and expeditious regulatory decisions when regulation is required;
> . . .
> (5) to foster sound economic conditions in transportation and to ensure effective competition and coordination between rail carriers and other modes;

1061. *Id.* § 14501(c)(2)(A) (Supp. 1999). Federal preemption of state and local restrictions on the routing of hazardous materials shipments under the Hazardous Materials Transportation Act, 49 U.S.C. § 5125 (1994), however, will not be defeated by § 14501(c)(2)(A). *See* Southern Blasting Servs., Inc. v. Wilkes County, 162 F. Supp. 2d 455 (W.D.N.C. 2001).

1062. *Compare Stucky*, 260 F.3d at 442-46, *Petrey*, 246 F.3d at 560-64, *Tocher*, 219 F.3d at 1050-51, R. Mayer of Atlanta, Inc. v. City of Atlanta, 158 F.3d 538 (11th Cir. 1998), *cert. denied*, 526 U.S. 1038 (1999), *and Garrett*, 2001 Ohio App. LEXIS 1422 (safety exemption applies only to states), *with* Ace Auto Body & Towing, Ltd. v. City of New York, 171 F.3d 765 (2d Cir.), *cert. denied*, 528 U.S. 868 (1999), People *ex rel.* Renne v. Servantes, 103 Cal. Rptr. 2d 870, 877, 880 (Cal. Ct. App. 2001), *review denied*, 2001 Cal. LEXIS 3297 (Cal. May 16, 2001) (safety exemption applies to municipalities as well as states).

1063. *See* 49 U.S.C. § 10101 *et seq.* (1994 & Supp. 1999).

1064. *See supra* note 1041.

1065. Pub. L. No. 94-210, 90 Stat. 31 (1976) (codified in scattered sections of 15, 31, 45, and 49 U.S.C.).

1066. Pub. L. No. 96-448, 94 Stat. 1895 (1980) (codified in scattered sections of 11, 45, and 49 U.S.C.). The constitutionality of the Staggers Rail Act's preemption of state rate regulation was upheld in *Texas v. United States*, 730 F.2d 339, 348-49 (5th Cir.), *cert. denied*, 469 U.S. 892 (1984), and *Illinois Commerce Comm'n v. ICC*, 749 F.2d 875, 885-86 (D.C. Cir. 1984), *cert. denied*, 474 U.S. 820 (1985).

(6) to maintain reasonable rates where there is an absence of effective competition and where rail rates provide revenues which exceed the amount necessary to maintain the rail system and to attract capital;

(7) to reduce regulatory barriers to entry into and exit from the industry;

. . .

(12) to prohibit predatory pricing and practices, to avoid undue concentrations of market power, and to prohibit unlawful discrimination.[1067]

The regulatory agencies have relied upon this statement of policy in applying other sections of the Interstate Commerce Act and the ICCTA.[1068] Moreover, consistency with the national rail transportation policy is a predicate for the Surface Transportation Board's exercise of its powers to grant exemptions from regulation[1069] and to approve rate bureau agreements.[1070]

b. AGENCY EXEMPTION AUTHORITY AND PREEMPTION
   OF OTHER LAW

The Staggers Rail Act substantially broadened the Interstate Commerce Commission's—and now the Surface Transportation Board's—authority to exempt a person, class of persons, or transaction or service from provisions of the Interstate Commerce Act. Section 10502 states that, with certain exceptions, the Surface Transportation Board "shall" exempt rail carriers, transactions, or services from continued regulation when it finds that (1) continued regulation is "not necessary to carry out the transportation policy of section 10101," and (2) either (a) "the transaction or service is of limited scope," or (b) continued regulation is "not needed to protect shippers from the abuse of market power."[1071] Courts construe this provision to confer "very broad authority" to eliminate all unnecessary regulation of railroads.[1072] The ICCTA reinforced this provision by directing the Surface Transportation Board to use its exemption authority "to the maximum extent" consistent with the rail provisions of the Interstate Commerce Act.[1073]

The regulatory agencies have exercised the rail exemption authority in a wide variety of areas. For example, many categories of railroad traffic are exempt from rate regulation,[1074] and the exemption authority has been used to relieve certain

---

1067. 49 U.S.C. § 10101 (Supp. 1999); *see also* H.R. REP. NO. 96-1430, at 88 (1980), *reprinted in* 1980 U.S.C.C.A.N. 4110, 4119.

1068. *See, e.g.*, Westmoreland Coal Sales Co. v. Denver & R.G.W.R.R., 5 I.C.C.2d 751, 756 (1989); Trailer Train Co.—Pooling of Car Serv. with Respect to Flatcars, 5 I.C.C.2d 552, 559-60 (1989); Union Pac. Corp., Union Pac. R.R. & Missouri Pac. R.R.—Control—Missouri-Kansas-Texas R.R., 4 I.C.C.2d 409, 426-27 (1988), *petition for review dismissed sub nom.* Railway Labor Executives Ass'n v. ICC, 883 F.2d 1079 (D.C. Cir. 1989); General Am. Transp. Corp. v. Indiana Harbor Belt R.R., 3 I.C.C.2d 599, 610-11 (1987), *aff'd sub nom.* General Am. Transp. Corp. v. ICC, 872 F.2d 1048 (D.C. Cir. 1989).

1069. 49 U.S.C. § 10502(a)(1) (Supp. 1999); *see* part J.2.b of this chapter.

1070. 49 U.S.C. § 10706(a)(2)(A) (Supp. 1999); *see* part J.2.d of this chapter.

1071. 49 U.S.C. § 10502(a)(1) & (2) (Supp. 1999).

1072. Coal Exporters Ass'n of the United States v. United States, 745 F.2d 76, 82 (D.C. Cir. 1984), *cert. denied*, 471 U.S. 1072 (1985); *see also* Simmons v. ICC, 760 F.2d 126, 132 (7th Cir. 1985) ("Congress wanted the exemption power to be wielded boldly."), *cert. denied*, 474 U.S. 1055 (1986).

1073. 49 U.S.C. § 10502(a) (Supp. 1999).

1074. *See, e.g.*, 49 C.F.R. § 1039.14 (2000) (boxcar traffic), upheld against challenge in Brae Corp. v. United States, 740 F.2d 1023, 1036-44 (D.C. Cir. 1984) (per curiam), *cert. denied*, 471 U.S. 1069

classes of rail-related transactions or services from statutory prior approval and other requirements.[1075] Exemptions also are routinely used in lieu of approval in uncontroversial control, abandonment, and other transactions.[1076] Parties are free to petition, modify, or revoke an exemption.[1077]

(1985), and expanded in Exemption From Regulation—Boxcar Traffic, 1 S.T.B. 42 (1996); 49 C.F.R. § 1090.2 (2000) (trailers and containers moving on flatcars), upheld against challenge in American Trucking Ass'ns v. ICC, 656 F.2d 1115, 1122-24 (5th Cir. 1981), and expanded in Improvement of TOFC/COFC Regulations (Railroad-Affiliated Motor Carriers & Other Motor Carriers), 3 I.C.C.2d 869, 885 (1987), and Improvement of TOFC/COFC Regulations (Pickup & Delivery), 6 I.C.C.2d 208, 226 (1989), aff'd sub nom. Central States Motor Freight Bureau v. ICC, 924 F.2d 1099 (D.C. Cir. 1991); 49 C.F.R. § 1039.10 (2000) (agricultural commodities except grain, soybeans, and sunflower seeds), adopted in, inter alia, Rail General Exemption Authority—Miscellaneous Agricultural Commodities, 367 I.C.C. 298, 311-12 (1983); 49 C.F.R. § 1039.11 (2000) (numerous miscellaneous commodities), adopted in, inter alia, Rail General Exemption Authority—Miscellaneous Manufactured Commodities, 6 I.C.C.2d 186, 205-07 (1989); Ex Parte No. 346 (Sub-No. 35), Rail General Exemption Authority—Exemption of Ferrous Recyclables, 1 S.T.B. 173 (1996); 49 C.F.R. § 1039.21 (2000) (ocean-rail international through rates), adopted in Railroad Exemption—International Joint Through Rates, 2 I.C.C.2d 121, 124-25 (1986). But see Coal Exporters Ass'n, 745 F.2d at 98-99 (vacating ICC's decision exempting export coal traffic from rate regulation).

1075. See, e.g., 49 C.F.R. §§ 1150.41-.45 (2000), adopted in Class Exemption for Acquisition or Operation of Rail Lines by Class III Rail Carriers Under 49 U.S.C. § 10902, 1 S.T.B. 95 (1996); 49 C.F.R. § 1150.36 (2000), adopted in Class Exemption for the Construction of Connecting Track Under 49 U.S.C. § 10901, 1 S.T.B. 75 (1996); 49 C.F.R. § 1185.1 (2000) (exemption from statutory prior approval requirements for certain interlocking directorates between rail carriers), adopted in Exemption from 49 U.S.C. 11322(a) for Certain Interlocking Directorates, 5 I.C.C.2d 7, 16 (1988), petition for review dismissed sub nom. United Transp. Union v. ICC, 891 F.2d 908 (D.C. Cir. 1989), cert. denied, 497 U.S. 1024 (1990); 49 C.F.R. § 1152.50 (2000) (exemption from statutory prior approval requirements for rail line abandonments and service and trackage rights discontinuances where no rail traffic has originated or terminated on rail line during the prior two years), adopted in Exemption of Out of Service Rail Lines, 2 I.C.C.2d 146, 159-60 (1986), aff'd sub nom. Illinois Commerce Comm'n v. ICC, 848 F.2d 1246 (D.C. Cir. 1988), cert. denied, 488 U.S. 1004 (1989); 49 C.F.R. § 1150.31 (2000) (exemption from statutory prior approval requirement of certain sales of railroad lines to new rail operators), adopted in Class Exemption for the Acquisition & Operation of Rail Lines Under 49 U.S.C. 10901, 1 I.C.C.2d 810, 820-21 (1985), review denied sub nom. Illinois Commerce Comm'n v. ICC, 817 F.2d 145 (D.C. Cir. 1987); 49 C.F.R. § 1180.2(d)(7) (2000) (exemption from statutory prior approval requirement of certain trackage rights agreements among rail carriers), adopted in Rail Consolidation Procedures—Trackage Rights Exemption, 1 I.C.C.2d 270, 282-83 (1985), aff'd sub nom. Illinois Commerce Comm'n v. ICC, 819 F.2d 311 (D.C. Cir. 1987); Common Carrier Status of States, State Agencies & Instrumentalities, & Political Subdivisions, 363 I.C.C. 132, 140-42 (1980) (partial exemption of state-operated rail carriers from common carrier certification and abandonment provisions), aff'd sub nom. Simmons v. ICC, 697 F.2d 326 (D.C. Cir. 1982); Exemption of Certain Designated Operators From Section 11343, 361 I.C.C. 379, 384 (1979) (exemption of "designated operators" conducting rail operations over portions of bankrupt Penn Central rail system from rail consolidation and interlocking directorate provisions), rev'd on other grounds sub nom. McGinness v. ICC, 662 F.2d 853 (D.C. Cir. 1981).

1076. See, e.g., Finance Dkt. No. 33813, RailAmerica, Inc.—Control Exemption—RailTex, Inc., Decision served Jan. 10, 2000, 2000 STB LEXIS 9 (2000).

1077. See, e.g., Association of Am. R.Rs.—Petition to Exempt Indus. Dev. Activities From 49 U.S.C. § 10761(a), 10761(a)(1), 11902, 11903, & 11904(a), 8 I.C.C.2d 365, 389 (1992); see also Mr. Sprout, Inc. v. United States, 8 F.3d 118, 122 (2d Cir. 1993) ("Once the ICC has decided to exempt a rail carrier from regulation, it retains the power to revoke that exemption, or reregulate the railroad."), cert. denied, 512 U.S. 1205 (1994).

Courts long held that the Interstate Commerce Act preempted various common-law remedies,[1078] but declined to hold that the act broadly displaced the antitrust laws.[1079] In certain cases, however, Congress has expressly exempted transactions and activities of rail carriers from antitrust scrutiny.[1080] In the Staggers Rail Act, Congress provided that the Interstate Commerce Commission's (now the Surface Transportation Board's) jurisdiction "over transportation by rail carriers, and the remedies provided in this part with respect to rates, classifications, rules ..., practices, routes, services, and facilities of such carriers ... is exclusive."[1081] Several courts held that this provision did not eliminate antitrust remedies.[1082]

The conference report for the ICCTA, however, indicates that this "exclusivity is limited to remedies with respect to rail regulation—not State and Federal law generally," and that, by way of example, "criminal statutes governing antitrust matters not preempted by this Act, and laws defining such criminal offenses as bribery and extortion, remain fully applicable unless specifically displaced, because they do not generally collide with the scheme of economic regulation (and deregulation) of rail transportation."[1083] Courts have construed the broad preemption language of the ICCTA as effecting a sweeping preemption of state economic regulation of railroads.[1084]

A significant issue is whether transactions or services lose whatever immunity they would otherwise have from the operation of other state and federal laws, including antitrust laws, when the agency exempts them from regulation pursuant to Section 10502. In a number of decisions exempting certain classes of rail traffic from rate regulation, the Interstate Commerce Commission announced that the exemption removed any antitrust immunity that would otherwise apply to the exempted rates pursuant to the Interstate Commerce Act's express immunization of rate bureau agreements.[1085] On the other hand, in the area of mergers and trackage

1078. *See, e.g.*, Chicago & N.W. Transp. Co. v. Kalo Brick & Tile Co., 450 U.S. 311 (1981) (state common-law remedy imposing service requirements preempted by Interstate Commerce Act); Texas & Pac. Ry. v. Abilene Cotton Oil Co., 204 U.S. 426 (1907) (common-law actions challenging rates established under the Interstate Commerce Act not available).

1079. *See, e.g.*, Georgia v. Pennsylvania R.R., 324 U.S. 439, 456-60 (1944); United States v. Trans-Missouri Freight Ass'n, 166 U.S. 290, 314-27 (1897).

1080. *See, e.g.*, 49 U.S.C. § 10706 (Supp. 1999) (rate agreements approved by STB); *id.* § 11321(a) (Supp. 1999) (merger or control transaction approved or exempted by STB). One court of appeals has suggested that 49 U.S.C. § 11321(a) would not bar a claim of predatory conduct by one railroad aimed at weakening another railroad and allowing it to be taken over. Springfield Terminal Ry. v. Canadian Pac. Ltd., 133 F.3d 103, 107 (1st Cir. 1997).

1081. 49 U.S.C. § 10501(b) (Supp. 1999). The statute further states that "the remedies provided under this part with respect to regulation of rail transportation are exclusive and preempt the remedies provided under Federal or State law." *Id.*

1082. *See, e.g.*, Alliance Shippers, Inc. v. Southern Pac. Transp. Co., 858 F.2d 567, 570 (9th Cir. 1988); Transkentucky Transp. R.R. v. Louisville & N.R.R., 581 F. Supp. 759, 763-65 (E.D. Ky. 1983).

1083. H.R. REP. NO. 104-422, at 167 (1995), *reprinted in* 1995 U.S.C.C.A.N. 850, 852.

1084. *See, e.g.*, City of Auburn v. United States, 154 F.3d 1025 (9th Cir. 1998); Burlington N. Santa Fe Corp. v. Anderson, 959 F. Supp. 1288 (D. Mont. 1997); CSX Transp., Inc. v. Georgia Pub. Serv. Comm'n, 944 F. Supp. 1573 (N.D. Ga. 1996).

1085. *See, e.g.*, Rail General Exemption Auth.—Lumber or Wood Products, 7 I.C.C.2d 673, 683 (1991); Rail General Exemption Auth.—Miscellaneous Manufactured Commodities, 6 I.C.C.2d 186, 197 (1989); Railroad Exemption—Export Coal, 367 I.C.C. 570, 595 & n.69 (1983), *vacated and remanded on other grounds sub nom.* Coal Exporters Ass'n v. United States, 745 F.2d 76 (D.C. Cir. 1984), *cert. denied*, 471 U.S. 1072 (1985); Exemption From Regulation—Boxcar Traffic, 367 I.C.C. 425, 446 (1983), *aff'd in pertinent part sub nom.* Brae Corp. v. United States, 740 F.2d 1023 (D.C. Cir. 1984) (per curiam), *cert. denied*, 471 U.S. 1069 (1985); Improvement of TOFC/COFC

rights, where a statutory provision expressly preempts the antitrust laws with respect to approved or exempted transactions,[1086] the regulators, after initial indications to the contrary,[1087] have concluded that transactions exempted from regulation under Section 10502 are still immune from the antitrust laws.[1088]

The Interstate Commerce Commission held that an exemption neither extinguishes the agency's exclusive jurisdiction nor permits the application of inconsistent federal or state laws to the exempted transaction or activity.[1089] In *G. & T. Terminal Packaging Co. v. Consolidated Rail Corp.*,[1090] a divided panel of the Third Circuit agreed with the agency's position[1091] and concluded that the Interstate Commerce Commission's exemption did not affect the Interstate Commerce Act's preemption of state common-law rights of action. In *Alliance Shippers, Inc. v. Southern Pacific Transportation Co.*,[1092] the Ninth Circuit concluded that the Interstate Commerce Commission's exemption of particular traffic did not revive state common-law and statutory discrimination remedies because these remedies would be inconsistent with the goals of the Staggers Rail Act, but that federal and state antitrust remedies "unquestionably survived" deregulation and apply to exempted traffic, presumably on the ground that they are not inconsistent with those goals.[1093]

c.   REGULATION OF ENTRY AND EXIT

The Staggers Rail Act eased entry requirements.[1094] Before 1980, the Interstate Commerce Commission could issue a certificate of public convenience and necessity authorizing new rail construction or the acquisition of a rail line by a noncarrier only if it found that the public convenience and necessity "require or will be enhanced by" the construction or acquisition.[1095] The Staggers Rail Act reduced the stringency of

Regulation, 364 I.C.C. 731, 736 & n.2 (1981), *aff'd sub nom.* American Trucking Ass'ns v. ICC, 656 F.2d 1115, 1126 (5th Cir. 1981). Rate bureaus are discussed in part J.2.d of this chapter.
1086. 49 U.S.C. § 11321(a) (Supp. 1999).
1087. Railroad Consolidation Procedures—Trackage Rights Exemption, 1 I.C.C.2d 270, 279 (1985), *aff'd sub nom.* Illinois Commerce Comm'n v. ICC, 819 F.2d 311 (D.C. Cir. 1987); *cf.* Finance Docket No. 29757, Colorado & S. Ry.—Merger Into Burlington N.R.R.—Exemption & Request for Determination of Fairness, Decision served Dec. 31, 1981 (exempted rail merger transaction not immune from operation of state corporation laws conferring rights on dissenting shareholders); Finance Docket No. 31035, Merger—Baltimore & O.R.R. & Chesapeake & O. Ry., Decision served Feb. 22, 1988 (same).
1088. Finance Docket No. 32133, Union Pac. Corp., Union Pac. R.R. & Missouri Pac. R.R.— Control— Chicago & N.W. Transp. Co. & Chicago & N.W. Ry., Decision served Mar. 7, 1995, 1995 ICC LEXIS 37, at *173-75 (1995), slip op. at 63-64; Finance Docket No. 30965 (Sub-Nos. 1 & 2), Delaware & H. Ry.—Lease & Trackage Rights—Springfield Terminal Ry., Decision served Apr. 21, 1993, 1993 ICC LEXIS 77, at *4 n.4 (1993), slip op. at 2 n.4.
1089. *See, e.g.*, Exemption of Railroads From Securities Regulation Under 49 U.S.C. § 11301, 1 I.C.C.2d 915, 916-18 (1985) (exemption of railroad securities transactions did not remove ICC's exclusive jurisdiction over, and did not permit federal or state authorities to regulate, such transactions).
1090. 830 F.2d 1230 (3d Cir. 1987), *cert. denied*, 485 U.S. 988 (1988).
1091. Consolidated Rail Corp.—Declaratory Order—Exemptions, 1 I.C.C.2d 895, 900-01 (1986).
1092. 858 F.2d 567 (9th Cir. 1988).
1093. *Id.* at 569-70; *see also* Association of Am. R.Rs.—Petition to Exempt Indus. Dev. Activities From 49 U.S.C. § 10761(a), 10761(a)(1), 11902, 11903, & 11904(a), 8 I.C.C.2d 365, 386 (1992) (exempted industrial development activities remain subject to antitrust laws).
1094. *See* H.R. REP. NO. 96-1430, at 115-16 (1980), *reprinted in* 1980 U.S.C.C.A.N. 4110, 4147-48.
1095. *See* Pub. L. No. 95-473, 92 Stat. 1402 (1978).

the requisite finding by substituting the word "permit" for the words "will be enhanced by."[1096] The ICCTA further liberalized the standard by providing that a certificate "shall" be issued by the Surface Transportation Board unless it finds that the construction or acquisition is "inconsistent with the public convenience and necessity."[1097] The Surface Transportation Board generally exempts new rail construction projects, subject only to environmental review,[1098] and most line sales to noncarriers are exempt.[1099]

The Staggers Rail Act also amended or repealed provisions of the Interstate Commerce Act to permit easier abandonment of lines. The statutory provisions, as further amended in 1995, place time limits on processing of abandonment applications and permit parties to make offers of financial assistance to avoid abandonment of a railroad line.[1100] The Surface Transportation Board has required rail carriers to make a substantial showing in connection with a request for authority to abandon a line.[1101]

1096. 49 U.S.C. § 10901(a) (1994).
1097. *Id.* § 10901(c) (Supp. 1999); *see also id.* § 10902 (Supp. 1999) (new provision regarding line purchases by smaller railroads); Class Exemption for Acquisition or Operation of Rail Lines by Class III Rail Carriers Under 49 U.S.C. § 10902, 1 S.T.B. 95 (1996).
1098. *See, e.g.*, Finance Docket No. 32571, Missouri Pac. R.R.—Construction & Operation Exemption—Harris & Chambers Counties, TX, Decision served June 30, 1995, 1995 ICC LEXIS 169 (1995). *See also* Finance Docket No. 33407, Dakota, M.& E.R.R. Construction Into the Powder River Basin, Final Environmental Impact Statement served Nov. 19, 2001. The STB, interpreting 49 U.S.C. § 10901(d) (Supp. 1999), has held that where a construction project involves crossing the line of another railroad, that railroad is not entitled to compensation for the opportunity cost of lost traffic. *See, e.g.*, Finance Docket No. 32630 (Sub-No. 1), Omaha Pub. Power Dist.—Petition Under 49 U.S.C. § 10901(d), Decision served Aug. 1, 1996, 1996 STB LEXIS 216 (1996). One court has rejected a shipper's antitrust challenge to a rail carrier's refusal to permit the shipper to construct new industrial track that would cross the carrier's line in order to reach the main line, on the ground that the shipper could not demonstrate antitrust injury. *See* Bar Techs. Inc. v. Conemaugh & Black Lick R.R., 73 F. Supp. 2d 512, 518-20 (W.D. Pa. 1999).
1099. 49 C.F.R. §§ 1150.31-.34 (2000).
1100. *See* 49 U.S.C. §§ 10903-10904 (Supp. 1999); Abandonment & Discontinuance of Rail Lines & Rail Transp. Under 49 U.S.C. § 10903, 1 S.T.B. 894 (1996) (new procedures to implement 1995 statutory changes); *id.*, 2 S.T.B. 311 (1997) (modifying rules), *dismissed on other grounds sub nom.* National Ass'n of Revisionary Property Owners v. STB, 158 F.3d 135 (D.C. Cir. 1998). Many cases discuss the standards used in reviewing railroad abandonment applications. *See, e.g.*, Chicago & N.W. Transp. Co. v. Kalo Brick & Tile Co., 450 U.S. 311 (1981); Southern Pac. Transp. Co. v. ICC, 871 F.2d 838, 843-44 (9th Cir. 1989); Busboom Grain Co. v. ICC, 856 F.2d 790 (7th Cir. 1988); Baltimore & O.R.R. v. ICC, 826 F.2d 1125, 1126 (D.C. Cir. 1987); Simmons v. ICC, 784 F.2d 242, 245-46 (7th Cir. 1985); Illinois Commerce Comm'n v. ICC, 776 F.2d 355 (D.C. Cir. 1985); Illinois v. ICC, 751 F.2d 903 (7th Cir. 1985); Glazer Steel Corp. v. ICC, 748 F.2d 1006, 1008 (5th Cir. 1984); Black v. ICC, 737 F.2d 643, 650-51 (7th Cir. 1984); Cartersville Elevator, Inc. v. ICC, 735 F.2d 1059, 1061 (8th Cir. 1984) (en banc); Georgia Pub. Serv. Comm'n v. United States, 704 F.2d 538, 541-42 (11th Cir. 1983); Illinois v. United States, 668 F.2d 923, 929-30 (7th Cir. 1981), *cert. denied*, 455 U.S. 100 (1982).
1101. *See, e.g.*, Dkt. No. AB-559 (Sub-No. IX), Gauley River R.R.—Abandonment & Discontinuance of Service—in Webster & Nicholas Counties, WV, Decision served June 16, 1999, 1999 STB LEXIS 345 (1999) (rejecting exemption petition because STB could not determine whether costs exceeded revenues from serving one shipper); Dkt. No. AB-6 (Sub-No. 382X), Burlington N. & S.F. Ry.—Abandonment of Chicago Area Trackage in Cook County, IL, Decision served Sept. 21, 1999, 1999 STB LEXIS 553 (1999) (rejecting petition because railroad did not provide enough information to establish losses on one portion of the line); Dkt. No. AB-57 (Sub-No. 48X), Soo Line R.R.—Abandonment Exemption—in Marshall & Roberts Counties, SD, Corrected Decision served Nov. 19, 1999, 1999 STB LEXIS 662 (1999) (rejecting petition for lack of supporting documentation and because railroad did not bifurcate data so that STB could separately evaluate

d.   REGULATION OF RATES AND AGREEMENTS

To regulate a rail rate as unreasonably high, the Surface Transportation Board must first find that the railroad has "market dominance" over the transportation to which the particular rate applies.[1102] If the agency determines that the railroad does not have market dominance, the railroad may establish any rate for transportation or other services.[1103] Regulation of minimum rates was repealed in 1995, and the setting of unduly low rates for predatory purposes is now subject to the antitrust laws.[1104]

Before it may determine that a carrier has market dominance, the Surface Transportation Board must make two findings. First, it must find that there is an "absence of effective competition from other rail carriers or modes of transportation for the transportation" to which the rate applies.[1105] Second, the agency also must find that the rate charged results in a revenue-to-variable-cost percentage of at least 180.[1106] If these findings cannot be made, the Surface Transportation Board lacks jurisdiction to determine whether the rate exceeds a maximum reasonable level.[1107]

In determining whether effective competition exists, the agency must evaluate the access of the shipper and the receiver to alternative transportation, the number of such alternatives, and the transportation costs associated with each alternative. The Surface Transportation Board examines both intramodal and intermodal competitive options. For many years, the agency also considered evidence that railroad rates are constrained by product or geographic competition.[1108] In December 1998, however, the Surface Transportation Board eliminated product and geographic competition from the types of competition it will consider in deciding whether a railroad has

---

contested portion of abandonment); San Joaquin Valley R.R.—Abandonment Exemption—In Kings & Fresno Counties, CA, 2 S.T.B. 270 (1997) (abandonment rejected for want of sufficient evidence of unprofitability); Dkt. No. AB-397 (Sub-No. 5X), Tulare Valley R.R.—Abandonment & Discontinuance Exemption—In Tulare & Kern Counties, CA, Decision served Feb. 21, 1997, 1997 STB LEXIS 37 (1997), recons. denied, Decision served Mar. 6, 1998 (same), 1998 STB LEXIS 76 (1998).

1102. 49 U.S.C. §§ 10701(d)(1), 10707(b) (Supp. 1999).

1103. Id. § 10701(c) (Supp. 1999); see Bessemer & L.E.R.R. v. ICC, 691 F.2d 1104, 1108 (3d Cir. 1982) (effect of market dominance provision was to end for most rail services ICC control over maximum rates and to permit carriers not having market dominance to set rates in response to their perception of market conditions), cert. denied, 462 U.S. 1110 (1983).

1104. See 49 U.S.C. § 10701(c) (Supp. 1999); H.R. REP. NO. 104-311, at 82-83 (1995), reprinted in 1995 U.S.C.C.A.N. 793, 794.

1105. 49 U.S.C. § 10707(a) (Supp. 1999).

1106. Id. § 10707(d) (Supp. 1999).

1107. Consolidated Papers, Inc. v. Chicago & N.W. Transp. Co., 7 I.C.C.2d 330, 332 (1991) (market dominance determination is a jurisdictional issue always subject to reexamination).

1108. See Market Dominance Determinations & Consideration of Prod. Competition, 365 I.C.C. 118, 135 (1981) (allowing consideration of product and geographic competition), aff'd sub nom. Western Coal Traffic League v. United States, 719 F.2d 772 (5th Cir. 1983) (en banc), cert. denied, 466 U.S. 953 (1984); Product & Geographic Competition, 2 I.C.C.2d 1, 18-22 (1985) (amending market dominance evidentiary guidelines, inter alia, to shift burden of proving product and geographic competition to the railroad defendants in rate complaint cases); Consolidated Papers, Inc. v. Chicago & N.W. Transp. Co., 7 I.C.C.2d 330 (1991) (applying factors); see also General Chem. Corp. v. United States, 817 F.2d 844, 855 (D.C. Cir. 1987) (per curiam); Salt River Project Agric. Improvement & Power Dist. v. United States, 762 F.2d 1053, 1059-60 (D.C. Cir. 1985); Aluminum Co. v. ICC, 761 F.2d 746, 750-51 (D.C. Cir. 1985); Arizona Pub. Serv. Co. v. United States, 742 F.2d 644, 649 (D.C. Cir. 1984). In Union Pac. R.R. v. ICC, 867 F.2d 646, 652-54 (D.C. Cir. 1989), the D.C. Circuit held that the ICC could not evade the market dominance test by treating an allegedly excessive rate level as an "unreasonable practice."

market dominance over particular traffic.[1109] It reaffirmed that decision on remand from the D.C. Circuit.[1110] It concluded that consideration of product and geographic competition "has placed unnecessary and exceedingly high obstacles in the path of the administrative rate complaint process."[1111] The agency has applied that decision to exclude evidence of product and geographic competition in several rate cases.[1112] In one of these cases, it held that, in deciding whether a railroad has market dominance over traffic on one segment of a route, it would consider evidence of modal competition only on that segment, not between origin and destination.[1113]

Even if the Surface Transportation Board determines that the rail carrier has market dominance, that finding does not establish a presumption that the rate in question is unreasonable.[1114] Instead, the agency must make a separate rate reasonableness determination. The test is whether the rate exceeds "a reasonable maximum" for the transportation to which it applies.[1115]

In determining whether a rate is unreasonably high, the Surface Transportation Board applies "constrained market pricing" principles that were adopted, after several false starts, in the *Coal Rate Guidelines* proceeding in 1985.[1116] These principles recognize that the railroads—because of their high fixed and common costs and the fact that much of their traffic has high demand elasticity and would be lost if the railroads charged a substantial mark-up above variable cost—must use differential pricing.[1117] The principal constraint on excessive rates is a "stand-alone cost" test, under which a railroad is not permitted to charge more than the full cost, including return to capital, of providing efficient rail service in a purely contestable market (i.e., one with no barriers to entry or exit).[1118]

1109. Ex Parte No. 627, Market Dominance Determinations—Prod. & Geographic Competition, Decision served Dec. 21, 1998, 1998 STB LEXIS 1003 (1998).

1110. Association of Am. R.Rs. v. STB, 237 F.3d 676 (D.C. Cir. 2001); Ex Parte 627, Market Dominance Determinations—Product & Geographic Competition, Corrected Decision served Apr. 6, 2001, 2001 STB LEXIS 341 (2001), *petition for review pending sub nom.* Association of Am. R.Rs. v. STB (D.C. Cir. No. 01-1213).

1111. Ex Parte No. 627 & Docket No. 42022, Market Dominance Determinations—Prod. & Geographic Competition; FMC Wyoming Corp. v. Union Pac. R.R., Decision served July 2, 1999, at 1, 1999 STB LEXIS 390, at *1 (1999).

1112. *Id.* (rejecting railroad's argument that exclusion of product and geographic competition evidence should not apply to a case that was filed prior to the time STB rendered its decision); Dkt. No. 42038, Minnesota Power, Inc. v. Duluth, M. & I.R. Ry., Decision served July 8, 1999, 1999 STB LEXIS 403 (1999) (declining to order discovery relating to what the STB characterized as a geographic alternative to the transportation at issue in the complaint).

1113. *Minnesota Power, supra* note 1112, 1999 STB LEXIS 403, at *7-12, slip op. at 4-6. The railroad had sought discovery relating to trucking of coal from a second plant owned by the shipper.

1114. *See* 49 U.S.C. § 10707(d)(2)(B) (Supp. 1999).

1115. *Id.*; *see also id.* § 10701(d)(1) (Supp. 1999).

1116. Coal Rate Guidelines, Nationwide, 1 I.C.C.2d 520, 522 (1985), *aff'd sub nom.* Consolidated Rail Corp. v. United States, 812 F.2d 1444 (3d Cir. 1987). The STB applies these principles in both coal and noncoal cases. *See* Burlington N.R.R. v. ICC, 985 F.2d 589, 596 (D.C. Cir. 1993); Dkt. No. 37809, McCarty Farms v. Burlington N., Inc., Decision served July 22, 1993, *aff'd sub nom.* McCarty Farms v. STB, 158 F.3d 1294 (D.C. Cir. 1998).

1117. A report prepared for the Federal Railroad Administration in 2000 endorsed this analysis. Eric Beshers, Hagler Bailly Services, Inc., Efficient Access Pricing for Rail Bottlenecks (2000), *available at* www.fra.dot.gov/pdf/bottlenecks.pdf.

1118. In a case involving pipeline rates, the STB applied a different test, the "revenue adequacy" constraint. Dkt. No. 41685, CF Indus., Inc. v. Koch Pipeline Co., Decision served May 9, 2000, 2000 STB LEXIS 260, *aff'd sub nom.* CF Indus., Inc. v. STB, 255 F.3d 816 (D.C. Cir. 2001).

The Surface Transportation Board was under a congressional mandate to adopt by the end of 1996 "a simplified and expedited method for determining the reasonableness of challenged rail rates in those cases in which a full stand-alone cost presentation is too costly, given the value of the case."[1119] It duly adopted regulations that look to various revenue/variable cost ratios as benchmarks for rate reasonableness in such cases.[1120] These regulations have not been applied in any subsequent proceeding. The D.C. Circuit dismissed a petition for review as unripe because the guidelines had not yet been applied.[1121]

In its so-called bottleneck decisions, the agency decided important issues concerning rate regulation for shippers served by only one railroad. In several consolidated cases, the shippers contended that they were entitled to secure separate rates for short "bottleneck" segments between a nearby interchange point and the generating plant.[1122] The shippers' goal was to limit those rates for the short bottleneck segments to the stand-alone cost level, and to secure bidding from competing railroads for the remainder of the movement. The railroads argued that the law does not require quotation of segment rates and limits rate challenges—and application of the stand-alone cost methodology—to the through, origin-to-destination rate.

The Surface Transportation Board generally resolved these issues in favor of the railroads,[1123] and the Eighth Circuit upheld one such decision.[1124] The court of appeals agreed that railroads were under no general obligation to provide segment rates. It dismissed as unripe the railroads' cross-appeal of the agency's related decision that railroads must publish separately challengeable rates for segments of through movements where the shipper and a connecting railroad have entered into a contract governing the remainder of each movement. The D.C. Circuit later upheld that exception.[1125]

The Staggers Rail Act added a new provision that authorized transportation services contracts between rail carriers and shippers and substantially deregulated traffic subject to such contracts. The ICCTA further curtailed the already limited review of contracts.[1126] A contract authorized by the statute may not subsequently be challenged before the Surface Transportation Board or in any court on the ground

---

1119. 49 U.S.C. § 10701(d)(3) (Supp. 1999).

1120. Rate Guidelines—Non-Coal Proceedings, 1 S.T.B 1004 (1996).

1121. Association of Am. R.Rs. v. STB, 146 F.3d 942 (D.C. Cir. 1998). An earlier D.C. Circuit decision overturned a methodology based on revenue-to-variable-cost ratios. *Burlington N.R.R.*, 985 F.2d 589.

1122. Use of the "bottleneck" label can be misleading. A bottleneck exists wherever one railroad serves a customer's facility. Some commentators have mistakenly assumed that bottlenecks automatically qualify as relevant markets subject to monopoly power without evaluating the proper relevant market.

1123. Dkt. No. 41242, Central Power & Light Co. v. Southern Pac. Transp. Co.; Dkt. No. 41295, Pennsylvania Power & Light Co. v. Consolidated Rail Corp.; Dkt. No. 41626, MidAmerican Energy Co. v. Union Pac. R.R. & Chicago & N.W. Ry., Decisions served Aug. 27, 1996 and Dec. 31, 1996, 1996 STB LEXIS 342 (1996), 1 S.T.B. 1059 (1996). The only exception was that, where a shipper secures a contract rate from one railroad for one segment of an interline movement and a common carrier rate from another railroad for the other segment, it can challenge the common carrier rate separately. 1 S.T.B. at 1074.

1124. MidAmerican Energy Co. v. STB, 169 F.3d 1099 (8th Cir.), *cert. denied*, 528 U.S. 950 (1999).

1125. Union Pac. R.R. v. STB, 202 F.3d 337 (D.C. Cir. 2000).

1126. 49 U.S.C. § 10709(g) (Supp. 1999).

that it violates a provision of the ICCTA.[1127] "If anticompetitive behavior is alleged, under this section, the antitrust laws are the appropriate and only remedy available."[1128]

The 4R Act and the Staggers Rail Act also narrowed the scope of antitrust exempt collective ratemaking by rail carriers under the Reed-Bulwinkle Act of 1948.[1129] Members of railroad rate bureaus may not discuss, participate in an agreement related to, or vote on single-line rates (i.e., a rate proposed by a single carrier for transportation over its own line)[1130] or on rates for interline movements (i.e., rates for transportation involving more than one railroad) unless each railroad involved in such activities "practicably participates" in such movements.[1131] Where there are multiple interline movements between two end points, members of a rate bureau may not discuss, participate in an agreement related to, or vote on any interline rates except those in which they can participate.[1132]

Railroads essentially no longer use rate bureau agreements in connection with transportation rates. Such agreements continue to have limited roles in other areas, such as car hire payments and arrangements for equipment repairs.

In *In re Lower Lake Erie Iron Ore Antitrust Litigation*,[1133] the Bessemer and Lake Erie Railroad (B&LE) appealed an adverse jury verdict based on allegations that the railroad companies serving the lower Lake Erie industrial region conspired to preclude potential competitors from entering the market for lake transport, dock handling, storage, and land transport of iron ore. The railroads allegedly conspired to exclude self-unloading vessels from the iron ore industry by denying dock facilities to self-unloaders, refusing to provide competitive inland rail service to nonrailroad-owned docks, and standardizing handling charges for unloading from bulkers (vessels requiring more costly unloading by cranes) and from self-unloaders.[1134] B&LE challenged the verdict on the ground of antitrust immunity, asserting that the railroads were authorized under the Reed-Bulwinkle Act to set rates jointly through rate bureaus, and also that the railroads' activity was protected by the

1127. *Id.* § 10709(c) (Supp. 1999).
1128. *See* H.R. REP. NO. 96-1035, at 58, *reprinted in* 1980 U.S.C.C.A.N. 3978, 4003.
1129. Ch. 491, 62 Stat. 472 (1948).
1130. 49 U.S.C. § 10706(a)(3)(A)(i) (Supp. 1999); *see* Western R.Rs.—Agreement, 364 I.C.C. 635, 642-43 (1981). Rate bureaus are associations of railroads allowed to discuss and set rates with antitrust immunity under certain circumstances. The ICC indicated that all contract rates would be viewed as "single-line rates," and therefore not a permissible subject of rate bureau agreements. 364 I.C.C. at 644.
1131. 49 U.S.C. § 10706(a)(3)(A)(ii) (Supp. 1999). Congress left the responsibility for defining "practicably participates" to the ICC. H.R. CONF. REP. NO. 96-1430, at 114 (1980), *reprinted in* 1980 U.S.C.C.A.N. 4110, 4146. In *Western Railroads*, the ICC declared: "Practicable participants in an interline movement are only those carriers who are direct connectors to a specific joint-line movement." 364 I.C.C. at 651; *see also* Petition to Delay Application of Direct Connector Requirement to Joint Rail Rates in General Increases, 367 I.C.C. 886, 893 (1983), *aff'd sub nom.* American Short Line R.R. Ass'n v. United States, 751 F.2d 107 (2d Cir. 1984).
1132. 49 U.S.C. § 10706(a)(3)(A)(iii) (Supp. 1999). *See Western Railroads*, 364 I.C.C. at 648. Rate bureaus also must prepare transcripts or sound recordings of all meetings and keep records of votes. These materials must be provided to the STB and other relevant federal agencies, but they are exempt from disclosure under the Freedom of Information Act. 49 U.S.C. § 10706(a)(3)(C) (Supp. 1999).
1133. 998 F.2d 1144 (3d Cir.), *cert. dismissed*, 510 U.S. 1021 & 1032 (1993), *cert. denied*, 510 U.S. 1091 (1994).
1134. *Id.* at 1151.

Keogh doctrine.[1135] The Third Circuit disagreed, holding that immunity extended no farther than activities specifically authorized by the Interstate Commerce Commission, such as joint setting of rates.[1136]

e.   COMPETITIVE ACCESS AND RELATED ISSUES

The Surface Transportation Board has several means at its disposal to prescribe "competitive access." The agency may (1) order railroads to participate in through routes and joint rates,[1137] (2) order a rail carrier to allow another rail carrier to operate over tracks within the first carrier's terminal facilities (referred to as terminal trackage rights),[1138] or (3) order a railroad to provide switching service for another railroad between a shipper's facility and the tracks of the other rail carrier (referred to as reciprocal switching).[1139] In each case, the agency must find the action to be "in the public interest."[1140] State competitive access remedies are preempted.[1141]

The Surface Transportation Board has promulgated competitive access rules (CARs) by means of through routes, joint rates, and reciprocal switching.[1142] In

---

1135. Keogh v. Chicago & Northwestern Ry., 260 U.S. 156 (1922). The *Keogh* doctrine is discussed in part D.2 of Chapter XIII. The future relevance of the *Keogh* doctrine to rail tariffs is questionable in light of the elimination, in the ICCTA, of provisions for the filing of rail tariffs. *See* 49 U.S.C. §§ 10761-10762, *repealed by* Pub. L. No. 104-88, § 102(a), 109 Stat. 803 (1995); H.R. REP. NO. 104-311, at 82 (1995), *reprinted in* 1995 U.S.C.C.A.N. 793, 794; Disclosure, Publication, & Notice of Change of Rates & Other Service Terms for Rail Common Carriage, 1 S.T.B. 153 (1996).

1136. 998 F.2d at 1156-61. The Third Circuit held that, while the plaintiff shippers' claim for damages was the difference between the ICC-approved rate and the rate that the plaintiff could have obtained absent the conspiracy, the mere fact that the measure of damages began with an ICC-approved rate did not define the nature of the conspiracy. *Id.* at 1160-61. The court also held that *Keogh* had no application to the damage claims of the plaintiff dock companies and trucking companies, who were competitors of the defendant railroads, because as a matter of law *Keogh* did not apply to claims of competitors. *Id.* at 1161.

1137. 49 U.S.C. § 10705(a)(1) (Supp. 1999).

1138. *Id.* § 11102(a) (Supp. 1999).

1139. *Id.* § 11102(c)(1) (Supp. 1999). On the possibility of prescribing bottleneck rates, see part J.2.d of this chapter.

1140. 49 U.S.C. §§ 10705(a)(1), 11102(a), (c)(1) (Supp. 1999). In addition, to impose either terminal trackage rights or reciprocal switching, the STB must find such arrangements to be "practicable." *Id.* § 11102(a), (c)(1).

1141. *See, e.g.,* Association of Am. R.Rs. v. Public Serv. Comm'n, 745 F. Supp. 1175 (S.D. W. Va.), *supplemented,* 745 F. Supp. 1188 (S.D. W. Va. 1989).

1142. Intramodal Rail Competition, 1 I.C.C.2d 822 (1985), *aff'd sub nom.* Baltimore Gas & Elec. Co. v. United States, 817 F.2d 108 (D.C. Cir. 1987) (codified at 49 C.F.R. pt. 1144 (2000)). The CARs provide that the STB will prescribe through routes and joint rates, and establish switching arrangements, only when necessary to remedy or prevent acts that are contrary to the competition aims of the national rail transportation policy or are otherwise anticompetitive. *See* Central Power & Light Co. v. Southern Pac. Transp. Co., 1 S.T.B. 1059, 1065-67 (1996). The CARs also address cancellation of through routes and joint rates. 49 C.F.R. §§ 1144.1-.4 (2000). However, the ICCTA repealed former 49 U.S.C. § 10705(e) (1994), relating to suspension and investigation of through route and joint rate cancellations. The ICC and the STB have more freely granted terminal trackage rights over nonapplicant railroads where necessary to effectuate competition-preserving merger conditions. *See* Union Pac. Corp., Union Pac. R.R. & Missouri Pac. R.R.—Control & Merger—Southern Pac. Rail Corp., Southern Pac. Transp. Co., St. Louis Southwestern Ry., SPCSL Corp., & Denver & R.G.W. R.R., 1 S.T.B. 233, 446-50 (1996), *aff'd sub nom.* Western Coal Traffic League v. STB, 169 F.3d 775 (D.C. Cir.) (1999); Union Pac. Corp., Pacific Rail Sys. & Union Pac. R.R.—Control—Missouri Pac. Corp. & Missouri Pac. R.R., 366 I.C.C. 459, 574-76

Midtec Paper Corp. v. Chicago & North Western Transportation Co.,[1143] the Interstate Commerce Commission also applied CARs to requests for terminal trackage rights. Interpreting CARs, the agency held in *Midtec* that a decision to order trackage rights or reciprocal switching will turn on "(i) whether the railroad has used its market power to extract unreasonable terms on through movements; or (ii) whether because of its monopoly position the railroad has shown a disregard for the shipper's needs by rendering inadequate service."[1144] In making these determinations, the Surface Transportation Board will consider evidence of intramodal, intermodal, and geographic competition.[1145]

In response to congressional requests, the Surface Transportation Board held two days of public hearings on competitive access issues in April 1998. Following the hearings, the agency issued a decision[1146] that, among other things, directed railroads and shippers to conduct discussions under the supervision of an administrative law judge regarding the interpretation of statutory provisions that empower the agency, where it is in the public interest, to mandate interline routes and rates,[1147] to grant trackage rights in terminals, and direct the switching of customers served by one railroad for the account of another railroad.[1148] In the mid-1980s, the Interstate Commerce Commission had ruled in *Midtec*[1149] that a showing of competitive abuse was a prerequisite for these remedies, and the agency had adopted rules, negotiated between railroad and shipper interests, to the same effect.[1150] Some shipper groups, however, sought a less restrictive approach. The 1998 discussions did not produce agreement, and in December the Surface Transportation Board advised Congress that the "differences between the railroads and the shippers on the Board's competitive access rules are fundamental, and they raise basic policy issues—concerning the appropriate role of competition, differential pricing, and how railroads earn revenues and structure their services—that are more appropriately resolved by Congress than by an administrative agency."[1151] Accordingly, the Surface Transportation Board did not "plan to initiate administrative action" to "revisit the competitive access rules at this time."[1152]

(1982), *aff'd in pertinent part sub nom.* Southern Pac. Transp. Co. v. ICC, 736 F.2d 708, 722-24 (D.C. Cir. 1984) (per curiam), *cert. denied*, 469 U.S. 1208 (1985).

1143. 3 I.C.C.2d 171 (1986), *aff'd sub nom.* Midtec Paper Corp. v. United States, 857 F.2d 1487 (D.C. Cir. 1988).

1144. *Id.* at 181. In a subsequent case, the ICC further clarified its test, indicating that it could impose terminal trackage rights if the railroad "has committed, or appears likely to commit, an act that is contrary to the competition policies of the rail transportation policy or is otherwise anticompetitive." Shenango, Inc. v. Pittsburgh, C & Y Ry., 5 I.C.C.2d 995, 1001 (1989).

1145. 3 I.C.C.2d at 181; *see also* Vista Chem. Co. v. Atchison, T. & S.F. Ry., 5 I.C.C.2d 331 (1989) (reciprocal switching).

1146. Ex Parte No. 575, Review of Rail Access & Competition Issues, Decision served Apr. 17, 1998, 1998 STB LEXIS 104 (1998).

1147. 49 U.S.C. § 10705(a) (Supp. 1999).

1148. *Id.* § 11102(a), (c)(1) (Supp. 1999).

1149. Midtec Paper Corp. v. Chicago & N.W. Transp. Co., 3 I.C.C.2d 171 (1986), *aff'd sub nom.* Midtec Paper Corp. v. United States, 857 F.2d 1487 (D.C. Cir. 1988).

1150. 49 C.F.R. § 1144.5 (2000), *adopted in* Intermodal Rail Competition, 1 I.C.C.2d 822 (1985), *aff'd sub nom.* Baltimore Gas & Elec. Co. v. United States, 817 F.2d 108 (D.C. Cir. 1987).

1151. Letter from Linda J. Morgan, Chairman, Surface Transportation Board, to Sens. McCain & Hutchison (Dec. 21, 1998).

1152. *Id.*

The Surface Transportation Board's April 1998 decision also urged the large and small railroads to seek agreements on points in issue between them, and this subsequently led to an agreement that includes, in addition to certain provisions related to rates, provisions for the relaxation in certain circumstances of contractual "paper barriers" that affect the ability of smaller railroads that were spun off or leased by large railroads to interchange traffic with alternative connections.[1153] The agency decided not to issue further rules relating to these paper barriers until it gained more experience under the 1998 agreement and continued to press the railroads to negotiate.[1154]

Several cases have addressed access issues under traditional antitrust principles. In *Laurel Sand & Gravel, Inc. v. CSX Transportation, Inc.*,[1155] a shipper and its prospective rail carrier filed suit in federal court to obtain trackage rights from CSX through the application of traditional antitrust principles. The plaintiff carrier alleged that CSX's refusal to grant the carrier trackage rights, which precluded the carrier from serving the shipper directly, violated Section 2 of the Sherman Act as a denial by a monopolist of access to an essential facility.[1156] The district court concluded that even if CSX had a monopoly in a relevant market and control of an essential facility, CSX had not violated Section 2 because it had offered reasonable access by means of a joint rate proposal that provided CSX little contribution (revenue in excess of variable costs),[1157] and it had no duty to offer trackage rights as it was not in the track-leasing business.[1158]

In *Delaware & Hudson Railway v. Consolidated Rail Corp.*,[1159] the Delaware & Hudson (D&H) sued Conrail under Section 2 of the Sherman Act alleging monopolization, denial of access to an essential facility, and attempted monopolization. The dispute centered on a "make or buy" policy under which Conrail would agree to participate in a joint rate only if it received the same contribution on the movement as it would have received if it had been the sole carrier. In reversing the district court's grant of summary judgment to Conrail on the monopolization and attempted monopolization claims, the Second Circuit held that there were genuine issues of material fact as to whether the make or buy policy was a legitimate business strategy or a plan willfully to acquire or maintain monopoly power.[1160] The fact that the make or buy policy was profit maximizing for Conrail did not necessarily shield the policy from Section 2.[1161] Similarly, the court held that there were genuine issues of fact as to whether Conrail had denied D&H the use of an essential facility insofar as Conrail's rates under the make or buy policy may have

---

1153. *Id.* at 1-2 & Addendum D.

1154. Ex Parte No. 575, Review of Rail Access and Competition Issues, Decision served Mar. 2, 1999, 1999 STB LEXIS 138 (1999).

1155. 704 F. Supp. 1309 (D. Md. 1989), *aff'd*, 924 F.2d 539 (4th Cir.), *cert. denied*, 502 U.S. 814 (1991).

1156. CSX had proposed a joint rate with the plaintiff rail carrier; however, the joint rate was allegedly too high to allow the plaintiff shipper to compete successfully. The plaintiffs then demanded trackage rights, which CSX refused to grant.

1157. The district court held that the reasonableness of CSX's proposed revenue division in the joint rate must be viewed from CSX's perspective in the rail transportation business rather than in terms of whether the rate allowed the shipper to be competitive in a desired market. 704 F. Supp. at 1323-24.

1158. *Id.* at 1324.

1159. 902 F.2d 174 (2d Cir. 1990), *cert. denied*, 500 U.S. 928 (1991).

1160. *Id.* at 178-79, 180.

1161. *Id.* at 178.

been so unreasonable as to constitute a denial, and whether Conrail possessed monopoly power in the relevant market.[1162]   The court contrasted Conrail's contribution, which had increased eightfold for the shipment in question under the make or buy policy, with the small CSX contribution in *Laurel Sand & Gravel*.[1163]

f.   MERGERS AND ACQUISITIONS

The Surface Transportation Board has exclusive jurisdiction over rail mergers, consolidations, and pooling transactions. Any rail carrier, corporation, or person participating in such a transaction that is approved or exempted by the agency "is exempt from the antitrust laws and from all other law, including State and municipal law, as necessary to let that rail carrier, corporation, or person carry out the transaction, hold, maintain, and operate property, and exercise control or franchises acquired through the transaction."[1164]   Mergers and consolidations of large railroads should be approved if the Surface Transportation Board finds the transaction to be "consistent with the public interest."[1165]   In considering such mergers, the agency must consider whether the transaction would have "an adverse effect on competition among rail carriers in the affected region or in the national rail system."[1166]   In rail merger proceedings not involving two large railroads, the Surface Transportation Board must grant its approval unless it determines that (1) "there is likely to be substantial lessening of competition, creation of a monopoly, or restraint of trade in freight surface transportation in any region of the United States; and (2) the anticompetitive effects of the transaction outweigh the public interest in meeting significant transportation needs."[1167]

Since enactment of the Staggers Rail Act in 1980, the Interstate Commerce Commission and the Surface Transportation Board have reviewed numerous important railroad mergers and consolidations. In a number of these cases,[1168] the

---

1162. *Id.* at 179-80.

1163. *Id.* at 180.

1164. 49 U.S.C. § 11321(a) (Supp. 1999).

1165. *Id.* § 11324(c) (Supp. 1999); *see* United States v. ICC, 396 U.S. 491, 508-13 (1970); Seaboard Air Line R.R. v. United States, 382 U.S. 154, 156-57 (1965) (per curiam); Minneapolis & St. L. Ry. v. United States, 361 U.S. 173, 186-88 (1959); Southern Pac. Transp. Co. v. ICC, 736 F.2d 708, 715-17 (D.C. Cir. 1984) (per curiam), *cert. denied*, 469 U.S. 1208 (1985); Missouri-Kansas-Texas R.R. v. United States, 632 F.2d 392, 395 (5th Cir. 1980), *cert. denied*, 451 U.S. 1017 (1981). In enacting the ICCTA, Congress rejected proposals to subject rail mergers to review under the antitrust laws or to change the public interest standard to one giving greater weight to competitive impacts and to accord the DOJ greater influence in the review process. *See, e.g.*, 141 CONG. REC. 34,563-69, 34,575 (1995).

1166. 49 U.S.C. § 11324(b)(5) (Supp. 1999).

1167. *Id.* § 11324(d) (Supp. 1999); *see* Illinois v. ICC, 687 F.2d 1047 (7th Cir. 1982).

1168. *See, e.g.*, Burlington N., Inc., & Burlington N. R.R.—Control & Merger—Santa Fe Pac. Corp. & Atchison, T. & S.F. Ry., 10 I.C.C.2d 661, 762-63, 771 (1995), *aff'd sub nom.* Western Resources, Inc. v. STB, 109 F.3d 782 (D.C. Cir. 1997); Union Pac. Corp., Union Pac. R.R. & Missouri Pac. R.R.—Control—Missouri-Kansas-Texas R.R., 4 I.C.C.2d 409, 437 (1988), *petition for review dismissed sub nom.* Railway Labor Executives Ass'n v. ICC, 883 F.2d 1079 (D.C. Cir. 1989); Chicago, M., St. P. & Pac. R.R.—Reorganization—Acquisition by Grand Trunk Corp., 2 I.C.C.2d 161 (1984), 2 I.C.C.2d 427 (1985), *appeal dismissed sub nom. In re* Chicago, M, St. P. & Pac. R.R., 799 F.2d 317 (7th Cir. 1986), *cert. denied*, 481 U.S. 1068 (1987); Union Pac. Corp., Pacific Rail Sys. & Union Pac. R.R.—Control—Missouri Pac. Corp. & Missouri Pac. R.R., 366 I.C.C. 459, 562-65 (1982), *aff'd in pertinent part sub nom.* Southern Pac. Transp. Co. v. ICC, 736 F.2d 708, 722-24 (D.C. Cir. 1984) (per curiam), *cert. denied*, 469 U.S. 1208 (1985).

agency exercised its statutory authority to condition its approval on the applicant railroads' acceptance of certain measures, such as trackage rights for other carriers, designed to alleviate potential adverse competitive effects of the transactions.[1169] In several cases, the consolidating railroads arranged settlements with other rail carriers and shippers, which the agency approved with or without modification as addressing competitive issues.[1170] The agency generally will not impose conditions requested by other rail carriers and shippers in lieu of settlement agreement provisions that adequately address the same potential adverse competitive effects of the proposed merger.[1171]

In one case, a proposed merger had too many competitive problems to allow even conditional approval. In *Santa Fe Southern Pacific Corp.—Control—Southern Pacific Transportation Co.*,[1172] the Interstate Commerce Commission rejected the proposed acquisition, concluding that the merger of the two railroads—whose rail lines were the only alternatives for significant long-haul traffic flows—would have significantly adverse effects on rail competition, that the potential public benefits of the transaction did not outweigh these anticompetitive effects, and that the poor financial health of one of the merging railroads did not justify approval of the transaction. The agency ordered the applicant holding company to divest itself of one of the two railroads, which had been operated separately during the pendency of the agency proceedings under an independent voting trust.[1173]

The late 1990s saw a series of rail mergers that resulted in significant industry consolidation. In August 1996, the Surface Transportation Board approved the merger of Union Pacific and Southern Pacific, reducing the number of major railroads in the West from three to two.[1174] The applicants entered into settlement agreements with their major competitor and a shipper group, the Chemical Manufacturers Association, that granted the competitor more than 4,000 miles of

---

1169. The ICCTA clarified that conditions can include line divestitures as well as awards of trackage rights and provided that conditions aimed at alleviating anticompetitive effects "shall provide for operating terms and compensation levels to ensure that such effects are alleviated." 49 U.S.C. § 11324(c) (Supp. 1999).

1170. *See, e.g.*, Burlington N., Inc., & Burlington N.R.R.—Control & Merger—Santa Fe Pac. Corp. & Atchison, T. & S.F. Ry., 10 I.C.C.2d 661, 761-68 (1995), *aff'd sub nom.* Western Resources, Inc. v. STB, 109 F.3d 782 (D.C. Cir. 1997); Union Pac. Corp., Union Pac. R.R. & Missouri Pac. R.R.—Control—Missouri-Kansas-Texas R.R., 4 I.C.C.2d 409, 417, 468, 480-83 (1988), *petition for review dismissed sub nom.* Railway Labor Executives Ass'n v. ICC, 883 F.2d 1079 (D.C. Cir. 1989).

1171. *See, e.g.*, Burlington N., Inc., & Burlington N. R.R.—Control & Merger—Santa Fe Pac. Corp. & Atchison, T. & S.F. Ry., 10 I.C.C.2d 661, 745-46 (1995), *aff'd sub nom.* Western Resources, Inc. v. STB, 109 F.3d 782 (D.C. Cir. 1997); Union Pac. Corp., Union Pac. R.R. & Missouri Pac. R.R.—Control—Missouri-Kansas-Texas R.R., 4 I.C.C.2d 409, 471-72 (1988), *petition for review dismissed sub nom.* Railway Labor Executives Ass'n v. ICC, 883 F.2d 1079 (D.C. Cir. 1989).

1172. 2 I.C.C.2d 709 (1986), *petition to reopen denied*, 3 I.C.C.2d 926 (1987).

1173. There were indications that the trust had been mishandled and the beneficial owner had improperly been allowed to influence operations of the trusteed railroad. Finance Dkt. No. 30400, Santa Fe S. Pac. Corp.—Control—Southern Pac. Transp. Co., Decision served Feb. 24, 1987. The ICC subsequently approved a plan of divestiture calling for the sale of Southern Pacific to another rail carrier. *See* Rio Grande Indus., SPTC Holding, Inc., & Denver & R.G.W.R.R.—Control—Southern Pac. Transp. Co., 4 I.C.C.2d 834 (1988), *aff'd sub nom.* Kansas City S. Indus. v. ICC, 902 F.2d 423 (5th Cir. 1990).

1174. Union Pac. Corp., Union Pac. R.R. & Missouri Pac. R.R.— Control & Merger—Southern Pac. Rail Corp., Southern Pac. Transp. Co., St. Louis Southwestern Ry., SPCSL Corp., & Denver & R.G.W.R.R., 1 S.T.B. 233 (1996), *aff'd sub nom.* Western Coal Traffic League v. STB, 169 F.3d 775 (D.C. Cir. 1999).

trackage rights and line sales.[1175]   The agency imposed additional conditions to preserve competition for shippers who would have lost rail competition but found that there would not be any significant reduction in competition for traffic that went from three railroad options to two.[1176] In this connection, the Surface Transportation Board found that there was no persuasive evidence that two railroads would tacitly collude to raise rates or degrade service.[1177]

In July 1998, the Surface Transportation Board approved the acquisition of Conrail by CSX and Norfolk Southern, reducing the number of major rail systems in the eastern United States from three to two.[1178] The agency's decision for the most part adhered to its long-standing policy of limiting competitive conditions in merger cases to those necessary to protect particular shippers or locations against the elimination of competition, and of declining to add competition.   However, the transaction that the parties had negotiated as the resolution of a takeover contest created new rail competition at several locations, including northern New Jersey, southern New Jersey/Philadelphia, and Detroit. The Surface Transportation Board imposed limited additional conditions aimed at restoring competition in New York that was lost when Conrail has been created in the 1970s. The agency took steps to ensure that the additional competition it anticipated from the transaction would be achieved by overriding "requirements" provisions of a long-term intermodal contract between Conrail and an intermodal subsidiary of CSX because it believed that the provisions would impede full competition in the Chicago-Northern New Jersey corridor.[1179]

In May 1999, the Surface Transportation Board approved Canadian National Railway's acquisition of Illinois Central.[1180] The decision endorsed the potential efficiency benefits of end-to-end railroad mergers that are not achievable through means short of merger. As it had in the past, the agency rejected requests for conditions based on asserted competitive harm that appeared to the agency to lack a causal connection to the merger or that were based on assertions that the merged railroad would foreclose shippers from access to more efficient interline routes by closing internal gateways.[1181]

1175. 1 S.T.B. at 252-55.

1176. *Id.* at 387-93.

1177. *Id.* at 570-75.

1178. Finance Dkt. No. 33388, CSX Corp. & CSX Transp., Inc.,—Norfolk S. Corp. & Norfolk S. Ry.— Control & Operating Leases/Agreements—Conrail, Inc., & Consolidated Rail Corp., Decision No. 89, served July 23, 1998, 1998 STB LEXIS 243 (1998). *See also* Decision No. 96, served Oct. 19, 1998, 1998 STB LEXIS 800 (1998) (resolving petitions for reconsideration).

1179. Decision No. 110, served Dec. 22, 1998, 1998 STB LEXIS 997, at *7-11 (1998), slip op. at 4-5. The agency also rejected proposals by CSX for compensation to be paid by Canadian Pacific for exercise of the "east-of-the-Hudson" trackage rights the STB had awarded to restore to New York City some of the rail competition that had been lost when Conrail was created. *Id.* Decision No. 109, served Dec. 18, 1998, 1998 STB LEXIS 981, at *11-13 (1998), slip op. at 6. In a subsequent decision, the STB revised trackage rights charges for Canadian Pacific's exercise of these rights. Decision No. 123, served May 20, 1999, 1999 STB LEXIS 297 (1999).

1180. Finance Dkt. No. 33556, Canadian Nat'l Ry., Grand Trunk Corp., & Grand Trunk W. R.R.— Control—Illinois Cent. Corp., Illinois Cent. R.R., Chicago, C. & P.R.R., & Cedar River R.R., Decision No. 37, served May 25, 1999, 1999 STB LEXIS 305 (1999).

1181. *Id.*, at *80-90, slip op. at 36-39. The STB also rejected an application filed by Kansas City Southern and an affiliate seeking terminal trackage rights near Springfield, Illinois, or in the alternative an override of restrictions in the subsidiary's existing trackage rights. Noting that the requested rights were not aimed at remedying anticompetitive effects of the merger or filling gaps in a consolidated Canadian National/Illinois Central system, the STB held that it lacked

In December 1999, the largest Canadian railroad, Canadian National, proposed to combine with Burlington Northern Santa Fe to form the largest North American railroad. This proposal resulted in the most sweeping reconsideration of rail merger policy since passage of the Staggers Rail Act in 1980. Following extensive hearings, the Surface Transportation Board imposed a fifteen-month moratorium on acceptance of applications for consolidation of large railroads.[1182] Acknowledging that its action was "unprecedented," the agency concluded that "mere consideration of any major merger now would likely generate responsive proposals that, if approved, could result in a North American duopoly."[1183] It decided that its merger rules and policies were outdated and unsuited for another round of major railroad mergers.

The Surface Transportation Board simultaneously instituted a fifteen-month rulemaking proceeding to revise those rules and policies[1184] and then promulgated new rules for such mergers in 2001.[1185] The new rules raise the threshold for approval of consolidations of Class I railroads and give the agency broader discretion to craft remedies in future proceedings. Citing concerns that future mergers may adversely affect competition in ways that the agency cannot easily remedy and that may disrupt rail service, the rules counsel applicants that they "should include provisions for enhanced competition."[1186] The Surface Transportation Board indicated that it will give substantial weight to competitive enhancements, such as creating new competition in terminal areas and new connections for smaller railroads.[1187] The agency also warned that it will not favor consolidations that reduce transportation alternatives, suggesting that it may preserve competitive options—such as three-carrier service to a shipper or city—that prior decisions did not preserve. Merger applicants must show how they will preserve major interline routes and opportunities for shippers to challenge bottleneck rates.[1188] Applicants must

---

jurisdiction to grant the requested relief because it was not necessary to carry out the merger. *Id.*, at *120-22, slip op. at 53.

1182. Ex Parte No. 582, Public Views on Major Rail Consolidations, Decision served Mar. 17, 2000, 2000 STB LEXIS 143 (2000). Shortly before imposing the moratorium, the STB allowed two systems of shortline railroads to join under common ownership. Agreeing with the applicants that the combination would not affect operations of the individual railroads or adversely affect rail competition, the STB authorized RailAmerica, Inc. to exercise control over the RailTex family of railroads. Finance Dkt. No. 33813, RailAmerica Inc.—Control Exception—RailTex, Inc., Decison served Jan. 10, 2000, 2000 STB LEXIS 9 (2000).

1183. Ex Parte No. 582, Public Views on Major Rail Consolidations, Decision served Mar. 17, 2000, 2000 STB LEXIS 143, at *16, *23 (2000), slip op. at 7, 10. A divided D.C. Circuit upheld the moratorium, ruling that the STB had sufficient statutory authority to impose the freeze and that its decision "reasonably interpreted the relevant statutes to accommodate a moratorium where necessary to carry out its duties to preserve competition and carry out the public interest." Western Coal Traffic League v. STB, 216 F.3d 1168, 1175 (D.C. Cir. 2000).

1184. Ex Parte No. 582 (Sub-No. 1), Major Rail Consolidation Procedures, Decision served Mar. 31, 2000, 2000 STB LEXIS 171 (2000).

1185. Ex Parte No. 582 (Sub-No. 1), Major Rail Consolidation Procedures, Decision served June 11, 2001, 2001 STB LEXIS 546 (2001). The STB determined that a potential transaction involving the smallest of the Class I railroads and another Class I carrier might not raise the same concerns and risks as would other potential mergers. It decided that proposals involving that railroad would be subject to the rules previously in effect unless the STB was persuaded to change its view in a particular case. 2001 STB LEXIS 546, at *26-28, slip op. at 15-16.

1186. *Id.* at *29, slip op. at 16.

1187. *Id.* at *32, slip op. at 17.

1188. *Id.* at *48-56, slip op. at 23-26.

evaluate the cumulative effects of their merger and "others like it" on the "evolving structure of the industry."[1189]

The Surface Transportation Board also adopted a "skeptical" attitude toward claims that mergers of Class I railroads generate public benefits.[1190] If benefits can be achieved without consolidation, the agency may discount them as benefits of the merger.[1191] The agency also announced its intention to impose conditions on merging parties in order to protect any element of the public interest, not merely to prevent loss of competition.[1192] Furthermore, because rail service temporarily declined after several recent mergers, the new rules require elaborate planning for and reporting on merger implementation. The Surface Transportation Board requires applicants to define a protocol for resolving claims of poor service, strongly recommending arbitration for such claims.[1193] If a merged carrier unreasonably fails to achieve projected benefits, the agency may require additional measures to remedy the failure.[1194]

The Surface Transportation Board also modified its treatment of voting trusts in rail mergers. Under the prior rules, one railroad could acquire a controlling interest in another before obtaining agency approval by placing the carrier's stock in a voting trust. The agency staff informally reviewed the trust agreement to ensure that it prevented unlawful control. Under the new rules, applicants must submit a proposed voting trust for review and comment by interested parties.[1195] The Surface Transportation Board expressed concern that the acquirer may no longer be able to divest the stock because the industry has become so concentrated.[1196]

g. INTERLOCKING DIRECTORATES

Common carriers, including railroads, are subject under Section 8 of the Clayton Act[1197] to the same interlock standards as other businesses. The Interstate Commerce Act also provides for Surface Transportation Board approval of director or officer interlocks between certain rail carriers.[1198] The agency has exempted all interlocks save those between large railroads.[1199]

3. Air Transportation

a. REGULATORY HISTORY AND FRAMEWORK

From 1938 to 1978, air carriers and foreign air carriers[1200] were subject to extensive regulation pursuant to the Civil Aeronautics Act of 1938 and the Federal

---

1189. *Id.* at *99-100, slip op. at 44.
1190. *Id.* at *20, slip op. at 12.
1191. *Id.* at *41-42, slip op. at 21.
1192. *Id.* at *66-68, slip op. at 30-31.
1193. *Id.* at *89-95, slip op. at 40-42.
1194. *Id.* at *43-48, slip op. at 21-23.
1195. *Id.* at * 61-62, *117-18, slip op. at 28, 51.
1196. *Id.* at *63-64, slip op. at 29.
1197. 15 U.S.C. § 19 (2000); *see* part G of Chapter III.
1198. 49 U.S.C. § 11328 (Supp. 1999).
1199. Revision of Regulations for Interlocking Rail Officers, 1 S.T.B. 1087 (1996).
1200. "Air carrier" means "a citizen of the United States undertaking by any means, directly or indirectly, to provide air transportation." 49 U.S.C. § 40102(2) (1994). "Foreign air carrier"

Aviation Act of 1958 (Aviation Act).[1201] The regulatory scheme was administered by the Civil Aeronautics Board, which had broad powers to regulate entry and exit;[1202] rates;[1203] consolidations, mergers, and acquisitions of control;[1204] interlocking relationships;[1205] methods of competition;[1206] and agreements among carriers.[1207]

The passage of the Airline Deregulation Act of 1978[1208] set in motion a continuing reduction in regulation of the industry. The Civil Aeronautics Board was terminated altogether on January 1, 1985, at which point the Department of Transportation took over the regulatory tasks that remained.[1209] As of 2001, the Department of Transportation had continuing regulatory responsibility in three principal areas.

First, the agency has the authority to approve and, in certain cases, to grant antitrust immunity to agreements between U.S. and foreign carriers.[1210] The Department of Transportation may approve such an agreement even when it substantially reduces or eliminates competition, so long as it finds that the agreement is necessary to meet a serious transportation need or to achieve important public benefits (which include foreign policy considerations). As discussed below, the agency has exercised this authority to promote "open skies" treaties between the United States and foreign countries that significantly reduce the regulation of international air transportation.

Second, the Department of Transportation has the authority purusant to Section 41712 to enjoin unfair or deceptive practices or methods of competition in the air transportation industry, both domestically and internationally:

> On the initiative of the Secretary of Transportation or the complaint of an air carrier, foreign air carrier, or travel agent, and if the Secretary considers it is in the public interest, the Secretary may investigate and decide whether an air carrier, foreign air carrier, or travel agent has been or is engaged in an unfair or deceptive practice or an unfair method of competition in air transportation or the sale of air transportation.[1211]

The Supreme Court has held that this provision is "modeled closely after § 5 of the Federal Trade Commission Act" and one "may profitably look to judicial

---

means "a person, not a citizen of the United States, undertaking by any means, directly or indirectly, to provide foreign air transportation." *Id.* § 40102(21) (1994).

1201. The Civil Aeronautics Act of 1938, 49 U.S.C. §§ 401-403, was repealed by the Federal Aviation Act, 49 U.S.C. App. §§ 1301-1387. In 1994, the Federal Aviation Act was recodified under Subtitle VII of Title 49, U.S. Code.

1202. 49 U.S.C. §§ 41101-41112 (1994 & Supp. 1999), *amended by* Pub. L. No. 106-181, 114 Stat. 165, 3267 (2000), Pub. L. No. 106-528, 114 Stat. 2522 (2000), Pub. L. No. 106-398, 114 Stat. 129-30, 1654 (2000); *see also* 49 U.S.C. §§ 41301-41310 (relating to foreign air carriers).

1203. 49 U.S.C. §§ 41501-41511 (1994 & Supp. 1999).

1204. *Id.* § 1378 (repealed by Pub. L. No. 103-272, § 7(b), 108 Stat. 1379) (1994)).

1205. *Id.* § 1379 (repealed by Pub. L. No. 103-272, § 7(b), 108 Stat. 1379) (1994)).

1206. *Id.* § 41712 (1994), amended by Pub. L. No. 106-181, 114 Stat. 102 (2000).

1207. *Id.* §§ 41309 (1994 & Supp. 1999), 42111 (1994).

1208. Pub. L. No. 95-504, 92 Stat. 1705 (1978).

1209. DOT authority initially included the power to regulate consolidations, mergers, and acquisitions of control, interlocking relationships, and agreements among carriers. On January 1, 1989, the DOT lost its power to approve mergers and interlocking relationships relating solely to domestic air transportation.

1210. 49 U.S.C. § 41308 (1994).

1211. *Id.* § 41712 (1994). This provision is unchanged from the authority previously held by the Civil Aeronautics Board (CAB).

interpretation of § 5 as an aid in the resolution of questions" presented under it.[1212] Department of Transportation authority in this area includes the exercise of rulemaking powers.[1213] Agency regulations promulgated pursuant to this provision govern oversales by air carriers,[1214] disclosure of the terms of air carriers' contracts of carriage with passengers,[1215] limitations on domestic baggage liability,[1216] the display of code-sharing arrangements in computer reservation systems (CRSs),[1217] and certain aspects of CRS operations by airline CRS owners.[1218] Air carriers are exempt from the jurisdiction of the Federal Trade Commission.[1219]

Third, the Department of Transportation has the authority to review certain "joint venture agreements."[1220] Carriers are required to submit any such proposed agreements to the Department of Transportation at least thirty days before the agreement may take effect. The agency may extend the waiting period by up to 150 days for code-sharing agreements, and by up to sixty days for other agreements. The agency also may require that other documents be submitted by major airlines desiring to enter into joint venture agreements.

In order to preserve the benefits of the deregulated, competition-driven regime inaugurated by the Airline Deregulation Act of 1978 (ADA), Congress included a preemption section preventing state and local governments from imposing their own economic regulations and policies on the airline industry to fill the regulatory voids resulting from deregulation at the federal level. Section 105(a) of the ADA, as re-codified in 1994, specifies:

> Except as provided in this subsection, a State, political subdivision of a State, or political authority of at least 2 States may not enact or enforce a law, regulation, or other provision having the force and effect of law related to a price, route, or service of an air carrier that may provide air transportation under this subpart.[1221]

This section has been held to preempt claims against an airline that relate to its fares, routes, or services and are based on state antitrust statutes, unfair business practice or consumer protection statutes, or common-law business torts.[1222] In

---

1212. American Airlines, Inc. v. North Am. Airlines, Inc., 351 U.S. 79, 82 (1956); *see also* Pan Am. World Airways v. United States, 371 U.S. 296, 303, 306-07 (1963) (relying on FTC Act § 5 precedent to interpret § 411 of the Civil Aeronautics Act); United Air Lines, Inc. v. CAB, 766 F.2d 1107, 1112 (7th Cir. 1985) (although the language of FTC Act § 5 and § 411 "is not identical, none of the differences seems deliberate, much less material").

1213. 49 U.S.C. § 40113(a) (1994).

1214. 14 C.F.R. pt. 250 (2001).

1215. *Id.* pt. 253 (2001).

1216. *Id.* pt. 254 (2001).

1217. *Id.* pt. 256 (2001).

1218. *Id.* pt. 255 (2001).

1219. 15 U.S.C. §§ 45(a)(2), 46(a), (b) (2000).

1220. 49 U.S.C. § 41720(a)(1) (Supp. 1999), *amended by* Pub. L. No. 106-181, 114 Stat. 108, 159 (2000), defines a "joint venture agreement" as "an agreement between two or more major carriers on or after January 1, 1998, with regard to (A) code-sharing, blocked-space arrangements, long-term wet leases . . . of aircraft, or frequent flyer programs; or (B) any other cooperative working arrangements between 2 or more major carriers that affects more than 15% of the total number of available seat miles offered by the major carriers."

1221. *Id.* § 41713(b)(1) (Supp. 1999). An exception is made for certain intrastate air transportation in Alaska. *Id.* § 41713(b)(2) (Supp. 1999).

1222. *See, e.g.*, Virgin Atl. Airways Ltd. v. British Airways PLC, 872 F. Supp. 52 (S.D.N.Y. 1994) (common-law unfair competition, tortious interference with contractual relations, and tortious

Morales v. Trans World Airlines, Inc.,[1223] the Supreme Court held that this section preempts the states from prohibiting allegedly deceptive airline fare advertisements through enforcement of their general consumer protection statutes. At issue were guidelines adopted by the National Association of Attorneys General containing detailed standards governing the content and format of airline advertising, the awarding of premiums to regular customers, and the payment of compensation to passengers who voluntarily surrender seats on an overbooked flight.

The *Morales* Court determined that the fare advertising provisions of these guidelines "obviously" related to airline fares.[1224] Accordingly, it held that enforcement of those provisions was preempted by the ADA.[1225] The Court rebuffed the argument that it was "set[ting] out on a road that leads to pre-emption of state laws against gambling and prostitution as applied to airlines."[1226] Instead, quoting *Shaw v. Delta Air Lines, Inc.,*[1227] the *Morales* Court left open the possibility that "'[s]ome state actions may affect [airline fares] in too tenuous, remote, or peripheral a manner' to have pre-emptive effect."[1228] Since *Morales*, courts generally have held state antitrust claims and state tortious interference with contract claims to be preempted.[1229]

Most courts have held, however, that the ADA does not preempt personal injury claims arising from air carrier "services" as opposed to air carrier "operations and maintenance."[1230] In addition, the ADA does not preempt breach of contract claims against an airline, even though the claims relate to its fares, routes, or services, where the airline has voluntarily assumed the contractual obligations it is alleged to have breached. In *American Airlines, Inc. v. Wolens,*[1231] participants in American's frequent flyer program brought a state court action challenging retroactive imposition of changes to the terms and conditions applicable to the program. The plaintiffs alleged that the changes violated the Illinois Consumer Fraud and Deceptive Practices Act and constituted a breach of contract. Rejecting American's argument

---

interference with prospective business relations claims preempted in suit alleging that defendant engaged in "dirty tricks" and other predatory conduct to eliminate competition from plaintiff in transatlantic air transportation market); Continental Airlines, Inc. v. American Airlines, Inc., 824 F. Supp. 689 (S.D. Tex. 1993) (common-law tortious interference with business relations and common-law unfair competition claims preempted in suit alleging predatory pricing); Frontier Airlines, Inc. v. United Air Lines, Inc., 758 F. Supp. 1399 (D. Colo. 1989) (claims under state antitrust and unfair practices statutes preempted in suit alleging monopolistic conduct relating to computer reservation system practices).

1223. 504 U.S. 374 (1992).
1224. *Id.* at 387.
1225. *Id.* at 392.
1226. *Id.* at 391.
1227. 463 U.S. 85, 100 n.21 (1983).
1228. 504 U.S. at 392.
1229. *See, e.g.,* Continental Airlines, Inc. v. United Air Lines, Inc., 120 F. Supp. 2d 556 (E.D. Va. 2000) (ADA preempted all state law claims for damages caused by agreement among multiple airlines to restrict the size of carry-on baggage at Dulles Airport).
1230. *See, e.g.,* Gee v. Southwest Airlines Co., 110 F.3d 1400, 1406-07 (9th Cir.) (suits for emotional distress allegedly caused by racial slurs uttered by intoxicated passengers who had been served alcoholic beverages and for failure to provide requested disability assistance were preempted, while suits for injuries allegedly sustained from swinging service cart door and suitcase falling from overhead bin were not preempted), *cert. denied,* 522 U.S. 915 (1997); Hodges v. Delta Air Lines, Inc., 44 F.3d 334 (5th Cir. 1995) (common-law negligence claim not preempted in personal injury suit against airline).
1231. 513 U.S. 219 (1995).

that the claims were preempted by the ADA, the Illinois Supreme Court held that they were not preempted because they were only tangentially or tenuously related to rates, routes, and services.[1232] The Supreme Court granted certiorari and reversed as to the claims under the state statute. The Court held that the Illinois Act

> serves as a means to guide and police the marketing practices of the airlines. . . . In light of the full text of the preemption clause, and of the ADA's purpose to leave largely to the airlines themselves, and not at all to the states, the selection and design of marketing mechanisms appropriate to the furnishing of air transportation services, we conclude that [the preemption clause] preempts plaintiffs' claims under the Illinois Consumer Fraud Act.[1233]

As to the plaintiffs' contract claims, however, the *Wolens* Court found no preemption. The Court distinguished between claims based on "state-imposed obligations," such as the Illinois consumer fraud statute, and claims based on obligations the airlines had voluntarily imposed on themselves through contract. "[T]erms and conditions airlines offer and passengers accept," the Court wrote, "are privately ordered obligations and thus do not amount to a State's 'enactment or enforcement [of] any law, rule, regulation, standard, or other provision having the force and effect of law' within the meaning of [the preemption clause]."[1234]

The ADA also expressly recognizes that airport proprietors, which are often municipalities, need the ability to address local issues and problems arising at and around their facilities. Thus, the ADA provides that its preemptive provision does not "limit a State, political subdivision of a State, or political authority of at least 2 States that owns or operates an airport . . . from carrying out its proprietary powers and rights."[1235] Courts generally have construed this proviso narrowly. In *American Airlines, Inc. v. DOT*,[1236] the Fifth Circuit held that local bond ordinances, which as enforced restricted the perimeter that could be served from Dallas Love Field, were not within the city of Dallas's proprietary powers because the reallocation of flights between Dallas Love Field and Dallas/Fort Worth International Airport was not a permissible goal, and the city of Dallas had not articulated another purpose for the regulation, such as relieving congestion at Dallas Love Field.[1237] Thus, although courts have held that airport owners and operators may enact regulations aimed at reducing noise, environmental concerns, and congestion, such regulations must be "reasonable, nonarbitrary, and nondiscriminatory rules that advance the local interest."[1238]

1232. American Airlines, Inc. v. Wolens, 626 N.E.2d 205, 208 (Ill. 1993).
1233. 513 U.S. at 229; *see also* Leonard v. Northwest Airlines, Inc., 605 N.W.2d 425 (Minn. Ct. App.) (state law breach of contract and unjust enrichment challenges to $75 ticket reissuance fee preempted), *cert. denied*, 531 U.S. 876 (2000).
1234. 513 U.S. at 228-29 (quoting amicus brief filed by United States).
1235. 49 U.S.C. § 41713(b)(3) (Supp. 1999).
1236. 202 F.3d 788 (5th Cir.), *cert. denied*, 530 U.S. 1284 (2000).
1237. The Fifth Circuit distinguished *Western Air Lines v. Port Auth. of New York and New Jersey*, 658 F. Supp. 952, 958 (S.D.N.Y. 1986) (upholding Port Authority 1,500 mile perimeter rule for New York LaGuardia Airport), on the grounds that a perimeter rule could be a reasonable means for alleviating congestion. 202 F.3d at 806-07. The Fifth Circuit criticized, and distinguished on factual grounds, *Arapahoe County Pub. Airport v. Centennial Express Airlines, Inc.*, 956 P.2d 587 (Colo. 1998) (upholding absolute ban on scheduled passenger service at Centennial Airport). 202 F.3d at 807.
1238. *Western Air Lines*, 658 F. Supp. at 958.

b.   MERGERS, ACQUISITIONS, AND JOINT VENTURES

(1) Airline Mergers and Acquisitions

While it held antitrust authority over the airline industry, the Civil Aeronautics Board decided a number of domestic consolidation and merger cases.[1239] In some cases it declined to exercise its discretion to grant antitrust immunity,[1240] and rather than relying exclusively on market share statistics as an indication of the potential effect of the transaction, it analyzed possible barriers to entry to determine whether a proposed acquisition "would substantially inhibit actual competition or the ability of potential entrants to respond to any attempt to exercise market power 'by decreasing service or raising fares above competitive levels in any relevant market.'"[1241]

Once vested with antitrust authority for the airline industry, the Department of Transportation considered a number of substantial transactions, issuing thirteen final orders approving twelve proposed mergers or acquisitions.[1242] Three applications were withdrawn.[1243] The Department of Transportation emphasized the competitive impact aspect of its jurisdiction, and did not approve any proposed merger on the ground that, although anticompetitive, it nevertheless met transportation needs and

---

1239. *See, e.g.*, Texas Int'l-Continental Acquisition Case, Order 81-10-66 (1981); Continental-Western Merger Case, Order 81-6-1/2 (1981); Republic-Airwest Acquisition Case, Order 80-9-65 (1980); Tiger Int'l-Seaboard World Acquisition Case, Order 80-7-20 (1980); Eastern-National Acquisition Case, Order 79-12-163/164/165 (1979); Continental-Western Merger Case, Order 79-9-185 (1979); North Central-Southern Merger Case, Order 79-6-6/8 (1979).

1240. *See, e.g.*, Texas Int'l-National and Pan American-National Acquisition Case, Order 79-12-163/164/165, at 75 (1979).

1241. Texas Int'l-Continental, Order 81-10-66, at 5 (citing Texas Int'l-National and Pan American-National); Continental-Western, Order 81-6-1/2, at 3-5. Although these decisions do not use the term "contestability," the quoted formulation of the CAB's test for antitrust analysis captures the essence of the contestability theory. In general, contestability theory examines the ease of "entry and exit in city pair markets" and the effect of "incumbents' fear of entry by other carriers" on fare levels. *See* Joint Application of Texas Air Corp. and People Express, Inc., Order 86-10-53, at 14, 1986 DOT Av. LEXIS 240 (1986).

1242. DOT review of mergers generally focused on transactions involving two large aircraft, scheduled passenger air carriers. *See* USAir's acquisition of Piedmont, Order 87-10-58, 1987 DOT Av. LEXIS 164 (1987); American Airlines's acquisition of AirCal, Order 87-3-8, 1987 DOT Av. LEXIS 792 (1987); USAir's acquisition of Pacific Southwest Airlines, Order 87-3-11, 1987 DOT Av. LEXIS 869 (1987); Texas Air's acquisition of People Express and Frontier, Order 86-10-53, 1986 DOT Av. LEXIS 240 (1986); Texas Air's acquisition of Eastern Air Lines, Order 86-10-2, 1986 DOT Av. LEXIS 287 (1986) (earlier, in Order 86-8-77, DOT had found that this proposed merger was likely to substantially reduce competition in the Washington-New York and New York-Boston shuttle markets, but rescinded its initial disapproval when Texas Air agreed to transfer enough additional slots to Pan Am to enable it to provide effective competition in those markets); Trans World Airlines's acquisition of Ozark Airlines, Order 86-9-29, 1986 DOT Av. LEXIS 414 (1986); Northwest Airlines's acquisition of Republic Airlines, Order 86-7-81, 1986 DOT Av. LEXIS 542 (1986); Horizon's acquisition of Cascade, Order 86-1-67, 1986 DOT Av. LEXIS 1055 (1986); Piedmont Aviation's acquisition of Empire Airlines, Order 86-1-45, 1986 DOT Av. LEXIS 1088 (1986); United Airlines's acquisition of Pan American World Airways's Int'l Pac. Operations, Order 85-11-67 (1985); Southwest Airlines's acquisition of Muse Air, Order 85-6-79 (1985); Midway's acquisition of Air Florida, Order 85-6-33 (1985). Section 408 exemptions granted by the DOT included approval for USAir's acquisition of Pennsylvania Commuter Airlines (Order 85-5-115 (1985)) and approval for Alaska Air Group's acquisition of Horizon Air (Order 86-12-61 (1986)).

1243. Texas Air's proposed acquisition of Trans World Airlines, Dkt. No. 43224; Texas Air Corp.'s proposed acquisition of Frontier Airlines, Dkt. No. 43413; TWA's proposed acquisition of USAir, Dkt. Nos. 44715, 44722.

secured public benefits that could not be met or obtained by any reasonably available, less anticompetitive transaction.[1244]

After the expiration of the Department of Transportation's authority over mergers and acquisitions,[1245] the Department of Justice assumed responsibility for reviewing mergers and acquisitions between domestic carriers.[1246] Initially, the Department of Justice focused its analysis on the impact of a proposed merger on national concentration levels.[1247] Since the early 1990s, however, the Department of Justice has focused on the competitive effects of a proposed transaction on individual city pairs, or on airlines' holdings or control of key assets.

In 1991, the Department of Justice announced that it would file a civil antitrust suit alleging that the proposed sale by Eastern Air Lines to United Air Lines of slots and gates at Washington National Airport would violate Section 1 of the Sherman Act by lessening competition in the provision of airline passenger service between Washington, D.C. and other U.S. cities.[1248] It observed that after Eastern's shutdown, United, through its hub at Dulles International Airport, and USAir, the largest carrier at Washington National, were the only carriers with nonstop service from Washington to many other cities. Moreover, "without a sufficiently large number of slots at National, it would be unlikely for another carrier to compete with United and USAir in many of these markets."[1249]

In 1998, Northwest Airlines announced its intention to acquire a controlling interest in Continental Airlines and to form a strategic alliance with Continental in which Northwest and Continental would code share on each other's flights and

1244. This ground for approval was set forth in 49 U.S.C. App. § 1378(b)(1)(B) (repealed by Pub. L. No. 103-272, § 7(b), 108 Stat. 1379 (1988)). The DOT did not grant antitrust immunity to any of the transactions it approved.

1245. *See supra* note 1209. Competitive issues are still raised in proceedings before the DOT under former § 401 of the Aviation Act, which includes provisions on transfers of certificates and continuing fitness. 49 U.S.C. App. § 1371 (1988). In addition, the DOT has cited competitive concerns in connection with the award of exemption slots for service to certain highly congested airports that are subject to the High Density Rule. *See* 49 U.S.C. §§ 41714, 41715, 41718 (Supp. 1999), *amended by* Pub. L. No. 106-181, 114 Stat. 106, 109, 112 (2000)); 14 C.F.R. §§ 93.121-.133 (2001); *see also* Order 2000-7-1, 2000 DOT Av. LEXIS 335 (July 4, 2000) (criteria for exemption to High Density Rule at Washington Reagan National Airport include increasing competition); Order 97-10-16, 1997 DOT Av. LEXIS 523 (Oct. 24, 1997) (exemptions to High Density Rule granted to new entrants based on public interest standard when DOT finds exceptional circumstances; "we have determined to define 'exceptional circumstances' more broadly by recognizing the need for competitive service in a market, especially low-fare competitive service"). With regard to domestic transactions, however, the DOT has indicated that the "primary concern over the antitrust implications of a merger is now the domain of the Department of Justice." Joint Application of Federal Express Corp. and Flying Tigers Line, Order 89-3-54, at 2, 1989 DOT Av. LEXIS 193 (1989).

1246. In addition, the DOJ has reviewed several acquisitions among fixed base operators (FBOs) which provide services such as sales of jet fuel and terminal services at airports. In 1992, the DOJ required modifications to avoid the elimination of rival FBO service at Boston Logan Airport. Restructure of Air Services Merger Lays to Rest Antitrust Concerns, 63 Antitrust & Trade Reg. Rep. (BNA) 263 (Aug. 27, 1992). In 1999, the DOJ required divestitures before approving Signature Flight Support Corporation's acquisition of AMR Combs. United States v. Signature Flight Support Corp., 1999-2 Trade Cas. (CCH) ¶ 72,611 (D.D.C. 1999) (final judgment).

1247. Remarks of Charles F. Rule, Ass't Att'y Gen., Antitrust Div., Before the International Aviation Club, Mar. 7, 1989, at 25-26.

1248. DOJ Press Release, No. 91-57 (Feb. 14, 1991).

1249. *Id.* The DOJ also rejected a failing firm argument related to Eastern (which was being sold by a bankruptcy trustee) because it concluded that there was a less anticompetitive purchaser available (Northwest Airlines). *Id.*

would allow full reciprocity between the two carriers' frequent flyer programs.[1250] The Department of Justice sued to enjoin Northwest from acquiring stock of Continental, alleging that the acquisition would give Northwest voting control over Continental, as well as a share in Continental's profits.[1251]   According to the complaint, Northwest's acquisition of Continental stock would have diminished substantially Northwest's and Continental's incentives to compete against each other on seven hub-to-hub routes, as well as on other routes.   In addition, the complaint alleged that the acquisition would have deterred Continental, which allegedly was poised to expand its Cleveland hub, from offering new service in competition with Northwest.   Although Northwest agreed to place its Continental voting stock in a voting trust for six years, the complaint alleged that this trust structure failed to prevent the acquisition from potentially harming competition.

Subsequent to the commencement of the action by the Department of Justice, Northwest and Continental modified the terms of their acquisition agreements and proceeded to consummate the acquisition.   The Department of Justice filed an amended complaint seeking, among other things, an order directing Northwest to divest the Continental stock it had acquired.[1252]   The amended complaint alleged that the modifications to the agreements implemented by Northwest did not remedy the anticompetitive effects of the acquisition. The Department of Justice did not challenge Northwest's and Continental's code sharing or frequent flyer program plans.   In 2000, the Department of Justice announced a settlement agreement pursuant to which Northwest would divest all but 7 percent of the voting interest in Continental and would be subject to significant restrictions upon its ability to vote its remaining stock.[1253]

Also in 2000, United Airlines and US Airways announced their agreement to merge.[1254]   The carriers expressly recognized that the merger would raise competition issues and proposed, as part of the merger transaction, to create a new carrier, DC Air, to be owned by a director of US Airways. Under the proposal, DC Air would acquire slots at Washington Reagan National Airport and would offer service from that airport to selected communities.[1255]   The merging parties and American Airlines subsequently entered into two transactions conditioned on the closing of the United-US Airways merger and intended to further address competitive concerns.   In the first transaction, American proposed to purchase from the combined United-US Airways gates and slots at airports including Washington Reagan National and New York LaGuardia, and multiple aircraft.   American further commited to fly a minimum number of daily flights on five United-US Airways hub-to-hub routes.   In addition, American and United proposed to operate the US Airways Shuttle jointly.[1256]   In the second transaction, American agreed to acquire 49 percent of the common stock of DC Air, to include DC Air as a participant in American's frequent flyer program, and to "wet lease" aircraft to DC Air.

1250. Northwest Airlines Press Release (Jan. 28, 1998).

1251. United States v. Northwest Airlines Corp., Civil Action No. 98-74611 (E.D. Mich. Oct. 23, 1998).

1252. United States v. Northwest Airlines Corp., Civil Action No. 98-74611 (E.D. Mich. Dec. 18, 1998).

1253. DOJ Press Release, Department Announces Tentative Settlement in Northwest-Continental Lawsuit (Nov. 6, 2000).

1254. United Air Lines Press Release (May 24, 2000).

1255. *Id.*

1256. American Airlines Press Release (Jan. 9, 2001).

In July 2001, the Department of Justice announced that it would seek to block the United-US Airways transaction. According to the agency, the proposed acquisition would violate the antitrust laws by reducing competition in hub-to-hub markets; Washington, D.C., and Baltimore, Maryland, nonstop markets; East Coast connect markets; and certain international routes.[1257] The Department of Justice also stated that the acquisition would reduce competition for corporate and government business travel and would "create or enhance dominance at may cities through the United States, including Boston, Washington and Philadelphia."[1258] The agency also concluded that the proposed remedial transactions would not adequately replace the competition being lost as a result of the proposed acquisition. United and US Airways subsequently abandoned their merger.

In 2001, American and Trans World Airlines (TWA) announced that TWA was filing for bankruptcy and that American proposed to purchase substantially all of the assets of TWA pursuant to a bankruptcy court auction process. TWA stated publicly that it was a "failed firm" and submitted testimony to the bankruptcy court that all competing offers to acquire TWA's assets or to restructure the company were inadequate, and that the failure to sell the bulk of its assets to American would result in the closing of the airline and loss of over 20,000 jobs. The bankruptcy court declared American the successful bidder for the bulk of TWA's assets and approved the sale of those assets to American.[1259] The Department of Justice determined not to challenge the American-TWA transaction, saying that its decision "came after a comprehensive investigation that included consideration of TWA's bankrupt condition."[1260]

(2) Airline Joint Ventures

In 1989, the Department of Justice challenged the proposed joint venture of the CRSs owned by American and Delta Air Lines,[1261] alleging that the proposed venture "would violate Section 7 of the Clayton Act and Section 1 of the Sherman Act because it would substantially lessen competition both in the sale of CRS services to travel agents and in the provision of scheduled airline passenger service."[1262] The agency found that there were only five CRSs in the United States and concluded that the elimination of one of the five competitors "could result in higher charges to travel agents for using CRS services."[1263] On the question of lessening competition in "the provision of scheduled airline passenger service," the Department of Justice offered the following analysis:

Travel agents using a particular CRS tend to sell a disproportionately high number of tickets on that CRS owner's airline. Because owner airlines sell more tickets when their CRS is used to book flights than they would if a neutral CRS were used,

---

1257. DOJ Press Release, Department of Justice and Several States Will Sue to Stop United Airlines From Acquiring US Airways (July 27, 2001).

1258. Id.

1259. In re Trans World Airlines, Inc., No. 01-056 (PJW) (Bankr. D. Del. Mar. 12, 2001).

1260. DOJ Press Release, Justice Department Announces It Won't Challenge American Airlines/TWA Acquisition (Mar. 16, 2001).

1261. DOJ Press Release, 89-191 (June 22, 1989).

1262. Id.

1263. Id.

competing airlines are less able to enter or expand service on city pairs in competition with airlines that also possess high CRS shares on that city pair.

The proposed transaction will increase CRS concentration on many city pairs and will combine high CRS market shares and the air transportation service of Delta or American on those city pairs. In city pair markets that are already highly concentrated, the effect of the joint venture could be both to increase concentration in those markets and make it more difficult for other airlines to enter the markets even if fares go up. As a result, in those city pairs, fares are likely to go up and service quality is likely to fall.[1264]

The transaction was abandoned in the face of this lawsuit.

Ten years later, five major domestic airlines (American, Continental, Delta, Northwest, and United) proposed to form Orbitz, an online travel agency that would, among other things, offer airlines rebates on certain fees if they would agree to become "charter associates." The charter associate agreement included a most favored nation provision requiring the charter associate airline to make available to Orbitz all of its publicly available fares, subject to certain conditions. The Departments of Justice and Transportation both commenced investigations of Orbitz. The areas of concern identified by the Department of Transportation were the possibility that Orbitz could be a vehicle for price or service collusion by airlines; whether the charter associate most favored nation provision unduly restricted charter associate airlines' ability to distribute their services via means other than Orbitz; and whether Orbitz would quickly attain a dominant position in the online travel agency business and thereby reduce competition among online agencies.[1265] The Department of Transportation concluded, however, that while it had "lingering concerns that Orbitz may *operate* in ways which might be anticompetitive and will monitor those concerns after launch," it had "concluded that it should neither block Orbitz from beginning operations nor compel it to change its business strategy at this time."[1266]

(3) International

International air travel requires the execution of treaties, bilateral agreements, or multilateral agreements by the nations involved. Historically, many of these treaties and bilateral agreements have been highly restrictive, often limiting the routes that may be flown, the number of carriers that may serve the route, and the number of flights each carrier could offer on each route. Since the early 1990s, the Department of Transportation, working with the Department of State, has pursued a policy of

1264. *Id.* In announcing the DOJ's opposition to the proposed American-Delta CRS deal, the Attorney General noted that the Secretary of Transportation had expressed concern that the transaction might have an adverse effect on competition in the airline industry and said that the DOJ was "pleased that the Department of Transportation shares our concern for competition in the industry." *Id.*
1265. Letter from Susan McDermott, Dep'y Ass't Sec. for Aviation and Int'l Affairs, Dep't of Transportation, and Samuel Podberesky, Ass't Gen. Counsel for Aviation Enforcement and Proceedings, Dep't of Transportation, to Jeffrey G. Katz, Chairman, President, and Chief Executive Officer, Orbitz (Apr. 13, 2001).
1266. *Id.* at 9. Orbitz was instructed to submit a report of marketplace operations six months after launch.

seeking to enter into open skies agreements that give carriers in the signatory nations virtually unlimited access to one another's international markets.[1267]

As a substantial inducement for nations to enter into open skies agreements, the Department of Transportation has exercised its authority to grant antitrust immunity to agreements between U.S. and foreign carriers. In 1993, coincident with the execution of an open skies agreement between the United States and the Netherlands, the Department of Transportation approved an agreement between Northwest Airlines and KLM Royal Dutch Airlines that allowed the two companies to integrate their services and operate as though they were a single carrier.[1268] The agency also granted the two airlines antitrust immunity to enable them to proceed under the agreement. The airlines' plan included an extensive code-sharing arrangement; integrated frequent flyer programs; and collaborative marketing, purchasing, scheduling, and pricing on transatlantic flights.

In mid-1996, the Department of Transportation granted antitrust immunity to three other alliances between U.S. and foreign air carriers: United Air Lines and Lufthansa; American Airlines and Canadian Airlines; and Delta Air Lines and Swissair, Sabena, and Austrian Airlines. Each of these alliances involved extensive code-sharing arrangements on international routes, other joint marketing and distribution activities, coordinated flight schedules, and revenue pooling and sharing on certain routes. In each case, the critical factors upon which the Department of Transportation relied in justifying its grants of antitrust immunity were the successful consummation of open skies agreements with the home countries of the foreign carriers (Germany, Canada, Switzerland, Belgium, and Austria), and the airlines' insistence that they would not consummate the proposed transactions in the absence of antitrust immunity.

The Department of Justice opposed the grant of immunity in each of these cases. Then-Assistant Attorney General of the Antitrust Division, Anne K. Bingaman, succinctly stated the Department of Justice's position:

> It is not necessary for code share partners to receive antitrust immunity for any agreement that would not violate the antitrust laws; and conduct that would violate the antitrust laws should not be permitted, much less immunized.[1269]

The Department of Transportation considered but rejected the Department of Justice's opposition with regard to the transactions for which it granted antitrust immunity.[1270]

1267. The DOT has defined an open skies agreement as containing, among other things, open entry on all routes, unrestricted capacity and frequency on all routes, unrestricted route and traffic rights, and open code-sharing opportunities. Order 92-8-13, 1992 DOT Av. LEXIS 568 (1992).

1268. Joint Application of Northwest Airlines, Inc. and KLM Royal Dutch Airlines for Approval and Antitrust Immunity of an Agreement Pursuant to Sections 412 and 414 of the Federal Aviation Act, Order 93-1-11, 1995 DOT Av. LEXIS 621 (1995).

1269. Anne K. Bingaman, Ass't Att'y Gen., Antitrust Div., Consolidation and Code Sharing: Antitrust Enforcement in the Airline Industry, Remarks Before the ABA Forum on Air and Space Law (Jan. 25, 1996), *available at* www.usdoj.gov/atr/public/speeches/speech.akb.htm.

1270. The DOJ has opposed even the approval of some nonimmunized alliances being considered by the DOT. In comments filed in connection with American Airlines's application to enter into a nonimmunized alliance with the TACA Group (a group of carriers serving Costa Rica, Guatemala, Honduras, and Nicaragua), the DOJ said:

Since 1996, the Department of Transportation has approved and granted antitrust immunity for several similar agreements, at times excluding from the grant of antitrust immunity any coordination between the two carriers with respect to certain categories of fares for nonstop flights on certain routes.[1271] The Department of Transportation also has declined to approve and grant antitrust immunity for proposed agreements between carriers in the absence of an open skies treaty.[1272]

In one instance, the Department of Justice challenged a transaction approved by the Department of Transportation. In 1993, the Department of Transportation approved the application of British Airways to acquire a stake in USAir Group. Pursuant to the airlines' agreement, British Airways purchased 20 percent of USAir stock (later raised to 24.6 percent). No antitrust immunity was sought or obtained for this transaction under the Aviation Act. The Department of Justice subsequently filed a Clayton Act Section 7 civil action and a proposed consent decree settling

---

With largely horizontal airline route combinations, the code-share partners' combined route network is not significantly larger than either of the existing networks. Consequently, they can jointly provide new on-line services to few city-pair markets currently served only by interline services, and they add significant competitive vigor to few city-pairs. The potential for code-share agreements between largely horizontal networks to create pro-competitive benefits and promote the public interest, therefore, is relatively low; and the risk to competition is relatively high.

Comments of the DOJ, American Airlines, Inc. and the TACA Group Reciprocal Code-Share Services Proceeding, Dkt. OST-96-1700-99 at 6 (Jan. 28, 1998).

1271. American Airlines, Swissair, and Sabena, Order 2000-5-13, 2000 DOT Av. LEXIS 244 (2000) (excluding from the grant of immunity full fare coach, business class, and first class fares for U.S. point-of-sale passengers flying nonstop between Chicago and Brussels, and between Chicago and Zurich); Alitalia Linee Aeree Italian, KLM Royal Dutch Airlines, and Northwest Airlines, Order 99-12-5, 1999 DOT Av. 655 (1999) (not authorizing the parties to operate under a common name); American Airlines and LanChile, Order 99-9-9, 1999 DOT Av. LEXIS 515 (1999) (excluding from the grant of immunity full fare coach, business class, and first class fares for U.S. point-of-sale passengers flying nonstop between Miami, Florida, and Santiago, Chile, and conditioning approval on the termination of exclusivity provisions in the parties' alliance agreements that would have precluded LanChile from entering into alliances with other U.S. carriers and American from entering into alliances with other South American carriers); United Airlines and Air Canada, Order 97-9-21, 1997 DOT Av. LEXIS 492 (1997) (excluding from immunity grant coordination between the two carriers with respect to certain categories of fares for nonstop flights between Chicago and Toronto, and between San Francisco and Toronto).

1272. See Order Terminating Proceedings, Order 99-7-22, 1999 DOT Av. LEXIS 446 (1999), terminating the DOT's review of the application of American Airlines and British Airways for approval of and antitrust immunity for the two airlines' proposed alliance agreement. The application, filed in January 1997, was expressly conditioned on the signing of an open skies treaty between the United States and the United Kingdom. Joint Application of American Airlines, Inc. and British Airways Plc under 49 U.S.C. §§ 41308-41309 for Approval of/and Antitrust Immunity for Alliance Agreement, Dkt No. OST 97 2058-1 (Jan. 10, 1997). As a result of separate investigations, the European Commission and the DOJ both called for American and British Airways to divest varying numbers of the slots they held for takeoffs and landings at London's Heathrow Airport. Commission Notice Concerning the Alliance between British Airways and American Airlines, Official Journal C239 at 10-16 (1998); Comments of the DOJ at 32-35, Dkt. No. OST-97-2058-222 (Jan. 10, 1997). The United States and the United Kingdom engaged in sporadic negotiation to replace the existing aviation treaty, known as Bermuda II, with an open skies treaty. Following a breakdown in the negotiations in early 1999, the DOT terminated the proceedings to review the proposed alliance, citing the failure of a "fundamental predicate" to the application—namely, the adoption of an open skies treaty. According to the DOT, the United Kingdom had not made "sufficient progress internally in resolving the issue of London airport access to permit the continuation of productive negotiation of an Open-Skies agreement." Order Terminating Proceedings, Order 99-7-22, 1999 DOT Av. LEXIS 446 (1999).

claims that the airlines' planned joint operations would substantially lessen competition in two markets: (1) scheduled connecting airline passenger service between interior U.S. points and London, and (2) scheduled nonstop airline passenger service in the Philadelphia-London and Baltimore/Washington-London markets. Competition would be reduced, according to the complaint, because USAir would be removed as an independent competitor for U.S.-London markets. Exacerbating the Department of Justice's competitive concern was the fact that carriers serving the U.S.-London markets were permitted to discuss and agree with one another on fares they would charge consumers through the International Air Transportation Association. Under the decree, USAir was required to divest its authority to provide scheduled passenger service to London from its Philadelphia, Baltimore/Washington, and Charlotte, North Carolina, gateways.[1273]

c. PRICE FIXING AND RELATED CONDUCT

When the domestic airline industry was heavily regulated, air carriers were required to file advance notice of fare increases with the Civil Aeronautics Board. With deregulation in the 1980s, air carriers continued to provide advance notice of fare increases through the Airline Tariff Publishing Company (ATPCo), to which all major airlines submit fare information electronically for distribution to CRSs and, through CRSs, to travel agents, other airlines, and the traveling public. Advance price increase notices typically were conveyed through the use of first and/or last ticket dates attached to particular fares to indicate when the fare would commence or expire.

In *United States v. Airline Tariff Publishing Co.*, the Department of Justice sued ATPCo and eight major airlines, alleging that the airlines used the ATPCo electronic fare submission and dissemination system to engage in unlawful price fixing. According to the complaint, the publication of first and last ticket dates allowed carriers to signal future pricing intentions in particular markets and facilitated electronic "negotiations" over future prices.[1274] If one carrier announced a future fare in a particular market or set of markets, and that fare was matched by other carriers, the Department of Justice claimed the proposed fare would likely take effect as of the posted first ticket date; if other carriers did not match, the initiating carrier was likely to withdraw its price increase before the effective date without ever subjecting itself to market risk. Two defendants settled the claims contemporaneously with the filing of the complaint.[1275] The other carriers and ATPCo defended the practice of advance price announcements through first and last ticket dates on various grounds, including that consumers benefited by being forewarned of price increases, allowing them to purchase lower fare tickets, and that each airline acted independently on the basis of the public information that was available to it. The remaining defendants also ultimately entered into a consent decree that included a general ban (with limited exceptions) on the defendants' use of first and last ticket dates.[1276]

1273. United States v. USAir Group, Inc., 1993-2 Trade Cas. (CCH) ¶ 70,416 (D.D.C. 1993) (final judgment).

1274. United States v. Airline Tariff Publ'g Co., Civ. No. 92-2854 (D.D.C. filed Dec. 21, 1992), *available at* www.usdoj.gov/atr/cases/f4700/4796.pdf.

1275. United States v. Airline Tariff Publ'g Co., 836 F. Supp. 9 (D.D.C. 1993) (final judgment).

1276. 1994-2 Trade Cas. (CCH) ¶ 70,687 (D.D.C. 1994) (final judgment). Related private class actions and a class action on behalf of state and local government purchasers of air travel also were filed.

More recently, private parties have challenged major carriers' fare rules as violations of Section 1. In *Chase v. Northwest Airlines, Inc.*,[1277] the plaintiffs survived a motion to dismiss their claims that Northwest and several unnamed competing airlines conspired through the Airlines Reporting Corporation to implement Northwest's refusal to permit consumers to use so-called hidden city tickets (where a passenger buys a ticket from travel from City A to City B continuing to City C but stops his or her travel at City B).

In addition to fares, major elements of airline costs also have been subject to scrutiny under Section 1 of the Sherman Act. In 1995, Delta Air Lines publicly announced a cap on the commissions it would pay travel agencies for bookings on Delta flights. Delta's cap was matched shortly thereafter by most of the other major domestic carriers. Travel agents subsequently sued these carriers for acting in concert to set commissions paid to travel agents.[1278] In addition to the "consciously parallel" airline conduct, the plaintiffs alleged the "plus factor" of private interairline communications about the commission cap prior to its implementation by most of the defendants. The case was settled in September 1996 for approximately $86 million. The settlement agreement did not provide for a uniform lifting of the commission cap, however, as any such agreement was itself viewed as unlawful.

d. MONOPOLIZATION

Airlines commonly enter into interline agreements which establish the terms and conditions on which airlines will, among other things, accept tickets issued by another carrier and agree to accept baggage associated with passengers connecting from another carrier so that passengers may book travel on multiple carriers under a single itinerary. Not all carriers have interline agreements with all other carriers, however. In 1985, the Department of Transportation rejected a claim by Continental Airlines that American Airlines's cancellation of an interline agreement with Continental represented an effort to preserve American's alleged monopoly position at Dallas/Fort Worth International Airport. Continental argued that American's conduct was barred by Section 411 of the Aviation Act even if it did not rise to the level of a Sherman Act § 2 violation. The Department of Transportation acknowledged that Section 411, the predecessor to what is now Section 41712, was not limited to practices prohibited by the antitrust laws, but said, "we are reluctant to

---

The private plaintiffs charged that seven major defendant airlines conspired, through the ATPCo electronic fare system, to eliminate price competition on routes to and from their hub airports. The class consisted of several million airline passengers who flew on the defendant carriers to, from, or through their hubs after January 1, 1988. The case was settled by means of a certificate program in which the defendant airlines contributed more than $400 million in certificates for discounts on future air transportation, each certificate being worth a maximum of 10% of the fare. *In re Domestic Air Transp. Antitrust Litig.*, 148 F.R.D. 297 (N.D. Ga. 1993). The state and local government class action, which alleged that the same group of airline defendants engaged in price fixing through the electronic publication of future pricing intentions, was settled contemporaneously with the filing of the complaint. The settlement provided that state and local government employees would receive a 10% discount on all official air travel on the defendant carriers (and on code-share flights involving the defendant carriers), up to a total of $40 million in discounts or for 18 months, whichever came first. *Colorado v. Airline Tariff Publ'g Co.*, 1995-2 Trade Cas. (CCH) ¶ 71,231 (D.D.C. 1995) (final judgment).

1277. 49 F. Supp. 2d 553 (E.D. Mich. 1999).

1278. *In re* Travel Agency Commission Antitrust Litig., 898 F. Supp. 685 (D. Minn. 1995) (refusing to dismiss complaint).

use general concepts of 'fairness' to proscribe competitive conduct as an unfair method of competition when such conduct does not constitute an actual or incipient violation of the antitrust laws and is not closely analogous to such a violation."[1279]

More recently, the Eleventh Circuit reversed a district court's dismissal of an action by Laker Airways seeking, among other things, to require British Airways to transfer slots at London's Gatwick airport to Laker and to enter into an interline agreement with Laker.[1280] The district court had dismissed the action on the grounds that Laker had failed to join an indispensable party. The Eleventh Circuit affirmed as to Laker's claims regarding the allocation of slots, but reversed as to Laker's claims regarding the interline agreement, as an interline agreement is "simply a contract between airline carriers and involves no other authorizing parties."[1281] The court expressly declined to opine on whether Laker's claims were subject to dismissal on grounds other than the failure to join an indispensable party.[1282]

In *Virgin Atlantic Airways Ltd. v. British Airways PLC*,[1283] the Second Circuit affirmed the district court's grant of summary judgment in favor of defendant British Airways on Virgin's claims that British Airways's practice of entering into incentive agreements with travel agents was part of an attempted monopolization or monopoly leveraging scheme in violation of Section 2 of the Sherman Act. The parties had stipulated for purposes of the motion that the relevant markets alleged in the complaint—Heathrow Airport, Gatwick Airport, and scheduled airline passenger services between city pairs and airport pairs—were properly identified as relevant markets.[1284] The court then focused on the opinion testimony offered by Virgin's retained expert, who opined that British Airways's travel agent incentive agreements, by which British Airways paid additional compensation to agents that met certain targets, unlawfully bundled competitive routes with monopoly routes. According to the expert, this constituted "predatory foreclosure,"[1285] which he characterized as (1) seeking to deter or delay a rival's entry or expansion, and (2) involving an immediate recoupment of any losses from sales at below-cost prices by setting prices substantially in excess of costs on other sales.[1286]

Both the Second Circuit and district court declined to decide whether Virgin's predatory foreclosure theory should be rejected as a matter of law, but the district court commented that under Virgin's theory, any volume price discount could be attacked, despite the fact that "deterring the market entry of some competitors is a natural product of legitimate competition where the nonentry results from their inability to compete efficiently on the merits."[1287] Instead, the courts found that Virgin had failed to present a factual basis for its predatory foreclosure theory.[1288]

Predatory pricing claims occasionally are brought against air carriers but they have rarely been successful because plaintifs have been unable to met the below-cost

1279. Continental Airlines, Inc. v. American Airlines, Inc., DOT Dkt. No. 42296, Order 85-12-69 (1985).
1280. Laker Airways, Inc. v. British Airways, PLC, 182 F.3d 843 (11th Cir. 1999).
1281. *Id.* at 850.
1282. *Id.*
1283. 257 F.3d 256 (2d Cir. 2001).
1284. 69 F. Supp. 2d 571, 573 (S.D.N.Y. 1999).
1285. 257 F.3d at 265.
1286. *Id.* at 266-72.
1287. 69 F. Supp. 2d at 577 n.2.
1288. 257 F.3d at 267-69; 69 F. Supp. 2d at 579-80.

standards set by the courts for predatory pricing.[1289] In *International Travel Arrangers, Inc. v. NWA, Inc.*,[1290] the Eighth Circuit reversed a jury verdict for the plaintiff wholesale tour operator against Northwest Airlines and an affiliated tour operator, Mainline Travel. The jury had found that the defendants monopolized and attempted to monopolize air transportation between Minneapolis and seven U.S. cities by selling seats below cost. In reversing, the Eighth Circuit confirmed its prior ruling in *Morgan v. Ponder*[1291] that objective cost analysis is the crucial component in a prima facie case of predatory pricing. It specified certain "cost markers" for determining whether a price is predatory: (1) prices above average total cost are legal per se; (2) at prices above average variable costs, the plaintiff must overcome a strong presumption of legality by showing other factors indicating that the price charged is anticompetitive; and (3) at prices below average variable costs, the burden of showing nonpredation falls on the defendant.[1292]

The Eighth Circuit found that the plaintiff's evidence failed to establish predatory pricing under this standard. The plaintiff's expert considered only those fares that supported his conclusion that the defendants sold below cost, and admitted that the higher fares he failed to consider exceeded Mainline's average total cost.[1293] The expert also failed to examine Mainline's overall price structure or its overall revenues.[1294] The Eighth Circuit concluded that the expert's failure to analyze the substantial number of seats sold at prices above average total cost undermined the validity of his conclusion.[1295] Even if some of Mainline's fares were below cost, *Morgan* required that a defendant's overall price structure be predatory.[1296] The Eighth Circuit also found that the plaintiff's proof was deficient because its expert compared Mainline's prices only to its average total cost, which was necessarily above Mainline's variable cost.[1297] Under *Morgan*, the plaintiff therefore was required to overcome a strong presumption of legality by showing other factors indicating that the price was anticompetitive. The court ruled that the plaintiff failed to meet this burden.[1298]

In *Continental Airlines, Inc. v. American Airlines, Inc.* and *Northwest Airlines, Inc. v. American Airlines, Inc.*,[1299] Continental and Northwest challenged American's implementation of its Value Pricing Plan in April 1992. The Value Pricing Plan reduced the categories of fares offered by American and reduced the price of first

---

1289. See part D.2 of Chapter II for a discussion of predatory pricing standards. In *Air Florida, Inc. v. Eastern Air Lines, Inc.*, Order 81-1-101, Dkt. 37313 (Jan. 21, 1981), the CAB ruled that a plaintiff must show not only that the defendant adopted below-cost prices, but also that the defendant had a reasonable expectation of recouping its short-term losses by reaping monopoly profits "for a sustained period after driving the target company from the market." *Id.* at 4. The CAB also adopted the approach of using the marginal cost of carrying an additional passenger as the appropriate cost against which to measure the allegedly predatory fares and observed that reducing fares in an effort to deter future competition is not anticompetitive but rather "the very result intended by Congress and the Board in the deregulation of air transportation." *Id.* at 5, 7, 9.

1290. 991 F.2d 1389 (8th Cir. 1993).

1291. 892 F.2d 1355 (8th Cir. 1989).

1292. 991 F.2d at 1394.

1293. *Id.* at 1395.

1294. *Id.*

1295. *Id.* at 1396.

1296. *Id.*

1297. *Id.*

1298. *Id.*

1299. 824 F. Supp. 689 (S.D. Tex. 1993).

class and coach tickets. The plaintiffs alleged that the plan was in fact a predatory pricing scheme designed to cause Continental and Northwest to incur substantial revenue losses and to allow American to charge monopoly prices in certain markets once plaintiffs were eliminated as competitors. The trial court in the consolidated cases rejected American's argument on summary judgment that the only appropriate test for evaluating predatory pricing claims was the marginal or average variable cost test. Within the Fifth Circuit, the court ruled, a plaintiff may prevail on a predatory pricing claim if it demonstrates that the defendant "at least sacrificed present revenues for the purpose of driving [the plaintiff] out of the market with the hope of recouping losses through subsequent higher prices."[1300] The jury ultimately returned a verdict in favor of American, finding that American lacked the specific intent to monopolize any of the eleven local, regional, and national markets defined by plaintiffs.

In 1999, the Department of Justice commenced an action alleging that American monopolized and attempted to monopolize airline passenger service on certain Dallas/Fort Worth city pairs.[1301] In particular, the complaint alleged that when small airlines enter routes to and from Dallas/Fort Worth International Airport, American and its affiliated regional carriers typically responded by increasing capacity and reducing fares "well beyond what makes business sense, except as a means of driving the new entrant out of the market."[1302] The complaint further alleged that the additional revenues American obtained as a result of adding capacity on certain Dallas/Fort Worth routes were less than American's costs of adding the flights.[1303]

The district court granted summary judgment for American.[1304] In opposing American's motion, the Department of Justice argued that the predatory pricing standards set forth in *Brooke Group Ltd. v. Brown & Williamson Corp.*[1305] did not apply because American's action involved capacity additions, not just price cuts.[1306] Characterizing the Department of Justice's argument as "a fundamentally flawed attempt to circumvent the high standards for proof of a predatory pricing claim by semantic sleight of hand,"[1307] the district court held the claims must "meet the standards of proof set forth in *Brooke Group:* the plaintiff must prove both that the defendant priced its product below an appropriate measure of cost, and that the defendant enjoyed a realistic prospect of recouping its losses by supra-competitive

---

1300. *Id.* at 698 (quoting International Air Indus., Inc. v. American Excelsior Co., 517 F.2d 714, 723 (5th Cir.), *cert. denied*, 424 U.S. 943 (1975)). In 1999, the Fifth Circuit stated that in light of the Supreme Court's decision in *Brooke Group Ltd. v. Brown & Williamson Tobacco Corp.*, 509 U.S. 209 (1993), its earlier decisions suggesting that prices above the monopolist's variable costs could be predatory under certain circumstances were no longer good law, and that to prevail in the Fifth Circuit "a plaintiff must show pricing below . . . average variable cost." Stearns Airport Equip. Co. v. FMC Corp., 170 F.3d 518, 532 (5th Cir. 1999).

1301. United States v. AMR Corp., No. 99-1180-JTM (D. Kan. filed May 13, 1999).

1302. Complaint at 1.

1303. *Id.* at 19.

1304. United States v. AMR Corp., 140 F. Supp. 2d 1141 (D. Kan. 2001).

1305. 509 U.S. 209 (1993).

1306. One court had already rejected the proposition that an airline's increased service constituted unlawful predatory conduct. In *Pacific Express, Inc. v. United Airlines, Inc.*, 959 F.2d 814 (9th Cir. 1992), the Ninth Circuit rejected claims that United's increase in service on routes served by Pacific Express was unlawful predation, observing that the intent to "vanquish a rival" does not establish an antitrust violation, at least as long as the effort to exclude the rival is based on the rival's relative efficiency, or lack thereof. *Id.* at 817-18.

1307. 140 F. Supp. 2d at 1194.

pricing."[1308] The court also concluded that the "claims of predatory pricing must be tested against American's average variable costs,"[1309] and that "uncontroverted evidence" established that American did not price its fares below its average variable costs on the four core routes for which the Department of Justice offered evidence on variable costs.[1310]

In opposing American's motion for summary judgment, the Department of Justice argued that the average variable cost test was not the proper test and proposed four alternative tests. The first test asked whether certain of American's route performance measures experienced a decline after a capacity change. The second and third tests compared revenues with fully allocated, rather than variable, costs at the route level. The fourth test sought to compare incremental revenues with incremental costs.[1311] The court rejected all of these tests, concluding that the first and fourth tests were improper "short-run tests for profit maximization," and in any event "failed to reliably measure" the costs of American's capacity additions.[1312] The court rejected the second and third tests because they were "the functional equivalent of applying an average total cost test to assess predation."[1313]

The district court also accepted American's assertion of the meeting competition defense, concluding that such a defense was appropriate in a Section 2 predatory pricing case, and that there was no evidence that American undercut its rivals' fares on the four core routes with a lower published fare during the alleged period of predation.[1314] The district court rejected the Department of Justice's argument that the meeting competition defense should not be applicable where the incumbent increases capacity:

> The ability to match prices implicitly but necessarily requires the ability to increase sales capacity. Granting an established competitor the "right" to reduce its prices in the face of new entrant competition, but simultaneously locking it into its current sales volume, prohibiting it from increasing its capacity to satisfy increased demand and indeed requiring it to turn away new, willing customers, drains all real meaning from the supposed "right" to match prices. Price matching inherently assumes a corresponding increase in output to compensate for the lower market price.[1315]

Finally, the court concluded that the Department of Justice had failed to establish that American had a dangerous probability of recouping its alleged losses through supracompetitive prices.[1316] According to the court, the evidence showed that Dallas/Fort Worth was not characterized by the sort of structural barriers that made supracompetitive pricing plausible, that the calculations of the Department of Justice's experts showed at most that after low-cost carriers left certain routes fares returned to close to their prior levels without showing that those levels were supracompetitive, and that the Department of Justice's argument that American was likely to recoup by charging higher fares on other routes because of a "reputation for

1308. *Id.* at 1195.
1309. *Id.* at 1199.
1310. *Id.* at 1196.
1311. *Id.* at 1200-01.
1312. *Id.* at 1201-02.
1313. *Id.* at 1203.
1314. *Id.* at 1203-09.
1315. *Id.* at 1208.
1316. *Id.* at 1208-17.

predation" was "fundamentally misguided, contrary to law, and unsupported by the uncontroverted facts."[1317]

The Department of Transportation also has been active in assessing alleged predatory pricing in the airline industry. In 1998, the agency published for public comment a *Proposed Statement of Enforcement Policy Regarding Unfair Exclusionary Conduct in the Air Transportation Industry*.[1318]   In its *Proposed Statement*, the Department of Transportation set forth a definition of "unfair exclusionary conduct" that it would consider a violation of the Aviation Act. According to the *Proposed Statement*, the Department of Transportation would consider a "major carrier" to violate Section 41712 of the Aviation Act "if in response to new entry into one or more of its local hub markets, [the major carrier] pursues a strategy of price cuts or capacity increases, or both, that either (1) causes it to forego more revenue than all of the new entrant's capacity could have diverted from it or (2) results in substantially lower operating profits—or greater operating losses—in the short run than would a reasonable alternative strategy for competing with the new entrant."[1319]   The *Proposed Statement* added that except when "strong reasons" suggest that Section 41712 has not been violated, the agency would commence enforcement proceedings if, in response to competition from a "new entrant"[1320] carrier,

> (1) the major carrier adds capacity and sells such a large number of seats at very low fares that the ensuing self-diversion of revenue results in lower local revenue than would a reasonable alternative response; (2) the number of local passengers that the major carrier carries at the new entrant's low fares (or at similar fares that are substantially below the major carrier's previous fares) exceeds the new entrant's total seat capacity, resulting, through self-diversion, in lower local revenue than would a reasonable alternative response; or (3) the number of local passengers that the major carrier carries at the new entrant's low fares (or at similar fares that are substantially below the major carrier's previous fares) exceeds the number of low-fare passengers carried by the new entrant, resulting, through self-diversion, in lower local revenue than would a reasonable alternative response.[1321]

The agency's expressed intent to depart from traditional antitrust analysis of predatory conduct generated more than 1,600 comments, both against and in favor of the *Proposed Statement*.   Congress subsequently requested the Transportation Research Board of the National Research Council of the National Academy of Sciences to study the *Proposed Statement*. The resulting report[1322] concluded that although opportunity costs were relevant in the assessment of whether conduct was predatory, the *Proposed Statement* was flawed and had the potential for undesirable consequences.[1323]   Among other things, the report observed that the Department of Transportation's proposal risked arbitrary enforcement, possibly favoring inefficient

---

1317. *Id.* at 1213.

1318. 63 Fed. Reg. 17,919 (DOT Apr. 10, 1998).

1319. *Id.* at 17,919-20.

1320. A "new entrant" is "an independent airline that has started jet service within the last ten years and pursues a competitive strategy of charging low fares." *Id.* at 17,920.

1321. *Id.* at 17,922.

1322. TRANSPORTATION RESEARCH BD., NAT'L RESEARCH COUNCIL, SPECIAL REPORT 255, ENTRY AND COMPETITION IN THE U.S. AIRLINE INDUSTRY: ISSUES AND OPPORTUNITIES (1999).

1323. *Id.* at 8.

competitors, and was inherently speculative because it called for a comparison of revenues actually earned with revenues that hypothetically would have been earned had the incumbent pursued a different course of action.[1324]   The Department of Transportation subsequently determined not to publish guidelines but to adopt a case-by-case approach.[1325]

e.   COMPUTER RESERVATIONS SYSTEMS

Shortly after the Airline Deregulation Act of 1978, CRSs came to play a central role in the distribution of air transportation. Individual carriers and groups of carriers formed CRSs as a means of displaying schedule, price, and availability information to thousands of travel agents around the country and the world. The CRSs also enabled travel agents to sell seats via electronic communication between the CRS computer network and the computer systems of individual carriers.

In 1984, the Civil Aeronautics Board adopted regulations governing certain aspects of CRS operations.[1326]   Those regulations prohibited the most blatant forms of computer screen bias and discrimination by CRSs, which were owned by the largest domestic airlines.   The agency determined that such bias and discrimination constituted deceptive and unfair practices, and cited Section 411 as support for its rulemaking authority in this area.[1327]   United Air Lines challenged the agency's authority to issue these CRS regulations on the basis of Section 411. The Seventh Circuit upheld the CRS regulations.[1328]   The court wrote that "[t]he resemblance of the conduct in this case to what has traditionally been regarded, whether rightly or wrongly, as monopolistic behavior is close enough" to justify regulation under Section 411.[1329]   Analogizing the Civil Aeronautics Board's authority under that section to "its progenitor, Section 5 of the Federal Trade Commission Act," the court held that "the Board can forbid anticompetitive practices before they become serious enough to violate the Sherman Act."[1330]

In 1992, the Department of Transportation issued modified and expanded rules governing CRS operations.[1331]   Some commenters again challenged the agency's authority to issue the CRS rules on the basis of Section 411, citing the Ninth Circuit decision in *Alaska Airlines, Inc. v. United Air Lines, Inc.*[1332]   In that case, the Ninth Circuit affirmed a lower court's ruling that United Air Lines and American Airlines, then owners of the two major CRSs (APOLLO and SABRE, respectively), did not violate the Sherman Act through their biasing of CRS display screens or the booking fees they charged other airlines which participated in their systems.   The court rejected the plaintiffs' arguments that, under the circumstances presented, each CRS constituted an essential facility to which participating carriers required reasonable

---

1324. *Id.*
1325. Findings and Conclusions on the Economic, Policy, and Legal Issues, DOT Dkt. OST-98-3713 (Jan. 17, 2001), *available at* ostpxweb.dot.gov/aviation/domestic-competition/compfindings.pdf.
1326. 49 Fed. Reg. 32,540 (CAB Aug. 15, 1984).
1327. Section 411 of the Federal Aviation Act was formerly codified at 49 U.S.C. § 1381. The DOT's authority to act against deceptive and unfair practices is now found in 49 U.S.C. § 41712 (1994), *amended by* Pub. L. No. 105-181, 114 Stat. 102 (2000).
1328. United Air Lines, Inc. v. CAB, 766 F.2d 1107 (7th Cir. 1985) (Posner, J.).
1329. *Id.* at 1133.
1330. *Id.*
1331. 14 C.F.R. pt. 255 (2001).
1332. 948 F.2d 536 (9th Cir. 1991).

access in order to compete effectively in the downstream air transportation market, and each CRS owner's market power with regard to its own CRS gave it an unfair competitive advantage in the air transportation market.[1333]   The Department of Transportation was not persuaded that the *Alaska* case vitiated its reliance on Section 411 as authority for the expanded CRS rules but relied on *United Air Lines, Inc. v. CAB* for the proposition that Section 411 may be used to prohibit conduct which does not by itself violate the Sherman Act.[1334]   No subsequent judicial challenge was made to the expanded CRS rules after their adoption by the Department of Transportation.

4. Ocean Shipping

Prior to 1996, marine cargo carriers were regulated primarily by three statutes which regulated carriers' rates and required filing of tariffs. The Shipping Act of 1916 (1916 Act) applied to "every common carrier by water in interstate commerce" and provided antitrust immunity for certain filed agreements or tariffs that were approved by the Shipping Board.[1335]   The Intracoastal Shipping Act of 1933 (1933 Act) applied to water carriers in noncontiguous domestic trades.[1336]   The Shipping Act of 1984 (1984 Act) restricted application of the 1916 Act to domestic offshore trades and superseded the 1916 Act with respect to ocean carriers in U.S. foreign commerce.[1337]   The 1984 Act exempted from coverage of the antitrust laws any agreement filed under the act or "any activity or agreement within the scope of this chapter, whether permitted under or prohibited by this chapter, undertaken or entered into with a reasonable basis to conclude" that it is pursuant to an agreement filed under the 1984 Act or which is exempt for filing under the act.[1338]   One purpose of the 1984 Act was to broaden the scope of the antitrust immunity that had been previously available under the 1916 Act.[1339]   Beginning in 1995, these legislative enactments were substantially revised.

The ICCTA[1340] repealed the 1933 Act and most of the 1916 Act. The ICCTA replaced the Interstate Commerce Commission with the Surface Transportation Board, which was given jurisdiction over most interstate coastwise water carriers.[1341]

1333. *Id.* at 542-46. The 1992 CRS Rules were scheduled to expire, by their terms, on December 31, 1997. In September 1997, the DOT issued an advance notice of proposed rulemaking inviting public comment on the existing rules and potential new rules. 62 Fed. Reg. 47,606 (DOT Sept. 10, 1997). According to the notice, the DOT's "preliminary position [is] that the [CRS] rules should be continued, probably with revisions." *Id.* In 2000, citing industry developments including the advent of Internet travel agencies such as Expedia, Travelocity, and Priceline, American's divestiture of its CRS, increased public ownership of other CRSs, and the announcement that several carriers had invested in a new Internet travel agency that proposed to book directly with carriers' computer networks thereby bypassing CRSs, the DOT invited interested parties to submit additional comments. 65 Fed. Reg. 45,551 (DOT July 24, 2000). The DOT has further extended the expiration date of the existing rules four times, currently to March 31, 2002. 62 Fed. Reg. 66,272 (DOT Dec. 18, 1997); 64 Fed. Reg. 15,127 (DOT Mar. 30, 1999); 65 Fed. Reg. 16,808 (DOT Mar. 30, 2000); 66 Fed. Reg. 13,860 (DOT Mar. 8, 2001).

1334. 57 Fed. Reg. 43,780 (DOT Sept. 22, 1992).

1335. *See generally* 46 U.S.C. § 817 (repealed by Pub. L. No. 104-88, 109 Stat. 954 (1995)).

1336. *See* 46 U.S.C. § 845a (repealed by Pub. L. No. 104-88, 109 Stat. 953 (1995)).

1337. 46 U.S.C. App. § 1703.

1338. *Id.* § 1706(a) (Supp. 1999).

1339. *See generally* H.R. REP. 98-53, pt. 1, at 11-12 (1984), *reprinted in* 1984 U.S.C.C.A.N. 167.

1340. Pub. L. No. 104-88, 109 Stat. 803 (1995).

1341. 49 U.S.C. § 13521 (Supp. 1999).

Under the ICCTA, coastwise carriers are required to file a tariff with the Surface Transportation Board if engaged in "noncontiguous domestic trade, except with regard to bulk cargo, forest products, recycled metal scrap, waste paper, and paper waste" or for movement of household goods.[1342] Except with respect to carriers of household goods, water carriers may move cargo pursuant to private written contracts expressly waiving certain rights or remedies under the act.[1343] The ICCTA does not provide antitrust immunity to water carriers.

The 1984 Act provided carriers in U.S. foreign commerce antitrust immunity but also provided a transparent tariff filing system. The 1984 Act was amended in 1998 (1998 Act)[1344] "to promote the growth and development of United States exports through competitive and efficient ocean transportation and by placing a greater reliance on the market place."[1345] Specifically, the 1998 Act (1) eliminated the tariff filing requirement, (2) increased the flexibility of ocean carriers and shippers to enter into service contracts, (3) expanded the role and regulation of "ocean transportation intermediaries," and (4) provided the Federal Maritime Comission with additional enforcement weapons.[1346]

Although the 1998 Act continued the antitrust immunity provided by the 1984 Act,[1347] "loyalty contracts" are subject to the antitrust laws.[1348] The 1998 Act redefined loyalty contract as a contract "by which a shipper obtains lower rates by committing all or a fixed portion of its cargo" to a particular carrier or carriers and "the contract provides for a deferred rebate arrangement."[1349]

Various portions of the regulatory scheme for ocean shipping involve pricing and vertical relationshps that have antitrust sensitivity.

a.   TARIFFS

Each common carrier or conference operating in U.S. foreign commerce must publish its tariff electronically through a private tariff bureau.[1350] There is no requirement of filing tariffs with the Federal Maritime Commission. The tariff must set forth the "rates, charges, classifications, rules and practices between all points or ports on its own route and on any through transportation route that has been established."[1351]

b.   SERVICE CONTRACTS

Service contracts offer shippers an alternative to tendering cargo under standard tariff terms. The 1998 Act liberalizes the use of service contracts "to provide

---

1342. *Id.* § 13702 (Supp. 1999).

1343. *See id.* § 14101 (Supp. 1999).

1344. Ocean Shipping Reform Act of 1998, Pub. L. No. 105-258, 112 Stat. 1902.

1345. 46 U.S.C. App. § 1701(4) (Supp. 1999).

1346. In addition, the 1998 Act includes a detailed revision of the prohibited acts enumerated in the 1984 Act. *Id.* § 1709 (Supp. 1999). The 1998 Act also gives the Federal Maritime Commission authority to prohibit—not just disapprove—unjust and unreasonable rates charged by controlled carriers. *Id.* § 1708(a) (Supp. 1999).

1347. *Id.* § 1706 (Supp. 1999).

1348. *Id.* § 1706(b)(4).

1349. *Id.* § 1702(13) (Supp. 1999).

1350. *Id.* § 1707(a)(2) (Supp. 1999).

1351. *Id.* § 1707(a)(1) (Supp. 1999).

shippers and common carriers with greater flexibility in entering into contractual arrangements."[1352]

The first major change concerns who may enter into a service contract. The 1998 Act (1) authorizes one or more shippers collectively to enter into a service contract, and (2) permits agreements between common carriers (aside from conferences) to enter into service contracts.[1353] Further, the 1998 Act permits members of common carrier agreements (as well as conferences) to enter into service contracts with shippers independent of any agreement (or conference).[1354] The 1998 Act also clarifies that agreements among ocean common carriers to engage in exclusive, preferential, or cooperative working arrangements with non-vessel-operating common carriers are to be treated as service contracts.[1355]

The 1998 Act provided for the confidential filing of service contracts with the Federal Maritime Commission.[1356] Under the new regime, only a few essential terms must be made available to the public.[1357] Moreover, the 1998 Act allows common carriers to negotiate different service contracts with similarly situated shippers.[1358] Thus, shippers can no longer demand "me too" discounts. A conference or group of two or more common carriers, however, may not discriminate based on a shipper's locality or port, or against a shippers' association or ocean transportation intermediary because of their status as such.[1359] These provisions are designed to promote competition and place a greater reliance on the marketplace.

1352. Report of the Senate Committee on Commerce, Science, and Transportation on S.414, S. REP. NO. 105-61, at 19 (1997).

1353. 46 U.S.C. App. §§ 1702 & 1704 (Supp. 1999).

1354. *Id.* § 1704(c) (Supp. 1999). The 1998 Act also shortens the notice period for taking independent action on a conference tariff from 10 to five days. *Id.* § 1704(b)(8) (Supp. 1999).

1355. *Id.* § 1703(a)(5); *see also* Report of the Senate Committee on Commerce, Science, and Transportation on S.414, S. REP. NO. 105-61, at 19 (1997).

1356. 46 U.S.C. App. § 1707(c)(2) (Supp. 1999).

1357. *Id.* § 1707(c)(3) (Supp. 1999).

1358. *Id.* § 1709(b) (Supp. 1999).

1359. *Id.* § 1709(c) (Supp. 1999).

APPENDIX A*

BASIC ANTITRUST AND TRADE REGULATION STATUTES

Sherman Act

Section 1

Every contract, combination in the form of trust or otherwise, or conspiracy, in restraint of trade or commerce among the several States, or with foreign nations, is declared to be illegal. Every person who shall make any contract or engage in any combination or conspiracy hereby declared to be illegal shall be deemed guilty of a felony, and, on conviction thereof, shall be punished by fine not exceeding $10,000,000 if a corporation, or, if any other person, $350,000, or by imprisonment not exceeding three years, or by both said punishments, in the discretion of the court. [15 U.S.C. § 1]

Section 2

Every person who shall monopolize, or attempt to monopolize, or combine or conspire with any other person or persons, to monopolize any part of the trade or commerce among the several States, or with foreign nations, shall be deemed guilty of a felony, and, on conviction thereof, shall be punished by fine not exceeding $10,000,000 if a corporation, or, if any other person, $350,000, or by imprisonment not exceeding three years, or by both said punishments, in the discretion of the court. [15 U.S.C. § 2]

Section 3

Every contract, combination in form of trust or otherwise, or conspiracy, in restraint of trade or commerce in any Territory of the United States or of the District of Columbia, or in restraint of trade or commerce between any such Territory and another, or between any such Territory or Territories and any State or States or the District of Columbia, or with foreign nations, or between the District of Columbia and any State or States or foreign nations, is declared illegal. Every person who shall make any such contract or engage in any such combination or conspiracy, shall be

---

deemed guilty of a felony, and, on conviction thereof, shall be punished by fine not exceeding $10,000,000 if a corporation, or, if any other person, $350,000, or by imprisonment not exceeding three years, or by both said punishments, in the discretion of the court. [15 U.S.C. § 3]

Section 4

The several district courts of the United States are invested with jurisdiction to prevent and restrain violations of [this Act]; and it shall be the duty of the several United States attorneys, in their respective districts, under the direction of the Attorney General, to institute proceedings in equity to prevent and restrain such violations. Such proceedings may be by way of petition setting forth the case and praying that such violation shall be enjoined or otherwise prohibited. When the parties complained of shall have been duly notified of such petition the court shall proceed, as soon as may be, to the hearing and determination of the case; and pending such petition and before final decree, the court may at any time make such temporary restraining order or prohibition as shall be deemed just in the premises. [15 U.S.C. § 4]

Section 5

Whenever it shall appear to the court before which any proceeding under section 4 of this [Act] may be pending, that the ends of justice require that other parties should be brought before the court, the court may cause them to be summoned, whether they reside in the district in which the court is held or not; and subpoenas to that end may be served in any district by the marshal thereof. [15 U.S.C. § 5]

Section 6

Any property owned under any contract or by any combination, or pursuant to any conspiracy (and being the subject thereof) mentioned in section 1 of this [Act], and being in the course of transportation from one State to another, or to a foreign country, shall be forfeited to the United States, and may be seized and condemned by like proceedings as those provided by law for the forfeiture, seizure, and condemnation of property imported into the United States contrary to law. [15 U.S.C. § 6]

*Section 6a**

[This Act] shall not apply to conduct involving trade or commerce (other than import trade or import commerce) with foreign nations unless—

---

*   This is the Export Trading Company Act, Pub. L. No. 97-290, 96 Stat. 1246 (1982), amendment to the Sherman Act.

(1) such conduct has a direct, substantial, and reasonably foreseeable effect—

(A) on trade or commerce which is not trade or commerce with foreign nations, or on import trade or import commerce with foreign nations; or

(B) on export trade or export commerce with foreign nations, of a person engaged in such trade or commerce in the United States; and

(2) such effect gives rise to a claim under the provisions of [this Act], other than this section.

If [this Act applies] to such conduct only because of the operation of paragraph (1)(B), then [this Act] shall apply to such conduct only for injury to export business in the United States. [15 U.S.C. § 6a]

Section 7

The word "person," or "persons," wherever used in [this Act] shall be deemed to include corporations and associations existing under or authorized by the laws of either the United States, the laws of any of the Territories, the laws of any State, or the laws of any foreign country. [15 U.S.C. § 7]

Clayton Act

Section 1

(a) "Antitrust laws," as used herein, includes the Act entitled "An Act to protect trade and commerce against unlawful restraints and monopolies," approved July second, eighteen hundred and ninety; sections seventy-three to seventy-seven, inclusive, of an Act entitled "An Act to reduce taxation, to provide revenue for the Government, and for other purposes," of August twenty-seventh, eighteen hundred and ninety-four; an Act entitled "An Act to amend sections seventy-three and seventy-six of the Act of August twenty-seventh, eighteen hundred and ninety-four, entitled 'An Act to reduce taxation, to provide revenue for the Government, and for other purposes,'" approved February twelfth, nineteen hundred and thirteen; and also this Act.

"Commerce," as used herein, means trade or commerce among the several States and with foreign nations, or between the District of Columbia or any Territory of the United States and any State, Territory, or foreign nation, or between any insular possessions or other places under the jurisdiction of the United States, or between any such possession or place and any State or Territory of the United States or the District of Columbia or any foreign nation, or within the District of Columbia or any Territory or any insular possession or other place under the jurisdiction of the United States: Provided, That nothing in this Act contained shall apply to the Philippine Islands.

The word "person" or "persons" wherever used in this Act shall be deemed to include corporations and associations existing under or authorized by the laws of either the United States, the laws of any of the Territories, the laws of any State, or the laws of any foreign country.

(b) This Act may be cited as the "Clayton Act". [15 U.S.C. § 12]

*Section 2**

(a)   It shall be unlawful for any person engaged in commerce, in the course of such commerce, either directly or indirectly, to discriminate in price between different purchasers of commodities of like grade and quality, where either or any of the purchases involved in such discrimination are in commerce, where such commodities are sold for use, consumption, or resale within the United States or any Territory thereof or the District of Columbia or any insular possession or other place under the jurisdiction of the United States, and where the effect of such discrimination may be substantially to lessen competition or tend to create a monopoly in any line of commerce, or to injure, destroy, or prevent competition with any person who either grants or knowingly receives the benefit of such discrimination, or with customers of either of them: Provided, That nothing herein contained shall prevent differentials which make only due allowance for differences in the cost of manufacture, sale, or delivery resulting from the differing methods or quantities in which such commodities are to such purchasers sold or delivered: Provided, however, That the Federal Trade Commission may, after due investigation and hearing to all interested parties, fix and establish quantity limits, and revise the same as it finds necessary, as to particular commodities or classes of commodities, where it finds that available purchasers in greater quantities are so few as to render differentials on account thereof unjustly discriminatory or promotive of monopoly in any line of commerce; and the foregoing shall then not be construed to permit differentials based on differences in quantities greater than those so fixed and established: And provided further, That nothing herein contained shall prevent persons engaged in selling goods, wares, or merchandise in commerce from selecting their own customers in bona fide transactions and not in restraint of trade: And provided further, That nothing herein contained shall prevent price changes from time to time where in response to changing conditions affecting the market for or the marketability of the goods concerned, such as but not limited to actual or imminent deterioration of perishable goods, obsolescence of seasonal goods, distress sales under court process, or sales in good faith in discontinuance of business in the goods concerned.   [15 U.S.C. § 13(a)]

(b)   Upon proof being made, at any hearing on a complaint under this section, that there has been discrimination in price or services or facilities furnished, the burden of rebutting the prima-facie case thus made by showing justification shall be upon the person charged with a violation of this section, and unless justification shall be affirmatively shown, the Commission is authorized to issue an order terminating the discrimination: Provided, however, That nothing herein contained shall prevent a seller rebutting the prima-facie case thus made by showing that his lower price or the furnishing of services or facilities to any purchaser or purchasers was made in good faith to meet an equally low price of a competitor, or the services or facilities furnished by a competitor.   [15 U.S.C. § 13(b)]

(c)   It shall be unlawful for any person engaged in commerce, in the course of such commerce, to pay or grant, or to receive or accept, anything of value as a

---

*   Robinson-Patman Act amendments to the Clayton Act.

commission, brokerage, or other compensation, or any allowance or discount in lieu thereof, except for services rendered in connection with the sale or purchase of goods, wares, or merchandise, either to the other party to such transaction or to an agent, representative, or other intermediary therein where such intermediary is acting in fact for or in behalf, or is subject to the direct or indirect control, of any party to such transaction other than the person by whom such compensation is so granted or paid. [15 U.S.C. § 13(c)]

(d)   It shall be unlawful for any person engaged in commerce to pay or contract for the payment of anything of value to or for the benefit of a customer of such person in the course of such commerce as compensation or in consideration for any services or facilities furnished by or through such customer in connection with the processing, handling, sale, or offering for sale of any products or commodities manufactured, sold, or offered for sale by such person, unless such payment or consideration is available on proportionally equal terms to all other customers competing in the distribution of such products or commodities. [15 U.S.C. § 13(d)]

(e)   It shall be unlawful for any person to discriminate in favor of one purchaser against another purchaser or purchasers of a commodity bought for resale, with or without processing, by contracting to furnish or furnishing, or by contributing to the furnishing of, any services or facilities connected with the processing, handling, sale, or offering for sale of such commodity so purchased upon terms not accorded to all purchasers on proportionally equal terms. [15 U.S.C. § 13(e)]

(f)   It shall be unlawful for any person engaged in commerce, in the course of such commerce, knowingly to induce or receive a discrimination in price which is prohibited by this section. [15 U.S.C. § 13(f)]

Section 3

It shall be unlawful for any person engaged in commerce, in the course of such commerce, to lease or make a sale or contract for sale of goods, wares, merchandise, machinery, supplies, or other commodities, whether patented or unpatented, for use, consumption, or resale within the United States or any Territory thereof or the District of Columbia or any insular possession or other place under the jurisdiction of the United States, or fix a price charged therefor, or discount from, or rebate upon, such price, on the condition, agreement, or understanding that the lessee or purchaser thereof shall not use or deal in the goods, wares, merchandise, machinery, supplies, or other commodities of a competitor or competitors of the lessor or seller, where the effect of such lease, sale, or contract for sale or such condition, agreement, or understanding may be to substantially lessen competition or tend to create a monopoly in any line of commerce. [15 U.S.C. § 14]

Section 4

(a)   Except as provided in subsection (b) of this section, any person who shall be injured in his business or property by reason of anything forbidden in the antitrust laws may sue therefor in any district court of the United States in the district in which the defendant resides or is found or has an agent, without respect to the amount in controversy, and shall recover threefold the damages by him sustained, and the cost of suit, including a reasonable attorney's fee. The court may award under this section, pursuant to a motion by such person promptly made, simple interest on actual damages for the period beginning on the date of service of such person's pleading setting forth a claim under the antitrust laws and ending on the date of judgment, or for any shorter period therein, if the court finds that the award of such interest for such period is just in the circumstances. In determining whether an award of interest under this section for any period is just in the circumstances, the court shall consider only—

(1)   whether such person or the opposing party, or either party's representative, made motions or asserted claims or defenses so lacking in merit as to show that such party or representative acted intentionally for delay, or otherwise acted in bad faith;

(2)   whether, in the course of the action involved, such person or the opposing party, or either party's representative, violated any applicable rule, statute, or court order providing for sanctions for dilatory behavior or otherwise providing for expeditious proceedings; and

(3)   whether such person or the opposing party, or either party's representative, engaged in conduct primarily for the purpose of delaying the litigation or increasing the cost thereof. [15 U.S.C. § 15(a)]

(b)(1)   Except as provided in paragraph (2), any person who is a foreign state may not recover under subsection (a) of this section an amount in excess of the actual damages sustained by it and the cost of suit, including a reasonable attorney's fee.

(2)   Paragraph (1) shall not apply to a foreign state if –

(A)   such foreign state would be denied, under section 1605(a)(2) of Title 28, immunity in a case in which the action is based upon a commercial activity, or an act, that is the subject matter of its claim under this section;

(B)   such foreign state waives all defenses based upon or arising out of its status as a foreign state, to any claims brought against it in the same action;

(C)   such foreign state engages primarily in commercial activities; and

(D)   such foreign state does not function, with respect to the commercial activity, or the act, that is the subject matter of its claim under this section as a procurement entity for itself or for another foreign state. [15 U.S.C. § 15(b)]

(c)   For purposes of this section—

(1)   the term "commercial activity" shall have the meaning given it in section 1603(d) of Title 28, and

(2)   the term "foreign state" shall have the meaning given it in section 1603(a) of Title 28. [15 U.S.C. § 15(c)]

Section 4A

Whenever the United States is hereafter injured in its business or property by reason of anything forbidden in the antitrust laws it may sue therefor in the United States district court for the district in which the defendant resides or is found or has an agent, without respect to the amount in controversy, and shall recover threefold the damages by it sustained and the cost of suit. The court may award under this section, pursuant to a motion by the United States promptly made, simple interest on actual damages for the period beginning on the date of service of the pleading of the United States setting forth a claim under the antitrust laws and ending on the date of judgment, or for any shorter period therein, if the court finds that the award of such interest for such period is just in the circumstances. In determining whether an award of interest under this section for any period is just in the circumstances, the court shall consider only—

(1) whether the United States or the opposing party, or either party's representative, made motions or asserted claims or defenses so lacking in merit as to show that such party or representative acted intentionally for delay or otherwise acted in bad faith;

(2) whether, in the course of the action involved, the United States or the opposing party, or either party's representative, violated any applicable rule, statute, or court order providing for sanctions for dilatory behavior or otherwise providing for expeditious proceedings;

(3) whether the United States or the opposing party, or either party's representative, engaged in conduct primarily for the purpose of delaying the litigation or increasing the cost thereof; and

(4) whether the award of such interest is necessary to compensate the United States adequately for the injury sustained by the United States. [15 U.S.C. § 15a]

Section 4B

Any action to enforce any cause of action under sections [4, 4A, or 4C] of this [Act] shall be forever barred unless commenced within four years after the cause of action accrued. No cause of action barred under existing law on the effective date of this Act shall be revived by this Act. [15 U.S.C. § 15b]

Section 4C

(a)(1) Any attorney general of a State may bring a civil action in the name of such State, as parens patriae on behalf of natural persons residing in such State, in any district court of the United States having jurisdiction of the defendant, to secure monetary relief as provided in this section for injury sustained by such natural persons to their property by reason of any violation of [the Sherman Act]. The court shall exclude from the amount of monetary relief awarded in such action any amount of monetary relief (A) which duplicates amounts which have been awarded for the same injury, or (B) which is properly allocable to (i) natural persons who have excluded their claims pursuant to subsection (b)(2) of this section, and (ii) any business entity.

(2) The court shall award the State as monetary relief threefold the total damage sustained as described in paragraph (1) of this subsection, and the cost of suit, including a reasonable attorney's fee. The court may award under this paragraph, pursuant to a motion by such State promptly made, simple interest on the total damage for the period beginning on the date of service of such State's pleading setting forth a claim under the antitrust laws and ending on the date of judgment, or for any shorter period therein, if the court finds that the award of such interest for such period is just in the circumstances. In determining whether an award of interest

under this paragraph for any period is just in the circumstances, the court shall consider only—

(A)   whether such State or the opposing party, or either party's representative, made motions or asserted claims or defenses so lacking in merit as to show that such party or representative acted intentionally for delay or otherwise acted in bad faith;

(B)   whether, in the course of the action involved, such State or the opposing party, or either party's representative, violated any applicable rule, statute, or court order providing for sanctions for dilatory behavior or otherwise providing for expeditious proceedings; and

(C)   whether such State or the opposing party, or either party's representative, engaged in conduct primarily for the purpose of delaying the litigation or increasing the cost thereof.

(b)(1)   In any action brought under subsection (a)(1) of this section, the State attorney general shall, at such times, in such manner, and with such content as the court may direct, cause notice thereof to be given by publication. If the court finds that notice given solely by publication would deny due process of law to any person or persons, the court may direct further notice to such person or persons according to the circumstances of the case.

(2)   Any person on whose behalf an action is brought under subsection (a)(1) of this section may elect to exclude from adjudication the portion of the State claim for monetary relief attributable to him by filing notice of such election with the court within such time as specified in the notice given pursuant to paragraph (1) of this subsection.

(3)   The final judgement in an action under subsection (a)(1) of this section shall be res judicata as to any claim under section [4 of this Act] by any person on behalf of whom such action was brought and who fails to give such notice within the period specified in the notice given pursuant to paragraph (1) of this subsection.

(c)   An action under subsection (a)(1) of this section shall not be dismissed or compromised without the approval of the court, and notice of any proposed dismissal or compromise shall be given in such manner as the court directs.

(d)   In any action under subsection (a) of this section—

(1)   the amount of the plaintiffs' attorney's fee, if any, shall be determined by the court; and

(2)   the court may, in its discretion, award a reasonable attorney's fee to a prevailing defendant upon a finding that the State attorney general has acted in bad faith, vexatiously, wantonly, or for oppressive reasons [15 U.S.C. § 15c]

Section 4D

In any action under section [4C](a)(1) of this [Act], in which there has been a determination that a defendant agreed to fix prices in violation of [the Sherman Act], damages may be proved and assessed in the aggregate by statistical or sampling methods, by the computation of illegal overcharges, or by such other reasonable system of estimating aggregate damages as the court in its discretion may permit without the necessity of separately proving the individual claim of, or amount of damage to, persons on whose behalf the suit was brought. [15 U.S.C. § 15d]

Section 4E

Monetary relief recovered in an action under section [4C](a)(1) of this [Act] shall—

(1) be distributed in such manner as the district court in its discretion may authorize; or

(2) be deemed a civil penalty by the court and deposited with the State as general revenues;

subject in either case to the requirement that any distribution procedure adopted afford each person a reasonable opportunity to secure his appropriate portion of the net monetary relief. [15 U.S.C. § 15e]

Section 4F

(a) Whenever the Attorney General of the United States has brought an action under the antitrust laws, and he has reason to believe that any State attorney general would be entitled to bring an action under this Act based substantially on the same alleged violation of the antitrust laws, he shall promptly give written notification thereof to such State attorney general.

(b) To assist a State attorney general in evaluating the notice or in bringing any action under this Act, the Attorney General of the United States shall, upon request by such State attorney general, make available to him, to the extent permitted by law, any investigative files or other materials which are or may be relevant or material to the actual or potential cause of action under this Act. [15 U.S.C. § 15f]

Section 4G

For the purposes of sections [4C, 4D, 4E, and 4F] of this [Act]:

(1) The term "State attorney general" means the chief legal officer of a State, or any other person authorized by State law to bring actions under section [4C] of this [Act], and includes the Corporation Counsel of the District of Columbia, except that such term does not include any person employed or retained on—

(A) a contingency fee based on a percentage of the monetary relief awarded under this section; or

(B) any other contingency fee basis, unless the amount of the award of a reasonable attorney's fee to a prevailing plaintiff is determined by the court under section [4C](d)(1) of this [Act].

(2) The term "State" means a State, the District of Columbia, the Commonwealth of Puerto Rico, and any other territory or possession of the United States.

(3) The term "natural persons" does not include proprietorships or partnerships. [15 U.S.C. § 15g]

Section 4H

Sections [4C, 4D, 4E, 4F, and 4G] of this [Act] shall apply in any State, unless such State provides by law for its nonapplicability in such State. [15 U.S.C. § 15h]

Section 5

(a)   A final judgment or decree heretofore or hereafter rendered in any civil or criminal proceeding brought by or on behalf of the United States under the antitrust laws to the effect that a defendant has violated said laws shall be prima facie evidence against such defendant in any action or proceeding brought by any other party against such defendant under said laws as to all matters respecting which said judgment or decree would be an estoppel as between the parties thereto: Provided, That this section shall not apply to consent judgments or decrees entered before any testimony has been taken.   Nothing contained in this section shall be construed to impose any limitation on the application of collateral estoppel, except that, in any action or proceeding brought under the antitrust laws, collateral estoppel effect shall not be given to any finding made by the Federal Trade Commission under the antitrust laws or under section [5 of the Federal Trade Commission Act] which could give rise to a claim for relief under the antitrust laws.

(b)   Any proposal for a consent judgment submitted by the United States for entry in any civil proceeding brought by or on behalf of the United States under the antitrust laws shall be filed with the district court before which such proceeding is pending and published by the United States in the Federal Register at least 60 days prior to the effective date of such judgment. Any written comments relating to such proposal and any responses by the United States thereto, shall also be filed with such district court and published by the United States in the Federal Register within such sixty-day period. Copies of such proposal and any other materials and documents which the United States considered determinative in formulating such proposal, shall also be made available to the public at the district court and in such other districts as the court may subsequently direct.   Simultaneously with the filing of such proposal, unless otherwise instructed by the court, the United States shall file with the district court, publish in the Federal Register, and thereafter furnish to any person upon request, a competitive impact statement which shall recite—

(1)   the nature and purpose of the proceeding;

(2)   a description of the practices or events giving rise to the alleged violation of the antitrust laws;

(3)   an explanation of the proposal for a consent judgment, including an explanation of any unusual circumstances giving rise to such proposal or any provision contained therein, relief to be obtained thereby, and the anticipated effects on competition of such relief;

(4)   the remedies available to potential private plaintiffs damaged by the alleged violations in the event that such proposal for the consent judgment is entered in such proceeding;

(5)   a description of the procedures available for modification of such proposal; and

(6) a description and evaluation of alternatives to such proposal actually considered by the United States.

(c) The United States shall also cause to be published, commencing at least 60 days prior to the effective date of the judgment described in subsection (b) of this section, for 7 days over a period of 2 weeks in newspapers of general circulation of the district in which the case has been filed, in the District of Columbia, and in such other districts as the court may direct—

  (i)   a summary of the terms of the proposal for consent judgment,

  (ii)   a summary of the competitive impact statement filed under subsection (b) of this section,

  (iii)   and a list of the materials and documents under subsection (b) of this section which the United States shall make available for purposes of meaningful public comment, and the place where such materials and documents are available for public inspection.

(d) During the 60-day period as specified in subsection (b) of this section, and such additional time as the United States may request and the court may grant, the United States shall receive and consider any written comments relating to the proposal for the consent judgment submitted under subsection (b) of this section. The Attorney General or his designee shall establish procedures to carry out the provisions of this subsection, but such 60-day time period shall not be shortened except by order of the district court upon a showing that (1) extraordinary circumstances require such shortening and (2) such shortening is not adverse to the public interest. At the close of the period during which such comments may be received, the United States shall file with the district court and cause to be published in the Federal Register a response to such comments.

(e) Before entering any consent judgment proposed by the United States under this section, the court shall determine that the entry of such judgment is in the public interest. For the purpose of such determination, the court may consider—

  (1) the competitive impact of such judgment, including termination of alleged violations, provisions for enforcement and modification, duration or relief sought, anticipated effects of alternative remedies actually considered, and any other considerations bearing upon the adequacy of such judgment;

  (2) the impact of entry of such judgment upon the public generally and individuals alleging specific injury from the violations set forth in the complaint including consideration of the public benefit, if any, to be derived from a determination of the issues at trial.

(f) In making its determination under subsection (e) of this section, the court may—

  (1) take testimony of Government officials or experts or such other expert witnesses, upon motion of any party or participant or upon its own motion, as the court may deem appropriate;

  (2) appoint a special master and such outside consultants or expert witnesses as the court may deem appropriate; and request and obtain the views, evaluations, or

advice of any individual, group or agency of government with respect to any aspects of the proposed judgment or the effect of such judgment, in such manner as the court deems appropriate;

(3)   authorize full or limited participation in proceedings before the court by interested persons or agencies, including appearance amicus curiae, intervention as a party pursuant to the Federal Rules of Civil Procedure, examination of witnesses or documentary materials, or participation in any other manner and extent which serves the public interest as the court may deem appropriate;

(4)   review any comments including any objections filed with the United States under subsection (d) of this section concerning the proposed judgment and the responses of the United States to such comments and objections; and

(5)   take such other action in the public interest as the court may deem appropriate.

(g)   Not later than 10 days following the date of the filing of any proposal for a consent judgment under subsection (b) of this section, each defendant shall file with the district court a description of any and all written or oral communications by or on behalf of such defendant, including any and all written or oral communications on behalf of such defendant, or other person, with any officer or employee of the United States concerning or relevant to such proposal, except that any such communications made by counsel of record alone with the Attorney General or the employees of the Department of Justice alone shall be excluded from the requirements of this subsection.   Prior to the entry of any consent judgment pursuant to the antitrust laws, each defendant shall certify to the district court that the requirements of this subsection have been complied with and that such filing is a true and complete description of such communications known to the defendant or which the defendant reasonably should have known.

(h)   Proceedings before the district court under subsections (e) and (f) of this section, and the competitive impact statement filed under subsection (b) of this section, shall not be admissible against any defendant in any action or proceeding brought by any other party against such defendant under the antitrust laws or by the United States under section [4A] of this [Act] nor constitute a basis for the introduction of the consent judgment as prima facie evidence against such defendant in any such action or proceeding.

(i)   Whenever any civil or criminal proceeding is instituted by the United States to prevent, restrain, or punish violations of any of the antitrust laws, but not including an action under section [4A] of this [Act], the running of the statute of limitations in respect to every private or State right of action arising under said laws and based in whole or in part on any matter complained of in said proceeding shall be suspended during the pendency thereof and for one year thereafter: Provided, however, That whenever the running of the statute of limitations in respect of a cause of action arising under section [4] or [4C] of this [Act] is suspended hereunder, any action to enforce such cause of action shall be forever barred unless commenced either within the period of suspension or within four years after the cause of action accrued. [15 U.S.C. § 16]

Section 6

The labor of a human being is not a commodity or article of commerce. Nothing contained in the antitrust laws shall be construed to forbid the existence and operation of labor, agricultural, or horticultural organizations, instituted for the purposes of mutual help, and not having capital stock or conducted for profit, or to forbid or restrain individual members of such organizations from lawfully carrying out the legitimate objects thereof; nor shall such organizations, or the members thereof, be held or construed to be illegal combinations or conspiracies in restraint of trade, under the antitrust laws. [15 U.S.C. § 17]

Section 7

No person engaged in commerce or in any activity affecting commerce shall acquire, directly or indirectly, the whole or any part of the stock or other share capital and no person subject to the jurisdiction of the Federal Trade Commission shall acquire the whole or any part of the assets of another person engaged also in commerce or in any activity affecting commerce, where in any line of commerce or in any activity affecting commerce in any section of the country, the effect of such acquisition may be substantially to lessen competition, or to tend to create a monopoly.

No person shall acquire, directly or indirectly, the whole or any part of the stock or other share capital and no person subject to the jurisdiction of the Federal Trade Commission shall acquire the whole or any part of the assets of one or more persons engaged in commerce or in any activity affecting commerce, where in any line of commerce or in any activity affecting commerce in any section of the country, the effect of such acquisition, of such stocks or assets, or of the use of such stock by the voting or granting of proxies or otherwise, may be substantially to lessen competition, or to tend to create a monopoly.

This section shall not apply to persons purchasing such stock solely for investment and not using the same by voting or otherwise to bring about, or in attempting to bring about, the substantial lessening of competition. Nor shall anything contained in this section prevent a corporation engaged in commerce or in any activity affecting commerce from causing the formation of subsidiary corporations for the actual carrying on of their immediate lawful business, or the natural and legitimate branches or extensions thereof, or from owning and holding all or a part of the stock of such subsidiary corporations, when the effect of such formation is not to substantially lessen competition.

Nor shall anything herein contained be construed to prohibit any common carrier subject to the laws to regulate commerce from aiding in the construction of branches or short lines so located as to become feeders to the main line of the company so aiding in such construction or from acquiring or owning all or any part of the stock of such branch lines, nor to prevent any such common carrier from acquiring and owning all or any part of the stock of a branch or short line constructed by an independent company where there is no substantial competition between the company owning the branch line so constructed and the company owning the main line acquiring the property or an interest therein, nor to prevent such common carrier from extending any of its lines through the medium of the acquisition of stock or otherwise of any other common carrier where there is no substantial competition between the company extending its lines and the company whose stock, property, or an interest therein is so acquired.

Nothing contained in this section shall be held to affect or impair any right heretofore legally acquired: Provided, That nothing in this section shall be held or construed to authorize or make lawful anything heretofore prohibited or made illegal by the antitrust laws, nor to exempt any person from the penal provisions thereof or the civil remedies therein provided.

Nothing contained in this section shall apply to transactions duly consummated pursuant to authority given by the Secretary of Transportation, Federal Power Commission, Surface Transportation Board, the Securities and Exchange Commission in the exercise of its jurisdiction under section [10 of the Public Utility Holding Company Act of 1955], the United States Maritime Commission, or the Secretary of Agriculture under any statutory provision vesting such power in such Commission, Board, or Secretary. [15 U.S.C. § 18]

Section 7A *

(a)   Except as exempted pursuant to subsection (c) of this section, no person shall acquire, directly or indirectly, any voting securities or assets of any other person, unless both persons (or in the case of a tender offer, the acquiring person) file notification pursuant to rules under subsection (d)(1) of this section and the waiting period described in subsection (b)(1) of this section has expired, if—

(1)   the acquiring person, or the person whose voting securities or assets are being acquired, is engaged in commerce or in any activity affecting commerce; and

(2)   as a result of such acquisition, the acquiring person would hold an aggregate amount of the voting securities and assets of the acquired person—

(A)   in excess of $200,000,000 (as adjusted and published for each fiscal year beginning after September 30, 2004, in the same manner as provided in section 8(a)(5) [of the Act] to reflect the percentage change in the gross national product for such fiscal year compared to the gross national product for the year ending September 30, 2003); or

(B)(i)   in excess of $50,000,000 (as so adjusted and published) but not in excess of $200,000,000 (as so adjusted and published); and

(ii) I.   any voting securities or assets of a person engaged in manufacturing which has annual net sales or total assets of $10,000,000 (as so adjusted and published) or more are being acquired by any person which has total assets or annual net sales of $100,000,000 (as so adjusted and published) or more;

II.   any voting securities or assets of a person not engaged in manufacturing which has total assets of $10,000,000 (as so adjusted and published) or more are being acquired by any person which has total assets or annual net sales of $100,000,000 (as so adjusted and published) or more; or

III.   any voting securities or assets of a person with annual net sales or total assets of $100,000,000 (as so adjusted and published) or more are being

---

* Hart-Scott-Rodino Antitrust Improvements Act amendments to the Clayton Act.

acquired by any person with total assets or annual net sales of $10,000,000 (as
so adjusted and published) or more.

In the case of a tender offer, the person whose voting securities are sought to be acquired by a person required to file notification under this subsection shall file notification pursuant to rules under subsection (d) of this section.

(b)(1)   The waiting period required under subsection (a) of this section shall—

(A)   begin on the date of the receipt by the Federal Trade Commission and the Assistant Attorney General in charge of the Antitrust Division of the Department of Justice (hereinafter referred to in this section as the "Assistant Attorney General") of—

(i)   the completed notification required under subsection (a) of this section, or

(ii)   if such notification is not completed, the notification to the extent completed and a statement of the reasons for such noncompliance, from both persons, or, in the case of a tender offer, the acquiring person; and

(B)   end on the thirtieth day after the date of such receipt (or in the case of a cash tender offer, the fifteenth day), or on such later date as may be set under subsection (e)(2) or (g)(2) of this section.

(2)   The Federal Trade Commission and the Assistant Attorney General may, in individual cases, terminate the waiting period specified in paragraph (1) and allow any person to proceed with any acquisition subject to this section, and promptly shall cause to be published in the Federal Register a notice that neither intends to take any action within such period with respect to such acquisition.

(3)   As used in this section—

(A)   The term "voting securities" means any securities which at present or upon conversion entitle the owner or holder thereof to vote for the election of directors of the issuer or, with respect to unincorporated issuers, persons exercising similar functions.

(B)   The amount or percentage of voting securities or assets of a person which are acquired or held by another person shall be determined by aggregating the amount or percentage of such voting securities or assets held or acquired by such other person and each affiliate thereof.

(c)   The following classes of transactions are exempt from the requirements of this section—

(1)   acquisitions of goods or realty transferred in the ordinary course of business;

(2)   acquisitions of bonds, mortgages, deeds of trust, or other obligations which are not voting securities;

(3)   acquisitions of voting securities of an issuer at least 50 per centum of the voting securities of which are owned by the acquiring person prior to such acquisition;

(4)   transfers to or from a Federal agency or a State or political subdivision thereof;

(5)   transactions specifically exempted from the antitrust laws by Federal statute;

(6)   transactions specifically exempted from the antitrust laws by Federal statute if approved by a Federal agency, if copies of all information and documentary

material filed with such agency are contemporaneously filed with the Federal Trade Commission and the Assistant Attorney General;

(7) transactions which require agency approval under [§ 301 of the Financial Institutions Reform, Recovery, and Enforcement Act, 12 U.S.C. § 1467a(e), § 18(c) of the Federal Deposit Insurance Act, 12 U.S.C. § 1828(c), or § 3 of the Bank Holding Company Act of 1956, 12 U.S.C. § 1842], except that a portion of such a transaction is not exempt under this paragraph if such portion of the transaction

(A) is subject to [§ 103(a) of the Gramm-Leach-Bliley Act, 12 U.S.C. § 1843(k)]; and

(B) does not require agency approval under [§ 3 of the Bank Holding Company Act of 1956, 12 U.S.C. § 1842];

(8) transactions which require agency approval under [§ 4 of the Bank Holding Company Act of 1956, 12 U.S.C. § 1843, or § 5 of the Home Owners' Loan Act of 1933, 12 U.S.C. § 1464], if copies of all information and documentary material filed with any such agency are contemporaneously filed with the Federal Trade Commission and the Assistant Attorney General at least 30 days prior to consummation of the proposed transaction, except that a portion of such a transaction is not exempt under this paragraph if such portion of the transaction

(A) is subject to [§ 103(a) of the Gramm-Leach-Bliley Act, 12 U.S.C. § 1843(k)]; and

(B) does not require agency approval under [§ 3 of the Bank Holding Company Act of 1956, 12 U.S.C. § 1842];

(9) acquisitions, solely for the purpose of investment, of voting securities, if, as a result of such acquisition, the securities acquired or held do not exceed 10 per centum of the outstanding voting securities of the issuer;

(10) acquisitions of voting securities, if, as a result of such acquisition, the voting securities acquired do not increase, directly or indirectly, the acquiring person's per centum share of outstanding voting securities of the issuer;

(11) acquisitions, solely for the purpose of investment, by any bank, banking association, trust company, investment company, or insurance company, of

(A) voting securities pursuant to a plan of reorganization or dissolution; or

(B) assets in the ordinary course of its business; and

(12) such other acquisitions, transfers, or transactions, as may be exempted under subsection (d)(2)(B) of this section.

(d) The Federal Trade Commission, with the concurrence of the Assistant Attorney General and by rule in accordance with section 553 of Title 5, consistent with the purposes of this section—

(1) shall require that the notification required under subsection (a) of this section be in such form and contain such documentary material and information relevant to a proposed acquisition as is necessary and appropriate to enable the Federal Trade Commission and the Assistant Attorney General to determine whether such acquisition may, if consummated, violate the antitrust laws; and

(2) may—

(A) define the terms used in this section;

(B) exempt, from the requirements of this section, classes of persons, acquisitions, transfers, or transactions which are not likely to violate the antitrust laws; and

(C) prescribe such other rules as may be necessary and appropriate to carry out the purposes of this section.

(e)(1)(A) The Federal Trade Commission or the Assistant Attorney General may, prior to the expiration of the 30-day waiting period (or in the case of a cash tender offer, the 15-day waiting period) specified in subsection (b)(1) of this section, require the submission of additional information or documentary material relevant to the proposed acquisition, from a person required to file notification with respect to such acquisition under subsection (a) of this section prior to the expiration of the waiting period specified in subsection (b)(1) of this section, or from any officer, director, partner, agent, or employee of such person.

(B)(i) The Assistant Attorney General and the Federal Trade Commission shall each designate a senior official who does not have direct responsibility for the review of any enforcement recommendation under this section concerning the transaction at issue, to hear any petition filed by such person to determine—

(I) whether the request for additional information or documentary material is unreasonably cumulative, unduly burdensome, or duplicative; or

(II) whether the request for additional information or documentary material has been substantially complied with by the petitioning person.

(ii) Internal review procedures for petitions filed pursuant to clause (i) shall include reasonable deadlines for expedited review of such petitions, after reasonable negotiations with investigative staff, in order to avoid undue delay of the merger review process.

(iii) Not later than 90 days after December 21, 2000, the Assistant Attorney General and the Federal Trade Commission shall conduct an internal review and implement reforms of the merger review process in order to eliminate unnecessary burden, remove costly duplication, and eliminate undue delay, in order to achieve a more effective and more efficient merger review process.

(iv) Not later than 120 days after December 21, 2000, the Assistant Attorney General and the Federal Trade Commission shall issue or amend their respective industry guidance, regulations, operating manuals and relevant policy documents, to the extent appropriate, to implement each reform in this subparagraph.

(v) Not later than 180 days after December 21, 2000, the Assistant Attorney General and the Federal Trade Commission shall each report to Congress—

(I) which reforms each agency has adopted under this subparagraph;

(II) which steps each has taken to implement such internal reforms; and

(III) the effects of such reforms.

(2) The Federal Trade Commission or the Assistant Attorney General, in its or his discretion, may extend the 30-day waiting period (or in the case of a cash tender offer, the 15-day waiting period) specified in subsection (b)(1) of this section for an additional period of not more than 30 days (or in the case of a cash tender offer, 10 days) after the date on which the Federal Trade Commission or the Assistant Attorney General, as the case may be, receives from any person to whom a request is made under paragraph (1), or in the case of tender offers, the acquiring person, (A)

all the information and documentary material required to be submitted pursuant to such a request, or (B) if such request is not fully complied with, the information and documentary material submitted and a statement of the reasons for such noncompliance. Such additional period may be further extended only by the United States district court, upon an application by the Federal Trade Commission or the Assistant Attorney General pursuant to subsection (g)(2) of this section.

(f) If a proceeding is instituted or an action is filed by the Federal Trade Commission, alleging that a proposed acquisition violates [§7] of this [Act], or [§5 of the Federal Trade Commission Act], or an action is filed by the United States, alleging that a proposed acquisition violates such [§7] of this [Act], or section 1 or 2 of this [Act], and the Federal Trade Commission or the Assistant Attorney General (1) files a motion for a preliminary injunction against consummation of such acquisition pendente lite, and (2) certifies the United States district court for the judicial district within which the respondent resides or carries on business, or in which the action is brought, that it or he believes that the public interest requires relief pendente lite pursuant to this subsection, then upon the filing of such motion and certification, the chief judge of such district court shall immediately notify the chief judge of the United States court of appeals for the circuit in which such district court is located, who shall designate a United States district judge to whom such action shall be assigned for all purposes.

(g)(1) Any person, or any officer, director, or partner thereof, who fails to comply with any provision of this section shall be liable to the United States for a civil penalty of not more than $10,000 for each day during which such person is in violation of this section. Such penalty may be recovered in a civil action brought by the United States.

    (2) If any person, or any officer, director, partner, agent, or employee thereof, fails substantially to comply with the notification requirement under subsection (a) of this section or any request for the submission of additional information or documentary material under subsection (e)(1) of this section within the waiting period specified in subsection (b)(1) of this section and as may be extended under subsection (e)(2) of this section, the United States district court—

        (A) may order compliance;

        (B) shall extend the waiting period specified in subsection (b)(1) of this section and as may have been extended under subsection (e)(2) of this section until there has been substantial compliance, except that, in the case of a tender offer, the court may not extend such waiting period on the basis of a failure, by the person whose stock is sought to be acquired, to comply substantially with such notification requirement or any such request; and

        (C) may grant such other equitable relief as the court in its discretion determines necessary or appropriate, upon application of the Federal Trade Commission or the Assistant Attorney General.

(h) Any information or documentary material filed with the Assistant Attorney General or the Federal Trade Commission pursuant to this section shall be exempt from disclosure under section 552 of title 5, and no such information or documentary material may be made public, except as may be relevant to any administrative or judicial action or proceeding. Nothing in this section is intended to prevent disclosure to either body of Congress or to any duly authorized committee or subcommittee of the Congress.

(i)(1)   Any action taken by the Federal Trade Commission or the Assistant Attorney General or any failure of the Federal Trade Commission or the Assistant Attorney General to take any action under this section shall not bar any proceeding or any action with respect to such acquisition at any time under any other section of this Act or any other provision of law.

(2)   Nothing contained in this section shall limit the authority of the Assistant Attorney General or the Federal Trade Commission to secure at any time from any person documentary material, oral testimony, or other information under the Antitrust Civil Process Act [15 U.S.C. §§ 1311 et seq.], the Federal Trade Commission Act [15 U.S.C. §§ 41 et seq.], or any other provision of law.

(j)   Reserved.

(k)   If the end of any period of time provided in this section falls on a Saturday, Sunday, or legal public holiday (as defined in section 6103(a) of title 5), then such period shall be extended to the end of the next day that is not a Saturday, Sunday, or legal public holiday. [15 U.S.C. § 18a]

Section 8

(a)(1)   No person shall, at the same time, serve as a director or officer in any two corporations (other than banks, banking associations, and trust companies) that are—
   (A)   engaged in whole or in part in commerce; and
   (B)   by virtue of their business and location of operation, competitors, so that the elimination of competition by agreement between them would constitute a violation of any of the antitrust laws;
if each of the corporations has capital, surplus, and undivided profits aggregating more than $10,000,000 as adjusted pursuant to paragraph (5) of this subsection.

(2)   Notwithstanding the provisions of paragraph (1), simultaneous service as a director or officer in any two corporations shall not be prohibited by this section if—
   (A)   the competitive sales of either corporation are less than $1,000,000, as adjusted pursuant to paragraph (5) of this subsection;
   (B)   the competitive sales of either corporation are less than 2 per centum of that corporation's total sales; or
   (C)   the competitive sales of each corporation are less than 4 per centum of that corporation's total sales.
For purposes of this paragraph, "competitive sales" means the gross revenues for all products and services sold by one corporation in competition with the other, determined on the basis of annual gross revenues for such products and services in that corporation's last completed fiscal year. For the purposes of this paragraph, "total sales" means the gross revenues for all products and services sold by one corporation over that corporation's last completed fiscal year.

(3)   The eligibility of a director or officer under the provisions of paragraph (1) shall be determined by the capital, surplus and undivided profits, exclusive of

dividends declared but not paid to stockholders, of each corporation at the end of that corporation's last completed fiscal year.

(4)   For purposes of this section, the term "officer" means an officer elected or chosen by the Board of Directors.

(5)   For each fiscal year commencing after September 30, 1990, the $10,000,000 and $1,000,000 thresholds in this subsection shall be increased (or decreased) as of October 1 each year by an amount equal to the percentage increase (or decrease) in the gross national product, as determined by the Department of Commerce or its successor, for the year then ended over the level so established for the year ending September 30, 1989. As soon as practicable, but not later than January 31 of each year, the Federal Trade Commission shall publish the adjusted amounts required by this paragraph.

(b)   When any person elected or chosen as a director or officer of any corporation subject to the provisions hereof is eligible at the time of his election or selection to act for such corporation in such capacity, his eligibility to act in such capacity shall not be affected by any of the provisions hereof by reason of any change in the capital, surplus and undivided profits, or affairs of such corporation from whatever cause, until the expiration of one year from the date on which the event causing ineligibility occurred. [15 U.S.C. § 19]

Section 11

(a)   Authority to enforce compliance with sections [2, 3, 7, and 8] of this [Act] by the persons respectively subject thereto is vested in the Surface Transportation Board where applicable to common carriers subject to subtitle IV of Title 49; in the Federal Communications Commission where applicable to common carriers engaged in wire or radio communication or radio transmission of energy; in the Secretary of Transportation where applicable to air carriers and foreign air carriers subject to part A of subtitle VII of title 49; in the Board of Governors of the Federal Reserve System where applicable to banks, banking associations, and trust companies; and in the Federal Trade Commission where applicable to all other character of commerce to be exercised as follows:

(b)   Whenever the Commission, Board, or Secretary vested with jurisdiction thereof shall have reason to believe that any person is violating or has violated any of the provisions of sections [2, 3, 7, and 8] of this [Act], it shall issue and serve upon such person and the Attorney General a complaint stating its charges in that respect, and containing a notice of a hearing upon a day and at a place therein fixed at least thirty days after the service of said complaint. The person so complained of shall have the right to appear at the place and time so fixed and show cause why an order should not be entered by the Commission, Board, or Secretary requiring such person to cease and desist from the violation of the law so charged in said complaint. The Attorney General shall have the right to intervene and appear in said proceeding and any person may make application, and upon good cause shown may be allowed by the Commission, Board, or Secretary, to intervene and appear in said proceeding by counsel or in person. The testimony in any such proceeding shall be reduced to writing and filed in the office of the Commission, Board, or Secretary. If upon such hearing the Commission, Board, or Secretary, as the case may be, shall be of the opinion that any of the provisions of said sections have been or are being violated, it shall make a report in writing, in which it shall state its findings as to the facts, and shall issue and cause to be served on such person an order requiring such person to cease and desist from such violations, and divest itself of the stock, or other share capital, or assets, held or rid itself of the directors chosen contrary to the provisions of sections [7 and 8] of this [Act], if any there be, in the manner and within the time fixed by said order. Until the expiration of the time allowed for filing a petition for review, if no such petition has been duly filed within such time, or, if a petition for review has been filed within such time then until the record in the proceeding has been filed in a court of appeals of the United States, as hereinafter provided, the Commission, Board, or Secretary may at any time, upon such notice and in such manner as it shall deem proper, modify or set aside, in whole or in part, any report or any order made or issued by it under this section. After the expiration of the time allowed for filing a petition for review, if no such petition has been duly filed within such time, the Commission, Board, or Secretary may at any time, after notice and opportunity for hearing, reopen and alter, modify, or set aside, in whole or in part, any report or order made or issued by it under this section, whenever in the opinion of the Commission, Board, or Secretary conditions of fact or of law have so changed as to require such action or if the public interest shall so require: Provided however, That the said person may, within sixty days after service upon him or it of said report or order entered after such a reopening, obtain a review thereof in the appropriate court of appeals of the United States, in the manner provided in subsection (c) of this section.

(c) Any person required by such order of the commission, board or Secretary to cease and desist from any such violation may obtain a review of such order in the court of appeals of the United States for any circuit within which such violation occurred or within which such person resides or carries on business, by filing in the court, within sixty days after the date of the service of such order, a written petition praying that the order of the commission, board, or Secretary be set aside. A copy of such petition shall be forthwith transmitted by the clerk of the court to the commission, board, or Secretary, and thereupon the commission, board, or Secretary shall file in the court the record in the proceeding, as provided in section 2112 of Title 28, [of the U.S. Code]. Upon such filing of the petition the court shall have jurisdiction of the proceeding and of the question determined therein concurrently with the commission, board, or Secretary until the filing of the record, and shall have power to make and enter a decree affirming, modifying, or setting aside the order of the commission, board, or Secretary, and enforcing the same to the extent that such order is affirmed, and to issue such writs as are ancillary to its jurisdiction or are necessary in its judgment to prevent injury to the public or to competitors pendente lite. The findings of the commission, board, or Secretary as to the facts, if supported by substantial evidence, shall be conclusive. To the extent that the order of the commission, board, or Secretary is affirmed, the court shall issue its own order commanding obedience to the terms of such order of the commission, board, or Secretary. If either party shall apply to the court for leave to adduce additional evidence, and shall show to the satisfaction of the court that such additional evidence is material and that there were reasonable grounds for the failure to adduce such evidence in the proceeding before the commission, board, or Secretary, the court may order such additional evidence to be taken before the commission, board, or Secretary, and to be adduced upon the hearing in such manner and upon such terms and conditions as to the court may seem proper. The commission, board, or Secretary may modify its findings as to the facts, or make new findings, by reason of the additional evidence so taken, and shall file such modified or new findings, which if supported by substantial evidence, shall be conclusive, and its recommendation, if any, for the modification or setting aside of its original order, with the return of such additional evidence. The judgment and decree of the court shall be final, except that the same shall be subject to review by the Supreme Court upon certiorari, as provided in section 1254 of Title 28 [of the U.S. Code].

(d)   Upon the filing of the record with its jurisdiction of the court of appeals to affirm, enforce, modify, or set aside orders of the commission, board, or Secretary shall be exclusive.

(e)   No order of the commission, board, or Secretary or judgment of the court to enforce the same shall in anyway relieve or absolve any person from any liability under the antitrust laws.

(f)   Complaints, orders, and other processes of the commission, board, or Secretary under this section may be serviced by anyone duly authorized by the commission, board, or Secretary, either (1) by delivering a copy thereof to the person to be served, or to a member of the partnership to be served, or to the president, secretary, or other executive officer or a director of the corporation to be served; or (2) by leaving a copy thereof at the residence or the principal office or place of business of such person; or (3) by mailing by registered or certified mail a copy thereof addressed to such person at his or its residence or principal office or place of business. The verified return by the person so serving said complaint, order, or other process setting forth the manner of said service shall be proof of the same, and the return post office receipt for said complaint, order, or other process mailed by registered or certified mail as aforesaid shall be proof of the service of the same.

(g)   Any order issued under subsection (b) of this section shall become final—

   (1)   upon the expiration of the time allowed for filing a petition for review, if no such petition has been duly filed within such time; but the commission, board, or Secretary may thereafter modify or set aside its order to the extent provided in the last sentence of subsection (b) of this section; or

   (2)   upon the expiration of the time allowed for filing a petition for certiorari, if the order of the commission, board, or Secretary has been affirmed, or the petition for review has been dismissed by the court of appeals, and no petition for certiorari has been duly filed; or

   (3)   upon the denial of a petition for certiorari, if the order of the commission, board, or Secretary has been affirmed or the petition for review has been dismissed by the court of appeals; or

   (4)   upon the expiration of thirty days from the date of issuance of the mandate of the Supreme Court, if such Court directs that the order of the commission, board, or Secretary be affirmed or the petition for review be dismissed.

(h)   If the Supreme Court directs that the order of the commission, board, or Secretary be modified or set aside, the order of the commission, board, or Secretary rendered in accordance with the mandate of the Supreme Court shall become final upon the expiration of thirty days from the time it was rendered, unless within such thirty days either party has instituted proceedings to have such order corrected to accord with the mandate, in which event the order of the commission, board, or Secretary shall become final when so corrected.

(i)   If the order of the commission, board, or Secretary is modified or set aside by the court of appeals, and if (1) the time allowed for filing a petition for certiorari has expired and no such petition has been duly filed, or (2) the petition for certiorari has been denied, or (3) the decision of the court has been affirmed by the Supreme Court, then the order of the commission, board, or Secretary rendered in accordance with the mandate of the court of appeals shall become final on the expiration of thirty days from the time such order of the commission, board, or Secretary was rendered, unless within such thirty days either party has instituted proceedings to have such order corrected so that it will accord with the mandate, in which event the order of the commission, board, or Secretary shall become final when so corrected.

(j)   If the Supreme Court orders a rehearing; or if the case is remanded by the court of appeals to the commission, board, or Secretary for a rehearing, and if (1) the time allowed for filing a petition for certiorari has expired, and no such petition has been duly filed, or (2) the petition for certiorari has been denied, or (3) the decision of the court has been affirmed by the Supreme Court, then the order of the commission, board, or Secretary rendered upon such rehearing shall become final in the same manner as though no prior order of the commission, board, or Secretary had been rendered.

(k)   As used in this section the term "mandate," in case a mandate has been recalled prior to the expiration of thirty days from the date of issuance thereof, means the final mandate.

(l)   Any person who violates any order issued by the commission, board, or Secretary under subsection (b) of this section after such order has become final, and while such order is in effect, shall forfeit and pay to the United States a civil penalty of not more than $5,000 for each violation, which shall accrue to the United States and may be recovered in a civil action brought by the United States. Each separate violation of any such order shall be a separate offense, except that in the case of a violation through continuing failure or neglect to obey a final order of the commission, board, or Secretary each day of continuance of such failure or neglect shall be deemed a separate offense. [15 U.S.C. § 21(a)-(l)]

Section 12

Any suit, action, or proceeding under the antitrust laws against a corporation may be brought not only in the judicial district whereof it is an inhabitant, but also in any district wherein it may be found or transacts business; and all process in such cases may be served in the district of which it is an inhabitant, or wherever it may be found. [15 U.S.C. § 22]

Section 13

In any suit, action, or proceeding brought by or on behalf of the United States subpoenas for witnesses who are required to attend a court of the United States in any judicial district in any case, civil or criminal, arising under the antitrust laws may run into any other district: Provided, That in civil cases no writ of subpoena shall issue for witnesses living out of the district in which the court is held at a greater distance than one hundred miles from the place of holding the same without the permission of the trial court being first had upon proper application and cause shown. [15 U.S.C. § 23]

Section 14

Whenever a corporation shall violate any of the penal provisions of the antitrust laws, such violation shall be deemed to be also that of the individual directors, officers, or agents of such corporation who shall have authorized, ordered, or done any of the acts constituting in whole or part such violation, and such violation shall be deemed a misdemeanor, and upon conviction therefor of any such director, officer, or agent he shall be punished by a fine of not exceeding $5,000 or by imprisonment for not exceeding one year, or by both, in the discretion of the court. [15 U.S.C. § 24]

Section 15

The several district courts of the United States are invested with jurisdiction to prevent and restrain violations of this Act, and it shall be the duty of the several United States attorneys, in their respective districts, under the direction of the Attorney General, to institute proceedings in equity to prevent and restrain such violations. Such proceedings may be by way of petition setting forth the case and praying that such violation shall be enjoined or otherwise prohibited. When the parties complained of shall have been duly notified of such petition, the court shall proceed, as soon as may be, to the hearing and determination of the case; and pending such petition, and before final decree, the court may at any time make such temporary restraining order or prohibition as shall be deemed just in the premises. Whenever it shall appear to the court before which any such proceeding may be pending that the ends of justice require that other parties should be brought before the court, the court may cause them to be summoned whether they reside in the district in which the court is held or not, and subpoenas to that end may be served in any district by the marshal thereof. [15 U.S.C. § 25]

Section 16

Any person, firm, corporation, or association shall be entitled to sue for and have injunctive relief, in any court of the United States having jurisdiction over the parties, against threatened loss or damage by a violation of the antitrust laws, including sections [2, 3, 7, and 8] of this [Act], when and under the same conditions and principles as injunctive relief against threatened conduct that will cause loss or damage is granted by courts of equity, under the rules governing such proceedings, and upon the execution of proper bond against damages for an injunction improvidently granted and a showing that the danger of irreparable loss or damage is immediate, a preliminary injunction may issue: Provided, That nothing herein contained shall be construed to entitle any person, firm, corporation, or association, except the United States, to bring suit for injunctive relief against any common carrier subject to the jurisdiction of the Surface Transportation Board under subtitle IV of Title 49. In any action under this section in which the plaintiff substantially prevails, the court shall award the cost of suit, including a reasonable attorney's fee, to such plaintiff. [15 U.S.C. § 26]

Robinson-Patman Act (excerpt)

Section 3

It shall be unlawful for any person engaged in commerce, in the course of such commerce, to be a party to, or assist in, any transaction of sale, or contract to sell, which discriminates to his knowledge against competitors of the purchaser, in that, any discount, rebate, allowance, or advertising service charge is granted to the purchaser over and above any discount, rebate, allowance, or advertising service charge available at the time of such transaction to said competitors in respect of a sale of goods of like grade, quality, and quantity; to sell, or contract to sell, goods in any way part of the United States at prices lower than those exacted by said person elsewhere in the United States for the purpose of destroying competition, or eliminating a competitor in such part of the United States; or, to sell, or contract to sell, goods at unreasonably low prices for the purpose of destroying competition or eliminating a competitor.

Any person violating any part of the provisions of this section shall, upon conviction thereof, be fined not more than $5,000 or imprisoned not more than one year, or both.
[15 U.S.C. § 13a. Unlike Section 1, this section of the Robinson-Patman Act is not part of the Clayton Act. Robinson-Patman Act Sections 2 and 4 are not reprinted herein.]

Federal Trade Commission Act (excerpts)

Section 5

(a)(1) Unfair methods of competition in or affecting commerce, and unfair or deceptive acts or practices in or affecting commerce, are declared unlawful.

(2) The Commission is empowered and directed to prevent persons, partnerships, or corporations, except banks, savings and loan institutions described in section 57a(f)(3) of this title, Federal credit unions described in section 57a(f)(4) of this title, common carriers subject to the Acts to regulate commerce, air carriers and foreign air carriers subject to the Federal Aviation Act of 1958 [49 App. U.S.C. §§ 1301 et seq.], and persons, partnerships, or corporations insofar as they are subject

to the Packers and Stockyards Act, 1921, as amended [7 U.S.C. §§ 181 et seq.], except as provided in section 406(b) of said Act [7 U.S.C. § 227(b)], from using unfair methods of competition in or affecting commerce and unfair or deceptive acts or practices in or affecting commerce.

(3)   This subsection shall not apply to unfair methods of competition involving commerce with foreign nations (other than import commerce) unless—

(A)   such methods of competition have a direct, substantial, and reasonably foreseeable effect—

(i)   on commerce which is not commerce with foreign nations, or on import commerce with foreign nations; or

(ii)   on export commerce with foreign nations, of a person engaged in such commerce in the United States; and

(B)   such effect gives rise to a claim under the provisions of this subsection, other than this paragraph.

If this subsection applies to such methods of competition only because of the operation of subparagraph (A)(ii), this subsection shall apply to such conduct only for injury to export business in the United States.

(b)   Whenever the Commission shall have reason to believe that any such person, partnership, or corporation has been or is using any unfair method of competition or unfair or deceptive act or practice in or affecting commerce, and if it shall appear to the Commission that a proceeding by it in respect thereof would be to the interest of the public, it shall issue and serve upon such persons, partnership, or corporation a complaint stating its charges in that respect and containing a notice of a hearing upon a day and at a place therein fixed at least thirty days after the service of said complaint. The person, partnership, or corporation so complained of shall have the right to appear at the place and time so fixed and show cause why an order should not be entered by the Commission requiring such person, partnership, or corporation to cease and desist from the violation of the law so charged in said complaint. Any person, partnership, or corporation may make application, and upon good cause shown may be allowed by the Commission to intervene and appear in said proceeding by counsel or in person. The testimony in any such proceeding shall be reduced to writing and filed in the office of the Commission. If upon such hearing the Commission shall be of the opinion that the method of competition or the act or practice in question is prohibited by this subchapter, it shall make a report in writing in which it shall state its findings as to the facts and shall issue and cause to be served on such person, partnership, or corporation an order requiring such person, partnership, or corporation to cease and desist from using such method of competition or such act or practice. Until the expiration of the time allowed for filing a petition for review, if no such petition has been duly filed within such time, or, if a petition for review has been filed within such time then until the record in the proceeding has been filed in a court of appeals of the United States, as hereinafter provided, the Commission may at any time, upon such notice and in such manner as it shall deem proper, modify or set aside, in whole or in part, any report or any order made or issued by it under this section. After the expiration of the time allowed for filing a petition for review, if no such petition has been duly filed within such time, the Commission may at any time, after notice, and opportunity for hearing, reopen and alter, modify, or set aside, in whole or in part, any report or order made or issued by it under this section, whenever in the opinion of the Commission conditions of fact or of law have so changed as to require such action or if the public interest shall so require, except that (1) the said person, partnership, or corporation may, within sixty days after service upon him or it of said report or order entered after such a reopening, obtain a review thereof in the appropriate court of appeals in the United States, in the manner provided in subsection (c) of this section; and (2) in the case of an order, the Commission shall reopen any such order to consider whether such order (including any affirmative relief provision contained in such order) should be altered, modified, or set aside, in whole or in part, if the person, partnership, or corporation involved files a request with the Commission which makes a satisfactory showing that changed conditions of law or fact require such order to be altered, modified, or set aside, in whole or in part. The Commission shall determine whether to alter, modify, or set aside any order of the Commission in response to a request made by a person, partnership, or corporation under paragraph[1] (2) not later than 120 days after the date of the filing of such request.

(c)   Any person, partnership, or corporation required by an order of the Commission to cease and desist from using any method of competition or act or practice may obtain a review of such order in the court of appeals of the United States, within any circuit where the method of competition or the act or practice in question was used or where such person, partnership, or corporation resides or carries on business, by filing in the court, within sixty days from the date of the service of such order, a written petition praying that the order of the Commission be set aside. A copy of such petition shall be forthwith transmitted by the clerk of the court to the Commission, and thereupon the Commission shall file in the court the record in the proceeding, as provided in section 2112 of Title 28 [the U.S. Code]. Upon such filing of the petition the court shall have jurisdiction of the proceeding and of the question determined therein concurrently with the Commission until the filing of the record and shall have the power to make and enter a decree affirming, modifying, or setting aside the order of the Commission, and enforcing the same to the extent that such order is affirmed and to issue such writs as are ancillary to its jurisdiction or are necessary in its judgment to prevent injury to the public or to competitors pendente lite. The findings of the Commission as to the facts, if supported by evidence, shall be conclusive. To the extent that the order of the Commission is affirmed, the court shall thereupon issue its own order commending obedience to the terms of such order of the Commission. If either party shall apply to the court for leave to adduce additional evidence, and shall show to the satisfaction of the court that such additional evidence is material and that there were reasonable grounds for the failure to adduce such evidence in the proceeding before the Commission, the court may order such additional evidence to be taken before the Commission and to be adduced upon the hearing in such manner and upon such terms and conditions as to the court may seem proper. The Commission may modify its findings as to the facts, or make new findings, by reason of the additional evidence so taken, and it shall file such modified or new findings, which, if supported by evidence, shall be conclusive, and its recommendation, if any, for the modification or setting aside of its original order, with the return of such additional evidence. The judgment and decree of the court

---

1.   So in original. Probably should be "clause."

shall be final, except that the same shall be subject to review by the Supreme Court upon certiorari, as provided in section 347 of Title 28 [of the U.S. Code].

(d) Upon the filing of the record with it the jurisdiction of the court of appeals of the United States to affirm, enforce, modify, or set aside orders of the Commission shall be exclusive.

(e) No order of the Commission or judgment of court to enforce the same shall be anyway relieve or absolve any person, partnership, or corporation from any liability under the Antitrust Acts.

(f) Complaints, orders, and other processes of the Commission under this section may be served by anyone duly authorized by the Commission, either (a) by delivering a copy thereof to the person to be served, or to a member of the partnership to be served, or the president, secretary, or other executive officer or a director of the corporation to be served; or (b) by leaving a copy thereof at the residence or the principal office or place of business of such person, partnership, or corporation; or (c) by mailing a copy thereof by registered mail or by certified mail addressed to such person, partnership, or corporation at his or its residence or principal office or place of business. The verified return by the person so serving said complaint, order, or other process setting forth the manner of said service shall be proof of the same, and the return post office receipt of said complaint, order, or other process mailed by registered mail or by certified mail as aforesaid shall be proof of the service of the same.

(g) An order of the Commission to cease and desist shall become final—
 (1) Upon the expiration of the time allowed for filing a petition for review, if no such petition has been duly filed within such time; but the Commission may thereafter modify or set aside its order to the extent provided in the last sentence of subsection (b) of this section.
 (2) Except as to any order provision subject to paragraph (4), upon the sixtieth day after such order is served, if a petition for review has been duly filed; except that any such order may be stayed, in whole or in part and subject to such conditions as may be appropriate, by—
  (A) the Commission;
  (B) an appropriate court of appeals of the United States, if (i) a petition for review of such order is pending in such court, and (ii) an application for such a stay was previously submitted to the Commission and the Commission, within the 30-day period beginning on the date the application was received by the Commission, either denied the application or did not grant or deny the application; or
  (C) the Supreme Court, if an applicable petition for certiorari is pending.
 (3) For purposes of subsection (m)(1)(B) of this section and of section 57b(a)(2) of this title, if a petition for review of the order of the Commission has been filed—
  (A) upon the expiration of the time allowed for filing a petition for certiorari, if the order of the Commission has been affirmed or the petition for review has been dismissed by the court of appeals and no petition for certiorari has been duly filed;

(B)   upon the denial of a petition for certiorari, if the order of the Commission has been affirmed or the petition for review has been dismissed by the court of appeals; or

(C)   upon the expiration of 30 days from the date of issuance of a mandate of the Supreme Court directing that the order of the Commission be affirmed or the petition for review be dismissed.

(4)   In the case of an order provision requiring a person, partnership, or corporation to divest itself of stock, other share capital, or assets, if a petition for review of such order of the Commission has been filed—

(A)   upon the expiration of the time allowed for filing a petition for certiorari, if the order of the Commission has been affirmed or the petition for review has been dismissed by the court of appeals and no petition for certiorari has been duly filed;

(B)   upon the denial of a petition for certiorari, if the order of the Commission has been affirmed or the petition for review has been dismissed by the court of appeals; or

(C)   upon the expiration of 30 days from the date of issuance of a mandate of the Supreme Court directing that the order of the Commission be affirmed or the petition for review be dismissed.

(h)   If the Supreme Court directs that the order of the Commission be modified or set aside, the order of the Commission rendered in accordance with the mandate of the Supreme Court shall become final upon the expiration of thirty days from the time it was rendered, unless within such thirty days either party has instituted proceedings to have such order corrected to accord with the mandate, in which event the order of the Commission shall become final when so corrected.

(i)   If the order of the Commission is modified or set aside by the court of appeals, and if (1) the time allowed for filing a petition for certiorari has expired and no such petition has been duly filed, or (2) the petition for certiorari has been denied, or (3) the decision of the court has been affirmed by the Supreme Court, then the order of the Commission rendered in accordance with the mandate of the court of appeals shall become final on the expiration of thirty days from the time such order of the Commission was rendered, unless within such thirty days either party has instituted proceedings to have such order corrected so that it will accord with the mandate, in which event the order of the Commission shall become final when so corrected.

(j)   If the Supreme Court orders a rehearing; or if the case is remanded by the court of appeals to the Commission for a rehearing; and if (1) the time allowed for filing a petition for certiorari has expired, and no such petition has been duly filed, or (2) the petition for certiorari has been denied, or (3) the decision of the court has been affirmed by the Supreme Court, then the order of the Commission rendered upon such rehearing shall become final in the same manner as though no prior order of the Commission had been rendered.

(k)   As used in this section the term "mandate", in case a mandate has been recalled prior to the expiration of thirty days from the date of issuance thereof, means the final mandate.

(l)   Any person, partnership, or corporation who violates an order of the Commission after it has become final, and while such order is in effect, shall forfeit and pay to the United States a civil penalty of not more than $10,000 for each violation, which shall accrue to the United States and may be recovered in a civil action brought by the Attorney General of the United States. Each separate violation of such an order shall be a separate offense, except that in a case of a violation through continuing failure to obey or neglect to obey a final order of the Commission, each day of continuance of such failure or neglect shall be deemed a separate offense. In such actions, the United States district courts are empowered to grant mandatory injunctions and such other and further equitable relief as they deem appropriate in the enforcement of such final orders of the Commission.

(m)(1)(A)   The Commission may commence a civil action to recover a civil penalty in a district court of the United States against any person, partnership, or corporation which violates any rule under this chapter respecting unfair or deceptive acts or practices (other than an interpretive rule or a rule violation of which the Commission has provided is not an unfair or deceptive act or practice in violation of subsection (a)(1) of this section) with actual knowledge or knowledge fairly implied on the basis of objective circumstances that such act is unfair or deceptive and is prohibited by such rule. In such action, such person, partnership, or corporation shall be liable for a civil penalty of not more then $10,000 for each violation.

    (B)   If the Commission determines in a proceeding under subsection (b) of this section that any act or practice is unfair or deceptive, and issues a final cease and desist order, other than a consent order with respect to such act or practice, then the Commission may commence a civil action to obtain a civil penalty in a district court of the United States against any person, partnership, or corporation which engages in such act or practice—

        (1)   after such cease and desist order becomes final (whether or not such person, partnership, or corporation was subject to such cease and desist order), and

        (2)   with actual knowledge that such act or practice is unfair or deceptive and is unlawful under subsection (a)(1) of this section.

    In such action, such person, partnership, or corporation shall be liable for a civil penalty of not more than $10,000 for each violation.

    (C)   In the case of a violation through continuing failure to comply with a rule or with subsection (a)(1) of this section, each day of continuance of such failure shall be treated as` a separate violation, for purposes of subparagraph (A) and (B). In determining the amount of such a civil penalty, the court shall take into account the degree of culpability, any history of prior such conduct, ability to pay, effect on ability to continue to do business, and such other matters as justice may require.

    (2)   If the cease and desist order establishing that the act or practice is unfair or deceptive was not issued against the defendant in a civil penalty action under paragraph (1)(B) the issues of fact in such action against such defendant shall be tried de novo. Upon request of any party to such an action against such defendant, the court shall also review the determination of law made by the Commission in the proceeding under subsection (b) of this section that the act or practice which was the subject of such proceeding constituted an unfair or deceptive act or practice in violation of subsection (a) of this section.

(3)   The Commission may compromise or settle any action for a civil penalty if such compromise or settlement is accompanied by public statement of its reasons and is approved by the court.

(n)   The Commission shall have no authority under this section or section 57a of this title to declare unlawful an act or practice on the grounds that such act or practice is unfair unless the act or practice causes or is likely to cause substantial injury to consumers which is not reasonably avoidable by consumers themselves and not outweighed by countervailing benefits to consumers or to competition.   In determining whether an act or practice is unfair, the Commission may consider established public policies as evidence to be considered with all other evidence. Such public policy considerations may not serve as a primary basis for such determination. [15 U.S.C. § 45]

Section 13(b)

(b)   Whenever the Commission has reason to believe—
    (1)   that any person, partnership, or corporation is violating, or is about to violate, any provision of law enforced by the Federal Trade Commission, and
    (2)   that the enjoining thereof pending the issuance of a complaint by the Commission and until such complaint is dismissed by the Commission or set aside by the court on review, or until the order of the Commission made thereon has become final, would be in the interest of the public—
the Commission by any of its attorneys designated by it for such purpose may bring suit in a district court of the United States to enjoin any such act or practice. Upon a proper showing that, weighing the equities and considering the Commission's likelihood of ultimate success, such action would be in the public interest, and after notice to the defendant, a temporary restraining order or a preliminary injunction may be granted without bond: Provided, however, That if a complaint is not filed within such period (not exceeding 20 days) as may be specified by the court after issuance of the temporary restraining order or preliminary injunction, the order or injunction shall be dissolved by the court and be of no further force and effect: Provided further, That in proper cases the Commission may seek, and after proper proof, the court may issue, a permanent injunction. Any suit may be brought where such person, partnership, or corporation resides or transacts business, or wherever venue is proper under section 1391 of Title 28. In addition, the court may, if the court determines that the interests of justice require that any other person, partnership, or corporation should be a party in such suit, cause such other person, partnership, or corporation to be added as a party without regard to whether venue is otherwise proper in the district in which the suit is brought. In any suit under this section, process may be served on any person, partnership, or corporation wherever it may be found. [15 U.S.C. § 53(b)]

Section 18

(a)(1)   Except as provided in subsection (h) of this section, the Commission may prescribe—

(A) interpretive rules and general statements of policy with respect to unfair or deceptive acts or practices in or affecting commerce (within the meaning of section [5(a)(1) of this Act]), and

(B) rules which define with specificity acts or practices which are unfair or deceptive acts or practices in or affecting commerce (within the meaning of section [5(a)(1) of this Act]), except that the Commission shall not develop or promulgate any trade rule or regulation with regard to the regulation of the development and utilization of the standards and certification activities pursuant to this section. Rules under this subparagraph may include requirements prescribed for the purpose of preventing such acts or practices.

(2) The Commission shall have no authority under [this Act], other than its authority under this section, to prescribe any rule with respect to unfair or deceptive acts or practices in or affecting commerce (within the meaning of section [5(a)(1) of this Act]). The preceding sentence shall not affect any authority of the Commission to prescribe rules (including interpretive rules), and general statements of policy, with respect to unfair methods of competition in or affecting commerce.

(b)(1) When prescribing a rule under subsection (a)(1)(B) of this section, the Commission shall proceed in accordance with section 553 of Title 5 (without regard to any reference in such section to sections 556 and 557 of such title), and shall also (A) publish a notice of proposed rulemaking stating with particularity the text of the rule, including any alternatives, which the Commission proposes to promulgate, and the reason for the proposed rule; (B) allow interested persons to submit written data, views, and arguments, and make all such submissions publicly available; (C) provide an opportunity for an informal hearing in accordance with subsection (c) of this section; and (D) promulgate, if appropriate, a final rule based on the matter in the rulemaking record (as defined in subsection (e)(1)(B) of this section), together with a statement of basis and purpose.

(2)(A) Prior to the publication of any notice of proposed rulemaking pursuant to paragraph (1)(A), the Commission shall publish an advance notice of proposed rulemaking in the Federal Register. Such advance notice shall—

(i)   contain a brief description of the area of inquiry under consideration, the objectives which the Commission seeks to achieve, and possible regulatory alternatives under consideration by the Commission; and

(ii)   invite the response of interested parties with respect to such proposed rulemaking, including any suggestions or alternative methods for achieving such objectives.

(B) The Commission shall submit such advance notice of proposed rulemaking to the Committee on Commerce, Science, and Transportation of the Senate and to the Committee on Energy and Commerce of the House of Representatives. The Commission may use such additional mechanisms as the Commission considers useful to obtain suggestions regarding the content of the area of inquiry before the publication of a general notice of proposed rulemaking under paragraph (1)(A).

(C) The Commission shall, 30 days before the publication of a notice of proposed rulemaking pursuant to paragraph (1)(A), submit such notice to the Committee on Commerce, Science, and Transportation of the Senate and to the Committee on Energy and Commerce of the House of Representatives.

(3)   The Commission shall issue a notice of proposed rulemaking pursuant to paragraph (1)(A) only where it has reason to believe that the unfair or deceptive acts or practices which are the subject of the proposed rulemaking are prevalent. The Commission shall make a determination that unfair or deceptive acts or practices are prevalent under this paragraph only if—

(A)   it has issued cease and desist orders regarding such acts or practices, or

(B)   any other information available to the Commission indicates a widespread pattern of unfair or deceptive acts or practices.

(c)   The Commission shall conduct any informal hearings required by subsection (b)(1)(C) of this section in accordance with the following procedure:

(1)(A)   The Commission shall provide for the conduct of proceedings under this subsection by hearing officers who shall perform their functions in accordance with the requirements of this subsection.

(B)   The officer who presides over the rulemaking proceedings shall be responsible to a chief presiding officer who shall not be responsible to any other officer or employee of the Commission.   The officer who presides over the rulemaking proceeding shall make a recommended decision based upon the findings and conclusions of such officer as to all relevant and material evidence, except that such recommended decision may be made by another officer if the officer who presided over the proceeding is no longer available to the Commission.

(C)   Except as required for the disposition of ex parte matters as authorized by law, no presiding officer shall consult any person or party with respect to any fact in issue unless such officer gives notice and opportunity for all parties to participate.

(2)   Subject to paragraph (3) of this subsection, an interested person is entitled—

(A)   to present his position orally or by documentary submissions (or both), and

(B)   if the Commission determines that there are disputed issues of material fact it is necessary to resolve, to present such rebuttal submissions and to conduct (or have conducted under paragraph (3)(B)) such cross-examination of persons as the Commission determines (i) to be appropriate, and (ii) to be required for a full and true disclosure with respect to such issues.

(3)   The Commission may prescribe such rules and make such rulings concerning proceedings in such hearings as may tend to avoid unnecessary costs or delay.   Such rules or rulings may included (A) imposition of reasonable time limits on each interested person's oral presentations, and (B) requirements that any cross-examination to which a person may be entitled under paragraph (2) be conducted by the Commission on behalf of that person in such manner as the Commission determines (i) to be appropriate, and (ii) to be required for a full and true disclosure with respect to disputed issues of material fact.

(4)(A)   Except as provided in subparagraph (B), if a group of persons each of whom under paragraphs (2) and (3) would be entitled to conduct (or have conducted) cross-examination and who are determined by the Commission to have the same or similar interests in the proceeding cannot agree upon a single representative of such interests for purposes of cross-examination, the Commission may make rules and rulings (i) limiting the representation of such interest, for such purposes, and (ii) governing the manner in which such cross-examination shall be limited.

(B)   When any person who is a member of a group with respect to which the Commission has made a determination under subparagraph (A) is unable to agree upon group representation with the other members of the group, then such person shall not be denied under the authority of subparagraph (A) the opportunity to conduct (or have conducted) cross-examination as to issues affecting his particular interests if (i) he satisfies the Commission that he has made a reasonable and good faith effort to reach agreement upon group representation with the other members of the group and (ii) the Commission determines that there are substantial and relevant issues which are not adequately presented by the group representative.

(5)   A verbatim transcript shall be taken of any oral presentation, and cross-examination, in an informal hearing to which this subsection applies. Such transcript shall be available to the public.

(d)(1)   The Commission's statement of basis and purpose to accompany a rule promulgated under subsection (a)(1)(B) of this section shall include (A) a statement as to the prevalence of the acts or practices treated by the rule; (B) a statement as to the manner and context in which such acts or practices are unfair or deceptive; and (C) a statement as to the economic effect of the rule, taking into account the effect on small business and consumers.

(2)(A)   The term "Commission" as used in this subsection and subsections (b) and (c) of this section includes any person authorized to act in behalf of the Commission in any part of the rulemaking proceeding.

(B)   A substantive amendment to, or repeal of, a rule promulgated under subsection (a)(1)(B) of this section shall be prescribed, and subject to judicial review, in the same manner as a rule prescribed under such subsection. An exemption under subsection (g) of this section shall not be treated as an amendment or repeal of a rule.

(3)   When any rule under subsection (a)(1)(B) of this section takes effect a subsequent violation thereof shall constitute an unfair or deceptive act or practice in violation of [§ 5(a)(1) of this Act], unless the Commission otherwise expressly provides in such rule.

(e)(1)(A)   Not later than 60 days after a rule is promulgated under subsection (a)(1)(B) of this section by the Commission, any interested person (including a consumer or consumer organization) may file a petition, in the United States Court of Appeals for the District of Columbia circuit or for the circuit in which such person resides or has his principal place of business, for judicial review of such rule. Copies of the petition shall be forthwith transmitted by the clerk of the court to the Commission or other officer designated by it for that purpose. The provisions of section 2112 of Title 28 shall apply to the filing of the rulemaking record of proceedings on which the Commission based its rule and to the transfer of proceedings in the courts of appeals.

(B)   For purpose of this section, the term "rulemaking record" means the rule, its statement of basis and purpose, the transcript required by subsection (c)(5) of this section, any written submissions, and any other information which the Commission considers relevant to such rule.

(2)   If the petitioner or the Commission applies to the court for leave to make additional oral submissions or written presentations and shows to the satisfaction of

the court that such submissions and presentations would be material and that there were reasonable grounds for the submissions and failure to make such submissions and presentations in the proceeding before the Commission, the court may order the Commission to provide additional opportunity to make such submissions and presentations. The Commission may modify or set aside its rule or make a new rule by reason of the additional submissions and presentations and shall file such modified or new rule, and the rule's statement of basis of purpose, with the return of such submissions and presentations. The court shall thereafter review such new or modified rule.

(3)   Upon the filing of the petition under paragraph (1) of this subsection, the court shall have jurisdiction to review the rule in accordance with chapter 7 of Title 5 and to grant appropriate relief, including interim relief, as provided in such chapter. The court shall hold unlawful and set aside the rule on any ground specified in subparagraphs (A),(B),(C), or (D) of section 706(2) of Title 5 (taking due account of the rule of prejudicial error), or if—

(A)   the court finds that the Commission's action is not supported by substantial evidence in the rulemaking record (as defined in paragraph (1)(B) of this subsection) taken as a whole, or

(B)   the court finds that—

(i)   a Commission determination under subsection (c) of this section that the petitioner is not entitled to conduct cross-examination or make rebuttal submissions, or

(ii)   a Commission rule or ruling under subsection (c) of this sectionlimiting the petitioner's cross-examination or rebuttal submissions, has precluded disclosure of disputed material facts which was necessary for fair determination by the Commission of the rulemaking proceeding taken as a whole.

The term "evidence", as used in this paragraph, means any matter in the rulemaking record.

(4)   The judgment of the court affirming or setting aside, in whole or in part, any such rule shall be final, subject to review by the Supreme Court of the United States upon certiorari or certification, as provided in section 1254 of Title 28

(5)(A)   Remedies under the preceding paragraphs of this subsection are in addition to and not in lieu of any other remedies provided by law.

(B)   The United States Courts of Appeal shall have exclusive jurisdiction of any action to obtain judicial review (other than in an enforcement proceeding) of a rule prescribed under subsection (a)(1)(B) of this section, if any district court of the United States would have had jurisdiction of such action but for this subparagraph. Any such action shall be brought in the United States Court of Appeals for the District of Columbia circuit, or for any circuit which includes a judicial district in which the action could have been brought but for this subparagraph.

(C)   A determination, rule, or ruling of the Commission described in paragraph (3)(B)(i) or (ii) may be reviewed only in a proceeding under this subsection and only in accordance with paragraph (3)(B). Section 706(2)(E) of Title 5 shall not apply to any rule promulgated under subsection (a)(1)(B) of this section. The contents and adequacy of any statement required by subsection (b)(1)(D) of this section shall not be subject to judicial review in any respect.

(f)(1) In order to prevent unfair or deceptive acts or practices in or affecting commerce (including acts or practices which are unfair or deceptive to consumers) by banks or savings and loan institutions described in paragraph (3), each agency specified in paragraph (2) or (3) of this subsection shall establish a separate division of consumer affairs which shall receive and take appropriate action upon complaints with respect to such acts or practices by banks or savings and loan institutions described in paragraph (3) subject to its jurisdiction. The Board of Governors of the Federal Reserve System (with respect to banks) and the Federal Home Loan Bank Board (with respect to savings and loan institutions described in paragraph (3)) and the National Credit Union Administration Board (with respect to Federal credit unions described in paragraph (4)) shall prescribe regulations to carry out the purposes of this section, including regulations defining with specificity such unfair or deceptive acts or practices, and containing requirements prescribed for the purpose of preventing such acts or practices. Whenever the Commission prescribes a rule under subsection (a)(1)(B) of this section, then within 60 days after such rule takes effect each such Board shall promulgate substantially similar regulations prohibiting acts or practices of banks or savings and loan institutions described in paragraph (3), or Federal credit unions described in paragraph (4), as the case may be, which are substantially similar to those prohibited by rules of the Commission and which impose substantially similar requirements, unless (A) any such Board finds that such acts or practices of banks or savings and loan institutions described in paragraph (3), or Federal credit unions described in paragraph (4), as the case may be, are not unfair or deceptive, or (B) the Board of Governors of the Federal Reserve System finds that implementation of similar regulations with respect to banks, savings and loan institutions or Federal credit unions would seriously conflict with essential monetary and payments systems policies of such Board, and publishes any such finding, and the reasons therefor, in the Federal Register.

(2) Compliance with regulations prescribed under this subsection shall be enforced under [§ 8 of the Federal Deposit Insurance Act, 12 U.S.C. § 1818], in the case of—

(A) national banks and banks operating under the code of law for the District of Columbia, and Federal branches and Federal agencies of foreign banks, by the division of consumer affairs established by the Office of the Comptroller of the Currency;

(B) member banks of the Federal Reserve System (other than national banks and banks operating under the code of law for the District of Columbia), branches and agencies of foreign banks (other than Federal branches, Federal agencies, and insured State branches of foreign banks), commercial lending companies owned or controlled by foreign banks, and organizations operating under section 25 or 25(a) of the Federal Reserve Act [12 U.S.C. §§ 601 et seq., 611 et seq.], by the division of consumer affairs established by the Board of Governors of the Federal Reserve System; and

(C) banks insured by the Federal Deposit Insurance Corporation (other banks[2] referred to in subparagraph (A) or (B)) and insured State branches of foreign banks, by the division of consumer affairs established by the Board of Directors of the Federal Deposit Insurance Corporation.

---

2.   So in original. Probably should be "other than banks."

(3) Compliance with regulations prescribed under this subsection shall be enforced under [§ 8 of the Federal Deposit Insurance Act, 12 U.S.C. § 1818] with respect to savings associations as defined in [§ 3 of the Federal Deposit Insurance Act, 12 U.S.C. § 1813].

(4) Compliance with regulations prescribed under this subsection shall be enforced with respect to Federal credit unions under [§§ 120 and 206 of the Federal Credit Union Act 12 U.S.C. §§ 1766 and 1786].

(5) For the purpose of the exercise by any agency referred to paragraph (2) of its powers under any Act referred to in that paragraph, a violation of any regulation prescribed under this subsection shall be deemed to be a violation of a requirement imposed under that Act. In addition to its powers under any provision of law specifically referred to in paragraph (2), each of the agencies referred to in that paragraph may exercise, for the purpose of enforcing compliance with any regulation prescribed under this subsection, any other authority conferred on it by law.

(6) The authority of the Board of Governors of the Federal Reserve System to issue regulations under this subsection does not impair the authority of any other agency designated in this subsection to make rules respecting its own procedures in enforcing compliance with regulations prescribed under this subsection.

(7) Each agency exercising authority under this subsection shall transmit to the Congress each year a detailed report on its activities under this paragraph during the preceding calendar year.

(g)(1) Any person to whom a rule under subsection (a)(1)(B) of this section applies may petition the Commission for an exemption from such rule.

(2) If, on its own motion or on the basis of a petition under paragraph (1), the Commission finds that the application of a rule prescribed under subsection (a)(1)(B) of this section to any person or class or[3] persons is not necessary to prevent the unfair or deceptive act or practice to which the rule relates, the Commission may exempt such person or class from all or part of such rule. Section 553 of Title 5 shall apply to action under this paragraph.

(3) Neither the pendency of a proceeding under this subsection respecting an exemption from a rule, nor the pendency of judicial proceedings to review the Commission's action or failure to act under this subsection, shall stay the applicability of such rule under subsection (a)(1)(B) of this section.

(h) The Commission shall not have any authority to promulgate any rule in the children's advertising proceeding pending on May 28, 1980, or in any substantially similar proceeding on the basis of a determination by the Commission that such advertising constitutes an unfair act or practice in or affecting commerce.

(i)(1) For purposes of this subsection, the term outside party" means any person other than (A) a Commissioner; (B) an officer or employee of the Commission; or (C) any person who has entered into a contract or any other agreement or arrangement with the Commission to provide any goods or services (including consulting services) to the Commission.

---

3.   So in original. Probably should be "of."

(2)   Not later than 60 days after May 28, 1980, the Commission shall publish a proposed rule, and not later than 180 days after May 28, 1980, the Commission shall promulgate a final rule, which shall authorize the Commission or any Commissioner to meet with any outside party concerning any rulemaking proceeding of the Commission. Such rule shall provide that—

(A)   notice of any such meeting shall be included in any weekly calendar prepared by the Commission, and

(B)   a verbatim record or a summary of any such meeting, or of any communication relating to any such meeting, shall be kept, made available to the public, and included in the rulemaking record.

(j)   Not later than 60 days after May 28, 1980, the Commission shall publish a proposed rule, and not later than 180 days after May 28, 1980, the Commission shall promulgate a final rule, which shall prohibit any officer, employee, or agent of the Commission with any investigative responsibility or other responsibility relating to any rulemaking proceeding within any operating bureau of the Commission, from communicating or causing to be communicated to any Commissioner or to the personal staff of any Commissioner any fact which is relevant to the merits of such proceeding and which is not on the rulemaking record of such proceeding, unless such communications is made available to the public and is included in the rulemaking record.   The provisions of this subsection shall not apply to any communication to the extent such communication is required for the disposition of ex parte matters as authorized by law. [15 U.S.C. § 57a]

Section 19

(a)(1)   If any person, partnership, or corporation violates any rule under this chapter respecting unfair or deceptive acts or practices (other than an interpretive rule, or a rule violation of which the Commission has provided is not an unfair or deceptive act or practice in violation of [section 5(a)]), then the Commission may commence a civil action against such person, partnership, or corporation for relief under subsection (b) of this section in a United States district court or in any court of competent jurisdiction of a State.

(2)   If any person, partnership, or corporation engages in any unfair or deceptive act or practice (within the meaning of section [5(a)(1)] of this title) with respect to which the Commission has issued a final cease and desist order which is applicable to such person, partnership, or corporation, then the Commission may commence a civil action against such person, partnership, or corporation in a United States district court or in any court of competent jurisdiction of a State. If the Commission satisfies the court that the act or practice to which the cease and desist order relates is one which a reasonable man would have known under the circumstances was dishonest or fraudulent, the court may grant relief under subsection (b) of this section.

(b)   The court in an action under subsection (a) of this section shall have jurisdiction to grant such relief as the court finds necessary to redress injury to consumers or other persons, partnerships, and corporations resulting from the rule violation or the unfair or deceptive act or practice, as the case may be. Such relief may include, but shall not be limited to, rescission or reformation of contracts, the refund of money or return of property, the payment of damages, and public notification respecting the rule violation or the unfair or deceptive act or practice, as the case may be; except that nothing in this subsection is intended to authorize the imposition of any exemplary or punitive damages.

(c)(1)   If (A) a cease and desist order issued under [section 5(b)] has become final under [section 5(g)] with respect to any person's, partnership's, or corporation's rule violation or unfair or deceptive act or practice, and (B) an action under this section is brought with respect to such person's, partnership's, or corporation's rule violation or act or practice, then the findings of the Commission as to the material facts in the proceeding under [section 5(b)] with respect to such person's, partnership's, or corporation's rule violation or act or practice, shall be conclusive until (i) the terms of such cease and desist order expressly provide that the Commission's findings shall not be conclusive, or (ii) the order becomes final by reason of [section 5(g)(1)], in which case such finding shall be conclusive if supported by evidence.

(2)   The court shall cause notice of an action under this section to be given in a manner which is reasonably calculated, under all of the circumstances, to apprise the persons, partnerships, and corporations allegedly injured by the defendant's rule violation or act or practice of the pendency of such action. Such notice may, in the discretion of the court, be given by publication.

(d)   No action may be brought by the Commission under this section more than 3 years after the rule violation by which an action under subsection (a)(1) of this section relates, or the unfair or deceptive act or practice to which an action under subsection (a)(2) of this section relates; except that if a cease and desist order with respect to any person's, partnership's, or corporation's rule violation or unfair or deceptive act or practice has become final and such order was issued in a proceeding under [section 5(b)] which was commenced not later than 3 years after the rule violation or act or practice occurred, a civil action may be commenced under this section against such person, partnership, or corporation at any time before the expiration of one year after such order becomes final.

(e)   Remedies provided in this section are in addition to, and not in lieu of, any other remedy or right of action provided by State or Federal law. Nothing in this section shall be construed to affect any authority of the Commission under any other provision of law. [15 U.S.C. § 57b].

1984 DEPARTMENT OF JUSTICE MERGER GUIDELINES (EXCERPTS)

1. Purpose and Underlying Policy Assumptions

1.0 These *Guidelines* state in outline form the present enforcement of the U.S. Department of Justice ("Department") concerning acquisition and mergers ("mergers") subject to section 7 of the Clayton Act[1] or to section 1 of the Sherman Act.[2] They describe the general principles and specific standards normally used by the Department in analyzing mergers.[3] By stating its policy as simply and clearly as possible, the Department hopes to reduce the uncertainty associated with enforcement of the antitrust laws in this area.

Although the *Guidelines* should improve the predictability of the Department's merger enforcement policy, it is not possible to remove the exercise of judgment from the evaluation of mergers under the antitrust laws. Because the specific standards set forth in the *Guidelines* must be applied to a broad range of possible factual circumstances, strict application of those standards may provide misleading answers to the economic questions raised under the antitrust laws. Moreover, the picture of competitive conditions that develops from historical evidence may provide an incomplete answer to the forward-looking inquiry of the *Guidelines*. Therefore, the Department will apply the standards of the *Guidelines* reasonably and flexibly to the particular facts and circumstances of each proposed merger.

The *Guidelines* are designed primarily to indicate when the Department is likely to challenge mergers, not how it will conduct the litigation of cases that it decides to bring. Although relevant in the latter context, the factors contemplated in the standards do not exhaust the range of evidence that the Department may introduce in court.[4]

The unifying theme of the *Guidelines* is that mergers should not be permitted to create or enhance "market power" or to facilitate its exercise. A sole seller (a

---

1. 15 U.S.C. § 18 (1982). Mergers subject to section 7 are prohibited if their effect "may be substantially to lessen competition, or to tend to create a monopoly."
2. 15 U.S.C. § 1 (1982). Mergers subject to section 1 are prohibited if they constitute a "contract, combination . . . , or conspiracy in restraint of trade."
3. They update the *Guidelines* issued by the Department in 1982. The Department may from time to time revise the *Merger Guidelines* as necessary to reflect any significant changes in enforcement policy or to clarify aspects of existing policy.
4. Parties seeking more specific advance guidance concerning the Department's enforcement intentions with respect to any particular merger should consider using the Business Review Procedure, 28 [C.F.R. § 50.6].

"monopolist") of a product with no good substitutes can maintain a selling price that is above the level that would prevail if the market were competitive. Where only a few firms account for most of the sales of a product, those firms can in some circumstances either explicitly or implicitly coordinate their actions in order to approximate the performance of a monopolist. This ability of one or more firms profitably to maintain prices above competitive levels for a significant period of time is termed "market power." Sellers with market power also may eliminate rivalry on variables other than price. In either case, the result is a transfer of wealth from buyers to sellers and a misallocation of resources.

"Market power" also encompasses the ability of a single buyer or group of buyers to depress the price paid for a product to a level that is below the competitive price. The exercise of market power by buyers has wealth transfer and resource misallocation effects analogous to those associated with the exercise of market power by sellers.

Although they sometimes harm competition, mergers generally play an important role in a free enterprise economy. They can penalize ineffective management and facilitate the efficient flow of investment capital and the redeployment of existing productive assets. While challenging competitively harmful mergers, the Department seeks to avoid unnecessary interference with that larger universe of mergers that are either competitively beneficial or neutral. In attempting to mediate between these dual concerns, however, the *Guidelines* reflect the congressional intent that merger enforcement should interdict competitive problems in their incipiency.

* * *

4. Horizontal Effect from Non-Horizontal Mergers

4.0 By definition, non-horizontal mergers involve firms that do not operate in the same market. It necessarily follows that such mergers produce no immediate change in the level of concentration in any relevant market as defined in Section 2 of these *Guidelines*. Although non-horizontal mergers are less likely than horizontal mergers to create competitive problems, they are invariably innocuous. This section describes the principal theories under which the Department is likely to challenge non-horizontal mergers.

4.1 Elimination of Specific Potential Entrants

4.11 THE THEORY OF POTENTIAL COMPETITION

In some circumstances, the non-horizontal merger[5] of a firm already in a market (the "acquired firm") with a potential entrant to that market (the "acquiring firm")[6] may adversely affect competition in the market. If the merger effectively removes the acquiring firm from the edge of the market, it could have either of the following effects.

---

5. Under traditional usage, such a merger could be characterized as either "vertical" or "conglomerate," but the label adds nothing to the analysis.

6. The terms "acquired" and "acquiring" refer to the relationship of the firms to the market of interest, not to the way the particular transaction is formally structured.

4.111 Harm to "Perceived Potential Competition"

By eliminating a significant present competitive threat that constrains the behavior of the firms already in the market, the merger could result in an immediate deterioration in market performance. The economic theory of limiting pricing suggests that monopolists and groups of colluding firms may find it profitable to restrain their pricing in order to deter new entry that is likely to push prices even lower by adding capacity to the market. If the acquiring firm had unique advantages in entering the market, the firms in the market might be able to set a new and higher price after the threat of entry by the acquiring firm was eliminated by the merger.

4.112 Harm to "Actual Potential Competition"

By eliminating the possibility of entry by the acquiring firm in a more procompetitive manner, the merger could result in a lost opportunity for improvement in market performance resulting from the addition of a significant competitor. The more procompetitive alternatives include both new entry and entry through a "toehold" acquisition of a present small competitor.

4.12 RELATION BETWEEN PERCEIVED AND ACTUAL POTENTIAL COMPETITION

If it were always profit-maximizing for incumbent firms to set price in such a way that all entry was deterred and if information and coordination were sufficient to implement this strategy, harm to perceived potential competition would be the only competitive problem to address. In practice, however, actual potential competition has independent importance. Firms already in the market may not find it optimal to set price low enough to deter all entry; moreover, those firms may misjudge the entry advantages of a particular firm and, therefore, the price necessary to deter its entry.[7]

4.13 ENFORCEMENT STANDARDS

Because of the close relationship between perceived potential competition and actual potential competition, the Department will evaluate mergers that raise either type of potential competition concern under a single structural analysis analogous to that applied to horizontal mergers. The Department first will consider a set of objective factors designed to identify cases in which harmful effects are plausible. In such cases, the Department then will conduct a more focused inquiry to determine whether the likelihood and magnitude of the possible harm justify a challenge to the merger. In this context, the Department will consider any specific evidence presented by the merging parties to show that the inferences of competitive harm drawn from the objective factors are unreliable.

The factors that the Department will consider are as follows:

---

7. When collusion is only tacit, the problem of arriving at and enforcing the correct limit price is likely to be particularly difficult.

4.131 Market Concentration

Barriers to entry are unlikely to affect market performance if the structure of the market is otherwise not conducive to monopolization or collusion. Adverse competitive effects are likely only if overall concentration, or the largest firm's market share, is high. The Department is unlikely to challenge a potential competition merger unless overall concentration of the acquired firm's market is above 1800 HHI (a somewhat lower concentration will suffice if one or more of the factors discussed in Section 3.4 indicate that effective collusion in the market is particularly likely). Other things being equal, the Department is increasingly likely to challenge a merger as this threshold is exceeded.

4.132 Conditions of Entry Generally

If entry to the market is generally easy, the fact that entry is marginally easier for one or more firms is unlikely to affect the behavior of the firms in the market. The Department is unlikely to challenge a potential competition merger when new entry into the acquiring firm's market can be accomplished by firms without any specific entry advantages under the conditions stated in Section 3.3. Other things being equal, the Department is increasingly likely to challenge a merger as the difficulty of entry increases above that threshold.

4.133 The Acquiring Firm's Entry Advantage

If more than a few firms have the same or a comparable advantage in entering the acquired firm's market, the elimination of one firm is unlikely to have any adverse competitive effect. The other similarly situated firm or firms would continue to exert a present restraining influence, or, if entry would be profitable, would recognize the opportunity and enter. The Department is unlikely to challenge a potential competition merger if the entry advantage ascribed to the acquiring firm (or another advantage of comparable importance) is also possessed by three or more other firms. Other things being equal, the Department is increasingly likely to challenge a merger as the number of other similarly situated firms decreases below three and as the extent of the entry advantage over non-advantaged firms increases.

If the evidence of likely actual entry by the acquiring firm is particularly strong,[8] however, the Department may challenge a potential competition merger, notwithstanding the presence of three or more firms that are objectively similarly situated. In such cases, the Department will determine the likely scale of entry, using either the firm's own documents or the minimum efficient scale in the industry. The Department will then evaluate the merger much as it would a horizontal merger between a firm the size of the likely scale of entry and the acquired firm.

4.134 The Market Share of the Acquired Firm

Entry through the acquisition of a relatively small firm in the market may have a competitive effect comparable to new entry. Small firms frequently play peripheral

---

8.   For example, the firm already may have moved beyond the stage of consideration and have made significant investments demonstrating an actual decision to enter.

roles in collusive interactions, and the particular advantages of the acquiring firm may convert a fringe firm into a significant factor in the market.[9] The Department is unlikely to challenge a potential competition merger when the acquired firm has a market share of five percent or less. Other things being equal, the Department is increasingly likely to challenge a merger as the market share of the acquired firm increases above that threshold. The Department is likely to challenge any merger satisfying the other conditions in which the acquired firm has a market share of 20 percent or more.

4.135 *Efficiencies*

As in the case of horizontal mergers, the Department will consider expected efficiencies in determining whether to challenge a potential competition merger. *See* Section 3.5 (Efficiencies).

4.2   *Competitive Problems from Vertical Mergers*

4.21   BARRIERS TO ENTRY FROM VERTICAL MERGERS

In certain circumstances, the vertical integration resulting from vertical mergers could create competitively objectionable barriers to entry. Stated generally, three conditions are necessary (but not sufficient) for this problem to exist. First, the degree of vertical integration between the two markets must be so extensive that entrants to one market (the "primary market") also would have to enter the other market (the "secondary market")[10] simultaneously. Second, the requirement of entry at the secondary level must make entry at the primary level significantly more difficult and less likely to occur. Finally, the structure and other characteristics of the primary market must be otherwise so conducive to noncompetitive performance that the increased difficulty of entry is likely to affect its performance. The following standards state the criteria by which the Department will determine whether these conditions are satisfied.

4.211 *Need for Two-Level Entry*

If there is sufficient unintegrated capacity[11] in the secondary market, new entrants to the primary market would not have to enter both markets simultaneously. The

---

9.   Although a similar effect is possible with the acquisition of larger firms, there is an increased danger that the acquiring firm will choose to acquiesce in monopolization or collusion because of the enhanced profits that would result from its own disappearance from the edge of the market.

10.   This competitive problem could result from either upstream or downstream integration, and could affect competition in either the upstream market or the downstream market. In the text, the term "primary market" refers to the market in which the competitive concerns are being considered, and the term "secondary market" refers to the adjacent market.

11.   Ownership integration does not necessarily mandate two-level entry by new entrants to the primary market. Such entry is most likely to be necessary where the primary and secondary markets are completely integrated by ownership and each firm in the primary market uses all of the capacity of its associated firm in the secondary market. In many cases of ownership integration, however, the functional fit between vertically integrated firms is not perfect, and an outside market exists for the sales (purchases) of the firms in the secondary market. If that market is sufficiently large and diverse, new entrants to the primary market may be able to participate without simultaneous entry

Department is unlikely to challenge a merger on this ground where post-merger sales (or purchases) by unintegrated firms in the secondary market would be sufficient to service two minimum-efficient-scale plants in the primary market. When the other conditions are satisfied, the Department is increasingly likely to challenge a merger as the unintegrated capacity declines below this level.

4.212 Increased Difficulty of Simultaneous Entry of Both Markets

The relevant question is whether the need for simultaneous entry to the secondary market gives rise to a substantial incremental difficulty as compared to entry into the primary market alone. If entry at the secondary level is easy in absolute terms, the requirement of simultaneous entry to that market is unlikely adversely to affect entry to the primary market. Whatever the difficulties of entry into the primary market may be, the Department is unlikely to challenge a merger on this ground if new entry into the secondary market can be accomplished under the conditions stated in Section 3.3.[12] When entry is not possible under those conditions, the Department is increasingly concerned about vertical mergers as the difficulty of entering the secondary market increases. The Department, however, will invoke this theory only where the need for secondary market entry significantly increases the costs (which may take the form of risks) of primary market entry.

More capital is necessary to enter two markets than to enter one. Standing alone, however, this additional capital requirement does not constitute a barrier to entry to the primary market. If the necessary funds were available at a cost commensurate with the level of risk in the secondary market, there would be no adverse effect. In some cases, however, lenders may doubt that would-be entrants to the primary market have the necessary skills and knowledge to succeed in the secondary market and, therefore, in the primary market. In order to compensate for this risk of failure, lenders might charge a higher rate for the necessary capital. This problem becomes increasingly significant as a higher percentage of the capital assets in the secondary market are long-lived and specialized to that market and, therefore, difficult to recover in the event of failure. In evaluating the likelihood of increased barriers to entry resulting from increased cost of capital, therefore, the Department will consider both the degree of similarity in the essential skills in the primary and secondary markets and the economic life and degree of specialization of the capital assets in the secondary market.

Economies of scale in the secondary market may constitute an additional barrier to entry to the primary market in some situations requiring two-level entry. The problem could arise if the capacities of minimum-efficient-scale plants in the primary and secondary markets differ significantly. For example, if the capacity of a minimum-efficient-scale plant in the secondary market were significantly greater than the needs of a minimum-efficient-scale plant in the primary market, entrants would have to choose between inefficient operation at the secondary level (because of operating an efficient plant at an inefficient output or because of operating an

---

to the secondary market. In considering the adequacy of this alternative, the Department will consider the likelihood of predatory price or supply "squeezes" by the integrated firms against their unintegrated rivals.

12. Entry into the secondary market may be greatly facilitated in that an assured supplier (customer) is provided by the primary market entry.

inefficiently small plant) or a larger than necessary scale at the primary level. Either of these effects could cause a significant increase in the operating costs of the entering firm.[13]

4.213 Structure and Performance of the Primary Market

Barriers to entry are unlikely to affect performance if the structure of the primary market is otherwise not conducive to monopolization or collusion.[14] The Department is unlikely to challenge a merger on this ground unless overall concentration of the primary market is above 1800 HHI (a somewhat lower concentration will suffice if one or more of the factors discussed in Section 3.4 indicate that effective collusion is particularly likely). Above that threshold, the Department is increasingly likely to challenge a merger that meets the other criteria set forth above as the concentration increases.

4.22 FACILITATING COLLUSION THROUGH VERTICAL MERGERS

4.221 Vertical Integration to the Retail Level

A high level of vertical integration by upstream firms into the associated retail market may facilitate collusion in the upstream market by making it easier to monitor price. Retail prices are generally more visible than prices in upstream markets, and vertical mergers may increase the level of vertical integration to the point at which the monitoring effect becomes significant. Adverse competitive consequences are unlikely unless the upstream market is generally conducive to collusion and a larger percentage of the products produced there are sold through vertically integrated retail outlets.

The Department is unlikely to challenge a merger on this ground unless (1) overall concentration of the upstream market is above 1800 HHI (a somewhat lower concentration will suffice if one or more of the factors discussed in Section 3.4 indicate that effective collusion is particularly likely), and (2) a large percentage of the upstream product would be sold through vertically-integrated retail outlets after the merger. Where the stated thresholds are met or exceeded, the Department's decision whether to challenge a merger on this ground will depend upon an individual evaluation of its likely competitive effect.

4.222 Elimination of a Disruptive Buyer

The elimination by vertical merger of a particularly disruptive buyer in a downstream market may facilitate collusion in the upstream market. If upstream firms view sales to a particular buyer as sufficiently important, they may deviate from the terms of a collusive agreement in an effort to secure that business, thereby disrupting the operation of the agreement. The merger of such a buyer with an

---

13. It is important to note, however, that this problem would not exist if a significant outside market exists at the secondary level. In that case, entrants could enter with the appropriately scaled plants at both levels, and sell or buy in the market as necessary.

14. For example, a market with 100 firms of equal size would perform competitively despite a significant increase in entry barriers.

upstream firm may eliminate that rivalry, making it easier for the upstream firms to collude effectively. Adverse competitive consequences are unlikely unless the upstream market is generally conducive to collusion and the disruptive firm is significantly more attractive to sellers than the other firms in its market.

The Department is unlikely to challenge a merger on this ground unless (1) overall concentration of the upstream market is 1800 HHI or above (a somewhat lower concentration will suffice if one or more of the factors discussed in Section 3.4 indicate that effective collusion is particularly likely), and (2) the allegedly disruptive firm differs substantially in volume of purchases or other relevant characteristics from the other firms in its market. Where the stated thresholds are met or exceeded, the Department's decision whether to challenge a merger on this ground will depend upon an individual evaluation of its likely competitive effect.

4.23 EVASION OF RATE REGULATION

Non-horizontal mergers may be used by monopoly public utilities subject to rate regulation as a tool for circumventing that regulation. The clearest example is the acquisition by a regulated utility of a supplier of its fixed or variable inputs. After the merger, the utility would be selling to itself and might be able arbitrarily to inflate the prices of internal transactions. Regulators may have great difficulty in policing these practices, particularly if there is no independent market for the product (or service) purchased from the affiliate.[15] As a result, inflated prices could be passed along to consumers as "legitimate" costs. In extreme cases, the regulated firm may effectively preempt the adjacent market, perhaps for the purpose of suppressing observable market transactions, and may distort resource allocation in that adjacent market as well as in the regulated market. In such cases, however, the Department recognizes that genuine economies of integration may be involved. The Department will consider challenging mergers that create substantial opportunities for such abuses.[16]

4.24 EFFICIENCIES

As in the case of horizontal mergers, the Department will consider expected efficiencies in determining whether to challenge a vertical merger. *See* Section 3.5 (Efficiencies). An extensive pattern of vertical integration may constitute evidence that substantial economies are afforded by vertical integration. Therefore, the Department will give relatively more weight to expected efficiencies in determining whether to challenge a vertical merger than in determining whether to challenge a horizontal merger.

---

15. A less severe, but nevertheless serious, problem can arise when a regulated utility acquires a firm that is not vertically related. The use of common facilities and managers may create an insoluable cost allocation problem and provide the opportunity to charge utility customers for non-utility costs, consequently distorting resource allocation in the adjacent as well as the regulated market.

16. Where a regulatory agency has the responsibility for approving such mergers, the Department may express its concerns to that agency in its role as competition advocate.

1992 DEPARTMENT OF JUSTICE AND FEDERAL TRADE COMMISSION HORIZONTAL MERGER GUIDELINES

0. Purpose, Underlying Policy Assumptions and Overview

These *Guidelines* outline the present enforcement policy of the Department of Justice and the Federal Trade Commission (the Agency) concerning horizontal acquisitions and mergers (mergers) subject to section 7 of the Clayton Act,[1] to section 1 of the Sherman Act,[2] or to section 5 of the FTC Act.[3] They describe the analytical framework and specific standards normally used by the Agency in analyzing mergers.[4] By stating its policy as simply and clearly as possible, the Agency hopes to reduce the uncertainty associated with enforcement of the antitrust laws in this area.

Although the *Guidelines* should improve the predictability of the Agency's merger enforcement policy, it is not possible to remove the exercise of judgment from the evaluation of mergers under the antitrust laws. Because the specific standards set forth in the *Guidelines* must be applied to a broad range of possible factual circumstances, mechanical application of those standards may provide misleading answers to the economic questions raised under the antitrust laws. Moreover, information is often incomplete and the picture of competitive conditions that develops from historical evidence may provide an incomplete answer to the forward-looking inquiry of the *Guidelines*. Therefore, the Agency will apply the standards of the *Guidelines* reasonably and flexibly to the particular facts and circumstances of each proposed merger.

---

1. 15 U.S.C. § 18 (1988). Mergers subject to section 7 are prohibited if their effect "may be substantially to lessen competition, or to tend to create a monopoly."
2. 15 U.S.C. § 1 (1988). Mergers subject to section 1 are prohibited if they constitute a "contract, combination . . . , or conspiracy in restraint of trade."
3. 15 U.S.C. § 45 (1988). Mergers subject to section 5 are prohibited if they constitute an "unfair method of competition."
4. These *Guidelines* update the *Merger Guidelines* issued by the U.S. Department of Justice in 1984 and the Statement of Federal Trade Commission Concerning Horizontal Mergers issued in 1982. The *Merger Guidelines* may be revised from time to time as necessary to reflect any significant changes in enforcement policy or to clarify aspects of existing policy.

0.1   Purpose and Underlying Policy Assumptions of the Guidelines

The *Guidelines* are designed primarily to articulate the analytical framework the Agency applies in determining whether a merger is likely substantially to lessen competition, not to describe how the Agency will conduct the litigation of cases that it decides to bring. Although relevant in the latter context, the factors contemplated in the *Guidelines* neither dictate nor exhaust the range of evidence that the Agency must or may introduce in litigation. Consistent with their objective, the *Guidelines* do not attempt to assign the burden of proof, or the burden of coming forward with evidence, on any particular issue. Nor do the *Guidelines* attempt to adjust or reapportion burdens of proof or burdens of coming forward as those standards have been established by the courts.[5] Instead, the *Guidelines* set forth a methodology for analyzing issues once the necessary facts are available. The necessary facts may be derived from the documents and statements of both the merging firms and other sources.

Throughout the *Guidelines*, the analysis is focused on whether consumers or producers "likely would" take certain actions, that is, whether the action is in the actor's economic interest. References to the profitability of certain actions focus on economic profits rather than accounting profits. Economic profits may be defined as the excess of revenues over costs where costs include the opportunity cost of invested capital.

Mergers are motivated by the prospect of financial gains. The possible sources of the financial gains from mergers are many, and the *Guidelines* do not attempt to identify all possible sources of gain in every merger. Instead, the *Guidelines* focus on the one potential source of gain that is of concern under the antitrust laws: market power.

The unifying theme of the *Guidelines* is that mergers should not be permitted to create or enhance market power or to facilitate its exercise. Market power to a seller is the ability profitably to maintain prices above competitive levels for a significant period of time.[6] In some circumstances, a sole seller (a monopolist) of a product with no good substitutes can maintain a selling price that is above the level that would prevail if the market were competitive. Similarly, in some circumstances, where only a few firms account for most of the sales of a product, those firms can exercise market power, perhaps even approximating the performance of a monopolist, by either explicitly or implicitly coordinating their actions. Circumstances also may permit a single firm, not a monopolist, to exercise market power through unilateral or non-coordinated conduct—conduct the success of which does not rely on the concurrence of other firms in the market or on coordinated responses by those firms. In any case, the result of the exercise of market power is a transfer of wealth from buyers to sellers or a misallocation of resources.

Market power also encompasses the ability of a single buyer (a "monopsonist"), a coordinating group of buyers, or a single buyer, not a monopsonist, to depress the price paid for a product to a level that is below the competitive price and thereby depress output. The exercise of market power by buyers ("monopsony power") has

---

5.   For example, the burden with respect to efficiency and failure continues to reside with the proponents of the merger.

6.   Sellers with market power also may lessen competition on dimensions other than price, such as product quality, service, or innovation.

adverse effects comparable to those associated with the exercise of market power by sellers. In order to assess potential monopsony concerns, the Agency will apply an analytical framework analogous to the framework of these *Guidelines*.

While challenging competitively harmful mergers, the Agency seeks to avoid unnecessary interference with the larger universe of mergers that are either competitively beneficial or neutral. In implementing this objective, however, the *Guidelines* reflect the congressional intent that merger enforcement should interdict competitive problems in their incipiency.

0.2   Overview

The *Guidelines* describe the analytical process that the Agency will employ in determining whether to challenge a horizontal merger. First, the Agency assesses whether the merger would significantly increase concentration and result in a concentrated market, properly defined and measured. Second, the Agency assesses whether the merger, in light of market concentration and other factors that characterize the market, raises concern about potential adverse competitive effects. Third, the Agency assesses whether entry would be timely, likely and sufficient either to deter or to counteract the competitive effects of concern. Fourth, the Agency assesses any efficiency gains that reasonably cannot be achieved by the parties through other means. Finally the Agency assesses whether, but for the merger, either party to the transaction would be likely to fail, causing its assets to exit the market. The process of assessing market concentration, potential adverse competitive effects, entry, efficiency and failure is a tool that allows the Agency to answer the ultimate inquiry in merger analysis: whether the merger is likely to create or enhance market power or to facilitate its exercise.

1.   Market Definition, Measurement and Concentration

1.0   Overview

A merger is unlikely to create or enhance market power or to facilitate its exercise unless it significantly increases concentration and results in a concentrated market, properly defined and measured. Mergers that either do not significantly increase concentration or do not result in a concentrated market ordinarily require no further analysis.

The analytic process described in this section ensures that the Agency evaluates the likely competitive impact of a merger within the context of economically meaningful markets—i.e., markets that could be subject to the exercise of market power. Accordingly, for each product or service (hereafter product) of each merging firm, the Agency seeks to define a market in which firms could effectively exercise market power if they were able to coordinate their actions.

Market definition focuses solely on demand substitution factors—i.e., possible consumer responses. Supply substitution factors—i.e., possible production responses—are considered elsewhere in the *Guidelines* in the identification of firms that participate in the relevant market and the analysis of entry. *See* Sections 1.3 and 3. A market is defined as a product or group of products and a geographic area in which it is produced or sold such that a hypothetical profit-maximizing firm, not subject to price regulation, that was the only present and future producer or seller of those products in that area likely would impose at least a "small but significant and nontransitory" increase in price, assuming the terms of sale of all other products are held constant. A relevant market is a group of products and a geographic area that is no bigger than necessary to satisfy this test. The "small but significant and non-transitory" increase in price is employed solely as a methodological tool for the analysis of mergers: it is not a tolerance level for price increases.

Absent price discrimination, a relevant market is described by a product or group of products and a geographic area. In determining whether a hypothetical monopolist would be in a position to exercise market power, it is necessary to evaluate the likely demand responses of consumers to a price increase. A price increase could be made unprofitable by consumers either switching to other products or switching to the same product produced by firms at other locations. The nature and magnitude of these two types of demand responses respectively determine the scope of the product market and the geographic market.

In contrast, where a hypothetical monopolist likely would discriminate in prices charged to different groups of buyers, distinguished, for example, by their uses or locations, the Agency may delineate different relevant markets corresponding to each such buyer group. Competition for sales to each such group may be affected differently by a particular merger and markets are delineated by evaluating the demand response of each such buyer group. A relevant market of this kind is described by a collection of products for sale to a given group of buyers.

Once defined, a relevant market must be measured in terms of its participants and concentration. Participants include firms currently producing or selling the market's products in the market's geographic area. In addition, participants may include other firms depending on their likely supply responses to a "small but significant and nontransitory" price increase. A firm is viewed as a participant if, in response to a "small but significant and nontransitory" price increase, it likely would enter rapidly into production or sale of a market product in the market's area, without incurring significant sunk costs of entry and exit. Firms likely to make any of these supply responses are considered to be "uncommitted" entrants because their supply response would create new production or sale in the relevant market and because that production or sale could be quickly terminated without significant loss.[7] Uncommitted entrants are capable of making such quick and uncommitted supply responses that they likely influenced the market premerger, would influence it post-merger, and accordingly are considered as market participants at both times. This analysis of market definition and market measurement applies equally to foreign and domestic firms.

If the process of market definition and market measurement identifies one or more relevant markets in which the merging firms are both participants, then the merger is considered to be horizontal. Sections 1.1 through 1.5 describe in greater

---

7.   Probable supply responses that require the entrant to incur significant sunk costs of entry and exit are not part of market measurement, but are included in the analysis of the significance of entry. *See* Section 3. Entrants that must commit substantial sunk costs are regarded as "committed" entrants because those sunk costs make entry irreversible in the short term without foregoing that investment; thus the likelihood of their entry must be evaluated with regard to their long-term profitability.

detail how product and geographic markets will be defined, how market shares will be calculated and how market concentration will be assessed.

1.1   *Product Market Definition*

The Agency will first define the relevant product market with respect to each of the products of each of the merging firms.[8]

1.11   GENERAL STANDARDS

Absent price discrimination, the Agency will delineate the product market to be a product or group of products such that a hypothetical profit-maximizing firm that was the only present and future seller of those products (monopolist) likely would impose at least a "small but significant and nontransitory" increase in price. That is, assuming that buyers likely would respond to an increase in price for a tentatively identified product group only by shifting to other products, what would happen? If the alternatives were, in the aggregate, sufficiently attractive at their existing terms of sale, an attempt to raise prices would result in a reduction of sales large enough that the price increase would not prove profitable, and the tentatively identified product group would prove to be too narrow.

Specifically, the Agency will begin with each product (narrowly defined) produced or sold by each merging firm and ask what would happen if a hypothetical monopolist of that product imposed at least a "small but significant and nontransitory" increase in price, but the terms of sale of all other products remained constant. If, in response to the price increase, the reduction in sales of the product would be large enough that a hypothetical monopolist would not find it profitable to impose such an increase in price, then the Agency will add to the product group the product that is the next-best substitute for the merging firm's product.[9]

In considering the likely reaction of buyers to a price increase, the Agency will take into account all relevant evidence, including, but not limited to, the following:

(1)   evidence that buyers have shifted or have considered shifting purchases between products in response to relative changes in price or other competitive variables;

(2)   evidence that sellers base business decisions on the prospect of buyer substitution between products in response to relative changes in price or other competitive variables;

(3)   the influence of downstream competition faced by buyers in their output markets; and

(4)   the timing and costs of switching products.

The price increase question is then asked for a hypothetical monopolist controlling the expanded product group. In performing successive iterations of the

---

8.   Although discussed separately, product market definition and geographic market definition are interrelated. In particular, the extent to which buyers of a particular product would shift to other products in the event of a "small but significant and nontransitory" increase in price must be evaluated in the context of the relevant geographic market.

9.   Throughout the *Guidelines*, the term "next best substitute" refers to the alternative which, if available in unlimited quantities at constant prices, would account for the greatest value of diversion of demand in response to a "small but significant and nontransitory" price increase.

price increase test, the hypothetical monopolist will be assumed to pursue maximum profits in deciding whether to raise the prices of any or all of the additional products under its control. This process will continue until a group of products is identified such that a hypothetical monopolist over that group of products would profitably impose at least a "small but significant and nontransitory" increase, including the price of a product of one of the merging firms. The Agency generally will consider the relevant product market to be the smallest group of products that satisfies this test.

In the above analysis, the Agency will use prevailing prices of the products of the merging firms and possible substitutes for such products, unless premerger circumstances are strongly suggestive of coordinated interaction, in which case the Agency will use a price more reflective of the competitive price.[10] However, the Agency may use likely future prices, absent the merger, when changes in the prevailing prices can be predicted with reasonable reliability. Changes in price may be predicted on the basis of, for example, changes in regulation which affect price either directly or indirectly by affecting costs or demand.

In general, the price for which an increase will be postulated will be whatever is considered to be the price of the product at the stage of the industry being examined.[11] In attempting to determine objectively the effect of a "small but significant and nontransitory" increase in price, the Agency, in most contexts, will use a price increase of five percent lasting for the foreseeable future. However, what constitutes a "small but significant and nontransitory" increase in price will depend on the nature of the industry, and the Agency at times may use a price increase that is larger or smaller than five percent.

1.12   PRODUCT MARKET DEFINITION IN THE PRESENCE OF PRICE DISCRIMINATION

The analysis of product market definition to this point has assumed that price discrimination—charging different buyers different prices for the same product, for example—would not be profitable for a hypothetical monopolist. A different analysis applies where price discrimination would be profitable for a hypothetical monopolist.

Existing buyers sometimes will differ significantly in their likelihood of switching to other products in response to a "small but significant and nontransitory" price increase. If a hypothetical monopolist can identify and price differently to those buyers (targeted buyers) who would not defeat the targeted price increase by substituting to other products in response to a "small but significant and nontransitory" price increase for the relevant product, and if other buyers likely would not purchase the relevant product and resell to targeted buyers, then a hypothetical monopolist would profitably impose a discriminatory price increase on

---

10.   The terms of sale of all other products are held constant in order to focus market definition on the behavior of consumers. Movements in the terms of sale for other products, as may result from the behavior of producers of those products, are accounted for in the analysis of competitive effects and entry. *See* Sections 2 and 3.

11.   For example, in a merger between retailers, the relevant price would be the retail price of a product to consumers. In the case of a merger among oil pipelines, the relevant price would be the tariff— the price of the transportation service.

sales to targeted buyers. This is true regardless of whether a general increase in price would cause such significant substitution that the price increase would not be profitable. The Agency will consider additional relevant product markets consisting of a particular use or uses by groups of buyers of the product for which a hypothetical monopolist would profitably and separately impose at least a "small but significant and nontransitory" increase in price.

1.2   *Geographic Market Definition*

For each product market in which both merging firms participate, the Agency will determine the geographic market or markets in which the firms produce or sell. A single firm may operate in a number of different geographic markets.

1.21   GENERAL STANDARDS

Absent price discrimination, the Agency will delineate the geographic market to be a region such that a hypothetical monopolist that was the only present or future producer of the relevant product at locations in that region would profitably impose at least a "small but significant and nontransitory" increase in price, holding constant the terms of sale for all products produced elsewhere. That is, assuming that buyers likely would respond to a price increase on products produced within the tentatively identified region only by shifting to products produced at locations of production outside the region, what would happen? If those locations of production outside the region were, in the aggregate, sufficiently attractive at their existing terms of sale, an attempt to raise price would result in a reduction in sales large enough that the price increase would not prove profitable, and the tentatively identified geographic area would prove to be too narrow.

In defining the geographic market or markets affected by a merger, the Agency will begin with the location of each merging firm (or each plant of a multiplant firm) and ask what would happen if a hypothetical monopolist of the relevant product at that point imposed at least a "small but significant and nontransitory" increase in price, but the terms of sale at all other locations remained constant. If, in response to the price increase, the reduction in sales of the product at that location would be large enough that a hypothetical monopolist producing or selling the relevant product at the merging firm's location would not find it profitable to impose such an increase in price, then the Agency will add the location from which production is the next-best substitute for production at the merging firm's location.

In considering the likely reaction of buyers to a price increase, the Agency will take into account all relevant evidence, including, but not limited to, the following:

(1)   evidence that buyers have shifted or have considered shifting purchases between different geographic locations in response to relative changes in price or other competitive variables;

(2)   evidence that sellers base business decisions on the prospect of buyer substitution between geographic locations in response to relative changes in price or other competitive variables;

(3)   the influence of downstream competition faced by buyers in their output markets; and

(4)   the timing and costs of switching suppliers.

The price increase question is then asked for a hypothetical monopolist controlling the expanded group of locations. In performing successive iterations of the price increase test, the hypothetical monopolist will be assumed to pursue maximum profits in deciding whether to raise the price at any or all of the additional locations under its control. This process will continue until a group of locations is identified such that a hypothetical monopolist over that group of locations would profitably impose at least a "small but significant and nontransitory" increase, including the price charged at a location of one of the merging firms.

The "smallest market" principle will be applied as it is in product market definition. The price for which an increase will be postulated, what constitutes a "small but significant and nontransitory" increase in price, and the substitution decisions of consumers all will be determined in the same way in which they are determined in product market definition.

1.22   GEOGRAPHIC MARKET DEFINITION IN THE PRESENCE OF PRICE DISCRIMINATION

The analysis of geographic market definition to this point has assumed that geographic price discrimination—charging different prices net of transportation costs for the same product to buyers in different areas, for example—would not be profitable for a hypothetical monopolist. However, if a hypothetical monopolist can identify and price differently to buyers in certain areas ("targeted buyers") who would not defeat the targeted price increase by substituting to more distant sellers in response to a "small but significant and nontransitory" price increase for the relevant product, and if other buyers likely would not purchase the relevant product and resell to targeted buyers,[12] then a hypothetical monopolist would profitably impose a discriminatory price increase. This is true even where a general price increase would cause such significant substitution that the price increase would not be profitable. The Agency will consider additional geographic markets consisting of particular locations of buyers for which a hypothetical monopolist would profitably and separately impose at least a "small but significant and nontransitory" increase in price.

1.3   *Identification of Firms That Participate in the Relevant Market*

1.31   CURRENT PRODUCERS OR SELLERS

The Agency's identification of firms that participate in the relevant market begins with all firms that currently produce or sell in the relevant market. This includes vertically integrated firms to the extent that such inclusion accurately reflects their competitive significance in the relevant market prior to the merger. To the extent

---

12.   This arbitrage is inherently impossible for many services and is particularly difficult where the product is sold on a delivered basis and where transportation costs are a significant percentage of the final cost.

that the analysis under Section 1.1 indicates that used, reconditioned or recycled goods are included in the relevant market, market participants will include firms that produce or sell such goods and that likely would offer those goods in competition with other relevant products.

1.32 FIRMS THAT PARTICIPATE THROUGH SUPPLY RESPONSE

In addition, the Agency will identify other firms not currently producing or selling the relevant product in the relevant area as participating in the relevant market if their inclusion would more accurately reflect probable supply responses. These firms are termed "uncommitted entrants." These supply responses must be likely to occur within one year and without the expenditure of significant sunk costs of entry and exit, in response to a "small but significant and nontransitory" price increase. If a firm has the technological capability to achieve such an uncommitted supply response, but likely would not (e.g., because difficulties in achieving product acceptance, distribution, or production would render such a response unprofitable), that firm will not be considered to be a market participant. The competitive significance of supply responses that require more time or that require firms to incur significant sunk costs of entry and exit will be considered in entry analysis. *See* Section 3.[13]

Sunk costs are the acquisition costs of tangible and intangible assets that cannot be recovered through the redeployment of these assets outside the relevant market, i.e., costs uniquely incurred to supply the relevant product and geographic market. Examples of sunk costs may include market-specific investments in production facilities, technologies, marketing (including product acceptance), research and development, regulatory approvals, and testing. A significant sunk cost is one which would not be recouped within one year of the commencement of the supply response, assuming a "small but significant and nontransitory" price increase in the relevant market. In this context, a "small but significant and nontransitory" price increase will be determined in the same way in which it is determined in product market definition, except the price increase will be assumed to last one year. In some instances, it may be difficult to calculate sunk costs with precision. Accordingly, when necessary, the Agency will make an overall assessment of the extent of sunk costs for firms likely to participate through supply responses.

These supply responses may give rise to new production of products in the relevant product market or new sources of supply in the relevant geographic market. Alternatively, where price discrimination is likely so that the relevant market is defined in terms of a targeted group of buyers, these supply responses serve to identify new sellers to the targeted buyers. Uncommitted supply responses may occur in several different ways: by the switching or extension of existing assets to production or sale in the relevant market; or by the construction or acquisition of assets that enable production or sale in the relevant market.

---

13. If uncommitted entrants likely would also remain in the market and would meet the entry tests of timeliness, likelihood and sufficiency, and thus would likely deter anticompetitive mergers or deter or counteract the competitive effects of concern (*see* Section 3, *infra*), the Agency will consider the impact of those firms in the entry analysis.

1.321 Production Substitution and Extension: The Switching or Extension of Existing Assets to Production or Sale in the Relevant Market

The productive and distributive assets of a firm sometimes can be used to produce and sell either the relevant products or products that buyers do not regard as good substitutes. Production substitution refers to the shift by a firm in the use of assets from producing and selling one product to producing and selling another. Production extension refers to the use of those assets, for example, existing brand names and reputation, both for their current production and for production of the relevant product. Depending upon the speed of that shift and the extent of sunk costs incurred in the shift or extension, the potential for production substitution or extension may necessitate treating as market participants firms that do not currently produce the relevant product.[14]

If a firm has existing assets that likely would be shifted or extended into production and sale of the relevant product within one year, and without incurring significant sunk costs of entry and exit, in response to a "small but significant and nontransitory" increase in price for only the relevant product, the Agency will treat that firm as a market participant. In assessing whether a firm is such a market participant, the Agency will take into account the costs of substitution or extension relative to the profitability of sales at the elevated price, and whether the firm's capacity is elsewhere committed or elsewhere so profitably employed that such capacity likely would not be available to respond to an increase in price in the market.

1.322 Obtaining New Assets for Production or Sale of the Relevant Product

A firm may also be able to enter into production or sale in the relevant market within one year and without the expenditure of significant sunk costs of entry and exit, in response to a "small but significant and nontransitory" increase in price for only the relevant product, even if the firm is newly organized or is an existing firm without products or productive assets closely related to the relevant market. If new firms, or existing firms without closely related products or productive assets, likely would enter into production or sale in the relevant market within one year without the expenditure of significant sunk costs of entry and exit, the Agency will treat those firms as market participants.

---

14.   Under other analytical approaches, production substitution sometimes has been reflected in the description of the product market. For example, the product market for stamped metal products such as automobile hub caps might be described as "light metal stamping," a production process rather than a product. The Agency believes that the approach described in the text provides a more clearly focused method of incorporating this factor in merger analysis. If production substitution among a group of products is nearly universal among the firms selling one or more of those products, however, the Agency may use an aggregate description of those markets as a matter of convenience.

1.4 Calculating Market Shares

1.41 GENERAL APPROACH

The Agency normally will calculate market shares for all firms (or plants) identified as market participants in Section 1.3 based on the total sales or capacity currently devoted to the relevant market together with that which likely would be devoted to the relevant market in response to a "small but significant and nontransitory" price increase. Market shares can be expressed either in dollar terms through measurement of sales, shipments, or production, or in physical terms through measurement of sales, shipments, production, capacity, or reserves.

Market shares will be calculated using the best indicator of firms' future competitive significance. Dollar sales or shipments generally will be used if firms are distinguished primarily by differentiation of their products. Unit sales generally will be used if firms are distinguished primarily on the basis of their relative advantages in serving different buyers or groups of buyers. Physical capacity or reserves generally will be used if it is these measures that most effectively distinguish firms.[15] Typically, annual data are used, but where individual sales are large and infrequent so that annual data may be unrepresentative, the Agency may measure market shares over a longer period of time.

In measuring a firm's market share, the Agency will not include its sales or capacity to the extent that the firm's capacity is committed or so profitably employed outside the relevant market that it would not be available to respond to an increase in price in the market.

1.42 PRICE DISCRIMINATION MARKETS

When markets are defined on the basis of price discrimination (Sections 1.12 and 1.22), the Agency will include only sales likely to be made into, or capacity likely to be used to supply, the relevant market in response to a "small but significant and nontransitory" price increase.

1.43 SPECIAL FACTORS AFFECTING FOREIGN FIRMS

Market shares will be assigned to foreign competitors in the same way in which they are assigned to domestic competitors. However, if exchange rates fluctuate significantly, so that comparable dollar calculations on an annual basis may be unrepresentative, the Agency may measure market shares over a period longer than one year.

If shipments from a particular country to the United States are subject to a quota, the market shares assigned to firms in that country will not exceed the amount of shipments by such firms allowed under the quota.[16] In the case of restraints that limit imports to some percentage of the total amount of the product sold in the United States (i.e., percentage quotas), a domestic price increase that reduced domestic

15. Where all firms have, on a forward-looking basis, an equal likelihood of securing sales, the Agency will assign firms equal shares.
16. The constraining effect of the quota on the importer's ability to expand sales is relevant to the evaluation of potential adverse competitive effects. *See* Section 2.

consumption also would reduce the volume of imports into the United States. Accordingly, actual import sales and capacity data will be reduced for purposes of calculating market shares. Finally, a single market share may be assigned to a country or group of countries if firms in that country or group of countries act in coordination.

1.5   *Concentration and Market Shares*

Market concentration is a function of the number of firms in a market and their respective market shares. As an aid to the interpretation of market data, the Agency will use the Herfindahl-Hirschman Index ("HHI") of market concentration. The HHI is calculated by summing the squares of the individual market shares of all the participants.[17] Unlike the four-firm concentration ratio, the HHI reflects both the distribution of the market shares of the top four firms and the composition of the market outside the top four firms. It also gives proportionately greater weight to the market shares of the larger firms, in accord with their relative importance in competitive interactions.

The Agency divides the spectrum of market concentration as measured by the HHI into three regions that can be broadly characterized as unconcentrated (HHI below 1000), moderately concentrated (HHI between 1000 and 1800), and highly concentrated (HHI above 1800). Although the resulting regions provide a useful framework for merger analysis, the numerical divisions suggest greater precision than is possible with the available economic tools and information. Other things being equal, cases falling just above and just below a threshold present comparable competitive issues.

1.51   GENERAL STANDARDS

In evaluating horizontal mergers, the Agency will consider both the post-merger market concentration and the increase in concentration resulting from the merger.[18] Market concentration is a useful indicator of the likely potential competitive effect of a merger. The general standards for horizontal mergers are as follows:

a) *Post-Merger HHI Below 1000.* The Agency regards markets in this region to be unconcentrated. Mergers resulting in unconcentrated markets are unlikely to have adverse competitive effects and ordinarily require no further analysis.

b) *Post-Merger HHI Between 1000 and 1800.* The Agency regards markets in this region to be moderately concentrated. Mergers producing an increase in the HHI

---

17.   For example, a market consisting of four firms with market shares of 30 percent, 30 percent, 20 percent and 20 percent has an HHI of 2600 ($30^2 + 30^2 + 20^2 + 20^2 = 2600$). The HHI ranges from 10,000 (in the case of a pure monopoly) to a number approaching zero (in the case of an atomistic market). Although it is desirable to include all firms in the calculation, lack of information about small firms is not critical because such firms do not affect the HHI significantly.

18.   The increase in concentration as measured by the HHI can be calculated independently of the overall market concentration by doubling the product of the market shares of the merging firms. For example, the merger of firms with shares of 5 percent and 10 percent of the market would increase the HHI by 100 (5 x 10 x 2 = 100). The explanation for this technique is as follows: In calculating the HHI before the merger, the market shares of the merging firms are squared individually: $(a)^2 + (b)^2$. After the merger, the sum of those shares would be squared: $(a + b)^2$, which equals $a^2 + 2ab + b^2$. The increase in the HHI therefore is represented by 2ab.

of less than 100 points in moderately concentrated markets post-merger are unlikely to have adverse competitive consequences and ordinarily require no further analysis. Mergers producing an increase in the HHI of more than 100 points in moderately concentrated markets post-merger potentially raise significant competitive concerns depending on the factors set forth in Sections 2-5 of the *Guidelines*.

c) *Post-Merger HHI Above 1800.* The Agency regards markets in this region to be highly concentrated. Mergers producing an increase in the HHI of less than 50 points, even in highly concentrated markets post-merger, are unlikely to have adverse competitive consequences and ordinarily require no further analysis. Mergers producing an increase in the HHI of more than 50 points in highly concentrated markets post-merger potentially raise significant competitive concerns, depending on the factors set forth in Sections 2-5 of the *Guidelines*. Where the post-merger HHI exceeds 1800, it will be presumed that mergers producing an increase in the HHI of more than 100 points are likely to create or enhance market power or facilitate its exercise. The presumption may be overcome by a showing that factors set forth in Sections 2-5 of the *Guidelines* make it unlikely that the merger will create or enhance market power or facilitate its exercise, in light of market concentration and market shares.

1.52　FACTORS AFFECTING THE SIGNIFICANCE OF MARKET SHARES AND CONCENTRATION

The post-merger level of market concentration and the change in concentration resulting from a merger affect the degree to which a merger raises competitive concerns. However, in some situations, market share and market concentration data may either understate or overstate the likely future competitive significance of a firm or firms in the market or the impact of a merger. The following are examples of such situations.

1.521　Changing Market Conditions

Market concentration and market share data of necessity are based on historical evidence. However, recent or ongoing changes in the market may indicate that the current market share of a particular firm either understates or overstates the firm's future competitive significance. For example, if a new technology that is important to long-term competitive viability is available to other firms in the market, but is not available to a particular firm, the Agency may conclude that the historical market share of that firm overstates its future competitive significance. The Agency will consider reasonably predictable effects of recent or ongoing changes in market conditions in interpreting market concentration and market share data.

1.522　Degree of Difference Between the Products and Locations in the Market and Substitutes Outside the Market

All else equal, the magnitude of potential competitive harm from a merger is greater if a hypothetical monopolist would raise price within the relevant market by substantially more than a "small but significant and nontransitory" amount. This may occur when the demand substitutes outside the relevant market, as a group, are not close substitutes for the products and locations within the relevant market. There thus may be a wide gap in the chain of demand substitutes at the edge of the product and geographic market. Under such circumstances, more market power is at stake in the relevant market than in a market in which a hypothetical monopolist would raise price by exactly five percent.

2.   The Potential Adverse Competitive Effects of Mergers

2.0   Overview

Other things being equal, market concentration affects the likelihood that one firm, or a small group of firms, could successfully exercise market power. The smaller the percentage of total supply that a firm controls, the more severely it must restrict its own output in order to produce a given price increase, and the less likely it is that an output restriction will be profitable. If collective action is necessary for the exercise of market power, as the number of firms necessary to control a given percentage of total supply decreases, the difficulties and costs of reaching and enforcing an understanding with respect to the control of that supply might be reduced. However, market share and concentration data provide only the starting point for analyzing the competitive impact of a merger. Before determining whether to challenge a merger, the Agency also will assess the other market factors that pertain to competitive effects, as well as entry, efficiencies and failure.

This section considers some of the potential adverse competitive effects of mergers and the factors in addition to market concentration relevant to each. Because an individual merger may threaten to harm competition through more than one of these effects, mergers will be analyzed in terms of as many potential adverse competitive effects as are appropriate. Entry, efficiencies, and failure are treated in Sections 3-5.

2.1   Lessening of Competition through Coordinated Interaction

A merger may diminish competition by enabling the firms selling in the relevant market more likely, more successfully, or more completely to engage in coordinated interaction that harms consumers. Coordinated interaction is comprised of actions by a group of firms that are profitable for each of them only as a result of the accommodating reactions of the others. This behavior includes tacit or express collusion, and may or may not be lawful in and of itself.

Successful coordinated interaction entails reaching terms of coordination that are profitable to the firms involved and an ability to detect and punish deviations that would undermine the coordinated interaction. Detection and punishment of deviations ensure that coordinating firms will find it more profitable to adhere to the terms of coordination than to pursue short-term profits from deviating, given the costs of reprisal. In this phase of the analysis, the Agency will examine the extent to which post-merger market conditions are conducive to reaching terms of coordination, detecting deviations from those terms, and punishing such deviations. Depending upon the circumstances, the following market factors, among others, may be relevant: the availability of key information concerning market conditions, transactions and individual competitors; the extent of firm and product heterogeneity; pricing or marketing practices typically employed by firms in the market; the characteristics of buyers and sellers; and the characteristics of typical transactions.

Certain market conditions that are conducive to reaching terms of coordination also may be conducive to detecting or punishing deviations from those terms. For example, the extent of information available to firms in the market, or the extent of homogeneity, may be relevant to both the ability to reach terms of coordination and to detect or punish deviations from those terms. The extent to which any specific market condition will be relevant to one or more of the conditions necessary to coordinated interaction will depend on the circumstances of the particular case.

It is likely that market conditions are conducive to coordinated interaction when the firms in the market previously have engaged in express collusion and when the salient characteristics of the market have not changed appreciably since the most recent such incident. Previous express collusion in another geographic market will have the same weight when the salient characteristics of that other market at the time of the collusion are comparable to those in the relevant market.

In analyzing the effect of a particular merger on coordinated interaction, the Agency is mindful of the difficulties of predicting likely future behavior based on the types of incomplete and sometimes contradictory information typically generated in merger investigations. Whether a merger is likely to diminish competition by enabling firms more likely, more successfully or more completely to engage in coordinated interaction depends on whether market conditions, on the whole, are conducive to reaching terms of coordination and detecting and punishing deviations from those terms.

2.11 CONDITIONS CONDUCIVE TO REACHING TERMS OF COORDINATION

Firms coordinating their interactions need not reach complex terms concerning the allocation of the market output across firms or the level of the market prices but may, instead, follow simple terms such as a common price, fixed price differentials, stable market shares, or customer or territorial restrictions. Terms of coordination need not perfectly achieve the monopoly outcome in order to be harmful to consumers. Instead, the terms of coordination may be imperfect and incomplete— inasmuch as they omit some market participants, omit some dimensions of competition, omit some customers, yield elevated prices short of monopoly levels, or lapse into episodic price wars—and still result in significant competitive harm. At some point, however, imperfections cause the profitability of abiding by the terms of coordination to decrease and, depending on their extent, may make coordinated interaction unlikely in the first instance.

Market conditions may be conducive to or hinder reaching terms of coordination. For example, reaching terms of coordination may be facilitated by product or firm homogeneity and by existing practices among firms, practices not necessarily themselves antitrust violations, such as standardization of pricing or product variables on which firms could compete. Key information about rival firms and the market may also facilitate reaching terms of coordination. Conversely, reaching terms of coordination may be limited or impeded by product heterogeneity or by firms having substantially incomplete information about the conditions and prospects of their rivals' businesses, perhaps because of important differences among their current business operations. In addition, reaching terms of coordination may be limited or impeded by firm heterogeneity, for example, differences in vertical integration or the production of another product that tends to be used together with the relevant product.

2.12   CONDITIONS CONDUCIVE TO DETECTING AND PUNISHING DEVIATIONS

Where market conditions are conducive to timely detection and punishment of significant deviations, a firm will find it more profitable to abide by the terms of coordination than to deviate from them. Deviation from the terms of coordination will be deterred where the threat of punishment is credible. Credible punishment, however, may not need to be any more complex than temporary abandonment of the terms of coordination by other firms in the market.

Where detection and punishment likely would be rapid, incentives to deviate are diminished and coordination is likely to be successful. The detection and punishment of deviations may be facilitated by existing practices among firms, themselves not necessarily antitrust violations, and by the characteristics of typical transactions. For example, if key information about specific transactions or individual price or output levels is available routinely to competitors, it may be difficult for a firm to deviate secretly. If orders for the relevant product are frequent, regular and small relative to the total output of a firm in a market, it may be difficult for the firm to deviate in a substantial way without the knowledge of rivals and without the opportunity for rivals to react. If demand or cost fluctuations are relatively infrequent and small, deviations may be relatively easy to deter.

By contrast, where detection or punishment is likely to be slow, incentives to deviate are enhanced and coordinated interaction is unlikely to be successful. If demand or cost fluctuations are relatively frequent and large, deviations may be relatively difficult to distinguish from these other sources of market price fluctuations, and, in consequence, deviations may be relatively difficult to deter.

In certain circumstances, buyer characteristics and the nature of the procurement process may affect the incentives to deviate from terms of coordination. Buyer size alone is not the determining characteristic. Where large buyers likely would engage in long-term contracting, so that the sales covered by such contracts can be large relative to the total output of a firm in the market, firms may have the incentive to deviate. However, this only can be accomplished where the duration, volume and profitability of the business covered by such contracts are sufficiently large as to make deviation more profitable in the long term than honoring the terms of coordination, and buyers likely would switch suppliers.

In some circumstances, coordinated interaction can be effectively prevented or limited by maverick firms—firms that have a greater economic incentive to deviate from the terms of coordination than do most of their rivals (e.g., firms that are unusually disruptive and competitive influences in the market). Consequently, acquisition of a maverick firm is one way in which a merger may make coordinated interaction more likely, more successful, or more complete. For example, in a market where capacity constraints are significant for many competitors, a firm is more likely to be a maverick the greater is its excess or divertable capacity in relation to its sales or its total capacity, and the lower are its direct and opportunity costs of expanding sales in the relevant market.[19] This is so because a firm's incentive to deviate from price-elevating and output-limiting terms of coordination is greater the more the firm is able profitably to expand its output as a proportion of the sales it would obtain if it adhered to the terms of coordination and the smaller is the base of sales on which it enjoys elevated profits prior to the price cutting deviation.[20] A firm also may be a maverick if it has an unusual ability secretly to expand its sales in relation to the sales it would obtain if it adhered to the terms of coordination. This ability might arise from opportunities to expand captive production for a downstream affiliate.

2.2 Lessening of Competition through Unilateral Effects

A merger may diminish competition even if it does not lead to increased likelihood of successful coordinated interaction, because merging firms may find it profitable to alter their behavior unilaterally following the acquisition by elevating price and suppressing output. Unilateral competitive effects can arise in a variety of different settings. In each setting, particular other factors describing the relevant market affect the likelihood of unilateral competitive effects. The settings differ by the primary characteristics that distinguish firms and shape the nature of their competition.

2.21 FIRMS DISTINGUISHED PRIMARILY BY DIFFERENTIATED PRODUCTS

In some markets the products are differentiated, so that products sold by different participants in the market are not perfect substitutes for one another. Moreover, different products in the market may vary in the degree of their substitutability for one another. In this setting, competition may be non-uniform (i.e., localized), so that individual sellers compete more directly with those rivals selling closer substitutes.[21]

A merger between firms in a market for differentiated products may diminish competition by enabling the merged firm to profit by unilaterally raising the price of

---

19. But excess capacity in the hands of non-maverick firms may be a potent weapon with which to punish deviations from the terms of coordination.
20. Similarly, in a market where product design or quality is significant, a firm is more likely to be an effective maverick the greater is the sales potential of its products among customers of its rivals, in relation to the sales it would obtain if it adhered to the terms of coordination. The likelihood of expansion responses by a maverick will be analyzed in the same fashion as uncommitted entry or committed entry (see Sections 1.3 and 3) depending on the significance of the sunk costs entailed in expansion.
21. Similarly, in some markets sellers are primarily distinguished by their relative advantages in serving different buyers or groups of buyers, and buyers negotiate individually with sellers. Here, for example, sellers may formally bid against one another for the business of a buyer, or each buyer may elicit individual price quotes from multiple sellers. A seller may find it relatively inexpensive to meet the demands of particular buyers or types of buyers, and relatively expensive to meet others' demands. Competition, again, may be localized: sellers compete more directly with those rivals having similar relative advantages in serving particular buyers or groups of buyers. For example, in open outcry auctions, price is determined by the cost of the second lowest-cost seller. A merger involving the first and second lowest-cost sellers could cause prices to rise to the constraining level of the next lowest-cost seller.

1498 ANTITRUST LAW DEVELOPMENTS (FIFTH)

one or both products above the premerger level. Some of the sales loss due to the price rise merely will be diverted to the product of the merger partner and, depending on relative margins, capturing such sales loss through merger may make the price increase profitable even though it would not have been profitable premerger. Substantial unilateral price elevation in a market for differentiated products requires that there be a significant share of sales in the market accounted for by consumers who regard the products of the merging firms as their first and second choices, and that repositioning of the non-parties' product lines to replace the localized competition lost through the merger be unlikely. The price rise will be greater the closer substitutes are the products of the merging firms, i.e., the more the buyers of one product consider the other product to be their next choice.

2.211 Closeness of the Products of the Merging Firms

The market concentration measures articulated in Section 1 may help assess the extent of the likely competitive effect from a unilateral price elevation by the merged firm notwithstanding the fact that the affected products are differentiated. The market concentration measures provide a measure of this effect if each product's market share is reflective of not only its relative appeal as a first choice to consumers of the merging firms' products but also its relative appeal as a second choice, and hence as a competitive constraint to the first choice.[22] Where this circumstance holds, market concentration data fall outside the safeharbor regions of Section 1.5, and the merging firms have a combined market share of at least thirty-five percent, the Agency will presume that a significant share of sales in the market are accounted for by consumers who regard the products of the merging firms as their first and second choices.

Purchasers of one of the merging firms' products may be more or less likely to make the other their second choice than market shares alone would indicate. The market shares of the merging firms' products may understate the competitive effect of concern, when, for example, the products of the merging firms are relatively more similar in their various attributes to one another than to other products in the relevant market. On the other hand, the market shares alone may overstate the competitive effects of concern when, for example, the relevant products are less similar in their attributes to one another than to other products in the relevant market.

Where market concentration data fall outside the safeharbor regions of Section 1.5, the merging firms have a combined market share of at least thirty-five percent, and where data on product attributes and relative product appeal show that a significant share of purchasers of one merging firm's product regard the other as their second choice, then market share data may be relied upon to demonstrate that there is a significant share of sales in the market accounted for by consumers who would be adversely affected by the merger.

---

22. Information about consumers' actual first and second product choices may be provided by marketing surveys, information from bidding structures, or normal course of business documents from industry participants.

2.212 Ability of Rival Sellers to Replace Lost Competition

A merger is not likely to lead to unilateral elevation of prices of differentiated products if, in response to such an effect, rival sellers likely would replace any localized competition lost through the merger by repositioning their product lines.[23]

In markets where it is costly for buyers to evaluate product quality, buyers who consider purchasing from both merging parties may limit the total number of sellers they consider. If either of the merging firms would be replaced in such buyers' consideration by an equally competitive seller not formerly considered, then the merger is not likely to lead to a unilateral elevation of prices.

2.22   FIRMS DISTINGUISHED PRIMARILY BY THEIR CAPACITIES

Where products are relatively undifferentiated and capacity primarily distinguishes firms and shapes the nature of their competition, the merged firm may find it profitable unilaterally to raise price and suppress output. The merger provides the merged firm a larger base of sales on which to enjoy the resulting price rise and also eliminates a competitor to which customers otherwise would have diverted their sales. Where the merging firms have a combined market share of at least thirty-five percent, merged firms may find it profitable to raise price and reduce joint output below the sum of their premerger outputs because the lost markups on the foregone sales may be outweighed by the resulting price increase on the merged base of sales.

This unilateral effect is unlikely unless a sufficiently large number of the merged firm's customers would not be able to find economical alternative sources of supply, i.e., competitors of the merged firm likely would not respond to the price increase and output reduction by the merged firm with increases in their own outputs sufficient in the aggregate to make the unilateral action of the merged firm unprofitable. Such non-party expansion is unlikely if those firms face binding capacity constraints that could not be economically relaxed within two years or if existing excess capacity is significantly more costly to operate than capacity currently in use.[24]

3.   Entry Analysis

3.0   Overview

A merger is not likely to create or enhance market power or to facilitate its exercise, if entry into the market is so easy that market participants, after the merger, either collectively or unilaterally could not profitably maintain a price increase above premerger levels. Such entry likely will deter an anticompetitive merger in its incipiency, or deter or counteract the competitive effects of concern.

---

23. The timeliness and likelihood of repositioning responses will be analyzed using the same methodology as used in analyzing uncommitted entry or committed entry (*see* Sections 1.3 and 3), depending on the significance of the sunk costs entailed in repositioning.

24. The timeliness and likelihood of non-party expansion will be analyzed using the same methodology as used in analyzing uncommitted or committed entry (*see* Sections 1.3 and 3) depending on the significance of the sunk costs entailed in expansion.

Entry is that easy if entry would be timely, likely, and sufficient in its magnitude, character and scope to deter or counteract the competitive effects of concern. In markets where entry is that easy (i.e., where entry passes these tests of timeliness, likelihood, and sufficiency), the merger raises no antitrust concern and ordinarily requires no further analysis.

The committed entry treated in this Section is defined as new competition that requires expenditure of significant sunk costs of entry and exit.[25] The Agency employs a three step methodology to assess whether committed entry would deter or counteract a competitive effect of concern.

The first step assesses whether entry can achieve significant market impact within a timely period. If significant market impact would require a longer period, entry will not deter or counteract the competitive effect of concern.

The second step assesses whether committed entry would be a profitable and, hence, a likely response to a merger having competitive effects of concern. Firms considering entry that requires significant sunk costs must evaluate the profitability of the entry on the basis of long term participation in the market, because the underlying assets will be committed to the market until they are economically depreciated. Entry that is sufficient to counteract the competitive effects of concern will cause prices to fall to their premerger levels or lower. Thus, the profitability of such committed entry must be determined on the basis of premerger market prices over the long-term.

A merger having anticompetitive effects can attract committed entry, profitable at premerger prices, that would not have occurred premerger at these same prices. But following the merger, the reduction in industry output and increase in prices associated with the competitive effect of concern may allow the same entry to occur without driving market prices below premerger levels. After a merger that results in decreased output and increased prices, the likely sales opportunities available to entrants at premerger prices will be larger than they were premerger, larger by the output reduction caused by the merger. If entry could be profitable at premerger prices without exceeding the likely sales opportunities—opportunities that include pre-existing pertinent factors as well as the merger-induced output reduction—then such entry is likely in response to the merger.

The third step assesses whether timely and likely entry would be sufficient to return market prices to their premerger levels. This end may be accomplished either through multiple entry or individual entry at a sufficient scale. Entry may not be sufficient, even though timely and likely, where the constraints on availability of essential assets, due to incumbent control, make it impossible for entry profitably to achieve the necessary level of sales. Also, the character and scope of entrants' products might not be fully responsive to the localized sales opportunities created by the removal of direct competition among sellers of differentiated products. In assessing whether entry will be timely, likely, and sufficient, the Agency recognizes that precise and detailed information may be difficult or impossible to obtain. In such instances, the Agency will rely on all available evidence bearing on whether entry will satisfy the conditions of timeliness, likelihood, and sufficiency.

---

25.   Supply responses that require less than one year and insignificant sunk costs to effectuate are analyzed as uncommitted entry in Section 1.3.

3.1   Entry Alternatives

The Agency will examine the timeliness, likelihood, and sufficiency of the means of entry (entry alternatives) a potential entrant might practically employ, without attempting to identify who might be potential entrants.   An entry alternative is defined by the actions the firm must take in order to produce and sell in the market. All phases of the entry effort will be considered, including, where relevant, planning, design, and management; permitting, licensing, and other approvals; construction, debugging, and operation of production facilities; and promotion (including necessary introductory discounts), marketing, distribution, and satisfaction of customer testing and qualification requirements.[26] Recent examples of entry, whether successful or unsuccessful, may provide a useful starting point for identifying the necessary actions, time requirements, and characteristics of possible entry alternatives.

3.2   Timeliness of Entry

In order to deter or counteract the competitive effects of concern, entrants quickly must achieve a significant impact on price in the relevant market.   The Agency generally will consider timely only those committed entry alternatives that can be achieved within two years from initial planning to significant market impact.[27] Where the relevant product is a durable good, consumers, in response to a significant commitment to entry, may defer purchases by making additional investments to extend the useful life of previously purchased goods and in this way deter or counteract for a time the competitive effects of concern.   In these circumstances, if entry only can occur outside of the two year period, the Agency will consider entry to be timely so long as it would deter or counteract the competitive effects of concern within the two year period and subsequently.

3.3   Likelihood of Entry

An entry alternative is likely if it would be profitable at premerger prices, and if such prices could be secured by the entrant.[28] The committed entrant will be unable to secure prices at premerger levels if its output is too large for the market to absorb without depressing prices further.   Thus, entry is unlikely if the minimum viable scale is larger than the likely sales opportunity available to entrants.

Minimum viable scale is the smallest average annual level of sales that the committed entrant must persistently achieve for profitability at premerger prices.[29]

---

26.   Many of these phases may be undertaken simultaneously.
27.   Firms which have committed to entering the market prior to the merger generally will be included in the measurement of the market.   Only committed entry or adjustments to pre-existing entry plans that are induced by the merger will be considered as possibly deterring or counteracting the competitive effects of concern.
28.   Where conditions indicate that entry may be profitable at prices below premerger levels, the Agency will assess the likelihood of entry at the lowest price at which such entry would be profitable.
29.   The concept of minimum viable scale (MVS) differs from the concept of minimum efficient scale (MES).   While MES is the smallest scale at which average costs are minimized, MVS is the smallest scale at which average costs equal the premerger price.

Minimum viable scale is a function of expected revenues, based upon premerger prices,[30] and all categories of costs associated with the entry alternative, including an appropriate rate of return on invested capital given that entry could fail and sunk costs, if any, will be lost.[31]

Sources of sales opportunities available to entrants include: (a) the output reduction associated with the competitive effect of concern,[32] (b) entrants' ability to capture a share of reasonably expected growth in market demand,[33] (c) entrants' ability securely to divert sales from incumbents, for example, through vertical integration or through forward contracting, and (d) any additional anticipated contraction in incumbents' output in response to entry.[34] Factors that reduce the sales opportunities available to entrants include: (a) the prospect that an entrant will share in a reasonably expected decline in market demand, (b) the exclusion of an entrant from a portion of the market over the long term because of vertical integration or forward contracting by incumbents, and (c) any anticipated sales expansion by incumbents in reaction to entry, either generalized or targeted at customers approached by the entrant, that utilizes prior irreversible investments in excess production capacity. Demand growth or decline will be viewed as relevant only if total market demand is projected to experience long-lasting change during at least the two year period following the competitive effect of concern.

3.4   Sufficiency of Entry

Inasmuch as multiple entry generally is possible and individual entrants may flexibly choose their scale, committed entry generally will be sufficient to deter or counteract the competitive effects of concern whenever entry is likely under the analysis of Section 3.3. However, entry, although likely, will not be sufficient if, as a result of incumbent control, the tangible and intangible assets required for entry are not adequately available for entrants to respond fully to their sales opportunities. In addition, where the competitive effect of concern is not uniform across the relevant market, in order for entry to be sufficient, the character and scope of entrants' products must be responsive to the localized sales opportunities that include the output reduction associated with the competitive effect of concern. For example, where the concern is unilateral price elevation as a result of a merger between producers of differentiated products, entry, in order to be sufficient, must involve a product so close to the products of the merging firms that the merged firm will be

---

30.   The expected path of future prices, absent the merger, may be used if future price changes can be predicted with reasonable reliability.

31.   The minimum viable scale of an entry alternative will be relatively large when the fixed costs of entry are large, when the fixed costs of entry are largely sunk, when the marginal costs of production are high at low levels of output, and when a plant is underutilized for a long time because of delays in achieving market acceptance.

32.   Five percent of total market sales typically is used because where a monopolist profitably would raise price by five percent or more across the entire relevant market, it is likely that the accompanying reduction in sales would be no less than five percent.

33.   Entrants' anticipated share of growth in demand depends on incumbents' capacity constraints and irreversible investments in capacity expansion, as well as on the relative appeal, acceptability and reputation of incumbents' and entrants' products to the new demand.

34.   For example, in a bidding market where all bidders are on equal footing, the market share of incumbents will contract as a result of entry.

unable to internalize enough of the sales loss due to the price rise, rendering the price increase unprofitable.

4.   Efficiencies[*]

Competition usually spurs firms to achieve efficiencies internally. Nevertheless, mergers have the potential to generate significant efficiencies by permitting a better utilization of existing assets, enabling the combined firm to achieve lower costs in producing a given quantity and quality than either firm could have achieved without the proposed transaction. Indeed, the primary benefit of mergers to the economy is their potential to generate such efficiencies.

Efficiencies generated through merger can enhance the merged firm's ability and incentive to compete, which may result in lower prices, improved quality, enhanced service, or new products. For example, merger-generated efficiencies may enhance competition by permitting two ineffective (e.g., high cost) competitors to become one effective (e.g., lower cost) competitor. In a coordinated interaction context (see Section 2.1), marginal cost reductions may make coordination less likely or effective by enhancing the incentive of a maverick to lower price or by creating a new maverick firm. In a unilateral effects context (see Section 2.2), marginal cost reductions may reduce the merged firm's incentive to elevate price. Efficiencies also may result in benefits in the form of new or improved products, and efficiencies may result in benefits even when price is not immediately and directly affected. Even when efficiencies generated through merger enhance a firm's ability to compete, however, a merger may have other effects that may lessen competition and ultimately may make the merger anticompetitive.

The Agency will consider only those efficiencies likely to be accomplished with the proposed merger and unlikely to be accomplished in the absence of either the proposed merger or another means having comparable anticompetitive effects. These are termed *merger-specific efficiencies*.[35] Only alternatives that are practical in the business situation faced by the merging firms will be considered in making this determination; the Agency will not insist upon a less restrictive alternative that is merely theoretical.

Efficiencies are difficult to verify and quantify, in part because much of the information relating to efficiencies is uniquely in the possession of the merging firms. Moreover, efficiencies projected reasonably and in good faith by the merging firms may not be realized. Therefore, the merging firms must substantiate efficiency claims so that the Agency can verify by reasonable means the likelihood and magnitude of each asserted efficiency, how and when each would be achieved (and any costs of doing so), how each would enhance the merged firm's ability and incentive to compete, and why each would be merger-specific. Efficiency claims will not be considered if they are vague or speculative or otherwise cannot be verified by reasonable means.

---

[*]   Revised Section 4 issued by the U.S. Department of Justice and the Federal Trade Commission (Apr. 8, 1997).

35.   The Agency will not deem efficiencies to be merger-specific if they could be preserved by practical alternatives that mitigate competitive concerns, such as divestiture or licensing. If a merger affects not whether but only when an efficiency would be achieved, only the timing advantage is a merger-specific efficiency.

Cognizable efficiencies are merger-specific efficiencies that have been verified and do not arise from anticompetitive reductions in output or service. Cognizable efficiencies are assessed net of costs produced by the merger or incurred in achieving those efficiencies.

The Agency will not challenge a merger if cognizable efficiencies are of a character and magnitude such that the merger is not likely to be anticompetitive in any relevant market.[36] To make the requisite determination, the Agency considers whether cognizable efficiencies likely would be sufficient to reverse the merger's potential to harm consumers in the relevant market, e.g., by preventing price increases in that market. In conducting this analysis,[37] the Agency will not simply compare the magnitude of the cognizable efficiencies with the magnitude of the likely harm to competition absent the efficiencies. The greater the potential adverse competitive effect of a merger—as indicated by the increase in the HHI and post-merger HHI from Section 1, the analysis of potential adverse competitive effects from Section 2, and the timeliness, likelihood, and sufficiency of entry from Section 3—the greater must be cognizable efficiencies in order for the Agency to conclude that the merger will not have an anticompetitive effect in the relevant market. When the potential adverse competitive effect of a merger is likely to be particularly large, extraordinarily great cognizable efficiencies would be necessary to prevent the merger from being anticompetitive.

In the Agency's experience, efficiencies are most likely to make a difference in merger analysis when the likely adverse competitive effects, absent the efficiencies, are not great. Efficiencies almost never justify a merger to monopoly or near-monopoly.

The Agency has found that certain types of efficiencies are more likely to be cognizable and substantial than others. For example, efficiencies resulting from shifting production among facilities formerly owned separately, which enable the merging firms to reduce the marginal cost of production, are more likely to be susceptible to verification, merger-specific, and substantial, and are less likely to result from anticompetitive reductions in output. Other efficiencies, such as those relating to research and development, are potentially substantial but are generally less susceptible to verification and may be the result of anticompetitive output reductions. Yet others, such as those relating to procurement, management, or capital cost are less likely to be merger-specific or substantial, or may not be cognizable for other reasons.

---

36.   Section 7 of the Clayton Act prohibits mergers that may substantially lessen competition "in any line of commerce . . . in any section of the country." Accordingly, the Agency normally assesses competition in each relevant market affected by a merger independently and normally will challenge the merger if it is likely to be anticompetitive in any relevant market. In some cases, however, the Agency in its prosecutorial discretion will consider efficiencies not strictly in the relevant market, but so inextricably linked with it that a partial divestiture or other remedy could not feasibly eliminate the anticompetitive effect in the relevant market without sacrificing the efficiencies in the other market(s). Inextricably linked efficiencies rarely are a significant factor in the Agency's determination not to challenge a merger. They are most likely to make a difference when they are great and the likely anticompetitive effect in the relevant market(s) is small.

37.   The result of this analysis over the short term will determine the Agency's enforcement decision in most cases. The Agency also will consider the effects of cognizable efficiencies with no short-term, direct effect on prices in the relevant market. Delayed benefits from efficiencies (due to delay in the achievement of, or the realization of consumer benefits from, the efficiencies) will be given less weight because they are less proximate and more difficult to predict.

5.   Failure and Exiting Assets

5.0   Overview

Notwithstanding the analysis of Sections 1-4 of the *Guidelines*, a merger is not likely to create or enhance market power or to facilitate its exercise, if imminent failure, as defined below, of one of the merging firms would cause the assets of that firm to exit the relevant market. In such circumstances, post-merger performance in the relevant market may be no worse than market performance had the merger been blocked and the assets left the market.

5.1   Failing Firm

A merger is not likely to create or enhance market power or facilitate its exercise if the following circumstances are met: (1) the allegedly failing firm would be unable to meet its financial obligations in the near future; (2) it would not be able to reorganize successfully under Chapter 11 of the Bankruptcy Act;[38] (3) it has made unsuccessful good-faith efforts to elicit reasonable alternative offers of acquisition of the assets of the failing firm[39] that would both keep its tangible and intangible assets in the relevant market and pose a less severe danger to competition than does the proposed merger; and (4) absent the acquisition, the assets of the failing firm would exit the relevant market.

5.2   Failing Division

A similar argument can be made for "failing" divisions as for failing firms. First, upon applying appropriate cost allocation rules, the division must have a negative cash flow on an operating basis. Second, absent the acquisition, it must be that the assets of the division would exit the relevant market in the near future if not sold. Due to the ability of the parent firm to allocate costs, revenues, and intracompany transactions among itself and its subsidiaries and divisions, the Agency will require evidence, not based solely on management plans that could be prepared solely for the purpose of demonstrating negative cash flow or the prospect of exit from the relevant market. Third, the owner of the failing division also must have complied with the competitively-preferable purchaser requirement of Section 5.1.

---

38.   11 U.S.C. §§ 1101-1174 (1988).
39.   Any offer to purchase the assets of the failing firm for a price above the liquidation value of those assets—the highest valued use outside the relevant market or equivalent offer to purchase the stock of the failing firm—will be regarded as a reasonable alternative offer.

1995 DEPARTMENT OF JUSTICE AND FEDERAL TRADE COMMISSION ANTITRUST ENFORCEMENT GUIDELINES FOR INTERNATIONAL OPERATIONS

1. Introduction

For more than a century, the U.S. antitrust laws have stood as the ultimate protector of the competitive process that underlies our free market economy. Through this process, which enhances consumer choice and promotes competitive prices, society as a whole benefits from the best possible allocation of resources.

Although the federal antitrust laws have always applied to foreign commerce, that application is particularly important today. Throughout the world, the importance of antitrust law as a means to ensure open and free markets, protect consumers, and prevent conduct that impedes competition is becoming more apparent. The Department of Justice ("the Department") and the Federal Trade Commission ("the Commission" or "FTC") (when referred to collectively, "the Agencies"), as the federal agencies charged with the responsibility of enforcing the antitrust laws, thus have made it a high priority to enforce the antitrust laws with respect to international operations and to cooperate wherever appropriate with foreign authorities regarding such enforcement. In furtherance of this priority, the Agencies have revised and updated the Department's 1988 *Antitrust Enforcement Guidelines for International Operations*, which are hereby withdrawn.[1]

The 1995 *Antitrust Enforcement Guidelines for International Operations* (hereinafter "*Guidelines*") are intended to provide antitrust guidance to businesses engaged in international operations on questions that relate specifically to the

---

1. The U.S. DEPARTMENT OF JUSTICE AND FEDERAL TRADE COMMISSION ANTITRUST GUIDELINES FOR THE LICENSING OF INTELLECTUAL PROPERTY (1995), the U.S. DEPARTMENT OF JUSTICE AND FEDERAL TRADE COMMISSION HORIZONTAL MERGER GUIDELINES (1992), and the STATEMENTS OF ANTITRUST ENFORCEMENT POLICY AND ANALYTICAL PRINCIPLES RELATING TO HEALTH CARE AND ANTITRUST, Jointly Issued by the U.S. Department of Justice and Federal Trade Commission (1994), are not qualified, modified, or otherwise amended by the issuance of these *Guidelines*.

Agencies' international enforcement policy.[2]   They do not, therefore, provide a complete statement of the Agencies' general enforcement policies.   The topics covered include the Agencies' subject matter jurisdiction over conduct and entities outside the United States and the considerations, issues, policies, and processes that govern their decision to exercise that jurisdiction; comity; mutual assistance in international antitrust enforcement; and the effects of foreign governmental involvement on the antitrust liability of private entities.   In addition, the *Guidelines* discuss the relationship between antitrust and international trade initiatives.   Finally, to illustrate how these principles may operate in certain contexts, the *Guidelines* include a number of examples.

As is the case with all guidelines, users should rely on qualified counsel to assist them in evaluating the antitrust risk associated with any contemplated transaction or activity.   No set of guidelines can possibly indicate how the Agencies will assess the particular facts of every case.   Persons seeking more specific advance statements of enforcement intentions with respect to the matters treated in these *Guidelines* should use the Department's Business Review procedure,[3] the Commission's Advisory Opinion procedure,[4] or one of the more specific procedures described below for particular types of transactions.

2.   Antitrust Laws Enforced by the Agencies

Foreign commerce cases can involve almost any provision of the antitrust laws. The Agencies do not discriminate in the enforcement of the antitrust laws on the basis of the nationality of the parties.   Nor do the Agencies employ their statutory authority to further non-antitrust goals.   Once jurisdictional requirements, comity, and doctrines of foreign governmental involvement have been considered and satisfied, the same substantive rules apply to all cases.

The following is a brief summary of the laws enforced by the Agencies that are likely to have the greatest significance for international transactions.

2.1   Sherman Act

Section 1 of the Sherman Act, 15 U.S.C. § 1, sets forth the basic antitrust prohibition against contracts, combinations, and conspiracies "in restraint of trade or commerce among the several States or with foreign nations."   Section 2 of the Act, 15 U.S.C. § 2, prohibits monopolization, attempts to monopolize, and conspiracies to monopolize "any part of trade or commerce among the several States or with foreign nations."   Section 6a of the Sherman Act, 15 U.S.C. § 6a, defines the jurisdictional reach of the Act with respect to non-import foreign commerce.

Violations of the Sherman Act may be prosecuted as civil or criminal offenses. Conduct that the Department prosecutes criminally is limited to traditional *per se* offenses of the law, which typically involve price-fixing, customer allocation, bid-rigging or other cartel activities that would also be violations of the law in many

---

2.   Readers should separately evaluate the risk of private litigation by competitors, consumers and suppliers, as well as the risk of enforcement by state prosecutors under state and federal antitrust laws.

3.   28 C.F.R. § 50.6 (1994).

4.   16 C.F.R. §§ 1.1-1.4 (1994).

countries. Criminal violations of the Act are punishable by fines and imprisonment. The Sherman Act provides that corporate defendants may be fined up to $10 million, other defendants may be fined up to $350,000, and individuals may be sentenced to up to 3 years imprisonment.[5] The Department has sole responsibility for the criminal enforcement of the Sherman Act. In a civil proceeding, the Department may obtain injunctive relief against prohibited practices. It may also obtain treble damages if the U.S. government is the purchaser of affected goods or services.[6] Private plaintiffs may also obtain injunctive and treble damage relief for violations of the Sherman Act.[7] Before the Commission, conduct that violates the Sherman Act may be challenged pursuant to the Commission's power under Section 5 of the Federal Trade Commission Act, described below.

2.2   *Clayton Act*

The Clayton Act, 15 U.S.C. § 12 *et seq.*, expands on the general prohibitions of the Sherman Act and addresses anticompetitive problems in their incipiency.[8] Section 7 of the Clayton Act, 15 U.S.C. § 18, prohibits any merger or acquisition of stock or assets "where in any line of commerce or in any activity affecting commerce in any section of the country, the effect of such acquisition may be substantially to lessen competition, or to tend to create a monopoly."[9] Section 15 of the Clayton Act empowers the Attorney General, and Section 13(b) of the FTC Act empowers the Commission, to seek a court order enjoining consummation of a merger that would violate Section 7. In addition, the Commission may seek a cease and desist order in an administrative proceeding against a merger under Section 11 of the Clayton Act, Section 5 of the FTC Act, or both. Private parties may also seek injunctive relief under 15 U.S.C. § 26.

Section 3 of the Clayton Act prohibits any person engaged in commerce from conditioning the lease or sale of goods or commodities upon the purchaser's agreement not to use the products of a competitor, if the effect may be "to substantially lessen competition or to tend to create a monopoly in any line of commerce."[10] In evaluating transactions, the trend of recent authority is to use the same analysis employed in the evaluation of tying under Section 1 of the Sherman Act to assess a defendant's liability under Section 3 of the Clayton Act.[11] Section 2

---

5.   Defendants may be fined up to twice the gross pecuniary gain or loss caused by their offense in lieu of the Sherman Act fines, pursuant to 18 U.S.C. § 3571(d) (1988 & Supp. 1993). In addition, the U.S. Sentencing Commission Guidelines provide further information about possible criminal sanctions for individual antitrust defendants in § 2R1.1 and for organizational defendants in Chapter 8.

6.   *See* 15 U.S.C. § 4 (1988) (injunctive relief); 15 U.S.C. § 15(a) (1988 & Supp. 1993) (damages).

7.   *See* 15 U.S.C. §§ 16, 26 (1988).

8.   Under the Clayton Act, "commerce" includes "trade or commerce among the several States and with foreign nations." "Persons" include corporations or associations existing under or authorized either by the laws of the United States or any of its states or territories, or by the laws of any foreign country. 15 U.S.C. § 12 (1988 & Supp. 1993).

9.   15 U.S.C. § 18 (1988). The asset acquisition clause applies to "person[s] subject to the jurisdiction of the Federal Trade Commission" under the Clayton Act.

10.   15 U.S.C. § 14 (1988).

11.   *See, e.g.*, Mozart Co. v. Mercedes-Benz of N. Am., Inc., 833 F.2d 1342, 1352 (9th Cir. 1987), *cert. denied*, 488 U.S. 870 (1988).

of the Clayton Act, known as the Robinson-Patman Act,[12] prohibits price discrimination in certain circumstances. In practice, the Commission has exercised primary enforcement responsibility for this provision.

2.3 Federal Trade Commission Act

Section 5 of the Federal Trade Commission Act ("FTC Act") declares unlawful "unfair methods of competition in or affecting commerce, and unfair or deceptive acts or practices in or affecting commerce."[13] Pursuant to its authority over unfair methods of competition, the Commission may take administrative action against conduct that violates the Sherman Act and the Clayton Act, as well as anticompetitive practices that do not fall within the scope of the Sherman or Clayton Acts. The Commission may also seek injunctive relief in federal court against any such conduct under Section 13(b) of the FTC Act. Although enforcement at the Commission relating to international deceptive practices has become increasingly important over time, these *Guidelines* are limited to the Commission's antitrust authority under the unfair methods of competition language of Section 5.

2.4 Hart-Scott-Rodino Antitrust Improvements Act of 1976

Title II of the Hart-Scott-Rodino Antitrust Improvements Act of 1976 ("HSR Act"), 15 U.S.C. § 18a, provides the Department and the Commission with several procedural devices to facilitate enforcement of the antitrust laws with respect to anticompetitive mergers and acquisitions.[14] The HSR Act requires persons engaged in commerce or in any activity affecting commerce to notify the Agencies of proposed mergers or acquisitions that would exceed statutory size-of-party and size-of-transaction thresholds,[15] to provide certain information relating to reportable

---

12. 15 U.S.C. §§ 13-13b, 21a (1988). The Robinson-Patman Act applies only to purchases involving commodities "for use, consumption, or resale within the United States." *Id.* at § 13. It has been construed not to apply to sales for export. *See, e.g.*, General Chem., Inc. v. Exxon Chem. Co., 625 F.2d 1231, 1234 (5th Cir. 1980). Intervening domestic sales, however, would be subject to the Act. *See* Raul Int'l Corp. v. Sealed Power Corp., 586 F. Supp. 349, 351-55 (D.N.J. 1984).
13. 15 U.S.C. § 45 (1988 & Supp. 1993).
14. The scope of the Agencies' jurisdiction under Clayton § 7 exceeds the scope of those transactions subject to the premerger notification requirements of the HSR Act. Whether or not the HSR Act premerger notification thresholds are satisfied, either Agency may request the parties to a merger affecting U.S. commerce to provide information voluntarily concerning the transaction. In addition, the Department may issue Civil Investigative Demands ("CIDs") pursuant to the Antitrust Civil Process Act, 15 U.S.C. §§ 1311-1314 (1988), and the Commission may issue administrative CIDs pursuant to the Act of Aug. 26, 1994, Pub. L. No. 103-312, § 7, 108 Stat. 1691 (1994). The Commission may also issue administrative subpoenas and orders to file special reports under Sections 9 and 6(b) of the FTC Act, respectively. 15 U.S.C. §§ 49, 46(b) (1988). Authority in particular cases is allocated to either the Department or the Commission pursuant to a voluntary clearance protocol. *See* Antitrust & Trade Reg. Daily (BNA), Dec. 6, 1993, *and* U.S. Department of Justice and Federal Trade Commission, Hart-Scott-Rodino Premerger Program Improvements (March 23, 1995).
15. Unless exempted pursuant to the HSR Act, the parties must provide premerger notification to the Agencies if (1) the acquiring person, or the person whose voting securities or assets are being acquired, is engaged in commerce or any activity affecting commerce; and (2)(a) any voting securities or assets of a person engaged in manufacturing which has annual net sales or total assets of $10 million or more are being acquired by any person which has total assets or annual net sales of $100 million or more, or (b) any voting securities or assets of a person not engaged in

transactions, and to wait for a prescribed period-15 days for cash tender offers and 30 days for most other transactions-before consummating the transaction.[16] The Agency may, before the end of the waiting period, request additional information concerning a transaction (make a "Second Request") and thereby extend the waiting period beyond the initial one prescribed, to a specified number of days after the receipt of the material required by the Second Request—10 days for cash tender offers and 20 days for most other transactions.[17]

The HSR Act and the FTC rules implementing the HSR Act[18] exempt from the premerger notification requirements certain international transactions (typically those having little nexus to U.S. commerce) that otherwise meet the statutory thresholds.[19] Failure to comply with the HSR Act is punishable by court-imposed civil penalties of up to $10,000 for each day a violation continues. The court may also order injunctive relief to remedy a failure substantially to comply with the HSR Act. Businesses may seek an interpretation of their obligations under the HSR Act from the Commission.[20]

2.5 National Cooperative Research and Production Act

The National Cooperative Research and Production Act ("NCRPA"), 15 U.S.C. §§ 4301-06, clarifies the substantive application of the U.S. antitrust laws to joint research and development ("R&D") activities and joint production activities. Originally drafted to encourage research and development by providing a special antitrust regime for research and development joint ventures, the NCRPA requires U.S. courts to judge the competitive effects of a challenged joint R&D or joint production venture, or a combination of the two, in properly defined relevant markets and under a rule-of-reason standard. The statute specifies that the conduct "shall be judged on the basis of its reasonableness, taking into account all relevant factors affecting competition, including, but not limited to, effects on competition in properly defined, relevant research, development, product, process, and service

---

manufacturing which has total assets of $10 million or more are being acquired by any person which has total assets or annual sales of $100 million or more; or (c) any voting securities or assets of a person with annual net sales or total assets of $100 million or more are being acquired by any person with total assets or annual net sales of $ 10 million or more; and (3) as a result of such acquisition, the acquiring person would hold (a) 15 percent or more of the voting securities or assets of the acquired person, or (b) an aggregate total amount of the voting securities and assets of the acquired person of $15 million. 15 U.S.C. § 18a(a) (1988). The size of the transaction test set forth in (3) must be read in conjunction with 16 C.F.R. § 802.20 (1994). This Section exempts asset acquisitions valued at $15 million or less. It also exempts voting securities acquisitions of $15 million or less unless, if as a result of the acquisition, the acquiring person would hold 50 percent or more of the voting securities of an issuer that has annual net sales or total assets of $25 million or more. The HSR rules are necessarily technical, contain other exemptions, and should be consulted, rather than relying on this summary.

16. 15 U.S.C. § 18a(b) (1988 & Supp. 1993); 16 C.F.R. § 803.1 (1994); *see also* 11 U.S.C. § 363(b)(2).
17. 15 U.S.C. § 18a(e) (1988).
18. 16 C.F.R. §§ 801-803 (1994).
19. 16 C.F.R. §§ 801.1(e), (k), 802.50-52 (1994). *See infra* at Section 4.22.
20. *See* 16 C.F.R. § 803.30 (1994).

markets."[21] This approach is consistent with the Agencies' general analysis of joint ventures.[22]

The NCRPA also establishes a voluntary procedure pursuant to which the Attorney General and the FTC may be notified of a joint R&D or production venture. The statute limits the monetary relief that may be obtained in private civil suits against the participants in a notified venture to actual rather than treble damages, if the challenged conduct is within the scope of the notification. With respect to joint production ventures, the National Cooperative Production Amendments of 1993[23] provide that the benefits of the limitation on recoverable damages for claims resulting from conduct within the scope of a notification are not available unless (1) the principal facilities for the production are located within the United States or its territories, and (2) "each person who controls any party to such venture (including such party itself) is a United States person, or a foreign person from a country whose law accords antitrust treatment no less favorable to United States persons than to such country's domestic persons with respect to participation in joint ventures for production."[24]

2.6   Webb-Pomerene Act

The Webb-Pomerene Act, 15 U.S.C. §§ 61-65, provides a limited antitrust exemption for the formation and operation of associations of otherwise competing businesses to engage in collective export sales. The exemption applies only to the export of "goods, wares, or merchandise."[25] It does not apply to conduct that has an anticompetitive effect in the United States or that injures domestic competitors of the members of an export association. Nor does it provide any immunity from prosecution under foreign antitrust laws.[26] Associations seeking an exemption under the Webb-Pomerene Act must file their articles of agreement and annual reports with the Commission, but pre-formation approval from the Commission is not required.

2.7   Export Trading Company Act of 1982

The Export Trading Company Act of 1982 (the "ETC Act"), Pub. L. No. 97-290, 96 Stat. 1234, is designed to increase U.S. exports of goods and services. It addresses that goal in several ways. First, in Title II, it encourages more efficient

---

21.   15 U.S.C. § 4302 (1988 & Supp. 1993).
22.   *See, e.g.*, U.S. DEPARTMENT OF JUSTICE AND FEDERAL TRADE COMMISSION ANTITRUST GUIDELINES FOR THE LICENSING OF INTELLECTUAL PROPERTY, § 4 (1995); STATEMENTS OF ANTITRUST ENFORCEMENT POLICY AND ANALYTICAL PRINCIPLES RELATING TO HEALTH CARE AND ANTITRUST, Jointly Issued by the U.S. Department of Justice and the Federal Trade Commission (1994), Statement 2 (outlining a four-step approach for joint venture analysis). *See generally* National Collegiate Athletic Ass'n v. Board of Regents of Univ. of Okla., 468 U.S. 85 (1984); Federal Trade Comm'n v. Indiana Fed'n of Dentists, 476 U.S. 447 (1986). *See also* Massachusetts Board of Registration in Optometry, 110 F.T.C. 549 (1988).
23.   Pub. L. No. 103-42, 107 Stat. 117, 119 (1993).
24.   15 U.S.C. § 4306 (2) (Supp. 1993).
25.   15 U.S.C. § 61 (1988).
26.   *See, e.g.*, Cases 89/85, etc., A. Ahlstrom Osakeyhtio v. Commission ("Wood Pulp"), 1988 E.C.R. 5193, [1987-1988 Transfer Binder] Common Mkt. Rep. (CCH) ¶ 14,491 (1988).

provision of export trade services to U.S. producers and suppliers by reducing restrictions on trade financing provided by financial institutions.[27] Second, in Title III, it reduces uncertainty concerning the application of the U.S. antitrust laws to export trade through the creation of a procedure by which persons engaged in U.S. export trade may obtain an export trade certificate of review ("ETCR").[28] Third, in Title IV, it clarifies the jurisdictional rules applicable to non-import cases brought under the Sherman Act and the FTC Act.[29] The Title III certificates are discussed briefly here; the jurisdictional rules are treated below in Section 3.1.

Export trade certificates of review are issued by the Secretary of Commerce with the concurrence of the Attorney General. Persons named in the ETCR obtain limited immunity from suit under both state and federal antitrust laws for activities that are specified in the certificate and that comply with the terms of the certificate. To obtain an ETCR, an applicant must show that proposed export conduct will:

(1)   result in neither a substantial lessening of competition or restraint of trade within the United States nor a substantial restraint of the export trade of any competitor of the applicant;

(2)   not unreasonably enhance, stabilize, or depress prices in the United States of the class of goods or services covered by the application;

(3)   not constitute unfair methods of competition against competitors engaged in the export of the class of goods or services exported by the applicant; and

(4)   not include any act that may reasonably be expected to result in the sale for consumption or resale in the United States of such goods or services.[30]

Congress intended that these standards "encompass the full range of the antitrust laws," as defined in the ETC Act.[31]

Although an ETCR provides significant protection under the antitrust laws, it has certain limitations. First, conduct that falls outside the scope of a certificate remains fully subject to private and governmental enforcement actions. Second, an ETCR that is obtained by fraud is void from the outset and thus offers no protection under the antitrust laws. Third, any person that has been injured by certified conduct may recover actual (though not treble) damages if that conduct is found to violate any of the statutory criteria described above. In any such action, certified conduct enjoys a presumption of legality, and the prevailing party is entitled to recover costs and attorneys' fees.[32] Fourth, an ETCR does not constitute, explicitly or implicitly, an endorsement or opinion by the Secretary of Commerce or by the Attorney General concerning the legality of such business plans under the laws of any foreign country.

The Secretary of Commerce may revoke or modify an ETCR if the Secretary or the Attorney General determines that the applicant's export activities have ceased to comply with the statutory criteria for obtaining a certificate. The Attorney General may also bring suit under Section 15 of the Clayton Act to enjoin conduct that

---

27.   *See* 12 U.S.C. §§ 372, 635 a-4, 1841, 1843 (1988 & Supp. 1993) (Because Title II does not implicate the antitrust laws, it is not discussed further in these *Guidelines*.).

28.   15 U.S.C. §§ 4011-21 (1988 & Supp. 1993).

29.   15 U.S.C. § 6a (1988); 15 U.S.C. § 45(a)(3) (1988).

30.   15 U.S.C. § 4013(a) (1988).

31.   H.R. Rep. No. 924, 97th Cong., 2d Sess. 26 (1982). *See* 15 U.S.C. § 4021(6).

32.   *See* 15 U.S.C. § 4016(b)(1) (1988) (injured party) *and* § 4016(b)(4) (1988) (party against whom claim is brought).

threatens "a clear and irreparable harm to the national interest,"[33] even if the conduct has been pre-approved as part of an ETCR.

The Commerce Department, in consultation with the Department, has issued guidelines setting forth the standards used in reviewing ETCR applications.[34] The ETC Guidelines contain several examples illustrating application of the certification standards to specific export trade conduct, including the use of vertical and horizontal restraints and technology licensing arrangements. In addition, the Commerce Department's Export Trading Company Guidebook[35] provides information on the functions and advantages of establishing or using an export trading company, including factors to consider in applying for an ETCR. The Commerce Department's Office of Export Trading Company Affairs provides advice and information on the formation of export trading companies and facilitates contacts between producers of exportable goods and services and firms offering export trade services.

2.8   Other Pertinent Legislation

2.81   WILSON TARIFF ACT

The Wilson Tariff Act, 15 U.S.C. §§ 8-11, prohibits "every combination, conspiracy, trust, agreement, or contract" made by or between two or more persons or corporations, either of whom is engaged in importing any article from a foreign country into the United States, where the agreement is intended to restrain trade or increase the market price in any part of the United States of the imported articles, or of "any manufacture into which such imported article enters or is intended to enter." Violation of the Act is a misdemeanor, punishable by a maximum fine of $5,000 or one year in prison. The Act also provides for seizure of the imported articles.[36]

2.82   ANTIDUMPING ACT OF 1916

The Revenue Act of 1916, better known as the Antidumping Act, 15 U.S.C. §§ 71-74, is not an antitrust statute, but its subject matter is closely related to the antitrust rules regarding predation. It is a trade statute that creates a private claim against importers who sell goods into the United States at prices substantially below the prices charged for the same goods in their home market. In order to state a claim, a plaintiff must show both that such lower prices were commonly and systematically charged, and that the importer had the specific intent to injure or destroy an industry in the United States, or to prevent the establishment of an industry. Dumping cases are more commonly brought using the administrative procedures of the Tariff Act of 1930, discussed below.

---

33.   15 U.S.C. § 4016(b)(5) (1988); see 15 U.S.C. § 25 (1988).
34.   See DEPARTMENT OF COMMERCE, INTERNATIONAL TRADE ADMINISTRATION, GUIDELINES FOR THE ISSUANCE OF EXPORT TRADE CERTIFICATES OF REVIEW (2d ed.), 50 Fed. Reg. 1786 (1985) (hereinafter "ETC Guidelines").
35.   U.S. DEPARTMENT OF COMMERCE, INTERNATIONAL TRADE ADMINISTRATION, THE EXPORT TRADING COMPANY GUIDEBOOK (1984).
36.   15 U.S.C. § 11 (1988).

2.83   TARIFF ACT OF 1930

A comprehensive discussion of the trade remedies available under the Tariff Act is beyond the scope of these *Guidelines*. However, because antitrust questions sometimes arise in the context of trade actions, it is appropriate to describe these laws briefly.

2.831 Countervailing Duties

Pursuant to Title VII.A of the Tariff Act,[37] U.S. manufacturers, producers, wholesalers, unions, and trade associations may petition for the imposition of offsetting duties on subsidized foreign imports.[38] The Department of Commerce's International Trade Administration ("ITA") must make a determination that the foreign government in question is subsidizing the imports, and in almost all cases the International Trade Commission ("ITC") must determine that a domestic industry is materially injured or threatened with material injury by reason of these imports.

2.832 Antidumping Duties

Pursuant to Title VII.B of the Tariff Act,[39] parties designated in the statute (the same parties as in the countervailing duties provision) may petition for antidumping duties, which must be imposed on foreign merchandise that is being, or is likely to be, sold in the United States at "less than fair value" ("LTFV"), if the U.S. industry is materially injured or threatened with material injury by imports of the foreign merchandise. The ITA makes the LTFV determination, and the ITC is responsible for the injury decision.

2.833 Section 337

Section 337 of the Tariff Act, 19 U.S.C. § 1337, prohibits "unfair methods of competition and unfair acts in the importation of articles into the United States," if the effect is to destroy or substantially injure a U.S. industry, or where the acts relate to importation of articles infringing U.S. patents, copyrights, trademarks, or registered mask works.[40] Complaints are filed with the ITC. The principal remedies under Section 337 are an exclusion order directing that any offending goods be excluded from entry into the United States, and a cease and desist order directed toward any offending U.S. firms and individuals.[41] The ITC is required to give the Agencies an opportunity to comment before making a final determination.[42] In

---

37. *See* 19 U.S.C. § 1671 *et seq.* (1988 & Supp. 1993), *amended by* Uruguay Round Agreements Act, Pub. L. No. 103-465, 108 Stat. 4809 (1994).

38. Some alternative procedures exist under Tariff Act § 701(c) for countries that have not subscribed to the World Trade Organization ("WTO") Agreement on Subsidies and Countervailing Measures or measures equivalent to it. 19 U.S.C. § 1671(c) (1988 & Supp. 1993), *amended by* the Uruguay Round Agreements Act, Pub. L. No. 103-465, 108 Stat. 4809 (1994).

39. *See* 19 U.S.C. § 1673 *et seq.* (1988).

40. 19 U.S.C. § 1337 (1988), *amended by* the Uruguay Round Agreements Act, Pub. L. No. 103-465, 108 Stat. 4809 (1994).

41. 19 U.S.C. §§ 1337(d), (f) (1988).

42. 19 U.S.C. § 1337(b)(2) (1988).

addition, the Department participates in the interagency group that prepares recommendations for the President to approve, disapprove, or allow to take effect the import relief proposed by the ITC.

2.84   TRADE ACT OF 1974

2.841   Section 201

Section 201 of the Trade Act of 1974, 19 U.S.C. § 2251 *et seq.*, provides that American businesses claiming serious injury due to significant increases in imports may petition the ITC for relief or modification under the so-called "escape clause." If the ITC makes a determination that "an article is being imported into the United States in such increased quantities as to be a substantial cause of serious injury, or the threat thereof, to the domestic industry producing an article like or directly competitive with the imported article," and formulates its recommendation for appropriate relief, the Department participates in the interagency committee that conducts the investigations and advises the President whether to adopt, modify, or reject the import relief recommended by the ITC.

2.842   Section 301

Section 301 of the Trade Act of 1974, 19 U.S.C. § 2411, provides that the U.S. Trade Representative ("USTR"), subject to the specific direction, if any, of the President, may take action, including restricting imports, to enforce rights of the United States under any trade agreement, to address acts inconsistent with the international legal rights of the United States, or to respond to unjustifiable, unreasonable or discriminatory practices of foreign governments that burden or restrict U.S. commerce. Interested parties may initiate such actions through petitions to the USTR, or the USTR may itself initiate proceedings.[43] Of particular interest to antitrust enforcement is Section 301(d)(3)(B)(i)(IV), which includes among the "unreasonable" practices of foreign governments that might justify a proceeding the "toleration by a foreign government of systematic anticompetitive activities by enterprises or among enterprises in the foreign country that have the effect of restricting . . . access of United States goods or services to a foreign market."[44] The Department participates in the interagency committee that makes recommendations to the President on what actions, if any, should be taken.

2.9   *Relevant International Agreements*

To further the twin goals of promoting enforcement cooperation between the United States and foreign governments and of reducing any tensions that may arise in particular proceedings, the Agencies have developed close relationships with antitrust and competition policy officials of many different countries. In some

---

43.   19 U.S.C. § 2412 (a), (b) (1988), *amended by* the Uruguay Round Agreements Act, Pub. L. No. 103-465, 108 Stat. 4809 (1994); *see also* Identification of Trade Expansion Priorities, Exec. Order No. 12,901, 59 Fed. Reg. 10,727 (1994).

44.   19 U.S.C. § 2411(d)(3)(B)(i)(IV) (1988), *amended by* the Uruguay Round Agreements Act, Pub. L. No. 103-465, 108 Stat. 4809 (1994), § 314(c).

instances, understandings have been reached with respect to notifications, consultations, and cooperation in antitrust matters.[45] In other instances, more general rules endorsed by multilateral organizations such as the Organization for Economic Cooperation and Development ("OECD") provide the basis for the Agencies' cooperative policies. Finally, even in the absence of specific or general international understandings or recommendations, the Agencies often seek cooperation with foreign authorities.

2.91   BILATERAL COOPERATION AGREEMENTS

Formal written bilateral arrangements exist between the United States and the Federal Republic of Germany, Australia, and Canada.[46] International antitrust cooperation can also occur through mutual legal assistance treaties ("MLATs"), which are treaties of general application pursuant to which the United States and a foreign country agree to assist one another in criminal law enforcement matters. MLATs currently are in force with over one dozen countries, and many more are in the process of ratification or negotiation. However, only the MLAT with Canada has been used to date to obtain assistance in antitrust investigations.[47] The Agencies also hold regular consultations with the antitrust officials of Canada, the European Commission, and Japan, and have close, informal ties with the antitrust authorities of many other countries. Since 1990, the Agencies have cooperated closely with countries in the process of establishing competition agencies, assisted by funding provided by the Agency for International Development.

On November 2, 1994, President Clinton signed into law the International Antitrust Enforcement Assistance Act of 1994,[48] which authorizes the Agencies to enter into antitrust mutual assistance agreements in accordance with the legislation.

---

45.   Chapter 15 of the North American Free Trade Agreement ("NAFTA") addresses competition policy matters and commits the Parties to cooperate on antitrust matters. North American Free Trade Agreement Between the Government of the United States of America, the Government of Canada and the Government of the United Mexican States, 32 I.L.M. 605, 663 (1993), *reprinted in* H.R. Doc. No. 159, 103d Cong., 1st Sess. 712, 1170-1174 (1993).

46.   *See* Agreement Relating to Mutual Cooperation Regarding Restrictive Business Practices, June 23, 1976, U.S.-Federal Republic of Germany, 27 U.S.T. 1956, T.I.S. No. 8291, *reprinted in* 4 Trade Reg. Rep. (CCH) ¶ 13,501; Agreement Between the Government of the United States of America and the Government of Australia Relating to Cooperation on Antitrust Matters, June 29, 1982, U.S.-Australia, T.I.A.S. No. 10365, *reprinted in* 4 Trade Reg. Rep. (CCH) ¶ 13,502; *and* Memorandum of Understanding as to Notification, Consultation, and Cooperation with Respect to the Application of National Antitrust Laws, March 9, 1984, U.S.-Canada, *reprinted in* 4 Trade Reg. Rep. (CCH) ¶ 13,503. The Agencies also signed a similar agreement with the Commission of the European Communities in 1991. *See* Agreement Between the Government of the United States of America and the Commission of the European Communities Regarding the Application of Their Competition Laws, Sept. 23, 1991, 30 I.L.M. 1491 (Nov. 1991), *reprinted in* 4 Trade Reg. Rep. (CCH) ¶ 13,504. However, on August 9, 1994, the European Court of Justice ruled that the conclusion of the Agreement did not comply with institutional requirements of the law of the European Union ("EU"). Under the Court's decision, action by the EU Council of Ministers is necessary for this type of agreement. *See* French Republic v. Commission of European Communities (No. C-327/91) (Aug. 9, 1994).

47.   Treaty with Canada on Mutual Legal Assistance in Criminal Matters, S. Treaty Doc. No. 28, 100th Cong., 2d Sess. (1988).

48.   Pub. L. No. 103-438, 108 Stat. 4597 (1994).

2.92   INTERNATIONAL GUIDELINES AND RECOMMENDATIONS

The Agencies have agreed with respect to member countries of the OECD to consider the legitimate interests of other nations in accordance with relevant OECD recommendations.[49] Under the terms of a 1986 recommendation, the United States agency with responsibility for a particular case notifies a member country whenever an antitrust enforcement action may affect important interests of that country or its nationals.[50] Examples of potentially notifiable actions include requests for documents located outside the United States, attempts to obtain information from potential witnesses located outside the United States, and cases or investigations with significant foreign conduct or involvement of foreign persons.

3.   Threshold International Enforcement Issues

3.1   Jurisdiction

Just as the acts of U.S. citizens in a foreign nation ordinarily are subject to the law of the country in which they occur, the acts of foreign citizens in the United States ordinarily are subject to U.S. law. The reach of the U.S. antitrust laws is not limited, however, to conduct and transactions that occur within the boundaries of the United States. Anticompetitive conduct that affects U.S. domestic or foreign commerce may violate the U.S. antitrust laws regardless of where such conduct occurs or the nationality of the parties involved.

Under the Sherman Act and the FTC Act, there are two principal tests for subject matter jurisdiction in foreign commerce cases. With respect to foreign import commerce, the Supreme Court has recently stated in *Hartford Fire Insurance Co. v. California* that "the Sherman Act applies to foreign conduct that was meant to produce and did in fact produce some substantial effect in the United States."[51] There has been no such authoritative ruling on the scope of the FTC Act, but both Acts apply to commerce "with foreign nations" and the Commission has held that

---

49. *See* Revised Recommendation of the OECD Council Concerning Cooperation Between Member Countries on Restrictive Business Practices Affecting International Trade, OECD Doc. No. C(86)44 (Final) (May 21, 1986). The Recommendation also calls for countries to consult with each other in appropriate situations, with the aim of promoting enforcement cooperation and minimizing differences that may arise.

50. The OECD has 25 member countries and the European Commission takes part in its work. The OECD's membership includes many of the most advanced market economies in the world. The OECD also has several observer nations, which have made rapid progress toward open market economies. The Agencies follow recommended OECD practices with respect to all member countries.

51. 113 S. Ct. 2891, 2909 (1993). In a world in which economic transactions observe no boundaries, international recognition of the "effects doctrine" of jurisdiction has become more widespread. In the context of import trade, the "implementation" test adopted in the European Court of Justice usually produces the same outcome as the "effects" test employed in the United States. *See* Cases 89/85, etc., Ahlstrom v. Commission, *supra* at note 26. The merger laws of the European Union, Canada, Germany, France, Australia, and the Czech and Slovak Republics, among others, take a similar approach.

terms used by both Acts should be construed together.[52] Second, with respect to foreign commerce other than imports, the Foreign Trade Antitrust Improvements Act of 1982 ("FTAIA") applies to foreign conduct that has a direct, substantial, and reasonably foreseeable effect on U.S. commerce.[53]

3.11   JURISDICTION OVER CONDUCT INVOLVING IMPORT COMMERCE

Imports into the United States by definition affect the U.S. domestic market directly, and will, therefore, almost invariably satisfy the intent part of the *Hartford Fire* test. Whether they in fact produce the requisite substantial effects will depend on the facts of each case.

ILLUSTRATIVE EXAMPLE A[54]

Situation: A, B, C, and D are foreign companies that produce a product in various foreign countries. None has any U.S. production, nor any U.S. subsidiaries. They organize a cartel for the purpose of raising the price for the product in question. Collectively, the cartel members make substantial sales into the United States, both in absolute terms and relative to total U.S. consumption.

Discussion: These facts present the straightforward case of cartel participants selling products directly into the United States. In this situation, the transaction is unambiguously an import into the U.S. market, and the sale is not complete until the goods reach the United States. Thus, U.S. subject matter jurisdiction is clear under the general principles of antitrust law expressed most recently in *Hartford Fire*. The facts presented here demonstrate actual and intended participation in U.S. commerce.[55] The separate question of personal jurisdiction under the facts presented here would be analyzed using the principles discussed *infra* in Section 4.1.

3.12   JURISDICTION OVER CONDUCT INVOLVING OTHER FOREIGN COMMERCE

With respect to foreign commerce other than imports, the jurisdictional limits of the Sherman Act and the FTC Act are delineated in the FTAIA. The FTAIA amended the Sherman Act to provide that it:

> shall not apply to conduct involving trade or commerce (other than import trade or commerce) with foreign nations unless
> (1)   such conduct has a direct, substantial, and reasonably foreseeable effect:
>   (A)   on trade or commerce which is not trade or commerce with foreign nations, or on import trade or import commerce with foreign nations; or

---

52.   *In re* Massachusetts Bd. of Registration in Optometry, 110 F.T.C. 598, 609 (1988).
53.   15 U.S.C. § 6a (1988) (Sherman Act) and § 45(a)(3) (1988) (FTC Act).
54.   The examples incorporated into the text are intended solely to illustrate how the Agencies would apply the principles articulated in the *Guidelines* in differing fact situations. In each case, of course, the ultimate outcome of the analysis, *i.e.* whether or not a violation of the antitrust laws has occurred, would depend on the specific facts and circumstances of the case. These examples, therefore, do not address many of the factual and economic questions the Agencies would ask in analyzing particular conduct or transactions under the antitrust laws. Therefore, certain hypothetical situations presented here may, when fully analyzed, not violate any provision of the antitrust laws.
55.   *See infra* at Section 3.12.

(B)   on export trade or export commerce with foreign nations, of a person engaged in such trade or commerce in the United States;[56]

(2)   such effect gives rise to a claim under the provisions of [the Sherman Act], other than this section.

The FTAIA uses slightly different statutory language for the FTC Act,[57] but produces the same jurisdictional outcomes.

3.121 Jurisdiction in Cases under Subsection 1(A) of the FTAIA

To the extent that conduct in foreign countries does not "involve" import commerce but does have an "effect" on either import transactions or commerce within the United States, the Agencies apply the "direct, substantial, and reasonably foreseeable" standard of the FTAIA. That standard is applied, for example, in cases in which a cartel of foreign enterprises, or a foreign monopolist, reaches the U.S. market through any mechanism that goes beyond direct sales, such as the use of an unrelated intermediary, as well as in cases in which foreign vertical restrictions or intellectual property licensing arrangements have an anticompetitive effect on U.S. commerce.

ILLUSTRATIVE EXAMPLE B

Situation: As in Illustrative Example A, the foreign cartel produces a product in several foreign countries. None of its members has any U.S. production, nor do any of them have U.S. subsidiaries. They organize a cartel for the purpose of raising the price for the product in question. Rather than selling directly into the United States, however, the cartel sells to an intermediary outside the United States, which they know will resell the product in the United States. The intermediary is not part of the cartel.

Discussion: The jurisdictional analysis would change slightly from the one presented in Example A, because not only is the conduct being challenged entered into by cartelists in a foreign country, but it is also initially implemented through a sale made in a foreign country. Despite the different test, however, the outcome on these facts would in all likelihood remain the same. The fact that the illegal conduct occurs prior to the import would trigger the application of the FTAIA. The Agencies would have to determine whether the challenged conduct had "direct, substantial and reasonably foreseeable effects" on U.S. domestic or import commerce. Furthermore, since "the essence of any violation of Section 1 [of the Sherman Act] is the illegal agreement itself—rather than the overt acts performed in furtherance of it,"[58] the Agencies would focus on the potential harm that would ensue if the conspiracy were

---

56.   If the Sherman Act applies to such conduct only because of the operation of paragraph (1)(B), then that Act shall apply to such conduct only for injury to export business in the United States. 15 U.S.C. § 6a (1988).

57.   *See* 15 U.S.C. § 45(a)(3) (1988).

58.   Summit Health, Ltd. v. Pinhas, 500 U.S. 322, 330-31 (1991).

successful, not on whether the actual conduct in furtherance of the conspiracy had in fact the prohibited effect upon interstate or foreign commerce.

ILLUSTRATIVE EXAMPLE C

Situation: Variant (1): Widgets are manufactured in both the United States and various other countries around the world. The non-U.S. manufacturers meet privately outside the United States and agree among themselves to raise prices to specified levels. Their agreement clearly indicates that sales in or into the United States are not within the scope of the agreement, and thus that each participant is free independently to set its prices for the U.S. market. Over time, the cartel members begin to sell excess production into the United States. These sales have the effect of stabilizing the cartel for the foreign markets. In the U.S. market, these "excess" sales are priced at levels below those that would have prevailed in the U.S. market but for the cartel, but there is no evidence that the prices are predatory. As a result of these events, several U.S. widget manufacturers curtail their production, overall domestic output falls, and remaining manufacturers fail to invest in new or improved capacity.

Variant (2): Assume now that the cartel agreement specifically provides that cartel members will set agreed prices for the U.S. market at levels designed to soak up excess quantities that arise as a result of price increases in foreign markets. The U.S. price level is set at periodic meetings where each participant indicates how much it must off-load in this way. Thus, the cartel members sell goods in the U.S. market at fixed prices that undercut prevailing U.S. price levels, with consequences similar to those in Variant 1.

Discussion: Variant (1): The jurisdictional issue is whether the predictable economic consequences of the original cartel agreement and the independent sales into the United States are sufficient to support jurisdiction. The mere fact that the existence of U.S. sales or the level of U.S. prices may ultimately be affected by the cartel agreement is not enough for either *Hartford Fire* jurisdiction or the FTAIA.[59] Furthermore, in the absence of an agreement with respect to the U.S. market, sales into the U.S. market at non-predatory levels do not raise antitrust concerns.[60]

Variant (2): The critical element of a foreign price-fixing agreement with direct, intended effects in the United States is now present. The fact that the cartel believes its U.S. prices are "reasonable," or that it may be exerting downward pressure on U.S. price levels, does not exonerate it.[61] Variant 2 presents a case where the Agencies would need clear evidence of the prohibited agreement before they would consider moving forward. They would be particularly cautious if the apparent effects in the U.S. market appeared to be beneficial to consumers.

---

59. If the Agencies lack jurisdiction under the FTAIA to challenge the cartel, the facts of this example would nonetheless lend themselves well to cooperative enforcement action among antitrust agencies. Virtually every country with an antitrust law prohibits horizontal cartels and the Agencies would willingly cooperate with foreign authorities taking direct action against the cartel in the countries where the agreement has raised the price of widgets to the extent such cooperation is allowed under U.S. law and any agreement executed pursuant to U.S. law with foreign agencies or governments.

60. *Cf.* Matsushita Elec. Indus. Co. v. Zenith Radio Corp., 475 U.S. 574 (1986).

61. *Cf.* Arizona v. Maricopa County Medical Soc'y, 457 U.S. 332 (1982); United States v. Socony-Vacuum Oil Co., 310 U.S. 150 (1940); United States v. Trenton Potteries Co., 273 U.S. 392 (1927).

3.122 Jurisdiction in Cases under Subsection 1(B) of the FTAIA

Two categories of "export cases" fall within the FTAIA's jurisdictional test. First, the Agencies may, in appropriate cases, take enforcement action against anticompetitive conduct, wherever occurring, that restrains U.S. exports, if (1) the conduct has a direct, substantial, and reasonably foreseeable effect on exports of goods or services from the United States, and (2) the U.S. courts can obtain jurisdiction over persons or corporations engaged in such conduct.[62] As Section 3.2 below explains more fully, if the conduct is unlawful under the importing country's antitrust laws as well, the Agencies are also prepared to work with that country's authorities if they are better situated to remedy the conduct, and if they are prepared to take action that will address the U.S. concerns, pursuant to their antitrust laws.

Second, the Agencies may in appropriate cases take enforcement action against conduct by U.S. exporters that has a direct, substantial, and reasonably foreseeable effect on trade or commerce within the United States, or on import trade or commerce. This can arise in two principal ways. First, if U.S. supply and demand were not particularly elastic, an agreement among U.S. firms accounting for a substantial share of the relevant market, regarding the level of their exports, could reduce supply and raise prices in the United States.[63] Second, conduct ostensibly export-related could affect the price of products sold or resold in the United States. This kind of effect could occur if, for example, U.S. firms fixed the price of an input used to manufacture a product overseas for ultimate resale in the United States.

ILLUSTRATIVE EXAMPLE D

Situation: Companies E and F are the only producers of product Q in country Epsilon, one of the biggest markets for sales of Q in the world. E and F together account for 99 percent of the sales of product Q in Epsilon.[64] In order to prevent a competing U.S. producer from entering the market in Epsilon, E and F agree that neither one of them will purchase or distribute the U.S. product, and that they will take "all feasible" measures to keep the U.S. company out of their market. Without specifically discussing what other measures they will take to carry out this plan, E and F meet with their distributors and, through a variety of threats and inducements, obtain agreement of all of the distributors not to carry the U.S. product. There are no commercially feasible substitute distribution channels available to the U.S. producer. Because of the actions of E and F, the U.S. producer cannot find any distributors to carry its product and is unable to make any sales in Epsilon.

Discussion: The agreement between E and F not to purchase or distribute the U.S. product would clearly have a direct and reasonably foreseeable effect on U.S. export commerce, since it is aimed at a U.S. exporter. The substantiality of the

---

62. *See* U.S. Department of Justice Press Release dated April 3, 1992 (announcing enforcement policy that would permit the Department to challenge foreign business conduct that harms U.S. exports when the conduct would have violated U.S. antitrust laws if it occurred in the United States).

63. One would need to show more than indirect price effects resulting from legitimate export efforts to support an antitrust challenge. *See* ETC Guidelines, *supra* at note 34, 50 Fed. Reg. at 1791.

64. That E and F together have an overwhelmingly dominant share in Epsilon may or may not, depending on the market conditions for Q, satisfy the requirement of "substantial effect on U.S. exports" as required by the FTAIA. Foreclosure of exports to a single country, such as Epsilon, may satisfy the statutory threshold if that country's market accounts for a significant part of the export opportunities for U.S. firms.

effects on U.S. exports would depend on the significance of E and F as purchasers and distributors of Q, although on these facts the virtually total foreclosure from Epsilon would almost certainly qualify as a substantial effect for jurisdictional purposes. However, if the Agencies believe that they may encounter difficulties in establishing personal jurisdiction or in obtaining effective relief, the case may be one in which the Agencies would seek to resolve their concerns by working with other authorities who are examining the transaction.

ILLUSTRATIVE EXAMPLE E

Situation: Companies P, Q, R, and S, organized under the laws of country Alpha, all manufacture and distribute construction equipment. Much of that equipment is protected by patents in the various countries where it is sold, including Alpha. The companies all belong to a private trade association, which develops industry standards that are often (although not always) adopted by Alpha's regulatory authorities. Feeling threatened by competition from the United States, the companies agree at a trade association meeting (1) to refuse to adopt any U.S. company technology as an industry standard, and (2) to boycott the distribution of U.S. construction equipment. The U.S. companies have taken all necessary steps to protect their intellectual property under the law of Alpha.

Discussion: In this example, the collective activity impedes U.S. companies in two ways: their technology is boycotted (even if U.S. companies are willing to license their intellectual property) and they are foreclosed from access to distribution channels. The jurisdictional question is whether these actions create a direct, substantial, and reasonably foreseeable effect on the exports of U.S. companies. The mere fact that only the market of Alpha appears to be foreclosed is not enough to defeat such an effect. Only if exclusion from Alpha as a quantitative measure were so *de minimis* in terms of actual volume of trade that there would not be a substantial effect on U.S. export commerce would jurisdiction be lacking. Given that this example involves construction equipment, a generally highly priced capital good, the exclusion from Alpha would probably satisfy the substantiality requirement for FTAIA jurisdiction. This arrangement appears to have been created with particular reference to competition from the United States, which indicates that the effects on U.S. exports are both direct and foreseeable.

3.13   JURISDICTION WHEN U.S. GOVERNMENT FINANCES OR PURCHASES

The Agencies may, in appropriate cases, take enforcement action when the U.S. Government is a purchaser, or substantially funds the purchase, of goods or services for consumption or use abroad. Cases in which the effect of anticompetitive conduct with respect to the sale of these goods or services falls primarily on U.S. taxpayers may qualify for redress under the federal antitrust laws.[65] As a general matter, the

---

65. *Cf.* United States v. Concentrated Phosphate Export Ass'n, 393 U.S. 199, 208 (1968) ("[A]lthough the fertilizer shipments were consigned to Korea and although in most cases Korea formally let the contracts, American participation was the overwhelmingly dominant feature. The burden of noncompetitive pricing fell, not on any foreign purchaser, but on the American taxpayer. The United States was, in essence, furnishing fertilizer to Korea. . . . The foreign elements in the transaction were, by comparison, insignificant."); United States v. Standard Tallow Corp., 1988-1 Trade Cas. (CCH) ¶ 67,913 (S.D.N.Y. 1988) (consent decree) (barring suppliers from fixing prices or rigging bids for the sale of tallow financed in whole or in part through grants or loans by the

Agencies consider there to be a sufficient effect on U.S. commerce to support the assertion of jurisdiction if, as a result of its payment or financing, the U.S. Government bears more than half the cost of the transaction. For purposes of this determination, the Agencies apply the standards used in certifying export conduct under the ETC Act of 1982, 15 U.S.C. §§ 4011-21(1982).[66]

ILLUSTRATIVE EXAMPLE F

Situation: A combination of U.S. firms and local firms in country Beta create a U.S.-based joint venture for the purpose of building a major pollution control facility for Beta's Environmental Control Agency ("BECA"). The venture has received preferential funding from the U.S. Government, which has the effect of making the present value of expected future repayment of the principal and interest on the loan less than half its face value. Once the venture has begun work, it appears that its members secretly have agreed to inflate the price quoted to BECA, in order to secure more funding.

Discussion: The fact that the U.S. Government bears more than half the financial risk of the transaction is sufficient for jurisdiction. With jurisdiction established, the Agencies would proceed to investigate whether the apparent bid-rigging actually occurred.[67]

ILLUSTRATIVE EXAMPLE G

Situation: The United States has many military bases and other facilities located in other countries. These facilities procure substantial goods and services from suppliers in the host country. In country X, it comes to the attention of the local U.S. military base commander that bids to supply certain construction services have been rigged.

Discussion: Sales made by a foreign party to the U.S. Government, including to a U.S. facility located in a foreign country, are within U.S. antitrust jurisdiction when they fall within the rule of Section 3.13. Bid-rigging of sales to the U.S. Government represents the kind of conduct that can lead to an antitrust action. Indeed, in the United States this type of behavior is normally prosecuted by the Department as a criminal offense. In practice, the Department has whenever possible worked closely with the host country antitrust authorities to explore remedies under local law. This has been successful in a number of instances.[68]

U.S. Government); United States v. Anthracite Export Ass'n, 1970 Trade Cas. (CCH) ¶ 73,348 (M.D. Pa. 1970) (consent decree) (barring price-fixing, bid-rigging, and market allocation in Army foreign aid program).

66. *See* ETC Guidelines, *supra* at note 34, 50 Fed. Reg. at 1799-1800. The requisite U.S. Government involvement could include the actual purchase of goods by the U.S. Government for shipment abroad, a U.S. Government grant to a foreign government that is specifically earmarked for the transaction, or a U.S. Government loan specifically earmarked for the transaction that is made on such generous terms that it amounts to a grant. U.S. Government interests would not be considered to be sufficiently implicated with respect to a transaction that is funded by an international agency, or a transaction in which the foreign government received non-earmarked funds from the United States as part of a general government-to-government aid program.

67. Such conduct might also violate the False Claims Act, 31 U.S.C. §§ 3729-3733 (1988 & Supp. 1993).

68. If, however, local law does not provide adequate remedies, or the local authorities are not prepared to take action, the Department will weigh the comity factors, discussed *infra* at Section 3.2, and take such action as is appropriate.

3.14   JURISDICTION UNDER SECTION 7 OF THE CLAYTON ACT

Section 7 of the Clayton Act applies to mergers and acquisitions between firms that are engaged in commerce or in any activity affecting commerce. The Agencies would apply the same principles regarding their foreign commerce jurisdiction to Clayton Section 7 cases as they would apply in Sherman Act cases.

ILLUSTRATIVE EXAMPLE H

Situation: Two foreign firms, one in Europe and the other in Canada, account together for a substantial percentage of U.S. sales of a particular product through direct imports. Both firms have sales offices and are subject to personal jurisdiction in the United States, although neither has productive assets in the United States. They enter into an agreement to merge.

Discussion: The express language of Section 7 of the Clayton Act reaches the stock and asset acquisitions of persons engaged in trade and commerce "with foreign nations."[69] Thus, in assessing jurisdiction for this merger outside the United States the Agencies could establish U.S. subject matter jurisdiction based on its effect on U.S. imports.

If the facts stated above were modified to show that the proposed merger would have effects on U.S. export commerce, as opposed to import trade, then in assessing jurisdiction under the Clayton Act the Agencies would analyze the question of effects on commerce in a manner consistent with the FTAIA: that is, they would look to see whether the effects on U.S. domestic or import commerce are direct, substantial, and reasonably foreseeable.[70] It is appropriate to do so because the FTAIA sheds light on the type of effects Congress considered necessary for foreign commerce cases, even though the FTAIA did not amend the Clayton Act.

In both these situations, the Agencies would conclude that Section 7 jurisdiction technically exists. However, if effective relief is difficult to obtain, the case may be one in which the Agencies would seek to coordinate their efforts with other authorities who are examining the transaction.[71]

3.2   *Comity*

In enforcing the antitrust laws, the Agencies consider international comity. Comity itself reflects the broad concept of respect among co-equal sovereign nations and plays a role in determining "the recognition which one nation allows within its territory to the legislative, executive or judicial acts of another nation."[72] Thus, in determining whether to assert jurisdiction to investigate or bring an action, or to seek particular remedies in a given case, each Agency takes into account whether significant interests of any foreign sovereign would be affected.[73]

---

69.   Clayton Act § 1, 15 U.S.C. § 12 (1988).
70.   *See supra* at Section 3.121.
71.   Through concepts such as "positive comity," one country's authorities may ask another country to take measures that address possible harm to competition in the requesting country's market.
72.   Hilton v. Guyot, 159 U.S. 113, 164 (1895).
73.   The Agencies have agreed to consider the legitimate interests of other nations in accordance with the recommendations of the OECD and various bilateral agreements, *see supra* at Section 2.9.

In performing a comity analysis, the Agencies take into account all relevant factors. Among others, these may include (1) the relative significance to the alleged violation of conduct within the United States, as compared to conduct abroad; (2) the nationality of the persons involved in or affected by the conduct; (3) the presence or absence of a purpose to affect U.S. consumers, markets, or exporters; (4) the relative significance and foreseeability of the effects of the conduct on the United States as compared to the effects abroad; (5) the existence of reasonable expectations that would be furthered or defeated by the action; (6) the degree of conflict with foreign law or articulated foreign economic policies; (7) the extent to which the enforcement activities of another country with respect to the same persons, including remedies resulting from those activities, may be affected; and (8) the effectiveness of foreign enforcement as compared to U.S. enforcement action.[74]

The relative weight that each factor should be given depends on the facts and circumstances of each case. With respect to the factor concerning conflict with foreign law, the Supreme Court made clear in *Hartford Fire*[75] that no conflict exists for purposes of an international comity analysis in the courts if the person subject to regulation by two states can comply with the laws of both. Bearing this in mind, the Agencies first ask what laws or policies of the arguably interested foreign jurisdictions are implicated by the conduct in question. There may be no actual conflict between the antitrust enforcement interests of the United States and the laws or policies of a foreign sovereign. This is increasingly true as more countries adopt antitrust or competition laws that are compatible with those of the United States. In these cases, the anticompetitive conduct in question may also be prohibited under the pertinent foreign laws, and thus the possible conflict would relate to enforcement practices or remedy. If the laws or policies of a foreign nation are neutral, it is again possible for the parties in question to comply with the U.S. prohibition without violating foreign law.

The Agencies also take full account of comity factors beyond whether there is a conflict with foreign law. In deciding whether or not to challenge an alleged antitrust violation, the Agencies would, as part of a comity analysis, consider whether one country encourages a certain course of conduct, leaves parties free to choose among different strategies, or prohibits some of those strategies. In addition, the Agencies take into account the effect of their enforcement activities on related enforcement activities of a foreign antitrust authority. For example, the Agencies would consider whether their activities would interfere with or reinforce the objectives of the foreign proceeding, including any remedies contemplated or obtained by the foreign antitrust authority.

The Agencies also will consider whether the objectives sought to be obtained by the assertion of U.S. law would be achieved in a particular instance by foreign enforcement. In lieu of bringing an enforcement action, the Agencies may consult with interested foreign sovereigns through appropriate diplomatic channels to attempt to eliminate anticompetitive effects in the United States. In cases where the United States decides to prosecute an antitrust action, such a decision represents a determination by the Executive Branch that the importance of antitrust enforcement

---

74. The first six of these factors are based on previous Department *Guidelines*. The seventh and eighth factors are derived from considerations in the U.S.-EC Antitrust Cooperation Agreement. *See supra* at note 46.

75. 113 S. Ct. 2891, 2910.

outweighs any relevant foreign policy concerns.[76] The Department does not believe that it is the role of the courts to "second-guess the executive branch's judgment as to the proper role of comity concerns under these circumstances."[77] To date, no Commission cases have presented the issue of the degree of deference that courts should give to the Commission's comity decisions.[78] It is important also to note that in disputes between private parties, many courts are willing to undertake a comity analysis.[79]

ILLUSTRATIVE EXAMPLE I

Situation: A group of buyers in one foreign country decide that they will agree on the price that they will offer to U.S. suppliers of a particular product. The agreement results in substantial loss of sales and capacity reductions in the United States.

Discussion: From a jurisdictional point of view, the FTAIA standard appears to be satisfied because the effects on U.S. exporters presented here are direct and the percentage of supply accounted for by the buyers' cartel is substantial given the fact that the U.S. suppliers are "major." The Agencies, however, would also take into consideration the comity aspects presented before deciding whether or not to proceed.

Consistent with their consideration of comity and its obligations under various international agreements, the Agencies would ordinarily notify the antitrust authority in the cartel's home country. If that authority were in a better position to address the competitive problem, and were prepared to take effective action to address the adverse effects on U.S. commerce, the Agencies would consider working cooperatively with the foreign authority or staying their own remedy pending enforcement efforts by the foreign country. In deciding whether to proceed, the Agencies would weigh the factors relating to comity set forth above. Factors weighing in favor of bringing such an action include the substantial and purposeful harm caused by the cartel to the United States.

ILLUSTRATIVE EXAMPLE J

Situation: A and B manufacture a consumer product for which there are no readily available substitutes in ten different countries around the world, including the United States, Canada, Mexico, Spain, Australia, and others. When they decide to merge, it becomes necessary for them to file premerger notifications in many of these countries, and to subject themselves to the merger law of all ten.[80]

Discussion: Under the 1986 OECD Recommendation, OECD countries notify one another when a proceeding such as a merger review is underway that might

---

76. Foreign policy concerns may also lead the United States not to prosecute a case. *See, e.g.,* U.S. Department of Justice Press Release dated Nov. 19, 1984 (announcing the termination, based on foreign policy concerns, of a grand jury investigation into passenger air travel between the United States and the United Kingdom).

77. United States v. Baker Hughes, Inc., 731 F. Supp. 3, 6 n.5 (D.D.C. 1990), *aff'd,* 908 F.2d 981 (D.C. Cir. 1990).

78. Like the Department, the Commission considers comity issues and consults with foreign antitrust authorities, but the Commission is not part of the Executive Branch.

79. *See, e.g.,* Timberlane Lumber Co. v. Bank of America, 549 F.2d 597 (9th Cir. 1976).

80. Not every country has compulsory premerger notification, and the events triggering duties to notify vary from country to country.

affect the interests of other countries. Within the strict limits of national confidentiality laws, agencies attempt to cooperate with one another in processing these reviews. This might extend to exchanges of publicly available information, agreements to let the other agencies know when a decision to institute a proceeding is taken, and to consult for purposes of international comity with respect to proposed remedial measures and investigatory methods. The parties can facilitate faster resolution of these cases if they are willing voluntarily to waive confidentiality protections and to cooperate with a joint investigation. At present, confidentiality provisions in U.S. and foreign laws do not usually permit effective coordination of a single international investigation in the absence of such waivers.

3.3   Effects of Foreign Government Involvement

Foreign governments may be involved in a variety of ways in conduct that may have antitrust consequences. To address the implications of such foreign governmental involvement, Congress and the courts have developed four special doctrines: the doctrine of foreign sovereign immunity; the doctrine of foreign sovereign compulsion; the act of state doctrine; and the application of the *Noerr-Pennington* doctrine to immunize the lobbying of foreign governments. Although these doctrines are interrelated, for purposes of discussion the *Guidelines* discuss each one individually.

3.31   FOREIGN SOVEREIGN IMMUNITY

The scope of immunity of a foreign government or its agencies and instrumentalities (hereinafter foreign government)[81] from the jurisdiction of the U.S. courts for all causes of action, including antitrust, is governed by the Foreign Sovereign Immunities Act of 1976 ("FSIA").[82] Subject to the treaties in place at the time of FSIA's enactment, a foreign government is immune from suit except where designated in the FSIA.[83]

Under the FSIA, a U.S. court has jurisdiction if the foreign government has:
(a)   waived its immunity explicitly or by implication,
(b)   engaged in commercial activity as described in the statute,
(c)   expropriated property in violation of international law,
(d)   acquired rights to U.S. property,
(e)   committed certain torts within the United States, or agreed to arbitration of a dispute.[84]

---

81.   Section 1603(b) of the Foreign Sovereign Immunities Act of 1976 defines an "agency or instrumentality of a foreign state" to be any entity "(1) which is a separate legal person, corporate or otherwise; and (2) which is an organ of a foreign state or political subdivision thereof, or a majority of whose shares or other ownership interest is owned by a foreign state or political subdivision thereof; and (3) which is neither a citizen of a State of the United States as defined in Section 1332(c) and (d) of [Title 28, U.S. Code], nor created under the laws of any third country." 28 U.S.C. § 1603(b) (1988). It is not uncommon in antitrust cases to see state-owned enterprises meeting this definition.
82.   28 U.S.C. § 1602 *et seq.* (1988).
83.   28 U.S.C. § 1604 (1988 & Supp. 1993).
84.   28 U.S.C. § 1605(a)(1-6) (1988).

The commercial activities exception is a frequently invoked exception to sovereign immunity under the FSIA. Under the FSIA, a foreign government is not immune in any case:

> in which the action is based upon a commercial activity carried on in the United States by the foreign state; or upon an act performed in the United States in connection with a commercial activity of the foreign state elsewhere; or upon an act outside the territory of the United States in connection with a commercial activity of the foreign state elsewhere and that act causes a direct effect in the United States.[85]

"Commercial activity of the foreign state" is not defined in the FSIA, but is to be determined by the "nature of the course of conduct or particular transaction or act, rather than by reference to its purpose."[86] In attempting to differentiate commercial from sovereign activity, courts have considered whether the conduct being challenged is customarily performed for profit[87] and whether the conduct is of a type that only a sovereign government can perform.[88] As a practical matter, most activities of foreign government-owned corporations operating in the commercial marketplace will be subject to U.S. antitrust laws to the same extent as the activities of foreign privately-owned firms.

The commercial activity also must have a substantial nexus with the United States before a foreign government is subject to suit. The FSIA sets out three different standards for meeting this requirement. First, the challenged conduct by the foreign government may occur in the United States.[89] Alternatively, the challenged commercial activity may entail an act performed in the United States in connection with a commercial activity of the foreign government elsewhere.[90] Or, finally, the challenged commercial activity of a foreign government outside of the United States may produce a direct effect within the United States, i.e., an effect which follows "as an immediate consequence of the defendant's . . . activity."[91]

---

85. 28 U.S.C. § 1605(a)(2) (1988).
86. 28 U.S.C. § 1603(d) (1988).
87. *See, e.g.*, Republic of Argentina v. Weltover, Inc., 112 S. Ct. 2160 (1992); Schoenberg v. Exportadora de Sal, S.A. de C.V., 930 F.2d 777 (9th Cir. 1991); Rush-Presbyterian-St. Luke's Medical Ctr. v. Hellenic Republic, 877 F.2d 574, 578 n.4 (7th Cir.), *cert. denied*, 493 U.S. 937 (1989).
88. *See, e.g.*, Saudi Arabia v. Nelson, 113 S. Ct. 1471 (1993); de Sanchez v. Banco Central de Nicaragua, 770 F.2d 1385 (5th Cir. 1985); Letelier v. Republic of Chile, 748 F.2d 790, 797-98 (2d Cir. 1984), *cert. denied*, 471 U.S. 1125 (1985); International Ass'n of Machinists & Aerospace Workers v. Organization of Petroleum Exporting Countries, 477 F. Supp. 553 (C.D. Cal. 1979), *aff'd on other grounds*, 649 F.2d 1354 (9th Cir. 1981), *cert. denied*, 454 U.S. 1163 (1982).
89. 28 U.S.C. § 1603(e) (1988).
90. *See* H.R. Rep. No. 1487, 94th Cong., 2d Sess. 18-19 (1976), *reprinted in* 1976 U.S.C.C.A.N. 6604, 6617-18 (providing as an example the wrongful termination in the United States of an employee of a foreign state employed in connection with commercial activity in a third country). *But see* Filus v. LOT Polish Airlines, 907 F.2d 1328, 1333 (2d Cir. 1990) (holding as too attenuated the failure to warn of a defective product sold outside of the United States in connection with an accident outside the United States.)
91. *Republic of Argentina*, 112 S. Ct. at 2168. This test is similar to proximate cause formulations adopted by other courts. *See* Martin v. Republic of South Africa, 836 F.2d 91, 95 (2d Cir. 1987) (a direct effect is one with no intervening element which flows in a straight line without deviation or interruption), quoting Upton v. Empire of Iran, 459 F. Supp. 264, 266 (D.D.C. 1978), *aff'd mem.*, 607 F.2d 494 (D.C. Cir. 1979).

3.32 FOREIGN SOVEREIGN COMPULSION

Although U.S. antitrust jurisdiction extends to conduct and parties in foreign countries whose actions have the required effects on U.S. commerce, as discussed above, those parties may find themselves subject to conflicting requirements from the other country (or countries) where they are located.[92] Under *Hartford Fire*, if it is possible for the party to comply both with the foreign law and the U.S. antitrust laws, the existence of the foreign law does not provide any legal excuse for actions that do not comply with U.S. law. However, a direct conflict may arise when the facts demonstrate that the foreign sovereign has compelled the very conduct that the U.S. antitrust law prohibits.

In these circumstances, at least one court has recognized a defense under the U.S. antitrust laws, and the Agencies will also recognize it.[93] There are two rationales underlying the defense of foreign sovereign compulsion. First, Congress enacted the U.S. antitrust laws against the background of well recognized principles of international law and comity among nations, pursuant to which U.S. authorities give due deference to the official acts of foreign governments. A defense for actions taken under the circumstances spelled out below serves to accommodate two equal sovereigns. Second, important considerations of fairness to the defendant require some mechanism that provides a predictable rule of decision for those seeking to conform their behavior to all pertinent laws.

Because of the limited scope of the defense, the Agencies will refrain from enforcement actions on the ground of foreign sovereign compulsion only when certain criteria are satisfied. First, the foreign government must have compelled the anticompetitive conduct under circumstances in which a refusal to comply with the foreign government's command would give rise to the imposition of penal or other severe sanctions. As a general matter, the Agencies regard the foreign government's formal representation that refusal to comply with its command would have such a result as being sufficient to establish that the conduct in question has been compelled, as long as that representation contains sufficient detail to enable the Agencies to see precisely how the compulsion would be accomplished under local law.[94] Foreign

---

92. Conduct by private entities not required by law is entirely outside of the protections afforded by this defense. *See* Continental Ore Co. v. Union Carbide & Carbon Corp., 370 U.S. 690, 706 (1962); United States v. Watchmakers of Switzerland Info. Ctr., Inc., 1963 Trade Cas. (CCH) ¶ 70,600 at 77,456-57 (S.D.N.Y. 1962) ("[T]he fact that the Swiss Government may, as a practical matter, approve the effects of this private activity cannot convert what is essentially a vulnerable private conspiracy into an unassailable system resulting from a foreign government mandate.") *See supra* at Section 3.2.

93. Interamerican Refining Corp. v. Texaco Maracaibo, Inc., 307 F. Supp. 1291 (D. Del. 1970) (defendant, having been ordered by the government of Venezuela not to sell oil to a particular refiner out of favor with the current political regime, held not subject to antitrust liability under the Sherman Act for an illegal group boycott). The defense of foreign sovereign compulsion is distinguished from the federalism-based state action doctrine. The state action doctrine applies not just to the actions of states and their subdivisions, but also to private anticompetitive conduct that is both undertaken pursuant to clearly articulated state policies, and is actively supervised by the state. *See* Federal Trade Comm'n v. Ticor Title Insurance Co., 112 S. Ct. 2169 (1992); California Retail Liquor Dealers Ass'n v. Midcal Aluminum, Inc., 445 U.S. 97, 105 (1980); Parker v. Brown, 317 U.S. 341 (1943).

94. For example, the Agencies may not regard as dispositive a statement that is ambiguous or that on its face appears to be internally inconsistent. The Agencies may inquire into the circumstances

government measures short of compulsion do not suffice for this defense, although they can be relevant in a comity analysis.

Second, although there can be no strict territorial test for this defense, the defense normally applies only when the foreign government compels conduct which can be accomplished entirely within its own territory. If the compelled conduct occurs in the United States, the Agencies will not recognize the defense.[95] For example, no defense arises when a foreign government requires the U.S. subsidiaries of several firms to organize a cartel in the United States to fix the price at which products would be sold in the United States, or when it requires its firms to fix mandatory resale prices for their U.S. distributors to use in the United States.

Third, with reference to the discussion of foreign sovereign immunity in Section 3.31 above, the order must come from the foreign government acting in its governmental capacity. The defense does not arise from conduct that would fall within the FSIA commercial activity exception.

ILLUSTRATIVE EXAMPLE K

Situation: Greatly increased quantities of commodity X have flooded into the world market over the last two or three years, including substantial amounts indirectly coming into the United States. Because they are unsure whether they would prevail in an antidumping and countervailing duty case, U.S. industry participants have refrained from filing trade law petitions. The officials of three foreign countries meet with their respective domestic firms and urge them to "rationalize" production by cooperatively cutting back. Going one step further, one of the interested governments orders cutbacks from its firms, subject to substantial penalties for non-compliance. Producers from the other two countries agree among themselves to institute comparable cutbacks, but their governments do not require them to do so.

Discussion: Assume for the purpose of this example that the overseas production cutbacks have the necessary effects on U.S. commerce to support jurisdiction. As for the participants from the two countries that did not impose any penalty for a failure to reduce production, the Agencies would not find that sovereign compulsion precluded prosecution of this agreement.[96] As for participants from the country that did compel production cut-backs through the imposition of severe penalties, the Agencies would acknowledge a defense of sovereign compulsion.

3.33 ACTS OF STATE

The act of state doctrine is a judge-made rule of federal common law.[97] It is a doctrine of judicial abstention based on considerations of international comity and separation of powers, and applies only if the specific conduct complained of is a public act of the foreign sovereign within its territorial jurisdiction on matters

---

underlying the statement and they may also request further information if the source of the power to compel is unclear.
95. *See* Linseman v. World Hockey Ass'n, 439 F. Supp. 1315, 1325 (D. Conn. 1977).
96. As in all such cases, the Agencies would consider comity factors as part of their analysis. *See supra* at Section 3.2.
97. Banco Nacional de Cuba v. Sabbatino, 376 U.S. 398, 421-22 n.21 (1964) (noting that other countries do not adhere in any formulaic way to an act of state doctrine).

pertaining to its governmental sovereignty. The act of state doctrine arises when the validity of the acts of a foreign government is an unavoidable issue in a case.[98]

Courts have refused to adjudicate claims or issues that would require the court to judge the legality (as a matter of U.S. law or international law) of the sovereign act of a foreign state.[99] Although in some cases the sovereign act in question may compel private behavior, such compulsion is not required by the doctrine.[100] While the act of state doctrine does not compel dismissal as a matter of course, judicial abstention is appropriate in a case where the court must "declare invalid, and thus ineffective as a rule of decision in the U.S. courts, . . . the official act of a foreign sovereign."[101]

When a restraint on competition arises directly from the act of a foreign sovereign, such as the grant of a license, award of a contract, expropriation of property, or the like, the Agencies may refrain from bringing an enforcement action based on the act of state doctrine. For example, the Agencies will not challenge foreign acts of state if the facts and circumstances indicate that: (1) the specific conduct complained of is a public act of the sovereign, (2) the act was taken within the territorial jurisdiction of the sovereign, and (3) the matter is governmental, rather than commercial.

3.34   PETITIONING OF SOVEREIGNS

Under the *Noerr-Pennington* doctrine, a genuine effort to obtain or influence action by governmental entities in the United States is immune from application of the Sherman Act, even if the intent or effect of that effort is to restrain or monopolize trade.[102] Whatever the basis asserted for *Noerr-Pennington* immunity (either as an application of the First Amendment or as a limit on the statutory reach of the Sherman Act, or both), the Agencies will apply it in the same manner to the petitioning of foreign governments and the U.S. Government.

ILLUSTRATIVE EXAMPLE L

Situation: In the course of preparing an antidumping case, which requires the U.S. industry to demonstrate that it has been injured through the effects of the dumped imports, producers representing 75 percent of U.S. output exchange the

---

98.   *See* W.S. Kirkpatrick & Co. v. Environmental Tectonics Corp., 493 U.S. 400 (1990).
99.   International Ass'n of Machinists and Aerospace Workers v. Organization of Petroleum Exporting Countries, 649 F.2d 1354, 1358 (9th Cir. 1981), *cert. denied*, 454 U.S. 1163 (1982).
100.   *See Timberlane*, *supra* at n.79, 549 F.2d at 606-08.
101.   *Kirkpatrick*, 493 U.S. at 405, quoting Ricaud v. American Metal Co., 246 U.S. 304, 310 (1918).
102.   *See* Eastern R.R. Presidents Conference v. Noerr Motor Freight, Inc., 365 U.S. 127 (1961); United Mine Workers of Am. v. Pennington, 381 U.S. 657 (1965); California Motor Transp. Co. v. Trucking Unlimited, 404 U.S. 508 (1972) (extending protection to petitioning before "all departments of Government," including the courts); Professional Real Estate Investors, Inc. v. Columbia Pictures Indus., 113 S. Ct. 1920 (1993). However, this immunity has never applied to "sham" activities, in which petitioning "ostensibly directed toward influencing governmental action, is a mere sham to cover . . . an attempt to interfere directly with the business relationships of a competitor." *Professional Real Estate Investors*, 113 S. Ct. at 1926, quoting *Noerr*, 365 U.S. at 144. *See also* USS-Posco Indus. v. Contra Costa Cty. Bldg. Constr. Council, AFL-CIO, 31 F.3d 800 (9th Cir. 1994).

information required for the adjudication. All the information is exchanged indirectly through third parties and in an aggregated form that makes the identity of any particular producer's information impossible to discern.

Discussion: Information exchanged by competitors within the context of an antidumping proceeding implicates the *Noerr-Pennington* petitioning immunity. To the extent that these exchanges are reasonably necessary in order for them to prepare their joint petition, which is permitted under the trade laws, *Noerr* is available to protect against antitrust liability that would otherwise arise. On these facts the parties are likely to be immunized by *Noerr* if they have taken the necessary measures to ensure that the provision of sensitive information called for by the Commerce Department and the ITC cannot be used for anticompetitive purposes. In such a situation, the information exchange is incidental to genuine petitioning and is not subject to the antitrust laws. Conversely, were the parties directly to exchange extensive information relating to their costs, the prices each has charged for the product, pricing trends, and profitability, including information about specific transactions that went beyond the scope of those facts required for the adjudication, such conduct would go beyond the contemplated protection of *Noerr* immunity.

3.4   *Antitrust Enforcement and International Trade Regulation*

There has always been a close relationship between the international application of the antitrust laws and the policies and rules governing the international trade of the United States. Restrictions such as tariffs or quotas on the free flow of goods affect market definition, consumer choice, and supply options for U.S. producers. In certain instances, the U.S. trade laws set forth specific procedures for settling disputes under those laws, which can involve price and quantity agreements by the foreign firms involved. When those procedures are followed, an implied antitrust immunity results.[103] However, agreements among competitors that do not comply with the law, or go beyond the measures authorized by the law, do not enjoy antitrust immunity. In the absence of legal authority, the fact, without more, that U.S. or foreign government officials were involved in or encouraged measures that would otherwise violate the antitrust laws does not immunize such arrangements.[104]

If a particular voluntary export restraint does not qualify for express or implied immunity from the antitrust laws, then the legality of the arrangement would depend

---

103. *See, e.g.*, Letter from Charles F. Rule, Acting Assistant Attorney General, Antitrust Division, Department of Justice, to Mr. Makoto Kuroda, Vice-Minister for International Affairs, Japanese Ministry of International Trade and Industry, July 30, 1986 (concluding that a suspension agreement did not violate U.S. antitrust laws on the basis of factual representations that the agreement applied only to products under investigation, that it did not require pricing above levels needed to eliminate sales below foreign market value, and that assigning weighted-average foreign market values to exporters who were not respondents in the investigation was necessary to achieve the purpose of the antidumping law).

104. *Cf.* United States v. Socony-Vacuum Oil Co., 310 U.S. 150, 226 (1940) ("Though employees of the government may have known of those programs and winked at them or tacitly approved them, no immunity would have thereby been obtained. For Congress had specified the precise manner and method of securing immunity [in the National Industrial Recovery Act]. None other would suffice."); *see also* Otter Tail Power Co. v. United States, 410 U.S. 366, 378-79 (1973).

upon the existence of the ordinary elements of an antitrust offense, such as whether or not a prohibited agreement exists or whether defenses such as foreign sovereign compulsion can be invoked.

ILLUSTRATIVE EXAMPLE M

Situation: Six U.S. producers of product Q have initiated an antidumping action alleging that imports of Q from country Sigma at less than fair value are causing material injury to the U.S. Q industry. The ITC has made a preliminary decision that there is a reasonable indication that the U.S. industry is suffering material injury from Q imported from Sigma. The Department of Commerce has preliminarily concluded that the foreign market value of Q imported into the United States by Sigma's Q producers exceeds the price at which they are selling Q in this country by margins of 10 to 40 percent. Sigma's Q producers jointly initiate discussions with the Department of Commerce that lead to suspension of the investigation in accordance with Section 734 of the Tariff Act of 1930, 19 U.S.C. § 1673c. The suspension agreement provides that each of Sigma's Q producers will sell product Q in the United States at no less than its individual foreign market value, as determined periodically by the Department of Commerce in accordance with the Tariff Act. Before determining to suspend the investigation, the Department of Commerce provides copies of the proposed agreement to the U.S. Q producers, who jointly advise the Department that they do not object to the suspension of the investigation on the terms proposed. The Department also determines that suspension of the investigation would be in the public interest. As a result of the suspension agreement, prices in the United States of Q imported from Sigma rise by an average of 25 percent from the prices that prevailed before the antidumping action was initiated.

Discussion: While an unsupervised agreement among foreign firms to raise their U.S. sales prices ordinarily would violate the Sherman Act, the suspension agreement outlined above qualifies for an implied immunity from the antitrust laws. As demonstrated here, the parties have engaged only in conduct contemplated by the Tariff Act and none of the participants have engaged in conduct beyond what is necessary to implement that statutory scheme.

ILLUSTRATIVE EXAMPLE N

Situation: The Export Association is a Webb-Pomerene association that has filed the appropriate certificates and reports with the Commission. The Association exports a commodity to markets around the world, and fixes the price at which all of its members sell the commodity in the foreign markets. Nearly 80 percent of all U.S. producers of the commodity belong to the Association, and on a world-wide level, the Association's members account for approximately 40 percent of annual sales.

Discussion. The Webb-Pomerene Act addresses only the question of antitrust liability under U.S. law. Although the U.S. antitrust laws confer an immunity on such associations, the Act does not purport to confer immunity under the law of any foreign country, nor does the Act compel the members of a Webb-Pomerene association to act in any particular way. Thus, a foreign government retains the ability to initiate proceedings if such an association allegedly violates that country's competition law.

4. Personal Jurisdiction and Procedural Rules

4.1 Personal Jurisdiction and Venue

The Agencies will bring suit only if they conclude that personal jurisdiction exists under the due process clause of the U.S. Constitution.[105] The Constitution requires that the defendant have affiliating or minimum contacts with the United States, such that the proceeding comports with "fair play and substantial justice."[106]

Section 12 of the Clayton Act, 15 U.S.C. § 22, provides that any suit under the antitrust laws against a corporation may be brought in the judicial district where it is an inhabitant, where it may be found, or where it transacts business. The concept of transacting business is interpreted pragmatically by the Agencies. Thus, a company may transact business in a particular district directly through an agent, or through a related corporation that is actually the "alter ego" of the foreign party.[107]

4.2 Investigatory Practice Relating to Foreign Nations

In conducting investigations that require documents that are located outside the United States, or contacts with persons located outside the United States, the Agencies first consider requests for voluntary cooperation when practical and consistent with enforcement objectives. When compulsory measures are needed, they seek whenever possible to work with the foreign government involved. U.S. law also provides authority in some circumstances for the use of compulsory measures directed to parties over whom the courts have personal jurisdiction, which the Agencies may use when other efforts to obtain information have been exhausted or would be unavailing.[108]

Conflicts can arise, however, where foreign statutes purport to prevent persons from disclosing documents or information for use in U.S. proceedings. However, the mere existence of such statutes does not excuse noncompliance with a request for information from one of the Agencies.[109] To enable the Agencies to obtain evidence located abroad more effectively, as noted in Section 2.91 above, Congress recently

---

105. *See also* International Shoe Co. v. Washington, 326 U.S. 310 (1945); Asahi Metal Industry Co. Ltd. v. Superior Court, 480 U.S. 102 (1987).

106. Go-Video, Inc. v. Akai Elec. Co., Ltd., 885 F.2d 1406, 1414 (9th Cir. 1989); Wells Fargo & Co. v. Wells Fargo Express Co., 556 F.2d 406, 418 (9th Cir. 1977). To establish jurisdiction, parties must also be served in accordance with the Federal Rules of Civil Procedure or other relevant authority. FED. R. CIV. P. 4(k); 15 U.S.C. §§ 22, 44.

107. *See, e.g.*, Letter from Donald S. Clark, Secretary of the Federal Trade Commission, to Caswell O. Hobbs, Esq., Morgan, Lewis & Bockius, Jan. 17, 1990 (Re: Petition to Quash Subpoena Nippon Sheet Glass, *et al.*, File No. 891-0088, at page 3) ("The Commission . . . may exercise jurisdiction over and serve process on, a foreign entity that has a related company in the United States acting as its agent or alter ego."); *see also* FED. R. CIV. P. 4; Volkswagenwerk AG v. Schlunk, 486 U.S. 694, 707-708 (1988); United States v. Scophony Corp., 333 U.S. 795, 810-818 (1948).

108. For example, 28 U.S.C. § 1783(a) (1988) authorizes a U.S. court to order the issuance of a subpoena "requiring the appearance as a witness before it, or before a person or body designated by it, of a national or resident of the United States who is in a foreign country, or requiring the production of a specified document or other thing by him," under circumstances spelled out in the statute.

109. *See* Societe Internationale pour Participations Industrielles et Commerciales, S.A. v. Rogers, 357 U.S. 197 (1958).

has enacted legislation authorizing the Agencies to negotiate bilateral agreements with foreign governments or antitrust enforcement agencies to facilitate the exchange of documents and evidence in civil and criminal investigations.[110]

4.22 HART-SCOTT-RODINO: SPECIAL FOREIGN COMMERCE RULES

As noted above in Section 2.4, qualifying mergers and acquisitions, defined both in terms of size of party and size of transaction, must be reported to the Agencies, along with certain information about the parties and the transaction, prior to their consummation, pursuant to the HSR Amendments to the Clayton Act, 15 U.S.C. § 18a.

In some instances, the HSR implementing regulations exempt otherwise reportable foreign transactions.[111] First, some acquisitions by U.S. persons are exempt. Acquisitions of foreign assets by a U.S. person are exempt when (i) no sales in or into the United States are attributable to those assets, or (ii) some sales in or into the United States are attributable to those assets, but the acquiring person would not hold assets of the acquired person to which $25 million or more of such sales in the acquired person's most recent fiscal year were attributable.[112] Acquisitions by a U.S. person of voting securities of a foreign issuer are exempt unless the issuer holds assets in the United States having an aggregate book value of $15 million or more, or made aggregate sales in or into the United States of $25 million or more in its most recent fiscal year.[113]

Second, some acquisitions by foreign persons are exempt. An exemption exists for acquisitions by foreign persons if (i) the acquisition is of voting securities of a foreign issuer and would not confer control of a U.S. issuer having annual net sales or total assets of $25 million or more, or of any issuer with assets located in the United States having a book value of $15 million or more; or (ii) the acquired person is also a foreign person and the aggregate annual net sales of the merging firms in or into the United States is less than $110 million and their aggregate total assets in the United States are less than $110 million.[114] In addition, an acquisition by a foreign person of assets located outside the United States is exempt. Acquisitions by foreign persons of U.S. issuers or assets are not exempt.

Finally, acquisitions are exempt if the ultimate parent entity of either the acquiring or the acquired person is controlled by a foreign state, and the acquisition is of assets located within that foreign state, or of voting securities of an issuer organized under its laws.[115] The HSR rules are necessarily technical, and should be consulted rather than relying on the summary description herein.

---

110. International Antitrust Enforcement Assistance Act of 1994, Pub. L. No. 103-438, 108 Stat. 4597 (1994).
111. *See* 16 C.F.R. §§ 802.50-52 (1994).
112. *See* 16 C.F.R. § 802.50(a) (1994).
113. *See* 16 C.F.R. § 802.50(b) (1994).
114. *See* 16 C.F.R. § 802.51 (1994).
115. *See* 16 C.F.R. § 802.52 (1994).

1995 DEPARTMENT OF JUSTICE AND FEDERAL TRADE COMMISSION ANTITRUST GUIDELINES FOR THE LICENSING OF INTELLECTUAL PROPERTY

1. Intellectual Property Protection and the Antitrust Laws

1.0 These *Guidelines* state the antitrust enforcement policy of the U.S. Department of Justice and the Federal Trade Commission (individually, "the Agency," and collectively, "the Agencies") with respect to the licensing of intellectual property protected by patent, copyright, and trade secret law, and of know-how.[1] By stating their general policy, the Agencies hope to assist those who need to predict whether the Agencies will challenge a practice as anticompetitive. However, these *Guidelines* cannot remove judgment and discretion in antitrust law enforcement. Moreover, the standards set forth in these *Guidelines* must be applied in unforeseeable circumstances. Each case will be evaluated in light of its own facts, and these *Guidelines* will be applied reasonably and flexibly.[2]

In the United States, patents confer rights to exclude others from making, using, or selling in the United States the invention claimed by the patent for a period of seventeen years from the date of issue.[3] To gain patent protection, an invention (which may be a product, process, machine, or composition of matter) must be novel,

---

1. These *Guidelines* do not cover the antitrust treatment of trademarks. Although the same general antitrust principles that apply to other forms of intellectual property apply to trademarks as well, these *Guidelines* deal with technology transfer and innovation-related issues that typically arise with respect to patents, copyrights, trade secrets, and know-how agreements, rather than with product-differentiation issues that typically arise with respect to trademarks.
2. As is the case with all guidelines, users should rely on qualified counsel to assist them in evaluating the antitrust risk associated with any contemplated transaction or activity. No set of guidelines can possibly indicate how the Agencies will assess the particular facts of every case. Parties who wish to know the Agencies' specific enforcement intentions with respect to any particular transaction should consider seeking a Department of Justice business review letter pursuant to 28 C.F.R. § 50.6 or a Federal Trade Commission Advisory Opinion pursuant to 16 C.F.R. §§ 1.1-1.4.
3. *See* 35 U.S.C. § 154 (1988). Section 532(a) of the Uruguay Round Agreements Act, Pub. L. No. 103-465, 108 Stat. 4809, 4983 (1994) would change the length of patent protection to a term beginning on the date at which the patent issues and ending twenty years from the date on which the application for the patent was filed.

nonobvious, and useful. Copyright protection applies to original works of authorship embodied in a tangible medium of expression.[4] A copyright protects only the expression, not the underlying ideas.[5] Unlike a patent, which protects an invention not only from copying but also from independent creation, a copyright does not preclude others from independently creating similar expression. Trade secret protection applies to information whose economic value depends on its not being generally known.[6] Trade secret protection is conditioned upon efforts to maintain secrecy and has no fixed term. As with copyright protection, trade secret protection does not preclude independent creation by others.

The intellectual property laws and the antitrust laws share the common purpose of promoting innovation and enhancing consumer welfare.[7] The intellectual property laws provide incentives for innovation and its dissemination and commercialization by establishing enforceable property rights for the creators of new and useful products, more efficient processes, and original works of expression. In the absence of intellectual property rights, imitators could more rapidly exploit the efforts of innovators and investors without compensation. Rapid imitation would reduce the commercial value of innovation and erode incentives to invest, ultimately to the detriment of consumers. The antitrust laws promote innovation and consumer welfare by prohibiting certain actions that may harm competition with respect to either existing or new ways of serving consumers.

2.   General Principles

2.0   These *Guidelines* embody three general principles: (a) for the purpose of antitrust analysis, the Agencies regard intellectual property as being essentially comparable to any other form of property; (b) the Agencies do not presume that intellectual property creates market power in the antitrust context; and (c) the Agencies recognize that intellectual property licensing allows firms to combine complementary factors of production and is generally procompetitive.

2.1   Standard Antitrust Analysis Applies to Intellectual Property

The Agencies apply the same general antitrust principles to conduct involving intellectual property that they apply to conduct involving any other form of tangible or intangible property. That is not to say that intellectual property is in all respects the same as any other form of property. Intellectual property has important characteristics, such as ease of misappropriation, that distinguish it from many other

---

4.   *See* 17 U.S.C. § 102 (1988 & Supp. V 1993). Copyright protection lasts for the author's life plus
     50 years, or 75 years from first publication (or 100 years from creation, whichever expires first) for
     works made for hire. *See* 17 U.S.C. § 302 (1988). The principles stated in these *Guidelines* also
     apply to protection of mask works fixed in a semiconductor chip product (*see* 17 U.S.C. § 901 *et
     seq.* (1988)), which is analogous to copyright protection for works of authorship.
5.   *See* 17 U.S.C. § 102(b) (1988).
6.   Trade secret protection derives from state law. *See generally* Kewanee Oil Co. v. Bicron Corp.,
     416 U.S. 470 (1974).
7.   "[T]he aims and objectives of patent and antitrust laws may seem, at first glance, wholly at odds.
     However, the two bodies of law are actually complementary, as both are aimed at encouraging
     innovation, industry and competition." Atari Games Corp. v. Nintendo of America, Inc., 897 F.2d
     1572, 1576 (Fed. Cir. 1990).

forms of property. These characteristics can be taken into account by standard antitrust analysis, however, and do not require the application of fundamentally different principles.[8]

Although there are clear and important differences in the purpose, extent, and duration of protection provided under the intellectual property regimes of patent, copyright, and trade secret, the governing antitrust principles are the same. Antitrust analysis takes differences among these forms of intellectual property into account in evaluating the specific market circumstances in which transactions occur, just as it does with other particular market circumstances.

Intellectual property law bestows on the owners of intellectual property certain rights to exclude others. These rights help the owners to profit from the use of their property. An intellectual property owner's rights to exclude are similar to the rights enjoyed by owners of other forms of private property. As with other forms of private property, certain types of conduct with respect to intellectual property may have anticompetitive effects against which the antitrust laws can and do protect. Intellectual property is thus neither particularly free from scrutiny under the antitrust laws, nor particularly suspect under them.

The Agencies recognize that the licensing of intellectual property is often international. The principles of antitrust analysis described in these *Guidelines* apply equally to domestic and international licensing arrangements. However, as described in the 1995 *Department of Justice and Federal Trade Commission Antitrust Enforcement Guidelines for International Operations*, considerations particular to international operations, such as jurisdiction and comity, may affect enforcement decisions when the arrangement is in an international context.

2.2 Intellectual Property and Market Power

Market power is the ability profitably to maintain prices above, or output below, competitive levels for a significant period of time.[9] The Agencies will not presume that a patent, copyright, or trade secret necessarily confers market power upon its owner. Although the intellectual property right confers the power to exclude with respect to the *specific* product, process, or work in question, there will often be sufficient actual or potential close substitutes for such product, process, or work to prevent the exercise of market power.[10] If a patent or other form of intellectual

---

8. As with other forms of property, the power to exclude others from the use of intellectual property may vary substantially, depending on the nature of the property and its status under federal or state law. The greater or lesser legal power of an owner to exclude others is also taken into account by standard antitrust analysis.

9. Market power can be exercised in other economic dimensions, such as quality, service, and the development of new or improved goods and processes. It is assumed in this definition that all competitive dimensions are held constant except the ones in which market power is being exercised; that a seller is able to charge higher prices for a higher-quality product does not alone indicate market power. The definition in the text is stated in terms of a seller with market power. A buyer could also exercise market power (e.g., by maintaining the price below the competitive level, thereby depressing output).

10. The Agencies note that the law is unclear on this issue. *Compare* Jefferson Parish Hospital District No. 2 v. Hyde, 466 U.S. 2, 16 (1984) (expressing the view in dictum that if a product is protected by a patent, "it is fair to presume that the inability to buy the product elsewhere gives the seller market power"), *with id.* at 37 n.7 (O'Connor, J., concurring) ("[A] patent holder has no market power in any relevant sense if there are close substitutes for the patented product."). *Compare also*

property does confer market power, that market power does not by itself offend the antitrust laws. As with any other tangible or intangible asset that enables its owner to obtain significant supracompetitive profits, market power (or even a monopoly) that is solely "a consequence of a superior product, business acumen, or historic accident" does not violate the antitrust laws.[11] Nor does such market power impose on the intellectual property owner an obligation to license the use of that property to others. As in other antitrust contexts, however, market power could be illegally acquired or maintained, or, even if lawfully acquired and maintained, would be relevant to the ability of an intellectual property owner to harm competition through unreasonable conduct in connection with such property.

2.3   *Procompetitive Benefits of Licensing*

Intellectual property typically is one component among many in a production process and derives value from its combination with complementary factors. Complementary factors of production include manufacturing and distribution facilities, workforces, and other items of intellectual property. The owner of intellectual property has to arrange for its combination with other necessary factors to realize its commercial value. Often, the owner finds it most efficient to contract with others for these factors, to sell rights to the intellectual property, or to enter into a joint venture arrangement for its development, rather than supplying these complementary factors itself.

Licensing, cross-licensing, or otherwise transferring intellectual property (hereinafter "licensing") can facilitate integration of the licensed property with complementary factors of production. This integration can lead to more efficient exploitation of the intellectual property, benefiting consumers through the reduction of costs and the introduction of new products. Such arrangements increase the value of intellectual property to consumers and to the developers of the technology. By potentially increasing the expected returns from intellectual property, licensing also can increase the incentive for its creation and thus promote greater investment in research and development.

Sometimes the use of one item of intellectual property requires access to another. An item of intellectual property "blocks" another when the second cannot be practiced without using the first. For example, an improvement on a patented machine can be blocked by the patent on the machine. Licensing may promote the coordinated development of technologies that are in a blocking relationship.

Field-of-use, territorial, and other limitations on intellectual property licenses may serve procompetitive ends by allowing the licensor to exploit its property as efficiently and effectively as possible. These various forms of exclusivity can be used to give a licensee an incentive to invest in the commercialization and distribution of products embodying the licensed intellectual property and to develop

---

Abbott Laboratories v. Brennan, 952 F.2d 1346, 1354-55 (Fed. Cir. 1991) (no presumption of market power from intellectual property right), *cert. denied*, 112 S. Ct. 2993 (1992), *with* Digidyne Corp. v. Data General Corp., 734 F.2d 1336, 1341-42 (9th Cir. 1984) (requisite economic power is presumed from copyright), *cert. denied*, 473 U.S. 908 (1985).

11.   United States v. Grinnell Corp., 384 U.S. 563, 571 (1966); *see also* United States v. Aluminum Co. of America, 148 F.2d 416, 430 (2d Cir. 1945) (Sherman Act is not violated by the attainment of market power solely through "superior skill, foresight and industry").

additional applications for the licensed property. The restrictions may do so, for example, by protecting the licensee against free-riding on the licensee's investments by other licensees or by the licensor. They may also increase the licensor's incentive to license, for example, by protecting the licensor from competition in the licensor's own technology in a market niche that it prefers to keep to itself. These benefits of licensing restrictions apply to patent, copyright, and trade secret licenses, and to know-how agreements.

EXAMPLE 1[12]

Situation: ComputerCo develops a new, copyrighted software program for inventory management. The program has wide application in the health field. ComputerCo licenses the program in an arrangement that imposes both field of use and territorial limitations. Some of ComputerCo's licenses permit use only in hospitals; others permit use only in group medical practices. ComputerCo charges different royalties for the different uses. All of ComputerCo's licenses permit use only in specified portions of the United States and in specified foreign countries.[13] The licenses contain no provisions that would prevent or discourage licensees from developing, using, or selling any other program, or from competing in any other good or service other than in the use of the licensed program. None of the licensees are actual or likely potential competitors of ComputerCo in the sale of inventory management programs.

Discussion: The key competitive issue raised by the licensing arrangement is whether it harms competition among entities that would have been actual or likely potential competitors in the absence of the arrangement. Such harm could occur if, for example, the licenses anticompetitively foreclose access to competing technologies (in this case, most likely competing computer programs), prevent licensees from developing their own competing technologies (again, in this case, most likely computer programs), or facilitate market allocation or price-fixing for any product or service supplied by the licensees. (*See* section 3.1.) If the license agreements contained such provisions, the Agency evaluating the arrangement would analyze its likely competitive effects as described in parts 3-5 of these *Guidelines*. In this hypothetical, there are no such provisions and thus the arrangement is merely a subdivision of the licensor's intellectual property among different fields of use and territories. The licensing arrangement does not appear likely to harm competition among entities that would have been actual or likely potential competitors if ComputerCo had chosen not to license the software program. The Agency therefore would be unlikely to object to this arrangement. Based on these facts, the result of the antitrust analysis would be the same whether the technology was protected by patent, copyright, or trade secret. The Agency's conclusion as to likely competitive effects could differ if, for example, the license barred licensees from using any other inventory management program.

---

12.   The examples in these *Guidelines* are hypothetical and do not represent judgments about, or analysis of, any actual market circumstances of the named industries.

13.   These *Guidelines* do not address the possible application of the antitrust laws of other countries to restraints such as territorial restrictions in international licensing arrangements.

3.   Antitrust Concerns and Modes of Analysis

3.1   Nature of the Concerns

While intellectual property licensing arrangements are typically welfare-enhancing and procompetitive, antitrust concerns may nonetheless arise.   For example, a licensing arrangement could include restraints that adversely affect competition in goods markets by dividing the markets among firms that would have competed using different technologies. *See, e.g.*, Example 7.   An arrangement that effectively merges the research and development activities of two of only a few entities that could plausibly engage in research and development in the relevant field might harm competition for development of new goods and services. *See* section 3.2.3.   An acquisition of intellectual property may lessen competition in a relevant antitrust market. *See* section 5.7.   The Agencies will focus on the actual effects of an arrangement, not on its formal terms.

The Agencies will not require the owner of intellectual property to create competition in its own technology.   However, antitrust concerns may arise when a licensing arrangement harms competition among entities that would have been actual or likely potential competitors[14] in a relevant market in the absence of the license (entities in a "horizontal relationship").   A restraint in a licensing arrangement may harm such competition, for example, if it facilitates market division or price-fixing. In addition, license restrictions with respect to one market may harm such competition in another market by anticompetitively foreclosing access to, or significantly raising the price of, an important input,[15] or by facilitating coordination to increase price or reduce output.   When it appears that such competition may be adversely affected, the Agencies will follow the analysis set forth below. *See generally* sections 3.4 and 4.2.

3.2   Markets Affected by Licensing Arrangements

Licensing arrangements raise concerns under the antitrust laws if they are likely to affect adversely the prices, quantities, qualities, or varieties of goods and services[16] either currently or potentially available.   The competitive effects of licensing arrangements often can be adequately assessed within the relevant markets for the goods affected by the arrangements.   In such instances, the Agencies will delineate and analyze only goods markets.   In other cases, however, the analysis may require the delineation of markets for technology or markets for research and development (innovation markets).

---

14.   A firm will be treated as a likely potential competitor if there is evidence that entry by that firm is reasonably probable in the absence of the licensing arrangement.

15.   As used herein, "input" includes outlets for distribution and sales, as well as factors of production. *See, e.g.*, sections 4.1.1 and 5.3-5.5 for further discussion of conditions under which foreclosing access to, or raising the price of, an input may harm competition in a relevant market.

16.   Hereinafter, the term "goods" also includes services.

3.2.1 Goods Markets

A number of different goods markets may be relevant to evaluating the effects of a licensing arrangement. A restraint in a licensing arrangement may have competitive effects in markets for final or intermediate goods made using the intellectual property, or it may have effects upstream, in markets for goods that are used as inputs, along with the intellectual property, to the production of other goods. In general, for goods markets affected by a licensing arrangement, the Agencies will approach the delineation of relevant market and the measurement of market share in the intellectual property area as in section 1 of the *U.S. Department of Justice and Federal Trade Commission Horizontal Merger Guidelines.*[17]

3.2.2 Technology Markets

Technology markets consist of the intellectual property that is licensed (the "licensed technology") and its close substitutes—that is, the technologies or goods that are close enough substitutes significantly to constrain the exercise of market power with respect to the intellectual property that is licensed.[18] When rights to intellectual property are marketed separately from the products in which they are used,[19] the Agencies may rely on technology markets to analyze the competitive effects of a licensing arrangement.

EXAMPLE 2

Situation: Firms Alpha and Beta independently develop different patented process technologies to manufacture the same off-patent drug for the treatment of a particular disease. Before the firms use their technologies internally or license them to third parties, they announce plans jointly to manufacture the drug, and to assign their manufacturing processes to the new manufacturing venture. Many firms are capable of using and have the incentive to use the licensed technologies to manufacture and distribute the drug; thus, the market for drug manufacturing and distribution is competitive. One of the Agencies is evaluating the likely competitive effects of the planned venture.

Discussion: The Agency would analyze the competitive effects of the proposed joint venture by first defining the relevant markets in which competition may be affected and then evaluating the likely competitive effects of the joint venture in the identified markets. (*See* Example 4 for a discussion of the Agencies' approach to joint venture analysis.) In this example, the structural effect of the joint venture in

---

17. U.S. DEPARTMENT OF JUSTICE AND FEDERAL TRADE COMMISSION, HORIZONTAL MERGER GUIDELINES (April 2, 1992) (hereinafter "1992 *Horizontal Merger Guidelines*"). As stated in section 1.41 of the 1992 *Horizontal Merger Guidelines*, market shares for goods markets "can be expressed either in dollar terms through measurement of sales, shipments, or production, or in physical terms through measurement of sales, shipments, production, capacity or reserves."

18. For example, the owner of a process for producing a particular good may be constrained in its conduct with respect to that process not only by other processes for making that good, but also by other goods that compete with the downstream good and by the processes used to produce those other goods.

19. Intellectual property is often licensed, sold, or transferred as an integral part of a marketed good. An example is a patented product marketed with an implied license permitting its use. In such circumstances, there is no need for a separate analysis of technology markets to capture relevant competitive effects.

the relevant goods market for the manufacture and distribution of the drug is unlikely to be significant, because many firms in addition to the joint venture compete in that market. The joint venture might, however, increase the prices of the drug produced using Alpha's or Beta's technology by reducing competition in the relevant market for technology to manufacture the drug.

The Agency would delineate a technology market in which to evaluate likely competitive effects of the proposed joint venture. The Agency would identify other technologies that can be used to make the drug with levels of effectiveness and cost per dose comparable to that of the technologies owned by Alpha and Beta. In addition, the Agency would consider the extent to which competition from other drugs that are substitutes for the drug produced using Alpha's or Beta's technology would limit the ability of a hypothetical monopolist that owned both Alpha's and Beta's technology to raise its price. To identify a technology's close substitutes and thus to delineate the relevant technology market, the Agencies will, if the data permit, identify the smallest group of technologies and goods over which a hypothetical monopolist of those technologies and goods likely would exercise market power—for example, by imposing a small but significant and nontransitory price increase.[20] The Agencies recognize that technology often is licensed in ways that are not readily quantifiable in monetary terms.[21] In such circumstances, the Agencies will delineate the relevant market by identifying other technologies and goods which buyers would substitute at a cost comparable to that of using the licensed technology.

In assessing the competitive significance of current and likely potential participants in a technology market, the Agencies will take into account all relevant evidence. When market share data are available and accurately reflect the competitive significance of market participants, the Agencies will include market share data in this assessment. The Agencies also will seek evidence of buyers' and market participants' assessments of the competitive significance of technology market participants. Such evidence is particularly important when market share data are unavailable, or do not accurately represent the competitive significance of market participants. When market share data or other indicia of market power are not available, and it appears that competing technologies are comparably efficient,[22] the Agencies will assign each technology the same market share. For new technologies, the Agencies generally will use the best available information to estimate market acceptance over a two-year period, beginning with commercial introduction.

3.2.3 RESEARCH AND DEVELOPMENT: INNOVATION MARKETS

If a licensing arrangement may adversely affect competition to develop new or improved goods or processes, the Agencies will analyze such an impact either as a separate competitive effect in relevant goods or technology markets, or as a

---

20. This is conceptually analogous to the analytical approach to goods markets under the 1992 *Horizontal Merger Guidelines*. *Cf.* § 1.11. Of course, market power also can be exercised in other dimensions, such as quality, and these dimensions also may be relevant to the definition and analysis of technology markets.

21. For example, technology may be licensed royalty-free in exchange for the right to use other technology, or it may be licensed as part of a package license.

22. The Agencies will regard two technologies as "comparably efficient" if they can be used to produce close substitutes at comparable costs.

competitive effect in a separate innovation market. A licensing arrangement may have competitive effects on innovation that cannot be adequately addressed through the analysis of goods or technology markets. For example, the arrangement may affect the development of goods that do not yet exist.[23] Alternatively, the arrangement may affect the development of new or improved goods or processes in geographic markets where there is no actual or likely potential competition in the relevant goods.[24]

An innovation market consists of the research and development directed to particular new or improved goods or processes, and the close substitutes for that research and development. The close substitutes are research and development efforts, technologies, and goods[25] that significantly constrain the exercise of market power with respect to the relevant research and development, for example by limiting the ability and incentive of a hypothetical monopolist to retard the pace of research and development. The Agencies will delineate an innovation market only when the capabilities to engage in the relevant research and development can be associated with specialized assets or characteristics of specific firms.

In assessing the competitive significance of current and likely potential participants in an innovation market, the Agencies will take into account all relevant evidence. When market share data are available and accurately reflect the competitive significance of market participants, the Agencies will include market share data in this assessment. The Agencies also will seek evidence of buyers' and market participants' assessments of the competitive significance of innovation market participants. Such evidence is particularly important when market share data are unavailable or do not accurately represent the competitive significance of market participants. The Agencies may base the market shares of participants in an innovation market on their shares of identifiable assets or characteristics upon which innovation depends, on shares of research and development expenditures, or on shares of a related product. When entities have comparable capabilities and incentives to pursue research and development that is a close substitute for the research and development activities of the parties to a licensing arrangement, the Agencies may assign equal market shares to such entities.

EXAMPLE 3

Situation: Two companies that specialize in advanced metallurgy agree to cross-license future patents relating to the development of a new component for aircraft jet turbines. Innovation in the development of the component requires the capability to work with very high tensile strength materials for jet turbines. Aspects of the

---

23. *E.g.*, Sensormatic, FTC Inv. No. 941-0126, 60 Fed. Reg. 5428 (accepted for comment Dec. 28, 1994); Wright Medical Technology, Inc., FTC Inv. No. 951-0015, 60 Fed. Reg. 460 (accepted for comment Dec. 8, 1994); American Home Products, FTC Inv. No. 941-0116, 59 Fed. Reg. 60,807 (accepted for comment Nov. 28, 1994); Roche Holdings Ltd., 113 F.T.C. 1086 (1990); United States v. Automobile Mfrs. Ass'n, 307 F. Supp. 617 (C.D. Cal. 1969), *appeal dismissed sub nom.* City of New York v. United States, 397 U.S. 248 (1970), *modified sub nom.* United States v. Motor Vehicles Mfrs. Ass'n, 1982-83 Trade Cas. (CCH) ¶ 65,088 (C.D. Cal. 1982).

24. *See* Complaint, United States v. General Motors Corp., Civ. No. 93-530 (D. Del., filed Nov. 16, 1993).

25. For example, the licensor of research and development may be constrained in its conduct not only by competing research and development efforts but also by other existing goods that would compete with the goods under development.

licensing arrangement raise the possibility that competition in research and development of this and related components will be lessened. One of the Agencies is considering whether to define an innovation market in which to evaluate the competitive effects of the arrangement.

Discussion: If the firms that have the capability and incentive to work with very high tensile strength materials for jet turbines can be reasonably identified, the Agency will consider defining a relevant innovation market for development of the new component. If the number of firms with the required capability and incentive to engage in research and development of very high tensile strength materials for aircraft jet turbines is small, the Agency may employ the concept of an innovation market to analyze the likely competitive effects of the arrangement in that market, or as an aid in analyzing competitive effects in technology or goods markets. The Agency would perform its analysis as described in parts 3-5.

If the number of firms with the required capability and incentive is large (either because there are a large number of such firms in the jet turbine industry, or because there are many firms in other industries with the required capability and incentive), then the Agency will conclude that the innovation market is competitive. Under these circumstances, it is unlikely that any single firm or plausible aggregation of firms could acquire a large enough share of the assets necessary for innovation to have an adverse impact on competition.

If the Agency cannot reasonably identify the firms with the required capability and incentive, it will not attempt to define an innovation market.

EXAMPLE 4

Situation: Three of the largest producers of a plastic used in disposable bottles plan to engage in joint research and development to produce a new type of plastic that is rapidly biodegradable. The joint venture will grant to its partners (but to no one else) licenses to all patent rights and use of know-how. One of the Agencies is evaluating the likely competitive effects of the proposed joint venture.

Discussion: The Agency would analyze the proposed research and development joint venture using an analysis similar to that applied to other joint ventures.[26] The Agency would begin by defining the relevant markets in which to analyze the joint venture's likely competitive effects. In this case, a relevant market is an innovation market—research and development for biodegradable (and other environmentally friendly) containers. The Agency would seek to identify any other entities that would be actual or likely potential competitors with the joint venture in that relevant market. This would include those firms that have the capability and incentive to undertake research and development closely substitutable for the research and development proposed to be undertaken by the joint venture, taking into account such firms' existing technologies and technologies under development, R&D facilities, and other relevant assets and business circumstances. Firms possessing such capabilities and incentives would be included in the research and development market even if they are not competitors in relevant markets for related goods, such as

---

26. *See, e.g.*, U.S. DEPARTMENT OF JUSTICE AND FEDERAL TRADE COMMISSION, STATEMENTS OF ENFORCEMENT POLICY AND ANALYTICAL PRINCIPLES RELATING TO HEALTH CARE AND ANTITRUST 20-23, 37-40, 72-74 (September 27, 1994). This type of transaction may qualify for treatment under the National Cooperative Research and Production Act of 1993, 15 U.S.C.A. §§ 4301-05.

the plastics currently produced by the joint venturers, although competitors in existing goods markets may often also compete in related innovation markets.

Having defined a relevant innovation market, the Agency would assess whether the joint venture is likely to have anticompetitive effects in that market. A starting point in this analysis is the degree of concentration in the relevant market and the market shares of the parties to the joint venture. If, in addition to the parties to the joint venture (taken collectively), there are at least four other independently controlled entities that possess comparable capabilities and incentives to undertake research and development of biodegradable plastics, or other products that would be close substitutes for such new plastics, the joint venture ordinarily would be unlikely to adversely affect competition in the relevant innovation market (*cf.* section 4.3). If there are fewer than four other independently controlled entities with similar capabilities and incentives, the Agency would consider whether the joint venture would give the parties to the joint venture an incentive and ability collectively to reduce investment in, or otherwise to retard the pace or scope of, research and development efforts. If the joint venture creates a significant risk of anticompetitive effects in the innovation market, the Agency would proceed to consider efficiency justifications for the venture, such as the potential for combining complementary R&D assets in such a way as to make successful innovation more likely, or to bring it about sooner, or to achieve cost reductions in research and development.

The Agency would also assess the likelihood that the joint venture would adversely affect competition in other relevant markets, including markets for products produced by the parties to the joint venture. The risk of such adverse competitive effects would be increased to the extent that, for example, the joint venture facilitates the exchange among the parties of competitively sensitive information relating to goods markets in which the parties currently compete or facilitates the coordination of competitive activities in such markets. The Agency would examine whether the joint venture imposes collateral restraints that might significantly restrict competition among the joint venturers in goods markets, and would examine whether such collateral restraints were reasonably necessary to achieve any efficiencies that are likely to be attained by the venture.

3.3   *Horizontal and Vertical Relationships*

As with other property transfers, antitrust analysis of intellectual property licensing arrangements examines whether the relationship among the parties to the arrangement is primarily horizontal or vertical in nature, or whether it has substantial aspects of both. A licensing arrangement has a vertical component when it affects activities that are in a complementary relationship, as is typically the case in a licensing arrangement. For example, the licensor's primary line of business may be in research and development, and the licensees, as manufacturers, may be buying the rights to use technology developed by the licensor. Alternatively, the licensor may be a component manufacturer owning intellectual property rights in a product that the licensee manufactures by combining the component with other inputs, or the licensor may manufacture the product, and the licensees may operate primarily in distribution and marketing.

In addition to this vertical component, the licensor and its licensees may also have a horizontal relationship. For analytical purposes, the Agencies ordinarily will treat a relationship between a licensor and its licensees, or between licensees, as horizontal when they would have been actual or likely potential competitors in a relevant market in the absence of the license.

The existence of a horizontal relationship between a licensor and its licensees does not, in itself, indicate that the arrangement is anticompetitive. Identification of such relationships is merely an aid in determining whether there may be anticompetitive effects arising from a licensing arrangement. Such a relationship need not give rise to an anticompetitive effect, nor does a purely vertical relationship assure that there are no anticompetitive effects.

The following examples illustrate different competitive relationships among a licensor and its licensees.

EXAMPLE 5

Situation: AgCo, a manufacturer of farm equipment, develops a new, patented emission control technology for its tractor engines and licenses it to FarmCo, another farm equipment manufacturer. AgCo's emission control technology is far superior to the technology currently owned and used by FarmCo, so much so that FarmCo's technology does not significantly constrain the prices that AgCo could charge for its technology. AgCo's emission control patent has a broad scope. It is likely that any improved emissions control technology that FarmCo could develop in the foreseeable future would infringe AgCo's patent.

Discussion: Because FarmCo's emission control technology does not significantly constrain AgCo's competitive conduct with respect to its emission control technology, AgCo's and FarmCo's emission control technologies are not close substitutes for each other. FarmCo is a consumer of AgCo's technology and is not an actual competitor of AgCo in the relevant market for superior emission control technology of the kind licensed by AgCo. Furthermore, FarmCo is not a likely potential competitor of AgCo in the relevant market because, even if FarmCo could develop an improved emission control technology, it is likely that it would infringe AgCo's patent. This means that the relationship between AgCo and FarmCo with regard to the supply and use of emissions control technology is vertical. Assuming that AgCo and FarmCo are actual or likely potential competitors in sales of farm equipment products, their relationship is horizontal in the relevant markets for farm equipment.

EXAMPLE 6

Situation: FarmCo develops a new valve technology for its engines and enters into a cross-licensing arrangement with AgCo, whereby AgCo licenses its emission control technology to FarmCo and FarmCo licenses its valve technology to AgCo. AgCo already owns an alternative valve technology that can be used to achieve engine performance similar to that using FarmCo's valve technology and at a comparable cost to consumers. Before adopting FarmCo's technology, AgCo was using its own valve technology in its production of engines and was licensing (and continues to license) that technology for use by others. As in Example 5, FarmCo does not own or control an emission control technology that is a close substitute for the technology licensed from AgCo. Furthermore, as in Example 5, FarmCo is not likely to develop an improved emission control technology that would be a close substitute for AgCo's technology, because of AgCo's blocking patent.

Discussion: FarmCo is a consumer and not a competitor of AgCo's emission control technology. As in Example 5, their relationship is vertical with regard to this technology. The relationship between AgCo and FarmCo in the relevant market that includes engine valve technology is vertical in part and horizontal in part. It is vertical in part because AgCo and FarmCo stand in a complementary relationship, in which AgCo is a consumer of a technology supplied by FarmCo. However, the relationship between AgCo and FarmCo in the relevant market that includes engine valve technology is also horizontal in part, because FarmCo and AgCo are actual competitors in the licensing of valve technology that can be used to achieve similar engine performance at a comparable cost. Whether the firms license their valve technologies to others is not important for the conclusion that the firms have a horizontal relationship in this relevant market. Even if AgCo's use of its valve technology were solely captive to its own production, the fact that the two valve technologies are substitutable at comparable cost means that the two firms have a horizontal relationship.

As in Example 5, the relationship between AgCo and FarmCo is horizontal in the relevant markets for farm equipment.

3.4 *Framework for Evaluating Licensing Restraints*

In the vast majority of cases, restraints in intellectual property licensing arrangements are evaluated under the rule of reason. The Agencies' general approach in analyzing a licensing restraint under the rule of reason is to inquire whether the restraint is likely to have anticompetitive effects and, if so, whether the restraint is reasonably necessary to achieve procompetitive benefits that outweigh those anticompetitive effects. *See Federal Trade Commission v. Indiana Federation of Dentists*, 476 U.S. 447 (1986); *NCAA v. Board of Regents of the University of Oklahoma*, 468 U.S. 85 (1984); *Broadcast Music, Inc. v. Columbia Broadcasting System, Inc.*, 441 U.S. 1 (1979); 7 Phillip E. Areeda, *Antitrust Law* § 1502 (1986). *See also* part 4.

In some cases, however, the courts conclude that a restraint's "nature and necessary effect are so plainly anticompetitive" that it should be treated as unlawful per se, without an elaborate inquiry into the restraint's likely competitive effect. *Federal Trade Commission v. Superior Court Trial Lawyers Association*, 493 U.S. 411, 433 (1990); *National Society of Professional Engineers v. United States*, 435 U.S. 679, 692 (1978). Among the restraints that have been held per se unlawful are naked price-fixing, output restraints, and market division among horizontal competitors, as well as certain group boycotts and resale price maintenance.

To determine whether a particular restraint in a licensing arrangement is given per se or rule of reason treatment, the Agencies will assess whether the restraint in question can be expected to contribute to an efficiency-enhancing integration of economic activity. *See Broadcast Music*, 441 U.S. at 16-24. In general, licensing arrangements promote such integration because they facilitate the combination of the licensor's intellectual property with complementary factors of production owned by the licensee. A restraint in a licensing arrangement may further such integration by, for example, aligning the incentives of the licensor and the licensees to promote the development and marketing of the licensed technology, or by substantially reducing transactions costs. If there is no efficiency-enhancing integration of economic activity and if the type of restraint is one that has been accorded per se treatment, the Agencies will challenge the restraint under the per se rule. Otherwise, the Agencies will apply a rule of reason analysis.

Application of the rule of reason generally requires a comprehensive inquiry into market conditions. (*See* sections 4.1-4.3.) However, that inquiry may be truncated in certain circumstances. If the Agencies conclude that a restraint has no likely anticompetitive effects, they will treat it as reasonable, without an elaborate analysis of market power or the justifications for the restraint. Similarly, if a restraint facially appears to be of a kind that would always or almost always tend to reduce output or increase prices,[27] and the restraint is not reasonably related to efficiencies, the Agencies will likely challenge the restraint without an elaborate analysis of particular industry circumstances.[28] *See Indiana Federation of Dentists*, 476 U.S. at 459-60; *NCAA*, 468 U.S. at 109.

EXAMPLE 7

Situation: Gamma, which manufactures Product X using its patented process, offers a license for its process technology to every other manufacturer of Product X, each of which competes world-wide with Gamma in the manufacture and sale of X. The process technology does not represent an economic improvement over the available existing technologies. Indeed, although most manufacturers accept licenses from Gamma, none of the licensees actually uses the licensed technology. The licenses provide that each manufacturer has an exclusive right to sell Product X manufactured using the licensed technology in a designated geographic area and that no manufacturer may sell Product X, however manufactured, outside the designated territory.

Discussion: The manufacturers of Product X are in a horizontal relationship in the goods market for Product X. Any manufacturers of Product X that control technologies that are substitutable at comparable cost for Gamma's process are also horizontal competitors of Gamma in the relevant technology market. The licensees of Gamma's process technology are technically in a vertical relationship, although that is not significant in this example because they do not actually use Gamma's technology.

The licensing arrangement restricts competition in the relevant goods market among manufacturers of Product X by requiring each manufacturer to limit its sales to an exclusive territory. Thus, competition among entities that would be actual competitors in the absence of the licensing arrangement is restricted. Based on the facts set forth above, the licensing arrangement does not involve a useful transfer of technology, and thus it is unlikely that the restraint on sales outside the designated territories contributes to an efficiency-enhancing integration of economic activity. Consequently, the evaluating Agency would be likely to challenge the arrangement under the per se rule as a horizontal territorial market allocation scheme and to view

27. Details about the Federal Trade Commission's approach are set forth in *Massachusetts Board of Registration in Optometry*, 110 F.T.C. 549, 604 (1988). In applying its truncated rule of reason inquiry, the FTC uses the analytical category of "inherently suspect" restraints to denote facially anticompetitive restraints that would always or almost always tend to decrease output or increase prices, but that may be relatively unfamiliar or may not fit neatly into traditional per se categories.
28. Under the FTC's *Mass. Board* approach, asserted efficiency justifications for inherently suspect restraints are examined to determine whether they are plausible and, if so, whether they are valid in the context of the market at issue. *Mass. Board*, 110 F.T.C. at 604.

the intellectual property aspects of the arrangement as a sham intended to cloak its true nature.

If the licensing arrangement could be expected to contribute to an efficiency-enhancing integration of economic activity, as might be the case if the licensed technology were an advance over existing processes and used by the licensees, the Agency would analyze the arrangement under the rule of reason applying the analytical framework described in this section.

In this example, the competitive implications do not generally depend on whether the licensed technology is protected by patent, is a trade secret or other know-how, or is a computer program protected by copyright; nor do the competitive implications generally depend on whether the allocation of markets is territorial, as in this example, or functional, based on fields of use.

4.   General Principles Concerning the Agencies' Evaluation of Licensing Arrangements under the Rule of Reason

4.1   *Analysis of Anticompetitive Effects*

The existence of anticompetitive effects resulting from a restraint in a licensing arrangement will be evaluated on the basis of the analysis described in this section.

4.1.1   MARKET STRUCTURE, COORDINATION, AND FORECLOSURE

When a licensing arrangement affects parties in a horizontal relationship, a restraint in that arrangement may increase the risk of coordinated pricing, output restrictions, or the acquisition or maintenance of market power. Harm to competition also may occur if the arrangement poses a significant risk of retarding or restricting the development of new or improved goods or processes.   The potential for competitive harm depends in part on the degree of concentration in, the difficulty of entry into, and the responsiveness of supply and demand to changes in price in the relevant markets. *Cf.* 1992 *Horizontal Merger Guidelines* §§ 1.5, 3.

When the licensor and licensees are in a vertical relationship, the Agencies will analyze whether the licensing arrangement may harm competition among entities in a horizontal relationship at either the level of the licensor or the licensees, or possibly in another relevant market.   Harm to competition from a restraint may occur if it anticompetitively forecloses access to, or increases competitors' costs of obtaining, important inputs, or facilitates coordination to raise price or restrict output.   The risk of anticompetitively foreclosing access or increasing competitors' costs is related to the proportion of the markets affected by the licensing restraint; other characteristics of the relevant markets, such as concentration, difficulty of entry, and the responsiveness of supply and demand to changes in price in the relevant markets; and the duration of the restraint. A licensing arrangement does not foreclose competition merely because some or all of the potential licensees in an industry choose to use the licensed technology to the exclusion of other technologies. Exclusive use may be an efficient consequence of the licensed technology having the lowest cost or highest value.

Harm to competition from a restraint in a vertical licensing arrangement also may occur if a licensing restraint facilitates coordination among entities in a horizontal relationship to raise prices or reduce output in a relevant market. For example, if owners of competing technologies impose similar restraints on their licensees, the licensors may find it easier to coordinate their pricing. Similarly, licensees that are competitors may find it easier to coordinate their pricing if they are subject to common restraints in licenses with a common licensor or competing licensors. The risk of anticompetitive coordination is increased when the relevant markets are concentrated and difficult to enter. The use of similar restraints may be common and procompetitive in an industry, however, because they contribute to efficient exploitation of the licensed property.

4.1.2 LICENSING ARRANGEMENTS INVOLVING EXCLUSIVITY

A licensing arrangement may involve exclusivity in two distinct respects. First, the licensor may grant one or more *exclusive licenses*, which restrict the right of the licensor to license others and possibly also to use the technology itself. Generally, an exclusive license may raise antitrust concerns only if the licensees themselves, or the licensor and its licensees, are in a horizontal relationship. Examples of arrangements involving exclusive licensing that may give rise to antitrust concerns include cross-licensing by parties collectively possessing market power (*see* section 5.5), grantbacks (*see* section 5.6), and acquisitions of intellectual property rights (*see* section 5.7).

A non-exclusive license of intellectual property that does not contain any restraints on the competitive conduct of the licensor or the licensee generally does not present antitrust concerns even if the parties to the license are in a horizontal relationship, because the non-exclusive license normally does not diminish competition that would occur in its absence.

A second form of exclusivity, *exclusive dealing*, arises when a license prevents or restrains the licensee from licensing, selling, distributing, or using competing technologies. *See* section 5.4. Exclusivity may be achieved by an explicit exclusive dealing term in the license or by other provisions such as compensation terms or other economic incentives. Such restraints may anticompetitively foreclose access to, or increase competitors' costs of obtaining, important inputs, or facilitate coordination to raise price or reduce output, but they also may have procompetitive effects. For example, a licensing arrangement that prevents the licensee from dealing in other technologies may encourage the licensee to develop and market the licensed technology or specialized applications of that technology. *See, e.g.,* Example 8. The Agencies will take into account such procompetitive effects in evaluating the reasonableness of the arrangement. *See* section 4.2.

The antitrust principles that apply to a licensor's grant of various forms of exclusivity to and among its licensees are similar to those that apply to comparable vertical restraints outside the licensing context, such as exclusive territories and exclusive dealing. However, the fact that intellectual property may in some cases be misappropriated more easily than other forms of property may justify the use of some restrictions that might be anticompetitive in other contexts.

As noted earlier, the Agencies will focus on the actual practice and its effects, not on the formal terms of the arrangement. A license denominated as non-exclusive (either in the sense of exclusive licensing or in the sense of exclusive dealing) may nonetheless give rise to the same concerns posed by formal exclusivity. A non-exclusive license may have the effect of exclusive licensing if it is structured so that the licensor is unlikely to license others or to practice the technology itself. A license that does not explicitly require exclusive dealing may have the effect of exclusive dealing if it is structured to increase significantly a licensee's cost when it uses competing technologies. However, a licensing arrangement will not automatically raise these concerns merely because a party chooses to deal with a single licensee or licensor, or confines his activity to a single field of use or location, or because only a single licensee has chosen to take a license.

EXAMPLE 8

Situation: NewCo, the inventor and manufacturer of a new flat panel display technology, lacking the capability to bring a flat panel display product to market, grants BigCo an exclusive license to sell a product embodying NewCo's technology. BigCo does not currently sell, and is not developing (or likely to develop), a product that would compete with the product embodying the new technology and does not control rights to another display technology. Several firms offer competing displays, BigCo accounts for only a small proportion of the outlets for distribution of display products, and entry into the manufacture and distribution of display products is relatively easy. Demand for the new technology is uncertain and successful market penetration will require considerable promotional effort. The license contains an exclusive dealing restriction preventing BigCo from selling products that compete with the product embodying the licensed technology.

Discussion: This example illustrates both types of exclusivity in a licensing arrangement. The license is exclusive in that it restricts the right of the licensor to grant other licenses. In addition, the license has an exclusive dealing component in that it restricts the licensee from selling competing products.

The inventor of the display technology and its licensee are in a vertical relationship and are not actual or likely potential competitors in the manufacture or sale of display products or in the sale or development of technology. Hence, the grant of an exclusive license does not affect competition between the licensor and the licensee. The exclusive license may promote competition in the manufacturing and sale of display products by encouraging BigCo to develop and promote the new product in the face of uncertain demand by rewarding BigCo for its efforts if they lead to large sales. Although the license bars the licensee from selling competing products, this exclusive dealing aspect is unlikely in this example to harm competition by anticompetitively foreclosing access, raising competitors' costs of inputs, or facilitating anticompetitive pricing because the relevant product market is unconcentrated, the exclusive dealing restraint affects only a small proportion of the outlets for distribution of display products, and entry is easy. On these facts, the evaluating Agency would be unlikely to challenge the arrangement.

4.2 Efficiencies and Justifications

If the Agencies conclude, upon an evaluation of the market factors described in section 4.1, that a restraint in a licensing arrangement is unlikely to have an anticompetitive effect, they will not challenge the restraint. If the Agencies conclude that the restraint has, or is likely to have, an anticompetitive effect, they will consider whether the restraint is reasonably necessary to achieve procompetitive efficiencies.

If the restraint is reasonably necessary, the Agencies will balance the procompetitive efficiencies and the anticompetitive effects to determine the probable net effect on competition in each relevant market.

The Agencies' comparison of anticompetitive harms and procompetitive efficiencies is necessarily a qualitative one. The risk of anticompetitive effects in a particular case may be insignificant compared to the expected efficiencies, or vice versa. As the expected anticompetitive effects in a particular licensing arrangement increase, the Agencies will require evidence establishing a greater level of expected efficiencies.

The existence of practical and significantly less restrictive alternatives is relevant to a determination of whether a restraint is reasonably necessary. If it is clear that the parties could have achieved similar efficiencies by means that are significantly less restrictive, then the Agencies will not give weight to the parties' efficiency claim. In making this assessment, however, the Agencies will not engage in a search for a theoretically least restrictive alternative that is not realistic in the practical prospective business situation faced by the parties.

When a restraint has, or is likely to have, an anticompetitive effect, the duration of that restraint can be an important factor in determining whether it is reasonably necessary to achieve the putative procompetitive efficiency. The effective duration of a restraint may depend on a number of factors, including the option of the affected party to terminate the arrangement unilaterally and the presence of contract terms (e.g., unpaid balances on minimum purchase commitments) that encourage the licensee to renew a license arrangement. Consistent with their approach to less restrictive alternative analysis generally, the Agencies will not attempt to draw fine distinctions regarding duration; rather, their focus will be on situations in which the duration clearly exceeds the period needed to achieve the procompetitive efficiency.

The evaluation of procompetitive efficiencies, of the reasonable necessity of a restraint to achieve them, and of the duration of the restraint, may depend on the market context. A restraint that may be justified by the needs of a new entrant, for example, may not have a procompetitive efficiency justification in different market circumstances. *Cf. United States v. Jerrold Electronics Corp.*, 187 F. Supp. 545 (E.D. Pa. 1960), *aff'd per curiam*, 365 U.S. 567 (1961).

4.3 Antitrust "Safety Zone"

Because licensing arrangements often promote innovation and enhance competition, the Agencies believe that an antitrust "safety zone" is useful in order to provide some degree of certainty and thus to encourage such activity.[29] Absent extraordinary circumstances, the Agencies will not challenge a restraint in an intellectual property licensing arrangement if (1) the restraint is not facially anticompetitive[30] and (2) the licensor and its licensees collectively account for no more than twenty percent of each relevant market significantly affected by the

---

29. The antitrust "safety zone" does not apply to restraints that are not in a licensing arrangement, or to restraints that are in a licensing arrangement but are unrelated to the use of the licensed intellectual property.

30. "Facially anticompetitive" refers to restraints that normally warrant per se treatment, as well as other restraints of a kind that would always or almost always tend to reduce output or increase prices. *See* section 3.4.

restraint. This "safety zone" does not apply to those transfers of intellectual property rights to which a merger analysis is applied. *See* section 5.7.

Whether a restraint falls within the safety zone will be determined by reference only to goods markets unless the analysis of goods markets alone would inadequately address the effects of the licensing arrangement on competition among technologies or in research and development.

If an examination of the effects on competition among technologies or in research development is required, and if market share data are unavailable or do not accurately represent competitive significance, the following safety zone criteria will apply. Absent extraordinary circumstances, the Agencies will not challenge a restraint in an intellectual property licensing arrangement that may affect competition in a technology market if (1) the restraint is not facially anticompetitive and (2) there are four or more independently controlled technologies in addition to the technologies controlled by the parties to the licensing arrangement that may be substitutable for the licensed technology at a comparable cost to the user. Absent extraordinary circumstances, the Agencies will not challenge a restraint in an intellectual property licensing arrangement that may affect competition in an innovation market if (1) the restraint is not facially anticompetitive and (2) four or more independently controlled entities in addition to the parties to the licensing arrangement possess the required specialized assets or characteristics and the incentive to engage in research and development that is a close substitute of the research and development activities of the parties to the licensing agreement.[31]

The Agencies emphasize that licensing arrangements are not anticompetitive merely because they do not fall within the scope of the safety zone. Indeed, it is likely that the great majority of licenses falling outside the safety zone are lawful and procompetitive. The safety zone is designed to provide owners of intellectual property with a degree of certainty in those situations in which anticompetitive effects are so unlikely that the arrangements may be presumed not to be anticompetitive without an inquiry into particular industry circumstances. It is not intended to suggest that parties should conform to the safety zone or to discourage parties falling outside the safety zone from adopting restrictions in their license arrangements that are reasonably necessary to achieve an efficiency-enhancing integration of economic activity. The Agencies will analyze arrangements falling outside the safety zone based on the considerations outlined in parts 3-5.

The status of a licensing arrangement with respect to the safety zone may change over time. A determination by the Agencies that a restraint in a licensing arrangement qualifies for inclusion in the safety zone is based on the factual circumstances prevailing at the time of the conduct at issue.[32]

5. Application of General Principles

5.0 This section illustrates the application of the general principles discussed above to particular licensing restraints and to arrangements that involve the cross-

---

31. This is consistent with congressional intent in enacting the National Cooperative Research Act. *See* H.R. Conf. Rpt. No. 1044, 98th Cong., 2d Sess., 10, *reprinted in* 1984 U.S.C.C.A.N. 3105, 3134-35.

32. The conduct at issue may be the transaction giving rise to the restraint or the subsequent implementation of the restraint.

licensing, pooling, or acquisition of intellectual property. The restraints and arrangements identified are typical of those that are likely to receive antitrust scrutiny; however, they are not intended as an exhaustive list of practices that could raise competitive concerns.

5.1   *Horizontal Restraints*

The existence of a restraint in a licensing arrangement that affects parties in a horizontal relationship (a "horizontal restraint") does not necessarily cause the arrangement to be anticompetitive. As in the case of joint ventures among horizontal competitors, licensing arrangements among such competitors may promote rather than hinder competition if they result in integrative efficiencies. Such efficiencies may arise, for example, from the realization of economies of scale and the integration of complementary research and development, production, and marketing capabilities.

Following the general principles outlined in section 3.4, horizontal restraints often will be evaluated under the rule of reason. In some circumstances, however, that analysis may be truncated; additionally, some restraints may merit per se treatment, including price fixing, allocation of markets or customers, agreements to reduce output, and certain group boycotts.

EXAMPLE 9

Situation: Two of the leading manufacturers of a consumer electronic product hold patents that cover alternative circuit designs for the product. The manufacturers assign their patents to a separate corporation wholly owned by the two firms. That corporation licenses the right to use the circuit designs to other consumer product manufacturers and establishes the license royalties. None of the patents is blocking; that is, each of the patents can be used without infringing a patent owned by the other firm. The different circuit designs are substitutable in that each permits the manufacture at comparable cost to consumers of products that consumers consider to be interchangeable. One of the Agencies is analyzing the licensing arrangement.

Discussion: In this example, the manufacturers are horizontal competitors in the goods market for the consumer product and in the related technology markets. The competitive issue with regard to a joint assignment of patent rights is whether the assignment has an adverse impact on competition in technology and goods markets that is not outweighed by procompetitive efficiencies, such as benefits in the use or dissemination of the technology. Each of the patent owners has a right to exclude others from using its patent. That right does not extend, however, to the agreement to assign rights jointly. To the extent that the patent rights cover technologies that are close substitutes, the joint determination of royalties likely would result in higher royalties and higher goods prices than would result if the owners licensed or used their technologies independently. In the absence of evidence establishing efficiency-enhancing integration from the joint assignment of patent rights, the Agency may conclude that the joint marketing of competing patent rights constitutes horizontal price fixing and could be challenged as a per se unlawful horizontal restraint of trade. If the joint marketing arrangement results in an efficiency-enhancing integration, the Agency would evaluate the arrangement under the rule of reason. However, the Agency may conclude that the anticompetitive effects are sufficiently apparent, and the claimed integrative efficiencies are sufficiently weak or not reasonably related to the restraints, to warrant challenge of the arrangement without an elaborate analysis of particular industry circumstances (*see* section 3.4).

5.2 Resale Price Maintenance

Resale price maintenance is illegal when "commodities have passed into the channels of trade and are owned by dealers." *Dr. Miles Medical Co. v. John D. Park & Sons Co.*, 220 U.S. 373, 408 (1911). It has been held per se illegal for a licensor of an intellectual property right in a product to fix a licensee's *resale* price of that product. *United States v. Univis Lens Co.*, 316 U.S. 241 (1942); *Ethyl Gasoline Corp. v. United States*, 309 U.S. 436 (1940).[33] Consistent with the principles set forth in section 3.4, the Agencies will enforce the per se rule against resale price maintenance in the intellectual property context.

5.3 Tying Arrangements

A "tying" or "tie-in" or "tied sale" arrangement has been defined as "an agreement by a party to sell one product . . . on the condition that the buyer also purchases a different (or tied) product, or at least agrees that he will not purchase that [tied] product from any other supplier." *Eastman Kodak Co. v. Image Technical Services, Inc.*, 112 S. Ct. 2072, 2079 (1992). Conditioning the ability of a licensee to license one or more items of intellectual property on the licensee's purchase of another item of intellectual property or a good or a service has been held in some cases to constitute illegal tying.[34] Although tying arrangements may result in anticompetitive effects, such arrangements can also result in significant efficiencies and procompetitive benefits. In the exercise of their prosecutorial discretion, the Agencies will consider both the anticompetitive effects and the efficiencies attributable to a tie-in. The Agencies would be likely to challenge a tying arrangement if: (1) the seller has market power in the tying product,[35] (2) the arrangement has an adverse effect on competition in the relevant market for the tied product, and (3) efficiency justifications for the arrangement do not outweigh the

---

33. *But cf.* United States v. General Electric Co., 272 U.S. 476 (1926) (holding that an owner of a product patent may condition a license to manufacture the product on the fixing of the *first* sale price of the patented product). Subsequent lower court decisions have distinguished the *GE* decision in various contexts. *See, e.g.,* Royal Indus. v. St. Regis Paper Co., 420 F.2d 449, 452 (9th Cir. 1969) (observing that *GE* involved a restriction by a patentee who also manufactured the patented product and leaving open the question whether a nonmanufacturing patentee may fix the price of the patented product); Newburgh Moire Co. v. Superior Moire Co., 237 F.2d 283, 293-94 (3rd Cir. 1956) (grant of multiple licenses each containing price restrictions does not come within the *GE* doctrine); Cummer-Graham Co. v. Straight Side Basket Corp., 142 F.2d 646, 647 (5th Cir.) (owner of an intellectual property right in a process to manufacture an unpatented product may not fix the sale price of that product), *cert. denied*, 323 U.S. 726 (1944); Barber-Colman Co. v. National Tool Co., 136 F.2d 339, 343-44 (6th Cir. 1943) (same).
34. *See, e.g.,* United States v. Paramount Pictures, Inc., 334 U.S. 131, 156-58 (1948) (copyrights); International Salt Co. v. United States, 332 U.S. 392 (1947) (patent and related product).
35. *Cf.* 35 U.S.C. § 271(d) (1988 & Supp. V 1993) (requirement of market power in patent misuse cases involving tying).

anticompetitive effects.[36] The Agencies will not presume that a patent, copyright, or trade secret necessarily confers market power upon its owner.

Package licensing—the licensing of multiple items of intellectual property in a single license or in a group of related licenses—may be a form of tying arrangement if the licensing of one product is conditioned upon the acceptance of a license of another, separate product. Package licensing can be efficiency enhancing under some circumstances.   When multiple licenses are needed to use any single item of intellectual property, for example, a package license may promote such efficiencies. If a package license constitutes a tying arrangement, the Agencies will evaluate its competitive effects under the same principles they apply to other tying arrangements.

5.4   Exclusive Dealing

In the intellectual property context, exclusive dealing occurs when a license prevents the licensee from licensing, selling, distributing, or using competing technologies. Exclusive dealing arrangements are evaluated under the rule of reason. *See Tampa Electric Co. v. Nashville Coal Co.*, 365 U.S. 320 (1961) (evaluating legality of exclusive dealing under section 1 of the Sherman Act and section 3 of the Clayton Act); *Beltone Electronics Corp.*, 100 F.T.C. 68 (1982) (evaluating legality of exclusive dealing under section 5 of the Federal Trade Commission Act).   In determining whether an exclusive dealing arrangement is likely to reduce competition in a relevant market, the Agencies will take into account the extent to which the arrangement (1) promotes the exploitation and development of the licensor's technology and (2) anticompetitively forecloses the exploitation and development of, or otherwise constrains competition among, competing technologies.

The likelihood that exclusive dealing may have anticompetitive effects is related, inter alia, to the degree of foreclosure in the relevant market, the duration of the exclusive dealing arrangement, and other characteristics of the input and output markets, such as concentration, difficulty of entry, and the responsiveness of supply and demand to changes in price in the relevant markets. (*See* sections 4.1.1 and 4.1.2.) If the Agencies determine that a particular exclusive dealing arrangement may have an anticompetitive effect, they will evaluate the extent to which the restraint encourages licensees to develop and market the licensed technology (or specialized applications of that technology), increases licensors' incentives to develop or refine the licensed technology, or otherwise increases competition and enhances output in a relevant market. (*See* section 4.2 and Example 8.)

5.5   Cross-Licensing and Pooling Arrangements

Cross-licensing and pooling arrangements are agreements of two or more owners of different items of intellectual property to license one another or third parties. These arrangements may provide procompetitive benefits by integrating complementary technologies, reducing transaction costs, clearing blocking positions,

---

36.   As is true throughout these *Guidelines*, the factors listed are those that guide the Agencies' internal analysis in exercising their prosecutorial discretion. They are not intended to circumscribe how the Agencies will conduct the litigation of cases that they decide to bring.

and avoiding costly infringement litigation. By promoting the dissemination of technology, cross-licensing and pooling arrangements are often procompetitive.

Cross-licensing and pooling arrangements can have anticompetitive effects in certain circumstances. For example, collective price or output restraints in pooling arrangements, such as the joint marketing of pooled intellectual property rights with collective price setting or coordinated output restrictions, may be deemed unlawful if they do not contribute to an efficiency-enhancing integration of economic activity among the participants. *Compare NCAA*, 468 U.S. at 114 (output restriction on college football broadcasting held unlawful because it was not reasonably related to any purported justification), *with Broadcast Music*, 441 U.S. at 23 (blanket license for music copyrights found not per se illegal because the cooperative price was necessary to the creation of a new product). When cross-licensing or pooling arrangements are mechanisms to accomplish naked price fixing or market division, they are subject to challenge under the per se rule. *See United States v. New Wrinkle, Inc.*, 342 U.S. 371 (1952) (price fixing).

Settlements involving the cross-licensing of intellectual property rights can be an efficient means to avoid litigation and, in general, courts favor such settlements. When such cross-licensing involves horizontal competitors, however, the Agencies will consider whether the effect of the settlement is to diminish competition among entities that would have been actual or likely potential competitors in a relevant market in the absence of the cross-license. In the absence of offsetting efficiencies, such settlements may be challenged as unlawful restraints of trade. *Cf. United States v. Singer Manufacturing Co.*, 374 U.S. 174 (1963) (cross-license agreement was part of broader combination to exclude competitors).

Pooling arrangements generally need not be open to all who would like to join. However, exclusion from cross-licensing and pooling arrangements among parties that collectively possess market power may, under some circumstances, harm competition. *Cf. Northwest Wholesale Stationers, Inc. v. Pacific Stationery & Printing Co.*, 472 U.S. 284 (1985) (exclusion of a competitor from a purchasing cooperative not per se unlawful absent a showing of market power). In general, exclusion from a pooling or cross-licensing arrangement among competing technologies is unlikely to have anticompetitive effects unless (1) excluded firms cannot effectively compete in the relevant market for the good incorporating the licensed technologies and (2) the pool participants collectively possess market power in the relevant market. If these circumstances exist, the Agencies will evaluate whether the arrangement's limitations on participation are reasonably related to the efficient development and exploitation of the pooled technologies and will assess the net effect of those limitations in the relevant market. *See* section 4.2.

Another possible anticompetitive effect of pooling arrangements may occur if the arrangement deters or discourages participants from engaging in research and development, thus retarding innovation. For example, a pooling arrangement that requires members to grant licenses to each other for current and future technology at minimal cost may reduce the incentives of its members to engage in research and development because members of the pool have to share their successful research and development and each of the members can free ride on the accomplishments of other pool members. *See generally United States v. Mfrs. Aircraft Ass'n, Inc.*, 1976-1 Trade Cas. (CCH) ¶ 60,810 (S.D.N.Y. 1975); *United States v. Automobile Mfrs. Ass'n*, 307 F. Supp. 617 (C.D. Cal 1969), *appeal dismissed sub nom. City of New*

York v. United States, 397 U.S. 248 (1970), *modified sub nom. United States v. Motor Vehicle Mfrs. Ass'n,* 1982-83 Trade Cas. (CCH) ¶ 65,088 (C.D. Cal. 1982). However, such an arrangement can have procompetitive benefits, for example, by exploiting economies of scale and integrating complementary capabilities of the pool members, (including the clearing of blocking positions), and is likely to cause competitive problems only when the arrangement includes a large fraction of the potential research and development in an innovation market. *See* section 3.2.3 and Example 4.

EXAMPLE 10

Situation: As in Example 9, two of the leading manufacturers of a consumer electronic product hold patents that cover alternative circuit designs for the product. The manufacturers assign several of their patents to a separate corporation wholly owned by the two firms. That corporation licenses the right to use the circuit designs to other consumer product manufacturers and establishes the license royalties. In this example, however, the manufacturers assign to the separate corporation only patents that are blocking. None of the patents assigned to the corporation can be used without infringing a patent owned by the other firm.

Discussion: Unlike the previous example, the joint assignment of patent rights to the wholly owned corporation in this example does not adversely affect competition in the licensed technology among entities that would have been actual or likely potential competitors in the absence of the licensing arrangement. Moreover, the licensing arrangement is likely to have procompetitive benefits in the use of the technology. Because the manufacturers' patents are blocking, the manufacturers are not in a horizontal relationship with respect to those patents. None of the patents can be used without the right to a patent owned by the other firm, so the patents are not substitutable. As in Example 9, the firms are horizontal competitors in the relevant goods market. In the absence of collateral restraints that would likely raise price or reduce output in the relevant goods market or in any other relevant antitrust market and that are not reasonably related to an efficiency-enhancing integration of economic activity, the evaluating Agency would be unlikely to challenge this arrangement.

5.6 *Grantbacks*

A grantback is an arrangement under which a licensee agrees to extend to the licensor of intellectual property the right to use the licensee's improvements to the licensed technology. Grantbacks can have procompetitive effects, especially if they are nonexclusive. Such arrangements provide a means for the licensee and the licensor to share risks and reward the licensor for making possible further innovation based on or informed by the licensed technology, and both promote innovation in the first place and promote the subsequent licensing of the results of the innovation. Grantbacks may adversely affect competition, however, if they substantially reduce the licensee's incentives to engage in research and development and thereby limit rivalry in innovation markets.

A non-exclusive grantback allows the licensee to practice its technology and license it to others. Such a grantback provision may be necessary to ensure that the licensor is not prevented from effectively competing because it is denied access to improvements developed with the aid of its own technology. Compared with an exclusive grantback, a non-exclusive grantback, which leaves the licensee free to license improvements technology to others, is less likely to have anticompetitive effects.

The Agencies will evaluate a grantback provision under the rule of reason, *see generally Transparent-Wrap Machine Corp. v. Stokes & Smith Co.*, 329 U.S. 637, 645-48 (1947) (grantback provision in technology license is not per se unlawful), considering its likely effects in light of the overall structure of the licensing arrangement and conditions in the relevant markets. An important factor in the Agencies' analysis of a grantback will be whether the licensor has market power in a relevant technology or innovation market. If the Agencies determine that a particular grantback provision is likely to reduce significantly licensees' incentives to invest in improving the licensed technology, the Agencies will consider the extent to which the grantback provision has offsetting procompetitive effects, such as (1) promoting dissemination of licensees' improvements to the licensed technology, (2) increasing the licensors' incentives to disseminate the licensed technology, or (3) otherwise increasing competition and output in a relevant technology or innovation market. *See* section 4.2. In addition, the Agencies will consider the extent to which grantback provisions in the relevant markets generally increase licensors' incentives to innovate in the first place.

5.7 Acquisition of Intellectual Property Rights

Certain transfers of intellectual property rights are most appropriately analyzed by applying the principles and standards used to analyze mergers, particularly those in the 1992 *Horizontal Merger Guidelines*. The Agencies will apply a merger analysis to an outright sale by an intellectual property owner of all of its rights to that intellectual property and to a transaction in which a person obtains through grant, sale, or other transfer an exclusive license for intellectual property (i.e., a license that precludes all other persons, including the licensor, from using the licensed intellectual property).[37] Such transactions may be assessed under section 7 of the Clayton Act, sections 1 and 2 of the Sherman Act, and section 5 of the Federal Trade Commission Act.

EXAMPLE 11
Situation: Omega develops a new, patented pharmaceutical for the treatment of a particular disease. The only drug on the market approved for the treatment of this disease is sold by Delta. Omega's patented drug has almost completed regulatory approval by the Food and Drug Administration. Omega has invested considerable sums in product development and market testing, and initial results show that Omega's drug would be a significant competitor to Delta's. However, rather than enter the market as a direct competitor of Delta, Omega licenses to Delta the right to manufacture and sell Omega's patented drug. The license agreement with Delta is nominally nonexclusive. However, Omega has rejected all requests by other firms to

---

37. The safety zone of section 4.3 does not apply to transfers of intellectual property such as those described in this section.

obtain a license to manufacture and sell Omega's patented drug, despite offers by those firms of terms that are reasonable in relation to those in Delta's license.

Discussion: Although Omega's license to Delta is nominally nonexclusive, the circumstances indicate that it is exclusive in fact because Omega has rejected all reasonable offers by other firms for licenses to manufacture and sell Omega's patented drug. The facts of this example indicate that Omega would be a likely potential competitor of Delta in the absence of the licensing arrangement, and thus they are in a horizontal relationship in the relevant goods market that includes drugs for the treatment of this particular disease. The evaluating Agency would apply a merger analysis to this transaction, since it involves an acquisition of a likely potential competitor.

6.   Enforcement of Invalid Intellectual Property Rights

The Agencies may challenge the enforcement of invalid intellectual property rights as antitrust violations. Enforcement or attempted enforcement of a patent obtained by fraud on the Patent and Trademark Office or the Copyright Office may violate section 2 of the Sherman Act, if all the elements otherwise necessary to establish a section 2 charge are proved, or section 5 of the Federal Trade Commission Act. *Walker Process Equipment, Inc. v. Food Machinery & Chemical Corp.*, 382 U.S. 172 (1965) (patents); *American Cyanamid Co.*, 72 F.T.C. 623, 684-85 (1967), *aff'd sub. nom. Charles Pfizer & Co.*, 401 F.2d 574 (6th Cir. 1968), *cert. denied*, 394 U.S. 920 (1969) (patents); *Michael Anthony Jewelers, Inc. v. Peacock Jewelry, Inc.*, 795 F. Supp. 639, 647 (S.D.N.Y. 1992) (copyrights). Inequitable conduct before the Patent and Trademark Office will not be the basis of a section 2 claim unless the conduct also involves knowing and willful fraud and the other elements of a section 2 claim are present. *Argus Chemical Corp. v. Fibre Glass-Evercoat, Inc.*, 812 F.2d 1381, 1384-85 (Fed. Cir. 1987). Actual or attempted enforcement of patents obtained by inequitable conduct that falls short of fraud under some circumstances may violate section 5 of the Federal Trade Commission Act, *American Cyanamid Co., supra.* Objectively baseless litigation to enforce invalid intellectual property rights may also constitute an element of a violation of the Sherman Act. *See Professional Real Estate Investors, Inc. v. Columbia Pictures Industries, Inc.*, 113 S. Ct. 1920, 1928 (1993) (copyrights); *Handgards, Inc. v. Ethicon, Inc.*, 743 F.2d 1282, 1289 (9th Cir. 1984), *cert. denied*, 469 U.S. 1190 (1985) (patents); *Handgards, Inc. v. Ethicon, Inc.*, 601 F.2d 986, 992-96 (9th Cir. 1979), *cert. denied*, 444 U.S. 1025 (1980) (patents); *CVD, Inc. v. Raytheon Co.*, 769 F.2d 842 (1st Cir. 1985) (trade secrets), *cert. denied*, 475 U.S. 1016 (1986).

1996 DEPARTMENT OF JUSTICE AND FEDERAL TRADE COMMISSION STATEMENTS OF ANTITRUST ENFORCEMENT POLICY IN HEALTH CARE

Introduction

In September 1993, the Department of Justice and the Federal Trade Commission (the "Agencies") issued six statements of their antitrust enforcement policies regarding mergers and various joint activities in the health care area. The six policy statements addressed: (1) hospital mergers; (2) hospital joint ventures involving high-technology or other expensive medical equipment; (3) physicians' provision of information to purchasers of health care services; (4) hospital participation in exchanges of price and cost information; (5) health care providers' joint purchasing arrangements; and (6) physician network joint ventures. The Agencies also committed to issuing expedited Department of Justice business reviews and Federal Trade Commission advisory opinions in response to requests for antitrust guidance on specific proposed conduct involving the health care industry.

The 1993 policy statements and expedited specific Agency guidance were designed to advise the health care community in a time of tremendous change, and to address, as completely as possible, the problem of uncertainty concerning the Agencies' enforcement policy that some had said might deter mergers, joint ventures, or other activities that could lower health care costs. Sound antitrust enforcement, of course, continued to protect consumers against anticompetitive activities.

When the Agencies issued the 1993 health care antitrust enforcement policy statements, they recognized that additional guidance might be desirable in the areas covered by those statements as well as in other health care areas, and committed to issuing revised and additional policy statements as warranted. In light of the comments the Agencies received on the 1993 statements and the Agencies' own experience, the Agencies revised and expanded the health care antitrust enforcement policy statements in September 1994. The 1994 statements, which superseded the 1993 statements, added new statements addressing hospital joint ventures involving specialized clinical or other expensive health care services, providers' collective provision of fee-related information to purchasers of health care services, and analytical principles relating to a broad range of health care provider networks (termed "multiprovider networks"), and expanded the antitrust "safety zones" for several other statements.

Since issuance of the 1994 statements, health care markets have continued to evolve in response to consumer demand and competition in the marketplace. New arrangements and variations on existing arrangements involving joint activity by health care providers continue to emerge to meet consumers', purchasers', and payers' desire for more efficient delivery of high quality health care services. During this period, the Agencies have gained additional experience with arrangements involving joint provider activity. As a result of these developments, the Agencies have decided to amplify the enforcement policy statement on physician network joint ventures and the more general statement on multiprovider networks.

In these revised statements, the Agencies continue to analyze all types of health care provider networks under general antitrust principles. These principles are sufficiently flexible to take into account the particular characteristics of health care markets and the rapid changes that are occurring in those markets. The Agencies emphasize that it is not their intent to treat such networks either more strictly or more leniently than joint ventures in other industries, or to favor any particular procompetitive organization or structure of health care delivery over other forms that consumers may desire. Rather, their goal is to ensure a competitive marketplace in which consumers will have the benefit of high quality, cost-effective health care and a wide range of choices, including new provider-controlled networks that expand consumer choice and increase competition.

The revisions to the statements on physician network joint ventures and multiprovider networks are summarized below. In addition to these revisions, various changes have been made to the language of both statements to improve their clarity. No revisions have been made to any of the other statements.

Physician Network Joint Ventures

The revised statement on physician network joint ventures provides an expanded discussion of the antitrust principles that apply to such ventures. The revisions focus on the analysis of networks that fall outside the safety zones contained in the existing statement, particularly those networks that do not involve the sharing of substantial financial risk by their physician participants. The revised statement explains that where physicians' integration through the network is likely to produce significant efficiencies, any agreements on price reasonably necessary to accomplish the venture's procompetitive benefits will be analyzed under the rule of reason.

The revised statement adds three hypothetical examples to further illustrate the application of these principles: (1) a physician network joint venture that does not involve the sharing of substantial financial risk, but receives rule of reason treatment due to the extensive integration among its physician participants; (2) a network that involves both risk-sharing and non-risk-sharing activities, and receives rule of reason treatment; and (3) a network that involves little or no integration among its physician participants, and is per se illegal.

The safety zones for physician network joint ventures remain unchanged, but the revised statement identifies additional types of financial risk-sharing arrangements that can qualify a network for the safety zones. It also further emphasizes two points previously made in the 1994 statements. First, the enumeration in the statements of particular examples of substantial financial risk sharing does not foreclose consideration of other arrangements through which physicians may share substantial financial risk. Second, a physician network that falls outside the safety zones is not necessarily anticompetitive.

Multiprovider Networks

In 1994, the Agencies issued a new statement on multiprovider health care networks that described the general antitrust analysis of such networks. The revised statement on multiprovider networks emphasizes that it is intended to articulate general principles relating to a wide range of health care provider networks. Many of the revisions to this statement reflect changes made to the revised statement on physician network joint ventures. In addition, four hypothetical examples involving PHOs ("physician-hospital organizations"), including one involving "messenger model" arrangements, have been added.

Safety Zones and Hypothetical Examples

Most of the nine statements give health care providers guidance in the form of antitrust safety zones, which describe conduct that the Agencies will not challenge under the antitrust laws, absent extraordinary circumstances. The Agencies are aware that some parties have interpreted the safety zones as defining the limits of joint conduct that is permissible under the antitrust laws. This view is incorrect. The inclusion of certain conduct within the antitrust safety zones does not imply that conduct falling outside the safety zones is likely to be challenged by the Agencies. Antitrust analysis is inherently fact-intensive. The safety zones are designed to require consideration of only a few factors that are relatively easy to apply, and to provide the Agencies with a high degree of confidence that arrangements falling within them are unlikely to raise substantial competitive concerns. Thus, the safety zones encompass only a subset of provider arrangements that the Agencies are unlikely to challenge under the antitrust laws. The statements outline the analysis the Agencies will use to review conduct that falls outside the safety zones.

Likewise, the statements' hypothetical examples concluding that the Agencies would not challenge the particular arrangement do not mean that conduct varying from the examples is likely to be challenged by the Agencies. The hypothetical examples are designed to illustrate how the statements' general principles apply to specific situations. Interested parties should examine the business review letters issued by the Department of Justice and the advisory opinions issued by the Federal Trade Commission and its staff for additional guidance on the application and interpretation of these statements. Copies of those letters and opinions and summaries of the letters and opinions are available from the Agencies at the mailing and Internet addresses listed at the end of the statements.

The statements also set forth the Department of Justice's business review procedure and the Federal Trade Commission's advisory opinion procedure under which the health care community can obtain the Agencies' antitrust enforcement intentions regarding specific proposed conduct on an expedited basis. The statements continue the commitment of the Agencies to respond to requests for business reviews or advisory opinions from the health care community no later than 90 days after all necessary information is received regarding any matter addressed in the statements, except requests relating to hospital mergers outside the antitrust safety zone and multiprovider networks. The Agencies also will respond to business review or advisory opinion requests regarding multiprovider networks or other non-merger health care matters within 120 days after all necessary information is received. The Agencies intend to work closely with persons making requests to clarify what information is necessary and to provide guidance throughout the process. The Agencies continue this commitment to expedited review in an effort to reduce antitrust uncertainty for the health care industry in what the Agencies recognize is a time of fundamental change.

The Agencies recognize the importance of antitrust guidance in evolving health care contexts. Consequently, the Agencies continue their commitment to issue additional guidance as warranted.

1. Statement of Department of Justice and Federal Trade Commission Enforcement Policy on Mergers among Hospitals

Introduction

Most hospital mergers and acquisitions ("mergers") do not present competitive concerns. While careful analysis may be necessary to determine the likely competitive effect of a particular hospital merger, the competitive effect of many hospital mergers is relatively easy to assess. This statement sets forth an antitrust safety zone for certain mergers in light of the Agencies' extensive experience analyzing hospital mergers. Mergers that fall within the antitrust safety zone will not be challenged by the Agencies under the antitrust laws, absent extraordinary circumstances.[1] This policy statement also briefly describes the Agencies' antitrust analysis of hospital mergers that fall outside the antitrust safety zone.

A. Antitrust Safety Zone: Mergers of Hospitals That Will Not Be Challenged, Absent Extraordinary Circumstances, by the Agencies

The Agencies will not challenge any merger between two general acute-care hospitals where one of the hospitals (1) has an average of fewer than 100 licensed beds over the three most recent years, and (2) has an average daily inpatient census

---

1. The Agencies are confident that conduct falling within the antitrust safety zones contained in these policy statements is very unlikely to raise competitive concerns. Accordingly, the Agencies anticipate that extraordinary circumstances warranting a challenge to such conduct will be rare.

of fewer than 40 patients over the three most recent years, absent extraordinary circumstances. This antitrust safety zone will not apply if that hospital is less than 5 years old.

The Agencies recognize that in some cases a general acute care hospital with fewer than 100 licensed beds and an average daily inpatient census of fewer than 40 patients will be the only hospital in a relevant market. As such, the hospital does not compete in any significant way with other hospitals. Accordingly, mergers involving such hospitals are unlikely to reduce competition substantially.

The Agencies also recognize that many general acute care hospitals, especially rural hospitals, with fewer than 100 licensed beds and an average daily inpatient census of fewer than 40 patients are unlikely to achieve the efficiencies that larger hospitals enjoy. Some of those cost-saving efficiencies may be realized, however, through a merger with another hospital.

B.   The Agencies' Analysis of Hospital Mergers That Fall outside the Antitrust Safety Zone

Hospital mergers that fall outside the antitrust safety zone are not necessarily anticompetitive, and may be procompetitive. The Agencies' analysis of hospital mergers follows the five steps set forth in the Department of Justice/Federal Trade Commission 1992 *Horizontal Merger Guidelines*.

Applying the analytical framework of the Merger Guidelines to particular facts of specific hospital mergers, the Agencies often have concluded that an investigated hospital merger will not result in a substantial lessening of competition in situations where market concentration might otherwise raise an inference of anticompetitive effects. Such situations include transactions where the Agencies found that: (1) the merger would not increase the likelihood of the exercise of market power either because of the existence post-merger of strong competitors or because the merging hospitals were sufficiently differentiated; (2) the merger would allow the hospitals to realize significant cost savings that could not otherwise be realized; or (3) the merger would eliminate a hospital that likely would fail with its assets exiting the market.

Antitrust challenges to hospital mergers are relatively rare. Of the hundreds of hospital mergers in the United States since 1987, the Agencies have challenged only a handful, and in several cases sought relief only as to part of the transaction. Most reviews of hospital mergers conducted by the Agencies are concluded within one month.

* * *

If hospitals are considering mergers that appear to fall within the antitrust safety zone and believe they need additional certainty regarding the legality of their conduct under the antitrust laws, they can take advantage of the Department's business review procedure (28 C.F.R. § 50.6 (1992)) or the Federal Trade Commission's advisory opinion procedure (16 C.F.R. §§ 1.1-1.4 (1993)). The Agencies will respond to business review or advisory opinion requests on behalf of hospitals considering mergers that appear to fall within the antitrust safety zone within 90 days after all necessary information is submitted.

2. **Statement of Department of Justice and Federal Trade Commission Enforcement Policy on Hospital Joint Ventures Involving High-Technology or Other Expensive Health Care Equipment**

Introduction

Most hospital joint ventures to purchase or otherwise share the ownership cost of, operate, and market high-technology or other expensive health care equipment and related services do not create antitrust problems. In most cases, these collaborative activities create procompetitive efficiencies that benefit consumers. These efficiencies include the provision of services at a lower cost or the provision of services that would not have been provided absent the joint venture. Sound antitrust enforcement policy distinguishes those joint ventures that on balance benefit the public from those that may increase prices without providing a countervailing benefit, and seeks to prevent only those that are harmful to consumers. The Agencies have never challenged a joint venture among hospitals to purchase or otherwise share the ownership cost of, operate and market high-technology or other expensive health care equipment and related services.

This statement of enforcement policy sets forth an antitrust safety zone that describes hospital high-technology or other expensive health care equipment joint ventures that will not be challenged, absent extraordinary circumstances, by the Agencies under the antitrust laws. It then describes the Agencies' antitrust analysis of hospital high-technology or other expensive health care equipment joint ventures that fall outside the antitrust safety zone. Finally, this statement includes examples of its application to hospital high-technology or other expensive health care equipment joint ventures.

A. Antitrust Safety Zone: Hospital High-Technology Joint Ventures That Will Not Be Challenged, Absent Extraordinary Circumstances, by the Agencies

The Agencies will not challenge under the antitrust laws any joint venture among hospitals to purchase or otherwise share the ownership cost of, operate, and market the related services of, high-technology or other expensive health care equipment if the joint venture includes only the number of hospitals whose participation is needed to support the equipment, absent extraordinary circumstances.[2] This applies to joint ventures involving purchases of new equipment as well as to joint ventures involving existing equipment.[3] A joint venture that includes additional hospitals also will not be challenged if the additional hospitals could not support the equipment on their

---

2. A hospital or group of hospitals will be considered able to support high-technology or other expensive health care equipment for purposes of this antitrust safety zone if it could recover the costs of owning, operating, and marketing the equipment over its useful life. If the joint venture is limited to ownership, only the ownership costs are relevant. If the joint venture is limited to owning and operating, only the owning and operating costs are relevant.

3. Consequently, the safety zone would apply in a situation in which one hospital had already purchased the health care equipment, but was not recovering the costs of the equipment and sought a joint venture with one or more hospitals in order to recover the costs of the equipment.

own or through the formation of a competing joint venture, absent extraordinary circumstances.

For example, if two hospitals are each unlikely to recover the cost of individually purchasing, operating, and marketing the services of a magnetic resonance imager (MRI) over its useful life, their joint venture with respect to the MRI would not be challenged by the Agencies. On the other hand, if the same two hospitals entered into a joint venture with a third hospital that independently could have purchased, operated, and marketed an MRI in a financially viable manner, the joint venture would not be in this antitrust safety zone. If, however, none of the three hospitals could have supported an MRI by itself, the Agencies would not challenge the joint venture.[4]

Information necessary to determine whether the costs of a piece of high-technology health care equipment could be recovered over its useful life is normally available to any hospital or group of hospitals considering such a purchase. This information may include the cost of the equipment, its expected useful life, the minimum number of procedures that must be done to meet a machine's financial breakeven point, the expected number of procedures the equipment will be used for given the population served by the joint venture and the expected price to be charged for the use of the equipment. Expected prices and costs should be confirmed by objective evidence, such as experiences in similar markets for similar technologies.

B. The Agencies' Analysis of Hospital High-Technology or Other Expensive Health Care Equipment Joint Ventures That Fall outside the Antitrust Safety Zone

The Agencies recognize that joint ventures that fall outside the antitrust safety zone do not necessarily raise significant antitrust concerns. The Agencies will apply a rule of reason analysis in their antitrust review of such joint ventures.[5] The objective of this analysis is to determine whether the joint venture may reduce competition substantially, and, if it might, whether it is likely to produce procompetitive efficiencies that outweigh its anticompetitive potential. This analysis is flexible and takes into account the nature and effect of the joint venture, the characteristics of the venture and of the hospital industry generally, and the reasons for, and purposes of, the venture. It also allows for consideration of efficiencies that will result from the venture. The steps involved in a rule of reason analysis are set forth below.[6]

---

4.   The antitrust safety zone described in this statement applies only to the joint venture and agreements reasonably necessary to the venture. The safety zone does not apply to or protect agreements made by participants in a joint venture that are related to a service not provided by the venture. For example, the antitrust safety zone that would apply to the MRI joint venture would not apply to protect an agreement among the hospitals with respect to charges for an overnight stay.

5.   This statement assumes that the joint venture arrangement is not one that uses the joint venture label but is likely merely to restrict competition and decrease output. For example, two hospitals that independently operate profitable MRI services could not avoid charges of price fixing by labeling as a joint venture their plan to obtain higher prices through joint marketing of their existing MRI services.

6.   Many joint ventures that could provide substantial efficiencies also may present little likelihood of competitive harm. Where it is clear initially that any joint venture presents little likelihood of

Step one: Define the relevant market. The rule of reason analysis first identifies what is produced through the joint venture. The relevant product and geographic markets are then properly defined. This process seeks to identify any other provider that could offer what patients or physicians generally would consider a good substitute for that provided by the joint venture. Thus, if a joint venture were to purchase and jointly operate and market the related services of an MRI, the relevant market would include all other MRIs in the area that are reasonable alternatives for the same patients, but would *not* include providers with only traditional X-ray equipment.

Step two: Evaluate the competitive effects of the venture. This step begins with an analysis of the structure of the relevant market. If many providers would compete with the joint venture, competitive harm is unlikely and the analysis would continue with step four described below.

If the structural analysis of the relevant market showed that the joint venture would eliminate an existing or potentially viable competing provider and that there were few competing providers of that service, or that cooperation in the joint venture market may spill over into a market in which the parties to the joint venture are competitors, it then would be necessary to assess the extent of the potential anticompetitive effects of the joint venture. In addition to the number and size of competing providers, factors that could restrain the ability of the joint venture to raise prices either unilaterally or through collusive agreements with other providers would include: (1) characteristics of the market that make anticompetitive coordination unlikely; (2) the likelihood that other providers would enter the market; and (3) the effects of government regulation.

The extent to which the joint venture restricts competition among the hospitals participating in the venture is evaluated during this step. In some cases, a joint venture to purchase or otherwise share the cost of high-technology equipment may not substantially eliminate competition among the hospitals in providing the related service made possible by the equipment. For example, two hospitals might purchase a mobile MRI jointly, but operate and market MRI services separately. In such instances, the potential impact on competition of the joint venture would be substantially reduced.[7]

Step three: Evaluate the impact of procompetitive efficiencies. This step requires an examination of the joint venture's potential to create procompetitive efficiencies, and the balancing of these efficiencies against any potential anticompetitive effects. The greater the venture's likely anticompetitive effects, the greater must be the venture's likely efficiencies. In certain circumstances, efficiencies can be substantial because of the need to spread the cost of expensive equipment over a large number of patients and the potential for improvements in

---

competitive harm, the step-by-step analysis described in the text below will not be necessary. For example, when two hospitals propose to merge existing expensive health care equipment into a joint venture in a properly defined market in which many other hospitals or other health care facilities operate the same equipment, such that the market will be unconcentrated, then the combination is unlikely to be anticompetitive and further analysis ordinarily would not be required. *See* DEPARTMENT OF JUSTICE/FEDERAL TRADE COMMISSION 1992 HORIZONTAL MERGER GUIDELINES.

7.   If steps one and two reveal no competitive concerns with the joint venture, step three is unnecessary, and the analysis continues with step four described below.

quality to occur as providers gain experience and skill from performing a larger number of procedures.

Step four: Evaluate collateral agreements. This step examines whether the joint venture includes collateral agreements or conditions that unreasonably restrict competition and are unlikely to contribute significantly to the legitimate purposes of the joint venture. The Agencies will examine whether the collateral agreements are reasonably necessary to achieve the efficiencies sought by the joint venture. For example, if the participants in a joint venture formed to purchase a mobile lithotripter also agreed on the daily room rate to be charged lithotripsy patients who required overnight hospitalization, this collateral agreement as to room rates would not be necessary to achieve the benefits of the lithotripter joint venture. Although the joint venture itself would be legal, the collateral agreement on hospital room rates would not be legal and would be subject to challenge.

C.   *Examples of Hospital High-Technology Joint Ventures*

The following are examples of hospital joint ventures that are unlikely to raise significant antitrust concerns. Each is intended to demonstrate an aspect of the analysis that would be used to evaluate the venture.

1.   NEW EQUIPMENT THAT CAN BE OFFERED ONLY BY A JOINT VENTURE

All the hospitals in a relevant market agree that they jointly will purchase, operate and market a helicopter to provide emergency transportation for patients. The community's need for the helicopter is not great enough to justify having more than one helicopter operating in the area and studies of similarly sized communities indicate that a second helicopter service could not be supported. This joint venture falls within the antitrust safety zone. It would make available a service that would not otherwise be available, and for which duplication would be inefficient.

2.   JOINT VENTURE TO PURCHASE EXPENSIVE EQUIPMENT

All five hospitals in a relevant market agree to jointly purchase a mobile health care device that provides a service for which consumers have no reasonable alternatives. The hospitals will share equally in the cost of maintaining the equipment, and the equipment will travel from one hospital to another and be available one day each week at each hospital. The hospitals' agreement contains no provisions for joint marketing of, and protects against exchanges of competitively sensitive information regarding, the equipment.[8] There are also no limitations on the prices that each hospital will charge for use of the equipment, on the number of procedures that each hospital can perform, or on each hospital's ability to purchase the equipment on its own. Although any combination of two of the hospitals could afford to purchase the equipment and recover their costs within the equipment's useful life, patient volume from all five hospitals is required to maximize the efficient use of the equipment and lead to significant cost savings. In addition, patient demand would be satisfied by provision of the equipment one day each week

---

8.   Examples of such information include prices and marketing plans.

at each hospital. The joint venture would result in higher use of the equipment, thus lowering the cost per patient and potentially improving quality.

This joint venture does not fall within the antitrust safety zone because smaller groups of hospitals could afford to purchase and operate the equipment and recover their costs. Therefore, the joint venture would be analyzed under the rule of reason. The first step is to define the relevant market. In this example, the relevant market consists of the services provided by the equipment, and the five hospitals all potentially compete against each other for patients requiring this service.

The second step in the analysis is to determine the competitive effects of the joint venture. Because the joint venture is likely to reduce the number of these health care devices in the market, there is a potential restraint on competition. The restraint would not be substantial, however, for several reasons. First, the joint venture is limited to the purchase of the equipment and would not eliminate competition among the hospitals in the provision of the services. The hospitals will market the services independently, and will not exchange competitively sensitive information. In addition, the venture does not preclude a hospital from purchasing another unit should the demand for these services increase.

Because the joint venture raises some competitive concerns, however, it is necessary to examine the potential efficiencies associated with the venture. As noted above, by sharing the equipment among the five hospitals significant cost savings can be achieved. The joint venture would produce substantial efficiencies while providing access to high quality care. Thus, this joint venture would on balance benefit consumers since it would not lessen competition substantially, and it would allow the hospitals to serve the community's need in a more efficient manner. Finally, in this example the joint venture does not involve any collateral agreements that raise competitive concerns. On these facts, the joint venture would not be challenged by the Agencies.

3.   JOINT VENTURE OF EXISTING EXPENSIVE EQUIPMENT WHERE
       ONE OF THE HOSPITALS IN THE VENTURE ALREADY
       OWNS THE EQUIPMENT

Metropolis has three hospitals and a population of 300,000. Mercy and University Hospitals each own and operate their own magnetic resonance imaging device ("MRI"). General Hospital does not. Three independent physician clinics also own and operate MRIs. All of the existing MRIs have similar capabilities. The acquisition of an MRI is not subject to review under a certificate of need law in the state in which Metropolis is located.

Managed care plans have told General Hospital that, unless it can provide MRI services, it will be a less attractive contracting partner than the other two hospitals in town. The five existing MRIs are slightly underutilized—that is, the average cost per scan could be reduced if utilization of the machines increased. There is insufficient demand in Metropolis for six fully-utilized MRIs.

General has considered purchasing its own MRI so that it can compete on equal terms with Mercy and University Hospitals. However, it has decided based on its analysis of demand for MRI services and the cost of acquiring and operating the equipment that it would be better to share the equipment with another hospital.

General proposes forming a joint venture in which it will purchase a 50 percent share in Mercy's MRI, and the two hospitals will work out an arrangement by which each hospital has equal access to the MRI. Each hospital in the joint venture will independently market and set prices for those MRI services, and the joint venture agreement protects against exchanges of competitively sensitive information among the hospitals. There is no restriction on the ability of each hospital to purchase its own equipment.

The proposed joint venture does not fall within the antitrust safety zone because General apparently could independently support the purchase and operation of its own MRI. Accordingly, the Agencies would analyze the joint venture under a rule of reason.

The first step of the rule of reason analysis is defining the relevant product and geographic markets. Assuming there are no good substitutes for MRI services, the relevant product market in this case is MRI services. Most patients currently receiving MRI services are unwilling to travel outside of Metropolis for those services, so the relevant geographic market is Metropolis. Mercy, University, and the three physician clinics are already offering MRI services in this market. Because General intends to offer MRI services within the next year, even if there is no joint venture, it is viewed as a market participant.

The second step is determining the competitive impact of the joint venture. Absent the joint venture, there would have been six independent MRIs in the market. This raises some competitive concerns with the joint venture. The fact that the joint venture will not entail joint price setting or marketing of MRI services to purchasers reduces the venture's potential anticompetitive effect. The competitive analysis would also consider the likelihood of additional entry in the market. If, for example, another physician clinic is likely to purchase an MRI in the event that the price of MRI services were to increase, any anticompetitive effect from the joint venture becomes less likely. Entry may be more likely in Metropolis than other areas because new entrants are not required to obtain certificates of need.

The third step of the analysis is assessing the likely efficiencies associated with the joint venture. The magnitude of any likely anticompetitive effects associated with the joint venture is important; the greater the venture's likely anticompetitive effects, the greater must be the venture's likely efficiencies. In this instance, the joint venture will avoid the costly duplication associated with General purchasing an MRI, and will allow Mercy to reduce the average cost of operating its MRI by increasing the number of procedures done. The competition between the Mercy/General venture and the other MRI providers in the market will provide some incentive for the joint venture to operate the MRI in as low-cost a manner as possible. Thus, there are efficiencies associated with the joint venture that could not be achieved in a less restrictive manner.

The final step of the analysis is determining whether the joint venture has any collateral agreements or conditions that reduce competition and are not reasonably necessary to achieve the efficiencies sought by the venture. For example, if the joint venture required managed care plans desiring MRI services to contract with both joint venture participants for those services, that condition would be viewed as anticompetitive and unnecessary to achieve the legitimate procompetitive goals of the joint venture. This example does not include any unnecessary collateral restraints.

On balance, when weighing the likelihood that the joint venture will significantly reduce competition for these services against its potential to result in efficiencies, the Agencies would view this joint venture favorably under a rule of reason analysis.

4.   JOINT VENTURE OF EXISTING EQUIPMENT WHERE BOTH HOSPITALS
      IN THE VENTURE ALREADY OWN THE EQUIPMENT

Valley Town has a population of 30,000 and is located in a valley surrounded by mountains. The closest urbanized area is over 75 miles away. There are two hospitals in Valley Town: Valley Medical Center and St. Mary's. Valley Medical Center offers a full range of primary and secondary services. St. Mary's offers primary and some secondary services. Although both hospitals have a CT scanner, Valley Medical Center's scanner is more sophisticated. Because of its greater sophistication, Valley Medical Center's scanner is more expensive to operate, and can conduct fewer scans in a day. A physician clinic in Valley Town operates a third CT scanner that is comparable to St. Mary's scanner and is not fully utilized.

Valley Medical Center has found that many of the scans that it conducts do not require the sophisticated features of its scanner. Because scans on its machine take so long, and so many patients require scans, Valley Medical Center also is experiencing significant scheduling problems. St. Mary's scanner, on the other hand, is underutilized, partially because many individuals go to Valley Medical Center because they need the more sophisticated scans that only Valley Medical Center's scanner can provide. Despite the underutilization of St. Mary's scanner, and the higher costs of Valley Medical Center's scanner, neither hospital has any intention of discontinuing its CT services.

Valley Medical Center and St. Mary's are proposing a joint venture that would own and operate both hospitals' CT scanners. The two hospitals will then independently market and set the prices they charge for those services, and the joint venture agreement protects against exchanges of competitively sensitive information between the hospitals. There is no restriction on the ability of each hospital to purchase its own equipment.

The proposed joint venture does not qualify under the Agencies' safety zone because the participating hospitals can independently support their own equipment. Accordingly, the Agencies would analyze the joint venture under a rule of reason. The first step of the analysis is to determine the relevant product and geographic markets. As long as other diagnostic services such as conventional X-rays or MRI scans are not viewed as a good substitute for CT scans, the relevant product market is CT scans. If patients currently receiving CT scans in Valley Town would be unlikely to switch to providers offering CT scans outside of Valley Town in the event that the price of CT scans in Valley Town increased by a small but significant amount, the relevant geographic market is Valley Town. There are three participants in this relevant market: Valley Medical Center, St. Mary's, and the physician clinic.

The second step of the analysis is determining the competitive effect of the joint venture. Because the joint venture does not entail joint pricing or marketing of CT services, the joint venture does not effectively reduce the number of market participants. This reduces the venture's potential anticompetitive effect. In fact, by increasing the scope of the CT services that each hospital can provide, the joint venture may increase competition between Valley Medical Center and St. Mary's since now both hospitals can provide sophisticated scans. Competitive concerns with this joint venture would be further ameliorated if other health care providers were likely to acquire CT scanners in response to a price increase following the formation of the joint venture.

The third step is assessing whether the efficiencies associated with the joint venture outweigh any anticompetitive effect associated with the joint venture. This joint venture will allow both hospitals to make either the sophisticated CT scanner or the less sophisticated, but less costly, CT scanner available to patients at those hospitals.

Thus, the joint venture should increase quality of care by allowing for better utilization and scheduling of the equipment, while also reducing the cost of providing that care, thereby benefitting the community. The joint venture may also increase quality of care by making more capacity available to Valley Medical Center; while Valley Medical Center faced capacity constraints prior to the joint venture, it can now take advantage of St. Mary's underutilized CT scanner. The joint venture will also improve access by allowing patients requiring routine scans to be moved from the sophisticated scanner at Valley Medical Center to St. Mary's scanner where the scans can be performed more quickly.

The last step of the analysis is to determine whether there are any collateral agreements or conditions associated with the joint venture that reduce competition and are not reasonably necessary to achieve the efficiencies sought by the joint venture. Assuming there are no such agreements or conditions, the Agencies would view this joint venture favorably under a rule of reason analysis.

As noted in the previous example, excluding price setting and marketing from the scope of the joint venture reduces the probability and magnitude of any anticompetitive effect of the joint venture, and thus reduces the likelihood that the Agencies will find the joint venture to be anticompetitive. If joint price setting and marketing were, however, a part of that joint venture, the Agencies would have to determine whether the cost savings and quality improvements associated with the joint venture offset the loss of competition between the two hospitals.

Also, if neither of the hospitals in Valley Town had a CT scanner, and they proposed a similar joint venture for the purchase of two CT scanners, one sophisticated and one less sophisticated, the Agencies would be unlikely to view that joint venture as anticompetitive, even though each hospital could independently support the purchase of its own CT scanner. This conclusion would be based upon a rule of reason analysis that was virtually identical to the one described above.

* * *

Hospitals that are considering high-technology or other expensive equipment joint ventures and are unsure of the legality of their conduct under the antitrust laws can take advantage of the Department's expedited business review procedure for joint ventures and information exchanges announced on December 1, 1992 (58 Fed. Reg. 6132 (1993)) or the Federal Trade Commission's advisory opinion procedure contained at 16 C.F.R. §§ 1.1-1.4 (1993). The Agencies will respond to a business review or advisory opinion request on behalf of hospitals that are considering a high-technology joint venture within 90 days after all necessary information is submitted. The Department's December 1, 1992 announcement contains specific guidance as to the information that should be submitted.

3.   Statement of Department of Justice and Federal Trade Commission Enforcement Policy on Hospital Joint Ventures Involving Specialized Clinical or Other Expensive Health Care Services

Introduction

Most hospital joint ventures to provide specialized clinical or other expensive health care services do not create antitrust problems. The Agencies have never challenged an integrated joint venture among hospitals to provide a specialized clinical or other expensive health care service.

Many hospitals wish to enter into joint ventures to offer these services because the development of these services involves investments—such as the recruitment and training of specialized personnel—that a single hospital may not be able to support. In many cases, these collaborative activities could create procompetitive efficiencies that benefit consumers, including the provision of services at a lower cost or the provision of a service that would not have been provided absent the joint venture. Sound antitrust enforcement policy distinguishes those joint ventures that on balance benefit the public from those that may increase prices without providing a countervailing benefit, and seeks to prevent only those that are harmful to consumers.

This statement of enforcement policy sets forth the Agencies' antitrust analysis of joint ventures between hospitals to provide specialized clinical or other expensive health care services and includes an example of its application to such ventures. It does not include a safety zone for such ventures since the Agencies believe that they must acquire more expertise in evaluating the cost of, demand for, and potential benefits from such joint ventures before they can articulate a meaningful safety zone. The absence of a safety zone for such collaborative activities does not imply that they create any greater antitrust risk than other types of collaborative activities.

A.   The Agencies' Analysis of Hospital Joint Ventures Involving Specialized Clinical or Other Expensive Health Care Services

The Agencies apply a rule of reason analysis in their antitrust review of hospital joint ventures involving specialized clinical or other expensive health care services.[9] The objective of this analysis is to determine whether the joint venture may reduce competition substantially, and if it might, whether it is likely to produce procompetitive efficiencies that outweigh its anticompetitive potential. This analysis is flexible and takes into account the nature and effect of the joint venture, the characteristics of the services involved and of the hospital industry generally, and the

---

9.   This statement assumes that the joint venture is not likely merely to restrict competition and decrease output. For example, if two hospitals that both profitably provide open heart surgery and a burn unit simply agree without entering into an integrated joint venture that in the future each of the services will be offered exclusively at only one of the hospitals, the agreement would be viewed as an illegal market allocation.

reasons for, and purposes of, the venture. It also allows for consideration of efficiencies that will result from the venture. The steps involved in a rule of reason analysis are set forth below.[10]

Step one: Define the relevant market. The rule of reason analysis first identifies the service that is produced through the joint venture. The relevant product and geographic markets that include the service are then properly defined. This process seeks to identify any other provider that could offer a service that patients or physicians generally would consider a good substitute for that provided by the joint venture. Thus, if a joint venture were to produce intensive care neonatology services, the relevant market would include only other neonatal intensive care nurseries that patients or physicians would view as reasonable alternatives.

Step two: Evaluate the competitive effects of the venture. This step begins with an analysis of the structure of the relevant market. If many providers compete with the joint venture, competitive harm is unlikely and the analysis would continue with step four described below. If the structural analysis of the relevant market showed that the joint venture would eliminate an existing or potentially viable competing provider of a service and that there were few competing providers of that service, or that cooperation in the joint venture market might spill over into a market in which the parties to the joint venture are competitors, it then would be necessary to assess the extent of the potential anticompetitive effects of the joint venture. In addition to the number and size of competing providers, factors that could restrain the ability of the joint venture to act anticompetitively either unilaterally or through collusive agreements with other providers would include: (1) characteristics of the market that make anticompetitive coordination unlikely; (2) the likelihood that others would enter the market; and (3) the effects of government regulation.

The extent to which the joint venture restricts competition among the hospitals participating in the venture is evaluated during this step. In some cases, a joint venture to provide a specialized clinical or other expensive health care service may not substantially limit competition. For example, if the only two hospitals providing primary and secondary acute care inpatient services in a relevant geographic market for such services were to form a joint venture to provide a tertiary service, they would continue to compete on primary and secondary services. Because the geographic market for a tertiary service may in certain cases be larger than the geographic market for primary or secondary services, the hospitals may also face substantial competition for the joint-ventured tertiary service.[11]

Step three: Evaluate the impact of procompetitive efficiencies. This step requires an examination of the joint venture's potential to create procompetitive efficiencies, and the balancing of these efficiencies against any potential anticompetitive effects. The greater the venture's likely anticompetitive effects, the greater must be the venture's likely efficiencies. In certain circumstances, efficiencies can be substantial because of the need to spread the cost of the investment associated with the recruitment and training of personnel over a large

---

10.   Many joint venturers that could provide substantial efficiencies also may present little likelihood of competitive harm. Where it is clear initially that any joint venture presents little likelihood of competitive harm, it will not be necessary to complete all steps in the analysis to conclude that the joint venture should not be challenged. *See* note 7, above.

11.   If steps one and two reveal no competitive concerns with the joint venture, step three is unnecessary, and the analysis continues with step four described below.

number of patients and the potential for improvement in quality to occur as providers gain experience and skill from performing a larger number of procedures. In the case of certain specialized clinical services, such as open heart surgery, the joint venture may permit the program to generate sufficient patient volume to meet well-accepted minimum standards for assuring quality and patient safety.

Step four: Evaluate collateral agreements. This step examines whether the joint venture includes collateral agreements or conditions that unreasonably restrict competition and are unlikely to contribute significantly to the legitimate purposes of the joint venture. The Agencies will examine whether the collateral agreements are reasonably necessary to achieve the efficiencies sought by the venture. For example, if the participants in a joint venture to provide highly sophisticated oncology services were to agree on the prices to be charged for all radiology services regardless of whether the services are provided to patients undergoing oncology radiation therapy, this collateral agreement as to radiology services for non-oncology patients would be unnecessary to achieve the benefits of the sophisticated oncology joint venture. Although the joint venture itself would be legal, the collateral agreement would not be legal and would be subject to challenge.

B.   Example—Hospital Joint Venture for New Specialized Clinical Service Not Involving Purchase of High-Technology or Other Expensive Health Care Equipment

Midvale has a population of about 75,000, and is geographically isolated in a rural part of its state. Midvale has two general acute care hospitals, Community Hospital and Religious Hospital, each of which performs a mix of basic primary, secondary, and some tertiary care services. The two hospitals have largely non-overlapping medical staffs. Neither hospital currently offers open-heart surgery services, nor has plans to do so on its own. Local residents, physicians, employers, and hospital managers all believe that Midvale has sufficient demand to support one local open-heart surgery unit.

The two hospitals in Midvale propose a joint venture whereby they will share the costs of recruiting a cardiac surgery team and establishing an open-heart surgery program, to be located at one of the hospitals. Patients will be referred to the program from both hospitals, who will share expenses and revenues of the program. The hospitals' agreement protects against exchanges of competitively sensitive information.

As stated above, the Agencies would analyze such a joint venture under a rule of reason. The first step of the rule of reason analysis is defining the relevant product and geographic markets. The relevant product market in this case is open-heart surgery services, because there are no reasonable alternatives for patients needing such surgery. The relevant geographic market may be limited to Midvale. Although patients now travel to distant hospitals for open-heart surgery, it is significantly more costly for patients to obtain surgery from them than from a provider located in Midvale. Physicians, patients, and purchasers believe that after the open heart surgery program is operational, most Midvale residents will choose to receive these services locally.

The second step is determining the competitive impact of the joint venture. Here, the joint venture does not eliminate any existing competition, because neither of the two hospitals previously was providing open-heart surgery. Nor does the joint venture eliminate any potential competition, because there is insufficient patient volume for more than one viable open-heart surgery program. Thus, only one such program could exist in Midvale, regardless of whether it was established unilaterally or through a joint venture.

Normally, the third step in the rule of reason analysis would be to assess the procompetitive effects of, and likely efficiencies associated with, the joint venture. In this instance, this step is unnecessary, since the analysis has concluded under step two that the joint venture will not result in any significant anticompetitive effects.

The final step of the analysis is to determine whether the joint venture has any collateral agreements or conditions that reduce competition and are not reasonably necessary to achieve the efficiencies sought by the venture. The joint venture does not appear to involve any such agreements or conditions; it does not eliminate or reduce competition between the two hospitals for any other services, or impose any conditions on use of the open-heart surgery program that would affect other competition.

Because the joint venture described above is unlikely significantly to reduce competition among hospitals for open-heart surgery services, and will in fact increase the services available to consumers, the Agencies would view this joint venture favorably under a rule of reason analysis.

* * *

Hospitals that are considering specialized clinical or other expensive health care services joint ventures and are unsure of the legality of their conduct under the antitrust laws can take advantage of the Department of Justice's expedited business review procedure announced on December 1, 1992 (58 Fed. Reg. 6132 (1993)) or the Federal Trade Commission's advisory opinion procedure contained at 16 C.F.R. §§ 1.1-1.4 (1993). The Agencies will respond to a business review or advisory opinion request on behalf of hospitals that are considering jointly providing such services within 90 days after all necessary information is submitted. The Department's December 1, 1992 announcement contains specific guidance as to the information that should be submitted.

4. Statement of Department of Justice and Federal Trade Commission Enforcement Policy on Providers' Collective Provision of Non-Fee-Related Information to Purchasers of Health Care Services

Introduction

The collective provision of non-fee-related information by competing health care providers to a purchaser in an effort to influence the terms upon which the purchaser deals with the providers does not necessarily raise antitrust concerns. Generally, providers' collective provision of certain types of information to a purchaser is likely either to raise little risk of anticompetitive effects or to provide procompetitive benefits.

This statement sets forth an antitrust safety zone that describes providers' collective provision of non-fee-related information that will not be challenged by the Agencies under the antitrust laws, absent extraordinary circumstances.[12]   It also describes conduct that is expressly excluded from the antitrust safety zone.

A.   Antitrust Safety Zone: Providers' Collective Provision of Non-Fee-Related Information That Will Not Be Challenged, Absent Extraordinary Circumstances, by the Agencies

Providers' collective provision of underlying medical data that may improve purchasers' resolution of issues relating to the mode, quality, or efficiency of treatment is unlikely to raise any significant antitrust concern and will not be challenged by the Agencies, absent extraordinary circumstances. Thus, the Agencies will not challenge, absent extraordinary circumstances, a medical society's collection of outcome data from its members about a particular procedure that they believe should be covered by a purchaser and the provision of such information to the purchaser.   The Agencies also will not challenge, absent extraordinary circumstances, providers' development of suggested practice parameters—standards for patient management developed to assist providers in clinical decisionmaking— that also may provide useful information to patients, providers, and purchasers. Because providers' collective provision of such information poses little risk of restraining competition and may help in the development of protocols that increase quality and efficiency, the Agencies will not challenge such activity, absent extraordinary circumstances.

In the course of providing underlying medical data, providers may collectively engage in discussions with purchasers about the scientific merit of that data. However, the antitrust safety zone excludes any attempt by providers to coerce a purchaser's decisionmaking by implying or threatening a boycott of any plan that does not follow the providers' joint recommendation. Providers who collectively threaten to or actually refuse to deal with a purchaser because they object to the purchaser's administrative, clinical, or other terms governing the provision of services run a substantial antitrust risk. For example, providers' collective refusal to provide X-rays to a purchaser that seeks them before covering a particular treatment regimen would constitute an antitrust violation.   Similarly, providers' collective attempt to force purchasers to adopt recommended practice parameters by threatening to or actually boycotting purchasers that refuse to accept their joint recommendation also would risk antitrust challenge.

* * *

Competing providers who are considering jointly providing non-fee-related information to a purchaser and are unsure of the legality of their conduct under the

---

12.   This statement addresses only providers' collective activities. As a general proposition, providers acting individually may provide any information to any purchaser without incurring liability under federal antitrust law. This statement also does not address the collective provision of information through an integrated joint venture or the exchange of information that necessarily occurs among providers involved in legitimate joint venture activities. Those activities generally do not raise antitrust concerns.

antitrust laws can take advantage of the Department of Justice's expedited business review procedure announced on December 1, 1992 (58 Fed. Reg. 6132 (1993)) or the Federal Trade Commission's advisory opinion procedure contained at 16 C.F.R. §§ 1.1-1.4 (1993). The Agencies will respond to a business review or advisory opinion request on behalf of providers who are considering jointly providing such information within 90 days after all necessary information is submitted. The Department's December 1, 1992 announcement contains specific guidance as to the information that should be submitted.

5.   **Statement of Department of Justice and Federal Trade Commission Enforcement Policy on Providers' Collective Provision of Fee-Related Information to Purchasers of Health Care Services**

Introduction

The collective provision by competing health care providers to purchasers of health care services of factual information concerning the fees charged currently or in the past for the providers' services, and other factual information concerning the amounts, levels, or methods of fees or reimbursement, does not necessarily raise antitrust concerns. With reasonable safeguards, providers' collective provision of this type of factual information to a purchaser of health care services may provide procompetitive benefits and raise little risk of anticompetitive effects.

This statement sets forth an antitrust safety zone that describes collective provision of fee-related information that will not be challenged by the Agencies under the antitrust laws, absent extraordinary circumstances.[13] It also describes types of conduct that are expressly excluded from the antitrust safety zone, some clearly unlawful, and others that may be lawful depending on the circumstances.

A.   *Antitrust Safety Zone: Providers' Collective Provision of Fee-Related Information That Will Not Be Challenged, Absent Extraordinary Circumstances, by the Agencies*

Providers' collective provision to purchasers of health care services of factual information concerning the providers' current or historical fees or other aspects of reimbursement, such as discounts or alternative reimbursement methods accepted (including capitation arrangements, risk-withhold fee arrangements, or use of all-inclusive fees), is unlikely to raise significant antitrust concern and will not be challenged by the Agencies, absent extraordinary circumstances. Such factual information can help purchasers efficiently develop reimbursement terms to be

---

13.   This statement addresses only providers' collective activities. As a general proposition, providers acting individually may provide any information to any purchaser without incurring liability under federal antitrust law. This statement also does not address the collective provision of information through an integrated joint venture or the exchange of information that necessarily occurs among providers involved in legitimate joint venture activities. Those activities generally do not raise antitrust concerns.

offered to providers and may be useful to a purchaser when provided in response to a request from the purchaser or at the initiative of providers.

In assembling information to be collectively provided to purchasers, providers need to be aware of the potential antitrust consequences of information exchanges among competitors. The principles expressed in the Agencies' statement on provider participation in exchanges of price and cost information are applicable in this context. Accordingly, in order to qualify for this safety zone, the collection of information to be provided to purchasers must satisfy the following conditions:

(1) the collection is managed by a third party (e.g., a purchaser, government agency, health care consultant, academic institution, or trade association);

(2) although current fee-related information may be provided to purchasers, any information that is shared among or is available to the competing providers furnishing the data must be more than three months old; and

(3) for any information that is available to the providers furnishing data, there are at least five providers reporting data upon which each disseminated statistic is based, no individual provider's data may represent more than 25 percent on a weighted basis of that statistic, and any information disseminated must be sufficiently aggregated such that it would not allow recipients to identify the prices charged by any individual provider.

The conditions that must be met for an information exchange among providers to fall within the antitrust safety zone are intended to ensure that an exchange of price or cost data is not used by competing providers for discussion or coordination of provider prices or costs. They represent a careful balancing of a provider's individual interest in obtaining information useful in adjusting the prices it charges or the wages it pays in response to changing market conditions against the risk that the exchange of such information may permit competing providers to communicate with each other regarding a mutually acceptable level of prices for health care services or compensation for employees.

B.   The Agencies' Analysis of Providers' Collective Provision of Fee-Related Information That Falls outside the Antitrust Safety Zone

The safety zone set forth in this policy statement does not apply to collective negotiations between unintegrated providers and purchasers in contemplation or in furtherance of any agreement among the providers on fees or other terms or aspects of reimbursement,[14] or to any agreement among unintegrated providers to deal with purchasers only on agreed terms. Providers also may not collectively threaten, implicitly or explicitly, to engage in a boycott or similar conduct, or actually undertake such a boycott or conduct, to coerce any purchaser to accept collectively-determined fees or other terms or aspects of reimbursement. These types

---

14.   Whether communications between providers and purchasers will amount to negotiations depends on the nature and context of the communications, not solely the number of such communications.

of conduct likely would violate the antitrust laws and, in many instances, might be per se illegal.

Also excluded from the safety zone is providers' collective provision of information or views concerning prospective fee-related matters. In some circumstances, the collective provision of this type of fee-related information also may be helpful to a purchaser and, as long as independent decisions on whether to accept a purchaser's offer are truly preserved, may not raise antitrust concerns. However, in other circumstances, the collective provision of prospective fee-related information or views may evidence or facilitate an agreement on prices or other competitively significant terms by the competing providers. It also may exert a coercive effect on the purchaser by implying or threatening a collective refusal to deal on terms other than those proposed, or amount to an implied threat to boycott any plan that does not follow the providers' collective proposal.

The Agencies recognize the need carefully to distinguish possibly procompetitive collective provision of prospective fee-related information or views from anticompetitive situations that involve unlawful price agreements, boycott threats, refusals to deal except on collectively determined terms, collective negotiations, or conduct that signals or facilitates collective price terms. Therefore, the collective provision of such prospective fee-related information or views will be assessed on a case-by-case basis. In their case-by-case analysis, the Agencies will look at all the facts and circumstances surrounding the provision of the information, including, but not limited to, the nature of the information provided, the nature and extent of the communications among the providers and between the providers and the purchaser, the rationale for providing the information, and the nature of the market in which the information is provided.

In addition, because the collective provision of prospective fee-related information and views can easily lead to or accompany unlawful collective negotiations, price agreements, or the other types of collective conduct noted above, providers need to be aware of the potential antitrust consequences of information exchanges among competitors in assembling information or views concerning prospective fee-related matters. Consequently, such protections as the use of a third party to manage the collection of information and views, and the adoption of mechanisms to assure that the information is not disseminated or used in a manner that facilitates unlawful agreements or coordinated conduct by the providers, likely would reduce antitrust concerns.

* * *

Competing providers who are considering collectively providing fee-related information to purchasers, and are unsure of the legality of their conduct under the antitrust laws, can take advantage of the Department of Justice's expedited business review procedure announced on December 1, 1992 (58 Fed. Reg. 6132 (1993)) or the Federal Trade Commission's advisory opinion procedure contained at 16 C.F.R. §§ 1.1-1.4 (1993). The Agencies will respond to a business review or advisory opinion request on behalf of providers who are considering collectively providing fee-related information within 90 days after all necessary information is submitted. The Department's December 1, 1992 announcement contains specific guidance as to the information that should be submitted.

6.   Statement of Department of Justice and Federal Trade Commission Enforcement Policy on Provider Participation in Exchanges of Price and Cost Information

Introduction

Participation by competing providers in surveys of prices for health care services, or surveys of salaries, wages or benefits of personnel, does not necessarily raise antitrust concerns. In fact, such surveys can have significant benefits for health care consumers. Providers can use information derived from price and compensation surveys to price their services more competitively and to offer compensation that attracts highly qualified personnel. Purchasers can use price survey information to make more informed decisions when buying health care services. Without appropriate safeguards, however, information exchanges among competing providers may facilitate collusion or otherwise reduce competition on prices or compensation, resulting in increased prices, or reduced quality and availability of health care services. A collusive restriction on the compensation paid to health care employees, for example, could adversely affect the availability of health care personnel.

This statement sets forth an antitrust safety zone that describes exchanges of price and cost information among providers that will not be challenged by the Agencies under the antitrust laws, absent extraordinary circumstances. It also briefly describes the Agencies' antitrust analysis of information exchanges that fall outside the antitrust safety zone.

A.   *Antitrust Safety Zone: Exchanges of Price and Cost Information among Providers That Will Not Be Challenged, Absent Extraordinary Circumstances, by the Agencies*

The Agencies will not challenge, absent extraordinary circumstances, provider participation in written surveys of (a) prices for health care services,[15] or (b) wages, salaries, or benefits of health care personnel, if the following conditions are satisfied:

(1)   the survey is managed by a third-party (e.g, a purchaser, government agency, health care consultant, academic institution, or trade association);

(2)   the information provided by survey participants is based on data more than 3 months old; and

(3)   there are at least five providers reporting data upon which each disseminated statistic is based, no individual provider's data represents more than 25 percent on a weighted basis of that statistic, and any information disseminated is sufficiently aggregated such that it would not allow recipients to identify the prices charged or compensation paid by any particular provider.

The conditions that must be met for an information exchange among providers to fall within the antitrust safety zone are intended to ensure that an exchange of price or cost data is not used by competing providers for discussion or coordination of provider prices or costs. They represent a careful balancing of a provider's

---

15.   The "prices" at which providers offer their services to purchasers can take many forms, including billed charges for individual services, discounts off billed charges, or per diem, capitated, or diagnosis related group rates.

individual interest in obtaining information useful in adjusting the prices it charges or the wages it pays in response to changing market conditions against the risk that the exchange of such information may permit competing providers to communicate with each other regarding a mutually acceptable level of prices for health care services or compensation for employees.

B.   The Agencies' Analysis of Provider Exchanges of Information That Fall outside the Antitrust Safety Zone

Exchanges of price and cost information that fall outside the antitrust safety zone generally will be evaluated to determine whether the information exchange may have an anticompetitive effect that outweighs any procompetitive justification for the exchange. Depending on the circumstances, public, non-provider initiated surveys may not raise competitive concerns. Such surveys could allow purchasers to have useful information that they can use for procompetitive purposes.

Exchanges of future prices for provider services or future compensation of employees are very likely to be considered anticompetitive. If an exchange among competing providers of price or cost information results in an agreement among competitors as to the prices for health care services or the wages to be paid to health care employees, that agreement will be considered unlawful per se.

* * *

Competing providers that are considering participating in a survey of price or cost information and are unsure of the legality of their conduct under the antitrust laws can take advantage of the Department's expedited business review procedure announced on December 1, 1992 (58 Fed. Reg. 6132 (1993)) or the Federal Trade Commission's advisory opinion procedure contained at 16 C.F.R. §§ 1.1-1.4 (1993). The Agencies will respond to a business review or advisory opinion request on behalf of providers who are considering participating in a survey of price or cost information within 90 days after all necessary information is submitted. The Department's December 1, 1992 announcement contains specific guidance as to the information that should be submitted.

7.   Statement of Department of Justice and Federal Trade Commission Enforcement Policy on Joint Purchasing Arrangements among Health Care Providers

Introduction

Most joint purchasing arrangements among hospitals or other health care providers do not raise antitrust concerns. Such collaborative activities typically allow the participants to achieve efficiencies that will benefit consumers. Joint purchasing arrangements usually involve the purchase of a product or service used in providing the ultimate package of health care services or products sold by the participants. Examples include the purchase of laundry or food services by hospitals, the purchase of computer or data processing services by hospitals or other groups of providers, and the purchase of prescription drugs and other pharmaceutical products. Through such joint purchasing arrangements, the participants frequently can obtain volume discounts, reduce transaction costs, and have access to consulting advice that may not be available to each participant on its own.

Joint purchasing arrangements are unlikely to raise antitrust concerns unless (1) the arrangement accounts for so large a portion of the purchases of a product or service that it can effectively exercise market power[16] in the purchase of the product or service, or (2) the products or services being purchased jointly account for so large a proportion of the total cost of the services being sold by the participants that the joint purchasing arrangement may facilitate price fixing or otherwise reduce competition. If neither factor is present, the joint purchasing arrangement will not present competitive concerns.[17]

This statement sets forth an antitrust safety zone that describes joint purchasing arrangements among health care providers that will not be challenged, absent extraordinary circumstances, by the Agencies under the antitrust laws. It also describes factors that mitigate any competitive concerns with joint purchasing arrangements that fall outside the antitrust safety zone.[18]

A. Antitrust Safety Zone: Joint Purchasing Arrangements among Health Care Providers That Will Not Be Challenged, Absent Extraordinary Circumstances, by the Agencies

The Agencies will not challenge, absent extraordinary circumstances, any joint purchasing arrangement among health care providers where two conditions are present: (1) the purchases account for less than 35 percent of the total sales of the purchased product or service in the relevant market; and (2) the cost of the products and services purchased jointly accounts for less than 20 percent of the total revenues from all products or services sold by each competing participant in the joint purchasing arrangement.

The first condition compares the purchases accounted for by a joint purchasing arrangement to the total purchases of the purchased product or service in the relevant market. Its purpose is to determine whether the joint purchasing arrangement might be able to drive down the price of the product or service being purchased below competitive levels. For example, a joint purchasing arrangement may account for all or most of the purchases of laundry services by hospitals in a particular market, but represent less than 35 percent of the purchases of all commercial laundry services in that market. Unless there are special costs that cannot be easily recovered associated with providing laundry services to hospitals, such a purchasing arrangement is not likely to force prices below competitive levels. The same principle applies to joint

---

16. In the case of a purchaser, this is the power to drive the price of goods or services purchased below competitive levels.

17. An agreement among purchasers that simply fixes the price that each purchaser will pay or offer to pay for a product or service is not a legitimate joint purchasing arrangement and is a per se antitrust violation. Legitimate joint purchasing arrangements provide some integration of purchasing functions to achieve efficiencies.

18. This statement applies to purchasing arrangements through which the participants acquire products or services for their own use, not arrangements in which the participants are jointly investing in equipment or providing a service. Joint ventures involving investment in equipment and the provision of services are discussed in separate policy statements.

purchasing arrangements for food services, data processing, and many other products and services.

The second condition addresses any possibility that a joint purchasing arrangement might result in standardized costs, thus facilitating price fixing or otherwise having anticompetitive effects. This condition applies only where some or all of the participants are direct competitors. For example, if a nationwide purchasing cooperative limits its membership to one hospital in each geographic area, there is not likely to be any concern about reduction of competition among its members. Even where a purchasing arrangement's membership includes hospitals or other health care providers that compete with one another, the arrangement is not likely to facilitate collusion if the goods and services being purchased jointly account for a small fraction of the final price of the services provided by the participants. In the health care field, it may be difficult to determine the specific final service in which the jointly purchased products are used, as well as the price at which that final service is sold.[19] Therefore, the Agencies will examine whether the cost of the products or services being purchased jointly accounts, in the aggregate, for less than 20 percent of the total revenues from all health care services of each competing participant.

B. *Factors Mitigating Competitive Concerns with Joint Purchasing Arrangements That Fall outside the Antitrust Safety Zone*

Joint purchasing arrangements among hospitals or other health care providers that fall outside the antitrust safety zone do not necessarily raise antitrust concerns. There are several safeguards that joint purchasing arrangements can adopt to mitigate concerns that might otherwise arise. First, antitrust concern is lessened if members are not required to use the arrangement for all their purchases of a particular product or service. Members can, however, be asked to commit to purchase a voluntarily specified amount through the arrangement so that a volume discount or other favorable contract can be negotiated. Second, where negotiations are conducted on behalf of the joint purchasing arrangement by an independent employee or agent who is not also an employee of a participant, antitrust risk is lowered. Third, the likelihood of anticompetitive communications is lessened where communications between the purchasing group and each individual participant are kept confidential, and not discussed with, or disseminated to, other participants.

These safeguards will reduce substantially, if not completely eliminate, use of the purchasing arrangement as a vehicle for discussing and coordinating the prices of health care services offered by the participants.[20] The adoption of these safeguards also will help demonstrate that the joint purchasing arrangement is intended to achieve economic efficiencies rather than to serve an anticompetitive purpose. Where there appear to be significant efficiencies from a joint purchasing arrangement, the Agencies will not challenge the arrangement absent substantial risk of anticompetitive effects.

---

19. This especially is true because some large purchasers negotiate prices with hospitals and other providers that encompass a group of services, while others pay separately for each service.

20. Obviously, if the members of a legitimate purchasing group engage in price fixing or other collusive anticompetitive conduct as to services sold by the participants, whether through the arrangement or independently, they remain subject to antitrust challenge.

The existence of a large number and variety of purchasing groups in the health care field suggests that entry barriers to forming new groups currently are not great. Thus, in most circumstances at present, it is not necessary to open a joint purchasing arrangement to all competitors in the market. However, if some competitors excluded from the arrangement are unable to compete effectively without access to the arrangement, and competition is thereby harmed, antitrust concerns will exist.

C.   *Example—Joint Purchasing Arrangement Involving Both Hospitals in Rural Community That the Agencies Would Not Challenge*

Smalltown is the county seat of Rural County. There are two general acute care hospitals, County Hospital ("County") and Smalltown Medical Center ("SMC"), both located in Smalltown. The nearest other hospitals are located in Big City, about 100 miles from Smalltown.

County and SMC propose to join a joint venture being formed by several of the hospitals in Big City through which they will purchase various hospital supplies— such as bandages, antiseptics, surgical gowns, and masks. The joint venture will likely be the vehicle for the purchase of most such products by the Smalltown hospitals, but under the joint venture agreement, both retain the option to purchase supplies independently.

The joint venture will be an independent corporation, jointly owned by the participating hospitals. It will purchase the supplies needed by the hospitals and then resell them to the hospitals at average variable cost plus a reasonable return on capital. The joint venture will periodically solicit from each participating hospital its expected needs for various hospital supplies, and negotiate the best terms possible for the combined purchases. It will also purchase supplies for its member hospitals on an ad hoc basis.

COMPETITIVE ANALYSIS

The first issue is whether the proposed joint purchasing arrangement would fall within the safety zone set forth in this policy statement. In order to make this determination, the Agencies would first inquire whether the joint purchases would account for less than 35 percent of the total sales of the purchased products in the relevant markets for the sales of those products. Here, the relevant hospital supply markets are likely to be national or at least regional in scope. Thus, while County and SMC might well account for more than 35 percent of the total sales of many hospital supplies in Smalltown or Rural County, they and the other hospitals in Big City that will participate in the arrangement together would likely not account for significant percentages of sales in the actual relevant markets. Thus, the first criterion for inclusion in the safety zone is likely to be satisfied.

The Agencies would then inquire whether the supplies to be purchased jointly account for less than 20 percent of the total revenues from all products and services sold by each of the competing hospitals that participate in the arrangement. In this case, County and SMC are competing hospitals, but this second criterion for inclusion in the safety zone is also likely to be satisfied, and the Agencies would not challenge the joint purchasing arrangement.

* * *

Hospitals or other health care providers that are considering joint purchasing arrangements and are unsure of the legality of their conduct under the antitrust laws can take advantage of the Department of Justice's expedited business review procedure for joint ventures and information exchanges announced on December 1, 1992 (58 Fed. Reg. 6132 (1993)) or the Federal Trade Commission's advisory opinion procedure contained at 16 C.F.R. §§ 1.1-1.4 (1993). The Agencies will respond to a business review or advisory opinion request on behalf of health care providers considering a joint purchasing arrangement within 90 days after all necessary information is submitted. The Department's December 1, 1992 announcement contains specific guidance as to the information that should be submitted.

8. Statement of Department of Justice and Federal Trade Commission Enforcement Policy on Physician Network Joint Ventures

Introduction

In recent years, health plans and other purchasers of health care services have developed a variety of managed care programs that seek to reduce the costs and assure the quality of health care services. Many physicians and physician groups have organized physician network joint ventures, such as individual practice associations ("IPAs"), preferred provider organizations ("PPOs"), and other arrangements to market their services to these plans.[21] Typically, such networks contract with the plans to provide physician services to plan subscribers at predetermined prices, and the physician participants in the networks agree to controls aimed at containing costs and assuring the appropriate and efficient provision of high quality physician services. By developing and implementing mechanisms that encourage physicians to collaborate in practicing efficiently as part of the network, many physician network joint ventures promise significant procompetitive benefits for consumers of health care services.

As used in this statement, a physician network joint venture is a physician-controlled venture in which the network's physician participants collectively agree on prices or price-related terms and jointly market their services.[22] Other types of health care network joint ventures are not directly addressed by this statement.[23]

---

21.   An IPA or PPO typically provides medical services to the subscribers of health plans but does not act as their insurer. In addition, an IPA or PPO does not require complete integration of the medical practices of its physician participants. Such physicians typically continue to compete fully for patients who are enrolled in health plans not served by the IPA or PPO, or who have indemnity insurance or pay for the physician's services directly "out of pocket."

22.   Although this statement refers to IPAs and PPOs as examples of physician network joint ventures, the Agencies' competitive analysis focuses on the substance of such arrangements, not on their formal titles. This policy statement applies, therefore, to all entities that are substantively equivalent to the physician network joint ventures described in this statement.

23.   The physician network joint ventures discussed in this statement are one type of the multiprovider network joint ventures discussed below in the Agencies' Statement of Enforcement Policy on

This statement of enforcement policy describes the Agencies' antitrust analysis of physician network joint ventures, and presents several examples of its application to specific hypothetical physician network joint ventures. Before describing the general antitrust analysis, the statement sets forth antitrust safety zones that describe physician network joint ventures that are highly unlikely to raise substantial competitive concerns, and therefore will not be challenged by the Agencies under the antitrust laws, absent extraordinary circumstances.

The Agencies emphasize that merely because a physician network joint venture does not come within a safety zone in no way indicates that it is unlawful under the antitrust laws. On the contrary, such arrangements may be procompetitive and lawful, and many such arrangements have received favorable business review letters or advisory opinions from the Agencies.[24] The safety zones use a few factors that are relatively easy to apply, to define a category of ventures for which the Agencies presume no anticompetitive harm, without examining competitive conditions in the particular case. A determination about the lawfulness of physician network joint ventures that fall outside the safety zones must be made on a case-by-case basis according to general antitrust principles and the more specific analysis described in this statement.

A.   Antitrust Safety Zones

This section describes those physician network joint ventures that will fall within the antitrust safety zones designated by the Agencies. The antitrust safety zones differ for "exclusive" and "non-exclusive" physician network joint ventures. In an "exclusive" venture, the network's physician participants are restricted in their ability to, or do not in practice, individually contract or affiliate with other network joint ventures or health plans. In a "non-exclusive" venture, on the other hand, the physician participants in fact do, or are available to, affiliate with other networks or contract individually with health plans. This section explains how the Agencies will determine whether a physician network joint venture is exclusive or non-exclusive. It also illustrates types of arrangements that can involve the sharing of substantial

---

Multiprovider Networks. That statement also covers other types of networks, such as networks that include both hospitals and physicians, and networks involving non-physician health professionals. In addition, that statement, and Example 7 of this statement, address networks that do not include agreements among competitors on prices or price-related terms, through use of various "messenger model" arrangements. Many of the issues relating to physician network joint ventures are the same as those that arise and are addressed in connection with multiprovider networks generally, and the analysis often will be very similar for all such arrangements.

24.   For example, the Agencies have approved a number of non-exclusive physician or provider networks in which the percentage of participating physicians or providers in the market exceeded the 30% criterion of the safety zone. See, e.g., Letter from Anne K. Bingaman, Assistant Attorney General, Department of Justice, to John F. Fischer (Oklahoma Physicians Network, Inc.) (Jan. 17, 1996) ("substantially more" than 30% of several specialties in a number of local markets, including more than 50% in one specialty); Letter from Anne K. Bingaman to Melissa J. Fields (Dermnet, Inc.) (Dec. 5, 1995) (44% of board-certified dermatologists); Letter from Anne K. Bingaman to Dee Hartzog (International Chiropractor's Association of California) (Oct. 27, 1994) (up to 50% of chiropractors); Letter from Mark Horoschak, Assistant Director, Federal Trade Commission, to Stephen P. Nash (Eastern Ohio Physicians Organization) (Sept. 28, 1995) (safety zone's 30% criterion exceeded for primary care physicians by a small amount, and for certain subspecialty fields "to a greater extent"); Letter from Mark Horoschak to John A. Cook (Oakland Physician Network) (Mar. 28, 1995) (multispecialty network with 44% of physicians in one specialty).

financial risk among a network's physician participants, which is necessary for a network to come within the safety zones.

1.   EXCLUSIVE PHYSICIAN NETWORK JOINT VENTURES THAT THE AGENCIES
      WILL NOT CHALLENGE, ABSENT EXTRAORDINARY CIRCUMSTANCES

The Agencies will not challenge, absent extraordinary circumstances, an exclusive physician network joint venture whose physician participants share substantial financial risk and constitute 20 percent or less of the physicians[25] in each physician specialty with active hospital staff privileges who practice in the relevant geographic market.[26]   In relevant markets with fewer than five physicians in a particular specialty, an exclusive physician network joint venture otherwise qualifying for the antitrust safety zone may include one physician from that specialty, on a non-exclusive basis, even though the inclusion of that physician results in the venture consisting of more than 20 percent of the physicians in that specialty.

2.   NON-EXCLUSIVE PHYSICIAN NETWORK JOINT VENTURES THAT THE
      AGENCIES WILL NOT CHALLENGE, ABSENT EXTRAORDINARY
      CIRCUMSTANCES

The Agencies will not challenge, absent extraordinary circumstances, a non-exclusive physician network joint venture whose physician participants share substantial financial risk and constitute 30 percent or less of the physicians in each physician specialty with active hospital staff privileges who practice in the relevant geographic market.   In relevant markets with fewer than four physicians in a particular specialty, a non-exclusive physician network joint venture otherwise qualifying for the antitrust safety zone may include one physician from that specialty, even though the inclusion of that physician results in the venture consisting of more than 30 percent of the physicians in that specialty.

3.   INDICIA OF NON-EXCLUSIVITY

Because of the different market share thresholds for the safety zones for exclusive and non-exclusive physician network joint ventures, the Agencies caution physician participants in a non-exclusive physician network joint venture to be sure that the network is non-exclusive in fact and not just in name. The Agencies will determine whether a physician network joint venture is exclusive or non-exclusive by its physician participants' activities, and not simply by the terms of the contractual relationship. In making that determination, the Agencies will examine the following indicia of non-exclusivity, among others:
      (1) that viable competing networks or managed care plans with adequate physician participation currently exist in the market;

---

25.   For purposes of the antitrust safety zones, in calculating the number of physicians in a relevant
      market and the number of physician participants in a physician network joint venture, each
      physician ordinarily will be counted individually, whether the physician practices in a group or
      solo practice.
26.   Generally, relevant geographic markets for the delivery of physician services are local.

(2)   that physicians in the network actually individually participate in, or contract with, other networks or managed care plans, or there is other evidence of their willingness and incentive to do so;

(3)   that physicians in the network earn substantial revenue from other networks or through individual contracts with managed care plans;

(4)   the absence of any indications of significant departicipation from other networks or managed care plans in the market; and

(5)   the absence of any indications of coordination among the physicians in the network regarding price or other competitively significant terms of participation in other networks or managed care plans.

Networks also may limit or condition physician participants' freedom to contract outside the network in ways that fall short of a commitment of full exclusivity. If those provisions significantly restrict the ability or willingness of a network's physicians to join other networks or contract individually with managed care plans, the network will be considered exclusive for purposes of the safety zones.

4.   SHARING OF SUBSTANTIAL FINANCIAL RISK BY PHYSICIANS IN A PHYSICIAN NETWORK JOINT VENTURE

To qualify for either antitrust safety zone, the participants in a physician network joint venture must share substantial financial risk in providing all the services that are jointly priced through the network.[27] The safety zones are limited to networks involving substantial financial risk sharing not because such risk sharing is a desired end in itself, but because it normally is a clear and reliable indicator that a physician network involves sufficient integration by its physician participants to achieve significant efficiencies.[28] Risk sharing provides incentives for the physicians to cooperate in controlling costs and improving quality by managing the provision of services by network physicians.

The following are examples of some types of arrangements through which participants in a physician network joint venture can share substantial financial risk:[29]

(1)   agreement by the venture to provide services to a health plan at a "capitated" rate;[30]

---

27.   Physician network joint ventures that involve both risk-sharing and non-risk-sharing arrangements do not fall within the safety zones. For example, a network may have both risk-sharing and non-risk-sharing contracts. It also may have contracts that involve risk sharing, but not all the physicians in the network participate in risk sharing or not all of the services are paid for on a risk-sharing basis. The Agencies will consider each of the network's arrangements separately, as well as the activities of the venture as a whole, to determine whether the joint pricing with respect to the non-risk-sharing aspects of the venture is appropriately analyzed under the rule of reason. *See infra* Example 2. The mere presence of some risk-sharing arrangements, however, will not necessarily result in rule of reason analysis of the non-risk-sharing aspects of the venture.

28.   The existence of financial risk sharing does not depend on whether, under applicable state law, the network is considered an insurer.

29.   Physician participants in a single network need not all be involved in the same risk-sharing arrangement within the network to fall within the safety zones. For example, primary care physicians may be capitated and specialists subject to a withhold, or groups of physicians may be in separate risk pools.

30.   A "capitated" rate is a fixed, predetermined payment per covered life (the "capitation") from a health plan to the joint venture in exchange for the joint venture's (not merely an individual physician's) providing and guaranteeing provision of a defined set of covered services to covered individuals for a specified period, regardless of the amount of services actually provided.

(2) agreement by the venture to provide designated services or classes of services to a health plan for a predetermined percentage of premium or revenue from the plan;[31]

(3) use by the venture of significant financial incentives for its physician participants, as a group, to achieve specified cost-containment goals. Two methods by which the venture can accomplish this are:

(a) withholding from all physician participants in the network a substantial amount of the compensation due to them, with distribution of that amount to the physician participants based on group performance in meeting the cost-containment goals of the network as a whole; or

(b) establishing overall cost or utilization targets for the network as a whole, with the network's physician participants subject to subsequent substantial financial rewards or penalties based on group performance in meeting the targets; and

(4) agreement by the venture to provide a complex or extended course of treatment that requires the substantial coordination of care by physicians in different specialities offering a complementary mix of services, for a fixed, predetermined payment, where the costs of that course of treatment for any individual patient can vary greatly due to the individual patient's condition, the choice, complexity, or length of treatment, or other factors.[32]

The Agencies recognize that new types of risk-sharing arrangements may develop. The preceding examples do not foreclose consideration of other arrangements through which the participants in a physician network joint venture may share substantial financial risk in the provision of medical services through the network.[33] Organizers of physician networks who are uncertain whether their proposed arrangements constitute substantial financial risk sharing for purposes of this policy statement are encouraged to take advantage of the Agencies' expedited business review and advisory opinion procedures.

B. The Agencies' Analysis of Physician Network Joint Ventures That Fall outside the Antitrust Safety Zones

Physician network joint ventures that fall outside the antitrust safety zones also may have the potential to create significant efficiencies, and do not necessarily raise substantial antitrust concerns. For example, physician network joint ventures in which the physician participants share substantial financial risk, but which involve a higher percentage of physicians in a relevant market than specified in the safety

---

31. This is similar to a capitation arrangement, except that the amount of payment to the network can vary in response to changes in the health plan's premiums or revenues.

32. Such arrangements are sometimes referred to as "global fees" or "all-inclusive case rates." Global fee or all-inclusive case rate arrangements that involve financial risk sharing as contemplated by this example will require that the joint venture (not merely an individual physician participant) assume the risk or benefit that the treatment provided through the network may either exceed, or cost less than, the predetermined payment.

33. The manner of dividing revenues among the network's physician participants generally does not raise antitrust issues so long as the competing physicians in a network share substantial financial risk. For example, capitated networks may distribute income among their physician participants using fee-for-service payment with a partial withhold fund to cover the risk of having to provide more services than were originally anticipated.

zones, may be lawful if they are not anticompetitive on balance.[34] Likewise, physician network joint ventures that do not involve the sharing of substantial financial risk also may be lawful if the physicians' integration through the joint venture creates significant efficiencies and the venture, on balance, is not anticompetitive.

The Agencies emphasize that it is not their intent to treat such networks either more strictly or more leniently than joint ventures in other industries, or to favor any particular procompetitive organization or structure of health care delivery over other forms that consumers may desire. Rather, their goal is to ensure a competitive marketplace in which consumers will have the benefit of high quality, cost-effective health care and a wide range of choices, including new provider-controlled networks that expand consumer choice and increase competition.

1.   DETERMINING WHEN AGREEMENTS AMONG PHYSICIANS IN A PHYSICIAN NETWORK JOINT VENTURE ARE ANALYZED UNDER THE RULE OF REASON

Antitrust law treats naked agreements among competitors that fix prices or allocate markets as per se illegal. Where competitors economically integrate in a joint venture, however, such agreements, if reasonably necessary to accomplish the procompetitive benefits of the integration, are analyzed under the rule of reason.[35] In accord with general antitrust principles, physician network joint ventures will be analyzed under the rule of reason, and will not be viewed as per se illegal, if the physicians' integration through the network is likely to produce significant efficiencies that benefit consumers, and any price agreements (or other agreements that would otherwise be per se illegal) by the network physicians are reasonably necessary to realize those efficiencies.[36]

Where the participants in a physician network joint venture have agreed to share substantial financial risk as defined in Section A.4. of this policy statement, their risk-sharing arrangement generally establishes both an overall efficiency goal for the venture and the incentives for the physicians to meet that goal. The setting of price is integral to the venture's use of such an arrangement and therefore warrants evaluation under the rule of reason.

---

34.   See infra Examples 5 and 6. Many such physician networks have received favorable business review or advisory opinion letters from the Agencies. The percentages used in the safety zones define areas in which the lack of anticompetitive effects ordinarily will be presumed.

35.   In a network limited to providers who are not actual or potential competitors, the providers generally can agree on the prices to be charged for their services without the kinds of economic integration discussed below.

36.   In some cases, the combination of the competing physicians in the network may enable them to offer what could be considered to be a new product producing substantial efficiencies, and therefore the venture will be analyzed under the rule of reason. See Broadcast Music, Inc. v. Columbia Broadcasting System, Inc., 441 U.S. 1, 21-22 (1979) (competitors' integration and creation of a blanket license for use of copyrighted compositions results in efficiencies so great as to make the blanket license a "different product" from the mere combination of individual competitors and, therefore, joint pricing of the blanket license is subject to rule of reason analysis, rather than the per se rule against price fixing). The Agencies' analysis will focus on the efficiencies likely to be produced by the venture, and the relationship of any price agreements to the achievement of those efficiencies, rather than on whether the venture creates a product that can be labeled "new" or "different."

Physician network joint ventures that do not involve the sharing of substantial financial risk may also involve sufficient integration to demonstrate that the venture is likely to produce significant efficiencies. Such integration can be evidenced by the network implementing an active and ongoing program to evaluate and modify practice patterns by the network's physician participants and create a high degree of interdependence and cooperation among the physicians to control costs and ensure quality. This program may include: (1) establishing mechanisms to monitor and control utilization of health care services that are designed to control costs and assure quality of care; (2) selectively choosing network physicians who are likely to further these efficiency objectives; and (3) the significant investment of capital, both monetary and human, in the necessary infrastructure and capability to realize the claimed efficiencies.

The foregoing are not, however, the only types of arrangements that can evidence sufficient integration to warrant rule of reason analysis, and the Agencies will consider other arrangements that also may evidence such integration. However, in all cases, the Agencies' analysis will focus on substance, rather than form, in assessing a network's likelihood of producing significant efficiencies. To the extent that agreements on prices to be charged for the integrated provision of services are reasonably necessary to the venture's achievement of efficiencies, they will be evaluated under the rule of reason.

In contrast to integrated physician network joint ventures, such as these discussed above, there have been arrangements among physicians that have taken the form of networks, but which in purpose or effect were little more than efforts by their participants to prevent or impede competitive forces from operating in the market. These arrangements are not likely to produce significant procompetitive efficiencies. Such arrangements have been, and will continue to be, treated as unlawful conspiracies or cartels, whose price agreements are per se illegal.

Determining that an arrangement is merely a vehicle to fix prices or engage in naked anticompetitive conduct is a factual inquiry that must be done on a case-by-case basis to determine the arrangement's true nature and likely competitive effects. However, a variety of factors may tend to corroborate a network's anticompetitive nature, including: statements evidencing anticompetitive purpose; a recent history of anticompetitive behavior or collusion in the market, including efforts to obstruct or undermine the development of managed care; obvious anticompetitive structure of the network (e.g., a network comprising a very high percentage of local area physicians, whose participation in the network is exclusive, without any plausible business or efficiency justification); the absence of any mechanisms with the potential for generating significant efficiencies or otherwise increasing competition through the network; the presence of anticompetitive collateral agreements; and the absence of mechanisms to prevent the network's operation from having anticompetitive spillover effects outside the network.

2.   APPLYING THE RULE OF REASON

A rule of reason analysis determines whether the formation and operation of the joint venture may have a substantial anticompetitive effect and, if so, whether that potential effect is outweighed by any procompetitive efficiencies resulting from the joint venture. The rule of reason analysis takes into account characteristics of the particular physician network joint venture, and the competitive environment in which it operates, that bear on the venture's likely effect on competition.

A determination about the lawfulness of a network's activity under the rule of reason sometimes can be reached without an extensive inquiry under each step of the analysis. For example, a physician network joint venture that involves substantial clinical integration may include a relatively small percentage of the physicians in the relevant markets on a non-exclusive basis. In that case, the Agencies may be able to conclude expeditiously that the network is unlikely to be anticompetitive, based on the competitive environment in which it operates. In assessing the competitive environment, the Agencies would consider such market factors as the number, types, and size of managed care plans operating in the area, the extent of physician participation in those plans, and the economic importance of the managed care plans to area physicians. *See infra* Example 1. Alternatively, for example, if a restraint that facially appears to be of a kind that would always or almost always tend to reduce output or increase prices, but has not been considered per se unlawful, is not reasonably necessary to the creation of efficiencies, the Agencies will likely challenge the restraint without an elaborate analysis of market definition and market power.[37]

The steps ordinarily involved in a rule of reason analysis of physician network joint ventures are set forth below.

Step one: Define the relevant market. The Agencies evaluate the competitive effects of a physician network joint venture in each relevant market in which it operates or has substantial impact. In defining the relevant product and geographic markets, the Agencies look to what substitutes, as a practical matter, are reasonably available to consumers for the services in question.[38] The Agencies will first identify the relevant services that the physician network joint venture provides. Although all services provided by each physician specialty might be a separate relevant service market, there may be instances in which significant overlap of services provided by different physician specialties, or in some circumstances, certain nonphysician health care providers, justifies including services from more than one physician specialty or category of providers in the same market. For each relevant service market, the relevant geographic market will include all physicians (or other providers) who are good substitutes for the physician participants in the joint venture.

Step two: Evaluate the competitive effects of the physician joint venture. The Agencies examine the structure and activities of the physician network joint venture and the nature of competition in the relevant market to determine whether the formation or operation of the venture is likely to have an anticompetitive effect. Two key areas of competitive concern are whether a physician network joint venture could raise the prices for physician services charged to health plans above competitive levels, or could prevent or impede the formation or operation of other networks or plans.

In assessing whether a particular network arrangement could raise prices or exclude competition, the Agencies will examine whether the network physicians collectively have the ability and incentive to engage in such conduct. The Agencies will consider not only the proportion of the physicians in any relevant market who

---

37. *See* FTC v. Indiana Federation of Dentists, 476 U.S. 447, 459-60 (1986).
38. A more extensive discussion of how the Agencies define relevant markets is contained in the Agencies' 1992 *Horizontal Merger Guidelines*.

are in the network, but also the incentives faced by physicians in the network, and whether different groups of physicians in a network may have significantly different incentives that would reduce the likelihood of anticompetitive conduct. The Department of Justice has entered into final judgments that permit a network to include a relatively large proportion of physicians in a relevant market where the percentage of physicians with an ownership interest in the network is strictly limited, and the network subcontracts with additional physicians under terms that create a sufficient divergence of economic interest between the subcontracting physicians and the owner physicians so that the owner physicians have an incentive to control the costs to the network of the subcontracting physicians.[39] Evaluating the incentives faced by network physicians requires an examination of the facts and circumstances of each particular case. The Agencies will assess whether different groups of physicians in the network actually have significantly divergent incentives that would override any shared interest, such as the incentive to profit from higher fees for their medical services. The Agencies will also consider whether the behavior of network physicians or other market evidence indicates that the differing incentives among groups of physicians will not prevent anticompetitive conduct.

If, in the relevant market, there are many other networks or many physicians who would be available to form competing networks or to contract directly with health plans, it is unlikely that the joint venture would raise significant competitive concerns. The Agencies will analyze the availability of suitable physicians to form competing networks, including the exclusive or non-exclusive nature of the physician network joint venture.

The Agencies recognize that the competitive impact of exclusive arrangements or other limitations on the ability of a network's physician participants to contract outside the network can vary greatly. For example, in some circumstances exclusivity may help a network serve its subscribers and increase its physician participants' incentives to further the interests of the network. In other situations, however, the anticompetitive risks posed by such exclusivity may outweigh its procompetitive benefits. Accordingly, the Agencies will evaluate the actual or likely effects of particular limitations on contracting in the market situation in which they occur.

An additional area of possible anticompetitive concern involves the risk of "spillover" effects from the venture. For example, a joint venture may involve the exchange of competitively sensitive information among competing physicians and thereby become a vehicle for the network's physician participants to coordinate their activities outside the venture. Ventures that are structured to reduce the likelihood of such spillover are less likely to result in anticompetitive effects. For example, a network that uses an outside agent to collect and analyze fee data from physicians for use in developing the network's fee schedule, and avoids the sharing of such sensitive information among the network's physician participants, may reduce concerns that the information could be used by the network's physician participants to set prices for services they provide outside the network.

---

39. *See, e.g.*, Competitive Impact Statements in United States v. Health Choice of Northwest Missouri, Inc., Case No. 95-6171-CV-SJ-6 (W.D. Mo., filed Sept. 13, 1995), 60 Fed. Reg. 51808, 51815 (Oct. 3, 1995); United States and State of Connecticut v. HealthCare Partners, Inc., Case No. 395-CV-01946-RNC (D. Conn., filed Sept. 13, 1995), 60 Fed. Reg. 52018, 52020 (Oct. 4, 1995).

Step three: Evaluate the impact of procompetitive efficiencies.[40] This step requires an examination of the joint venture's likely procompetitive efficiencies, and the balancing of these efficiencies against any likely anticompetitive effects. The greater the venture's likely anticompetitive effects, the greater must be the venture's likely efficiencies. In assessing efficiency claims, the Agencies focus on net efficiencies that will be derived from the operation of the network and that result in lower prices or higher quality to consumers. The Agencies will not accept claims of efficiencies if the parties reasonably can achieve equivalent or comparable savings through significantly less anticompetitive means. In making this assessment, however, the Agencies will not search for a theoretically least restrictive alternative that is not practical given business realities.

Experience indicates that, in general, more significant efficiencies are likely to result from a physician network joint venture's substantial financial risk sharing or substantial clinical integration. However, the Agencies will consider a broad range of possible cost savings, including improved cost controls, case management and quality assurance, economies of scale, and reduced administrative or transaction costs. In assessing the likelihood that efficiencies will be realized, the Agencies recognize that competition is one of the strongest motivations for firms to lower prices, reduce costs, and provide higher quality. Thus, the greater the competition facing the network, the more likely it is that the network will actually realize potential efficiencies that would benefit consumers.

Step four: Evaluation of collateral agreements. This step examines whether the physician network joint venture includes collateral agreements or conditions that unreasonably restrict competition and are unlikely to contribute significantly to the legitimate purposes of the physician network joint venture. The Agencies will examine whether the collateral agreements are reasonably necessary to achieve the efficiencies sought by the joint venture. For example, if the physician participants in a physician network joint venture agree on the prices they will charge patients who are not covered by the health plans with which their network contracts, such an agreement plainly is not reasonably necessary to the success of the joint venture and is an antitrust violation.[41] Similarly, attempts by a physician network joint venture to exclude competitors or classes of competitors of the network's physician participants from the market could have anticompetitive effects, without advancing any legitimate, procompetitive goal of the network. This could happen, for example, if the network facilitated agreements among the physicians to refuse to deal with such competitors outside the network, or to pressure other market participants to refuse to deal with such competitors or deny them necessary access to key facilities.

C.   Examples of Physician Network Joint Ventures

The following are examples of how the Agencies would apply the principles set forth in this statement to specific physician network joint ventures. The first three are new examples: 1) a network involving substantial clinical integration, that is unlikely to raise significant competitive concerns under the rule of reason; 2) a

---

40.   If steps one and two reveal no competitive concerns with the physician network joint venture, step three is unnecessary, and the analysis continues with step four, below.

41.   This analysis of collateral agreements also applies to physician network joint ventures that fall within the safety zones.

network involving both substantial financial risk-sharing and non-risk-sharing arrangements, which would be analyzed under the rule of reason; and 3) a network involving neither substantial financial risk-sharing nor substantial clinical integration, and whose price agreements likely would be challenged as per se unlawful. The last four examples involve networks that operate in a variety of market settings and with different levels of physician participants; three are networks that involve substantial financial risk-sharing and one is a network in which the physician participants do not jointly agree on, or negotiate, price.

1.   PHYSICIAN NETWORK JOINT VENTURE INVOLVING CLINICAL INTEGRATION

Charlestown is a relatively isolated, medium-sized city. For the purposes of this example, the services provided by primary care physicians and those provided by the different physician specialties each constitute a relevant product market; and the relevant geographic market for each of them is Charlestown.

Several HMOs and other significant managed care plans operate in Charlestown. A substantial proportion of insured individuals are enrolled in these plans, and enrollment in managed care is expected to increase. Many physicians in each of the specialties participate in more than one of these plans. There is no significant overlap among the participants on the physician panels of many of these plans.

A group of Charlestown physicians establishes an IPA to assume greater responsibility for managing the cost and quality of care rendered to Charlestown residents who are members of health plans. They hope to reduce costs while maintaining or improving the quality of care, and thus to attract more managed care patients to their practices.

The IPA will implement systems to establish goals relating to quality and appropriate utilization of services by IPA participants, regularly evaluate both individual participants' and the network's aggregate performance with respect to those goals, and modify individual participants' actual practices, where necessary, based on those evaluations. The IPA will engage in case management, preauthorization of some services, and concurrent and retrospective review of inpatient stays. In addition, the IPA is developing practice standards and protocols to govern treatment and utilization of services, and it will actively review the care rendered by each doctor in light of these standards and protocols.

There is a significant investment of capital to purchase the information systems necessary to gather aggregate and individual data on the cost, quantity, and nature of services provided or ordered by the IPA physicians; to measure performance of the group and the individual doctors against cost and quality benchmarks; and to monitor patient satisfaction. The IPA will provide payers with detailed reports on the cost and quantity of services provided, and on the network's success in meeting its goals.

The IPA will hire a medical director and a support staff to perform the above functions and to coordinate patient care in specific cases. The doctors also have invested appreciable time in developing the practice standards and protocols, and will continue actively to monitor care provided through the IPA. Network participants who fail to adhere to the network's standards and protocols will be subject to remedial action, including the possibility of expulsion from the network.

The IPA physicians will be paid by health plans on a fee-for-service basis; the physicians will not share substantial financial risk for the cost of services rendered to covered individuals through the network. The IPA will retain an agent to develop a fee schedule, negotiate fees, and contract with payers on behalf of the venture. Information about what participating doctors charge non-network patients will not be disseminated to participants in the IPA, and the doctors will not agree on the prices they will charge patients not covered by IPA contracts.

The IPA is built around three geographically dispersed primary care group practices that together account for 25 percent of the primary care doctors in Charlestown. A number of specialists to whom the primary care doctors most often refer their patients also are invited to participate in the IPA. These specialists are selected based on their established referral relationships with the primary care doctors, the quality of care provided by the doctors, their willingness to cooperate with the goals of the IPA, and the need to provide convenient referral services to patients of the primary care doctors. Specialist services that are needed less frequently will be provided by doctors who are not IPA participants. Participating specialists constitute from 20 to 35 percent of the specialists in each relevant market, depending on the specialty. Physician participation in the IPA is non-exclusive. Many IPA participants already do and are expected to continue to participate in other managed care plans and earn substantial income from those plans.

COMPETITIVE ANALYSIS

Although the IPA does not fall within the antitrust safety zone because the physicians do not share substantial financial risk, the Agencies would analyze the IPA under the rule of reason because it offers the potential for creating significant efficiencies and the price agreement is reasonably necessary to realize those efficiencies. Prior to contracting on behalf of competing doctors, the IPA will develop and invest in mechanisms to provide cost-effective quality care, including standards and protocols to govern treatment and utilization of services, information systems to measure and monitor individual physician and aggregate network performance, and procedures to modify physician behavior and assure adherence to network standards and protocols. The network is structured to achieve its efficiencies through a high degree of interdependence and cooperation among its physician participants. The price agreement, under these circumstances, is subordinate to and reasonably necessary to achieve these objectives.[42]

Furthermore, the Agencies would not challenge under the rule of reason the doctors' agreement to establish and operate the IPA. In conducting the rule of reason analysis, the Agencies would evaluate the likely competitive effects of the venture in each relevant market. In this case, the IPA does not appear likely to limit competition in any relevant market either by hampering the ability of health plans to contract individually with area physicians or with other physician network joint ventures, or by enabling the physicians to raise prices above competitive levels. The IPA does not appear to be overinclusive: many primary care physicians and

42. Although the physicians in this example have not directly agreed with one another on the prices to be charged for services rendered through the network, the venture's use of an agent, subject to its control, to establish fees and to negotiate and execute contracts on behalf of the venture amounts to a price agreement among competitors. However, the use of such an agent should reduce the risk of the network's activities having anticompetitive spillover effects on competition among the physicians for non-network patients.

specialists are available to other plans, and the doctors in the IPA have been selected to achieve the network's procompetitive potential. Many IPA participants also participate in other managed care plans and are expected to continue to do so in the future. Moreover, several significant managed care plans are not dependent on the IPA participants to offer their products to consumers. Finally, the venture is structured so that physician participants do not share competitively sensitive information, thus reducing the likelihood of anticompetitive spillover effects outside the network where the physicians still compete, and the venture avoids any anticompetitive collateral agreements.

Since the venture is not likely to be anticompetitive, there is no need for further detailed evaluation of the venture's potential for generating procompetitive efficiencies. For these reasons, the Agencies would not challenge the joint venture. However, they would reexamine this conclusion and do a more complete analysis of the procompetitive efficiencies if evidence of actual anticompetitive effects were to develop.

2.   PHYSICIAN NETWORK JOINT VENTURE INVOLVING RISK-SHARING AND
      NON-RISK-SHARING CONTRACTS

An IPA has capitation contracts with three insurer-developed HMOs. Under its contracts with the HMOs, the IPA receives a set fee per member per month for all covered services required by enrollees in a particular health plan. Physician participants in the IPA are paid on a fee-for-service basis, pursuant to a fee schedule developed by the IPA. Physicians participate in the IPA on a non-exclusive basis. Many of the IPA's physicians participate in managed care plans outside the IPA, and earn substantial income from those plans.

The IPA uses a variety of mechanisms to assure appropriate use of services under its capitation contracts so that it can provide contract services within its capitation budgets. In part because the IPA has managed the provision of care effectively, enrollment in the HMOs has grown to the point where HMO patients are a significant share of the IPA doctors' patients.

The three insurers that offer the HMOs also offer PPO options in response to the request of employers who want to give their employees greater choice of plans. Although the capitation contracts are a substantial majority of the IPA's business, it also contracts with the insurers to provide services to the PPO programs on a fee-for-service basis. The physicians are paid according to the same fee schedule used to pay them under the IPA's capitated contracts. The IPA uses the same panel of providers and the same utilization management mechanisms that are involved in the HMO contracts. The IPA has tracked utilization for HMO and PPO patients, which shows similar utilization patterns for both types of patients.

COMPETITIVE ANALYSIS

Because the IPA negotiates and enters into both capitated and fee-for-service contracts on behalf on its physicians, the venture is not within a safety zone. However, the IPA's HMO contracts are analyzed under the rule of reason because they involve substantial financial risk-sharing. The PPO contracts also are analyzed under the rule of reason because there are significant efficiencies from the capitated arrangements that carry over to the fee-for-service business. The IPA's procedures for managing the provision of care under its capitation contracts and its related fee schedules produce significant efficiencies; and since those same procedures and fees are used for the PPO contracts and result in similar utilization patterns, they will likely result in significant efficiencies for the PPO arrangements as well.

3.   PHYSICIAN NETWORK THAT IS PER SE UNLAWFUL

A group of physicians in Clarksville forms an IPA to contract with managed care plans. There is some limited managed care presence in the area, and new plans have announced their interest in entering. The physicians agree that the only way they can effectively combat the power of the plans and protect themselves from low fees and intrusive utilization review is to organize and negotiate with the plans collectively through the IPA, rather than individually.

Membership in the IPA is open to any licensed physician in Clarksville. Members contribute $2,000 each to fund the legal fees associated with incorporating the IPA and its operating expenses, including the salary of an executive director who will negotiate contracts on behalf of the IPA. The IPA will enter only into fee-for-service contracts. The doctors will not share substantial financial risk under the contracts. The Contracting Committee, in consultation with the executive director, develops a fee schedule.

The IPA establishes a Quality Assurance and Utilization Review Committee. Upon recommendation of this committee, the members vote to have the IPA adopt two basic utilization review parameters: strict limits on documentation to be provided by physicians to the payers, and arbitration of disputes regarding plan utilization review decisions by a committee of the local medical society. The IPA refuses to contract with plans that do not accept these utilization review parameters. The IPA claims to have its own utilization review/quality assurance programs in development, but has taken very few steps to create such a program. It decides to rely instead on the hospital's established peer review mechanisms.

Although there is no formal exclusivity agreement, IPA physicians who are approached by managed care plans seeking contracts refer the plans to the IPA. Except for some contracts predating the formation of the IPA, the physicians do not contract individually with managed care plans on terms other than those set by the IPA.

COMPETITIVE ANALYSIS

This IPA is merely a vehicle for collective decisions by its physicians on price and other significant terms of dealing. The physicians' purpose in forming the IPA is to increase their bargaining power with payers. The IPA makes no effort to selectively choose physicians who are likely to further the network's achievement of efficiencies, and the IPA involves no significant integration, financial or otherwise. IPA physicians' participation in the hospital's general peer review procedures does not evidence integration by those physicians that is likely to result in significant efficiencies in the provision of services through the IPA. The IPA does not manage the provision of care or offer any substantial potential for significant procompetitive efficiencies. The physicians are merely collectively agreeing on prices they will receive for services rendered under IPA contracts and not to accept certain aspects of utilization review that they do not like.

The physicians' contribution of capital to form the IPA does not make it a legitimate joint venture. In some circumstances, capital contributions by an IPA's participants can indicate that the participants have made a significant commitment to the creation of an efficiency-producing competitive entity in the market.[43] Capital contributions, however, can also be used to fund a cartel. The key inquiry is whether the contributed capital is being used to further the network's capability to achieve substantial efficiencies. In this case, the funds are being used primarily to support the joint negotiation, and not to achieve substantial procompetitive efficiencies. Thus, the physicians' agreement to bargain through the joint venture will be treated as per se illegal price fixing.

4.   EXCLUSIVE PHYSICIAN NETWORK JOINT VENTURE WITH FINANCIAL RISK-SHARING AND COMPRISING MORE THAN TWENTY PERCENT OF PHYSICIANS WITH ACTIVE ADMITTING PRIVILEGES AT A HOSPITAL

County Seat is a relatively isolated, medium-sized community of about 350,000 residents. The closest town is 50 miles away. County Seat has five general acute care hospitals that offer a mix of basic primary, secondary, and tertiary care services.

Five hundred physicians have medical practices based in County Seat, and all maintain active admitting privileges at one or more of County Seat's hospitals. No physician from outside County Seat has any type of admitting privileges at a County Seat hospital. The physicians represent 10 different specialties and are distributed evenly among the specialties, with 50 doctors practicing each specialty.

One hundred physicians (also distributed evenly among specialties) maintain active admitting privileges at County Seat Medical Center. County Seat's other 400 physicians maintain active admitting privileges at other County Seat hospitals.

Half of County Seat Medical Center's 100 active admitting physicians propose to form an IPA to market their services to purchasers of health care services. The physicians are divided evenly among the specialties. Under the proposed arrangement, the physicians in the network joint venture would agree to meaningful cost containment and quality goals, including utilization review, quality assurance, and other measures designed to reduce the provision of unnecessary care to the plan's subscribers, and a substantial amount (in this example 20 percent) of the compensation due to the network's physician participants would be withheld and distributed only if these measures are successfully met. This physician network joint venture would be exclusive: Its physician participants would not be free to contract individually with health plans or to join other physician joint ventures.

A number of health plans that contract selectively with hospitals and physicians already operate in County Seat. These plans and local employers agree that other County Seat physicians, and the hospitals to which they admit, are good substitutes for the active admitting physicians and the inpatient services provided at County Seat Medical Center. Physicians with medical practices based outside County Seat, however, are not good substitutes for area physicians, because such physicians would find it inconvenient to practice at County Seat hospitals due to the distance between their practice locations and County Seat.

---

43.   *See supra* Example 1.

COMPETITIVE ANALYSIS

A key issue is whether a physician network joint venture, such as this IPA, comprising 50 percent of the physicians in each specialty with active privileges at one of five comparable hospitals in County Seat would fall within the antitrust safety zone. The physicians within the joint venture represent less than 20 percent of all the physicians in each specialty in County Seat.

County Seat is the relevant geographic market for purposes of analyzing the competitive effects of this proposed physician joint venture. Within each specialty, physicians with admitting privileges at area hospitals are good substitutes for one another. However, physicians with practices based elsewhere are not considered good substitutes.

For purposes of analyzing the effects of the venture, all of the physicians in County Seat should be considered market participants. Purchasers of health care services consider all physicians within each specialty, and the hospitals at which they have admitting privileges, to be relatively interchangeable. Thus, in this example, any attempt by the joint venture's physician participants collectively to increase the price of physician services above competitive levels would likely lead third-party purchasers to recruit non-network physicians at County Seat Medical Center or other area hospitals.

Because physician network joint venture participants constitute less than 20 percent of each group of specialists in County Seat and agree to share substantial financial risk, this proposed joint venture would fall within the antitrust safety zone.

5.   PHYSICIAN NETWORK JOINT VENTURE WITH FINANCIAL RISK-SHARING AND A LARGE PERCENTAGE OF PHYSICIANS IN A RELATIVELY SMALL COMMUNITY

Smalltown has a population of 25,000, a single hospital, and 50 physicians, most of whom are family practitioners. All of the physicians practice exclusively in Smalltown and have active admitting privileges at the Smalltown hospital. The closest urban area, Big City, is located some 35 miles away and has a population of 500,000. A little more than half of Smalltown's working adults commute to work in Big City. Some of the health plans used by employers in Big City are interested in extending their network of providers to Smalltown to provide coverage for subscribers who live in Smalltown, but commute to work in Big City (coverage is to include the families of commuting subscribers). However, the number of commuting Smalltown subscribers is a small fraction of the Big City employers' total workforce.

Responding to these employers' needs, a few health plans have asked physicians in Smalltown to organize a non-exclusive IPA large enough to provide a reasonable choice to subscribers who reside in Smalltown, but commute to work in Big City. Because of the relatively small number of potential enrollees in Smalltown, the plans prefer to contract with such a physician network joint venture, rather than engage in what may prove to be a time-consuming series of negotiations with individual Smalltown physicians to establish a panel of physician providers there.

A number of Smalltown physicians have agreed to form a physician network joint venture. The joint venture will contract with health plans to provide physician services to subscribers of the plans in exchange for a monthly capitation fee paid for each of the plans' subscribers. The physicians forming this joint venture would constitute about half of the total number of physicians in Smalltown. They would represent about 35 percent of the town's family practitioners, but higher percentages of the town's general surgeons (50 percent), pediatricians (50 percent), and obstetricians (67 percent). The health plans that serve Big City employers say that the IPA must have a large percentage of Smalltown physicians to provide adequate coverage for employees and their families in Smalltown and in a few scattered rural communities in the immediate area and to allow the doctors to provide coverage for each other.

In this example, other health plans already have entered Smalltown, and contracted with individual physicians. They have made substantial inroads with Smalltown employers, signing up a large number of enrollees. None of these plans has had any difficulty contracting with individual physicians, including many who would participate in the proposed joint venture.

Finally, the evidence indicates that Smalltown is the relevant geographic market for all physician services. Physicians in Big City are not good substitutes for a significant number of Smalltown residents.

COMPETITIVE ANALYSIS

This proposed physician network joint venture would not fall within the antitrust safety zone because it would comprise over 30 percent of the physicians in a number of relevant specialties in the geographic market. However, the Agencies would not challenge the joint venture because a rule of reason analysis indicates that its formation would not likely hamper the ability of health plans to contract individually with area physicians or with other physician network joint ventures, or enable the physicians to raise prices above competitive levels. In addition, the joint venture's agreement to accept capitated fees creates incentives for its physicians to achieve cost savings.

That health plans have requested formation of this venture also is significant, for it suggests that the joint venture would offer additional efficiencies. In this instance, it appears to be a low-cost method for plans to enter an area without investing in costly negotiations to identify and contract with individual physicians.

Moreover, in small markets such as Smalltown, it may be necessary for purchasers of health care services to contract with a relatively large number of physicians to provide adequate coverage and choice for enrollees. For instance, if there were only three obstetricians in Smalltown, it would not be possible for a physician network joint venture offering obstetrical services to have less than 33 percent of the obstetricians in the relevant area. Furthermore, it may be impractical to have less than 67 percent in the plan, because two obstetricians may be needed in the venture to provide coverage for each other.

Although the joint venture has a relatively large percentage of some specialties, it appears unlikely to present competitive concerns under the rule of reason because of three factors: (1) the demonstrated ability of health plans to contract with physicians individually; (2) the possibility that other physician network joint ventures could be formed; and (3) the potential benefits from the coverage to be provided by this physician network joint venture. Therefore, the Agencies would not challenge the joint venture.

6.   PHYSICIAN NETWORK JOINT VENTURE WITH FINANCIAL RISK SHARING AND A
      LARGE PERCENTAGE OF PHYSICIANS IN A SMALL, RURAL COUNTY

Rural County has a population of 15,000, a small primary care hospital, and ten physicians, including seven general and family practitioners, an obstetrician, a pediatrician, and a general surgeon. All of the physicians are solo practitioners. The nearest urban area is about 60 miles away in Big City, which has a population of 300,000, and three major hospitals to which patients from Rural County are referred or transferred for higher levels of hospital care. However, Big City is too far away for most residents of Rural County routinely to use its physicians for services available in Rural County.

Insurance Company, which operates throughout the state, is attempting to offer managed care programs in all areas of the state, and has asked the local physicians in Rural County to form an IPA to provide services under the program to covered persons living in the County. No other managed care plan has attempted to enter the County previously.

Initially, two of the general practitioners and two of the specialists express interest in forming a network, but Insurance Company says that it intends to market its plan to the larger local employers, who need broader geographic and specialty coverage for their employees. Consequently, Insurance Company needs more of the local general practitioners and the one remaining specialist in the IPA to provide adequate geographic, specialty, and backup coverage to subscribers in Rural County. Eventually, four of the seven general practitioners and the one remaining specialist join the IPA and agree to provide services to Insurance Company's subscribers, under contracts providing for capitation. While the physicians' participation in the IPA is structured to be non-exclusive, no other managed care plan has yet entered the local market or approached any of the physicians about joining a different provider panel. In discussing the formation of the IPA with Insurance Company, a number of the physicians have made clear their intention to continue to practice outside the IPA and have indicated they would be interested in contracting individually with other managed care plans when those plans expand into Rural County.

COMPETITIVE ANALYSIS

This proposed physician network joint venture would not fall within the antitrust safety zone because it would comprise over 30 percent of the general practitioners in the geographic market. Under the circumstances, a rule of reason analysis indicates that the Agencies would not challenge the formation of the joint venture, for the reasons discussed below.

For purposes of this analysis, Rural County is considered the relevant geographic market. Generally, the Agencies will closely examine joint ventures that comprise a large percentage of physicians in the relevant market. However, in this case, the establishment of the IPA and its inclusion of more than half of the general practitioners and all of the specialists in the network is the result of the payer's expressed need to have more of the local physicians in its network to sell its product in the market. Thus, the level of physician participation in the network does not appear to be overinclusive, but rather appears to be the minimum necessary to meet the employers' needs.

Although the IPA has more than half of the general practitioners and all of the specialists in it, under the particular circumstances this does not, by itself, raise sufficient concerns of possible foreclosure of entry by other managed care plans, or of the collective ability to raise prices above competitive levels, to warrant antitrust challenge to the joint venture by the Agencies. Because it is the first such joint venture in the county, there is no way absolutely to verify at the outset that the joint venture in fact will be non-exclusive. However, the physicians' participation in the IPA is formally non-exclusive, and they have expressed a willingness to consider joining other managed care programs if they begin operating in the area. Moreover, the three general practitioners who are not members of the IPA are available to contract with other managed care plans. The IPA also was established with participation by the local area physicians at the request of Insurance Company, indicating that this structure was not undertaken as a means for the physicians to increase prices or prevent entry of managed care plans.

Finally, the joint venture can benefit consumers in Rural County through the creation of efficiencies. The physicians have jointly put themselves at financial risk to control the use and cost of health care services through capitation. To make the capitation arrangement financially viable, the physicians will have to control the use and cost of health care services they provide under Insurance Company's program. Through the physicians' network joint venture, Rural County residents will be offered a beneficial product, while competition among the physicians outside the network will continue.

Given these facts, the Agencies would not challenge the joint venture. If, however, it later became apparent that the physicians' participation in the joint venture in fact was exclusive, and consequently other managed care plans that wanted to enter the market and contract with some or all of the physicians at competitive terms were unable to do so, the Agencies would re-examine the joint venture's legality. The joint venture also would raise antitrust concerns if it appeared that participation by most of the local physicians in the joint venture resulted in anticompetitive effects in markets outside the joint venture, such as uniformity of fees charged by the physicians in their solo medical practices.

7.   PHYSICIAN NETWORK JOINT VENTURE WITH NO PRICE AGREEMENT AND
      INVOLVING ALL OF THE PHYSICIANS IN A SMALL, RURAL COUNTY

Rural County has a population of 10,000, a small primary care hospital, and six physicians, consisting of a group practice of three family practitioners, a general practitioner, an obstetrician, and a general surgeon. The nearest urban area is about 75 miles away in Big City, which has a population of 200,000, and two major hospitals to which patients from Rural County are referred or transferred for higher levels of hospital care. Big City is too far away, however, for most residents of Rural County to use for services available in Rural County.

HealthCare, a managed care plan headquartered in another state, is thinking of marketing a plan to the larger employers in Rural County. However, it finds that the cost of contracting individually with providers, administering the system, and overseeing the quality of care in Rural County is too high on a per capita basis to allow it to convince employers to switch from indemnity plans to its plan.

HealthCare believes its plan would be more successful if it offered higher quality and better access to care by opening a clinic in the northern part of the county where no physicians currently practice.

All of the local physicians approach HealthCare about contracting with their recently-formed, non-exclusive, IPA. The physicians are willing to agree through their IPA to provide services at the new clinic that HealthCare will establish in the northern part of the county and to implement the utilization review procedures that HealthCare has adopted in other parts of the state.

HealthCare wants to negotiate with the new IPA. It believes that the local physicians collectively can operate the new clinic more efficiently than it can from its distant headquarters, but HealthCare also believes that collectively negotiating with all of the physicians will result in it having to pay higher fees or capitation rates. Thus, it encourages the IPA to appoint an agent to negotiate the non-fee related aspects of the contracts and to facilitate fee negotiations with the group practice and the individual doctors. The group practice and the individual physicians each will sign and negotiate their own individual contracts regarding fees and will unilaterally determine whether to contract with HealthCare, but will agree through the IPA to provide physician, administrative, and utilization review services. The agent will facilitate these individual fee negotiations by discussing separately and confidentially with each physician the physician's fee demands and presenting the information to HealthCare. No fee information will be shared among the physicians.

COMPETITIVE ANALYSIS

For purposes of this analysis, Rural County is considered the relevant geographic market. Generally, the Agencies are concerned with joint ventures that comprise all or a large percentage of the physicians in the relevant market. In this case, however, the joint venture appears on balance to be procompetitive. The potential for competitive harm from the venture is not great and is outweighed by the efficiencies likely to be generated by the arrangement.

The physicians are not jointly negotiating fees or engaging in other activities that would be viewed as per se antitrust violations. Therefore, the IPA would be evaluated under the rule of reason. Any possible competitive harm would be balanced against any likely efficiencies to be realized by the venture to see whether, on balance, the IPA is anticompetitive or procompetitive.

Because the IPA is non-exclusive, the potential for competitive harm from foreclosure of competition is reduced. Its physicians are free to contract with other managed care plans or individually with HealthCare if they desire. In addition, potential concerns over anticompetitive pricing are minimized because physicians will continue to negotiate prices individually. Although the physicians are jointly negotiating non-price terms of the contract, agreement on these terms appears to be necessary to the successful operation of the joint venture. The small risk of anticompetitive harm from this venture is outweighed by the substantial procompetitive benefits of improved quality of care and access to physician services that the venture will engender. The new clinic in the northern part of the county will make it easier for residents of that area to receive the care they need. Given these facts, the Agencies would not challenge the joint venture.

* * *

Physicians who are considering forming physician network joint ventures and are unsure of the legality of their conduct under the antitrust laws can take advantage of the Department of Justice's expedited business review procedure announced on December 1, 1992 (58 Fed. Reg. 6132 (1993)) or the Federal Trade Commission's advisory opinion procedure contained at 16 C.F.R. §§ 1.1-1.4 (1993). The Agencies will respond to a business review or advisory opinion request on behalf of physicians who are considering forming a network joint venture within 90 days after all necessary information is submitted.   The Department's December 1, 1992 announcement contains specific guidance about the information that should be submitted.

9.   Statement of Department of Justice and Federal Trade Commission Enforcement Policy on Multiprovider Networks

Introduction

The health care industry is changing rapidly as it looks for innovative ways to control costs and efficiently provide quality services.   Health care providers are forming a wide range of new relationships and affiliations, including networks among otherwise competing providers, as well as networks of providers offering complementary or unrelated services.[44]   These affiliations, referred to herein as multiprovider networks, can offer significant procompetitive benefits to consumers. They also can present antitrust questions, particularly if the network includes otherwise competing providers.

As used in this statement, multiprovider networks are ventures among providers that jointly market their health care services to health plans and other purchasers. Such ventures may contract to provide services to subscribers at jointly determined prices and agree to controls aimed at containing costs and assuring quality. Multiprovider networks vary greatly regarding the providers they include, the contractual relationships among those providers, and the efficiencies likely to be realized by the networks.   Competitive conditions in the markets in which such networks operate also may vary greatly.

In this statement, the Agencies describe the antitrust principles that they apply in evaluating multiprovider networks, address some issues commonly raised in connection with the formation and operation of such networks, and present examples of the application of antitrust principles to hypothetical multiprovider networks. Because multiprovider networks involve a large variety of structures and relationships among many different types of health care providers, and new

---

44.   The multiprovider networks covered by this statement include all types and combinations of health care providers, such as networks involving just a single type of provider (e.g., dentists or hospitals) or a single provider specialty (e.g., orthodontists), as well as networks involving more than one type of provider (e.g., physician-hospital organizations or networks involving both physician and non-physician professionals).   Networks containing only physicians, which are addressed in detail in the preceding enforcement policy statement, are a particular category of multiprovider network. Many of the issues relating to multiprovider networks in general are the same as those that arise, and are addressed, in connection with physician network joint ventures, and the analysis often will be very similar for all such arrangements.

arrangements are continually developing, the Agencies are unable to establish a meaningful safety zone for these entities.

A.   Determining When Agreements among Providers in a Multiprovider Network Are Analyzed under the Rule of Reason

Antitrust law condemns as per se illegal naked agreements among competitors that fix prices or allocate markets. Where competitors economically integrate in a joint venture, however, such agreements, if reasonably necessary to accomplish the procompetitive benefits of the integration, are analyzed under the rule of reason.[45] In accord with general antitrust principles, multiprovider networks will be evaluated under the rule of reason, and will not be viewed as per se illegal, if the providers' integration through the network is likely to produce significant efficiencies that benefit consumers, and any price agreements (or other agreements that would otherwise be per se illegal) by the network providers are reasonably necessary to realize those efficiencies.[46]

In some multiprovider networks, significant efficiencies may be achieved through agreement by the competing providers to share substantial financial risk for the services provided through the network.[47] In such cases, the setting of price would be integral to the network's use of such an arrangement and, therefore, would warrant evaluation under the rule of reason.

The following are examples of some types of arrangements through which substantial financial risk can be shared among competitors in a multiprovider network:

(1)   agreement by the venture to provide services to a health plan at a "capitated" rate;[48]

(2)   agreement by the venture to provide designated services or classes of services to a health plan for a predetermined percentage of premium or revenue from the plan;[49]

---

45.   In a network limited to providers who are not actual or potential competitors, the providers generally can agree on the prices to be charged for their services without the kinds of economic integration discussed below.

46.   In some cases, the combination of the competing providers in the network may enable them to offer what could be considered to be a new product producing substantial efficiencies, and therefore the venture will be analyzed under the rule of reason. *See* Broadcast Music, Inc. v. Columbia Broadcasting System, Inc., 441 U.S. 1 (1979) (competitors' integration and creation of a blanket license for use of copyrighted compositions result in efficiencies so great as to make the blanket license a "different product" from the mere combination of individual competitors and, therefore, joint pricing of the blanket license is subject to rule of reason analysis, rather than the per se rule against price fixing). The Agencies' analysis will focus on the efficiencies likely to be produced by the venture, and the relationship of any price agreements to the achievement of those efficiencies, rather than on whether the venture creates a product that can be labeled "new" or "different."

47.   The existence of financial risk sharing does not depend on whether, under applicable state law, the network is considered an insurer.

48.   A "capitated" rate is a fixed, predetermined payment per covered life (the "capitation") from a health plan to the joint venture in exchange for the joint venture's (not merely an individual provider's) furnishing and guaranteeing provision of a defined set of covered services to covered individuals for a specified period, regardless of the amount of services actually provided.

49.   This is similar to a capitation arrangement, except that the amount of payment to the network can vary in response to changes in the health plan's premiums or revenues.

(3) use by the venture of significant financial incentives for its provider participants, as a group, to achieve specified cost-containment goals. Two methods by which the venture can accomplish this are:

(a) withholding from all provider participants a substantial amount of the compensation due to them, with distribution of that amount to the participants based on group performance in meeting the cost-containment goals of the network as a whole; or

(b) establishing overall cost or utilization targets for the network as a whole, with the provider participants subject to subsequent substantial financial rewards or penalties based on group performance in meeting the targets; and

(4) agreement by the venture to provide a complex or extended course of treatment that requires the substantial coordination of care by different types of providers offering a complementary mix of services, for a fixed, predetermined payment, where the costs of that course of treatment for any individual patient can vary greatly due to the individual patient's condition, the choice, complexity, or length of treatment, or other factors.[50]

The Agencies recognize that new types of risk-sharing arrangements may develop. The preceding examples do not foreclose consideration of other arrangements through which the participants in a multiprovider network joint venture may share substantial financial risk in the provision of health care services or products through the network.[51] Organizers of multiprovider networks who are uncertain whether their proposed arrangements constitute substantial financial risk sharing for purposes of this policy statement are encouraged to take advantage of the Agencies' expedited business review and advisory opinion procedures.

Multiprovider networks that do not involve the sharing of substantial financial risk may also involve sufficient integration to demonstrate that the venture is likely to produce significant efficiencies. For example, as discussed in the Statement Of Enforcement Policy On Physician Network Joint Ventures, substantial clinical integration among competing physicians in a network who do not share substantial financial risk may produce efficiency benefits that justify joint pricing.[52] However, given the wide range of providers who may participate in multiprovider networks, the types of clinical integration and efficiencies available to physician network joint ventures may not be relevant to all multiprovider networks. Accordingly, the Agencies will consider the particular nature of the services provided by the network in assessing whether the network has the potential for producing efficiencies that warrant rule of reason treatment. In all cases, the Agencies' analysis will focus on

---

50. Such arrangements are sometimes referred to either as "global fees" or "all-inclusive case rates." Global fee or all-inclusive case rate arrangements that involve financial risk sharing as contemplated by this example will require that the joint venture (not merely an individual provider participant) assume the risk or benefit that the treatment provided through the network may either exceed, or cost less than, the predetermined payment.

51. The manner of dividing revenues among the network's provider participants generally does not raise antitrust issues so long as the competing providers in a network share substantial financial risk. For example, capitated networks frequently distribute income among their participants using fee-for-service payment with a partial withhold fund to cover the risk of having to provide more services than were originally anticipated.

52. See Section B(1) of the Agencies' Statement of Enforcement Policy on Physician Network Joint Ventures.

substance, not form, in assessing a network's likelihood of producing significant efficiencies. To the extent that agreements on prices to be charged for the integrated provision of services promote the venture's achievement of efficiencies, they will be evaluated under the rule of reason.

A multiprovider network also might include an agreement among competitors on service allocation or specialization. The Agencies would examine the relationship between the agreement and efficiency-enhancing joint activity. If such an agreement is reasonably necessary for the network to realize significant procompetitive benefits, it similarly would be subject to rule of reason analysis.[53] For example, competing hospitals in an integrated multiprovider network might need to agree that only certain hospitals would provide certain services to network patients in order to achieve the benefits of the integration.[54] The hospitals, however, would not necessarily be permitted to agree on what services they would provide to non-network patients.[55]

B.   Applying the Rule of Reason

A rule of reason analysis determines whether the formation and operation of the joint venture may have a substantial anticompetitive effect and, if so, whether that potential effect is outweighed by any procompetitive efficiencies resulting from the venture. The rule of reason analysis takes into account characteristics of the particular multiprovider network and the competitive environment in which it operates to determine the network's likely effect on competition.

A determination about the lawfulness of a multiprovider network's activity under the rule of reason sometimes can be reached without an extensive inquiry under each step of the analysis. For example, a multiprovider network that involves substantial integration may include a relatively small percentage of the providers in each relevant product market on a non-exclusive basis. In that case, the Agencies may be able to conclude expeditiously that the network is unlikely to be anticompetitive, based on the competitive environment in which it operates. In assessing the competitive environment, the Agencies would consider such market factors as the number, type, and size of managed care plans operating in the area, the extent of provider participation in those plans, and the economic importance of the managed care plans to area providers. Alternatively, for example, if a restraint that facially

---

53.   A unilateral decision to eliminate a service or specialization, however, does not generally present antitrust issues. For example, a hospital or other provider unilaterally may decide to concentrate on its more profitable services and not offer other less profitable services, and seek to enter a network joint venture with competitors that still provides the latter services. If such a decision is made unilaterally, rather than pursuant to an express or implied agreement, the arrangement would not be considered a per se illegal market allocation.

54.   Hospitals, even if they do not belong to a multiprovider network, also could agree jointly to develop and operate new services that the participants could not profitably support individually or through a less inclusive joint venture, and to decide where the jointly operated services are to be located. Such joint ventures would be analyzed by the Agencies under the rule of reason. The Statement of Enforcement Policy on Hospital Joint Ventures Involving Specialized Clinical or Other Expensive Health Care Services offers additional guidance on joint ventures among hospitals to provide such services.

55.   The Agencies' analysis would take into account that agreements among multiprovider network participants relating to the offering of services might be more likely than those relating to price to affect participants' competition outside the network, and to persist even if the network is disbanded.

appears to be of a kind that would always or almost always tend to reduce output or increase prices, but has not been considered per se unlawful, is not reasonably necessary to the creation of efficiencies, the Agencies will likely challenge the restraint without an elaborate analysis of market definition and market power.[56]

The steps ordinarily involved in a rule of reason analysis of multiprovider networks are set forth below.

1.   MARKET DEFINITION

The Agencies will evaluate the competitive effects of multiprovider networks in each of the relevant markets in which they operate or have substantial impact. In defining the relevant product and geographic markets, the Agencies look to what substitutes, as a practical matter, are reasonably available to consumers for the services in question.[57]

A multiprovider network can affect markets for the provision of hospital, medical, and other health care services, and health insurance/financing markets. The possible product markets for analyzing the competitive effects of multiprovider networks likely would include both the market for such networks themselves, if there is a distinct market for such networks, and the markets for service components of the network that are, or could be, sold separately outside the network. For example, if two hospitals formed a multiprovider network with their medical and other health care professional staffs, the Agencies would consider potential competitive effects in each market affected by the network, including but not necessarily limited to the markets for inpatient hospital services, outpatient services, each physician and non-physician health care service provided by network members, and health insurance/financing markets whose participants may deal with the network and its various types of health care providers.

The relevant geographic market for each relevant product market affected by the multiprovider network will be determined through a fact-specific analysis that focuses on the location of reasonable alternatives. The relevant geographic markets may be broader for some product markets than for others.

2.   COMPETITIVE EFFECTS

In applying the rule of reason, the Agencies will examine both the potential "horizontal" and "vertical" effects of the arrangement. Agreements between or among competitors (e.g., competing hospitals or competing physicians) are considered "horizontal" under the antitrust laws. Agreements between or among parties that are not competitors (such as a hospital and a physician in a physician-hospital organization ("PHO")), may be considered "vertical" in nature.

a.   Horizontal Analysis

In evaluating the possible horizontal competitive effects of multiprovider networks, the Agencies will define the relevant markets (as discussed earlier) and

---

56.   *See* FTC v. Indiana Federation of Dentists, 476 U.S. 447, 459-60 (1986).

57.   A more extensive discussion of how the Agencies define relevant markets is contained in the Agencies' 1992 *Horizontal Merger Guidelines*.

evaluate the network's likely overall competitive effects considering all market conditions. Determining market share and concentration in the relevant markets is often an important first step in analyzing a network's competitive effects. For example, in analyzing a PHO, the Agencies will consider the network's market share (and the market concentration) in such service components as inpatient hospital services (as measured by such indicia as number of institutions, number of hospital beds, patient census, and revenues), physician services (in individual physician specialty or other appropriate service markets),[58] and any other services provided by competing health care providers, institutional or noninstitutional, participating in the network.

If a particular multiprovider network had a substantial share of any of the relevant service markets, it could, depending on other factors, increase the price of such services above competitive levels. For example, a network that included most or all of the surgeons in a relevant geographic market could create market power in the market for surgical services and thereby permit the surgeons to increase prices.

If there is only one hospital in the market, a multiprovider network, by definition, cannot reduce any existing competition among hospitals. Such a network could, however, reduce competition among other providers, for example, among physicians in the network and, thereby, reduce the ability of payers to control the costs of both physician and hospital services.[59] It also could reduce competition between the hospital and non-hospital providers of certain services, such as outpatient surgery.

Although market share and concentration are useful starting points in analyzing the competitive effects of multiprovider networks, the Agencies' ultimate conclusion is based upon a more comprehensive analysis. This will include an analysis of collateral agreements and spillover effects.[60] In addition, in assessing the likely competitive effects of a multiprovider network, the Agencies are particularly interested in the ability and willingness of health plans and other purchasers of health care services to switch between different health care providers or networks in response to a price increase, and the factors that determine the ability and willingness of plans to make such changes. The Agencies will consider not only the proportion of the providers in any relevant market who are in the network, but also the incentives faced by providers in the network, and whether different groups of providers in a network may have significantly different incentives that would reduce the likelihood of anticompetitive conduct.[61] If plans can contract at competitive terms with other networks or with individual providers, and can obtain a similar quality and range of services for their enrollees, the network is less likely to raise competitive concerns.

In examining a multiprovider network's overall competitive effect, the Agencies will examine whether the competing providers in the network have agreed among themselves to offer their services exclusively through the network or are otherwise

---

58. Although all services provided by each physician specialty or category of non-physician provider might be a separate relevant service market, there may be instances in which significant overlap of services provided by different physician specialties or categories of providers justifies including services from more than one physician specialty or provider category in the same market.
59. By aligning itself with a large share of physicians in the market, a monopoly hospital may effectively be able to insulate itself from payer efforts to control utilization of its services and thus protect its monopoly profits.
60. *See* Statement of Enforcement Policy on Physician Network Joint Ventures.
61. *See* discussion in Statement of Enforcement Policy on Physician Network Joint Ventures.

operating, or are likely to operate, exclusively. Such exclusive arrangements are not necessarily anticompetitive.[62] Exclusive networks, however, mean that the providers in the network are not available to join other networks or contract individually with health plans, and thus, in some circumstances, exclusive networks can impede or preclude competition among networks and among individual providers. In determining whether an exclusive arrangement of this type raises antitrust concerns, the Agencies will examine the market share of the providers subject to the exclusivity arrangement; the terms of the exclusive arrangement, such as its duration and providers' ability and financial incentives or disincentives to withdraw from the arrangement; the number of providers that need to be included for the network and potentially competing networks to compete effectively; and the justification for the exclusivity arrangement.

Networks also may limit or condition provider participants' freedom to contract outside the network in ways that fall short of a commitment of full exclusivity. The Agencie's recognize that the competitive impact of exclusive arrangements or other limitations on the ability of a network's provider participants to contract outside the network can vary greatly.

b.   *Vertical Analysis*

In addition to the horizontal issues discussed above, multiprovider networks also can raise vertical issues. Generally, vertical concerns can arise if a network's power in one market in which it operates enables it to limit competition in another market.

Some multiprovider networks involve "vertical" exclusive arrangements that restrict the providers in one market from dealing with non-network providers that compete in a different market, or that restrict network provider participants' dealings with health plans or other purchasers. For example, a multiprovider network owned by a hospital and individually contracting with its participating physicians might limit the incentives or ability of those physicians to participate in other networks. Similarly, a hospital might use a multiprovider network to block or impede other hospitals from entering a market or from offering competing services.

In evaluating whether such exclusive arrangements raise antitrust concerns, the Agencies will examine the degree to which the arrangement may limit the ability of other networks or health plans to compete in the market. The factors the Agencies will consider include those set forth in the discussion of exclusive arrangements [in Statement 8.C.4], above.

For example, if the multiprovider network has exclusive arrangements with only a small percentage of the physicians in a relevant market, and there are enough suitable alternative physicians in the market to allow other competing networks to form, the exclusive arrangement is unlikely to raise antitrust concerns. On the other hand, a network might contract exclusively with a large percentage of physicians in a relevant market, for example general surgeons. In that case, if purchasers or payers could not form a satisfactory competing network using the remaining general surgeons in the market, and could not induce new general surgeons to enter the market, those purchasers and payers would be forced to use this network, rather than put together a panel consisting of those providers of each needed service who offer

---

62.   For example, an exclusive arrangement may help ensure the multiprovider network's ability to serve its subscribers and increase its providers' incentives to further the interests of the network.

the most attractive combination of price and quality. Thus, the exclusive arrangement would be likely to restrict competition unreasonably, both among general surgeons (the horizontal effect) and among health care providers in other service markets and payers (the vertical effects).

The Agencies recognize that exclusive arrangements, whether they are horizontal or vertical, may not be explicit, so that labeling a multiprovider network as "non-exclusive" will not be determinative. In some cases, providers will refuse to contract with other networks or purchasers, even though they have not entered into an agreement specifically forbidding them from doing so. For example, if a network includes a large percentage of physicians in a certain market, those physicians may perceive that they are likely to obtain more favorable terms from plans by dealing collectively through one network, rather than as individuals.

In determining whether a network is truly non-exclusive, the Agencies will consider a number of factors, including the following:

(1) that viable competing networks or managed care plans with adequate provider participation currently exist in the market;

(2) that providers in the network actually individually participate in, or contract with, other networks or managed care plans, or there is other evidence of their willingness and incentive to do so;

(3) that providers in the network earn substantial revenue from other networks or through individual contracts with managed care plans;

(4) the absence of any indications of substantial departicipation from other networks or managed care plans in the market; and

(5) the absence of any indications of coordination among the providers in the network regarding price or other competitively significant terms of participation in other networks or managed care plans.

c.   Exclusion of Particular Providers

Most multiprovider networks will contract with some, but not all, providers in an area. Such selective contracting may be a method through which networks limit their provider panels in an effort to achieve quality and cost-containment goals, and thus enhance their ability to compete against other networks. One reason often advanced for selective contracting is to ensure that the network can direct a sufficient patient volume to its providers to justify price concessions or adherence to strict quality controls by the providers. It may also help the network create a favorable market reputation based on careful selection of high quality, cost-effective providers. In addition, selective contracting may be procompetitive by giving non-participant providers an incentive to form competing networks. A rule of reason analysis usually is applied in judging the legality of a multiprovider network's exclusion of providers or classes of providers from the network, or its policies on referring enrollees to network providers. The focus of the analysis is not on whether a particular provider has been harmed by the exclusion or referral policies, but rather whether the conduct reduces competition among providers in the market and thereby harms consumers. Where other networks offering the same types of services exist or could be formed, there are not likely to be significant competitive concerns associated with the exclusion of particular providers by particular networks. Exclusion or referral policies may present competitive concerns, however, if providers or classes of providers are unable to compete effectively without access to the network, and competition is thereby harmed. In assessing such situations, the Agencies will consider whether there are procompetitive reasons for the exclusion or referral policies.

3.   EFFICIENCIES

Finally, the Agencies will balance any potential anticompetitive effects of the multiprovider network against the potential efficiencies associated with its formation and operation. The greater the network's likely anticompetitive effects, the greater must be the network's likely efficiencies. In assessing efficiency claims, the Agencies focus on net efficiencies that will be derived from the operation of the network and that result in lower prices or higher quality to consumers. The Agencies will not accept claims of efficiencies if the parties reasonably can achieve equivalent or comparable savings through significantly less anticompetitive means. In making this assessment, however, the Agencies will not search for a theoretically least restrictive alternative that is not practical given business realities.

Experience indicates that, in general, more significant efficiencies are likely to result from a multiprovider network joint venture's substantial financial risk-sharing or substantial clinical integration. However, the Agencies will consider a broad range of possible cost savings, including improved cost controls, case management and quality assurance, economies of scale, and reduced administrative or transaction costs.

In assessing the likelihood that efficiencies will be realized, the Agencies recognize that competition is one of the strongest motivations for firms to lower prices, reduce costs, and provide higher quality. Thus, the greater the competition facing the network, the more likely the network will actually realize potential efficiencies that would benefit consumers.

4.   INFORMATION USED IN THE ANALYSIS

In conducting a rule of reason analysis, the Agencies rely upon a wide variety of data and information, including the information supplied by the participants in the multiprovider network, purchasers, providers, consumers, and others familiar with the market in question. The Agencies may interview purchasers of health care services, including self-insured employers and other employers that offer health benefits, and health plans (such as HMOs and PPOs), competitors of the providers in the network, and any other parties who may have relevant information for analyzing the competitive effects of the network.

The Agencies do not simply count the number of parties who support or oppose the formation of the multiprovider network. Instead, the Agencies seek information concerning the competitive dynamics in the particular community where the network is forming. For example, in defining relevant markets, the Agencies are likely to give substantial weight to information provided by purchasers or payers who have attempted to switch between providers in the face of a price increase. Similarly, an employer or payer with locations in several communities may have had experience with a network comparable to the proposed network, and thus be able to provide the

Agencies with useful information about the likely effect of the proposed network, including its potential competitive benefits.

In assessing the information provided by various parties, the Agencies take into account the parties' economic incentives and interests. In addition, the Agencies attach less significance to opinions that are based on incomplete, biased, or inaccurate information, or opinions of those who, for whatever reason, may be simply indifferent to the potential for anticompetitive harm.

C. Arrangements That Do Not Involve Horizontal Agreements on Prices or Price-Related Terms

Some networks that are not substantially integrated use a variety of "messenger model" arrangements to facilitate contracting between providers and payers and avoid price-fixing agreements among competing network providers. Arrangements that are designed simply to minimize the costs associated with the contracting process, and that do not result in a collective determination by the competing network providers on prices or price-related terms, are not per se illegal price fixing.[63]

Messenger models can be organized and operate in a variety of ways. For example, network providers may use an agent or third party to convey to purchasers information obtained individually from the providers about the prices or price-related terms that the providers are willing to accept.[64] In some cases, the agent may convey to the providers all contract offers made by purchasers, and each provider then makes an independent, unilateral decision to accept or reject the contract offers. In others, the agent may have received from individual providers some authority to accept contract offers on their behalf. The agent also may help providers understand the contracts offered, for example by providing objective or empirical information about the terms of an offer (such as a comparison of the offered terms to other contracts agreed to by network participants).

The key issue in any messenger model arrangement is whether the arrangement creates or facilitates an agreement among competitors on prices or price-related terms. Determining whether there is such an agreement is a question of fact in each case. The Agencies will examine whether the agent facilitates collective decision-making by network providers, rather than independent, unilateral, decisions.[65] In particular, the Agencies will examine whether the agent coordinates the providers' responses to a particular proposal, disseminates to network providers the views or intentions of other network providers as to the proposal, expresses an opinion on the terms offered, collectively negotiates for the providers, or decides whether or not to convey an offer based on the agent's judgment about the

---

63. *See infra* Example 4.

64. Guidance about the antitrust standards applicable to collection and exchange of fee information can be found in the Statement of Enforcement Policy on Providers' Collective Provision of Fee-Related Information to Purchasers of Health Care Services, and the Statement of Enforcement Policy on Provider Participation in Exchanges of Price and Cost Information.

65. Use of an intermediary or "independent" third party to convey collectively determined price offers to purchasers or to negotiate agreements with purchasers, or giving to individual providers an opportunity to "opt" into, or out of, such agreements does not negate the existence of an agreement.

attractiveness of the prices or price-related terms. If the agent engages in such activities, the arrangement may amount to a per se illegal price-fixing agreement.

D. *Examples of Multiprovider Network Joint Ventures*

The following are four examples of how the Agencies would apply the principles set forth in this statement to specific multiprovider network joint ventures, including: 1) a PHO involving substantial clinical integration, that does not raise significant competitive concerns under the rule of reason; 2) a PHO providing services on a per case basis, that would be analyzed under the rule of reason; 3) a PHO involving substantial financial risk sharing and including all the physicians in a small rural county, that does not raise competitive concerns under the rule of reason; and 4) a PHO that does not involve horizontal agreements on price.

1. PHO INVOLVING SUBSTANTIAL CLINICAL INTEGRATION

Roxbury is a relatively isolated, medium-sized city. For the purposes of this example, the services provided by primary care physicians and those provided by the different physician specialists each constitute a relevant product market; and the relevant geographic market for each of them is Roxbury.

Several HMOs and other significant managed care plans operate in Roxbury. A substantial proportion of insured individuals are enrolled in these plans, and enrollment in managed care is expected to increase. Many physicians in each of the specialties and Roxbury's four hospitals participate in more than one of these plans. There is no significant overlap among the participants on the physician panels of many of these plans, nor among the active medical staffs of the hospitals, except in a few specialties. Most plans include only 2 or 3 of Roxbury's hospitals, and each hospital is a substitute for any other.

One of Roxbury's hospitals and the physicians on its active medical staff establish a PHO to assume greater responsibility for managing the cost and quality of care rendered to Roxbury residents who are members of health plans. They hope to reduce costs while maintaining or improving the quality of care, and thus to attract more managed care patients to the hospital and their practices.

The PHO will implement systems to establish goals relating to quality and appropriate utilization of services by PHO participants, regularly evaluate both the hospital's and each individual doctor's and the network's aggregate performance concerning those goals, and modify the hospital's and individual participants' actual practices, where necessary, based on those evaluations. The PHO will engage in case management, preadmission authorization of some services, and concurrent and retrospective review of inpatient stays. In addition, the PHO is developing practice standards and protocols to govern treatment and utilization of services, and it will actively review the care rendered by each doctor in light of these standards and protocols.

There is a significant investment of capital to purchase the information systems necessary to gather aggregate and individual data on the cost, quantity, and nature of services provided or ordered by the hospital and PHO physicians; to measure performance of the PHO, the hospital, and the individual doctors against cost and quality benchmarks; and to monitor patient satisfaction. The PHO will provide payers with detailed reports on the cost and quantity of services provided, and on the network's success in meeting its goals.

The PHO will hire a medical director and support staff to perform the above functions and to coordinate patient care in specific cases. The doctors and the hospital's administrative staff also have invested appreciable time in developing the practice standards and protocols, and will continue actively to monitor care provided through the PHO. PHO physicians who fail to adhere to the network's standards and protocols will be subject to remedial action, including the possibility of expulsion from the network.

Under PHO contracts, physicians will be paid by health plans on a fee-for-service basis; the hospital will be paid a set amount for each day a covered patient is in the hospital, and will be paid on a fee-for-service basis for other services. The physicians will not share substantial financial risk for the cost of services rendered to covered individuals through the network. The PHO will retain an agent to develop a fee schedule, negotiate fees, and contract with payers. Information about what participating doctors charge non-network patients will not be disseminated to participants of the PHO, and the doctors will not agree on the prices they will charge patients not covered by PHO contracts.

All members of the hospital's medical staff join the PHO, including its three geographically dispersed primary care group practices that together account for about 25 percent of the primary care doctors in Roxbury. These primary care doctors generally refer their patients to specialists on the hospital's active medical staff. The PHO includes all primary care doctors and specialists on the hospital's medical staff because of those established referral relationships with the primary care doctors, the admitting privileges all have at the hospital, the quality of care provided by the medical staff, their commitment to cooperate with the goals of the PHO, and the need to provide convenient referral services to patients of the primary care doctors. Participating specialists include from 20 to 35 percent of specialists in each relevant market, depending on the specialty. Hospital and physician participation in the PHO is non-exclusive. Many PHO participants, including the hospital, already do and are expected to continue to participate in other managed care plans and earn substantial income from those plans.

COMPETITIVE ANALYSIS

The Agencies would analyze the PHO under the rule of reason because it offers the potential for creating significant efficiencies and the price agreement among the physicians is reasonably necessary to realize those efficiencies. Prior to contracting on behalf of competing physicians, the PHO will develop mechanisms to provide cost-effective, quality care, including standards and protocols to govern treatment and utilization of services, information systems to measure and monitor both the individual performance of the hospital and physicians and aggregate network performance, and procedures to modify hospital and physician behavior and assure adherence to network standards and protocols. The network is structured to achieve its efficiencies through a high degree of interdependence and cooperation among its participants. The price agreement for physician services, under these circumstances, is subordinate to and reasonably necessary to achieve these objectives.[66]

---

66. Although the physicians have not directly agreed among themselves on the prices to be charged, their use of an agent subject to the control of the PHO to establish fees and to negotiate and

Furthermore, the Agencies would not challenge establishment and operation of the PHO under the rule of reason. In conducting the rule of reason analysis, the Agencies would evaluate the likely competitive effects of the venture in each relevant market. In this case, the PHO does not appear likely to limit competition in any relevant market either by hampering the ability of health plans to contract individually with area hospitals or physicians or with other network joint ventures, or by enabling the hospital or physicians to raise prices above competitive levels. The PHO does not appear to be overinclusive: many primary care physicians as well as specialists are available to other plans, and the doctors in the PHO have been included to achieve the network's procompetitive potential. Many PHO doctors also participate in other managed care plans and are expected to continue to do so in the future. Moreover, several significant managed care plans are not dependent on the PHO doctors to offer their products to consumers. Finally, the venture is structured so that physician participants do not share competitively sensitive information, thus reducing the likelihood of anticompetitive spillover effects outside the network where the physicians still compete, and the venture avoids any anticompetitive collateral agreements.

Since the venture is not likely to be anticompetitive, there is no need for further detailed evaluation of the venture's potential for generating procompetitive efficiencies. For these reasons, the Agencies would not challenge the joint venture. They would reexamine this conclusion, however, and do a more complete analysis of the procompetitive efficiencies if evidence of actual anticompetitive effects were to develop.

2.   PHO THAT PROVIDES SERVICES ON A PER CASE BASIS

Goodville is a large city with a number of hospitals. One of Goodville's hospitals, together with its oncologists and other relevant health care providers, establishes a joint venture to contract with health plans and other payers of health care services to provide bone marrow transplants and related cancer care for certain types of cancers based on an all inclusive per case payment. Under these contracts, the venture will receive a single payment for all hospital, physician, and ancillary services rendered to covered patients requiring bone marrow transplants. The venture will be responsible for paying for and coordinating the various forms of care provided. At first, it will pay its providers using a fee schedule with a withhold to cover unanticipated losses on the case rate. Based on its operational experience, the venture intends to explore other payment methodologies that may most effectively provide the venture's providers with financial incentives to allocate resources efficiently in their treatment of patients.

COMPETITIVE ANALYSIS

The joint venture is a multiprovider network in which competitors share substantial financial risk, and the price agreement among members of the venture will be analyzed under the rule of reason. The per case payment arrangement

execute contracts on behalf of the venture would amount to a price agreement among competitors. The use of such an agent, however, should reduce the risk of the PHO's activities having anticompetitive spillover effects on competition among provider participants for non-network patients.

involves the sharing of substantial financial risk because the venture will receive a single, predetermined payment for a course of treatment that requires the substantial coordination of care by different types of providers and can vary significantly in cost and complexity from patient to patient. The venture will pay its provider participants in a way that gives them incentives to allocate resources efficiently, and that spreads among the participants the risk of loss and the possibility of gain on any particular case. The venture adds to the market another contracting option for health plans and other payers that is likely to result in cost savings because of its use of a per case payment method. Establishment of the case rate is an integral part of the risk sharing arrangement.

3.   PHO WITH ALL THE PHYSICIANS IN A SMALL, RURAL COUNTY

Frederick County has a population of 15,000, and a 50-bed hospital that offers primary and some secondary services. There are 12 physicians on the active medical staff of the hospital (six general and family practitioners, one internist, two pediatricians, one otolaryngologist, and two general surgeons) as well as a part-time pathologist, anesthesiologist, and radiologist. Outside of Frederick County, the nearest hospitals are in Big City, 25 miles away. Most Frederick County residents receive basic physician and hospital care in Frederick County, and are referred or transferred to the Big City physician specialists and hospitals for higher levels of care.

No managed care plans currently operate in Frederick County. Nor are there any large employers who selectively contract with Frederick County physicians. Increasingly, Frederick County residents who work for employers in Big City are covered under managed care contracts that direct Frederick County residents to hospitals and to numerous primary care and specialty physicians in Big City. Providers in Frederick County who are losing patients to hospitals and doctors in Big City want to contract with payers and employers so that they can retain these patients. However, the Frederick County hospital and doctors have been unsuccessful in their efforts to obtain contracts individually; too few potential enrollees are involved to justify payers' undertaking the expense and effort of individually contracting with Frederick County providers and administering a utilization review and quality assurance program for a provider network in Frederick County.

The hospital and all the physicians in Frederick County want to establish a PHO to contract with managed care plans and employers operating in Big City. Managed care plans have expressed interest in contracting with all Frederick County physicians under a single risk-sharing contract. The PHO also will offer its network to employers operating in Frederick County.

The PHO will market the services of the hospital on a per diem basis, and physician services on the basis of a fee schedule that is significantly discounted from the doctors' current charges. The PHO will be eligible for a bonus of up to 20 percent of the total payments made to it, depending on the PHO's success in meeting utilization targets agreed to with the payers. An employee of the hospital will develop a fee schedule, negotiate fees, and contract with payers on behalf of the PHO. Information about what participating doctors charge non-PHO patients will not be disseminated to the doctors, and they will not agree on the prices they will charge patients not covered by PHO contracts.

Physicians' participation in the PHO is structured to be non-exclusive. Because no other managed care plans operate in the area, PHO physicians do not now participate in other plans and have not been approached by other plans. The PHO physicians have made clear their intention to continue to practice outside the PHO and to be available to contract individually with any other managed care plans that expand into Frederick County.

COMPETITIVE ANALYSIS

The agreement of the physicians on the prices they will charge through the PHO would be analyzed under the rule of reason, because they share substantial financial risk through the use of a pricing arrangement that provides significant financial incentives for the physicians, as a group, to achieve specified cost-containment goals. The venture thus has the potential for creating significant efficiencies, and the setting of price promotes the venture's use of the risk-sharing arrangement.

The Agencies would not challenge formation and operation of the PHO under the rule of reason. Under the rule of reason analysis, the Agencies would evaluate the likely competitive effects of the venture. The venture does not appear likely to limit competition in any relevant market. Managed care plans' current practice of directing patients from Frederick County to Big City suggests that the physicians in the PHO face significant competition from providers and managed care plans that operate in Big City. Moreover, the absence of managed care contracting in Frederick County, either now or in the foreseeable future, indicates that the network is not likely to reduce any actual or likely competition for patients who do not travel to Big City for care.

While the venture involves all of the doctors in Frederick County, this was necessary to respond to competition from Big City providers. It is not possible to verify at the outset that the venture will in fact be non-exclusive, but the physicians' participation in the venture is structured to be non-exclusive, and the doctors have expressed a willingness to consider joining other managed care plans if they begin operating in the area.

For these reasons, the Agencies would not challenge the joint venture. However, if it later became apparent that the physicians' participation in the PHO was exclusive in fact, and consequently managed care plans or employers that wanted to contract with some or all of the physicians at competitive terms were unable to do so, or that the PHO doctors entered into collateral agreements that restrained competition for services furnished outside the PHO, the Agencies likely would challenge the joint venture.

4.   PHO THAT DOES NOT INVOLVE HORIZONTAL AGREEMENTS ON PRICE

A hospital and doctors and other health care providers on its medical staff have established a PHO to market their services to payers, including employers with self-funded health benefits plans. The PHO contracts on a fee-for-service basis. The physicians and other health care providers who are participants in the PHO do not share substantial financial risk or otherwise integrate their services so as to provide significant efficiencies. The payers prefer to continue to use their existing third-party administrators for contract administration and utilization management, or to do it in-house.

There is no agreement among the PHO's participants to deal only through the PHO, and many of them participate in other networks and HMOs on a variety of terms. Some payers have chosen to contract with the hospital and some or all of the PHO physicians and other providers without going through the PHO, and a significant proportion of the PHO's participants contract with payers in this manner.

In an effort to avoid horizontal price agreements among competing participants in the PHO while facilitating the contracting process, the PHO considers using the following mechanisms:

A. An agent of the PHO, not otherwise affiliated with any PHO participant, will obtain from each participant a fee schedule or conversion factor that represents the minimum payment that participant will accept from a payer. The agent is authorized to contract on the participants' behalf with payers offering prices at this level or better. The agent does not negotiate pricing terms with the payer and does not share pricing information among competing participants. Price offers that do not meet the authorized fee are conveyed to the individual participant.

B. The same as option A, with the added feature that the agent is authorized, for a specified time, to bind the participant to any contract offers with prices equal, to or better than, those in a contract that the participant has already approved.

C. The same as option A, except that in order to assist payers in developing contract offers, the agent takes the fee authorizations of the various participants and develops a schedule that can be presented to a payer showing the percentages of participants in the network who have authorized contracts at various price levels.

D. The venture hires an agent to negotiate prices with payers on behalf of the PHO's participants. The agent does not disclose to the payer the prices the participants are willing to accept, as in option C, but attempts to obtain the best possible prices for all the participants. The resulting contract offer then is relayed to each participant for acceptance or rejection.

COMPETITIVE ANALYSIS

In the circumstances described in options A through D, the Agencies would determine whether there was a horizontal agreement on price or any other competitively significant terms among PHO participants. The Agencies would determine whether such agreements were subject to the per se rule or the rule of reason, and evaluate them accordingly.

The existence of an agreement is a factual question. The PHO's use of options A through C does not establish the existence of a horizontal price agreement. Nor is there sharing of price information or other evidence of explicit or implicit agreements among network participants on price. The agent does not inform PHO participants about others' acceptance or rejection of contract offers; there is no agreement or understanding that PHO participants will only contract through the PHO; and participants deal outside the network on competitive terms.

The PHO's use of option D amounts to a per se unlawful price agreement. The participants' joint negotiation through a common agent confronts the payer with the combined bargaining power of the PHO participants, even though they ultimately have to agree individually to the contract negotiated on their behalf.

2000 DEPARTMENT OF JUSTICE AND FEDERAL TRADE COMMISSION ANTITRUST GUIDELINES FOR COLLABORATIONS AMONG COMPETITORS

Preamble

In order to compete in modern markets, competitors sometimes need to collaborate. Competitive forces are driving firms toward complex collaborations to achieve goals such as expanding into foreign markets, funding expensive innovation efforts, and lowering production and other costs.

Such collaborations often are not only benign but procompetitive. Indeed, in the last two decades, the federal antitrust agencies have brought relatively few civil cases against competitor collaborations. Nevertheless, a perception that antitrust laws are skeptical about agreements among actual or potential competitors may deter the development of procompetitive collaborations.[1]

To provide guidance to business people, the Federal Trade Commission ("FTC") and the U.S. Department of Justice ("DOJ") (collectively, "the Agencies") previously issued guidelines addressing several special circumstances in which antitrust issues related to competitor collaborations may arise.[2] But none of these *Guidelines* represents a general statement of the Agencies' analytical approach to competitor collaborations. The increasing varieties and use of competitor collaborations have yielded requests for improved clarity regarding their treatment under the antitrust laws.

The new *Antitrust Guidelines for Collaborations among Competitors* ("*Competitor Collaboration Guidelines*") are intended to explain how the Agencies

---

1. Congress has protected certain collaborations from full antitrust liability by passing the National Cooperative Research Act of 1984 ("NCRA") and the National Cooperative Research and Production Act of 1993 ("NCRPA") (codified together at 15 U.S.C. §§ 4301-06).

2. The *Statements of Antitrust Enforcement Policy in Health Care* ("*Health Care Statements*") outline the Agencies' approach to certain health care collaborations, among other things. The *Antitrust Guidelines for the Licensing of Intellectual Property* ("*Intellectual Property Guidelines*") outline the Agencies' enforcement policy with respect to intellectual property licensing agreements among competitors, among other things. The 1992 *DOJ/FTC Horizontal Merger Guidelines*, as amended in 1997 ("*Horizontal Merger Guidelines*"), outline the Agencies' approach to horizontal mergers and acquisitions, and certain competitor collaborations.

analyze certain antitrust issues raised by collaborations among competitors. Competitor collaborations and the market circumstances in which they operate vary widely. No set of guidelines can provide specific answers to every antitrust question that might arise from a competitor collaboration. These *Guidelines* describe an analytical framework to assist businesses in assessing the likelihood of an antitrust challenge to a collaboration with one or more competitors. They should enable businesses to evaluate proposed transactions with greater understanding of possible antitrust implications, thus encouraging procompetitive collaborations, deterring collaborations likely to harm competition and consumers, and facilitating the Agencies' investigations of collaborations.

Section 1: Purpose, Definitions, and Overview

1.1   Purpose and Definitions

These *Guidelines* state the antitrust enforcement policy of the Agencies with respect to competitor collaborations. By stating their general policy, the Agencies hope to assist businesses in assessing whether the Agencies will challenge a competitor collaboration or any of the agreements of which it is comprised.[3] However, these *Guidelines* cannot remove judgment and discretion in antitrust law enforcement. The Agencies evaluate each case in light of its own facts and apply the analytical framework set forth in these *Guidelines* reasonably and flexibly.[4]

A "competitor collaboration" comprises a set of one or more agreements, other than merger agreements, between or among competitors to engage in economic activity, and the economic activity resulting therefrom.[5] "Competitors" encompasses both actual and potential competitors.[6] Competitor collaborations involve one or more business activities, such as research and development ("R&D"), production, marketing, distribution, sales or purchasing. Information sharing and various trade association activities also may take place through competitor collaborations.

These *Guidelines* take into account neither the possible effects of competitor collaborations in foreclosing or limiting competition by rivals not participating in a collaboration nor the possible anticompetitive effects of standard setting in the

---

3.   These *Guidelines* neither describe how the Agencies litigate cases nor assign burdens of proof or production.

4.   The analytical framework set forth in these *Guidelines* is consistent with the analytical frameworks in the *Health Care Statements* and the *Intellectual Property Guidelines*, which remain in effect to address issues in their special contexts.

5.   These *Guidelines* use the terms "anticompetitive harm," "procompetitive benefit," and "overall competitive effect" in analyzing the competitive effects of agreements among competitors. All of these terms include actual and likely competitive effects. The *Guidelines* use the term "anticompetitive harm" to refer to an agreement's adverse competitive consequences, without taking account of offsetting procompetitive benefits. Conversely, the term "procompetitive benefit" refers to an agreement's favorable competitive consequences, without taking account of its anticompetitive harm. The terms "overall competitive effect" or "competitive effect" are used in discussing the combination of an agreement's anticompetitive harm and procompetitive benefit.

6.   Firms also may be in a buyer-seller or other relationship, but that does not eliminate the need to examine the competitor relationship, if present. A firm is treated as a potential competitor if there is evidence that entry by that firm is reasonably probable in the absence of the relevant agreement, or that competitively significant decisions by actual competitors are constrained by concerns that anticompetitive conduct likely would induce the firm to enter.

context of competitor collaborations. Nevertheless, these effects may be of concern to the Agencies and may prompt enforcement actions.

1.2 Overview of Analytical Framework

Two types of analysis are used by the Supreme Court to determine the lawfulness of an agreement among competitors: per se and rule of reason.[7] Certain types of agreements are so likely to harm competition and to have no significant procompetitive benefit that they do not warrant the time and expense required for particularized inquiry into their effects. Once identified, such agreements are challenged as per se unlawful.[8] All other agreements are evaluated under the rule of reason, which involves a factual inquiry into an agreement's overall competitive effect. As the Supreme Court has explained, rule of reason analysis entails a flexible inquiry and varies in focus and detail depending on the nature of the agreement and market circumstances.[9]

This overview briefly sets forth questions and factors that the Agencies assess in analyzing an agreement among competitors. The rest of the *Guidelines* should be consulted for the detailed definitions and discussion that underlie this analysis.

Agreements Challenged as Per Se Illegal. Agreements of a type that always or almost always tends to raise price or to reduce output are per se illegal. The Agencies challenge such agreements, once identified, as per se illegal. Types of agreements that have been held per se illegal include agreements among competitors to fix prices or output, rig bids, or share or divide markets by allocating customers, suppliers, territories, or lines of commerce. The courts conclusively presume such agreements, once identified, to be illegal, without inquiring into their claimed business purposes, anticompetitive harms, procompetitive benefits, or overall competitive effects. The Department of Justice prosecutes participants in hard-core cartel agreements criminally.

Agreements Analyzed under the Rule of Reason. Agreements not challenged as per se illegal are analyzed under the rule of reason to determine their overall competitive effect. These include agreements of a type that otherwise might be considered per se illegal, provided they are reasonably related to, and reasonably necessary to achieve procompetitive benefits from, an efficiency-enhancing integration of economic activity.

Rule of reason analysis focuses on the state of competition with, as compared to without, the relevant agreement. The central question is whether the relevant agreement likely harms competition by increasing the ability or incentive profitably to raise price above or reduce output, quality, service, or innovation below what likely would prevail in the absence of the relevant agreement.

Rule of reason analysis entails a flexible inquiry and varies in focus and detail depending on the nature of the agreement and market circumstances. The Agencies focus on only those factors, and undertake only that factual inquiry, necessary to

---

7. *See* National Soc'y of Prof'l Eng'rs v. United States, 435 U.S. 679, 692 (1978).
8. *See* FTC v. Superior Court Trial Lawyers Ass'n, 493 U.S. 411, 432-36 (1990).
9. *See* California Dental Ass'n v. FTC, 119 S. Ct. 1604, 1617-18 (1999); FTC v. Indiana Fed'n of Dentists, 476 U.S. 447, 459-61 (1986); National Collegiate Athletic Ass'n v. Board of Regents of the Univ. of Okla., 468 U.S. 85, 104-13 (1984).

make a sound determination of the overall competitive effect of the relevant agreement. Ordinarily, however, no one factor is dispositive in the analysis.

The Agencies' analysis begins with an examination of the nature of the relevant agreement. As part of this examination, the Agencies ask about the business purpose of the agreement and examine whether the agreement, if already in operation, has caused anticompetitive harm. In some cases, the nature of the agreement and the absence of market power together may demonstrate the absence of anticompetitive harm. In such cases, the Agencies do not challenge the agreement. Alternatively, where the likelihood of anticompetitive harm is evident from the nature of the agreement, or anticompetitive harm has resulted from an agreement already in operation, then, absent overriding benefits that could offset the anticompetitive harm, the Agencies challenge such agreements without a detailed market analysis.

If the initial examination of the nature of the agreement indicates possible competitive concerns, but the agreement is not one that would be challenged without a detailed market analysis, the Agencies analyze the agreement in greater depth. The Agencies typically define relevant markets and calculate market shares and concentration as an initial step in assessing whether the agreement may create or increase market power or facilitate its exercise. The Agencies examine the extent to which the participants and the collaboration have the ability and incentive to compete independently. The Agencies also evaluate other market circumstances, e.g. entry, that may foster or prevent anticompetitive harms.

If the examination of these factors indicates no potential for anticompetitive harm, the Agencies end the investigation without considering procompetitive benefits. If investigation indicates anticompetitive harm, the Agencies examine whether the relevant agreement is reasonably necessary to achieve procompetitive benefits that likely would offset anticompetitive harms.

1.3   *Competitor Collaborations Distinguished from Mergers*

The competitive effects from competitor collaborations may differ from those of mergers due to a number of factors. Most mergers completely end competition between the merging parties in the relevant market(s). By contrast, most competitor collaborations preserve some form of competition among the participants. This remaining competition may reduce competitive concerns, but also may raise questions about whether participants have agreed to anticompetitive restraints on the remaining competition.

Mergers are designed to be permanent, while competitor collaborations are more typically of limited duration. Thus, participants in a collaboration typically remain potential competitors, even if they are not actual competitors for certain purposes (e.g., R&D) during the collaboration. The potential for future competition between participants in a collaboration requires antitrust scrutiny different from that required for mergers.

Nonetheless, in some cases, competitor collaborations have competitive effects identical to those that would arise if the participants merged in whole or in part. The Agencies treat a competitor collaboration as a horizontal merger in a relevant market and analyze the collaboration pursuant to the *Horizontal Merger Guidelines* if appropriate, which ordinarily is when: (a) the participants are competitors in that relevant market; (b) the formation of the collaboration involves an efficiency-enhancing integration of economic activity in the relevant market; (c) the integration eliminates all competition among the participants in the relevant market; and (d) the collaboration does not terminate within a sufficiently limited period[10] by its own specific and express terms.[11] Effects of the collaboration on competition in other markets are analyzed as appropriate under these *Guidelines* or other applicable precedent. *See* Example 1.[12]

Section 2: General Principles for Evaluation Agreements among Competitors

2.1 Potential Procompetitive Benefits

The Agencies recognize that consumers may benefit from competitor collaborations in a variety of ways. For example, a competitor collaboration may enable participants to offer goods or services that are cheaper, more valuable to consumers, or brought to market faster than would be possible absent the collaboration. A collaboration may allow its participants to better use existing assets, or may provide incentives for them to make output-enhancing investments that would not occur absent the collaboration. The potential efficiencies from competitor collaborations may be achieved though a variety of contractual arrangements including joint ventures, trade or professional associations, licensing arrangements, or strategic alliances.

Efficiency gains from competitor collaborations often stem from combinations of different capabilities or resources. For example, one participant may have special technical expertise that usefully complements another participant's manufacturing process, allowing the latter participant to lower its production cost or improve the quality of its product. In other instances, a collaboration may facilitate the attainment of scale or scope economies beyond the reach of any single participant. For example, two firms may be able to combine their research or marketing activities to lower their cost of bringing their products to market, or reduce the time needed to develop and begin commercial sales of new products. Consumers may benefit from these collaborations as the participants are able to lower prices, improve quality, or bring new products to market faster.

2.2 Potential Anticompetitive Harms

Competitor collaborations may harm competition and consumers by increasing the ability or incentive profitably to raise price above or reduce output, quality, service, or innovation below what likely would prevail in the absence of the relevant agreement. Such effects may arise through a variety of mechanisms. Among other things, agreements may limit independent decision making or combine the control of

10. In general, the Agencies use ten years as a term indicating sufficient permanence to justify treatment of a competitor collaboration as analogous to a merger. The length of this term may vary, however, depending on industry-specific circumstances, such as technology life cycles.
11. This definition, however, does not determine obligations arising under the Hart-Scott-Rodino Antitrust Improvements Act of 1976, 15 U.S.C. § 18a.
12. Examples illustrating this and other points set forth in these *Guidelines* are included in the Appendix.

or financial interests in production, key assets, or decisions regarding price, output, or other competitively sensitive variables, or may otherwise reduce the participants' ability or incentive to compete independently.

Competitor collaborations also may facilitate explicit or tacit collusion through facilitating practices such as the exchange or disclosure of competitively sensitive information or through increased market concentration. Such collusion may involve the relevant market in which the collaboration operates or another market in which the participants in the collaboration are actual or potential competitors.

2.3   Analysis of the Overall Collaboration and the Agreements of Which It Consists

A competitor collaboration comprises a set of one or more agreements, other than merger agreements, between or among competitors to engage in economic activity, and the economic activity resulting therefrom. In general, the Agencies assess the competitive effects of the overall collaboration and any individual agreement or set of agreements within the collaboration that may harm competition. For purposes of these *Guidelines*, the phrase "relevant agreement" refers to whichever of these three —the overall collaboration, an individual agreement, or a set of agreements—the evaluating Agency is assessing. Two or more agreements are assessed together if their procompetitive benefits or anticompetitive harms are so intertwined that they cannot meaningfully be isolated and attributed to any individual agreement. *See* Example 2.

2.4   Competitive Effects Are Assessed as of the Time of Possible Harm to Competition

The competitive effects of a relevant agreement may change over time, depending on changes in circumstances such as internal reorganization, adoption of new agreements as part of the collaboration, addition or departure of participants, new market conditions, or changes in market share. The Agencies assess the competitive effects of a relevant agreement as of the time of possible harm to competition, whether at formation of the collaboration or at a later time, as appropriate. *See* Example 3. However, an assessment after a collaboration has been formed is sensitive to the reasonable expectations of participants whose significant sunk cost investments in reliance on the relevant agreement were made before it became anticompetitive.

Section 3:   Analytical Framework for Evaluating Agreements among Competitors

3.1   Introduction

Section 3 sets forth the analytical framework that the Agencies use to evaluate the competitive effects of a competitor collaboration and the agreements of which it consists. Certain types of agreements are so likely to be harmful to competition and to have no significant benefits that they do not warrant the time and expense required for particularized inquiry into their effects.[13] Once identified, such agreements are challenged as per se illegal.[14]

Agreements not challenged as per se illegal are analyzed under the rule of reason. Rule of reason analysis focuses on the state of competition with, as compared to without, the relevant agreement. Under the rule of reason, the central question is whether the relevant agreement likely harms competition by increasing the ability or incentive profitably to raise price above or reduce output, quality, service, or innovation below what likely would prevail in the absence of the relevant agreement. Given the great variety of competitor collaborations, rule of reason analysis entails a flexible inquiry and varies in focus and detail depending on the nature of the agreement and market circumstances. Rule of reason analysis focuses on only those factors, and undertakes only the degree of factual inquiry, necessary to assess accurately the overall competitive effect of the relevant agreement.[15]

3.2 Agreements Challenged as Per Se Illegal

Agreements of a type that always or almost always tends to raise price or reduce output are per se illegal.[16] The Agencies challenge such agreements, once identified, as per se illegal. Typically these are agreements not to compete on price or output. Types of agreements that have been held per se illegal include agreements among competitors to fix prices or output, rig bids, or share or divide markets by allocating customers, suppliers, territories or lines of commerce.[17] The courts conclusively presume such agreements, once identified, to be illegal, without inquiring into their claimed business purposes, anticompetitive harms, procompetitive benefits, or overall competitive effects. The Department of Justice prosecutes participants in hard-core cartel agreements criminally.

If, however, participants in an efficiency-enhancing integration of economic activity enter into an agreement that is reasonably related to the integration and reasonably necessary to achieve its procompetitive benefits, the Agencies analyze the agreement under the rule of reason, even if it is of a type that might otherwise be considered per se illegal.[18] See Example 4. In an efficiency-enhancing integration, participants collaborate to perform or cause to be performed (by a joint venture entity created by the collaboration or by one or more participants or by a third party acting on behalf of other participants) one or more business functions, such as production, distribution, marketing, purchasing or R&D, and thereby benefit, or potentially benefit, consumers by expanding output, reducing price, or enhancing quality, service, or innovation. Participants in an efficiency-enhancing integration typically combine, by contract or otherwise, significant capital, technology, or other complementary assets to achieve procompetitive benefits that the participants could not achieve separately. The mere coordination of decisions on price, output,

---

13. *See* Continental TV, Inc. v. GTE Sylvania Inc., 433 U.S. 36, 50 n.16 (1977).
14. *See Superior Court Trial Lawyers Ass'n*, 493 U.S. at 432-36.
15. *See California Dental Ass'n*, 119 S. Ct. at 1617-18; *Indiana Fed'n of Dentists*, 476 U.S. at 459-61; *NCAA*, 468 U.S. at 104-13.
16. *See* Broadcast Music, Inc. v. Columbia Broadcasting Sys., 441 U.S. 1, 19-20 (1979).
17. *See, e.g.*, Palmer v. BRG of Georgia, Inc., 498 U.S. 46 (1990) (market allocation); United States v. Trenton Potteries Co., 273 U.S. 392 (1927) (price fixing).
18. *See* Arizona v. Maricopa County Medical Soc'y, 457 U.S. 332, 339 n.7, 356-57 (1982) (finding no integration).

customers, territories, and the like is not integration, and cost savings without integration are not a basis for avoiding per se condemnation. The integration must be of a type that plausibly would generate procompetitive benefits cognizable under the efficiencies analysis set forth in Section 3.36 below. Such procompetitive benefits may enhance the participants' ability or incentives to compete and thus may offset an agreement's anticompetitive tendencies. *See* Examples 5 through 7.

An agreement may be "reasonably necessary" without being essential. However, if the participants could achieve an equivalent or comparable efficiency-enhancing integration through practical, significantly less restrictive means, then the Agencies conclude that the agreement is not reasonably necessary.[19] In making this assessment, except in unusual circumstances, the Agencies consider whether practical, significantly less restrictive means were reasonably available when the agreement was entered into, but do not search for a theoretically less restrictive alternative that was not practical given the business realities.

Before accepting a claim that an agreement is reasonably necessary to achieve procompetitive benefits from an integration of economic activity, the Agencies undertake a limited factual inquiry to evaluate the claim.[20] Such an inquiry may reveal that efficiencies from an agreement that are possible in theory are not plausible in the context of the particular collaboration. Some claims—such as those premised on the notion that competition itself is unreasonable—are insufficient as a matter of law,[21] and others may be implausible on their face. In any case, labeling an arrangement a "joint venture" will not protect what is merely a device to raise price or restrict output;[22] the nature of the conduct, not its designation, is determinative.

3.3   Agreements Analyzed under the Rule of Reason

Agreements not challenged as per se illegal are analyzed under the rule of reason to determine their overall competitive effect. Rule of reason analysis focuses on the state of competition with, as compared to without, the relevant agreement. The central question is whether the relevant agreement likely harms competition by increasing the ability or incentive profitably to raise price above or reduce output, quality, service, or innovation below what likely would prevail in the absence of the relevant agreement.[23]

Rule of reason analysis entails a flexible inquiry and varies in focus and detail depending on the nature of the agreement and market circumstances.[24] The Agencies

19. *See id.* at 352-53 (observing that even if a maximum fee schedule for physicians' services were desirable, it was not necessary that the schedule be established by physicians rather than by insurers); *Broadcast Music*, 441 U.S. at 20-21 (setting of price "necessary" for the blanket license).

20. *See Maricopa*, 457 U.S. at 352-53, 356-57 (scrutinizing the defendant medical foundations for indicia of integration and evaluating the record evidence regarding less restrictive alternatives).

21. *See Indiana Fed'n of Dentists*, 476 U.S. at 463-64; *NCAA*, 468 U.S. at 116-17; *Prof'l Eng'rs*, 435 U.S. at 693-96. Other claims, such as an absence of market power, are no defense to per se illegality. *See Superior Court Trial Lawyers Ass'n*, 493 U.S. at 434-36; United States v. Socony-Vacuum Oil Co., 310 U.S. 150, 224-26 & n.59 (1940).

22. *See* Timken Roller Bearing Co. v. United States, 341 U.S. 593, 598 (1951).

23. In addition, concerns may arise where an agreement increases the ability or incentive of buyers to exercise monopsony power. *See infra* Section 3.31(a).

24. *See California Dental Ass'n*, 119 S. Ct. at 1612-13, 1617 ("What is required . . . is an enquiry meet for the case, looking to the circumstances, details, and logic of a restraint."); *NCAA*, 468 U.S. 109 n.39 ("the rule of reason can sometimes be applied in the twinkling of an eye") (quoting PHILLIP F.

focus on only those factors, and undertake only that factual inquiry, necessary to make a sound determination of the overall competitive effect of the relevant agreement. Ordinarily, however, no one factor is dispositive in the analysis.

Under the rule of reason, the Agencies' analysis begins with an examination of the nature of the relevant agreement, since the nature of the agreement determines the types of anticompetitive harms that may be of concern. As part of this examination, the Agencies ask about the business purpose of the agreement and examine whether the agreement, if already in operation, has caused anticompetitive harm.[25] If the nature of the agreement and the absence of market power[26] together demonstrate the absence of anticompetitive harm, the Agencies do not challenge the agreement. *See* Example 8. Alternatively, where the likelihood of anticompetitive harm is evident from the nature of the agreement,[27] or anticompetitive harm has resulted from an agreement already in operation[28] then, absent overriding benefits that could offset the anticompetitive harm, the Agencies challenge such agreements without a detailed market analysis.[29]

If the initial examination of the nature of the agreement indicates possible competitive concerns, but the agreement is not one that would be challenged without a detailed market analysis, the Agencies analyze the agreement in greater depth. The Agencies typically define relevant markets and calculate market shares and concentration as an initial step in assessing whether the agreement may create or increase market power[30] or facilitate its exercise and thus poses risks to competition.[31] The Agencies examine factors relevant to the extent to which the participants and the collaboration have the ability and incentive to compete independently, such as whether an agreement is exclusive or non-exclusive and its duration.[32] The Agencies also evaluate whether entry would be timely, likely, and sufficient to deter or

---

AREEDA, THE "RULE OF REASON" IN ANTITRUST ANALYSIS: GENERAL ISSUES 37-38 (Federal Judicial Center, June 1981)).

25. *See* Board of Trade of the City of Chicago v. United States, 246 U.S. 231, 238 (1918).
26. That market power is absent may be determined without defining a relevant market. For example, if no market power is likely under any plausible market definition, it does not matter which one is correct. Alternatively, easy entry may indicate an absence of market power.
27. *See California Dental Ass'n*, 119 S. Ct. at 1612-13, 1617 (an "obvious anticompetitive effect" would warrant quick condemnation); *Indiana Fed'n of Dentists*, 476 U.S. at 459; *NCAA*, 468 U.S. at 104, 106-10.
28. *See Indiana Fed'n of Dentists*, 476 U.S. at 460-61 ("Since the purpose of the inquiries into market definition and market power is to determine whether an arrangement has the potential for genuine adverse effects on competition, 'proof of actual detrimental effects, such as a reduction of output,' can obviate the need for an inquiry into market power, which is but a 'surrogate for detrimental effects.'") (quoting 7 PHILLIP E. AREEDA, ANTITRUST LAW ¶ 1511, at 424 (1986)); *NCAA*, 468 U.S. at 104-08, 110 n.42.
29. *See Indiana Fed'n of Dentists*, 476 U.S. at 459-60 (condemning without "detailed market analysis" an agreement to limit competition by withholding x-rays from patients' insurers after finding no competitive justification).
30. Market power to a seller is the ability profitably to maintain prices above competitive levels for a significant period of time. Sellers also may exercise market power with respect to significant competitive dimensions other than price, such as quality, service, or innovation. Market power to a buyer is the ability profitably to depress the price paid for a product below the competitive level for a significant period of time and thereby depress output.
31. *See* Eastman Kodak Co. v. Image Technical Services, Inc., 504 U.S. 451, 464 (1992).
32. *Compare NCAA*, 468 U.S. at 113-15, 119-20 (noting that colleges were not permitted to televise their own games without restraint), *with Broadcast Music*, 441 U.S. at 23-24 (finding no legal or practical impediment to individual licenses).

counteract any anticompetitive harms. In addition, the Agencies assess any other market circumstances that may foster or impede anticompetitive harms.

If the examination of these factors indicates no potential for anticompetitive harm, the Agencies end the investigation without considering procompetitive benefits. If investigation indicates anticompetitive harm, the Agencies examine whether the relevant agreement is reasonably necessary to achieve procompetitive benefits that likely would offset anticompetitive harms.[33]

3.31   NATURE OF THE RELEVANT AGREEMENT: BUSINESS PURPOSE, OPERATION IN THE MARKETPLACE AND POSSIBLE COMPETITIVE CONCERNS

The nature of the agreement is relevant to whether it may cause anticompetitive harm. For example, by limiting independent decision making or combining control over or financial interests in production, key assets, or decisions on price, output, or other competitively sensitive variables, an agreement may create or increase market power or facilitate its exercise by the collaboration, its participants, or both. An agreement to limit independent decision making or to combine control or financial interests may reduce the ability or incentive to compete independently. An agreement also may increase the likelihood of an exercise of market power by facilitating explicit or tacit collusion,[34] either through facilitating practices such as an exchange of competitively sensitive information or through increased market concentration.

In examining the nature of the relevant agreement, the Agencies take into account inferences about business purposes for the agreement that can be drawn from objective facts. The Agencies also consider evidence of the subjective intent of the participants to the extent that it sheds light on competitive effects.[35] The Agencies do not undertake a full analysis of procompetitive benefits pursuant to Section 3.36 below, however, unless an anticompetitive harm appears likely. The Agencies also examine whether an agreement already in operation has caused anticompetitive harm.[36] Anticompetitive harm may be observed, for example, if a competitor collaboration successfully mandates new, anticompetitive conduct or successfully eliminates procompetitive pre-collaboration conduct, such as withholding services that were desired by consumers when offered in a competitive market. If anticompetitive harm is found, examination of market power ordinarily is not required. In some cases, however, a determination of anticompetitive harm may be informed by consideration of market power.

The following sections illustrate competitive concerns that may arise from the nature of particular types of competitor collaborations. This list is not exhaustive. In addition, where these sections address agreements of a type that otherwise might be

---

33. *See NCAA*, 468 U.S. at 113-15 (rejecting efficiency claims when production was limited, not enhanced); *Prof'l Eng'rs*, 435 U.S. at 696 (dictum) (distinguishing restraints that promote competition from those that eliminate competition); *Chicago Bd. of Trade*, 246 U.S. at 238 (same).

34. As used in these *Guidelines*, "collusion" is not limited to conduct that involves an agreement under the antitrust jaws.

35. Anticompetitive intent alone does not establish an antitrust violation, and procompetitive intent does not preclude a violation. *See, e.g., Chicago Bd. of Trade*, 246 U.S. at 238. But extrinsic evidence of intent may aid in evaluating market power, the likelihood of anticompetitive harm, and claimed procompetitive justifications where an agreement's effects are otherwise ambiguous.

36. *See id.*

considered per se illegal, such as agreements on price, the discussion assumes that the agreements already have been determined to be subject to rule of reason analysis because they are reasonably related to, and reasonably necessary to achieve procompetitive benefits from, an efficiency-enhancing integration of economic activity. *See supra* Section 3.2.

3.31(a) Relevant Agreements That Limit Independent Decision Making or Combine Control or Financial Interests

The following is intended to illustrate but not exhaust the types of agreements that might harm competition by eliminating independent decision making or combining control or financial interests.

Production Collaborations. Competitor collaborations may involve agreements jointly to produce a product sold to others or used by the participants as an input. Such agreements are often procompetitive.[37] Participants may combine complementary technologies, know-how, or other assets to enable the collaboration to produce a good more efficiently or to produce a good that no one participant alone could produce. However, production collaborations may involve agreements on the level of output or the use of key assets, or on the price at which the product will be marketed by the collaboration, or on other competitively significant variables, such as quality, service, or promotional strategies, that can result in anticompetitive harm. Such agreements can create or increase market power or facilitate its exercise by limiting independent decision making or by combining in the collaboration, or in certain participants, the control over some or all production or key assets or decisions about key competitive variables that otherwise would be controlled independently.[38] Such agreements could reduce individual participants' control over assets necessary to compete and thereby reduce their ability to compete independently, combine financial interests in ways that undermine incentives to compete independently or both.

Marketing Collaborations. Competitor collaborations may involve agreements jointly to sell, distribute, or promote goods or services that are either jointly or individually produced. Such agreements may be procompetitive, for example, where a combination of complementary assets enables products more quickly and efficiently to reach the marketplace. However, marketing collaborations may involve agreements on price, output, or other competitively significant variables, or on the use of competitively significant assets, such as an extensive distribution network, that can result in anticompetitive harm. Such agreements can create or increase market

---

37. The NCRPA accords rule of reason treatment to certain production collaborations. However, the statute permits per se challenges, in appropriate circumstances, to a variety of activities, including agreements to jointly market the goods or services produced or to limit the participants' independent sale of goods or services produced outside the collaboration. NCRPA, 15 U.S.C. §§ 4301-02.

38. For example, where output resulting from a collaboration is transferred to participants for independent marketing, anticompetitive harm could result if that output is restricted or if the transfer takes place at a supracompetitive price. Such conduct could raise participants' marginal costs through inflated per-unit charges on the transfer of the collaboration's output. Anticompetitive harm could occur even if there is vigorous competition among collaboration participants in the output market, since all the participants would have paid the same inflated transfer price.

power or facilitate its exercise by limiting independent decision making; by combining in the collaboration, or in certain participants, control over competitively significant assets or decisions about competitively significant variables that otherwise would be controlled independently; or by combining financial interests in ways that undermine incentives to compete independently. For example, joint promotion might reduce or eliminate comparative advertising, thus harming competition by restricting information to consumers on price and other competitively significant variables.

Buying Collaborations. Competitor collaborations may involve agreements jointly to purchase necessary inputs. Many such agreements do not raise antitrust concerns and indeed may be procompetitive. Purchasing collaborations, for example, may enable participants to centralize ordering, to combine warehousing or distribution functions more efficiently, or to achieve other efficiencies. However, such agreements can create or increase market power (which, in the case of buyers, is called "monopsony power") or facilitate its exercise by increasing the ability or incentive to drive the price of the purchased product, and thereby depress output, below what likely would prevail in the absence of the relevant agreement. Buying collaborations also may facilitate collusion by standardizing participants' costs or by enhancing the ability to project or monitor a participant's output level through knowledge of its input purchases.

Research & Development Collaborations. Competitor collaborations may involve agreements to engage in joint research and development ("R&D"). Most such agreements are procompetitive, and they typically are analyzed under the rule of reason.[39] Through the combination of complementary assets, technology, or know-how, an R&D collaboration may enable participants more quickly or more efficiently to research and develop new or improved goods, services, or production processes. Joint R&D agreements, however, can create or increase market power or facilitate its exercise by limiting independent decision making or by combining in the collaboration, or in certain participants, control over competitively significant assets or all or a portion of participants' individual competitive R&D efforts. Although R&D collaborations also may facilitate tacit collusion on R&D efforts, achieving, monitoring, and punishing departures from collusion is sometimes difficult in the R&D context.

An exercise of market power may injure consumers by reducing innovation below the level that otherwise would prevail, leading to fewer or no products for consumers to choose from, lower quality products, or products that reach consumers more slowly than they otherwise would. An exercise of market power also may injure consumers by reducing the number of independent competitors in the market for the goods, services, or production processes derived from the R&D collaboration, leading to higher prices or reduced output, quality, or service. A central question is whether the agreement increases the ability or incentive anticompetitively to reduce R&D efforts pursued independently or through the collaboration, for example, by slowing the pace at which R&D efforts are pursued. Other considerations being equal, R&D agreements are more likely to raise competitive concerns when the

---

39. Aspects of the antitrust analysis of competitor collaborations involving R&D are governed by provisions of the NCRPA, 15 U.S.C. §§ 4301-02.

collaboration or its participants already possess a secure source of market power over an existing product and the new R&D efforts might cannibalize their supracompetitive earnings.   In addition, anticompetitive harm generally is more likely when R&D competition is confined to firms with specialized characteristics or assets, such as intellectual property, or when a regulatory approval process limits the ability of late-comers to catch up with competitors already engaged in the R&D.

3.31(b)   Relevant Agreements That May Facilitate Collusion

Each of the types of competitor collaborations outlined above can facilitate collusion. Competitor collaborations may provide an opportunity for participants to discuss and agree on anticompetitive terms, or otherwise to collude anticompetitively, as well as a greater ability to detect and punish deviations that would undermine the collusion.   Certain marketing, production, and buying collaborations, for example, may provide opportunities for their participants to collude on price, output, customers, territories, or other competitively sensitive variables. R&D collaborations, however, may be less likely to facilitate collusion regarding R&D activities since R&D often is conducted in secret, and it thus may be difficult to monitor an agreement to coordinate R&D. In addition, collaborations can increase concentration in a relevant market and thus increase the likelihood of collusion among all firms, including the collaboration and its participants.

Agreements that facilitate collusion sometimes involve the exchange or disclosure of information. The Agencies recognize that the sharing of information among competitors may be procompetitive and is often reasonably necessary to achieve the procompetitive benefits of certain collaborations; for example, sharing certain technology, know-how, or other intellectual property may be essential to achieve the procompetitive benefits of an R&D collaboration. Nevertheless, in some cases, the sharing of information related to a market in which the collaboration operates or in which the participants are actual or potential competitors may increase the likelihood of collusion on matters such as price, output, or other competitively sensitive variables. The competitive concern depends on the nature of the information shared. Other things being equal, the sharing of information relating to price, output, costs, or strategic planning is more likely to raise competitive concern than the sharing of information relating to less competitively sensitive variables. Similarly, other things being equal, the sharing of information on current operating and future business plans is more likely to raise concerns than the sharing of historical information. Finally, other things being equal, the sharing of individual company data is more likely to raise concern than the sharing of aggregated data that does not permit recipients to identify individual firm data.

3.32   RELEVANT MARKETS AFFECTED BY THE COLLABORATION

The Agencies typically identify and assess competitive effects in all of the relevant product and geographic markets in which competition may be affected by a competitor collaboration, although in some cases it may be possible to assess competitive effects directly without defining a particular relevant market(s). Markets affected by a competitor collaboration include all markets in which the economic integration of the participants' operations occurs or in which the collaboration operates or will operate,[40] and may also include additional markets in which any participant is an actual or potential competitor.[41]

3.32(a) Goods Markets

In general, for goods[42] markets affected by a competitor collaboration, the Agencies approach relevant market definition as described in Section 1 of the *Horizontal Merger Guidelines*. To determine the relevant market, the Agencies generally consider the likely reaction of buyers to a price increase and typically ask, among other things, how buyers would respond to increases over prevailing price levels. However, when circumstances strongly suggest that the prevailing price exceeds what likely would have prevailed absent the relevant agreement, the Agencies use a price more reflective of the price that likely would have prevailed. Once a market has been defined, market shares are assigned both to firms currently in the relevant market and to firms that are able to make "uncommitted" supply responses. *See* Sections 1.31 and 1.32 of the *Horizontal Merger Guidelines*.

3.32(b) Technology Markets

When rights to intellectual property are marketed separately from the products in which they are used, the Agencies may define technology markets in assessing the competitive effects of a competitor collaboration that includes an agreement to license intellectual property. Technology markets consist of the intellectual property that is licensed and its close substitutes; that is, the technologies or goods that are close enough substitutes significantly to constrain the exercise of market power with respect to the intellectual property that is licensed. The Agencies approach the definition of a relevant technology market and the measurement of market share as described in Section 3.2.2 of the *Intellectual Property Guidelines*.

3.32(c) Research and Development: Innovation Markets

In many cases, an agreement's competitive effects on innovation are analyzed as a separate competitive effect in a relevant goods market. However, if a competitor collaboration may have competitive effects on innovation that cannot be adequately addressed through the analysis of goods or technology markets, the Agencies may define and analyze an innovation market as described in Section 3.2.3 of the *Intellectual Property Guidelines*. An innovation market consists of the research and development directed to particular new or improved goods or processes and the close substitutes for that research and development. The Agencies define an innovation market only when the capabilities to engage in the relevant research and development can be associated with specialized assets or characteristics of specific firms.

---

40. For example, where a production joint venture buys inputs from an upstream market to incorporate in products to be sold in a downstream market, both upstream and downstream markets may be "markets affected by a competitor collaboration."

41. Participation in the collaboration may change the participants' behavior in this third category of markets, for example, by altering incentives and available information, or by providing an opportunity to form additional agreements among participants.

42. The term "goods" also includes services.

3.33   *Market Shares and Market Concentration*

Market share and market concentration affect the likelihood that the relevant agreement will create or increase market power or facilitate its exercise. The creation, increase, or facilitation of market power will likely increase the ability and incentive profitably to raise price above or reduce output, quality, service, or innovation below what likely would prevail in the absence of the relevant agreement.

Other things being equal, market share affects the extent to which participants or the collaboration must restrict their own output in order to achieve anticompetitive effects in a relevant market. The smaller the percentage of total supply that a firm controls, the more severely it must restrict its own output in order to produce a given price increase, and the less likely it is that an output restriction will be profitable. In assessing whether an agreement may cause anticompetitive harm, the Agencies typically calculate the market shares of the participants and of the collaboration.[43] The Agencies assign a range of market shares to the collaboration. The high end of that range is the sum of the market shares of the collaboration and its participants. The low end is the share of the collaboration in isolation. In general, the Agencies approach the calculation of market share as set forth in Section 1.4 of the *Horizontal Merger Guidelines*.

Other things being equal, market concentration affects the difficulties and costs of achieving and enforcing collusion in a relevant market. Accordingly, in assessing whether an agreement may increase the likelihood of collusion, the Agencies calculate market concentration. In general, the Agencies approach the calculation of market concentration as set forth in Section 1.5 of the *Horizontal Merger Guidelines*, ascribing to the competitor collaboration the same range of market shares described above.

Market share and market concentration provide only a starting point for evaluating the competitive effect of the relevant agreement. The Agencies also examine other factors outlined in the *Horizontal Merger Guidelines* as set forth below:

The Agencies consider whether factors such as those discussed in Section 1.52 of the *Horizontal Merger Guidelines* indicate that market share and concentration data overstate or understate the likely competitive significance of participants and their collaboration.

In assessing whether anticompetitive harm may arise from an agreement that combines control over or financial interests in assets or otherwise limits independent decision making, the Agencies consider whether factors such as those discussed in Section 2.2 of the *Horizontal Merger Guidelines* suggest that anticompetitive harm is more or less likely.

In assessing whether anticompetitive harms may arise from an agreement that may increase the likelihood of collusion, the Agencies consider whether factors such as those discussed in Section 2.1 of the *Horizontal Merger Guidelines* suggest that anticompetitive harm is more or less likely.

---

43.   When the competitive concern is that a limitation on independent decision making or a combination of control or financial interests may yield an anticompetitive reduction of research and development, the Agencies typically frame their inquiries more generally, looking to the strength, scope, and number of competing R&D efforts and their close substitutes. *See supra* Sections 3.31(a) and 3.32(c).

In evaluating the significance of market share and market concentration data and interpreting the range of market shares ascribed to the collaboration, the Agencies also examine factors beyond those set forth in the *Horizontal Merger Guidelines*. The following section describes which factors are relevant and the issues that the Agencies examine in evaluating those factors.

3.34   FACTORS RELEVANT TO THE ABILITY AND INCENTIVE OF THE PARTICIPANTS AND THE COLLABORATION TO COMPETE

Competitor collaborations sometimes do not end competition among the participants and the collaboration. Participants may continue to compete against each other and their collaboration, either through separate, independent business operations or through membership in other collaborations. Collaborations may be managed by decision makers independent of the individual participants. Control over key competitive variables may remain outside the collaboration, such as where participants independently market and set prices for the collaboration's output.

Sometimes, however, competition among the participants and the collaboration may be restrained through explicit contractual terms or through financial or other provisions that reduce or eliminate the incentive to compete. The Agencies look to the competitive benefits and harms of the relevant agreement, not merely the formal terms of agreements among the participants.

Where the nature of the agreement and market share and market concentration data reveal a likelihood of anticompetitive harm, the Agencies more closely examine the extent to which the participants and the collaboration have the ability and incentive to compete independent of each other. The Agencies are likely to focus on six factors: (a) the extent to which the relevant agreement is non-exclusive in that participants are likely to continue to compete independently outside the collaboration in the market in which the collaboration operates; (b) the extent to which participants retain independent control of assets necessary to compete; (c) the nature and extent of participants' financial interests in the collaboration or in each other; (d) the control of the collaboration's competitively significant decision making; (e) the likelihood of anticompetitive information sharing; and (f) the duration of the collaboration.

Each of these factors is discussed in further detail below. Consideration of these factors may reduce or increase competitive concern. The analysis necessarily is flexible: the relevance and significance of each factor depends upon the facts and circumstances of each case, and any additional factors pertinent under the circumstances are considered. For example, when an agreement is examined subsequent to formation of the collaboration, the Agencies also examine factual evidence concerning participants' actual conduct.

3.34(a)   Exclusivity

The Agencies consider whether, to what extent, and in what manner the relevant agreement permits participants to continue to compete against each other and their collaboration, either through separate, independent business operations or through membership in other collaborations. The Agencies inquire whether a collaboration is non-exclusive in fact as well as in name and consider any costs or other impediments to competing with the collaboration. In assessing exclusivity when an agreement already is in operation, the Agencies examine whether, to what extent, and in what manner participants actually have continued to compete against each other and the collaboration. In general, competitive concern likely is reduced to the extent that participants actually have continued to compete, either through separate, independent business operations or through membership in other collaborations, or are permitted to do so.

3.34(b) Control over Assets

The Agencies ask whether the relevant agreement requires participants to contribute to the collaboration significant assets that previously have enabled or likely would enable participants to be effective independent competitors in markets affected by the collaboration. If such resources must be contributed to the collaboration and are specialized in that they cannot readily be replaced, the participants may have lost all or some of their ability to compete against each other and their collaboration, even if they retain the contractual right to do so.[44] In general, the greater the contribution of specialized assets to the collaboration that is required, the less the participants may be relied upon to provide independent competition.

3.34(c) Financial Interests in the Collaboration or in Other Participants

The Agencies assess each participant's financial interest in the collaboration and its potential impact on the participant's incentive to compete independently with the collaboration. The potential impact may vary depending on the size and nature of the financial interest (e.g., whether the financial interest is debt or equity). In general, the greater the financial interest in the collaboration, the less likely is the participant to compete with the collaboration.[45] The Agencies also assess direct equity investments between or among the participants. Such investments may reduce the incentives of the participants to compete with each other. In either case, the analysis is sensitive to the level of financial interest in the collaboration or in another participant relative to the level of the participant's investment in its independent business operations in the markets affected by the collaboration.

3.34(d) Control of the Collaboration's Competitively Significant Decision Making

The Agencies consider the manner in which a collaboration is organized and governed in assessing the extent to which participants and their collaboration have the ability and incentive to compete independently. Thus, the Agencies consider the extent to which the collaboration's governance structure enables the collaboration to act as an independent decision maker. For example, the Agencies ask whether participants are allowed to appoint members of a board of directors for the collaboration, if incorporated, or otherwise to exercise significant control over the operations of the collaboration. In general, the collaboration is less likely to compete

---

44. For example, if participants in a production collaboration must contribute most of their productive capacity to the collaboration, the collaboration may impair the ability of its participants to remain effective independent competitors regardless of the terms of the agreement.

45. Similarly, a collaboration's financial interest in a participant may diminish the collaboration's incentive to compete with that participant.

independently as participants gain greater control over the collaboration's price, output, and other competitively significant decisions.[46]

To the extent that the collaboration's decision making is subject to the participants' control, the Agencies consider whether that control could be exercised jointly. Joint control over the collaboration's price and output levels could create or increase market power and raise competitive concerns. Depending on the nature of the collaboration, competitive concern also may arise due to joint control over other competitively significant decisions, such as the level and scope of R&D efforts and investment. In contrast, to the extent that participants independently set the price and quantity[47] of their share of a collaboration's output and independently control other competitively significant decisions, an agreement's likely anticompetitive harm is reduced.[48]

3.34(e) Likelihood of Anticompetitive Information Sharing

The Agencies evaluate the extent to which competitively sensitive information concerning markets affected by the collaboration likely would be disclosed. This likelihood depends on, among other things, the nature of the collaboration, its organization and governance, and safeguards implemented to prevent or minimize such disclosure. For example, participants might refrain from assigning marketing personnel to an R&D collaboration, or, in a marketing collaboration, participants might limit access to competitively sensitive information regarding their respective operations to only certain individuals or to an independent third party. Similarly, a buying collaboration might use an independent third party to handle negotiations in which its participants' input requirements or other competitively sensitive information could be revealed. In general, it is less likely that the collaboration will facilitate collusion on competitively sensitive variables if appropriate safeguards governing information sharing are in place.

3.34(f) Duration of the Collaboration

The Agencies consider the duration of the collaboration in assessing whether participants retain the ability and incentive to compete against each other and their collaboration. In general, the shorter the duration, the more likely participants are to compete against each other and their collaboration.

---

46. Control may diverge from financial interests. For example, a small equity investment may be coupled with a right to veto large capital expenditures and, thereby, to effectively limit output. The Agencies examine a collaboration's actual governance structure in assessing issues of control.

47. Even if prices to consumers are set independently, anticompetitive harms may still occur if participants jointly set the collaboration's level of output. For example, participants may effectively coordinate price increases by reducing the collaboration's level of output and collecting their profits through high transfer prices, i.e., through the amounts that participants contribute to the collaboration in exchange for each unit of the collaboration's output. Where a transfer price is determined by reference to an objective measure not under the control of the participants (e.g., average price in a different unconcentrated geographic market), competitive concern may be less likely.

48. Anticompetitive harm also is less likely if individual participants may independently increase the overall output of the collaboration.

3.35 ENTRY

Easy entry may deter or prevent profitably maintaining price above, or output, quality, service or innovation below, what likely would prevail in the absence of the relevant agreement. Where the nature of the agreement and market share and concentration data suggest a likelihood of anticompetitive harm that is not sufficiently mitigated by any continuing competition identified through the analysis in Section 3.34, the Agencies inquire whether entry would be timely, likely, and sufficient in its magnitude, character and scope to deter or counteract the anticompetitive harm of concern. If so, the relevant agreement ordinarily requires no further analysis.

As a general matter, the Agencies assess timeliness, likelihood, and sufficiency of committed entry under principles set forth in Section 3 of the *Horizontal Merger Guidelines*.[49] However, unlike mergers, competitor collaborations often restrict only certain business activities, while preserving competition among participants in other respects, and they may be designed to terminate after a limited duration. Consequently, the extent to which an agreement creates and enables identification of opportunities that would induce entry and the conditions under which ease of entry may deter or counteract anticompetitive harms may be more complex and less direct than for mergers and will vary somewhat according to the nature of the relevant agreement. For example, the likelihood of entry may be affected by what potential entrants believe about the probable duration of an anticompetitive agreement. Other things being equal, the shorter the anticipated duration of an anticompetitive agreement, the smaller the profit opportunities for potential entrants, and the lower the likelihood that it will induce committed entry. Examples of other differences are set forth below.

For certain collaborations, sufficiency of entry may be affected by the possibility that entrants will participate in the anticompetitive agreement. To the extent that such participation raises the amount of entry needed to deter or counteract anticompetitive harms, and assets required for entry are not adequately available for entrants to respond fully to their sales opportunities, or otherwise renders entry inadequate in magnitude, character or scope, sufficient entry may be more difficult to achieve.[50]

---

49. Committed entry is defined as new competition that requires expenditure of significant sunk costs of entry and exit. *See* Section 3.0 of the *Horizontal Merger Guidelines*.

50. Under the same principles applied to production and marketing collaborations, the exercise of monopsony power by a buying collaboration may be deterred or counteracted by the entry of new purchasers. To the extent that collaborators reduce their purchases, they may create an opportunity for new buyers to make purchases without forcing the price of the input above pre-relevant agreement levels. Committed purchasing entry, defined as new purchasing competition that requires expenditure of significant sunk costs of entry and exit—such as a new steel factory built in response to a reduction in the price of iron ore—is analyzed under principles analogous to those articulated in Section 3 of the *Horizontal Merger Guidelines*. Under that analysis, the Agencies assess whether a monopsonistic price reduction is likely to attract committed purchasing entry, profitable at pre-relevant agreement prices, that would not have occurred before the relevant agreement at those same prices. (Uncommitted new buyers are identified as participants in the relevant market if their demand responses to a price decrease are likely to occur within one year and without the expenditure of significant sunk costs of entry and exit. *See id.* at Sections 1.32 and 1.41.)

In the context of research and development collaborations, widespread availability of R&D capabilities and the large gains that may accrue to successful innovators often suggest a high likelihood that entry will deter or counteract anticompetitive reductions of R&D efforts. Nonetheless, such conditions do not always pertain, and the Agencies ask whether entry may deter or counteract anticompetitive R&D reductions, taking into account the likelihood, timeliness, and sufficiency of entry.

To be timely, entry must be sufficiently prompt to deter or counteract such harms. The Agencies evaluate the likelihood of entry based on the extent to which potential entrants have (1) core competencies (and the ability to acquire any necessary specialized assets) that give them the ability to enter into competing R&D and (2) incentives to enter into competing R&D. The sufficiency of entry depends on whether the character and scope of the entrants' R&D efforts are close enough to the reduced R&D efforts to be likely to achieve similar innovations in the same time frame or otherwise to render a collaborative reduction of R&D unprofitable.

3.36   IDENTIFYING PROCOMPETITIVE BENEFITS OF THE COLLABORATION

Competition usually spurs firms to achieve efficiencies internally. Nevertheless, as explained above, competitor collaborations have the potential to generate significant efficiencies that benefit consumers in a variety of ways. For example, a competitor collaboration may enable firms to offer goods or services that are cheaper, more valuable to consumers, or brought to market faster than would otherwise be possible. Efficiency gains from competitor collaborations often stem from combinations of different capabilities or resources. *See supra* Section 2.1. Indeed, the primary benefit of competitor collaborations to the economy is their potential to generate such efficiencies.

Efficiencies generated through a competitor collaboration can enhance the ability and incentive of the collaboration and its participants to compete, which may result in lower prices, improved quality, enhanced service, or new products. For example, through collaboration, competitors may be able to produce an input more efficiently than any one participant could individually; such collaboration-generated efficiencies may enhance competition by permitting two or more ineffective (e.g., high cost) participants to become more effective, lower cost competitors. Even when efficiencies generated through a competitor collaboration enhance the collaboration's or the participants' ability to compete, however, a competitor collaboration may have other effects that may lessen competition and ultimately may make the relevant agreement anticompetitive.

If the Agencies conclude that the relevant agreement has caused, or is likely to cause, anticompetitive harm, they consider whether the agreement is reasonably necessary to achieve "cognizable efficiencies." "Cognizable efficiencies" are efficiencies that have been verified by the Agencies, that do not arise from anticompetitive reductions in output or service, and that cannot be achieved through practical, significantly less restrictive means. *See infra* Sections 3.36(a) and 3.36(b). Cognizable efficiencies are assessed net of costs produced by the competitor collaboration or incurred in achieving those efficiencies.

3.36(a) Cognizable Efficiencies Must Be Verifiable and Potentially Procompetitive

Efficiencies are difficult to verify and quantify, in part because much of the information relating to efficiencies is uniquely in the possession of the collaboration's participants. The participants must substantiate efficiency claims so that the Agencies can verify by reasonable means the likelihood and magnitude of each asserted efficiency; how and when each would be achieved; any costs of doing so; how each would enhance the collaboration's or its participants' ability and incentive to compete; and why the relevant agreement is reasonably necessary to achieve the claimed efficiencies (*see* Section 3.36(b)). Efficiency claims are not considered if they are vague or speculative or otherwise cannot be verified by reasonable means.

Moreover, cognizable efficiencies must be potentially procompetitive. Some asserted efficiencies, such as those premised on the notion that competition itself is unreasonable, are insufficient as a matter of law. Similarly, cost savings that arise from anticompetitive output or service reductions are not treated as cognizable efficiencies. *See* Example 9.

3.36(b) Reasonable Necessity and Less Restrictive Alternatives

The Agencies consider only those efficiencies for which the relevant agreement is reasonably necessary. An agreement may be "reasonably necessary" without being essential. However, if the participants could have achieved or could achieve similar efficiencies by practical, significantly less restrictive means, then the Agencies conclude that the relevant agreement is not reasonably necessary to their achievement. In making this assessment, the Agencies consider only alternatives that are practical in the business situation faced by the participants; the Agencies do not search for a theoretically less restrictive alternative that is not realistic given business realities.

The reasonable necessity of an agreement may depend upon the market context and upon the duration of the agreement. An agreement that may be justified by the needs of a new entrant, for example, may not be reasonably necessary to achieve cognizable efficiencies in different market circumstances. The reasonable necessity of an agreement also may depend on whether it deters individual participants from undertaking free riding or other opportunistic conduct that could reduce significantly the ability of the collaboration to achieve cognizable efficiencies. Collaborations sometimes include agreements to discourage any one participant from appropriating an undue share of the fruits of the collaboration or to align participants' incentives to encourage cooperation in achieving the efficiency goals of the collaboration. The Agencies assess whether such agreements are reasonably necessary to deter opportunistic conduct that otherwise would likely prevent the achievement of cognizable efficiencies. *See* Example 10.

3.37 OVERALL COMPETITIVE EFFECT

If the relevant agreement is reasonably necessary to achieve cognizable efficiencies, the Agencies assess the likelihood and magnitude of cognizable efficiencies and anticompetitive harms to determine the agreement's overall actual or likely effect on competition in the relevant market. To make the requisite determination, the Agencies consider whether cognizable efficiencies likely would be sufficient to offset the potential of the agreement to harm consumers in the relevant market, for example, by preventing price increases.[51]

The Agencies' comparison of cognizable efficiencies and anticompetitive harms is necessarily an approximate judgment. In assessing the overall competitive effect of an agreement, the Agencies consider the magnitude and likelihood of both the anticompetitive harms and cognizable efficiencies from the relevant agreement. The likelihood and magnitude of anticompetitive harms in a particular case may be insignificant compared to the expected cognizable efficiencies, or vice versa. As the expected anticompetitive harm of the agreement increases, the Agencies require evidence establishing a greater level of expected cognizable efficiencies in order to avoid the conclusion that the agreement will have an anticompetitive effect overall. When the anticompetitive harm of the agreement is likely to be particularly large, extraordinarily great cognizable efficiencies would be necessary to prevent the agreement from having an anticompetitive effect overall.

Section 4: Antitrust Safety Zones

4.1   Overview

Because competitor collaborations are often procompetitive, the Agencies believe that "safety zones" are useful in order to encourage such activity. The safety zones set out below are designed to provide participants in a competitor collaboration with a degree of certainty in those situations in which anticompetitive effects are so unlikely that the Agencies presume the arrangements to be lawful without inquiring into particular circumstances. They are not intended to discourage competitor collaborations that fall outside the safety zones.

The Agencies emphasize that competitor collaborations are not anticompetitive merely because they fall outside the safety zones. Indeed, many competitor collaborations falling outside the safety zones are procompetitive or competitively neutral. The Agencies analyze arrangements outside the safety zones based on the principles outlined in Section 3 above.

The following sections articulate two safety zones. Section 4.2 sets out a general safety zone applicable to any competitor collaboration.[52] Section 4.3 establishes a safety zone applicable to research and development collaborations whose competitive effects are analyzed within an innovation market. These safety zones are

---

51.   In most cases, the Agencies' enforcement decisions depend on their analysis of the overall effect of the relevant agreement over the short term. The Agencies also will consider the effects of cognizable efficiencies with no short-term, direct effect on prices in the relevant market. Delayed benefits from the efficiencies (due to delay in the achievement of, or the realization of consumer benefits from, the efficiencies) will be given less weight because they are less proximate and more difficult to predict.

52.   See Sections 1.1 and 1.3 above.

intended to supplement safety zone provisions in the Agencies' other guidelines and statements of enforcement policy.[53]

4.2   Safety Zone for Competitor Collaborations in General

Absent extraordinary circumstances, the Agencies do not challenge a competitor collaboration when the market shares of the collaboration and its participants collectively account for no more than twenty percent of each relevant market in which competition may be affected.[54] The safety zone, however, does not apply to agreements that are per se illegal, or that would be challenged without a detailed market analysis,[55] or to competitor collaborations to which a merger analysis is applied.[56]

4.3   Safety Zone for Research and Development Competition Analyzed in Terms of Innovation Markets

Absent extraordinary circumstances, the Agencies do not challenge a competitor collaboration on the basis of effects on competition in an innovation market where three or more independently controlled research efforts in addition to those of the collaboration possess the required specialized assets or characteristics and the incentive to engage in R&D that is a close substitute for the R&D activity of the collaboration. In determining whether independently controlled R&D efforts are close substitutes, the Agencies consider, among other things, the nature, scope, and magnitude of the R&D efforts; their access to financial support; their access to intellectual property, skilled personnel, or other specialized assets; their timing; and their ability, either acting alone or through others, to successfully commercialize innovations. The antitrust safety zone does not apply to agreements that are per se illegal, or that would be challenged without a detailed market analysis,[57] or to competitor collaborations to which a merger analysis is applied.[58]

---

53.   The Agencies have articulated antitrust safety zones in *Health Care Statements* 7 and 8 and the *Intellectual Property Guidelines*, as well as in the *Horizontal Merger Guidelines*. The antitrust safety zones in these other guidelines relate to particular facts in a specific industry or to particular types of transactions.

54.   For purposes of the safety zone, the Agencies consider the combined market shares of the participants and the collaboration. For example, with a collaboration among two competitors where each participant individually holds a 6 percent market share in the relevant market and the collaboration separately holds a 3 percent market share in the relevant market, the combined market share in the relevant market for purposes of the safety zone would be 15 percent. This collaboration, therefore, would fall within the safety zone. However, if the collaboration involved three competitors, each with a 6 percent market share in the relevant market, the combined market share in the relevant market for purposes of the safety zone would be 21 percent, and the collaboration would fall outside the safety zone. Including market shares of the participants takes into account possible spillover effects on competition within the relevant market among the participants and their collaboration.

55.   *See supra* notes 27-29 and accompanying text in Section 3.3.

56.   *See* Section 1.3 above.

57.   *See supra* notes 27-29 and accompanying text in Section 3.3.

58.   *See* Section 1.3 above.

APPENDIX

Section 1.3

EXAMPLE 1 (COMPETITOR COLLABORATION/MERGER)

Facts: Two oil companies agree to integrate all of their refining and refined product marketing operations. Under terms of the agreement, the collaboration will expire after twelve years; prior to that expiration date, it may be terminated by either participant on six months' prior notice. The two oil companies maintain separate crude oil production operations.

Analysis: The formation of the collaboration involves an efficiency-enhancing integration of operations in the refining and refined product markets, and the integration eliminates all competition between the participants in those markets. The evaluating Agency likely would conclude that expiration after twelve years does not constitute termination "within a sufficiently limited period." The participants' entitlement to terminate the collaboration at any time after giving prior notice is not termination by the collaboration's "own specific and express terms." Based on the facts presented, the evaluating Agency likely would analyze the collaboration under the *Horizontal Merger Guidelines,* rather than as a competitor collaboration under these *Guidelines.* Any agreements restricting competition on crude oil production would be analyzed under these *Guidelines.*

Section 2.3

EXAMPLE 2 (ANALYSIS OF INDIVIDUAL AGREEMENTS/SET OF AGREEMENTS)

Facts: Two firms enter a joint venture to develop and produce a new software product to be sold independently by the participants. The product will be useful in two areas, biotechnology research and pharmaceuticals research, but doing business with each of the two classes of purchasers would require a different distribution network and a separate marketing campaign. Successful penetration of one market is likely to stimulate sales in the other by enhancing the reputation of the software and by facilitating the ability of biotechnology and pharmaceutical researchers to use the fruits of each other's efforts. Although the software is to be marketed independently by the participants rather than by the joint venture, the participants agree that one will sell only to biotechnology researchers and the other will sell only to pharmaceutical researchers. The participants also agree to fix the maximum price that either firm may charge. The parties assert that the combination of these two requirements is necessary for the successful marketing of the new product. They argue that the market allocation provides each participant with adequate incentives to commercialize the product in its sector without fear that the other participant will free-ride on its efforts and that the maximum price prevents either participant from unduly exploiting its sector of the market to the detriment of sales efforts in the other sector.

Analysis: The evaluating Agency would assess overall competitive effects associated with the collaboration in its entirety and with individual agreements, such as the agreement to allocate markets, the agreement to fix maximum prices, and any of the sundry other agreements associated with joint development and production and independent marketing of the software. From the facts presented, it appears that the agreements to allocate markets and to fix maximum prices may be so intertwined that their benefits and harms "cannot meaningfully be isolated." The two agreements arguably operate together to ensure a particular blend of incentives to achieve the potential procompetitive benefits of successful commercialization of the new product. Moreover, the effects of the agreement to fix maximum prices may mitigate the price effects of the agreement to allocate markets. Based on the facts presented, the evaluating Agency likely would conclude that the agreements to allocate markets and to fix maximum prices should be analyzed as a whole.

Section 2.4

EXAMPLE 3 (TIME OF POSSIBLE HARM TO COMPETITION)

Facts: A group of 25 small-to-mid-size banks formed a joint venture to establish an automatic teller machine network. To ensure sufficient business to justify launching the venture, the joint venture agreement specified that participants would not participate in any other ATM networks. Numerous other ATM networks were forming in roughly the same time period.

Over time, the joint venture expanded by adding more and more banks, and the number of its competitors fell. Now, ten years after formation, the joint venture has 900 member banks and controls 60% of the ATM outlets in a relevant geographic market. Following complaints from consumers that ATM fees have rapidly escalated, the evaluating Agency assesses the rule barring participation in other ATM networks, which now binds 900 banks.

Analysis: The circumstances in which the venture operates have changed over time, and the evaluating Agency would determine whether the exclusivity rule now harms competition. In assessing the exclusivity rule's competitive effect, the evaluating Agency would take account of the collaboration's substantial current market share and any procompetitive benefits of exclusivity under present circumstances, along with other factors discussed in Section 3. The Agencies would consider whether significant sunk investments were made in reliance on the exclusivity rule.

Section 3.2

EXAMPLE 4 (AGREEMENT NOT TO COMPETE ON PRICE)

Facts: Net-Business and Net-Company are two start-up companies. They independently developed, and have begun selling in competition with one another, software for the networks that link users within a particular business to each other and, in some cases, to entities outside the business. Both Net-Business and Net-Company were formed by computer specialists with no prior business expertise, and they are having trouble implementing marketing strategies, distributing their inventory, and managing their sales forces. The two companies decide to form a partnership joint venture, NET-FIRM, whose sole function will be to market and distribute the network software products of Net-Business and Net-Company. NET-FIRM will be the exclusive marketer of network software produced by Net-Business and Net-Company. Net-Business and Net-Company will each have 50% control of NET-FIRM, but each will derive profits from NET-FIRM in proportion to the revenues from sales of that partner's products. The documents setting up NET-

FIRM specify that Net-Business and Net-Company will agree on the prices for the products that NET-FIRM will sell.

Analysis: Net-Business and Net-Company will agree on the prices at which NET-FIRM will sell their individually-produced software. The agreement is one "not to compete on price," and it is of a type that always or almost always tends to raise price or reduce output. The agreement to jointly set price may be challenged as per se illegal, unless it is reasonably related to, and reasonably necessary to achieve procompetitive benefits from, an efficiency-enhancing integration of economic activity.

EXAMPLE 5 (SPECIALIZATION WITHOUT INTEGRATION)

Facts: Firm A and Firm B are two of only three producers of automobile carburetors. Minor engine variations from year to year, even within given models of a particular automobile manufacturer, require re-design of each year's carburetor and re-tooling for carburetor production. Firms A and B meet and agree that henceforth Firm A will design and produce carburetors only for automobile models of even-numbered years and Firm B will design and produce carburetors only for automobile models of odd-numbered years. Some design and re-tooling costs would be saved, but automobile manufacturers would face only two suppliers each year, rather than three.

Analysis: The agreement allocates sales by automobile model year and constitutes an agreement "not to compete on ... output." The participants do not combine production; rather, the collaboration consists solely of an agreement *not* to produce certain carburetors. The mere coordination of decisions on output is not integration, and cost-savings without integration, such as the costs saved by refraining from design and production for any given model year, are not a basis for avoiding per se condemnation. The agreement is of a type so likely to harm competition and to have no significant benefits that particularized inquiry into its competitive effect is deemed by the antitrust laws not to be worth the time and expense that would be required. Consequently, the evaluating Agency likely would conclude that the agreement is per se illegal.

EXAMPLE 6 (EFFICIENCY-ENHANCING INTEGRATION PRESENT)

Facts: Compu-Max and Compu-Pro are two major producers of a variety of computer software. Each has a large, world-wide sales department. Each firm has developed and sold its own word-processing software. However, despite all efforts to develop a strong market presence in word processing, each firm has achieved only slightly more than a 10% market share, and neither is a major competitor to the two firms that dominate the word-processing software market.

Compu-Max and Compu-Pro determine that in light of their complementary areas of design expertise they could develop a markedly better word-processing program together than either can produce on its own. Compu-Max and Compu-Pro form a joint venture, WORD-FIRM, to jointly develop and market a new word-processing program, with expenses and profits to be split equally. Compu-Max and Compu-Pro both contribute to WORD-FIRM software developers experienced with word processing.

Analysis: Compu-Max and Compu-Pro have combined their word-processing design efforts, reflecting complementary areas of design expertise, in a common endeavor to develop new word-processing software that they could not have developed separately. Each participant has contributed significant assets—the time and know-how of its word-processing software developers—to the joint effort. Consequently, the evaluating Agency likely would conclude that the joint word-processing software development project is an efficiency-enhancing integration of economic activity that promotes procompetitive benefits.

EXAMPLE 7 (EFFICIENCY-ENHANCING INTEGRATION ABSENT)

Facts: Each of the three major producers of flashlight batteries has a patent on a process for manufacturing a revolutionary new flashlight battery—the Century Battery—that would last 100 years without requiring recharging or replacement. There is little chance that another firm could produce such a battery without infringing one of the patents. Based on consumer surveys, each firm believes that aggregate profits will be less if all three sold the Century Battery than if all three sold only conventional batteries, but that any one firm could maximize profits by being the first to introduce a Century Battery. All three are capable of introducing the Century Battery within two years, although it is uncertain who would be first to market.

One component in all conventional batteries is a copper widget. An essential element in each producers' Century Battery would be a zinc, rather than a copper widget. Instead of introducing the Century Battery, the three producers agree that their batteries will use only copper widgets. Adherence to the agreement precludes any of the producers from introducing a Century Battery.

Analysis: The agreement to use only copper widgets is merely an agreement not to produce any zinc-based batteries, in particular, the Century Battery. It is "an agreement not to compete on . . . output" and is "of a type that always or almost always tends to raise price or reduce output." The participants do not collaborate to perform any business functions, and there are no procompetitive benefits from an efficiency-enhancing integration of economic activity. The evaluating Agency likely would challenge the agreement to use only copper widgets as per se illegal.

Section 3.3

EXAMPLE 8 (RULE-OF-REASON: AGREEMENT QUICKLY EXCULPATED)

Facts: Under the facts of Example 4, Net-Business and Net-Company jointly market their independently-produced network software products through NET-FIRM. Those facts are changed in one respect: rather than jointly setting the prices of their products, Net-Business and Net-Company will each independently specify the prices at which its products are to be sold by NET-FIRM. The participants explicitly agree that each company will decide on the prices for its own software independently of the other company. The collaboration also includes a requirement that NET-FIRM compile and transmit to each participant quarterly reports summarizing any comments received from customers in the course of NET-Firm's marketing efforts regarding the desirable/undesirable features of and desirable improvements to (1) that participant's product and (2) network software in general. Sufficient provisions are included to prevent the company-specific information reported to one participant from being disclosed to the other, and those provisions are followed. The information pertaining to network software in general is to be reported simultaneously to both participants.

Analysis: Under these revised facts, there is no agreement "not to compete on price or output." Absent any agreement of a type that always or almost always tends to raise price or reduce output, and absent any subsequent conduct suggesting that the firms did not follow their explicit agreement to set prices independently, no aspect of the partnership arrangement might be subjected to per se analysis. Analysis would continue under the rule of reason.

The information disclosure arrangements provide for the sharing of a very limited category of information: customer-response data pertaining to network software in general. Collection and sharing of information of this nature is unlikely to increase the ability or incentive of Net-Business or Net-Company to raise price or reduce output, quality, service, or innovation. There is no evidence that the disclosure arrangements have caused anticompetitive harm and no evidence that the prohibitions against disclosure of firm-specific information have been violated. Under any plausible relevant market definition, Net-Business and Net-Company have small market shares, and there is no other evidence to suggest that they have market power. In light of these facts, the evaluating Agency would refrain from further investigation.

Section 3.36(a)

EXAMPLE 9 (COST SAVINGS FROM ANTICOMPETITIVE OUTPUT OR SERVICE REDUCTIONS)

Facts: Two widget manufacturers enter a marketing collaboration. Each will continue to manufacture and set the price for its own widget, but the widgets will be promoted by a joint sales force. The two manufacturers conclude that through this collaboration they can increase their profits using only half of their aggregate pre-collaboration sales forces by (1) taking advantage of economies of scale—presenting both widgets during the same customer call—and (2) refraining from time-consuming demonstrations highlighting the relative advantages of one manufacturer's widgets over the other manufacturer's widgets. Prior to their collaboration, both manufacturers had engaged in the demonstrations.

Analysis: The savings attributable to economies of scale would be cognizable efficiencies. In contrast, eliminating demonstrations that highlight the relative advantages of one manufacturer's widgets over the other manufacturer's widgets deprives customers of information useful to their decision making. Cost savings from this source arise from an anticompetitive output or service reduction and would not be cognizable efficiencies.

EXAMPLE 10 (EFFICIENCIES FROM RESTRICTIONS ON COMPETITIVE INDEPENDENCE)

Facts: Under the facts of Example 6, Compu-Max and Compu-Pro decide to collaborate on developing and marketing word-processing software. The firms agree that neither one will engage in R&D for designing word-processing software outside of their WORD-FIRM joint venture. Compu-Max papers drafted during the negotiations cite the concern that absent a restriction on outside word-processing R&D, Compu-Pro might withhold its best ideas, use the joint venture to learn

Compu-Max's approaches to design problems, and then use that information to design an improved word-processing software product on its own. Compu-Pro's files contain similar documents regarding Compu-Max.

Compu-Max and Compu-Pro further agree that neither will sell its previously designed word-processing program once their jointly developed product is ready to be introduced. Papers in both firms' files, dating from the time of the negotiations, state that this latter restraint was designed to foster greater trust between the participants and thereby enable the collaboration to function more smoothly. As further support, the parties point to a recent failed collaboration involving other firms who sought to collaborate on developing and selling a new spread-sheet program while independently marketing their older spread-sheet software.

Analysis: The restraints on outside R&D efforts and on outside sales both restrict the competitive independence of the participants and could cause competitive harm. The evaluating Agency would inquire whether each restraint is reasonably necessary to achieve cognizable efficiencies. In the given context, that inquiry would entail an assessment of whether, by aligning the participants' incentives, the restraints in fact are reasonably necessary to deter opportunistic conduct that otherwise would likely prevent achieving cognizable efficiency goals of the collaboration.

With respect to the limitation on independent R&D efforts, possible alternatives might include agreements specifying the level and quality of each participant's R&D contributions to WORD-FIRM or requiring the sharing of all relevant R&D. The evaluating Agency would assess whether any alternatives would permit each participant to adequately monitor the scope and quality of the other's R&D contributions and whether they would effectively prevent the misappropriation of the other participant's know-how. In some circumstances, there may be no "practical, significantly less restrictive" alternative.

Although the agreement prohibiting outside sales might be challenged as per se illegal if not reasonably necessary for achieving the procompetitive benefits of the integration discussed in Example 6, the evaluating Agency likely would analyze the agreement under the rule of reason if it could not adequately assess the claim of reasonable necessity through limited factual inquiry. As a general matter, participants' contributions of marketing assets to the collaboration could more readily be monitored than their contributions of know-how, and neither participant may be capable of misappropriating the other's marketing contributions as readily as it could misappropriate know-how. Consequently, the specification and monitoring of each participant's marketing contributions could be a "practical, significantly less restrictive" alternative to prohibiting outside sales of pre-existing products. The evaluating Agency, however, would examine the experiences of the failed spread-sheet collaboration and any other facts presented by the parties to better assess whether such specification and monitoring would likely enable the achievement of cognizable efficiencies.

APPENDIX H

1993 HORIZONTAL MERGER GUIDELINES OF THE NATIONAL ASSOCIATION OF ATTORNEYS GENERAL

1. Purpose and Scope of the *Guidelines*

These *Guidelines* explain the general enforcement policy of the state and territorial attorneys general ("the Attorneys General") who comprise the National Association of Attorneys General[1] ("NAAG") concerning horizontal acquisitions and mergers[2] (collectively "mergers") subject to section 7 of the Clayton Act,[3] sections 1 and 2 of the Sherman Act[4] and analogous provisions of the antitrust laws of those states which have enacted them.[5]

The state attorney general is the primary or exclusive public enforcer of the antitrust law in most states. The Attorneys General also represent their states and the natural person citizens of their states in federal antitrust litigation.[6]

These *Guidelines* embody the general enforcement policy of the Attorneys General. Individual attorneys general may vary or supplement this general policy in recognition of variations in precedents among the federal circuits and differences in state antitrust laws and in the exercise of their individual prosecutorial discretion.

These *Guidelines* serve three principal purposes. First, they provide a uniform framework for the states to evaluate the facts of a particular horizontal merger and the dynamic conditions of an industry. Second, they inform businesses of the substantive standards used by the Attorneys General to review, and when

---

1. The Attorneys General of American Samoa, Guam, the Commonwealth of Northern Marianas Islands, the Commonwealth of Puerto Rico and the Virgin Islands are members of NAAG.
2. A horizontal merger involves firms that are actually or potentially in both the same product and geographic markets, as those markets are defined in Section 3 of these *Guidelines*.
3. Section 7 of the Clayton Act, 15 U.S.C. § 18, prohibits mergers if their effect "may be substantially to lessen competition or to tend to create a monopoly."
4. Section 1 of the Sherman Act, 15 U.S.C. § 1, prohibits mergers which constitute an unreasonable "restraint of trade." Section 2 of the Sherman Act, 15 U.S.C. § 2, prohibits mergers which create a monopoly or constitute an attempt, combination or conspiracy to monopolize.
5. The antitrust laws of the states are set forth in 6 Trade Reg. Rep. (CCH) ¶ 30,000 *et seq.*
6. The authority of the Attorneys General to invoke section 7 of the Clayton Act to enjoin a merger injurious to the general welfare and economy of the State was first articulated in *Georgia v. Pennsylvania R.R.*, 324 U.S. 439 (1945). *California v. American Stores*, 110 S. Ct. 1853 (1990), confirms Attorneys General's authority to enforce section 7 and confirms the availability of the divestiture remedy to Attorneys General.

appropriate, challenge specific mergers. They help businesses to assess the legality of potential transactions and therefore are useful as a business planning tool. Third, the *Guidelines* are designed primarily to articulate the analytical framework the states apply in determining whether a merger is likely substantially to lessen competition, not to describe how the states will conduct litigation. As such, the *Guidelines* do not purport to provide a complete restatement of existing merger law. Rather, the *Guidelines* put forward a framework for the analysis of horizontal mergers which relies upon an accurate characterization of relevant markets and which is grounded in and consistent with the purposes and meaning of section 7 of the Clayton Act, as amended by the Celler-Kefauver Act of 1950 ("section 7"), and as reflected in its legislative history and interpretation by the United States Supreme Court.

The organizing principle of the *Guidelines* is the application of facts concerning the marketplace and widely accepted economic theory to these authoritative sources of the law's meaning.

2.   Policies Underlying These *Guidelines*

The federal antitrust law provisions relevant to horizontal mergers, most specifically section 7 and analogous state law provisions,[7] have one primary and several subsidiary purposes. The central purpose of the law is to prevent firms from attaining either market or monopoly power,[8] because firms possessing such power can raise prices to consumers above competitive levels, thereby effecting a transfer of wealth from consumers to such firms.[9]

Congress determined that highly concentrated industries were characterized by and conducive to the exercise of market power and prohibited mergers which may substantially lessen competition. Such mergers were prohibited even prior to the parties actual attainment or exercise of market power, that is, when the trend to harmful concentration was incipient.

These *Guidelines* deal only with these competitive consequences of horizontal mergers, and challenges will be instituted only against mergers that may lead to detrimental economic effects. Mergers may also have other consequences that are relevant to the social and political goals of section 7. For example, mergers may affect the opportunities for small and regional business to survive and compete. Although such consequences are beyond the scope of these *Guidelines*, they may affect the Attorneys General's ultimate exercise of prosecutorial discretion and may

---

7.   For example, see statutes of Hawaii, Maine, Mississippi, Nebraska, New Jersey, Ohio, Oklahoma, Texas, Washington and Puerto Rico for provisions analogous to section 7. *See* 6 Trade Reg. Rep. (CCH) ¶ 30,000 *et seq.* However, all states with a provision analogous to section 1 of the Sherman Act may also challenge mergers under such authority. *See* note 6 concerning state enforcement of section 7. Appendix A contains copies of the NAAG Voluntary Pre-Merger Disclosure Compact, the Protocol for Coordinating Federal-State Merger Probes and the FTC's Call for Comments on Merger Cooperation Program. [Editors' Note: Appendix A is not included in this treatise.]

8.   Market power is the ability of one or more firms to maintain prices above a competitive level, or to prevent prices from decreasing to a lower competitive level, or to limit output or entry.

9.   A buyer or group of buyers may similarly attain and exercise the power to drive prices below a competitive level for a significant period of time. This is usually termed an exercise of "monopsony power." When the terms "buyer(s)" or "groups of buyers" are used herein they are deemed to include "seller(s)" or "groups of sellers" adversely affected by the exercise of market or monopsony power.

help the states decide which of the possible challenges that are justified on economic grounds should be instituted.

Goals such as productive and allocative efficiency are generally consistent with, though subsidiary to, the central goal of preventing wealth transfers from consumers to firms possessing market power. When the productive efficiency of a firm increases (its cost of production is lowered), a firm in a highly competitive industry may pass on some of the savings to consumers in the form of lower prices. However, to the extent that a merger increases market power, there is less likelihood that any productive efficiencies would be passed along to consumers.

To the extent that Congress was concerned with productive efficiency in enacting these laws, it prescribed the prevention of high levels of market concentration as the means to this end.[10] Furthermore, the Supreme Court has clearly ruled that any conflict between the goal of preventing anticompetitive mergers and that of increasing efficiency must be resolved in favor of the former explicit and predominant concern of the Congress.[11]

Although Congress was apparently unaware of allocative efficiency when it enacted section 7 and the other antitrust laws,[12] preserving allocative efficiency is generally considered an additional benefit realized by the prevention of market power, because the act of restricting output has the concomitant effect of raising prices to consumers.[13]

---

10. There is vigorous debate whether firms in industries with high concentration are on average more or less efficient than those in industries with moderate or low levels of concentration.

   The theory of "x-inefficiency" predicts that firms constrained by vigorous competition have lower production costs than firms in an industry with little or no competition. Various economists have attempted to quantify production cost increases due to x-inefficiency and the theory is the subject of ongoing debate.

11. In *FTC v. Procter & Gamble Co.*, 386 U.S. 568, 580 (1967), the Court stated: "Possible economies cannot be used as a defense to illegality. Congress was aware that some mergers which lessen competition may also result in economies but it struck the balance in favor of protecting competition."

   In *United States v. Philadelphia National Bank*, 374 U.S. 321, 371 (1963), the Court stated:
   We are clear, however, that a merger the effect of which "may be substantially to lessen competition" is not saved because, on some ultimate reckoning of social or economic debits and credits, it may be deemed beneficial. A value choice of such magnitude is beyond the ordinary limits of judicial competence, and in any event has been made for us already, by Congress when it enacted the amended § 7. Congress determined to preserve our traditionally competitive economy. It therefore proscribed anticompetitive mergers, the benign and the malignant alike, fully aware, we must assume, that some price might have to be paid.

12. Perfect "allocative efficiency" or "pareto optimality" is a state of equilibrium on the "utility-possibility frontier" in which no person can be made better off without making someone else worse off. Allocative efficiency can be achieved in an economy with massive inequalities of income and distribution, e.g., one percent of the population can receive ninety-nine percent of the economy's wealth and ninety-nine percent of the population can receive one percent. A massive transfer of wealth from consumers to a monopolist does not of itself decrease allocative efficiency. However, when a monopolist restricts its output, the total wealth of society is diminished, thereby reducing allocative efficiency. Economists term this loss of society's wealth the "deadweight loss." The term of art "consumer welfare," often used when discussing the efficiency effects of mergers and restraints of trade, refers to the concept of allocative efficiency, not the welfare of consumers who purchase the monopolist's product. Consumer welfare is diminished when a monopolist restricts output.

13. In most mergers creating market power, the dollar magnitude of the wealth transfer from consumers would be greater than the monetary measure of loss in allocative efficiency (dead weight loss). *See* note 12. It is, moreover, important to understand that a transfer of wealth from

2.1   *The Economic Effects of Mergers*

Mergers may have negative or positive competitive consequences. The following is a summary description of the most common competitive effects of mergers relevant to enforcement of section 7.

2.11   ACQUISITION OF MARKET POWER AND WEALTH TRANSFERS

When two firms, neither possessing market power, cease competing and merge, the inevitable consequence is the elimination of the competition between them. More significantly, however, the merged entity may now possess market power, an anticompetitive outcome.

A merger may also increase the concentration level in an industry to a point at which the remaining firms can effectively engage in active collusion or implicitly coordinate their actions and thus collectively exercise market power.

When a firm or firms exercise market power by profitably maintaining prices above competitive levels for a significant period of time, a transfer of wealth from consumers to those firms occurs.[14] This transfer of wealth is the major evil sought to be addressed by section 7.[15]

The wealth transfer orientation of section 7 is the same as that of the Sherman Act. The major difference between the two provisions, and reason for the enactment of section 7, is the "incipiency" standard of section 7, which permits antitrust intervention at a point when the anticompetitive consequences of a merger are not manifest but are likely to occur absent intervention. The Celler-Kefauver amendments retained and strengthened the "incipiency" standard by extending the coverage of the law to acquisitions of assets. In Section 4 of these *Guidelines* the Attorneys General specifically attempt to give expression to the statutory concern of "incipiency."

2.12   PRODUCTIVE EFFICIENCY

A merger may increase or decrease the costs of the parties to the merger and thus increase or decrease productive efficiency. A merger which increases productive efficiency and does not produce a firm or firms capable of exercising market power should lower prices paid by consumers. An inefficient merger in an unconcentrated industry is generally of no competitive concern. The efficiency effects of mergers are easy to speculate about but hard to accurately predict. There is much

---

consumers to firms with market power can decrease the well-being of consumers without any decrease in so-called "consumer welfare."

14. Tacit or active collusion on terms of trade other than price also produces wealth transfer effects. This would include, for example, an agreement to eliminate rivalry on service features or to limit the choices otherwise available to consumers.

15. The predominant concern with wealth transfers was evidenced in the statements of both supporters and opponents of the Celler-Kefauver amendments. *See, e.g.*, 95 Cong. Rec. 11,506 (1949) (remarks of Rep. Bennett); *id.* at 11,492 (remarks of Rep. Carroll); *id.* at 11,506 (remarks of Rep. Byrne); Hearings Before the Subcomm. on the Judiciary, 81st Cong., 1st and 2d Sess., note 260 at 180 (remarks of Sen. Kilgore); 95 Cong. Rec. 11,493 (1949) (remarks of Rep. Yates); *id.* at 11,490-91 (remarks of Rep. Goodwin); 95 Cong. Rec. 16,490 (1949) (colloquy of Sen. Kefauver and Sen. Wiley).

disagreement among economists as to whether merged firms usually perform well and whether, on average, mergers have been shown to produce significant efficiencies. However, most efficiencies and those most quantitatively significant will be realized in mergers involving small firms. Such mergers do not raise any concern under the enforcement standards adopted in Section 4 of these *Guidelines*. Furthermore, the concentration thresholds adopted in Section 4 are usually sufficient to enable firms to obtain the most significant efficiencies likely to result from growth through merger as opposed to growth through internal expansion.[16]

2.13 ALLOCATIVE EFFICIENCY

A merger which facilitates the exercise of market power results in a decrease in allocative efficiency. When firms with market power restrict their output, the total wealth of society diminishes. This effect is universally condemned by economists, and its prevention, while not a concern of the Congress which enacted section 7, is a goal consistent with the purposes of the antitrust laws.

2.14 RAISING RIVALS' COSTS

In certain circumstances, a merger may raise the costs of the competitors of the parties to the merger. For example, a merger could increase the power of a firm to affect the price that rivals must pay for inputs or the conditions under which they must operate, in a manner that creates a relative disadvantage for the rivals. If the market structure is such that these increased costs can be passed on to consumers, then the prevention of this effect is consistent with the goals of the antitrust laws. Preventing such effect will also prevent a decrease in allocative and productive efficiency.

3.   Market Definition

These *Guidelines* are concerned with horizontal mergers, that is, mergers involving firms that are actual or potential competitors in the same product and geographic markets. The primary analytical tool utilized in the *Guidelines* is the measurement of concentration in a particular market and increase in concentration in that market resulting from a merger. The market shares used to compute these concentration factors will depend upon the market definition adopted.[17] The reasonable delineation of these market boundaries is critical to realizing the objectives of the *Guidelines* and the antitrust laws. If the market boundaries chosen are seriously distorted in relation to the actual workings of the marketplace, an enforcement error is likely.[18] An overly restricted product or geographic market

---

16. There may be rare instances where the minimum efficient scale of production and output constitutes a significant percentage of the relevant market.

17. For example, consider the proposed merger of two firms producing the same product. Each has a fifty percent share of the sales of this product in a certain state but only one percent of national sales. If the proper geographic market is the state, then the competitive consequences of the merger will be far different than if the geographic market is the entire country.

18. Governmental challenge of a merger which is not likely to lessen competition substantially is frequently termed "Type I error." The failure to challenge a merger which is likely to lessen competition substantially is termed "Type II error." Type I error can be corrected by the court

definition may trigger antitrust intervention when the merger would not significantly harm competition or in other circumstances result in the failure to challenge an anticompetitive merger. An overly expansive market definition, on the other hand, may result in the failure to challenge a merger with serious anticompetitive consequences.[19] Markets should be defined from the perspective of those interests section 7 was primarily enacted to protect, i.e., the classes of consumers (or suppliers) who may be adversely affected by an anticompetitive merger. The Attorneys General will utilize historical data to identify these classes of consumers ("the protected interest group"), their sources of supply, suitable substitutes for the product and alternative sources of the product and its substitutes. The market thus defined will be presumed correct unless rebutted by empirical evidence that supply responses within a reasonable period of time will render unprofitable an attempted exercise of market power.[20]

The following sections detail how these general principles will be applied to define product and geographic markets and to calculate the market shares of firms determined to be within the relevant market.

3.1   *Product Market Definition*

The Attorneys General will determine the customers who purchase the products or services ("products") of the merging firms. Each product produced in common by the merging parties will constitute a provisional product market. However, if a market is incorrectly defined too narrowly, the merger may appear to be not horizontal when there may be a horizontal anticompetitive effect in a broader market.[21] In short, the provisional product market will be expanded to include

---

which determines the validity of the challenge. Type II error will most likely go uncorrected, since the vast majority of merger challenges are mounted by the government. In other areas of antitrust law, private actions predominate and can correct Type II error. Consumers, whose interests were paramount in the enactment of section 7 and section 1 of the Sherman Act, suffer the damage of Type II error.

19.   Consider, for example, the market(s) for flexible wrapping materials. These materials include clear plastic, metallic foils, waxed paper and others. Firms A and B each produce thirty percent of the clear plastic wrap and five percent of all flexible wrapping material in a relevant geographic market. Firm C produces seventy percent of the metallic foil and sixty percent of all flexible wrap. If the proper market definition is all flexible wrapping materials, then treating clear plastic and metallic foils as separate markets may lead to an unwarranted challenge to a merger between firms A and B. The same incorrect market definition may also result in the failure to challenge a merger between Firm C and either Firm A or Firm B because of the incorrect assumption that metallic foil and clear plastic wrap do not compete. However, if the correct market definition is clear plastic wrap but the more expansive market definition of all flexible materials is chosen, this may result in the failure to challenge an anticompetitive merger of firms A and B.

20.   Empirical evidence, as contrasted with expert opinion, speculation, or economic theories, is generally grounded in demonstrable, historical fact. Empirical evidence of a probable supply response would include a factual showing that this response had occurred in the past when prices increased significantly. A mere prediction based on a theoretical possibility that a manufacturer would or could shift his production from one product to another to capitalize on a price increase, when unsupported by evidence of previous similar responses or other factual information of comparable probative weight, is not considered "empirical evidence."

21.   For example, suppose there are two beer producers and two malt liquor producers and the merger involves the acquisition of one of the malt liquor firms by one of the beer producers. If the relevant market is defined as "beer," the merger would not be horizontal. The provisional market should be defined as "beverages containing X percent alcohol."

suitable substitutes for the product which are comparably priced.[22] A comparably priced substitute will be deemed suitable and thereby expand the product market definition if, and only if, considered suitable by customers accounting for seventy-five percent of the purchases.

Actual substitution by customers in the past will presumptively establish that a product is considered a suitable substitute for the provisionally defined product. However, other evidence offered by the parties probative of the assertion that customers deem a product to be a suitable substitute will also be considered.[23]

3.11 CONSUMERS WHO MAY BE VULNERABLE TO PRICE DISCRIMINATION

Notwithstanding the determination in Section 3.1 that a product is a suitable substitute for the provisional product pursuant to application of the seventy-five percent rule, there may be small, but significant, groups of consumers who cannot substitute or can do so only with great difficulty. These consumers may be subject to price discrimination and thus may be particularly adversely affected by a merger. In addition, some markets may contain differentiated products which are not perfect substitutes for one another but are not sufficiently differentiated to warrant separate markets. If the products of the merging firms are closer substitutes, i.e., the more the buyers of one product consider the other product to be their next choice, the consumers of these products may be more subject to an exercise of market power. Similarly, the existence of distinct prices, unique production facilities, a product's peculiar characteristics and uses, distinct customers, and specialized vendors may support the definition of narrower product markets.[24]

Evidence of the commercial reality of such a market includes price discrimination, inelasticity of demand and industry or public recognition of a distinct market.

3.2 *Geographic Market Definition*

Utilizing the product market(s) defined in Section 3.1, the Attorneys General will define the relevant geographic market. First, the Attorneys General will determine

---

22. The existence of a functionally suitable substitute which is significantly more expensive than the relevant product will not discipline an exercise of market power until the price of the relevant product has been raised to a level comparable to the substitute. The Attorneys General will also seek to ascertain whether current price comparability of two products resulted from an exercise of market power. For example, suppose that the provisionally defined product recently cost twenty percent less than a possible substitute, but its price has recently risen twenty percent as a result of the exercise of market power. Rather than serving as a basis for broadening the product market to include the possible substitute, this finding will provide compelling evidence that any further concentration through merger will only exacerbate the market power which already exists. To ascertain whether the price comparability of two possibly interchangeable products was the result of an exercise of market power over one product, the appropriate question to ask may be "what would happen if the price of the product in question dropped?" If a significant price decrease does not substantially increase sales, then a previous exercise of market power has likely been detected, and the two products should probably be considered to be in separate product markets. *See* United States v. E.I. duPont de Nemours & Co., 351 U.S. 377, 399-400 (1956).

23. Recycled or reconditioned goods will be considered suitable substitutes if they meet the requirements of this section.

24. *See* Brown Shoe Co. v. United States, 370 U.S. 294, 325 (1962).

the sources and locations where the customers of the merging parties readily turn for their supply of the relevant product. These will include the merging parties and other sources of supply. To this group of suppliers and their locations will be added suppliers or buyers closely proximate to the customers of the merging parties. In determining those suppliers to whom the protected interest group readily turn for supply of the relevant product, the Attorneys General will include all sources of supply within the past two years still present in the market.

Utilizing the locations from which supplies of the relevant product are obtained by members of the protected interest group, the geographic market will be defined as the area encompassing the production locations from which this group purchases seventy-five percent of their supplies of the relevant product.

The product and geographic markets as defined above will be utilized in calculating market shares and concentration levels unless additional sources of supply are recognized by application of the procedures specified in Section 3.3.

3.21   GEOGRAPHIC MARKETS SUBJECT TO PRICE DISCRIMINATION

The Attorneys General may define additional narrower geographic markets when there is strong evidence that sellers are able to discriminate among buyers in separate locations within the geographic market(s) defined in Section 3.2. The Attorneys General will evaluate evidence concerning discrimination on price, terms of credit and delivery, and priority of shipment.[25]

3.3   Principles for Recognizing Potential Competition

Where there is relevant empirical evidence of profitable supply and demand responses which will be likely to occur within one year of any attempted exercise of market power, the Attorneys General will calculate market shares and concentration levels, incorporating both sources of potential supply and the firms identified as being in the market defined by the procedures outlined in Sections 3.1 and 3.11.

The Attorneys General will evaluate empirical evidence of the following sources of potential competition:

1)   That current suppliers of the product will produce additional supplies for the relevant market by utilizing excess capacity;

2)   That new sources of the product will be readily available from firms outside the geographic market with excess capacity.

3.31   EXPANSION OF OUTPUT

The Attorneys General will identify current suppliers of the product that will expand their output by utilization of excess capacity within one year of any attempted exercise of market power. Proof of probable utilization of excess capacity addresses the issues of: (i) The cost of bringing the excess capacity on line; (ii) the amount of excess capacity; (iii) prior history of supplying this market or present

---

25.   The Attorneys General welcome submissions by buyers concerning such discrimination or any other non-speculative evidence that a proposed merger will adversely affect them.

intention to do so; and (iv) how much prices would have to rise to likely induce this supply response.

3.32 NEW SOURCES OF ADDITIONAL SUPPLY

The Attorneys General will identify firms not currently supplying the product in the geographic market but which will expand their output by utilization of excess capacity within one year of any attempted exercise of market power. Proof of probable utilization of excess capacity addresses the issues of: (i) The cost of bringing the excess capacity on line; (ii) the amount of excess capacity; (iii) prior history of supplying this market or present intention to do so; and (iv) how much prices would have to rise to likely induce this supply response.

3.4 *Calculating Market Shares*

Using the product and geographic markets defined in Sections 3.1 and 3.2, the firms supplying the market and any additional sources of supply recognized under Section 3.3, the shares of all firms determined to be in the market will be calculated.[26]

The market shares of firms presently supplying the market shall be based upon actual data from the relevant market. If there has been a demonstration of a probable supply response as defined in Section 3.3, the market shares of firms already selling in the market will be adjusted to account for the proven probable supply response. Similarly, market shares will be assigned to firms not currently supplying the market who have been shown to be likely to expand output to provide additional sources of supply as discussed in Sections 3.32 and 3.33. The assigned market shares of such firms will be based upon the amount of the product these firms would supply. The Attorneys General will utilize dollar sales, unit sales, capacity measures or other appropriate sales measurements to quantify actual market activity.

3.41 FOREIGN FIRMS

Foreign firms presently supplying the relevant market will be assigned market shares in the same manner as domestic firms, according to their actual current sales in the relevant market. Foreign firms and their productive capacity are inherently a less reliable check on market power by domestic firms because foreign firms face a variety of barriers to continuing sales or increasing their sales. These barriers include import quotas, voluntary quantitative restrictions, tariffs and fluctuations in exchange rates. When such barriers exist, market share based upon historical sales data will be reduced appropriately.

---

26. In some situations, market share and market concentration data may either understate or overstate the likely future competitive significance of a firm or firms in the market or the impact of a merger. The Attorneys General will consider empirical evidence of recent or ongoing changes in market conditions or in a particular firm and may make appropriate adjustments to the market concentration and market share data. *See* United States v. General Dynamics Corp., 415 U.S. 486 (1974).

A single market share will be assigned to the firms of any foreign country or group of countries which in fact coordinate their sales.[27]

3.411 *Alternative Method for Defining Markets Utilizing the Methodology of the United States Department of Justice/ Federal Trade Commission Merger Guidelines*

Any party presenting a position concerning the likely competitive consequences of a merger to one or more Attorneys General may present its position and analysis using the market definition principles and methodology set forth in the *Merger Guidelines of the United States Department of Justice and the Federal Trade Commission*, released on April 2, 1992 (*DOJ/FTC Guidelines*), 62 Antitrust & Trade Reg. Rep. Special Supp. (April 2, 1992). This method will only be considered where, in the opinion of the state Attorney General, sufficient evidence is available to implement the methodology workably and without speculation. In most situations, both the NAAG and DOJ/FTC market definition methodologies will produce the same result. In the event that the two tests produce different results, the Attorneys General will rely on the test that appears most accurately to reflect the market and is based on the most reliable evidence.

There are two purposes for permitting such alternative method for defining markets. First, many of the mergers which the Attorneys General may analyze using these *Guidelines* will also be subject to scrutiny by either the Antitrust Division of the United States Department of Justice or the Federal Trade Commission. Parties may desire to present positions concerning the likely competitive consequences of a particular transaction to both federal and state antitrust enforcement agencies. Such parties will benefit from the ability to utilize a single market definition methodology in presenting their position concerning a particular transaction. Second, the Attorneys General seek to facilitate the joint or coordinated analysis of mergers by state and federal enforcement agencies.

Consistent with these principles, the Attorneys General may utilize the market definition methodology set forth in the *DOJ/FTC Guidelines* as an additional or alternative method in analyzing the competitive consequences of particular transactions.

4.   Measurement of Concentration

The primary tool utilized by the Attorneys General to determine whether a specific horizontal merger is likely to substantially harm competition is a measurement of the level of concentration in each market defined in Section 3 or 3A. Concentration is a measurement of the number of firms in a market and their market shares. The *Guidelines* employ the Herfindahl-Hirschman Index ("HHI") to calculate the level of concentration in an industry before and after a merger and, therefore, the increase in concentration which would result from the merger.[28]

---

27. For example, an import quota may be established for a particular foreign country and the foreign government may then apportion the quota among firms engaged in the import of the relevant product.

28. The HHI is computed by summing the numerical squares of the market shares of all the firms in the market. For example, a market with four firms each having a market share of 25% has an HHI

Unlike the traditional four firm concentration ratio ("CR4") which was formerly used by enforcement agencies and courts to measure market concentration,[29] the HHI reflects both the distribution of the market shares of all the leading firms in the market and the composition of the market beyond the leading firms.[30]

The predominant concern of the Congress in enacting section 7 was the prevention of high levels of industrial concentration because it believed that such structure was likely to produce anticompetitive consequences. Foremost among these expected anticompetitive effects of high concentration is the exercise of market power by one or more firms. The HHI levels which trigger presumptions that mergers are likely to create or enhance market power should be set at the concentration levels likely to predict a substantial lessening of competition.[31]

Furthermore, an important component of the scholarly economic inquiry into the competitive consequences of mergers has been the correlation of concentration levels with various indicia of competition. Other theories which predict the competitive effects of mergers based upon factors other than market concentration are valuable adjuncts to market concentration analysis. The most important of the supplemental inquiries concerns "ease of entry" into the markets affected by the merger.[32]

The Attorneys General divide the spectrum of market concentration into the same three numerical regions utilized by the United States Department of Justice. They are characterized in these *Guidelines* as "unconcentrated" (HHI below 1000) "moderately concentrated" (HHI between 1000 and 1800) and "highly concentrated" (HHI above 1800).[33]

4.1   *General Standards*

The Attorneys General will calculate the post-merger concentration level in the market and the increase in concentration caused by the merger.

---

of 2500 calculated as follows: $25^2 + 25^2 + 25^2 + 25^2 = 2500$. A market with a pure monopolist, i.e., a firm with 100 percent of the market has an HHI of 10,000 calculated as $100^2 = 10,000$. If the market has four firms, each having a market share of twenty-five percent and two of these four firms merge, the increase in the HHI is computed as follows: Pre-merger $25^2 + 25^2 + 25^2 + 25^2 = 2500$. Post-merger $50^2 + 25^2 + 25^2 = 3750$. The increase in the HHI due to the merger is 1250, i.e., $3750 - 2500 = 1250$. The increase is also equivalent to twice the product of the market shares of the merging firms, i.e., 25 x 25 x 2 = 1250.

29.   The CR4 is the sum of the market shares of the top four firms in the market. A CR4 cannot be converted into any single HHI but rather includes a possible range of HHI levels. For example, consider two markets with CR4 of 100 percent. The first is comprised of four firms; each with a market share of twenty-five percent. This yields an HHI of 2500, i.e., $25^2 + 25^2 + 25^2 + 25^2 = 2500$. The second market is comprised of four firms with market shares of 70%, 10%, 10% and 10%. This yields an HHI of 5200, i.e., $70^2 + 10^2 + 10^2 + 10^2 = 5200$.

30.   The HHI also gives significantly greater weight to the market shares of the largest firms, which properly reflects the leading roles which such firms are likely to play in a collusive agreement or other exercise of market power. A single dominant firm's likely role as the price leader in an oligopolistic market is also reflected in the HHI. For these reasons, the HHI is now the generally preferred measure of concentration.

31.   Other characteristics of the particular industry, such as barriers to entry, may indicate that concentration measures either overstate or understate the competitive significance of the merger.

32.   *See* Section 5.1.

33.   Mergers resulting in a post-merger HHI of less than 1,000 do not create a presumption that the merger will have significant anticompetitive impact.

While it may be justifiable to challenge any merger above the threshold of market concentration where successful tacit or express collusion and interdependent behavior are significantly facilitated (HHI 1000) the Attorneys General are unlikely to challenge mergers which do not significantly increase concentration. This policy recognizes section 7's prohibition of mergers whose effect "may be substantially to lessen competition." When the threshold of very high concentration is exceeded (HHI 1800), the likelihood of anticompetitive effects are greatly increased and the increase in concentration likely to substantially lessen competition concomitantly reduced. The concentration increases which trigger presumptions that mergers are likely to create or enhance market power have been adopted in reasonable accommodation of both the "substantiality" requirement of section 7 and the need objectively to factor in the dynamic conditions in an industry.[34]

4.2   Post-Merger HHI between 1000 and 1800

A merger that increases the HHI by more than 100 to a level in excess of 1,000 creates a presumption that the merger will result in significant anticompetitive effects. This presumption may be overcome if the merging parties are able to demonstrate, upon consideration of all of the other factors contained in these *Guidelines*, that the merger is not likely significantly to lessen competition. The greater the HHI increase and level, the less likely that these factors will overcome this presumption.

4.3   Post-Merger HHI above 1800

A merger that increases the HHI by more than fifty to a level in excess of 1,800 creates a presumption that the merger will result in significant anticompetitive effects. This presumption may be overcome if the merging parties are able to demonstrate, upon consideration of all of the other factors contained in these *Guidelines*, that the merger is not likely significantly to lessen competition. The greater the HHI increase and level, the less likely that these factors will overcome this presumption.[35]

4.4   Mergers Involving the Leading Firm or a New,
Innovative Firm in a Market

The merger of a dominant firm with a small firm in the market may create or increase the market power of the dominant firm yet increase the HHI by an amount

---

34. The decision whether or not to bring suit is ultimately within the sole discretion of each Attorney General. In addition to the economic impact of a merger on a state, Attorneys General may consider numerous other factors in deciding whether to challenge a merger that raises competitive concerns. For example, Attorneys General are more likely to be concerned about mergers in industries exhibiting a significant trend towards concentration. The existence of an in-depth examination of the merger by other antitrust enforcement agencies may be relevant to the action of an Attorney General with respect to a merger that otherwise raises competitive concerns.

35. For example, this presumption will be rarely overcome if the increase exceeds 200 and the resulting HHI level exceeds 2,500.

less than the levels set forth in Sections 4.2 and 4.3. Similarly, the merger of a new, innovative firm with an existing significant competitor in the market may substantially reduce competition yet increase the HHI by an amount less than the levels set forth in Sections 4.2 and 4.3. Therefore, mergers presumptively create or enhance market power if the proposed merger involves either a leading firm with a market share of at least thirty-five percent and a firm with a market share of one percent or more, or a firm with a market share of twenty percent or more and a new, innovative firm in a market or attempting to enter a market that is moderately or highly concentrated, unless assessment of the factors discussed in Sections 5.1 and/or 5.3 clearly compels the conclusion that the merger is not likely substantially to lessen competition.

5. Additional Factors That May Be Considered in Determining Whether to Challenge a Merger

There are additional factors aside from market share and market concentration that may make a merger more or less likely substantially to lessen competition. While the assessment of these factors would increase the flexibility of these *Guidelines*, overemphasis on these other factors, given the current state of economic knowledge, would significantly vitiate the predictability and the consistency of enforcement under the *Guidelines* and would greatly reduce their value as a planning and risk assessment tool for the business community.

The present state of economic theory, especially where there is an absence of supporting empirical work, is generally insufficient to overcome the usual presumption that increases in market concentration will increase the likelihood and degree to which industry performance is adversely affected. Increased concentration may allow the industry's constituent firms to coordinate pricing in a variety of ways, to neutralize the potential benefits of increased efficiency through output reduction and to forestall entry.

For example, many theories have been offered regarding the extent to which a particular factor may tend to increase or decrease the likelihood of collusion. In an actual merger analysis, however, a relevant market is likely to be characterized by several of these factors pointing in opposite directions, and economics offers little guidance on how the individual factors should be judged in combination. Even the significance of isolated factors remains in doubt. Many states have discovered bid-rigging among highway contractors, for example, when the characteristics of the industry might lead some to predict theoretically that collusion would be extremely difficult, if not impossible.

Because of this, the merging parties will bear a heavy burden of showing that the normal presumption of anticompetitive effect should not be applied in a particular case. This heavy burden will increase further with higher levels of concentration and increases in concentration, particularly to the extent the post-merger HHI would be greater than 1800 and the increase in HHI greater than 50.

While maintaining primary reliance on the concentration and market share analysis discussed in Section 4, the Attorneys General will, in appropriate circumstances, assess four additional factors. These are ease of entry, collusive behavior, powerful or sophisticated buyers and efficiencies.

5.1   *Ease of Entry*

5.11   OVERVIEW

A merger is not likely to create or enhance market power or to facilitate its exercise if entry into the market is so easy that market participants, after the merger, either collectively or unilaterally could not profitably maintain a price increase above premerger levels. Such entry likely will deter an anticompetitive merger in its incipiency, or deter or counteract the competitive effects of concern.

Entry is that easy if entry would be timely, likely and sufficient in its magnitude, character and scope to deter or counteract the competitive effects of concern. In markets where entry is that easy (i.e., where entry passes these tests of timeliness, likelihood, and sufficiency), the merger raises no antitrust concern and ordinary requires no further analysis.

The entry treated in this section is defined as new competition that requires expenditure of significant sunk costs of entry and exit ("committed entry"). The Attorneys General will employ a three-step methodology to assess whether committed entry would deter or counteract a competitive effect of concern.

This first step assesses whether entry can achieve significant market impact within a timely period. If significant market impact would require a longer period, entry will not deter or counteract the competitive effect of concern.

The second step assesses whether committed entry would be a profitable and, hence, a likely response to a merger having competitive effects of concern. Firms considering entry that requires significant sunk costs must evaluate that profitability of the entry on the basis of long-term participation in the market, because the underlying assets will be committed to the market until they are economically depreciated. Entry that is sufficient to counteract the competitive effects of concern will cause prices to fall to their premerger levels or lower. Thus, the profitability of such committed entry must be determined on the basis of pre-merger market prices over the long term.

A merger having anticompetitive effects can attract committed entry, profitable at premerger prices, that would not have occurred premerger at these same prices. But following the merger, the reduction in industry output and increase in prices associated with the competitive effect of concern may allow the same entry to occur without driving market prices below premerger levels. After a merger that results in decreased output and increased prices, the likely sales opportunities available to entrants at premerger prices will be larger than they were premerger, larger by the output reduction caused by the merger. If entry could be profitable at premerger prices without exceeding the likely sales opportunities—opportunities that include pre-existing pertinent factors as well as the merger-induced output reduction—then such entry is likely in response to the merger.

The third step assesses whether timely and likely entry would be sufficient to return market prices to their premerger levels. This end may be accomplished either through multiple entry or individual entry at a sufficient scale. Entry may not be sufficient, even though timely and likely, where the constraints on availability of essential assets, due to incumbent control, make it impossible for entry profitably to achieve the necessary level of sales. Also, the character and scope of entrants' products might not be fully responsive to the localized sales opportunities created by the removal of direct competition among sellers of differentiated products. In assessing whether entry will be timely, likely, and sufficient, the Attorneys General recognize that precise and detailed information may be difficult or impossible to obtain. In such instances, the Attorneys General will rely on all available evidence bearing on whether entry will satisfy the conditions of timeliness, likelihood, and sufficiency.

5.12   TIMELINESS OF ENTRY

In order to deter or counteract the competitive effects of concern, entrants quickly must achieve a significant impact on price in the relevant market. The Attorneys General generally will consider timely only those committed entry alternatives that can be achieved within two years from initial planning to significant market impact.[36] Where the relevant product is a durable good, consumers, in response to a significant commitment to entry, may defer purchases by making additional investments to extend the useful life of previously purchased goods and in this way deter or counteract for a time the competitive effects of concern. In these circumstances, if entry only can occur outside of the two year period, the Attorneys General will consider entry to be timely so long as it would deter or counteract the competitive effects of concern within the two year period and subsequently.

5.13   LIKELIHOOD OF ENTRY

An entry alternative is likely if it would be profitable at premerger prices, and if such prices could be secured by the entrant.[37] The committed entrant will be unable to secure prices at premerger levels if its output is too large for the market to absorb without depressing prices further. Thus, entry is unlikely if the minimum viable scale is larger than the likely sales opportunity available to entrants.

Minimum viable scale is the smallest average annual level of sales that the committed entrant must persistently achieve for profitability at premerger prices.[38] Minimum viable scale is a function of expected revenues, based upon premerger prices,[39] and all categories of costs associated with the entry alternative, including an appropriate rate of return on invested capital given that entry could fail and sunk costs, if any, will be lost.[40]

---

36. Firms which have committed to entering the market prior to the merger generally will be included in the measurement of the market. Only committed entry or adjustments to pre-existing entry plans that are induced by the merger will be considered as possibly deterring or counteracting the competitive effects of concern.

37. Where conditions indicate that entry may be profitable at prices below premerger levels, the Attorneys General will assess the likelihood of entry at the lowest price at which such entry would be profitable.

38. The concept of minimum viable scale ("MVS") differs from the concept of minimum efficient scale ("MES"). While MES is the smallest scale at which average costs are minimized, MVS is the smallest scale at which average costs equal the premerger price.

39. The expected path of future prices, absent the merger, may be used if future price changes can be predicted with reasonable reliability.

40. The minimum viable scale of an entry alternative will be relatively large when the fixed costs of entry are large, when the fixed costs of entry are largely sunk, when the marginal costs of production are high at low levels of output, and when a plant is underutilized for a long time because of delays in achieving market acceptance.

Sources of sales opportunities available to entrants include: (a) The output reduction associated with the competitive effect of concern;[41] (b) entrants' ability to capture a share of reasonably expected growth in market demand;[42] (c) entrants' ability securely to divert sales from incumbents, for example, through vertical integration or through forward contracting; and (d) any additional anticipated contraction in incumbents' output in response to entry.[43] Factors that reduce the sales opportunities available to entrants include: (a) The prospect that an entrant will share in a reasonably expected decline in market demand; (b) the exclusion of an entrant from a portion of the market over the long term because of vertical integration or forward contracting by incumbents; and (c) any anticipated strategic reaction, including but not limited to, sales expansion by incumbents in reaction to entry, either generalized or targeted at customers approached by the entrant, that utilized prior irreversible investments in excess production capacity. Demand growth or decline will be viewed as relevant only if total market demand is projected to experience long-lasting change during at least the two year period following the competitive effect of concern.

5.14 SUFFICIENCY OF ENTRY

Inasmuch as multiple entry generally is possible and individual entrants may flexibly choose their scale, committed entry generally will be sufficient to deter or counteract the competitive effects of concern whenever entry is likely under the analysis of Section 5.1. However, entry, although likely, will not be sufficient if, as a result of incumbent control, the tangible and intangible assets required for entry are not adequately available for entrants to respond fully to their sales opportunities. In addition, where the competitive effect of concern is not uniform across the relevant market, in order for entry to be sufficient, the character and scope of entrants' products must be responsive to the localized sales opportunities that include the output reduction associated with the competitive effect of concern. For example, where the concern is unilateral price elevation as a result of a merger between producers of differentiated products, entry, in order to be sufficient, must involve a product so close to the products of the merging firms that the merged firm will be unable to internalize enough of the sales loss due to the price rise, rendering the price increase unprofitable.

5.15 ENTRY ALTERNATIVES

The Attorneys General will examine the timeliness, likelihood, and sufficiency of the means of entry (entry alternatives) a potential entrant might practically employ, without attempting to identify who might be potential entrants. An entry alternative is defined by the actions the firm must take in order to produce and sell in the market.

---

41. Five percent of total market sales typically is used because where a monopolist profitability would raise price by five percent or more across the entire relevant market, it is likely that the accompanying reduction in sales would be no less than five percent.

42. Entrant's anticipated share of growth in demand depends on incumbents' capacity constraints and irreversible investments in capacity expansion, as well as on the relative appeal, acceptability and reputation of incumbents' and entrants' products to the new demand.

43. For example, in a bidding market where all bidders are on equal footing, the market share of incumbents will contract as a result of entry.

All phases of the entry effort will be considered, including, where relevant, planning, design, and management; permitting, licensing, and other approvals, construction, debugging, and operation of production facilities; and promotion (including necessary introductory discounts), marketing, distribution and satisfaction of customer testing and qualification requirements.[44] Recent examples of entry, whether successful or unsuccessful, may provide a useful starting point for identifying the necessary actions, time requirements, and characteristics of possible entry alternatives. Entry may be by diversion of existing supplies into the market or by new production sources of supply. The Attorneys General will evaluate empirical evidence of the following sources of entry.

5.15A Diversion of Existing Supplies into the Market

The parties to a merger may produce evidence that firms will divert supplies of the product into the market in response to a price increase or restriction of output. The Attorneys General will analyze proof concerning such probable diversions of supplies currently exported from the relevant market, supplies internally consumed by vertically integrated firms in the market and additional supplies from firms currently shipping part of their production into the market.

5.15A(1) Exports

A firm currently exporting the product from the relevant market may divert the supply back into the market in response to a price increase or restriction of output.

This response is unlikely from an exporter who is a party to the merger, since it is unlikely to discipline its own attempted exercise of market power. It is also unlikely if the exporter is an oligopolist likely to benefit from the collective exercise of market power.

Although parties wishing to prove this supply response are free to produce any empirical evidence, the most persuasive proof will be historical shipping patterns showing past diversion of exports in response to price increases or restricted supply. In addition, the parties should, at a minimum, address the following questions: Are the exports contractually committed and for what term? Are the exports otherwise obligated to current buyers?

5.15A(2) Internal Consumption

A vertically integrated firm producing the product for internal consumption may divert this supply to the open market. Diversion is unlikely if there are no suitable and economical substitutes for the product and/or the firm has contractual or other obligations for the goods utilizing the relevant product. The most persuasive proof of such diversion will be evidence that a vertically integrated firm already sells some of the product on the open market and has a history of transferring production intended for internal consumption to the open market.

---

44. Many of these phases may be undertaken simultaneously.

5.15A(3) Increased Importation

A firm shipping part of its output of the product into the relevant market may respond to an attempted exercise of market power by diverting additional production into the relevant market. In order to address the impact of such a response, the parties should, at a minimum, address the factual issues of whether and for what terms these additional supplies are contractually or otherwise obligated to buyers outside the relevant market, the percentage of the suppliers' production now sent into the market and their historical shipping patterns.

5.15B New Production Sources of Additional Supply

The parties to a merger may produce evidence that firms not currently supplying the product will do so within two years of any attempted exercise of market power. This might be shown for firms with production flexibility, firms who will erect new production facilities and firms engaging in arbitrage.

5.15B(1) Production Flexibility

The Attorneys General will evaluate proof concerning firms with flexible production facilities who are capable of switching to the production of the relevant product within two years and are likely to do so. A history of such switching in the past will be the most persuasive evidence that this response is probable.

5.15B(2) Construction of New Facilities

A party may attempt to demonstrate that firms not presently supplying the product will erect new plant facilities (or establish new service facilities) within two years of an attempted exercise of market power.

5.15B(3) Arbitrage

Firms proximate to the relevant market may respond to an exercise of market power by buying the product outside the market and reselling it inside the market. This potential source of supply is unlikely if the relevant product is a service or combined product and service. A history of arbitrage in the industry will be most probative that this potential response is probable.

5.2   *Collusion and Oligopolistic Behavior*

If there is evidence of past collusion or anticompetitive behavior,[45] the presumptions set forth in Section 4 will rarely be overcome and a proposed merger falling below the numerical thresholds set forth in Section 4 may also be examined more closely where such evidence is present. In the face of indications that collusion

---

45.   An oligopolistic market will usually be moderately to highly concentrated or very highly concentrated and will exhibit one or more of the following practices: (1) price leadership; (2) pre-announced price changes; (3) relative price rigidity in response to excess capacity or diminished demand; (4) public pronouncements regarding price; and (5) price discrimination.

or oligopolistic behavior is likely to be presently occurring, the Attorneys General will not consider other factors offered for the purpose of showing that the presumptions in Section 4 are overcome.

The absence of current or past collusion or oligopolistic behavior will not diminish the presumptions set forth in Section 4.

5.3   *Efficiencies*

To the extent that efficiency was a concern of the Congress in enacting section 7, that concern was expressed in the legislative finding that less industrial concentration would further that goal.[46]   The Attorneys General find that there is no substantial empirical support for the assertion that mergers involving firms of sufficient size to raise concerns under the standards set forth in Section 4, usually or on average result in substantial efficiencies.   Furthermore, the concentration thresholds adopted in Section 4 are generally high enough to enable firms to obtain the most significant efficiencies likely to result from growth through merger.

Even in those rare situations where significant efficiencies can be demonstrated, rather than merely predicted, this showing cannot constitute a defense to an otherwise unlawful merger.[47]   Accordingly, efficiencies will only be considered when the merging parties can demonstrate by clear and convincing evidence that the merger will lead to significant efficiencies.   Moreover, the merging parties must demonstrate that the efficiencies will ensure that consumer prices will not increase despite any increase in market power due to the merger.   In highly concentrated markets, even a merger which produces efficiencies will tend to create or enhance market power and will likely increase consumer prices.   In addition, the Attorneys General will reject claims of efficiencies unless the merging parties can demonstrate that equivalent or comparable savings can not be achieved through other means and that such cost savings will persist over the long run.[48]

5.4   *Powerful or Sophisticated Buyers*

Tacit or express collusion can be frustrated by the presence of powerful and sophisticated buyers if these are appropriately situated to force firms in the primary market to negotiate secretly or offer substantial concessions for large purchasers.   In most circumstances, however, the Attorneys General find that the presence of powerful or sophisticated buyers is unlikely to prevent anticompetitive effects from

---

46.   For example, see 95 Cong. Rec. 11,487 (1949) (statement of Rep. Celler, co-author of legislation). "Bigness does not mean efficiency, a better product, or lower prices." 95 Cong. Rec. 11,495-98 (1949) (statement of Rep. Boggs); Corporate Mergers and Acquisitions: Hearings on H.R. 2734 Before a Subcomm. of the Senate Comm. on the Judiciary, 81st Cong. lst & 2nd Sess. 206, 308 (1950) (statement of James L. Donnelly).

47.   *See* note 11.

48.   Example: In an industry with a one percent profit margin, proven cost savings of three percent would be significant. If a merger which produces cost savings of the magnitude specified does not simultaneously facilitate the exercise of market power, these savings should reduce consumer prices, an effect consistent with the purposes of section 7. However, if the merger simultaneously produces these efficiencies and creates or enhances market power, there is less likelihood that consumer prices will be reduced. In such circumstances consumer prices likely will rise as a result of the exercise of market power.

occurring.[49] Thus, the presence of powerful or sophisticated buyers will only be considered when the buyers are uniquely positioned to enter the primary market in response to collusive pricing, or to finance or otherwise facilitate the entry of others.

6.   Failing Firm Defense

The failing firm doctrine, which has been recognized by the United States Supreme Court, may be a defense to an otherwise unlawful merger.[50] Because it may allow anticompetitive mergers, the defense will be strictly construed.

The Attorneys General will only consider a failing firm defense to an anticompetitive merger where the proponents of the merger satisfy their burden of showing the following three elements: (1) That the resources of the allegedly failing firm are so depleted and the prospect of rehabilitation is so remote that the firm faces a high probability of a business failure;[51] (2) that it had made reasonable good faith efforts and had failed to find another reasonable prospective purchaser; and (3) that there is no less anticompetitive alternative available.[52]

---

49.   For example, if some but not all of the buyers in a market are powerful and sophisticated, the former may be able to achieve price concessions while the less powerful buyers will not. In that case the merger should be evaluated by its impact on the less powerful buyers. Similarly, powerful buyers may often find it more profitable to preserve the monopoly in the primary market and share in its profits than to force competition there. This is most likely when both buyer and seller market levels are highly concentrated and each side has significant power to force the other side to behave competitively. In that case forbearance on both sides, which results in preservation of the monopoly and sharing of its profits, is a more profitable result than aggressive behavior that will eliminate monopoly profits at both levels.

50.   United States v. General Dynamics Corp., 415 U.S. 486, 507 (1974); United States v. Greater Buffalo Press, Inc., 402 U.S. 549, 555 (1971).

51.   Evidence showing that the putative failing firm would not be able to reorganize successfully under Chapter 11 of the Bankruptcy Act, 11 U.S.C. §§ 1101-1174 (1988), would be highly relevant.

52.   The Attorneys General may exercise their prosecutorial discretion by declining to challenge a merger which will sustain a failing division of an otherwise viable firm. Since the failing division claim is highly susceptible to manipulation and abuse, the Attorneys General will require the three elements of the "failing firm" defense to be proven by clear and convincing evidence.

1995 VERTICAL RESTRAINTS GUIDELINES OF THE NATIONAL ASSOCIATION OF ATTORNEYS GENERAL

1. Purpose and Scope of the *Guidelines*

These *Guidelines* explain the general enforcement policy of the fifty state attorneys general who comprise the National Association of Attorneys General ("NAAG")[1] concerning resale price maintenance agreements and non-price vertical restraints of trade subject to Sections 1 and 2 of the Sherman Act,[2] Section 3 of the Clayton Act[3] and analogous provisions of the antitrust laws of those States which have enacted them.[4]

In most states the Attorney General is the primary or exclusive public enforcer of the state's antitrust laws. The Attorneys General also represent their states and the natural person citizens of their states in federal antitrust litigation.[5]

Vertical restraints are arrangements among businesses operating at different levels of an industry, e.g., between a manufacturer and a distributor or between a wholesaler and a retailer. They restrain the way, or price at which, these firms may buy, sell or resell goods and services. These *Guidelines* focus primarily on resale

---

1. The Attorneys General of American Samoa, Guam, the Northern Mariana Islands, Puerto Rico, and the Virgin Islands, and the Corporation Counsel of the District of Columbia are also members of NAAG.
2. Sherman Act Section 1, 15 U.S.C. § 1, prohibits concerted activity in restraint of trade. Section 2, 15 U.S.C. § 2, prohibits monopolization, attempts to monopolize and conspiracies to monopolize any part of trade or commerce.
3. Clayton Act Section 3, 15 U.S.C. § 14, states in pertinent part "It shall be unlawful . . . to lease or make a sale or contract for sale of . . . commodities . . . on the condition, agreement or understanding that the lessee or purchaser thereof shall not use or deal in the commodities of a competitor or competitors of the seller or lessor where the effect . . . may be to substantially lessen competition or tend to create a monopoly in any line of commerce."
4. Citations to the antitrust laws of the States are set forth in 6 Trade Reg. Rep. (CCH) ¶ 30,000 *et seq.*
5. Clayton Act Section 4C, 15 U.S.C. § 15c, states in pertinent part:
   (1) Any attorney general of a State may bring a civil action in the name of such State, as parens patriae on behalf of natural persons residing in such State, in any district court of the United States having jurisdiction of the defendant, to secure monetary relief as provided in this section for injury sustained by such natural persons to their property by reason of any violation of sections 1 to 7 of this title.

price maintenance agreements, as well as exclusive dealing arrangements[6] and other foreclosure restraints such as tie-ins, which condition the sale of one product or service on the purchase of a second distinct product or service.

These *Guidelines* embody a general enforcement policy of NAAG and its members. Individual Attorneys General may vary or supplement this general policy to allow for variations in precedents among the federal circuits, differences in state antitrust laws and the exercise of their individual prosecutorial discretion. The *Guidelines* are not a substitute for properly submitted amici curiae briefs, which focus on the facts of particular cases. The "rule of reason" inquiry which the Supreme Court requires to determine the legality of non-price restraints is complicated and contextual.[7] That is, the contours of the rule of reason inquiry appropriate for a particular vertical restraint will depend on specific market and industry factors not reducible to any broadly applicable formula. Attorneys General may file briefs amici curiae in vertical restraint cases where such participation is warranted or requested by any federal or state court.

The *Guidelines* serve two primary purposes. First, the *Guidelines* clearly mark the boundaries between horizontal agreements and resale price maintenance agreements that are per se unlawful and those purely non-price vertical agreements subject to a rule of reason analysis. Second, the *Guidelines* describe and explain the factors that are relevant to the Attorneys General in conducting a rule of reason analysis of a non-price vertical restraint.

Neither these *Guidelines* nor any other generalized statement of enforcement policy can assure businesses that a particular restraint will or will not be held lawful in court. Real cases present market and industry variables too numerous to be measured adequately in general formulae. Furthermore, no public enforcement policy can or should inhibit private litigation. Private parties have been and will continue to be the primary enforcers of the antitrust laws. In many cases the superior knowledge and experience of business litigants may result in better enforcement decisions than can be made by prosecutors whose knowledge is based only on theory and inquiry. Finally, although federal and state enforcement agencies can characterize the law, it remains for Congress to make those laws and for the judiciary to interpret the law.

---

6. Exclusive dealing arrangements, as the term is used in these *Guidelines*, include agreements that a seller deal exclusively with a particular buyer or group of buyers or that a buyer deal exclusively with a particular seller or group of sellers. Examples of exclusive dealing arrangements are exclusive distributorships (also referred to as "exclusive distribution territories"), requirements contracts and exclusive outlet provisions. These restraints, especially when air-tight, completely or substantially foreclose intrabrand competition.

    Other vertical restraints such as location clauses, customer restrictions, areas of primary responsibility and profit pass-over arrangements may unreasonably restrain trade, but have less tendency to do so. For example, the imposition of areas of primary responsibility will allow a supplier to realize most of the objectives of an exclusive distributorship without extinguishing intrabrand competition. In particular cases these less suspect restraints may be imposed with anticompetitive intent or may unreasonably restrain trade. A location clause may effectively foreclose any intrabrand competition. A pass-over arrangement may have no purpose other than the penalization of extraterritorial sales with no countervailing interbrand benefit. *See, e.g.*, Eiberger v. Sony Corp. of America, 622 F.2d 1068, 1076-81 (2d Cir. 1980). In such cases the analysis detailed in Section 4 will be applied.

    It should be noted that no case has held that any non-price vertical restraint is per se lawful.

7. Continental T.V. Inc. v. GTE Sylvania, Inc., 433 U.S. 36 (1977) ("*Sylvania*").

2. Categorization of Restraints

A literal reading of Section 1 of the Sherman Act would condemn all concerted activity which restrains trade or commerce among the States, including conduct as innocuous and necessary as a simple contract to sell and buy.[8] However, the Supreme Court has interpreted the prohibition of the Act to reach only those concerted restraints of trade which are "unreasonable."[9] After nearly a century of interpretation, the Court has further refined the doctrine prohibiting unreasonable restraints of trade into two broad categories of arrangements: those which are per se unlawful and those whose legality (reasonableness) are to be determined under the so-called "rule of reason" analysis. In the per se category are restraints of trade such as price-fixing, whose anticompetitive effects are so uniform and unequivocal that the Courts will condemn them without any inquiry into the actual economic effects of the practice in a given case. Restraints which are not per se unlawful are subject to a rule of reason inquiry into their expected or actual market effects. Among these practices are non-price vertical restraints.

The foregoing doctrines require a threshold determination of whether a restraint is per se unlawful or subject to the far reaching market effect analysis which is detailed below. Per se or rule of reason categorization will in turn often depend upon whether a restraint is horizontal[10] or vertical in nature, and if vertical, whether the arrangement restrains pricing decisions or non-price aspects of the marketing process. This initial characterization of restraints is especially important when firms engage in more than one restraint or when they exert pressure or coercion at one level of an industry that ultimately imposes a restraint at another level.

If it is unstructured, a full rule of reason analysis can be inherently cumbersome, protracted and imprecise. In addition to expressing a judgment on the social and economic value of certain restraints, per se rules provide the business community with the certainty and predictability that are conducive to rational decision making.[11] However, the distinctions between per se and rule of reason standards adopted in the *Guidelines* are rooted in settled case law and do not represent any independent policy choice between such rules.

2.1 Categorizing Price and Non-Price Vertical Restraints

Resale price maintenance agreements ("RPM"), also called vertical price-fixing agreements, are per se unlawful and have been so since the 1911 Supreme Court decision in *Dr. Miles Medical Co. v. John D. Park & Sons Co.*, 220 U.S. 373. *Dr. Miles* also discussed the per se illegality of single brand horizontal price-fixing arrangements and equated the conclusively presumed anticompetitive effects of both practices.[12]

---

8.   *See, e.g.*, United States v. Trans-Missouri Freight Ass'n, 166 U.S. 290 (1897).
9.   Standard Oil Co. v. United States, 221 U.S. 1 (1911).
10. Horizontal agreements restrain trade among comptitors at the same level of an industry, e.g., competing wholesalers agree to fix their prices.
11. In *United States v. Topco, Inc.*, 405 U.S. 596, 609-10 (1972), the Court stated: "Without the per se rules, businessmen would be left with little to aid them in predicting in any particular case what courts will find to be legal and illegal under the Sherman Act."
12. "And where commodities have passed into the channels of trade and are owned by dealers, the validity of agreements to prevent competition and to maintain prices is not to be determined

RPM can be prosecuted as a crime under the federal antitrust laws. Although such criminal challenges have been infrequent, RPM may be prosecuted as such by the Attorneys General in appropriate cases where state antitrust laws provide for criminal sanctions.[13]

An RPM agreement is reached when two or more independent firms at different levels in the distribution system agree to fix, raise, lower, maintain or stabilize the price at which goods or services will be resold.[14] There need not be any agreement on specific resale prices or price levels.[15] A practice under which a supplier's obligation to provide some benefit to a distributor, when it depends at least in part, on the price at which the distributor resells the supplier's product, may be viewed as a type of RPM agreement.

Non-price vertical restraints may have the effect of raising the prices at which goods or services are resold. However, a purely non-price vertical restraint, such as an exclusive distributorship, should not be treated as an RPM agreement merely because it may have an effect on price.

A more significant issue of categorization is raised when a supplier and its distributors have adopted both RPM and other non-price vertical restraints of trade. While in such cases the RPM agreement is per se illegal, questions have arisen as to whether the non-price restraints should then also be treated as per se unlawful.[16]

The Attorneys General will treat the issue as one of fact, i.e., are the non-price restraints adopted to reinforce or assure the success of the price-fixing arrangement or is such their predominant effect? If so, the non-price restraints will be treated as per se unlawful. In conducting the factual inquiry necessary to determine whether non-price restraints were adopted to reinforce an RPM agreement, the Attorneys General will be cognizant of several general principles germane to this issue. First, firms engaging in RPM are already willfully violating a long established and well understood aspect of the antitrust laws.

Second, the reselling parties to an RPM agreement have incentives to cheat on the conspiracy by engaging in indirect forms of price competition.[17] The adoption of non-price vertical restraints may help maintain the discipline and effectiveness of the RPM agreement.

Finally, it is widely recognized that one of the potential harmful effects of RPM is to help maintain a suppliers' cartel. The adoption of non-price vertical restraints,

---

by the circumstance whether they were produced by several manufacturers or by one, or whether they were previously owned by one or many."
Dr. Miles, 220 U.S. at 408 09.
13. Citations to the antitrust laws of the States are set forth in 6 Trade Reg. Rep. (CCH) ¶ 30,000 *et seq.*
14. United States v. Parke, Davis & Co., 362 U.S. 29, 47 (1960).
15. United States v. Parke, Davis & Co., 362 U.S. 29 (1960). In *Business Electronics, Inc. v. Sharp Electronics, Inc.*, 485 U.S. 717, 722 (1988), the Supreme Court determined that to render illegal per se a vertical agreement between a manufacturer and a dealer to terminate sales to a second dealer, the first dealer "must expressly or implicitly agree to set its prices at some level, though not a specific one" quoting the decision below. 780 F.2d 1212, 1218 (5th Cir. 1986).
16. Monsanto Co. v. Spray-Rite Service Corp., 465 U.S. 752, 759 n.6 (1984).
17. These include rebates, the provision of free goods and tie-in sales, favorable credit terms, absorption of transportation costs and expanded warranties.

especially exclusive distributorships, may reinforce the cartel maintaining properties for which the RPM schemes were initially adopted.[18]

2.2 Categorizing Horizontal and Vertical Restraints

In accordance with settled and longstanding Supreme Court precedent, the Attorneys General will treat all naked horizontal agreements to fix prices or allocate customers, markets or territories as per se violations of Sherman Act Section 1 and analogous state law provisions. The Supreme Court has held that both intrabrand and interbrand competition are protected by the law.[19] Accordingly, the Court has consistently held horizontal agreements per se unlawful whether the conspirators are competitors selling different brands or the same brand.[20]

An issue of categorization may arise when a manufacturer (or distributor) and dealers agree or form a combination to fix prices or price advertising and it appears that each dealer agrees to so restrict its pricing or price advertising upon the condition that other dealers act accordingly or with knowledge that other dealers are so acting. In *Business Electronics, Inc. v. Sharp Electronics, Inc.*, 108 S. Ct. 1515, 1525 (1988), the Court characterized such a combination as horizontal in nature. Therefore, in accordance with the teaching of *Sharp Electronics*, the Attorneys General will evaluate vertical price fixing agreements and combinations to determine whether they are also properly characterized as being horizontal in nature.

2.3 Dual Distribution

Dual distribution occurs when a supplier of a product also acts as a dealer of the product in actual or potential competition with independent distributors of the product. Because of the competitive presence of the supplier at the dealer level, issues of categorization arise when a dual distributing supplier imposes vertical restraints which diminish or limit its competition with independent dealers.[21]

If the restraint takes the form of a vertical price-fixing agreement, the categorization issue is less significant in the sense that both vertical and horizontal price-fixing agreements are per se unlawful.

The mere fact that a supplier is a dual distributor should not automatically cause a non-price vertical restraint to be characterized as a horizontal agreement. A dual distributing supplier may impose a vertical restraint with the intent that it efficiently organize its dealers to engage in interbrand competition and without primary regard to the supplier's presence at the dealer level. Such a restraint will be evaluated under the rule of reason analysis specified in Section 4.

---

18. *See* Ornstein, *Resale Price Maintenance and Cartels*, 30 ANTITRUST BULL. 401, 407 (1985), *and* Telser, *Why Should Manufacturers Want Fair Trade?*, 3 J.L. ECON. 86 (1960).
19. *Sylvania*, 433 U.S. at 51.
20. United States v. General Motors Corp., 384 U.S. 127 (1966); *Dr. Miles, supra*, 220 U.S. at 408-09. *See also* United States v. Topco, 405 U.S. 596 (1972) (an agreement among competitors effectuated by an association's licensing agreements will also be considered horizontal); United States v. Sealy, 388 U.S. 350 (1967) (an agreement among competitors effectuated by a manufacturer's distributor agreements will also be treated as horizontal).
21. For example, the dual distributor may keep a certain class of customer for itself, e.g., government contracts, or impose traditional exclusive distributorships by geographical territory.

If the intent or predominant effect of the restraint is to prevent competition for the firm in its dealer capacity, the restraint will be treated as horizontal in nature and effect. When actual intent to restrain competition for the firm acting as dealer is found, this factor will be dispositive.

The following factors will be evaluated by the Attorneys General in determining whether to treat a vertical restraint imposed by a dual distributor as horizontal:

1) Whether a high percentage of the brand's sales at the dealer level are made by company owned outlets.[22]

2) Whether the non-price restriction diminishes interbrand competition because it restrains competing dealers who sell both the supplier's brand and competing brands.[23]

3) Whether the competing independent dealers are also interbrand competitors of the firm at the supplier level.[24]

3.   The Potential Effects of Non-Price Vertical Restraints of Trade

In the 1977 *Sylvania* decision, the Supreme Court determined that the legality of non-price vertical restraints of trade would be judged under a rule of reason analysis, thereby abandoning the previous rule that such restraints were conclusively presumed to be unreasonable, i.e., illegal per se. The basis of the Court's ruling was its recognition of a growing body of economic literature which had theorized that in certain situations vertical restraints might enhance efficiency and spur competition among manufacturers or suppliers of competing brands. The Court required a rule of reason inquiry to balance any pro-competitive interbrand effects against the diminution or elimination of intrabrand competition, which vertical restraints always intentionally cause.

3.1   Economic Theories Concerning the Effects of Vertical Restraints

It is difficult to generalize about the application of economic theory in this area because markets often deviate from the model of perfect competition in significant ways. However, models which properly account for market variations can usefully inform policy and enforcement decisions provided fidelity to the facts is maintained when modelling assumptions are developed.[25] Models which do not account for the market imperfections likely to be present will often lead to inaccurate or incomplete enforcement decisions.

---

22.   *See, e.g.*, Graphic Products Distributors, Inc. v. Itek Corp., 717 F.2d 1560 (11th Cir. 1983).

23.   *See, e.g.*, American Motor Inns, Inc. v. Holiday Inns, Inc., 521 F.2d 1230 (3rd Cir. 1975).

24.   *See, e.g.*, Hobart Bros. Co. v. Malcolm T. Gilliland, Inc., 471 F.2d 894 (5th Cir. 1973), *cert. denied*, 412 U.S. 923 (1973).

25.   For example, the existence of market imperfections can cause many consumers to be unaware of either the existence of certain options or the fact that these options are cost effective substitutes for the product in question. *See* Eastman Kodak Co. v. Image Technical Services, Inc., 112 S. Ct. 2072, 2086 (1992). *See* Lande, *Chicago Takes it on the Chin: Imperfect Information Could Play a Crucial Role in the Post-Kodak World*, 62 ANTITRUST L.J. 193 (1993).

Application of the traditional model of perfect competition can be both inconclusive and flawed.[26]   Similarly, the wholesale application of vertical integration theory to the analysis of vertical restraints can be misleading.[27]   It must also be recognized that those theorists who extol the efficiency enhancing properties of vertical restraints often premise such support on the assumption that a given market will *ultimately* expunge vertical restraints which decrease efficiency and are anticompetitive. But this is only likely to happen if the market workably conforms to certain assumptions underlying the model of perfect competition. These assumptions include, for example, that consumers make rational decisions based upon perfect knowledge of the marketplace, without the distortions introduced by misleading or misinformative advertising or market power at the producer or retailer level. Today's markets rarely comport with this ideal situation. Indeed, if markets were perfectly competitive in this sense, producers and retailers would have no incentive to adopt vertical restraints to certify quality, prevent free-riding or induce retailers to undertake greater promotional effort.

Furthermore, the view that markets will expunge market inefficiencies in the long run is nothing more than an extension of the observation that the market will ultimately destroy all cartels, all monopolies and all collusion.   However, the Congress and state legislatures have adopted antitrust laws because they were unwilling to wait for ultimate market cure and the inefficiency and consumer welfare losses attendant upon waiting for this lengthy process to run its course.[28]

3.2   Pro-Competitive Effects of Non-Price Vertical Restraints

Non-price vertical restraints of trade can enhance efficiency and consumer welfare in a number of ways.[29]   The Attorneys General will consider these benefits only if the parties demonstrate that these benefits are likely to exist, that they will be significant in magnitude, that they will outweigh all of the anticompetitive effects of the restraints, and that the benefits will be passed on to consumers. The Attorneys General will not presume that such benefits are present.   Although there are numerous variations to each of these theories, the principal theories are as follows.

---

26.   Grimes, *The Seven Myths of Vertical Price Fixing: The Politics and Economics of a Century-Long Debate*, 21 S.W.U. L. REV. 1285 (1992).

27.   Scherer, *The Economics of Vertical Restraints*, 52 ANTITRUST L.J. 687 (1983).   Vertical integration theory, in this context, deals with potential gains in efficiency which result when, for example, a supplier becomes its own dealer or a dealer its own supplier.

28.   The "long run" is loosely defined as the period of time necessary for effective entry to occur. Depending on the nature of the industry and the magnitude of entry barriers, this could mean from several months (e.g., service industry with minimal capital and skill requirements) to many years (e.g., capital intensive manufacturing or services that require highly specialized skills).

29.   The theorists who contend that vertical restraints increase efficiency are usually referring to allocative efficiency or "Pareto efficiency." Perfect allocative efficiency is a state of equilibrium on the so-called "utility-possibility frontier" in which no person can be made better off without making someone else worse off.   Allocative efficiency can be achieved in an economy with massive inequities of income and distribution, i.e., 1% of the population can receive 99% of the economy's utility and 99% of the population can receive 1%.   In contrast to the concept of allocative efficiency is "production efficiency." This type of efficiency is achieved by minimizing the costs of producing a given unit of a good or service.

3.2A INCREASING INTERBRAND COMPETITION

By diminishing or extinguishing intrabrand competition, a supplier may provide existing or new dealers with the incentive to devote additional effort to advertising, services and other forms of product enhancement and differentiation. These additional services may enable the product to compete effectively in the interbrand struggle, even as it diminishes intrabrand competition.

This argument is premised, in part, on the assumption that a rational supplier acting unilaterally may have no interest in strengthening the power of its dealers, and in some sense, his interests are consistent with ultimate consumers. Therefore, when a vertical restraint is unilaterally imposed and enhances dealer power it may be intended to strengthen the product in the interbrand market.[30]

3.2B ELIMINATING FREE-RIDING

A second theoretical benefit resulting from vertical restraints may be the reduction of "free-riding." Free-riding is said to occur when discount or off-price dealers, who neither advertise, service or otherwise enhance a product, reap the benefits of such services performed by other dealers who must charge a higher price for the product. Similarly, "vertical or interbrand free-riding" occurs when a dealer utilizes the services provided to it by one manufacturer to sell the products of another manufacturer. An exclusive dealership may prevent such activity from occurring and thereby induce retailers to undertake a host of pre and post-sale service and promotional activities.

The free-ride phenomenon is much disputed among theorists, especially with regard to certain products for which servicing or product enhancement is highly unlikely.[31] Others have argued that free-riding could be eliminated through less restrictive means such as contract provisions or promotional fees.[32] Also, some have argued that retailer promotional activities can be misleading especially, where consumers assume that the retailer is neutral as to various brands.[33]

---

30. Recent empirical studies have cast some doubt on the oft-stated generalization that the net welfare effect of lessening intrabrand competition will be favorable. Mueller, *The Sealy Restraints: Restrictions on Free Riding or Output?*, 1989 WIS. L. REV. 1255 (1989) (elimination of vertical restraints produced lower retail prices and higher output); Steiner, *Sylvania Economics—A Critique*, 60 ANTITRUST L.J. 41 (1991) (elimination of resale price fixing in two industries, toys and jeans, produced lower prices and higher output). These and similar studies suggest that producers have little incentive to impose vertical restraints on major categories of products enjoying substantial brand loyalty because downstream players will want to carry products that the consumers will select regardless of any downstream promotion. In these situations, it is likely that vertical restraints reflect "the triumph of retail leverage over common producer and consumer interests in a more competitive retail segment." Grimes, *supra* note 26, at 1305.
31. *See, e.g.*, Scherer, *supra* note 27, at 694; MARVEL & MCCAFFERTY, RESALE PRICE MAINTENANCE (Ohio State Univ., Oct. 1982). "In many cases, the results of the search [for additional dealer services] have been fruitless, even ludicrous; and as a consequence have led many to question whether special services can explain the incidence and use of RPM." *See also* Mueller, *supra* note 30; Marvel & McCafferty, *Resale Price Maintenance and Quality Certification*, 15 RAND J. ECON. 27 (1984).
32. *Id.*
33. *See* Grimes, *Spiff, Polish and Consumer Deception: Vertical Price Restraints Revisited*, 80 CAL. L. REV. 817 (1992).

3.2C RETAILER CERTIFICATION OF QUALITY

Certain retailers develop reputations for only carrying high quality products. Consumers may rely on such retailers to in effect "certify" that products they carry are of high quality thereby reducing consumer search costs. In some cases, the certification process can be costly to the retailer. Hence, retailers may be less likely to carry or "certify" a producer's product where other retailers are permitted a free-ride on the certifying retailer's efforts.[34]

Although the argument may have validity in some markets, it relies on the assumption that consumers are unable to evaluate product quality. Only where such certification serves as a surrogate for accurate, relevant product information may consumers benefit sufficiently to offset the likely adverse impact from reduced intrabrand competition caused by such restraints.

Also, quality certification can often be achieved more efficiently through producer-level image advertising or directly purchased through promotional fees.[35]

3.2D NEW ENTRY

Finally, in some circumstances a vertical restraint may facilitate the entry of a new product into the market. An exclusive distributorship may give dealers the incentive to carry and promote a new product and assure a level of advertising or servicing necessary to win acceptance for a new product. As with the foregoing potential benefits of non-price vertical restraints, this benefit is not presumed. Their existence or likelihood must be demonstrated.

3.3 *Anticompetitive Effects of Non-Price Vertical Restraints*

3.3A ELIMINATION OF INTRABRAND COMPETITION

The most obvious and inevitable effect of most non-price vertical restraints of trade is the diminution or elimination of intrabrand competition. Intrabrand competition can be a strong counterweight to limited interbrand competition. As previously discussed, the Supreme Court has clearly held that the antitrust laws protect this kind of competition and require a balancing of anticompetitive effects in the intrabrand market against any pro-competitive interbrand effects in determining the legality of a restraint.

3.3B FACILITATION OF COLLUSION

A second possible anticompetitive effect of vertical restraints is the facilitation of collusion among suppliers and or dealers, when certain market conditions exist.

When most or all of the competing suppliers in a concentrated industry limit the number and geographical reach of their dealers, a dealer's cartel will be shielded from competitive prices from outside the cartel's region. Similarly, direct collusion among suppliers or collusion with dealers acting as surrogates is facilitated.

---

34. Marvel & McCafferty, *Resale Price Maintenance and Quality Certification*, 15 RAND J. ECON. 346 (1984).
35. *See* Grimes, *supra* note 33.

Furthermore, the widespread use of such restraints facilitates the policing of a conspiracy, by strictly controlling the number of outlets that must be monitored for compliance.

3.3C EXCLUSION OF COMPETITORS

Vertical restraints can raise entry barriers, erect new barriers and force competitors to operate inefficiently. When the dominant firms in a concentrated market bind available dealers to exclusive dealing arrangements, rivals of the dominant firms or potential entrants may have difficulty arranging for the distribution of their products. Potential entrants may be forced to enter the market at two levels rather than one, making entry significantly more costly. Existing competitors may be forced to vertically integrate or find new independent dealers. Either option may be more costly than distributing through the now foreclosed dealers.

A firm may contract for the exclusive right to purchase an important component in the manufacturing or distribution process. If the exclusive arrangement leaves insufficient quantities of the important component for competitors, potential or existing, entry barriers may be raised and costs of production increased. This will occur if the competing firms must integrate into the production of the component, and this is more costly, or if they are forced to substitute a less cost-effective or suitable component.

3.3D ALLOCATIVE INEFFICIENCY FROM RETAIL PROMOTION INDUCED BY VERTICAL RESTRAINTS

When vertical restraints operate at the retail level and affect multi-brand retailers, these retailers have a financial incentive to promote a particular brand over others that they sell. Consumers, not knowing this, may continue to regard the multi-brand retailer as an objective advice-giver. The consumer may buy a brand not consistent with the consumer's preferences because of this promotion, a result inconsistent with the allocation of resources expected from a workably competitive market.

3.3E REINFORCEMENT OF OLIGOPOLISTIC BEHAVIOR

In an oligopolistic market the previously discussed tendency of vertical restraints to facilitate overt collusion and raise entry barriers, also facilitates tacit collusion and reinforces patterns of consciously parallel behavior. Also, erosion of the oligopoly is retarded by making entry more costly.

4. The Rule of Reason Analysis of Non-Price Vertical Restraints of Trade

The decision to challenge a particular vertical restraint will be made after an analysis of the arrangement under the factors listed in this section and in Section 3 above. Although certain factors may be deemed more important in certain contexts, no single factor is dispositive. That is, there are no arbitrary cutoff points which can be said to assure that a restraint will or will not definitely be challenged. Such arbitrary tests, while useful in other contexts, and appealing because of the certainty they seemingly provide, are of little utility in reaching a reasoned determination or enforcing the law in this complex area.

4.1   Intrabrand Effects

The factors in Section 4 have as their primary function, the prediction or assessment of the competitive effects of a vertical sales restraint in the *interbrand* market, although certain intrabrand effects will be noted. Vertical restraints are always intended to diminish or eliminate intrabrand competition. Where a specific restraint or attribute of a restraint tends to ameliorate these anticompetitive intrabrand effects, it will be noted.

4.2   Fungible and Highly Differentiated Products

The competitive effects of a particular restraint will be influenced by whether the product involved is fungible or highly differentiated.

High product differentiation produces less elastic demand for the product in the near term, that is the demand is less sensitive to price changes in the short run. The dealers of such a product may be able to raise prices significantly without customer defection to other brands. In essence, high product differentiation produces greater market power.

It has also been demonstrated that the additional services, advertising or product differentiation which may result from restraints such as territorial restrictions may only be valued by the marginal consumers of established, highly differentiated products. If some consumers of the product do not want the additional service or place little value on it, the loss of consumer welfare to such consumers may well exceed any welfare gains to marginal consumers.[36]

In contrast, a fungible product, or one for which there is easy and suitable substitution, will produce a market with highly elastic demand and vigorous interbrand price competition. However, fungible products are subject to less product enhancement by dealers. The prevention of "free-riding" is generally inapposite. Furthermore, a restraint which truly induces additional dealer services may cause interbrand free-riding effects, an inefficient result. Collusion is also more likely to be successful in the markets for fungible products, but this effect will depend upon market concentration and coverage factors discussed in Section 4.8.

4.3   Multiple Exclusive Distributorships

If a dealer is granted the exclusive right to distribute two or more competing products in the same geographical territory, interbrand competition is substantially eliminated for those brands. The greater the number and market share of brands exclusively distributed by a single dealer with a territorial monopoly the greater will

---

36.   Comanor, *Vertical Price-Fixing, Vertical Market Restrictions, and the New Antitrust Policy*, 98 HARVARD L. REV. 983 (1985). *See also* Spence, *Monopoly, Quality and Regulation*, 6 BELL J. ECON. 417 (1975).

be the anticompetitive effect in the interbrand market. Collusion will also be greatly facilitated.

4.4   Dealer Involvement in the Imposition of a Restraint

The unilateral imposition of a vertical restraint by a supplier may be motivated by the desire to enhance the competitiveness of a product in the interbrand market.

An intrabrand agreement among dealers which is imposed upon or adopted and policed by a supplier is per se unlawful, as discussed in Section 2.2.

However, between unilateral imposition of a vertical restraint and horizontal conspiracy, there are varying levels of dealer participation or coercion which may cause a supplier to impose a restraint. This participation is a relevant factor in assessing whether a particular restraint is likely to serve any procompetitive purpose in the interbrand market.

At one extreme, a supplier may have received sporadic, uncoordinated requests by individual dealers that a restraint be imposed. At the other end of the spectrum, a group of dealers may have actually engaged in an intrabrand conspiracy by jointly petitioning a manufacturer to impose a restraint.

The Attorneys General will consider the role that dealer pressure played in the institution of a vertical restraint. It will be considered in terms of its magnitude, frequency and the level of its coordination. The more frequent and more forceful the pressure, the less likely that the supplier imposed the restraint for pro-competitive reasons and the more likely that the supplier merely bowed to dealer pressure, motivated by the dealers' shortsighted desire to reap monopoly profits.[37]

The phenomenon of dealer pressure that has, arguably, not reached the point of conspiracy, also occurs among multibrand dealers.[38] When such pressure leads to the adoption of vertical restraints by many suppliers, not only is the pro-competitive interbrand rationale absent, but results similar to interbrand collusion are achieved.[39]

---

37.   In *Monsanto*, the Court recognized the prevalence and legitimacy of communications between dealers and suppliers which inform a supplier whether or not there is compliance with a vertical restraint which the supplier had independently imposed. 465 U.S. at 762. This practice, where dealers monitor compliance with a restraint unilaterally imposed by the supplier, contrasts sharply with dealer pressure aimed at persuading or coercing a supplier to impose a restraint which will enhance the dealers' power, arguably at the expense of both the supplier and consumer. Restraints imposed because of such pressure may also have consequences similar to an interbrand agreement. For example, dealer pressure may cause a supplier of Product A to grant territorial exclusivity, thereby eliminating competing dealers who discount. Using this as a model, the dealers of Product B exert pressure for the imposition of similar exclusive distributorships. B is less likely to resist once its competitor has adopted the restraint. This process can continue until a significant portion of the market is covered by the restraint. Discounts are eliminated over a broad range of the market. The outcome is similar to an interbrand agreement. This "leadership" pattern, observed recently by the Attorneys General in several industries is not evidence of free markets functioning, but rather the political economy of groups or institutional behavior. The interbrand effect is especially likely if the dealer pressure emanates from trade associations whose members are interbrand competitors.

38.   For example, a group of large multibrand retail or wholesale chains meet and announce *individually* that they will only deal with suppliers who employ certain restraints. The restraints are thereafter imposed *unilaterally* by several suppliers.

39.   This discussion is distinct from the evidentiary standards utilized in proving actual intrabrand or interbrand agreements. *See* [Section 2.1], *supra* and *Monsanto*, 465 U.S. at 762-768.

4.5 The Requirement and Performance of Additional Services under Vertical Restraints

One rationale for the imposition of vertical restraints is that they are necessary to induce and assure the advertising, services and product enhancement which will allow a product to compete effectively in the interbrand market.

The Attorneys General will consider whether a supplier imposing a vertical restraint requires dealers to perform additional advertising, pre-sale demonstration, post-sale servicing and other forms of product enhancement and monitors compliance with those requirements. The nature of the additional services will also be considered.[40]

In the case of a restraint which has already been in effect, the Attorneys General will also assess to what extent these additional services were actually provided after the restraint was imposed.

4.6 Natural Longevity v. Contractual Longevity of Restraints

Natural market forces tend to expunge anticompetitive restraints. Therefore, in certain circumstances, the fact that a particular type of restraint has existed for a long time may prove that the restraint is not anticompetitive. On the other hand contractual provisions can keep anticompetitive restraints in force for a longer period than natural market forces would normally permit. Thus the fact that a particular type of restraint has existed for a long time can lead to two inferences:

1) that the restraint has existed a long time because it is generally procompetitive.

2) that the restraint is anticompetitive but successful and has been kept in place by long contractual periods and its exclusionary effect.

The Attorneys General will look carefully at market structure, the length of contract terms containing restraints and the ease of entry and exit from the market to determine which of the above inferences is appropriate.

4.7 Concentration and Coverage of the Markets

The tendency of vertical restraints to facilitate collusion among suppliers or dealers and exclusion of rivals increases with the concentration of the markets and coverage[41] of a particular restraint or different restraints having the same effect.[42] The Attorneys General will attempt to ascertain the concentration levels in the

---

40. For example, if a supplier requires its dealers to buy shirts for local sports teams or to display its product in a certain showcase, the requirement may have little procompetitive benefit, such as, providing consumers better quality, a greater selection, or lower prices. However, the anticompetitive consequences of such a restraint, if any, may also be insignificant.
41. "Coverage" of a restraint refers generally to the percentage of sales in a market sold subject to the restraint in question.
42. For example, one firm may adopt exclusive distributorships. A competing firm adopts coterminous areas of primary responsibility and simultaneously adopts a profit or warranty pass-over arrangement which penalizes extraterritorial sales so harshly that the restraints have the same effect as exclusive distributorships.

supplier and dealer markets and the market shares of firms employing the vertical restraint under scrutiny.

A determination of the extent to which a vertical restraint may facilitate collusion or exclusion will be made in accordance with the following precepts:

(a)   If the supplier and dealer markets are not concentrated or the restraint is not utilized by firms with a large market share, collusion or exclusion is not significantly facilitated by the restraint.

(b)   If either the dealer or supplier market is concentrated and highly covered by a restraint, collusion in the concentrated market will be facilitated. The absence of exclusion will not be considered an ameliorating factor, since the threat of a new entrant into a concentrated market does not prevent collusion.

(c)   If one market is both highly concentrated and highly covered by a restraint and the other market is highly covered, collusion and exclusion will be facilitated in the first market.

(d)   If both supplier and dealer markets are concentrated and covered by a restraint, collusion and exclusion will be facilitated in both markets.

The higher the actual concentration and coverage figures, the more pronounced will be the tendency to facilitate collusion and/or exclusion. There are various ways of measuring concentration and coverage which can be utilized when accurate market share data is available.[43]

Certain specific values have become associated with the concept of a "concentrated industry."[44] While these are useful guideposts, no hard and fast cut-off point will be applied in these *Guidelines*. Nevertheless, the Attorneys General will be unlikely to challenge a non-price vertical restraint when the markets involved, in all of the relevant levels of distribution, have HHI's less than 1000, or when all of the relevant parties to a non-price vertical agreement have less than 10 percent of their respective markets.

4.8   *Indicia of Tacit Collusion or Conscious Parallelism*

Related to the tendency of widely adopted vertical restraints to facilitate collusion and exclusion in concentrated markets is their tendency to reinforce patterns of consciously parallel or tacitly collusive behavior in oligopolistic markets.

When a restraint covers a high percentage of an oligopolistic market, it will tend to reinforce anticompetitive oligopolistic behavior. In turn a market will be considered oligopolistic if it is highly concentrated and some or all of the following practices are common to the industry:

---

43.   For these purposes, the market share of a supplier will be its share of all sales to firms in the dealer market under scrutiny. Furthermore, vertically integrated firms will be included in the market share calculations and deemed to be employing the restraint. Partially integrated firms will be included and deemed to be employing the restraint for that percentage of products transferred internally to the dealer market rather than purchased in the market. Coverage may be computed by summing the market shares of all firms employing the restraint in the suppliers' market ("SM") and dealers' market ("DM"). Concentration can be measured by use of the Herfindahl-Hirschman Index ("HHI") which is the sum of the squares of the market shares of all of the firms in the industry.

44.   For example, a four firm concentration ratio of 60% or an HHI in the range of 1000-1800 for a concentrated market and above 1800 for a highly concentrated market. *See* NAAG HORIZONTAL MERGER GUIDELINES at §§ 4.2, 4.3.

1)   Price leadership
2)   Pre-announced price changes
3)   Price rigidity in response to excess capacity or diminished demand
4)   Public pronouncements and discussions of the "right price" for the industry[45]
5)   Systematic price discrimination
6)   Past collusion regarding prices or marketing practices.

4.9   Entry Barriers

Barriers to enter the industry where the restraint is imposed will be evaluated.

A vertical restraint may be utilized by an entrant to encourage dealers to distribute a new product and elicit the level of advertising and service essential to assure the product's acceptance with consumers. These are procompetitive goals.

As discussed in Section 4.9, widely adopted vertical restraints in concentrated industries may, however, facilitate exclusion by tying up available dealers or monopolizing a component necessary to manufacture or market a product.

The Attorneys General will also assess entry barriers in an industry which are unrelated to the restraint itself, because the length of time necessary for market forces to purge an anticompetitive restraint will be determined by such conditions.

The Attorneys General will be less likely to challenge a restraint deemed anticompetitive after full analysis, if entry barriers are low. Artificial barriers, such as government regulation and licensing, will also be considered because they may erect obstacles to entry which market forces are powerless to correct.

4.10   Effect on Consumer Choice

There is virtual consensus among economists that a competitive market will produce a wide range of price/quality options. Vertical restraints can increase or decrease the number of price/quality options. The Attorneys General will consider the actual or likely effect that a restraint has on such consumer choice in assessing a restraint.

4.11   Miscellaneous Factors

In the assessment of particular restraints, additional miscellaneous factors may become relevant to the inquiry. Among these factors would be the regulatory climate in an industry, a history of collusion in the industry or evidence disclosing the actual competitive intent of the responsible officials of a firm imposing a vertical restraint.

5.   Tying Arrangements

Tying arrangements condition the sale of one distinct product or service ("the tying product") on the buyer's agreement to purchase a second distinct product or

---

45.   Posner, *Oligopoly and The Antitrust Laws: A Suggested Approach*, 21 STANFORD LAW REV. 1579 (1969).

service ("the tied product") or agreement not to purchase the tied product or service from any other supplier.[46]

Some tying arrangements are explicit, but others must be inferred from inducements short of a formal requirement. For example, when a firm sells two products separately but offers a steep discount when both products are purchased, a tying arrangement may be inferred. Similarly, when a firm significantly curtails service of one product unless another product is purchased, fails to cooperate with the purchaser in other respects, or fails to offer the buyer new products unless it also buys the product in question, an effective tie may be inferred.

Tying arrangements can unreasonably restrain trade and lead to anti-competitive effects by permitting a firm to exploit a dominant position in the market for the tying product by diminishing competition on the merits in the market for the tied product.[47] Inferior tied products may be insulated from competition and entry of new competitors is made more difficult. In other cases, tying arrangements may represent an efficient means of packaging products or services which attract, rather than force consumers to purchase the tied products.

The Supreme Court has ruled on the characteristics which make a tying arrangement per se unlawful.[48] In cases where the tying arrangements are not deemed per se unlawful, an abbreviated form of the rule of reason analysis specified in Section 4 will be utilized to determine whether a particular arrangement will be challenged.

5.1   Tying Arrangements Which Are Per Se Unlawful

The Supreme Court held, and the Attorneys General will deem, a tying arrangement per se unlawful if it has the following characteristics:

1)   The tying and tied products (services) are distinct;

2)   The arrangement forecloses a "substantial volume of commerce" or there is a "substantial potential" of such impact on competition.[49]

3)   The firm tying the products has sufficient "market power" in the tying product to make anticompetitive "forcing . . . probable."[50]

---

46.   Eastman Kodak Co. v. Image Technical Services, Inc., 112 S. Ct. 2072, 2079 (1992).
47.   Tying also can enable a firm to engage in price discrimination. This has the effect of making certain customers (and consumers as a whole) pay more for their products. IBM Corp. v. United States, 298 U.S. 131 (1936). This transfer of wealth from consumers to a firm with market power is an undesirable outcome that the antitrust laws were designed to prevent.
48.   Jefferson Parish Hospital District No. 2 v. Hyde, 466 U.S. 2 (1984). The above discussion and *Jefferson Parish* concern tying arrangements challenged under Section 1 of the Sherman Act. The standards applicable to tying arrangements challenged under Section 3 of the Clayton Act were discussed by the Supreme Court in *Times-Picayune Publishing Co. v. United States*, 345 U.S. 594 (1953).
49.   *Jefferson Parish*, 466 U.S. at 16.
50.   The Court has described this requirement as follows:
      "Per se condemnation—condemnation without inquiry into actual market conditions—is only appropriate if the existence of forcing is probable. Thus application of the per se rule focuses on the probability of anticompetitive consequences. Of course, as a threshold matter there must be a substantial potential for impact on competition in order to justify per se condemnation."
      Jefferson Parish, at 15-16.

5.1A DISTINCT PRODUCTS

The requirement that the tying and tied products be distinct is satisfied if the two products can be provided separately and there is a distinct demand for each of the products.[51] Distinct demand can be shown from actual separate sales or requests for such separate sales.[52]

5.1B IMPACT ON COMMERCE

The requirement that the arrangements have the potential for affecting a substantial amount of commerce or have actually foreclosed a substantial amount of commerce, is satisfied when it can be shown that substantial separate sales would occur absent the tying arrangement.[53]

5.1C MARKET POWER SUFFICIENT TO MAKE "FORCING" A PROBABLE OUTCOME

The final requirement for per se treatment of a tying arrangement is that the firm possess sufficient "market power" in the tying product to create the probability that consumers will be forced to buy the tied product, thereby diminishing "merit" competition for sales of the tied product.[54]

Market power is sufficient to make forcing a probable outcome if the firm employing the arrangement has a monopoly over the tying product (including a patent), a dominant position in the market for the tying product or offers a "unique product that competitors are not able to offer."[55] Such market power can be present in aftermarkets where the seller has a relatively small share of the original equipment market, but substantial leverage in aftermarkets as the result of information problems.[56] Market power can additionally be inferred in part from a large defendant market share, or it can be present even if the defendant's market share is smaller due to the existence of significant market imperfections.[57]

---

51. Evidence of two separate products with separate demands exists when two products are used in variable proportions. Goods used in variable proportions also can sometimes be the subject of a tie whose purpose is price discrimination. *See Jefferson Parish*, 466 U.S. at 13-15.
52. The Court stated that ". . . the question whether one or two products are involved turns *not on the functional relation between them*, but rather on the character of the *demand* for the two items." *Jefferson Parish*, 466 U.S. at 19 (emphasis supplied).
53. This threshold requirement is distinct from the issue of "forcing." If the amount of commerce affected or likely to be affected is de minimis, a restraint will not be unlawful under a per se test, even if there is "forcing." Nor can it be held unreasonable under a rule of reason test. This requirement is analogous to the predicate in all Sherman Act cases that a "not insubstantial amount" of interstate commerce be affected.
54. Forcing is not demonstrated merely by showing that a buyer formerly purchased the products separately or would do so if the products were not tied. Such purchases may be the result of the attractiveness of the items as packaged. Such proof is relevant to the issue of the probability of a substantial effect on commerce discussed in Section 5.1B. Forcing requires more, i.e., the diminution or elimination of "merit" competition for sale of the tied product.
55. 466 U.S. at 17, e.g., unique real property.
56. Eastman Kodak Co. v. Image Technical Services, Inc., 112 S. Ct. 2072 (1992).
57. *Eastman Kodak Co. v. Image Technical Services, Inc.*, 112 S. Ct. 2072 (1992), shows how imperfect information can enable a firm without a conventionally defined monopoly share to use a tying arrangement that prevents consumers from making optimal purchasing decisions. Market imperfections can substitute for traditional market share based market power and enable a firm in a market that otherwise appears competitive to harm consumers.

In any event, actual proof of substantial anticompetitive forcing will satisfy the test of market power.

5.2   Analysis of Tying Arrangements under the Rule of Reason

When a seller employing tie-in sales has insufficient market power to "force" the purchase of the tied product, analysis under the rule of reason is required to determine whether the arrangement unreasonably restrains trade.[58]   The analysis requires an inquiry into the effect of the arrangement on the quality, supply and demand for both the tying and tied products, but focuses primarily on the market for the tied product.[59]   Efficiencies, business justifications,[60] and actual competitive intent, when ascertainable, will also be evaluated.   Because many of the factors utilized in the analysis of other non-price vertical restraints have little relevance in analyzing the competitive consequences of tying, an abbreviated form of the analysis discussed in Section 4 will be applied.

5.2A   DEGREE OF PRODUCT DIFFERENTIATION OF THE TYING PRODUCT

A product may not be so highly differentiated as to be "unique," (thereby not satisfying the market power test for per se treatment) yet be sufficiently differentiated so as to approach, but not reach, a position of "market power."   The more highly differentiated a tying product, the more likely a tying arrangement will tend to diminish merit competition for sales of the tied product.

5.2B   COVERAGE AND ENTRY BARRIERS

If all or most of the firms in the market for the tying product adopt similar tying arrangements and the barriers for entry into that market are high, the arrangements will have a greater adverse impact on merit competition in the market for the tied product.   This would also substantially limit buyer choice in terms of the number of packaging options.   However, if as a result of the tying arrangement, the tying and tied products are now available in a greater variety of packages, separate or tied, buyer choice is increased and the tying arrangement may enhance consumer welfare.

6.   Market Definition

In analyzing purely non-price vertical restraints of trade in accordance with the factors discussed in Sections 4 and 5, the Attorneys General will utilize the market

---

58.   As in per se cases, threshold findings of distinct products and probable or actual effect on a substantial amount of commerce must be made.   *See* discussion in Sections 5.1A and 5.1B.

59.   For example, the Supreme Court indicated in *Kodak* that ties have the ability to obscure and complicate the buyer's transaction thereby undercutting the welfare and efficiency benefits of competition.   *See generally* Grimes, *Antitrust Tie-In Analysis After Kodak: Understanding the Role of Market Imperfections*, 62 ANTITRUST L.J. 263, 273-79 (1994); Lande, *supra* note 25.

60.   Efficiencies or business justifications, although easy to allege and difficult to prove convincingly, may be considered as a defense to a tying arrangement.   United States v. Jerrold Electronic Corp., 365 U.S. 567 (1961).

definition principles set forth in the 1993 *Horizontal Merger Guidelines of the National Association of Attorneys General*. (*See* Sections 3.1, 3.11, 3.2 and 3.21 of the *Guidelines*.) The product and geographic market should be analyzed separately for each product subject to the restraint.

TABLE OF CASES

A

Aztec Steel Co. v. Florida Steel Corp., 691 F.2d 480 (11th Cir. 1982), *cert. denied*, 460 U.S. 1040 (1983), 989

B

Babbit v. United Farm Workers Nat'l Union, 442 U.S. 289 (1978), 1011
Babcock & Wilcox Co. v. United Techs. Corp., 435 F. Supp. 1249 (N.D. Ohio 1977), 369, 398, 399, 869
Baby Food Antitrust Litig., *In re*, 166 F.3d 112 (3d Cir. 1999), 6, 10, 11, 14, 95, 919, 920
Bacchus Indus., Inc. v. Arvin Indus., Inc., 939 F.2d 887 (10th Cir. 1991), 584
Bacon v. Texaco, Inc., 503 F.2d 946 (5th Cir. 1974), *cert. denied*, 420 U.S. 1005 (1975), 457, 458, 459
Baglio v. Baska, 940 F. Supp. 819 (W.D. Pa. 1996), *aff'd*, 116 F.3d 467 (3d Cir. 1997), 848
Baglio v. Baska, 116 F.3d 467 (3d Cir. 1997), 1338
Bailey's Bakery, Ltd. v. Continental Baking Co., 235 F. Supp. 705 (D. Haw. 1964), *aff'd*, 401 F.2d 182 (9th Cir. 1968), *cert. denied*, 393 U.S. 1086 (1969), 138, 876
Bailey's, Inc. v. Windsor Am., Inc., 948 F.2d 1018 (6th Cir. 1991), 162, 311
Baim & Blank, Inc. v. Philco Corp., 148 F. Supp. 541 (E.D.N.Y. 1957), 467, 468
Bain v. Henderson, 621 F.2d 959 (9th Cir. 1980), 45
Baker v. Chagrin Valley Med. Corp., 1985-1 Trade Cas. (CCH) ¶ 66,622 (N.D. Ohio 1985), 893, 1330
Baker v. F & F Inv., 420 F.2d 1191 (7th Cir.), *cert. denied*, 400 U.S. 821 (1970), 902, 903, 904
Baker v. Simmons Co., 307 F.2d 458 (1st Cir. 1962), *cert. denied*, 382 U.S. 820 (1965), 207
Baker-Cammack Hosiery Mills, Inc. v. Davis Co., 181 F.2d 550 (4th Cir.), *cert. denied*, 340 U.S. 824 (1950), 1080
Baker's Aid v. Hussmann Foodservice Co., No. CV 87-0937, 1988 WL 138254 (E.D.N.Y. Dec. 19, 1988), 983
Baker's Aid v. Hussmann Foodservice Co., 730 F. Supp. 1209 (E.D.N.Y. 1990), 305
Baker's Carpet Gallery, Inc. v. Mohawk Indus., Inc., 942 F. Supp. 1464 (N.D. Ga. 1996), 139
Bakers Franchise Corp. v. FTC, 302 F.2d 258 (3d Cir. 1962), 626, 656
Balaklaw v. Lovell, 14 F.3d 793 (2d Cir. 1994), 66, 70, 225, 847, 850, 1337, 1338
Baldree v. Cargill, Inc., 758 F. Supp. 704 (M.D. Fla. 1990), *aff'd without op.*, 925 F.2d 1474 (11th Cir. 1991), 1253
Baldwin v. Loew's, Inc., 312 F.2d 387 (7th Cir. 1963), 899
Baldwin-Lima-Hamilton Corp. v. Tatnall Measuring Sys., 169 F. Supp. 1 (E.D. Pa. 1958), *aff'd per curiam*, 268 F.2d 395 (3d Cir.), *cert. denied*, 361 U.S. 894 (1959), 1071
Balian Ice Cream Co. v. Arden Farms Co., 231 F.2d 356 (9th Cir. 1955), *cert. denied*, 350 U.S. 991 (1956), 483, 493
Ballard v. Blue Shield, 543 F.2d 1075 (4th Cir. 1976), *cert. denied*, 430 U.S. 922 (1977), 44
Ball Mem'l Hosp., Inc. v. Mutual Hosp. Ins., Inc., 603 F. Supp. 1077 (S.D. Ind. 1985), *aff'd*, 784 F.2d 1325 (7th Cir. 1986), 131
Ball Mem'l Hosp., Inc. v. Mutual Hosp. Ins., Inc., 784 F.2d 1325 (7th Cir. 1986), 65, 68, 69, 237, 239, 251, 252, 469
Balmoral Cinema, Inc. v. Allied Artists Pictures Corp., 885 F.2d 313 (6th Cir. 1989), 52, 54, 55, 112
Baltimore & O.R.R. v. ICC, 826 F.2d 1125 (D.C. Cir. 1987), 1397
Baltimore Luggage Co. v. Samsonite Corp., 1992-2 Trade Cas. (CCH) ¶ 69,998 (4th Cir. 1992), 1007
Baltimore Metro. Pharm. Ass'n, 117 F.T.C. 95 (1994), 1360
Baltimore Scrap Corp. v. David J. Joseph Co., 81 F. Supp. 2d 602 (D. Md. 2000), *aff'd*, 237 F.3d 394 (4th Cir.), *cert. denied*, 121 S. Ct. 2521 (2001), 1233

C

D

D & N Auto Parts Co., 55 F.T.C. 1279 (1959), *aff'd sub nom.* Mid-South Distribs. v. FTC, 287 F.2d 512 (5th Cir.), *cert. denied*, 368 U.S. 838 (1961), 492, 516, 517

D & R Distrib. Co. v. Chambers Corp., 608 F. Supp. 1290 (E.D. Cal. 1984), 172

D & S Redi-Mix v. Sierra Redi-Mix & Contracting Co., 692 F.2d 1245 (9th Cir. 1982), 872, 873

Daniel v. American Bd. of Emergency Med., 988 F. Supp. 112 (W.D.N.Y. 1997), 893

Daniels v. Amerco, 1982-2 Trade Cas. (CCH) ¶ 64,794 (S.D.N.Y 1982), 952, 953

Daniels v. Amerco, 1983-1 Trade Cas. (CCH) ¶ 65,274 (S.D.N.Y. 1983), 902, 929, 931, 933, 944, 946, 950

Daniels v. Pipefitters' Ass'n Local Union No. 597, 983 F.2d 800 (7th Cir. 1993), 992

Danielson Food Prods., Inc. v. Poly-Clip Sys., 120 F. Supp. 2d 1142 (N.D. Ill. 2000), 166

Danik, Inc. v. Hartmarx Corp., 875 F.2d 890 (D.C. Cir. 1989), *aff'd sub nom.* Cooter & Gell v. Hartmarx Corp., 496 U.S. 384 (1990), 1023

Danko v. Shell Oil Co., 115 F. Supp. 886 (E.D.N.Y. 1953), 466

Dannon Co., 121 F.T.C. 136 (1996), 627

Danny Kresky Enters. Corp. v. Magid, 716 F.2d 206 (3d Cir. 1983), 876

Darda, Inc. USA v. Majorette Toys (U.S.) Inc., 627 F. Supp. 1121 (S.D. Fla. 1986),*aff'd in part and rev'd in part*, 824 F.2d 976 (Fed. Cir. 1987), 1050

Dart Drug Corp. v. Corning Glass Works, 480 F. Supp. 1091 (D. Md. 1979), 855, 868, 965

Dart Drug Corp. v. Parke, Davis & Co., 344 F.2d 173 (D.C. Cir. 1965), 1006

Dart Indus. v. Banner, 200 U.S.P.Q. (BNA) 656 (D.D.C. 1978), *rev'd*, 636 F.2d 684 (D.C. Cir. 1980), 1031

Dart Indus. v. Plunkett Co., 704 F.2d 496 (10th Cir. 1983), 157, 498

DataGate, Inc. v. Hewlett-Packard Co., 60 F.3d 1421 (9th Cir. 1995), *cert. denied*, 517 U.S. 1115 (1996), 190, 204

Data Gen. Corp. Antitrust Litig., *In re*, 490 F. Supp. 1089 (N.D. Cal. 1980), 181, 193, 195

Data Gen. Corp. Antitrust Litig., *In re*, 529 F. Supp. 801 (N.D. Cal. 1981), *aff'd in part and rev'd in part sub nom.* Digidyne Corp. v. Data Gen. Corp., 734 F.2d 1336 (9th Cir. 1984), *cert. denied*, 473 U.S. 908 (1985), 193

Data Gen. Corp. v. Digidyne Corp., 473 U.S. 908 (1985), 198, 1068

Data Gen. Corp. v. Grumman Sys. Support Corp., 761 F. Supp. 185 (D. Mass. 1991), *aff'd*, 36 F.3d 1147 (1st Cir. 1994), 208, 1113

Data Gen. Corp. v. Grumman Sys. Support Corp., 36 F.3d 1147 (1st Cir. 1994), 182, 192, 243, 248, 249, 277, 286, 1069, 1070, 1077, 1099, 1100, 1101

Dataphase Sys. v. CL Sys., 640 F.2d 109 (8th Cir. 1981), 886

Data Processing Fin. & Gen. Corp. v. IBM, 430 F.2d 1277 (8th Cir. 1970), *aff'g* Control Data Corp. v. IBM, 306 F. Supp. 839 (D. Minn. 1969), 761

Daubert v. Merrell Dow Pharmaceuticals, Inc., 509 U.S. 579 (1993), 598, 600, 1008, 1009

Daugherty v. Pall, 43 F.R.D. 329 (C.D. Cal. 1967), 961

Dauro Advert. Inc. v. General Motors Corp., 75 F. Supp. 2d 1165 (D. Colo. 1999), 181, 188, 540

Davenport Grain Co. v. J. Lynch & Co., 109 F.R.D. 256 (D. Neb. 1985), 987, 990

David L. Aldridge Co. v. Microsoft Corp., 995 F. Supp. 728 (S.D. Tex. 1998), 295, 850, 852

David R. McGeorge Car Co. v. Leyland Motor Sales, Inc., 504 F.2d 52 (4th Cir. 1974), *cert. denied*, 420 U.S. 992 (1975), 507

Davies v. Genesis Med. Ctr., 994 F. Supp. 1078 (S.D. Iowa 1998), 535, 560, 850

Davis v. FTC, 1997-1 Trade Cas. (CCH) ¶ 71,790 (S.D.N.Y. 1997), 689, 690

Davis v. Marathon Oil Co., 528 F.2d 395 (6th Cir. 1975), *cert. denied*, 429 U.S. 823 (1976), 168, 191, 205

Davis v. Northside Realty Assoc., Inc., 95 F.R.D. 39 (N.D. Ga. 1982), 931, 932, 934, 948, 952

Davis v. Southern Bell Tel. & Tel. Co., 755 F. Supp. 1532 (S.D. Fla. 1991), 1215

Davis v. Southern Bell Tel. & Tel. Co., 149 F.R.D. 666 (S.D. Fla. 1993), 804, 809

Davis v. Southern Bell Tel. & Tel. Co., 1994-1 Trade Cas. (CCH) ¶ 70,510 (S.D. Fla. 1994), 239, 240, 288, 294

E

Essential Communs. Sys. v. AT&T, 610 F.2d 1114 (3d Cir. 1979), 1242
Estate Constr. Co. v. Miller & Smith Holding Co., 14 F.3d 213 (4th Cir. 1994), 3
Estee Lauder, Inc. v. Fragrance Counter, Inc., 189 F.R.D. 269 (S.D.N.Y. 1999), 1104
E.T. Barwick Indus. v. Walter E. Heller & Co., 692 F. Supp. 1331 (N.D. Ga. 1987), *aff'd without op.*, 891 F.2d 906 (11th Cir. 1989), 226, 566
Ethicon, Inc. v. Aetna Cas. & Sur. Co., 737 F. Supp. 1320 (S.D.N.Y. 1990), 1025
Ethyl Corp., 101 F.T.C. 425 (1983), *vacated sub nom.* E.I. duPont de Nemours & Co. v. FTC, 729 F.2d 128 (2d Cir. 1984), 614, 615
Ethyl Corp. v. Hercules Powder Co., 232 F. Supp. 453 (D. Del. 1963), 1058
Eubanks v. Getty Oil Co., 896 F.2d 960 (5th Cir. 1990), 1007
Euramca Ecosystems, Inc. v. Roediger Pittsburgh, Inc., 581 F. Supp. 415 (N.D. Ill. 1984), 498
Eureka Urethane, Inc. v. PBA, Inc., 746 F. Supp. 915 (E.D. Mo. 1990), *aff'd*, 935 F.2d 990 (8th Cir. 1991), 247, 248, 279
Eurim-Pharm GmbH v. Pfizer, Inc., 593 F. Supp. 1102 (S.D.N.Y. 1984), 1087, 1119, 1120
Euromepa v. R. Esmerian, Inc., 154 F.3d 24 (2d Cir. 1998), 1191
European Body Concepts, Inc., 119 F.T.C. 947 (1995), 628
European Rail Pass Antitrust Litig., *In re*, 166 F. Supp. 2d 836 (S.D.N.Y. 2001), 527
Evac, LLC v. Pataki, 89 F. Supp. 2d 250 (N.D.N.Y. 2000), 591, 593, 1329
Evanns v. AT&T Corp., 229 F.3d 837 (9th Cir. 2000), 1241
Evans v. S.S. Kresge Co., 544 F.2d 1184 (3d Cir. 1976), *cert. denied*, 433 U.S. 908 (1977), 42, 44
Evans Prods. Co., [F.T.C. Complaints & Orders 1983-1987 Transfer Binder] Trade Reg. Rep. (CCH) ¶ 22,372 (W.D. Wash. June 17, 1986), 669
Evans Prods. Co., 1986-1 Trade Cas. (CCH) ¶ 67,113 (S.D. Fla. 1986), 639
Everhart v. United Ref. Co., 1980-81 Trade Cas. (CCH) ¶ 63,788 (N.D. Ohio 1981), 136
Everseal Waterproofing Corp., 89 F.T.C. 110 (1977), 657
Eversharp, Inc., 77 F.T.C. 686 (1970), 641
Eversharp, Inc. v. Fisher Pen Co., 204 F. Supp. 649 (N.D. Ill. 1961), 1074
Ewald Bros v. Mid-America Dairymen, Inc., 877 F.2d 1384 (8th Cir. 1989), 1250
E.W. French & Sons v. General Portland, Inc., 885 F.2d 1392 (9th Cir. 1989), 899, 900
Excel Handbag Co. v. Edison Bros. Stores, 630 F.2d 379 (5th Cir. 1980), 503
Excell Mortgage Corp., 115 F.T.C. 171 (1992), 709
Ex-Cell-O Corp., 82 F.T.C. 38 (1973), 627
Execu-Tech Bus. Sys. v. Appleton Papers, Inc., 743 So. 2d 19 (Fla. Dist. Ct. App. 1999), 855
Exemption from 49 U.S.C. § 11322(a) for Certain Interlocking Directorates, 5 I.C.C.2d 7 (1988), *petition for review dismissed sub nom.* United Transp. Union v. ICC, 891 F.2d 908 (D.C. Cir. 1989), *cert. denied*, 497 U.S. 1024 (1990), 1394
Exemption From Regulation—Boxcar Traffic, 367 I.C.C. 425 (1983), *aff'd in pertinent part sub nom.* United States v. Brae Corp., 740 F.2d 1023 (D.C. Cir. 1984) (per curiam), *cert. denied*, 471 U.S. 1069 (1985), 1395
Exemption of Certain Designated Operators From Section 11343, 361 I.C.C. 379 (1979), *rev'd sub nom.* McGinness v. ICC, 662 F.2d 853 (D.C. Cir. 1981), 1394
Exemption of Out of Service Rail Lines, 2 I.C.C.2d 146 (1986), *aff'd sub nom.* Illinois Commerce Comm'n v. ICC, 848 F.2d 1246 (D.C. Cir. 1988), *cert. denied*, 488 U.S. 1004 (1989), 1394
Exhibitors Poster Exch. v. National Screen Serv. Corp., 441 F.2d 560 (5th Cir. 1971), 887
Exhibitors' Serv. v. American Multi-Cinema, Inc., 583 F. Supp. 1186 (C.D. Cal. 1984), *rev'd*, 788 F.2d 574 (9th Cir. 1986), 1015, 1018
Exhibitors' Serv. v. American Multi-Cinema, Inc., 788 F.2d 574 (9th Cir. 1986), 866
Eximco v. Trane Co., 737 F.2d 505 (5th Cir. 1984), 467
Ex parte Republic of Peru, 318 U.S. 578 (1943), 1136
Ex parte Rice, 67 So. 2d 825 (Ala. 1953), 811
Export Liquor Sales, Inc. v. Ammex Warehouse Co., 426 F.2d 251 (6th Cir. 1970), *cert. denied*, 400 U.S. 1000 (1971), 466

F

Fulton v. Hecht, 580 F.2d 1243 (5th Cir. 1978), *cert. denied*, 440 U.S. 981 (1979), 722
Fund for Constitutional Gov't v. National Archives, 656 F.2d 856 (D.C. Cir. 1981), 971
Funtes v. South Hills Cardiology, 946 F.2d 196 (3d Cir. 1991), 1328
Furlong v. Long Island Coll. Hosp., 710 F.2d 922 (2d Cir. 1983), 40, 45
Fusco v. Xerox Corp., 676 F.2d 332 (8th Cir. 1982), 465, 467
Futurevision Cable Sys. v. Multivision Cable TV Corp., 789 F. Supp. 760 (S.D. Miss. 1992),
    aff'd without op., 986 F.2d 1418 (5th Cir. 1993), 4, 78, 171, 452, 567, 1278

G

Gabriel & Assocs. v. Invisible Fence Co., 1993-2 Trade Cas. (CCH) ¶ 70,440 (D. Md. 1993),
    465
Gaetzi v. Carling Brewing Co., 205 F. Supp. 615 (E.D. Mich. 1962), 902, 904
GAF Corp. v. Circle Floor Co., 329 F. Supp. 823 (S.D.N.Y. 1971), *aff'd*, 463 F.2d 752 (2d
    Cir. 1972), *cert. dismissed*, 413 U.S. 901 (1973), 170
GAF Corp. v. Eastman Kodak Co., 519 F. Supp. 1203 (S.D.N.Y. 1981), 293, 1003, 1077
Gaines v. Budget Rent-A-Car Corp., 1972 Trade Cas. (CCH) ¶ 73,860 (N.D. Ill. 1972), 934
Gaines v. NCAA, 746 F. Supp. 738 (M.D. Tenn. 1990), 248
Gainesville Utils. Dep't v. Florida Power & Light Co., 573 F.2d 292 (5th Cir.), *cert. denied*,
    439 U.S. 966 (1978), 5, 104, 1296
Galavan Supplements, Ltd. v. Archer Daniels Midland Co., No. C97-3259 FMS, 1997 U.S.
    Dist. LEXIS 18585 (N.D. Cal. Nov. 18, 1997), 1124
Gall v. Home Box Office, Inc., 1992-2 Trade Cas. (CCH) ¶ 69,949 (S.D.N.Y. 1992), *aff'd*
    without op., 9 F.3d 1538 (2d Cir. 1993), 469, 567, 592, 1282
Gallagher v. Mazda Motor of Am., Inc., 781 F. Supp. 1079 (E.D. Pa. 1992), 1166
Gallant v. BOC Group, Inc., 886 F. Supp. 202 (D. Mass. 1995), 521, 866
Galloway v. American Brands, Inc., 81 F.R.D. 580 (E.D.N.C. 1978), 909
G. & T. Terminal Packaging Co. v. Consolidated Rail Corp., 830 F.2d 1230 (3d Cir. 1987),
    cert. denied, 485 U.S. 988 (1988), 1396
Gantt v. Clemson Agricultural Coll., 208 F. Supp. 416 (D.S.C. 1962), 888
Gardco Mfg. v. Herst Lighting Co., 820 F.2d 1209 (Fed. Cir. 1987), 1111
Gardiner Stone Hunter Int'l v. Iberia Lineas Aereas de Espana, S.A., 896 F. Supp. 125
    (S.D.N.Y. 1995), 1138, 1143
Gardner v. Clark, 101 F. Supp. 2d 468 (N.D. Miss. 2000), 1051
Garment Dist., Inc. v. Belk Stores Servs., Inc., 617 F. Supp. 944 (W.D.N.C. 1985), *aff'd*, 799
    F.2d 905 (4th Cir. 1986), *cert. denied*, 486 U.S. 1005 (1988), 172
Garment Dist., Inc. v. Belk Stores Servs., Inc., 799 F.2d 905 (4th Cir. 1986), *cert. denied*, 486
    U.S. 1005 (1988), 18, 20, 168
Garot Anderson Agencies v. Blue Cross & Blue Shield United, 1993-1 Trade Cas. (CCH)
    ¶ 70,235 (N.D. Ill. 1993), 79, 104
Garshman v. Universal Resources Holding, Inc., 625 F. Supp. 737 (D.N.J. 1986), 4, 131
Garshman v. Universal Resources Holding, Inc., 824 F.2d 223 (3d Cir. 1987), 27
Gas-A-Tron of Ariz. v. American Oil Co., 1977-2 Trade Cas. (CCH) ¶ 61,789 (D. Ariz. 1977),
    856, 859
Gassett v. Nissan N.A., Inc., 877 F. Supp. 974 (D.V.I. 1994), *aff'd without op.*, 66 F.3d 311
    (3d Cir. 1995), 507
Gates v. Victor Fine Foods, 54 F.3d 1457 (9th Cir.), *cert. denied*, 516 U.S. 869 (1995), 1143
Gates Rubber Co., [FTC Complaints & Orders 1970-1973 Transfer Binder] Trade Reg. Rep.
    (CCH) ¶ 19,657 (F.T.C. 1971), 396
Gateway Eastern Ry. Co. v. Terminal R.R. Ass'n, 35 F.3d 1134 (7th Cir. 1994), 888
Gateway, Inc., 2001 F.T.C. LEXIS 107 (2001), 621, 631
Gateway 2000, Inc., 126 F.T.C. 888 (1998), 633, 717

Gucci v. Gucci Shops, 651 F. Supp. 194 (S.D.N.Y. 1986), 28
Guerine v. J & W Inv., Inc., 544 F.2d 863 (5th Cir. 1977), 938
Guernsey v. Rich Plan, 408 F. Supp. 582 (N.D. Ind. 1976), 722
Guild Mortgage Co., 113 F.T.C. 1183 (1990), 709
Gulf & W. Indus. v. Great Atl. & Pac. Tea Co., 476 F.2d 687 (2d Cir. 1973), 319, 320
Gulf Oil Corp. v. Copp Paving Co., 419 U.S. 186 (1974), 37, 38, 456, 457, 462
Gulf Oil Corp. v. Gilbert, 330 U.S. 501 (1947), 1178
Gulf Oil Corp. v. Gulf Can. Ltd., [1980] 2 S.C.R. 39, 1980-1 Trade Cas. (CCH) ¶ 63,285 (Can. 1980), 1184
Gulf States Land & Dev., Inc. v. Premier Bank, 956 F.2d 502 (5th Cir. 1992), 4, 919
Gulf States Utils. Co. v. FPC, 411 U.S. 747 (1973), 1296
Gulfstream III Assocs. v. Gulfstream Aerospace Corp., 789 F. Supp. 1288 (D.N.J. 1992), 1017
Gulfstream III Assocs. v. Gulfstream Aerospace Corp., 995 F.2d 425 (3d Cir. 1993), 856, 874, 889
Gulf Wandes Corp. v. General Elec. Co., 62 F.R.D. 377 (E.D. La. 1974), 947
Gupta v. Penn Jersey Corp., 582 F. Supp. 1058 (E.D. Pa. 1984), 955, 961
Guyott Co. v. Texaco, Inc., 261 F. Supp. 942 (D. Conn. 1966), 463, 464, 499
Guzowski v. Hartman, 969 F.2d 211 (6th Cir. 1992), cert. denied, 506 U.S. 1053 (1993), 26, 28
GVF Cannery, Inc. v. California Tomato Growers Ass'n, 511 F. Supp. 711 (N.D. Cal. 1981), 1248
Gypsum Antitrust Cases, In re, 565 F.2d 1123 (9th Cir. 1977), 962
Gypsum Cases, In re, 386 F. Supp. 959 (N.D. Cal. 1974), aff'd sub nom. In re Gypsum Antitrust Cases, 565 F.2d 1123 (9th Cir. 1977), 949, 958
Gypsum Wallboard, In re, 297 F. Supp. 1350 (J.P.M.L. 1969), 926

H

Häagen-Dazs Co., 119 F.T.C. 762 (1995), 621, 627
H.A. Artists & Assoc., Inc. v. Actors' Equity Ass'n, 451 U.S. 704 (1981), 1376, 1377, 1378
Haas v. Pittsburgh Nat'l Bank, 526 F.2d 1083 (3d Cir. 1975), 909
Hack v. President and Fellows of Yale Coll., 237 F.3d 81 (2d Cir. 2000), cert. denied, 122 S. Ct. 201 (2001), 196, 201, 205, 232, 245, 534
Haff v. Jewelmont Corp., 594 F. Supp. 1468 (N.D. Cal. 1984), 521, 866
Hahn v. Oregon Physicians' Serv., 868 F.2d 1022 (9th Cir. 1988), cert. denied, 493 U.S. 846 (1989), 52, 61, 72, 88, 105, 110, 124, 453, 922, 1346, 1347
Hahn v. Oregon Physicians Serv., 689 F.2d 840 (9th Cir. 1982), cert. denied, 462 U.S. 1133 (1983), 39, 1372
Hairsten v. Pacific-10 Conf., 893 F. Supp. 1485 (W.D. Wash. 1994), aff'd, 101 F.3d 1315 (9th Cir. 1996), 888
Hale v. Henkel, 201 U.S. 43 (1906), 741
Hall v. Cole, 412 U.S. 1 (1973), 1012, 1019
Hall v. NCAA, No. 94-2392-KHV, 1997 U.S. Dist. LEXIS 9452 (D. Kan. June 19, 1997), 989
Halliburton Co. v. Schlumberger Tech. Corp., 925 F.2d 1435 (Fed. Cir. 1991), 1046
Hallmark Indus. v. Reynolds Metals Co., 489 F.2d 8 (9th Cir. 1973), cert. denied, 417 U.S. 932 (1974), 168
Halverson v. Convenient Food Mart, Inc., 69 F.R.D. 331 (N.D. Ill. 1974), 946
Halverson v. Convenient Food Mart, Inc., 458 F.2d 927 (7th Cir. 1972), 938
Hamburg Bros., 54 F.T.C. 1450 (1958), 489
Hamilton Chapter of Alpha Delta Phi, Inc. v. Hamilton College, 106 F. Supp. 2d 406 (N.D.N.Y. 2000), 534, 564

Hennegan v. Pacifico Creative Serv., 674 F. Supp. 303 (D. Guam 1987), 504, 505

Hennegan v. Pacifico Creative Serv., 787 F.2d 1299 (9th Cir.), *cert. denied*, 479 U.S. 886 (1986), 893, 901

Hennessey v. NCAA, 564 F.2d 1136 (5th Cir. 1977), 119, 842

Hennessy Indus. Inc. v. FMC Corp., 779 F.2d 402 (7th Cir. 1985), 167, 1041, 1060, 1064

Henry v. A.B. Dick Co., 224 U.S. 1 (1912), 1097

Henry v. Chloride, Inc., 809 F.2d 1334 (8th Cir. 1987), 264, 474, 475, 476, 538

Henry Rosenfeld, Inc., 52 F.T.C. 1535 (1956), 506

Hensley v. Eckerhart, 461 U.S. 424 (1983), 1014, 1016

Hensley Equip. Co. v. Esco Corp., 383 F.2d 252 (5th Cir.), *modified per curiam*, 386 F.2d 442 (1967), 1074, 1096

Henson v. East Lincoln Township, 814 F.2d 410 (7th Cir. 1987), 931

Herbert R. Gibson, Sr., 95 F.T.C. 553, *modified*, 96 F.T.C. 126 (1980), *aff'd*, 682 F.2d 554 (5th Cir. 1982), *cert. denied*, 460 U.S. 1068 (1983), 500, 501, 504, 505, 506, 507

Hercules, Inc., 84 F.T.C. 605 (1974), *modified*, 86 F.T.C. 1236 (1975), 628

Herman v. William Brooks Shoe Co., 49 U.S.P.Q.2d (BNA) 1361 (S.D.N.Y. 1998), 1045

Herman Schwabe, Inc. v. United Shoe Mach. Corp., 297 F.2d 906 (2d Cir.), *cert. denied*, 369 U.S. 865 (1962), 878, 880

Hertz Corp. v. City of New York, 1 F.3d 121 (2d Cir. 1993), *cert. denied*, 510 U.S. 1111 (1994), 76, 1218

Heublein, Inc., 96 F.T.C. 385 (1980), 340, 354, 355, 356, 359, 360, 369, 554

Heublein, Inc. v. FTC, 539 F. Supp. 123 (D. Conn. 1982), 374

Hew Corp. v. Tandy Corp., 480 F. Supp. 758 (D. Mass. 1979), 1015

Hewitt v. Joyce Beverages of Wis., Inc., 721 F.2d 625 (7th Cir. 1983), 946, 952

Hewlett-Packard Co., 2001 F.T.C. LEXIS 37 (2001), 621

Hewlett-Packard Co. v. Arch Assocs. Corp., 908 F. Supp. 265 (E.D. Pa. 1995), 4, 506, 569, 591

Hewlett-Packard Co. v. Bausch & Lomb, Inc., 882 F.2d 1556 (Fed. Cir. 1989), *cert. denied*, 493 U.S. 1076 (1990), 1040

Hewlett-Packard Co. v. Boston Scientific Corp., 77 F. Supp. 2d 189 (D. Mass. 1999), 305

Hewlett-Packard Co. v. Genrad, Inc., 882 F. Supp. 1141 (D. Mass. 1995), 1001, 1111, 1114

Hickman v. Taylor, 329 U.S. 495 (1946), 982

Hicks v. Bekins Moving & Storage Co., 87 F.2d 583 (9th Cir. 1937), 1025

Hi-Co Enters. v. Conagra, Inc., 75 F.R.D. 628 (S.D. Ga. 1976), 929, 946, 951

Higgins v. Medical Coll., 849 F. Supp. 1113 (E.D. Va. 1994), 61, 915, 1336, 1338

Higgins v. New York Stock Exch., 942 F.2d 829 (2d Cir. 1991), 892, 893, 907, 908

High Fructose Corn Syrup Antitrust Litig., *In re*, 156 F. Supp. 2d 1017 (C.D. Ill. 2001), 11, 919, 921, 992

High Pressure Laminate Antitrust Litig., *In re*, 2000-2 Trade Cas. (CCH) ¶ 73,094 (J.P.M.L. 2000), 925, 926

Highspire, Inc. v. UKF Am., Inc., 469 F. Supp. 1009 (S.D.N.Y. 1979), 465

High Strength Steel, Inc. v. Svenskt Stal Aktiebolag, 1985-2 Trade Cas. (CCH) ¶ 66,884 (N.D. Ill. 1985), 1179

High Tech. Careers v. San Jose Mercury News, 996 F.2d 987 (9th Cir. 1993), 229, 276, 277, 924

High Tech Communs. v. Panasonic Co., 1995-1 Trade Cas. (CCH) ¶ 70,977 (E.D. La. 1995), 485

Hill v. A-T-O, Inc., 535 F.2d 1349 (2d Cir. 1976), 192, 203

Hill Aircraft & Leasing Corp. v. Fulton County, 561 F. Supp. 667 (N.D. Ga. 1982), *aff'd without op.*, 729 F.2d 1467 (11th Cir. 1984), 308

Hillis Motors, Inc. v. Hawaii Auto. Dealers' Ass'n, 997 F.2d 581 (9th Cir. 1993), 836

Hillsborough County v. Automated Med. Lab., 471 U.S. 707 (1985), 818

Hillside Amusement Co. v. Warner Bros. Pictures, 7 F.R.D. 260 (S.D.N.Y. 1944), 963

Hydranautics v. FilmtTec Corp., 70 F.3d 533 (9th Cir. 1995), *cert. denied*, 519 U.S. 814 (1996), 1043, 1114, 1233

Hydranautics v. FilmTec Corp., 204 F.3d 880 (9th Cir. 2000), 1224

Hydro Air of Conn., Inc. v. Versa Techs., Inc., 599 F. Supp. 1119 (D. Conn. 1984), 171

Hydrolevel Corp. v. American Soc'y of Mech. Eng'rs, 635 F.2d 118 (2d Cir. 1980), *aff'd*, 456 U.S. 556 (1982), 876

Hygrade Milk & Cream Co. v. Tropicana Prods., Inc., 1994 U.S. Dist. LEXIS 1091 (S.D.N.Y. Feb. 4, 1994), 516

Hygrade Milk & Cream Co. v. Tropicana Prods., Inc., 1996-1 Trade Cas. (CCH) ¶ 71,438 (S.D.N.Y. 1996), 485, 498, 506, 507, 508, 512

I

Iams Co. v. Falduti, 974 F. Supp. 1263 (E.D. Mo. 1997), 139, 468

IBM Peripheral EDP Devices Antitrust Litig., *In re*, 459 F. Supp. 626 (N.D. Cal. 1978), 261

IBM Peripheral EDP Devices Antitrust Litig., *In re*, 481 F. Supp. 965 (N.D. Cal. 1979), *aff'd sub nom.* Transamerica Computer Co. v. IBM, 698 F.2d 1377 (9th Cir.), *cert. denied*, 464 U.S. 955 (1983), 186, 242, 243, 290, 291, 292, 552, 554

IBP, Inc. v. Glickman, 187 F.3d 974 (8th Cir. 1999), 1253

Icon Indus. Controls Corp. v. Cimetrix, Inc., 921 F. Supp. 375 (W.D. La. 1996), 1164

Idaho Potato Comm'n v. M&M Produce Farms & Sales, 95 F. Supp. 2d 150 (S.D.N.Y. 2000), *aff'd sub nom.* Hapco Farms, Inc. v. Idaho Potato Comm'n, 283 F.3d 468 (2d Cir. 2001), 1090

Ideal Dairy Farms v. John Labatt, Ltd., 90 F.3d 737 (3d Cir. 1996), 232, 283

Ideal Plumbing Co. v. Benco, Inc., 382 F. Supp. 1161 (W.D. Ark. 1974), *aff'd*, 529 F.2d 972 (8th Cir. 1976), 470

Ideal Plumbing Co. v. Benco, Inc., 529 F.2d 972 (8th Cir. 1976), 499, 501

Ideal Toy Corp., 64 F.T.C. 297 (1964), 641

I. Haas Trucking Corp. v. New York Fruit Auction Corp., 364 F. Supp. 868 (S.D.N.Y. 1973), 205

ILC Peripherals Leasing Corp. v. IBM, 458 F. Supp. 423 (N.D. Cal. 1977), *aff'd per curiam sub nom.* Memorex Corp. v. IBM, 636 F.2d 1188 (9th Cir. 1980), *cert. denied*, 452 U.S. 972 (1981), 186, 269, 285, 290, 291, 293, 294, 874, 999

Illinois v. Abbott & Assocs., 460 U.S. 557 (1983), 973, 974

Illinois v. Ampress Brick Co., 67 F.R.D. 461 (N.D. Ill. 1975), 853

Illinois v. Ampress Brick Co., 536 F.2d 1163 (7th Cir. 1976), 853

Illinois v. Borg, Inc., 548 F. Supp. 972 (N.D. Ill. 1982), 857

Illinois v. Borg, Inc., 564 F. Supp. 96 (N.D. Ill. 1983), 973, 975

Illinois v. Bristol-Myers Co., 470 F.2d 1276 (D.C. Cir. 1972), 804

Illinois v. Brunswick Corp., 32 F.R.D. 453 (N.D. Ill. 1963), 804

Illinois v. F.E. Moran, Inc., 740 F.2d 533 (7th Cir. 1984), 973, 974, 975

Illinois v. General Paving Co., 590 F.2d 680 (7th Cir.), *cert. denied*, 444 U.S. 679 (1979), 1001, 1005

Illinois v. ICC, 687 F.2d 1047 (7th Cir. 1982), 1405

Illinois v. ICC, 751 F.2d 903 (7th Cir. 1985), 1397

Illinois v. Ralph Vancil, Inc., 1976-2 Trade Cas. (CCH) ¶ 61,025 (S.D. Ill. 1976), 902, 903, 913

Illinois v. Sangamo Constr., 657 F.2d 855 (7th Cir. 1981), 1012, 1018

Illinois v. Sarbaugh, 552 F.2d 768 (7th Cir.), *cert. denied*, 434 U.S. 889 (1977), 780, 973, 976

Illinois v. Sperry Rand Corp., 237 F. Supp. 520 (N.D. Ill. 1965), 903, 1004

Illinois Bell Tel. Co. v. Haines & Co., 905 F.2d 1081 (7th Cir. 1990), *vacated*, 499 U.S. 944 (1991), 283

Independent Sch. Dist. No. 89 v. Bolain Equip., Inc., 90 F.R.D. 245 (W.D. Okla. 1980), 929
Independent Serv. Orgs. Antitrust Litig., *In re*, 1995-2 Trade Cas. (CCH) ¶ 71,099 (D. Kan. 1995), 993
Independent Serv. Orgs. Antitrust Litig., *In re*, 1996-1 Trade Cas. (CCH) ¶ 71,269 (D. Kan. 1995), 989
Independent Serv. Orgs. Antitrust Litig., *In re*, 161 F.R.D. 107 (D. Kan. 1995), 912
Independent Serv. Orgs. Antitrust Litig., *In re*, 910 F. Supp. 1537 (D. Kan. 1995), 885
Independent Serv. Orgs. Antitrust Litig., *In re*, 174 F.R.D. 104 (D. Kan. 1997), 990
Independent Serv. Orgs. Antitrust Litig., *In re*, 964 F. Supp. 1479 (D. Kan. 1997), 1060
Independent Serv. Orgs. Antitrust Litig., *In re*, 85 F. Supp. 2d 1130 (D. Kan. 2000), 188, 1101, 1102
Independent Serv. Orgs. Antitrust Litig., *In re*, 114 F. Supp. 2d 1070 (D. Kan.), *aff'd*, 203 F.3d 1322 (Fed. Cir. 2000), *cert. denied*, 531 U.S. 1143 (2001), 297, 1078
Independent Serv. Orgs. Antitrust Litig., *In re*, 203 F.3d 1322 (Fed. Cir. 2000), *cert. denied*, 531 U.S. 1143 (2001), 240, 252, 285, 286, 297, 1048, 1069, 1077, 1078, 1079, 1111, 1232
Independent Taxicab Drivers' Employees v. Greater Houston Transp. Co., 760 F.2d 607 (5th Cir.) *cert. denied*, 474 U.S. 903 (1985), 1236
Indiana Fed'n of Dentists, 101 F.T.C. 47 (1983), 63
Indiana Fed'n of Dentists v. FTC, 745 F.2d 1124 (7th Cir. 1984), 63, 123
Indiana Grocery Co. v. Super Valu Stores, 647 F. Supp. 254 (S.D. Ind. 1986), 459
Indiana Grocery Co. v. Super Valu Stores, 684 F. Supp. 561 (S.D. Ind. 1988), *aff'd*, 864 F.2d 1409 (7th Cir. 1989), 252
Indiana Grocery Co. v. Super Valu Stores, 864 F.2d 1409 (7th Cir. 1989), 133, 238, 239, 305, 307, 476, 919
Indiana Manufactured Hous. Ass'n v. FTC, 641 F.2d 481 (7th Cir. 1981), 697, 701
Indian Coffee Corp. v. Procter & Gamble Co., 752 F.2d 891 (3d Cir.), *cert. denied*, 474 U.S. 863 (1985), 266, 463, 872
Indian Head, Inc. v. Allied Tube & Conduit Corp., 817 F.2d 938 (2d Cir. 1987), *aff'd*, 486 U.S. 492 (1988), 82
Indium Corp. of Am. v. Semi-Alloys, Inc., 566 F. Supp. 1344 (N.D.N.Y. 1983), 863
Indium Corp. of Am. v. Semi-Alloys, Inc., 611 F. Supp. 379 (N.D.N.Y.), *aff'd*, 781 F.2d 879 (Fed. Cir. 1985), *cert. denied*, 479 U.S. 820 (1986), 843, 1041
Indium Corp. of Am. v. Semi-Alloys, Inc., 781 F.2d 879 (Fed. Cir. 1985), *cert. denied*, 479 U.S. 820 (1986), 1041
Individualized Catalogues, Inc., 65 F.T.C. 48 (1964), *rescinded*, 76 F.T.C. 80 (1969), 509
Industrial Bldg. Materials, Inc. v. Interchem. Corp., 437 F.2d 1336 (9th Cir. 1970), 171, 917
Industrial Diamonds Antitrust Litig., *In re*, 167 F.R.D. 374 (S.D.N.Y. 1996), 928, 930, 932, 943, 945, 948
Industrial Gas Antitrust Litig., *In re*, 681 F.2d 514 (7th Cir. 1982), *cert. denied*, 460 U.S. 1016 (1983), 866
Industrial Inv. Dev. Corp. v. Mitsui & Co., 594 F.2d 48 (5th Cir. 1979), *cert. denied*, 445 U.S. 903 (1980), 1145, 1148
Industrial Inv. Dev. Corp. v. Mitsui & Co., 671 F.2d 876 (5th Cir. 1982), *vacated and remanded*, 460 U.S. 1007, *reaff'd*, 704 F.2d 785 (5th Cir.), *cert. denied*, 464 U.S. 961 (1983), 1125, 1126, 1178
Industrial Inv. Dev. Corp. v. Mitsui & Co., 704 F.2d 785 (5th Cir.), *cert. denied*, 464 U.S. 961 (1983), 863
Industrial Silicon Antitrust Litig., *In re*, 1998-2 Trade Cas. (CCH) ¶ 72,348 (W.D. Pa. 1998), 1009
Industria Siciliana Asfalti, Bitumi, SpA v. Exxon Research & Eng'g Co., 1977-1 Trade Cas. (CCH) ¶ 61,256 (S.D.N.Y. 1977), 227, 1164
Infant Formula Antitrust Litig., *In re*, MDL No. 878, 1992 U.S. Dist. LEXIS 21981 (N.D. Fla. Jan. 13, 1992), 804
Information Exch. Sys. v. First Bank Nat'l Ass'n, 994 F.2d 478 (8th Cir. 1993), 892

Intermountain Ford Tractor Sales Co. v. Massey-Ferguson Ltd., 210 F. Supp. 930 (D. Utah 1962), *aff'd per curiam*, 325 F.2d 713 (10th Cir. 1963), *cert. denied*, 377 U.S. 931 (1964), 1176

International Air Indus., Inc. v. American Excelsior Co., 517 F.2d 714 (5th Cir. 1975), *cert. denied*, 424 U.S. 943 (1976), 260, 261, 474, 475, 483, 1425

International Ass'n of Heat & Frost Insulators v. United Contractors Ass'n, 483 F.2d 384 (3d Cir. 1973), *modified*, 494 F.2d 1353 (3d Cir. 1974), 842

International Ass'n of Machinists v. OPEC, 477 F. Supp. 553 (C.D. Cal. 1979), *aff'd*, 649 F.2d 1354 (9th Cir. 1981), *cert. denied*, 454 U.S. 1163 (1982), 1142

International Ass'n of Machinists v. OPEC, 649 F.2d 1354 (9th Cir. 1981), *cert. denied*, 454 U.S. 1163 (1982), 1142, 1144, 1145, 1146, 1148, 1152

International Audiotext Network v. AT&T, 893 F. Supp. 1207 (S.D.N.Y. 1994), *aff'd*, 62 F.3d 69 (2d Cir. 1995), 235, 238, 281, 289

International Bhd. of Teamsters, Local 734 v. Philip Morris Inc., 34 F. Supp. 2d 656 (N.D. Ill. 1998), *aff'd*, 196 F.3d 818 (7th Cir. 1999), 854

International Bhd. of Teamsters, Local 734 v. Philip Morris Inc., 196 F.3d 818 (7th Cir. 1999), 848

International Distrib. Ctrs. v. Walsh Trucking Co., 812 F.2d 786 (2d Cir.), *cert. denied*, 482 U.S. 915 (1987), 16, 126, 231, 235, 237, 307, 309, 310

International Harvester Co., 104 F.T.C. 949 (1984), 618, 622, 623, 649

International Harvester Co. of Am. v. Kentucky, 234 U.S. 216 (1914), 819, 820

International Harvester Co. of Am. v. Missouri, 234 U.S. 199 (1914), 819

International House of Pancakes Franchise Litig., *In re*, 331 F. Supp. 556 (J.P.M.L. 1971), 926

International House of Pancakes Franchise Litig., *In re*, 1972 Trade Cas. (CCH) ¶ 73,864 (W.D. Mo. 1972), 955

International Logistics Group, Ltd. v. Chrysler Corp., 884 F.2d 904 (6th Cir. 1989), *cert. denied*, 494 U.S. 1066 (1990), 23, 155, 160, 166, 566, 586

International Mfg. Co. v. Landon, Inc., 336 F.2d 723 (9th Cir. 1964), *cert. denied*, 379 U.S. 988 (1965), 181, 1073, 1080

International Nickel Co. v. Ford Motor Co., 166 F. Supp. 551 (S.D.N.Y. 1958), 1038, 1039

International Raw Materials, Ltd. v. Stauffer Chem. Co., 716 F. Supp. 188 (E.D. Pa. 1989), *vacated*, 898 F.2d 946 (3d Cir. 1990), 1159, 1160, 1161

International Raw Materials, Ltd. v. Stauffer Chem. Co., 978 F.2d 1318 (3d Cir. 1992), 1159

International Rys. of Cent. Am. v. United Brands Co., 532 F.2d 231 (2d Cir.), *cert. denied*, 429 U.S. 835 (1976), 173, 277, 322

International Rys. of Cent. Am. v. United Fruit Co., 373 F.2d 408 (2d Cir.), *cert. denied*, 387 U.S. 921 (1967), 916

International Salt Co. v. Ohio Turnpike Comm'n, 392 F.2d 579 (8th Cir.), *cert. dismissed per stipulation*, 393 U.S. 947 (1968), 1006

International Serv. Indus., 84 F.T.C. 408 (1974), 637

International Shoe Co. v. FTC, 280 U.S. 291 (1930), 348, 349

International Shoe Co. v. Washington, 326 U.S. 310 (1945), 795, 1139, 1170, 1171, 1175

International Shoe Mach. Corp. v. United Shoe Mach. Corp., 315 F.2d 449 (1st Cir.), *cert. denied*, 375 U.S. 820 (1963), 1004, 1006, 1007

International Sys. & Controls Corp., *In re*, 693 F.2d 1235 (5th Cir. 1982), 983

International Tech. Consul. v. Pilkington PLC, 137 F.3d 1382 (9th Cir. 1998), 1008

International Travel Arrangers v. NWA, Inc., 1990-2 Trade Cas. (CCH) ¶ 69,112 (D. Minn. 1990), 891

International Travel Arrangers v. NWA, Inc., 991 F.2d 1389 (8th Cir.), *cert. denied*, 510 U.S. 932 (1993), 27, 251, 258, 264, 1424

International Travel Arrangers, Inc. v. Western Airlines, 623 F.2d 1255 (8th Cir.), *cert. denied*, 449 U.S. 1063 (1980), 22, 294, 874, 914, 1014, 1015, 1243

J

Jack Faucett Assocs. v. AT&T, 1983-1 Trade Cas. (CCH) ¶ 65,285 (D.D.C. 1983), 938

Jack Faucett Assocs. v. AT&T, 1986-1 Trade Cas. (CCH) ¶ 66,904 (D.D.C. 1985), 956

Jack Faucett Assocs. v. AT&T, 744 F.2d 118 (D.C. Cir. 1984), *cert. denied*, 469 U.S. 1196 (1985), 1237

Jack Frost Lab. v. Physicians & Nurses Mfg., 901 F. Supp. 718 (S.D.N.Y. 1995), *aff'd without op.*, 124 F.3d 229 (Fed. Cir. 1997), 1040

Jack Kahn Music Co. v. Baldwin Piano & Organ Co., 604 F.2d 755 (2d Cir. 1979), 158, 888

Jack La Lanne Mgmt. Corp., 84 F.T.C. 1139 (1974), 637

Jackshaw Pontiac, Inc. v. Cleveland Press Publ'g Co., 102 F.R.D. 183 (N.D. Ohio 1984), 929, 933, 937, 938, 939

Jackson v. Radcliffe, 795 F. Supp. 197 (S.D. Tex. 1992), 1333

Jackson v. Swift Eckrich, Inc., 53 F.3d 1452 (8th Cir. 1995), 1252

Jack Walters & Sons Corp. v. Morton Bldg., Inc., 737 F.2d 698 (7th Cir.), *cert. denied*, 469 U.S. 1018 (1984), 68, 133, 138, 143, 180, 181, 185, 202, 1105

Jack Winter, Inc. v. Koratron Co., 375 F. Supp. 1 (N.D. Cal. 1974), 1043, 1092

Jacob Siegel Co. v. FTC, 327 U.S. 608 (1946), 654, 656, 696

Jacobson & Co. v. Armstrong Cork Co., 433 F. Supp. 1210 (S.D.N.Y. 1977), 168

Jacobson & Co. v. Armstrong Cork Co., 548 F.2d 438 (2d Cir. 1977), 887

Jacobs, Visconsi & Jacobs, Co. v. City of Lawrence, 927 F.2d 1111 (10th Cir. 1991), 1220

Jade Aircraft Sales v. Bridgeport, 1990-2 Trade Cas. (CCH) ¶ 69,225 (D. Conn. 1990), 843

Jaffee v. Horton Mem'l Hosp., 680 F. Supp. 125 (S.D.N.Y. 1988), 40, 1328

J. Allen Ramey, M.D., Inc. v. Pacific Found. for Med. Care, 999 F. Supp. 1355 (S.D. Cal. 1998), 850, 1348

Jamesbury Corp. v. Kitamura Valve Mfg. Co., 484 F. Supp. 533 (S.D. Tex. 1980), 1172

James L. McElhaney, M.D., 116 F.T.C. 1137 (1993), 629, 630

James M. King & Assocs. v. G.D. Van Wagenen Co., 1987-1 Trade Cas. (CCH) ¶ 67,534 (D. Minn. 1987), 400

James R. Snyder Co. v. Associated Gen. Contractors of Am., 677 F.2d 1111 (6th Cir.), *cert. denied*, 459 U.S. 1015 (1982), 42

Jamison v. FTC, 628 F. Supp. 1548 (D.D.C. 1986), 697

J & R Research Corp., 2000 F.T.C. LEXIS 90 (2000), 630

J & S Oil, Inc. v. Irving Oil Corp., 63 F. Supp. 2d 62 (D. Me. 1999), 477, 595

Janel Sales Corp. v. Lanvin Parfums, Inc., 396 F.2d 398 (2d Cir.), *cert. denied*, 393 U.S. 938 (1968), 146, 152

Janich Bros. v. American Distilling Co., 570 F.2d 848 (9th Cir. 1977), *cert. denied*, 439 U.S. 829 (1978), 258, 260, 262

Janini v. Kuwait Univ., 43 F.3d 1534 (D.C. Cir. 1995), 1141

Japanese Elec. Prod. Antitrust Litig., *In re*, 631 F.2d 1069 (3d Cir. 1980), 999

Japanese Elec. Prods. Antitrust Litig., *In re*, 723 F.2d 238 (3d Cir. 1983), *rev'd sub nom.* Matsushita Elec. Indus. Co. v. Zenith Radio Corp., 475 U.S. 574 (1986), 313, 461, 1132

Japan Gas Lighter Ass'n v. Ronson Corp., 257 F. Supp. 219 (D.N.J. 1966), 1170

Jarrow Formulas, Inc. v. International Nutrition Co., Civ. 3:01CV00478, 2001 U.S. Dist. LEXIS 19414 (D. Conn. Nov. 16, 2001), 1049

Jaurequi v. Carter Mfg. Co., 173 F.3d 1076 (8th Cir. 1999), 1009

Javelin Corp. v. Uniroyal, Inc., 546 F.2d 276 (9th Cir. 1976), *cert. denied*, 431 U.S. 938 (1977), 842, 914

Jayco Sys., Inc. v. Savin Bus. Mach. Corp., 777 F.2d 306 (5th Cir. 1985), *cert. denied*, 479 U.S. 816 (1986), 232, 568, 586

Jay Norris Corp., 91 F.T.C. 751 (1978), *enforced as modified*, 598 F.2d 1244 (2d Cir.), *cert. denied*, 444 U.S. 980 (1979), 625, 637, 652

Jay Norris, Inc. v. FTC, 598 F.2d 1244 (2d Cir.), *cert. denied*, 444 U.S. 980 (1979), 654, 660

K

L

L. Heller & Son v. FTC, 191 F.2d 954 (7th Cir. 1951), 657

Liamuiga Tours v. Travel Impressions, Ltd., 617 F. Supp. 920 (E.D.N.Y. 1985), 1121

Liang v. Hunt, 477 F. Supp. 891 (N.D. Ill. 1979), 865

Libbey-Owens-Ford Glass Co. v. FTC, 352 F.2d 415 (6th Cir. 1965), 640, 654

Liberty Fin. Cos., Inc., 1999 F.T.C. LEXIS 99 (1999), 642

Liberty Lake Invs., Inc. v. Magnuson, 12 F.3d 155 (9th Cir. 1993), *cert. denied*, 513 U.S. 818 (1994), 1043, 1233

Liberty Lincoln Mercury, Inc. v. Ford Motor Co., 134 F.3d 557 (3d Cir. 1998), 463

Liberty Trucking Co., Ext.-Gen'l Commodities, 131 M.C.C. 573 (1979), 1389

Lie v. St. Joseph Hosp., 964 F.2d 567 (6th Cir. 1992), 60, 67, 68, 849, 919, 1333

Lieberman v. FTC, 771 F.2d 32 (2d Cir. 1985), 377, 691, 828

Lifemark Hosps. v. Liljeberg Enters., 1993-2 Trade Cas. (CCH) ¶ 70,437 (E.D. La. 1993), 1024, 1025

Lifescan, Inc. v. Polymer Tech. Int'l Corp., 35 U.S.P.Q.2d (BNA) 1225 (W.D. Wash. 1995), 1098

Lifschultz Fast Freight, Inc. v. Consolidated Freightways Corp., 805 F. Supp. 1277 (D.S.C. 1992), *aff'd*, 998 F.2d 1009 (4th Cir.), *cert. denied*, 510 U.S. 993 (1993), 1242

Liggett & Myers, Inc., 87 F.T.C. 1074 (1976), *aff'd*, 567 F.2d 1273 (4th Cir. 1977), 339, 536, 541, 547, 555

Liggett & Myers, Inc. v. FTC, 567 F.2d 1273 (4th Cir. 1977), 550

Liggett Group v. Brown & Williamson Tobacco Corp., 964 F.2d 335 (4th Cir. 1992), *aff'd sub nom.* Brooke Group Ltd. v. Brown & Williamson Tobacco Corp., 509 U.S. 209 (1993), 266

Lighthouse Rug Co. v. FTC, 35 F.2d 163 (7th Cir. 1929), 635

Lindsley v. Natural Carbonic Gas Go., 220 U.S. 61 (1911), 819

Lindy Bros. Builders v. American Radiator & Standard Sanitary Corp., 487 F.2d 161 (3d Cir. 1973) *aff'd in part and vacated in part*, 540 F.2d 102 (3d Cir. 1976), 1013, 1014

Lindy Bros. Builders v. American Radiator & Standard Sanitary Corp., 540 F.2d 102 (3d Cir. 1976), 1014, 1016

Linen Supply Cos., *In re*, 15 F.R.D. 115 (S.D.N.Y. 1953), 741

Linerboard Antitrust Litig., *In re*, 203 F.R.D. 197 (E.D. Pa. 2001), 934

Link v. Mercedes-Benz of N. Am., Inc., 550 F.2d 860 (3d Cir.), *cert. denied*, 431 U.S. 933 (1977), 954

Link v. Mercedes-Benz of N. Am., Inc., 788 F.2d 918 (3d Cir. 1986), 854, 855, 859

Linseman v. World Hockey Ass'n, 439 F. Supp. 1315 (D. Conn. 1977), 1145, 1154

L'Invincible, 14 U.S. (1 Wheat.) 238 (1816), 1136

Lippa & Co. v. Lenox Inc., 305 F. Supp. 175 (D. Vt. 1969), 1166

Lippa's, Inc. v. Lenox, Inc., 305 F. Supp. 182 (D. Vt. 1969), 896

Liquilux Gas Servs. v. Tropical Gas Co., 303 F. Supp. 414 (D.P.R. 1969), 456

Litman v. A. Barton Hepburn Hosp., 679 F. Supp. 196 (N.D.N.Y. 1988), 40

Little Caesar Enters. v. Smith, 895 F. Supp. 884 (E.D. Mich. 1995), 189, 845, 894, 946

Little Caesar Enters. v. Smith, 172 F.R.D. 236 (E.D. Mich. 1997), 946, 1001

Little Caesar Enters. v. Smith, 34 F. Supp. 2d 459 (E.D. Mich. 1998), 182, 203, 245, 1105

Little Carnegie Theatre v. Columbia Pictures Corp., 1958 Trade Cas. (CCH) ¶ 69,215 (S.D.N.Y. 1958), 888

Littlejohn v. Shell Oil Co., 483 F.2d 1140 (5th Cir.), *cert. denied*, 414 U.S. 1116 (1973), 460

Litton Indus., Inc., 82 F.T.C. 793 (1973), 332

Litton Indus., Inc., 97 F.T.C. 1, 70 (1981), *enforced as modified*, 676 F.2d 364 (9th Cir. 1982), 621

Litton Indus., Inc. v. FTC, 676 F.2d 364 (9th Cir. 1982), 654, 660, 661, 695, 696

Litton Indus. Prods. v. Solid State Sys., 755 F.2d 158 (Fed. Cir. 1985), 1044

Litton Sys. v. AT&T, 91 F.R.D. 574 (S.D.N.Y. 1981), *aff'd*, 700 F.2d 785 (2d Cir. 1983), *cert. denied*, 464 U.S. 1073 (1984), 990, 1012

M

Minnesota Power, Inc. v. Duluth, M. & I.R. Ry., Decision served July 8, 1999, 1999 STB LEXIS 403 (1999), 1399

Minnesota Twins P'ship v. State *ex rel.* Hatch, 592 N.W.2d 847 (Minn.), *cert. denied*, 528 U.S. 1013 (1999), 1387

Minolta Camera Prods. Antitrust Litig., *In re*, 668 F. Supp. 456 (D. Md. 1987), 132, 809

Minpeco, S.A. v. ContiCommodity Servs., 116 F.R.D. 517 (S.D.N.Y.), *aff'd sub nom.* Korwek v. Hunt, 827 F.2d 874 (2d Cir. 1987), 1188

Minpeco, S.A. v. ContiCommodity Servs., 1988-1 Trade Cas. (CCH) ¶ 67,885 (S.D.N.Y. 1988), 1026

Mir v. Little Co. of Mary Hosp., 844 F.2d 646 (9th Cir. 1988), 873, 908, 1330

Miranda v. Arizona, 384 U.S. 436 (1966), 743

Miranda v. Michigan, 141 F. Supp. 2d 747 (E.D. Mich. 2001), 1241

Miriam Maschek, Inc., 85 F.T.C. 536 (1975), 657

Misco, Inc. v. United States Steel Corp., 784 F.2d 198 (6th Cir. 1986), 457

Mission Hills Condominium Ass'n M-1 v. Corley, 570 F. Supp. 453 (N.D. Ill. 1983), 836

Mississippi River Corp. v. FTC, 454 F.2d 1083 (8th Cir. 1972), 346, 363

Mississippi River Fuel Corp., 69 F.T.C. 1186 (1966), 691

Missouri v. American Cyanamid Co., Dkt. No. 97-4024-CV-C-SOW (W.D. Mo. Jan. 30, 1997), 830

Missouri v. Hunter, 459 U.S. 359 (1983), 785

Missouri v. Jenkins, 491 U.S. 274 (1989), 1018

Missouri v. National Org. for Women, 620 F.2d 1301 (8th Cir.), *cert. denied*, 449 U.S. 842 (1980), 124

Missouri v. United Tel. Co., No. Civ. 4414-CV-C-66BA, 1995 WL 792066 (W.D. Mo. Nov. 15, 1995), 1005

Missouri Pac. R.R.—Construction & Operation Exemption— Harris & Chambers Counties, TX, Decision served June 30, 1995, 1995 ICC LEXIS 169 (1995), 1397

Missouri Portland Cement Co. v. Cargill, Inc., 498 F.2d 851 (2d Cir.), *cert. denied*, 419 U.S. 883 (1974), 355, 357, 361, 368

Mitchael v. Intracorp., Inc., 179 F.3d 847 (10th Cir. 1999), 7, 14

Mitchell v. Frank R. Howard Mem'l Hosp., 853 F.2d 762 (9th Cir. 1988), *cert. denied*, 489 U.S. 1013 (1989), 44

Mitchell Bros. Film Group v. Cinema Adult Theater, 604 F.2d 852 (5th Cir. 1979), *cert. denied*, 445 U.S. 917 (1980), 1100

Mitek Surgical Prods. v. Arthrex, Inc., 21 F. Supp. 2d 1309 (D. Utah 1998), *aff'd without op.*, 230 F.3d 1383 (Fed. Cir. 2000), 1050

Mitel Corp. v. A&A Connections, Inc., 1998-1 Trade Cas. (CCH) ¶ 72,120 (E.D. Pa. 1998), 571

Mitsubishi Elec. Corp. v. IMS Tech. Inc., 44 U.S.P.Q.2d (BNA) 1904 (N.D. Ill. 1997), 34, 1041

Mitsubishi Motor Sales of Am., Inc., 123 F.T.C. 288 (1997), 710

Mitsubishi Motors Corp. v. Soler Chrysler-Plymouth, Inc., 473 U.S. 614 (1985), 1020, 1021, 1179, 1203

Miyano Mach. USA, Inc. v. Zonar, 1993-1 Trade Cas. (CCH) ¶ 70,145 (N.D. Ill. 1993), 499, 521

Mizlou Television Network, Inc. v. NBC, 603 F. Supp. 677 (D.D.C. 1984), 128, 1172

M.L.C., Inc. v. North Am. Philips Corp., 109 F.R.D. 134 (S.D.N.Y. 1986), 990

MLC, Inc. v. North Am. Philips Corp., 671 F. Supp. 246 (S.D.N.Y. 1987), 16, 151, 167, 172

M. Leff Radio Parts, Inc. v. Mattel, Inc., 706 F. Supp. 387 (W.D. Pa. 1988), 197, 205, 210

Mobil Oil Corp., 116 F.T.C. 113 (1993), 627

Mobil Oil Corp. v. W.R. Grace & Co., 367 F. Supp. 207 (D. Conn. 1973), 1060

Modern Mktg. Serv., 71 F.T.C. 1676 (1967), 500

Modern Mktg. Serv., [F.T.C. Complaints & Orders 1983-1987 Transfer Binder] Trade Reg. Rep. ¶ 22,158 (F.T.C. May 21, 1984), *dismissed*, Dkt. 3783 (Aug. 28, 1984), 504

N

O

P

Q

R

S

Sablosky v. Paramount Film Distrib. Corp., 137 F. Supp. 929 (E.D. Pa. 1955), 1006

Sabre Shipping Corp. v. American President Lines, 285 F. Supp. 949 (S.D.N.Y. 1968), *cert. denied*, 407 F.2d 173 (2d Cir.), *cert. denied*, 395 U.S. 922 (1969), 1117, 1156

Safeway Stores, Inc., 91 F.T.C. 975 (1978), 639

Safeway Stores, Inc. v. Freeman, 369 F.2d 952 (1966), 1251

Safeway Stores, Inc. v. Oklahoma Retail Grocers Ass'n, 360 U.S. 334 (1959), 819

Safeway Stores, Inc. v. Vance, 355 U.S. 389 (1958), 838

Sage Int'l, Ltd. v. Cadillac Gage Co., 534 F. Supp. 896 (E.D. Mich. 1981), 1146, 1148, 1152

Sage Realty Corp. v. ISS Cleaning Servs. Group, Inc., 936 F. Supp. 130 (S.D.N.Y. 1996), 847, 1382

Sager Glove Corp. v. Commissioner, 311 F.2d 210 (7th Cir. 1962), *cert. denied*, 373 U.S. 910 (1963), 1027

Sahm v. V-1 Oil Co., 402 F.2d 69 (10th Cir. 1968), 140

Salco Corp. v. General Motors Corp., 517 F.2d 567 (10th Cir. 1975), 158, 311, 312, 528

Salerno v. American League of Prof'l Baseball Clubs, 429 F.2d 1003 (2d Cir. 1970), *cert. denied*, 400 U.S. 1001 (1971), 1386, 1387

Sales Mktg. Servs., 82 F.T.C. 1519 (1973), 461

Salts v. Moore, 107 F. Supp. 2d 732 (N.D. Miss. 2000), 7

Sample, Inc. v. Pendelton Woolen Mills, Inc., 704 F. Supp. 498 (S.D.N.Y. 1989), 141, 167

Samuel v. Herrick Mem'l Hosp., 201 F.3d 830 (6th Cir. 2000), 885, 888

Samuel Silverman, 5 F.T.C. 294 (1922), 635

San Antonio Tel. Co. v. AT&T, 68 F.R.D. 435 (W.D. Tex. 1975), 938, 949

San Antonio Tel. Co. v. AT&T, 499 F.2d 349 (5th Cir. 1974), 1166, 1167

Sandcrest Outpatient Servs. v. Cumberland County Hosp. Sys., 853 F.2d 1139 (4th Cir. 1988), 1219, 1330

Sanders v. Levy, 558 F.2d 636 (2d. Cir. 1976), *rev'd sub nom.* Oppenheimer Fund, Inc. v. Sanders, 437 U.S. 340 (1978), 994, 996, 997

Sanderson v. Winner, 507 F.2d 477 (10th Cir. 1974), *cert. denied*, 421 U.S. 914 (1975), 938

San Diego Gas & Elec. Co. and Enova Energy, Inc., 79 F.E.R.C. (CCH) ¶ 61,372 (1997), *reh'g denied*, 85 F.E.R.C. (CCH) ¶ 61,199 (1998), 1305

Sandoz Pharms., 115 F.T.C. 625 (1992), 176

Sandura Co. v. FTC, 339 F.2d 847 (6th Cir. 1964), 655, 656

S & W Constr. & Materials Co. v. Dravo Basic Materials Co., 813 F. Supp. 1214 (S.D. Miss. 1992), *aff'd without op.*, 1 F.3d 1238 (5th Cir. 1993), 479

Sandy River Nursing Care Ctr. v. Aetna Cas. & Sur. Co., 985 F.2d 1138 (1st Cir.), *cert. denied*, 510 U.S. 818 (1993), 111, 1214, 1222, 1228, 1369

San Francisco Seals, Ltd. v. NHL, 379 F. Supp. 966 (C.D. Cal. 1974), 438

Sanjuan v. American Bd. of Psychiatry and Neurology, Inc., 40 F.3d 247 (7th Cir. 1994), 845, 913, 1020, 1179

San Juan Cement, Inc. v. Puerto Rican Cement Co., 922 F. Supp. 716 (D.P.R. 1996), 39

San Marino Elec. Corp. v. George J. Meyer Mfg. Co., 155 U.S.P.Q. (BNA) 617 (C.D. Cal. 1967), *aff'd*, 422 F.2d 1285 (9th Cir. 1970), 1062

San-Mar Labs., Inc., 95 F.T.C. 236 (1980), 668

Sanner v. Board of Trade, 62 F.3d 918 (7th Cir. 1995), 836, 861

Sanofi, S.A. v. Med-Tech Veterinarian Prods., 222 U.S.P.Q. (BNA) 143 (D. Kan. 1983), 1055

Sano Petroleum Corp. v. American Oil Co., 187 F. Supp. 345 (E.D.N.Y. 1960), 498, 499, 508

Santa Clara Valley Distrib. Co. v. Pabst Brewing Co., 556 F.2d 942 (9th Cir. 1977), 138, 142, 159

Santa Cruz Med. Clinic v. Dominican Santa Cruz Hosp., 1995-1 Trade Cas. (CCH) ¶ 70,915 (N.D. Cal. 1994), 399

Schenker v. Pepperidge Farm, 1963 Trade Cas. (CCH) ¶ 70,974 (S.D.N.Y. 1963), 964, 966, 968

Scherbatskoy v. Halliburton Co., 52 U.S.P.Q.2d (BNA) 1461 (Fed. Cir. 1999), 1109

Schering Corp., 118 F.T.C. 1030 (1994), 619, 627

Schering-Plough Healthcare Prods., Inc., 123 F.T.C. 1301 (1997), 626

Scheuer v. Rhodes, 416 U.S. 232 (1974), 590

Schilling v. Rogers, 363 U.S. 666 (1960), 1011

Schlafly v. Caro-Kann Corp., 1998-1 Trade Cas. (CCH) ¶ 72,138 (Fed. Cir. 1998), 1068, 1095

Schlafly v. Public Key Partners, No. 94-20512 SW, 1997 U.S. Dist. LEXIS 15287 (N.D. Cal. Aug. 29, 1997), 594

Schlegel Mfg. Co. v. USM Corp., 525 F.2d 775 (6th Cir. 1975), *cert. denied*, 425 U.S. 912 (1976), 1075

Schmidt v. Columbia Pictures Indus., 1986-2 Trade Cas. (CCH) ¶ 67,323 (D. Nev. 1986), 966, 967, 968

Schmidt v. Polish People's Republic, 579 F. Supp. 23 (S.D.N.Y), *aff'd*, 742 F.2d 67 (2d Cir. 1984), 1169, 1170

Schnabel v. Volkswagen of Am., Inc., 185 F. Supp. 122 (N.D. Iowa 1960), 838

Schnapps Shop, Inc. v. H.W. Wright & Co., 377 F. Supp. 570 (D. Md. 1973), 140

School Asbestos Litig., *In re*, 789 F.2d 996 (3d Cir.), *cert. denied*, 479 U.S. 852 (1986), 954

School Dist. v. Harper & Row Publishers, 267 F. Supp. 1001 (E.D. Pa. 1967), 960

School Dist. v. Kurtz Bros., 240 F. Supp. 361 (E.D. Pa. 1965), 1167

Schreiber v. NCAA, 916 F. Supp. 1105 (D. Kan. 1996), 868, 889

Schuler v. Better Equip. Launder Ctr., Inc., 74 F.R.D. 85 (D. Mass. 1977), 946

Schuylkill Energy Resources, Inc. v. Pennsylvania Power & Light Co., 113 F.3d 405 (3d Cir.), *cert. denied*, 522 U.S. 977 (1997), 844, 864

Schwartz v. Hospital of the Univ. of Pa., 1993-1 Trade Cas. (CCH) ¶ 70,222 (E.D. Pa. 1993), 12, 13, 16, 40, 45, 46

Schwartz v. Jamesway Corp., 660 F. Supp. 138 (E.D.N.Y. 1987), 1022

Schwartz v. Sun Oil Co., No. 96-72862, 1999 U.S. Dist. LEXIS 22257 (E.D. Mich. Dec. 9, 1999), 522

Schwegmann Bros. v. Calvert Distillers Corp., 341 U.S. 384 (1951), 132

Schwimmer v. Sony Corp. of Am., 471 F. Supp. 793 (E.D.N.Y. 1979), *aff'd*, 637 F.2d 41 (2d Cir. 1980), 1210

Schwimmer v. Sony Corp. of Am., 637 F.2d 41 (2d Cir. 1980), 468, 856

Sciambra v. Graham News, 841 F.2d 651 (5th Cir.), *cert. denied*, 488 U.S. 855 (1988), 875, 876, 989

Sciambra v. Graham News, 892 F.2d 411 (5th Cir. 1990), 840, 1012

Science Prods. Co. v. Chevron Chem. Co., 384 F. Supp. 793 (N.D. Ill. 1974), 554

Scientific Mfg. Co. v. FTC, 124 F.2d 640 (3d Cir. 1941), 635

S.C. Johnson, Inc. v. Carter-Wallace, Inc., 225 U.S.P.Q. (BNA) 968 (S.D.N.Y. 1985), *aff'd in part and vacated in part*, 228 U.S.P.Q. (BNA) 367 (Fed. Cir. 1986), 1031

SCM Corp. v. Brother Int'l Corp., 316 F. Supp. 1328 (S.D.N.Y. 1970), 1168

SCM Corp. v. FTC, 565 F.2d 807 (2d Cir. 1977), *appeal after remand*, 612 F.2d 707 (2d Cir.), *cert. denied*, 449 U.S. 821 (1980), 406, 407, 889

SCM Corp. v. RCA, 318 F. Supp. 433 (S.D.N.Y. 1970), 1065

SCM Corp. v. Xerox Corp., 463 F. Supp. 983 (D. Conn. 1978), *remanded*, 599 F.2d 32 (2d Cir. 1979), 896, 1036, 1055

SCM Corp. v. Xerox Corp., 645 F.2d 1195 (2d Cir. 1981), *cert. denied*, 455 U.S. 1016 (1982), 286, 319, 322, 1035, 1036, 1076, 1077

Scotch Whiskey, *In re*, 299 F. Supp. 543 (J.P.M.L. 1969), 925

Scott Med. Supply Co. v. Bedsole Surgical Supplies, Inc., 488 F.2d 934 (5th Cir. 1974), 170

Scott Paper Co., 63 F.T.C. 2240 (1963), 683

Scranton Constr. Co. v. Litton Indus. Leasing Corp., 494 F.2d 778 (5th Cir. 1974), *cert. denied*, 419 U.S. 1105 (1975), 43

Systemcare, Inc. v. Wang Lab. Corp., 117 F.3d 1137 (10th Cir. 1997), 176

Syufy Enters. v. American Multicinema, Inc., 793 F.2d 990 (9th Cir. 1986), *cert. denied*, 479 U.S. 1031 (1987), 309, 310, 311, 536, 542, 601, 877

T

Tacker v. Wilson, 830 F. Supp. 422 (W.D. Tenn. 1993), 4, 722

Taffett v. Southern Co., 967 F.2d 1483 (11th Cir.), *cert. denied*, 506 U.S. 1021 (1992), 1241, 1242

Taggart v. Rutledge, 657 F. Supp. 1420 (D. Mont. 1987), *aff'd without op.*, 852 F.2d 1290 (9th Cir. 1988), 194, 215, 457, 460

Tahan v. Hodgson, 662 F.2d 862 (D.C. Cir. 1981), 1202

Talbot v. Saipem A.G., 835 F. Supp. 352 (S.D. Tex. 1993), 1143

Taleigh Corp., 119 F.T.C. 835 (1995), 628

Tamaron Distrib. Corp. v. Weiner, 418 F.2d 137 (7th Cir. 1969), 34, 135

Tambone v. Memorial Hosp., 635 F. Supp. 508 (N.D. Ill. 1986), *aff'd*, 825 F.2d 1132 (7th Cir. 1987), 1215

Tambone v. Memorial Hosp., 825 F.2d 1132 (7th Cir. 1987), 1368

Tambone v. Simpson, 414 N.E.2d 533 (Ill. 1980), 823

TAM, Inc. v. Gulf Oil Corp., 553 F. Supp. 499 (E.D. Pa. 1983), 222

Tampa Elec. Co. v. Nashville Coal Co., 365 U.S. 320 (1961), 215, 216, 224, 225, 233, 529, 577, 578, 585

Tanaka v. University of S. Cal., 252 F.3d 1059 (9th Cir. 2001), 60, 67, 443, 527, 540, 590, 591

T&N PLC, 113 F.T.C. 1016 (1990), 384

T&T Geotechnical, Inc. v. Union Pac. Res. Co., 944 F. Supp. 1317 (N.D. Tex. 1996), 1041, 1048

Tank Insulation Int'l v. Insultherm, Inc., 104 F.3d 83 (5th Cir.), *cert. denied*, 522 U.S. 907 (1997), 1114

Tarabishi v. McAlester Reg'l Hosp., 951 F.2d 1558 (10th Cir. 1991), *cert. denied*, 505 U.S. 1206 (1992), 1327

Tarleton v. Meharry Med. College, 717 F.2d 1523 (6th Cir. 1983), 37, 44, 46

Tarrant Serv. Agency v. American Standard, Inc., 12 F.3d 609 (6th Cir. 1993), *cert. denied*, 512 U.S. 1221 (1994), 230, 550, 566

Tashof v. FTC, 437 F.2d 707 (D.C. Cir. 1970), 657

Tasty Baking Co. v. Ralston Purina, Inc., 653 F. Supp. 1250 (E.D. Pa. 1987), 234, 303, 336, 398, 557, 581, 582, 583, 584, 867

Taxi Weekly, Inc. v. Metropolitan Taxicab Bd. of Trade, 539 F.2d 907 (2d Cir. 1976), 873, 876

Taylor Publ'g Co. v. Jostens, Inc., 216 F.3d 465 (5th Cir. 2000), 257, 259, 261, 297, 475, 477

TCA Bldg. Co. v. Northwestern Resources Co., 861 F. Supp. 1366 (S.D. Tex. 1994), 40

TCA Bldg. Co. v. Northwestern Resources Co., 873 F. Supp. 29 (S.D. Tex. 1995), 280, 281, 582, 594

Tchacosh Co. v. Rockwell Int'l Corp., 766 F.2d 1333 (9th Cir. 1985), 1151

TCH Corp., 118 F.T.C. 368 (1994), 380

Teamsters Local Unions Nos. 75 & 200 v. Barry Trucking, Inc., 176 F.3d 1004 (7th Cir. 1999), 886

TEC Cogeneration Inc. v. Florida Power & Light Co., 76 F.3d 1560 (11th Cir.), *modified*, 86 F.3d 1028 (11th Cir. 1996), 1215, 1236, 1237, 1300

Technical Chem. Co. v. IG-LO Prods., 812 F.2d 222 (5th Cir. 1987), 987, 989

TechniCAL, Inc. v. Allpax Prods., 786 F. Supp. 581 (E.D. La.), *aff'd without op.*, 977 F.2d 578 (5th Cir. 1992), 80

Technical Learning Collective, Inc. v. Daimler-Benz A.G., 1980-1 Trade Cas. (CCH) ¶ 63,006 (D. Md. 1979), 932

Technical Learning Collective, Inc. v. Daimler-Benz A.G., 1980-81 Trade Cas. (CCH) ¶ 63,612 (D. Md. 1980), 859, 913

Technical Resource Serv., Inc. v. Dornier Medical Sys., Inc., 134 F.3d 1458 (11th Cir. 1998), 248

Technicon Instr. Corp. v. Alpkem Corp., 866 F.2d 417 (Fed. Cir. 1989), 297, 1041

Technograph Printed Circuits, Ltd. v. Bendix Aviation Corp., 218 F. Supp. 1 (D. Md. 1963), *aff'd per curiam*, 327 F.2d 497 (4th Cir.), *cert. denied*, 379 U.S. 826 (1964), 1061, 1107

Tekton, Inc. v. Builders Bid Serv., 676 F.2d 1352 (10th Cir. 1982), 86

Telecomm Tech. Servs., Inc. v. Siemens Rolm Communs., 172 F.R.D. 532 (N.D. Ga. 1997), 934, 946

Telecomm Tech. Servs., Inc. v. Siemens Rolm Communs., 66 F. Supp. 2d 1306 (N.D. Ga. 1998), 1101

Tele-Communications, Inc., 119 F.T.C. 593 (1993), 365

Tele-Communications, Inc. & Liberty Media Corp., 9 F.C.C.R. 4783 (1994), 1276

Telecommunications Research & Action Ctr. v. FCC, 750 F.2d 70 (D.C. Cir. 1984), 697

Telecom Plus v. Local No. 3, 719 F.2d 613 (2d Cir. 1983), 1243

Telectronics Proprietary, Ltd. v. Medtronic, Inc., 687 F. Supp. 832 (S.D.N.Y. 1988), 310, 319, 914

Teleflex Indus. Prods. v. Brunswick Corp., 293 F. Supp. 106 (E.D. Pa. 1968), *order vacated*, 410 F.2d 380 (3d Cir. 1969), 207, 208

Teleo, Inc. v. Ford Indus., 587 P.2d 1360 (Okla. 1978), 811

Telerate Sys. v. Caro, 689 F. Supp. 221 (S.D.N.Y. 1988), 179, 183, 188, 193, 204, 233, 243, 554

Telex Corp. v. IBM, 367 F. Supp. 258 (N.D. Okla. 1973), *rev'd*, 510 F.2d 894 (10th Cir.), *cert. dismissed*, 423 U.S. 802 (1975), 186, 291

Telex Corp. v. IBM, 510 F.2d 894 (10th Cir. 1975), *rev'g* 367 F. Supp. 258 (N.D. Okla. 1973), *cert. dismissed*, 423 U.S. 802 (1975), 248, 291, 533, 547, 554, 1106

Tel-Phonic Serv. v. TBS Int'l, Inc., 975 F.2d 1134 (5th Cir. 1992), 508

Tempkin v. Lewis-Gale Hosp., 1989-2 Trade Cas. (CCH) ¶ 68,865 (W.D. Va. 1989), 123

Tempo Music, Inc. v. Myers, 407 F.2d 503 (4th Cir. 1969), 761, 1098

Tennant Co. v. Hako Minuteman, Inc., 651 F. Supp. 945 (N.D. Ill. 1986), 1048

Tenneco, Inc., 98 F.T.C. 464 (1981), *rev'd*, 689 F.2d 346 (2d Cir. 1982), 354, 355, 357, 555

Tenneco, Inc. v. FTC, 689 F.2d 346 (2d Cir. 1982), 316, 354, 355, 357, 358, 359

Tennessee *ex rel.* Burson v. Joe Stewart Body Shop, 1992-1 Trade Cas. (CCH) ¶ 69,748 (W.D. Tenn. 1992), 805

Tennessee *ex rel.* Burson v. Pet Inc., 1993-2 Trade Cas. (CCH) ¶ 70,303 (M.D. Tenn.) (final judgment filed June 23, 1993), 804

Tennessee *ex rel.* Leech v. Highland Mem'l Cemetery, 489 F. Supp. 65 (E.D. Tenn. 1980), 87, 809

Terazosin Hydrochloride Antitrust Litig., *In re*, No. 99-MDL-1317, 2000 U.S. Dist. LEXIS 20477 (S.D. Fla. Dec. 13, 2000), 1087

Terrell v. Household Goods Carriers' Bureau, 494 F.2d 16 (5th Cir.), *cert. dismissed*, 419 U.S. 987 (1974), 879

Terry's Floor Fashions, Inc. v. Burlington Indus., 763 F.2d 604 (4th Cir. 1985), 20, 465

Texaco, Inc., [F.T.C. Complaints & Orders 1983-1987 Transfer Binder] Trade Reg. Rep. (CCH) ¶ 22,146 (F.T.C. 1984), 376

Texaco, Inc., 104 F.T.C. 241 (1984), 383, 384, 385

Texaco Inc. v. Hasbrouck, 496 U.S. 543 (1990), 463, 471, 478, 481, 486, 495

Texaco Puerto Rico, Inc. v. Medina, 834 F.2d 242 (1st Cir. 1987), 922

Texas v. Allan Constr. Co., 851 F.2d 1526 (5th Cir. 1988), 899, 900, 902, 905

Texas v. Mid-America Dairymen, Inc., 1997-2 Trade Cas. (CCH) ¶ 71,930 (Tex. Dist. Ct. 1997), 326

United States v. Finnell, 535 F. Supp. 410 (D. Kan. 1982), 736

United States v. First City Fin. Corp., 1988-1 Trade Cas. (CCH) ¶ 67,967 (D.D.C. 1988), 377

United States v. First City Nat'l Bank, 386 U.S. 361 (1967), 1318, 1319

United States v. First Fed. Credit Control, Inc., Antitrust & Trade Reg. Rep. (BNA) No. 1062, 864 (N.D. Ohio Mar. 11, 1982), 715

United States v. First Hawaiian, Inc., Civ. No. 90-00904 DAE (D. Haw. filed Dec. 28, 1990), 562

United States v. First Nat'l Bank, 310 F. Supp. 157 (D. Md. 1970), 346, 1318

United States v. First Nat'l Bank, 699 F.2d 341 (7th Cir. 1983), 1190

United States v. First Nat'l Bank & Trust Co., 376 U.S. 665 (1964), 316, 756, 1313

United States v. First Nat'l Bank of Jackson, 301 F. Supp. 1161 (S.D. Miss. 1969), 346

United States v. First Nat'l City Bank, 396 F.2d 897 (2d Cir. 1968), 1182, 1188

United States v. First Nat'l State Bancorp., 499 F. Supp. 793 (D.N.J. 1980), 355, 357, 562, 577, 584

United States v. Fischbach & Moore, Inc., 576 F. Supp. 1384 (W.D. Pa. 1983), 778, 779, 780, 781

United States v. Fischbach & Moore, Inc., 1984-1 Trade Cas. (CCH) ¶ 65,874 (W.D. Wash. 1983), 774

United States v. Fischbach & Moore, Inc., 750 F.2d 1183 (3d Cir. 1984), *cert. denied*, 470 U.S. 1029 (1985), *and cert. denied*, 470 U.S. 1085 (1985), 38, 40, 43, 44

United States v. Fischbach & Moore, Inc., 776 F.2d 839 (9th Cir. 1985), 974, 978

United States v. Fitapelli, 786 F.2d 1461 (11th Cir. 1986), 38, 773

United States v. Fleet/Norstar Fin. Group, Civ. No. 91-0021-P (D. Me. filed July 5, 1991), 562, 1321

United States v. Flanagan, 465 U.S. 259 (1984), 753

United States v. Flemmi, 245 F.3d 24 (1st Cir.), *cert. denied*, 531 U.S. 1170 (2001), 742

United States v. Flintkote Co., 1991-2 U.S. Tax Cas. (CCH) ¶ 50,435 (N.D. Cal. 1991), *aff'd*, 7 F.3d 870 (9th Cir. 1993), 1028

United States v. Flintkote Co., 7 F.3d 870 (9th Cir. 1993), 899

United States v. Floersheim, 1980-2 Trade Cas. (CCH) ¶ 63,368 (C.D. Cal. 1980), *aff'd*, No. 80-5444 (9th Cir. July 23, 1981), 663

United States v. Flom, 558 F.2d 1179 (5th Cir. 1977), 781

United States v. Florida Power Corp., 1971 Trade Cas. (CCH) ¶ 73,637 (M.D. Fla. 1971), 1297

United States v. Florida Rock Indus., Inc., 2000-1 Trade Cas. (CCH) ¶ 72,858 (M.D. Fla. 1999), 388

United States v. Florists Tel. Delivery Ass'n, 1996-1 Trade Cas. (CCH) ¶ 71,394 (E.D. Mich. 1990), 433

United States v. FMC Corp., 306 F. Supp. 1106 (E.D. Pa. 1969), 94

United States v. Foley, 598 F.2d 1323 (4th Cir. 1979), *cert. denied*, 444 U.S. 1043 (1980), 5, 40, 779

United States v. Ford Motor Co., 24 F.R.D. 65 (D.D.C. 1959), 781

United States v. Ford Motor Co., 315 F. Supp. 372 (E.D. Mich. 1970), *aff'd*, 405 U.S. 562 (1972), 396

United States v. Ford Motor Co., 335 U.S. 303 (1948), 764, 765

United States v. Ford Motor Co., 405 U.S. 562 (1972), 346, 363, 395, 756

United States v. Foremost-McKesson, Inc., 1976-2 Trade Cas. (CCH) ¶ 61,165 (D. Nev. 1976), 393

United States v. Forman, 767 F.2d 875 (Fed. Cir. 1985), 1111

United States v. Fortner Enters. Steel Corp., 394 U.S. 495 (1969), 177, 180, 204, 526

United States v. Friedman, 532 F.2d 928 (3d Cir. 1976), 986

United States v. Friedrick, 842 F.2d 382 (D.C. Cir. 1988), 749

United States v. Frito-Lay, Inc., 1975-1 Trade Cas. (CCH) ¶ 60,265 (C.D. Cal. 1975), 764

United States v. GAF Corp., 596 F.2d 10 (2d Cir. 1979), 734

United States v. McKesson & Robbins, Inc., 351 U.S. 305 (1956), 160
United States v. McPartlin, 595 F.2d 1321 (7th Cir.), *cert. denied*, 444 U.S. 833 (1979), 746
United States v. McVeigh, 896 F. Supp. 1549 (W.D. Okla. 1995), 741
United States v. Mechanik, 475 U.S. 66 (1986), 744
United States v. Medical Mutual of Ohio, 1999-1 Trade Cas. (CCH) ¶ 72,465 (N.D. Ohio 1999), 148
United States v. Medina, 992 F.2d 573 (6th Cir. 1993), *cert. denied*, 501 U.S. 1109 (1994), 782
United States v. Melvin, 650 F.2d 641 (5th Cir. 1981), 746
United States v. Memphis Retail Appliance Dealers Ass'n, 1957 Trade Cas. (CCH) ¶ 68,704 (W.D. Tenn. 1957), 84
United States v. Menichino, 32 F.3d 569 (6th Cir. 1994), 776
United States v. Mercedes-Benz of N. Am., Inc., 517 F. Supp. 1369 (N.D. Cal. 1981), 203, 204, 207
United States v. Mercedes-Benz of N. Am., Inc., 547 F. Supp. 399 (N.D. Cal. 1982), 760
United States v. Merck & Co., 1980-81 Trade Cas. (CCH) ¶ 63,682 (S.D. Cal. 1980), 384
United States v. Mercury PCS II, L.L.C., 1999-2 Trade Cas. (CCH) ¶ 72,707 (D.D.C. 1999), 757, 1274
United States v. Mercy Health Servs., 902 F. Supp. 968 (N.D. Iowa 1995), *vacated as moot*, 107 F.3d 632 (8th Cir. 1997), 328, 579, 589, 1362, 1363, 1364
United States v. Mercy Health Servs., 107 F.3d 632 (8th Cir. 1997), 885
United States v. Michaelson, 552 F.2d 472 (2d Cir. 1977), 771
United States v. Microsoft Corp., 1995-2 Trade Cas. (CCH) ¶ 71,096 (D.D.C. 1995), 254, 1060
United States v. Microsoft Corp., 159 F.R.D. 318 (D.D.C.), *rev'd and remanded*, 56 F.3d 1448 (D.C. Cir. 1995), 293, 760, 762, 763, 1060
United States v. Microsoft Corp., 980 F. Supp. 537 (D.D.C. 1997), 183
United States v. Microsoft Corp., 1998-2 Trade Cas. (CCH) ¶ 72,261 (D.D.C. 1998), 289
United States v. Microsoft Corp., 65 F. Supp. 2d 1 (D.D.C. 1999), *aff'd*, 253 F.3d 34 (D.C. Cir.), *cert. denied*, 122 S. Ct. 350 (2001), 300
United States v. Microsoft Corp., 84 F. Supp. 2d 9 (D.D.C. 1999), 1101
United States v. Microsoft Corp., 87 F. Supp. 2d 30 (D.D.C. 2000), *aff'd in part, rev'd in part*, 253 F.3d 34 (D.C. Cir.), *cert. denied*, 122 S. Ct. 350 (2001), 183, 188, 189, 223, 302, 833
United States v. Microsoft Corp., 97 F. Supp. 2d 59 (D.D.C. 2000), *aff'd, rev'd, and remanded in part*, 253 F.3d 34 (D.C. Cir.), *cert. denied*, 122 S. Ct. 350 (2001), 833
United States v. Microsoft Corp., 56 F.3d 1448 (D.C. Cir. 1995), 387, 760, 1060
United States v. Microsoft Corp., 147 F.3d 935 (D.C. Cir. 1998), 183, 390, 762
United States v. Microsoft Corp., 165 F.3d 952 (D.C. Cir. 1999), 767
United States v. Microsoft Corp., 253 F.3d 34 (D.C. Cir.), *cert. denied*, 122 S. Ct. 350 (2001), 48, 67, 178, 179, 183, 184, 186, 210, 215, 232, 233, 234, 235, 238, 242, 243, 249, 250, 251, 253, 254, 255, 257, 292, 298, 299, 303, 307, 528, 536, 537, 538, 551, 552, 589, 833, 1056, 1070, 1071, 1078, 1079
United States v. Mid-America Dairymen, Inc., 1977-1 Trade Cas. (CCH) ¶ 61,508 (W.D. Mo. 1977), 760
United States v. Middlebrooks, 618 F.2d 273 (5th Cir.), *cert. denied*, 449 U.S. 984 (1980), 6
United States v. Milikowsky, 65 F.3d 4 (2d Cir. 1995), 788
United States v. Miller, 771 F.2d 1219 (9th Cir. 1985), 730, 773, 776, 779
United States v. Miller, 871 F.2d 488 (4th Cir. 1989), 786
United States v. Milliken, 769 F. Supp. 1023 (W.D. Tenn. 1991), 772
United States v. Minneapolis & St. L. Ry., 361 U.S. 173 (1959), 1405
United States v. Minnesota Mining & Mfg. Co., 92 F. Supp. 947 (D. Mass. 1950), 1160, 1161
United States v. Minnesota Mining & Mfg. Co., 1950-51 Trade Cas. (CCH) ¶ 62,724 (D. Mass. 1950), 1113
United States v. Misle Bus & Equip. Co., 967 F.2d 1227 (8th Cir. 1992), 89

V

W

X

Y

Yaffe v. Detroit Steel Corp., 50 F.R.D. 481 (N.D. Ill. 1970), 955

Yaffe v. Powers, 454 F.2d 1362 (1st Cir. 1972), 950

Yamaha Motor Co. v. FTC, 657 F.2d 971 (8th Cir. 1981), *affirming in part and modifying in part* Brunswick Corp., 94 F.T.C. 1174 (1979), *cert. denied*, 456 U.S. 915 (1982), 316, 358, 359, 411, 419, 449, 450, 610

Yanai v. Frito-Lay, Inc., 61 F.R.D. 349 (N.D. Ohio 1973), 949, 950

Y & Y Popcorn Supply Co. v. ABC Vending Corp., 263 F. Supp. 709 (E.D. Pa. 1967), 1004, 1006

Yarn Processing Patent Validity Litig., *In re*, 472 F. Supp. 178 (S.D. Fla. 1979), 912

Yarn Processing Patent Validity Litig., *In re*, 541 F.2d 1127 (5th Cir. 1976), *cert. denied*, 433 U.S. 910 (1977), 1057, 1063, 1065

Yarn Process Patent Validity & Antitrust Litig., *In re*, 398 F. Supp. 31 (S.D. Fla. 1974), *aff'd in part and rev'd in part*, 541 F.2d 1127 (5th Cir. 1976), *cert. denied*, 433 U.S. 910 (1977), 1036

Yeager's Fuel, Inc. v. Pennsylvania Power & Light Co., 1995-1 Trade Cas. (CCH) ¶ 70,974 (E.D. Pa. 1995), 935

Yeager's Fuel, Inc. v. Pennsylvania Power & Light Co., 953 F. Supp. 617 (E.D. Pa. 1997), 288, 305, 500, 504, 594, 1301

Yeager's Fuel, Inc. v. Pennsylvania Power & Light Co., 22 F.3d 1260 (3d Cir. 1994), 1214, 1301

Yeager v. Waste Mgmt., Inc., 1995-1 Trade Cas. (CCH) ¶ 70,882 (N.D. Ohio 1994), 470, 892

Yellow Pages Cost Consultants v. GTE Directories Corp., 951 F.2d 1158 (9th Cir. 1991), *cert. denied*, 504 U.S. 913 (1992), 863, 867, 881

Yellow Page Solutions, Inc. v. Bell Atl. Yellow Pages Co., 2001 U.S. Dist. LEXIS 18831 (S.D.N.Y. Nov. 19, 2001), 466, 470, 534, 546, 592, 849

Yentsch v. Texaco, Inc., 630 F.2d 46 (2d Cir. 1980), 139, 141, 165, 176, 179, 188, 195, 201, 205, 206

YKK (U.S.A.) Inc., 116 F.T.C. 628 (1993), 613

YKK (U.S.A.) Inc., [F.T.C. Complaints & Orders 1993-1997 Transfer Binder] Trade Reg. Rep. (CCH) ¶ 23,355 (F.T.C. July 1, 1993), 100

Yoder Bros. v. California-Florida Plant Corp., 537 F.2d 1347 (5th Cir. 1976), *cert. denied*, 429 U.S. 1094 (1977), 108, 236, 537, 547, 551, 554, 836, 895, 898, 899

Young v. Katz, 447 F.2d 431 (5th Cir. 1971), 959

Young v. Lehigh Corp., 1989-2 Trade Cas. (CCH) ¶ 68,790 (N.D. Ill. 1989), 875

Young & Rubicam/Zemp, Inc., 105 F.T.C. 317 (1985), 627

Younger v. Jensen, 605 P.2d 813 (Cal. 1980), 816

Z

Zachair, Ltd. v. Driggs, 967 F. Supp. 741 (D. Md. 1997), 980

Zahn v. International Paper Co., 414 U.S. 291 (1973), 941

Zajicek v. KoolVent Metal Awning Corp. of Am., 283 F.2d 127 (9th Cir. 1960), *cert. denied*, 365 U.S. 859 (1961), 1039

Zamanian v. Christian Health Ministry, Civ. A. No. 94-1781, 1994 WL 396179 (E.D. La. July 22, 1994), 1335

Zapata Gulf Marine Corp. v. Puerto Rico Mar. Shipping Auth., No. CIV.A.86-2911, 1989 WL 143151 (E.D. La. Nov. 15, 1989), 241, 258

Zapata Gulf Marine Corp. v. Puerto Rico Mar. Shipping Auth., 133 F.R.D. 481 (E.D. La. 1990), *appeal dismissed*, 925 F.2d 812 (5th Cir.), *cert. denied*, 501 U.S. 1262 (1991), 882

Z Channel Ltd. v. Home Box Office, 931 F.2d 1338 (9th Cir. 1991), 1278

INDEX

ABA SECTION OF ANTITRUST LAW
COMMITMENT TO QUALITY

The Section of Antitrust Law is committed to the highest standards of scholarship and continuing legal education. To that end, each of our books and treatises is subjected to rigorous quality control mechanisms throughout the design, drafting, editing, and peer review processes. Each Section publication is drafted and edited by leading experts on the topics covered and then rigorously peer reviewed by the Section's Books and Treatises Committee, at least two Council members, and then other officers and experts. Because the Section's quality commitment does not stop at publication, we encourage you to provide any comments or suggestions you may have for future editions of this book or other publications.